GLOBAL MARKETING

EIGHTH EDITION
GLOBAL EDITION

Warren J. Keegan

Lubin Graduate School of Business
Pace University
New York City and
Westchester, New York

Mark C. Green

Department of Business Administration
and Economics
Simpson College
Indianola, Iowa

Tippie College of Business
University of Iowa
Iowa City, Iowa

Boston   Columbus   Indianapolis   New York   San Francisco   Upper Saddle River
Amsterdam   Cape Town   Dubai   London   Madrid   Milan   Munich   Paris   Montréal
Toronto   Delhi   Mexico City   São Paulo   Sydney   Hong Kong   Seoul   Singapore   Taipei   Tokyo

Editor in Chief: Stephanie Wall
Acquisitions Editor: Mark Gaffney
Senior Acquisitions Editor,
    Global Editions: Steven Jackson
Project Editor, Global Editions: Suchismita Ukil
Program Manager Team Lead: Ashley Santora
Program Manager: Jennifer M. Collins
Editorial Assistant: Daniel Petrino
Director of Marketing: Maggie Moylan
Executive Marketing Manager: Anne Fahlgren
Project Manager Team Lead: Judy Leale
Project Manager: Becca Groves
Head of Learning Asset Acquisition,
    Global Editions: Laura Dent
Media Producer, Global Editions: M. Vikram Kumar

Associate Print and Media Editor,
    Global Editions: Anuprova Dey Chowdhuri
Senior Manufacturing Controller, Production,
    Global Editions: Trudy Kimber
Creative Director: Blair Brown
Senior Art Director: Janet Slowik
Manager of Central Design, Cover: Jayne Conte
Designer, Cover: Karen Salzbach
Cover Image: © My Life Graphic/Shutterstock
VP, Director of Digital Strategy & Assessment: Paul Gentile
Digital Editor: Brian Surette
Digital Development Manager: Robin Lazrus
Digital Project Manager: Alana Coles
MyLab Product Manager: Joan Waxman
Digital Production Project Manager: Lisa Rinaldi

Credits and acknowledgments borrowed from other sources and reproduced, with permission, in this textbook appear on the appropriate page within the text.

Pearson Education Limited
Edinburgh Gate
Harlow
Essex CM20 2JE
England

and Associated Companies throughout the world

Visit us on the World Wide Web at: www.pearsonglobaleditions.com

© Pearson Education Limited 2015

ISBN 10: 1-292-01738-4
ISBN 13: 978-1-292-01738-9

British Library Cataloguing-in-Publication Data
A catalogue record for this book is available from the British Library

10 9 8 7 6 5 4 3 2
20 19 18 17 16 15

Typeset in 10/12 Times by Integra
Printed and bound by Courier Kendallville in The United States of America

To Cynthia, my wife, best friend,
and partner in living life creatively.

—WJK

In memoriam:
Peter Nathaniel Green 1964–2013

—MCG

Brief Contents

Contents

Preface

Global Marketing, Eighth Edition, builds on the worldwide success of the previous editions of *Principles of Global Marketing* and *Global Marketing*. Those books took an environmental and strategic approach by outlining the major dimensions of the global business environment. The authors also provided a set of conceptual and analytical tools that prepared students to successfully apply the four Ps to global marketing.

Our goal for all eight editions has been the same: to write a book that is authoritative in content yet relaxed and assured in style and tone. Here's what students have to say:

- "An excellent textbook with many real-life examples."
- "The authors use simple language and clearly state the important points."
- "This is the best textbook that I am using this term."
- "The authors have done an excellent job of writing a text that can be read easily."

When *Principles of Global Marketing* first appeared in 1996, we invited readers to "look ahead" to such developments as the ending of America's trade embargo with Vietnam, Europe's new single market, Daimler AG's Smart car, Volkswagen's global ambitions, and Whirlpool's expansion into emerging markets. These topics represented "big stories" in the global marketing arena and continue to receive press coverage on a regular basis.

Guided by our experience using the text in undergraduate and graduate classrooms and in corporate training seminars, we have revised, updated, and expanded *Global Marketing*, Eighth Edition. We have benefited tremendously from readers' feedback and input; we also continue to draw on our direct experience in the Americas, Asia, Europe, Africa, and the Middle East. The result is a text that addresses your needs and the needs of instructors in every part of the world. *Global Marketing* has been adopted at scores of colleges and universities in the United States; international use of the English-language Global Edition is found in Australia, Canada, China, Ireland, Italy, Japan, Malaysia, Saudi Arabia, South Korea, Spain, and Sri Lanka. The text is also available in Albanian, Chinese (simplified and traditional), Japanese, Korean, Macedonian, Portuguese, Spanish, and Turkish editions.

What's New to the Eighth Edition

Thunderclap Newman once sang,

> "Call out the instigator,
> there's something in the air . . .
> we've got to get together sooner or later,
> because the revolution's here."

Indeed, something *is* in the air. Two specific geopolitical developments that formed the backdrop to the Seventh Edition continue to dominate the headlines as this revision goes to press. First, after popular uprisings in North Africa upended the long-entrenched political order, the region is still in transition. Tensions remain especially high in Egypt and Syria. Second, the sovereign debt crisis in the euro zone, while still not resolved, is not as acute today as it was in 2011. High on the EU's agenda now are broader concerns about high unemployment levels and stagnant demand in Greece, Italy, and elsewhere.

More generally, the global economic crisis continues to impact global marketing strategies. Virtually every industry sector, company, and country has been affected by the downturn. Although the North American auto industry is rebounding, Europe's automakers are plagued by excess capacity. The lack of credit remains a key issue that is still squeezing companies and consumers. Among the bright spots: Real estate values in the United States appear to have bottomed out, and the uptick in the demand for housing provides grounds for optimism. Also, Wall Street continues to rebound, with some stocks hitting record highs.

Although all of these storylines continue to unfold as this edition goes to press, we have tried to offer up-to-date, original insights into the complexities and subtleties of these shifts in the external environment and their implications for global marketers. Other specific updates and revisions include:

- Fifty percent of the chapter-opening cases and related end-of-chapter cases are new to the Eighth Edition. Holdover cases have been revised and updated.
- All tables containing key company, country, and industry data have been updated. Examples include Table 2-3, "Index of Economic Freedom"; all the income and population tables in Chapters 3 and 7; Table 10-2, "The World's Most Valuable Brands"; Table 13-1, "Top 25 Global Marketers"; and Table 13-2, "Top 20 Global Advertising Agency Companies."
- The discussion of BRIC nations has been expanded to talk about the BRICS countries, reflecting South Africa's increasing importance as an emerging market.
- New discussion of social media is integrated throughout the Eighth Edition. Chapter 15, "Global Marketing and the Digital Revolution," has been completely revised and updated to include discussion of location-based mobile platforms, cloud computing, tablets, and other emerging topics.
- A new sidebar, Innovation, Entrepreneurship, and the Global Startup, presents profiles of visionary business leaders from around the world.
- Income and population data in Chapter 3 have been reorganized for improved clarity and comparability.
- A new emphasis on developing critical thinking skills when analyzing chapter-ending cases has been included in the Eighth Edition.
- To supplement the use of *Global Marketing*, Eighth Edition, faculty and students can access author updates and comments on Twitter, the microblogging Web site. In addition, the authors have archived nearly 2,000 articles pertaining to global marketing on Delicious.com, the social bookmarking site (www.delicious.com/MarkCGreen).

Time marches on. As this edition goes to press in 2013, some iconic global brands and companies celebrate golden anniversaries. Among them: the Beatles! Fifty years ago, the Beatles topped the charts in the United Kingdom before fundamentally revolutionizing popular music. Also 50 years ago, the first hypermarket opened in France. Turning 40 this year is the mobile phone; Motorola's DynaTec mobile handset was the first shot fired in the nascent telecommunications revolution. It was 30 years ago, in 1983, that Theodore Levitt's classic article "The Globalization of Markets" was published in *Harvard Business Review*. That same year, the compact disc player was introduced, ushering in a new era of digital music. And, in April 2013, Apple's game-changing iTunes store turned 10.

Unifying themes in earlier editions included the growing impact of emerging nations in general and Brazil, Russia, India, and China in particular. To those four BRIC countries we add South Africa in this edition. Also in earlier editions, we explored the marketing strategies used by global companies such as Embraer (Brazil), Lukoil (Russia), Cemex (Mexico), Lenovo (China), and India's Big Three—Wipro, Infosys, and Tata—to build scale and scope on the global stage. We then broadened our view to examine emerging markets as a whole. We noted that, prior to the world wide economic downturn, Mexico, Indonesia, Nigeria, and Turkey (the so-called MINTs) and a handful of other emerging nations were rapidly approaching the tipping point in terms of both competitive vigor and marketing opportunity.

In the Seventh Edition previously, we charted the path of the nascent economic recovery and the resulting shifts in global market opportunities and threats. New phrases such as *austerity, capital flight, currency wars, double-dip recession, global imbalances, global rebalancing, quantitative easing (QE)*, and *sovereign-debt crisis* were introduced into the discourse. The crisis in the euro zone was, and remains, one of the top stories of the year. Greece, Ireland, Italy, Portugal, and Spain bear especially close observation; this is the opening case in Chapter 3. Meanwhile, the big news in Asia was China's overtaking Japan as the world's second-largest economy. China has also surpassed the United States as the world's leading manufacturer.

The aforementioned trends are central to the Eighth Edition as well. As noted previously, unprecedented social and political change is underway in North Africa. Sub-Saharan Africa's economies are rebounding from the global financial crisis at a rapid pace. Every day the business press contains another announcement that a global company plans to enter Africa or expand operations there. Bharti-Airtel, Coca-Cola, Ford, IBM, Nestlé, and Walmart are among the companies that have joined the "final gold rush" into the world's last untapped market. "Africa 3.0," the lead-in case to Chapter 15, explores the way mobile phones are transforming business and home life across the continent. This is clearly a region that bears watching.

Current research findings have been integrated into each chapter of *Global Marketing*, Eighth Edition. For example, we have incorporated key insights from Seung Ho Park and Wilfried R. Vanhonacker's article "The Challenge for Multinational Corporations in China: Think Local, Act Global," which appeared in *MIT Sloan Management Review* in 2007. Similarly, we found Arindam K. Bhattacharya and David C. Michael's 2008 *Harvard Business Review* article "How Local Companies Keep Multinationals at Bay" to be extremely insightful.

Similarly, our thinking about the global/local market paradox has been influenced by John Quelch's 2012 book, *All Business Is Local*. We have added scores of current examples of global marketing practice as well as quotations from global marketing practitioners and industry experts. Throughout the text, organizational Web sites are referenced for further student study and exploration. A companion Web site (www.pearsonglobaleditions.com/keegan) is integrated with the text as well.

End-of-Chapter Cases and Chapter Sidebars

Each chapter opens with a brief case study introducing a company, a country, a product, or a global marketing issue that directly relates to the chapter's themes and content. The cases vary in length from a few hundred words to more than 2,600 words, yet they are all short enough to be covered in a single class period. The cases were written with the same objectives in mind: to raise issues that will encourage student interest and learning; to stimulate class discussion; to give students a chance to apply theory and concepts while developing critical thinking skills; and to enhance the classroom experience for students and instructors alike. Every chapter and case has been classroom-tested in both undergraduate and graduate courses.

The end-of-chapter cases strike a balance between revisions and updates of cases from the Seventh Edition and cases that are new to this edition. Revised and updated cases include Case 1-2, "McDonald's Expands Globally While Adjusting Its Local Recipe"; Case 7-1, "Global Companies Target Low-Income Consumers"; Case 15-1, "Africa 3.0"; and Case 16-1, "Volkswagen Aims for the Top."

New cases in the Eighth Edition include Case 1-3, "Apple Versus Samsung: The Battle for Smartphone Supremacy Heats Up"; Case 3-1, "Global Trading Partners Look East and West for Economic Growth"; Case 4-1, "Will Tourism Ruin Venice?"; Case 5-1, "Mr. President—Free Pussy Riot!"; Case 8-1, "East-Asian countries: Export-led Growth for Economic Success"; Case 9-1, "Mo'men Launches Franchises in UAE"; Case 12-1, "Carrefour's Entry in Dubai"; and Case 14-1, "Red Bull."

In addition, every chapter contains two or more sidebars on three themes: Emerging Markets Briefing Book; Innovation, Entrepreneurship, and the Global Startup; and The Cultural Context. Among the entrepreneurs profiled are Kevin Plank (Under Armour), Reed Hastings (Netflix), and Diego Della Valle (Tod's).

Teaching Aids for Instructors on the Instructor's Resource Center

At www.pearsonglobaleditions.com/keegan, instructors can access a variety of print, digital, and presentation resources available with this text in downloadable format. Registration is simple and gives you immediate access to new titles and new editions. As a registered faculty member, you can download resource files and receive immediate access and instructions for installing course management content on your campus server.

If you need assistance, our dedicated technical support team is ready to help with the media supplements that accompany this text. Visit http://247pearsoned.custhelp.com for answers to frequently asked questions and toll-free user-support phone numbers.

The following supplements are available to adopting instructors (for detailed descriptions, please visit www.pearsonglobaleditions.com/keegan):

- **Instructor's Manual.** This downloadable instructor's manual includes sample syllabi, lecture outlines, answers to all end-of-chapter questions and case questions, and additional activities and assignments for your students. This manual is available for download by visiting www.pearsonglobaleditions.com/keegan.
- **Test Item File.** This downloadable Test Item File contains over 1,600 questions, including multiple-choice, true/false, and essay-type questions. Each question is followed by the correct answer, the learning objective it ties to, the AACSB category when appropriate, the question type (concept, application, critical thinking, or synthesis), and a difficulty rating.
- **PowerPoints.** These downloadable PowerPoint slides are available from www.pearson globaleditions.com/keegan. PowerPoints include the basic outlines and key points with corresponding figures and art from each chapter. These PowerPoint slides are completely customizable for individual course needs or are ready to use as is. The notes section of each slide provides additional explanations written for your students.
- **TestGen.** Pearson Education's test-generating software is available from www.pearson globaleditions.com/keegan. The software is PC/Mac compatible and preloaded with all of the Test Item File questions. You can manually or randomly view test questions and drag-and-drop to create a test. You can also add or modify test bank questions as needed.

Video Library

Videos illustrating the most important topics can be accessed at:

MyMarketingLab—available for instructors and students, provides round-the-clock, instant access to videos and corresponding assessments and simulations for Pearson textbooks.

CourseSmart*   CourseSmart*

CourseSmart eTextbooks were developed for students looking to save on required or recommended textbooks. Students simply select their eText by title or author and purchase immediate access to the content for the duration of the course using any major credit card. With a CourseSmart eText, students can search for specific keywords or page numbers, take notes online, print out reading assignments that incorporate lecture notes, and bookmark important passages for later review. For more information or to purchase a CourseSmart eTextbook, visit www.coursesmart.co.uk.

One of our challenges in writing new editions of this textbook is the rate of change in the global business environment. Yesterday's impossibility becomes today's reality; new companies explode onto the scene; company leadership changes abruptly. In short, any book can be quickly outdated by current events. Even so, we set out to create a compelling narrative that captures the unfolding drama that is inherent in marketing in the globalization era. The authors are passionate about the subject of global marketing; if our readers detect a note of enthusiasm in our writing, then we have been successful. We believe that you will find *Global Marketing*, Eighth Edition, to be the most engaging, up-to-date, relevant, and useful text of its kind.

---

*This product may not be available in all markets. For more details, please visit www.coursesmart.co.uk or contact your local Pearson representative.

Acknowledgments

This book reflects the contributions, labor, and insights of many persons.

I would like to thank my students, colleagues, associates, and clients for sharing their insights and understanding of global marketing theory and practice. It is impossible to single out everyone who has contributed to this edition, but I would especially like to thank:

Stephen Blank, Lawrence G. Bridwell, Steve Burgess, John Dory, Bob Fulmer, Donald Gibson, Pradeep Gopalakrisna, Jim Gould, David Heenan, Hermawan Kartajaya, Suren Kaushik, Bodo B. Schlegelmilch, Jim Stoner, John Stopford, Barbara Stöttinger, Michael Szenberg, Martin Topol, Robert Vambery, and Dominique Xardel.

I also wish to acknowledge the many contributions of the students in my doctoral seminar on global strategic marketing. The Pace doctoral students are a remarkable group of experienced executives who have decided to pursue a doctoral degree while working full time.

My associates at Keegan & Company—Eli Seggev, Mark Keegan, and Anthony Donato—are outstanding expert consultants. Their collective backgrounds include doctoral degrees in marketing, and law and a master's degree in public administration. The cross-fertilization of their training and experience and challenging client assignments addressing contemporary marketing issues is a continuing source of new ideas and insights on global strategic marketing.

Special thanks are due the superb librarians at Pace University: Michelle Lang, head, Graduate Center Library, and Anne B. Campbell, reference librarian, have a remarkable ability to find anything. Like the Canadian Mounties who always get their man, Michelle and Anne always get the document. My admiration for their talent and appreciation for their effort are unbounded.

Elyse Arno Brill, my coauthor for *Offensive Marketing* (Butterworth Heinemann), has provided invaluable assistance in researching, writing, and teaching. Her energy and creativity are unbounded. I am in awe of her ability to juggle a large and growing family, community service, a working farm, and our joint projects. She is an original and creative thinker with an impressive ability to identify important new directions and insights in marketing.

Stephanie Wall, Editor in Chief at Pearson, and Mark Gaffney, Acquisitions Editor, were quick to endorse and support the Eighth Edition. Becca Groves, Production Project Manager; and Daniel Petrino, Editorial Assistant, kept the revision process on track and on schedule. Michelle Dellinger, Senior Project Manager at Integra, shepherded the manuscript through the final stages of the publication process. We are also grateful for the continuing support at Pearson.

Finally, I wish to thank my wife, Dr. Cynthia MacKay, who is a constant source of inspiration, support, and delight, as well as my companion in global market field research trips (many by motorcycle).

Warren J. Keegan
September 2013

I am indebted to the many colleagues and friends who carefully read and critiqued individual manuscript sections and chapters. Their comments improved the clarity and readability of the text. In particular, I would like to thank James A. Baggett, Hunter Clark, Frank Colella, Dave Collins, Diana Dickinson, Mark Freyberg, Alexandre Gilfanov, Carl Halgren, Kathy Hill, Mark Juffernbruch, David Kochel, Peter Kvetko, Keith Miller, Gayle Moberg, James Palmieri, Alexandre Plokhov, Yao Lu Swanson, Wendy Vasquez, David Wolf, and Thomas Wright.

Many individuals were instrumental in helping us secure permissions, and I want to acknowledge everyone who "went the extra mile" in supporting this revision. I would especially like to thank Bill Becker, John Deere; Veronique Bellett, McArthurGlen; Janon Costley, Total Apparel Group; Kirk Edmondson, Lexus Advanced Business Development; Travis Edmonson, Pollo Campero; Anita Gambill, STIHL USA; Monica Gartner, Bang & Olufsen; Jeffrey Hipps, Theta Digital/ATI; Lou Ireland, DuPont Pioneer; Kim Isele, NAVTEQ; Bob Johnsen, 5B Artist Management; Mary Jubb, Kikkoman; Denise Lavoie, Henkel; Ilana McCabe, QVC Inc.; Daniel McDonnell, Forrester Research; Pat McFadden, Nucor; Brad Miller, New Balance Athletic Shoe, Inc.; Kerry Ann Miller, Subaru of America; Morgan Molinoff, Edelman; Jenni Moyer, Consumer Electronics Association; Kerry Moyer, Consumer Electronics Association; Ciarra O'Sullivan, Global Call to Action Against Poverty; Ramiro Pindeda, Bridgestone Americas Tire Operations, LLC; Lenore Rice, Seibert & Rice; Vivian Santangelo, Meredith Corporation; Mara Seibert, Seibert & Rice; Micaela Shaw, BSH Home Appliances Corporation; Naomi Starkman, Slow Food Nation; Corey Taylor, Slipknot; Kathleen Tepfer, Scottish Development International; and Terri Wilsie, CSX.

Colleagues at several institutions contributed material to this revision. The authors are indebted to Keith Miller, Ellis and Nelle Levitt Distinguished Professor of Law at Drake University Law School, for expanding and revising Case 5-3, "Gambling Goes Global on the Internet." Dominic Standish, a colleague at CIMBA Italy, organized the panel discussion "Death in Venice: Is Tourism Killing or Saving the City?" in fall 2011. That panel, our subsequent discussions, and Dominic's book *Venice in Environmental Peril? Myth and Reality* were key resources for the opening case in Chapter 4. Yao Lu Swanson, my marketing colleague at Simpson, kindly provided expert answers and clarifications in response to my questions about China.

I would also like to thank the many present and former students at Simpson College and the University of Iowa who have offered feedback on previous editions of *Global Marketing,* contributed case studies, and suggested improvements. These include Devin Linn's case on the wine industry in Argentina. Simpson alumna Beth Dorrell graciously offered her expertise on export documentation. Mikkel Jakobsen provided source material on Denmark for "The Cultural Context" sidebar in Chapter 4. Caleb Hegna supplied important data about the white-goods market in Germany. My conversations with Michael Schwoll also helped shaped the text treatment of marketing practices in Germany.

The students in my international marketing course at CIMBA Italy worked collaboratively on the issue of tourism in Venice; Case 4-1 represents, in part, a mashup of the various team efforts. Hats off to Kaleb Beckett, Luci Boat, Leslie Bourland, Lauren Camerieri, Lucas Commodore, Jeff Dellinger, Chris Duncan, Jacque Ford, Brian Fry, Glynis Gallagher, Katie Greif, Kim Halamicek, Harper Hier, Jake Hirsch, Mike Johnson, Sarah Jones, Josh Kroll, Sean Miller, Chris Nucero, Mark Parmalee, Jack Roeder, Chris Shonkwiler, Slava Sinitsyn, and Chloe Suh. All were enthusiastic participants in the project and our work together in Italy made a lasting impression on me. Indeed, the whiteboard that these students filled while reviewing for a midterm exam served as the inspiration and springboard for the cover design of the Eighth Edition.

It was a great pleasure working with the Pearson team that managed the production of this edition. Let me echo Warren's thanks to all members of the Pearson team, and especially to Meeta Pendharkar, our Editorial Project Manager, and Becca Groves, Senior Project Manager.

Stephanie Wall, Editor in Chief, encouraged us to integrate MyMarketingLab into this revision. Mark Gaffney, Acquisitions Editor, Marketing, was instrumental in moving the project along. The production moved along smoothly through the summer of 2013 thanks to Michelle Dellinger, Senior Project Manager at Integra. Kudos also to our photo researcher, Nicole Solano, for demonstrating once again that "every picture tells a story." Nicole also handled permissions research on ads and other content elements. Thanks to the entire Pearson sales team for helping promote the book in the field. I additionally want to acknowledge the contributions of Mahmood Kahn, Virginia Tech, for expertly creating this edition's Test Item File, Kerry Walsh, University of South Florida, for her fine work on the Instructor's Manual and Jill Solomon, University of South Florida, for preparing a new set of PowerPoint slides.

Mark C. Green

September 2013

Pearson would like to thank and acknowledge the following people for their work on the Global Edition:

Contributors

Ali Hallak, Head of Digital Marketing, Samsung Gulf Electronics, UAE; Hamed Shamma, American University in Cairo, Egypt; Ronan Jouan de Kervenoael, Sabanci University, Turkey; Soo Jiuan Tan, National University of Singapore, Singapore; Stefania Paladini, Coventry University, UK; Yosra Sourour, University of Manchester, UK

Reviewers

A. Ercan Gegez, Marmara University, Turkey; Christine Prince, ISG International Business School, France; Norizan Mohd. Kassim, King Abdulaziz University, Saudi Arabia; Shohab Sikandar Desai, American University in the Emirates, UAE

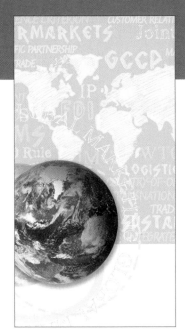

1
Introduction to Global Marketing

CASE 1-1
The Global Marketplace Is Also Local

Consider the following proposition: *We live in a global marketplace.* Apple iPhones, McDonald's restaurants, Samsung HDTVs, LEGO toys, Swatch watches, Burberry trench coats, and Caterpillar earthmoving equipment are found practically everywhere on the planet. Global companies are fierce rivals in key markets. For example, American auto industry giants General Motors and Ford are locked in a competitive struggle with Toyota, Hyundai, and other global Asian rivals as well as European companies such as Volkswagen. U.S.-based Intel, the world's largest chip maker, competes with South Korea's Samsung. In the global cell phone market, Nokia (Finland), Apple (United States), Motorola (United States), and Samsung are key players. Appliances from Whirlpool and Electrolux compete for precious retail space with products manufactured and marketed by Germany's Bosch, China's Haier Group, and South Korea's LG.

Exhibit 1-1 Salvatore Ferragamo, based in Florence, Italy, is one of the world's leading fashion brands. Emerging markets represent important opportunities for luxury goods marketers. As Ferruccio Ferragamo notes, "We cannot make enough to keep up with demand from the Chinese. They want their shoes not just 'Made in Italy' but often 'Made in Florence.'"

To show its support for socially responsible initiatives, Ferragamo recently introduced a new shoe line called Ferragamo WORLD that utilizes eco-friendly production processes. A portion of the proceeds from every pair sold supports Acumen Fund's anti-poverty efforts in East Africa, India, and Pakistan.

Source: Roussel Bernard/Alamy.

Now consider a second proposition: *We live in a world in which markets are local.* In China, for example, Yum! Brands' East Dawning fast-food chain competes with local restaurants such as New Asia Snack and Haidi Lao.[1] France's domestic film industry generates about 40 percent of local motion picture box office receipts; U.S.-made movies account for about 50 percent. In Turkey, local artists such as Sertab account for more than 80 percent of recorded music sales. *Kiki*, a Japanese magazine for teenage girls, competes for newsstand sales with *Vogue Girl*, *Cosmo Girl*, and other titles from Western publishers. In Germany, the children's television powerhouse Nickelodeon competes with local broadcaster Super RTL. In Brazil, many consumers are partial to Guaraná Antarctica and other local soft drink brands made from guaraná, a berry that grows in the Amazon region.

The "global marketplace versus local markets" paradox lies at the heart of this text book. In later chapters, we will investigate the nature of local markets in more detail. For now, however, we will focus on the first part of the paradox. Think for a moment about brands and products that are found throughout the world. Ask the average consumer where this global "horn of plenty" comes from, and you'll likely hear a variety of answers. It's certainly true that some brands—McDonald's, Dos Equis, Swatch, Waterford, Ferragamo, and Burberry, for instance—are strongly identified with a particular country. In much of the world, Coca-Cola and McDonald's are recognized as iconic American brands, just as Ferragamo and Versace are synonymous with classic Italian style (see Exhibit 1-1).

However, for many other products, brands, and companies, the sense of identity with a particular country is becoming blurred.

Which brands are Japanese? American? Korean? German? Indian? Where is Nokia headquartered? When is a German car *not* a German car? Can a car be both German *and* American? Consider:

- An American-built Ford Mustang has 65 percent American and Canadian content; an American-built Toyota Sienna XLE mini-van has 90 percent American and Canadian content.[2]
- China's Shanghai Automotive (SAIC) owns the rights to the MG, the legendary two-seat British sports car. In 2008, SAIC began manufacturing a limited-edition TF model at a plant in Longbridge, UK. In 2011, production of the MG6 sedan began in Birmingham.[3] India's Tata Group recently paid $2.4 billion to acquire Land Rover and Jaguar from Ford.
- German carmaker BMW exports the X5 sport-utility vehicle that it builds in Spartanville, South Carolina, to more than 100 countries.

At the end of this chapter, you will find the rest of Case 1-1. Taken together, the two parts give you the opportunity to learn more about the global marketplace and test your knowledge of current issues in global marketing. You may be surprised at what you learn!

---

[1]Laurie Burkitt, "China Loses Its Taste for Yum," *The Wall Street Journal* (December 3, 2012), p. B9.
[2]Jathon Sapsford and Norihiko Shirouzu, "Mom, Apple Pie and…Toyota?" *The Wall Street Journal* (May 11, 2006), p. B1.
[3]Norihiko Shirouzu, "Homecoming Is Set for MG," *The Wall Street Journal* (March 16, 2011), p. B8.

LEARNING OBJECTIVES

1 Use the product/market growth matrix to explain the various ways a company can expand globally.

2 Describe how companies in global industries pursue competitive advantage.

3 Compare and contrast single-country marketing strategy with global marketing strategy (GMS).

4 Identify the companies at the top of the Global 500 rankings.

5 Explain the stages a company goes through as its management orientation evolves from domestic and ethnocentric to global and geocentric.

6 Discuss the driving and restraining forces affecting global integration today.

Introduction and Overview

As the preceding examples illustrate, the global marketplace finds expression in many ways. Some are quite subtle; others are not. While shopping, you may have noticed more multilanguage labeling on your favorite products and brands. Your local gas station may have changed its name from Getty to Lukoil, reflecting the Russian energy giant's expanding global reach. On the highway, you may have seen a semitrailer truck from FedEx's Global Supply Chain Services fleet. Or perhaps you took advantage of Radiohead's offer to set your own price when you downloaded *In Rainbows* from the Internet. When you pick up a pound of whole-bean Central American coffee at your favorite coffee café, you will find that some beans are labeled Fair Trade Certified. Your toll-free telephone call to a software technical support service or an airline customer service center may be answered in Bangalore or Mumbai. *Slumdog Millionaire*, which received an Oscar in 2009 for Best Picture, was filmed on location in and around Mumbai. You have surely followed media reports about the Occupy Wall Street movement in New York City and related protests in Great Britain, Germany, Greece, and Italy.

The growing importance of global marketing is one aspect of a sweeping transformation that has profoundly affected the people and industries of many nations during the past 160 years. International trade has existed for centuries; beginning in 200 B.C., for example, the legendary Silk Road was a land route connecting China with Mediterranean Europe. From the mid-1800s to the early 1920s, with Great Britain the dominant economic power in the world, international trade flourished. However, a series of global upheavals, including World War I, the Bolshevik Revolution, and the Great Depression, brought that era to an end. Then, following World War II, a new era began. Unparalleled expansion into global markets by companies that previously served only customers located in their respective home countries is one hallmark of this new global era.

Four decades ago, the phrase *global marketing* did not exist. Today, businesspeople use global marketing to realize their companies' full commercial potential. That is why, no matter whether you live in Asia, Europe, North America, or South America, you may be familiar with the brands mentioned in the opening paragraphs. However, there is another, even more critical reason why companies need to take global marketing seriously: survival. A management team that fails to understand the importance of global marketing risks losing its domestic business to competitors with lower costs, more experience, and better products.

But what is global marketing? How does it differ from "regular" marketing as it is typically practiced and taught in an introductory course? **Marketing** can be defined as the activity, set of institutions, and processes for creating, communicating, delivering, and exchanging offerings that have value for customers, clients, partners, and society at large.[5] Marketing activities center on an organization's efforts to satisfy customer wants and needs with products and services that offer competitive value. The **marketing mix** (the four Ps of product, price, place, and promotion) comprises a contemporary marketer's primary tools. Marketing is a universal discipline, as applicable in Argentina as it is in Zimbabwe.

This book is about *global marketing*. An organization that engages in **global marketing** focuses its resources and competencies on global market opportunities and threats. A fundamental difference between regular marketing and global marketing is the scope of activities. A company that engages in global marketing conducts important business activities outside the home-country market. The scope issue can be conceptualized in terms of the familiar product/market matrix of growth strategies (see Table 1-1). Some companies pursue a *market development strategy*; this involves seeking new customers by introducing existing products or services to a new market segment or to a new geographical market. Global marketing can also take the form of a *diversification strategy* in which a company creates new product or service offerings targeting a new segment, a new country, or a new region.

Starbucks provides a good case study of a global marketer that can simultaneously execute all four of the growth strategies shown in Table 1-1:

- **Market penetration:** Starbucks is building on its loyalty card and rewards program in the United States with a smartphone app that enables customers to pay for purchases electronically. The app displays a bar code that the barista can scan.
- **Market development:** Starbucks is entering India via an alliance with the Tata Group. Phase 1 calls for sourcing coffee beans in India and marketing them at Starbucks stores throughout the world. The next phase will likely involve opening Starbucks outlets in Tata's upscale Taj hotels in India.[6]
- **Product development:** Starbucks created a brand of instant coffee, Via, to enable its customers to enjoy coffee at the office and other locations where brewed coffee is not

---

[4]Jin Jing, "Hotpot Chain Haidi Lao Places Emphasis on Very Personal Customer Service," *Shanghai Daily* (August 18, 2011).
[5]American Marketing Association. http://www.marketingpower.com/AboutAMA/ Pages/ DefinitionofMarketing.aspx. Accessed March 1, 2011.
[6]Paul Beckett, "Starbucks Brews Coffee Plan for India," *The Wall Street Journal* (January 14, 2011), p. B8.

TABLE 1-1 Product/Market Growth Matrix

		Product Orientation	
		Existing Products	New Products
Market Orientation	**Existing markets**	1. Market penetration strategy	2. Product development strategy
	New markets	3. Market development strategy	4. Diversification strategy

available. After a successful launch in the United States, Starbucks rolled out Via in Great Britain, Japan, South Korea, and several other Asian countries. Starbucks also recently introduced its first coffee machine. The Versimo allows Starbucks' customers to "prepare their favorite beverages at home."

- **Diversification:** Starbucks has launched several new ventures, including music CDs and movie production. Next up: Revamping stores so they can serve as wine bars and attract new customers in the evening.[7]

To get some practice applying Table 1-1, create a product/market growth matrix for another global company. IKEA, LEGO, and Walt Disney are all good candidates for this type of exercise.

Companies that engage in global marketing frequently encounter unique or unfamiliar features in specific countries or regions of the world. In China, for example, product counterfeiting and piracy are rampant. Companies doing business there must take extra care to protect their intellectual property and deal with "knockoffs." In some regions of the world, bribery and corruption are deeply entrenched. A successful global marketer understands specific concepts and has a broad and deep understanding of the world's varied business environments. He or she also must understand the strategies that, when skillfully implemented in conjunction with universal marketing fundamentals, increase the likelihood of market success. And, as John Quelch and Katherine Jocz assert, "The best global brands are also the best local brands." That is, managers at global companies understand the importance of local excellence.[8] This book concentrates on the major dimensions of global marketing. A brief overview of marketing is presented next, although the authors assume that the reader has completed an introductory marketing course or has equivalent experience.

Principles of Marketing: A Review

As defined in the previous section, marketing is one of the functional areas of a business, distinct from finance and operations. Marketing can also be thought of as a set of activities and processes that, along with product design, manufacturing, and transportation logistics, comprise a firm's **value chain**. Decisions at every stage, from idea conception to support after the sale, should be assessed in terms of their ability to create value for customers.

For any organization operating anywhere in the world, the essence of marketing is to surpass the competition at the task of creating perceived value—that is, a superior value proposition—for customers. The **value equation** is a guide to this task:

$$\text{Value} = \text{Benefits/Price (money, time, effort, etc.)}$$

The marketing mix is integral to the equation because benefits are a combination of the product, the promotion, and the distribution. As a general rule, value, as the customer perceives it, can be increased in these ways. Markets can offer customers an improved bundle of benefits or lower prices (or both!). Marketers may strive to improve the product itself, to design new channels of distribution, to create better communications strategies, or a combination of all three. Marketers may also seek to increase value by finding ways to cut costs and prices. Nonmonetary costs are also a factor, and marketers may be able to decrease the time and effort that customers

---

[7]Bruce Horovitz, "Starbucks Remakes Its Future with an Eye on Wine and Beer," *USA Today* (October 22, 2010), p. 1B.
[8]John Quelch and Katherine Jocz, *All Business Is Local* (New York: Portfolio/Penguin, 2012).

must expend to learn about or seek out the product.[9] Companies that use price as a competitive weapon may scour the globe to ensure an ample supply of low-wage labor or access to cheap raw materials. Companies can also reduce prices if costs are low because of process efficiencies in manufacturing or because of economies of scale associated with high production volumes.

Recall the definition of a market: *people or organizations that are both able and willing to buy.* In order to achieve market success, a product or brand must measure up to a threshold of acceptable quality and be consistent with buyer behavior, expectations, and preferences. If a company is able to offer a combination of superior product, distribution, or promotion benefits *and* lower prices than the competition's, it should enjoy an extremely advantageous position. Toyota, Nissan, and other Japanese automakers made significant gains in the American market in the 1980s by creating a superior value proposition: They offered cars with higher quality, better mileage, and lower prices than those made by General Motors, Ford, and Chrysler. Today, the auto industry is shifting its attention to emerging markets such as India and Africa. Renault and its rivals are racing to offer middle-class consumers a new value proposition: high-quality vehicles that sell for the equivalent of $10,000 or less. On the heels of Renault's success with the Dacia Logan come the $2,500 Nano from India's Tata Motors and a $3,000 Datsun from Nissan (see Case 11-1).

Achieving success in global marketing often requires persistence and patience. Following World War II, some of Japan's initial auto exports were market failures. In the late 1960s, for example, Subaru of America began importing the Subaru 360 automobile and selling it for $1,297. After *Consumer Reports* judged the 360 to be unacceptable, sales ground to a halt. Similarly, the Yugo automobile achieved a modest level of U.S. sales in the 1980s (despite a "don't buy" rating from a consumer magazine) because its sticker price of $3,999 made it the cheapest new car available. Low quality was the primary reason for the market failure of both the Subaru 360 and the Yugo.[10] The Subaru story does have a happy ending, however, due in no small measure to the company's decades-long efforts to improve its vehicles. In fact, in 2012 *Consumer Reports* put Subaru at the top of its quality rankings, surpassing Mazda, Toyota, Honda, and Nissan.[11] History has not been so kind to the Yugo, however; it ended up on *Time* magazine's list of the "50 Worst Cars of All Time."

Even some of the world's biggest, most successful companies stumble while pursuing global opportunities. Walmart's recent exit from the German market was due, in part, to the fact that German shoppers could find lower prices at stores known as "hard discounters." In addition, many German consumers prefer to go to several small shops rather than seek out the convenience of a single, "all-in-one" store located outside a town center. Likewise, United Kingdom (UK)–based Tesco's attempts to enter the U.S. market with its Fresh & Easy stores failed, in part, because U.S. consumers were unfamiliar with the private-label goods that make up much of the merchandise stock (see Case 12-2).

Competitive Advantage, Globalization, and Global Industries

When a company succeeds in creating more value for customers than its competitors do, that company is said to enjoy **competitive advantage** in an industry.[12] Competitive advantage is measured relative to rivals in a given industry. For example, your local laundromat is in a local industry; its competitors are local. In a national industry, competitors are national. In a global industry—consumer electronics, apparel, automobiles, steel, pharmaceuticals, furniture, and dozens of other sectors—the competition is, likewise, global (and, in many industries, local as well). Global marketing is essential if a company competes in a global industry or one that is globalizing.

---

[9]With certain categories of differentiated goods, including designer clothing and other luxury products, higher price is often associated with increased value.

[10]The history of the Subaru 360 is documented in Randall Rothman, *Where the Suckers Moon: The Life and Death of an Advertising Campaign* (New York: Vintage Books, 1994), p. 4.

[11]"Who Makes the Best Cars?" *Consumer Reports* (April 2012), pp. 14–18.

[12]Jay Barney notes that "a firm is said to have a competitive advantage when it is implementing a value-creating strategy not simultaneously being implemented by any current or potential competitors." See Jay Barney, "Firm Resources and Sustained Competitive Advantage," *Journal of Management* 17, no. 1 (1991), p. 102.

The transformation of formerly local or national industries into global ones is part of a broader economic process of *globalization*, which Jagdish Bhagwati defines as follows:

> Economic globalization constitutes integration of national economies into the international economy through trade, direct foreign investment (by corporations and multinationals), short-term capital flows, international flows of workers and humanity generally, and flows of technology.[13]

From a marketing point of view, globalization presents companies with tantalizing opportunities—and challenges—as executives decide whether to offer their products and services everywhere. At the same time, globalization presents companies with unprecedented opportunities to reconfigure themselves; as John Micklethwait and Adrian Wooldridge put it, the same global bazaar that allows consumers to buy the best that the world can offer also allows producers to find the best partners.[14] For example, globalization is presenting significant marketing opportunities for professional sports organizations such as the National Basketball Association, the National Football League, and Major League Soccer (Exhibit 1-2). As Major League Soccer commissioner Don Garber noted, "In the global culture the universal language is soccer. That's the sweet spot. If it weren't for the shrinking world caused by globalization, we wouldn't have the opportunity we have today."[15]

Is there more to a global industry than simply "global competition"? Definitely. As defined by management guru Michael Porter, a **global industry** is one in which competitive advantage can be achieved by integrating and leveraging operations on a worldwide scale. Put another way, an industry is global to the extent that a company's industry position in one country is interdependent with its industry position in other countries. Indicators of globalization include the ratio of cross-border trade to total worldwide production, the ratio of cross-border investment to total capital investment, and the proportion of industry revenue generated by companies that compete in all key world regions.[16] One way to determine the degree of globalization in an industry sector is to calculate the ratio of the annual

Exhibit 1-2 The National Football League (NFL) promotes American football globally. The NFL is focusing on a handful of key markets, including Canada, China, Germany, Japan, Mexico, and the United Kingdom. In fall 2010 guitar legend Jeff Beck performed "God Save the Queen" at Wembley Stadium in London prior to an NFL exhibition game between the San Francisco 49ers and the Denver Broncos. The final score: 49ers 24, Broncos 16.
Sources: Michael Zagaris/Getty Images and James Starling/Alamy.

---

[13]Jagdish Bhagwati, *In Defense of Globalization* (New York: Oxford University Press, 2004), p. 3.
[14]John Micklethwait and Adrian Wooldridge, *A Future Perfect: The Challenge and Hidden Promise of Globalization* (New York: Crown Publishers, 2000), p. xxvii.
[15]Grant Wahl, "Football vs. Fútbol," *Sports Illustrated* (July 5, 2004), pp. 68–72.
[16]Vijay Govindarajan and Anil Gupta, "Setting a Course for the New Global Landscape," *Financial Times—Mastering Global Business*, part I (1998), p. 3.

"We believe a company can only think in one set of terms. If you are premium, you have to focus on it."[18]

—Helmut Panke, former chairman, Bayerische Motoren Werke (BMW) AG

value of global trade in the sector—including the value of components shipped to various countries during the production process—to the annual value of industry sales. In terms of these metrics, the consumer electronics, apparel, automobile, and steel industries are highly globalized.[17]

Achieving competitive advantage in a global industry requires executives and managers to maintain a well-defined strategic focus. **Focus** is simply the concentration of attention on a core business or competence. The importance of focus for a global company is evident in the following comment by Helmut Maucher, former chairman of Nestlé SA:

> Nestlé is focused: We are food and beverages. We are not running bicycle shops. Even in food we are not in all fields. There are certain areas we do not touch. For the time being we have no biscuits [cookies] in Europe and the United States for competitive reasons, and no margarine. We have no soft drinks because I have said we either buy Coca-Cola or we leave it alone. This is focus.[19]

However, company management may choose to initiate a change in focus as part of an overall strategy shift. Even Coca-Cola has been forced to sharpen its focus on its core beverage brands. Following sluggish sales in 2000 and 2001, former chairman and chief executive Douglas Daft formed a new alliance with Nestlé that jointly developed and marketed coffees and teas. Daft also set about the task of transforming Coca-Cola's Minute Maid unit into a global division that markets a variety of juice brands worldwide. As Daft explained:

> We're a network of brands and businesses. You don't just want to be a total beverage company. Each brand has a different return on investment, is sold differently, drunk for different reasons, and has different managing structures. If you mix them all together, you lose the focus.[20]

Examples abound of corporate executives addressing the issue of focus, often in response to changes in the global business environment. In recent years, Bertelsmann, Colgate, Danone, Electrolux, Fiat, Ford, Fortune Brands, General Motors, Harley-Davidson, Henkel, LEGO, McDonald's, Royal Philips Electronics, Toshiba, and many other companies have stepped up efforts to sharpen their strategic focus on core businesses and brands. Specific actions can take a number of different forms besides alliances, including mergers, acquisitions, divestitures, and folding some businesses into other company divisions.[21]

Value, competitive advantage, and the focus required to achieve them are universal in their relevance, and they should guide marketing efforts in any part of the world. Global marketing requires attention to these issues on a worldwide basis and utilization of a business intelligence system capable of monitoring the globe for opportunities and threats. A fundamental premise of this book can be stated as follows: Companies that understand and engage in global marketing can offer more overall value to customers than companies that do not have that understanding. There are many who share this conviction. In the mid-1990s, for example, C. Samuel Craig and Susan P. Douglas noted:

> Globalization is no longer an abstraction but a stark reality.... Choosing not to participate in global markets is no longer an option. All firms, regardless of their size, have to craft strategies in the broader context of world markets to anticipate, respond, and adapt to the changing configuration of these markets.[22]

---

[17]Diana Farrell, "Assessing Your Company's Global Potential," *Harvard Business Review* 82, no. 12 (December 2004), p. 85.

[18]Scott Miller, "BMW Bucks Diversification to Focus on Luxury Models," *The Wall Street Journal* (March 20, 2002), p. B4.

[19]Elizabeth Ashcroft, "Nestlé and the Twenty-First Century," Harvard Business School Case 9-595-074, 1995. See also Ernest Beck, "Nestlé Feels Little Pressure to Make Big Acquisitions," *The Wall Street Journal* (June 22, 2000), p. B4.

[20]Betsy McKay, "Coke's 'Think Local' Strategy Has Yet to Prove Itself," *The Wall Street Journal* (March 1, 2001), p. B6.

[21]Robert A. Guth, "How Japan's Toshiba Got Its Focus Back," *The Wall Street Journal* (December 12, 2000), p. A6.

[22]C. Samuel Craig and Susan P. Douglas, "Responding to the Challenges of Global Markets: Change, Complexity, Competition, and Conscience," *Columbia Journal of World Business* 31, no. 4 (Winter 1996), pp. 6–18.

Evidence is mounting that companies in a range of industries are getting the message. For example, three Italian furniture companies have joined together to increase sales outside of Italy and ward off increased competition from Asia. Luxury goods purveyors such as LVMH and Prada Group provided the model for the new business entity, which unites Poltrona Frau, Cassina, and Cappellini.[23] Hong Kong's Tai Ping Carpets International is also globalizing. Top managers have been dispersed to different parts of the world; while the finance and technology functions are still in Hong Kong, the marketing chief is based in New York City and the head of operations is in Singapore. As company director John Ying noted, "We're trying to create a minimultinational."[24]

Global Marketing: What It Is and What It Isn't

The discipline of marketing is universal. It is natural, however, that marketing practices will vary from country to country for the simple reason that the countries and peoples of the world are different. These differences mean that a marketing approach that has proven successful in one country will not *necessarily* succeed in another country. Customer preferences, competitors, channels of distribution, and communication media may differ. An important managerial task in global marketing is learning to recognize the extent to which it is possible to extend marketing plans and programs worldwide, as well as the extent to which adaptation is required.

The way a company addresses this task is a reflection of its **global marketing strategy (GMS)**. In single-country marketing, strategy development addresses two fundamental issues: choosing a target market and developing a marketing mix. The same two issues are at the heart of a firm's GMS, although they are viewed from a somewhat different perspective (see Table 1-2). *Global market participation* is the extent to which a company has operations in major world markets. *Standardization versus adaptation* is the extent to which each marketing mix element is standardized (i.e., executed the same way) or adapted (i.e., executed in different ways) in various country markets. For example, Nike recently adopted the slogan "Here I am" for its pan-European clothing advertising targeting women. The decision to drop the famous "Just do it" tagline in the region was based on research indicating that college-age women in Europe are not as competitive about sports as men are.[25]

GMS has three additional dimensions that pertain to marketing management. First, *concentration of marketing activities* is the extent to which activities related to the marketing mix (e.g., promotional campaigns or pricing decisions) are performed in one or a few country locations. *Coordination of marketing activities* refers to the extent to which marketing activities

TABLE 1-2 Comparison of Single-Country Marketing Strategy and Global Marketing Strategy (GMS)

Single-Country Marketing Strategy	Global Marketing Strategy
Target market strategy	Global market participation
Marketing mix development	Marketing mix development
Product	Product adaptation or standardization
Price	Price adaptation or standardization
Promotion	Promotion adaptation or standardization
Place	Place adaptation or standardization
	Concentration of marketing activities
	Coordination of marketing activities
	Integration of competitive moves

[23]Gabriel Kahn, "Three Italian Furniture Makers Hope to Create a Global Luxury Powerhouse," *The Wall Street Journal* (October 31, 2006), p. B1.

[24]Phred Dvorak, "Big Changes Drive Small Carpet Firm," *The Wall Street Journal* (October 30, 2006), p. B3.

[25]Aaron O. Patrick, "Softer Nike Pitch Woos Europe's Women," *The Wall Street Journal* (September 11, 2008), p. B6.

→ **THE CULTURAL CONTEXT**

50th Anniversary of Great Britain's Greatest Cultural Export

SYNC • THINK • LEARN

MyMarketingLab

How did rock and roll start? In the 1950s, American artists such as Buddy Holly, Elvis Presley, Chuck Berry, and Ray Charles began pushing the boundaries of popular music. However, it was four young men from Liverpool, England, who perfected the form and, starting in the early 1960s, brought new momentum to the music scene. As MTV Networks executive Bill Flanagan puts it, the result of John Lennon, Paul McCartney, George Harrison, and Ringo Starr playing together was "the greatest sound music has ever produced."

In the 1960s, England's exports to the world included the Beatles as well as music by other "British Invasion" bands such as the Animals, the Kinks, and the Rolling Stones. Whether you view the breakthrough year as 1962 (first Beatles single released in the United Kingdom), 1963 (the Beatles top the charts in the United Kingdom), or 1964 (America succumbs to Beatlemania after the band appears on *The Ed Sullivan Show*), it is safe to say that the Fab Four have reached their golden anniversary.

At home, Beatles records were released by Parlophone, a record label owned by Electrical and Musical Industries Ltd. EMI, as the parent company is known, also owned the famous Abbey Roads studios where the Beatles recorded with producer George Martin. Internationally, Beatles records were released under licensing agreements with various other companies on a country-by-country basis. Although EMI had acquired Los Angeles–based Capitol Records in the 1950s, company executives passed on the opportunity to release Beatles records in the United States. And so, the first few Beatles singles and one LP, "Introducing the Beatles," were released by Vee-Jay Records. As the group's popularity surged, however, Capitol Records obtained the rights to subsequent Beatles singles and LPs. The rest, as they say, is history (see Exhibit 1-3).

From a global marketing perspective, the history of the Beatles' records is an interesting case study in both product adaptation and product extension. Although many people don't realize it, the early albums released in the United Kingdom differed from releases in the United States and other countries. EMI sent master tapes to various countries, often customizing them at the request of the local company. At home, for example, the first Beatles LP was titled "Please Please Me," not "Introducing the Beatles." Capitol Records' first Beatles LP, "Meet the Beatles," was released in January 1964. However, it was actually the Beatles' *second* UK long player (the original title was "With the Beatles").

In addition, U.S. album releases by the Fab Four had fewer tracks than the UK releases, had different track sequences, and also included singles and B-sides that were generally not found on the British LPs. In France, the preferred format was known as "extended play" (EP), generally with two songs on each side.

There were other differences as well. In an effort to "Americanize" the sound of the Beatles' recordings, a studio effect known as reverb was added to some tracks. Reverb makes a "dry" (unprocessed) sound "wetter" by adding an echo-like effect. Another studio tool, compression, was used to add sizzle to high-end sounds such as the cymbals on Ringo Starr's drum kit. In addition, some of the original mono and stereo tracks were remixed for the American market.

Sources: George Martin, *All You Need Is Ears* (New York: St. Martin's Press, 1979); special thanks to Douglas Hinman, Piers Hemmingsen, and James McVeety for additional research.

Exhibit 1-3 It has been 50 years since four lads from Liverpool, England—Ringo Starr, Paul McCartney, George Harrison, and John Lennon—burst onto the global music scene and left an indelible mark on global culture. Ringo and Paul, the two surviving members of the band, continue to record and tour as solo artists. Who was *your* favorite Beatle?

Source: Popperfoto / Getty Images.

related to the marketing mix are planned and executed interdependently around the globe. Finally, *integration of competitive moves* is the extent to which a firm's competitive marketing tactics in different parts of the world are interdependent. The GMS should enhance the firm's performance on a worldwide basis.[26]

The decision to enter one or more particular markets outside the home country depends on a company's resources, its managerial mind-set, and the nature of opportunities and threats. Today, most observers agree that Brazil, Russia, India, China, and South Africa—five emerging markets known collectively as BRICS—represent significant growth opportunities. Mexico, Indonesia, Nigeria, and Turkey—the so-called MINTs—also hold great potential. Throughout this text, marketing issues in these countries are highlighted in "Emerging Markets Briefing Book" boxes.

We can use Burberry as a case study in global marketing strategy. The UK-based luxury brand is available in scores of countries, and Burberry's current expansion plans emphasize several geographical areas (Exhibit 1-4). First are the BRICS nations, where growing numbers of middle-class consumers are developing a taste for luxury brands. Second is the United States, dotted with shopping malls whose managers are anxious to entice crowd-pulling luxury goods retailers by sharing fit-out costs and offering attractive, rent-free periods. Burberry's marketing mix strategy includes the following:

- **Product:** Boost sales of handbags, belts, and accessories—products whose sales are less cyclical than clothing's.
- **Price:** More expensive than Coach, less expensive than Prada. "Affordable luxury" is central to the value proposition.
- **Place:** Burberry intends to open more independent stores in key cities including New York, London, and Hong Kong. Such locations generate more than half the company's revenue and profit.[27]
- **Promotion:** Roll out a new logo to reduce "plaid overexposure." Use social media such as Twitter and www.artofthetrench.com. Launch Burberry Acoustic, a project to provide exposure for emerging music talent via http://live.burberry.com.

Exhibit 1-4 England's Burberry Group celebrated its 150th anniversary in 2006. Burberry's trademark is registered in more than 90 countries. The company's signature plaid pattern—often referred to as "the check"—is incorporated into a wide range of apparel items and accessories. The Burberry brand is enjoying renewed popularity throughout the world; sales in Asia are particularly strong. New CEO Angela Ahrendts wants to broaden the brand's appeal. To do this, she intends to introduce two new logos: an equestrian knight and the cursive signature of company founder Thomas Burberry.
Source: Oli Scarff/Getty Images.

---

[26]Shaoming Zou and S. Tamer Cavusgil, "The GMS: A Broad Conceptualization of Global Marketing Strategy and Its Effect on Performance," *Journal of Marketing* 66, no. 4 (October 2002), pp. 40–56.
[27]Paul Sonne and Kathy Gordon, "Burberry Refocusing on World's Big Cities," *The Wall Street Journal* (November 8, 2012), p. B9.

As you can see in Table 1-2, the next part of the GMS involves the concentration and coordination of marketing activities. At Burberry, haphazard growth had led to a federation of individual operations. Company units in some parts of the world didn't talk to each other. In some cases they competed *against* each other, and sometimes designed their own products for their own markets and wouldn't share ideas with other parts of the business. To address this issue, CEO Angela Ahrendts has been very clear that she wants to *leverage* the Burberry franchise. Her mantra is: One company, one brand. Ahrendts faces other challenges as well. She must maintain momentum in the face of difficult economic conditions worldwide and avoid diluting the brand while ramping up expansion.

The issue of standardization versus adaptation in global marketing has been at the center of a long-standing controversy among both academicians and business practitioners. Much of the controversy dates back to Professor Theodore Levitt's 1983 article "The Globalization of Markets" in the *Harvard Business Review*. Levitt argued that marketers were confronted with a "homogeneous global village." He advised organizations to develop standardized, high-quality world products and market them around the globe by using standardized advertising, pricing, and distribution. Some well-publicized failures by Parker Pen and other companies that had tried to follow Levitt's advice brought his proposals into question. The business press frequently quoted industry observers who disputed Levitt's views. As Carl Spielvogel, chairman and CEO of the Backer Spielvogel Bates Worldwide advertising agency, told *The Wall Street Journal* in the late 1980s, "Theodore Levitt's comment about the world becoming homogenized is bunk. There are about two products that lend themselves to global marketing—and one of them is Coca-Cola."[28]

Global marketing is the key to Coke's worldwide success. However, that success was *not* based on a total standardization of marketing mix elements. For example, Coca-Cola achieved success in Japan by spending a great deal of time and money to become an insider; that is, the company built a complete local infrastructure with its sales force and vending machine operations. Coke's success in Japan is a function of its ability to achieve global localization, by being as much of an insider as a local company but still reaping the benefits that result from world-scale operations. Although the Coca-Cola Company has experienced a recent sales decline in Japan, it remains a key market that accounts for about 20 percent of total worldwide operating revenues.[29]

What does the phrase *global localization* really mean? In a nutshell, it means that a successful global marketer must have the ability to "think globally and act locally." Kenichi Ohmae summed up this paradox as follows:

> The essence of being a global company is to maintain a kind of tension within the organization without being undone by it. Some companies say the new world requires homogeneous products—"one size fits all"—everywhere. Others say the world requires endless customization—special products for every region. The best global companies understand it's neither and it's both. They keep the two perspectives in mind simultaneously.[30]

As we will see many times in this book, *global* marketing may include a combination of standard (e.g., the actual product itself) and nonstandard (e.g., distribution or packaging) approaches. A global product may be the same product everywhere and yet different. Global marketing requires marketers to think and act in a way that is both global *and* local by responding to similarities and differences in world markets.

But it is important to bear in mind that "global localization" is a two-way street, and that there is more to the story than "think globally, act locally." Many companies are learning that it is equally important to *think locally and act globally.* In practice, this means that companies are discovering the value of leveraging innovations that occur far from headquarters and transporting them back home. For example, McDonald's restaurants in France don't look like McDonald's restaurants elsewhere. Décor colors are muted, and the golden arches are displayed more subtly. After seeing the sales increases posted in France, some American franchisees began undertaking similar renovations. As *Burger Business* newsletter editor Scott Hume has noted, "Most of the

[28]Joanne Lipman, "Ad Fad: Marketers Turn Sour on Global Sales Pitch Harvard Guru Makes," *The Wall Street Journal* (May 12, 1988), p. 1.
[29]Chad Terhune, "Coke Tries to Pop Back in Vital Japan Market," *The Wall Street Journal* (July 11, 2006), pp. C1, C3.
[30]William C. Taylor and Alan M. Webber, *Going Global: Four Entrepreneurs Map the New World Marketplace* (New York: Penguin Books USA, 1996), pp. 48, 49.

TABLE 1-3 Think Locally/Act Globally

Company/Headquarters Country	Product
Cinnabon/USA	Cinnabon customers in Central and South America prefer dulce de leche. Products developed for those regions are being introduced in the United States, where the Hispanic population is a key segment.[31]
Starbucks/USA	Starbucks opened an experimental store in Amsterdam that serves as a testing ground for new design concepts such as locally sourced and recycled building materials. The best concepts will be extended to other parts of Europe. *Fast Company* magazine included Liz Muller, Director of Creative Design at Starbucks, in its "Most Creative People 2013" ranking.
Kraft Foods/USA	Tang drink powder became a $1 billion brand as regional managers in Latin America and the Middle East moved beyond orange (the top-seller) into popular local flavors such as mango and pineapple. Kraft plans to reboot Tang in the U.S. market using lessons learned abroad.[32]

interesting ideas of McDonald's are coming from *outside* the U.S. McDonald's is becoming a European chain with stores in the U.S."[33] (see Case 1-2).

These reverse flows of innovation are not occurring just between developed regions such as Western Europe and North America. The growing economic power of China, India, and other emerging markets means that many innovations originate there (see Table 1-3). For example, Nestlé, Procter & Gamble, Unilever, and other consumer products companies are learning that low-cost products with less packaging developed for low-income consumers also appeal to cost-conscious consumers in, say, Spain and Greece (see Exhibit 1-5).[34]

Exhibit 1-5 For Nestlé, innovation is the key to an expanded presence in emerging markets such as Thailand, Sri Lanka, and Mali. The consumer-goods giant is headquartered in Switzerland, but one-third of its research and development centers are located in emerging markets. Recently, Nestlé introduced mobile coffee carts from which vendors sell single servings of Nescafé brand coffee. In a textbook example of "Think locally, act globally," some of these innovations are being transferred to high-income countries in Europe and elsewhere.
Source: adrian arbib/Alamy.

[31]Leslie Kwoh, "Cinnabon Finds Sweet Success in Russia, Mideast," *The Wall Street Journal* (December 26, 2012), p. B5.
[32]E. J. Schultz, "To the Moon and Back: How Tang Grew to Be a Billion-Dollar Global Brand," *Advertising Age* (June 16, 2011).
[33]Greg Farrell, "McDonald's Relies on Europe for Growth," *Financial Times* (April 20, 2010).
[34]Louise Lucas, "New Accent on Consumer Tastes," *Financial Times* (December 14, 2010), p. 14.

The Coca-Cola Company supports its Coke, Fanta, and Powerade brands with marketing mix elements that are both global and local. Dozens of other companies also have successfully pursued global marketing by creating strong global brands. This has been accomplished in various ways. In consumer electronics, Apple is synonymous with hardware and software integration, ease of use, cutting-edge innovation, and high-tech design. In appliances, Germany's reputation for engineering and manufacturing excellence is a source of competitive advantage for Bosch (see Exhibit 1-6). Italy's Benetton utilizes a sophisticated distribution system to quickly deliver the latest fashions to its worldwide network of stores. The backbone of Caterpillar's global success is a network of dealers who support a promise of "24-hour parts and service" anywhere in the world. As these examples indicate, there are many different paths to success in global markets. In this book, we do *not* propose that global marketing is a knee-jerk attempt to impose a totally standardized approach on marketing around the world. A

Exhibit 1-6 Bosch, Germany's largest privately held industrial group, celebrated its 125th anniversary in 2011. Bosch competes in a variety of sectors including automotive and industrial technology and consumer products. The company uses the slogan "Invented for life" in its advertising and has more than 350 subsidiaries and a market presence in more than 150 countries.
Source: Courtesy of BSH Home Appliance Corporation.

The quietest dishwasher, even with a jam-packed upper deck.

The quietest dishwasher brand[1] in the U.S. introduces a new third rack for more capacity and flexibility.

Invented to change the game. Leave it to Bosch to figure out a way to make a good thing better. Our third rack[2] adds up to 30% more loading area[3], to fit more steak knives, more burger spatulas, more bbq tongs, more silverware. And we accomplished all this while still delivering German-engineered machines as quiet as 39 dBA[4]. They're dishwashers that are rewriting the rules. They're dishwashers invented for your life. See yours at your nearest Bosch retailer. www.bosch-home.com/us

BOSCH
Invented for life

© 2013 BSH Home Appliances. [1]Based on an average of sound ratings on major brands' websites. Major brands defined as Traqline Top 10 Brands, December 2012. [2]500 series and up models only. [3]Compared to a Bosch dishwasher with two racks. [4]Model SH_9PT57UC/XXX. Ask your Bosch dealer for details, or visit bosch-home.com/us

TABLE 1-4 Examples of Effective Global Marketing—McDonald's

Marketing Mix Element	Standardized	Localized
Product	Big Mac	McAloo Tikka potato burger (India)
Promotion	Brand name	Slang nicknames, for example, Mickey D's (USA, Canada), Macky D's (UK, Ireland), Macca's (Australia), Mäkkäri (Finland), MakDo (Philippines), McDo (France)
	Advertising slogan "i'm lovin' it"	*"Venez comme vous êtes"* ("Come as you are") television ad campaign in France. Various executions show individuals expressing different aspects of their respective personalities. One features a young man dining with his father. The ad's creative strategy centers on sexual freedom and rebellion: The father does not realize that his son is gay.
Place	Free-standing restaurants in high-traffic public areas	McDonald's Switzerland operates themed dining cars on the Swiss national rail system; McDonald's is served on the Stena Line ferry from Helsinki to Oslo; home delivery (India)
Price	Average price of Big Mac is $4.20 (United States)	$6.79 (Norway); $2.44 (China)

central issue in global marketing is how to tailor the global marketing concept to fit particular products, businesses, and markets.[35]

As shown in Table 1-4, McDonald's global marketing strategy is based on a combination of global and local marketing mix elements. For example, a vital element in McDonald's business model is a restaurant system that can be set up virtually anywhere in the world. McDonald's offers core menu items—hamburgers, French fries, and soft drinks—in most countries, and the company also customizes menu offerings in accordance with local eating customs. The average price of a Big Mac in the United States is $4.20. By contrast, in China Big Macs sell for the equivalent of $2.44. In absolute terms, Chinese Big Macs are cheaper than American ones. But is it a fair comparison? Real estate costs vary from country to country, as do per capita incomes.

The particular approach to global marketing that a company adopts will depend on industry conditions and its source or sources of competitive advantage. For example:

- Harley-Davidson's motorcycles are perceived around the world as *the* all-American bike. Should Harley-Davidson start manufacturing motorcycles in a low-wage country such as Mexico?
- The success of Honda and Toyota in world markets was initially based on exporting cars from factories in Japan. Today, both companies operate manufacturing and assembly facilities in the Americas, Asia, and Europe. From these sites, the automakers supply customers in the local market and also export to the rest of the world. For example, each year Honda exports tens of thousands of Accords and Civics from U.S. plants to Japan and dozens of other countries. Will European consumers continue to buy Honda vehicles exported from America? Will American consumers continue to snap up American-built Toyotas?
- Uniqlo, a division of Japan's Fast Retailing, operates about 850 stores in Japan and 300 stores in 12 overseas countries. The company sources 90 percent of its clothing from China. Uniqlo currently has 6 stores in the United States; plans call for a total of 200 U.S. stores by 2020. Can the company achieve its goal of reaching $50 billion in sales by 2020, thus becoming the world's number 1 apparel retailer?

[35]John A. Quelch and Edward J. Hoff, "Customizing Global Marketing," *Harvard Business Review* 64, no. 3 (May–June 1986), p. 59.

Exhibit 1-7 Japan's Fast Retailing competes with global companies such as Inditex (Spain), H&M (Sweden), and GAP (United States). By aggressively pursuing overseas expansion for the Uniqlo chain of shops, Fast Retailing founder Tadashi Yanai intends to create the world's biggest apparel retail operation by 2020. Even as the company expands globally, management must ensure that it remains profitable in Japan.

The answer to these questions is: It all depends. Because Harley-Davidson's competitive advantage is based, in part, on its "Made in the USA" positioning, shifting production outside the United States is not advisable. The company has opened a new production facility in Kansas, and ceased production of Buell Motorcycles. It also sold MV Augusta, an Italian motorcycle manufacturer that it had acquired in 2008.

Toyota's success in the United States was originally attributable to its ability to transfer world-class manufacturing skills—"the Toyota Way"—to America while using advertising to inform prospective customers that American workers build the Avalon, Camry, and Tundra models, with many components purchased from American suppliers. The U.S. market generates approximately two-thirds of Toyota's profits. However, in its drive to become the world's top automaker, Toyota's insular corporate culture and focus on cost cutting compromised overall product quality. The big question facing Toyota today is whether its reputation and sales will fully recover following much-publicized problems such as sudden acceleration that resulted in embarrassing product recalls.

As noted, about one-quarter of Uniqlo's 1,200 stores are located outside Japan; key country markets include the United States, China, Russia, Singapore, and South Korea. Shoppers have responded favorably to Uniqlo's colorful designs and the high service standards for which Japanese retailers are famous. According to A. T. Kearney's 2011 Global Retail Development Index for Apparel, China is the number 1–ranked emerging market opportunity for apparel. In China, Uniqlo's management team selectively targets cities with high population densities such as Beijing and Shanghai (see Exhibit 1-7).[36]

The Importance of Global Marketing

The largest single market in the world in terms of national income is the United States, representing roughly 25 percent of the total world market for all products and services. U.S. companies that wish to achieve maximum growth potential must "go global," because 75 percent of world market potential is outside their home country. Management at Coca-Cola clearly understands this; about 75 percent of the company's operating income and two-thirds of its operating revenue

[36]Mayumi Negishi, Dana Mattioli, and Ryan Dezember, "Japan's Uniqlo Sets Goal: No. 1 in the U.S.," *The Wall Street Journal* (April 12, 2013), p. B7. See also Hiroyuki Kachi and Kenneth Maxwell, "Uniqlo Woos the World but Falters at Home," *The Wall Street Journal* (October 12, 2012), p. B8.

are generated outside North America. Non-U.S. companies have an even greater motivation to seek market opportunities beyond their own borders; their opportunities include the 300 million people in the United States. For example, even though the dollar value of the home market for Japanese companies is the third largest in the world (after the United States and China), the market *outside* Japan is 90 percent of the world potential for Japanese companies. For European countries, the picture is even more dramatic. Even though Germany is the largest single-country market in Europe, 94 percent of the world market potential for German companies is outside Germany.

Many companies have recognized the importance of conducting business activities outside their home country. Industries that were essentially national in scope only a few years ago are dominated today by a handful of global companies. In most industries, the companies that will survive and prosper in the twenty-first century will be global enterprises. Some companies that fail to formulate adequate responses to the challenges and opportunities of globalization will be absorbed by more dynamic, visionary enterprises. Others will undergo wrenching transformations and, if their efforts succeed, will emerge from the process greatly transformed. Some companies will simply disappear.

Each year, *Fortune* magazine compiles a ranking of the 500 largest service and manufacturing companies by revenues.[37] Royal Dutch Shell stands atop the 2012 Global 500 rankings, with revenues of $484 billion. In all, 8 companies in the top 10 compete in the oil or energy sectors. Walmart, the world's biggest retailer, occupies the number 3 position; it currently generates only about one-third of its revenues outside the United States. However, global expansion is key to the company's growth strategy. Toyota, the only global automaker and the only other nonenergy company in the top 10, has faced unprecedented challenges over the past few years, including quality-control issues that forced it to recall millions of vehicles.

Examining the size of individual product markets, measured in terms of annual sales, provides another perspective on global marketing's importance. Many of the companies identified in the *Fortune* rankings are key players in the global marketplace. Annual sales in select global industry sector markets are shown in Table 1-5.

TABLE 1-5 How Big Is the Market? Consumer Products

Product or Service	Size of Market	Key Players and Brands
Cigarettes	$295 billion	Philip Morris International (USA); British American Tobacco (UK); Japan Tobacco (Japan)
Luxury goods	$230 billion	LVMH Group (France); Richemont (Switzerland); Kering (France)
Cosmetics	$200 billion	L'Oréal SA (France); Estée Lauder (USA); Shiseido (Japan); Procter & Gamble (USA)
Personal computers	$175 billion	Hewlett-Packard (USA); Lenovo (China); Dell (USA); Acer (Taiwan)
Flat-screen TVs	$100 billion	Samsung (South Korea); Sony (Japan); LG (South Korea)
Bottled water	$100 billion	Nestlé (Switzerland); Groupe Danone (France); Coca-Cola (USA); PepsiCo (USA)
Home appliances	$85 billion	Whirlpool (USA); Electrolux (Sweden); Bosch-Siemens (Germany)
Cell phones	$60 billion	Nokia (Finland); Motorola (USA); Apple (USA); Samsung (South Korea)
Video games	$43 billion	Nintendo (Japan); Sony (Japan); Microsoft (USA)
Recorded music	$32 billion	Sony BMG (Japan); Warner Music Group (USA); Universal Music Group (France)

Source: Compiled by the authors.

---

[37]The complete list can be found online at: http://money.cnn.com/magazines/fortune/global500/2012/full_list

Management Orientations

The form and substance of a company's response to global market opportunities depend greatly on management's assumptions or beliefs—both conscious and unconscious—about the nature of the world. The worldview of a company's personnel can be described as ethnocentric, polycentric, regiocentric, or geocentric.[38] Management at a company with a prevailing ethnocentric orientation may consciously make a decision to move in the direction of geocentricism. The orientations are collectively known as the EPRG framework.

Ethnocentric Orientation

A person who assumes that his or her home country is superior to the rest of the world is said to have an **ethnocentric orientation**. Ethnocentrism is sometimes associated with attitudes of national arrogance or assumptions of national superiority; it can also manifest itself as indifference to marketing opportunities outside the home country. Company personnel with an ethnocentric orientation see only similarities in markets and *assume* that products and practices that succeed in the home country will succeed anywhere. At some companies, the ethnocentric orientation means that opportunities outside the home country are largely ignored. Such companies are sometimes called *domestic companies*. Ethnocentric companies that conduct business outside the home country can be described as *international companies*; they adhere to the notion that the products that succeed in the home country are superior. This point of view leads to a **standardized** or **extension approach** to marketing based on the premise that products can be sold everywhere without adaptation.

As the following examples illustrate, an ethnocentric orientation can take a variety of forms:

- Nissan's earliest exports were cars and trucks that had been designed for mild Japanese winters; the vehicles were difficult to start in many parts of the United States during the cold winter months. In northern Japan, many car owners would put blankets over the hoods of their cars. Nissan's assumption was that Americans would do the same thing. As a Nissan spokesman said, "We tried for a long time to design cars in Japan and shove them down the American consumer's throat. That didn't work very well."[39]
- Until the 1980s, Eli Lilly and Company operated as an ethnocentric company: Activity outside the United States was tightly controlled by headquarters, and the focus was on selling products originally developed for the U.S. market.[40]
- For many years, executives at California's Robert Mondavi Corporation operated the company as an ethnocentric international entity. As former CEO Michael Mondavi explained, "Robert Mondavi was a local winery that thought locally, grew locally, produced locally, and sold globally.... To be a truly global company, I believe it's imperative to grow and produce great wines in the world in the best wine-growing regions of the world, regardless of the country or the borders." [41]
- The cell phone divisions of Toshiba, Sharp, and other Japanese companies prospered by focusing on the domestic market. When handset sales in Japan slowed a few years ago, the Japanese companies realized that Nokia, Motorola, and Samsung already dominated key world markets. Atsutoshi Nishida, president of Toshiba, noted, "We were thinking only about Japan. We really missed our chance."[42]

In the ethnocentric international company, foreign operations or markets are typically viewed as being secondary or subordinate to domestic ones. (We are using the term *domestic* to mean the country in which a company is headquartered.) An ethnocentric company operates

---

[38]Adapted from Howard Perlmutter, "The Tortuous Evolution of the Multinational Corporation," *Columbia Journal of World Business* (January–February 1969).
[39]Norihiko Shirouzu, "Tailoring World's Cars to U.S. Tastes," *The Wall Street Journal* (January 1, 2001), pp. B1, B6.
[40]T. W. Malnight, "Globalization of an Ethnocentric Firm: An Evolutionary Perspective," *Strategic Management Journal* 16, no. 2 (February 1995), p. 125.
[41]Robert Mondavi, *Harvests of Joy: My Passion for Excellence* (New York: Harcourt Brace & Company, 1998), p. 333.
[42]Martin Fackler, "A Second Chance for Japanese Cell Phone Makers," *The New York Times* (November 17, 2005), p. C1.

under the assumption that headquarters' "tried-and-true" knowledge and organizational capabilities can be applied in other parts of the world. Although this assumption can sometimes work to a company's advantage, valuable managerial knowledge and experience in local markets may go unnoticed. Even if customer needs or wants differ from those in the home country, those differences are ignored at headquarters.

Sixty years ago, most business enterprises—and especially those located in a large country like the United States—could operate quite successfully with an ethnocentric orientation. Today, however, ethnocentrism is one of the major internal weaknesses that must be overcome if a company is to transform itself into an effective global competitor.

Polycentric Orientation

The **polycentric orientation** is the opposite of ethnocentrism. The term *polycentric* describes management's belief or assumption that each country in which a company does business is unique. This assumption lays the groundwork for each subsidiary to develop its own unique business and marketing strategies in order to succeed; the term *multinational company* is often used to describe such a structure. This point of view leads to a **localized** or **adaptation approach** that assumes that products must be adapted in response to different market conditions. Examples of companies with a polycentric orientation include the following:

- Until the mid-1990s, Citicorp operated on a polycentric basis. James Bailey, a former Citicorp executive, explains, "We were like a medieval state. There was the king and his court and they were in charge, right? No. It was the land barons who were in charge. The king and his court might declare this or that, but the land barons went and did their thing."[44] Realizing that the financial services industry was globalizing, then-CEO John Reed attempted to achieve a higher degree of integration between Citicorp's operating units.

- Unilever, the Anglo-Dutch consumer products company, once exhibited a polycentric orientation. For example, its Rexona deodorant brand had 30 different package designs and 48 different formulations. Advertising was also executed on a local basis. Top management has spent the last decade changing Unilever's strategic orientation by implementing a reorganization plan that centralizes authority and reduces the power of local country managers.[45]

Regiocentric Orientation

In a company with a **regiocentric orientation**, a region becomes the relevant geographic unit; management's goal is to develop an integrated regional strategy. What does *regional* mean in this context? A U.S. company that focuses on the countries included in the North American Free Trade Agreement (NAFTA)—namely, the United States, Canada, and Mexico—has a regiocentric orientation. Similarly, a European company that focuses its attention on Europe is regiocentric. Some companies serve markets throughout the world, but do so on a regional basis. Such a company could be viewed as a variant of the multinational model discussed previously. For decades, a regiocentric orientation prevailed at General Motors: Executives in different parts of the world—Asia-Pacific and Europe, for example—were given considerable autonomy when designing vehicles for their respective regions. Company engineers in Australia, for example, developed models for sale in the local market. One result of this approach: A total of 270 different types of radios were being installed in GM vehicles around the world. As GM Vice Chairman Robert Lutz told an interviewer in 2004, "GM's global product plan used to be four regional plans stapled together."[46]

> "What unites us through our brands, markets, and businesses is the group's identity, which we refer to as 'a worldwide business with local presence.' Everywhere we operate, our priority is to create or develop a strong brand that reflects consumer needs in that market as closely as possible."[43]
>
> Franck Riboud, Chairman and CEO of Groupe Danone

[43]Franck Riboud, "Think Global, Act Local," *Outlook* no. 3 (2003), p. 8.
[44]Saul Hansell, "Uniting the Feudal Lords at Citicorp," *The New York Times* (January 16, 1994), Sec. 3, p. 1.
[45]Deborah Ball, "Too Many Cooks: Despite Revamp, Unwieldy Unilever Falls Behind Rivals," *The Wall Street Journal* (January 3, 2005), pp. A1, A5.
[46]Lee Hawkins, Jr., "New Driver: Reversing 80 Years of History, GM Is Reining in Global Fiefs," *The Wall Street Journal* (October 6, 2004), pp. A1, A14.

"These days everyone in the Midwest is begging Honda to come into their hometown. It is no longer viewed as a 'Japanese' company, but a 'pro-American-worker corporation' flush with jobs, jobs, jobs."[48]

Douglas Brinkley, Professor of History, Tulane University

Geocentric Orientation

A company with a **geocentric orientation** views the entire world as a potential market and strives to develop integrated global strategies. A company whose management has adopted a geocentric orientation is sometimes known as a *global* or *transnational company*.[47] During the past several years, long-standing regiocentric policies at GM, such as those just discussed, have been replaced by a geocentric approach. Among other changes, the new policy calls for engineering jobs to be assigned on a worldwide basis, with a global council based in Detroit determining the allocation of the company's $7 billion annual product development budget. One goal of the geocentric approach: Save 40 percent in radio costs by using a total of 50 different radios.

It is a positive sign that, at many companies, management realizes the need to adopt a geocentric orientation. However, the transition to new structures and organizational forms can take time to bear fruit. As new global competitors emerge on the scene, management at long-established industry giants such as GM must face up to the challenge of organizational transformation. More than a decade ago, Louis R. Hughes, a GM executive, said, "We are on our way to becoming a transnational corporation." Basil Drossos, former president of GM de Argentina, echoed his colleague's words, noting, "We are talking about becoming a global corporation as opposed to a multinational company; that implies that the centers of expertise may reside anywhere they best reside."[49] For the moment, GM is still the world's number 1 automaker in terms of revenue. In 2008, Toyota sold more vehicles worldwide than GM for the first time. As GM emerged from bankruptcy in 2009, it did so as a smaller, leaner company.

A global company can be further described as one that either pursues a strategy of serving world markets from a single country, or sources globally for the purposes of focusing on select country markets. In addition, global companies tend to retain their association with a particular headquarters country. Harley-Davidson serves world markets from the United States exclusively. Similarly, all the production for luxury goods marketer Tod's takes place in Italy. By contrast, Uniqlo sources its apparel from low-wage countries; a sophisticated supply chain ensures timely delivery to its network of stores. Benetton pursues a mixed approach, sourcing some of its apparel from Italy and some from low-wage countries. Harley-Davidson, Tod's, Uniqlo, and Benetton may all be thought of as global companies.

Transnational companies serve global markets and use global supply chains, which often results in a blurring of national identity. A true transnational would be characterized as "stateless." Toyota and Honda are two examples of companies that exhibit key characteristics of transnationality. At global and transnational companies, management uses a combination of standardized (extension) and localized (adaptation) elements in the marketing program. A key factor that distinguishes global and transnational companies from international or multinational companies is *mind-set*: At global and transnational companies, decisions regarding extension and adaptation are not based on assumptions. Rather, such decisions are made on the basis of ongoing research into market needs and wants.

One way to assess a company's "degree of transnationality" is to compute an average of three ratios: (1) sales outside the home country to total sales, (2) assets outside the home country to total assets, and (3) employees outside the home country to total employees. Viewed in terms of these metrics, Nestlé, Unilever, Royal Philips Electronics, GlaxoSmithKline, and the News Corporation can also be categorized as transnational companies. Each is headquartered in a relatively small home-country market, a fact of life that has compelled management to adopt regiocentric or geocentric orientations to achieve revenue and profit growth.

---

[47]Although the definitions provided here are important, to avoid confusion we will use the term *global marketing* when describing the general activities of global companies. Another note of caution is in order: Usage of the terms *international*, *multinational*, and *global* varies widely. Alert readers of the business press are likely to recognize inconsistencies; usage does not always reflect the definitions provided here. In particular, companies that are (in the view of the authors as well as numerous other academics) global are often described as *multinational enterprises* (abbreviated MNEs) or *multinational corporations* (abbreviated MNCs). The United Nations prefers the term *transnational company* rather than *global company*. When we refer to an "international company" or a "multinational," we will do so in a way that maintains the distinctions described in the text.

[48]Douglas Brinkley, "Hoosier Honda," *The Wall Street Journal* (July 18, 2006), p. A14.

[49]Rebecca Blumenstein, "Global Strategy: GM Is Building Plants in Developing Nations to Woo New Markets," *The Wall Street Journal* (August 4, 1997), p. A4.

INNOVATION, ENTREPRENEURSHIP, AND THE GLOBAL STARTUP

Kevin Plank, Under Armour

Kevin Plank is an entrepreneur. He developed an innovative product, created a brand, and started a company to manufacture and market it. By applying the basic tools and principles of modern marketing, Plank achieved remarkable success. As is true with many entrepreneurs, Plank's idea was based on his own needs and wants. As a football player at the University of Maryland, Plank was dissatisfied with the traditional cotton T-shirts he wore during practice. Convinced that "there had to be something better," Plank's insight was to adapt the type of synthetic material used to make women's lingerie—typically a polyester/Lycra blend—for a new purpose: athletic performance. The lightweight fabric holds its shape, wicks moisture away from the body, dries quickly, and offers a snug, glove-like fit.

During his senior year, Plank bought a bolt of material and hired a tailor to sew some T-shirts. He then gave them away to teammates at Maryland and to friends who had joined the NFL. After graduation in 1996, Plank set up shop in a townhouse his family owned in Georgetown. After giving away several hundred shirts to equipment managers at various universities, Plank booked his first order: Georgia Tech bought 200 shirts for $12 each. Less than 20 years later, Plank's company is on track to reach $2.0 billion in sales.

Under Armour is a contender in the $37 billion sports apparel industry that is dominated by industry titans Nike and Adidas. Moreover, Plank's company is the dominant player in the specialty category known as compression wear. As the owner of a rival manufacturer notes admiringly, "Whether product innovation, packaging, or 'right-time, right-place,' or all of the above, they basically were able to light the fuse." Or, as another industry observer puts it, "They saw something no one else saw and built a business around it." In Plank's own words, "All we're trying to do is change the way people think about fitness."

Evidence of the company's ongoing commitment to innovation can be seen in recent product introductions. For example, Spine is a lightweight running shoe that was launched in 2012. Nike dominates the running-shoe market; to jump-start Under Armour's shoe business, Plank hired Gene McCarthy as senior vice president of footwear and Dave Dombrow as creative director. Both McCarthy and Dombrow came from Nike. Spine is designed to work like, well, the human spine: It can be rigid or flexible depending on the wearer's needs. Also on tap is the E39 shirt, with sensors that monitor the wearer's heart rate, breathing, and other key performance measures. The UA Highlight is a football cleat that eliminates the need to tape a player's ankles. And, for college students who shun raincoats and umbrellas while walking around campus in bad weather, there is the Storm Cotton waterproof sweatshirt line.

Plank is unwavering in his strategic intention of building Under Armour into "the biggest brand in the land!" To do this, he must expand his company's global presence. In 2012, only 6 percent of Under Armour's revenues were generated outside North America. By contrast, 60 percent of Nike's business is international; for Germany-based Adidas, 60 percent of sales come from outside Europe. Some industry observers think Under Armour is planning significant global product introductions timed to coincide with the 2016 Summer Olympic Games in Brazil.

Sources: John Kell, "Under Armour Arrives on Global Stage," *The Wall Street Journal* (June 3, 2013), p. B2; Bruce Horovitz, "Under Armour Races to Discover Innovative Fitness Gear," *USA Today* (July 6, 2012), pp. 1B, 2B.

Exhibit 1-8 Innovation and global expansion are central to Under Armour founder Kevin Plank's strategic vision for increasing annual sales from $2 billion to $3 billion. In pursuit of the "third billion," Under Armour's product development teams are working on water-repelling sweatshirts and fitness gear that monitors heart rate and other athletic performance data.
Source: Washington Post / Getty Images.

The geocentric orientation represents a synthesis of ethnocentrism and polycentrism; it is a "worldview" that sees similarities and differences in markets and countries and seeks to create a global strategy that is fully responsive to local needs and wants. A regiocentric manager might be said to have a worldview on a regional scale; the world outside the region of interest will be viewed with an ethnocentric or a polycentric orientation, or a combination of the two. However, research suggests that many companies are seeking to strengthen their regional competitiveness rather than move directly to develop global responses to changes in the competitive environment.[50]

The ethnocentric company is centralized in its marketing management; the polycentric company is decentralized; and the regiocentric and geocentric companies are integrated on a regional and global scale, respectively. A crucial difference among the orientations is the underlying assumption for each. The ethnocentric orientation is based on a belief in home-country superiority. The underlying assumption of the polycentric approach is that there are so many differences in cultural, economic, and marketing conditions in the world that it is futile to attempt to transfer experience across national boundaries. A key challenge facing organizational leaders today is managing a company's evolution beyond an ethnocentric, polycentric, or regiocentric orientation to a geocentric one. As noted in one highly regarded book on global business, "The multinational solution encounters problems by ignoring a number of organizational impediments to the implementation of a global strategy and underestimating the impact of global competition."[51]

Forces Affecting Global Integration and Global Marketing

The remarkable growth of the global economy over the past 65 years has been shaped by the dynamic interplay of various driving and restraining forces. During most of those decades, companies from different parts of the world in different industries achieved great success by pursuing international, multinational, or global strategies. During the 1990s, changes in the business environment presented a number of challenges to established ways of doing business. Today, despite calls for protectionism as a response to the economic crisis, global marketing continues to grow in importance. This is due to the fact that, even today, driving forces have more momentum than restraining forces. The forces affecting global integration are shown in Figure 1-1.

Regional economic agreements, converging market needs and wants, technology advances, pressure to cut costs, pressure to improve quality, improvements in communication and transportation technology, global economic growth, and opportunities for leverage all represent important driving forces; any industry subject to these forces is a candidate for globalization.

Multilateral Trade Agreements

A number of multilateral trade agreements have accelerated the pace of global integration. NAFTA is expanding trade among the United States, Canada, and Mexico. The General Agreement on Tariffs and Trade (GATT), which was ratified by more than 120 nations in 1994,

FIGURE 1-1

Driving and Restraining Forces Affecting Global Integration

[50]Allan J. Morrison, David A. Ricks, and Kendall Roth, "Globalization Versus Regionalization: Which Way for the Multinational?" *Organizational Dynamics* (Winter 1991), p. 18.

[51]Michael A. Yoshino and U. Srinivasa Rangan, *Strategic Alliances: An Entrepreneurial Approach to Globalization* (Boston: Harvard Business School Press, 1995), p. 64.

created the World Trade Organization (WTO) to promote and protect free trade. In Europe, the expanding membership of the European Union is lowering boundaries to trade within the region. The creation of a single currency zone and the introduction of the euro have led to increased intra-European trade in the twenty-first century.

Converging Market Needs and Wants and the Information Revolution

A person studying markets around the world will discover cultural universals as well as differences. The common elements in human nature provide an underlying basis for the opportunity to create and serve global markets. The word *create* is deliberate. Most global markets do not exist in nature; marketing efforts must create them. For example, no one *needs* soft drinks, and yet today in some countries, per capita soft drink consumption *exceeds* water consumption. Marketing has driven this change in behavior, and today the soft drink industry is a truly global one. Evidence is mounting that consumer needs and wants around the world are converging today as never before. This creates an opportunity for global marketing. Multinational companies pursuing strategies of product adaptation run the risk of failing to be successful against global competitors that have recognized opportunities to serve global customers.

The information revolution—what some refer to as the "democratization of information"—is one reason for the trend toward convergence. The revolution is fueled by a variety of technologies, products, and services, including satellite dishes; globe-spanning TV networks such as CNN and MTV; widespread access to broadband Internet; and Facebook, Twitter, YouTube, and other social media. Taken together, these communication tools mean that people in the remotest corners of the globe can compare their own lifestyles and standards of living with those of people in other countries. In regional markets such as Europe and Asia, the increasing overlap of advertising across national boundaries and the mobility of consumers have created opportunities for marketers to pursue pan-regional product positioning. The Internet is an even stronger driving force: When a company establishes a site on the Internet, the company automatically becomes global. In addition, the Internet allows people everywhere in the world to reach out, buying and selling a virtually unlimited assortment of products and services.

Transportation and Communication Improvements

The time and cost barriers associated with distance have fallen tremendously over the past 100 years. The jet airplane revolutionized communication by making it possible for people to travel around the world in less than 48 hours. Tourism enables people from many countries to see and experience the newest products sold abroad. In 1970, 75 million passengers traveled internationally; according to figures compiled by the International Air Transport Association, that figure increased to nearly 980 million passengers in 2011. One essential characteristic of the effective global business is face-to-face communication among employees and between a company and its customers. Modern jet travel made such communication feasible. Today's information technology allows airline alliance partners such as United and Lufthansa to sell seats on each other's flights, thereby making it easier for travelers to get from point to point. Meanwhile, the cost of international data, voice, and video communication has fallen dramatically over the past several decades. Today, Skype, Google+, and Cisco Telepresence are powerful new communication channels. They are the latest in a series of innovations—including fax, e-mail, video teleconferencing, Wi-Fi, and broadband Internet—that enable managers, executives, and customers to link up electronically from virtually any part of the world without traveling at all.

A similar revolution has occurred in transportation technology. The costs associated with physical distribution, in terms of both money and time, have been greatly reduced as well. The per-unit cost of shipping automobiles from Japan and Korea to the United States by specially designed auto-transport ships is less than the cost of overland shipping from Detroit to either U.S. coast. Another key innovation has been the increased utilization of 20- and 40-foot metal containers that can be transferred from trucks to railroad cars to ships.

Product Development Costs

The pressure for globalization is intense when new products require major investments and long periods of development time. The pharmaceutical industry provides a striking illustration of this

TABLE 1-6 World Pharmaceutical Market by Region

	2011	2007–2011	2012–2016
	Market Size (US$ billions)	*CAGR %	Forecast CAGR %
North America	$347.1	3.5%	1–4%
Europe	265.4	4.9	0–3
Asia/Africa/Australia	165.2	15.5	10–13
Japan	111.2	3.9	1–4
Latin America	66.7	12.3	10–13
Total world	995.5	6.1	3–6

*Compound annual growth rate
Source: Based on IMS Health Market Prognosis. Courtesy of IMS Health.

driving force. According to the Pharmaceutical Research and Manufacturers Association, the cost of developing a new drug in 1976 was $54 million. Today, the process of developing a new drug and securing regulatory approval to market it can take 14 years, and the average total cost of bringing a new drug to market is estimated to exceed $400 million.[52] Such costs must be recovered in the global marketplace, because no single national market is likely to be large enough to support investments of this size. Thus, Pfizer, Merck, GlaxoSmithKline, Novartis, Bristol-Myers Squibb, Sanofi-Aventis, and other leading pharmaceutical companies have little choice but to engage in global marketing. As noted earlier, however, global marketing does not necessarily mean operating everywhere; in the pharmaceutical industry, for example, seven countries account for 75 percent of sales. As shown in Table 1-6, demand for pharmaceuticals in Asia is expected to exhibit double-digit growth in the next few years. In an effort to tap that opportunity and to reduce development costs, Novartis and its rivals are establishing research and development (R&D) centers in China.[53]

Quality

Global marketing strategies can generate greater revenue and greater operating margins that, in turn, support design and manufacturing quality. A global and a domestic company may each spend 5 percent of sales on R&D, but the global company may have many times the total revenue of the domestic company because it serves the world market. It is easy to understand how John Deere, Nissan, Matsushita, Caterpillar, and other global companies have achieved world-class quality (see Exhibit 1-9). Global companies "raise the bar" for all competitors in an industry. When a global company establishes a benchmark in quality, competitors must quickly make their own improvements and come up to par. For example, the U.S. auto manufacturers have seen their market share erode over the past four decades as Japanese manufacturers built reputations for quality and durability. Despite making great strides in quality, Detroit now faces a new threat: Sales, revenues, and profits have plunged in the wake of the economic crisis. Even before the crisis, the Japanese had invested heavily in hybrid vehicles that are increasingly popular with eco-conscious drivers. The runaway success of the Toyota Prius is a case in point.

World Economic Trends

Prior to the global economic crisis that began in 2008, economic growth had been a driving force in the expansion of the international economy and in the growth of global marketing for three reasons. First, economic growth in key developing countries creates market opportunities that provide a major incentive for companies to expand globally. Thanks to rising per capita incomes

---

[52]Joseph A. DiMasi, Ronald W. Hansen, and Henry G. Grabowski, "The Price of Innovation: New Estimates of Drug Development Costs," *Journal of Health Economics* 22, no. 2 (March 2003), p. 151.
[53]Nicholas Zamiska, "Novartis to Establish Drug R&D Center in China," *The Wall Street Journal* (November 11, 2006), p. A3.

您需要更多的投资回报

现在就购买约翰迪尔5000系列拖拉机吧!

JOHN DEERE

JohnDeere.com.cn

Exhibit 1-9 With annual sales of $26 billion, Moline, Illinois–based Deere & Company is the world's leading manufacturer of farm equipment. The company also produces equipment for the construction, forestry, and lawn care industries. Deere has benefited from booming worldwide demand for agricultural commodities; demand for tractors has been especially strong in Brazil, China, India, and other emerging markets.
Source: Courtesy of John Deere.

in India, China, and elsewhere, the growing ranks of middle-class consumers have more money to spend than in the past. At the same time, slow growth in industrialized countries has compelled management to look abroad for opportunities in nations or regions with high rates of growth.

Second, economic growth has reduced resistance that might otherwise have developed in response to the entry of foreign firms into domestic economies. When a country such as China is experiencing rapid economic growth, policymakers are likely to look more favorably on outsiders. A growing country means growing markets; there is often plenty of opportunity for everyone. It is thus possible for a "foreign" company to enter a domestic economy and establish itself without threatening the existence of local firms. The latter can ultimately be strengthened by the new competitive environment. Without economic growth, however, global enterprises may take business away from domestic ones. Domestic businesses are more likely to seek governmental intervention to protect their local positions if markets are not growing. Predictably, the recent economic crisis creates new pressure on policymakers in emerging markets to protect domestic markets.

The worldwide movement toward free markets, deregulation, and privatization is a third driving force. The trend toward privatization is opening up formerly closed markets; tremendous opportunities are being created as a result. In their book, Daniel Yergin and Joseph Stanislaw described these trends as follows:

> It is the greatest sale in the history of the world. Governments are getting out of businesses by disposing of what amounts to trillions of dollars of assets. Everything is going—from steel plants and phone companies and electric utilities to airlines and railroads to hotels, restaurants, and nightclubs. It is happening not only in the former Soviet Union, Eastern Europe, and China but also in Western Europe, Asia, Latin America, and Africa—and in the United States.[54]

For example, when a nation's telephone company is a state monopoly, the government can require it to buy equipment and services from national companies. An independent company that needs to maximize shareholder value has the freedom to seek vendors that offer the best overall value proposition, regardless of nationality. Privatization of telephone systems around the world created significant opportunities for telecommunications equipment suppliers such as Sweden's

---

[54]Daniel Yergin and Joseph Stanislaw, *The Commanding Heights* (New York: Simon & Schuster, 1998), p. 13.

Ericsson; Alcatel-Lucent, a Franco-American company; and Canada-based Nortel Networks. After years of growth, however, most telecom suppliers experienced slower growth as customers cut spending in the face of the global recession. In 2009, Nortel Networks filed for bankruptcy; it auctioned thousands of patents to an alliance of companies including Apple and Microsoft.

Leverage

> "If we were going to be world-class, we needed to pull together and leverage our global assets around the world to create a powerhouse 'One Ford.' It's exactly why we are here."[55]
>
> —Alan Mulally, CEO, Ford Motor Company

A global company possesses the unique opportunity to develop leverage. In the context of global marketing, **leverage** means some type of advantage that a company enjoys by virtue of the fact that it has experience in more than one country. Leverage allows a company to conserve resources when pursuing opportunities in new geographical markets. In other words, leverage enables a company to expend less time, less effort, and/or less money. Four important types of leverage are experience transfers, scale economies, resource utilization, and global strategy.

EXPERIENCE TRANSFERS A global company can leverage its experience in any market in the world. It can draw upon management practices, strategies, products, advertising appeals, or sales or promotional ideas that have been market tested in one country or region and apply them in other comparable markets. For example, Whirlpool has considerable experience in the United States dealing with powerful retail buyers such as Sears and Best Buy. The majority of European appliance retailers have plans to establish their own cross-border "power" retailing systems; as former Whirlpool CEO David Whitwam explained, "When power retailers take hold in Europe, we will be ready for it. The skills we've developed here are directly transferable."[56]

Chevron is another example of a global company that gains leverage through experience transfers. As H. F. Iskander, general manager of Chevron's Kuwait office, explains:

> Chevron is pumping oil in different locations all over the world. There is no problem we have not confronted and solved somewhere. There isn't a rock we haven't drilled through. We centralize all that knowledge at our headquarters, analyze it, sort it out, and that enables us to solve any oil-drilling problem anywhere. As a developing country you may have a national oil company that has been pumping your own oil for 20 years. But we tell them, "Look, you have 20 years of experience, but there's no diversity. It is just one year of knowledge 20 times over." When you are operating in a multitude of countries, like Chevron, you see a multitude of different problems and you have to come up with a multitude of solutions. You have to, or you won't be in business. All those solutions are then stored in Chevron's corporate memory. The key to our business now is to tap that memory, and bring out the solution that we used to solve a problem in Nigeria in order to solve the same problem in China or Kuwait.[57]

SCALE ECONOMIES The global company can take advantage of its greater manufacturing volume to obtain traditional scale advantages within a single factory. Also, finished products can be manufactured by combining components manufactured in scale-efficient plants in different countries. Japan's giant Matsushita Electric Company is a classic example of global marketing in action; it achieved scale economies by exporting VCRs, televisions, and other consumer electronics products throughout the world from world-scale factories in Japan. The importance of manufacturing scale has diminished somewhat as companies implement flexible manufacturing techniques and invest in factories outside the home country. However, scale economies were a cornerstone of Japanese success in the 1970s and 1980s.

Leverage from scale economies is not limited to manufacturing. Just as a domestic company can achieve economies in staffing by eliminating duplicate positions after an acquisition, a global company can achieve the same economies on a global scale by centralizing functional activities. The larger scale of the global company also creates opportunities to improve corporate staff competence and quality.

[55]Bill Vlasic, "Ford's Bet: It's A Small World After All," *The New York Times* (January 9, 2010), p. B1.
[56]William C. Taylor and Alan M. Webber, *Going Global: Four Entrepreneurs Map the New World Marketplace* (New York: Penguin USA, 1996), p. 18.
[57]Thomas L. Friedman, *The Lexus and the Olive Tree* (New York: Anchor Books, 2000), pp. 221–222.

RESOURCE UTILIZATION A major strength of the global company is its ability to scan the entire world to identify people, money, and raw materials that will enable it to compete most effectively in world markets. For a global company, it is not problematic if the value of the "home" currency rises or falls dramatically, because there really is no such thing as a home currency. The world is full of currencies, and a global company seeks financial resources on the best available terms. In turn, it uses them where there is the greatest opportunity to serve a need at a profit.

GLOBAL STRATEGY The global company's greatest single advantage can be its global strategy. A global strategy is built on an information system that scans the world business environment to identify opportunities, trends, threats, and resources. When opportunities are identified, the global company adheres to the three principles identified earlier: It leverages its skills and focuses its resources to create superior perceived value for customers and achieve competitive advantage. *The global strategy is a design to create a winning offering on a global scale.* This takes great discipline, much creativity, and constant effort. The reward is not just success, it's survival. For example, French automaker Renault operated for many years as a regional company. During that time, its primary struggle was a two-way race with Peugeot Citroën for dominance in the French auto industry. However, in an industry dominated by Toyota and other global competitors, Chairman Louis Schweitzer had no choice but to formulate a global strategy. Initiatives include acquiring a majority stake in Nissan Motor and Romania's Dacia. Schweitzer has also invested $1 billion in a plant in Brazil and is spending hundreds of millions of dollars in South Korea.[58]

A note of caution is in order: A global strategy is no guarantee of ongoing organizational success. Companies that cannot formulate or successfully implement a coherent global strategy may lose their independence. InBev's acquisition of Anheuser-Busch at the end of 2008 is a case in point. Some globalization strategies do not yield the expected results, as seen in the unraveling of the DaimlerChrysler merger and the failure of Deutsche Post's DHL unit to penetrate the U.S. domestic package delivery market.

The severe downturn in the business environment in the early years of the twenty-first century wreaked havoc with strategic plans. This proved true for established global firms as well as newcomers from emerging markets that had only recently come to prominence on the world stage. For example, at Swiss-based ABB, Mexico's Cemex, and UK supermarket chain Tesco, the ambitious global visions of the respective chief executives were undermined by expensive strategic bets that did not pay off.[59] Although all three companies survived, they are smaller, more focused entities than they had been previously.

Restraining Forces

Despite the impact of the driving forces identified previously, several restraining forces may slow a company's efforts to engage in global marketing. In addition to the market differences discussed earlier, important restraining forces include management myopia, organizational culture, national controls, and opposition to globalization. As we have noted, however, in today's world the driving forces predominate over the restraining forces. That is why the importance of global marketing is steadily growing.

MANAGEMENT MYOPIA AND ORGANIZATIONAL CULTURE In many cases, management simply ignores opportunities to pursue global marketing. A company that is "nearsighted" and ethnocentric will not expand geographically. Anheuser-Busch, the brewer of Budweiser beer, lost its independence after years of focusing primarily on the domestic U.S. market. Myopia is also a recipe for market disaster if headquarters attempts to dictate when it should listen. Global marketing does not work without a strong local team that can provide information about local market conditions.

In companies where subsidiary management "knows it all," there is no room for vision from the top. In companies where headquarters management is all-knowing, there is no room for local initiative or an in-depth knowledge of local needs and conditions. Executives and managers at

---

[58]John Tagliabue, "Renault Pins Its Survival on a Global Gamble," *The New York Times* (July 2, 2000), Section 3, pp. 1, 6; Don Kirk and Peter S. Green, "Renault Rolls the Dice on Two Auto Projects Abroad," *The New York Times* (August 29, 2002), pp. W1, W7.

[59]Joel Millman, "The Fallen: Lorenzo Zambrano; Hard Times for Cement Man," *The Wall Street Journal* (December 11, 2008), p. A1.

successful global companies have learned how to integrate global vision and perspective with local market initiative and input. A striking theme emerged during interviews conducted by one of the authors with executives of successful global companies. That theme was respect for local initiative and input by headquarters executives, and the corresponding respect for headquarters' vision by local executives.

NATIONAL CONTROLS Every country protects the commercial interests of local enterprises by maintaining control over market access and entry into both low- and high-tech industries. Such control ranges from a monopoly controlling access to tobacco markets to national government control of broadcast, equipment, and data transmission markets. Today, tariff barriers have been largely removed in high-income countries, thanks to the WTO, GATT, NAFTA, and other economic agreements. However, **nontariff barriers (NTBs)** are still very much in evidence. NTBs are nonmonetary restrictions on cross-border trade, such as the proposed "Buy American" provision in Washington's economic stimulus package, food safety rules, and other bureaucratic obstacles. NTBs have the potential to make it difficult for companies to gain access to some individual country and regional markets.

OPPOSITION TO GLOBALIZATION To many people around the world, globalization and global marketing represent a threat. The term *globaphobia* is sometimes used to describe an attitude of hostility toward trade agreements, global brands, or company policies that appear to result in hardship for some individuals or countries while benefiting others. Globaphobia manifests itself in various ways, including protests or violence directed at policymakers or well-known global companies (see Exhibit 1-10). Opponents of globalization include labor unions, college and university students, national and international nongovernmental organizations (NGOs), and others. *Shock Doctrine* author Naomi Klein has been an especially outspoken critic of globalization.

In the United States, some people believe that globalization has depressed the wages of American workers and resulted in the loss of both blue- and white-collar jobs. Protectionist sentiment has increased in the wake of the recent economic crisis. In many developing countries, there is a growing suspicion that the world's advanced countries—starting with the United States—are reaping most of the rewards of free trade. As an unemployed miner in Bolivia put it, "Globalization is just another name for submission and domination. We've had to live with that here for 500 years and now we want to be our own masters."[60]

Exhibit 1-10 American fashion icon Ralph Lauren created the official uniforms that Team USA wore at the opening and closing ceremonies of the 2012 Olympics in China. Controversy erupted after it was revealed that the uniforms—navy blazers, white trousers and skirts, and berets—were "Made in China" rather than in the United States. Critics linked the outsourcing story to the broader issue of the loss of manufacturing jobs in America.

In response, a Ralph Lauren spokesperson released a statement pledging that the 2014 Olympics uniforms will be "Made in the USA." Still, some observers believe that America's competitive advantage lies in innovation, design, and marketing rather than low-wage manufacturing. According to this view, America's economy actually benefits from outsourcing. What do you think?

Source: ASSOCIATED PRESS.

---

[60]Larry Rohter, "Bolivia's Poor Proclaim Abiding Distrust of Globalization," *The New York Times* (October 17, 2003), p. A3.

Outline of This Book

This book has been written for students and businesspeople interested in global marketing. Throughout the book, we present and discuss important concepts and tools specifically applicable to global marketing.

The book is divided into five parts. Part 1 consists of Chapter 1, an overview of global marketing and the basic theory of global marketing. Chapters 2 through 5 comprise Part 2, in which we cover the environments of global marketing. Chapters 2 and 3 examine economic and regional market characteristics, including the locations of income and population, patterns of trade and investment, and stages of market development. In Chapter 4, we examine social and cultural elements, and in Chapter 5 we present the legal, political, and regulatory dimensions. We devote Part 3 to topics that must be considered when approaching global markets. We cover marketing information systems and research in Chapter 6. Chapter 7 discusses market segmentation, targeting, and positioning. Chapter 8 surveys the basics of importing, exporting, and sourcing. We devote Chapter 9 to various aspects of global strategy, including strategy alternatives for market entry and expansion. We devote Part 4 to the global context of marketing mix decisions. Guidelines for making product, price, channel, and marketing communications decisions in response to global market opportunities and threats are presented in detail in Chapters 10 through 14. Chapter 15 explores the ways that the Internet, e-commerce, and other aspects of the digital revolution are creating new opportunities and challenges for global marketers. The two chapters in Part 5 address issues of corporate strategy and leadership, in the twenty-first century. Chapter 16 includes an overview of strategy and competitive advantage. Chapter 17 addresses some of the leadership challenges facing the chief executives of global companies. In addition, the chapter examines the organization and control of global marketing programs as well as the issue of corporate social responsibility.

Summary

Marketing is an organizational function and a set of processes for creating, communicating, and delivering value to customers and for managing customer relationships in ways that benefit the organization and its stakeholders. A company that engages in **global marketing** focuses its resources on global market opportunities and threats. Successful global marketers such as Nestlé, Coca-Cola, and Honda use familiar **marketing mix** elements—the four Ps—to create global marketing programs. Marketing, R&D, manufacturing, and other activities comprise a firm's **value chain**; firms configure these activities to create superior customer value on a global basis. The **value equation** ($V = B/P$) expresses the relationship between value and the marketing mix.

Global companies also maintain strategic **focus** while relentlessly pursuing **competitive advantage**. The marketing mix, value chain, competitive advantage, and focus are universal in their applicability, irrespective of whether a company does business only in the home country or has a presence in many markets around the world. However, in a **global industry**, companies that fail to pursue global opportunities risk being pushed aside by stronger global competitors.

A firm's **global marketing strategy (GMS)** can enhance its worldwide performance. The GMS addresses several issues. First is the nature of the marketing program in terms of the balance between a **standardized (extension) approach** to the marketing mix elements and a **localized (adaptation) approach** that is responsive to country or regional differences. Second is the *concentration of marketing activities* in a few countries or the dispersal of such activities across many countries. Companies that engage in global marketing can also engage in *coordination of marketing activities*. Finally, a firm's GMS addresses the issue of *global market participation*.

The importance of global marketing today can be seen in the company rankings compiled by *The Wall Street Journal*, *Fortune*, the *Financial Times*, and other publications. Whether ranked by revenues or some other measure, most of the world's major corporations are active regionally or globally. The size of global markets for individual industries or product categories helps explain why companies "go global." Global markets for some product categories represent hundreds of billions of dollars in annual sales; other markets are much smaller. Whatever the size of the opportunity, successful industry competitors find that increasing revenues and profits means seeking markets outside the home country.

Company management can be classified in terms of its orientation toward the world: **ethnocentric**, **polycentric**, **regiocentric**, or **geocentric**. The terms reflect progressive levels of development or evolution. An ethnocentric orientation characterizes *domestic* and *international companies*; international companies pursue marketing opportunities outside the home market by extending various elements of the marketing mix. A polycentric worldview predominates at a *multinational company*, where country managers operating autonomously adapt the marketing mix. When management moves to integrate and coordinate activities on a regional basis, the decision reflects a regiocentric orientation. Managers at *global* and *transnational companies* are geocentric in their orientation and pursue both extension and adaptation strategies in global markets.

The dynamic interplay of several driving and restraining forces shapes the importance of global marketing. Driving forces include market needs and wants, technology, transportation and communication improvements, product costs, quality, world economic trends, and a recognition of opportunities to develop **leverage** by operating globally. Restraining forces include market differences, management myopia, organizational culture, and national controls such as **nontariff barriers (NTBs)**.

MyMarketingLab

Go to **mymktlab.com** for the following Assisted-graded writing questions:

1-1. Discuss the differences between the global marketing strategies of Harley-Davidson and Toyota.

1-2. UK-based Burberry is a luxury fashion brand that appeals to both genders and to all ages. To improve Burberry's competitiveness in the luxury goods market, CEO Angela Ahrendts recently unveiled a new strategy that includes all the elements of the marketing mix. The strategy also addresses key markets that Burberry will participate in, as well as the integration and coordination of marketing activities. Search for recent articles about Burberry and discuss Burberry's GMS.

1-3. Mymarketinglab Only – comprehensive writing assignment for this chapter.

MyMarketingLab

Go to **mymktlab.com** to complete the problems marked with this icon .

Discussion Questions

1-4. What are the basic goals of marketing? Are these goals relevant to global marketing?

1-5. What is meant by "global localization"? Is Coca-Cola a global product? Explain.

1-6. A company's global marketing strategy (GMS) is a crucial competitive tool. Discuss some of the global marketing strategies available to companies. Give examples of companies that use the different strategies.

1-7. UK-based Burberry is a luxury fashion brand that appeals to both genders and to all ages. To improve Burberry's competitiveness in the luxury goods market, CEO Angela Ahrendts recently unveiled a new strategy that includes all the elements of the marketing mix. The strategy also addresses key markets that Burberry will participate in, as well as the integration and coordination of marketing activities. Search for recent articles about Burberry and discuss Burberry's GMS.

1-8. Discuss the differences between the global marketing strategies of Harley-Davidson and Toyota.

⭐ **1-9.** Describe the differences among ethnocentric, polycentric, regiocentric, and geocentric management orientations.

1-10. Identify and briefly describe some of the forces that have resulted in increased global integration and the growing importance of global marketing.

1-11. Define *leverage* and explain the different types of leverage available to companies with global operations.

1-12. Each July, *Fortune* publishes its Global 500 listing of the world's largest companies. You can find the current rankings online at: http://money.cnn.com/magazines/fortune /global500/2012/full_list/. Alternatively, you can consult the print edition of *Fortune*. Browse through the list and choose any company that interests you. Compare its 2012 ranking with the most recent ranking. Has the company's ranking changed? Consult additional sources (e.g., magazine articles, annual reports, the company's Web site) to get a better understanding of the factors and forces that contributed to the company's move up or down in the rankings. Write a brief summary of your findings.

⭐ **1-13.** There's a saying in the business world that "nothing fails like success." Take Gap, for example. How can a fashion retailer that was once *the* source for wardrobe staples such as chinos and white T-shirts suddenly lose its marketing edge? Motorola also fell victim to its own success. The company's Razr cell phone was a huge hit, but Motorola struggled to leverage that success. Now, Google owns Motorola Mobility. Also, Starbucks CEO Howard Shultz recently warned that his company and brand risk becoming commoditized. And, as noted in Case 1-3, some industry observers are saying that Apple has "lost its cool." If you were to make separate recommendations to management at each of these companies, what would you say?

CASE 1-1 CONTINUED (REFER TO PAGE 24)

The Global Marketplace

Now that you have an overview of global marketing, it's time to test your knowledge of global current events. Some well-known companies and brands are listed in the left-hand column. The question is: In what country is the parent corporation located? Possible answers are shown in the right-hand column. Write the letter corresponding to the country of your choice in the space provided; each country can be used more than once. Answers follow.

_____	1. Firestone Tire & Rubber	a. Germany
_____	2. Ray-Ban	b. France
_____	3. Rolls-Royce	c. Japan
_____	4. RCA	d. Great Britain
_____	5. Budweiser	e. United States
_____	6. Ben & Jerry's Homemade	f. Switzerland
_____	7. Gerber	g. Italy
_____	8. Miller Beer	h. Sweden
_____	9. Rollerblade	i. Finland
_____	10. Case New Holland	j. China
_____	11. Weed Eater	k. Netherlands
_____	12. Holiday Inn	l. Belgium
_____	13. Wild Turkey bourbon	m. India
_____	14. ThinkPad	n. Brazil
_____	15. Wilson Sporting Goods	o. South Korea
_____	16. Right Guard	
_____	17. BFGoodrich	
_____	18. Jaguar	
_____	19. Burger King	
_____	20. Jenny Craig	
_____	21. The Body Shop	
_____	22. Titleist	
_____	23. Swift	
_____	24. Gaggia	
_____	25. Church's English shoes	

Answers:

1. Japan (Bridgestone) **2.** Italy (Luxottica SpA) **3.** Germany (Volkswagen) **4.** China (TTE) **5.** Belgium (Anheuser-Busch InBev) **6.** Great Britain/Netherlands (Unilever) **7.** Switzerland (Nestlé) **8.** Great Britain (SABMiller) **9.** Italy (Benetton) **10.** Italy (Fiat) **11.** Sweden (AB Electrolux) **12.** Great Britain (InterContinental Hotels Group PLC) **13.** Italy (Campari) **14.** China (Lenovo) **15.** Finland (Amer Group) **16.** Germany (Henkel) **17.** France (Michelin) **18.** India (Tata Motors) **19.** Brazil (3G Capital) **20.** Switzerland (Nestlé) **21.** France (L'Oréal) **22.** South Korea (Fila Korea) **23.** Brazil (JBS) **24.** Netherlands (Philips) **25.** Italy (Prada Group)

Discussion Questions

1-14. Anheuser-Busch (A-B), which has been described as "an American icon," is now under the ownership of a company based in Belgium. Responding to reports that some consumers planned to boycott Budweiser products to protest the deal, one industry observer said, "Brand nationality is all about where it was born, and also the ingredients of that beer and how they make the beer. Basically, it doesn't matter who owns it. We are in a global world right now." Do you agree?

1-15. Anheuser-Busch has long enjoyed a reputation as a very desirable place to work. Executives were awarded well-appointed corporate suites and traveled on corporate jets; many had secretaries as well as executive assistants. When managers took commercial flights, they flew first class. Most employees received beer for free and could count on donations of beer and merchandise for community events. Tickets to Cardinals home games were also used as a marketing tool. A-B spent heavily on advertising and promotion; various advertising agencies produced about 100 new ads for A-B each year. Given these facts, what changes, if any, would you expect A-B's new owners to make? Why?

1-16. In 2009, Italy's Fiat acquired a 20 percent stake in Chrysler, another iconic American company. Are you familiar with Fiat? What do you think CEO Sergio Marchionne hoped to accomplish with this deal? How might Chrysler benefit from the alliance?

1-17. Ben & Jerry's Homemade is a quirky ice cream marketer based in Burlington, Vermont. Founders Ben Cohen and Jerry Greenfield are legendary for their enlightened business practices, which include a three-part mission statement: product mission, financial mission, and social mission. When the company was acquired by consumer products giant Unilever, some of the brand's loyal customers were alarmed. What do you think was the source of their concern?

CASE 1-2
McDonald's Expands Globally While Adjusting Its Local Recipe

McDonald's Corporation is a fast-food legend whose famous golden arches can be found in 118 different countries. The company is the undisputed leader in the quick-service restaurant (QSR) segment of the hospitality industry, with more than twice the system-wide revenues of Burger King. McDonald's built its reputation by promising and delivering three things to customers: inexpensive food with consistent taste regardless of location; quick service; and a clean, familiar environment.

The company was also a pioneer in the development of convenience-oriented features such as drive-through windows and indoor playgrounds for children. Today, thanks to memorable advertising and intensive promotion efforts, McDonald's is one of the world's most valuable brands: In 2012, Interbrand ranked it as the world's number 7 brand overall (Coca-Cola is number 1). The golden arches are said to be the second-most-recognized symbol in the world, behind the Olympic rings. In the United States alone, McDonald's typically spends about twice as much on advertising as Burger King and Wendy's.

Today, however, the company faces competitive attacks from several directions. During the 1990s, a wide range of upscale food and beverage purveyors arrived on the scene. For example, consumers began flocking to Starbucks coffee bars, where they spend freely on lattes and other coffee-based specialty drinks. The "fast-casual" segment of the industry, which includes companies such as Panera Bread, Cosi, and Baja Fresh, is attracting customers seeking higher-quality menu items in more comfortable surroundings. Meanwhile, Subway overtook McDonald's as the restaurant chain with the most outlets in the United States. Some industry observers suggested that, in terms of both food offerings and marketing, McDonald's was losing touch with modern American lifestyles.

Exhibit 1-11
Source: Hasan Jamali/AP Wide World Photos.

Until recently, the picture appeared brighter outside the United States. Thanks to changing lifestyles around the globe, more people are embracing the Western-style fast-food culture. McDonald's responded to the opportunity by stepping up its rate of new unit openings. McDonald's International is organized into three geographic regions: (1) Europe; (2) Asia/Pacific, Middle East, and Africa (APMEA); and (3) Other Countries. In 2005, the offices of the country heads for Europe and Asia were moved from the U.S. headquarters to their respective regions; now, for example, the head of APMEA manages his business from Hong Kong. Commenting on the change, Ken Koziol, vice president of worldwide restaurant innovation, explained, "McDonald's was built on a strong foundation of a core menu that we took around the world but we need to make sure we are more locally relevant. Taste profiles and desires are changing."

Asia-Pacific

The Indian market appears to hold huge potential for McDonald's. In fall 1996, the company opened its first restaurants in New Delhi and Bombay. In Delhi, McDonald's competes with Nirula's, a QSR chain with several dozen outlets; in addition, there are hundreds of smaller regional chains throughout India. The U.S.-based Subway chain opened its first Indian location in 2001; Pizza Hut, KFC, and Domino's Pizza have also entered the market. The Pizza Hut on Juhu Road in Bombay is housed in a three-story-tall building with large plate glass windows and central air conditioning. On most nights a long line of customers forms outside.

Indian demand for meals from the major food chains is growing at a double-digit rate; annual total sales exceed $1 billion. With those trends in mind, McDonald's identifies strategic locations in areas with heavy pedestrian traffic, such as the shopping street in Bandra in the Bombay suburbs. Other restaurant locations include a site near a college in Vile Parle and another opposite the Andheri train station; in all, McDonald's India operated more than 250 locations at the end of 2012. Prices are lower than in other countries; most sandwiches cost about 40 rupees (less than $1). Drinks cost 15 rupees, and a packet of French fries is 25 rupees. A complete meal costs the equivalent of about $2.

Because the Hindu religion prohibits eating beef, McDonald's developed the Chicken Maharaja Mac specifically for India. Despite protests from several Hindu nationalist groups, the first McDonald's attracted huge crowds to its site near the Victoria railway terminal; customers included many tourists from across India and from abroad as well as locals commuting to and from work. In short order, however, Hindu activists renewed their protests, this time accusing the company of using beef tallow in its cooking. Management responded by posting signs reading, "No beef or beef products sold here," but the doubts raised by the controversy kept many potential customers away.

Since that time, McDonald's has worked steadily to prove that it is sensitive to Indian tastes and traditions. As is true throughout the world, McDonald's emphasizes that most of the food ingredients it uses—as much as 95 percent—are produced locally. In addition, to accommodate vegetarians, each restaurant has two separate food preparation areas. The "green" kitchen is devoted to vegetarian fare such as the spicy McAloo Tikka potato burger, Pizza McPuff, and Paneer Salsa McWrap. Meat items are prepared on the red side. Even the mayonnaise is made without eggs. Some of the new menu items developed for India are now being introduced in Europe and the United States.

China is currently home to the world's largest McDonald's; China is also the fastest-growing market in terms of the number of new restaurant openings. The first Chinese location opened in mid-1992 in central Beijing, a few blocks from Tiananmen Square. Despite having a 20-year lease for the site, McDonald's found itself in the middle of a dispute between the central government and Beijing's city government. City officials decided to build a new $1.2 billion commercial complex in the city center and demanded that McDonald's vacate the site. McDonald's was forced to abandon the location. Despite the turbulent start, McDonald's now has more than 1,500 restaurants in China. The restaurants purchase 95 percent of their supplies, including lettuce, from local sources.

> "The tastes of the urban, upwardly mobile Indian are evolving, and more Indians are looking to eat out and experiment. The potential Indian customer base for a McDonald's or a Subway is larger than the size of entire developed countries."
>
> —Sapna Nayak, food analyst at Raobank India

In Asia and elsewhere, McDonald's protects itself from currency fluctuations by purchasing as much as possible from local suppliers. For example, the company's Singapore locations now buy chicken patties from Thailand rather than from the United States. However, French fries must still be imported from Australia or the United States. To help offset higher costs, McDonald's offers customers the choice of rice as a side dish at a lower price.

Western Europe

The golden arches are a familiar sight in Europe, particularly in France, Germany, and the United Kingdom. There is even a four-star Golden Arch hotel in Zurich. Overall, Europe contributes about 40 percent of both revenue and operating income, making it a key world region.

France's tradition of culinary excellence makes it a special case in Europe; French dining options range from legendary three-star Michelin restaurants to humble neighborhood bistros. From the time McDonald's opened its first French outlet in 1972, policymakers and media commentators have voiced concerns about the impact of fast food on French culture. Even so, with more than 1,200 locations, France today represents McDonald's second-largest market (the United States ranks number 1).

However, controversy has kept the company in the public eye. For example, some French citizens objected when McDonald's became the official food of the World Cup finals that were held in France in 1998. In August 1999, a sheep farmer named Jose Bové led a protest against construction of the 851st French McDonald's near the village of Millau. The group used construction tools to dismantle the partially finished structure. Bové told the press that the group had singled out McDonald's because, in his words, it is a symbol of America, "the place where they not only promote globalization and industrially produced food but also unfairly penalize our peasants." Ten years ago, executives at McDonald's France even ran an ad in *Femme Actuelle* magazine suggesting that children should eat only one meal at McDonald's per week.

McDonald's French franchisees experience some of the same competitive pressures facing the U.S. units; there are also key differences. For example, local bistro operators have enjoyed great success selling fresh-baked baguettes filled with ham and brie, effectively neutralizing McDonald's advantage of fast service and low prices. In response, executives hired an architecture firm to develop new restaurant designs and reimage the French operations.

A total of eight different themes were developed; many of the redesigned restaurants have hardwood floors and exposed brick walls. Signs are in muted colors rather than the chain's signature red and yellow, and the golden arches are displayed more subtly. Overall, the restaurants don't look like McDonald's restaurants elsewhere. The first redesigned restaurant is located on the Champs-Élysées on a site previously occupied by a Burger King; called "Music," the restaurant provides diners with the opportunity to listen to music on iPods and watch music videos on TV monitors. In some locations, lime green Danish designer armchairs have replaced plastic seats. As McDonald's locations in France undergo style makeovers, some franchisees report sales increases of 10 to 20 percent. Encouraged by these results, McDonald's has embarked on an ambitious program to refurbish several thousand outlets in various countries.

Central and Eastern Europe

January 31, 2010, marked the 20th anniversary of McDonald's arrival in the Soviet Union. The first Moscow McDonald's was built on Pushkin Square, near a major metro station just a few blocks from the Kremlin. It has 700 indoor seats and another 200 outside. It boasts 800 employees and features a 70-foot counter with 27 cash registers, equivalent to 20 ordinary McDonald's restaurants rolled into one. For its 20th-birthday celebration, the Pushkin Square location offered customers a "buy one, get one free" hamburger promotion; accordion-wielding musicians provided background music.

Khamzat Khazbulatov was selected to manage the first restaurant; today, he is director of McDonald's operations for all of Russia. At present, there are 235 McDonald's restaurants in Russia, and the company employs more than 25,000 people. To ensure a steady supply of high-quality raw materials, the company built McComplex, a huge, $50 million processing facility on the outskirts of Moscow. McDonald's also worked closely with local farmers to boost yields and quality. Now the facility has been turned over to private companies that today provide 80 percent of the ingredients used in Russia. For example, Wimm-Bill-Dann supplies dairy products to McDonald's; in 2002, it became the first Russian company to be listed on the New York Stock Exchange. Overall, 100,000 people are employed by companies in McDonald's supply chain.

Ukraine and Belarus are among the other members of the Commonwealth of Independent States with newly opened restaurants. The first Ukrainian McDonald's opened in Kiev in 1997; by 2007, the chain had expanded to 57 locations in 16 cities. Plans call for up to 100 restaurants, for a total investment of $120 million.

McDonald's has also set its sights on Central Europe, where plans call for hundreds of new restaurants to be opened in Croatia, Slovakia, Romania, and other countries. In 2010, McDonald's Czech Republic restaurants featured a special lineup of New York–themed sandwiches that were promoted with the iconic "I Heart NY" logo. Advertisements promised, "Another burger each week"; the offerings included Wall Street Beef ("grilled beef, cheese, crispy bacon, fresh lettuce and onion with BBQ sauce on an oval bun topped with sesame seeds"); Broadway Chicken; SoHo Grande; Manhattan Grilled Chicken; and Brooklyn Classic.

> "McDonald's comes off as uncool. If you want to be chic, you eat sushi. Indian food is even more cutting edge. McDonald's is like white bread."
>
> —Daniel, a 26-year-old architectural draftsman in San Francisco

Refocusing on the U.S. Market

Disappointing financial results led to a management shakeup in 2002, and Jim Cantalupo became CEO. Cantalupo was a retired vice chairman whose 28-year career at McDonald's included considerable international experience. He vowed to get the company back on track by focusing on the basics, namely, customer service, clean restaurants, and reliable food. Unhappy with the company's "Smile" advertising theme, Cantalupo took the extraordinary step of calling a summit meeting of senior creative personnel from 14 advertising agencies representing McDonald's 10 largest international markets. Foremost among them was New York–based DDB Worldwide, the lead agency on the McDonald's account that handles advertising in 34 countries, including Australia, the United States, and Germany. In addition, Leo Burnett is responsible for ads targeting children. McDonald's marketing and advertising managers from key countries were also summoned to the meeting at company headquarters in Oak Brook, Illinois.

As Larry Light, then-global chief marketing officer for McDonald's, noted:

> Creative talent is a rare talent, and creative people don't belong to geographies, to Brazil or France or Australia. We're going to challenge our agencies to be more open-minded about sharing between geographies.

Charlie Bell, a former executive at McDonald's Europe who was promoted to chief operating officer, didn't mince words about the company's advertising. "For one of the world's best brands, we have missed the mark," he said before the summit meeting. In June 2002, the company announced that it had picked the phrase "i'm lovin' it" as its new global marketing theme; the copy was proposed by Heye & Partner, a DDB Worldwide unit located in Germany. Tragically, within a few months, both Cantalupo and Bell died unexpectedly.

Jim Skinner, who then became the company's chief executive officer, instituted a "Plan to Win" initiative to increase McDonald's momentum. The core idea was to make McDonald's "better, not just bigger." Skinner identified five main drivers of McDonald's: people, products, place, price, and promotion.

Even as McDonald's executives attempted to come to grips with the problems facing their company, various business experts were offering advice of their own. In the mid-1990s, one market analyst said, "McDonald's is similar to Coca-Cola 10 years ago. It's on the verge of becoming an international giant, with the United States as a major market, but overseas as the driving force." Adrian J. Slywotzky, author of *Value Migration*, noted, "McDonald's needs to move the question from 'How can we sell more hamburgers?' to 'What does our brand allow us to consider selling to our customers?'" Mark DiMassimo, chief executive of a New York–based company that specializes in brand advertising, called McDonald's "a large lost organization that is searching for a strategy." In his view, "The company must focus, focus, focus, and stand for one thing."

There is ample evidence that, 11 years after its implementation, the Plan to Win strategy has been a success. *Consumer Reports* lauded the company's efforts to upgrade its coffee program. Consumers have embraced "better-for-you" menu items such as salads and sandwiches. The company is also seeking ways to be more environmentally conscious by using less plastic packaging and recycling more. Denis Hennequin, the executive in charge of European operations, is pleased with the results of his reimaging campaign. He said, "I'm changing the story. We've got to be loyal to our roots, we have to be affordable, we have to be convenient…but we have to add new dimensions."

> **"For a market leader, they've been really aggressive in a pretty fundamental way, but at the same time not losing the core of who McDonald's is."**
>
> —Kevin Lane Keller, Professor of Marketing
> Tuck School of Business, Dartmouth College

Despite the challenging economic environment, McDonald's total stock return for the three-year period 2007 through 2009 was the highest among the 30 companies that comprise the Dow Jones Industrial Average. The company's strong financial results have given it the resources to move forward with a remodeling initiative for restaurants in the United States. The price tag: A whopping $1 billion. The upgrades are partly a response to the positive results from revamped European operations; the makeover also reflects an appreciation for the retail design principles used by Apple, Starbucks, and other trendsetters. By 2015, most of McDonald's 14,000 U.S. restaurants will be updated.

McDonald's executives intend to create a modern, streamlined environment that will encourage customers to stay longer and spend more. Some of the changes are dramatic: Gone are the red roofs and splashes of neon yellow that many associate with iconic spokes-clown Ronald McDonald. The new color palette includes subtle shades of orange, yellow, and green. Also on tap: softer lighting and comfortable, stylish new furniture. As Jim Carras, a senior U.S. executive, noted, "McDonald's has to change with the times. And we have to do so faster than we ever have before."

Discussion Questions

1-18. Identify the key elements in McDonald's global marketing strategy. In particular, how does McDonald's approach the issue of standardization? Does McDonald's think globally and act locally? Does it also think locally and act globally?

1-19. Do you think government officials in developing countries such as Russia, China, and India welcome McDonald's? Do consumers in these countries welcome McDonald's? Why or why not?

1-20. The Plan to Win initiative is built around five factors that drive McDonald's business: people, products, place, price, and promotion. As a student of marketing, what can you say about these factors?

1-21. Is it realistic to expect that McDonald's—or any well-known company—can expand globally without occasionally making mistakes or generating controversy? Why do antiglobalization protesters around the world frequently target McDonald's?

Visit the Web Site

See www.mcdonalds.com
for a directory to country-specific sites.

Sources: Maureen Morrison, "Is McDonald's Losing That Lovin' Feeling?" *Advertising Age* (February 20, 2012), pp. 1, 20; Bruce Horovitz, "McDonald's Revamps Stores to Look More Upscale," *USA Today* (May 8, 2011), pp. 1B, 2B; Andrew E. Kramer, "Russia's Evolution, as Seen Through the Golden Arches," *The New York Times* (February 2, 2010), p. B3; Janet Adamy, "As Burgers Boom in Russia, McDonald's Touts Discipline," *The Wall Street Journal* (October 16, 2007), pp. A1, A17; Jenny Wiggins, "Burger, Fries, and a Shake-Up," *Financial Times* (January 27, 2007), p. 7; Steven Gray, "Beyond Burgers: McDonald's Menu Upgrade Boosts Meal Prices and Results," *The Wall Street Journal* (February 18–19, 2006), pp. A1, A7; Jeremy Grant, "Golden Arches Bridge Local Tastes," *Financial Times* (February 9, 2006), p. 10; Saritha Rai, "Tastes of India in U.S. Wrappers," *The New York Times* (April 29, 2003), pp. W1, W7; Bruce Horovitz, "It's Back to Basics for McDonald's," *USA Today* (May 21, 2003), pp. 1B, 2B; Sherri Day, "After Years at Top, McDonald's Strives to Regain Ground," *The New York Times* (March 3, 2003), pp. A1, A19; Sherri Day and Stuart Elliot, "At McDonald's, an Effort to Restore Lost Luster," *The New York Times* (April 8, 2003), pp. B1, B4; Shirley Leung and Suzanne Vranica, "Happy Meals Are No Longer Bringing Smiles at McDonald's," *The Wall Street Journal* (January 31, 2003), p. B1; Shirley Leung and Ron Lieber, "The New Menu Option at McDonald's: Plastic," *The Wall Street Journal* (November 26, 2002), pp. D1, D2; Shirley Leung, "McHaute Cuisine: Armchairs, TVs and Espresso—Is It McDonald's?" *The Wall Street Journal* (August 30, 2002), pp. A1, A6; Bruce Horovitz, "McDonald's Tries a New Recipe to Revive Sales," *USA Today* (July 10, 2001), pp. 1A, 2A; Geoff Winestock and Yaroslav Trofimov, "McDonald's Reassures Italians About Beef," *The Wall Street Journal* (January 16, 2001), pp. A3, A6.

CASE 1-3
Apple versus Samsung: The Battle for Smartphone Supremacy Heats Up

When Steve Jobs died in October 2011, the world lost one of the towering figures of the modern business era. Apple, the company Jobs cofounded, was a pioneer in the consumer electronics world; key product introductions included the Apple II (1977), the Macintosh (1984), the iPod and iTunes (2001), the Apple Store (2001), the iPhone (2007), and the iPad (2009). At the time of Jobs's death, Apple was the most valuable tech company in the world. By September 2012, Apple stock had soared to record levels, briefly rising above $700 per share. In addition, Apple had amassed more than $100 billion in cash, most of it held abroad as foreign earnings. Meanwhile, once-dominant tech industry giants such as Nokia, Sony, Dell, and BlackBerry were struggling.

Despite strong 2012 sales for the iPhone 5, however, industry observers began to wonder whether Apple's hot streak of hit product introductions was starting to cool. Apple's reputation was based on its proven ability to disrupt existing markets (for example, the music and telecommunications industries) and create new markets with technical and design innovations. However, in some circles the 2012 launch of the iPhone 5 was viewed as an evolutionary, rather than a revolutionary, breakthrough. In fact, many consumers opted to buy the slower, cheaper iPhone 4 or 4S rather than upgrade to the iPhone 5.

As growth in the key smartphone sector began to slow, Apple was being challenged by various competitors. First and foremost was Samsung Electronics, a division of Korean industrial giant Samsung Group, whose products range from semiconductors to household appliances to smartphones. Samsung's popular Galaxy series of phones are powered by Android, an operating system developed by Google. Some Galaxy models, including the Galaxy Note (also known as a "phablet"), have larger screens than the iPhone, a point of difference that has helped drive sales. The rivalry has been heated, with the two sides squaring off in court over alleged patent infringement.

China and Europe are two of Samsung's key markets; in 2012, Samsung launched the Galaxy S III in Europe. In 2013, Samsung staged a lavish event at Radio City Music Hall in New York to launch the Galaxy S 4. Why the change? As J.K. Shin, the executive in charge of Samsung's mobile business, noted, "We're a global player in the smartphone market and a global company, and the U.S. is an important market for us...I'm not satisfied with our U.S. market share."

In many developing countries, there is strong demand for inexpensive mobile phones. Some Android-based models from Samsung and other companies sell for much less than the iPhone 5. Apple does not offer a lower-cost version of the iPhone. In the United States, wireless carriers such as Verizon and AT&T usually subsidize the price of the iPhone for consumers who sign a multiyear service contract. That's why an American iPhone 5 sells for $199. By contrast, in other countries consumers pay the full price of the iPhone but are not tied to a contract. Moreover, the iPhone 5 is the same in every world market. By contrast, Samsung makes several versions of the Galaxy S 4—using different processors, for example—to suit the needs of different regions.

Exhibit 1-12 Apple co-founder Steve Jobs wore many hats during his illustrious career, including inventor, entrepreneur, CEO, and visionary technologist. He was also a master showman, a storyteller, and marketing genius. His appearances at product launches are the stuff of legend, and under his guidance Apple's must-have products—including the iPod, the iPhone, and the iPad—were, simply put, the epitome of "cool."

As Silicon Valley venture capitalist Roger McNamee has pointed out, there was another side to Jobs. In McNamee's words, "Steve's the last of the great builders. What makes him different is he's creating jobs and economic activity out of thin air while just about every other CEO in America is working out ways to cut costs and lay people off."

Source: Bloomberg via Getty Images.

Not surprisingly, smartphone makers are setting their sights on China, India, and other emerging markets. For example, Greater China, which includes China, Hong Kong, and Taiwan, is now Apple's second-largest market. While Apple currently commands almost a 50 percent share of the market for phones selling for $480 and up, CEO Tim Cook is not satisfied. Distribution is critical, and Cook is aggressively expanding the number of outlets in China that sell iPhones. Negotiations are ongoing with China Mobile, the largest carrier in the region and the world's largest carrier overall.

As growth in China and Europe slows, India, the number 3 smartphone market, is becoming increasingly important. Here, however, Apple lags far behind Samsung in terms of smartphone shipments. Samsung offers an Android phone for about $100; by contrast, Indian consumers pay $500 for an iPhone 4 and about $850 for the iPhone 5.

Famously, Steve Jobs downplayed the importance of formal market research, saying that consumers don't know what they want. By contrast, Samsung Electronics relies heavily on market research; 60,000 staff members work in dozens of research centers in China, Great Britain, India, Japan, the United States, and elsewhere. Samsung designers have backgrounds in such diverse disciplines as psychology, sociology, and engineering. Researchers track trends in fashion and interior design. Also, Samsung spends more on advertising and promotion than Apple. For example, Samsung has a major presence at the SXSW Interactive, Film, and Music conference held each March in Austin, Texas. In 2013, Samsung sponsored the TechSet Blogger Lounge and presented a concert showcase by Prince; Samsung users got preferred access to tickets. Although many SXSW attendees use iPhones and iPads, Apple has no visible corporate presence at the conference.

Discussion Questions

1-22. Do you own a smartphone? If so, which brand did you buy, and why?

1-23. Should Apple introduce a lower-cost iPhone to attract consumers who are not willing or able to pay a premium for an Apple device?

1-24. Do you think Apple can continue to grow by developing breakthrough products that create new markets, as it did with the iPod, iPhone, and iPad?

1-25. How has Samsung's global marketing strategy enabled it to compete so effectively against Apple?

Sources: Sam Grobart, "Think Colossal: How Samsung Became the World's No. 1 Smartphone Maker," Cover Story, *Bloomberg Businessweek* (April 1–7, 2013), pp. 58–64; Yun-Hee Kim, "Samsung Targets Apple's Home Turf," *The Wall Street Journal* (March 15, 2013), pp. B1, B4; Dhanya Ann Thoppil, "In India, iPhone Lags Far Behind," *The Wall Street Journal* (February 27, 2013), pp. B1, B4; Brian X. Chen, "Challenging Apple's Cool," *The New York Times* (February 11, 2013), pp. B1, B6; Anton Troianovski, "Fight to Unseat iPhone Intensifies," *The Wall Street Journal* (January 25, 2013), pp. B1, B6; Rolfe Winkler, "Apple's Power Within," *The Wall Street Journal* (December 7, 2013), p. C1.

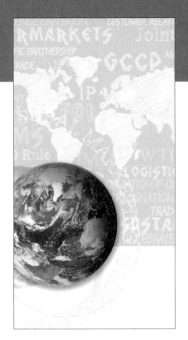

2

The Global Economic Environment

CASE 2-1
A New Front in the Battle of Ideas

The history of twentieth-century world economic thought has been called a "battle of ideas." Following the Bolshevik Revolution of 1917, the leaders of the Soviet Union established a centrally planned economy and put themselves in charge. In the West, by contrast, free market capitalism was the order of the day. After the stock market collapse of 1925 and the Great Depression of the 1930s, however, the wisdom of laissez-faire economic policies and free markets was called into question. Maybe the Soviet model was the best one? Should the government, in fact, play a central role in the economy?

To reboot the world economy in the 1930s, governments heeded the advice of economist John Maynard Keynes and embarked on massive spending programs (see Exhibit 2-1). In the United

Exhibit 2-1 John Maynard Keynes (left) and Friedrich August von Hayek were two of the twentieth century's most important economists. Keynes advocated government intervention in markets; by contrast, Hayek believed that markets should function without government interference. This "battle of ideas" is at the heart of the current policy debate about solving the global economic crisis.
Sources: Paul J. Richards/AFP/Newscom and Album/Oronoz/Newscom.

States, for example, President Franklin Roosevelt launched the Works Progress Administration (WPA) and put millions of Americans back to work. Fiscal stimulus programs were also the order of the day in Europe, Latin America, and especially in Germany and Japan, where governments were preparing for war. Government leaders were willing to accept moderate inflation rates provided unemployment was kept down. The results were impressive: Economic growth began to accelerate. The outbreak of World War II required massive increases in manufacturing output, and high unemployment gave way to full employment and worker shortages.

The Cold War decades that followed World War II saw the East and the West jockeying for geopolitical advantage. In the 1970s, Western economies were suffering from "stagflation": high inflation *and* high unemployment. The Soviet Union, led by an aging Leonid Brezhnev, was also hobbled by economic stagnation and malaise. In the 1980s, U.S. President Ronald Reagan and Prime Minister Margaret Thatcher of Great Britain took bold steps to revive their respective countries' economies, but this time the approach was different. Both leaders substantially *reduced* the role of government in their respective countries. Suddenly, Friedrich von Hayek's economic theories were in vogue.

As Western economies rebounded, Mikhail Gorbachev launched an economic restructuring program in the Soviet Union known as *perestroika*. But it was too little, too late. Within the space of just a few short years, the Berlin Wall came down, the two Germanys were reunited, and the Soviet Union broke apart into 15 separate countries. As the twenty-first century began, it appeared as though free market ideology had prevailed over the central-planning model.

By 2008, however, an economic crisis that had its roots in lax subprime mortgage lending practices and greed-driven deal making in unregulated financial markets began to spread around the globe. In the United States, where the crisis began, economic misery was widespread: The housing market collapsed, real estate values plummeted, credit tightened, and job growth slowed. The story was repeated around the globe, in Greece, Ireland, Italy, Spain, and elsewhere. Case 2-1 describes the challenges of the recent economic slowdown in more detail. (When you are done reading the chapter, study the case and answer the discussion questions.) Needless to say, the recent economic downturn has created both challenges and opportunities for global marketers.

The global economic crisis illustrates vividly the dynamic, integrated nature of today's economic environment. Recall the basic definition of a market: people or organizations with needs and wants and the willingness and ability to buy or sell. As noted in Chapter 1, many companies engage in global marketing in an effort to reach new customers outside their home countries and thereby increase sales, profits, and market share. Brazil, Russia, India, China, and South Korea deserve special mention; collectively referred to as BRICS, these five country markets are especially dynamic and represent important opportunities.[1] The BRICS nations and other emerging markets are also home to companies that are challenging established global giants at home and abroad.

This chapter will identify the most salient characteristics of the world economic environment, starting with an overview of the world economy. We then present a survey of economic system types, a discussion of the stages of market development, and an explanation of balance of payments. Foreign exchange is discussed in the final section of the chapter. Throughout the chapter, we will discuss the implications of the recent worldwide economic downturn on global marketing strategies.

---

[1] The "BRIC" designation first appeared in a 2001 report published by Goldman Sachs, the New York–based investment bank, hedge fund, and private equity firm. Investment strategists and developmental economists have advanced proposals for expanding the framework. For example, BRIC-IT includes Indonesia, the fourth-most-populous country in the world and one of the fastest growing. "T" is for Turkey, a candidate for membership in the European Union and another fast-growing country that is the envy of the Arab world. Both Turkey and Indonesia are Islamic countries and have demonstrated that Islam is not incompatible with democracy and growth.

LEARNING OBJECTIVES

1 Identify and briefly explain the major changes in the world economy that have occurred during the past few decades.

2 Compare and contrast the main types of economic systems that are found in different regions of the world.

3 Explain the categories of economic development used by the World Bank and identify the key emerging country markets at each stage of development.

4 Discuss the significance of balance of payments statistics for the world's major economies.

5 Identify the countries that are the world's leading exporters.

6 Briefly explain how exchange rates impact a company's opportunities in different parts of the world.

The World Economy—An Overview

The world economy has changed profoundly since World War II.[2] Perhaps the most fundamental change is the emergence of global markets; responding to new opportunities, global competitors have steadily displaced or absorbed local competitors. Concurrently, the integration of the world economy has increased significantly. Economic integration stood at 10 percent at the beginning of the twentieth century; today, it is approximately 50 percent. Integration is particularly striking in the European Union (EU) and the North American Free Trade Area.

Just 65 years ago, the world was far less integrated than it is today. As evidence of the changes that have taken place, consider the automobile. Cars with European nameplates such as Renault, Citroën, Peugeot, Morris, Volvo, and others were radically different from the American cars from Chevrolet, Ford, or Plymouth or the Japanese models from Toyota or Nissan. These were local cars built by local companies, mostly destined for local or regional markets. Even today, global and regional auto companies make cars for their home-country car buyers that are not marketed abroad. However, it is also true that the global car is a reality for BMW, Ford, Honda, Hyundai, Kia, and Toyota. Product changes reflect organizational changes as well: The world's largest automakers have, for the most part, evolved into global companies. Ford is a case in point: In 2008, the company unveiled an updated version of the Fiesta that is being marketed throughout the world. As Mark Fields, an executive vice president at Ford, explained, "We've had cars with the same name, like Escort and Focus, but the products themselves were very regional. This is a real shift point for us in that it's a real global car."[3]

During the past two decades, the world economic environment has become increasingly dynamic; change has been dramatic and far-reaching. To achieve success, executives and marketers must take into account the following new realities:[4]

- Capital movements have replaced trade as the driving force of the world economy.
- Production has become "uncoupled" from employment.
- The world economy dominates the scene; individual country economies play a subordinate role.
- The struggle between capitalism and socialism that began in 1917 is over.
- The growth of e-commerce diminishes the importance of national barriers and forces companies to reevaluate their business models.

The first change is the increased volume of capital movements. The dollar value of world trade in goods and services was $25 trillion in 2009. However, the Bank for International Settlements has calculated that foreign exchange transactions worth approximately $4 trillion are booked *every day*. This works out to more than $1 quadrillion annually, a figure that far surpasses the dollar value of world trade in goods and services.[5] An inescapable conclusion resides in these data: Global capital movements far exceed the dollar volume of global trade. In other words, *currency trading represents the world's largest market.*

The second change concerns the relationship between productivity and employment. To illustrate this relationship, it is necessary to review some basic macroeconomics. **Gross domestic product (GDP)**, a measure of a nation's economic activity, is calculated by adding consumer spending (*C*), investment spending (*I*), government purchases (*G*), and net exports (*NX*):

$$C + I + G + NX = GDP$$

Economic growth, as measured by GDP, reflects increases in a nation's productivity. Until the recent economic crisis, employment in manufacturing had remained steady or declined

---

[2]Numerous books and articles survey this subject, for example, Lowell Bryan et al., *Race for the World: Strategies to Build a Great Global Firm* (Boston: Harvard Business School Press, 1999).
[3]Bill Vlasic, "Ford Introduces One Small Car for a World of Markets," *The New York Times* (February 15, 2008), p. C3.
[4]William Greider offers a thought-provoking analysis of these new realities in *One World, Ready or Not: The Manic Logic of Global Capitalism* (New York: Simon & Schuster, 1997).
[5]Tom Lauricella, "Currency Trading Soars," *The Wall Street Journal* (September 1, 2010), p. A1.

while productivity continued to grow. Employment rates declined in countries where a bubble economy of misallocated resources in housing and real estate collapsed. In the United States, manufacturing's share of GDP declined from 19.2 percent in 1989 to 13 percent in 2009.[6] In 2011, manufacturing employment accounted for about 9 percent of the U.S. workforce; in 1971, the figure was 26 percent. During that 40-year period, productivity increased dramatically. Similar trends can be found in many other major industrial economies as well. In the United Kingdom, for example, manufacturing's share of jobs is only 8 percent, compared with 24 percent in 1980.[7] One recent study of 20 large economies found that between 1995 and 2002, more than 22 million factory jobs were eliminated. Manufacturing is not in decline—it is *employment* in manufacturing that is in decline.[8] Creating new jobs is one of the most important tasks facing policymakers today.

The third major change is the emergence of the world economy as the dominant economic unit. Company executives and national leaders who recognize this have the greatest chance of success. For example, the real secret of the economic success of Germany and Japan is the fact that business leaders and policymakers focus on world markets and their respective countries' competitive positions in that world economy. This change has brought two questions to the fore: How does the global economy work, and who is in charge? Unfortunately, the answers to these questions are not clear-cut.

The fourth change is the end of the Cold War. The demise of communism as an economic and political system can be explained in a straightforward manner: Communism is not an effective economic system. The overwhelmingly superior performance of the world's market economies has given leaders in socialist countries little choice but to renounce their ideology. A key policy change in such countries has been the abandonment of futile attempts to manage national economies with a single central plan. This policy change frequently goes hand in hand with governmental efforts to foster increased public participation in matters of state by introducing democratic reforms.[10]

Finally, the personal computer revolution and the advent of the Internet era have in some ways diminished the importance of national boundaries. Worldwide, an estimated 1 billion people use personal computers. In the so-called Information Age, barriers of time and place have been subverted by a transnational cyberworld that functions "24/7." Amazon.com, eBay, Facebook, Google, Groupon, iTunes, Priceline, Twitter, and YouTube are just a few of the companies that are pushing the envelope in this brave new world.

> "Only an outbreak of protectionist policies or a sharp rise in international shipping costs could slow or temporarily reverse manufacturing's declining share of employment in the United States."[9]
>
> —Steven J. Davis, Professor of Economics, University of Chicago

Economic Systems

Traditionally, economists identified four main types of economic systems: market capitalism, centrally planned socialism, centrally planned capitalism, and market socialism. As shown in Figure 2-1, this classification was based on the dominant method of resource allocation (market versus command) and the dominant form of resource ownership (private versus state). Thanks to

---

[6]Another economic indicator, *gross national income* (GNI), comprises GDP plus income generated from nonresident sources. A third metric, *gross national product* (GNP), is the total value of all final goods and services produced in a country by its residents and domestic business enterprises, plus the value of output produced by citizens working abroad, plus income generated by capital held abroad, minus transfers of net earnings by global companies operating in the country. GDP also measures economic activity; however, GDP includes *all* income produced within a country's borders by its residents and domestic enterprises as well as foreign-owned enterprises. Income earned by citizens working abroad is *not* included. For example, Ireland has attracted a great deal of foreign investment, and foreign-owned firms account for nearly 90 percent of Ireland's exports. This helps explain the fact that, in 2010, Ireland's GDP totaled €155 billion ($204 billion) while GNP was €128 billion ($168 billion). However, as a practical matter, GNP, GDP, and GNI figures for many countries will be roughly the same.

[7]Brian Groom, "Balance and Power," *Financial Times* (July 22, 2010), p. 7.

[8]Jon E. Hilsenrath and Rebecca Buckman, "Factory Employment Is Falling World-Wide," *The Wall Street Journal* (October 20, 2003), p. A2. Some companies have cut employment by outsourcing or subcontracting nonmanufacturing activities such as data processing, accounting, and customer service.

[9]Tracey Taylor, "A Label of Pride That Pays," *The New York Times* (April 23, 2009), p. B4.

[10]Marcus W. Brauchli, "Poll Vaults: More Nations Embrace Democracy—and Find It Can Often Be Messy," *The Wall Street Journal* (June 25, 1996), pp. A1, A6.

FIGURE 2-1

Economic Systems

Resource Allocation

	Market	Command
Private	Market capitalism	Centrally planned capitalism
State	Market socialism	Centrally planned socialism

Resource Ownership

globalization, however, economic systems are harder to categorize within the confines of a four-cell matrix. Alternatively, more robust, descriptive criteria include the following:[11]

- *Type of economy.* Is the nation an advanced industrial state, an emerging economy, a transition economy, or a developing nation?
- *Type of government.* Is the nation ruled by a monarchy, a dictatorship, or a tyrant? Is there an autocratic, one-party system? Is the nation dominated by another state, or is it a democracy with a multiparty system? Is it an unstable or terrorist nation?
- *Trade and capital flows.* Is the nation characterized by almost completely free trade or incomplete free trade, and is it part of a trading bloc? Is there a currency board, or are there exchange controls? Is there no trade, or does the government dominate trade possibilities?
- *The commanding heights* (e.g., the transportation, communications, and energy sectors). Are these sectors state owned and operated? Is there a mix of state and private ownership? Are they all private, with or without controlled prices?
- *Services provided by the state and funded through taxes.* Are pensions, health care, and education provided? Pensions and education but not health care? Do privatized systems dominate?
- *Institutions.* Is the nation characterized by transparency, standards, the absence of corruption, and the presence of a free press and strong courts? Or is corruption a fact of life and the press controlled by the government? Are standards ignored and the court system compromised?
- *Markets.* Does the nation have a free market system characterized by high-risk/high-reward entrepreneurial dynamism? Is it a free market that is dominated by monopolies, cartels, and concentrated industries? Is it a socialized market with cooperation among business, government, and labor (but with little entrepreneurial support)? Or is planning, including price and wage controls, dominated by the government?

Market Capitalism

Market capitalism is an economic system in which individuals and firms allocate resources and production resources are privately owned. Simply put, consumers decide what goods they desire and firms determine what and how much of those goods to produce; the role of the state in market capitalism is to promote competition among firms and to ensure consumer protection. Today, market capitalism is widely practiced around the world, most notably in North America and the EU (see Table 2-1).

It would be a gross oversimplification, however, to assume that all market-oriented economies function in an identical manner. Economist Paul Krugman has remarked that the United States is distinguished by its competitive, "wild free-for-all," and decentralized initiative. By contrast, outsiders sometimes refer to Japan as "Japan Inc." The label can be interpreted in different ways, but it basically refers to a tightly run, highly regulated economic system that is also market oriented.

---

[11]The authors are indebted to Professor Emeritus Francis J. Colella, Department of Economics, Simpson College, for suggesting these criteria.

TABLE 2-1 Western Market Systems

Type of System	Key Characteristics	Countries
Anglo-Saxon model	Private ownership; free enterprise economy; capitalism; minimal social safety net; highly flexible employment policies	United States, Canada, Great Britain
Social market economy model	Private ownership; "social partners" orientation that includes employer groups, unions, and banks; unions and corporations are involved in government, and vice versa; inflexible employment policies	Germany, France, Italy
Nordic model	Mix of state ownership and private ownership; high taxes; some market regulation; generous social safety net	Sweden, Norway

Centrally Planned Socialism

At the opposite end of the spectrum from market capitalism is **centrally planned socialism**. In this type of economic system, the state has broad powers to serve the public interest as it sees fit. State planners make "top-down" decisions about what goods and services are produced and in what quantities; consumers can spend their money on what is available. Government ownership of entire industries as well as individual enterprises is characteristic of centrally planned socialism. Because demand typically exceeds supply, the elements of the marketing mix are not used as strategic variables.[13] Little reliance is placed on product differentiation, advertising, or promotion; to eliminate "exploitation" by intermediaries, the government also controls distribution.

The clear superiority of market capitalism in delivering the goods and services that people need and want has led to its adoption in many formerly socialist countries. This socialist ideology, developed in the nineteenth century by Marx and perpetuated in the twentieth century by Lenin and others, has been resoundingly refuted. As William Greider writes:

> Marxism is utterly vanquished, if not yet entirely extinct, as an alternative economic system. Capitalism is triumphant. The ideological conflict first joined in the mid-nineteenth century in response to the rise of industrial capitalism, the deep argument that has preoccupied political imagination for 150 years, is ended.[14]

For decades, the economies of China, the former Soviet Union, and India functioned according to the tenets of centrally planned socialism. All three countries are now engaged in economic reforms characterized, in varying proportions, by increased reliance on market-allocation and private ownership. Even as China's leaders attempt to maintain control over society, they acknowledge the importance of economic reform (see Exhibit 2-2). At a recent assembly, the Chinese Communist Party said that reform "is an inevitable road for invigorating the country's economy and promoting social progress, and a great pioneering undertaking without parallel in history."

Centrally Planned Capitalism and Market Socialism

In reality, market capitalism and centrally planned socialism do not exist in "pure" form. In most countries, to a greater or lesser degree, command and market resource allocation are practiced simultaneously, as are private and state resource ownership. The role of government in modern market economies varies widely. An economic system in which command resource allocation is utilized extensively in an overall environment of private resource ownership can be

> "Countries with planned economies have never been part of economic globalization. China's economy must become a market economy."[12]
>
> —Long Yongtu, chief WTO negotiator for China

---

[12]Nicholas R. Lardy, *Integrating China into the Global Economy* (Washington, D.C.: The Brookings Institution, 2003), p. 21.

[13]Peggy A. Golden, Patricia M. Doney, Denise M. Johnson, and Jerald R. Smith, "The Dynamics of a Marketing Orientation in Transition Economies: A Study of Russian Firms," *Journal of International Marketing* 3, no. 2 (1995), pp. 29–49.

[14]William Greider, *One World, Ready or Not: The Manic Logic of Global Capitalism* (New York: Simon & Schuster, 1997), p. 37.

Exhibit 2-2 In 2003, the Rolling Stones' "40 Licks" CD was released in China. However, some of the band's most famous hits —"Brown Sugar," "Beast of Burden," "Honky Tonk Women," and "Let's Spend the Night Together"— were left off because officials viewed them as promoting social permissiveness. The Stones were scheduled to bring their fortieth anniversary tour to Beijing and Shanghai in 2003. However, the concerts were postponed due to the SARS outbreak.

Overall, the Licks tour grossed $311 million, and the band played to an audience of nearly 3.5 million people. When Mick, Keith and company finally did perform in China in 2006, government officials ordered the band to omit five songs from its set list.
Source: AP Images.

called **centrally planned capitalism**. A fourth variant, **market socialism**, is also possible. In such a system, market-allocation policies are permitted within an overall environment of state ownership.

In Sweden, for example, where the government controls two-thirds of all expenditures, resource allocation is more "voter" oriented than "market" oriented. Also, as indicated in Table 2-2, the Swedish government has significant holdings in key business sectors. Thus, Sweden's so-called "welfare state" has a hybrid economic system that incorporates elements of both centrally planned socialism and capitalism. The Swedish government is embarking on a privatization plan that calls for selling its stakes in some of the businesses listed in Table 2-2.[15] For example, in 2008 Vin & Spirit was sold to France's Pernod Ricard for $8.34 billion.

As noted previously, China is an example of state-directed socialism. However, China's Communist leadership has given considerable freedom to businesses and individuals in the Guangdong Province to operate within a market system. Today, China's private sector accounts for approximately 70 percent of national output. Even so, state enterprises still receive more than two-thirds of the credit available from the country's banks.

Market reforms and nascent capitalism in many parts of the world are creating opportunities for large-scale investments by global companies. Indeed, Coca-Cola returned to India in 1994, two decades after being forced out by the government. A new law allowing 100 percent foreign ownership of enterprises helped pave the way. By contrast, Cuba stands as one of the last

TABLE 2-2 Examples of Government Resource Ownership in Sweden

Company	Industry Sector	State Ownership %
TeliaSonera	Telecom	45
SAS	Airline	21
Nordea	Banking	20
OMX	Stock exchange	7
Vin & Spirit	Alcohol	100*

*Sold in 2008.

[15]Joel Sherwood and Terence Roth, "Defeat of Sweden's Ruling Party Clears Way for Sales of State Assets," *The Wall Street Journal* (September 19, 2006), p. A8.

bastions of the command allocation approach. Daniel Yergin and Joseph Stanislaw sum up the situation this way:

> Socialists are embracing capitalism, governments are selling off companies they had nationalized, and countries are seeking to entice multinational corporations expelled just two decades earlier. Today, politicians on the left admit that their governments can no longer afford the expansive welfare state. . . . The decamping of the state from the "commanding heights" marks a great divide between the twentieth and twenty-first centuries. It is opening the doors of many formerly closed countries to trade and investment, and vastly increasing the global market.[16]

The Washington, D.C.–based Heritage Foundation, a conservative think tank, takes a more conventional approach to classifying economies: It compiles a survey of more than 175 countries ranked by degree of economic freedom (Table 2-3). A number of key economic variables are considered: trade policy, taxation policy, government consumption of economic output, monetary policy, capital flows and foreign investment, banking policy, wage and price controls, property rights, regulations, and the black market. Hong Kong and Singapore are ranked first and second in terms of economic freedom; Zimbabwe, Cuba, and North Korea are ranked lowest (see Exhibit 2-3). Coincidentally, Cuba and North Korea are the only two countries where Coca-Cola is not available through authorized channels!

A high correlation exists between the degree of economic freedom and the extent to which a nation's mixed economy is market oriented. However, the criteria for the ranking have been subject to some debate. For example, author William Greider has observed that the authoritarian state capitalism practiced in Singapore deprives the nation's citizens of free speech, a free press, and free assembly. Indeed, Singapore once banned the import, manufacture, and sale of chewing gum, because discarded wads of gum were making a mess in public places. Today, gum is available at pharmacies; before buying a pack, however, consumers must register their names and addresses. Greider notes, "Singaporeans are comfortably provided for by a harshly autocratic government that administers paranoid control over press and politics and an effective welfare state that keeps everyone well housed and fed, but not free."[17] As Greider's observation makes clear, some aspects of "free economies" bear more than a passing resemblance to command-style economic systems.

Exhibit 2-3 For decades, Singapore has been an important trade hub in Asia. The city-state is now being remade as a cultural destination. Leaders have embarked upon an ambitious real estate development program designed to keep Singapore up to date and competitive with Doha, Dubai, and other popular tourist centers. Sentosa Cove, a mixed-use, integrated resort, features thousands of apartments and villas, as well as hotels, a casino complex, and numerous retail shops. Unfortunately, many development projects are now in jeopardy, victims of the global recession.
Source: Tim Brown/Getty Images.

[16]Daniel Yergin and Joseph Stanislaw, "Sale of the Century," *Financial Times Weekend* (January 24–25, 1998), p. I.
[17]William Greider, *One World, Ready or Not: The Manic Logic of Global Capitalism* (New York: Simon & Schuster, 1997), pp. 36–37. See also John Burton, "Singapore's Social Contract Shows Signs of Strain," *Financial Times* (August 19–20, 2006), p. 3.

TABLE 2-3 Index of Economic Freedom—2013 Rankings

1. Hong Kong	46. Spain	90. Morocco	136. China
2. Singapore	47. Malta	91. Lebanon	137. Guinea
3. Australia	48. Hungary	92. The Gambia	138. Guinea-Bissau
4. New Zealand	49. Costa Rica	93. Zambia	139. Russia
5. Switzerland	50. Mexico	94. Serbia	140. Vietnam
6. Canada	51. Israel	95. Cambodia	141. Nepal
7. Chile	52. Jamaica	96. Honduras	142. Central African
8. Mauritius	53. El Salvador	97. The Philippines	Republic
9. Denmark	54. Saint Vincent and	98. Tanzania	143. Micronesia
10. United States	the Grenadines	99. Gabon	144. Laos
11. Ireland	55. Latvia	100. Brazil	
12. Bahrain	56. Malaysia	101. Benin	**Repressed**
13. Estonia	57. Poland	102. Belize	145. Algeria
14. United Kingdom	58. Albania	103. Bosnia and Herzegovina	146. Ethiopia
15. Luxembourg	59. Romania	104. Swaziland	147. Liberia
16. Finland	60. Bulgaria	105. Fiji	148. Burundi
17. The Netherlands	61. Thailand	106. Samoa	149. Maldives
18. Sweden	62. France	107. Tunisia	150. Togo
19. Germany	63. Rwanda	108. Indonesia	151. Sierra Leone
20. Taiwan	64. Dominica	109. Vanuatu	152. Haiti
21. Georgia	65. Cape Verde	110. Nicaragua	153. São Tomé and
22. Lithuania	66. Kuwait	111. Mali	Príncipe
23. Iceland	67. Portugal	112. Tonga	154. Belarus
24. Japan	68. Kazakhstan	113. Yemen	155. Lesotho
25. Austria	69. Turkey	114. Kenya	156. Bolivia
26. Macau	70. Montenegro	115. Moldova	157. Comoros
27. Qatar	71. Panama	116. Senegal	158. Angola
28. United Arab Emirates	72. Trinidad and Tobago	117. Greece	159. Ecuador
29. Czech Republic	73. Madagascar	118. Malawi	160. Argentina
30. Botswana	74. South Africa	119. India	161. Ukraine
31. Norway	75. Mongolia	120. Nigeria	162. Uzbekistan
32. Saint Lucia	76. Slovenia	121. Pakistan	163. Kiribati
33. Jordan	77. Ghana	122. Bhutan	164. Chad
34. South Korea	78. Croatia	123. Mozambique	165. Solomon Islands
35. The Bahamas	79. Uganda	124. Seychelles	166. Timor-Leste
	80. Paraguay	125. Egypt	167. Republic of Congo
Moderately Free	81. Sri Lanka	126. Côte d'Ivoire	168. Iran
36. Uruguay	82. Saudi Arabia	127. Djibouti	169. Turkmenistan
37. Colombia	83. Italy	128. Niger	170. Equatorial Guinea
38. Armenia	84. Namibia	129. Guyana	171. Democratic Republic
39. Barbados	85. Guatemala	130. Papua New Guinea	of Congo
40. Belgium		131. Tajikistan	172. Burma
41. Cyprus	**Mostly Unfree**	132. Bangladesh	173. Eritrea
42. Slovakia	86. Burkina Faso	133. Cameroon	174. Venezuela
43. Macedonia	87. Dominican Republic	134. Mauritania	175. Zimbabwe
44. Peru	88. Azerbaijan	135. Suriname	176. Cuba
45. Oman	89. Kyrgyz Republic		177. North Korea

NOT RANKED

Afghanistan	Kosovo	Liechtenstein	Sudan
Iraq	Libya	Somalia	Syria

Source: Terry Miller and Kim R. Holmes, *2013 Index of Economic Freedom* (Washington, D.C.: The Heritage Foundation and Dow Jones & Company, Inc., 2013), available at: www.heritage.org/index (accessed February 1, 2013).

Venezuela after Chávez

MyMarketingLab   SYNC • THINK • LEARN

The death of Venezuelan President Hugo Chávez in March 2013 marked the end of an era. After assuming the presidency in 1999, Chávez toyed with the idea of pursuing a "third way" to economic growth. That approach, suggested by then–British Prime Minister Tony Blair, was a mashup of socialism and capitalism—i.e., "capitalism with a human face." However, it wasn't long before Chávez began espousing socialist policies for his country while vilifying the United States. Venezuela's rich oil reserves provided resources for Chávez to rally popular support in his own country. Chávez also provided Cuba and other Latin American neighbors with aid, mostly in the form of cheap oil through an energy pact known as Petrocaribe.

American filmmaker Oliver Stone has spent a significant part of his career documenting Latin America's political environment. Some observers criticized Stone's 2003 film *Comandante* for making an anti-American statement while painting a sympathetic portrait of Cuban leader Fidel Castro as a moral individual. Stone's most recent documentary is titled *South of the Border*. This time around, the filmmaker turned his camera on several South American leaders, including President Chávez and Bolivia's Evo Morales. Stone objected to media descriptions of Chávez and his peers as "dictators." On the contrary, the director portrayed these leaders as champions of the poor who worked to return their respective nations' natural resources "back to the people" (see Exhibit 2-4).

Chávez, a former military officer, minced few words when expressing his disdain for American politicians and American-style, free market economic policies. Speaking about former U.S. President George W. Bush in *South of the Border*, Chávez says, "You are a donkey, Mr. Bush." In an interview Chávez remarked, "I'm not loved by [former U.S. Secretary of State] Hillary Clinton . . . and I don't love her either." Why didn't Mrs. Clinton love President Chávez? For one, Chávez's economic policies included nationalization of international companies and the imposition of currency controls. Meanwhile, in Chávez's words,

"U.S. capitalism is broken . . . we need to change the system . . . the future of capitalism in Venezuela is in the cemetery."

Chávez had plenty more to say about capitalism. "It is not a temporary crisis of the capitalist system—it is a structural crisis," he said. "When you live in a democracy in such an unequal region as Latin America, you need to have a socialist vision. I believe in economies with markets—not in market economies. There is a difference."

Guillermo Zuloaga, owner of the Globovision television station, has a different view. Globovision reaches nearly half of Venezuela's television households, and Zuloaga is proud that his station has an independent voice. As he told *The Wall Street Journal*, "The quality of Venezuelan life is deteriorating considerably. . . . We have problems with electricity, problems with water, the highest crime rate of any place. . . . The Chávez government has infringed almost every article of the constitution." As a result of his willingness to speak critically about the Chávez government, Zuloaga was arrested and charged with slander.

What was daily life like in Venezuela like after 15 years under Chávez? The government allowed many import permits to expire, resulting in shortages of food and other necessities. Foreign exchange controls meant that importers lacked the dollars necessary to bring in a variety of consumer goods. Venezuela shares nearly 1,400 miles of border with Colombia; many goods had to be transshipped by trucks from Colombia's ports because ports in Puerto Cabello and elsewhere had deteriorated. One positive: The government subsidized gasoline production, so a gallon of premium gas cost only about 5.6 cents.

Sources: Ángel González, "Almost-Free Gas Comes at a High Cost," *The Wall Street Journal* (April 12, 2013), pp. A1, 12; "Hugo Chávez," Editorial, *The Wall Street Journal* (March 6, 2013), p. A20; Sara Schaefer Munoz, "Chávez's Stamp Most Keenly Felt on Farms," *The Wall Street Journal* (October 6–7, 2012), p. A7; Mary Anastasia O'Grady, "Chávez's Assault on the Press," *The Wall Street Journal* (July 12, 2010), p. A13; Matthew Garrahan, "When Hugo Met Oliver," *Financial Times* (June 19/20, 2010), pp. 1, 2; Matthew Garrahan, "Chávez Attacks Economic Critics," *Financial Times* (June 17, 2010), p. 2; Mary Anastasia O'Grady, "Chavismo Meets the Market," *The Wall Street Journal* (June 7, 2010), p. A17.

Exhibit 2-4 Motion picture director Oliver Stone (right) with Venezuelan President Hugo Chávez. Chávez was proud of his accomplishments as president, noting that Venezuela's economy grew under his leadership. Even so, some observers at home and abroad were alarmed by the president's economic policies. It is unclear what direction the country will take after elections in April 2013.
Source: © Allstar Picture Library/Alamy.

Stages of Market Development

At any point in time, individual country markets are at different stages of economic development. The World Bank has developed a four-category classification system that uses per capita **gross national income (GNI)** as a base. The income definition for each of the stages is derived from the World Bank's lending categories, and countries within a given category generally have a number of characteristics in common. Thus, the stages provide a useful basis for global market segmentation and target marketing. The categories are shown in Table 2-4.

A decade ago, a number of countries in Central Europe, Latin America, and Asia were expected to experience rapid economic growth. Known as *big emerging markets* (BEMs), the list included China, India, Indonesia, South Korea, Brazil, Mexico, Argentina, South Africa, Poland, and Turkey.[18] Today, much attention is focused on opportunities in Brazil, Russia, India, China, and South Africa. As previously noted, these five countries are collectively known as BRICS. Experts predict that the BRICS nations will be key players in global trade even as their track records on human rights, environmental protection, and other issues come under closer scrutiny by their trading partners. The BRICS government leaders will also come under pressure at home as their developing market economies create greater income disparity. For each of the stages of economic development discussed here, special attention is given to the BRICS countries.

Low-Income Countries

Low-income countries have a GNI per capita of $1,025 or less. The general characteristics shared by countries at this income level are:

1. Limited industrialization and a high percentage of the population engaged in agriculture and subsistence farming
2. High birth rates, short life expectancy
3. Low literacy rates
4. Heavy reliance on foreign aid
5. Political instability and unrest
6. Concentration in Africa south of the Sahara

About 13 percent of the world's population is included in this economic category. Many low-income countries have such serious economic, social, and political problems that they represent extremely limited opportunities for investment and operations. Some are no-growth economies, such as Burundi and Rwanda, with a high percentage of the population living at the

TABLE 2-4 Stages of Market Development

Income Group by per Capita GNI	2011 GDP ($ millions)	2011 GNI per Capita ($)	World GDP (%)	2011 Population (millions)
High-income countries (OECD)				
GNI per capita ≥$12,476	43,890,000	41,225	62	1,039
High-income countries (non-OECD)				
GNI per capita ≥$12,476	2,752,000	25,372	3	96
Upper-middle countries				
GNI per capita ≥$4,036 to ≤$12,475	18,240,000	6,563	26	2,489
Lower-middle-income countries				
GNI per capita ≥$1,026 but ≤$4,035	4,768,000	1,764	7	2,533
Low-income countries				
GNI per capita ≤$1,025	472.8	569	.67	816

---

[18]For an excellent discussion of BEMs, see Jeffrey E. Garten, *The Big Ten: The Big Emerging Markets and How They Will Change Our Lives* (New York: Basic Books, 1997).
[19]Sarah Theodore, "Beer Has Big Changes on Tap," *Beverage Industry* (September 2008), p. 24.

national poverty line. Others were once relatively stable countries with growing economies that have become divided by political struggles. The result is an unstable environment characterized by civil strife, flat income, and considerable danger to residents. Countries embroiled in civil wars are dangerous areas; most companies find it prudent to avoid them.

Other low-income countries represent genuine market opportunities. Bangladesh is a case in point: GNI per capita is approximately $780, and the garment industry is enjoying burgeoning exports. Finished clothing exports doubled between 2004 and 2009; buyers include Gap, H&M, Tesco, Walmart, Zara, and other retailers. Garments represent fully 80 percent of the country's exports; the president of the Bangladesh Garment Manufacturers and Exporters Association expected that exports would total $25 billion by 2013. Despite that, workers in Bangladesh currently have the lowest wages in the global garment industry. In fall 2010, the government-mandated minimum wage was raised from $24 per month to $44. An estimated 3 million Bangladeshis—mostly women—work in the industry. Bangladesh's garment sector has benefited from labor unrest, rising wages, and a stronger currency in China.[20] Tragically, there has been a rash of fatal accidents at clothing factories in Bangladesh in recent years. In January 2013, seven workers were killed when fire broke out at a factory in Dhaka operated by Smart Export Garments. Labor activists are renewing calls for increased oversight and improved safety standards.[21]

Some of the smaller countries from the former Soviet Union, including Tajikistan and Uzbekistan, fall into the low- and lower-middle income categories. Sometimes referred to collectively as "the Stans," they present marketers with an interesting challenge. Incomes are low, there is considerable economic hardship, and the potential for disruption is certainly high. Are they problem cases, or are they attractive opportunities with good potential for economic growth? These countries present an interesting risk–reward trade-off; some companies have taken the plunge, but many others are still assessing whether to take the risk.

Lower-Middle-Income Countries

The United Nations designates 50 countries in the bottom ranks of the low-income category as **least-developed countries (LDCs)**; the term is sometimes used to indicate a contrast with **developing** (i.e., upper ranks of low-income plus lower-middle- and upper-middle-income) **countries** and **developed** (high-income) **countries**. **Lower-middle-income countries** are those with a GNI per capita between $1,026 and $4,035. Consumer markets in these countries are expanding rapidly. Countries such as Indonesia and Thailand represent an increasing competitive threat as they mobilize their relatively cheap—and often highly motivated—labor forces to serve target markets in the rest of the world. The developing countries in the lower-middle-income category have a major competitive advantage in mature, standardized, labor-intensive light industry sectors such as footwear, textiles, and toys.

With a 2011 GNI per capita of $1,410, India has transitioned out of the low-income category and now is classified as a lower-middle-income country. In 2007, India commemorated the 60th anniversary of its independence from Great Britain. For many decades, economic growth was weak. As the 1990s began, India was in the throes of an economic crisis: Inflation was high, and foreign exchange reserves were low. Country leaders opened India's economy to trade and investment and dramatically improved market opportunities. Manmohan Singh was placed in charge of India's economy. Singh, former governor of the Indian central bank and finance minister, believed that India had been taking the wrong road. Accordingly, he set about dismantling the planned economy by eliminating import licensing requirements for many products, reducing tariffs, easing restrictions on foreign investment, and liberalizing the rupee.

Yashwant Sinha, the country's former finance minister, once declared that the twenty-first century would be "the century of India." His words appear prescient; India is now home to a number of world-class companies with growing global reach, including Infosys, Mahindra & Mahindra, Tata, and Wipro. Meanwhile, the list of global companies operating in India is

> "As the saying goes, if you are not manufacturing in China or selling in India, you are as good as finished."[22]
>
> —Dipankar Halder, Associate Director, KSA Technopak, India

> "It may feel like the temperature has only risen a couple of degrees so far, but this heralds the end of India's economic Ice Age."[23]
>
> —Vivek Paul, Vice Chairman, Wipro

---

[20]Vikas Bajaj, "Bangladesh, with Low Pay, Moves in on China," *The New York Times* (July 17, 2010), p. A1; see also Mahtab Haider, "Defying Predictions, Bangladesh's Garment Factories Thrive," *The Christian Science Monitor* (February 7, 2006), p. 4.

[21]Julfikar Ali Manik and Jim Yardley, "Bangladesh Clothing Factory, Site of Fire that Killed 7, Made European Brands," *The New York Times* (January 18, 2013), p. A5.

[22]Saritha Rai, "Tastes of India in U.S. Wrappers," *The New York Times* (April 29, 2003), p. W7.

[23]Manjeet Kirpalani, "The Factories Are Humming," *Businessweek* (October 18, 2004), pp. 54–55.

EMERGING MARKETS BRIEFING BOOK

Myanmar Is Open for Business

Myanmar is a low-income country in Southeast Asia with a population of 52 million people. After gaining independence from Great Britain in 1948, the country was ruled for decades by a military junta. In 2011, however, the country formerly known as Burma abruptly changed course. For starters, Myanmar's citizens elected a president, Thein Sein. Other political and economic changes swiftly followed: Political prisoners have been released, and press censorship has been abolished (see Exhibit 2-5).

Encouraged by Myanmar's transition from dictatorship toward economic openness and democracy, many Western governments lifted sanctions such as bans on the country's imports. These actions opened the doors to global companies, and Coca-Cola, General Electric (GE), MasterCard, Mitsubishi, Nestlé, Visa, and many others have begun setting up operations. Indeed, foreign investment has skyrocketed, from a modest $208 million in 2000 to $850 million in 2011.

However, those global giants will be playing catch-up. Why? During years of Western sanctions, companies in China, Japan, and other Asian countries maintained a presence in Myanmar. That fact is paying dividends today; Mitsubishi is a case in point. The company established an export office in Yangon years ago. As Mitsuo Ido, Mitsubishi's general manager, notes, "Japan and Myanmar have had a long relationship, and Japanese companies are now very interested in increasing their involvement here. Myanmar people are very similar to Japanese in some ways."

U.S. President Barack Obama made a quick visit to the country at the end of 2012. Even now, however, some sanctions remain in place. These include sanctions targeting "Specially Designated Nationals," who had ties to the former military regime such as businessman Zaw Zaw.

Much remains to be done. Ethnic conflict is rife; the fledgling government is struggling to achieve peace and stability in the face of protests. In addition, Myanmar's economic and physical infrastructures are seriously underdeveloped. The legal system is undeveloped, and workers lack training. Mobile telecommunications networks need upgrades; most Western cell phones don't work in Myanmar. According to the Asian Development Bank, only about one-quarter of Myanmar's population has access to reliable electricity, and power shortages and outages are not unusual. Despite these obstacles, the country's rich gas and oil reserves represent a major opportunity for GE; Total, a French energy giant; and other companies.

It remains to be seen whether the "gold rush" yields big successes. Years ago, some companies that attempted to capitalize on new opportunities in Russia and Vietnam ended up losing a lot of money. Corruption is rampant, and many former military leaders have secured licenses in banking and other services. Global soft drinks titan Coca-Cola finds itself competing with inexpensive soft drinks such as Blue Mountain Cola and Fantasy Orange. Even so, some business owners in Myanmar worry that foreigners will dominate key business sectors. An executive at a New York–based investment firm summed up the opportunity this way: "If I was 25 years old and single, I'd just go there. It's just ready for takeoff."

Sources: Laura Meckler, "Obama Challenges Myanmar on Visit," *The Wall Street Journal* (November 20, 2012), p. A8; Patrick Barta, "Final Frontier: Firms Flock to Newly Opened Myanmar," *The Wall Street Journal* (November 12, 2012), p. A1; Michiyo Nakamoto and Gwen Robinson, "Japan Looks for Early Lead in Myanmar Race," *Financial Times* (October 1, 2012), p. 6; Patrick Barta, "Myanmar Concerns Remain, U.S. Envoy Says," *The Wall Street Journal* (August 20, 2012), p. A7; "Myanmar Is Next Real Thing for Coke," *Financial Times* (June 15, 2012), p. 16; Simon Hall, "Energy Titans Look to Myanmar," *The Wall Street Journal* (June 8, 2012), p. B6; David Pilling and Gwen Robinson, "Myanmar: A Nation Rises," *Financial Times* (December 3, 2010), p. 6.

Exhibit 2-5 An employee takes a call as customers purchase jewelry at a gold shop in Yangon, the former capital of Myanmar. Myanmar's economy expanded 6.5 percent in 2012 and is set for further growth as sweeping political, economic, and financial reforms raise hopes of a renaissance for the impoverished nation. Now that trade sanctions have been lifted, global companies in a variety of industries are moving quickly to formulate and implement market-entry strategies. For example, less than 10 percent of Myanmar's citizens currently own mobile phones. The government hopes to increase mobile phone penetration to 80 percent of the population by 2016. This represents an enormous market opportunity for mobile operators and other technology companies.
Source: AFP / Getty Images.

growing longer. They include Benetton, Cadbury, Coca-Cola, DuPont, Ericsson, Fujitsu, IBM, L'Oréal, MTV, Staples, Unilever, and Walmart. India's huge population base also presents attractive opportunities for automakers. Suzuki, Hyundai, General Motors, and Ford are among the global car manufacturers doing business in India.

Table 2-3 ranks the former Soviet republic of Uzbekistan quite low in terms of economic freedom. This is one indication of a risky business environment in a lower-middle-income country. Even so, there are market opportunities in this country. In fact, GM's sales in Uzbekistan for 2010 were up 41 percent over 2009, making this Central Asian country GM's 10th-largest market! Russia itself, whose economy is in the upper-middle-income category, slipped to number 139 in the 2013 rankings. The pace of Russia's economic recovery has lagged that in other emerging markets, and the Kremlin's search for new sources of revenue to fund its budget outlays has created tension between government ministries and business. In fact, some observers have asked whether Russia should still be included in the BRICS grouping.

Upper-Middle-Income Countries

Upper-middle-income countries, also known as *industrializing* or *developing countries*, are those with GNI per capita ranging from $4,036 to $12,475. In these countries, the percentage of the population engaged in agriculture drops sharply as people move to the industrial sector and the degree of urbanization increases. Chile, Malaysia, Mexico, Venezuela, and many other countries in this stage are rapidly industrializing (see Exhibit 2-6). They have high literacy rates and strong education systems; wages are rising, but they are still significantly lower than in the advanced countries. Innovative local companies can become formidable competitors and help contribute to their nations' rapid, export-driven economic growth.

Brazil ($10,720 GNI per capita in 2011), Russia ($10,730), China ($4,940), and South Africa ($6,960) are the four BRICS nations that currently fall into the upper-middle-income category. Russia's economic situation improves and declines as the price of oil fluctuates. Strong local companies have appeared on the scene, including Wimm-Bill-Dann Foods, Russia's largest dairy company. However, corruption is pervasive, and the bureaucracy often means a mountain of red tape for companies such as Diageo, Mars, McDonald's, Nestlé, and SAB Miller. Still, the market opportunity is enticing: Wages have increased dramatically in recent years, and consumers are showing a tendency to spend rather than save.[24]

Exhibit 2-6 With per capita GNI of $11,820, Venezuela is classified as an upper-middle-income country. Venezuela is one of the world's top oil-producing nations and an important source of U.S. oil imports. State-owned Petróleos de Venezuela S.A. (PDVSA) has operations in many different countries. For example, its CITGO Petroleum subsidiary operates 13,000 filling stations in the United States. A new initiative, CITGO-Venezuela Energy Efficient Lighting Program, is distributing 500,000 compact fluorescent light bulbs to help 50,000 low-income U.S. households save energy.
Source: Used with permission of CITGO.

[24]Jenny Wiggins, "Brands Make a Dash into Russia," *Financial Times* (September 4, 2008), p. 10.

Brazil is the largest country in Latin America in terms of the size of its economy, population, and geographic territory. Brazil also boasts the richest reserves of natural resources in the hemisphere; China, Brazil's top trading partner, has an insatiable appetite for iron ore and other commodities. Government policies aimed at stabilizing Brazil's macroeconomy have yielded impressive results: Brazil's GNI has grown at an average annual rate of 4 percent over the past eight years. During the same time period, nearly 50 million Brazilians have joined the middle class as incomes and living standards have risen.[25] Needless to say, this trend has been a boon to global companies doing business in Brazil, which include Electrolux, Fiat, Ford, General Motors, Nestlé, Nokia, Raytheon, Toyota, Unilever, and Whirlpool (see Exhibit 2-7).

Typical of countries at this stage of development, Brazil is a study in contrasts. Grocery distribution companies use logistics software to route their trucks; meanwhile, horse-drawn carts are still a common sight on many roads. To keep pace with the volatile financial environment of the early 1990s, many local retailers invested in sophisticated computer and communications systems. They use sophisticated inventory management software to maintain financial control. Thanks to Brazil's strength in computers, the country's outsourcing sector is growing rapidly.[26] Former French President Jacques Chirac underscored Brazil's importance on the world trade scene when he noted, "Geographically, Brazil is part of America. But it's European because of its culture and global because of its interests."[27]

China is the third BRICS nation in the upper-middle-income category; GNI per capita was $4,940 in 2011. China represents the largest single destination for foreign investment in the developing world. Attracted by the country's vast size and market potential, companies in Asia, Europe, and North and South America are making China a key country in their global strategies. Shenzhen and other special economic zones have attracted billions of dollars in foreign investment. However, despite ongoing market reforms, Chinese society does not have democratic

Exhibit 2-7 In 2007, Brazil's president Luiz Inacio Lula da Silva spoke at opening ceremonies for Nestlé's $48 million plant in Feira de Santana. The facility produces 50,000 tons of coffee, cookies, and other items each year; most are adapted to suit Brazilian tastes and pocketbooks. As Ivan Zurita, president of Nestlé do Brasil, noted, "In our country there are 30 million people considered too poor to be consumers, and we have come to the conclusion that regionalization will speed up our competitiveness in terms of cost and greater operational efficiency." Source: REUTERS/Jamil Bittar.

[25]Joe Leahy, "Brazil Needs to Be Wary as It Enjoys Success Amid 'Insanity,'" *Financial Times* (August 3, 2011), p. 2.
[26]Antonio Regalado, "Soccer, Samba and Outsourcing?" *The Wall Street Journal* (January 25, 2007), p. B1.
[27]Matt Moffett and Helene Cooper, "Silent Invasion: In Backyard of the U.S., Europe Gains Ground in Trade, Diplomacy," *The Wall Street Journal* (September 18, 1997), pp. A1, A8.

Exhibit 2-8 Leaders of the BRICS nations met at a summit in South Africa in 2013. They are (from left): Indian Prime minister Manmohan Singh, Chinese President Xi Jinping, South African President Jacob Zuma, Brazilian President Dilma Rousseff, and Russian President Vladimir Putin.
Source: AFP / Getty Images.

foundations. Although China joined the World Trade Organization (WTO) in 2001, trading partners are still concerned about human rights, intellectual property rights, and other issues. The country's leaders must thus deal with China's sprawling bureaucracy while reforming the state's enterprise sector. To ensure that the nation's export-led economic transformation is sustained, policymakers have launched hundreds of infrastructure projects. These include airports, cargo ports, highways, and railroads. Avon, Coca-Cola, Dell, Ford, General Motors, Honda, HSBC, JPMorgan Chase, McDonald's, Motorola, Procter & Gamble, Samsung, Siemens AG, Toyota, and Volkswagen are among the scores of global companies that are actively pursuing opportunities in China.

South Africa joined the BRICS group in 2011. In 2013, South African President Jacob Zuma welcomed leaders from the other four BRICS nations to a summit in Durban (see Exhibit 2-8). One important item on the agenda: How to increase trade and investment among the five nations. In addition, President Zuma hopes to attract more direct investment in the African continent as a whole.[28]

Lower-middle- and upper-income countries that achieve the highest sustained rates of economic growth are sometimes referred to collectively as **newly industrializing economies (NIEs)**. Overall, NIEs are characterized by greater industrial output than developing economies; heavy manufactures and refined products make up an increasing proportion of their exports. Goldman Sachs, the firm that developed the original BRIC framework more than a decade ago, has identified a new country grouping called Next-11 (N11). Five of the N11 countries are considered NIEs. These include three lower-middle-income countries: Egypt, Indonesia, and the Philippines. Mexico and Turkey are N11 NIEs from the ranks of the upper-middle-income category. Among these five countries, Egypt, Indonesia, and the Philippines have posted positive GDP growth over the past several years.

Marketing Opportunities in LDCs and Developing Countries

Despite many problems in LDCs and developing countries, it is possible to nurture long-term market opportunities. Today, Nike produces and sells only a small portion of its output in China, but when the firm refers to China as a "two-billion-foot market," it clearly has the future in mind.

---

[28]Patrick McGroarty, "South Africa Trade Hits Bump," *The Wall Street Journal* (March 25, 2013), p. A11.

C. K. Prahalad and Allen Hammond have identified several assumptions and misconceptions about the "bottom of the pyramid" (BOP) that need to be corrected:[29]

- Mistaken assumption #1: *The poor have no money.* In fact, the aggregate buying power of poor communities can be substantial. In rural Bangladesh, for example, villagers spend considerable sums to use village phones operated by local entrepreneurs.
- Mistaken assumption #2: *The poor are too concerned with fulfilling basic needs to "waste" money on nonessential goods.* In fact, consumers who are too poor to purchase a house do buy "luxury" items such as television sets and gas stoves to improve their lives.
- Mistaken assumption #3: *The goods sold in developing markets are so inexpensive that there is no room for a new market entrant to make a profit.* In fact, because the poor often pay higher prices for many goods, there is an opportunity for efficient competitors to realize attractive margins by offering quality and low prices.
- Mistaken assumption #4: *People in BOP markets cannot use advanced technology.* In fact, residents of rural areas can and do quickly learn to use cell phones, PCs, and similar devices.
- Mistaken assumption #5: *Global companies that target BOP markets will be criticized for exploiting the poor.* In fact, the informal economies in many poor countries are highly exploitative. A global company offering basic goods and services that improve a country's standard of living can earn a reasonable return while benefiting society.

Despite the difficult economic conditions in parts of Southeast Asia, Latin America, Africa, and Eastern Europe, many nations in these regions will evolve into attractive markets. One of marketing's roles in developing countries is to focus resources on the task of creating and delivering products that are best suited to local needs and incomes. Appropriate marketing communications techniques can also be applied to accelerate acceptance of these products. Marketing can be the link that relates resources to opportunity and facilitates need satisfaction on the consumer's terms.

An interesting debate in marketing is whether it has any relevance to the process of economic development. Some people believe that marketing is relevant only in affluent, industrialized countries, where the major problem is directing society's resources into ever-changing output or production to satisfy a dynamic marketplace. In the less-developed country, the argument goes, the major problem is the allocation of scarce resources toward obvious production needs. Efforts should therefore focus on production and how to increase output, not on customer needs and wants.

Conversely, it can be argued that the process of focusing an organization's resources on environmental opportunities is a process of universal relevance. The role of marketing—to identify people's needs and wants and to focus individual and organizational efforts to respond to those needs and wants—is the same in all countries, irrespective of the level of economic development. When global marketers respond to the needs of rural residents in emerging markets such as China and India, they are also more likely to gain all-important government support and approval.

For example, pursuing alternative energy sources is important for two reasons: the lack of coal reserves in many countries and the concerns that heavy reliance on fossil fuels contributes to global warming. Similarly, people everywhere need affordable, safe drinking water. Recognizing this fact, Nestlé launched Pure Life bottled water in Pakistan. The price was set at about 35 cents a bottle, and advertising promised, "Pure safety. Pure trust. The ideal water." Pure Life quickly captured 50 percent of the bottled water market in Pakistan; the brand has since been rolled out in dozens of other low-income countries.[30] The Coca-Cola Company recently began to address dietary and health needs in low-income countries by developing Vitango, a beverage product that can help fight anemia, blindness, and other ailments related to malnutrition.

---

[29]Adapted from C. K. Prahalad and Allen Hammond, "Serving the World's Poor, Profitably," *Harvard Business Review* 80, no. 9 (September 2002), pp. 48–57.
[30]Ernest Beck, "Populist Perrier? Nestlé Pitches Bottled Water to World's Poor," *The Asian Wall Street Journal* (June 18, 1999), p. B1.

There is also an opportunity to help developing countries join the Internet economy. Intel Chairman Craig Barrett has been visiting villages in China and India and launching programs to provide Internet access and computer training. One aspect of Intel's World Ahead initiative is the development of a $550 computer that is powered by a car battery. Similarly, Hewlett-Packard engineers are working to develop solar-powered communication devices that can link remote areas to the Internet.[32] Meanwhile, an initiative called One Laptop Per Child embarked on a program to develop a laptop computer that governments in developing countries can buy for $100.

Global companies can also contribute to economic development by finding creative ways to preserve old-growth forests and other resources while creating economic opportunities for local inhabitants. In Brazil, for example, Daimler AG works with a cooperative of farmers who transform coconut husks into natural rubber to be used in auto seats, headrests, and sun visors. French luxury goods marketer Hermès International has created a line of handbags called "Amazonia" made of latex extracted by traditional rubber tappers. Both Daimler and Hermès are responding to the opportunity to promote themselves as environmentally conscious while appealing to "green"-oriented consumers. As Isabela Fortes, director of a company in Rio de Janeiro that retrains forest workers, notes, "You can only prevent forest people from destroying the jungle by giving them viable economic alternatives."[33]

High-Income Countries

High-income countries, also known as *advanced, developed, industrialized,* or *postindustrial countries*, are those with a GNI per capita of $12,476 or higher. With the exception of a few oil-rich nations, the countries in this category reached their present income level through a process of sustained economic growth.

The phrase *postindustrial countries* was first used by Daniel Bell of Harvard to describe the United States, Sweden, Japan, and other advanced, high-income societies. In his 1973 book *The Coming of the Post-Industrial Society*, Bell drew a distinction between the industrial and the postindustrial stages of country development that went beyond mere measures of income. Bell's thesis was that the sources of innovation in postindustrial societies are derived increasingly from the codification of theoretical knowledge rather than from "random" inventions. The service sector accounts for more than half of national output, the processing and exchange of information become increasingly important, and knowledge trumps capital as the key strategic resource. In addition, in a postindustrial society, intellectual technology is more important than machine technology, and scientists and professionals play a more dominant role than engineers and semi-skilled workers. Further, postindustrial societies exhibit an orientation toward the future and stress the importance of interpersonal relationships in the functioning of society. Taken together, these forces and factors spell big sociological changes for the work and home lives of the residents of postindustrial nations.

Product and market opportunities in a postindustrial society are heavily dependent upon new products and innovations. Ownership levels for basic products are extremely high in most households. Organizations seeking to grow often face a difficult task if they attempt to expand their share of existing markets. Alternatively, they can endeavor to create new markets. Today, for example, global companies in a range of communication-related industries are seeking to create new e-commerce markets for interactive forms of electronic communication. A case in point is Barry Diller's IAC/InterActiveCorp, which owns search engine Ask.com, the Match.com dating site, the Web magazine *Daily Beast*, and other Internet businesses.

In 2009, the Financial Times Stock Exchange (FTSE) upgraded South Korea's economic status from "emerging" to "developed." The change is consistent with the World Bank's ranking and reflects South Korea's emergence as a global powerhouse. It is the 15th-largest economy by GDP, the 7th-largest exporter, and the 10th-largest importer. South Korea is home to Samsung Electronics, LG Group, Kia Motors Corporation, Daewoo Corporation, Hyundai Corporation, and other well-known global enterprises. In place of substantial barriers to free trade, South

> "Sustainable energy pioneers who focus on the base of the pyramid could set the stage for one of the biggest bonanzas in the history of commerce, since extensive adoption and experience in developing markets would almost certainly lead to dramatic improvements in cost and quality."[31]
>
> —Stuart L. Hart and Clayton M. Christensen

---

[31]Stuart L. Hart and Clayton M. Christensen, "The Great Leap: Driving Innovation from the Base of the Pyramid," *MIT Sloan Management Review* 44, no. 1 (Fall 2002), p. 56.
[32]Jason Dean and Peter Wonacott, "Tech Firms Woo 'Next Billion' Users," *The Wall Street Journal* (November 3, 2006), p. A2. See also David Kirkpatrick, "Looking for Profits in Poverty," *Fortune* (February 5, 2001), pp. 174–176.
[33]Miriam Jordan, "From the Amazon to Your Armrest," *The Wall Street Journal* (May 1, 2001), pp. B1, B4.

Korea initiated major reforms in its political and economic systems in response to the "Asian flu." Even so, investors note the political risk posed by North Korea's aggressiveness in recent months. Another concern is inconsistent treatment of foreign investors by the government. For example, authorities recently raided the local offices of French retailer Carrefour.

Seven high-income countries—the United States, Japan, Germany, France, Britain, Canada, and Italy—comprise the **Group of Seven (G-7)**. Finance ministers, central bankers, and heads of state from the seven nations have worked together for more than a quarter of a century in an effort to steer the global economy in the direction of prosperity and to ensure monetary stability. Whenever a global crisis looms—be it the Latin American debt crisis of the 1980s or Russia's struggle to transform its economy in the 1990s—representatives from the G-7 nations gather and try to coordinate policy. Starting in the mid-1990s, Russia began attending the G-7 summit meetings. In 1998, Russia became a full participant, giving rise to the **Group of Eight (G-8)** (see Exhibit 2-9). The **Group of Twenty (G-20)** was established in 1999; it is comprised of finance ministers and central bank governors from 19 countries plus the European Union. The G-20 includes developing nations such as Brazil, India, Indonesia, and Turkey.

Another institution composed of high-income countries is the **Organization for Economic Cooperation and Development** (**OECD**; www.oecd.org). The 34 nations that belong to the OECD believe in market-allocation economic systems and pluralistic democracy. The organization has been variously described as an "economic think tank" and a "rich-man's club"; in any event, the OECD's fundamental task is to "enable its members to achieve the highest sustainable economic growth and improve the economic and social well-being of their populations." Today's organization is based in Paris and evolved from a group of European nations that worked together after World War II to rebuild the region's economy. Canada and the United States have been members since 1961; Japan joined in 1964. Evidence of the increasing importance of the BRICS group is the fact that Brazil, Russia, India, and China have all formally announced their intention to join the OECD. Applicants must demonstrate progress toward economic reform.

Representatives from OECD member nations work together in committees to review economic and social policies that affect world trade. The secretary-general presides over a council that meets regularly and has decision-making power. Committees of specialists from member countries provide a forum for discussion of trade and other issues. Consultation, peer pressure, and diplomacy are the keys to helping member nations candidly assess their own economic policies and actions. The OECD publishes country surveys and an annual economic outlook. Recently, the OECD has become more focused on global issues, social policy, and labor market deregulation. For example, the OECD has addressed the vexing problem of bribery; in 1997, it passed a convention that requires members to cooperate when pursuing bribery allegations. In the 15+ years since the agreement entered into force, Germany, France, and other countries have adopted antibribery laws. Prosecutors from various countries are doing a better job of collaborating across borders; one case against Siemens AG resulted in a record ($1.6 billion) fine.[34]

The Triad

The ascendancy of the global economy has been noted by many observers in recent decades. One of the most astute is Kenichi Ohmae, former chairman of McKinsey & Company Japan. His 1985 book *Triad Power* represented one of the first attempts to develop a coherent conceptualization of the new emerging order. Ohmae argued that successful global companies had to be equally strong in Japan, Western Europe, and the United States. These three regions, which Ohmae collectively called the **Triad**, represent the dominant economic centers of the world. Today, nearly 75 percent of world income as measured by GNP is located in the Triad. Ohmae has recently revised his view of the world; in the **expanded Triad**, the Japanese leg encompasses the entire Pacific region, the American leg includes Canada and Mexico, and the boundary in Europe is moving eastward. Coca-Cola is a perfect illustration of a company with a balanced revenue stream. About 7 percent of the company's revenues are generated in Eurasia and Africa; another 13 percent come from Europe; and Latin America accounts for 11 percent. The Pacific region contributes 14 percent, and North America accounts for about 31 percent. The balance comes from the company's bottling investments.

---

[34]Russell Gold and David Crawford, "U.S., Other Nations Step Up Bribery Battle," *The Wall Street Journal* (September 12, 2008), pp. B1, B6.

Exhibit 2-9 When the world's leaders meet to discuss policy issues, nongovernmental organizations (NGOs) often take advantage of the opportunity to make their voices heard. This print ad was timed to coincide with the 2008 G-8 summit in Japan. The ad was paid for by Oxfam International, Whiteband, Save the Children, One, and Avaaz.org. The copy urges G8 leaders to keep their aid promises, to provide health care and education for everyone, and to address the issue of climate change.
Source: Used by permission.

Marketing Implications of the Stages of Development

The stages of economic development described previously can serve as a guide to marketers in evaluating **product saturation levels**, or the percentage of potential buyers or households that own a particular product. George David is the former CEO of United Technologies; its business units include Otis Elevators. David explained the significance of product saturation to his former business as follows:

> We measure elevator populations in countries as units installed per thousand people. And in China, the number today is about one half an elevator per thousand people. In most countries of the world outside of the U.S., people live in elevator and storied apartment houses. It's true all over Europe, all over Asia, South America, certainly true in China. And in a mature market like Europe, the installed population is about six elevators per thousand people. And so we're on our way to some portion of six.[35]

As this comment suggests, product saturation levels for many products are low in emerging markets. For example, India's teledensity—a measure of ownership of private telephones—is only about 20 percent of the population. In China, saturation levels of private motor vehicles and personal computers (PCs) are quite low; there is only 1 car or light truck for every 43,000 Chinese, and only 1 PC for every 6,000 people. In Poland in 2001, there were 21 cars per 100 people compared with 49 per 100 people in the EU. In 2002 Poland had 11 PCs per 100 people; in the EU, the ratio was 34 PCs per 100 people.[36] In India, just 8 out of every 1,000 adults own a car.[37] In Russia, 200 people out of 1,000 own cars; in Germany, the figure is 565 out of 1,000.[38] Low levels of vehicle ownership are one reason Myanmar represents an attractive market opportunity for global automakers (see Myanmar Is Open for Business on p. 72).

Balance of Payments

The **balance of payments** is a record of all economic transactions between the residents of a country and the rest of the world. U.S. balance of payments statistics for the period 2007 to 2011 are shown in Table 2-5. International trade data for the United States is available from the U.S. Bureau of Economic Analysis (www.bea.gov); the bureau's interactive Web site enables users to generate customized reports. The International Monetary Fund's *Balance of Payments Statistics Yearbook* provides trade statistics and summaries of economic activity for all countries in the world.[39]

TABLE 2-5 U.S. Balance of Payments, 2007–2011 (US$ millions)

	2007	2008	2009	2010	2011
A. Current Account	**−731,214**	**−668,854**	**−376,551**	**−470,898**	**−465,926**
1. Goods Exports	1,148,481	1,304,896	1,069,491	1,288,882	1,497,406
2. Goods Imports	−1,976,853	−2,139,548	−1,575,400	−1,934,006	−2,235,819
3. *Balance on Goods*	*−819,373*	*−834,652*	*−505,910*	*−645,124*	*−738,413*
4. Services: Credit	497,245	534,166	505,547	553,603	605,961
5. Services: Debit	−378,130	−398,266	−380,909	−403,216	−427,428
6. *Balance on Services*	119,115	135,850	124,637	150,387	178,533
7. *Balance on Goods and Services*	*−700,258*	*−698,802*	*−381,272*	*−494,737*	*−559,880*
B. Capital Account	**−1,842**	**6,010**	**−140**	**−152**	**−1,159**

Source: www.bea.gov.

---

[35]Ron Insana, "United Tech Outperforms Peers Year After Year," *USA Today* (April 4, 2005), p. 3B.
[36]Stefan Wagstyl, "The Next Investment Wave: Companies in East and West Prepare for the Risks and Opportunities of an Enlarged EU," *Financial Times* (April 27, 2004), p. 13.
[37]Amy Chozik, "Nissan Races to Make Smaller, Cheaper Cars," *The Wall Street Journal* (October 22, 2007), p. A12.
[38]Lukas I. Alpert, "Russia's Auto Market Shines," *The Wall Street Journal* (August 30, 2012), p. B3.
[39]Balance of payments data are available from a number of different sources, each of which may show slightly different figures for a given line item.

The balance of payments is divided into the current and the capital accounts. The **current account** is a broad measure that includes **merchandise trade** (i.e., manufactured goods) and **services trade** (i.e., intangible, experience-based economic output) plus certain categories of financial transfers such as humanitarian aid. A country with a negative current account balance has a **trade deficit**; that is, the outflow of money to pay for imports exceeds the inflow of money from sales of exports. Conversely, a country with a positive current account balance has a **trade surplus**. The **capital account** is a record of all long-term direct investment, portfolio investment, and other short- and long-term capital flows. The minus signs signify outflows of cash; for example, in Table 2-5 line 2 shows an outflow of $2.2 trillion in 2011 that represents payment for U.S. merchandise imports. (Entries not shown in Table 2-5 represent changes in net errors and omissions, foreign liabilities, and reserves.) These are the entries that comprise the balance of payments balance. In general, a country accumulates reserves when the net of its current and capital account transactions shows a surplus; it gives up reserves when the net shows a deficit. The important fact to recognize about the overall balance of payments is that it is always in balance, although imbalances do occur in subsets of the overall balance. For example, a commonly reported balance is the trade balance on goods (line 3 in Table 2-5).

A close examination of Table 2-5 reveals that the United States regularly posts deficits in both the current account and the trade balance in goods. The U.S. trade deficit reflects a number of factors, including increased imports from China, a seemingly insatiable consumer demand for imported goods, and the enormous cost of military operations in the Middle East and Afghanistan. Table 2-6 shows a record of goods and services trade between the United States and the BRIC countries for 2011. A comparison of lines 4 and 5 in the two tables shows a bright spot from the U.S. perspective: The United States has maintained a services trade surplus with the much of the rest of the world. Overall, however, the United States posts balance of payments deficits while important trading partners, such as China, have surpluses.

China has more than $3 trillion in foreign reserves, more than any other nation. It offsets its trade surpluses with an outflow of capital, while the United States offsets its trade deficit with an inflow of capital. China and other countries with healthy trade surpluses are setting up *sovereign wealth funds* to invest some of the money. As trading partners, U.S. consumers and businesses own an increasing quantity of foreign products, while foreign investors own more U.S. land, real estate, and government securities. In 2005, the United States borrowed 6 percent of its output in goods and services from foreign countries.[40] Foreign-owned U.S. assets total $2.5 trillion; China currently owns $1.1 trillion in U.S. treasury bonds. As Ha Jiming, an economist with China's largest investment bank, noted, "One trillion is a big amount, but it is also a hot potato."[41] Some policymakers in Washington are alarmed about the U.S. trade deficit with China, which reached $280 billion in 2011.

TABLE 2-6 U.S. Goods and Services Trade with Brazil, India, and China, 2011 (US$ millions)

	China	India	Brazil	Russia
1. U.S. Goods Exports to	105,263	21,616	42,821	8,384
2. Goods Imports from	−400,642	−36,338	−31,549	−34,652
3. *Balance on Goods*	−295,378	−14,722	*11,272*	−26,268
4. U.S. Services Exports to	26,731	11,108	21,721	na
5. Services Imports from	−11,395	−16,921	−6,970	na
6. *U.S. Balance on Services*	15,335	−5,814	14,751	na
7. *U.S. Balance on Goods and Services*	−280,043	−20,536	26,022	na

Source: www.bea.gov.

[40]David Wessel, "Counting on a Miracle with U.S. Debt," *The Wall Street Journal* (September 29, 2005), p. A2.
[41]Richard McGregor, "The Trillion Dollar Question: China is Grappling with How to Deploy Its Foreign Exchange Riches," *Financial Times* (September 25, 2006).

Trade in Merchandise and Services

Thanks in part to the achievements of General Agreement on Tariffs and Trade (GATT) and the WTO, world merchandise trade has grown at a faster rate than world production since the end of World War II. Put differently, import and export growth has outpaced the rate of increase in GNI. According to figures compiled by the WTO, the dollar value of world merchandise trade in 2009 totaled $11.8 trillion. However, as the world slipped into recession in 2008, annual world trade growth slowed to about 6 percent. The top exporting and importing countries are shown in Table 2-7.

In 2003, Germany surpassed the United States as the world's top exporter. German manufacturers of all sizes have benefited from global economic growth because they provide the motors, machines, vehicles, and other capital goods that are required to build factories and country infrastructures; worldwide, machinery and transport equipment constitute approximately one-third of global exports. Overall, about two-thirds of Germany's exports go to other EU nations; France is the number 1 country destination, while the United States ranks second. Today, exports generate 40 percent of Germany's gross domestic product, and 9 million jobs are export related. In addition, annual sales by the foreign subsidiaries of German-based companies are $1.5 billion.[42]

In 2009, China leapfrogged Germany in the global merchandise export rankings (see Table 2-7). China's top-place ranking underscores its role as an export powerhouse; the country has demonstrated continued economic strength by achieving double-digit export growth. Chinese exports have surged since China joined the WTO in 2001; in fact, policymakers in several countries are pressuring Beijing to boost the value of the yuan in an effort to stem the tide of imports.

The fastest-growing sector of world trade is trade in services. Services include travel and entertainment; education; business services such as accounting, advertising, engineering, investment banking, and legal services; and royalties and license fees that represent payments for intellectual property. One of the major issues in trade relations between the high- and lower-income countries is trade in services. As a group, low-, lower-middle, and even upper-middle-income countries are lax in enforcing international copyrights and protecting intellectual property and patent laws. As a result, countries that export service products such as computer software, music, and video entertainment suffer a loss of income. According to the Global Software Piracy Study conducted each year by the Business Software Alliance, annual worldwide losses due to software piracy amount to approximately $50 billion. In China alone, software piracy cost the industry an estimated $7.6 billion in lost sales in 2009.

The United States is a major service trader. As shown in Figure 2-2, U.S. services exports in 2012 totaled nearly $649 billion. This represents about one-third of total U.S. exports. The U.S. services surplus (service exports minus imports) stood at $207 billion. This surplus partially offset the U.S. merchandise trade deficit, which declined to $741 billion in 2012 from a record $835 billion in 2006. American Express, Walt Disney, IBM, Microsoft, and UPS are a few of the U.S. companies that have experienced rapid growth in demand for their services around the world.

TABLE 2-7 Top Exporters and Importers in World Merchandise Trade, 2009 (US$ billions)

Leading Exporters	2009	Leading Importers	2009
1. China	$1,202	1. United States	$1,605
2. Germany	1,126	2. China	1,006
3. United States	1,056	3. Germany	938
4. Japan	581	4. France	560
5. Netherlands	498	5. Japan	552

Source: WTO.

---

[42]Bertrand Benoit and Richard Milne, "Germany's Best-Kept Secret: How Its Exporters are Beating the World," *Financial Times* (May 19, 2006), p. 11.

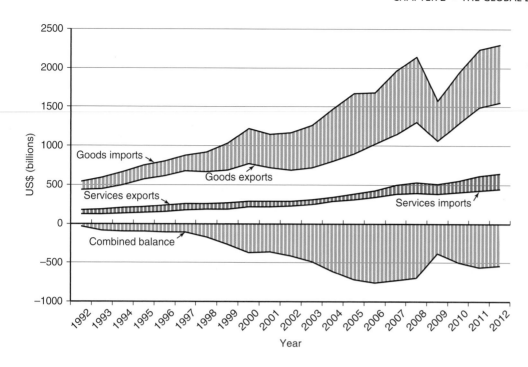

FIGURE 2-2

U.S. Trade Balance on Services and on Merchandise Trade (US$ billions)

Overview of International Finance

Foreign exchange makes it possible for a company in one country to conduct business in other countries with different currencies. However, foreign exchange is an aspect of global marketing that involves certain financial risks, decisions, and activities that are completely different from those facing a domestic marketer. Moreover, those risks can be even higher in developing markets such as Thailand, Malaysia, and South Korea. When a company conducts business within a single country or region with customers and suppliers paying in the same currency, there is no exchange risk. All prices, payments, receipts, assets, and liabilities are in the given currency. However, when conducting business across boundaries in countries with different currencies, a company is thrust into the turbulent world of exchange risk.

The foreign exchange market consists literally of a buyer's and a seller's market where currencies are traded for both spot and future delivery on a continuous basis. As noted earlier in the chapter, $4 trillion in currencies is traded every day. The *spot* market is for immediate delivery; the market for future delivery is called the *forward* market. This is a true market where prices are based on the combined forces of supply and demand that come into play at the moment of any transaction.

Who are the participants in this market? First, a country's central bank can intervene in currency markets by buying and selling currencies and government securities in an effort to influence exchange rates. Recall that China currently holds trillions of dollars in U.S. treasury securities. Such purchases help ensure that China's currency is relatively weak compared to the U.S. dollar.[43] Second, some of the trading in the foreign exchange market takes the form of transactions needed to settle accounts for the global trade in goods and services. For example, because Porsche is a German company, the dollars spent on Porsche automobiles by American car buyers must be converted to euros. Finally, currency speculators also participate in the foreign exchange market.

Devaluation can result from government action or an economic crisis; whatever the cause, devaluation is reduction in the value of a nation's currency against other currencies. For example, in August 1998 the Russian economy imploded. The ruble plunged in value, and the government defaulted on its foreign debt obligations. Many Russians faced wage cuts and layoffs; savings were wiped out as banks collapsed. In the decade that followed, however, Russia's economy

---

[43]Mark Whitehouse, "U.S. Foreign Debt Shows Its Teeth as Rates Climb," *The Wall Street Journal* (September 25, 2006), p. A9.

made a rapid recovery. Real GDP doubled, in part because import price increases caused by the ruble's devaluation stimulated local production. As one economist noted, "The crash of '98 really cleaned out the macroeconomy."[44]

To the extent that a country sells more goods and services abroad than it buys, there will be a greater demand for its currency and a tendency for it to appreciate in value—unless the government pursues foreign exchange policies that do not allow the currency to fluctuate. In international economics, such policies are called *mercantilism* or *competitive-currency politics* because they favor domestic industries at the expense of foreign competitors. During the past few years, the Chinese government has been criticized for keeping China's currency undervalued to support exports. Faced with escalating rhetoric from Washington and elsewhere, Beijing has responded by adopting a policy of **revaluation** to allow the yuan to strengthen against the dollar and other currencies.[45] Between 2006 and 2008, the yuan appreciated by about 20 percent.

What effect would a stronger Chinese currency have? The impact would be both domestic and global. In the broadest sense, a stronger renminbi (or yuan, as the Chinese currency is called) should help rebalance the global economy. In other words, China's economic growth would be less dependent on the United States and other countries continuing to snap up its exports. Chinese consumers and companies would enjoy increased purchasing power as imported goods become more affordable. This would put downward pressure on China's consumer price index, helping Beijing meet its goal of keeping inflation under control. Global automakers such as BMW, General Motors, and Volkswagen that assemble cars in China from imported parts would reap the benefits of lower costs.

Table 2-8 shows how fluctuating currency values can affect financial risk, depending on the terms of payment specified in the contract. Suppose, at the time a deal is made, the exchange rate is €1.10 equals $1.00. How is a U.S. exporter affected if the dollar strengthens against the euro (e.g., €1.25 equals $1.00) and the contract specifies payment in dollars? What happens if the dollar weakens (e.g., €0.85 equals $1.00)? Conversely, what if the European buyer contracts to pay in euros rather than dollars?

Given that currencies fluctuate in value, a reasonable question to ask is whether a particular currency is over- or undervalued compared with another currency. Recall from the chapter discussion that a currency's value can reflect government policy (as in the case of China) or market forces. One way to approach the question is to compare world prices for a single well-known product: McDonald's Big Mac hamburger. The so-called Big Mac Index is a "quick and dirty" way of determining which of the world's currencies are weak or strong. The underlying assumption is that the price of a Big Mac in any world currency should, after being converted to dollars, equal the price of a Big Mac in the United States. (Similar indexes have been proposed based on the price of Starbucks coffee and IKEA furniture.)[46]

A country's currency would be overvalued if the Big Mac price (converted to dollars) is higher than the U.S. price. Conversely, a country's currency would be undervalued if the converted Big Mac price is lower than the U.S. price. Economists use the concept of purchasing

TABLE 2-8 Exchange Risks and Gains in Foreign Transactions

Foreign Contract Exchange Rates	$1,000,000 Contract		€1,100,000 Contract	
	U.S. Seller Receives	European Buyer Pays	U.S. Seller Receives	European Buyer Pays
€1.25 = $1	$1,000,000	€1,250,000	$880,000	€1,100,000
€1.10 = $1	$1,000,000	€1,100,000	$1,000,000	€1,100,000
€1.00 = $1	$1,000,000	€1,000,000	$1,100,000	€1,100,000
€0.85 = $1	$1,000,000	€850,000	$1,294,118	€1,100,000

[44]David J. Lynch, "Russia Brings Revitalized Economy to the Table," *USA Today* (July 13, 2006).
[45]Damian Paletta and John W. Miller, "China, U.S. Square Off Over Yuan," *The Wall Street Journal* (October 7, 2010), p. A10.
[46]"When the Chips Are Down," Economist.com (accessed December 1, 2010).

power parity (PPP) when adjusting national income data to improve comparability. For example, let's take as given that the average U.S. price of a Big Mac is $3.73; in China, the price is 14.5 yuan. If we divide 14.5 by 6.65 (the yuan/dollar exchange rate), we get 2.18. Because this converted price is less than the U.S. price, the yuan must be undervalued. In other words, based on the U.S. price for a Big Mac, the yuan/dollar exchange rate ought to be 3.88/$1 rather than 6.65 to $1.[47] Make sure you understand that if the exchange rate changes from 6.65 to the dollar to 3.88 to the dollar, the yuan has strengthened relative to the dollar.

Economic Exposure

Economic exposure reflects the impact of currency fluctuations on a company's financial performance. Economic exposure can occur when a company's business transactions result in sales or purchases denominated in foreign currencies. Diageo, for example, faces economic exposure to the extent that it accepts payment for exports of Scotch whisky at one exchange rate but actually settles its accounts at a different exchange rate.[48] Obviously, economic exposure is a critical issue for Nestlé, with 98 percent of annual sales taking place outside Switzerland. Among countries in the euro zone, GlaxoSmithKline, Daimler AG, BP, Sanofi-Aventis, Royal Dutch Shell, AstraZeneca, and SAB Miller all generate more than one-third of total sales in the U.S. market. Given the current weakness of the dollar relative to the euro, all of these companies face potential economic exposure. By comparison, General Electric (GE) generates more than 50 percent of its revenues in the domestic U.S. market, so the relative extent of GE's exposure is less than that of the European companies just listed. Even so, as noted in its annual report, GE does face economic exposure:

> When countries or regions experience currency and/or economic stress, we often have increased exposure to certain risks, but also often have new profit opportunities. Potential increased risks include, among other things, high receivable delinquencies and bad debts, delays or cancellations of sales and orders principally related to power and aircraft equipment, higher local currency financing costs and slowdown in established financial services activities.[49]

In dealing with the economic exposure introduced by currency fluctuations, a key issue is whether the company can use price as a strategic tool for maintaining its profit margins. Can the company adjust prices in response to a rise or fall of foreign exchange rates in various markets? That depends on the price elasticity of demand. The less price-sensitive the demand, the greater the flexibility a company has in responding to exchange rate changes. In the late 1980s, for example, Porsche raised prices in the United States three times in response to the weak dollar. The result: Porsche's U.S. sales dropped precipitously, from 30,000 vehicles in 1986 to 4,500 vehicles in 1992. Clearly, U.S. luxury car buyers were exhibiting elastic demand curves for pricey German sports cars!

Managing Exchange Rate Exposure

It should be clear from this discussion that accurately forecasting exchange rate movements is a major challenge. Over the years, the search for ways of managing cash flows to eliminate or reduce exchange rate risks has resulted in the development of numerous techniques and financial strategies. For example, it may be desirable to sell products in the company's home country currency. When this is not possible, techniques are available to reduce both transaction and operating exposure.

Hedging exchange rate exposure involves establishing an offsetting currency position such that the loss or gain of one currency position is offset by a corresponding gain or loss in some other currency. The practice is common among global companies that sell products and maintain operations in different countries. Today, for example, Porsche relies on currency hedging rather than price increases to boost pretax profits on sales of its automobiles. Porsche manufactures all of its cars in Europe, but generates about 45 percent of its sales in the United States. Thus,

---

[47]The authors acknowledge that the PPP theory–based Big Mac Index is simplistic; as noted in this section, exchange rates are also affected by interest rate differentials and monetary and fiscal policies—not just prices.
[48]John Willman, "Currency Squeeze on Guinness," *Financial Times—Weekend Money* (September 27–28, 1997), p. 5.
[49]General Electric 2004 *Annual Report*, p. 58.

Porsche faces economic exposure stemming from the relative value of the dollar to the euro. Porsche is "fully hedged"; that is, it takes currency positions to protect all earnings from foreign exchange movements.[50]

If company forecasts indicate that the value of the foreign currency will weaken against the home currency, it can hedge to protect against potential transaction losses. Conversely, when it is anticipated that the foreign currency will appreciate (strengthen) against the home currency, then a gain, rather than a loss, can be expected on foreign transactions when revenues are converted into the home currency. Given this expectation, the best decision may be not to hedge at all. (The operative word is "may"; many companies hedge anyway unless management is convinced the foreign currency will strengthen.) Porsche has profited by (correctly) betting on a weak dollar.

External hedging methods for managing both transaction and translation exposure require companies to participate in the foreign currency market. Specific hedging tools include forward contracts and currency options. *Internal hedging methods* include price adjustment clauses and intracorporate borrowing or lending in foreign currencies. The **forward market** is a mechanism for buying and selling currencies at a preset price for future delivery. If it is known that a certain amount of foreign currency is going to be paid out or received at some future date, a company can insure itself against exchange loss by buying or selling forward. With a forward contract, the company can lock in a specific fixed exchange rate for a future date and thus immunize itself against the loss (or gain) caused by the exchange rate fluctuation. By consulting sources such as the *Financial Times, The Wall Street Journal*, or www.ozforex.com, it is possible to determine exchange rates on any given day. In addition to spot prices, 30-, 60-, and 180-day forward prices are quoted for dozens of world currencies.

Companies use the forward market when the currency exposure is known in advance (e.g., when a firm contract of sale exists). In some situations, however, companies are not certain about the future foreign currency cash inflow or outflow. Consider the risk exposure of a U.S. company that bids for a foreign project but won't know until sometime later if the project will be granted. The company needs to protect the dollar value of the contract by hedging the *potential* foreign currency cash inflow that will be generated if the company turns out to be the winning bidder. In such an instance, forward contracts are not the appropriate hedging tool.

A foreign currency **option** is best for such situations. A **put option** gives the buyer the right, not the obligation, to sell a specified number of foreign currency units at a fixed price, up to the option's expiration date. (Conversely, a **call option** is the right, but not the obligation, to buy the foreign currency.) In the example of bidding the foreign project, the company can take out a put option to sell the foreign currency for dollars at a set price in the future. In other words, the U.S. company locks in the value of the contract in dollars. Thus, if the project is granted, the future foreign currency cash inflow has been hedged by means of the put option. If the project is *not* granted, the company can trade the put option in the options market without exercising it; remember, options are rights, not obligations. The only money the company stands to lose is the difference between what it paid for the option and what it receives upon selling it.

Financial officers of global firms can avoid economic exposure altogether by demanding a particular currency as the payment for its foreign sales. As noted, a U.S-based company might demand U.S. dollars as the payment currency for its foreign sales. This, however, does not eliminate currency risk; it simply shifts that risk to the customers. In common practice, companies typically attempt to invoice exports (receivables) in strong currencies and invoice imports (payables) in weak currencies. However, in today's highly competitive world market, such practice may reduce a company's competitive edge.

Summary

The economic environment is a major determinant of global market potential and opportunity. In today's global economy, capital movements are the key driving force, production has become uncoupled from employment, and capitalism has vanquished communism. Based

---

[50]Stephen Power, "Porsche Powers Profit with Currency Play," *The Wall Street Journal* (December 8, 2004), p. C3.

on patterns of resource allocation and ownership, the world's national economies can be categorized as **market capitalism**, **centrally planned capitalism**, **centrally planned socialism**, and **market socialism**. The final years of the twentieth century were marked by a transition toward market capitalism in many countries that had been centrally controlled. However, great disparity still exists among the nations of the world in terms of economic freedom.

Countries can be categorized in terms of their stage of economic development: **low income**, **lower-middle income**, **upper-middle income**, and **high income**. **Gross domestic product (GDP)** and **gross national income (GNI)** are commonly used measures of economic development. The 50 poorest countries in the low-income category are sometimes referred to as **least-developed countries (LDCs)**. Upper-middle-income countries with high growth rates are often called **newly industrializing economies (NIEs)**. Several of the world's economies are notable for their fast growth; for example, the **BRICS** nations include Brazil (lower-middle income), Russia (upper-middle income), India (low income), China (lower-middle income), and South Africa (upper-middle income). The **Group of Seven (G-7)**, the **Group of Eight (G-8)**, the **Group of Twenty (G-20)**, and the **Organization for Economic Cooperation and Development (OECD)** represent efforts by high-income nations to promote democratic ideals and free market policies throughout the rest of the world. Most of the world's income is located in the **Triad**, which includes Japan, the United States, and Western Europe. Companies with global aspirations generally have operations in all three areas. Market potential for a product can be evaluated by determining **product saturation levels** in light of income levels.

A country's **balance of payments** is a record of its economic transactions with the rest of the world; this record shows whether a country has a **trade surplus** (value of exports exceeds value of imports) or a **trade deficit** (value of imports exceeds value of exports). Trade figures can be further divided into **merchandise trade** and **services trade** accounts; a country can run a surplus in both accounts, a deficit in both accounts, or a combination of the two. The U.S. merchandise trade deficit was $741 billion in 2012. However, the United States enjoys an annual service trade surplus. Overall, the United States is a debtor; China enjoys an overall trade surplus and serves as a creditor nation.

Foreign exchange provides a means for settling accounts across borders. The dynamics of international finance can have a significant impact on a nation's economy as well as the fortunes of individual companies. Currencies can be subject to **devaluation** or **revaluation** as a result of actions taken by a country's central bank. Currency trading by international speculators can also lead to devaluation. When a country's economy is strong or when demand for its goods is high, its currency tends to appreciate in value. When currency values fluctuate, global firms face various types of economic exposure. Firms can manage exchange rate exposure by **hedging**.

MyMarketingLab

Go to **mymktlab.com** for the following Assisted-graded writing questions:

2-1. Explain how market capitalism, centrally planned capitalism, centrally planned socialism, and market socialism differ. Give an example of a country that illustrates each type of system.

2-2. A manufacturer of satellite dishes is assessing the world market potential for his products. He asks you if he should consider developing countries as potential markets. Discuss what he should do.

2-3. Mymarketinglab Only – comprehensive writing assignment for this chapter.

MyMarketingLab

Go to **mymktlab.com** to complete the problems marked with this icon .

Discussion Questions

2-4. The seven criteria for describing a nation's economy introduced at the beginning of this chapter can be combined in a number of different ways. For example, the United States can be characterized as follows:

- *Type of economy:* Advanced industrial state
- *Type of government:* Democracy with a multiparty system
- *Trade and capital flows:* Incomplete free trade and part of a trading bloc
- *The commanding heights:* Mix of state and private ownership
- *Services provided by the state and funded through taxes:* Pensions and education, but not health care
- *Institutions:* Transparency, standards, no corruption, a free press, and strong courts
- *Markets:* Free market system characterized by high-risk/high-reward entrepreneurial dynamism

Use these seven criteria p. 64 to develop a profile of one of the BRICS nations, or any other country that interests you. What implications does this profile have for marketing opportunities in the country?

2-5. Why are Brazil, Russia, India, China, and South Africa (BRICS) highlighted in this chapter? Identify the current stage of economic development for each BRICS nation.

2-6. Turn to the Index of Economic Freedom (Table 2-3) and identify where the BRICS nations are ranked. How should global marketers use the Index as a guide to global market opportunities?

2-7. The Heritage Foundation's Index of Economic Freedom is not the only ranking that assesses countries in terms of successful economic policies. For example, the World Economic Forum (WEF; www.weforum.org) publishes an annual Global Competitiveness Report; in the 2010–2011 report, the United States ranked 4th, according to the WEF's metrics. By contrast, Sweden was in 2nd place. According to the Index of Economic Freedom's rankings, the United States and Sweden are in 10th and 18th place, respectively. Why are the rankings so different? What criteria does each index consider?

2-8. When the first edition of this textbook was published in 1996, the World Bank defined "low-income country" as one with per capita income of less than $501. In 2003, when the third edition of *Global Marketing* appeared, "low income" was defined as $785 or less in per capita income. As shown in Table 2-4 of this chapter, $1,025 is the current "low-income" threshold. The other stages of development have been revised upward in a similar manner. How do you explain the upward trend in the definition of income categories during the past 17+ years?

2-9. A friend is distressed to learn that America's merchandise trade deficit hit $735 billion in 2012. You want to cheer your friend up by demonstrating that the trade picture is not as bleak as it sounds. What do you say?

2-10. India is not included in the Big Mac Index. Can you explain why? Using the following data, compute the price of a Big Mac in Norway, Thailand, and Mexico. What is the equivalent price in dollars? Is it higher or lower than the U.S. price? How much is the kroner (or baht or peso) over- or undervalued?

- Norway price: Kroner 45; exchange rate: 6.25/$1
- Thailand price: Baht 70; exchange rate: 32.3/$1
- Mexico price: Peso 32; exchange rate: 12.8/$1

CASE 2-1   CONTINUED (REFER TO PAGE 60)

A New Front in the Battle of Ideas

As pain from the economic crisis spread around the globe, policymakers set about devising strategies to prevent a global economic meltdown. Various economic stimulus packages were passed, including "cash for clunkers" deals that encouraged consumers to trade in old gas guzzlers for newer, more fuel-efficient cars.

World leaders offered a variety of criticisms, perspectives, and proposals. Some denounced "American-style capitalism" at the annual General Assembly meeting at the United Nations. French President Nicolas Sarkozy called for greater oversight of the global financial system: "Let us rebuild together a regulated capitalism in which whole swatches of financial activity are not left to the sole judgment of market operators," he said. Brazilian President Luiz Inácio Lula da Silva, a former labor leader, called for the global community to create a new foundation for the world economic system that would prevent abuses and shrink the gap between the rich and poor. Mahmoud Ahmadinejad, president of Iran, told the Assembly that the financial crisis was a sign that the American empire was "reaching the end of its road."

Some observers noted that the rhetoric was breathing new life into the long-standing debate between two competing schools of economic thought. On one side of the debate was John Maynard Keynes, a British economist and the author of *The Economic Consequences of the Peace*. Published in 1919, the book explained why the post–World War I economy in Europe suffered from inflation and stagnation. In 1936, Keynes published *The General Theory of Employment, Interest and Money*. Keynes advocated giving the state broad powers to make decisions about a nation's economy.

While campaigning for president, then–U.S. Senator Obama promised that his economic policies would create between 2.5 million and 3.5 million new jobs. The Emergency Economic Stabilization Act of 2008, the $787 billion economic stimulus package passed by the U.S. Congress, was a textbook example of Keynesian principles designed to boost aggregate demand. According to the White House, every $1 of government spending would yield about $1.50 in gross national product (GDP). In Keynesian economics, this was known as a spending multiplier. Yet, as U.S. President Barack Obama expanded the government's role in health care, some began to see his policies as moving the country toward a central planning economic model. Some labeled his policies as socialist.

On the other side of the debate was Austrian economist Friedrich Hayek, who was a proponent of free markets. In his 1943 book *The Road to Serfdom*, Hayek argued that political freedom and economic freedom go hand in hand. He warned that expanding the government's role in the economy could have unintended consequences, such as reducing the role of the individual in society. Moreover, Hayek believed that collectivism can lead to tyranny; he held up the Soviet Union as a case in point. As the U.S. employment needle barely moved amid increased government spending and a burgeoning deficit, Hayek's name was invoked. Not surprisingly, Hayek's theories have caught on with conservatives. For example, Glenn Beck, a conservative Fox News personality, featured *The Road to Serfdom* on his talk show.

The battle of ideas described here is also being debated by a new generation of economists and analysts. For example, political risk consultant Ian Bremmer has written *The End of the Free Market: Who Wins the War Between the States and Corporations?* The impetus for the book came from an encounter with a Chinese diplomat who asked, "Now that the free market has failed, what do you think is the proper role for the state in the economy?" In his book, Bremmer argues that China and Russia are using state capitalism to promote the interests of their companies. State capitalism is an economic system in which markets are used for political gain. Meanwhile, in emerging markets such as Brazil, socialist-leaning leaders are steering their countries away from free market principles.

Bremmer explains how the economic environment has changed since the economic crisis began in 2008. In his view, the G-7 world was characterized by widespread agreement that prosperity depended on the rule of law, independent courts, transparency, and a free media. In that world, free market capitalism was the dominant ideology and global corporations were the principal economic heavyweights. These global players sought to maximize profit and thereby increase shareholder wealth. Bremmer notes that this consensus provided the engine driving 40 years of globalization.

So, what has changed? China has emerged from the global economic crisis in relatively good shape, yet China's leaders do not fully embrace free market economics. The courts are not independent, and the media is not free. Moreover, China is not a democracy. Under state capitalism, politicians become key economic actors; rather than making profit the number 1 goal, they seek first to achieve political goals. China's success has emboldened socialist-leaning ruling elites in other countries to pursue economic growth while solidifying their own bases of political power. This is creating friction between competing economic systems. As Bremmer explains, "There will be winners and losers, and the world's political and business leaders better begin to try to sort out who those winners and losers will be."

Discussion Questions

2-11. Does the recent global economic crisis signal that the American model of free market capitalism is fundamentally flawed?

2-12. Keynes and Hayek aren't necessarily household names, but they did get a boost when economist Russell Roberts created a rap video titled *Fear the Boom and Bust* with filmmaker John Papola. The video is available on YouTube. After viewing it, you should be able to answer the following questions: Are you a Keynesian? Or do you side with Hayek?

2-13. Policymakers in Japan, the world's third-largest economy, must transition their nation away from a manufacturing-dependent model for growth. What industry sectors might emerge as the new drivers of economic growth?

2-14. Do you think that the economic stimulus programs in the United States, Asia, and elsewhere were the right approach to pulling the world out of recession?

2-15. The case mentions China, Russia, and Latin America as countries and regions where state capitalism is present. Are there state capitalist powers in other parts of the world as well?

Sources: Russ Roberts, "Why Friedrich Hayek Is Making a Comeback," *The Wall Street Journal* (June 28, 2010), p. A21; Glenn Beck, "The One Thing: The Road to Serfdom," *Fox News* (June 9, 2009); Jason Dean and Marcus Walker, "Crisis Stirs Critics of Free Markets," *The Wall Street Journal* (September 25, 2008), p. A3; Jay Solomon, "Leaders Seek Global Response to Financial Crisis," *The Wall Street Journal* (September 24, 2008), p. A10; James Hookway, "Commodities Exporters Look to China for Growth as the West Sags," *The Wall Street Journal* (June 5, 2008), p. A12; Marcus Walker, James Hookway, John Lyons, and James T. Areddy, "U.S. Slump Takes Toll Across Globe," *The Wall Street Journal* (April 3, 2008), pp. A1, A13; Peter S. Goodman, "Trading Partners Fear U.S. Consumers Won't Continue Free-Spending Ways," *The New York Times* (January 25, 2008), pp. C1, C4; Keith Bradsher, "Throughout Asia, Exporters Brace for Tremors from a U.S. Pullback," *New York Times* (January 25, 2008), pp. C1, C4.

CASE 2-2
Argentina Uncorks Malbec; World Ready for a Glass

Argentina has been producing wine since the sixteenth century, but the country's winemakers did not start competing globally until recently. Argentina's sudden popularity in global markets is due in large part to Malbec, a grape variety that is now synonymous with Argentina. The Malbec grape originated in France, where it was once a crucial blending component in wines from the Bordeaux region. *Malbec* (French for "bad beak") has largely fallen out of popularity in France and is now only found mainly in wines from Cahors and the Loire.

Immigrants brought Malbec vines to Argentina during the first half of the nineteenth century, and the grape was cultivated with much more success than in Europe. Argentina currently boasts 278 wineries with 1,047 labels, with the vast majority operating in the Mendoza region. Terroir, which refers to the climate and soil, plays a fundamental role in cultivating Malbec successfully. Malbec vines grow extremely well in the desert landscapes and arid climate of Mendoza, which lies in the eastern slopes of the Andes Mountains. The vines' lifeline: an irrigation system that delivers glacial water from the Andes. Mendoza's vineyards are some of the highest in the world, pushing 5,000 feet above sea level, roughly 4,000 feet higher than those found in Napa Valley, California. The altitude ensures more sun with less heat and gives the grapes more acidity with softer tannins. This translates into wines with fresh flavors that don't need cellar aging.

Argentina is the fifth-largest wine-producing nation in the world. In 2009, Argentina produced approximately 1.4 billion liters of wine, exporting 430 million of those liters to 128 countries. The turnaround was remarkable: In 1990, Argentina produced inexpensive red, white, and rosé wines solely for its domestic market. At that time, neither differentiation nor quality was a goal—just quantity. In 1970, Argentina had an annual wine consumption rate of 92 liters per capita and very little competition, thanks to government protectionism. Even today, 95 percent of the wine consumed in Argentina is produced domestically, but consumption is dropping.

Consumers' tastes have changed in recent years, shifting toward soft drinks and other beverages. Wine consumption fell 20 percent, and the industry realized that it needed to shift its focus. Instead of high yields and large-scale production, winemakers began to concentrate on quality, on controlling and reducing yields, and on exporting specialized wines throughout the world. The transition was a success, and although 70 percent of Argentina's wine remains in the domestic market, Argentina has become the fourth-largest exporter of wine in the world, following only Italy, Australia, and France.

The target market for Argentina's wine exports is the United States rather than Europe. The strategy appears to be working; consumption of Malbec is growing in America. In 2003, Americans consumed 11 bottles of Australian wine to every 1 Argentine bottle. By 2008, Australian wines still outsold those from Argentina, but only by a 3-to-1 margin. In 2009, the value of Argentina's wine exports to the United States was $150 million, up from $101 million in 2006 (see Table 1).

What is Argentina delivering to the U.S. market that other imported wines fail to offer? The answer is simple: value. As Jose Alberto Zuccardi, director of the Zuccardi Winery in Mendoza, commented recently, "We are very optimistic, we think Argentina is growing in export sales and the reason is that we offer good value to consumers who may be looking to spend less money for the same or better quality." According to Nielsen, Malbec is the fastest-growing varietal in the United States market, where consumption tripled in 2009. Malbec-based wines can be found throughout the entire price spectrum, from $10 to $100. Although the expensive offerings can

TABLE 1 Fifteen-Most-Exported Brands of Argentine Wine

Brands	Value (thousands of dollars)	Volume (thousands of cases)
Fuzion (Familia Zuccardi)	20,433	1,063
Trivento (Trivento)	14,237	573
Catena (Catena Zapata)	13,158	197
Alamos (Catena Zapata)	12,366	374
Trapiche Reserva (Trapiche)	10,758	270
Trapiche (Trapiche)	10,463	423
Norton (Norton)	8,104	261
Finca Flichman (Finca Flichman)	7,635	337
Navarro Correas Colec. Privada (N. Correas)	7,626	158
Argento (Argento Wine Company)	7,545	414
Pascual Toso (Pascual Toso)	6,638	165
Astica (Trapiche)	6,442	374
Terrazas (Terrazas de los Andes)	6,066	143
Macus James (Fecovita)	5,719	457
Pampas del Sur (Trivento)	5,319	343

be excellent, most consumers are choosing the inexpensive bottles, which offer terrific value for the money and are good for everyday drinking.

The opportunities Argentina presents are attracting foreign investors from around the world. The ability to produce quality wines at a fraction of the cost of doing so in the United States gives Argentina a tremendous competitive advantage. An acre of land in Mendoza costs roughly $30,000, much less than the cost of an acre in Napa Valley, California. Vintners also have the autonomy to plant whichever variety they want, something rarely allowed in Europe. Michael Evans, an American who moved to Argentina in 2004, started the company Vines of Mendoza. Evans does not operate a winery per se, however. Instead, he leases plots to investors, who get to choose the varietal and develop the brand, while Evans does the rest.

Other, better-known winemakers have a presence in Argentina as well. Paul Hobbs (Viña Cobos) and Kendall-Jackson (Tapiz and Mariposa) both have vineyards in Mendoza, as do European vintners Château Lafite and Pernod Ricard. Perhaps the most surprising investor is LVMH Moët Hennessy-Louis Vuitton, which produces wines under the Terrazas de los Andes label.

Another facet of the opportunity in Argentina is represented by Château HANA in Mendoza. The enterprise is the brainchild of Aziz Abdul, a Muslim who was born in Vietnam, grew up in southern India, and learned to appreciate wine while studying mathematics in Paris. After accepting a buyout package from his employer in 2008, Abdul had the capital to invest in a winery. His aim is to produce wine in Argentina that represents a merging of the modern French style with the robust style of a typical Malbec. The wines of Château HANA (the name is a combination of the first initials from Abdul's first name and those of his wife and daughters) are relatively expensive compared with other local brands.

During his time in France, Abdul had the opportunity to visit Château Lafite, Château Latour, and other world-famous wine estates. Explaining what he learned from France's elite winemakers, Abdul recalls:

> They told me the aromas to avoid and how. I learned that after harvesting the grapes, it was better to leave them intact for as long as possible as that imparts more character. . . . There are thousands of wines in Argentina—why add another? You have to be distinctive. That's terroir—it's the land and the man together.

To date, Aziz has spent more than $500,000 to buy a vineyard in Mendoza, hire an experienced winemaker, and assemble a state-of-the-art production facility with an annual production capacity of more than 100,000 bottles. He has sold several hundred cases of his wine to upscale hotel restaurants in Buenos Aires. Abdul started exporting in 2012; his first target markets were the United States, China, and Brazil.

As can be inferred from these examples, times are good in Mendoza, but threats in Argentina's internal and external environments do exist. One potential risk is, ironically, Malbec's sudden popularity. Historically, varietals that gain sudden popularity tend to lose it sooner or later. Markets are often plagued with hundreds of labels with little differentiation and mediocre quality; Australia is a case in point.

Perhaps the biggest threat is Argentina itself. Its economy is infamous for being vulnerable to an economic crisis every 6 to 10 years. With these crises comes high inflation, which could greatly increase production costs. If prices rise, then value—Malbec's competitive advantage in the market—will decrease. Inflation is currently running at about 25 percent.

Other regions are also starting to experiment with Malbec-based wines. Argentina and Malbec are synonymous for now, but that identity could be lost. Argentina is currently working to build and maintain that identity by repositioning itself in the global market. Nicolas Catena, who is widely considered to be the founder of Argentina's emergence as a source of quality wine exports, expanded his U.S. marketing budget to more than $2 million after Argentina's economic crisis in 2001. Vines of Argentina, an industry marketing firm, spends approximately $3 million a year to increase awareness globally. Michael Halstrick, president of Norton Winery, commented, "We want people opening a bottle of wine to think of tango, of football, of the Andes. We are no longer just producing a commodity; we are a country that has arrived."

With savvy marketing and a dose of good luck, Argentina's wine industry will be able to find long-term global sustainability. Robert Parker, the world's foremost wine critic, believes that Argentina is approaching the tipping point in terms of popularity. Parker commented, "By the year 2015, the greatness of Argentinean wines made from the Malbec grape will be understood as a given." But while the Argentines wait, they will surely be sipping Malbec.

Discussion Questions

⭐ 2-16. Identify the marketing strategies that have helped Argentina's wine industry expand beyond its home market and reach consumers in all parts of the world.

2-17. Even though the Malbec grape is well known in Argentina, consumers in other countries are less familiar with it. What recommendations do you have to help increase consumer understanding of, and appreciation for, Malbec-based wines?

2-18. The forces of supply and demand affect many industries, and the wine industry is no exception. Currently the world is awash in an ocean of excess wine. Many winemakers in France, Australia, and other countries are struggling financially. Given this situation, what can Argentina's wine producers do to maintain or increase their market share?

This case was prepared by Research Assistant Devin Linn under the supervision of Professor Mark Green.

Sources: Jude Webber, "A Punt on a New Wine with Roots All Over the World," *Financial Times* (October 28, 2011), p. 12; James Molesworth, "Argentina's Hit or Miss Year," *Wine Spectator* (December 15, 2010); Eric Asimov, "Argentina Opens the Tap for Malbec," *The New York Times* (April 28, 2010); Laura Saieg, "Malbec Consumption Triples," *Wine Sur* (May 12, 2010); Dan Prescher, "Argentine Malbec Wine Bucks Trend to Shine in Sluggish Wine Market," *International Living* (April 29, 2010); Ana Tagua, "The 30 Most Exported Argentinean Brands," *Wine Sur* (April 7, 2010); Helen Coster, "Harvesting Profits in Argentina's Wine Country," *Forbes* (March 1, 2010); Mike Veseth, "Wine, Recession and Argentina," *The Wine Economist* (April 30, 2009); Dave McIntyre, "Argentina's Andes Advantage," *The Washington Post* (April 8, 2009); Candace Piette, "Argentina's Grapes of Success," *BBC News* (March 30, 2009); Andrew Jefford, "On the Roof of the Wine-Growing World," *Financial Times* (March 14, 2009); Dorothy J. Gaiter and John Brecher, "Malbec Beckons; Heed the Call; Argentina's Signature Red Deserves Its Wild Popularity, Offering Zing and Boldness for Modest Prices," *The Wall Street Journal* (January 24, 2009); Lance Cutler, "The California/Argentina Wine Connection," *Wine Business Monthly* (August 15, 2007); Dorothy J. Gaiter and John Brecher, "South America's Rising Star; Argentina's Malbec Makes a Big Splash; Living with Success," *The Wall Street Journal* (June 22, 2007); David J. Lynch, "Golden Days for Argentine Wine Could Turn Cloudy," *USA Today* (November 16, 2007); Jon Bonné, "The Mysteries of Argentinean Malbec," *MSNBC* (June 5, 2006); Mark Mazzetti, "Argentina on the Cheap," *Slate* (July 11, 2003).

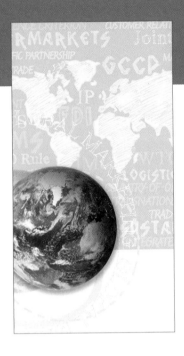

3

The Global Trade Environment

CASE 3-1
Global Trading Partners Look East and West for Economic Growth

Global trade talks have been taking on a distinctly bicoastal character lately. Looking east and west across the Pacific Ocean, the United States and several Asian countries are hammering out the details of a trade framework known as the Trans-Pacific Partnership (TPP). The goal is an ambitious one: to create a free trade area that will lead to long-term economic growth. Looking east and west across the Atlantic Ocean, the United States and the European Union (EU) are *also* in negotiations to create a separate free trade area. As with the TPP, the goal of the Transatlantic Trade and Investment Partnership (TTIP) is to kick-start economic growth among the member nations.

The United States and the EU have the world's largest trading relationship. In 2012, for example, two-way trade worth $927 billion—€450 billion in goods and another €250 billion in

Exhibit 3-1 Farmers stage a demonstration march during an anti-Trans-Pacific Partnership rally in Tokyo in April 2012. Thousands of farmers rallied against the Asia-Pacific free trade pact prior to a visit to the United States by Japanese Prime Minister Yoshihiko Noda.
Source: AFP / Getty Images.

services—crisscrossed the Atlantic Ocean. However, the share of trade between the regions has been declining for years, as both sides increasingly buy from and sell goods and services to China and other Asian countries.

Now, officials on both sides are attempting to forge an agreement that will reverse the decline and boost the volume of U.S.-EU two-way trade to even higher levels. What's the point, you ask? The answer is straightforward: A free trade agreement (FTA) that generates more trade will boost economies on both sides of the Atlantic. In the United States, business leaders are pressing President Barack Obama to pursue more trade deals. In Europe, German Chancellor Angela Merkel, British Prime Minister David Cameron, and other leaders are pushing for a new agreement that will create new avenues for job creation and economic growth in the respective countries.

Before an agreement can be reached, however, major differences will have to be worked out between the two sides. One sticking point is agriculture. For example, the EU restricts the import of most genetically modified crops, which are common in the United States. Tariff reduction is another key issue. Although tariffs between the trading partners currently average between 2 and 3 percent, further reduction could result in significant savings. A third issue concerns a variety of regulations that hamper cross-border investment and purchasing. Such regulations are sometimes called nontariff barriers, and many observers agree that they are harder to remove than tariff barriers. For example, the EU would like an easing of restrictions on U.S. government purchases of European goods. However, that matter is complicated because some of those buying decisions are made at the state level, and some states have passed "Buy American" laws.

How difficult will it be for the various sides to complete negotiations? At the end of this chapter, you will find the continuation of this case. Will the Americans and the Europeans be able to draw up an agreement? How about the United States and the Asia/Pacific countries?

Since World War II, nations have had tremendous interest in furthering the cause of economic cooperation and integration. Such agreements can be *bilateral* in nature; that is, a trade deal can be negotiated between two nations. However, trade agreements also occur at the regional and global levels. The euro zone, and the larger, 28-nation EU to which 18 euro zone countries also belong, exemplify regional economic integration. The TTIP and the TPP in Case 3-1 are also regional in scope.

Our survey of the world trade environment begins at the global level with the WTO and its predecessor, the General Agreement on Tariffs and Trade (GATT). Next, the four main types of bilateral and regional preferential trade agreements (PTAs) are identified and described. An introduction to individual countries in the world's major market regions follows; each section also includes detailed discussion of the specific preferential trade agreements in which those countries participate. Important marketing issues in each region are also discussed. Several important emerging country markets were described in Chapter 2; in this chapter, special attention will be given to individual country markets that were not previously discussed.

LEARNING OBJECTIVES

1 Explain the role of the World Trade Organization in facilitating global trade relations among nations.

2 Compare and contrast the four main categories of preferential trade agreements.

3 Explain the trade relationship dynamics among signatories of North American Free Trade Agreement (NAFTA).

4 Identify the four main preferential trade agreements in Latin America and the key members of each.

5 Identify the main preferential trade agreements in Asia.

6 Understand the rationale for the creation of both the European Union and the euro zone.

7 Describe the activities of the key regional organizations in the Middle East.

8 Explain the issues for global marketers wishing to expand in Africa.

The World Trade Organization and GATT

The year 2012 marked 65 years since the enactment of the **General Agreement on Tariffs and Trade (GATT)**, a treaty among nations whose governments agreed, at least in principle, to promote trade among members. GATT was intended to be a multilateral, global initiative, and GATT negotiators did succeed in liberalizing world merchandise trade. GATT was also an organization that handled 300 trade disputes—many involving food—during its half-century of existence.

TABLE 3-1 Recent WTO Cases

Countries Involved in Dispute	Nature of Dispute and Outcome
United States, European Union, and Canada versus China	In 2006, the complainants asked the DSB to consider Chinese tariffs on imported auto parts. The complainants argued that their auto manufacturers were at a disadvantage because Beijing required them to buy components locally or pay high tariffs. In 2008, the WTO ruled that China had violated trade rules.
United States versus Brazil	In 2003, Brazil filed a complaint against the United States, charging that cotton subsidies depressed prices and disadvantaged producers in emerging markets. In 2004, the DSB, in its first-ever ruling on agricultural subsidies, agreed that cotton subsidies violate international trade rules.
Antigua and Barbuda versus the United States	In 2003, Antigua filed suit charging that by prohibiting Internet gambling, the United States was violating global trade agreements. In 2004, the WTO ruled in favor of Antigua.
United States versus European Union (EU)	In 2002, U.S. President Bush imposed 30 percent tariffs on a range of steel imports for a period of three years. The EU lodged a protest, and in 2003 the WTO ruled that the tariffs were illegal. President Bush responded by lifting the tariffs.

GATT itself had no enforcement power (the losing party in a dispute was entitled to ignore the ruling), and the process of dealing with disputes sometimes stretched on for years. Little wonder, then, that some critics referred to GATT as the "General Agreement to Talk and Talk."

The successor to GATT, the **World Trade Organization (WTO)**, came into existence on January 1, 1995. From its base in Geneva, Switzerland, the WTO provides a forum for trade-related negotiations among its 157 members. The WTO's neutral trade experts also serve as mediators in global trade disputes. The WTO has a Dispute Settlement Body (DSB) that mediates complaints concerning unfair trade barriers and other issues among the WTO's member countries. During a 60-day consultation period, parties to a complaint are expected to engage in good-faith negotiations and reach an amicable resolution. If that fails, the complainant can ask the DSB appoint a three-member panel of trade experts to hear the case behind closed doors. After convening, the panel has 9 months within which to issue its ruling.[1] The DSB is empowered to act on the panel's recommendations. The losing party has the option of turning to a seven-member appellate body. If, after due process, a country's trade policies are found to violate WTO rules, it is expected to change those policies. If changes are not forthcoming, the WTO can authorize trade sanctions against the loser. Table 3-1 lists some recent cases that have been brought to the WTO.

Trade ministers representing the WTO member nations meet annually to work on improving world trade. It remains to be seen whether the WTO will live up to expectations when it comes to additional major policy initiatives on such vexing issues as foreign investment and agricultural subsidies. The current round of WTO negotiations began in 2001; the talks collapsed in 2005, and attempts to revive them in the years since have not been successful. That is one reason why the TAPA and the TPP negotiations are moving ahead.

> "For the WTO process to work, countries have to start liberalizing policies in politically sensitive sectors."[2]
>
> —Daniel Griswold, Center for Trade Policy Studies, Cato Institute

Preferential Trade Agreements

The WTO promotes free trade on a global basis; however, countries in each of the world's regions are seeking to liberalize trade within their own regions. A **preferential trade agreement (PTA)** is a mechanism that confers special treatment on select trading partners. By favoring certain

---

[1] Scott Miller, "Global Dogfight: Airplane Battle Spotlights Power of a Quirky Court," *The Wall Street Journal* (June 1, 2005), pp. A1, A14.
[2] Scott Miller, "Trade Talks Twist in the Wind," *The Wall Street Journal* (November 8, 2005), p. A14.

countries, such agreements frequently discriminate against other countries. For that reason, it is customary for countries to notify the WTO when they enter into preferential trade agreements. In recent years, the WTO has been notified of approximately 300 preferential trade agreements. Few fully conform to WTO requirements; none, however, has been disallowed.

Free Trade Area

A **free trade area (FTA)** is formed when two or more countries agree to eliminate tariffs and other barriers that restrict trade. When trading partners successfully negotiate a **free trade agreement** (also abbreviated **FTA**), the ultimate goal of which is to have zero duties on goods that cross borders between the partners, it creates a free trade area. In some instances, duties are eliminated on the day the agreement takes effect; in other cases, duties are phased out over a set period of time. Countries that belong to an FTA can maintain independent trade policies with respect to third countries. **Rules of origin** discourage the importation of goods into the member country with the lowest external tariff for transshipment to one or more FTA members with higher external tariffs; customs inspectors police the borders between members.

For example, because Chile and Canada established an FTA in 1997, a Canadian-built Caterpillar grader tractor imported into Chile would not be subject to duty. If the same piece of equipment was imported from a factory in the United States, the importer would pay about $13,000 in duties. Could Caterpillar send the U.S.-built tractor to Chile by way of Canada, thereby allowing the importer to avoid paying the duty? No, because the tractor would bear a "Made in the U.S.A." certificate of origin indicating it was subject to the duty. Little wonder, then, that the U.S. government negotiated its own bilateral free trade agreement with Chile that entered into force in 2003.

According to the Business Roundtable, an association composed of CEOs of leading U.S. companies, to date more than 300 FTAs have been negotiated globally. Overall, roughly 50 percent of global trade takes place among nations linked by FTAs. Additional examples of FTAs include the European Economic Area, a free trade area that includes the 28-nation EU plus Norway, Liechtenstein, and Iceland; the Group of Three (G-3), an FTA encompassing Colombia, Mexico, and Venezuela; and the Closer Economic Partnership Agreement, a FTA between China and Hong Kong. In October 2011, the U.S. Congress finally ratified the long-delayed FTAs with South Korea, Panama, and Colombia (see Exhibits 3-2 and 3-3).

Customs Union

A **customs union** represents the logical evolution of an FTA. In addition to eliminating internal barriers to trade, members of a customs union agree to the establishment of **common external tariffs (CETs)**. In 1996, for example, the EU and Turkey initiated a customs union in an effort to boost two-way trade above the average annual level of $20 billion. The arrangement called for the elimination of tariffs averaging 14 percent that added $1.5 billion each year to the cost of European goods imported by Turkey. Other customs unions discussed in this chapter are the Andean Community, the Central American Integration System (SICA), Mercosur, and CARICOM.

Common Market

A **common market** is the next level of economic integration. In addition to the removal of internal barriers to trade and the establishment of common external tariffs, the common market allows for free movement of factors of production, including labor and capital. The Andean Community, the SICA, and CARICOM, which currently function as customs unions, may ultimately evolve into true common markets.

Economic Union

An **economic union** builds upon the elimination of internal tariff barriers, the establishment of common external barriers, and the free flow of factors. It seeks to coordinate and harmonize economic and social policies within the union to facilitate the free flow of capital, labor, and goods and services from country to country. An economic union is a common marketplace not only for goods but also for services and capital. For example, if professionals are going to be able to work

Exhibit 3-2 Many small business owners are advocates of free trade agreements. Speaking on behalf of the Consumer Electronics Association, the CEO of electronics manufacturer Thiel notes, "Today we're a leading maker of high-performance speakers with 30 American employees and thousands of global trade partners. We're also one of 2,200 CEA members growing our economy thanks to free trade. Speak out for free trade. Support free trade agreements with Colombia, Panama, and South Korea."

Source: Used by permission of Consumer Electronic Association.

Exhibit 3-3 In November 2010, Ford Motor Company ran ads in 20 newspapers summarizing its objections to the proposed FTA with South Korea. The message was clear: for every 52 cars Korea exports to the United States, American carmakers export 1. A few weeks after the ad appeared, policymakers worked out changes to the proposed deal that would result in an immediate lifting of import tariffs on U.S. auto exports to Korea. As a result, representatives of the United Auto Workers union spoke out in favor of the FTA.

Source: Bloomberg via Getty Images.

TABLE 3-2 Forms of Regional Economic Integration

Stage of Integration	Elimination of Tariffs and Quotas Among Members	Common External Tariff (CET) and Quota System	Elimination of Restrictions on Factor Movements	Harmonization and Unification of Economic and Social Policies and Institutions
Free Trade Area	Yes	No	No	No
Customs Union	Yes	Yes	No	No
Common Market	Yes	Yes	Yes	No
Economic Union	Yes	Yes	Yes	Yes

anywhere in the EU, the members must harmonize their practice licensing so that a doctor or lawyer qualified in one country may practice in any other.[3]

The full evolution of an economic union would involve the creation of a unified central bank; the use of a single currency; and common policies on agriculture, social services, welfare, regional development, transport, taxation, competition, and mergers. A true economic union requires extensive political unity, which makes it similar to a nation. The further integration of nations that were members of fully developed economic unions would be the formation of a central government that would bring together independent political states into a single political framework. The EU is approaching its target of completing most of the steps required to become a full economic union, with one notable setback: Despite the fact that 16 member nations ratified a proposed European Constitution, the initiative was derailed after voters in France and the Netherlands voted against the measure. Table 3-2 and Figure 3-1 compare the various forms of regional economic integration.

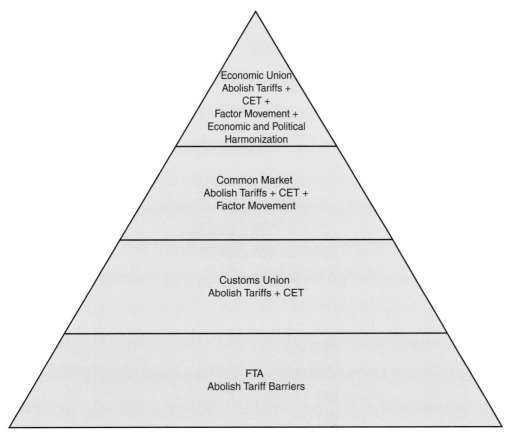

FIGURE 3-1

Hierarchy of Preferential Trade Agreements

---

[3] Gabriele Steinhauser, "A Rocky Road to Economic Union," *The Wall Street Journal* (June 9–10, 2010), p. A9.

North America

North America, which includes Canada, the United States, and Mexico, comprises a distinctive regional market. The United States combines great wealth, a large population, vast space, and plentiful natural resources in a single national economic and political environment and presents unique marketing characteristics. High product-ownership levels are associated with high income and relatively high receptivity to innovations and new ideas both in consumer and industrial products. The United States is home to more global industry leaders than any other nation in the world. For example, U.S. companies are the dominant producers in the computer, software, aerospace, entertainment, medical equipment, and jet engine industry sectors.

In 1988, the United States and Canada signed a free trade agreement (U.S.-Canada Free Trade Agreement, or CFTA), and the Canada-U.S. Free Trade Area formally came into existence in 1989. This helps explain the more than $400 billion per year in goods and services that flow between Canada and the United States, the biggest trading relationship between any two single nations. Canada takes 20 percent of U.S. exports and the United States buys approximately 85 percent of Canada's exports. Figure 3-2 illustrates the economic integration of North

FIGURE 3-2

United States' Top Import/Export Partners

Source: U.S. Bureau of the Census, www.census.gov.

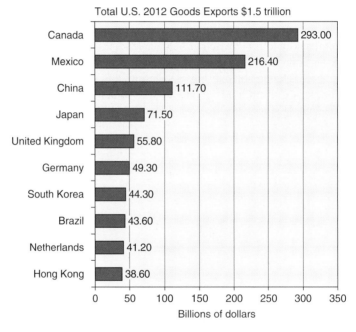

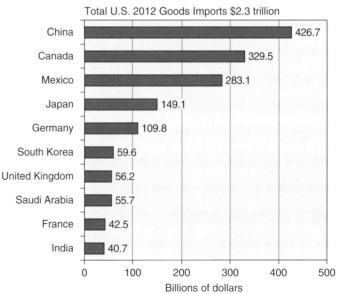

America: Canada is the United States' number 1 trading partner, Mexico is second, and China ranks third. American companies have more invested in Canada than in any other country. Many U.S. manufacturers, including General Electric (GE) and IBM, use their Canadian operations as major global suppliers for some product lines. By participating in the Canadian auto market, U.S. automakers gain greater economies of scale. The CFTA, which was fully implemented when all duties were eliminated effective January 1998, has created a true continental market for most products.

In 1992, representatives from the United States, Canada, and Mexico concluded negotiations for the **North American Free Trade Agreement (NAFTA)**. The agreement was approved by both houses of the U.S. Congress and became effective on January 1, 1994. The result is a free trade area with a combined population of more than 460 million people and a total gross domestic product (GDP) of almost $18 trillion (Figure 3-3).

Why does NAFTA create a free trade area as opposed to a customs union or a common market? The governments of all three nations pledge to promote economic growth through tariff elimination and expanded trade and investment. At present, however, there are no common external tariffs nor have restrictions on labor and other factor movements been eliminated. The issue of illegal immigration from Mexico into the United States remains a contentious one. Nevertheless, the benefits of continental free trade will enable all three countries to meet the economic challenges of the decades to come. The gradual elimination of barriers to the flow of goods, services, and investment, coupled with strong protection of intellectual property rights (patents, trademarks, and copyrights), will further benefit businesses, workers, farmers, and consumers.

The agreement does leave the door open for discretionary protectionism, however. For example, California avocado growers won government protection for a market worth $250 million; Mexican avocado growers can ship their fruit to the United States only during the winter months, and only to states in the northeast. Moreover, Mexican avocados are subject to quotas, so only $30 million worth of avocados reach the United States each year. Mexican farmer Ricardo Salgado complained, "The California growers want to control all of the supply—that way they get the best prices. We'd love to have a bigger selling season, but right now we have to wait for the U.S. Congress to give us permission."[4] Mexico engages in some protectionism of its own; for example, in 2003 a 98.8 percent tariff was imposed on chicken leg quarters beyond the first 50,000 metric tons imported. In addition, Mexico imposed a 46.6 percent tariff on Red and Golden Delicious apples.

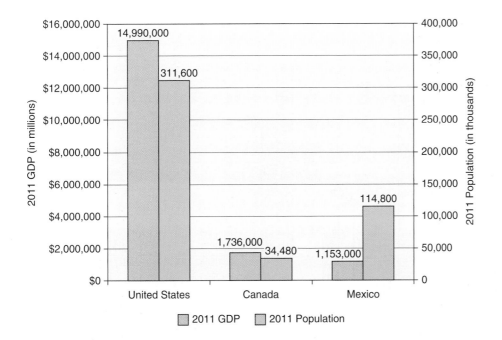

FIGURE 3-3

NAFTA Income and Population

[4] Joel Millman, "Bitter Fruit: Spats Persist Despite NAFTA," *The Wall Street Journal* (June 19, 2000), p. A23.

Latin America: SICA, Andean Community, Mercosur, and CARICOM

Latin America includes the Caribbean and Central and South America (because of NAFTA, Mexico is grouped with North America). The allure of the Latin American market has been its considerable size and huge resource base. After a decade of no growth, crippling inflation, increasing foreign debt, protectionism, and bloated government payrolls, the countries of Latin America have begun the process of economic transformation. Balanced budgets are a priority, and privatization is underway. Free markets, open economies, and deregulation have begun to replace the policies of the past. In many countries, tariffs that sometimes reached as high as 100 percent or more have been lowered to 10 to 20 percent.

With the exception of Cuba, most elected governments in Latin America are democratic. However, there is widespread skepticism about the benefits of participating fully in the global economy. As left-leaning politicians such as Venezuela's late President Hugo Chávez become more popular, concern is growing that free market forces may lose momentum in the region. Global corporations are watching developments closely. They are encouraged by import liberalization, the prospects for lower tariffs within subregional trading groups, and the potential for establishing more efficient regional production. Many observers envision a free trade area throughout the hemisphere. The four most important preferential trading arrangements in Latin America are the Central American Integration System (SICA), the Andean Community, the Common Market of the South (Mercosur), and the Caribbean Community and Common Market (CARICOM).

Central American Integration System

Central America is trying to revive its common market, which was set up in the early 1960s. The five original members—El Salvador, Honduras, Guatemala, Nicaragua, and Costa Rica—decided in July 1991 to reestablish the Central American Common Market (CACM). Efforts to improve regional integration gained momentum with the granting of observer status to Panama. In 1997, with Panama as a member, the group's name was changed to the **Central American Integration System** (*Sistema de la Integración Centroamericana*, or SICA; see Figure 3-4).

The Secretariat for Central American Economic Integration, headquartered in Guatemala City, helps to coordinate the progress toward a true Central American common market. Common rules of origin were also adopted, allowing for more free movement of goods among SICA countries. SICA countries agreed to conform to a CET of 5 to 20 percent for most goods by the

FIGURE 3-4

SICA Income and Population

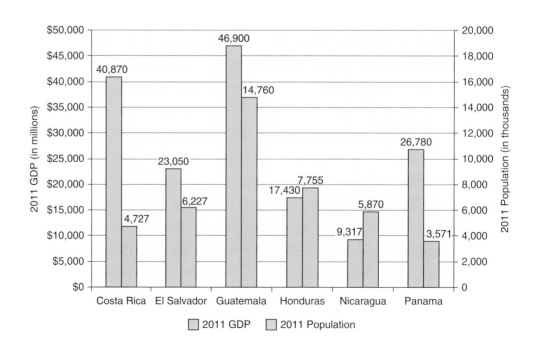

mid-1990s; many tariffs had previously exceeded 100 percent. Starting in 2000, import duties converged to a range of 0 to 15 percent.

Implementation of the Central American Free Trade Agreement with the United States created a free trade area known as DR-CAFTA that includes five SICA members (El Salvador, Honduras, Guatemala, Nicaragua, and Costa Rica; Panama is excluded) plus the Dominican Republic. Implementation has been slow, but some changes have already taken effect. For example, 80 percent of U.S. goods and more than half of U.S. agricultural products can now be imported into Central America on a duty-free basis. Benefits to Central American companies include a streamlining of export paperwork and the adoption of an online application process. The region will attract more direct foreign investment as foreign companies see reduced risk thanks to clearer rules. In addition, a significant number of companies in Central America operated in the "shadow economy," with many commercial transactions going unreported. Government tax revenues should increase as companies join the formal economy to take advantage of CAFTA's benefits.[5]

Despite progress, attempts to achieve integration in Central America have been described as uncoordinated, inefficient, and costly. Tariffs still exist on imports of products—sugar, coffee, and alcoholic beverages, for example—that are also produced in the importing country. As one Guatemalan analyst remarked more than a decade ago, "Only when I see Salvadoran beer on sale in Guatemala and Guatemalan beer on sale in El Salvador will I believe that trade liberalization and integration is a reality."[6]

Andean Community

The **Andean Community** (*Comunidad Andina de Naciones*, or CAN; see Figure 3-5) was formed in 1969 to accelerate the development of member states Bolivia, Chile, Colombia, Ecuador, Peru, and Venezuela through economic and social integration. Chile withdrew in 1976. The remaining five members agreed to lower tariffs on intragroup trade and to work together to decide what products each country should produce. At the same time, foreign goods and companies were kept out as much as possible. One Bolivian described the unfortunate result of this lack of competition in the following way: "We had agreed, 'You buy our overpriced goods and we'll buy yours.'"[7]

In 1988, the group members decided to get a fresh start. Beginning in 1992, the Andean Pact signatories agreed to form Latin America's first operating subregional free trade area. The pact abolished all foreign exchange, financial and fiscal incentives, and export subsidies at the end of 1992. Common external tariffs were established, marking the transition to a true customs union. Overall, however, the region's rural residents and urban poor became frustrated and impatient with the lack of progress. As one Andean scholar put it, "After 10 or 15 years of operating with free-market policies, paradise hasn't come. People start wondering if the gospel was as good as advertised."[8]

Blessed with a location near the equator, Ecuador's cut-flower industry generates hundreds of millions of dollars in sales each year. About 70 percent of Ecuador's flower harvest is exported to the United States; in all, about one-fourth of the cut roses sold in the United States come from Ecuador. For years, thanks to the Andean Trade Promotion and Drug Eradication Act, flowers from Ecuador, Colombia, Bolivia, and Peru were imported into the United States duty-free. The U.S. Congress passed the act to encourage Latin American farmers to cultivate ornamental flowers rather than plants that are part of the illegal drug trade. However, the act expired at the end of 2006; for Peru and Colombia, the flower trade is covered by bilateral trade agreements. Although Ecuador's duty-free status was extended, President Rafael Correa is opposed to free trade talks with the United States. His stance has prompted fears that flower production will plummet, resulting in thousands of lost jobs.

Competing ideologies help explain why intraregional trade is not yielding more benefits; Peru and Colombia are pursuing growth via capitalism, whereas the governments in Ecuador

> "The boom in the export of commodities to countries such as China and India has led to the emergence of Latin American countries with a large consumer demand. Agreements such as Mercosur facilitate trade within the region of products with higher levels of added value."[9]
>
> —Mauricio Claveria, Abeceb Consultancy, Argentina

[5] Adam Thomson, "Trade Deal Has Hidden Qualities," *Financial Times Special Report: Central America Finance & Investment* (September 19, 2008), p. 3.
[6] Johanna Tuckman, "Central Americans Start to Act Together," *Financial Times* (July 9, 1997), p. 4.
[7] "NAFTA Is Not Alone," *The Economist* (June 18, 1994), pp. 47–48.
[8] Marc Lifsher, "The Andean Arc of Instability," *The Wall Street Journal* (February 24, 2003), p. A13.
[9] Viñcent Bevins, "A Dream Disrupted," *Financial Times—International Business Insight, Part Four: Latin America* (November 23, 2010), p. 8.

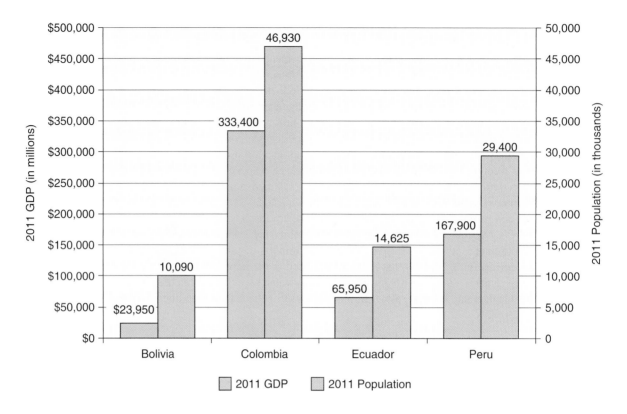

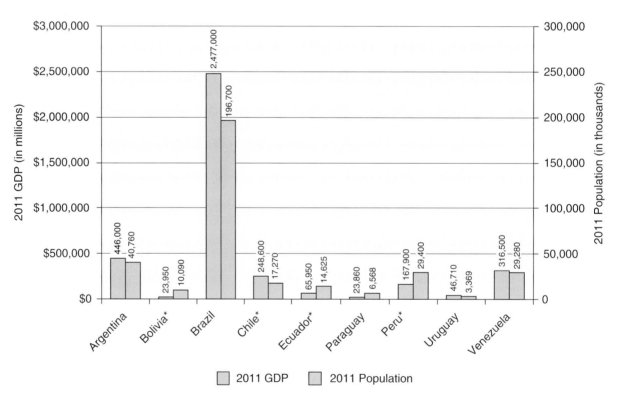

*Associate members that participate in free trade area only.

FIGURE 3-5

ANDEAN/Mercosur Income and Population

and Bolivia have socialist leanings. Venezuela withdrew from the Andean Community in 2006; President Hugo Chávez declared the community "dead" after Peru and Colombia began negotiating FTAs with the United States. Venezuela is currently in the process of becoming a full member of Mercosur.

Common Market of the South (Mercosur)

March 2011 marked the 20th anniversary of the signing of the Asunción Treaty. The treaty signified the agreement by the governments of Argentina, Brazil, Paraguay, and Uruguay to form the **Common Market of the South** (*Mercado Común del Sur*, or **Mercosur**; see Figure 3-5). The four countries agreed to begin phasing in tariff reform on January 1, 1995. Internal tariffs were eliminated, and CETs of 20 percent or less were established. In theory, goods, services, and factors of production will ultimately move freely throughout the member countries; until this goal is achieved, however, Mercosur will actually operate as a customs union rather than as a true common market. Today, about 90 percent of goods are traded freely; however, individual members of Mercosur can charge both internal and external tariffs when it suits the respective government.

Much depends on the successful outcome of this experiment in regional cooperation. The early signs were positive, as trade between the four full member nations grew dramatically during the 1990s. However, the region has experienced a series of financial crises; for example, Brazil's currency was devalued in 1995 and again in 1999.

Argentina provides a case study in how a country can emerge from an economic crisis as a stronger global competitor. Argentina's economy minister responded to the financial crisis of 2001–2002 by implementing emergency measures that included a 29 percent currency devaluation for exports and capital transactions. Argentina was allowed to break from the CET and raise duties on consumer goods. The crisis had a silver lining: Virtually overnight, Argentina's wine exports to the United States were worth four times more when dollar revenues were converted into pesos. The currency devaluation also made Argentine vineyard property cheaper for foreign buyers. Low prices for land, inexpensive labor, and ideal growing conditions for the Malbec grape have combined to make Argentina's wine industry a major player in world markets. As one winemaker noted, "You can make better wine here for less money than anywhere in the world." A new challenge looms, however; the dollar's weakness relative to the euro means that winemakers are paying 25 percent more for oak aging barrels imported from France.[10]

The trade agreement landscape in the region continues to evolve. In 1996, Chile became an associate member of Mercosur. Policymakers opted against full membership because Chile already had lower external tariffs than the rest of Mercosur; ironically, full membership would have required raising them. (In other words, Chile participates in the free trade area aspect of Mercosur, not the customs union.) Chile's export-driven success makes it a role model for the rest of Latin America as well as Central and Eastern Europe.

In 2004, Mercosur signed a cooperation agreement with the Andean Community; as a result, Bolivia, Colombia, Ecuador, and Peru have become associate members. The EU is Mercosur's number 1 trading partner; Mercosur is negotiating with the EU to establish a free trade area. Germany and France are opposed to such an agreement on the grounds that low-cost agricultural exports from South America will harm farmers in Europe.

Venezuela began the process of joining Mercosur in 2006, the same year that it withdrew from the Andean Community. For several years, Venezuela reaped the rewards of booming demand and high prices for oil; oil revenues account for 75 percent of its exports. Its late president, Hugo Chávez, was a self-proclaimed revolutionary firebrand. After being elected in 1998, he proclaimed that his vision for Venezuela was "socialism for the twenty-first century." Even so, Venezuela offers significant market opportunities for global companies. General Motors produces vehicles at a plant in Valencia; even running three shifts per day, it is unable to meet demand. Procter & Gamble's Latin American headquarters is located in Caracas. Other global companies with operations in Venezuela include Cargill, Chevron, ExxonMobil, Ford, Kellogg, 3M, and Toyota.[11]

---

[10] David J. Lynch, "Golden Days for Argentine Wine Could Turn a Bit Cloudy," *USA Today* (November 16, 2007), pp. 1B, 2B.
[11] David J. Lynch, "Venezuelan Consumers Gobble Up U.S. Goods," *USA Today* (March 28, 2007), pp. 1B, 2B.

➡ EMERGING MARKETS BRIEFING BOOK

Brazil

MyMarketingLab SYNC • THINK • LEARN

As the data in Figure 3-5 clearly show, Brazil is an economic powerhouse in South America. Brazil has the largest geographical territory and the largest population in the region. It has emerged on the world stage as a strong exporter. Rapid economic growth has given policymakers, including President Dilma Rousseff, a greater presence on the global stage and more clout at global trade talks.

One symbol of Brazil's new role in the global economy is Embraer, a jet aircraft manufacturer (see Exhibit 3-4). Specializing in regional jets that seat between 37 and 124 passengers, Embraer has won orders from Air Canada, Delta, JetBlue, Saudi Arabian Airlines, and other carriers. A cornerstone of Embraer's strategy is management's policy of sourcing the best components available anywhere in the world. This approach, known as reverse outsourcing, has proven its worth in the development of new models such as the E-170/175. In that program, more than one dozen partners, including GE and Honeywell, shared the development risks in exchange for a percentage of revenue from aircraft sales. In order to sell more regional jets to China, Embraer has also established a $50 million joint venture with China Aviation Industry Corporation.

In the United States alone, more than 850 Embraer jets are currently in service. The reason is simple: It is a huge market. As Paulo Cesar Silva, Embraer's top executive for Commercial Aviation, notes, "For us, North America is—and will continue to be—the most important market in terms of the potential to sell new products here. Aviation in North America is about 40 percent of aviation in the world." Embraer is also aggressively pursuing the defense sector with its light attack aircraft, the Super Tucano. The U.S. military has expressed interest, and orders have come in from Colombia, Indonesia, and other nations.

Brazil's agricultural sector is also a leading exporter. Brazil is the world's number 1 exporter of beef, coffee, orange juice (check the label on your orange juice carton), and sugar. Annual coffee bean production totals 40 million 60-kilo bags—one-third of the world total. JBS is the world's largest meat processor. Brazil is rapidly gaining a reputation as a producer of sugar-based ethanol, which can serve as

a sustainable substitute for expensive gasoline. As Ermor Zambello, manager of the Grupo Farias sugar mill, notes, "Globalization has made us think more about foreign markets. Now, we have more of a global outlook, and we are concerned about global production."

The central issue in the current, Doha Round of WTO negotiations is agriculture. Brazil and India are taking the lead of the Group of Twenty developing nations calling for agricultural sector reform. For example, the average tariff on Brazil's exports to the 34 Organisation for the Economic Co-operation and Development (OECD) nations is 27 percent. Government subsidies are also a key issue. In the EU, government spending accounts for about one-third of gross farm receipts; in the United States, the government provides about one-quarter of gross farm receipts. By contrast, Brazil's spending on farm support amounts to only about 3 percent of farm receipts.

Moving forward, Brazil faces a number of other challenges. Steady appreciation of Brazil's currency, the real, may require exporters to raise prices. Embraer faces tough competition from Canada's Bombardier. The country's infrastructure remains woefully underdeveloped; significant investment is required to improve highways, railroads, and ports. Businesspeople speak of "the Brazil cost," a phrase that refers to delays related to excessive red tape.

Trade with China is presenting both opportunities and threats. In 2009, China surpassed the United States as Brazil's top trading partner. China's explosive economic growth has created great demand for soybeans, iron ore, and other Brazilian commodity exports. However, Brazilian manufacturers in light-industry sectors such as toys, eyeglasses, and footwear are facing increased competition from low-priced Chinese imports.

Sources: Ben Mutzabaugh, "Brazil's Embraer Jets Are Sized Just Right," *USA Today* (July 6, 2012), pp. 1B, 2B; Joe Leahy, "In Search of More High-Flyers," *Financial Times* (April 17, 2012), p. 10; Joe Leahy, "The Brazilian Economy: A High-Flyer Now Flags," *Financial Times* (January 11, 2012), p. 7; Antonia Regalado, "Soccer, Samba, and Outsourcing?" *The Wall Street Journal* (January 25, 2007), pp. B1, B8; David J. Lynch, "Brazil Hopes to Build on Its Ethanol Success," *USA Today* (March 29, 2006), pp. 1B, 2B; David J. Lynch, "China's Growing Pull Puts Brazil in a Bind," *USA Today* (March 21, 2006), pp. 1B, 2B; David J. Lynch, "Comeback Kid Embraer Has Hot New Jet, and Fiery CEO to Match," *USA Today* (March 7, 2006), pp. 1B, 2B; David J. Lynch, "Brazil's Agricultural Exports Cast Long Shadow," *USA Today* (March 10, 2006), pp. 1B, 2B.

Exhibit 3-4 Embraer is the world's fourth-largest aircraft manufacturer; however, in the regional aircraft sector, Embraer is second only to Canada's Bombardier.
Source: Alexandre Meneghini/AP Images.

Caribbean Community and Common Market (CARICOM)

CARICOM was formed in 1973 as a movement toward unity in the Caribbean. It replaced the Caribbean Free Trade Association (CARIFTA) founded in 1965. The members are Antigua and Barbuda, Bahamas, Barbados, Belize, Dominica, Grenada, Guyana, Haiti, Jamaica, Montserrat, St. Kitts and Nevis, St. Lucia, St. Vincent and the Grenadines, Suriname, and Trinidad and Tobago. The population of the entire 15-member CARICOM is about 15 million; disparate levels of economic development can be seen by comparing gross national income (GNI) per capita in Dominica and Grenada with that of Haiti (see Table 3-3).

To date, CARICOM's main objective has been to achieve a deepening of economic integration by means of a Caribbean common market. However, CARICOM was largely stagnant during its first two decades of existence. At its annual meeting in July 1991, member countries agreed to speed integration; a customs union was established with common external tariffs. At the 1998 summit meeting, leaders from the 15 countries agreed to move quickly to establish an economic union with a common currency. A study of the issue suggested, however, that the limited extent of intraregional trade would limit the potential gains from lower transaction costs.[12]

A trade dispute between the United States and Antigua and Barbuda has raised some eyebrows. Until recently, Antigua's online gambling industry generated more than $3 billion annually. However, after Washington clamped down on Internet poker sites, Antigua's revenues slumped. Believing that the United States was violating international law, Antigua appealed to the WTO. The trade body ruled in favor of Antigua, and gave it the right to sell various types of U.S. intellectual property, including software and DVDs, without compensating the trademark and copyright owners.[13]

The English-speaking CARICOM members in the eastern Caribbean are also concerned with defending their privileged trading position with the United States. That status dates to the Caribbean Basin Initiative (CBI) of 1984, which promoted export production of certain products by providing duty-free U.S. market access to 20 countries, including members of CARICOM. Recently, CBI members requested that the CBI be expanded. The Caribbean Basin Trade Partnership Act, which

	2011 GDP (in millions)	2011 Population (in thousands)
Antigua and Barbuda	1,118	90
Bahamas	7,788	347
Barbados	3,685	274
Belize	1,448	357
Dominica	484	68
Grenada	816	105
Guyana	2,577	756
Haiti	7,346	10,120
Jamaica	14,440	2,709
Montserrat	Na	Na
St. Kitts and Nevis	688	53
St. Lucia	1,259	176
St. Vincent and Grenadines	688	109
Suriname	4,351	52
Trinidad and Tobago	22,400	1,346
Total	**$69,088**[a]	**16,562**[a]

TABLE 3-3

CARICOM Income and Population

[a]Excludes Montserrat.

---

[12] Myrvin L. Anthony and Andrew Hughes Hallett, "Is the Case for Economic and Monetary Union in the Caribbean Realistic?" *World Economy* 23, no. 1 (January 2000), pp. 119–144.
[13] Bruce Einhorn, "A Caribbean Headache for Obama's New Trade Rep," *Bloomberg Businessweek* (May 3, 2013).

went into effect on October 1, 2000, exempts textile and apparel exports from the Caribbean to the United States from duties and tariffs. CARICOM is shown in Figure 3-6.

Current Trade-Related Issues

One of the biggest trade-related issues in the Western Hemisphere is the creation of a Free Trade Area of the Americas (FTAA). However, leaders in several Latin American countries—Brazil in particular—are frustrated by Washington's tendency to dictate trade terms that will benefit special interests in the United States. For example, a bipartisan coalition of U.S. policymakers favors the inclusion of labor and other non-trade–related requirements in trade treaties such as the FTAA. Labor law enforcement was included in the texts of the FTAs that the United States signed with Jordan and Morocco. However, several Latin American leaders are opposed to including labor standards in the FTAA.

Now Brazil and its Mercosur partners are advocating a slower, three-stage approach to negotiations with the United States. The first stage would include discussions on business facilitation issues, such as standardized customs forms and industry deregulation; the second would focus on dispute settlement and rules of origin; and the third would focus on tariffs. Meanwhile, as previously noted, Mercosur, CARICOM, SICA, and the Andean Community are taking steps toward further intraregional integration and aligning with Europe.

Asia-Pacific: The Association of Southeast Asian Nations (ASEAN)

The **Association of Southeast Asian Nations** (**ASEAN**) was established in 1967 as an organization for economic, political, social, and cultural cooperation among its member countries. Brunei, Indonesia, Malaysia, the Philippines, Singapore, and Thailand were the original six members. Vietnam became the first Communist nation in the group when it was admitted to ASEAN in July 1995. Cambodia and Laos were admitted at the organization's 30th anniversary meeting in July 1997. Burma (known as Myanmar by the ruling military junta) joined in 1998, following delays related to the country's internal politics and human rights record (see Figure 3-6). The original six members are sometimes referred to as ASEAN-6.

FIGURE 3-6

ASEAN Income and Population

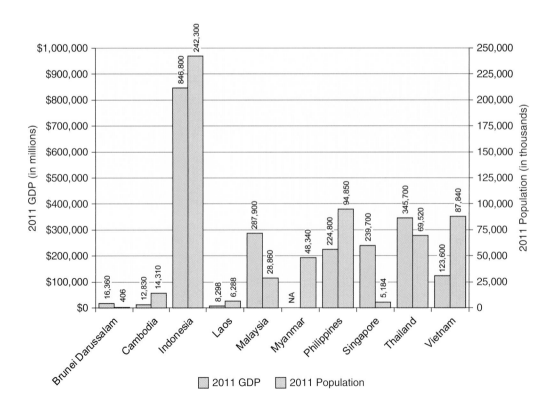

Individually and collectively, ASEAN countries are active in regional and global trade. ASEAN's top trading partners include Japan, the EU, China, and the United States. A few years ago, ASEAN officials realized that broad common goals were not enough to keep the association alive. Although the ASEAN member countries are geographically close, they have historically been divided in many respects. One problem was the strict need for consensus among all members before proceeding with any form of cooperative effort. An ASEAN Free Trade Area (AFTA) has finally become a reality, thanks to recent progress at achieving intraregional tariff reductions among the six founding ASEAN members. ASEAN's leaders are now working to establish a fully integrated, single-market ASEAN Economic Community by 2015.

Recently, Japan, China, and Korea were informally added to the member roster; some observers called this configuration "ASEAN plus three." When the roster expanded again to include Australia, New Zealand, and India, it was dubbed "ASEAN plus six." The latter is working to establish an East Asian Community, with the first step being the establishment of an East Asian Free Trade Area.[14] Although China's participation has met with some opposition, China's dynamic growth and increasing power in the region required a response. Rodolfo Collectively, ASEAN participants must seek new avenues for economic growth that are less dependent on exporting goods and services to the West. A central challenge is the fact that, despite generating roughly one-third of global GNP, the ASEAN countries represent widely varying stages of development.[15]

January 1, 2010, marked the formal establishment of a new China/ASEAN FTA. Encompassing 1.9 billion people, the new FTA removes tariffs on 90 percent of traded goods. Overall, the FTA should benefit the region; Malaysia, for example, should experience an increase in commodity exports such as palm oil and rubber. However, some ASEAN industry sectors could be also hurt by a flood of low-cost Chinese imports. Thailand's leaders were so concerned about the impact on the country's steel and textile industries that they asked for a delay in lifting tariffs.[16]

Singapore represents a special case among the ASEAN nations. In fewer than three decades, Singapore transformed itself from a British colony to a vibrant, 240-square-mile industrial power. Singapore has an extremely efficient infrastructure—the Port of Singapore is the world's second-largest container port (Hong Kong's ranks first)—and a standard of living second in the region only to Japan's. Singapore's 5 million citizens have played a critical role in the country's economic achievements by readily accepting the notion that "the country with the most knowledge will win" in global competition. Excellent training programs and a 95 percent literacy rate help explain why Singapore has more engineers per capita than the United States. Singapore's Economic Development Board has also actively recruited business interest in the nation. The manufacturing companies that have been attracted to Singapore read like a who's who of global marketing and include Hewlett-Packard, IBM, Philips, and Apple; in all, more than 3,000 companies have operations or investments in Singapore.

Singapore alone accounts for more than one-third of U.S. trading activities with ASEAN countries; U.S. merchandise exports to Singapore in 2012 totaled $30.7 billion, while imports totaled $20.6 billion. Singapore is closely tied with its neighbors; more than 32 percent of imports are reexported to other Asian countries. Singapore's efforts to fashion a civil society have gained the country some notoriety; crime is nearly nonexistent, thanks to the long-ruling People's Action Party's severe treatment of criminals.

Marketing Issues in the Asia-Pacific Region

Mastering the Japanese market takes flexibility, ambition, and a long-term commitment. Japan has changed from being a closed market to one that's just tough. There are barriers in Japan in terms of attitudes as well as laws. Any organization wishing to compete in Japan must be committed to providing top-quality products and services. In many cases, products and marketing must be tailored to local tastes. Repeat visits and extended socializing with distributors are necessary to build trust. Marketers must also master the *keiretsu* system of tightly knit corporate alliances.

---

[14] Bernard Gordon, "The FTA Fetish," *The Wall Street Journal* (November 17, 2005), p. A16.

[15] James Hookway, "Asian Nations Push Ideas for Trade," *The Wall Street Journal* (October 26, 2009), p. A12.

[16] Liz Gooch, "In Southeast Asia, Unease Over Free Trade Zone," *The New York Times* (December 28, 2009).

Bhutan and GNH (Gross National Happiness)

A sign hanging in Albert Einstein's office at Princeton University bore the inscription, "Not everything that counts can be counted, and not everything that can be counted counts." In this chapter and the last, national income data have been used to measure the total output of each of the world's economies. It has been argued, however, that indicators such as GDP and GNI per capita are inadequate. For example, China's GDP has doubled twice since 1990. However, according to data collected over that time period, ordinary Chinese citizens do not appear any happier today than they were when the country's leaders began transitioning to a free market economy. If increased income and consumption don't correlate with happiness, then what does? According to some economists and policymakers, supplemental indicators that measure things like social progress, quality of life, and sustainability are needed.

Bhutan, a kingdom of 700,000 people in the Himalaya mountains, is a case in point (see Exhibit 3-5). Per capita GNI is approximately $2,130; using this figure as a metric, Bhutan can be assigned to the lower-middle-income category of nations. However, for the past 40 years, Bhutan has relied on a measure besides economic growth, namely, Gross National Happiness (GNH).

The GNH Index includes both objective and subjective indicators: Psychological well-being, time use, community vitality, culture, health, education, environmental diversity, living standards, and governance. As Lyonpo Jigmi Thinley, home minister of Bhutan, explained, "We have to think of human well-being in broader terms. Material well-being is only one component. That doesn't ensure that you're at peace with your environment and in harmony with each other."

Not surprisingly, there is some disagreement among social scientists regarding the best way to define, track, and measure such

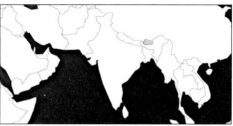

intangibles as happiness and quality of life. In Britain, for example, officials have developed a summary of "sustainable development indicators" that include measures of traffic, pollution, and crime. In another approach, survey participants report the feelings they experience as they go about their daily routines. These can include a range of activities from paying bills to participating in sports activities. In France, former President Nicolas Sarkozy established the Commission on the Measurement of Economic Performance and Social Progress.

Meanwhile, officials in Bhutan have launched a number of initiatives to promote happiness in the kingdom. For example, teachers are rotated between rural and urban areas to ensure all schoolchildren have access to a top-quality education. As Thakur S. Powdyel, an official at Bhutan's Ministry of Education, puts it, "The goal of life should not be limited to production, consumption, more production and more consumption. There is no necessary relationship between the level of possession and the level of well-being."

With the global economic crisis as a backdrop, a first-ever Happiness Congress was held in Madrid in the fall of 2010. The Congress was sponsored by the Coca-Cola Company, which uses the tagline "Open Happiness" in its global advertising. The global beverage giant also established the Coca-Cola Institute of Happiness in Spain after research indicated that Spanish consumers associate Coke with happiness more than any other brand. Minister Thinley from Bhutan was the keynote speaker at the Congress; his address was titled "Happiness in Difficult Times." As Mr. Thinley told attendees, "Our economic models are greatly, deeply flawed. They are not sustainable."

Sources: Richard Easterlin, "When Growth Outpaces Happiness," *The New York Times* (September 28, 2012), p. A31; Tim Harford, "Happiness: A Measure of Cheer," *Financial Times* (December 27, 2010), p. 5; Victor Mallet, "Bhutan and Coke Join Hands for Happiness," *Financial Times* (October 22, 2010); Andrew C. Revkin, "A New Measure of Well-Being from a Happy Little Kingdom," *The New York Times* (October 4, 2005), p. F1.

SYNC • THINK • LEARN

MyMarketingLab

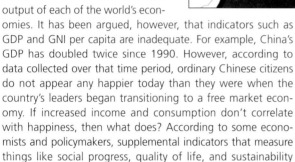

On the lighter side, it is worth noting that many consumer packaged goods marketed in Japan—including items that are not imported—have English, French, or German on the labels to suggest a cosmopolitan image and Western look. A Westerner may wonder, however, what the actual communication task is. For example, the label of City Original Coffee proclaims, "Ease Your Bosoms. This coffee has carefully selected high quality beans and roasted by our all the experience." The intended message: Drinking our coffee provides a relaxing break and "takes a load off your chest." Casual wear and sports apparel are also emblazoned with fractured messages. Japanese retailers do not seem at all concerned that the messages are syntactically suspect. As one shopkeeper explained, the point is that a message in English, French, or German can convey hipness and help sell a product. "I don't expect people to *read* it," she said.[17]

[17] Howard W. French, "To Grandparents, English Word Trend Isn't 'Naisu,'" *The New York Times* (October 23, 2002), p. A4.

Exhibit 3-5 GNH (gross national happiness), rather than GNP (gross national product) guides policy in Bhutan. However, some critics argue that promoting happiness in the Himalayan state has resulted in some negative consequences. For example, a compulsory dress code means that men must wear a knee-length wrap-around garment called a "gho." Women must wear ankle-length dresses known as "kira." Moreover, emphasis on the Buddhist culture shared by the majority of the population has caused resentment among the Nepalese minority living in the south.
Source: Getty Images and EyesWideOpen / Getty Images.

Western, Central, and Eastern Europe

The countries of Western Europe are among the most prosperous in the world. Despite the fact that there are significant differences in income between the north and the south and obvious differences in language and culture, the once-varied societies of Western Europe have grown remarkably alike. Still, enough differences remain that many observers view Western Europe in terms of three tiers. Many Britons view themselves as somewhat apart from the rest of the continent; Euro-skepticism is widespread, and the country still has problems finding common ground with historic rivals Germany and France. Meanwhile, across the English Channel, Greece, Italy, Portugal, and Spain have struggled mightily to overcome the stigma of being labeled "Club Med nations," "peripheral economies," and other derogatory descriptions by their northern neighbors. Indeed, as noted in the chapter-opening case (Case 3-1), these Southern European countries are at the center of the sovereign debt crisis.

The European Union (EU)

The origins of the EU can be traced back to the 1958 Treaty of Rome. The six original members of the European Community (EC), as the group was called then, were Belgium, France, Holland, Italy, Luxembourg, and West Germany. In 1973, Great Britain, Denmark, and Ireland were admitted, followed by Greece in 1981 and Spain and Portugal in 1986. Beginning in 1987, the 12 countries that were EC members set about the difficult task of creating a genuine single market in goods, services, and capital. In other words, the goal was to create a true economic union. Adopting the Single European Act by the end of 1992 was a major EC achievement; the Council of Ministers adopted more than 200 pieces of legislation and regulations to make the single market a reality.

FIGURE 3-7

EU Top 10 Trading Partners

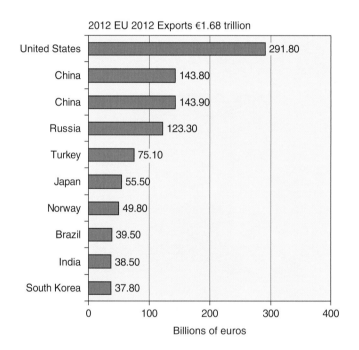

2012 EU 2012 Exports €1.68 trillion

	Billions of euros
United States	291.80
China	143.80
China	143.90
Russia	123.30
Turkey	75.10
Japan	55.50
Norway	49.80
Brazil	39.50
India	38.50
South Korea	37.80

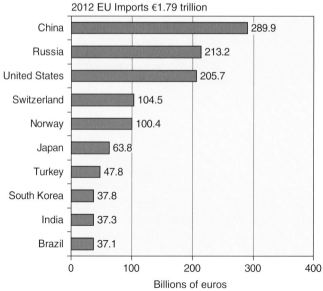

2012 EU Imports €1.79 trillion

	Billions of euros
China	289.9
Russia	213.2
United States	205.7
Switzerland	104.5
Norway	100.4
Japan	63.8
Turkey	47.8
South Korea	37.8
India	37.3
Brazil	37.1

The objective of the EU member countries is to harmonize national laws and regulations so that goods, services, people, and money can flow freely across national boundaries. December 31, 1992, marked the dawn of the new economic era in Europe. Finland, Sweden, and Austria officially joined the EU on January 1, 1995. (In November 1994, voters in Norway rejected a membership proposal.) Evidence that this is more than a free trade area, customs union, or common market is the fact that citizens of member countries are now able to freely cross borders within the union. The EU is encouraging the development of a community-wide labor pool; it is also attempting to shake up Europe's cartel mentality by handing down rules of competition patterned after U.S. antitrust law. Improvements to highway and rail networks are now being coordinated as well. The EU's top 10 trading partners are shown in Figure 3-7.

Further EU enlargement is part of the story in this region today. Cyprus, the Czech Republic, Estonia, Hungary, Poland, Latvia, Lithuania, Malta, the Slovak Republic, and Slovenia became full EU members on May 1, 2004. Bulgaria and Romania joined in 2007; Croatia, the newest member, joined on July 1, 2013. Collectively, the 28 nations of the EU are home to 500 million people and constitute the world's largest economy, with more than $15 trillion in combined GNI. Table 3-4 lists the EU member nations.

TABLE 3-4

The 28-Nation EU: Income and Population

	2011 GDP (in millions)	2011 Population (in thousands)
Austria	417,700	8,419
Belgium	513,700	11,010
Bulgaria	53,510	7,476
Croatia	56,440	4,267
Cyprus	24,690	1,117
Czech Republic	217,000	10,550
Denmark	333,600	5,574
Estonia	22,150	1,340
Finland	263,000	5,387
France	2,773,000	65,440
Germany	3,601,000	81,730
Greece	289,600	11,300
Hungary	128,964	10,022
Ireland	217,300	4,487
Italy	2,194,000	60,770
Latvia	28,250	2,220
Lithuania	42,730	3,203
Luxembourg	59,200	517
Malta	8,887	419
Netherlands	836,100	16,700
Poland	514,500	38,220
Portugal	237,400	10,640
Romania	179,800	21,390
Slovak Republic	895,990	5,440
Slovenia	98,540	2,052
Spain	1,477,000	46,240
Sweden	539,700	9,453
United Kingdom	2,445,000	62,640
Total	**$18,468,751**	**508,023**

The 1992 signing of the **Maastricht** (Netherlands) **Treaty** set the stage for the creation of an economic and monetary union that includes a European central bank and a single European currency known as the euro. The treaty entered into force in November, 1993; in May 1998, Austria, Belgium, Finland, Ireland, the Netherlands, France, Germany, Italy, Luxembourg, Portugal, and Spain were chosen as the 11 charter members of the **euro zone**.

The single-currency era, which officially began on January 1, 1999, has brought many benefits to companies in the euro zone, such as eliminating costs associated with currency conversion and exchange rate uncertainty. However, as noted in Case 3-1 at the beginning and end of this chapter, the euro zone is in crisis today. The euro existed as a unit of account until January 1, 2002, when actual coins and paper money were issued and national currencies such as the French franc were withdrawn from circulation. Greece joined in 2001; Slovenia became the 13th member on January 1, 2007. Cyrus and Malta joined in 2008, and Slovakia adopted the euro on January 1, 2009. On January 1, 2011, Estonia became the 17th EU nation to join the euro zone; Latvia joined in 2014. (see Exhibit 3-6). Today, the euro zone has 24 members in all; Andorra, Kosovo, Montenegro, Monaco, San Marino, and Vatican City use the euro but are not part of the EU.

Marketing Issues in the EU

The European Commission establishes directives and sets deadlines for their implementation by legislation in individual nations. The business environment in Europe has undergone considerable transformation since 1992, with significant implications for all elements of the marketing mix:[18]

- *Product:* **Harmonization** means that content and other product standards that varied among nations have been brought into alignment. As a result, companies have an opportunity to reap economies by reducing the number of product adaptations.
- *Price:* More competitive environment; improved **transparency** in the euro zone because the single currency makes it easier to compare prices for the same product in different countries.

Exhibit 3-6 Office buildings flashed out the news on January 1, 2011 as Estonia became the 17th EU country to join the euro zone. Estonia qualified for membership because the government kept inflation low and the budget deficit is below 3 percent of GDP. Slovakia joined in January 2009, Cyprus and Malta joined in 2008, and Slovenia (population 2 million) joined the euro zone on January 1, 2007. In all, 23 nations belong to the euro zone; the non-EU members are Andorra, Kosovo, Montenegro, Monaco, San Marino, and the Vatican City.
Source: AFP/Getty Images.

[18] G. Guido, "Implementing a Pan-European Marketing Strategy," *Long Range Planning* (Vol. 5, 1991), p. 32.

- *Promotion:* Common guidelines on TV broadcasting; uniform standards for TV commercials.
- *Distribution:* Simplification of transit documents; elimination of customs formalities at border crossings.

Case Europe, for example, manufactures and markets farm machinery. When it introduced the Magnum tractor in Europe in 1988, it offered 17 different versions because of different countries' regulations regarding placement of lights and brakes. Thanks to harmonization, Case offers the current model, the Magnum MX, in one version. However, because different types of implements and trailers are used in different countries, the MX is available with different kinds of hitches.[19]

The advent of the euro on January 1, 1999, brought about more changes. Direct comparability of prices in the euro zone forces companies to review pricing policies. The marketing challenge is to develop strategies to take advantage of opportunities in one of the largest, wealthiest, most stable markets in the world. Corporations must therefore assess the extent to which they can treat the region as one entity and how to change organizational policies and structures to adapt to and take advantage of a unified Europe.

The enlargement of the EU will further impact marketing strategies. For example, food safety laws in the EU are different from those in some Central European countries. As a result, Coca-Cola had to delay launching its Powerade sports drink and other beverage products. Specifically, Polish and EU food law require the use of different ingredients. In addition to the harmonization of laws, the very size of the expanded EU offers opportunities. For example, Procter & Gamble executives foresee that in the event of shortages in a particular country, they will be able to shift products from one market to another. A 28-nation EU also allows for more flexibility in the placement of factories. However, there will also be challenges. For example, South American banana growers now face 75 percent tariffs on exports to the new EU countries; previously, tariffs on bananas were virtually nonexistent. Also, because tariffs and quotas protect sugar production in the EU, both consumers and food producers such as Kraft will face rising costs.[20]

Because they are in transition, the markets of Central and Eastern Europe present interesting opportunities and challenges. Global companies view the region as an important new source of growth, and the first company to penetrate a country market often emerges as the industry leader. Exporting has been favored as a market-entry mode, but direct investment in the region is on the rise. With wage rates much lower than those in Spain, Portugal, and Greece, the region offers attractive locations for low-cost manufacturing. For consumer products, distribution is a critical marketing mix element because availability is the key to sales.

One study examined the approaches utilized by 3M International, McDonald's, Philips Electronics, Henkel, Südzucker AG, and several other companies operating in Central Europe. Consumers and businesses in the region are eagerly embracing well-known global brands that were once available only to government elites and others in privileged positions. The study found a high degree of standardization of marketing program elements; in particular, the core product and brand elements were largely unchanged from those used in Western Europe. Consumer companies generally target high-end segments of the market and focus on brand image and product quality; industrial marketers concentrate on opportunities to do business with the largest firms in a given country.[21]

[19] George Russell, "Marketing in the 'Old Country': The Diversity of Europe Presents Unique Challenges," *Agri Marketing* 37, no. 1 (January 1999), p. 38.

[20] Scott Miller, "Trading Partners Meet New EU," *The Wall Street Journal* (May 4, 2004), p. A17.

[21] Arnold Shuh, "Global Standardization as a Success Formula for Marketing in Central Eastern Europe," *Journal of World Business* 35, no. 2 (Summer 2000), pp. 133–148.

The Middle East

The Middle East includes 16 countries: Afghanistan, Bahrain, Cyprus, Egypt, Iran, Iraq, Israel, Jordan, Kuwait, Lebanon, Oman, Qatar, Saudi Arabia, Syria, the United Arab Emirates (which include Abu Dhabi and Dubai), and Yemen (see Exhibit 3-7). The majority of the population is Arab, a large percentage is Persian, and a small percentage is Jewish. Persians and most Arabs share the same religion, beliefs, and Islamic traditions, making the population 95 percent Muslim and 5 percent Christian and Jewish.

Despite this apparent homogeneity, many differences exist. Middle Eastern countries are distributed across the Index of Economic Freedom discussed in Chapter 2; Bahrain ranks the highest in terms of freedom, at 12; next is the United Arab Emirates, ranked at 28. Kuwait ranks 66th on the list; Saudi Arabia ranks 82nd. Moreover, the Middle East does not have a single societal type with a typical belief, behavior, and tradition. Each capital and major city in the Middle East has a variety of social groups that can be differentiated on the basis of religion, social class, education, and degree of wealth.

The price of oil drives business in the Middle East. Seven of the countries have high oil revenues: Bahrain, Iran, Iraq, Kuwait, Oman, Qatar, and Saudi Arabia hold significant world oil reserves. Oil revenues have widened the gap between poor and rich nations in the Middle East, and the disparities contribute to political and social instability in the area. Saudi Arabia, a monarchy with 22 million people and 25 percent of the world's known oil reserves, remains the most important market in this region.

In 2011 the region was rocked by demonstrations and protests that have been described as "the Arab awakening" and "the Arab spring." The governments of Tunisia and Egypt were overthrown, civil war broke out in Libya, and Syria's regime cracked down on insurgent activists. Elsewhere in the region, leaders were forced to make economic and political concessions. Prior to the uprisings, Syria had been a case study in the slow pace of change coming to the Middle East. Citing China's success at opening its economy while maintaining social control, President Bashar al-Assad took steps to move Syria away from a rigid socialist economic model. Private banks opened for business, a stock market was established, and possessing foreign currency became legal for Syrian citizens. Ties with the West began improving, too; U.S. President Barack Obama lifted some sanctions and named an ambassador to Syria. Entrepreneurs with ties to Syria began returning from Lebanon and the United States, a trend that helped spark a consumer culture. In Damascus, signs of economic rebirth included a Ford dealership, a KFC restaurant, and

Exhibit 3-7 Dubai is one of the seven emirates that make up the United Arab Emirates (UAE). Compared to its neighbors, Dubai's economy is relatively diversified: It is an important business hub for the manufacturing, IT, and finance sectors. Dubai has also become a popular tourism destination in the region. The global economic crisis has had a major impact on Dubai. Following six years of economic growth fueled by a building boom and lavish consumer spending, real estate prices have collapsed and major construction projects have been canceled. Workers—many of whom are expatriates—are losing their jobs and visas.
Source: Kamran Jebreili/AP Images.

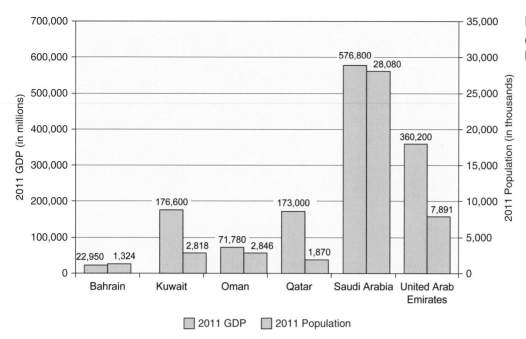

FIGURE 3-8

GCC Income and Population

Benetton boutiques.[22] Currently, however Syria is embroiled in a civil war as rebel forces try to overthrow President al-Assad.

Cooperation Council for the Arab States of the Gulf

The key regional organization, commonly referred to as the **Gulf Cooperation Council (GCC)**, was established in 1981 by Bahrain, Kuwait, Oman, Qatar, Saudi Arabia, and the United Arab Emirates (Figure 3-8). These six countries hold about 45 percent of the world's known oil reserves, but production is only about 18 percent of world oil output. Ironically, Saudi Arabia and several other Middle Eastern countries post current account deficits, largely because they must import most of the goods and services that their citizens consume. The countries are heavily dependent on oil revenues to pay for their imports; efforts toward economic diversification are underway. For example, Saudi Arabia has developed new businesses in the petrochemical, cement, and iron industries; Bahrain is expanding its banking and insurance sectors; and the United Arab Emirates is focusing on information technology, media, and telecommunications.[23]

The organization provides a means of realizing coordination, integration, and cooperation in all economic, social, and cultural affairs. Gulf finance ministers drew up an economic cooperation agreement covering investment, petroleum, the abolition of customs duties, harmonization of banking regulations, and financial and monetary coordination. GCC committees coordinate trade development in the region, industrial strategy, agricultural policy, and uniform petroleum policies and prices. Current goals include establishing an Arab common market and increasing trade ties with Asia.

The GCC is one of three newer regional organizations. In 1989, two other organizations were established. Morocco, Algeria, Mauritania, Tunisia, and Libya banded together in the Arab Maghreb Union (AMU); Egypt, Iraq, Jordan, and North Yemen created the Arab Cooperation Council (ACC). Many Arabs see their new regional groups—the GCC, ACC, and AMU—as embryonic economic communities that will foster the development of inter-Arab trade and investment. The newer organizations are likely to lead more quickly to economic integration and reform than the Arab League, which consists of 22 member states and has a constitution that requires unanimous decisions.

---

[22] Jay Solomon, "Syria Cracks Open Its Frail Economy," *The Wall Street Journal* (September 1, 2009), pp. A1, A12.
[23] Moin A. Siddiqi, "GCC: A Force to Be Reckoned With," *Middle East* (December 2003).

Marketing Issues in the Middle East

Connection is a key word in conducting business in the Middle East. Those who take the time to develop relationships with key business and government figures are more likely to cut through red tape than those who do not. A predilection for bargaining is culturally ingrained, and the visiting businessperson must be prepared for some old-fashioned haggling. Establishing personal rapport, mutual trust, and mutual respect are essentially the most important factors leading to a successful business relationship. Decisions are usually not made by correspondence or telephone. The Arab businessperson does business with the individual, not with the company. Also, most social customs are based on the Arab male-dominated society. Women are usually not part of the business or entertainment scene for traditional Muslim Arabs.

Africa

The African continent is an enormous landmass with a territory of 11.7 million square miles; the United States would fit inside Africa about three and a half times. It is not really possible to treat Africa as a single economic unit. The 54 nations on the continent can be divided into three distinct areas: the Republic of South Africa; North Africa; and sub-Saharan, or Black, Africa, which is located between the Sahara in the north and the Zambezi River in the south. With 1.3 percent of the world's wealth and 11.5 percent of its population, Africa is a developing region with an average per capita income of less than $600. Many African nations are former colonies of Europe, and the EU remains the continent's most important trading partner.

The Arabs living in North Africa are differentiated politically and economically from the populace in the rest of Africa. The six northern nations are richer and more developed than those located in the sub-Saharan region, and several—notably Libya, Algeria, and Egypt—benefit from large oil resources. The Middle East and North Africa are sometimes viewed as a regional entity known as "Mena"; as oil prices have soared, the International Monetary Fund (IMF) has encouraged Mena policymakers to invest the petrodollar windfall in infrastructure improvements as a way of sustaining economic growth.[24] Most governments in the area are working to reduce their reliance on oil revenues and their public aid levels. The economies of non-oil-based, "emerging Mena" countries, which include Jordan, Lebanon, Morocco, and Tunisia, have also performed well in recent years.

Economic Community of West African States (ECOWAS)

The Treaty of Lagos establishing the **Economic Community of West African States (ECOWAS)** was signed in May 1975 by 16 states with the object of promoting trade, cooperation, and self-reliance in West Africa. The original members were Benin, Burkina Faso, Cape Verde, Côte d'Ivoire, the Gambia, Ghana, Guinea, Guinea-Bissau, Liberia, Mali, Mauritania, Niger, Nigeria, Senegal, Sierra Leone, and Togo; Mauritania left the group in 2002 (Table 3-5). In 1980, the member countries agreed to establish a free trade area for unprocessed agricultural products and handicrafts. Tariffs on industrial goods were also to be abolished; however, there were implementation delays.

By January 1990, tariffs on 25 items manufactured in ECOWAS member states had been eliminated. The organization installed a computer system to process customs and trade statistics and to calculate the loss of revenue resulting from the liberalization of intercommunity trade. In June 1990, ECOWAS adopted measures to create a single monetary zone in the region by 1994. Despite such achievements, economic development has occurred unevenly in the region. In recent years, Ghana has performed impressively, propelled by deals related to its oil, gas, and mineral sectors. China has signed deals with the region that are worth $15 billion.[25] By contrast, Liberia and Sierra Leone are still experiencing political conflict and economic decline.

---

[24] Victoria Robson, "Window of Opportunity," *Middle East Economic Digest* 49, no. 18 (May 6, 2005), p. 6.

[25] Will Connors, "China Extends Africa Push with Loans, Deal in Ghana," *The Wall Street Journal* (September 24, 2010), p. A15.

TABLE 3-5

ECOWAS Income and Population

	2011 GDP (in millions)	2011 Population (in thousands)
Benin	$ 7,295	9,100
Burkina Faso	10,190	16,970
Cape Verde	1,901	501
Côte d'Ivoire	24,070	20,150
The Gambia	898	1,776
Ghana	39,200	24,970
Guinea	5,089	10,220
Guinea-Bissau	973	1,547
Liberia	1,545	4,129
Mali	10,590	15,840
Niger	6,017	16,070
Nigeria	244,000	162,500
Senegal	14,290	12,770
Sierra Leone	2,243	5,997
Togo	3,620	6,155
Total	**$371,921**	**308,695**

East African Community

Kenya, Uganda, Tanzania, Rwanda, and Burundi are the five nations that comprise the world's newest common market (see Figure 3-9). The East African Community's origins date back more than 40 years, but it has only been since 1999 that substantial progress has been made toward integration and cooperation. Today's East African Community has evolved through several of the stages listed in Table 3-2. In 2005, a customs union was implemented. The formation of the common market in 2010 resulted in the free movement of people, goods and services, and capital within the community. Members also intend to move swiftly to establish an economic union. The first step will be creating a monetary union; although negotiations were still ongoing in

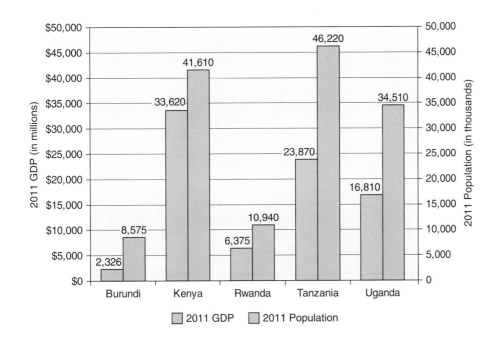

FIGURE 3-9

East Africa Community Income and Population

mid-2013, the goal is to introduce a common currency in 2015. There is even talk about forming a single nation. As one observer noted, "The idea of a United States of East Africa is less far-fetched than it was before."[26]

Southern African Development Community (SADC)

In 1992, the **Southern African Development Community** (**SADC**) superseded the South African Development Coordination Council as a mechanism by which the region's black-ruled states could promote trade, cooperation, and economic integration. The members are Angola, Botswana, Democratic Republic of Congo (formerly Zaire), Lesotho, Malawi, Mauritius, Mozambique, Namibia, South Africa, Seychelles, Swaziland, Tanzania, Zambia, and Zimbabwe (see Table 3-6). South Africa joined the community in 1994; it represents about 75 percent of the income in the region and 86 percent of intraregional exports. The SADC's ultimate goal is a fully developed customs union; in 2000, an 11-nation free trade area was finally established (Angola, the Democratic Republic of Congo, and Seychelles are not participants). South Africa and the EU signed a Trade, Development, and Cooperation Agreement (TDCA) in 2000; two-way trade and foreign direct investment have increased substantially since then. Meanwhile other SADC members are concerned that such an arrangement provides European global companies with a base from which to dominate the continent. South Africa, Botswana, Lesotho, Namibia, and Swaziland also belong to the Southern African Customs Union (SACU).

Marketing Issues in Africa

In 2000, U.S. President George W. Bush signed the African Growth and Opportunities Act (AGOA) into law (see www.agoa.gov). Created with the theme of "Trade, not Aid," the law is designed to support African nations that make significant progress toward economic liberalization. African companies will find it easier to gain access to financing from the U.S. Export-Import Bank; AGOA also represents a formal step toward a U.S.-Africa free trade area. One of the act's key provisions grants textile and apparel manufacturers in Kenya and Mauritius free access to the U.S. market up to $3.5 billion in exports each year. As Benjamin Kipkorir, Kenya's ambassador to the United States, observed a decade ago, "Every country that has industrialized, starting from England in the eighteenth century, began with textiles. We'd like to do the same thing."

TABLE 3-6

SADC Income and Population

	2011 GNI (in millions)	2011 Population (in thousands)
Angola	104,300	19,620
Botswana	17,330	2,031
Democratic Republic of Congo	15,650	67,760
Lesotho	2,426	2,194
Malawi	5,621	15,380
Mauritius	11,260	1,286
Mozambique	12,800	23,930
Namibia	12,300	2,324
Seychelles	1,007	86
South Africa	408,200	50,590
Swaziland	3,978	1,068
Tanzania	23,870	46,220
Zambia	19,210	13,470
Zimbabwe	9,656	12,750
Total	**$647,608**	**258,709**

[26] Josh Kron, "African Countries Form a Common Market," *The New York Times* (July 2, 2010), p. B2. See also William Wallis, "Enthusiasm for EAC Not Matched by Results," *Financial Times Special Report: Doing Business in Kenya* (November 26, 2010), p. 1.

Under the Agreement on Textiles and Clothing negotiated during the Uruguay Round of GATT negotiations, global textile quotas were eliminated in 2005. Nevertheless, the textile provision in AGOA is controversial. The United States imports nearly $100 billion in textiles and apparel each year. The largest share—more than 40 percent—originates in China, with the balance coming from other parts of Asia plus Latin America and Africa. Wary U.S. legislators from textile-producing states fear job losses among their constituents.

Despite such initiatives, only about 3 percent of annual foreign direct investment goes to Africa. Still, some Persian Gulf states are creating closer ties with Africa, investing billions of dollars in key sectors such as infrastructure, agriculture, and telecommunications. For example, Dubai World, a state-owned company, is negotiating a deal in Nigeria's energy sector that could be valued at several billion dollars. Dubai also funded construction of a container terminal that opened recently in Djibouti. The largest terminal of its kind in sub-Saharan Africa, it will be managed by DP World, a subsidiary of Dubai World. Such investments are welcome at a time when investors in Europe, stung by economic losses in the developed world, are cutting spending. As Djibouti President Ismail Guelleh noted, "What the Arabs are doing for us is what colonialists should have done for Africa."[27]

Summary

This chapter examines the environment for world trade, focusing on the institutions and regional cooperation agreements that affect trade patterns. The multilateral **World Trade Organization**, created in 1995 as the successor to the **General Agreement on Tariffs and Trade**, provides a forum for settling disputes among member nations and tries to set policy for world trade. The world trade environment is also characterized by **preferential trade agreements** among smaller numbers of countries on regional and subregional bases. These agreements can be conceptualized on a continuum of increasing economic integration.

Free trade areas such as the one created by the **North American Free Trade Agreement (NAFTA)** represent the lowest level of economic integration. The purpose of a **free trade agreement (FTA)** is to eliminate tariffs and quotas. **Rules of origin** are used to verify the country from which goods are shipped. A **customs union**, such as Mercosur, represents a further degree of integration in the form of **common external tariffs**. In a **common market**, such as the Central American Integration System (SICA) and the East African Community, restrictions on the movement of labor and capital are eased in an effort to further increase integration. An **economic union**, such as the EU, the highest level of economic integration, is achieved by unification of economic policies and institutions. **Harmonization**, the coming together of varying standards and regulations, is a key characteristic of the EU.

Other important cooperation arrangements include the Association of Southeast Asian Nations (ASEAN) and the Gulf Cooperation Council (GCC). In Africa, the two main cooperation agreements are the Economic Community of West African States (ECOWAS) and the South African Development Community (SADC).

MyMarketingLab

Go to **mymktlab.com** for the following Assisted-graded writing questions:

3-1. The creation of the single market in Europe has led to harmonization. What does this mean? How does harmonization affect a company's global marketing strategies?

3-2. Why are Greece, Ireland, Italy, Portugal, and Spain sometimes referred to as the euro zone's "peripheral countries"?

3-3. Mymarketinglab Only – comprehensive writing assignment for this chapter.

[27] Margaret Coker, "Persian Gulf States Bet on Africa Despite Downturn," *The Wall Street Journal* (February 24, 2009), p. A9.

MyMarketingLab

Go to **mymktlab.com** to complete the problems marked with this icon .

Discussion Questions

3-4. Explain the role of the World Trade Organization. Why has the Doha Round of trade talks stalled?

3-5. Describe the similarities and differences among a free trade area, a customs union, a common market, and an economic union. Give an example of each.

3-6. What are the criteria for joining the euro zone?

3-7. Identify a regional economic organization or agreement in each of the following areas: Latin America, Asia/Pacific, Western Europe, Central Europe, the Middle East, and Africa.

3-8. Several key dates mentioned in the chapter are listed here. Can you identify the event associated with each? (The answers follow.)

> January 1, 1994
> January 1, 1995
> January 1, 1999
> January 1, 2002
> May 1, 2004
> January 1, 2009
> January 1, 2011
> July 1, 2013

Answers: January 1, 1994—NAFTA becomes effective; January 1, 1995—WTO becomes the successor to GATT; January 1, 1999—introduction of the euro as a unit of account; January 1, 2002—euro currency goes into circulation; May 1, 2004—EU enlargement to 25 members; January 1, 2009—Slovakia becomes the 16th member of the euro zone; January 1, 2011—Estonia becomes the 17th member of the euro zone; July 1, 2013—Croatia joins the EU.

CASE 3-1 CONTINUED (REFER TO PAGE 92)

Will New Trade Partnerships Fuel East-West Growth?

As noted in Chapter 2, Europe desperately needs to find new sources of economic growth. What better way to do so than to sign an FTA with the United States? That's exactly what European leaders are asking as talks get underway between leaders on both sides of the Atlantic. Even though tariffs on goods imports and exports average only about 3 percent, the volume of two-way trade is very large—some $500 billion in goods alone. If tariffs were eliminated, even a small increase in trade could yield substantial benefits. As an executive at GE explained, "This could be the biggest, most valuable free-trade agreement by far, even if it produces only a marginal increase in trade."

Tariffs are only one part of the picture. Various types of nontariff restrictions create bureaucratic obstacles that affect a variety of industries. For example, Europe has blocked imports of genetically modified agricultural products such as corn and soy. Another issue concerns product labeling. Some food companies that market dairy products in the United States use terms such as "Parmesan" on their labeling. However, according to EU law, the name "Parmesan" should apply only to a cow's-milk cheese known as "Parmigiano-Reggiano" that is produced using traditional methods in the Parma/Reggio region of Italy. The Italian cheese bears symbols for Protected Geographic Indication (PGI) and Protected Designation of Origin (PDO). The only ingredients besides milk in true Parmigiano-Reggiano are salt and an enzyme. By contrast, Kraft 100% Grated Parmesan Cheese contains cellulose powder (for a smooth texture), potassium sorbate (a preservative), and other ingredients. Because of EU regulations, Kraft cannot sell its cheese in Europe.

Another contentious issue is also a cultural one. In parts of Europe, some hold the view that American cultural exports—Hollywood movies, for example—overwhelm the works of local film producers. This has prompted European policymakers to demand "carve-outs" that exempt certain industries from the trade pact. In France, for example, the motion picture industry receives state subsidies, and broadcasters are required to comply with quotas for the amount of programming that originates in Europe. Digital media would also be exempt. Not surprisingly, some critics have denounced the proposed carve-outs as blatant protectionism; however, supporters believe they are legitimate ways to preserve cultural diversity.

The Trans-Pacific Partnership

In 2005, Brunei, Chile, New Zealand, and Singapore signed an agreement pledging to eliminate all tariffs among the trade partners by 2015. Signatories to the free trade pact, known as the Trans-Pacific Partnership (TPP), now include Australia, Canada, Malaysia, Mexico, Peru, the United States, and Vietnam. Japan is currently negotiating to become the TPP's 12th member. According to the International Monetary Fund, goods exports by the eleven nations negotiating the TPP account for about 25 percent of the world total. If Japan were to join, the agreement would cover nearly 40 percent of world economic output.

Impetus for U.S. involvement gained momentum under President George W. Bush. U.S. President Barack Obama views the TPP as a means of increasing American exports. The president is also under pressure to create more jobs for U.S. workers. Ironically, however, implementation of the TPP could result in a loss of jobs. For example, New Balance Athletic Shoe produces 7 million pairs of athletic shoes annually at its plant in Maine. It is the only major company that still manufactures athletic shoes where its headquarters is located. Even so, the company must source more than 20 million pairs from factories in China, Indonesia, the United Kingdom, and Vietnam to meet the demand of its U.S. customers. As Matthew LeBretton, head of public affairs at New Balance, explains:

> If this is purely a business decision, then it's very clear that you make more profit by making shoes in Asia than in the United States. We aren't purists, but we are doing this for reasons that are other than financial impact. It's the right thing for us to do. We suffer as a country when we lose the ability to manufacture.

Another issue is Beijing's concern that TPP represents an American strategy of "containment," i.e., neutralizing China's growing influence in the Asia-Pacific region. This concern has increased as the likelihood grows that Japan will join the group. The U.S. position is that any nation—including China—can join, providing it meets standards pertaining to opening markets and limiting the amount of government assistance given to state-run companies. Meanwhile, to avoid the kinds of disconnects that are occurring in the U.S.-EU negotiations, agricultural issues are being negotiated separately from the main deal.

Discussion Questions

3-9. What critical thinking issues are raised by this case?

3-10. Are you in favor of dropping U.S. tariffs on footwear, even if it means some New Balance employees will lose their jobs?

3-11. Do you think Americans and Europeans can overcome deeply entrenched disagreements and reach an accord?

3-12. Japanese rice farmers are opposed to Japan joining the TPP. Why?

Sources: Brian Spegele and Thomas Catan, "China Suggests Shift on U.S.-Led Trade Pact," *The Wall Street Journal* (June 1–2, 2013), p. A6; James Kanter, "European Parliament Approves Resolution Limiting the Scope of a Free-Trade Pact," *The New York Times* (May 24, 2013), p. B7; David Dreier, "China Belongs in the Pacific Trade Talks," *The Wall Street Journal* (April 12, 2013), p. A11; Yuka Hayashi, "'Abenomics' Plan for Growth in Japan: Free-Trade Talks," *The Wall Street Journal* (March 15, 2013), p. A8; Hiroko Tabuchi, "Japan to Enter Talks on Pacific Trade," *The New York Times* (March 16, 2013), p. B3; Philip Stephens, "Transatlantic Free Trade Promises a Bigger Prize," *Financial Times* (February 15, 2013), p. 11; Stephen Fidler, "Trans-Atlantic Trading Partners Barter Over Rules," *The Wall Street Journal* (February 14, 2013), p. A11; Sudeep Reddy, "Broad Trade Deal on Table," *The Wall Street Journal* (February 14, 2013), p. A1; Matthew Dalton and Stephen Fidler, "U.S. Considers Opening Ambitious Trade Talks with EU," *The Wall Street Journal* (December 24, 2012), p. A7; Jack Ewing, "Trade Deal Between U.S. and Europe Resurfaces," *The New York Times* (November 26, 2012), p. B2; Larry Olmsted, "Most Parmesan Cheese in America Is Fake, Here's Why," *Forbes* (November 19, 2012); Eric Martin, "New Balance Wants Its Tariffs, Nike Doesn't," *Bloomberg Businessweek* (May 7, 2012), pp. 14–15; Yuka Hayashi and Tom Barkley, "Japan's Bid to Join Asian Trade Pact Faces a Leery U.S.," *The Wall Street Journal* (February 7, 2012), p. A9; John D. McKinnon, "Bush Pushes Trans-Pacific Free Trade," *The Wall Street Journal* (January 24, 2008), p. A3.

CASE 3-2
Will the Euro Survive? The Euro Zone Fights for Its Life

How do you fix one, two, or several broken economies? More specifically, how do you keep the euro zone intact? During the summer of 2012, Mario Draghi, the president of the European Central Bank (ECB), had an answer: "Within our mandate, the ECB is ready to do whatever it takes to preserve the euro. And believe me, it will be enough." With those words, Draghi declared that he intended to keep the euro zone from falling apart.

Following strong growth in the early years of the twenty-first century, the good times ended as one EU economy after another fell victim to the global economic crisis. At the heart of the problem was the fact that during the boom years, several countries had run up huge current account deficits. Governments were then obliged to borrow money to offset the deficits (see Exhibit 3-8).

In 2010, two years after the collapse of Lehman Brothers, Europe experienced a banking crisis of its own. Property values slumped—in other words, the so-called asset bubble burst—and the banks that

Exhibit 3-8 The European Central Bank (ECB), based in Frankfurt, Germany, establishes policy for the 23 nations that use the euro. Jean-Claude Trichet was the ECB president from 2003 to 2011, during which time he was sometimes referred to as "Mr. Euro." The ECB has been in crisis management mode for months, buying bonds from cash-strapped euro zone governments and providing liquidity for the euro zone financial system.
Source: Iain Masterton/Alamy

had provided the financing faced a cash crunch. As governments intervened to keep banks from failing, they piled up debt. Global investors in New York, London, and elsewhere worried that governments would default on their debt obligations.

In the twentieth century, when each European country had its own currency, government leaders could manipulate exchange rates by using devaluation. As you read in Chapter 2, a weaker currency has the effect of making exports more competitive. This, in turn, stimulates the economy. Everything changed in Europe a decade ago when a currency union was created. To date, 24 nations—18 EU members and 6 non-EU states—have adopted the euro. For them, devaluation is no longer an option.

Despite being members of Europe's single market, EU nations vary widely in terms of trading patterns and economic strength. To the north, Germany is Europe's largest economy. An export powerhouse, Germany's annual GDP exceeds $3.3 trillion, and its overall annual trade surplus is about $200 billion. German companies enjoy high productivity and are strong competitors in global markets. In the north, labor markets are relatively flexible, and employees typically exhibit strong work ethics. As a general rule, companies in the south are less competitive, and government labor regulations make it hard to lay off workers. European countries also vary widely in their taxing and spending policies. The German people have a reputation for thriftiness. By contrast, Greece and its Southern European neighbors have reputations as being big spenders.

Greece, for example, exports very little, and its economy is only one-tenth the size of Germany's. But Greece is not the only European country that is in crisis. Ireland, Spain, Italy, and Portugal are also at risk. As one Portuguese businessman put it, "The euro's great if you're traveling around, but it's an absurd idea to have the same currency in a country like Greece or Portugal as in Germany, which has totally different habits and culture."

Each year, the World Economic Forum (WEF) releases competitiveness ratings for more than 100 countries. In its report for 2012–2013, Greece, Italy, Portugal, Spain, and Ireland ranked lower than their EU neighbors in terms of infrastructure, business sophistication, macroeconomic environment, and other criteria. Little wonder, then, that these countries are sometimes referred to as the EU's "peripheral economies."

Faced with huge budget deficits, Europe's leaders have been forced to introduce sweeping economic reforms. They have instituted unprecedented austerity measures in order to rein in runaway government budgets. Desperate to prop up economies teetering on the brink of collapse, EU's leadership devised a €750 billion rescue package.

Greece

A significant amount of the bailout money—€110 billion/$150 billion—was earmarked for Greece. Ranked 83rd in the WEF's Global Competitive Index, Greece has a long history of deep-rooted economic problems including tax evasion; a bloated, inefficient administration; and widespread corruption. Even so, after adopting the euro in 2001, Greece experienced an economic boom buoyed by positive trends in consumer spending and housing.

However, the global financial crisis that began in 2008 hit Greece especially hard. As consumers and businesses in all parts of the world cut back on spending, Greek shipping companies lost business. Then, in summer 2009, tourist traffic from Northern Europe—an important source of revenue—slowed considerably. Greece's budget deficit then ballooned to 13.6 percent, far higher than the 3 percent limit mandated by the EU. Prime Minister George Papandreou had no choice but to impose tax increases, deep cuts in wages and pensions, and other austerity measures. Greek citizens responded with violent demonstrations, and workers went on strike.

As a condition for accepting the bailout package, Papandreou had to agree that the European Commission, the International Monetary Fund, and the European Central Bank would be allowed to monitor Greece's economic reform program. In an effort to raise €50 billion ($71 billion) by 2015, the Greek government intends to sell government-owned organizations and properties including the national post office and a telecommunications company.

Italy

Italy, ranked 48th in the WEF Global Competitiveness Index, is currently viewed as less "at risk" than Ireland and Portugal. In Italy, austerity is the order of the day. A three-year fiscal plan calls for €40 billion in budget cuts by 2014 to comply with euro zone rules. The government intends to have a balanced budget by 2014. By that time, it is hoped that Italy's debt-to-GDP ratio—currently second to Greece's—will have fallen from 120 percent to 112 percent. Unfortunately, Prime Minister Silvio Berlusconi's extravagant personal life, including well-publicized allegations of a sex scandal, have undermined public confidence in the government.

Portugal

Measured in terms of per capita GNI, Portugal is the poorest country in Western Europe; it ranks 46th in the WEF Index. In the darkest days of the financial crisis, Portugal's budget deficit was 9.3 percent of GDP. Portugal's foreign affairs minister noted that his country's debt situation could lead to its expulsion from the euro zone. However, Prime Minister José Sócrates took decisive action; he froze the pay of public employees, reduced military spending, and postponed infrastructure projects. Commenting on the infrastructure issue, Fernando Ulrich, head of one of Portugal's top banks, said, "We cannot afford to invest any more money in cement for the next 10 years. We have to spend all our available funds on improving the competitiveness of the export sector."

Spain

Spain, the euro zone's fourth-largest economy, ranks 42nd in the Global Competitive Index. Its 20 percent unemployment rate is the highest in the EU; generous unemployment benefits reduce the incentive for individuals to find and keep jobs and cause a drain on public funds. Construction activity ground to a halt as overbuilding resulted in the bursting of the real estate bubble. Under pressure to initiate reforms, Prime Minister José Luis Rodríguez Zapatero proposed changes to Spain's strict employment laws. Meanwhile, the Bank of Spain is moving to support *cajas*, regional savings banks that suffered huge losses in the housing market.

Ireland

Riding the wave of the technology boom of the late 1990s, Ireland's economy grew at an annual rate of 9.6 percent. The Celtic Tiger, as some called Ireland, was transformed into a preferred location for high-tech manufacturing. Foreign direct investment represented two-thirds of overall GDP, far above the 20 percent average in the EU as a whole. The first decade of the twenty-first century was a dizzying time for Ireland, as real estate prices soared.

Although Ireland is currently ranked 29th in terms of global competitiveness, the economic downturn directly affected some of the Emerald Isle's oldest and most iconic brands. For example, citing falling global demand and the real estate bust, Guinness canceled plans to invest €650 million ($1 billion) to build a superbrewery on the site of its 250-year-old St. James's Gate facility. Waterford Wedgwood, the venerable crystal and fine-china company, entered insolvency administration, and its owners put its assets up for sale.

Discussion Questions

3-13. Why did the European Commission bail out banks in Ireland and Greece? Why not let them default?

3-14. Investors demanded that Portugal's José Sócrates and other leaders make big spending cuts. However, Sócrates and other socialist prime ministers would prefer to generate economic growth via government spending. Does this make Sócrates, Zapatero, and like-minded leaders Keynesians? Or are they following Hayek's principles?

3-15. Why do citizens in France, Great Britain, and elsewhere stage protests when the government imposes austerity measures?

Sources: Lionel Barber and Michael Steen, "'Whatever It Takes': The Italian Determined to Save the Euro," *Financial Times* (December 14, 2012), p. 7; Charles Forelle, "Aging Greece Tries National Yard Sale," *The Wall Street Journal* (June 28, 2011), p. A1; Stephen Erlanger, "Euro Zone Is Imperiled by North–South Divide," *The New York Times* (December 3, 2010), p. A1; Victor Mallet and Peter Wise, "Peripheral Nerves," *Financial Times* (November 8, 2010), p. 11; Marcus Walker, "Irish Resist EU's Push to Accept a Rescue," *The Wall Street Journal* (November 15, 2010), p. A1; Bob Davis, "As Global Economy Shifts, Companies Rethink, Retool," *The Wall Street Journal* (November 8, 2010), pp. A1, A18; "French Protests, British Austerity Give U.S. Glimpse of Its Future" (Editorial), *USA Today* (October 25, 2010), p. 10A; Mark Mulligan, "Spain's Reforms Given Urgency by Debt Crisis," *Financial Times* (June 16, 2010), p. 3; Victor Mallet, "Europe Enters Era of Belt-Tightening," *Financial Times* (May 14, 2010).

4

Social and Cultural Environments

 CASE 4-1
Will Tourism Ruin Venice?

Venice is unique among the cities of the world. Located on the Adriatic Sea in northern Italy's Veneto region, Venice consists of more than 100 islands linked by a system of canals. Historically, the lagoon provided Venetians with a safe haven from Germanic and Hun invaders. In fact, the word "lagoon" itself originated in the local Venetian dialect. "Ghetto," "casino," "marzipan," "quarantine," and "scampi" are some other words that Venice has contributed to the English language.

Over the centuries, Venice became a vital commercial center for international trade, linking Europe with the Far East. Venetian prowess in manufacturing and commerce is legendary, and

Exhibit 4-1 A cruise ship docks in Venice, Italy. Venice is a popular port of call for passengers on ships operated by MSC, Norwegian, and other carriers. While Venice's economy is heavily dependent on free-spending visitors from around the globe, environmentalists and local residents worry that mass tourism is a threat to both the city and the surrounding lagoon.
Source: Courtesy of Manuel Silvestri.

includes glassmaking and shipbuilding. In addition, Venice was an important artistic and cultural center during the Renaissance Era.

Today, the Germanic hordes are no longer a threat. However, Venice is threatened by modern invaders: Venice is tied with Barcelona as top cruise destination in the Mediterranean. Despite the recent economic downturn, giant cruise ships arrive each week. They slowly navigate down the Guidecca Canal before disgorging passengers eager to visit such famous landmarks as the Realto Bridge, Piazza San Marco, Palazzo Ducale, and the Grand Canal. Locals complain that the ships cause the windows of the palazzos that line the canal to rattle and shake. In 1999, only about 100,000 visitors arrived by boat. Now, more than 1,000 cruise ships and ferries dock at Venice's main passenger terminal each year. As a result, the number of visitors who come for short-term stays can swell as high as 100,000 people per *day*.

Tourists also arrive by air, rail, and car; Marco Polo airport is less than 20 kilometers from Venice. In terms of nationality, Americans constitute the largest group of foreign tourists. Overall, tourism is the leading source of income in Venice, with approximately 15 million visitors arriving each year. By comparison, the year-round resident population of Venice is only about 59,000 people; that number has been steadily declining for years. Tourism gets a boost because Venice hosts important cultural events such as the International Film Festival and the Biennale International Art Exposition. Venice has also hosted the America's Cup World Series in 2012.

Concern is growing among the locals about the potentially detrimental effects of the cruise ships—specifically, air, water, and noise pollution—and possible damage to the submerged foundations that support Venice's famed architectural treasures. Not surprisingly, it is a divisive issue. Says one bar owner, "Everyone in Venice works with the cruise passengers, from taxis to bars to suppliers. The ships bring people, and the cruises can save a season." Even so, Europe's recent economic crisis was particularly hard on Italy. Even Harry's Bar, an iconic Venice fixture since the 1930s, fell on hard times and may close.

For those not in favor of the cruise ships, the potential benefits of tourist money flowing into the Venice economy do not offset the detrimental effects. As one resident complains, "Some days you have 10 ships coming in. It just isn't safe." There is even a sense among some locals that many visitors care less about Venice's cultural life and more about shopping for souvenirs. "And even if they did spend millions, is it worth the risk of destroying the city?" the resident asks.

The conflicting priorities of commerce and conservation in Venice illustrate the ways that differences in the social and cultural environments impact marketing opportunities and dynamics around the globe. This chapter focuses on the social and cultural forces that shape and affect individual, group, and corporate behavior in the marketplace. We start with a general discussion of the basic aspects of culture and society and the emergence of a twenty-first-century global consumer culture. Next, several useful conceptual frameworks for understanding culture are presented. These include Hall's concept of high- and low-context cultures, Maslow's hierarchy of needs, Hofstede's cultural typology, the self-reference criterion, and diffusion theory. The chapter also includes specific examples of the impact of culture and society on the marketing of both consumer and industrial products.

Clearly, Venice's cultural riches constitute a magnet for tourists. It remains to be seen, however, whether the rising tide of tourism and other commercial ventures is sustainable. You will have the opportunity to explore the issue in the continuation of this case on page 148. The discussion questions at the end of the case will give you a chance to reflect further on "lessons learned."

LEARNING OBJECTIVES

1 Define *culture* and identify the various expressions and manifestations of culture that can impact global marketing strategies.

2 Compare and contrast the key aspects of high- and low-context cultures.

3 Identify and briefly explain the major dimensions of Hofstede's social values typology.

4 Understand the importance of diffusion theory and its applicability to global marketing.

5 Explain the concept of environmental sensitivity and give contrasting examples of product categories that are deeply embedded in culture and those that are not.

Society, Culture, and Global Consumer Culture

Both differences and similarities characterize the world's cultures, meaning that the task of the global marketer is twofold. First, marketers must study and understand the cultures of the countries in which they will be doing business. Second, they must incorporate this understanding into the marketing planning process. In some instances, strategies and marketing programs will have to be adapted; however, marketers should also take advantage of shared cultural characteristics and avoid unneeded and costly adaptations of the marketing mix.

Any systematic study of a new geographic market requires a combination of tough-mindedness and openmindedness. While marketers should be secure in their own convictions and traditions, an open mind is required to appreciate the integrity and value of other ways of life and points of view. People must, in other words, overcome the prejudices that are a natural result of the human tendency toward ethnocentricity. Although "culture shock" is a normal human reaction to the new and unknown, successful global marketers strive to comprehend human experience from the local point of view. One reason cultural factors challenge global marketers is that many of these factors are hidden from view. Because culture is a learned behavior passed on from generation to generation, it can be difficult for the outsider to fathom. However, as they endeavor to understand cultural factors, outsiders gradually become insiders and develop cultural empathy. There are many different paths to the same goals in life. The global marketer understands this and revels in life's rich diversity.

Anthropologists and sociologists have offered scores of different definitions of culture. As a starting point, **culture** can be understood as "ways of living, built up by a group of human beings, that are transmitted from one generation to another." A culture acts out its ways of living in the context of *social institutions*, including family, educational, religious, governmental, and business institutions. Those institutions, in turn, function to reinforce cultural norms. Culture also includes both conscious and unconscious values, ideas, attitudes, and symbols that shape human behavior and that are transmitted from one generation to the next. Organizational anthropologist Geert Hofstede defines *culture* as "the collective programming of the mind that distinguishes the members of one category of people from those of another."[1] A particular "category of people" may constitute a nation, an ethnic group, a gender group, an organization, a family, or some other unit.

Some anthropologists and sociologists divide cultural elements into two broad categories: material culture and nonmaterial culture. The former is sometimes referred to as the *physical component* or *physical culture*, which includes physical objects and artifacts created by humans such as clothing and tools. Nonmaterial culture (also known as *subjective* or *abstract culture*) includes intangibles such as religion, perceptions, attitudes, beliefs, and values. It is generally agreed that the material and nonmaterial elements of culture are interrelated and interactive. Cultural anthropologist George P. Murdock studied material and nonmaterial culture and identified dozens of "cultural universals," including athletic sports, body adornment, cooking, courtship, dancing, decorative art, education, ethics, etiquette, family feasting, food taboos, language, marriage, mealtime, medicine, mourning, music, property rights, religious rituals, residence rules, status differentiation, and trade.[2]

It is against this background of traditional definitions that global marketers should understand the following worldwide sociocultural phenomenon of the early twenty-first century:[3] It has been argued that consumption has become the hallmark of postmodern society. As cultural information and imagery flow freely across borders via satellite TV, the Internet, and similar communication channels, new global consumer cultures are emerging. Persons who identify with these cultures share meaningful sets of consumption-related symbols. Some of these cultures are associated with specific product categories; marketers speak of "coffee culture," "credit-card culture," "fast-food culture," "pub culture," "soccer culture," and so on. This cosmopolitan culture, which is comprised of various segments, owes its existence in large part to a wired world in which there is increasing interconnectedness of various local cultures. It can be exploited by **global consumer culture positioning** (**GCCP**), a marketing tool that will be explained in more detail in Chapter 7. In particular, marketers can use advertising to communicate the notion that people everywhere consume a particular brand or to appeal to human universals.

---

[1] Geert Hofstede and Michael Harris Bond, "The Confucius Connection: From Cultural Roots to Economic Growth," *Organizational Dynamics* (Spring 1988), p. 5.

[2] George P. Murdock, "The Common Denominator of Culture," in *The Science of Man in the World Crisis*, Ralph Linton, ed. (New York: Columbia University Press, 1945), p. 145.

[3] The following discussion is adapted from Dana L. Alden, Jan-Benedict Steenkamp, and Rajeev Batra, "Brand Positioning through Advertising in Asia, North America, and Europe: The Role of Global Consumer Culture," *Journal of Marketing* 63, no. 1 (January 1999), pp. 75–87.

Attitudes, Beliefs, and Values

If we accept Hofstede's notion of culture as "the collective programming of the mind," then it makes sense to learn about culture by studying the attitudes, beliefs, and values shared by a specific group of people. An **attitude** is a learned tendency to respond in a consistent way to a given object or entity. Attitudes are clusters of interrelated beliefs. A **belief** is an organized pattern of knowledge that an individual holds to be true about the world. Attitudes and beliefs, in turn, are closely related to values. A **value** can be defined as an enduring belief or feeling that a specific mode of conduct is personally or socially preferable to another mode of conduct.[4] In the view of Hofstede and others, values represent the deepest level of a culture and are present in the majority of the members of that particular culture.

Some specific examples will allow us to illustrate these definitions by comparing and contrasting attitudes, beliefs, and values. The Japanese, for example, strive to achieve cooperation, consensus, self-denial, and harmony. Because these all represent feelings about modes of conduct, they are *values*. Japan's monocultural society reflects the *belief* among the Japanese that they are unique in the world. Many Japanese, especially young people, also believe that the West is the source of important fashion trends. As a result, many Japanese share a favorable *attitude* toward American brands. Within any large, dominant cultural group, there are likely to be **subcultures**; that is, smaller groups of people with their own shared subset of attitudes, beliefs, and values. Values, attitudes, and beliefs can also be surveyed at the level of any "category of people" that is embedded within a broad culture. For example, if you are a vegetarian, then eating meat represents a mode of conduct that you and others who share your views avoid. Subcultures often represent attractive niche marketing opportunities.

Religion

Religion is an important source of a society's beliefs, attitudes, and values. The world's major religions include Buddhism, Hinduism, Islam, Judaism, and Christianity; the latter includes Roman Catholicism and numerous Protestant denominations. Examples abound of religious tenets, practices, holidays, and histories directly impacting the way people of different faiths react to global marketing activities. For example, Hindus do not eat beef, which means that McDonald's does not serve hamburgers in India (see Case 1-2). In Muslim countries, Yum! Brands has successfully promoted KFC in conjunction with religious observances. In the Islamic world, Ramadan is a time of fasting that begins in the ninth month of the Islamic calendar. In Indonesia, home to the world's largest Muslim population, KFC uses Ramadan-themed outdoor advertising to encourage Indonesians to come to the restaurants at buka puasa, the end of each day's fast. Business at KFC Indonesia's 400 units is up as much as 20 percent during Ramadan.

When followers of a particular religion believe they have been offended, the response can take various forms (see Exhibit 4-2). In the aftermath of the September 2001 terrorist attacks in New York and Washington, D.C., and the subsequent American military actions in the Middle East and Afghanistan, some Muslims have tapped into anti-American sentiment by urging a boycott of American brands. One entrepreneur, Tunisian-born Tawfik Mathlouthi, launched a soft drink brand, Mecca-Cola, as an alternative to Coca-Cola for Muslims living in the United Kingdom and France. The brand's name is both an intentional reference to the holy city of Islam as well as an ironic swipe at Coca-Cola, which Mathlouthi calls "the Mecca of capitalism." London's *Sunday Times* called Mecca-Cola "the drink now seen as politically preferable to Pepsi or Coke."[5] In 2003, Qibla Cola (the name comes from an Arabic word for "direction") was launched in the United Kingdom. Founder Zahida Parveen hoped to reach a broader market than Mecca-Cola by positioning the brand "for any consumer with a conscience, irrespective of ethnicity or religion."[6]

Religious issues have also been at the heart of a dispute about whether references to God and Christianity should be included in a new European constitution, which will be adopted now that the European Union (EU) has expanded its membership from 15 to 27 countries. On one side of

---

[4] Milton Rokeach, *Beliefs, Attitudes, and Values* (San Francisco: Jossey-Bass, 1968), p. 160.
[5] Bill Britt, "Upstart Cola Taps Anti-War Vibe," *Advertising Age* (February 24, 2003), p. 1. See also Digby Lidstone, "Pop Idols," *Middle East Economic Digest* (August 22, 2003), p. 4.
[6] Meg Carter, "New Colas Wage Battle for Hearts and Minds," *Financial Times* (January 8, 2004), p. 9.

Exhibit 4-2 In 2006, protesters across the Muslim world demonstrated against the publication of cartoon images of Muhammed in a Danish newspaper. Many supermarkets in Cairo, the largest city in the Arab world, removed Danish products from their shelves.
Source: Khaled Desouki/Getty Images.

the dispute are Europe's Catholic countries, including Ireland, Spain, Italy, and Poland. As Italy's deputy prime minister said, "The Italian government believes that [Europe's] common religious heritage should be explicitly referred to with the values of Judeo-Christian tradition." By contrast, the official position in France and Belgium is one of church–state separation. According to this view, religion has no place in the founding documents of the enlarged EU. In addition, Muslims constitute a politically active minority in France and other countries; Turkey is predominately Muslim. Thus representatives of Europe's Muslim population are resisting any reference to Christianity in the new constitution.[7]

Aesthetics

Within every culture, there is an overall sense of what is beautiful and what is not beautiful, what represents good taste as opposed to tastelessness or even obscenity, and so on. Such considerations are matters of **aesthetics**. Global marketers must understand the importance of *visual aesthetics* embodied in the color or shape of a product, label, or package. Likewise, different parts of the world perceive *aesthetic styles*—various degrees of complexity, for example—differently. Aesthetic elements that are attractive, appealing, and in good taste in one country may be perceived oppositely in another country.

In some cases, a standardized color can be used in all countries; examples include Caterpillar Yellow, the trademark of the earthmoving equipment company and its licensed outdoor gear. Likewise, Cadbury has trademarked the color purple for its chocolate confectionary packaging. In surveys about color preferences, 50 percent of respondents indicate blue is their favorite—and it is favored by a wide margin over the next-preferred color. The use of blue dates back millennia; artisans in ancient Egypt, China, and Mayan civilizations all worked with the color after the advent of mining led to the extraction of minerals containing blue pigment. Because it was rare and expensive, blue came to be associated with royalty and divinity.[8] Today, Tiffany Blue is a trademarked color that the luxury goods marketer uses on its gift bags and boxes.

Because color perceptions can vary among cultures, adaptation to local preferences may be required. Such perceptions should be taken into account when making decisions about product

---

[7] Richard Bernstein, "Continent Wrings Its Hands Over Proclaiming Its Faith," *The New York Times* (November 12, 2003), p. A4. See also Brandon Mitchener, "Birth of a Nation? As Europe Unites, Religion, Defense Still Stand in Way," *The Wall Street Journal* (July 11, 2003), pp. A1, A6.

[8] Natalie Angier, "True Blue Stands Out in an Earthy Crowd," *The New York Times* (October 23, 2012), pp. D1, D3. See also Natalie Angier, "Blue Through the Centuries: Sacred and Sought After," *The New York Times* (October 23, 2012), p. D3.

packaging and other brand-related communications. In highly competitive markets, inappropriate or unattractive product packaging may put a company or brand at a disadvantage. New color schemes may also be needed because of a changing competitive environment.

There is nothing inherently "good" or "bad" about any color of the spectrum; all associations and perceptions regarding color arise from culture. Red is a popular color in most parts of the world; besides being the color of blood, in many countries red is tied to centuries-old traditions of viticulture and winemaking. One study of perceptions in eight countries found that red is associated with "active," "hot," and "vibrant"; in most countries studied, it also conveys meanings such as "emotional" and "sharp."[9] As such, red has positive connotations in many societies. However, red is poorly received in some African countries. Blue, because of its associations with sky and water, has an elemental connotation with undertones of dependability, constancy, and eternity. White connotes purity and cleanliness in the West, but it is associated with death in parts of Asia. In the Middle East, purple is associated with death. Another research team concluded that gray connotes inexpensive in China and Japan, whereas it is associated with high quality and high cost in the United States. The researchers also found that the Chinese associate brown with soft drink labels and associated the color with something being good tasting; South Korean and Japanese consumers associate yellow with soft drinks and something being good tasting. For Americans, the color red has those associations.[10]

Music is an aesthetic component of all cultures and is accepted as a form of artistic expression and a source of entertainment. In one sense, music represents a "transculture" that is not identified with any particular nation. For example, rhythm, or movement through time, is a universal aspect of music. However, music is also characterized by considerable stylistic variation with regional or country-specific associations. For example, bossa nova rhythms are associated with Argentina; samba with Brazil; salsa with Cuba; reggae with Jamaica; merengue with the Dominican Republic; and blues, driving rock rhythms, hip-hop, and rap with the United States. Sociologists have noted that national identity derives in part from a country's indigenous or popular music; a unique music style can "represent the uniqueness of the cultural entity and of the community."[11]

Music provides an interesting example of the "think globally, act locally" theme of this book. Musicians in different countries draw from, absorb, adapt, and synthesize transcultural music influences, as well as country-specific ones, as they create hybrid styles such as Polish reggae or Italian hip-hop. Motti Regev describes this paradox as follows:

> Producers of and listeners to these types of music feel, at one and the same time, participants in a specific contemporary, global-universal form of expression *and* innovators of local, national, ethnic, and other identities. A cultural form associated with American culture and with the powerful commercial interests of the international music industry is being used in order to construct a sense of local difference and authenticity.[12]

Because music plays an important role in advertising, marketers must understand what style is appropriate in a given national market. Although background music can be used effectively in broadcast commercials, the type of music appropriate for a commercial in one part of the world may not be acceptable or effective in another part. Government restrictions must also be taken into account. In China, authorities have the power to dictate which songs can be marketed and performed, as the Rolling Stones can attest. Rock music journalism must also conform to state mandates, as the publisher of *Rolling Stone* magazine learned (see Exhibit 4-3).

---

[9] Thomas J. Madden, Kelly Hewett, and Martin S. Roth, "Managing Images in Different Cultures: A Cross-National Study of Color Meanings and Preferences," *Journal of International Marketing* 8, no. 4 (2000), p. 98.

[10] Laurence E. Jacobs, Charles Keown, Reginald Worthley, and Kyung-I Ghymn, "Cross-Cultural Colour Comparisons: Global Marketers Beware!" *International Marketing Review* 8, no. 3 (1991), pp. 21–30.

[11] Martin Stokes, *Ethnicity, Identity, and Music: The Musical Construction of Place* (Oxford: Berg, 1994).

[12] Motti Regev, "Rock Aesthetics and Musics of the World," *Theory, Culture & Society* 14, no. 3 (August 1997), pp. 125–142.

Exhibit 4-3 The March 2006 inaugural issue of *Rolling Stone's* Chinese edition featured local rocker Cui Jian on the cover. Cui was one of the first Chinese musicians to incorporate Western rock stylings into his music; he is also famous for a song titled "Nothing to My Name" that was an anthem to Chinese students participating in the 1989 Tiananmen Square democracy protests. However, Chinese authorities had other concerns about the first issue; for one thing, they objected to the large *Rolling Stone* masthead on the magazine's cover. Regulators also disapproved of the U.S. magazine's choice of Audiovisual World as its local partner. A few months later, Rolling Stone reappeared with a new look and a new publishing partner: for the October 2006 issue, the Rolling Stone masthead was scaled down and the magazine itself was incorporated into Pop Times.

Source: Frederic J. Brown/Getty Images, Inc. AFP.

Dietary Preferences

Cultural influences are also quite apparent in food preparation and consumption patterns and habits. Need proof? Consider the following:

- Domino's Pizza, the world's largest pizza-delivery company, pulled out of Italy because Italians perceived its product to be "too American." In particular, the tomato sauce was too bold and the toppings were too heavy. Domino's had better luck in India, where it spiced up its recipes with offerings that include pizza keema do pyaaza, peppy paneer, and five peppers.[13]
- To successfully launch the Subway chain in India, it was necessary to educate consumers about the benefits of the company's sandwiches. Why? Because Indians do not normally consume bread.[14]

These examples underscore the fact that a solid understanding of food-related cultural preferences is important for any company that seeks to market food or beverage products globally. Titoo Ahluwalia, chairman of a market research firm in Mumbai, pointed out that local companies can also leverage superior cultural understanding to compete effectively with large foreign firms. He said, "Indian companies have an advantage when they are drawing from tradition. When it comes to food, drink, and medicine, you have to be culturally sensitive."[15] Companies that lack such sensitivity are bound to make marketing mistakes. When Subway expanded into India, the company chose two U.S.-educated Indian brothers to help open stores and supervise operations.

Although some food preferences remain deeply embedded in culture, plenty of evidence suggests that global dietary preferences are converging. For example, "fast food" is gaining increased acceptance around the world. Heads of families in many countries are pressed for time and are disinclined to prepare home-cooked meals. Also, young people are experimenting with different foods, and the global tourism boom has exposed travelers to pizza, pasta, and other ethnic foods. Shorter lunch hours and tighter budgets are forcing workers to find a place to grab a quick, cheap bite before returning to work.[16] As cultural differences become less relevant, such convenience products will be purchased in any country where consumers' disposable incomes are high enough.

---

[13] Amy Kamzin, "Domino's Deadline to Deliver," *Financial Times* (January 18, 2013), p. 10.
[14] Richard Gibson, "Foreign Flavors," *The Wall Street Journal* (September 25, 2006), p. R8.
[15] Fara Warner, "Savvy Indian Marketers Hold Their Ground," *The Wall Street Journal Asia* (December 1, 1997), p. 8.
[16] John Willman, "'Fast Food' Spreads as Lifestyles Change," *Financial Times* (March 27, 1998), p. 7.

→ THE CULTURAL CONTEXT

Can French Cuisine Regain Its Luster?

SYNC • THINK • LEARN

MyMarketingLab

For centuries, France has enjoyed a reputation as the epitome of the culinary arts. Terms such as *haute cuisine, cuisine classique*, and *nouvelle cuisine* have been used to describe various styles and eras of French cooking. Quiche, escargot, and Tournados Rossini are some of the French dishes that entered the culinary mainstream in the twentieth century. French restaurants that use luxury ingredients and boast highly coveted stars from the venerable Michelin guide have long been popular dining destinations among globe-trotting gourmands. The hit movies *Julie and Julia* and *Ratatouille* helped boost awareness of French gastronomy among the general population.

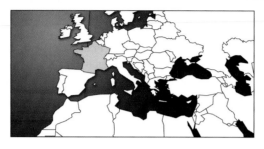

However, all is not well in the land of *haute cuisine*. Recently, a number of authors, journalists, and food critics have chronicled a disturbing trend: the decline in France's status as a culinary superpower. Several famous twentieth-century French master chefs have passed away, including legendary pâtissier Gaston Lenotre. Meanwhile, chefs in London, Japan, and Spain are breaking new ground in terms of cooking technology and food chemistry. A new generation of chefs, including Heston Blumenthal of The Fat Duck in Bray, England, and Ferran Adria of El Bulli in Spain, are celebrated for their forays into "molecular gastronomy" and other innovations (see Exhibit 4-4). Another Brit, Gordon Ramsay, is featured in the popular *Hell's Kitchen* reality TV show. In short, France is no longer universally viewed as cutting-edge.

The numbers tell part of the story: McDonald's is France's number 1 private-sector employer, and the number of cafés has shrunk to 40,000 from 200,000 half a century ago. While sales of the most expensive French wines are booming, thanks to strong demand in Asia, sales of French wines made for everyday drinking are declining around the world.

What is to be done? Plenty, it turns out. For example, Omnivore is an organization and magazine started by food writer Luc Dubanchet. The goal is to spread the word about *le jeune cuisine*, which is more casual than traditional French cuisine. Omnivore's sponsors include Groupe Danon's water division, which markets the Evian and Badoit brands. Another organization, Le Fooding, publishes a magazine and sponsors festivals featuring food prepared by top French chefs. Le Fooding's sponsors include Veuve Clicquot Champagne. Sponsors generally hope to generate increased awareness and sales among both chefs and restaurant patrons.

In addition, a French organization called the Interprofessional Council of Bordeaux Wine (CIVB) has launched a new program to promote Bordeaux wines in global markets. Dubbed Bordeaux Tomorrow, the program calls for opening "Bordeaux Bars" in London, Hong Kong, New York, and other key cities. Print ads will emphasize that wines from the Bordeaux region are fun to drink on a regular basis and are not just for wealthy connoisseurs and collectors. As Christophe Chateau, communications director of CIVB, explains, "We need to show people that you can get excellent value for [the] money from Bordeaux for between €3 and €10 a bottle. In restaurants, people often avoid Bordeaux because they think it will be too expensive."

Another suggestion comes from Donald Morisson, author of *The Death of French Culture*. Morrison argues that French chefs should forget about past glories; instead, they should spend more time abroad, where they can be exposed to new ideas. A recent gathering in Great Milton, England, is a perfect example of this approach. Top chefs from the United States, France, and Great Britain met for a weeklong conference called "The American Food Revolution." One attendee, Gérard Passédat of the Michelin-starred Petit Nice in Marseille, summed up the event this way: "Unfortunately, we [French] are too rigid. Food is so central to the French way of life. There are different cultures, different clienteles, as well as intellectual and psychological barriers. But meetings like this will help us to breach them."

Sources: Adam Sage, "Bordeaux Rescue Plan Goes Down-Market to Boost Sales," *The Australian* (January 10, 2011); Michael Steinberger, *Au Revoir to All That: Food, Wine, and the End of France* (New York: Bloomsbury, 2009); Katy McLaughlin, "French Food Fights Back," *The New York Times* (July 14, 2010); Donald Morrison, "Cordon Blues," *Financial Times* (June 6/7, 2009), p. 16; R. W. Apple, Jr., "Europe Borrows a Cup of Inspiration," *The New York Times* (April 21, 2004), pp. C1, C8.

Exhibit 4-4 Heston Blumenthal is a world-renowned chef working in the Southern England town of Bray; his restaurant, The Fat Duck, has received a coveted three-star rating from the Michelin Guide. The menu includes snail porridge and cod cooked with a blow torch and served with apple jelly and apple "snow." However, Blumenthal does not like the term "molecular gastronomy." "'Molecular' makes it sound complicated, and 'gastronomy' makes it sound elitist," he says.

Sources: Peter Titmuss/Alamy and Bon Appetit/Alamy.

As we have seen, however, such processes can provoke a nationalist backlash. To counteract the exposure of its young citizens to *le Big Mac* and other American-style fast foods, the French National Council of Culinary Arts designed a course on French cuisine and "good taste" for elementary school students. The director of the council is Alexandre Lazareff. In his book *The French Culinary Exception*, Lazareff warned that France's tradition of *haute cuisine* is under attack by the globalization of taste. More generally, Lazareff spoke out against perceived challenges to France's culinary identity and way of life. His concerns are real; while McDonald's continues to open new restaurants in France (today there are more than 1,100 outlets), the number of traditional bistros and cafés has declined steadily for years. Despite McDonald's success, the French have coined a new buzzword, *le fooding*, to express the notion that the nation's passion for food goes beyond mere gastronomy:

> To eat with feeling in France is to eat with your head and your spirit, with your nose, your eyes, and your ears, not simply your palate. *Le fooding* seeks to give witness to the modernity and new reality of drinking and eating in the twenty-first century....Everything is *fooding* so long as audacity, sense, and the senses mix.[17]

Language and Communication

The diversity of cultures around the world is also reflected in language. A person can learn a great deal about another culture without leaving home by studying its language and literature; such study is the next-best thing to actually living in another country. Linguists have divided the study of *spoken* or *verbal* language into four main areas: syntax (rules of sentence formation), semantics (system of meaning), phonology (system of sound patterns), and morphology (word formation). *Unspoken* or *nonverbal* communication includes gestures, touching, and other forms of body language that supplement spoken communication. (Nonverbal communication is sometimes called the silent language.) Both the spoken and unspoken aspects of language are included in the broader linguistic field of *semiotics*, which is the study of signs and their meanings.

In global marketing, language is a crucial tool for communicating with customers, suppliers, channel intermediaries, and others. The marketing literature is full of anecdotal references to costly blunders caused by incorrect or inept translations of product names and advertising copy. As you can see from Figure 4-1, pronunciation subtleties associated with certain Chinese characters can trip up well-meaning gift giving in China. For example, it would be a bad sign to give an umbrella to a business acquaintance because it would be the equivalent of hoping that his or her business fails. When British retail-development firm BAA McArthurGlen set up a U.S.-style factory outlet mall in Austria, local officials wanted to know, "Where's the factory?" To win approval for the project, McArthurGlen was forced to call its development a "designer outlet center."[18] Anheuser-Busch and Miller Brewing both experienced market failures in the United Kingdom; the problem was the phrase "light beer," which was understood as meaning "reduced alcohol levels" rather than "fewer calories." Now Miller Lite is marketed in Europe as "Miller Pilsner."[19]

book   umbrella   clock

FIGURE 4-1

In China, it is bad luck to give a book, an umbrella, or a clock as a gift. Why? The character for "book" is pronounced shu, which sounds like "I hope you lose (have bad luck)". "Umbrella" (san) sounds like "to break into pieces or fall apart." And "clock" (zhong) sounds like "death" or "the end."

---

[17] Jacqueline Friedrich, "All the Rage in Paris? Le Fooding," *The Wall Street Journal* (February 9, 2001), p. W11.
[18] Ernest Beck, "American-Style Outlet Malls in Europe Make Headway Despite Local Resistance," *The Wall Street Journal* (September 17, 1998), p. A17. A complete account of one man's efforts to bring outlet malls to Europe is found in J. Byrne Murphy, *Le Deal* (New York: St. Martins, 2008).
[19] Dan Bilefsky and Christopher Lawton, "In Europe, Marketing Beer as 'American' May Not Be a Plus," *The Wall Street Journal* (July 21, 2004), p. B1.

Before Hearst Corporation launched *Good Housekeeping* magazine in Japan, managers experimented with Japanese translations. The closest word in Japanese, *kaji*, means "domestic duties." However, that word can be interpreted as tasks performed by servants. In the end, the American title was retained, with the word "Good" in much larger type on the front cover than the word "Housekeeping." Inside the magazine, some of the editorial content is adapted to appeal to Japanese women; for example, the famous Seal of Approval was eliminated because the concept confused readers. Editor-in-chief Ellen Levine said, "We have no interest in trying to export our product exactly as it is. That would be cultural suicide."[20]

In China, Dell had to find a meaningful interpretation of "direct sales," the phrase that describes the company's powerful business model. A literal translation results in *zhi xiao*, which is the Chinese term for "illegal pyramid marketing schemes." To counteract the negative connotation, Dell's sales representatives began using the phrase *zhi xiao ding gou*, which translates as "direct orders."[21] Similarly, a team of translators was tasked with compiling a dictionary to help fans of American football in China understand the game (Figure 4-2).

Phonology and morphology can also come into play; Colgate discovered that in Spanish, *colgate* is a verb form that means "go hang yourself." Whirlpool spent considerable sums of money on brand advertising in Europe only to discover that consumers in Italy, France, and Germany had trouble pronouncing the company's name.[22] Conversely, Renzo Rosso deliberately chose "Diesel" for a new jeans brand because, as he once noted, "It's one of the few words pronounced the same in every language." Rosso has built Diesel into a successful global youth brand and one of Italy's top fashion success stories; annual sales revenues exceed $1.2 billion.[23]

Technology is providing interesting new opportunities for exploiting linguistics in the name of marketing. For example, young people throughout the world are using cell phones to send text messages; it turns out that certain number combinations have meanings in particular languages. For example, in Korean the phonetic pronunciation of the numerical sequence 8282, "Pal Yi Pal Yi," means "hurry up," and 7179 ("Chil Han Chil Gu") sounds like "close friend." Also, as many

blitz 突袭:猛撞 (四分卫)一种 防守技术	**capture and kill** '擒杀'
	successfully capture the quarterback 成功地擒抱四分卫
gambling kickoff 赌博踢	**play action** 假跑真传
short kick 短开球	**Hail Mary pass** 长传到达阵区
punt 凌空踢球	**touchdown** 持球触地

FIGURE 4-2

Thanks to a team of academics who compiled an encyclopedia of American football terms, Chinese sports fans should have a better understanding of NFL games. For example, the Chinese translation for blitz is "lightning war against the quarterback." Onside kick is rendered "gambling kickoff" or "short kick," while punt is "give up and kick it back." The authors of The American Football Encyclopedia also interpreted sack as "capture and kill" or "capture the quarterback"; play action is "pass after fake run." Hail Mary pass translates as "miracle long pass," and touchdown is "hold the ball and touch the ground."

[20] Yumiko Ono, "Will Good Housekeeping Translate into Japanese?" *The Wall Street Journal* (December 30, 1997), p. B1.
[21] Evan Ramstad and Gary McWilliams, "Computer Savvy: For Dell, Success in China Tells Tale of Maturing Market," *The Wall Street Journal* (July 5, 2005), pp. A1, A8.
[22] Greg Steinmetz and Carl Quintanilla, "Tough Target: Whirlpool Expected Easy Going in Europe, and It Got a Big Shock," *The Wall Street Journal* (April 10, 1998), pp. A1, A6.
[23] Alice Rawsthorn, "A Hipster on Jean Therapy," *Financial Times* (August 20, 1998), p. 8.

digital-savvy young teens in Korea can attest, 4 5683 968 can be interpreted as "I love you."[24] Korean marketers are using these and other numerical sequences in their advertising. After eBay boosted its presence in China by acquiring the EachNet auction site in 2003, it used rebates and other promotions to attract users. For example, EachNet offered credits of 68 yuan on purchases of 168 yuan or more. The figures were chosen for their linguistic properties: In Chinese, the word "six" is a homophone (has the same pronunciation) for the word "safe," and "eight" is pronounced the same as "prosperity."[25]

One impact of globalization on culture is the diffusion of the English language around the globe. Today, more people speak English as a second language than there are people whose native language is English. Nearly 85 percent of the teenagers in the EU are studying English. Despite the fact that Sony is headquartered in Japan, the company makes it clear to job applicants in any part of the world that it does not consider English to be a "foreign language." The same is true for Finland's Nokia. Matsushita introduced a policy that requires all managers to pass an English-language-competency test before being considered for promotion. Top management at Matsushita concluded that a staid corporate culture that was exclusively Japanese was eroding the company's competitiveness in the global market. The English-language requirement is a potent symbol that a Japanese company is globalizing.[26]

The challenges presented by nonverbal communication are perhaps even more formidable. For example, Westerners doing business in the Middle East must be careful not to reveal the soles of their shoes to hosts or pass documents with the left hand. In Japan, bowing is an important form of nonverbal communication that has many nuances. People who grow up in the West tend to be verbal; those from Asia exhibit behavior that places more weight on nonverbal aspects of interpersonal communication. In the East, it is expected that people will pick up on nonverbal cues and intuitively understand meanings without being told.[27] Westerners must pay close attention not only to what they hear but also to what they see when conducting business in such cultures.

Deep cultural understanding that is based in language can be an important source of competitive advantage for global companies. The aggressive expansion of Spain's Telefónica in Latin America provides a case in point. As Juan Villalonga, former chairman of Telefónica, noted, "It is not just speaking a common language. It is sharing a culture and understanding friendships in the same way."[28]

Several important communication issues may emerge. One is *sequencing*, which concerns whether the discussion goes directly from point A to point B or seems to go off on tangents. Another is *phasing*, which pertains to whether certain important agenda items are discussed immediately or after the parties have taken some time to establish rapport. According to two experts on international negotiations, several distinctly American tactics frequently emerge during negotiations. These tactics are often effective with other Americans, but may require modification when dealing with people from other cultural backgrounds. In any communication situation, speakers offer a variety of cues that can help astute observers understand the speaker's mind-set and mental programming. Here are some examples:[29]

- Americans typically want to "go it alone." As a result, they may be outnumbered in a negotiation situation.
- Many Americans like to "lay their cards on the table." However, in some contexts, it is important to build rapport and *not* "get to the point" immediately.
- Americans tend to talk too much and to talk when they should be listening and observing. In some cultures, long silences are valued. Nonverbal communication cues can be just as important as words.

---

[24] The authors are indebted to Professor Yong Tae Bang, Department of International Trade, College of Business Administration, Paichai University, South Korea, for his comments on this section. See also Meeyoung Song, "How to Sell in Korea? Marketers Count the Ways," *The Wall Street Journal* (August 24, 2001), p. A6.

[25] Mylene Mangalindan, "Hot Bidding: In a Challenging Market, eBay Confronts a Big New Rival," *The Wall Street Journal* (August 12, 2005), p. A1.

[26] Kevin Voigt, "At Matsushita, It's a New Word Order," *Asian Wall Street Journal Weekly* (June 18–24, 2001), p. 1.

[27] See Anthony C. Di Benedetto, Miriko Tamate, and Rajan Chandran, "Developing Strategy for the Japanese Marketplace," *Journal of Advertising Research* (January–February 1992), pp. 39–48.

[28] Tom Burns, "Spanish Telecoms Visionary Beholds a Brave New World," *Financial Times* (May 2, 1998), p. 24.

[29] John L. Graham and Roy A. Heberger, Jr., "Negotiators Abroad—Don't Shoot from the Hip," *Harvard Business Review* 61, no. 4 (July–August 1983), pp. 160–168.

Marketing's Impact on Culture

Universal aspects of the cultural environment represent opportunities for global marketers to standardize some or all elements of a marketing program. The astute global marketer often discovers that much of the apparent cultural diversity in the world turns out to be different ways of accomplishing the same thing. Shared preferences for convenience foods, disposable products, popular music, and movies in North America, Europe, Latin America, and Asia suggest that many consumer products have broad, even universal, appeal. Increasing travel and improving communications have contributed to a convergence of tastes and preferences in a number of product categories. The cultural exchange and the globalization of culture have been capitalized upon, and even significantly accelerated, by companies that have seized opportunities to find customers around the world. However, as noted at the beginning of this chapter, the impact of marketing and, more generally, of global capitalism on culture can be controversial. For example, sociologist George Ritzer and others lament the so-called "McDonaldization of culture" that, they say, occurs when global companies break down cultural barriers while expanding into new markets with their products. As Ritzer noted:

> Eating is at the heart of most cultures and for many it is something on which much time, attention and money are lavished. In attempting to alter the way people eat, McDonaldization poses a profound threat to the entire cultural complex of many societies.[31]

Fabien Ouaki is living proof that persons outside of academe and government have also joined the battle against McDonaldization. Ouaki is the managing director of Tati, a discount retailer based in France. Ouaki is opening new stores in select countries, including the United States. Ouaki claims that "personal revenge" is one motivation for entering the U.S. market. "As a Frenchman, it makes me sick to see kids crying to go see 'Titanic,' eat at McDonald's, or drink Coke. I want to see New Yorkers crying to have a Tati wedding dress," he said.[32] Similarly, the international Slow Food movement boasts 70,000 members in dozens of countries. Slow Food grew out of a 1986 protest over the opening of a McDonald's on a popular plaza in Rome; every two years, Slow Food stages a Salone del Gusto in Italy that showcases traditional food preparation. As a spokesperson said, "Slow Food is about the idea that things should not taste the same everywhere."[33] In 2008, Slow Food U.S.A. attracted 60,000 people to an event in San Francisco that featured a farmers' market and a speakers series called "Food for Thought" (see Exhibit 4-5).

> "A great cook tells his story, not that of his neighbor or what he has seen on television. The future is 'glocal' cooking, both global and local."[30]
>
> Alain Ducasse, Louis XV restaurant, Monaco

Exhibit 4-5 At Slow Food gatherings, participants can attend forums, workshops, and panels featuring writers such as Eric Schlosser (Fast Food Nation) and world-famous chefs such as Alice Waters. And, of course, there is the food: artisanal meats, cheeses, breads, and much more.
Source: slowfoodnation.org, © Slow Food USA.

[30] Rosa Jackson, "Michelin Men," *Financial Times* (November 24/25, 2012), p. R8.
[31] George Ritzer, *The McDonaldization Thesis* (London: Sage Publications, 1998), p. 8.
[32] Amy Barrett, "French Discounter Takes Cheap Chic World-Wide," *The Wall Street Journal* (May 27, 1998), p. B8.
[33] Christine Muhlke, "A Slow Food Festival Reaches Out to the Uncommitted," *The New York Times* (September 3, 2008), p. D12. See also Alexander Stille, "Slow Food's Pleasure Principles," *The Utne Reader* (May/June 2002), pp. 56–58.

High- and Low-Context Cultures

Edward T. Hall has suggested the concept of high and low context as a way of understanding different cultural orientations.[34] In a **low-context culture**, messages are explicit and specific; words carry most of the communication power. In a **high-context culture**, less information is contained in the verbal part of a message. Much more information resides in the context of communication, including the background, associations, and basic values of the communicators. In general, high-context cultures function with much less legal paperwork than is deemed essential in low-context cultures. Japan, Saudi Arabia, and other high-context cultures place a great deal of emphasis on a person's values and position or place in society. In such cultures, the granting of a business loan is more likely to be based on "who you are" than on formal analysis of pro forma financial documents.

In a low-context culture, such as the United States, Switzerland, or Germany, deals are made with much less information about the character, background, and values of the participants. Much more reliance is placed on the words and numbers in the loan application. By contrast, Japanese companies, such as Sony, traditionally paid a great deal of attention to the university background of a new hire; preference would be given to graduates of Tokyo University. Specific elements on a résumé were less important.

In a high-context culture, a person's word is his or her bond. There is less need to anticipate contingencies and provide for external legal sanctions because the culture emphasizes obligations and trust as important values. In these cultures, shared feelings of obligation and honor take the place of impersonal legal sanctions. This helps explain the importance of long and protracted negotiations that never seem to get to the point. Part of the purpose of negotiating, for a person from a high-context culture, is to get to know the potential partner.

For example, insisting on competitive bidding can cause complications in low-context cultures. In a high-context culture, the job is given to the person who will do the best work and whom one can trust and control. In a low-context culture, one tries to make the specifications so precise that the threat of legal sanction forces a builder, for example, to do a good job. As Hall has noted, a builder in Japan is likely to say, "What has that piece of paper got to do with the situation? If we can't trust each other enough to go ahead without it, why bother?"

Although countries can be classified as high or low context in their overall tendency, there are exceptions to the general tendency. These exceptions are found in subcultures. The United States is a low-context culture with subcultures that operate in the high-context mode. The world of the central banker, for example, is a "gentleman's" world; that is, a high-context culture. Even during the most hectic day of trading in the foreign exchange markets, a central banker's word is sufficient for him or her to borrow millions of dollars. In a high-context culture there is trust, a sense of fair play, and a widespread acceptance of the rules of the game as it is played. Table 4-1 summarizes some of the ways in which high- and low-context cultures differ.

TABLE 4-1 High- and Low-Context Cultures

Factors or Dimensions	High Context	Low Context
Lawyers	Less important	Very important
A person's word	Is his or her bond	Is not to be relied upon; "get it in writing"
Responsibility for organizational error	Taken by highest level	Pushed to lowest level
Space	People breathe on each other	People maintain a bubble of private space and resent intrusions
Time	Polychronic—everything in life must be dealt with in terms of its own time	Monochronic—time is money; linear— one thing at a time
Negotiations	Are lengthy—a major purpose is to allow the parties to get to know each other	Proceed quickly
Competitive bidding	Infrequent	Common
Country or regional examples	Japan, Middle East	United States, Northern Europe

---

[34] Edward T. Hall, "How Cultures Collide," *Psychology Today* (July 1976), pp. 66–97.

Hofstede's Cultural Typology

Organizational anthropologist Geert Hofstede was introduced earlier in this chapter in a discussion of his widely quoted definition of culture. Hofstede is also well known for research studies of social values that suggest that the cultures of different nations can be compared in terms of five dimensions.[35] Hofstede notes that three of the dimensions refer to expected social behavior, the fourth dimension is concerned with "man's search for Truth," and the fifth reflects the importance of time (for more information, visit www.geert-hofstede.com).

The first dimension, **power distance**, is the extent to which the less powerful members of a society accept—even expect—power to be distributed unequally. To paraphrase George Orwell, all societies are unequal, but some are more unequal than others. Hong Kong and France are both high power distance cultures; low power distance characterizes Germany, Austria, the Netherlands, and Scandinavia.

The second dimension is a reflection of the degree to which individuals in a society are integrated into groups. In **individualist cultures**, each member of society is primarily concerned with his or her own interests and those of his or her immediate family. In **collectivist cultures**, all of society's members are integrated into cohesive in-groups. High individualism is a general aspect of culture in the United States and Europe; low individualism is characteristic of Japanese and other Asian culture patterns.

Achievement, the third dimension, describes a society in which men are expected to be assertive, competitive, and concerned with material success and women fulfill the role of nurturer and are concerned with issues such as the welfare of children. **Nurturing**, by contrast, describes a society in which the social roles of men and women overlap, with neither gender exhibiting

TABLE 4-2 Hofstede's Five Dimensions of National Culture

1. ***Individualistic***–People look after their own and family interests
   Collectivistic–People expect the group to look after and protect them

Individualistic	← Japan →	*Collectivistic*
United States, Canada, Australia		Mexico, Thailand

2. ***High power distance***–Accepts wide differences in power; great deal of respect for those in authority
   Low power distance–Plays down inequalities; employees are not afraid to approach nor are in awe of the boss

High power distance	← Italy, Japan →	*Low power distance*
Mexico, Singapore, France		United States, Sweden

3. ***High uncertainty avoidance***–Threatened with ambiguity and experience high levels of anxiety
   Low uncertainty avoidance–Comfortable with risks; tolerant of different behavior and opinions

High uncertainty avoidance	← United Kingdom →	*Low uncertainty avoidance*
Italy, Mexico, France		Canada, United States, Singapore

4. ***Achievement***–Values such as assertiveness, acquiring money and goods, and competition prevail
   Nurturing–Values such as relationships and concern for others prevail

Achievement	← Canada, Greece →	*Nurturing*
United States, Japan, Mexico		France, Sweden

5. ***Long-term Orientation***–People look to the future and value thrift and persistence
   Short-term Orientation–People value tradition and the past

Short-term Orientation	← →	*Long-term Orientation*
Germany, Australia, United States, Canada		China, Taiwan, Japan

Source: Stephen P. Robbins and Mary Coulter, *Management*, 12e (Upper Saddle River, NJ: Pearson Education, 2014) p. 87.

---

[35] Geert Hofstede and Michael Harris Bond, "The Confucius Connection: From Cultural Roots to Economic Growth," *Organizational Dynamics* (Spring 1988), p. 5.

overly ambitious or competitive behavior. Japan and Austria rank highest in masculinity; Spain, Taiwan, the Netherlands, and the Scandinavian countries are among the lowest.

Uncertainty avoidance is the extent to which the members of a society are uncomfortable with unclear, ambiguous, or unstructured situations. Members of uncertainty-avoiding cultures may resort to aggressive, emotional, intolerant behavior; they are characterized by a belief in absolute truth. Members of uncertainty-accepting cultures (e.g., Denmark, Sweden, Ireland, and the United States) are more tolerant of persons whose opinions differ from their own.

Greece and Portugal score high in uncertainty avoidance; other Mediterranean countries and much of Latin America rank high in uncertainty avoidance as well. Acceptance of uncertainty generally manifests itself in behavior that is more contemplative, relativistic, and tolerant; these values are evident in Southeast Asia and India.

Hofstede's research convinced him that, although these four dimensions yield interesting and useful interpretations, they do not provide sufficient insight into possible cultural bases for economic growth. Hofstede was also disturbed by the fact that *Western* social scientists had developed the surveys used in the research. Because many economists had failed to predict the explosive economic development of Japan and the Asian tigers (i.e., South Korea, Taiwan, Hong Kong, and Singapore), Hofstede surmised that some cultural dimensions in Asia were eluding the researchers. This methodological problem was remedied by a Chinese Value Survey (CVS) developed by Chinese social scientists in Hong Kong and Taiwan.

The CVS data support the first three "social behavior" dimensions of culture: power distance, individualism/collectivism, and masculinity/femininity. Uncertainty avoidance, however, does not show up in the CVS. Instead, the CVS reveals a dimension, **long-term orientation (LTO)** versus **short-term orientation**, that had eluded Western researchers.[36] Hofstede interpreted this dimension as concerning "a society's search for virtue," rather than truth. The dimension assesses the sense of immediacy within a culture; that is, whether gratification should be immediate or deferred.

Long-term values include *persistence* (perseverance), defined as a general tenacity in the pursuit of a goal. *Ordering relationships* by status reflects the presence of societal hierarchies, and *observing this order* indicates the acceptance of complementary relations. *Thrift* manifests itself in high savings rates. Finally, *a sense of shame* leads to sensitivity in social contacts. Hofstede notes that these values are widely held within high-performing Asian countries such as Hong Kong, Taiwan, and Japan, but that the presence of these values by itself is not sufficient to lead to economic growth. Two other conditions are necessary: the existence of a market and the existence of a supportive political context. Although Hofstede determined that India ranks quite high on the LTO dimension, market restrictions and political forces have, until recently, held back that nation's economic growth.

By studying Hofstede's work, marketers gain insights that can guide them in a range of activities, including developing products, interacting with joint-venture partners, and conducting sales meetings. For example, understanding the time orientation of one's native culture compared to that of others is crucial (see Table 4-1). In Japan, Brazil, and India, building a relationship with a potential business partner takes precedence over transacting the deal. People from cultures that emphasize the short term must adapt to the slower pace of business in some countries. As noted earlier, language can offer some insights into cultural differences. For example, the phrase "in a New York minute" captures the urgent pace of American urban life.

Conversely, the Japanese notion of *gaman* ("persistence") provides insight into the willingness of Japanese corporations to pursue research and development (R&D) projects for which the odds of short-term success appear low. When Sony licensed the newly invented transistor from Bell Laboratories in the mid-1950s, for example, the limited high-frequency yield (sound output) of the device suggested to American engineers that the most appropriate application would be for a hearing aid. However, *gaman* meant that Sony engineers were not deterred by the slow progress of their efforts to increase the yield. As Sony cofounder Masaru Ibuka recalled, "To challenge the yield is a very interesting point for us. At that time no one recognized the importance of it." Sony's persistence was rewarded when company engineers eventually made the yield breakthrough that resulted in a wildly successful global product—the pocket-sized transistor radio.[37]

---

[36] In some articles, Hofstede refers to this dimension as "Confucian Dynamism" because it is highest in Japan, Hong Kong, and Taiwan.

[37] James Lardner, *Fast Forward: Hollywood, the Japanese, and the VCR Wars* (New York: NAL Penguin, 1987), p. 45.

By understanding the dimension of uncertainty avoidance, global marketers are better equipped to assess the amount of risk with which buyers are comfortable. In Japan and other Asian cultures characterized by a low tolerance for ambiguity, buyers will be conscious of brand names and are likely to exhibit high brand loyalty. Advertising copy in countries with high levels of uncertainty avoidance should provide reassurance by stressing warranties, money-back guarantees, and other risk-reducing features. Hong Kong has an even higher tolerance for ambiguity than the United States; Japan, however, ranks quite high in uncertainty avoidance, as do France and Spain.

The power distance dimension reflects the degree of trust among members of society. The higher the power distance (PDI), the lower the level of trust. Organizationally, high PDI finds expression in tall, hierarchical designs; a preference for centralization; and relatively more supervisory personnel. The PDI dimension also provides insights into the dynamics between superiors and subordinates. In cultures where respect for hierarchy is high, subordinates may have to navigate through several layers of assistants to get to the boss. In that case, the latter is likely to be isolated in an office with the door closed. In such cultures, superiors may easily intimidate lower-level employees. Research has suggested that, when evaluating alternatives for entering global markets, companies in high-PDI cultures prefer sole ownership of subsidiaries because it provides them with more control. Conversely, companies in low-PDI cultures are more apt to use joint ventures.[38] France and Hong Kong are qualify as countries with the highest PDI. Other countries with high PDI scores are Mexico and India.

The achievement—nurturing dimension is likely to manifest itself in the relative importance of achievement and possessions (masculine values) compared with a spirit of helpfulness and social support (feminine values). Overall, an aggressive, achievement-oriented salesperson is better matched to the culture of Austria, Japan, or Mexico than to that of Denmark. (Such a salesperson would also have to bear in mind that both Japan and Mexico rank high in LTO, a dimension that can be at odds with transaction-oriented assertiveness.) Similarly, a Western woman who is sent to make a presentation to a Japanese company will undoubtedly find that her audience consists of men. The Japanese managers may react negatively to a woman, especially if she is younger than they are.

The collective–individual orientation deserves special comment because there is wide agreement that it is an important component of culture. Knowing which cultures value the collective and which value the individual can help marketers in various ways. In Japan, for example, the team orientation and desire for *wa* ("harmony") means that singling out one person for distinction and praise in front of peers can be awkward for those involved. Again, language provides important clues about these cultural dimensions; as the saying goes in Japan, "The nail that sticks up gets hammered down." Throughout much of Asia, the collectivist orientation is dominant. In the highly individualist U.S. culture, however, a person whose individual accomplishments are publicly acknowledged is likely to be pleased by the recognition.[39]

Several teams of researchers have attempted to determine whether cross-national collective–individual differences are reflected in print and television advertisements. In theory, a global company's communication efforts should be adapted in accordance with a particular country's orientation. For example, in cultures where individualism is highly valued, ads would typically feature one person; in countries where individualism is less highly valued, ads would feature groups. Although one team[40] claimed to have found a strong correlation, the findings were not confirmed by a later study.[41] However, Bob Cutler argues that print advertising is, by its very nature, designed to communicate to an individual reader. This suggests that the individualism–collectivism distinction may be a moot issue in print advertising.

In highly collectivist cultures, however, products or services that enjoy an early word-of-mouth buzz among influential consumer groups can quickly achieve phenomenon status that then spreads to other countries. The Tamagotchi craze of the late 1990s is a perfect example. The

---

[38] Scott A. Shane, "The Effect of Cultural Differences in Perceptions of Transaction Costs on National Differences in the Preference for International Joint Ventures," *Asia Pacific Journal of Management* 10, no. 1 (1993), pp. 57–69.
[39] Adapted from Anne Macquin and Dominique Rouziès, "Selling Across the Culture Gap," *Financial Times— Mastering Global Business*, part 7 (1998), pp. 10–11.
[40] Katherine Toland Frith and Subir Sengupta, "Individualism: A Cross-Cultural Analysis of Print Advertisements from the U.S. and India," paper presented at 1991 Annual Conference of Advertising Division of Association for Education in Journalism and Mass Communication, Boston, MA.
[41] Bob D. Cutler, S. Altan Erdem, and Rajshekhar G. Javalgi, "Advertisers' Relative Reliance on Collectivism-Individualism Appeals," *Journal of International Consumer Marketing* 9, no. 3 (1997), pp. 43–55.

→ THE CULTURAL CONTEXT

Applying Hofstede's Typology to Denmark

MyMarketingLab SYNC • THINK • LEARN

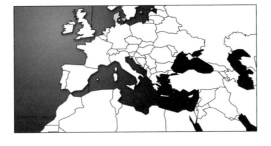

What is Denmark really like? The following profile captures Denmark in terms of Hofstede's cultural values framework (see Exhibit 4-6).

Future Orientation: The extent to which a society encourages and rewards future-oriented behaviors such as planning, investing in the future, and delaying gratification. Denmark scores high.

In the Danish business environment, it is normal to prepare and discuss five-year budgets and business plans that are then adjusted yearly. Also, the Danish population is aware of the importance of saving for retirement. The Ministry of Economic Affairs hopes to establish a world-class innovation center in Denmark. The center would elevate Denmark to the top ranks of countries with consumer-driven innovation.

Gender Differentiation: The extent to which a society maximizes gender role differences. Denmark scores low.

In Denmark, gender role differences are insignificant. Danish women are strong and believe they can do anything that a man can. Danish women are very focused on equality, both in the home and at work. It is very common for fathers to take equal part in cleaning and other duties around the house.

Uncertainty Avoidance: The extent to which the members of a society are accepting of ambiguous situations or comfortable with unfamiliar situations. Denmark scores low; in other words, it is an uncertainty-accepting society.

Danes generally are not afraid of taking chances; they are comfortable doing things that are not carefully thought out or planned. Denmark's "flexicurity" policy combines free labor markets (workers can be fired) with adjustable welfare benefits, including financial support and free job training for the unemployed. The Danish social system provides a close-knit safety system to fall back on. Society relies on and supports a system that is costly but provides a constant sense of security.

Power Distance: The degree to which members of a society expect power to be unequally shared. Denmark scores low, which results in very flat and informal organizational structures and the wide use of various matrix models.

Janteloven, or "the law of Jante," deeply affects how Scandinavian people act and are expected to act. The term originated with writer Aksel Sandemose, who wrote a novel about Jante, a village where one is not supposed to believe he or she is better or smarter than anyone else. Humility is important, and this limits power distance.

Individualism/Collectivism: The degree to which societal institutions encourage individuals to be integrated into groups within organizations and society. Denmark scores high on individualism.

In-Group Collectivism and Institutional Collectivism: The extent to which members of a society take pride in membership in small groups such as their families and circle of close friends and the organizations in which they are employed. Denmark scores high in institutional collectivism and low in in-group collectivism.

Sources: Justin Fox, "Why Denmark Loves Globalization," www.time.com (accessed June 1, 2008). Leila Abboud, "Power Play: How Denmark Paved Way to Energy Independence," *The Wall Street Journal* (April 16, 2007), p. A1; Jeffrey Stinson, "Denmark's 'Flexicurity' Blends Welfare State, Economic Growth," *USA Today* (March 7, 2007), pp. 1B, 2B.

Exhibit 4-6 Inspired by the Hans Christian Anderson tale, Denmark's Little Mermaid is a famous landmark in Copenhagen Harbor. However, in 2010, she was moved temporarily to the Danish pavilion at Shanghai Expo. **Source:** imago stock&people/Newscom.

virtual pets were test-marketed in central Tokyo in a shopping area frequented by teenage girls. *Kuchikomi* (word of mouth) was so strong among schoolgirls that toymaker Bandai was hard-pressed to keep up with demand. By the time Tamagotchi reached New York toy retailer F.A.O. Schwartz, the prerelease buzz ensured that the initial 10,000-unit shipment sold out immediately. Although Japanese teens also pay attention to print and television advertising, it is clear that marketers can reach this segment by providing selected youngsters with product samples.[42]

The Self-Reference Criterion and Perception

As we have shown, a person's perception of market needs is framed by his or her own cultural experience. A framework for systematically reducing perceptual blockage and distortion was developed by James Lee and published in the *Harvard Business Review* in 1966. Lee termed the unconscious reference to one's own cultural values the **self-reference criterion (SRC)**. To address this problem and eliminate or reduce cultural myopia, he proposed a systematic, four-step framework:

1. Define the problem or goal in terms of home-country cultural traits, habits, and norms.
2. Define the problem or goal in terms of host-country cultural traits, habits, and norms. Make no value judgments.
3. Isolate the SRC influence and examine it carefully to see how it complicates the problem.
4. Redefine the problem without the SRC influence and solve for the host-country market situation.[43]

The Walt Disney Company's decision to build a theme park in France provides an excellent vehicle for understanding SRC. As they planned their entry into the French market, how might Disney executives have done things differently had they used the steps of SRC?

Step 1 Disney executives believe there is virtually unlimited demand for American cultural exports around the world. Evidence includes the success of McDonald's, Coca-Cola, Hollywood movies, and American rock music. Disney has a stellar track record in exporting its American management system and business style. Tokyo Disneyland, a virtual carbon copy of the park in Anaheim, California, has been a runaway success (see Exhibit 4-7). Disney policies prohibit sale or consumption of alcohol inside its theme parks.

Exhibit 4-7 The year 2013 marked the 30th anniversary of Tokyo Disneyland Resort. In addition to the original theme park, there is now a Tokyo DisneySea attraction plus hotels and a shopping district. To commemorate "Happiness Year," Disney officials were joined by executives from development partner Oriental Land Company. **Source:** Bloomberg via Getty Images.

---

[42] Bethan Hutton, "Winning Word-of-Mouth Approval," *Financial Times* (September 8, 1997), p. 10.
[43] James A. Lee, "Cultural Analysis in Overseas Operations," *Harvard Business Review* (March–April 1966), pp. 106–114.

Step 2 Europeans in general, and the French in particular, are sensitive about American cultural imperialism. Consuming wine with the midday meal is a long-established custom. Europeans have their own real castles, and many popular Disney characters come from European folk tales.

Step 3 The significant differences revealed by comparing the findings in steps 1 and 2 suggest strongly that the needs upon which the American and Japanese Disney theme parks were based do not exist in France. A modification of this design is needed for European success.

Step 4 This would require the design of a theme park that is more in keeping with French and European cultural norms. Allow the French to put their own identity on the park.

The lesson that the SRC teaches is that a vital, critical skill of the global marketer is unbiased perception; that is, the ability to see what is so in a culture. Although this skill is as valuable at home as it is abroad, it is critical to the global marketer because of the widespread tendency toward ethnocentrism and the use of the SRC. The SRC can be a powerful negative force in global business, and forgetting to check for it can lead to misunderstanding and failure. While planning Euro Disney, former Disney Chairman Michael Eisner and other company executives were blinded by a potent combination of their own prior success and ethnocentrism. Avoiding the SRC requires a person to suspend assumptions based on prior experience and success and be prepared to acquire new knowledge about human behavior and motivation.

Diffusion Theory[44]

Hundreds of studies have described the process by which an individual adopts a new idea. Sociologist Everett Rogers reviewed these studies and discovered a pattern of remarkably similar findings. Rogers then distilled the research into three concepts that are extremely useful to global marketers: the adoption process, characteristics of innovations, and adopter categories. Taken together, these concepts constitute Rogers' **diffusion of innovation** framework.

An innovation is something new. When applied to a product, "new" can mean different things. In an absolute sense, once a product has been introduced anywhere in the world, it is no longer an innovation, because it is no longer new to the world. Relatively speaking, however, a product already introduced in one market may be an innovation elsewhere because it is new and different for the targeted market. Global marketing often entails just such product introductions. Managers find themselves marketing products that may be, simultaneously, innovations in some markets and mature or declining products in others.

The Adoption Process

One of the basic elements of Rogers' diffusion theory is the concept of an **adoption process**—the mental stages through which an individual passes from the time of his or her first knowledge of an innovation to the time of product adoption or purchase. Rogers suggests that an individual passes through five different stages in proceeding from first knowledge of a product to the final adoption or purchase of that product: awareness, interest, evaluation, trial, and adoption.

1. *Awareness:* In the first stage, the customer becomes aware for the first time of the product or innovation. Studies have shown that at this stage, impersonal sources of information such as mass media advertising are most important. An important early communication objective in global marketing is to create awareness of a new product through general exposure to advertising messages.
2. *Interest:* During this stage, the customer is interested enough to learn more. The customer has focused his or her attention on communications relating to the product and will engage in research activities and seek out additional information.
3. *Evaluation:* In this stage the individual mentally assesses the product's benefits in relation to present and anticipated future needs and, based on this judgment, decides whether to try it.
4. *Trial:* Most customers will not purchase expensive products without the "hands-on" experience marketers call a "trial." A good example of a product trial that does not involve purchase is the automobile test drive. For health care products and other inexpensive consumer packaged goods, a trial often involves actual purchase. Marketers frequently induce

---

[44] This section draws from Everett M. Rogers, *Diffusion of Innovations* (New York: Free Press, 1962).

a trial by distributing free samples. For inexpensive products, an initial single purchase is defined as a trial.

5. *Adoption:* At this point, the individual either makes an initial purchase (in the case of the more expensive product) or continues to purchase—adopts and exhibits brand loyalty to—the less expensive product. Studies show that as a person moves from evaluation through a trial to adoption, personal sources of information are more important than impersonal sources. It is during these stages that sales representatives and word of mouth become major persuasive forces affecting the decision to buy.

Characteristics of Innovations

In addition to describing the product adoption process, Rogers also identifies five major **characteristics of innovations**. These are the factors that affect the rate at which innovations are adopted: relative advantage, compatibility, complexity, divisibility, and communicability.

1. *Relative advantage:* How a new product compares with existing products or methods in the eyes of customers. The perceived relative advantage of a new product versus existing products is a major influence on the rate of adoption. If a product has a substantial relative advantage vis-à-vis the competition, it is likely to gain quick acceptance. When compact disc players were first introduced in the early 1980s, industry observers predicted that only audiophiles would care enough about digital sound—and have the money—to purchase them. However, the sonic advantages of CDs compared to LPs were obvious to the mass market; as prices for CD players plummeted, the 12-inch black vinyl LP was rendered virtually extinct in less than a decade.

2. *Compatibility:* The extent to which a product is consistent with existing values and past experiences of adopters. The history of innovations in international marketing is replete with failures caused by the lack of compatibility of new products in the target market. For example, the first consumer VCR, the Sony Betamax, ultimately failed because it could only record for 1 hour. Most buyers wanted to record movies and sports events; thus they shunned the Betamax in favor of VHS-format VCRs, which could record 4 hours of programming.

3. *Complexity:* The degree to which an innovation or new product is difficult to understand and use. Product complexity is a factor that can slow down the rate of adoption, particularly in developing country markets with low rates of literacy. In the 1990s, dozens of global companies developed new, interactive, multimedia consumer electronics products. Complexity was a key design issue; it was a standing joke that in most households, VCR clocks flashed "12:00" because users didn't know how to set them. To achieve mass success, new products have to be as simple to use as, for example, slipping a prerecorded DVD into a DVD player.

4. *Divisibility:* The ability of a product to be tried and used on a limited basis without great expense. Wide discrepancies in income levels around the globe result in major differences in preferred purchase quantities, serving sizes, and product portions. CPC International's Hellmann's mayonnaise was simply not selling in U.S.-size jars in Latin America. Sales took off after the company placed the mayonnaise in small plastic packets. The plastic packets were within the food budgets of local consumers, and they required no refrigeration—another plus.

5. *Communicability:* The degree to which benefits of an innovation or the value of a product may be communicated to a potential market. A new digital cassette recorder from Philips was a market failure, in part because advertisements did not clearly communicate the fact that the product could make CD-quality recordings using new cassette technology while still playing older, analog tapes.

Adopter Categories

Adopter categories are classifications of individuals within a market on the basis of the categories' innovativeness. Hundreds of studies of the diffusion of innovation demonstrate that, at least in the West, adoption is a social phenomenon that is characterized by a normal distribution curve, as shown in Figure 4-3.

Five categories have been assigned to the segments of this normal distribution. The first 2.5 percent of people to purchase a product are defined as innovators. The next 13.5 percent are early adopters, the next 34 percent are the early majority, the next 34 percent are the late majority,

FIGURE 4-3
Adopter Categories

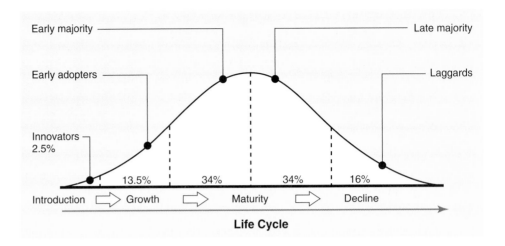

Life Cycle

and the final 16 percent are laggards. Studies show that innovators tend to be venturesome, more cosmopolitan in their social relationships, and wealthier than those who adopt later. Early adopters are the most influential people in their communities, even more so than the innovators. Thus the early adopters are a critical group in the adoption process, and they have great influence on the early and late majority, who comprise the bulk of the adopters of any product. Several characteristics of early adopters stand out. First, they tend to be younger, with higher social status, and in a more favorable financial position than later adopters. They must be responsive to mass media information sources and must learn about innovations from these sources, because they cannot simply copy the behavior of early adopters.

One of the major reasons for the normal distribution of adopter categories is the *interaction effect*; that is, the process through which individuals who have adopted an innovation influence others. Adoption of a new idea or product is the result of human interaction in a social system. If the first adopter of an innovation or new product discusses it with two other people, and each of these two adopters passes the new idea along to two other people, and so on, the resulting distribution yields a normal bell shape when plotted.[45]

Diffusion of Innovations in Pacific Rim Countries

In a cross-national comparison of the United States, Japan, South Korea, and Taiwan, Takada and Jain present evidence that different country characteristics—in particular, culture and communication patterns—affect diffusion processes for room air conditioners, washing machines, and calculators. Proceeding from the observation that Japan, South Korea, and Taiwan are high-context cultures with relatively homogeneous populations and the United States is a low-context, heterogeneous culture, Takada and Jain surmised that Asia would show faster rates of diffusion than the United States (see Figure 4-4). A second hypothesis supported by the research was that adoption would

FIGURE 4-4
Asian Hierarchy

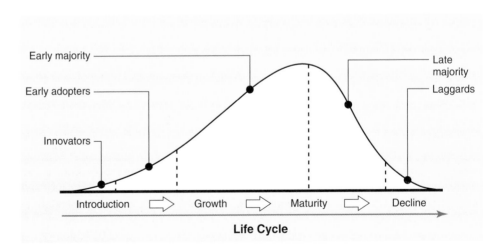

Life Cycle

[45] For an excellent application and discussion of adopter categories, see Malcolm Gladwell, *The Tipping Point* (New York: Little, Brown, and Company, 2000), Chapter 6.

proceed more quickly in markets where innovations were introduced relatively late. Presumably, the lag time would give potential consumers more opportunity to assess the relative advantages, compatibility, and other product attributes. Takada and Jain's research has important marketing implications. They note: "If a marketing manager plans to enter the newly industrializing countries (NICs) or other Asia markets with a product that has proved to be successful in the home market, the product's diffusion processes are likely to be much faster than in the home market."[46]

As noted before, there are likely to be fewer innovators in Japan and other Asian countries, where risk avoidance is high. However, as the Tamagotchi story illustrated, once consumers become aware that others have tried the product, they follow suit quickly so as not to be left behind.

Marketing Implications of Social and Cultural Environments

The various cultural factors described earlier can exert important influences on consumer and industrial products marketing around the globe. These factors must be recognized in formulating a global marketing plan. **Environmental sensitivity** reflects the extent to which products must be adapted to the culture-specific needs of different national markets. A useful approach is to view products on a continuum of environmental sensitivity. At one end of the continuum are environmentally insensitive products that do not require significant adaptation to the environments of various world markets. At the other end of the continuum are products that are highly sensitive to different environmental factors. A company with environmentally insensitive products will spend relatively less time determining the specific and unique conditions of local markets because the product is basically universal. The greater a product's environmental sensitivity, the greater the need for managers to address country-specific economic, regulatory, technological, social, and cultural environmental conditions.

The sensitivity of products can be represented on a two-dimensional scale, as shown in Figure 4-5. The horizontal axis shows environmental sensitivity, the vertical axis the degree for product adaptation needed. Any product exhibiting low levels of environmental sensitivity—integrated circuits, for example—belongs in the lower left of the figure. Intel has sold more than 100 million microprocessors because a chip is a chip anywhere around the world. Moving to the right on the horizontal axis, the level of sensitivity increases, as does the amount of adaptation. Computers exhibit moderate levels of environmental sensitivity; for example, variations in country voltage requirements require some adaptation. In addition, the computer's software documentation should be in the local language.

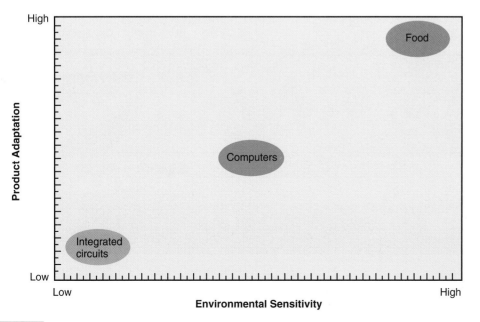

FIGURE 4-5
Environmental Sensitivity

[46] Hirokazu Takada and Dipak Jain, "Cross-National Analysis of Diffusion of Consumer Durable Goods in Pacific Rim Countries," *Journal of Marketing* 55 (April 1991), pp. 48–53.

At the upper right of Figure 4-5 are products with high environmental sensitivity. Food sometimes falls into this category because it is sensitive to climate and culture. As we saw in the McDonald's case at the end of Chapter 1, the fast-food giant has achieved great success outside the United States by adapting its menu items to local tastes. General Electric's turbine equipment may also appear on the high-sensitivity end of the continuum; in many countries, local equipment manufacturers receive preferential treatment when bidding on national projects.

Research studies show that, independent of social class and income, culture is a significant influence on consumption behavior and durable goods ownership.[47] Consumer products are probably more sensitive to cultural differences than are industrial products. Hunger is a basic physiological need in Maslow's hierarchy; everyone needs to eat, but what we want to eat can be strongly influenced by culture. Evidence from the front lines of the marketing wars suggests that food is probably the most sensitive category of consumer products. CPC International failed to win popularity for Knorr dehydrated soups among Americans. The U.S. soup market was dominated by the Campbell Soup Company; 90 percent of the soup consumed by households was canned. Knorr was a Swiss company acquired by CPC that had a major share of the European prepared-food market, where bouillon and dehydrated soups account for 80 percent of consumer soup sales. Despite CPC's failure to change the soup-eating habits of Americans, the company (now called Bestfoods and a unit of Unilever) is a successful global marketer with operations in more than 60 countries and sales in 110 countries.

Thirst also shows how needs differ from wants. Hydration is a universal physiological need (see Exhibit 4-8). As is the case with food and cooking, however, the particular liquids people *want* to drink can be strongly influenced by culture. Coffee is a beverage category that illustrates the point. On the European continent, coffee has been consumed for centuries. By contrast, Britain has historically been a nation of tea drinkers, and the notion of afternoon tea is firmly entrenched in British culture. In the 1970s, tea outsold coffee by a ratio of 4 to 1. Brits who did drink coffee tended to buy it in instant form, because the preparation of instant is similar to that of tea. By the 1990s, however, Britain was experiencing an economic boom and an explosion of new nightclubs and restaurants. Trendy Londoners looking for a nonpub "third place" found it in the form of Seattle Coffee Company cafés. An instant success after the first store was opened by coffee-starved Americans in 1995, by 1998 Seattle Coffee had 65 locations around London. Starbucks bought the business from Seattle Coffee's founders for $84 million. Today, Starbucks has overcome the challenge of high real estate prices and has more than 700 locations in the United Kingdom.[48]

Exhibit 4-8 In countries where water from the tap or well may be contaminated, bottled water is a convenient alternative. The fastest growth in the industry is occurring in developing countries; in the past five years, bottled water consumption has tripled in India and more than doubled in China. Many consumers also choose bottled water as an alternative to other beverage choices. However, the Earth Policy Institute and other groups view bottled water as an overpriced, wasteful extravagance. The International Bottled Water Association disagrees with that view. A spokesman said, "We're an on-the-go society demanding convenient packaging and consistent quality, and that's what bottled water provides."
Source: Gurinder Osan/AP Images.

[47] Charles M. Schaninger, Jacques C. Bourgeois, and Christian W. Buss, "French-English Canadian Subcultural Consumption Differences," *Journal of Marketing* 49 (Spring 1985), pp. 82–92.
[48] Deborah Ball, "Lattes Lure Brits to Coffee," *The Wall Street Journal* (October 20, 2005), pp. B1, B6. See also Marco R. della Cava, "Brewing a British Coup," *USA Today* (September 16, 1998), pp. D1, D2.

Summary

Culture, a society's "programming of the mind," has both a pervasive and a changing influence on each national market environment. Global marketers must recognize the influence of culture and be prepared to either respond to it or change it. Human behavior is a function of a person's own unique personality and that person's interaction with the collective forces of the particular society and culture in which he or she has lived. In particular, **attitudes**, **values**, and **beliefs** can vary significantly from country to country. Also, differences pertaining to religion, **aesthetics**, dietary customs, and language and communication can affect local reaction to a company's brands or products as well as the ability of company personnel to function effectively in different cultures. A number of concepts and theoretical frameworks provide insights into these and other cultural issues.

Cultures can be classified as **high** or **low context**; communication and negotiation styles can differ from country to country. Hofstede's social values typology helps marketers understand culture in terms of **power distance**, **individualism** versus **collectivism**, **achievement** versus **nurturing**, **uncertainty avoidance**, and **long-** versus **short-term orientation**. By understanding the **self-reference criterion**, global marketers can overcome people's unconscious tendency for perceptual blockage and distortion.

Rogers' classic study on the **diffusion of innovations** helps explain how products are adopted over time by different **adopter categories**. The **adoption process** that consumers go through can be divided into a multistage **hierarchy of effects**. Rogers' findings concerning the **characteristics of innovations** can also help marketers successfully launch new products in global markets. Research has suggested that Asian adopter categories differ from the Western model. An awareness of **environmental sensitivity** can help marketers determine whether consumer and industry products must be adapted to the needs of different markets.

MyMarketingLab

Go to **mymktlab.com** for the following Assisted-graded writing questions:

4-1. Discuss the contrast between the United States and Japan in terms of traditions and organizational behavior and norms.

4-2. Explain the self-reference criterion (SRC) and its significance to global marketers. Conduct exploratory research and find examples of product failures that might have been avoided through the application of the SRC.

4-3. Mymarketinglab Only – comprehensive writing assignment for this chapter.

MyMarketingLab

Go to **mymktlab.com** to complete the problems marked with this icon .

Discussion Questions

4-4. What are some of the elements that make up culture? How do these find expression in your native culture?

4-5. What is the difference between a low-context culture and a high-context culture? Name a country that is an example of each type and offer evidence for your answer.

4-6. How can Hofstede's cultural typologies help Western marketers better understand Asian culture?

4-7. Briefly explain the social research of Everett Rogers on the topics of diffusion of innovations, characteristics of innovations, and adopter categories. How does the adoption process in Asia differ from the traditional Western model?

CASE 4-1   CONTINUED (REFER TO PAGE 124)

Is Tourism the Savior or the Scourge of Venice?

Cruise ships are not the only marketing-related issue that has ruffled some feathers in Venice and resulted in public debate. Venice's unique setting results in severe seasonal flooding; in the winter, tide surges known as *acqua alta* ("high water") cause severe structural damage to buildings and make it hard for pedestrians to navigate the city's narrow streets. Water damage is one reason that several of the city's landmarks are in need of repair, but Italy's Ministry of Culture allocates roughly $47 million each year for historic renovation in the entire country. With only about $1.8 earmarked for the entire Veneto region, Venice itself receives less than $200,000 in renovation funds. Needless to say, this is far less than the amount needed for upkeep and repair.

In other parts of the country, water damage from flooding is not a problem. Even so, many ancient artifacts are crumbling. In the face of public budget shortfalls, owners of Italy's most famous fashion brands are footing the bill for historic renovations. For example, Diego Della Valle, the CEO of Tod's, is contributing about $34 million to the restoration of the Colosseum in Rome. Announcing the gift at a press conference in 2011, Della Valle said, "A monument that represents Italy in the world must be restored, and a company that represents 'Made in Italy' stepped forward to say, 'If you need us, we are here.'" Similarly, Brunello Cucinelli, the "King of Cashmere," is helping defray the cost of restoring the Arch of Augustus, an Etruscan artifact dating to the third century B.C. in Perugia, the capital of the Umbrian region.

To make up for the shortfall in Venice, corporate sponsors such as Coca-Cola and Bulgari are allowed to erect large billboards near tourist attractions; the city uses the advertising revenue to fund renovations (see Exhibit 4-9). For example, Coca-Cola billboards were recently put up near the Piazza San Marco. Renata Cordello, the official at the Ministry of Culture responsible for renovations, explains, "We're just not in a position to say 'no' to money, not for aesthetic reasons. I can't turn down the image of a bottle when there are pieces of the Palazzo Ducale falling to the ground."

As noted earlier, tourism in Venice has been the subject of considerable debate. Among the questions being raised are the following: Is Venice dying from too much tourism? Should tourism be limited? Should some kind of action be taken to attract a "different kind of tourist" and a "different kind of tourism" than the typical "daytripper" on a package tour? Or, does Venice need every dollar (or, euro, yuan, or ruble) it can get?

A sign of the times, literally and figuratively, are the billboards that have been erected on popular tourist landmarks undergoing renovation. Vicenzo Casali is a native of Venice and an architect who specializes in urban design projects. As Casali wryly observes, one

Exhibit 4-9 Bulgari and other well-known luxury brands are funding the restoration, renovation, and maintenance of famous Venetian landmarks. In exchange for financial support, companies are allowed to place billboard advertising on buildings that are popular tourist destinations. Although the Venice Foundation considers such funding sources to be crucial, critics say that Renaissance landmarks should not be used for commercial purposes.
Source: Marco Secchi / Getty Images.

recent billboard in Piazza San Marco promoted a designer shopping mall located outside the city; ironically, the billboard's message was that people who come to Venice should do an about face and *leave* Venice to do some shopping! Is it possible, Casali wonders, that such advertisers actually have no interest in restoration per se, but rather are using Venice for a different purpose—a purely commercial one?

Nathalie Salas, a marketing consultant living in Italy, believes that "passive tourism" poses a threat to the sustainability of Venice's tourist industry. But, rather than place the blame on the tourists themselves, Salas believes the problem arises in part from the way Venice is being positioned. The paradox of Venice, says Salas, is that while it is the most unique city in the world, it is also gradually becoming standardized. Like other cities, Venice offers branded entertainment such as Hard Rock Café (featuring "mouth-watering American classics") and global hotel chains. What does this lead to? Standardized tourists and standardized products, Salas says.

Salas proposes a shift from a style of tourism that focuses on tangible resources—e.g., landmarks such as the Rialto Bridge and Piazza San Marco—to one that emphasizes intangible resources such as lifestyle and image. Instead of the stereotypical sightseeing holiday, Salas suggests offering visitors a chance to experience everyday Venetian life with itineraries that are "off the beaten path" and that will allow visitors to interact with the city in a more sustainable way. She also believes tourism's outreach should be oriented less toward first-time customers and more toward repeat visitors. In short, Salas believes that an emphasis on quality instead of quantity is one way to address the tourism issue in Venice.

Jane da Mosto is a longtime Venice resident and an advisor to the Venice in Peril Fund, a British nongovernmental organization (NGO). On the issue of whether tourism is killing or saving Venice, she poses the following questions: What is the "real" Venice? And, what do we *want* it to be? Is it a unified city and lagoon whose symbiosis dates back 1,500 years? Or, is it simply a collection of monuments and landmarks in the middle of the city? As for those who complain about Venice being overrun with tourists, da Mosto reminds them that a virtuous cycle may be at work: Venice's cultural riches provide the energy and resources for socioeconomic development that attracts creative people. They, in turn, contribute to *further* socioeconomic development and economic prosperity that results in a revitalization of the existing culture.

Dominic Standish is the author of a new book in which he explores the problem of Venetian cultural conservation and economic development. Overall, Standish views tourism in Venice as more of an opportunity than a threat. While acknowledging some of the problems associated with tourism, Standish believes the root of the problem lies in city management and public policy. In his book, he argues for both modernization and development, and outlines a multi-point plan that addresses various pressing needs in these areas.

For example, there is a need to modernize accommodations for residents as well as develop new facilities to serve the needs of students and visitors. Speaking about local opposition to building new hotels on the mainland, Standish notes that this increases the likelihood that global chains will purchase historic palaces in Venice and convert them into hotels. Standish is opposed to such conversions. He does support plans to develop a new maritime passenger services facility that will allow cruise ships to dock further away from residential areas. Tessera City, a new mixed-use development near Marco Polo airport, should also relieve some of the tourism pressure on Venice. Standish supports plans to develop a subway system connecting the airport to Venice. And, he notes, Venice's sewage system badly needs upgrading, despite estimates that the cost could total €250 million.

Meanwhile, a massive effort dubbed the Moses Project is underway to prevent flooding. The name was chosen deliberately because of the Biblical account of Moses parting the Red Sea. Underwater flood barriers are being installed in the lagoon; consisting of huge steel sheets, the barrier can be raised to prevent flooding and then lowered back to the seabed when not needed. Environmentalists are concerned about the impact the barriers will have on the lagoon's fragile ecosystem. The system is scheduled to be operational in mid-2014.

Venice is not the only city struggling to balance commercial interests with the concerns of conservationists and preservationists. In Charleston, South Carolina, the proposed development of a new $35 million cruise ship terminal has many locals up in arms. Opponents are concerned about the new facility's impact on the historic district where the port is located. The mayor of Charleston thinks the plan's critics have it all wrong. He points out that some 1,700 vessels use the port each year but only 85 of them—5 percent—are cruise ships. "This is not a theme park," he said. "One of the authentic parts of Charleston is that we are an international port."

Discussion Questions:

4-8. What critical thinking issues are raised in the case?

4-9. The case presents various points of view on the issue of tourism in Venice. Whose perspective(s), if any, do you agree with?

4-10. Should companies that contribute to historic renovation projects be allowed to place advertising on the buildings?

4-11. In June 2011, city officials in Venice approved a tax on tourists staying in the city. Do you think this is a fair and effective way to generate revenue and limit the number of tourists?

4-12. Do you think that Venice's tourist officials should use marketing communications to provide information that would direct visitors to areas of the city that are "less touristy"?

Sources: Dominic Standish, *Venice in Environmental Peril? Myth and Reality* (Lanham, MD: University Press of America, 2012); "Saving Venice with Fellini Flicks," *The Wall Street Journal* (March 20, 2013), p. A21; Kim Severson, "This Charleston Harbor Battle Is Over the Impact of Cruise Ships," *The New York Times* (February 20, 2013), pp. A1, A17; Giovanni Legorano and Deborah Ball, "The Trouble with Harry's: Venice Bar Fights Last Call," *The Wall Street Journal* (December 17, 2012); "Tod's Founder to Restore Roman Colosseum," *Associated* Press (January 21, 2011); Elisabeta Povoledo, "Venice Tourist Ships Rattle Windows and Nerves," *The New York Times* (May 15, 2011), p. A16; Elisabetta Povoledo, "Behind Venice's Ads, the Restoration of Its Heritage," *The New York Times* (September 19, 2010), p. A20.

CASE 4-2
Soccer and the Fashion World

Soccer enjoys a reputation as "the world's sport" and "the beautiful game." As John Quelch and Katherine Jocz point out in a recent book, professional soccer teams such as Real Madrid have embraced the power of global marketing. They recruit players of different nationalities and use Web sites and social media to interact with fans.

These facts help explain why every four years, World Cup fever breaks out around the world. The 2010 World Cup, held in South Africa, was broadcast on 376 television channels in 214 countries and territories. It attracted a cumulative audience of 26 billion people; an estimated 1 billion people tuned in for the championship game between Spain and the Netherlands. ESPN and ABC, both units of Walt Disney, spent $100 million for the rights to broadcast the World Cup in 2010 and 2014. Global marketers, keen to capitalize on a huge television viewing audience, spend tens of millions of dollars as partners, sponsors, and advertisers (see Exhibit 4-10).

The Fédération Internationale de Football Association (FIFA), based in Zurich, is soccer's governing body. As noted at www.fifa.com, the organization's mission goes far beyond the World Cup. FIFA seeks to "broaden the appeal of football [soccer] across all walks of life." Among other things, FIFA oversees the licensing of logos and team mascots to companies such as Adidas and Electronic Arts. In 2006, when the World Cup finals were held in Germany, FIFA reaped the rewards after fans spent $2 billion on soccer memorabilia. Overall, the 2010 World Cup in South Africa generated more than $3 billion from commercial deals alone.

The problem is that after the championship, match sales—and FIFA's revenues—start to dwindle. To counteract this trend, FIFA is launching a new global fashion brand. The goal is to build and maintain awareness and interest in soccer in the years between World Cup matches. The United States is a key market for FIFA; the U.S. Soccer Federation governs professional organizations, including Major League Soccer (MLS), as well as youth and school competitions.

Marketers have already learned that there are big profits to be reaped from the connection between soccer and the fashion world. Soccer stars achieve celebrity status, are household names in many parts of the world, and enjoy seemingly universal appeal. Fans don clothes featuring team names and colors. Little wonder, then, that a recent print advertising campaign for luxury goods marketer Louis Vuitton featured football legends Zinedine Zindane (France), Pelé (Brazil), and Diego Maradona (Argentina).

Despite the fact that the American team advanced to the semifinals in South Africa, the game is much more popular in other parts of the world. In the words of one commentator, America is "the last major outpost of soccer apathy." MLS Commissioner Don Garber believes that it is important to teach Americans a new way of following the sport. "At their base level, sports are local and they are tribal," he says.

In the United States, 2010 World Cup merchandise such as T-shirts, hoodies, and Official Match Balls was available at Walmart, Sports Authority, and sports.com. FIFA chose Total Apparel Goup (TAG) to boost soccer's visibility and popularity among Americans. As TAG CEO Janon Costly noted, the task is to establish soccer's place in mainstream U.S. culture. He said, "Now sport and fashion and entertainment are interchangeable, and you have to strategize with that in mind. Clothes put the sport squarely in front of people who might not see it any other way."

In fall 2010, the FIFA collection was launched in the United States and 11 other countries. The collection's five separate lines target both men and women: 1904, Editions, Code, Essentials, and Trophy. The

Exhibit 4-10 Don Jones (left), chairman of Total Apparel Group (TAG), and Janon Costley, TAG's CEO, hope to boost soccer's visibility and popularity in the United States with a line of FIFA-themed clothing. As Costley notes, "If you buy the product, you participate in the sport in some way, so the garment itself becomes an educational platform."
Source: TAG/Janon Costley.

theme of the 1904 line is FIFA's founding that year in Paris. Following trends set by Yves Saint Laurent and other designers, the Paris address Rue St Honoré is embossed on the shirts. The fall 2010 collection also included limited-edition, retro-styled "FIFA Heritage Tees," with the shirts featuring original tournament logos and mascots. "Juanito," from the 1970 World Cup in Mexico, is one such design; it was chosen specifically to appeal to Mexican Americans.

Other sports organizations have attempted to launch branded clothing lines in the United States, with mixed success. Reebok tried, and failed, with its NFL Equipment line of performance-oriented gear. By contrast, Walmart succeeded with NBA-branded apparel that was aimed squarely at the mass market. A line of PGA Tour apparel generates about $50 million in annual wholesale turnover; however, it took nearly a decade to achieve that level. As Leo McCullagh, who was responsible for PGA Tour marketing and licensing for many years, explains, "It's extraordinarily hard to turn a sports league or governing body into a brand that works elsewhere. You have to combine the right price points with the right retailers and get the governing body to think about what their brand is really worth. And that's never easy."

FIFA is not the only global marketer seeking revenue growth by boosting soccer's popularity in America. For example, soccer superstar David Beckham was at the center of a splashy promotional campaign for Adidas. Beckham has now been a worldwide Adidas endorser for more than a decade. Following Beckham's highly publicized 2007 move from Real Madrid to the Los Angeles Galaxy, he signed a five-year, $250 million contract. Beckham has been featured prominently in a variety of media, including billboards and prime-time television ads. Adidas executives expect Beckham's endorsement to lead to increased sales of a variety of branded merchandise. As Stephen Pierpoint, vice president for brand marketing at Adidas, says, "The U.S. market has a real opportunity to grow. Football [soccer] has always been a core sport for Adidas. We hope David will be the catalyst for growth."

Discussion Questions

⭐ **4-13.** Is FIFA's "sartorial strategy" likely to influence Americans' perceptions of soccer?

4-14. Discuss your thoughts on whether soccer can be transformed into a mainstream sport in the United States.

4-15. With the 2010 World Cup in South Africa, FIFA faced a number of challenges pertaining to security, ticketing, and transportation. The 2014 World Cup will be held in Brazil, where key infrastructure areas such as telecommunications and airports are underdeveloped. What must FIFA do to ensure the 2014 World Cup is successful?

Sources: Matthew Futterman, "Is America Becoming a 'Football' Paradise?" *The Wall Street Journal* (December 1–2, 2012), p. A16; Brian Aguilar, "To Show Their Support, Soccer Fans in the U.S. Need to Master 'Tifo,'" *The Wall Street Journal* (September 14, 2012), pp. A1, A6; Simon Kuper, "Why We Follow Football," *Financial Times: Life & Arts* (April 28/29, 2012), p. 2; Joseph D'Hippolito, "Beckham Returns; Fans Turn," *The New York Times* (March 22, 2011), pp. B10, B13; Vanessa Friedman, "A Sartorial Strategy for Growth," *Financial Times* (June 10, 2010), p. 12; Terry Lefton, "Apparel Firm Tries to Help FIFA Get Foot in Door as Lifestyle Brand," *Sports Business Journal* (May 3–9, 2010), p. 9; Matthew Futterman and Nick Wingfield, "Are Americans Becoming Soccer Fans?" *The Wall Street Journal* (July 29, 2009), p. D8; Michael MacCambridge, "The Goal Is Popularity," *The Wall Street Journal* (July 15, 2009), p. A13; "Global Brands Kicks Off FIFA Fashion," *License! Global* 12, no. 4 (May 2009), p. 18; Jon Weinbach, "U.S. Soccer League Finally Hopes to Score," *The Wall Street Journal* (March 23, 2007), pp. B1, B2.

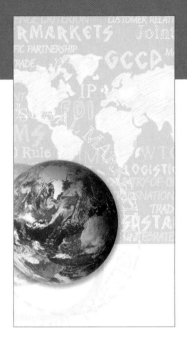

5

The Political, Legal, and Regulatory Environments

CASE 5-1
Mr. President—Free Pussy Riot!

Russia is being transformed by economic change. In Moscow, for example, affluent Russians can shop at boutiques that offer Versace, Burberry, Bulgari, and other exclusive brands. Although per capita gross national income (GNI) in Russia is only $10,731, Russian shoppers spend billions each year on luxury goods. In 2006, flush with dollars from oil exports, the Russian government lifted all currency controls and made the ruble freely convertible in world markets.

That same year, Russian President Vladimir Putin hosted the Group of Eight Summit in St. Petersburg. The moment marked Russia's arrival on the world stage. Putin took advantage of the opportunity to present his country to the world in a positive light. The PR effort included a two-hour television broadcast during which Putin answered questions submitted from around the world via the Internet. Putin was also *Time* magazine's 2007 "Man of the Year."

Exhibit 5-1 Disguised in bright balaclavas, the all-female art collective known as Pussy Riot appears on Red Square in Moscow. In 2012, after attempting to perform an anti-Kremlin song in an Orthodox cathedral, three of the activists were arrested and convicted of "anti-religious hooliganism." Two of the women were sent to prison; the third was released. The group's members maintain that their work is intended to transform Russian society for the better.
Source: REUTERS/Denis Sinyakov.

Despite the positive publicity, however, the phrases *managed democracy* and *state capitalism* have been used to describe the arbitrary exercise of state power in Russia. The Kremlin plans to limit foreign investment in strategic industries such as oil; the term *renationalization* has been applied to the process by which state-owned enterprises are acquiring rivals. *Kleptocracy* refers to rampant corruption and bribery. In 2008, Dmitry Medvedev was elected president, and Putin was named prime minister. The tandem leadership team ruled until the May 2012 presidential elections, when Putin was elected to another term.

By the end of 2012, the Putin government was generating global publicity again, but this time the issue was on a smaller, cultural level. Controversy erupted after members of feminist punk rock band Pussy Riot were arrested following a brief performance at the Christ the Savior cathedral in Moscow (see Exhibit 5-1). The band was known for its anti-Putin stance and provocative lyrics; one of the band's songs is titled "Holy Mary, Blessed Virgin, Drive Putin Away." Three of the band's members—Maria Alyokhina, Yekaterina Samutsevich, and Nadezhda Tolokonnikova—were charged with "hooliganism motivated by religious hatred." After a lengthy legal process, Ms. Alyokhina and Ms. Tolokonnikova were sentenced to two-year prison terms in a remote part of Siberia. Ms. Samutsevich was acquited.

Putin's Russia is a case study in the impact that the political, legal, and regulatory environments can have on international trade and global marketing activities. Each of the world's national governments regulates trade and commerce with other countries and attempts to control the access outside enterprises have to national resources. Every country has its own unique legal and regulatory system that affects the operations and activities of the global enterprise, including the global marketer's ability to address market opportunities and threats. Laws and regulations constrain the cross-border movement of products, services, people, money, and know-how. The global marketer must attempt to comply with each set of national—and, in some instances, regional—constraints. The fact that laws and regulations are frequently ambiguous and continually changing hampers these efforts.

In this chapter, we consider the basic elements of the political, legal, and regulatory environments of global marketing, including the most pressing current issues, and offer some suggestions for dealing with those issues. Some specific topics—such as rules for exporting and importing industrial and consumer products; standards for health and safety; and regulations regarding packaging, labeling, advertising, and promotion—are examined in later chapters devoted to individual marketing mix elements.

LEARNING OBJECTIVES

1 Understand the elements of a country's political environment that can impact global marketing activities.

2 Define *international law* and describe the main types of legal systems found in different parts of the world.

3 Understand the most important business issues that can lead to legal problems for global marketers.

4 Describe the available alternatives for conflict resolution and dispute settlement when doing business outside the home country.

5 In general terms, outline the regulatory environment in the European Union.

The Political Environment

Global marketing activities take place within the **political environment** of governmental institutions, political parties, and organizations through which a country's people and rulers exercise power. As we saw in Chapter 4, each nation has a unique culture that reflects its society. Each nation also has a *political culture* that reflects the relative importance of the government and legal system and provides a context within which individuals and corporations understand their relationship to the political system. Any company doing business outside its home country should carefully study the political culture in the target country and analyze salient issues arising from the political environment. These include the governing party's attitude toward sovereignty, political risk, taxes, the threat of equity dilution, and expropriation.

Nation-States and Sovereignty

Sovereignty can be defined as supreme and independent political authority. A century ago, U.S. Supreme Court Chief Justice Melville Fuller said, "Every sovereign state is bound to respect the independence of every other sovereign state, and the courts in one country will not sit in judgment on the acts of government of another done within its territory." More recently, Richard Stanley, president of the Stanley Foundation, offered the following concise description:

> A sovereign state was considered free and independent. It regulated trade, managed the flow of people into and out of its boundaries, and exercised undivided jurisdiction over all persons and property within its territory. It had the right, authority, and ability to conduct its domestic affairs without outside interference and to use its international power and influence with full discretion.[1]

Government actions taken in the name of sovereignty occur in the context of two important criteria: a country's stage of development and the political and economic systems in place in the country.

As outlined in Chapter 2, the economies of individual nations may be classified as industrialized, newly industrializing, or developing. Many governments in developing countries exercise control over their nations' economic development by passing protectionist laws and regulations. Their objective is to encourage economic development by protecting emerging or strategic industries. Government leaders can also engage in cronyism and provide favors for family members or "good friends." For example, former Indonesian President Suharto established a national car program that granted tax breaks and tariff privileges to a company established in South Korea by his youngest son. The United States, the European Union (EU), and Japan responded by taking the matter to the World Trade Organization (WTO).

Conversely, when many nations reach advanced stages of economic development, their governments declare that (in theory, at least) any practice or policy that restrains free trade is illegal. Antitrust laws and regulations are established to promote fair competition. Advanced-country laws often define and preserve a nation's social order; laws may extend to political, cultural, and even intellectual activities and social conduct. In France, for example, laws forbid the use of foreign words such as *le weekend* or *le marketing* in official documents. Also, a French law passed in 1996 requires that at least 40 percent of the songs played by popular radio stations be French. Companies that may be affected positively or negatively by legislative acts often use advertising as a vehicle for expressing their positions on issues (see Exhibit 5-2).

We also noted in Chapter 2 that most of the world's economies combine elements of market and nonmarket systems. The sovereign political power of a government in a predominantly nonmarket economy reaches quite far into the economic life of a country. By contrast, in a capitalist, market-oriented democracy, that power tends to be much more constrained. A current global phenomenon in both nonmarket and market structures is the trend toward privatization, which reduces direct governmental involvement as a supplier of goods and services in a given economy. In essence, each act of privatization moves a nation's economy further in the free market direction.

The trend can be traced to the late Margaret Thatcher's economic policies in the 1980s when she was British prime minister. British Airways, British Petroleum, British Steel, and Rolls-Royce were some of the companies that were privatized under so-called Thatcherite economics. The policy was highly controversial; some pilloried the prime minister for visiting misery on Great Britain; others hailed her for taking bold steps to spur the economy. More recently, the economic crisis in the EU has prompted Italy's government to consider possible sales of its stakes in Enel, the country's largest power utility, and Eni, an oil and gas company. Italy's debt totals more than $2 trillion, and the government is seeking ways to raise millions of euros.

Some observers believe global market integration is eroding national economic sovereignty. Economic consultant Neal Soss noted, "The ultimate resource of a government is power, and we've seen repeatedly that the willpower of governments can be overcome by persistent attacks from the marketplace."[2] Is this a disturbing trend? If the issue is framed in terms of marketing,

---

[1] See *Changing Concepts of Sovereignty: Can the United Nations Keep Pace?* (Muscatine, IA: The Stanley Foundation, 1992), p. 7.
[2] Cited in Karen Pennar, "Is the Nation-State Obsolete in a Global Economy?" *BusinessWeek* (July 17, 1995), p. 80.

Motherhood, apple pie and GATT

Quick, name something supported by Presidents Clinton, Bush and Reagan; 450 leading American economists, including four Nobel laureates; the National Governors Association; the Consumers Union; the Business Roundtable, and many others.

Motherhood? Apple pie? Well, probably. But there's no doubt that each of those individuals and organizations supports GATT, the General Agreement on Tariffs and Trade. What's known as the Uruguay Round of GATT, an accord that took 117 countries more than seven years to negotiate, is now awaiting approval by Congress.

The agreement will reduce import tariffs worldwide by an average of 40 percent and cover new areas such as agriculture, intellectual property and some services—areas of importance to the U.S. economy. It could generate as much as $5 trillion in new worldwide commerce by 2005.

In the words of former President Ronald Reagan: "In trade, everyone ends up a winner as markets grow." We've seen evidence of that this year since the North American Free Trade Agreement (NAFTA) went into effect January 1. Despite negative predictions to the contrary, trade is up, consumer prices are down and massive layoffs just haven't happened.

While the GATT tariff reductions are smaller than those for NAFTA, the number of countries involved and the size of their trade flows are much larger. GATT's effect on the U.S. alone will be five times that of NAFTA.

We hope the enacting legislation is approved before Congress adjourns for the year —and without any financing features that would hurt the companies GATT is intended to help.

What will GATT mean for the U.S.?

First, it's important to note that international trade represents about a quarter of U.S. gross domestic product, or GDP—the value of what the nation produces. Over the last five years, exports accounted for half of U.S. economic growth. More than 10.5 million U.S. workers owe their jobs directly or indirectly to the export of goods or services, and another 500,000 to 1.4 million jobs—at higher-than-average pay—are predicted from GATT.

The Treasury Department estimates that the long-range benefits of this GATT accord will amount to $100 billion to $200 billion a year in added income to the U.S., or $1,700 per family. Other studies predict increases to the GDP as high as 1.2 percent. Agricultural exports alone are expected to rise by as much as $8.5 billion a year in the next decade.

What makes GATT such a boon to the U.S.?

■ Foreign countries on average have more trade restrictions and tariffs on U.S. goods than the U.S. does on theirs. GATT will reduce tariffs and level the playing field.

■ GATT will, for the first time, protect "intellectual property" like patents, trademarks and copyrights. That'll help U.S. computer-software, entertainment, high-tech and pharmaceutical industries, to name a few.

■ Also for the first time, GATT will open markets for service industries like accounting, advertising, computer services, construction and engineering.

■ GATT will open markets for U.S. agricultural products.

So let's call our mothers, cut ourselves a slice of apple pie and let our senators and representatives know we want the GATT legislation passed this year.

Mobil®

Exhibit 5-2 Many global companies use corporate advertising to advocate their official position on trade-related issues. In the mid-1990s, Mobil mounted an ad campaign that addressed a number of topics of public interest, including trade issues, clean air, alternative fuels, and health care reform. This ad urged the U.S. Congress to approve GATT.

Source: Exxon Mobil Historical Collection, *The Center for American History*, The University of Texas at Austin.

the concept of exchange comes to the fore: Nations may be willing to give up sovereignty in return for something of value. If countries can increase their share of world trade and increase national income, perhaps they will be willing to cede some sovereignty. In Europe, the individual EU countries gave up the right to have their own currencies, ceded the right to set their own product standards, and have made other sacrifices in exchange for improved market access.

Political Risk

Political risk is the possibility of a change in a country's political environment or government policy that would adversely affect a company's ability to operate effectively and profitably. As Ethan Kapstein, a professor at INSEAD, has noted:

> Perhaps the greatest threats to the operations of global corporations, and those that are most difficult to manage, arise out of the political environment in which they conduct their business. One day, a foreign company is a welcome member of the local community; the next day, opportunistic politicians vilify it.[3]

Political risk can deter a company from investing abroad; to put it another way, when a high level of uncertainty characterizes a country's political environment, the country may have difficulty attracting foreign investment. However, as Professor Kapstein points out, executives often fail to conceptualize political risk because they have not studied political science. For this reason,

---

[3] Ethan Kapstein, "Avoiding Unrest in a Volatile Environment," *Financial Times—Mastering Uncertainty, Pt I* (March 17, 2006), p. 5.

they have not been exposed to the issues that students of politics ask about the activities of global companies. (A strong argument for a liberal arts education!) Current events must be part of the information agenda; for example, businesspeople need to stay apprised of the formation and evolution of political parties. Valuable sources of information include *The Economist*, the *Financial Times*, and other business periodicals. The Economist Intelligence Unit (EIU; www.eiu.com), the Geneva-based Business Environment Risk Intelligence (BERI; www.beri.com), and the PRS Group (www.prsgroup.com) publish up-to-date political risk reports on individual country markets. Note that these commercial sources vary somewhat in the criteria they consider to constitute political risk. For example, BERI focuses on societal and system attributes, whereas the PRS Group focuses more directly on government actions and economic functions (see Table 5-1).

As noted in the chapter-opening case, the political maneuverings of the Russian government create a high level of political risk. During his first two terms as Russia's president, Putin implemented reforms in an effort to pave the way for Russia's membership in the WTO and to attract foreign investment. In 2008, when Dmitry Medvedev was elected president, Putin became prime minister. It was generally perceived that Putin was the more powerful member of this "ruling tandem." The Russian government has a number of bills pending that, if adopted, will strengthen intellectual property and contract law. Meanwhile, the level of political risk remains high; compounding matters is the fact that Russia's economy was severely impacted by the global economic crisis. As Paul Melling, a partner at the law firm of Baker & McKenzie, explains, "Many multinationals are thinking long and hard about how big their company in Russia ought to be—the bigger the company, the bigger the risk."[4]

Meanwhile, the current political climate in the rest of Central and Eastern Europe is still characterized by varying degrees of uncertainty. As ranked by the Economic Intelligence Unit's Political Instability Index, Hungary, Albania, and Latvia represent moderate levels of risk. Hungary and Latvia have already achieved upper-middle-income status. Now that Latvia has joined the euro zone, it is expected that lower interest rates will promote further economic growth. Albania's progress in transitioning to a market economy has attracted investment from abroad. Moreover, products that are labeled "Made in Albania" are finding acceptance in global markets. The evidence can be seen in the success of DoniAnna, a shoe manufacturer that was founded by Albanian entrepreneur Donika Mici.[5] Diligent attention to risk assessment

TABLE 5-1 Categories of Political Risk

EIU	BERI	PRS Group
War	Fractionalization of the political spectrum	Political turmoil probability
Social unrest	Fractionalization by language, ethnic, and/or religious groups	Equity restrictions
Orderly political transfer	Restrictive/coercive measures required to retain power	Local operations restrictions
Politically motivated violence	Mentality (xenophobia, nationalism, corruption, nepotism)	Taxation discrimination
International disputes	Social conditions (including population density and wealth distribution)	Repatriation restrictions
Change in government/pro-business orientation	Organization and strength of forces for a radical government	Exchange controls
Institutional effectiveness	Dependence on and/or importance to a major hostile power	Tariff barriers
Bureaucracy	Negative influences of regional political forces	Other barriers
Transparency or fairness	Societal conflict involving demonstrations, strikes, and street violence	Payment delays
Corruption	Instability as perceived by assassinations and guerilla war	Fiscal or monetary expansion
Crime		Labor costs
		Foreign debt

Source: Adapted from Llewellyn D. Howell, *The Handbook of Country and Political Risk Analysis*, 2nd ed. (East Syracuse, NY: The PRS Group, Inc., 1998). Reprinted by permission.

---

[4] Courtney Weaver, "The Price of a Presence in Russia," *Financial Times* (July 26, 2010), p. 2B.
[5] Dan Bilefsky, "Intrepid Shoe Executive Casts Lot with Albania," *The New York Times* (October 8, 2009), p. B6.

throughout the region should be ongoing to determine when the risk has decreased to levels acceptable to management.

Companies can purchase insurance to offset potential risks arising from the political environment. In Japan, Germany, France, Britain, the United States, and other industrialized nations, various agencies offer investment insurance to corporations doing business abroad. The Overseas Private Investment Corporation (OPIC; www.opic.gov) provides various types of political risk insurance to U.S. companies; in Canada, the Export Development Corporation performs a similar function. OPIC's activities came under scrutiny in 1997 when the Bill Clinton administration proposed reauthorizing it, along with the Export-Import Bank. Some legislators wanted to dismantle both agencies as part of an effort to reduce government involvement in business. These legislators criticized the agencies for providing unnecessary subsidies to large corporations.[6]

Taxes

Governments rely on tax revenues for the funds necessary for social services, the military, and other expenditures. Unfortunately, government taxation policies on the sale of goods and services frequently motivate companies and individuals to profit by *not* paying taxes. For example, in China, import duties have dropped since the country joined the WTO. Even so, many goods are still subject to double-digit duties plus a 17 percent value-added tax (VAT). As a result, significant quantities of oil, cigarettes, photographic film, personal computers, and other products are smuggled into China. In some instances, customs documents are falsified to undercount goods in a shipment; the Chinese military has allegedly escorted goods into the country as well. Ironically, global companies can still profit from the practice; it has been estimated, for example, that 90 percent of the foreign cigarettes sold in China are smuggled in. For Philip Morris, this means annual sales of $100 million to distributors in Hong Kong who then smuggle the smokes across the border.[7] High excise and VAT taxes can also encourage legal cross-border shopping as consumers go abroad in search of good values. In Great Britain, for example, the Wine and Spirit Association estimates that, on average, cars returning from France are loaded with 80 bottles of wine.

Corporate taxation is another issue. The high level of political risk currently evident in Russia can be attributed in part to excessively high taxes on business operations. High taxes encourage many enterprises to engage in cash or barter transactions, which are off the books and sheltered from the eyes of tax authorities. This, in turn, has created a liquidity squeeze that prevents companies from paying wages to employees; unpaid, disgruntled workers can contribute to political instability. Meanwhile, the Russian government is pursuing a tough new tax policy in an effort to shrink Russia's budget deficit and qualify for loans from the International Monetary Fund (IMF). However, such policies should not have the effect of deterring foreign investment. As Bruce Bean, head of the American Chamber of Commerce in Moscow, summed up the situation:

> Change the name of the country, change the flag, change the border. Yes, this was done overnight. But build a market economy, introduce a meaningful tax system, create new accounting rules, accept the concept that companies which cannot compete should go bankrupt and the workers there lose their jobs? These things take time.[8]

Meanwhile, global companies are being caught up in the chaos. In July 1998, tax collectors seized dozens of automobiles belonging to Johnson & Johnson's (J&J) Russian division and froze the group's assets. The authorities claimed J&J owed $19 million in back taxes.

The diverse geographical activity of the global corporation also requires special attention given to tax laws. Many companies make efforts to minimize their tax liability by shifting the location of income. For example, it has been estimated that tax minimization by foreign companies doing business in the United States costs the U.S. government billions of dollars each year in lost revenue. In one approach called "earnings stripping," foreign companies reduce earnings by making loans to U.S. affiliates rather than using direct investment to finance U.S. activities. The U.S. subsidiary can then deduct the interest it pays on such loans and thereby reduce its tax burden.

[6] Nancy Dunne, "Eximbank and OPIC Face Survival Test in U.S.," *Financial Times* (May 8, 1997), p. 8.

[7] Craig S. Smith and Wayne Arnold, "China's Antismuggling Drive to Hurt U.S. Exporters That Support Crackdown," *The Wall Street Journal* (August 5, 1998), p. A12.

[8] Andrew Higgins, "Go Figure: At Russian Companies, Hard Numbers Often Hard to Come By," *The Wall Street Journal* (August 20, 1998), p. A9.

THE CULTURAL CONTEXT

Europe Says "No" to GMOs

SYNC • THINK • LEARN

MyMarketingLab

In 2008, prior to the onset of the global economic crisis, surging world demand caused the price of oil to spiral upward; cash-strapped consumers felt the economic pain every time they stopped at the gas pump. Adding to consumers' misery was the fact that prices for grocery staples were also going up, due in part to rising transportation costs as well as increased demand for food in China and other emerging markets. Meanwhile, the search for alternative fuel sources sparked interest in ethanol and other biofuels. The resulting increase in the demand for corn also contributed to record prices for agricultural commodities.

As prices soared, politicians in all parts of the world looked for solutions. Some countries banned food exports to ensure adequate domestic supply. In Asian countries, authorities battled rice hoarding in the face of surging prices. What else could be done? Officials at Bayer, DuPont, Syngenta, Monsanto, and other companies that market seeds and other agricultural products believed that the answer was, in part, plant biotechnology, including genetic engineering. Plants that have been genetically modified are known as *genetically modified organisms*, or GMOs. The first generation of GMO crops—primarily corn, cotton, soybeans, and canola—demonstrated increased resistance to insect pests and weeds. A new generation of GMOs currently under development could offer different benefits, such as drought tolerance or flood resistance.

The problem, however, is that a growing number of consumers around the world are deeply concerned about food products that have not been produced naturally. As a result, many are skeptical about GMOs and the benefits of eating food products that incorporate genetically engineered ingredients. As one French citizen noted,

"We have a very risk-averse society that has been completely traumatized by food scares."

In Europe, a number of activist groups, including Greenpeace and Friends of the Earth (FoE), have taken up the fight against GMOs (see Exhibit 5-3). They claim that GMOs pose threats to both people and the environment; terms such as *Frankenfoods* have been used to get the point across. The general public, already cynical thanks to perceived governmental mishandling of the "mad cow" scare, has been receptive.

Monsanto and other biotech companies have begun to work more closely with government regulators. The companies had already been supplying regulatory agencies with their research; now the companies are advocating certain changes in the U.S. Food and Drug Administration's policies concerning GMOs. The agribusiness companies are hoping that the FDA can help reassure consumers so that mandatory labeling along the lines of the European model won't be required. American companies are also frustrated by lengthy regulatory delays in Europe, where all EU governments are involved in the process of approving new food products for sale to the public. At the European Commission itself, five separate directorates are involved in biotechnology issues, and two—DG Sanco and DG Environment—have responsibility for assessing the safety of the food supply.

Sources: Clive Cookson, "A Time to Sow?" *Financial Times* (July 11, 2008), p. 5; John W. Miller, "Stalk-Raving Mad," *The Wall Street Journal* (October 12, 2006), pp. B1, B5; John Mason and David Firn, "Monsanto Sees Seeds of Food Revolution in Europe," *Financial Times* (March 19, 2004), p. 6; Alison Maitland, "An Ethical Answer to Consumers' Fears," *Financial Times* (December 4, 2003), p. 11; Tony Smith, "Brazil to Lift Ban on Crops with Genetic Modification," *The New York Times* (September 25, 2003), p. W1; Norman E. Borlaug, "Science vs. Hysteria," *The Wall Street Journal* (January 22, 2003), p. A14; Elizabeth Becker, "U.S. Threatens to Act Against Europeans Over Modified Foods," *The New York Times* (January 10, 2003), p. A4.

Exhibit 5-3 European consumers have faced a number of food-safety issues in recent years, including outbreaks of hoof-and-mouth disease and mad cow disease. Not surprisingly, many Europeans are skeptical about genetically modified organisms (GMOs) and the benefits of eating food products that incorporate genetically engineered ingredients. As one French citizen noted recently, "We have a very risk-averse society that has been completely traumatized by food scares."
Source: Pascal Parrot/ABACAPRESS.COM/Newscom.

Seizure of Assets

The ultimate threat a government can pose toward a company is seizing its assets. **Expropriation** refers to governmental action to dispossess a foreign company or investor. Compensation is generally provided, although often not in the "prompt, effective, and adequate" manner provided for by international standards. If no compensation is provided, the action is referred to as **confiscation**.[9] International law is generally interpreted as prohibiting any act by a government to take foreign property without compensation. **Nationalization** is generally broader in scope than expropriation; it occurs when the government takes control of some or all of the enterprises in a particular industry. International law recognizes nationalization as a legitimate exercise of government power, as long as the act satisfies a "public purpose" and is accompanied by "adequate payment" (i.e., payment that reflects fair market value of the property).

In 1959, for example, the newly empowered Castro government nationalized property belonging to American sugar producers in retaliation for new American import quotas on sugar. Cuban-owned production sources were not nationalized. Castro offered compensation in the form of Cuban government bonds, which was adequate under Cuban law. However, the U.S. State Department viewed this particular act of nationalization as discriminatory and the compensation offered as inadequate.[10] More recently, late Venezuelan President Hugo Chávez nationalized Electricidad de Caracas, a utility company, and CANTV, a telecommunications provider. The Venezuelan government paid AES Corporation $739.3 million for Electricidad de Caracas; Verizon Communications received $572 million for its stake in CANTV.[11]

Short of outright expropriation or nationalization, the phrase *creeping expropriation* has been applied to limitations on economic activities of foreign firms in particular countries. These limitations have involved repatriation of profits, dividends, royalties, and technical assistance fees from local investments or technology arrangements. Other issues include increased local content requirements, quotas for hiring local nationals, price controls, and other restrictions affecting return on investment. Global companies have also suffered discriminatory tariffs and nontariff barriers that limit market entry of certain industrial and consumer goods, as well as discriminatory laws on patents and trademarks. Intellectual property restrictions have had the practical effect of eliminating or drastically reducing protection of pharmaceutical products.

In the mid-1970s, J&J and other foreign investors in India had to submit to a host of government regulations to retain majority equity positions in companies already established. Many of these rules were later copied in whole or in part by Malaysia, Indonesia, the Philippines, Nigeria, and Brazil. By the late 1980s, after a "lost decade" in Latin America characterized by debt crises and low GNP growth, lawmakers reversed many of these restrictive and discriminatory laws. The goal was to again attract foreign direct investment and badly needed Western technology. The end of the Cold War and the restructuring of political allegiances contributed significantly to these changes.

When governments expropriate foreign property, a number of impediments can limit actions to reclaim that property. For example, according to the U.S. Act of State Doctrine, if the government of a foreign state is involved in a specific act, the U.S. courts will not get involved. However, representatives of expropriated companies may seek recourse through arbitration at the World Bank Investment Dispute Settlement Center. It is also possible to buy expropriation insurance from either a private company or a government agency such as OPIC. The expropriation of copper companies operating in Chile in the early 1970s shows the effect that companies can have on their own fate. Companies that strenuously resisted government efforts to introduce home-country nationals into the company management were expropriated outright; those companies that made genuine efforts to follow Chilean guidelines were allowed to remain under joint Chilean–U.S. management.

[9] Franklin R. Root, *Entry Strategies for International Markets* (New York: Lexington Books, 1994), p. 154.

[10] William R. Slomanson, *Fundamental Perspectives on International Law* (St. Paul, MN: West Publishing, 1990), p. 356.

[11] David J. Lynch, "Venezuelan Consumers Gobble up U.S. Goods Despite Political Tension," *USA Today* (March 28, 2007).

International Law

International law may be defined as the rules and principles that nation-states consider binding upon themselves. International law pertains to property, trade, immigration, and other areas that have traditionally been under the jurisdiction of individual nations. International law applies only to the extent that countries are willing to assume all rights and obligations in these areas. The roots of modern international law can be traced back to the seventeenth-century Peace of Westphalia. Early international law was concerned with waging war, establishing peace, and other political issues such as diplomatic recognition of new national entities and governments. Although elaborate international rules gradually emerged—covering, for example, the status of neutral nations—the creation of laws governing commerce proceeded on a state-by-state basis in the nineteenth century. International law still has the function of upholding order, although in a broader sense than laws dealing with problems arising from war. At first, international law was essentially an amalgam of treaties, covenants, codes, and agreements. As trade grew among nations, order in commercial affairs assumed increasing importance. The law had originally dealt only with nations as entities, but a growing body of law rejected the idea that only nations could be subject to international law.

Paralleling the expanding body of international case law in the twentieth and twenty-first centuries new international judiciary organizations have contributed to the creation of an established rule of international law: the Permanent Court of International Justice (1920–1945); the International Court of Justice (ICJ; www.icj-cij.org), which is the judicial arm of the United Nations and was founded in 1946; and the International Law Commission, established by the United States in 1947 (see Exhibit 5-4). Disputes arising between nations are issues of *public international law*, and they may be taken before the ICJ (also known as the World Court), located in The Hague. As described in the supplemental documents to the United Nations Charter, Article 38 of the ICJ Statute concerns international law:

> The Court, whose function is to decide in accordance with international law such disputes as are submitted to it, shall apply:
>
> **a.** international conventions, whether general or particular, establishing rules expressly recognized by the contesting states;
> **b.** international custom, as evidence of a general practice accepted as law;
> **c.** the general principles of law recognized by civilized nations;
> **d.** subject to the provisions of Article 59, judicial decisions and the teachings of the most highly qualified publicists of the various nations, as subsidiary means for the determination of rules of law.

Exhibit 5-4 Located in The Hague, the International Court of Justice (ICJ) is the judicial arm of the United Nations. The court's 15 judges are elected to 9-year terms. The primary function of the ICJ is to settle disputes among different countries according to international law. The ICJ also offers advice on legal issues submitted by various international agencies.
Source: U.N./Corbis.

Other sources of modern international law include treaties, international customs, judicial case decisions in the courts of law of various nations, and scholarly writings. What happens if a nation has allowed a case against it to be brought before the ICJ and then refuses to accept a judgment against it? The plaintiff nation can seek recourse through the United Nations Security Council, which can use its full range of powers to enforce the judgment.

Common Law Versus Civil Law

Private international law is the body of law that applies to disputes arising from commercial transactions between companies of different nations. As noted, laws governing commerce emerged gradually, leading to a major split in legal systems among various countries.[12] The story of law in the Western world can be traced to two sources: Rome, from which the continental European civil-law tradition originated, and English common law, from which the U.S. legal system originated.

A **civil-law country** is one in which the legal system reflects the structural concepts and principles of the Roman Empire in the sixth century.

> For complex historical reasons, Roman law was received differently and at vastly different times in various regions of Europe, and in the nineteenth century each European country made a new start and adopted its own set of national private-law codes, for which the *Code Napoleon* of 1804 was the prototype. But the new national codes drew largely on Roman law in conceptual structure and substantive content. In civil-law countries, the codes in which private law is cast are formulated in broad general terms and are thought of as completely comprehensive, that is, as the all-inclusive source of authority by reference to which every disputed case must be referred for decision.[13]

In a **common-law country**, many disputes are decided by reliance on the authority of past judicial decisions (cases). A common-law legal system is based on the concept of precedent, sometimes called *stare decisis*. Precedent is the notion that past judicial decisions on a particular issue are binding on a court when that same issue is presented later. This description is somewhat cryptic, because it is easier to observe the operation of precedent than to define it. Nevertheless, precedent and *stare decisis* represent the fundamental principles of common-law decision making. Although much of contemporary American and English law is legislative in origin, the law inferred from past judicial decisions is equal in importance to the law set down in codes. Common-law countries often rely on codification in certain areas—the U.S. Uniform Commercial Code is one example—but these codes are not the all-inclusive, systematic statements found in civil-law countries.

The Uniform Commercial Code (UCC), fully adopted by 49 U.S. states, codifies a body of specifically designed rules covering commercial conduct. (Louisiana has adopted parts of the UCC, but its laws are still heavily influenced by the French civil code.) The host country's legal system—that is, common or civil law—directly affects the form a legal business entity will take. In common-law countries, companies are legally incorporated by state authority. In civil-law countries, a contract between two or more parties who are fully liable for the actions of the company forms a company.

The United States, 9 of Canada's 10 provinces, and other former colonies with an Anglo-Saxon history founded their systems on common law. Historically, much of continental Europe was influenced by Roman law and, later, the Napoleonic Code (see Exhibit 5-5). Asian countries are split: India, Pakistan, Malaysia, Singapore, and Hong Kong are common-law jurisdictions. Japan, Korea, Thailand, Indochina, Taiwan, Indonesia, and China are civil-law jurisdictions. The legal systems in Scandinavia are mixed, displaying some civil-law attributes and some common-law attributes. Today, the majority of countries have legal systems based on civil-law traditions.

As various countries in Eastern and Central Europe wrestle with establishing legal systems in the post-Communist era, a struggle of sorts has broken out; consultants representing both common-law and civil-law countries are trying to influence the process. In much of Central Europe, including Poland, Hungary, and the Czech Republic, the German civil-law tradition prevails. As a result, banks not only take deposits and make loans but also engage in the buying and selling of securities. In Eastern Europe, particularly Russia, the United States has had greater

---

[12] Much of the material in this section is adapted from Randall Kelso and Charles D. Kelso, *Studying Law: An Introduction* (St. Paul, MN: West Publishing, 1984).
[13] Harry Jones, "Our Uncommon Common Law," *Tennessee Law Review* 30 (1975), p. 447.

Exhibit 5-5 In its origins, the legal system of the United States was substantially influenced by English law. The English and American systems are common law in nature; that is, the law is pronounced by courts when there are no statutes to follow.

Common-law systems are distinguishable from the civil-law systems found in much of Europe. Civil-law systems rely more heavily on statutes and codes, such as the Napoleonic Code of 1804, in deciding cases. From these code provisions, abstract principles are perceived and then applied in specific cases. By contrast, common-law courts find abstract principles in particular cases and then generalize what the law is from those principles.

Source: L F File/Shutterstock.com.

influence. Germany has accused the United States of promoting a system so complex that it requires legions of lawyers to interpret it. The U.S. response is that the German system is outdated.[14] In any event, the constant stream of laws and decrees issued by the Russian government creates an unpredictable, evolving legal environment. Specialized publications such as *The Russian and Commonwealth Business Law Report* are important resources for anyone doing business in Russia or in the 10 other nations that comprise the Commonwealth of Independent States.

Islamic Law

The legal system in many Middle Eastern countries is identified with the laws of Islam, which are associated with "the one and only one God, the Almighty."[15] In **Islamic law**, the *sharia* is a comprehensive code governing Muslim conduct in all areas of life, including business. The code is derived from two sources. First is the Koran, the Holy Book written in Arabic that is a record of the revelations made to the Prophet Mohammed by Allah. The second source is the Hadith, which is based on the life, sayings, and practices of Muhammad. In particular, the Hadith spells out the products and practices that are *haram* (forbidden). The orders and instructions found in the Koran are analogous to code laws; the guidelines of the Hadith correspond to common law. Any Westerner doing business in Malaysia or the Middle East should have, at minimum, a rudimentary understanding of Islamic law and its implications for commercial activities. Brewers, for example, must refrain from advertising beer on billboards or in local-language newspapers.

Sidestepping Legal Problems: Important Business Issues

Clearly, the global legal environment is very dynamic and complex. Therefore, the best course to follow is to get expert legal help. However, the astute, proactive marketer can do a great deal to prevent conflicts from arising in the first place, especially concerning issues such as establishment, jurisdiction, patents and trademarks, antitrust, licensing and trade secrets, bribery, and advertising and other promotion tools. Chapters 13 and 14 discuss regulation of specific promotion activities.

Jurisdiction

Company personnel working abroad should understand the extent to which they are subject to the jurisdiction of host-country courts. **Jurisdiction** pertains to global marketing insofar as it

---

[14] Mark M. Nelson, "Two Styles of Business Vie in East Europe," *The Wall Street Journal* (April 3, 1995), p. A14.
[15] This section is adapted from Mushtaq Luqmani, Ugur Yavas, and Zahir Quraeshi, "Advertising in Saudi Arabia: Content and Regulation," *International Marketing Review* 6, no. 1 (1989), pp. 61–63.

concerns a court's authority to rule on particular types of issues arising outside of a nation's borders or to exercise power over individuals or entities from different countries. Employees of foreign companies working in the United States must understand that U.S. courts have jurisdiction to the extent that the company can be demonstrated to be doing business in the state in which the court sits. The court may examine whether the foreign company maintains an office, solicits business, maintains bank accounts or other property, or has agents or other employees in the state in question. In one case, Revlon sued United Overseas Limited (UOL) in the U.S. District Court for the Southern District of New York. Revlon charged the British company with breach of contract, contending that UOL had failed to purchase some specialty shampoos as agreed. Claiming lack of jurisdiction, UOL asked the court to dismiss the complaint. Revlon countered with the argument that UOL was, in fact, subject to the court's jurisdiction; Revlon cited the presence of a UOL sign above the entrance to the offices of a New York company in which UOL had a 50 percent ownership interest. The court denied UOL's motion to dismiss.[16]

Jurisdiction also played an important role in two other trade-related disputes. One pitted Volkswagen AG against General Motors. After GM's worldwide head of purchasing, José Ignacio López de Arriortúa, was hired by Volkswagen in 1992, his former employer accused him of taking trade secrets. Volkswagen accepted U.S. court jurisdiction in the dispute, although the company's lawyers requested that the U.S. District Court in Detroit transfer the case to Germany. Jurisdiction was also an issue in a trade dispute that pitted Eastman Kodak against Fuji Photo Film. Kodak alleged that the Japanese government had helped Fuji in Japan by blocking the distribution of Kodak film. The U.S. government turned the case over to the WTO despite the opinion expressed by many experts that the WTO lacks jurisdiction in complaints over trade and competition policy.

Intellectual Property: Patents, Trademarks, and Copyrights

Patents and trademarks that are protected in one country are not necessarily protected in another, so global marketers must ensure that patents and trademarks are registered in each country where business is conducted. A **patent** is a formal legal document that gives an inventor the exclusive right to make, use, and sell an invention for a specified period of time. Typically, the invention represents an "inventive leap" that is "novel" or "nonobvious." A **trademark** is defined as a distinctive mark, motto, device, or emblem that a manufacturer affixes to a particular product or package to distinguish it from goods produced by other manufacturers (see Exhibits 5-6 and 5-7). A **copyright** establishes ownership of a written, recorded, performed, or filmed creative work.

Infringement of intellectual property can take a variety of forms. **Counterfeiting** is the unauthorized copying and production of a product. An *associative counterfeit*, or *imitation*, uses a product name that differs slightly from a well-known brand but is close enough that consumers

> "We have confidence in international law. When you invent something, it is necessary immediately to defend your creativity with intellectual patents. Italy has one of the poorest records in Europe with regard to patents. We need to educate businessmen about this."[17]
>
> —Mario Moretti Polegato, chairman, Geox (Italy's biggest shoe company)

Exhibit 5-6 Luxury goods marketer Louis Vuitton recently sued Carrefour, the French hypermarket operator, in China. Attorneys for Louis Vuitton alleged that a Shanghai Carrefour store sold counterfeit copies of Vuitton's handbags for 50 yuan, the equivalent of about $6. Genuine Louis Vuitton handbags sell for about $1,000 in China. China is experiencing an increase in lawsuits involving patents, trade secrets, and counterfeit goods.
Source: Eugene Hoshiko/AP Images.

[16] Joseph Ortego and Josh Kardisch, "Foreign Companies Can Limit the Risk of Being Subject to U.S. Courts," *National Law Journal* 17, no. 3 (September 19, 1994), p. C2.
[17] Tony Barber, "'Patents Are Key' to Taking on China," *Financial Times* (July 25, 2006), p. 2.

Exhibit 5-7 The Champagne region in France is world famous for producing sparkling wines. However, the word "Champagne" sometimes appears on labels of sparkling wines from the United States and other countries. The EU recently asked the WTO for permission to restrict the use of "Champagne" and certain other words associated with traditional European products. Such "geographic indicators" would assure consumers about the origin and authenticity of the products they buy; in other words, a wine labeled "Champagne" would be from Champagne, France. In 2005, representatives from several wine regions in the United States and the EU signed a Joint Declaration to Protect Wine Place & Origin. In addition, a Wine Accord signed by the United States and EU bans the misuse of 16 place names by marketers of wine products that do not originate in those places.
Source: Champagne, USA.

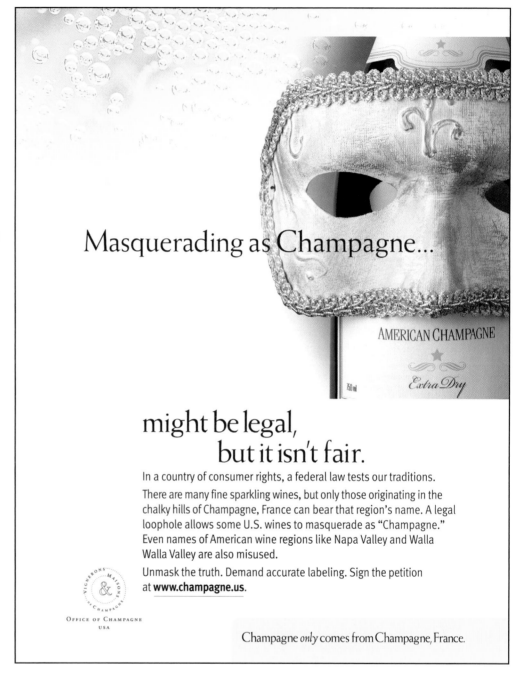

will mistake it for the genuine product (see Exhibit 5-8). A third type of counterfeiting is *piracy*, the unauthorized publication or reproduction of copyrighted work. Counterfeiting and piracy are particularly important in industries such as motion pictures, recorded music, computer software, and textbook publishing. Companies in these industries produce products that can be easily duplicated and distributed on a mass basis. The United States in particular has a vested interest in intellectual property protection around the globe because it is home to many companies in the industries just mentioned. However, the United States faces significant challenges in countries such as China. As one expert has noted:

> Current attempts to establish intellectual property law, particularly on the Chinese mainland, have been deeply flawed in their failure to address the difficulties of reconciling legal values, institutions, and forms generated in the West with the legacy of China's past and the constraints imposed by its present circumstances.[18]

---

[18] William P. Alford, *To Steal a Book Is an Elegant Offense: Intellectual Property Law in Chinese Civilization* (Stanford, CA: Stanford University Press, 1995), p. 2.

Exhibit 5-8 Budweiser is a registered trademark of Anheuser-Busch/InBev, the world's largest brewing company. At the present, however, AB/InBev can't use the Budweiser brand name on a global basis. That's because in 1895 the Budejovicky Budvar brewery was established in Budweis, Bohemia, and its beer was officially named Budweiser, "the beer of kings." In 2011, Europe's Court of First Instance ruled that both companies can use the Budweiser trademark in the United Kingdom.
Source: AP Wide World Photos.

In the United States, where patents, trademarks, and copyrights are registered with the Federal Patent Office, the patent holder retains all rights for the life of the patent even if the product is not produced or sold. The Trademark Act of 1946, also known as the Lanham Act, covers trademarks in the United States. President Ronald Reagan signed the Trademark Law Revision Act into law in November 1988. The law makes it easier for companies to register new trademarks. Patent and trademark protection in the United States is very good, and U.S. law relies on the precedent of previously decided court cases for guidance.

To register a patent in Europe, a company has the option of filing on a country-by-country basis or applying to the European Patent Office in Munich for patent registration in a specific number of countries. A third option will soon be available: The Community Patent Convention will make it possible for an inventor to file for a patent that is effective in the 27 signatory nations. Currently, patent procedures in Europe are quite expensive, in part because of the cost of translating technical documents into all the languages of the EU countries; as of mid-2004, the translation issue remained unresolved.[19] In July 1997, in response to complaints, the European Patent Office instituted a 19 percent reduction in the average cost of an eight-country patent registration. The United States recently joined the World Intellectual Property Organization (WIPO); governed by the Madrid agreement of 1891 and the more flexible 1996 **Madrid Protocol**, the system allows trademark owners to seek protection in as many as 74 countries with a single application and fee (see Exhibit 5-9).

Companies sometimes find ways to exploit loopholes or other unique opportunities offered by patent and trademark laws in individual nations. Sometimes, individuals register trademarks in local country markets before the actual corporate entity files for trademark protection. For example, Starbucks filed for trademark protection in 1997 in Russia but did not open any cafés there. Sergei Zuykov, an attorney in Moscow, filed a petition in court in 2002 to cancel Starbucks' claim to the brand name because it had not been used in commerce. Technically, Zuykov was merely taking advantage of provisions in Russia's civil code; even though he has been denounced as a "trademark squatter," he was not violating the law. Zuykov then offered to sell Seattle-based Starbucks its name back for $600,000![20]

Then there is the case of singer/songwriter Tom Waits. His distinctive vocal style—a gravelly growl—and songs about losers and dreamers have endeared him to his fans. Within the music industry, Waits is distinctive for another reason: Unlike a growing number of musicians, he refuses to license his songs to marketers for use in broadcast commercials. In addition, he aggressively pursues lawsuits against marketers who use "ringers"—soundalikes—in

[19] Frances Williams, "Call for Stronger EU Patent Laws," *Financial Times* (May 22, 1997).
[20] Andrew Kramer, "He Doesn't Make Coffee, but He Controls 'Starbucks' in Russia," *The New York Times* (October 12, 2005), pp. C1, C4.

Exhibit 5-9 Headquartered in Geneva, Switzerland, the World Intellectual Property Organization (WIPO) is one of 16 specialized subunits of the United Nations. WIPO's mission is to promote and protect intellectual property throughout the world. WIPO views intellectual property as a critical element in economic development; it has created illustrated booklets that explain trademarks, copyright, and other intellectual property issues in a straightforward, easy-to-understand manner. Local agencies can access and print the booklets directly from WIPO's Internet site.

Source: Reprinted with permission from the World Intellectual Property Organization, which owns the copyright.

their advertising. Twenty years ago Waits sued Frito-Lay for using a soundalike in a Doritos ad; he was awarded $2.5 million. Recently, the singer has pursued global marketers. For example, he sued Volkswagen's Audi division for a TV commercial that aired in Spain; Waits claimed that the music ripped off his song "Innocent When You Dream" and that the vocalist imitated his vocal style. An appeals court in Barcelona awarded Waits $43,000 for copyright infringement and $36,000 for violation of his "moral rights as an artist."

Waits says he does not mind when another singer imitates him as a form of artistic expression. As Waits explains, "I make a distinction between people who use the voice as a creative item and people who are selling cigarettes and underwear. It's a big difference. We all know the difference. And it's stealing. They get a lot out of standing next to me, and I just get big legal bills."[21]

International concern about intellectual property issues in the nineteenth century resulted in two important agreements. The first is the International Convention for the Protection of Industrial Property. Also known as the Paris Union or Paris Convention, the convention dates to 1883 and is now honored by nearly 100 countries. This treaty facilitates multicountry patent registrations by ensuring that once a company files in a signatory country, the company will be afforded a "right of priority" in other countries for 1 year from the date of the original filing. A U.S. company wishing to obtain foreign patent rights must apply to the Paris Union within 1 year of filing in the United States or risk a permanent loss of patent rights abroad.[22]

In 1886, the International Union for the Protection of Literary and Artistic Property was formed. Also known as the Berne Convention, this was a landmark agreement on copyright protection. References to the convention pop up in some unexpected places. For example, as the credits roll at the end of *The Late Show with David Letterman*, the following message appears:

> Worldwide Pants Incorporated is the author of this motion picture for purposes of the Berne Convention and all laws giving effect thereto. Unauthorized duplication, distribution, exhibition, or use may result in civil liabilities and/or criminal prosecution.

---

[21] Ben Sisario, "Still Fighting for the Right to His Voice," *The New York Times* (January 20, 2006), p. B3.
[22] Franklin R. Root, *Entry Strategies for International Markets* (New York: Lexington Books, 1994), p. 113.

Two other treaties deserve mention. The Patent Cooperation Treaty (PCT) has more than 100 contracting states, including Australia, Brazil, France, Germany, Japan, North Korea, South Korea, the Netherlands, Switzerland, the Russian Federation and other former Soviet republics, and the United States. The members constitute a union that provides certain technical services and cooperates in the filing, searching, and examination of patent applications in all member countries. The European Patent Office administers applications for the European Patent Convention, which is effective in the EU and Switzerland. An applicant can file a single patent application covering all the convention states; the advantage is that the application will be subject to only one procedure of grant. Although national patent laws remain effective under this system, approved patents are effective in all member countries for a period of 20 years from the filing date.

In recent years, the U.S. government has devoted considerable diplomatic effort to improving the worldwide environment for intellectual property protection. For example, China agreed to accede to the Berne Convention in 1992; on January 1, 1994, China became an official signatory of the PCT. After years of discussion, the United States and Japan have agreed to make changes in their respective patent systems; Japan has promised to speed up patent examinations, eliminate challenges to patent submissions, and allow patent applications to be filed in English.

Effective June 7, 1995, in accordance with the General Agreement on Tariffs and Trade (GATT), new U.S. patents are granted for a period of 20 years from the filing date. Previously, patents were valid for a 17-year term effective after being granted. Thus, U.S. patent laws now harmonize with those in the EU as well as Japan. Even with the changes, however, patents in Japan are narrower than those in the United States. As a result, companies such as Caterpillar have been unable to protect critical innovations in Japan because products very similar to those made by U.S. companies can be patented without fear of infringement.[23]

Another key issue is global patent protection for software. Although copyright law protects the computer code, it does not apply to the idea embodied in the software. Beginning in 1981, the U.S. Patent and Trademark Office extended patent protection to software; Microsoft has more than 500 software patents. In Europe, software patents were not allowed under the Munich Convention; in June 1997, however, the EU indicated it was ready to revise patent laws so they cover software.[24]

Table 5-2 ranks the 10 companies that received the most U.S. patents in 2009. IBM, which has topped the rankings every year since 1993, generates more than $1 billion in revenues by licensing patents and other forms of intellectual property. As illustrated in Exhibit 5-10, DuPont recently was awarded its 7 millionth patent.

TABLE 5-2 Companies Receiving the Most U.S. Patents, 2009

Company	No. of Patents
1. IBM	4,887
2. Samsung Electronics	3,592
3. Microsoft	2,901
4. Canon Kabushiki Kaisha	2,200
5. Panasonic	1,641
6. Toshiba	1,561
7. Sony	1,549
8. Intel	1,271
9. Seiko-Epson	1,328
10. Hewlett-Packard	1,269

Source: U.S. Patent and Trademark Office.

---

[23] John Carey, "Inching Toward a Borderless Patent," *BusinessWeek* (September 5, 1994), p. 35.
[24] Richard Pynder, "Intellectual Property in Need of Protection," *Financial Times* (July 7, 1998), p. 22.

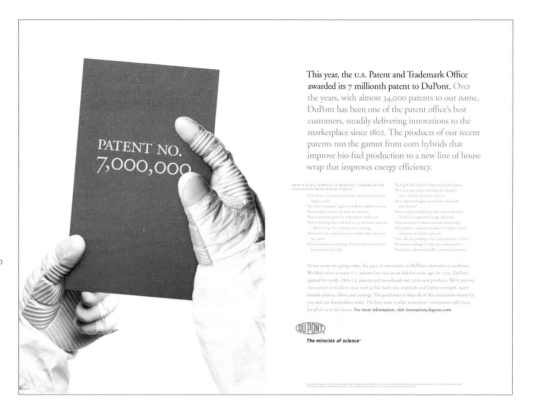

Antitrust

Antitrust laws in the United States and other countries are designed to combat restrictive business practices and to encourage competition. Agencies such as the U.S. Federal Trade Commission, Japan's Fair Trade Commission (FTC), and the European Commission enforce antitrust laws (see Exhibit 5-11). Some legal experts believe that the pressures of global competition have resulted in an increased incidence of price-fixing and collusion among companies. As then-FTC Chairman Robert Pitofsky said, "For years, tariffs and trade barriers blocked global trade. Now those are falling, and we are forced to confront the private anticompetitive behavior that often remains."[25]

A recent rash of antitrust actions brought in the United States against foreign companies has raised concerns that the United States is violating international law as well as the sovereignty of other nations. The U.S. antitrust laws are a legacy of the nineteenth-century trust-busting era and are intended to maintain free competition by limiting the concentration of economic power. The Sherman Act of 1890 prohibits certain restrictive business practices, including fixing prices, limiting production, allocating markets, and engaging in any other scheme designed to limit or avoid competition. The law applies to the activities of U.S. companies outside U.S. boundaries as well as to foreign companies conducting business in the United States. In a precedent-setting case, Nippon Paper Industries was found guilty in a U.S. court of conspiring with other Japanese companies to raise fax paper prices in the United States. The Japanese government denounced the U.S. indictment of Nippon Paper in December 1995 as a violation of international law and Japan's sovereignty. The meetings at which pricing strategies were allegedly discussed took place outside the United States; a U.S. federal judge struck down the indictment, ruling that the Sherman Act does not apply to foreign conduct. However, a federal appeals court in Boston reversed the decision. In his opinion, U.S. Circuit Judge Bruce Selya wrote, "We live in an age of international commerce, where decisions reached in one corner of the world can reverberate around the globe."[26]

For the past four decades, the competition authority of the European Commission has had the power to prohibit agreements and practices that prevent, restrict, and distort competition. The

[25] John R. Wilke, "Hunting Cartels: U.S. Trust-Busters Increasingly Target International Business," *The Wall Street Journal* (February 5, 1997), p. A10.
[26] John R. Wilke, "U.S. Court Rules Antitrust Laws Apply to Foreigners," *The Wall Street Journal* (March 19, 1997), p. B5.

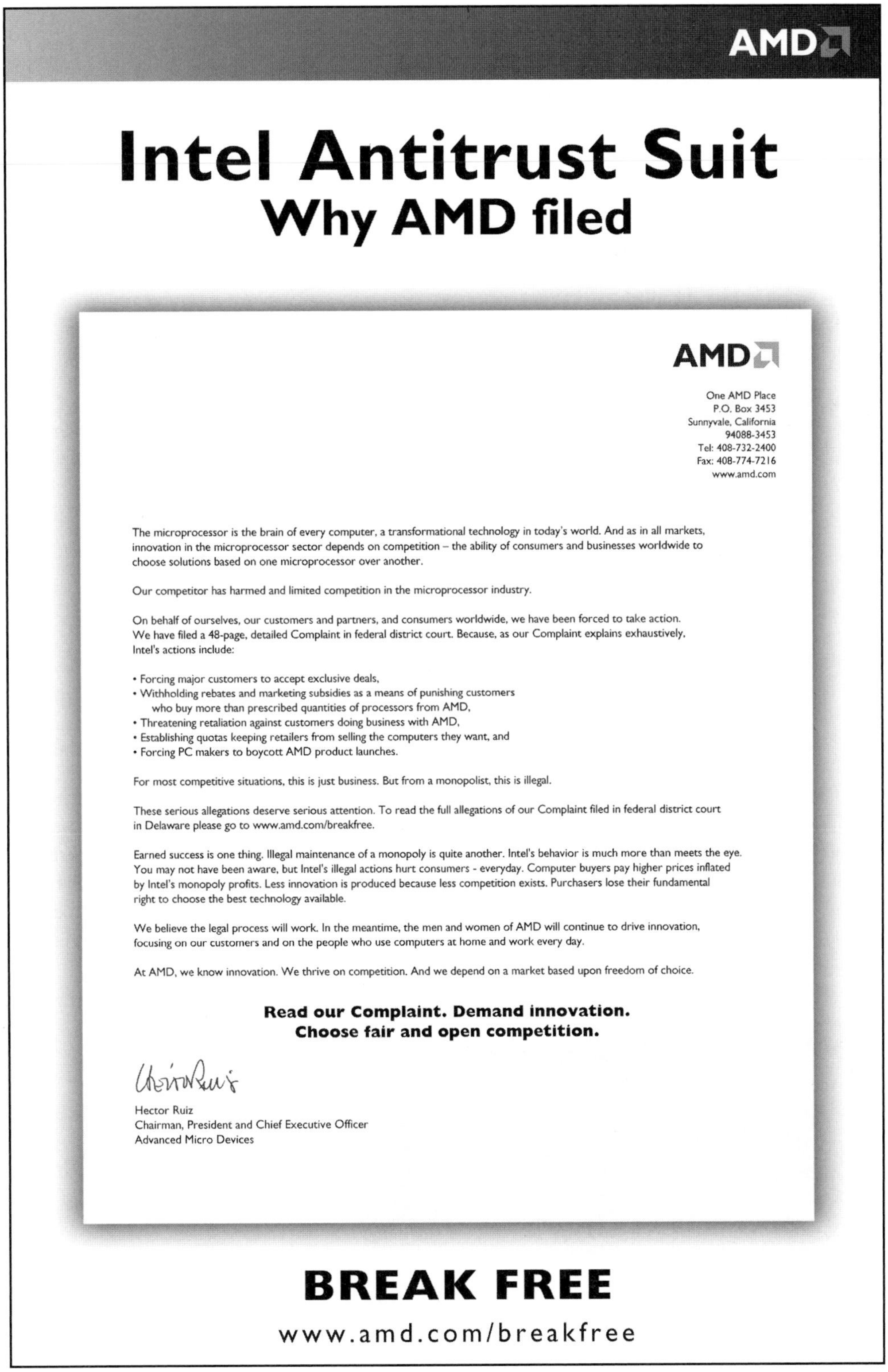

Exhibit 5-11 Advanced Micro Devices (AMD) is the world's second-largest supplier of microprocessors for PCs and servers and is recognized as a technology innovation leader. The dominant market leader, Intel, has held its market share constant in the 80%–90% range over the years. AMD filed a lawsuit against Intel in U.S. Federal Court, claiming Intel uses its dominant market power to stifle or exclude competition and engage in anticompetitive behavior around the globe. Full-page ads were deployed to describe Intel's conduct.
Source: AP Photo/Alexei Nikolsky.

commission has jurisdiction over European-based companies as well as non-European-based ones that generate significant revenues in Europe, such as Microsoft (see Exhibit 5-12). For example, the commission can block a proposed merger or joint venture, approve it with only minor modifications, or demand substantial concessions before granting approval. The commission begins with a preliminary study of a proposed deal; serious concerns can lead to an in-depth investigation lasting several months.

EMERGING MARKETS BRIEFING BOOK

BlackBerry in the Middle East

MyMarketingLab SYNC • THINK • LEARN

Research in Motion (RIM) is a Canadian company best known as the marketer behind the wildly successful BlackBerry. RIM markets BlackBerry devices in more than 175 countries and has more than 40 million subscribers. The BlackBerry Messenger is popular with politicians and businesspeople for a very simple reason: The BlackBerry Enterprise Server offers advanced encryption that provides superior data security. However, in some countries that advantage is actually a disadvantage, at least as far as officials are concerned.

In the Middle East, for example, governments typically maintain strict controls over the Internet for security reasons. In 2009, Etisalat, a telecommunications company in the United Arab Emirates (UAE), urged BlackBerry users to download a software upgrade; it turned out the upgrade contained spyware. The following year, UAE officials at the Telecommunications Regulatory Authority (TRA) threatened to suspend some services to the country's 500,000 BlackBerry users. The rationale: BlackBerry technology allows encrypted data to be sent abroad without going through a country's telecommunications infrastructure. According to government officials, this makes it easier for a variety of undesirable types—organized crime figures and drug smugglers, for example—to conduct "business" from the

UAE. BlackBerry's services, it was alleged, were "causing serious social, judicial and national security repercussions." In the end, however, the TRA relented and there was no service interruption. Few details were available to explain the about-face, however.

Saudi Arabia's Communication and Information Technology Commission (CITC) was also ready to restrict BlackBerry services, citing national security concerns. The issue in Saudi Arabia was tied to the location of RIM's servers: Canada. Unlike the UAE, where many BlackBerry users are expatriate businessmen and bankers, many of the 700,000 subscribers in Saudi Arabia are citizens of the kingdom. Some observers think the restrictions are intended to allow the government to maintain control over the social fabric of the nation. As one Saudi noted, "I think it's mainly a social issue. It's suddenly become trendy to have a BlackBerry … and it's now the most popular way to chat among Saudi youths."

Sources: Joe Leahy, "India Faces Games Chaos if It Curbs BlackBerry," *Financial Times* (August 21/22, 2010), p. 2; Abdullah Al-Shihri, "Saudi Arabia to Continue BlackBerry Service," *USA Today* (August 8, 2010); Misha Glenny, "BlackBerry Is But a Skirmish in the Battle for the Web," *Financial Times* (August 7/8, 2010), p. 7; Paul Taylor, "BlackBerry Faces Wrath of Mideast Spy Masters," *Financial Times* (August 7/8, 2010), p. 2; Andrew England, "Concern Over Crime Behind BlackBerry Plan," *Financial Times* (August 3, 2010), p. 4.

Beginning in the mid-1990s, the commission has taken an increasingly activist approach. Mario Monti, an Italian with an economics background, was Europe's antitrust chief during this period. Nicknamed "Super Mario" by the European press, Monti blocked the proposed merger of WorldCom and Sprint in 2000. He also demanded major concessions before allowing America Online to acquire Time Warner.[27] There have been calls for the EU to revamp its approach to

Exhibit 5-12 In the spring of 2006, attorneys for Microsoft and the European Commission appeared before a 13-judge panel at the European Court of First Instance in Luxembourg. Microsoft's lawyers argued that negligible sales of Edition N constituted evidence that the 2004 ruling was a failure.

In September 2007, the Court of First Instance upheld the European Commission's case against the software giant.
Source: Geert Vanden Wijngaert/AP Images.

----
[27] Anita Raghavan and Brandon Mitchener, "'Super Mario': EU's Antitrust Czar Isn't Afraid to Say No; Just Ask Time Warner," *The Wall Street Journal* (October 2, 2000), pp. A1, A10.

TABLE 5-3 Antitrust Rulings

Companies Involved	Global Antitrust Review	Antitrust Review in USA
Acquisition of Anheuser-Busch (United States) by InBev (Belgium/Brazil), 2008, $52 billion	Deal approved in China but company is prohibited from pursuing Huaran Snow or Beijing Yanjing.	Approved; InBev was required to sell Labatt USA.
Merger of Sony Music (Japan) and BMG (Germany), 2004	Approved by EU.	Approved.
Acquisition of Honeywell (United States) by GE (United States), 2001, $40 billion	Deal was vetoed on grounds that merged firm would be stronger than competitors in aviation equipment.	Deal was on track for approval, subject to conditions.
Joint venture between music businesses of EMI Group PLC (Great Britain) and Time Warner (United States), 2000, $20 billion	EU regulators expressed concern that the new EMI–Time Warner would dominate the growing market for digital music distribution.	Deal was scrapped in October 2000 before regulatory review began.

Source: Compiled by the authors.

antitrust issues and reduce its caseload. Any proposed changes will pit modernists against traditionalists. As one European attorney complained, "The commission is putting resources into regulating cases that don't actually restrict competition, which means that the cases that do need to be looked at are not being resolved efficiently."[28] Table 5-3 summarizes some recent joint ventures, mergers, and other global business deals that have been subject to review by antitrust authorities on both sides of the Atlantic.

Because the interstate-trade clause of the Treaty of Rome applies to trade with third countries, a company must be aware of the conduct of its affiliates. The commission also exempts certain cartels from Articles 85 and 86 of the treaty in an effort to encourage the growth of important businesses. The intent is to allow European companies to compete on an equal footing with Japan and the United States. In some instances, individual country laws in Europe apply to specific marketing mix elements. For example, some countries permit selective or exclusive product distribution. However, European Community law can take precedence.

In one case, Consten, a French company, had exclusive French rights to import and distribute consumer electronics products from the German company Grundig AG. Consten sued another French firm, charging the latter with bringing "parallel imports" into France illegally; that is, Consten charged that the competitor bought Grundig products from various foreign suppliers without Consten's knowledge and was selling them in France. Although Consten's complaint was upheld by two French courts, the Paris Court of Appeals suspended the judgment, pending a ruling by the European Commission on whether the Grundig–Consten arrangement violated Articles 85 and 86 of the Treaty of Rome. The commission eventually ruled against Consten on the grounds that "territorial protection proved to be particularly damaging to the realization of the Common Market."[29]

In some instances, companies or entire industries have been able to secure exemption from antitrust rules. In the airline industry, for example, KLM and Northwestern won an exemption from the U.S. government and now share computer codes and set prices jointly. Similarly, the European Commission permitted United International Pictures (UIP), a joint venture between Paramount, Universal, and MGM/UA, to cut costs by collaborating on motion picture distribution in Europe. However, in 1998, the commission reversed itself and notified the three studios that they had to distribute their films independently in Europe.[30] A **cartel** is a group of individual companies that collectively set prices, control output, or take other actions to maximize profits. For example, the group of oil-producing countries known as OPEC is a cartel.

In the United States, most cartels are illegal. One notable exception, however, has a direct impact on global marketing: A number of the world's major shipping lines, including the

[28] Emma Tucker, "Europe's Paper Mountain," *Financial Times* (February 11, 1998), p. 21.
[29] Detlev Vagts, *Transnational Business Problems* (Mineola, NY: The Foundation Press, 1986), pp. 285–291.
[30] Alice Rawsthorn and Emma Tucker, "Movie Studios May Have to Scrap Joint Distributor," *Financial Times* (February 6, 1998), p. 1.

U.S.-based Sea-Land Service and Denmark's A.P. Moller/Maersk line, have enjoyed exemptions from antitrust laws since the passage of the Shipping Act of 1916. The law was originally enacted to ensure reliability; today, it has been estimated that the cartel results in shipping prices that are 18 percent higher than they would be if shippers set prices independently. Attempts in recent years to change the law have been unsuccessful.[31]

Licensing and Trade Secrets

Licensing is a contractual agreement in which a licensor allows a licensee to use patents, trademarks, trade secrets, technology, or other intangible assets in return for royalty payments or other forms of compensation. U.S. laws do not regulate the licensing process per se as do technology-transfer laws in the EU, Australia, Japan, and many developing countries. The duration of the licensing agreement and the amount of royalties a company can receive are considered a matter of commercial negotiation between licensor and licensee, and there are no government restrictions on remittances of royalties abroad. Important considerations in licensing include what assets a firm may offer for license, how to price the assets, and whether to grant only the right to "make" the product or the rights to "use" and to "sell" the product as well. The right to sublicense is another important issue. As with distribution agreements, decisions must also be made regarding exclusive or nonexclusive arrangements and the size of the licensee's territory.

To prevent the licensee from using the licensed technology to compete directly with the licensor, the latter may try to limit the licensee to selling only in its home country. The licensor may also seek to contractually bind the licensee to discontinue use of the technology after the contract has expired. In practice, host-government laws and even U.S. antitrust laws may make such agreements impossible to obtain. Licensing is thus a potentially dangerous action: It may be instrumental in creating a competitor. Therefore, licensors should be careful to ensure that their own competitive positions remain advantageous. This requires constant innovation.

As noted, licensing agreements can come under antitrust scrutiny. In one case, Bayer AG granted an exclusive patent license for a new household insecticide to S.C. Johnson & Sons. The German firm's decision to license was based in part on the time required for approval by the Environmental Protection Agency (EPA), which had stretched to 3 years. Bayer decided it made better business sense to let the U.S. firm deal with regulatory authorities in return for a 5 percent royalty on sales. However, a class action suit filed against the companies alleged that the licensing deal would allow Johnson to monopolize the $450 million home insecticide market.

At this point, the U.S. Justice Department stepped in, calling the licensing agreement anticompetitive. In a statement, Anne Bingaman, then head of the Justice Department's antitrust unit, said, "The cozy arrangement that Bayer and Johnson maintained is unacceptable in a highly concentrated market." Bayer agreed to offer licenses to any interested company on better terms than the original contract with Johnson. Johnson agreed to notify the U.S. government of any future pending exclusive licensing agreements for household insecticides. Further, if Bayer was party to any such agreements, Bayer agreed that the Justice Department had the right to veto them. The reaction from the legal community was negative. One Washington lawyer who specializes in intellectual property law noted that the case "really attacks traditional licensing practices." As Melvin Jager, president of the Licensing Executives Society, explained, "An exclusive license is a very valuable tool to promote intellectual property and get it out into the marketplace."[32]

What happens if a licensee gains knowledge of the licensor's trade secrets? *Trade secrets* are confidential information or knowledge that has commercial value and is not in the public domain and for which steps have been taken to keep it secret. Trade secrets include manufacturing processes, formulas, designs, and customer lists. To prevent disclosure, the licensing of unpatented trade secrets should be linked to confidentiality contracts with each employee who has access to the protected information. In the United States, trade secrets are protected by state law rather than federal statute; most states have adopted the Uniform Trade Secrets Act (UTSA). The U.S. law provides trade secret liability against third parties that obtain confidential information through an intermediary. Remedies include damages and other forms of relief.

---

[31] Anna Wilde Mathews, "Making Waves: As U.S. Trade Grows, Shipping Cartels Get a Bit More Scrutiny," *The Wall Street Journal* (October 7, 1997), pp. A1, A8.
[32] Brigid McMenamin, "Eroding Patent Rights," *Forbes* (October 24, 1994), p. 92.

The 1990s saw widespread improvements in laws pertaining to trade secrets. Several countries adopted trade secret statutes for the first time. Mexico's first statute protecting trade secrets became effective on June 28, 1991; China's first trade secret law took effect on December 1, 1993. In both countries, the new laws were part of broader revisions of intellectual property laws. Japan and South Korea have also amended their intellectual property laws to include trade secrets. Many countries in Central and Eastern Europe enacted laws to protect trade secrets. When NAFTA became effective on January 1, 1994, it marked the first international trade agreement with provisions for protecting trade secrets. This milestone was quickly followed by the Agreement on Trade-Related Aspects of Intellectual Property Rights (TRIPs), which resulted from the Uruguay Round of GATT negotiations. The TRIPs agreement requires signatory countries to protect against acquisition, disclosure, or use of trade secrets "in a manner contrary to honest commercial practices."[33] Despite these formal legal developments, in practice, enforcement is the key issue. Companies transferring trade secrets across borders should apprise themselves not only of the existence of legal protection but also of the risks associated with lax enforcement.

Bribery and Corruption: Legal and Ethical Issues

History does not record a burst of international outrage when Charles M. Schwab, head of Bethlehem Steel at the beginning of the twentieth century, presented a $200,000 diamond and pearl necklace to the mistress of Czar Alexander III's nephew.[34] In return for that consideration, Bethlehem Steel won the contract to supply the rails for the Trans-Siberian railroad. Today, in the post-Soviet era, Western companies are again being lured by emerging opportunities in Central and Eastern Europe. As in the Middle East and other parts of the world, companies are finding that bribery is a way of life and that corruption is widespread. **Bribery** is the corrupt business practice of demanding or offering some type of consideration—typically a cash payment—when negotiating a cross-border deal. Employees of U.S. companies in particular are constrained by U.S. government policies of the post-Watergate age. Transparency International (www.transparency.org) compiles an annual report ranking countries in terms of a Corruption Perceptions Index (CPI). The "cleanest" score is 10. The 2010 ranking of the highest and lowest countries is shown in Table 5-4.

TABLE 5-4 2010 Corruption Rankings

Rank/Country	2010 CPI Score	Rank/Country	2010 CPI Score
1. Denmark	9.3	168. Equatorial Guinea	1.9
1. New Zealand	9.3	170. Burundi	1.8
1. Singapore	9.3	171. Chad	1.7
4. Finland	9.2	172. Sudan	1.6
4. Sweden	9.2	172. Turkmenistan	1.6
6. Canada	8.9	172. Uzbekistan	1.6
7. Netherlands	8.8	175. Iraq	1.5
8. Australia	8.7	176. Afghanistan	1.4
8. Switzerland	8.7	176. Myanmar	1.4
10. Norway	8.6	178. Somalia	1.1

Note: Transparency International's Corruption Perceptions Index scores countries on their perceived levels of public-sector corruption on a scale from 0 (highly corrupt) to 10 (very clean).

Source: Reprinted from 2010 Corruption Rankings. Copyright 2010 Transparency International: the global coalition against corruption. Used with permission. For more information, visit www.transparency.org.

---

[33] Salem M. Katsh and Michael P. Dierks, "Globally, Trade Secrets Laws Are All Over the Map," *The National Law Journal* 17, no. 36 (May 8, 1995), p. C12.
[34] Much of the material in this section is adapted from Daniel Pines, "Amending the Foreign Corrupt Practices Act to Include a Private Right of Action," *California Law Review* (January 1994), pp. 185–229.

In the United States, the **Foreign Corrupt Practices Act (FCPA)** is a legacy of the Watergate scandal during Richard Nixon's presidency. In the course of his investigation, the Watergate special prosecutor discovered that more than 300 American companies had made undisclosed payments to foreign officials, totaling hundreds of millions of dollars. Congress unanimously passed the act, and President Jimmy Carter signed the act into law on December 17, 1977. Administered by the Department of Justice and the SEC, the act was concerned with disclosure and prohibition. The disclosure part of the act required publicly held companies to institute internal accounting controls that would record all transactions. The prohibition part made it a crime for U.S. corporations to bribe an official of a foreign government or political party to obtain or retain business. Payments to third parties were also prohibited when the company had reason to believe that part or all of the money would be channeled to foreign officials.

The U.S. business community immediately began lobbying for changes to the act, complaining that the statute was too vague and so broad in scope that it threatened to severely curtail U.S. business activities abroad. President Ronald Reagan signed amendments to the statute into law in 1988 as part of the Omnibus Trade and Competitiveness Act. Among the changes were exclusions for "grease" payments to low-level officials to cut red tape and expedite "routine governmental actions" such as clearing shipments through customs, securing permits, or getting airport passport clearance to leave a country.

Convictions carry severe jail sentences and substantial fines. Johnson & Johnson, Tyson Foods, Chevron, Siemens, and Daimler are among the companies that have been slapped with sanctions in recent years. The law is worded quite broadly and has plenty of gray areas; even so, in 2009 and 2010 the U.S. Justice Department collected $2 billion in fines and penalties.[35] A company cannot pay or reimburse fines incurred by "rogue" employees; the rationale is that individuals commit such crimes. As noted on the Justice Department's Web site:

> The following criminal penalties may be imposed for violations of the FCPA's anti-bribery provisions: corporations and other business entities are subject to a fine of up to $2,000,000; officers, directors, stockholders, employees, and agents are subject to a fine of up to $100,000 and imprisonment for up to five years. Moreover, under the Alternative Fines Act, these fines may be actually quite higher—the actual fine may be up to twice the benefit that the defendant sought to obtain by making the corrupt payment. You should also be aware that fines imposed on individuals may not be paid by their employer or principal.[36]

It has also been made clear that the law will not let a person do indirectly (e.g., through an agent, joint venture partner, or other third party) what it prohibits directly.

Some critics of the FCPA decry it as a regrettable display of moral imperialism. At issue is the extraterritorial sovereignty of U.S. law. It is wrong, according to these critics, to impose U.S. laws, standards, values, and mores on American companies and citizens worldwide. As one legal expert pointed out, however, this criticism has one fundamental flaw: There is no nation in which the letter of the law condones bribery of government officials. Thus, the standard set by the FCPA is shared, in principle at least, by other nations.[37]

Another criticism of the FCPA is that it puts U.S. companies in a difficult position vis-à-vis foreign competitors, especially those in Japan and Europe. Several opinion polls and surveys of the business community have revealed the widespread perception that the act adversely affects U.S. businesses overseas. In contrast, some academic researchers have concluded that the FCPA has *not* negatively affected the export performance of U.S. industry. However, a U.S. Commerce Department report prepared with the help of U.S. intelligence services indicated that in 1994 alone, bribes offered by non-U.S. companies were a factor in 100 business deals valued at $45 billion. Foreign companies prevailed in 80 percent of those deals.[38] Although accurate statistics are hard to come by, the rankings shown in Table 5-4 highlight some areas of the world where bribery is still rampant.

---

[35] John Bussey, "The Rule of Law Finds Its Way Abroad—However Painfully," *The Wall Street Journal* (June 24, 2011), p. B1.

[36] www.justice.gov/criminal/fraud/fcpa/docs/lay-persons-guide.pdf (accessed June 1, 2011).

[37] Daniel Pines, "Amending the Foreign Corrupt Practices Act to Include a Private Right of Action," *California Law Review* (January 1994), p. 205.

[38] Amy Borrus, "Inside the World of Greased Palms," *BusinessWeek* (November 6, 1995), pp. 36–38.

The existence of bribery as a fact of life in world markets will not change just because the U.S. Congress condemns it. Bribery payments are considered a deductible business expense in many European countries. According to one estimate, the annual price tag for illegal payments by German firms alone is more than $5 billion. Still, increasing numbers of global companies are adopting codes of conduct designed to reduce illegal activities. Moreover, in May 1997 the Organisation for Economic Co-operation and Development (OECD) adopted a formal standard against bribery by drafting a binding international convention that makes it a crime for a company bidding on a contract to bribe foreign officials. The OECD's antibribery convention (officially known as the Convention on Combating Bribery of Foreign Public Officials in International Business Transactions) went into effect in 1999. The OECD is also working on a smaller scale to create so-called islands of integrity. The goal is to achieve transparency at the level of an individual deal, with all the players pledging not to bribe.[40]

Investigative reporters often file stories regarding bribery or other forms of malfeasance. In emerging countries, journalists may themselves become targets if they criticize the rich or powerful (see Case 5-1). When companies operate abroad in the absence of home-country legal constraints, they face a continuum of choices concerning company ethics. At one extreme, they can maintain home-country ethics worldwide with absolutely no adjustment or adaptation to local practice. At the other extreme, they can abandon any attempt to maintain company ethics and adapt entirely to local conditions and circumstances as they are perceived by company managers in each local environment. Between these extremes, one approach that companies may select is to utilize varying degrees of an extension of home-country ethics. Alternatively, they may adapt in varying degrees to local customs and practices.

What should a U.S. company do if competitors are willing to offer a bribe? Two alternative courses of action are possible. One is to ignore bribery and act as if it does not exist. The other is to recognize the existence of bribery and evaluate its effect on customers' purchase decisions as if it were just another element of the marketing mix. The overall value of a company's offer must be as good as, or better than, the competitor's overall offering, bribe included. It may be possible to offer a lower price, a better product, better distribution, or better advertising to offset the value added by the bribe. The best line of defense is to have a product that is clearly superior to that of the competition. In such a case, a bribe should not sway the purchase decision. Alternatively, clear superiority in service and in local representation may tip the scales.

> "Corruption is probably the most immediate threat and difficulty that any business faces in Russia—and the trend is increasing."[39]
>
> —Carlo Gallo, business risk consultant

Conflict Resolution, Dispute Settlement, and Litigation

The degree of legal cooperation and harmony in the EU is unique and stems, in part, from the existence of code law as a common bond. Other regional organizations have made far less progress toward harmonization. Countries vary in their approach toward conflict resolution. The United States has more lawyers than any other country in the world and is arguably the most litigious nation on earth. In part, this is a reflection of the low-context nature of American culture and the spirit of confrontational competitiveness. Other factors can contribute to differing attitudes toward litigation. For example, in many European nations class action lawsuits are not allowed. Also, European lawyers cannot undertake cases on a contingency fee basis. However, change is in the air, as Europe experiences a broad political shift away from the welfare state.[41]

Conflicts inevitably arise in business anywhere, especially when different cultures come together to buy, sell, establish joint ventures, compete, and cooperate in global markets. For American companies, the dispute with a foreign party is frequently in the home-country jurisdiction. The issue can be litigated in the United States, where the company and its attorneys might be said to enjoy "home-court" advantage. Litigation in foreign courts, however, becomes vastly

[39] Rebecca Bream and Neil Buckley, "Investors Still Drawn to Russia Despite Pitfalls," *Financial Times* (December 1, 2006), p. 21.

[40] José Ángel Gurría, "Rich Must Set the Example of Bribery," *Financial Times* (September 13, 2006), p. 5.

[41] Charles Fleming, "Europe Learns Litigious Ways," *The Wall Street Journal* (February 24, 2004), p. A17.

more complex, partly because of differences in language, legal systems, currencies, and traditional business customs and patterns.

In addition, problems arise from differences in procedures relating to discovery. In essence, *discovery* is the process of obtaining evidence to prove claims and determining which evidence may be admissible in which countries under which conditions. A further complication is the fact that judgments handed down in courts in another country may not be enforceable in the home country. For all these reasons, many companies prefer to pursue arbitration before proceeding to litigate.

Alternatives to Litigation for Dispute Settlement[42]

In 1995, the Cuban government abruptly cancelled contracts with Endesa, a Spanish utility company. Rather than seek restitution in a Cuban court, Endesa turned to the International Arbitration Tribunal in Paris, seeking damages of $12 million. Endesa's actions illustrate how alternative dispute resolution (ADR) methods allow parties to resolve international commercial disputes without resorting to the court system. Formal arbitration is one means of settling international business disputes outside the courtroom. **Arbitration** is a negotiation process that the two parties have, by prior agreement, committed themselves to using. It is a fair process in the sense that the parties using it have created it themselves. Generally, arbitration involves a hearing of the parties before a three-member panel; each party selects one panel member, and those two panel members in turn select the third member. The panel renders a judgment that the parties agree in advance to abide by.

The most important treaty regarding international arbitration is the 1958 United Nations Convention on the Recognition and Enforcement of Foreign Arbitral Awards. Also known as the New York Convention, the treaty has 107 signatory countries, including China. Brazil is notable among the big emerging markets for not being a signatory. The framework created by the New York Convention is important for several reasons. First, when parties enter into agreements that provide for international arbitration, the signatory countries can hold the parties to their pledge to use arbitration. Second, after arbitration has taken place and the arbitrators have made an award, the signatories recognize and can enforce the judgment. Third, the signatories agree that there are limited grounds for challenging arbitration decisions. The grounds that are recognized are different from the typical appeals that are permitted in a court of law.

Some firms and lawyers inexperienced in the practice of international commercial arbitration approach the arbitration clauses in a contract as "just another clause." However, the terms of every contract are different and, therefore, no two arbitration clauses should be the same. Consider, for example, the case of a contract between an American firm and a Japanese one. If the parties resort to arbitration, where will it take place? The American side will be reluctant to go to Japan; conversely, the Japanese side will not want to arbitrate in the United States. An alternative, "neutral" location—Singapore or London, for example—must be considered and specified in the arbitration clause. In what language will the proceedings be conducted? If no language is specified in the arbitration clause, the arbitrators themselves will choose.

In addition to location and language, other issues must be addressed as well. For example, if the parties to a patent-licensing arrangement agree in the arbitration clause that the validity of the patent cannot be contested, such a provision may not be enforceable in some countries. Which country's laws will be used as the standard for invalidity? Pursuing such an issue on a country-by-country basis would be inordinately time-consuming. In addition, there is the issue of acceptance: By law, U.S. courts must accept an arbitrator's decision in patent disputes; in other countries, however, there is no general rule of acceptance.

To reduce delays relating to such issues, one expert suggests drafting arbitration clauses with as much specificity as possible. To the extent possible, for example, patent policies in various countries should be addressed; arbitration clauses may also include a provision that all foreign patent issues will be judged according to the standard of home-country law. Another provision could forbid the parties from commencing separate legal actions in other countries. The goal is to help the arbitration tribunal zero in on the express intentions of the parties.[43]

[42] The authors are indebted to Louis B. Kimmelman of O'Melveny & Meyers LLP, New York City, New York, for his contributions to this section.

[43] Bruce Londa, "An Agreement to Arbitrate Disputes Isn't the Same in Every Language," *Brandweek* (September 26, 1994), p. 18. See also John M. Allen, Jr., and Bruce G. Merritt, "Drafters of Arbitration Clauses Face a Variety of Unforeseen Perils," *National Law Journal* 17, no. 33 (April 17, 1995), pp. C6–C7.

For decades, business arbitration has also been promoted through the International Court of Arbitration at the Paris-based International Chamber of Commerce (ICC; www.iccwbo.org). The ICC recently modernized some of its older rules. However, because it is such a well-known organization, it has an extensive backlog of cases. Overall, the ICC has gained a reputation for being slower, more expensive, and more cumbersome than some alternatives. As U.S. involvement in global commerce grew dramatically during the post–World War II period, the American Arbitration Association (AAA) also became recognized as an effective institution within which to resolve disputes. In 1992, the AAA signed a cooperation agreement with China's Beijing Conciliation Center.

Another agency for settling disputes is the Swedish Arbitration Institute of the Stockholm Chamber of Commerce. This agency frequently administered disputes between Western and Eastern European countries and has gained credibility for its evenhanded administration. However, a favorable ruling from the arbitration tribunal is one thing; an enforced ruling is another. For example, Canada's IMP Group took its case against a Russian hotel development partner to Stockholm and was awarded $9.4 million. When payment was not forthcoming, IMP's representatives took matters into their own hands: They commandeered an Aeroflot jet in Canada and released it only after the Russians paid up![44]

Other arbitration alternatives have proliferated in recent years. In addition to those mentioned, active centers for arbitration exist in Vancouver, Hong Kong, Cairo, Kuala Lumpur, Singapore, Buenos Aires, Bogotá, and Mexico City. A World Arbitration Institute was established in New York; in the United Kingdom, the Advisory, Conciliation and Arbitration Service (ACAS) has achieved great success in handling industrial disputes. An International Council for Commercial Arbitration (ICCA) was established to coordinate the far-flung activities of arbitration organizations. The ICCA meets in different locations around the world every 4 years.

The United Nations Conference on International Trade Law (UNCITRAL; www.uncitral.org) has also been a significant force in the area of arbitration. Its rules have become more or less standard, as many of the organizations just named have adopted them with some modifications. Many developing countries, for example, long held prejudices against the ICC, AAA, and other developed country organizations. Representatives of developing nations assumed that such organizations would be biased in favor of multinational corporations. Developing nations thus insisted on settlement in national courts, which was unacceptable to the multinational firms. This was especially true in Latin America, where the Calvo Doctrine required disputes arising with foreign investors to be resolved in national courts under national laws. The growing influence of the ICCA and UNCITRAL rules, coupled with the proliferation of regional arbitration centers, have contributed to changing attitudes in developing countries and resulted in the increased use of arbitration around the world.

The Regulatory Environment

The **regulatory environment** of global marketing consists of a variety of governmental and nongovernmental agencies that enforce laws or set guidelines for conducting business. These regulatory agencies address a wide range of marketing issues, including price control, valuation of imports and exports, trade practices, labeling, food and drug regulations, employment conditions, collective bargaining, advertising content, and competitive practices. As noted in *The Wall Street Journal*:

> Each nation's regulations reflect and reinforce its brand of capitalism—predatory in the U.S., paternal in Germany, and protected in Japan—and its social values. It's easier to open a business in the U.S. than in Germany because Germans value social consensus above risk-taking, but it's harder to hire people because Americans worry more about discrimination lawsuits. It's easier to import children's clothes in the U.S. than [in] Japan because Japanese bureaucrats defend a jumble of import restrictions, but it's harder to open bank branches across the U.S. because Americans strongly defend state prerogatives.[45]

---

[44] Dorothee J. Feils and Florin M. Sabac, "The Impact of Political Risk on the Foreign Direct Investment Decision: A Capital Budgeting Analysis," *Engineering* 45, no. 2 (2000), p. 129.
[45] Bob Davis, "Red-Tape Traumas: To All U.S. Managers Upset by Regulations: Try Germany or Japan," *The Wall Street Journal* (December 14, 1995), p. A1.

In most countries, the influence of regulatory agencies is pervasive, and an understanding of how they operate is essential to protect business interests and advance new programs. Executives at many global companies are realizing the need to hire lobbyists to represent their interests and to influence the direction of the regulatory process. For example, in the early 1990s McDonald's, Nike, and Toyota didn't have a single representative in Brussels. Today, each of the companies has several people representing its interests to the European Commission. U.S. law firms and consulting firms also have sharply increased their presence in Brussels; in an effort to gain insight into EU politics and access to its policymakers, some have hired EU officials. In all, there are currently approximately 15,000 lobbyists in Brussels representing about 1,400 companies and nonprofit organizations from around the world.[46]

Regional Economic Organizations: The EU Example

The overall importance of regional organizations such as the WTO and the EU was discussed in Chapter 3. The legal dimensions are important, however, and will be briefly mentioned here. The Treaty of Rome established the European Community (EC), the precursor to the EU. The treaty created an institutional framework in which a council (the Council of Ministers) serves as the main decision-making body, with each country member having direct representation. The other three main institutions of the community are the European Commission, the EU's executive arm; the European Parliament, the legislative body; and the European Court of Justice.

The 1987 Single European Act amended the Treaty of Rome and provided strong impetus for the creation of a single market beginning January 1, 1993. Although technically the target was not completely met, approximately 85 percent of the newer recommendations were implemented into national law by most member states by the target date, resulting in substantial harmonization. A relatively new body known as the European Council (a distinct entity from the Council of Ministers) was formally incorporated into the EC institutional structure by Article 2 of the 1987 act. Composed of heads of member states plus the president of the commission, the European Council's role is to define general political guidelines for the union and provide direction on integration-related issues such as monetary union.[47] Governments in Central and Eastern European countries that hope to join are currently getting their laws in line with those of the EU.

The Treaty of Rome contains hundreds of articles, several of which are directly applicable to global companies and global marketers. Articles 30 through 36 establish the general policy referred to as "Free Flow of Goods, People, Capital and Technology" among the member states. Articles 85 through 86 contain competition rules, as amended by various directives of the 20-member EU Commission. The commission is the administrative arm of the EU; from its base in Brussels, the commission proposes laws and policies, monitors the observance of EU laws, administers and implements EU legislation, and represents the EU to international organizations.[48] Commission members represent the union rather than their respective nations.

The laws, regulations, directives, and policies that originate in the commission must be submitted to the parliament for an opinion and then passed along to the council for a final decision. Once the council approves a prospective law, it becomes union law, which is somewhat analogous to U.S. federal law. Regulations automatically become law throughout the union; directives include a time frame for implementation by legislation in each member state. For example, in 1994 the commission issued a directive regarding use of trademarks in comparative advertising. Individual member nations of the EU worked to implement the directive; in the United Kingdom, the 1994 Trade Marks Act gave companies the right to apply for trademark

[46] Raphael Minder, "The Lobbyists Take Brussels by Storm," *Financial Times* (January 26, 2006), p. 7. See also Brandon Mitchener, "Standard Bearers: Increasingly, Rules of Global Economy Are Set in Brussels," *The Wall Street Journal* (April 23, 2002), p. A1.

[47] Klaus-Dieter Borchardt, *European Integration: The Origins and Growth of the European Union* (Luxembourg: Office for Official Publications of the European Communities, 1995), p. 30.

[48] Klaus-Dieter Borchardt, *The ABC of Community Law* (Luxembourg: Office for Official Publications of the European Communities, 1994), p. 25.

TABLE 5-5 Recent Cases Before the European Court of Justice/Court of First Instance

Country/Plaintiffs Involved	Issue
Chocoladefabriken Lindt & Sprüngli AG (Switzerland)/Franz Hauswirth GmbH (Austria)	Lindt markets gold-foil-wrapped chocolate Easter bunnies (Goldhase), for which it owns a trademark. Lindt sued Hauswirth for trademark infringement after the Austrian company began marketing its own foil-wrapped bunny. The Austrian Supreme Court asked the ECJ to rule on "bad faith" in trademark matters.[49]
L'Oréal (France)/Bellure (France)	Perfume marketer L'Oréal sued rival Bellure for marketing "knockoff" perfume that mimicked the bottles, packaging, and fragrances of L'Oréal's brands. The ECJ ruled in favor of L'Oréal on the grounds that the similarity of Bellure's products to L'Oréal's constituted an unfair advantage. The Court of Appeal later upheld the ECJ's decision.[50]
Italy/Monsanto, Syngenta, Pioneer Hi-Bred International	In 2000, fearing risk to human health, Italy banned foods containing four strains of genetically modified corn. The Italian court hearing the plaintiffs' appeal asked for ECJ intervention; in 2003, the ECJ ruled that the ban was not justified. The case was returned to Italy for a final ruling; the Italian court ruled that the government was not entitled to impose the ban.

protection of smells, sounds, and images and also provides improved protection against trademark counterfeiting.

With the rise of the single market, many industries are facing new regulatory environments. The European Court of Justice is the EU's highest legal authority. It is responsible for ensuring that EU laws and treaties are upheld throughout the union. Based in Luxembourg, it consists of two separate tribunals. The senior body is known as the Court of Justice; a separate entity, the Court of First Instance, hears cases involving commerce and competition (see Table 5-5).

Although the European Court of Justice plays a role similar to that of the U.S. Supreme Court, there are important differences. The European court cannot decide which cases it will hear, and it does not issue dissenting opinions. The court exercises jurisdiction over a range of civil matters involving trade, individual rights, and environmental law. For example, the court can assess damages against countries that fail to introduce directives by the date set. The court also hears disputes that arise among the 28 EU member nations on trade issues such as mergers, monopolies, trade barriers and regulations, and exports. The court is also empowered to resolve conflicts between national law and EU law. In most cases, the latter supersedes national laws of individual European countries.

Marketers must be aware, however, that national laws should always be consulted. National laws may be *stricter* than community law, especially in such areas as competition and antitrust. To the extent possible, community law is intended to harmonize national laws to promote the purposes defined in Articles 30 through 36. The goal is to bring the lax laws of some member states up to designated minimum standards. However, more restrictive positions may still exist in some national laws.

For example, Italy recently introduced the Reguzzoni-Versace Law. It is intended to regulate trade in textiles, leather, and footwear; it states that if at least two stages of production—there are four stages altogether—occur in Italy, a garment can be labeled "Made in Italy." In addition, the country or countries in which the remaining production stages took place must be identified. Reguzzoni-Versace was *supposed* to enter into force October 1, 2010. However, Brussels objected on grounds that the law conflicts with Article 34, which prohibits national measures providing restrictions to trade in the EU. EU regulators view Reguzzoni-Versace as "protectionist" and more stringent than EU law, which requires only that one main production stage take place in Europe.[51]

---

[49] Charles Forelle, "Europe's High Court Tries on a Bunny Suit Made of Chocolate," *The Wall Street Journal* (June 11, 2009), p. A1.
[50] Michael Peel, "L'Oréal in Legal Victory Over Rival," *Financial Times* (June 18, 2009).
[51] David Segal, "Is Italy Too Italian?" The New York Times (July 31, 2010), p. B1.

Summary

The political environment of global marketing is the set of governmental institutions, political parties, and organizations that are the expression of the people in the nations of the world. In particular, anyone engaged in global marketing should have an overall understanding of the importance of **sovereignty** to national governments. The political environment varies from country to country, and **political risk** assessment is crucial. It is also important to understand a particular government's actions with respect to taxes and seizures of assets. Historically, the latter have taken the form of **expropriation, confiscation**, and **nationalization**.

The legal environment consists of laws, courts, attorneys, legal customs, and practices. **International law** comprises the rules and principles that nation-states consider binding upon themselves. The countries of the world can be broadly categorized as having either **common-law** legal systems or **civil-law** legal systems. The United States and Canada and many former British colonies are common-law countries; most other countries are civil-law countries. A third system, **Islamic law**, predominates in the Middle East. Some of the most important legal issues pertain to **jurisdiction**, antitrust, and licensing. In addition, **bribery** is pervasive in many parts of the world; the **Foreign Corrupt Practices Act (FCPA)** applies to American companies operating abroad. Intellectual property protection is another critical issue. **Counterfeiting** is a major problem in global marketing; it often involves infringement of a company's **copyright, patent**, or **trademark** ownership. When legal conflicts arise, companies can pursue the matter in court or use **arbitration**.

The regulatory environment consists of agencies, both governmental and nongovernmental, that enforce laws or set guidelines for conducting business. Global marketing activities can be affected by a number of international or regional economic organizations; in Europe, for example, the EU makes laws governing member states. The WTO will have a broad impact on global marketing activities in the years to come. Although all three environments are complex, astute marketers plan ahead to avoid situations that might result in conflict, misunderstanding, or outright violation of national laws.

MyMarketingLab

Go to **mymktlab.com** for the following Assisted-graded writing questions:

5-1. What is sovereignty? Discuss your thoughts on what is an important consideration in the political environment of global marketing.

5-2. Discuss some of the differences between the legal environment of a country that embraces common law and one that observes civil law.

5-3. Mymarketinglab Only – comprehensive writing assignment for this chapter.

MyMarketingLab

Go to **mymktlab.com** to complete the problems marked with this icon .

Discussion Questions

 5-4. Describe some of the sources of political risk. Specifically, what forms can political risk take?

5-5. Global marketers can avoid legal conflicts by understanding the reasons conflicts arise in the first place. Identify and describe several legal issues that relate to global commerce.

5-6. You are an American traveling on business in the Middle East. As you are leaving country X, the passport control officer at the airport tells you there will be a passport "processing" delay of 12 hours. You explain that your plane leaves in 30 minutes, and the official suggests that a contribution of $50 would probably speed things up. If you comply with the suggestion, have you violated U.S. law? Explain.

 5-7. "See you in court" is one way to respond when legal issues arise. Why can that approach backfire when the issue concerns global marketing?

CASE 5-1   **CONTINUED (REFER TO PAGE 152)**
Mr. President—Free Pussy Riot!

Although Pussy Riot is generally associated with the opposition movement in Russia, the band members are quick to point out that they view themselves as artists rather than political activists. Not surprisingly, their cause has attracted considerable attention. At a concert in Moscow, pop star Madonna appeared with the words "Pussy Riot" on her back. A documentary film about the trial, *Pussy Riot: A Punk Prayer*, was screened at the 2013 South by Southwest Film, Interactive, and Music Festival in Austin, Texas.

There is other evidence that the political environment in Russia is precarious. Anna Politkovskaya, a reporter for Russia's *Novaya Gazeta* ("New Paper"), often filed stories critical of President Vladimir Putin. On October 7, 2006, Politkovskaya was gunned down by assailants as she returned from a shopping trip. Since 2000, more than a dozen journalists have been murdered in Russia. Observers note that Russia's independent press suffered as the Kremlin tightened control in anticipation of the 2008 presidential election.

Revenues from the fuel and energy sectors translate into government spending that comprises a whopping 40 percent of gross domestic product (GDP). A related problem is the fact that Russia's energy industry is dominated by a handful of huge conglomerates. The men who run these companies are known as *oligarchs*; at one time, Yukos Oil's Mikhail Khodorkovsky, Sibneft's Roman Abramovich, and their peers were among Russia's ultra-rich elite. However, there was widespread resentment among the Russian citizenry about the manner in which the oligarchs had gained control of their respective companies. In 2003, the Putin government sent a message to the oligarchs by arresting Khodorkovsky and several other oligarchs. In 2010, after having spent 7 years in prison, Khodorkovsky was sentenced to another 13.5 years of incarceration after a Moscow court found him guilty of money laundering and embezzlement.

Many observers viewed the verdict as evidence of the Russian government's desire to maintain an iron grip on the economy. There are other problems as well. Russia's entrenched bureaucracy is a barrier to increased economic freedom. Further, the banking system remains fragile and is in need of reform. Yevgeny Yasin, a former economy minister and an advocate of liberal reforms, noted recently, "The Russian economy is constrained by bureaucratic shackles. If the economy is to grow, these chains must be dropped. If we can overcome this feudal system of using power, we will create a stimulus for strong and sustainable economic growth and improve the standards of living."

Despite the political risk, a number of global companies are rolling the dice in an effort to capitalize on Russia's improved economic climate. For example, IKEA, the global furniture retailer, has opened dozens of new stores across Russia. However, after Russian bureaucrats allegedly sought bribes, the company had to lease diesel generators to ensure a stable supply of electricity. In 2010 IKEA announced that it was halting construction of a $1 billion mall and would focus on existing stores. France's Auchan and German retail chains Rewe and Metro are targeting the grocery market. By contrast, Carrefour and UK-based Tesco do not yet have a market presence due to the perceived risks. Walmart recently closed its Moscow office.

As the global economic downturn deepened and lending standards tightened around the globe, credit lines from Russia's banks dried up. Now, Russia's dependence on a single commodity for the bulk of its export earnings has turned out to be a liability. Despite talk of creating a Silicon Valley–type development in suburban Moscow, some observers have begun asking whether it is time to take the "R" out of "BRICS." Which emerging market should take its place? Indonesia is the top choice. The new acronym could be BIIC; an alternative would be BICI. As Richard Shaw, an investment advisor, notes, BICIS ("BEE-chees") "is catchy—kind of like an Italian purse."

Meanwhile, Washington's relationship with Moscow has been growing more strained. In December 2012, President Barack Obama

Exhibit 5-13 In 2012, Vladimir Putin was elected to a third term as president of Russia. Kremlin observers are concerned that liberal reforms begun under former president Dmitri Medvedev will be sidetracked as Putin consolidates his power and clamps down on protesters.

signed the Russia and Moldova Jackson-Vanik Repeal and Sergei Magnitsky Rule of Law Accountability Act. The first part of the law normalizes trade relations with Russia and Moldova by repealing Jackson-Vanik, a law dating to the mid-1970s. At that time, the Soviet Union was a non-market economy and restricted the right of its citizens to emigrate abroad; Jackson-Vanik denied most-favored-nation trading status to any country that blocked emigration rights. However, the Soviet Union broke apart in 1991, Russia has transitioned to a market economy, and today its citizens are free to travel abroad and emigrate. Moreover, Russia joined the WTO in 2012. For these reasons, Jackson-Vanik is no longer relevant.

The second part of the law is concerned with civil rights issues in Russia at the present time. Sergei Magnitsky was a Russian lawyer who uncovered evidence that Russian government officials had stolen $230 million in tax payments made by the Heritage Capital Management investment firm. When Magnitsky went public with his allegations in 2008, he was arrested. He died in jail under suspicious circumstances in November 2009. The law calls for the U.S. government to identify by name Russian officials believed to be complicit in Magnitsky's death; those persons will not be allowed to enter the United States and any assets held in the United States have been frozen.

Discussion Questions

5-8. Discuss why the Putin government decided to pursue legal action against the members of Pussy Riot.

5-9. What impact will the Magnitsky law have on the political and legal environment in Russia?

5-10. As the chief marketing officer of a global company, would you recommend establishing operations in Russia?

5-11. What response do you think the Russian government will make to passage of the Magnitsky law?

Sources: Courtney Weaver, "Freedom Fighter," *Financial Times Life & Arts* (December 15/16, 2012), p. 23; Melena Ryzik, "Carefully Calibrated for Protest," *The New York Times* (August 26, 2012), p. AR1; John Thornhill and Geoff Dyer, "Death of a Lawyer," *Financial Times Life & Arts* (July 28/29, 2012), pp. 2-3; Anatol Lieven, "How the Rule of Law May Come Eventually to Russia," *Financial Times* (December 6, 2010), p. 11; Roben Farzad, "The BRIC Debate: Drop Russia, Add Indonesia?" *BusinessWeek* (November 18, 2010); Neil Buckley, "From Shock Therapy to Retail Therapy: Russia's Middle Class Starts Spending," *Financial Times* (October 31, 2006), p. 13; David Lynch, "Russia Brings Revitalized Economy to the Table," *USA Today* (July 13, 2006), pp. 1B, 2B; Guy Chazan, "Kremlin Capitalism: Russian Car Maker Comes Under Sway of Old Pal of Putin," *The Wall Street Journal* (May 19, 2006), pp. A1, A7; Greg Hitt and Gregory L. White, "Hurdles Grow as Russia, U.S. Near Trade Deal," *The Wall Street Journal* (April 12, 2006), p. A4.

CASE 5-2
America's Cuban Conundrum

When Barack Obama was sworn in as the 44th president of the United States, he inherited a situation that had confounded his predecessors in the Oval Office for over half a century. The problem was Cuba, the tiny island nation in the Caribbean that, until recently, had been ruled by Fidel Castro. During his nearly 50 years in power, Fidel Castro remained unrepentant and clung to his socialist economic policies. In denouncing "neo-liberal globalization." Castro said, "The more contact we have with capitalism, the more repugnance I feel."

His health failing, Castro handed over the levers of power to his brother Raul. And, as President Obama set out an ambitious agenda for sweeping changes, many observers wondered whether it was time for a new era of trade, support, and cooperation with Cuba.

In the decades after Castro took power, America's trade embargo with the island nation was a matter of presidential policy. Then, in 1996, President Bill Clinton signed the Cuban Liberty and Democratic Solidarity Act, also known as the Helms-Burton Act. Clinton's action came after Cuban MiGs shot down two U.S. civilian airplanes, killing the four Cuban Americans who were on board. The act had two key provisions. First, it denied entry into the United States to corporate officers of companies from other countries doing business on U.S. property in Cuba that was confiscated by the Cuban government. Second, it allowed U.S. companies and citizens to sue foreign firms and investors doing business on U.S. property confiscated in Cuba. However, in July 1996 President Clinton ordered a 6-month moratorium on lawsuits. Washington pledged to keep the embargo in place until Castro held free elections and released political prisoners.

Cuba is a Communist outpost in the Caribbean where "socialism or death" is the national motto. After Castro came to power in 1959, his government took control of most private companies without providing compensation to the owners. American assets owned by both individuals and companies worth approximately $1.8 billion were among those expropriated; today, those assets are worth about $6 billion (see Table 1). President John F. Kennedy responded by imposing a trade embargo on the island nation. Five decades later, when Castro finally stepped down, no significant changes in policy were made.

In 1990, Castro opened his nation's economy to foreign investment; by the mid-1990s, foreign commitments to invest in Cuba totaled more than half a billion dollars. In 1993, Castro decreed that the U.S. dollar was legal tender although the peso would still be

Cuba's official currency. As a result, hundreds of millions of dollars were injected into Cuba's economy; Cuban exiles living in the United States were the source of much of the money. Cubans were able to spend the dollars in special stores that stocked imported foods and other hard-to-find products. In a country where doctors are among the highest-paid workers, with salaries equal to about $20 per month, the cash infusions significantly improved a family's standard of living. In 1994, *mercados agropecuarios* ("farmers' markets") were created as a mechanism to enable farmers to earn more money.

Cuba desperately needed investment and U.S. dollars, in part to compensate for the end of subsidies following the demise of the Soviet Union. Oil companies from Europe and Canada were among the first to seek potential opportunities in Cuba. Many American executives were concerned that lucrative opportunities would be lost as Spain, Mexico, Italy, Canada, and other countries moved aggressively into Cuba. Anticipating a softening in the U.S. government's stance,

Exhibit 5-14 Times are changing in Cuba. Under President Raúl Castro, decades of Soviet-style command-and-control economic policies are giving way to reform in agriculture and other sectors. Small-scale private businesses, including restaurants and car washes, are starting to appear now that many types of entrepreneurial activities have been legalized.
Source: Maisna/Shutterstock.

TABLE 1 American Companies Seeking Restitution from Cuba

Company	Amount of Claim (millions)
American Brands	$10.6
Coca-Cola	$27.5
General Dynamics	$10.4
ITT	$47.6
Lone Star Cement	$24.9
Standard Oil	$71.6
Texaco	$50.1

Source: U.S. Justice Department.

representatives from scores of U.S. companies visited Cuba regularly to meet with officials from state enterprises.

Throughout the 1990s, Cuba remained officially off-limits to all but a handful of U.S. companies. Some telecommunications and financial services were allowed; AT&T, Sprint, and other companies have offered direct-dial service between the United States and Cuba since 1994. Also, a limited number of charter flights were available each day between Miami and Havana. Sale of medicines was also permitted under the embargo. At a State Department briefing for business executives, Assistant Secretary of State for Inter-American Affairs Alexander Watson told his audience, "The Europeans and the Asians are knocking on the door in Latin America. The game is on and we can compete effectively, but it will be a big mistake if we leave the game to others." Secretary Watson was asked whether his comments on free trade applied to Cuba. "No, no. That simply can't be, not for now," Watson replied. "Cuba is a special case. This administration will maintain the embargo until major democratic changes take place in Cuba."

Within the United States, the government's stance toward Cuba had both supporters and opponents. Senator Jesse Helms pushed for a tougher embargo and sponsored a bill in Congress that would penalize foreign countries and companies for doing business with Cuba. The Cuban-American National Foundation actively engaged in anti-Cuba and anti-Castro lobbying. Companies that openly spoke out against the embargo included Carlson Companies, owner of the Radisson Hotel chain; grain-processing giant Archer Daniels Midland (ADM); and the Otis Elevator division of United Technologies. A spokesperson for Carlson noted, "We see Cuba as an exciting new opportunity—the forbidden fruit of the Caribbean." A number of executives, including Ron Perelman, whose corporate holdings include Revlon and Consolidated Cigar Corporation, were optimistic that the embargo would be lifted within a few years.

Meanwhile, opinion was divided on the question of whether the embargo was costing U.S. companies once-in-a-lifetime opportunities. Some observers argued that many European and Latin American investments in Cuba were short-term, high-risk propositions that would not create barriers to U.S. companies. The opponents of the embargo, however, pointed to evidence that some investments were substantial. Three thousand new hotel rooms were added by Spain's Grupo Sol Melia and Germany's LTI International Hotels. Both companies were taking advantage of the Cuban government's goal to increase tourism. Moreover, Italian and Mexican companies were snapping up contracts to overhaul the country's telecommunications infrastructure. Wayne Andreas, chairman of ADM, summed up the views of many American executives when he said, "Our embargo has been a total failure for 30 years. We ought to have all the Americans in Cuba doing all the business they can. It's time for a change."

The Helms-Burton Era

The Helms-Burton Act brought change, but not the type advocated by ADM's Andreas. The toughened U.S. stance signaled by Helms-Burton greatly concerned key trading partners even though Washington insisted that the act was consistent with international law. In particular, supporters noted that the "effects doctrine" of international law permits a nation to take "reasonable" measures to protect its interests when an act outside its boundaries produces a direct effect inside its boundaries. Unmoved by such rationalizations, the European Commission responded in mid-1996 by proposing legislation barring European companies from complying with Helms-Burton. Although such a "blocking statute" was permitted under Article 235 of the EU treaty, Denmark threatened to veto the action on the grounds that

issuing such a statute exceeded the European Commission's authority; Denmark's concerns were accommodated, and the legislation was adopted. Similarly, the Canadian government enacted legislation that would allow Canadian companies to retaliate against U.S. court orders regarding sanctions. Also, Canadian companies that complied with the U.S. sanctions could be fined $1 million for doing so.

In the fall of 1996, the WTO agreed to a request by the EU to convene a three-person trade panel that would determine whether Helms-Burton violated international trade rules. The official U.S. position was that Helms-Burton was a foreign policy measure designed to promote the transition to democracy in Cuba. The United States also hinted that, if necessary, it could legitimize Helms-Burton by invoking the WTO's national security exemption. That exemption, in turn, hinged on whether the United States faced "an emergency in international relations."

Meanwhile, efforts were underway to resolve the issue on a diplomatic basis. Sir Leon Brittan, trade commissioner for the EU, visited the United States in early November with an invitation for the United States and the EU to put aside misunderstandings and join forces in promoting democracy and human rights in Cuba. He noted:

> By opposing Helms-Burton, Europe is challenging one country's presumed right to impose its foreign policy on others by using the threat of trade sanctions. This has nothing whatever to do with human rights. We are merely attacking a precedent which the U.S. would oppose in many other circumstances, with the full support of the EU.

In January 1997, President Clinton extended the moratorium on lawsuits against foreign investors in Cuba. In the months following the Helms-Burton Act, a dozen companies ceased operating on confiscated U.S. property in Cuba. Stet, an Italian telecommunications company, agreed to pay ITT for confiscated assets, thereby exempting itself from possible sanctions. However, in some parts of the world, reaction to the president's action was lukewarm. The EU issued a statement noting that the action "falls short of the European Commission's hopes for a more comprehensive resolution of this difficult issue in trans-Atlantic relations." The EU also reiterated its intention of pursuing the case at the WTO. Art Eggleton, Canada's international trade minister, responded with a less guarded tone: "It continues to be unacceptable behavior by the United States in foisting its foreign policy onto Canada, and other countries, and threatening Canadian business and anybody who wants to do business legally with Cuba."

In February 1997, the WTO appointed the panel that would consider the dispute. However, Washington declared that it would boycott the panel proceedings on the grounds that the panel's members weren't competent to review U.S. foreign policy interests. Stuart Eizenstat, undersecretary for international trade at the U.S. Commerce Department, said, "The WTO was not created to decide foreign-policy and national-security issues." One expert on international trade law cautioned that the United States was jeopardizing the future of the WTO. Professor John Jackson of the University of Michigan School of Law said, "If the U.S. takes these kinds of unilateral stonewalling tactics, then it may find itself against other countries doing the same thing in the future."

The parties averted a confrontation at the WTO when the EU suspended its complaint in April, following President Clinton's pledge to seek congressional amendments to Helms-Burton. In particular, the president agreed to seek a waiver of the provision denying U.S. visas to employees of companies using expropriated property. A few days later, the EU and the United States announced plans to develop an agreement on property claims in Cuba with "common disciplines" designed to deter and inhibit investment in confiscated property.

The U.S. stance was seen in a new perspective following Pope John Paul II's visit to Cuba in January 1998. Many observers were heartened by Cuban authorities' decision to release nearly 300 political prisoners in February. In the fall of 2000, President Clinton signed a law that permitted Cuba to buy unlimited amounts of food and medicine from the United States. The slight liberalization of trade represented a victory for the U.S. farm lobby even though all purchases had to be made in cash.

In 2002, several pieces of legislation were introduced in the U.S. Congress that would have effectively undercut the embargo. One bill prohibited funding that would have been used to enforce sanctions on private sales of medicine and agricultural products. Another proposal would have had the effect of withholding budget money earmarked for enforcing both the ban on U.S. travel to Cuba and limits on monthly dollar remittances. Also in 2002, Castro began to clamp down on the growing democracy movement; about 70 writers and activists were jailed.

President George W. Bush responded by phasing out cultural travel exchanges between the United States and Cuba. In 2004, President Bush imposed new restrictions on Cuban Americans. Visits to immediate family members still living in Cuba were limited to one visit every 3 years. In addition, Cuban Americans wishing to send money to relatives could send no more than $1,200 per year.

The early months of Obama's administration saw a rollback of various restrictions. In April 2009, for example, the president lifted restrictions on family travel and money transfers. Although reactions to the announcement were mixed, a significant increase in travel on commercial airlines will not be possible until a bilateral aviation agreement is negotiated between the two nations.

At a Summit of the Americas meeting in Trinidad, President Obama declared, "The United States seeks a new beginning with Cuba. I know there is a longer journey that must be traveled in overcoming decades of mistrust, but there are critical steps we can take." Many observers were surprised by the conciliatory tone of Raul Castro's response to the U.S. president's overtures. Castro indicated a willingness to engage in dialogue about such seemingly intractable issues as human rights, political prisoners, and freedom of the press. "We could be wrong, we admit it. We're human beings. We're willing to sit down to talk, as it should be done," Castro said.

Raul's initial response to Obama's overture was indeed conciliatory, and in August 2009 the United States and Cuba held extended talks for the first time in at least 10 years. These talks included meetings between U.S. and Cuban governmental official and between U.S. officials and Cuban opposition figures. But the official position of the Cuban government, announced in September by Cuban Foreign Minister Bruno Rodriguez, was that the U.S. trade embargo should be lifted unilaterally without preconditions. Meanwhile, Obama, despite his overtures, appears to be linking any lifting of the embargo to Cuba's making progress on human rights.

Discussion Questions

5-12. What was the key issue that prompted the EU to take the Helms-Burton dispute to the WTO?

⭐ 5-13. Who benefits the most from an embargo of this type? Who suffers?

5-14. In light of the overtures U.S. President Barack Obama has made to Raul Castro, what is the likelihood that the United States and Cuba will resume diplomatic and trade relations during the Obama administration?

Sources: The authors are indebted to Hunter R. Clark, Professor of Law, Drake University Law School, for his contributions to this case. *Additional sources:* Alan Gomez, "U.S.-Cuba Relations: A Sea Change Today?" *USA Today* (January 14, 2013), pp. 1A, 2A; Damien Cave, "Cuba's Free-Market Farm Experiment Yields a Meager Crop," *The New York Times* (December 9, 2012), p. 5; John Paul Rathbone, "Cuba Reform Drive Brings Exiles to Homeland," *Financial Times* (January 28/29, 2012), p. 3; Laura Meckler, "Leaders' Comments Auger Warmer U.S.-Cuba Ties," *The Wall Street Journal* (April 18, 2009), p. A3; Alan Gomez, "Obama Could Change Relations with Cuba," *USA Today* (December 8, 2008), p. 4A; Jerry Perkins, "Making American Dollar Legal Tenderizes Tough Cuban Economy," *The Des Moines Register* (April 6, 2003), pp. 1D, 5D; Mary Anastasia O'Grady, "Threshing Out a Deal Between the Farmers and Fidel," *The Wall Street Journal* (September 20, 2002), p. A11; Pascal Fletcher, "Cuba Sees Itself as Shining Example Amid Global Troubles," *Financial Times* (September 19–20, 1998), p. 3; Carl Gershman, "Thanks to the Pope, Civil Society Stirs in Cuba," *The Wall Street Journal* (September 18, 1998), p. A11; Stuart E. Eizenstat, "A Multilateral Approach to Property Rights," *The Wall Street Journal* (April 11, 1997), p. A18; Therese Raphael, "U.S. and Europe Clash Over Cuba," *The Wall Street Journal* (March 31, 1997), p. A14.

CASE 5-3
Gambling Goes Global on the Internet

Mankind has engaged in gambling for many centuries. Archeologists have unearthed six-sided dice dating from around 3000 B.C. Ancient Egyptians played a game resembling backgammon. On the Indian subcontinent more than 3,500 years ago, there were public and private gambling houses, dice games, and betting on fights between animals. Farther east, Asian cultures also have a rich and long tradition of gambling. As cultural artifacts, playing cards had their primitive origins in Asia.

When Europeans arrived in North America, they found that the native peoples had been gambling in a variety of ways for centuries. Of course, the European settlers and colonists were no strangers to gambling themselves. They brought with them a penchant for gambling in various forms, including card playing, dice games, and lotteries. Even the Puritan settlers played cards.

Much of America's Revolutionary War was funded from lottery proceeds. Likewise, several of the young nation's new universities, including Columbia, Yale, and Princeton, were founded with substantial financial assistance from lotteries. America's connection to gambling has continued throughout its Civil War, two World Wars, and the emergence of Nevada as the icon of "Las Vegas–style" gambling.

Today, gambling has gone global. This is not surprising, given gambling's prevalence through time around the world. The Internet Age is creating new opportunities for gamblers as well as challenges for those wanting to limit the spread of and access to gambling. It is no longer necessary to be physically present in a casino or horse track to place bets on blackjack, sporting events, and horse racing. "Virtual" casinos now offer gamblers a wide range of online gaming opportunities.

In the 1990s, online casinos proliferated as Internet entrepreneurs sought to satisfy the worldwide demand for online gaming. Rodolphe Durand, a strategy professor and author of *The Pirate Organization*, has noted that, in Europe, these organizations originally operated in the "pirate space" as offshore activities because gambling "onshore" was illegal. Only later were the rules, regulations, and laws framed to allow a legitimate industry to flourish in Great Britain, France, and other European countries. Today, in fact, these gambling companies are based outside the United States because of questions about the legality of such activity under state and federal law. Some, including Gibraltar-based Party Digital Entertainment Plc and 888 Holdings Plc, are publicly traded corporations.

Despite its long history of gambling, the United States has also engaged in strict regulation of the industry. The surge in Internet gaming triggered efforts to ban such activity and to prosecute the principals of the so-called offshore online casinos. This regulatory action has angered governments in various countries, especially smaller countries where the online casinos are based. One country, Antigua and Barbuda (Antigua), filed a claim with the WTO in 2004 arguing that U.S. laws and policies pertaining to online gambling violate the terms of a fair trade agreement known as the General Agreement on Trade in Services (GATS).

Antigua claimed that the United States discriminated against foreign suppliers of "recreational services," including Internet gaming. The claim was based on the following argument: Even as it maintains a number of federal laws that prohibit offshore Internet gaming, the United States exempts off-track betting on horse races over the Internet from these same federal laws. According to the suit,

Exhibit 5-15 Jonathan Duhamel, winner of the "World Series of Poker" Main Event Championship. The 23-year-old Duhamel won more than $8 million in prize money.
Source: ROBYN BECK/AFP/Getty Images/Newscom.

this situation benefits domestic interests at the expense of offshore casinos.

In 2005, a WTO compliance panel ruled that the United States had, in fact, discriminated between foreign and domestic suppliers of gambling services. But the panel gave the United States an opportunity to show that the prevention of offshore betting was necessary as a means of protecting "public order and public morals." In March 2007, the WTO ruled that the continuing exemption for online betting on horse racing in the United States unfairly discriminated against foreign casinos. Further, the United States could restrict online gambling only as long as its laws were equally applied to American operators as well as to foreign operators, the ruling stated.

The WTO ruling allowed Antigua to seek trade sanctions against the United States. While Antigua may not have the economic muscle to bring about meaningful trade sanctions against the United States, it is possible that other countries affected by the United States ban, including Great Britain, may also petition the WTO for relief.

In 2006, U.S. authorities arrested David Caruthers, the British-born chief executive of Costa Rica–based BetonSports. Agents intercepted Caruthers while he was in the Dallas/Fort Worth airport en route from London to Costa Rica. In a 26-page indictment, the U.S. Department of Justice charged Caruthers and others with multiple counts of racketeering, conspiracy, and fraud. Caruthers was later convicted and sentenced to 33 months in prison.

The U.S. government has adopted a variety of measures to make Internet gambling in the United States illegal, or at least make access to it more difficult. For example, in the fall of 2006, U.S. President George W. Bush signed into law the SAFE Port Act, which includes the Unlawful Internet Gambling Enforcement Act (UIGEA). This measure prohibits U.S. banks, credit card companies, and other financial intermediaries from sending money to or receiving money from offshore casinos. Thus, the law makes it difficult for gamblers to fund their offshore accounts.

In summer 2010, U.S. Congressman Barney Frank sponsored a bill to legalize online poker. As Frank noted, "Some adults will spend their money foolishly, but it is not the purpose of the federal government to prevent them legally from doing it." The bill included provisions for taxing winnings from online poker; according to some estimates, this could yield some $40 billion in much-needed tax revenues over a 10-year period. Another rationale for removing the ban: Supporters of online poker are emphatic that poker is a game that involves skill; thus, it is not gambling.

The bill passed the House Financial Services Committee, but then, with midterm elections looming, lost momentum. Despite the prospect of generating much-needed revenue by taxing online poker, there was little interest in the issue on Capitol Hill. John Pappas is executive director of Poker Players Alliance (PPA), a lobbying group that is an advocate for legalization. "This won't be a priority of the Republican congress, and it wasn't a priority of the Democratic congress either," he said.

Adding to the complexity of online poker's legal status is the fact that, in 49 of the 50 American states, online poker is not illegal. Specifically, federal law allows states to legalize and regulate online poker games as long as the players and the virtual casinos are physically situated inside state borders. The State of Washington is the exception; in 2006, the state legislature passed a law that makes it a felony for the state's residents to play online poker.

Against this backdrop of legislative maneuvering, gray areas, and legal red tape, some online sites abandoned the U.S. market. Others, such as Full Tilt Poker and PokerStars, stayed. Ultimately, an estimated 1.8 million professional and amateur poker players in the United States were playing online each year. On a typical night, as many as 100,000 people logged on to Full Tilt Poker. Another 200,000 players were typically active on PokerStars.

In addition, large numbers of poker fans were tuning in to TV shows such as ESPN's *World Series of Poker* and *Poker After Dark* on NBC. Significant advertising dollars for these shows came from online poker companies. In addition, the online operators paid production costs for some of the programs; in the broadcast industry, such arrangements are known as "time buys."

The advertisers typically operated two types of Web sites. Commercials for "tutorial" or "educational" poker sites with the Internet suffix ".net" urged viewers to log on and "play for free." In addition, players who appeared on the shows were paid to wear hats, shirts, and other apparel displaying logos for the ".net" sites. By contrast, "dot.com" poker sites were not mentioned in the commercials. For example, online gaming operator PokerStars spent between $20 million and $30 million annually to advertise on ESPN. However, the ads were for PokerStars.net, an educational site, not PokerStars.com, the actual online gaming site. This tactic allowed the broadcasters to skirt federal laws that prohibit the promotion of illegal activities such as prostitution.

On April 15, 2011, the U.S. Department of Justice cracked down again. The agency unsealed indictments against the founders of the three-largest online poker companies. The indictments alleged that the defendants had engaged in bank fraud, money laundering, and other violations of the UIGEA. The Department of Justice also seized the Internet addresses of, and blocked access to, Full Tilt Poker and other sites.

The effects of what the industry has called "Black Friday" continue to develop. On July 26, 2011, Bodog announced that it was leaving the U.S. market at the end of 2011. Bodog has been a leading Internet poker site, and its exit from the United States indicated that few companies are willing to risk continuing online operations for U.S. residents.

Against this backdrop, there is the continuing effort in states to legalize intra-state Internet gambling. The New Jersey legislature approved a bill that would have made it the first state to allow intra-state Internet gambling, but Governor Chris Christie vetoed it. Iowa and Nevada are among the states contemplating the legalization of Internet gambling for their residents. In Iowa, for example, an estimated 150,000 residents play online poker. Legalized play through the state's 17 regulated casinos would generate an estimated $30 million to $35 million in annual tax revenues. U.S. Digital Gaming is a California company whose management has expressed an interest in operating Iowa's online poker network. As Kirk Uhler, the company's vice president of government affairs, noted, "What is driving this is the recognition that you have an existing activity that's already taking place in an unregulated environment, and the revenue is all flowing overseas."

Discussion Questions

5-15. Do you think that the UIGEA unfairly discriminates against offshore gaming companies?

5-16. How likely is it that legislative efforts to prevent people from gambling will be successful?

5-17. At a time when the U.S. government is desperate to generate revenues, would it make sense for policymakers to license, regulate, and tax Internet gambling? Do the results of the 2012 presidential election and the recent economic crisis create the conditions for tapping this new revenue source? Or, should concerns about the erosion of social values dominate the discussion of Internet gambling?

Sources: This case was prepared by Keith Miller, Ellis and Nelle Levitt Distinguished Professor of Law, Drake University Law School. *Additional sources:* Anthony N. Cabot and Keith C. Miller, *The Law of Gambling and Regulated Gaming* (Durham, NC: Carolina Academic Press Case Law Series, 2011); David Streitfeld, "Tech Industry Sets Its Sights on Gambling," *The New York Times* (February 18, 2013), pp. A1, A11; Sam Schechner and Alexandra Berzon, "Inside the TV Poker Machine," *The Wall Street Journal* (July 26, 2011), p. B1; Alexandra Berzon, "Online Poker Players Face Big Life Changes," *The Wall Street Journal* (April 18, 2011), p. B1; Ross Tieman, "Rock and Roll and Research," *Financial Times* (March 7, 2011), p. 11; Jennifer Jacobs, "Proposal Would Regulate, Legalize Online Poker," *The Des Moines Register* (February 25, 2011), p. 1; Michael Kaplan, "Gambling in the Gray," *Cigar Aficionado* (February 2011), pp. 112–114; Sewell Chan, "Congress Rethinks Its Ban on Internet Gambling," *The New York Times* (July 29, 2010), p. A1; Roger Blitz, "PartyGaming Eyes Place at the U.S. Online Table," *Financial Times* (April 8, 2009), p. 20; Blitz, "A Better Hand," *Financial Times* (February 4, 2009), p. 7; Blitz, "The Unlucky Gambler," *Financial Times* (July 23/23, 2006), p. 7; Blitz and Tom Braithwaite, "Online Operators Weigh Up the Odds," *Financial Times* (July 19, 2006), p. 21; Scott Miller and Christina Binkley, "Trade Body Rules Against U.S. Ban on Web Gambling," *The Wall Street Journal* (March 25, 2004), p. A2.

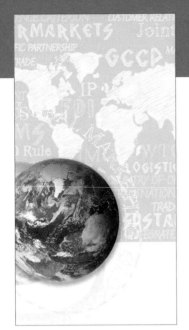

6

Global Information Systems and Market Research

 CASE 6-1
Nestlé's Middle East Investment in Market Research

For years, Nestlé Middle East has been known for innovation and creativity. The company motto, *"Good Food, Good Life"* is the promise that Nestlé is committed to delivering on every day, everywhere. Nestlé, with its wide range of products is known for high quality, taste and nutrition which include bottled water, ice cream, chocolate, dairy, and baby food among others. In the Middle East alone, Nestlé has over 60 products. Even with formidable competitors like Procter and Gamble (P&G), Coca-Cola and Unilever vying for the same space, Nestlé manages to retain a good market share by focusing on nutritional value and healthy lifestyle. How

Exhibit 6-1 Nestlé SA, a company more than 140 years old, has come a long way from its humble beginnings in the late 19th century in Vevey, Switzerland to becoming a global brand employing over 275,000 people in 481 factories, and with operations in nearly every country on the map. Nestlé, which has been operating successfully in the Middle East for the past 70 years, founded Nestlé Middle East in 1997 and has since invested more than US $400 million in the region, owning and operating 14 factories and 16 offices. Nestlé's products among others include Maggi, KitKat, Cerelac, and the eponymous Nescafé. The company today boasts of more than 5,500 cups of Nescafé instant coffee, in various flavors, and catering to different tastes and preferences, being consumed every second around the globe.

did Nestlé manage to maintain its position in the Middle East? Nestlé operates successfully in more than 80 countries with the help of intensified market research and subsequently, has developed a diversified portfolio of products. Nestlé, the Switzerland-based nutrition, health and wellness company, acts as a regional hub in the Middle East, catering to the needs of 13 countries in the vicinity. Nestlé Middle East was founded in 1997 in Jebel Ali Free Zone, Dubai and at present, it owns and operates 17 factories and 37 offices in the region, employing over 7,000 people across all operations. Nestlé Middle East has invested more than $400 million since its foundation, for establishing factories in high growth markets and research and development (R&D). To learn more about the way Nestlé invests and conducts research, turn to the continuation of Case 6-1 at the end of this chapter.

When researching any market, marketers must know where to go to obtain information, what subject areas to investigate and what data to seek, the different ways to acquire it, and the various types of analyses that will lead to a better understanding of consumers with important insights into their framework. It is the marketer's good luck that a veritable cornucopia of market information is available on the Internet. A few keystrokes can yield literally hundreds of articles, research findings, and Web sites that offer a wealth of information about particular country markets. Even so, marketers must do their homework if they are to make the most of modern information technology. First, they need to understand the importance of information technology and marketing information systems as strategic assets. Second, they should have a general understanding of the formal market research process. Finally, they should know how to manage the marketing information collection system and the marketing research effort. These topics are the focus of this chapter.

LEARNING OBJECTIVES

1 Discuss the role of information technology in a global company's decision-making processes.

2 Understand the importance of direct perception in the global marketing research process.

3 Explain some of the ways global marketers adapt the individual steps in the traditional market research process.

4 Compare the way a multinational firm organizes the marketing research effort with the way a global or transnational firm approaches the organizing issue.

5 Explain how information's role as a strategic asset affects the structure of global corporations.

Information Technology and Business Intelligence for Global Marketing

The phrase **information technology (IT)** refers to an organization's processes for creating, storing, exchanging, using, and managing information. A **management information system (MIS)** provides managers and other decision makers with a continuous flow of information about company operations. MIS is a broad term that can be used to refer to a system of hardware and software that a company uses to manage information. (The term can also be used to describe an IT department; in this case, it refers to people, hardware, and software.) An MIS should provide a means for gathering, analyzing, classifying, storing, retrieving, and reporting relevant data. The MIS should also cover important aspects of a company's external environment, including customers and competitors.

One component of a firm's MIS is a business intelligence (BI) network that helps managers make decisions; its major objective is:

…to enable interactive access to data, enable manipulation of these data, and to provide managers and analysts with the ability to conduct appropriate analysis. By analyzing historical and current data, situations, and performances, decision makers get valuable insights upon which they can base more informed and better decisions.[1]

Global competition intensifies the need for effective MIS and business intelligence that are accessible throughout the company. As Jean-Pierre Corniou, chief information officer (CIO) at Renault, noted:

> My vision is to design, build, sell, and maintain cars. Everything I do is directly linked to this, to the urgent need to increase turnover, margins, and brand image. Every single investment and expense in the IT field has to be driven by this vision of the automotive business.[2]

Caterpillar, GE, Boeing, FedEx, Diageo, Ford, Toyota, and many other companies with global operations have made significant investments in IT in recent years. Such investment is typically directed at upgrading a company's computer hardware and software. Microsoft, Sun Microsystems, SAP, Oracle, and IBM are some of the beneficiaries of this trend. All are global enterprises, and many of their customers are global as well. Vendors of complex software systems can find it difficult to achieve 100 percent customer satisfaction. Thomas Siebel, founder of Siebel Systems, explains how his company met this challenge:

> Siebel Systems is a global company, not a multinational company. I believe the notion of the multinational company—where a division is free to follow its own set of business rules—is obsolete, though there are still plenty around. Our customers—global companies like IBM, Zurich Financial Services, and Citicorp—expect the same high level of service and quality, and the same licensing policies, no matter where we do business with them around the world. Our human resources and legal departments help us create policies that respect local cultures and requirements worldwide, while at the same time maintaining the highest standards. We have one brand, one image, one set of corporate colors, one set of messages, across every place on the planet.[3]

Unlike the public Internet, an **intranet** is a private network that allows authorized company personnel or outsiders to share information electronically in a secure fashion without generating mountains of paper. Intranets allow a company's information system to serve as a 24-hour nerve center, enabling Amazon.com, Dell, and other companies to operate as *real time enterprises* (RTEs). The RTE model is expected to grow in popularity as wireless Internet access becomes more widely available.

An **electronic data interchange (EDI)** system allows a company's business units to submit orders, issue invoices, and conduct business electronically with other company units as well as with outside companies. One of the key features of EDI is that its transaction formats are universal. This enables computer systems at different companies to speak the same language. Walmart is legendary for its sophisticated EDI system; for years, vendors had received orders from the retailer on personal computers using dial-up modems connected to third-party transmission networks. In 2002, Walmart informed vendors that it was switching to an Internet-based EDI system. The switch has saved both time and money; the modem-based system was susceptible to transmission interruptions, and the cost was between $0.10 and $0.20 per thousand characters transmitted. Any vendor that now wishes to do business with Walmart must purchase and install the necessary computer software.[4]

Poor operating results can often be traced to insufficient data and information about events both inside and outside the company. For example, when a new management team took over the

---

[1] Efraim Turban, Ramesh Sharda, Jay E. Aronson, and David King, *Business Intelligence: A Managerial Approach* (Upper Saddle River, NJ: Pearson Education, 2008), p. 9.

[2] Jean-Pierre Corniou, "Bringing Business Technology Out into the Open," *Financial Times—Information Technology Review* (September 17, 2003), p. 2.

[3] Bronwyn Fryer, "High-Tech the Old-Fashioned Way: An Interview with Tom Siebel of Siebel Systems," *Harvard Business Review* (March 2001), pp. 118–125. In 2006, Siebel Systems merged with Oracle.

[4] Ann Zimmerman, "To Sell Goods to Walmart, Get on the Net," *The Wall Street Journal* (November 21, 2003), pp. B1, B6.

→ THE CULTURAL CONTEXT

Tesco's Clubcard

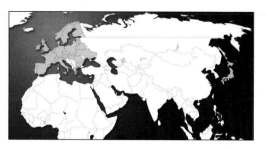

SYNC • THINK • LEARN

MyMarketingLab

As the UK's number 1 supermarket chain, Tesco is "the one to beat." Tesco's management team faces the constant challenge of staying ahead of fast-growing competitors. These include local chains such as Sainsbury as well as Asda, which is owned by retail giant Walmart.

One of the keys to Tesco's success is a loyalty program tied to its Clubcard. Signing up for the program is easy: Shoppers fill out applications (either at the store or online) that include questions regarding family demographics and dietary preferences. The 15 million households with Clubcards represent 80 percent of Tesco's customer base. Shoppers present their cards at checkout and are awarded two points for every £1 spent (see Exhibit 6-2).

For every 100 points accumulated, shoppers receive a £1 voucher that can be redeemed for future grocery purchases or used with airline frequent-flyer programs. Tesco partners with other retailers such as Pizza Express, where vouchers are worth four times their face value. Needless to say, the Clubcard is a hit with university students! Tesco also offers different incentives to different segments; for example, high spenders are offered vouchers that are worth triple points when redeemed on certain categories of merchandise.

But the Clubcard program does more than allow Tesco to reward its customers. It also provides Tesco's IT team with a clear picture of what is selling, what isn't selling, and where the gaps are in its product assortment. The Clubcard program is managed by Dunnhumby, an independent consultancy located near London. Each product in the database is scored on price and dozens of other dimensions. As an example of the value of the Clubcard program, Dunnhumby cofounder Clive Humby points to wine sales:

> In the wine department, we could see that people were trading up to stuff Tesco didn't stock. At Christmas, people wanted to buy 'posh' wine; those who usually bought cheap wine went from spending £2.99 a bottle to £5.99 a bottle—but

where were the people who should have been trading up from £5.99 to £7.99? They were at [specialty wine store] Oddbins because Tesco didn't have a full-enough range.

Dunnhumby groups Tesco customers into various clusters based on the similarity of the contents of their shopping carts. For example, analysts have dubbed one segment "Finer Foods"; it is comprised of time-deprived, affluent customers who choose upscale products. When the data indicated that these shoppers weren't buying fine wine or cheese at Tesco, the company upgraded its offerings and introduced a house brand bearing the "Tesco's Finest" label. By contrast, traditional shoppers are "Makers" who buy ingredients to prepare home-cooked meals. They gravitate toward Tesco's lower-priced "Tesco Value" products such as beer, baked beans, canned tomatoes, and noodles.

By combining household information with weekly purchase behavior data, Tesco is able to tailor promotions to specific customer segments. Did a shopper buy diapers for the first time? Tesco sends that household coupons for baby wipes and beer. Why beer? New dads who are staying home with the baby can't get out to the local pub as often as they once did. So, they stock up on beer to consume at home.

Clubcard also gives Tesco a tactical advantage over Walmart's Asda stores. Walmart's value proposition is very clear: Low prices. To prevent the most-value-conscious shoppers from defecting, Tesco mined its database to identify Clubcard users who bought the lowest-priced grocery items. Managers identified several hundred items that the value hunters bought regularly; prices on those items were then lowered. The result: The shoppers stayed with Tesco instead of switching to Asda. Tesco currently leads Asda in share of UK grocery sales by a margin of two to one.

Sources: Elizabeth Rigby, "Fresh Horizons Uneasily Scanned," *Financial Times* (September 19, 2010); Andrea Felsted, "Tesco Takes Clubcard Route to Buoyant Sales," *Financial Times* (January 12, 2010); Andrea Felsted, "Tesco Experiments with Clubcard," *Financial Times* (September 8, 2010); Cecilie Rohwedder, "Stores of Knowledge: No. 1 Retailer in Britain Uses 'Clubcard' to Thwart Wal-Mart," *The Wall Street Journal* (June 6, 2006), pp. A1, A16.

Exhibit 6-2 Tesco's Clubcard is a loyalty program that the UK-based grocery store chain uses to reward customers; shoppers receive points based on purchase amounts. Points are converted to voucher that can be redeemed for merchandise. Tesco also uses Clubcard to collect data on shopping preferences and patterns. Clubcard has been rolled out in many of Tesco's international locations, including Poland.
Source: AFP/Getty Images

U.S. unit of Adidas AG, the German athletic shoemaker, the team discovered that data were not available on normal inventory turnover rates. A new reporting system revealed that archrivals Reebok and Nike turned inventories five times a year, compared with twice a year at Adidas. This information was used to tighten the marketing focus on the best-selling Adidas products. In Japan, 7-Eleven's computerized distribution system provides it with a competitive advantage in the convenience store industry. Every 7-Eleven store is linked with every other store and with distribution centers. As one retail analyst noted:

> With the system they have established, whatever time you go, the shelves are never empty. If people come in at 4 A.M. and the stores don't have what they want, that will have a big impact on what people think of the store.[5]

Globalization puts increased pressure on companies to achieve as many economies as possible. IT provides a number of helpful tools. As noted previously, EDI links with vendors enable retailers to improve inventory management and restock hot-selling products in a timely, cost-effective manner. In addition to EDI, retailers are increasingly using a technique known as **efficient consumer response (ECR)** in an effort to work more closely with vendors on stock replenishment. ECR can be defined as a joint initiative of members of a supply chain working together to improve and optimize aspects of the supply chain to benefit customers. ECR systems utilize **electronic point of sale (EPOS)** data gathered by checkout scanners to help retailers identify product sales patterns and how consumer preferences vary with geography. Although currently more popular in the United States, the ECR system is gaining traction in Europe. Companies such as Carrefour, Metro, Coca-Cola, and Henkel have all embraced ECR. Supply-chain innovations such as radio frequency identification tags (RFID) are likely to provide increased momentum for the use of ECR.

EPOS, ECR, and other IT tools are also helping businesses improve their ability to target consumers and increase loyalty. The trend among retailers is to develop customer-focused strategies that will personalize and differentiate the business. In addition to point-of-sale (POS) scanner data, loyalty programs that use electronic smart cards provide retailers with important information about shopping habits. A new business tool that helps companies collect, store, and analyze customer data is called **customer relationship management (CRM)**. Although industry experts offer varying descriptions and definitions of CRM, the prevailing view is that CRM is a philosophy that values two-way communication between the company and the customer. Every point of contact ("touchpoint" in CRM-speak) that a company has with a consumer or business customer—via a Web site, a warranty card or sweepstakes entry, a payment on a credit card account, or an inquiry to a call center—is an opportunity to collect data. CRM tools allow companies such as American Express, Dell, HSBC, Sharp, and Sony to determine which customers are most valuable and to react in a timely manner with customized product and service offerings that closely match customer needs. If implemented correctly, CRM can make employees more productive and enhance corporate profitability; it also benefits customers by providing value-added products and services.

A company's use of CRM can manifest itself in various ways. Some are visible to consumers, others are not; some make extensive use of leading-edge information technology, others do not. In the hotel industry, for example, CRM can take the form of front desk staff who monitor, respond to, and anticipate the needs of repeat customers. A visitor to Amazon.com who buys the latest U2 CD encounters CRM when he or she gets the message "Customers who bought this title also bought Bruce Springsteen's *Working on a Dream.*" CRM can also be based on the click path that a Web site visitor follows. In this case, however, Internet users may be unaware that a company is tracking their behaviors and interests.

One challenge of using CRM is integrating data into a complete picture of the customer and his or her relationship to the company and its products or services. This is sometimes referred to as a "360-degree view of the customer." The challenge is compounded for global marketers. Subsidiaries in different parts of the world may use different customer data formats, and commercial CRM products may not support all the target languages. In view of such issues, industry experts recommend implementing global CRM programs in phases. The first phase could focus

---

[5] Bethan Hutton, "Japan's 7-Eleven Sets Store by Computer Links," *Financial Times* (March 17, 1998), p. 26.

on a specific task such as *sales force automation* (SFA); this term refers to a software system that automates routine aspects of sales and marketing functions such as lead assignment, contact follow-up, and opportunity reporting. An SFA system can also analyze the cost of sales and the effectiveness of marketing campaigns. Some SFA software can assist with quote preparation and management of other aspects of a sales campaign, such as mass mailings and conference or convention attendee follow-up.

For example, an important first step in implementing a CRM system could be to utilize SFA software from a company such as Oracle or Onyx Software. The objective at this stage of the CRM effort would be to provide sales representatives in all country locations with access via an Internet portal to sales activities throughout the organization. To simplify the implementation, the company could require that all sales activities be recorded in English. Subsequently, marketing, customer service, and other functions could be added to the system.[6]

Privacy issues also vary widely from country to country. In the EU, for example, a Directive on Data Collection has been in effect since 1998. Companies that use CRM to collect data about individual consumers must satisfy the regulations in each of the EU's 27 member countries. There are also restrictions about sharing such information across national borders. In 2000, the U.S. Department of Commerce and the EU concluded a Safe Harbor agreement that establishes principles for privacy protection for companies that wish to transfer data to the United States from Europe. The principles, which are posted in detail at www.export.gov/safeharbor, include:

- The purposes for which information is collected and used and the means by which individuals can direct inquiries to the company
- An "opt out" option to prevent the disclosure of personal information to third parties
- An agreement that information can only be transferred to third parties that are in compliance with Safe Harbor Principles
- Individuals must have access to information collected about them and must be able to correct or delete inaccurate information

Databases called **data warehouses** are frequently an integral part of a company's CRM system. Data warehouses can serve other purposes as well. For example, they can help retailers with multiple store locations fine-tune product assortments. Company personnel, including persons who are not computer specialists, can access data warehouses via standard Web browsers. Behind the familiar interfaces, however, is specialized software capable of performing multidimensional analyses that use sophisticated techniques such as linear programming and regression analysis. This enhances the ability of managers to respond to changing business conditions by adjusting marketing mix elements. MicroStrategy, an information services company in the United Kingdom, is one of several companies creating data warehouses for clients. As former Vice President Stewart Holness explains, "Many corporations have a vast amount of information which they have spent money accumulating, but they have not been able to distribute it. The Web is the perfect vehicle for it."[7]

As Holness' comment makes clear, the Internet is revolutionizing corporate information processing (see Chapter 15). Companies slow to recognize the revolution risk falling behind competitors. For example, Germany is home to the *Mittelstand*, a group of 3 million small and mid-size manufacturers that have traditionally been focused and successful global marketers. The *Mittelstand* are often cited as an illustration of how small companies can help propel economic growth and sustain prosperity. As Dietmar Hopp, chief executive of Germany's largest software firm, noted in the mid-1990s:

With globalization there is no difference now between the *Mittelstand* and big companies—the business processes are comparable. It is only a matter of time before foreign competitors use the Internet to strengthen their foothold in Germany. German companies should follow their example and build up their U.S. and Asian activities through electronic marketing and commerce.[8]

---

[6] Gina Fraone, "Facing Up to Global CRM," *eWeek* (July 30, 2001), pp. 37–41.
[7] Vanessa Houlder, "Warehouse Parties," *Financial Times* (October 23, 1996), p. 8. See also John W. Verity, "Coaxing Meaning Out of Raw Data," *BusinessWeek* (February 3, 1997), pp. 134+.
[8] Graham Bowley, "In the Information Technology Slow Lane," *Financial Times* (November 11, 1997), p. 14.

The evidence suggests that *Mittelstand* companies have gotten the message. According to a study conducted by IBM Germany and *Impulse*, a German magazine for entrepreneurs, most *Mittelstand* companies now have Web homepages. Approximately one-third use the Web for e-business activities such as ordering and cross-linking with suppliers.[9]

These examples show just some of the ways that IT is affecting global marketing. However, EDI, ECR, EPOS, SFA, CRM, and other aspects of IT do not simply represent marketing issues; rather, they are organizational imperatives. The tasks of designing, organizing, and implementing systems for business intelligence and information gathering must be coordinated in a coherent manner that contributes to the organization's overall strategic direction. Modern IT tools provide the means for a company's marketing information system and research functions to provide relevant information in a timely, cost-efficient, and actionable manner.

Overall, then, the global organization has the following needs:

- An efficient, effective system that will scan and digest published sources and technical journals in the headquarters country as well as in all countries in which the company has operations or customers.
- Daily scanning, translating, digesting, abstracting, and electronic inputting of information into a market intelligence system. Today, thanks to advances in IT, full-text versions of many sources are available online as PDF files. Print documents can easily be scanned, digitized, and added to a company's information system.
- Expanding information coverage in other regions of the world.

Sources of Market Information

Although environmental scanning is a vital source of information, research has shown that headquarters executives of global companies obtain as much as two-thirds of the information they need from *personal sources*. A great deal of external information comes from executives based abroad in company subsidiaries, affiliates, and branches. These executives are likely to have established communication with distributors, consumers, customers, suppliers, and government officials. A striking feature of the global corporation—and a major source of competitive strength—is the role that executives abroad play in acquiring and disseminating information about the world environment. Headquarters executives generally acknowledge that company executives overseas are the people who know best what is going on in their areas.

The information issue exposes one of the key weaknesses of a domestic company: Although more attractive opportunities may be present outside existing areas of operation, they are likely to go unnoticed by inside sources in a domestic company because the scanning horizon tends to end at the home-country border. Similarly, a company with limited geographical operations may be at risk because internal sources abroad tend to scan only the information about their own countries or regions.

Direct sensory perception provides a vital background for the information that comes from human and documentary sources. Direct perception gets all the senses involved. It means seeing, feeling, hearing, smelling, or tasting for oneself to find out what is going on in a particular country, rather than getting secondhand information by hearing or reading about a particular issue. Some information is easily available from other sources, but sensory experience of it is needed for it to sink in. Often, the background information or context one gets from observing a situation can help fill in the big picture. For example, Walmart's first stores in China stocked a number of products—extension ladders and giant bottles of soy sauce, for example—that were inappropriate for local customers. Joe Hatfield, Walmart's top executive for Asia, began roaming the streets of Shenzhen in search of ideas. His observations paid off; when Walmart's giant store in Dalian opened in April 2000, a million shoppers passed through its doors in the first week (see Exhibit 6-3). They snapped up products ranging from lunch boxes to pizza topped with corn and

---

[9] "E-Business in the *Mittelstand*," www.impulse.de (accessed January 23, 2002).

Exhibit 6-3 Joe Menzer, CEO and President of Walmart International, shakes hands with two employees of Beijing Walmart.
Source: © Lou Linwei / Alamy.

pineapple.[10] When Jim Stengel was chief marketing officer at Procter & Gamble, he moved his managers away from a preoccupation with research data to a wider view based on direct perception. As Stengel noted:

> We often find consumers can't articulate it. That's why we need to have a culture where we are understanding. There can't be detachment. You can't just live away from the consumer and the brand and hope to gain your insights from data or reading or talking to academics. You have to be experiential. And some of our best ideas are coming from people getting out there and experiencing and listening.[11]

Direct perception can also be important when a global player dominates a company's domestic market. Such was the case with Microsoft and its Xbox video game system, which was launched in a market dominated by Sony. Cindy Spodek-Dickey, Microsoft's group manager for national consumer promotions and sponsorships, took Xbox "on the road" with various promotional partners such as the Association of Volleyball Professionals (AVP). At AVP tournaments in different cities, spectators (and potential customers) had the opportunity to visit the Xbox hospitality tent to try out the new system. At one tournament event, Spodek-Dickey explained the importance of informal market research:

> What are the other sponsors doing? What's the crowd into? What brands are they wearing? How are they interacting with our property? I'll stop them as they come out of the tent and say: "What do you think? What do you like about Xbox? What do you think of your PlayStation?" It's mother-in-law research. I wouldn't want to stake a $10 million ad campaign on it, but I think it keeps you credible and real. When you start to hear the same feedback, three, four, five times, you'd better be paying attention....I believe it is part of any good marketer's job to be in touch with their audience and their product. There's no substitute for face-to-face, eye-to-eye, hand-to-hand.[13]

> "Case studies from the footwear industry show the importance of direct perception in identifying market opportunities. Diego Della Valle is CEO of Tod's; Mario Moretti Polegato heads Geox; and Blake Mycoskie founded TOMS. What they have in common is that all three were traveling abroad, viewing and experiencing the world, when inspiration struck."[12]
>
> —Mark C. Green, Professor of Marketing, Simpson College

---

[10] Peter Wonacott, "Walmart Finds Market Footing in China," *The Wall Street Journal* (July 17, 2000), p. A31.
[11] Gary Silverman, "How May I Help You?" *Financial Times* (February 4–5, 2006), p. W2.
[12] Mark C. Green, "Entrepreneurship, Italian Style." Paper presented at Schumptoberfest Conference on Innovation and Entrepreneurship in the Liberal Arts, Grinnell College (October 2012).
[13] Kenneth Hein, "We Know What Guys Want," *Brandweek* (November 14, 2002), p. M48.

Formal Market Research

Information is a critical ingredient in formulating and implementing a successful marketing strategy. As described earlier, a marketing information system should produce a continuous flow of information. **Market research**, by contrast, is the project-specific, systematic gathering of data. The American Marketing Association defines *marketing research* as "the activity that links the consumer, customer, and public to the marketer through information."[14] In **global market research**, this activity is carried out on a global scale. The challenge of global market research is to recognize and respond to the important national differences that influence the way information can be obtained. These include cultural, linguistic, economic, political, religious, historical, and market differences.

Michael Czinkota and Ilkka Ronkainen note that the objectives of international market research are the same as the objectives of domestic research. However, they have identified four specific environmental factors that may require international research efforts to be conducted differently than domestic research. First, researchers must be prepared for new parameters of doing business. Not only will there be different requirements, but the ways in which rules are applied may differ as well. Second, "cultural megashock" may occur as company personnel come to grips with a new set of culture-based assumptions about conducting business. Third, a company entering more than one new geographic market faces a burgeoning network of interacting factors; research may help prevent psychological overload. Fourth, company researchers may have to broaden their definition of competitors in international markets to include competitive pressures that would not be present in the domestic market.[15]

Market research can be conducted in two different ways. One is to design and implement a study with in-house staff. The other is to use an outside firm specializing in market research. In global marketing, a combination of in-house and outside research efforts is often advisable. Many outside firms have considerable international expertise; some specialize in particular industry segments. According to figures compiled by *Marketing News*, global market research revenues for the top 25 research companies totaled $22.4 billion in 2008.[16] The Nielsen Company is the world's largest market research organization; it is the source of the well-known Nielsen TV ratings for the U.S. market. Nielsen Media Research International also provides media measurement services in more than 40 global markets. Other research specialists are the Kantar Group (brand awareness and media analysis), IMS Health (pharmaceutical and health care industries), and Germany's GfK SE (custom research and consumer tracking).

The process of collecting data and converting it into useful information can be quite detailed, as shown in Figure 6-1. In the discussion that follows, we will focus on eight basic steps: information requirement, problem definition, choose unit of analysis, examine data availability, assess value of research, research design, data analysis, and interpretation and presentation.

Step 1: Information Requirement

The late Thomas Bata was a self-described "shoe salesman" who built the Bata Shoe Organization into a global empire that is now based in Switzerland. Legend has it that the Czech-born, Swiss-educated Bata once fired a salesman who, upon returning from Africa, reported that there was no opportunity to sell shoes there because everyone walked around barefoot. According to this story, Bata hired another salesman who understood that, in fact, Africa represented a huge untapped market for shoes. This anecdote underscores the fact that direct observation must be linked to unbiased perception and insight. However, as many marketers will acknowledge, it can be difficult to alter entrenched consumer behavior patterns.

Formal research often is undertaken after a problem or opportunity has been identified. A company may need to supplement direct perception with additional information to determine whether a particular country or regional market does, in fact, offer good growth potential. What proportion of potential customers can be converted into *actual* customers? Is a competitor making

> "Traditional research concentrated on the 'what.' Now we are trying to establish the 'why.' We are not asking what consumers think about products and ideas but focusing on what makes them tick."[17]
>
> —Simon Stewart, marketing director, Britvic

---

[14] Peter D. Bennett, ed., *Dictionary of Marketing Terms*, 2nd ed. (Chicago: American Marketing Association, 1995), p. 169.
[15] Michael R. Czinkota and Ilkka A. Ronkainen, "Market Research for Your Export Operations: Part I—Using Secondary Sources of Research," *International Trade Forum* 30, no. 3 (1994), pp. 22–33.
[16] "Top 25 Global Market Research Firms," *Marketing News* (August 15, 2009), pp. H4–H50.
[17] Louise Lucas, "Up Close and Personal Brands," *Financial Times* (October 14, 2010), p. 13.

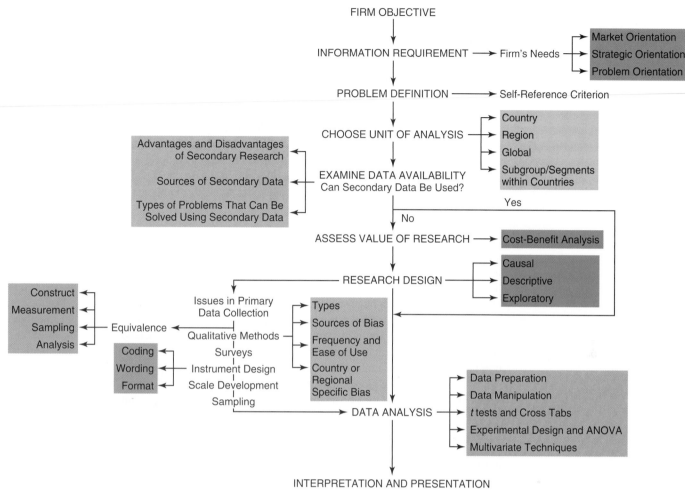

FIGURE 6-1 Market Research Process

Source: Kumar, V., *International Marketing Research,* 1st Edition, © 2000. Reprinted by permission of Pearson Education, Inc., Upper Saddle River, NJ

inroads in one or more important markets around the world? Is research on local taste preferences required to determine if a food product must be adapted? A truism of market research is that a problem well defined is a problem half-solved. Thus, regardless of the particular situation that sets the research effort in motion, the first two questions a marketer should ask are "What information do I need?" and "Why do I need this information?" Table 6-1 lists various subject categories that may require research.

TABLE 6-1 Subject Agenda Categories for a Global Marketing Information System

Category	Coverage
1. Market potential	Demand estimates, consumer behavior, review of products, channels, communication media
2. Competitor information	Corporate, business, and functional strategies; resources and intentions; capabilities
3. Foreign exchange	Balance of payments, interest rates, attractiveness of country currency, expectations of analysts
4. Prescriptive information	Laws, regulations, rulings concerning taxes, earnings, dividends in both host and home countries
5. Resource information	Availability of human, financial, physical, and information resources
6. General conditions	Overall review of sociocultural, political, and technological environments

Step 2: Problem Definition

As noted in Chapter 4, when a person's home-country values and beliefs influence the assessment of a foreign culture or country, the self-reference criterion (SRC) is at work. The SRC tendency underscores the importance of understanding the cultural environments of global markets, as the following examples illustrate:

- When Mattel first introduced Barbie in Japan, managers assumed that Japanese girls would find the doll's design just as appealing as American girls did. They didn't.
- When the Walt Disney Company opened Disneyland Paris, park employees were expected to comply with a detailed written code regarding personal appearance. The goal was to ensure that guests received the kind of experience associated with the Disney name. However, the French considered the code to be an insult to French culture, individualism, and privacy.

As these examples show, assumptions that managers make based on home-country marketing success can turn out to be wrong when applied globally. Marketers might also assume that a marketing program that is successful in one country market can be applied to other country markets in the region. Consider again the case of Disney's theme park business. Although Disneyland Japan was a huge success from opening day, the $3.2 billion Hong Kong Disneyland that opened in 2005 has been less successful. This is due, in part, to the fact that mainland Chinese have limited familiarity with traditional Disney "face characters" such as Snow White. As Jay Rasulo, president of Disney's park and resort division, noted, "People from the mainland don't show up with the embedded 'Disney software' like at other parks."[18]

When approaching global markets, it is best to have "eyes wide open." In other words, marketers must be aware of the impact that SRC and other cross-cultural assumptions can have. Such awareness can have several positive effects. First, it can enhance management's willingness to conduct market research in the first place. Second, an awareness of SRC can help ensure that the research effort is designed with minimal home-country or second-country bias. Third, it can enhance management's receptiveness to research findings—even if they contradict "tried-and-true" marketing experience in other markets.

Step 3: Choose Unit of Analysis

The next step involves the need to identify in what part(s) of the world the company should be doing business and to find out as much as possible about the business environment in the area(s) identified. These issues are reflected in the subject agenda categories in Table 6-1. The unit of analysis may be a single country; it may also be a region such as Europe or South America. In some instances, the marketer is interested in a segment that is global. Countrywide data are not required for all market-entry decisions. Rather, a specific city, state, or province may be the relevant unit of analysis. For example, a company that is considering entering China may focus initially on Shanghai. Located in the Jiangsu province, Shanghai is China's largest city and main seaport. Because Shanghai is a manufacturing center, has a well-developed infrastructure, and is home to a population with a relatively high per capita income, it would be the logical focus of a market research effort.

Step 4: Examine Data Availability

The first task at this stage is to answer several questions regarding the availability of data. What type of data should be gathered? Can **secondary data**—for example, data available in company files, the library, industry or trade journals, or online databases—be used? When does management need the information in order to make a decision regarding market entry? Marketers must address these issues before proceeding to the next step of the research process. Using data that are readily available saves both money and time: A formal market study can cost hundreds of thousands of dollars and take many months to complete.

A low-cost approach to market research and data collection begins with desk research. In other words, "The key to creating a cost-effective way of surveying foreign markets is to climb

---

[18] Merissa Marr and Geoffrey A. Fowler, "Chinese Lessons for Disney," *The Wall Street Journal* (June 12, 2006), p. B1.

on the shoulders of those who have gone before."[19] Suppose a marketer wants to assess the basic market potential for a particular product. To find the answer, secondary sources are a good place to start. Clipping services, company or public libraries, online databases, government census records, and trade associations are just a few of the data sources that can be tapped with minimal effort and cost. Data from these sources already exist. Such data are known as *secondary data* because they were not gathered for the specific project at hand. *Statistical Abstract of the United States* is just one of the annual publications issued by the U.S. government that contains myriad facts about international markets.

The U.S. government's most comprehensive source of world trade data is the National Trade Data Base (NTDB), an online resource from the Department of Commerce. The Bureau of Economic Analysis (www.bea.gov) and the Census Bureau (www.census.gov) are excellent online resources for foreign trade, economic indicators, and other current and historical data. Trade data for the European Union are available from Eurostat (epp.eurostat.ec.europa.eu). Most countries compile estimates of gross national product (GNP), gross domestic product (GDP), consumption, investment, government expenditures, and price levels. Demographic data indicating the population size, distribution of population by age category, and rates of population growth are also available. Market information from export census documents compiled by the Department of Commerce on the basis of shippers' export declarations (known as "ex-decs" or SEDs, these must be filled out for any export valued at $1,500 or more) is also available. Another important source of market data is the Foreign Commercial Service.

Many countries have set up Web sites to help small firms find opportunities in world markets. For example, the Virtual Trade Commissioner (www.infoexport.gc.ca) is a service of Canada's Department of Foreign Affairs and International Trade (DFAIT). The site is a computerized database containing the names of Canadian companies that export.

These do not exhaust the types of data available, however. A single source, *The Statistical Yearbook of the United Nations*, contains global data on agriculture, mining, manufacturing, construction, energy production and consumption, internal and external trade, railroad and air transport, wages and prices, health, housing, education, communication infrastructure, and availability of mass communication media. The U.S. Central Intelligence Agency publishes *The World Factbook*, which is revised yearly. Other important sources are the World Bank, the International Monetary Fund, and Japan's Ministry of International Trade and Industry (MITI). *The Economist* and the *Financial Times* regularly compile comprehensive surveys of regional and country markets and include them in their publications. Data from these sources are generally available in both print and electronic form.

How can such data be useful? Take industrial growth patterns as one example. Because they generally reveal consumption patterns, production patterns are helpful in assessing market opportunities. Additionally, trends in manufacturing production indicate potential markets for companies that supply manufacturing inputs. At the early stages of growth in a country, when per capita incomes are low, manufacturing centers on such necessities as food and beverages, textiles, and other forms of light industry. As incomes rise, the relative importance of these industries declines as heavy industry begins to develop.

A word of caution is in order at this point: Remember that data are compiled from various sources, some of which may not be reputable. Even when the sources are reputable, there is likely to be some variability from source to source. Anyone using data should be clear on exactly what the data are measuring. For example, studying income data requires understanding whether one is working with GNP or GDP figures. Also, anyone using the Internet as an information source should evaluate the credibility of the person(s) responsible for the Web site. Moreover, as Czinkota and Ronkainen note,[20] secondary data may support the decision to pursue a market opportunity outside the home country, but such data are unlikely to shed light on specific questions: What is the market potential for our furniture in Indonesia? How much does the typical Nigerian consumer spend on soft drinks? If a packaging change is made to ensure compliance with Germany's Green Dot Ordinance, what effect, if any, will the change have on consumer purchasing behavior?

---

[19] Michael R. Czinkota and Ilkka A. Ronkainen, "Market Research for Your Export Operations: Part I—Using Secondary Sources of Research," *International Trade Forum* 30, no. 3 (1994), p. 22.

[20] Michael R. Czinkota and Ilkka A. Ronkainen, "Market Research for Your Export Operations: Part II—Conducting Primary Marketing Research," *International Trade Forum* 31, no. 1 (1995), p. 16.

→ **THE CULTURAL CONTEXT**

Bikers Go "Hog" Wild

MyMarketingLab SYNC • THINK • LEARN

In 2013, Harley-Davidson (H-D) celebrated its 110th anniversary. The company has grown impressively during its first 100-plus years of operation; as the second decade of the twenty-first century got underway, H-D posted revenues of $4.1 billion. Savvy export marketing enabled H-D to dramatically increase worldwide sales of its heavyweight motorcycles. From Australia to Germany to Mexico City, H-D enthusiasts were paying the equivalent of up to $25,000 to own an American-built classic. In many countries, dealers put would-be buyers on a 6-month waiting list because of high demand.

H-D's international success came after years of neglecting overseas markets. The company was also slow to react to a growing threat from Japanese manufacturers. Early on, the company used an export-selling approach, symbolized by its underdeveloped dealer network. By the late 1980s, after recruiting dealers in the important Japanese and European markets, company executives discovered a basic principle of global marketing. "As the saying goes, we needed to think global but act local," said Jerry G. Wilke, vice president for worldwide marketing during that time. Managers began to adapt the company's international marketing to make it more responsive to local conditions.

In Japan, for example, H-D's rugged image and high quality helped make it the best-selling imported motorcycle. After learning that riders in Tokyo consider fashion and customized bikes to be essential, H-D opened stores specializing in clothing and bike accessories. Recently H-D has begun catering to Japanese women who enjoy riding (see Exhibit 6-4). Today, Japan generates 5.6 percent of company revenues

for motorcycles, parts, accessories, and merchandise.

In Europe, H-D discovered that an "evening out" means something different than it does in America. The company sponsored a rally in France, where beer and live rock music were available until midnight. Recalls Wilke, "People asked us why we were ending the rally just as the evening was starting. So I had to go persuade the band to keep playing and reopen the bar until 3 or 4 A.M."

Today, the company has a clear picture of its core European customers; as Klaus Stobel, European affairs director for Harley-Davidson Europe, explained, "The people who buy Harleys in Europe are like the people who buy BMWs in the U.S. They are dentists and lawyers." H-D currently ranks second in overall market share for the European heavyweight motorcycle segment; in 2010, Europe accounted for 16.7 percent of global revenues.

The global economic crisis cut into worldwide sales. The reason was straightforward: Credit was tight and, for many people, a motorcycle is a discretionary purchase, not a necessity. In 2010, the company shipped 210,494 motorcycles, down from about 350,000 units in 2006. Despite the slump in demand, in some years there are not enough bikes to go around. This is a situation that seems to suit company executives just fine. As former H-D President James H. Paterson once noted, "Enough motorcycles is too many motorcycles."

Sources: Harley-Davidson *Annual Report*, 2010; Stephen Wisnefski and Susan Carey, "Credit Squeeze Threatens 'Hog' Sales," *The Wall Street Journal* (October 17, 2010), p. A1; Jeremy Grand and Harold Ehren, "Harley-Davidson Eyes Europe," *Financial Times* (July 28, 2003), p. 17; Kevin Kelly and Karen Lowry Miller, "The Rumble Heard Round the World: Harleys," *BusinessWeek* (May 24, 1993), pp. 58, 60; Robert L. Rose, "Vrooming Back: After Nearly Stalling, Harley-Davidson Finds New Crowd of Riders," *The Wall Street Journal* (August 31, 1990), pp. A1, A6.

E: hibit 6-4 A top priority for Harley-Davidson chief executive Keith Wandell is expanding the company's global presence and reaching out to new market segments. New dealerships have been added in India, Russia, Mexico, and other emerging markets. Today, Harley has more full-service dealerships abroad than in the United States. Plans call for international sales to account for more than 40 percent of total sales by 2014, up from 25 percent in 2006. Harley-Davison is also diversifying its customer base by targeting female riders in key markets. And, with an eye to the needs of older consumers, Harley offers models with heated seats and handlebars and more comfortable riding positions.
Source: © Jay Goebel / Alamy.

TABLE 6-2 Global Market Research Reports from MarketResearch.com

Title of Study	Price	Publisher
Chinese Markets for Cosmetics	$4,000	Asia Market Information & Development Company
Online Music	$3,950	Global Industry Analysts
Whiskies—UK	$3,000	Mintel International Group Ltd.
Luxury Goods Retailing—Global	$2,990	Mintel International Group Ltd.
Pharmaceutical Markets in Brazil, Russia, India, and China	$2,500	Kalorama Information
Economic Crisis Response: U.S. [run up] Telecommunications 2008–2012	$2,000	IDC
Automotive Industry	$1,450	Global Industry Analysts
The 2009–2014 World Outlook for Laptop Computers	$795	Icon Group International, Inc.

Source: MarketResearch.com, accessed March 9, 2009. Used by permission.

Syndicated studies published by private research companies are another source of secondary data and information (the word *syndicated* comes from the newspaper industry and refers to the practice of selling articles, cartoons, or guest columns to a number of different organizations). For example, MarketResearch.com (www.marketresearch.com) sells reports on a wide range of global business sectors; the company partners with 350 research firms to offer a comprehensive set of reports. A sampling of reports available from MarketResearch.comon topics covered in this textbook is shown in Table 6-2; although a single report can cost thousands of dollars, a company may be able to get the market information it needs without incurring the greater costs associated with conducting primary research.

Step 5: Assess Value of Research

When data are not available through published statistics or studies, management may wish to conduct further study of the individual country market, region, or global segment. However, collecting information costs money. Thus, the marketing research plan should also spell out what this information is worth to the company in dollars (or euros, or yen, etc.) compared with what it would cost to collect it. What will the company gain by collecting these data? What would be the cost of not getting the data that could be converted into useful information? Research requires an investment of both money and managerial time, and it is necessary to perform a cost-benefit analysis before proceeding further. In some instances, a company will pursue the same course of action no matter what the research reveals. Even when more information is needed to ensure a high-quality decision, a realistic cost estimate of a formal study may reveal that the cost to perform research is simply too high.

The small markets around the world pose a special problem for the researcher. The relatively low profit potential in smaller markets justifies only modest expenditures for marketing research. Therefore, the global researcher must devise techniques and methods that keep expenditures in line with the market's profit potential. The researcher is often pressured to discover economic and demographic relationships that can lead to estimates of demand based on a minimum of information. It may also be necessary to use inexpensive survey research that sacrifices some elegance or statistical rigor to achieve results within the constraints of the smaller market research budget.

Step 6: Research Design

As indicated in Figure 6-1, if secondary data can be used, the researcher can go directly to the data analysis step. Suppose, however, that data are not available through published statistics or studies; in addition, suppose that the cost-benefit analysis indicated in step 5 has been performed and that the decision has been made to carry on with the research effort. **Primary data** are gathered through original research pertaining to the particular problem identified in step 1. At this point, it is time to establish a research design.

Global marketing guru David Arnold offers the following guidelines regarding data gathering:[21]

- Use multiple indicators rather than a single measure. This approach will decrease the level of uncertainty for decision makers. As the saying goes, "There are three sides to every story: your side, my side, and the truth." A land surveyor can pinpoint the location of a third object given the known location of two objects. This technique, known as *triangulation*, is equally useful in global market research.
- Individual companies should develop customized indicators specific to the industry, product market, or business model. Such indicators should leverage a company's previous experience in global markets. For example, in some developing markets Mary Kay Cosmetics uses the average wage of a female secretary as a basis for estimating income potential for its beauty consultants.
- Always conduct comparative assessments in multiple markets. Do not assess a particular market in isolation. Comparative assessment enables management to develop a "portfolio" approach in which alternative priorities and scenarios can be developed. For example, to better understand Czech consumers in general, a company might also conduct research in nearby Poland and Hungary. By contrast, if a brewing company wished to learn more about beer consumption patterns in the Czech Republic, it might also conduct research in Ireland and Germany, where per capita beer consumption is high.
- Observations of purchasing patterns and other behavior should be weighted more heavily than reports or opinions regarding purchase intention or price sensitivity. Particularly in developing markets, it is difficult to accurately survey consumer perceptions.

With these guidelines in mind, the marketer must address a new set of questions and issues in primary data collection. Should the research effort be geared toward quantitative, numerical data that can be subjected to statistical analysis, or should qualitative techniques be used? In global market research, it is advisable for the plan to call for a mix of techniques. For consumer products, qualitative research is especially well suited to accomplish the following tasks:[22]

- To provide consumer understanding; to "get close" to the consumer
- To describe the social and cultural contexts of consumer behavior, including cultural, religious, and political factors that impact decision making
- To identify core-brand equity and "get under the skin" of brands
- To "mine" the consumer and identify what people really feel

ISSUES IN DATA COLLECTION The research problem may be more narrowly focused on marketing issues, such as the need to adapt products and other mix elements to local tastes and to assess demand and profit potential. Demand and profit potential, in turn, depend in part on whether the market being studied can be classified as existing or potential. *Existing markets* are those in which customer needs are already being served by one or more companies. In many countries, data about the size of existing markets—in terms of dollar volume and unit sales—are readily available. In some countries, however, formal market research is a relatively new phenomenon and data are scarce. McKinsey & Company, Gartner Group Asia, and Grey China Advertising have been very active in China. For example, using focus groups and other techniques, Grey China gathers a wealth of information about attitudes and buying patterns that it publishes in its Grey China Base Annual Consumer Study. Recent findings point to growing concerns about the future, Westernization of grocery purchases, growing market saturation, increasingly discerning customers, and a rise in consumer willingness to try new products. Even so, data gathered by different sources may be inconsistent. What is the level of soft drink consumption in China? Euromonitor International estimates consumption at 23 billion liters, whereas Coca-Cola's in-house marketing research team places the figure at 39 billion liters. Likewise, CSM, a Chinese

---

[21] David Arnold, *The Mirage of Global Markets* (Upper Saddle River, NJ: Financial Times Prentice Hall, 2004), pp. 41–43.
[22] John Pawle, "Mining the International Consumer," *Journal of the Market Research Society* 41, no. 1 (1999), p. 20.

television-rating agency, estimates the TV-advertising market at $2.8 billion per year. According to Nielsen Media Research, the figure is closer to $7.5 billion.[23]

In such situations, and in countries where such data are not available, researchers must first estimate the market size, the level of demand, or the rate of product purchase or consumption. A second research objective in existing markets may be assessment of the company's overall competitiveness in terms of product appeal, price, distribution, and promotional coverage and effectiveness. Researchers may be able to pinpoint a weakness in the competitor's product or identify an under- or unserved market segment. The minivan and sport-utility vehicle segments of the auto industry illustrate the opportunity an existing market can present. For years, Chrysler dominated the U.S. minivan segment, for which annual sales at one time totaled about 1.2 million vehicles. Most global marketers compete in this segment, although a number of models have been discontinued due to declining sales. For example, Toyota introduced its Japanese-built Previa in the United States in 1991; critics mocked the teardrop styling and dismissed it as being underpowered. For the 1998 model year, the Previa was replaced with the American-built Sienna. To ensure that the Sienna suited American tastes, Toyota designers and engineers studied Chrysler minivans and duplicated key features such as numerous cup holders and a second sliding rear door on the driver's side.

In some instances, there is no existing market to research. Such *potential markets* can be further subdivided into latent and incipient markets. A **latent market** is, in essence, an undiscovered segment. It is a market in which demand would materialize *if* an appropriate product were made available. In a latent market, demand is zero before the product is introduced. In the case of existing markets such as the one for minivans previously described, the main research challenge is to understand the extent to which the competition fully meets customer needs. As J. Davis Illingworth, an executive at Toyota Motor Sales USA, explained, "I think the American public will look at Sienna as an American product that meets their needs."[24] With latent markets, initial success is not based on a company's competitiveness. Rather, it depends on the prime-mover advantage—a company's ability to uncover the opportunity and launch a marketing program that taps the latent demand. This is precisely what Chrysler achieved by single-handedly creating the minivan market.

Sometimes, traditional market research is not an effective means for identifying latent markets. As Peter Drucker has noted, the failure of American companies to successfully commercialize fax machines—an American innovation—can be traced to research that indicated no potential demand for such a product. The problem, in Drucker's view, stems from the typical survey question for a product targeted at a latent market. Suppose a researcher asks, "Would you buy a telephone accessory that costs upwards of $1,500 and enables you to send, for $1 a page, the same letter the post office delivers for $0.25?" On the basis of economics alone, the respondent most likely will answer, "No."

Drucker explained that Japanese companies are the leading sellers of fax machines today because their understanding of the market was not based on survey research. Instead, they reviewed the early days of mainframe computers, photocopy machines, cell phones, and other information and communications products. The Japanese realized that, judging only by the initial costs associated with buying and using these new products, the prospects of market acceptance were low. However, each of these products became a huge success after people began to use them. This realization prompted the Japanese to focus on the market for the *benefits* provided by fax machines, rather than the market for the machines themselves. By looking at the success of courier services such as FedEx, the Japanese realized that, in essence, the fax machine market already existed.[25]

To illustrate Drucker's point, consider the case of Red Bull energy drink. Dietrich Mateschitz hired a market research firm to assess the market potential for his creation. In the tests, consumers reacted negatively to the taste, the logo, and the brand name. Mateschitz ignored the research, and Red Bull is now a $2 billion brand. As Mateschitz explains, "When we first started, we said

> "At that time, Japanese women almost never used mascaras because, by nature, they have very straight, short and thin lashes. We designed mascara that was able to lengthen and curl lashes. It was a huge success. We would never have seen that in a focus group."[26]
>
> —Jean-Paul Agon, CEO, L'Oréal, discussing the decision to relaunch the Maybelline makeup brand in Japan with mascara

---

[23] Gabriel Kahn, "Chinese Puzzle: Spotty Consumer Data," *The Wall Street Journal* (October 15, 2003), p. B1.

[24] Kathleen Kerwin, "Can This Minivan Dent Detroit?" *BusinessWeek* (February 3, 1997), p. 37.

[25] Peter F. Drucker, "Marketing 101 for a Fast-Changing Decade," *The Wall Street Journal* (November 20, 1990), p. A17.

[26] Adam Jones, "How to Make up Demand," *Financial Times* (October 3, 2006), p. 8.

there is no existing market for Red Bull, but Red Bull will create it. And this is what finally became true."[27]

An **incipient market** is a market that will emerge if a particular economic, demographic, political, or sociocultural trend continues. A company is not likely to succeed if it offers a product in an incipient market before the trends have taken root. After the trends have had a chance to gain traction, the incipient market will become latent and, later, existing. The concept of incipient markets can also be illustrated by the impact of rising income on demand for automobiles and other expensive consumer durables. As per capita income rises in a country, the demand for automobiles will also rise. Therefore, if a company can predict a country's future rate of income growth, it can also predict the growth rate of its automobile market.

For example, to capitalize on China's rapid economic growth, Volkswagen, Peugeot, Chrysler, and other global automakers have established in-country manufacturing operations. China even has incipient demand for imported exotic cars; in early 1994 Ferrari opened its first showroom in Beijing. Because of a 150 percent import tax, China's first Ferrari buyers were entrepreneurs who had profited from China's increasing openness to Western-style marketing and capitalism. By the end of the 1990s, demand for luxury cars had grown at a faster rate than anticipated.[28] Today, there are 30 million cars and light trucks for China's 1.3 billion people. Clearly, China is a very attractive market opportunity for carmakers.

By contrast, some companies have concluded that China has limited potential at present. For example, in 1998 UK-based retailer Marks & Spencer closed its office in Shanghai and tabled plans to open a store in China. Commenting to the press, a company representative directly addressed the issue of whether China represented an incipient market:

> After 3 years of research, we have come to the conclusion that the timing is not right. The majority of our customers are from middle-income groups. But, our interest is in Shanghai, and the size of the middle-income group, although it is growing, is not yet at a level that would justify us opening a store there.[29]

RESEARCH METHODOLOGIES Survey research, interviews, consumer panels, observation, and focus groups are some of the tools used to collect primary market data. These are the same tools used by marketers whose activities are not global; however, some adaptations and special considerations for global marketing may be required.

Survey research utilizes questionnaires designed to elicit quantitative data ("How much would you buy?"), qualitative responses ("Why would you buy?"), or both. Survey research is often conducted by means of a questionnaire distributed through the mail, asked over the telephone, or asked in person. Many good marketing research textbooks provide details on questionnaire design and administration.

In global market research, a number of survey design and administration issues may arise. When using the telephone as a research tool, it is important to remember that what is customary in one country may be impossible in others because of infrastructure differences, cultural barriers, or other reasons. For example, telephone directories or lists may not be available; also, important differences may exist between urban dwellers and people in rural areas. In China, for example, the Ministry of Information Industry reports that 77 percent of households in coastal areas have at least one fixed-line telephone; in rural areas, the number is only 40 percent.

At a deeper level, culture shapes attitudes and values in a way that directly affects people's willingness to respond to interviewer questions. Open-ended questions may help the researcher identify a respondent's frame of reference. In some cultures, respondents may be unwilling to answer certain questions or they may intentionally give inaccurate answers.

Recall that step 2 of the global market research process calls for identifying possible sources of SRC bias. This issue is especially important in survey research: SRC bias can originate from the cultural backgrounds of those designing the questionnaire. For example, a survey designed and administered in the United States may be inappropriate in non-Western cultures even if it is

[27] Kerry A. Dolan, "The Soda with Buzz," *Forbes* (March 28, 2005), p. 126.

[28] Jason Leow and Gordon Fairclough, "Rich Chinese Fancy Luxury Cars," *The Wall Street Journal*, April 12, 2007, pp. B1, B2.

[29] James Harding, "Foreign Investors Face New Curbs on Ownership of Stores," *Financial Times* (November 10, 1998), p. 7.

carefully translated. This is especially true if the person designing the questionnaire is not familiar with the SRC. A technique known as *back translation* can help increase comprehension and validity; the technique requires that, after a questionnaire or survey instrument is translated into a particular target language, it is translated once again, this time into the original language by a different translator. For even greater accuracy, *parallel translations*—two versions by different translators—can be used as input to the back translation. The same techniques can ensure that advertising copy is accurately translated into different languages.

Personal interviews allow researchers to ask "why?" and then explore answers with the respondent on a face-to-face basis.

A **consumer panel** is a sample of respondents whose behavior is tracked over time. For example, a number of companies, including the Nielsen Media Research unit of Netherlands-based VNU, AGB, GfK, and TNS, conduct television audience measurement (TAM) by studying the viewing habits of household panels. Broadcasters use audience share data to set advertising rates; advertisers such as Procter & Gamble, Unilever, and Coca-Cola use the data to choose programs during which to advertise. In the United States, Nielsen has enjoyed a virtual monopoly on viewership research for half a century. For years, however, the four major U.S. television networks have complained that they lose advertising revenues because Nielsen's data collection methods undercount viewership. Nielsen has responded to these concerns by upgrading its survey methodology; the company now uses an electronic device known as a **peoplemeter** to collect national audience data. Peoplemeter systems are currently in use in dozens of countries around the world, including China; Nielsen is also rolling out peoplemeters to collect local audience viewership data in key metropolitan markets such as New York City.

> "You can't go out and ask people what they need or want because they don't know. The whole trick is to come out with a product and say, 'Have you thought of this?' and hear the consumer respond, 'Wow! No, I hadn't.' If you can do that, you're on."[30]
>
> —David Lewis, chief designer, Bang & Olufsen

When **observation** is used as a data collection method, one or more trained observers (or a mechanical device such as a video camera) watch and record the behavior of actual or prospective buyers. The research results are then used to guide marketing managers in their decision making. For example, after Volkswagen's U.S. sales began to slump, the company launched "Moonraker," an 18-month effort designed to help its engineers, marketers, and design specialists better understand American consumers. Despite the presence of a design center in California, decision makers at headquarters in Wolfsburg, Germany, generally ignored feedback from U.S. customers. As Stefan Liske, director of product strategy at VW, acknowledged, "We needed a totally different approach. We asked ourselves, 'Do we really know everything about this market?'" The Moonraker team visited the Mall of America in Minneapolis and the Rock and Roll Hall of Fame in Cleveland; they also spent spring break in Florida observing college students.

The experience was an eye-opener; as one designer explained, "In Germany, it's all about driving, but here, it's about everything *but* driving. People here want to use their time in other ways, like talk on their cell phone." Another member of the team, an engineer, shadowed a single mom as she took her kids to school and ran errands. The engineer noted that American drivers need a place to store a box of tissues and a place to put a bag of fast food picked up at a drive-through window. "I began thinking about what specific features her car needed. It was about living the customer's life and putting ourselves in their place," he said.[31]

A marketer of breakfast cereals might send researchers to preselected households at 6 A.M. to watch families go about their morning routines. The client could also assign a researcher to accompany family members to the grocery store to observe their behavior under actual shopping conditions. The client might wish to know about the shoppers' reactions to in-store promotions linked to an advertising campaign. The researcher could record comments or discretely take photographs. Of course, companies using observation as a research methodology must be sensitive to concerns about privacy issues. A second problem with observation is *reactivity*, which is the tendency of research subjects to behave differently for the simple reason that they know they are under study. Additional examples include the following:

- Hoping to gain insights for product and package design improvements, Procter & Gamble sent video crews into 80 households in the United Kingdom, Italy, Germany, and China. P&G's ultimate goal was to amass an in-house video library that can be directly accessed

[30] Deborah Steinborn, "Talking About Design," *The Wall Street Journal—The Journal Report: Product Design* (June 23, 2008), p. R6.
[31] Gina Chon, "VW's American Road Trip," *The Wall Street Journal* (January 4, 2006), pp. B1, B9.

EMERGING MARKETS BRIEFING BOOK

Market Research in Brazil

MyMarketingLab SYNC • THINK • LEARN

Emerging markets present a number of challenges to anyone conducting market research. First, the technology infrastructure may be undeveloped. In addition, there are geographic issues; in the BRICS nations, for example, many provincial areas are isolated and difficult to reach. Third, researchers may have to adapt their data-gathering methodologies to suit the country environment. Finally, privacy issues can present challenges.

Brazil is a case in point. The technological infrastructure for gathering market data is minimal. Government census reports are a poor source of population data. As a result, it can be difficult to obtain a representative sample; it is expensive to design a national probability sample. Compounding the problem is a lack of telephone penetration. Geographic issues also arise; this is not surprising, given the immensity of Brazil's territory. Marketers often find that, outside of major metropolitan areas, little EPOS data is available. It is very difficult to track what is selling, at what price, and who the customers are. This necessitates the use of field teams to gather data.

L'Oréal, the French cosmetics company, uses observation in Brazil and other emerging markets. Patricia Pineau is in charge of L'Oréal's consumer insights team. She explains, "It all starts with observation. Observing is necessary to decode exactly what

women are trying to get and what they are attracted to. Sometimes it is the gesture that will reveal something that they really want to gain." Among the insights L'Oréal gained in Brazil: Women change their nail polish daily to coordinate with outfits. Rather than taking care to apply polish only to the nails, they brush it on their fingers and use a cotton swab to clean off the excess.

A third problem is encountered when designing face-to-face interviews. If the research design calls for interviewing broad socioeconomic groups, the demographics of interviewers should match those of respondent groups. Street- or mall-intercept techniques can be used to good effect. Security issues require the use of teams. Researchers may offer a gift rather than cash as an incentive. Finally, privacy issues are very important, especially to affluent Brazilians. Wealthy respondents are unlikely to answer questions about personal finance. To ensure confidentiality, financial services companies may bring in interviewers based on a developed market. To gain trust, interviewers can ask respondents to recommend other potential interviewees.

Sources: Louise Luca, "Up Close and Personal Brands," *Financial Times* (October 14, 2010), p. 13; Arundhati Parmar, "Tailor Techniques to Each Audience in Latin Market," *Marketing News* (February 3, 2003), pp. 4–6. See also Harold L. Sirkin, James W. Hemerling, and Arindam K. Bhattacharya, *Globality: Competing with Everyone from Everywhere for Everything* (New York: Boston Consulting Group, 2008), pp. 117–118.

by keyword searches. Stan Joosten, an IT manager, noted, "You could search for 'eating snacks' and find all [the] clips from all over the world on that topic. Immediately, it gives you a global perspective on certain topics."[32]

- Michelle Arnau, a marketing manager for Nestlé's PowerBar brand, attended the 2004 New York City Marathon to see how runners were using single-serve packets of PowerGel, a concentrated, performance-boosting gel in a single-serving packet. Ms. Arnau observed that runners typically tore off the top with their teeth and attempted to consume the gel in a single squeeze without breaking their stride. Ms. Arnau was dismayed to see that the long neck of the packet sometimes prevented the gel from flowing out quickly. Designers at Nestlé then created an improved package with an upside-down, triangular-shaped top that is narrow enough to control the flow of the gel but also fits into the athlete's mouth.[33]

In **focus group** research, a trained moderator facilitates discussion of a product concept, a brand's image and personality, an advertisement, a social trend, or another topic with a group of 6 to 10 people. Global marketers can use focus groups to arrive at important insights. For example:

- In the mid-1990s, Whirlpool launched a European advertising campaign that featured fantasy characters such as a drying diva and a washing-machine goddess. The campaign's success prompted management to adapt it for use in the United States and Latin America. First, however, the company conducted focus groups to gauge reaction to the ads. Nick Mote, Whirlpool's worldwide account director at France's Publicis advertising agency, said, "We've had some incredible research results. It was just like somebody switched the lights on."[34]

---

[32] Emily Nelson, "P&G Checks Out Real Life," *The Wall Street Journal* (May 17, 2001), pp. B1, B4.

[33] Deborah Ball, "The Perils of Packaging: Nestlé Aims for Easier Openings," *The Wall Street Journal* (November 17, 2005), p. B1.

[34] Katheryn Kranhold, "Whirlpool Conjures Up Appliance Divas," *The Wall Street Journal* (April 27, 2000), p. B1.

- In Singapore, focus groups of young teens were used to help guide development of Coca-Cola's advertising program. As Karen Wong, Coke's country marketing director for Singapore, explained, "We tested everything from extreme to borderline boring: body-piercing all over, grungy kids in a car listening to rock music and head-banging all the way. Youth doing things that youth in America do." Some participants found much of Coke's imagery—for example, a shirtless young man crowd surfing at a rock concert and careening down a store aisle on a grocery cart—too rebellious. As one young Singaporean remarked, "They look like they're on drugs. And if they're on drugs, then how can they be performing at school?" Armed with the focus group results, Coca-Cola's managers devised an ad campaign for Singapore that was well within the bounds of societal approval.[35]

- When Blockbuster Video was planning its entry into Japan, the world's number 2 video rental market, the company convened focus groups to learn more about Japanese preferences and perceptions of existing video rental outlets. In the mid-1990s, most video stores in Japan were tiny operations with limited display space. Video titles were piled from the floor to the ceiling, making it difficult to find and retrieve individual titles. Acting on the information provided by the focus groups, Blockbuster designed its Japanese stores with 3,000 square feet of floor space and display shelves that were more accessible.[36]

A typical focus group meets at a facility equipped with recording equipment and a two-way mirror behind which representatives of the client company observe the proceedings. The moderator can utilize a number of approaches to elicit reactions and responses, including projective techniques, visualization, and role plays. When using a *projective technique*, the researcher presents open-ended or ambiguous stimuli to a subject. Presumably, when verbalizing a response, the subject will "project"—that is, reveal—his or her unconscious attitudes and biases. By analyzing the responses, researchers are better able to understand how consumers perceive a particular product, brand, or company.

For example, in a focus group convened to assess car-buying preferences among a segment comprised of twentysomethings, the researcher might ask participants to describe a party where various automotive brands are present. What is Nissan wearing, eating, and drinking? What kind of sneakers does Honda have on? What are their personalities like? Who's shy? Who's loud? Who gets the girl (or guy)? Interaction among group members can result in synergies that yield important qualitative insights that are likely to differ from those based on data gathered through more direct questioning. Even though focus group research is a technique that has grown in popularity, some industry observers caution that the technique has been used so much that participants, especially those who are used on a regular basis, have become overly familiar with its workings.

Nevertheless, focus group research yields qualitative data that do not lend themselves to statistical projection. Such data suggest rather than confirm hypotheses; also, qualitative data tend to be directional rather than conclusive. Such data are extremely valuable in the exploratory phase of a project and are typically used in conjunction with data gathered via observation and other methods.

SCALE DEVELOPMENT Market research requires assigning some type of measure, ranking, or interval to a response. To take a simple example of measurement, a *nominal scale* is used to establish the identity of a survey element. For example, male respondents could be labeled "1" and female respondents could be labeled "2." Scaling can also entail placing each response in some kind of continuum; a common example is the Likert scale, which asks respondents to indicate whether they "strongly agree" with a statement, "strongly disagree," or whether their attitude falls somewhere in the middle. In a multicountry research project, it is important to have *scalar equivalence*, which means that two respondents in different countries with the same value for a given variable receive equivalent scores on the same survey item.

Even with standard data-gathering techniques, the application of a particular technique may differ from country to country. Matthew Draper, vice president at New Jersey–based Total Research Corporation, cites "scalar bias" as a major problem: "There are substantial differences

---

[35] Cris Prystay, "Selling to Singapore's Teens Is Tricky," *The Wall Street Journal* (October 4, 2002), p. B4.
[36] Khanh T. L. Tran, "Blockbuster Finds Success in Japan That Eluded the Chain in Germany," *The Wall Street Journal* (August 28, 1998), p. A14.

in the way people use scales, and research data based on scales such as rating product usefulness on a scale of 1 to 10 is therefore frequently cluttered with biases disguising the truth." For example, while the typical American scale would equate a high number such as 10 with "most" or "best" and 1 with "least," Germans prefer scales in which 1 is "most/best." Also, while American survey items pertaining to spending provide a range of figures, Germans prefer the opportunity to provide an exact answer.[37]

SAMPLING When collecting data, researchers generally cannot administer a survey to every possible person in the designated group. A sample is a selected subset of a population that is representative of the entire population. The two best-known types of samples are probability samples and nonprobability samples. A probability sample is generated by following statistical rules that ensure that each member of the population under study has an equal chance—or probability—of being included in the sample. The results of a probability sample can be projected to the entire population with statistical reliability reflecting sampling error, degree of confidence, and standard deviation.

The results of a nonprobability sample cannot be projected with statistical reliability. One form of nonprobability sample is a *convenience sample*. As the name implies, researchers select people who are easy to reach. For example, in one study that compared consumer shopping attitudes in the United States, Jordan, Singapore, and Turkey, data for the latter three countries were gathered from convenience samples recruited by an acquaintance of the researcher. Although data gathered in this way are not subject to statistical inference, they may be adequate to address the problem defined in step 1. In this study, for example, the researchers were able to identify a clear trend toward cultural convergence in shopping attitudes and customs that cut across modern industrial countries, emerging industrial countries, and developing countries.[38]

To obtain a *quota sample*, the researcher divides the population under study into categories; a sample is then taken from each category. The term *quota* refers to the need to make sure that enough people are chosen in each category to reflect the overall makeup of the population. For example, assume a country's population is divided into six categories according to monthly income, as follows:

Percent of population	10%	15%	25%	25%	15%	10%
Earnings per month	0–9	10–19	20–39	40–59	60–69	70–100

If it is assumed that income is the characteristic that adequately differentiates the population for study purposes, then a quota sample would include respondents of different income levels in the same proportion as they occur in the population; that is, 15 percent with monthly earnings from 10 to 19, and so on.

Step 7: Data Analysis[39]

The data collected up to this point must be subjected to some form of analysis if they are to be useful to decision makers. Although a detailed discussion is beyond the scope of this text, a brief overview is in order. First, the data must be prepared—the term *cleaned* is sometimes used—before further analysis is possible. They must be logged and stored in a central location or database; when research has been conducted in various parts of the world, rounding up data can pose some difficulties. Are data comparable across samples so that multicountry analysis can be performed? Some amount of editing may be required; for example, some responses may be missing or difficult to interpret. Next, questionnaires must be coded. Simply put, coding involves identifying the respondents and the variables. Finally, some data adjustment may be required.

Data analysis continues with *tabulation*—that is, the arrangement of data in tabular form. Researchers may wish to determine various things: the mean, median, and mode; range and standard deviation; and the shape of the distribution (e.g., that of a normal curve or not). For nominally scaled variables such as "male" and "female," a simple cross-tabulation may be

---

[37] Jack Edmonston, "U.S., Overseas Differences Abound," *Business Marketing* (January 1998), p. 32.

[38] Eugene H. Fram and Riad Ajami, "Globalization of Markets and Shopping Stress: Cross-Country Comparisons," *Business Horizons* 37, no. 1 (January–February 1994), pp. 17–23.

[39] Parts of this section are adapted from Glen L. Urban, John R. Hauser, and Nikhilesh Dholakia, *Essentials of New Product Management* (Upper Saddle River, NJ: Prentice Hall, 1987), Chapters 6 and 7.

TABLE 6-3 Hypothetical Scales for Obtaining Consumer Perceptions of Nokia Smartphone

Instructions: *Please rate this product on the following product characteristics or benefits.*

	Rating				
	Low				High
Variables (Product Characteristics/Benefits)	**1**	**2**	**3**	**4**	**5**
1. Long battery life	____	____	____	____	____
2. Many apps available	____	____	____	____	____
3. 4G Internet access	____	____	____	____	____
4. Thin case	____	____	____	____	____
5. Intuitive interface	____	____	____	____	____
6. Music storage capacity	____	____	____	____	____
7. Large display screen	____	____	____	____	____
8. Fits hand comfortably	____	____	____	____	____
9. Works anywhere in the world	____	____	____	____	____
10. Different colors available	____	____	____	____	____

performed. Suppose, for example, that Nielsen Media Research surveyed video gamers to determine how they feel about products (e.g., soft drinks) and advertisements (e.g., a billboard for a cell phone) embedded in video games. Nielsen could use cross-tabulation to separately examine the responses of male and female subjects to see if their responses differ significantly. If females are equally or more positive in their responses than males, video game companies could use this information to persuade consumer products companies to pay to have select products targeted at women featured as integral parts of the games. Researchers can also use various relatively simple statistical techniques such as hypothesis testing and chi-square testing; advanced data analysis such as analysis of variance (ANOVA), correlation analysis, and regression analysis can also be used.

If the researcher is interested in the interaction among variables, *interdependence techniques* such as factor analysis, cluster analysis, and multidimensional scaling can be used. **Factor analysis** can be used to transform large amounts of data into manageable units; specialized computer programs perform data reduction by "distilling out" from a multitude of survey responses a few meaningful factors that underlie attitudes and perceptions. Factor analysis is useful in psychographic segmentation studies; it can also be used to create perceptual maps. In this form of analysis, variables are not classified as dependent or independent. Instead, subjects are asked to rate specific product benefits on five-point scales; Table 6-3 shows a hypothetical scale that Nokia might use to assess consumer perceptions of a new combination smartphone. Although the scale shown in Table 6-3 lists 10 characteristics/benefits, factor analysis will generate *factor loadings* that enable the researcher to determine two or three factors that underlie the benefits. That is why it is said that factor analysis results in data reduction. For the smartphone, the researcher might label the factors "easy to use" and "stylish." The computer will also output *factor scores* for each respondent; respondent 1 might have a factor score of .35 for the factor identified as "easy to use"; respondent 2 might have .42, and so on. When all respondents' factor scores are averaged, Nokia's position on a perceptual map can be determined (see Figure 6-2). Similar determinations can be made for other smartphone brands.

Large number of variables (e.g., "large display screen" and other key product attributes)— how do they interact?	→	Computer generates *factor loadings* for each variable so that a smaller number of factors (e.g., "easy to use") can be inferred by the researcher.	→	Computer generates *factor scores* for each respondent, which are used to create perceptual maps.

FIGURE 6-2

How Factor Analysis Works

TABLE 6-4 MDS Study Inputs: Similarity Judgment Scales for Pairs of Luxury Brands

	Very Similar				Very Different
	1	2	3	4	5
Burberry/Gucci	____	____	____	____	____
Burberry/Coach	____	____	____	____	____
Burberry/Michael Kors	____	____	____	____	____
Burberry/Tod's	____	____	____	____	____
Burberry/Dolce & Gabbana	____	____	____	____	____
Burberry/Dior	____	____	____	____	____
Burberry/Bottega Veneta	____	____	____	____	____
Gucci/Coach	____	____	____	____	____
Gucci/Michael Kors	____	____	____	____	____
Gucci/Tod's	____	____	____	____	____
Gucci/Dolce & Gabbana	____	____	____	____	____
Gucci/Dior	____	____	____	____	____
Gucci/Bottega Veneta	____	____	____	____	____

Cluster analysis allows the researcher to group variables into clusters that maximize within-group similarities and between-group differences. Cluster analysis shares some characteristics of factor analysis: It does not classify variables as dependent or independent, and it can be used in psychographic segmentation. Cluster analysis is well suited to global market research because similarities and differences can be established among local, national, and regional markets of the world. Cluster analysis can also be used to perform benefit segmentation and to identify new product opportunities.

Multidimensional scaling (MDS) is another technique for creating perceptual maps. When the researcher is using MDS, the respondent is given the task of comparing products or brands, one pair at a time, and judging them in terms of similarity. The researcher then infers the dimensions that underlie the judgments. MDS is particularly useful when there are many alternatives from which to choose—soft drink, toothpaste, or automotive brands, for instance—and when consumers may have difficulty verbalizing their perceptions. To create a well-defined perceptual map, a minimum of eight products or brands should be used.

For example, suppose that a luxury goods marketer such as Coach initiates a study of consumer perceptions of global luxury brands. There are many luxury brands to choose from; some (including Coach) have outlet stores featuring discounted merchandise, and some offer "flash sales" offering select styles for a limited time. Some brands, including Michael Kors and Ralph Lauren, offer lower-priced but highly profitable "diffusion" lines in addition to high-end collections. Some luxury goods firms, including Louis Vuitton, distribute their goods exclusively through company-owned retail stores; for Burberry and other brands, channel strategy includes wholesale operations.

Consumers may differentiate one designer brand from another in various ways: how easy it is to purchase each brand, how visible each brand is, whether or not the brand offers diffusion lines, and so on. To the researcher, this might represent an underlying perceptual dimension of "ubiquitous versus rare." Table 6-4 shows a five-point similarity judgment scale for eight designer brands. Figure 6-3 shows the position of the eight brands on the "ubiquity" dimension for a hypothetical respondent. The figure shows that Burberry and Coach are perceived as the most similar while Coach and Dior are the farthest apart.

The responses help marketers understand which brands in a particular category—luxury fashion brands in this example—are in direct competition with each other and which are not. The responses are inputted into a computer running an MDS program; the output is a perceptual

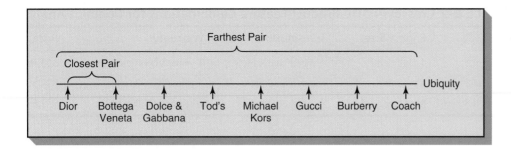

FIGURE 6-3
Hypothetical One-Dimensional Illustration of Similarity Judgments for Luxury Brands

map such as that shown in Figure 6-4. Once the computer has generated the map, the marketer examines the positions of different brands and infers the dimensions, which in this case are "ubiquity/rarity" and "exclusivity/accessibility." Coach's high ranking in terms of accessibility could be attributed in part to a pricing strategy that includes the lowest-priced entry-level handbag. Coach's position on the ubiquity dimension would be a function of the brand's multiple company-owned retail and outlet stores, wide availability at department stores, and the Poppy diffusion line.

This type of study could help Coach and other luxury goods marketers respond to new industry realities, which include a shift in the perception of what constitutes luxury and the increasing fragmentation of consumer tastes. Some of these changes in the market are driven by increasing opportunities in China and other emerging markets.[40] Such a map would also be helpful to, say, an up-and-coming fashion designer hoping to launch a new line. Perhaps the designer could find an optimal ubiquity/accessibility balance and fit in the gap between Burberry, Coach, and Ralph Lauren.

Dependence techniques assess the interdependence of two or more dependent variables with one or more independent variables. Conjoint analysis is an example of a dependence technique that is useful in both single market and global market research. Let us illustrate this with an example from the SUV category of the automotive industry. Suppose Kia's new product team has performed an MDS study and created a perceptual map similar to the one shown in Figure 6-4. The next task is to select an ideal position and then identify specific product features that will deliver that positioning. The researchers want to determine the relative importance of a product's *salient attributes* in consumer decision making; that is, the relevance or importance that

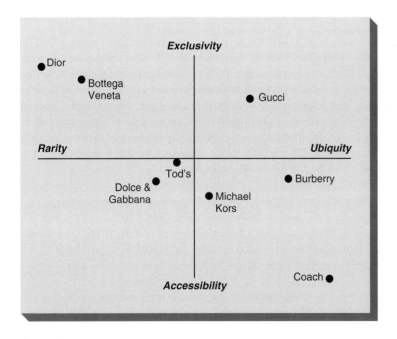

FIGURE 6-4
Hypothetical MDS-Based Perceptual Map for Luxury Fashion Brands

[40] Parts of this section were adapted from Vanessa Friedman, Rachel Sanderson, and Scheherazade Daneshkhu, "Luxury's New Look," *Financial Times* (December 24, 2012), p. 5.

TABLE 6-5 Crossover SUV Product Feature Combinations for Conjoint Analysis

	Engine Size	Transmission	Warranty	Price
Level 1	4-cylinder	4-speed automatic	3 years/50,000 miles	$22,500
Level 2	6-cylinder	6-speed automatic	5 years/75,000 miles	$27,500
Level 3	8-cylinder	8-speed automatic	10 years/100,000 miles	$32,500

consumers attach to a product's qualities or properties. If the target position is "smooth, carlike ride with sports handling," the team must determine relevant physical product characteristics (e.g., 6-cylinder engine, 6-speed transmission). The team must also determine other characteristics (e.g., price, mileage, warranty, etc.) that consumers most prefer. Each attribute should be available in different levels, for example, 5-year or 10-year warranty.

Conjoint analysis is a tool that researchers can use to gain insights into the combination of features that will be most attractive to consumers; it is assumed that features affect both perception and preferences. Table 6-5 shows a listing of possible features; a total of 36 combinations are possible. In a full-profile approach, each of these combinations (e.g., 6-cylinder engine, 6-speed automatic transmission, 5-year warranty, $27,500) is printed on an index card, and consumers are asked to rank them in order by preference. Conjoint analysis then determines the values or *utilities* of the various levels of product features and plots them graphically. Because the number of combinations can overwhelm subjects and lead to fatigue, it is sometimes preferable to use a pair-wise approach that allows subjects to consider two attributes at a time.

Better marketing research might have helped Nokia in its struggle to maintain leadership in the highly competitive global cellular phone market. Nokia focused on the functionality and features of its phones, even as consumer tastes and preferences were shifting to trendy styling and features such as cameras and large color screens. For years, Nokia manufactured only so-called "candy bar" phones; because executives believed that the shape was a signature of the Nokia brand, the company did not offer flip (clamshell), slide, or swivel styles. Meanwhile, Sony, LG, Samsung, and Motorola were offering sleek new designs. In Europe, Nokia's market share fell from 51 percent in 2002 to about 33 percent in 2004. "Nokia didn't have the coolness factor," says industry consultant Jack Gold. "They didn't really do flip phones; they were a little late with cameras, and they didn't push them. Coolness in the consumer space is a big deal, and they were stodgy." Ansii Vanjoki, Nokia's head of multimedia, acknowledges, "We read the signs in the marketplace a bit wrong. The competition was emphasizing factors such as color richness and screen size. That's attractive at the point of sale. We missed that one."[41]

COMPARATIVE ANALYSIS AND MARKET ESTIMATION BY ANALOGY One of the unique opportunities in global marketing analysis is to conduct comparisons of market potential and marketing performance in different country or regional markets at the same point in time. A common form of comparative analysis is the intracompany cross-national comparison. For example, general market conditions in two or more countries (as measured by income, stage of industrialization, or some other indicator) may be similar. If there is a significant discrepancy between per capita sales of a given product in the countries, the marketer might reasonably research it and determine what actions need to be taken. Consider the following examples:

- Campbell is the world's largest soup company, commanding about 80 percent of the U.S. canned soup market. However, the company has a presence in only 6 percent of the world's soup markets. Russians eat 32 billion servings of soup each year, and the Chinese consume *300* billion! By contrast, Americans eat 15 billion servings each year. Sensing a huge opportunity, Campbell CEO Douglas Conant dispatched teams to observe Russian and Chinese habits.[42]
- Cadbury, the British confectionary company, estimates that the chocolate market in India is worth about $465 million per year. By contrast, annual chocolate sales are $4.89 billion in

---

[41] Nelson D. Schwartz and Joan M. Levinstein, "Has Nokia Lost It?" *Fortune* (January 24, 2005), pp. 98–106.
[42] Bruce Horovitz, "CEO Nears 10-Year Goal to Clean up a Soupy Mess," *USA Today* (January 26, 2009), pp. 1B, 2B.

Britain, which has one-tenth the population of India. Cadbury executives believe the Indian market for confections and chocolate will grow at more than 12 percent annually.[43]

- In India, only about 10 percent of men who shave use Gillette razors. Worldwide, 50 percent of male shavers use Gillette products. To achieve greater penetration in India, Gillette rolled out a no-frills brand that costs 15 rupees—about 34 cents. The Gillette Guard® has a lighter handle that is cheaper to produce. It also lacks the lubrication strip found in Gillette's more expensive razors, and replacement blades cost only 5 rupees (11 cents).[44]

In these examples, data are, for the most part, available. However, global marketers may find that certain types of desired data are unavailable for a particular country market. This is especially true in developing-country markets. If this is the case, it is sometimes possible to estimate market size or potential demand by analogy. Drawing an *analogy* is simply stating a partial resemblance. For example, Germany and Italy both have flagship automakers, namely, Volkswagen and Fiat, respectively. A less-well-known flagship automaker is Russia's AvtoVAZ. So, we could say that "AvtoVAZ is to Russia what Volkswagen is to Germany and Fiat is to Italy." Statements such as this are analogies. Analogy reduces the unknown by highlighting the "commonness" of two different things."[45]

David Arnold notes that there are four possible approaches to forecasting by analogy:[46]

- Data are available on a comparable product in the same country.
- Data are available on the same product in a comparable country.
- Data are available on the same product from an independent distributor in a neighboring country.
- Data are available about a comparable company in the same country.

Time-series displacement is an analogy technique based on the assumption that an analogy between markets exists in different time periods. Displacing time is a useful form of market analysis when data are available for two markets at different levels of development. The time-displacement method requires a marketer to estimate when two markets are at similar stages of development. For example, the market for Polaroid instant cameras in Russia at the present time is comparable to the instant camera market in the United States in the mid-1960s. By obtaining data on the factors associated with demand for instant cameras in the United States in 1964 and in Russia today, as well as actual U.S. demand in 1964, one could estimate current potential in Russia.

Step 8: Interpretation and Presentation

The report based on the market research must be useful to managers as input to the decision-making process. Whether the report is presented in written form, orally, or electronically via video, it must relate clearly to the problem or opportunity identified in step 1. Generally, it is advisable for major findings to be summarized concisely in a memo that indicates the answer or answers to the problem first proposed in step 1. Many managers are uncomfortable with research jargon and complex quantitative analysis. Results should thus be clearly stated and provide a basis for managerial action. Otherwise, the report may end up on the shelf, where it will gather dust and serve as a reminder of wasted time and money. As the data provided by a corporate information system and market research become increasingly available on a worldwide basis, it becomes possible to analyze marketing expenditure effectiveness across national boundaries. Managers can then decide where they are achieving the greatest marginal effectiveness for their marketing expenditures and can adjust expenditures accordingly.

---

[43] Sonya Misquitta, "Cadbury Redefines Cheap Luxury," *The Wall Street Journal* (June 8, 2009), p. B4.

[44] Ellen Byron, "Gillette's Latest Innovation in Razors: The 11-Cent Blade," *The Wall Street Journal* (October 1, 2010), p. B1.

[45] Ikujiro Nonaka and Hirotaka Takeuchi, *The Knowledge-Creating Company* (Cambridge, MA: Harvard Business School Press, 1995), p. 67. As Nonaka and Takeuchi explain, "Metaphor and analogy are often confused. Association of two things through metaphor is driven mostly by intuition and holistic imagery and does not aim to find differences between them. On the other hand, association through analogy is carried out by rational thinking and focuses on structural/functional similarities between two things....Thus analogy helps us understand the unknown through the known."

[46] David Arnold, *The Mirage of Global Markets* (Upper Saddle River, NJ: Financial Times Prentice Hall, 2004), pp. 41–43.

Headquarters' Control of Market Research

An important issue for the global company is where to locate control of the organization's research capability. The difference between a multinational, polycentric company and a global, geocentric company on this issue is significant. In the multinational company, responsibility for research is delegated to the operating subsidiary. The global company delegates responsibility for research to operating subsidiaries but retains overall responsibility and control of research as a headquarters' function. A key difference between single-country market research and global market research is the importance of comparability. In practice, this means that the global company must ensure that research is designed and executed so as to yield comparable data.

Simply put, *comparability* means that the results can be used to make valid comparisons between the countries covered by the research.[47] To achieve this, the company must inject a level of control and review of marketing research at the global level. The director of worldwide marketing research must respond to local conditions as he or she develops a research program that can be implemented on a global basis. The research director must pay particular attention to whether data gathered are based on emic analysis or etic analysis. These terms, which come from anthropology, refer to the perspective taken in the study of another culture. **Emic analysis** is similar to ethnography in that it attempts to study a culture from within, using its own system of meanings and values. **Etic analysis** is "from the outside"; in other words, it is a more detached perspective that is often used in comparative or multicountry studies. In a particular research study, an etic scale would entail using the same set of items across all countries. This approach enhances comparability, but some precision is lost. By contrast, an emic study would be tailored to fit a particular country; inferences about cross-cultural similarities based on emic research have to be made subjectively. A good compromise is to use a survey instrument that incorporates elements of both types of analysis. It is likely that the marketing director will end up with a number of marketing programs tailored to clusters of countries that exhibit within-group similarities. The agenda of a coordinated worldwide research program might look like the one in Table 6-6.

The director of worldwide research should not simply direct the efforts of country research managers. His or her job is to ensure that the corporation achieves maximum results worldwide from the total allocation of its research resources. Achieving this requires that personnel in each country are aware of research being carried out in the rest of the world and are involved in influencing the design of their own in-country research as well as the overall research program. Ultimately, the director of worldwide research is responsible for the overall research design and program. It is his or her job to take inputs from the entire world and produce a coordinated research strategy that generates the information needed to achieve global sales and profit objectives.

The Marketing Information System as a Strategic Asset

The advent of the transnational enterprise means that boundaries between the firm and the outside world are dissolving. Marketing has historically been responsible for managing many of the relationships across that boundary. The boundary between marketing and other functions is also dissolving, and the traditional notion of marketing as a distinct functional area within the firm may be giving way to a new model. The process of marketing decision making is also changing, largely because of the changing role of information from a support tool to a wealth-generating, strategic asset.

TABLE 6-6 Worldwide Marketing Research Plan

Research Objective	Country Cluster A	Country Cluster B	Country Cluster C
Identify market potential			X
Appraise competitive intentions		X	X
Evaluate product appeal	X	X	X
Study market response to price	X		
Appraise distribution channels	X	X	X

---

[47] V. Kumar, *International Marketing Research* (Upper Saddle River, NJ: Prentice Hall, 1999), p. 15.

Many global firms are creating flattened organizations with less hierarchical and less centralized decision-making structures. Such organizations facilitate the exchange and flow of information among departments that previously may have operated as autonomous "silos." The more information-intensive the firm, the greater the degree to which marketing is involved in activities traditionally associated with other functional areas. In such firms there is parallel processing of information.

Information intensity in the firm has an impact on perceptions of market attractiveness, competitive position, and organizational structure. The greater a company's information intensity, the more the traditional product and market boundaries shift. In essence, companies increasingly face new sources of competition from other firms in historically noncompetitive industries, particularly if those other firms are also information intensive. Diverse firms now find themselves in direct competition with each other. They offer essentially the same products as a natural extension and redefinition of traditional product lines and marketing activities. Today, when marketers speak of "value added," the chances are they are not referring to unique product features. Rather, the emphasis is on the information exchanged as part of customer transactions, much of which cuts across traditional product lines.

Summary

Information is one of the most basic ingredients of a successful marketing strategy. A company's **management information system (MIS)** and **intranet** provide decision makers with a continuous flow of information. **Information technology** is profoundly affecting global marketing activities by allowing managers to access and manipulate data to assist in decision making. **Electronic data interchange (EDI), electronic point of sale (EPOS)** data, **efficient consumer response (ECR), customer relationship management (CRM)**, and **data warehouses** are some of the new tools and techniques available. The global marketer must scan the world for information about opportunities and threats and make information available via a management information system.

Formal **market research**—the project-specific, systematic gathering of data—is often required before marketers make key decisions. **Global market research** links customers and marketers through information gathered on a global scale. The research process begins when marketers define the problem and set research objectives; this step may entail assessing whether a particular market should be classified as **latent** or **incipient**. A research plan specifies the relative amounts of qualitative and quantitative information desired. Information is collected using either primary or **secondary data** sources. In today's wired world, the Internet has taken its place alongside more traditional channels as an important secondary information source. In some instances, the cost of collecting primary data may outweigh the potential benefits. Secondary sources are especially useful for researching a market that is too small to justify a large commitment of time and money.

If collection of primary data can be justified on a cost-benefit basis, research can be conducted via **survey research, personal interviews, consumer panels, observation**, and **focus groups**. Before collecting data, researchers must determine whether a probability sample is required. In global marketing, careful attention must be paid to issues such as eliminating cultural bias in research, accurately translating surveys, and ensuring data comparability in different markets. A number of techniques are available for analyzing survey data, including **factor analysis, cluster analysis, multidimensional scaling (MDS)**, and **conjoint analysis**. Research findings and recommendations must be presented clearly. A final issue is how much control headquarters will have over research and the overall management of the organization's information system. To ensure comparability of data, the researcher should utilize both **emic** and **etic** approaches.

MyMarketingLab

Go to **mymktlab.com** for the following Assisted-graded writing questions:

6-1. Discuss how existing, latent, and incipient demand differ. How might these differences affect the design of a marketing research project?

6-2. In light of the recent global economic downturn, should Lew Frankfort's strategy for expanding in China be revised?

6-3. Mymarketinglab Only – comprehensive writing assignment for this chapter.

MyMarketingLab

Go to **mymktlab.com** to complete the problems marked with this icon .

Discussion Questions

6-4. Explain how information technology puts powerful tools in the hands of global marketers.

6-5. Assume that you have been asked by the president of your organization to devise a systematic approach to scanning. The president does not want to be surprised by major market or competitive developments. What would you recommend?

6-6. Outline the basic steps of the market research process.

6-7. Describe some of the analytical techniques used by global marketers. When is it appropriate to use each technique?

6-8. Coach has often been cited as an example on how to revitalize a brand. The same could be said for Burberry, the British fashion goods company discussed in Chapter 1. Locate some articles about Burberry and read about the research its management has conducted and the formula it used to polish the brand. Are the approaches evident at Burberry and Coach similar? Are they competitors?

6-9. Below is a table similar to Table 6-4 that contains eight sports sedan nameplates. You can perform a rudimentary analysis along the lines of multidimensional scaling by ranking them by similarity. Do some research on the different models and see which pair you find to be the most similar. Which pair is the most different? Using these eight brands, create a rough perceptual map. What dimensions would you use to label the axes?

MDS Study Inputs: Similarity Judgment Scales for Pairs of Sport Sedans

	Very Similar				Very Different
	1	2	3	4	5
BMW328i/Volvo S60	____	____	____	____	____
BMW328i/Acura TL	____	____	____	____	____
BMW328i/Cadillac ATS	____	____	____	____	____
BMW328i /Audi A4	____	____	____	____	____
BMW328i/Mercedes-Benz C250	____	____	____	____	____
BMW328i/Lexus IS	____	____	____	____	____
BMW328i/Infiniti G37	____	____	____	____	____
Volvo S60/Acura TL	____	____	____	____	____
Volvo S60/Cadillac ATS	____	____	____	____	____
Volvo S60/Audi A4	____	____	____	____	____
Volvo S60/Mercedes-Benz C250	____	____	____	____	____
Volvo S60/Lexus IS	____	____	____	____	____
Volvo S60/Infiniti G37	____	____	____	____	____

CASE 6-1   CONTINUED (REFER TO PAGE 188)
CONTINUED (REFER TO PAGE 188)

Nestlé's Middle East Investment in Market Research

In 2009, Nestlé Middle East's total revenue from a range of 60 products, as mentioned earlier, accounted for $1.4 billion. Nestlé gains consumer trust not only by considering serious concerns over the quality of food and the variety it serves to its consumers, but also by investing in research labs to ensure they exceed the food safety quality requirements. Nestlé Middle East is an important market globally, and has been identified as a potential growth market with a lot of opportunities. In 2009, Nestlé's state-of-the-art Regional Microbiological Laboratory located in Dubai, United Arab Emirates became well-known for carrying out a wide range of tests for the analysis of salmonella. The new facility is also used for training several government bodies. Another recent investment is the advanced Sensory Lab Unit for Renovation-Innovation of Products (SLURP), also located in Dubai. This lab is fitted with high-end technological facilities to serve as a center of expertise for advanced sensory profiling analyses on shelf-stable dairy, coffee and confectionery products.

Nestlé believes investing in factories is very important because they support and facilitate research in various ways. Manufacturing products locally allows Nestlé to adapt to the cultural needs and preferences of the local market, and accelerate the delivery of fresher products to the market and the consumer. Thus, new information gathered from the market can be implemented effectively in a timely manner. According to Nestlé, doing so gives them a prime advantage over their competition, a practice they have followed for many of their manufacturing plants in the Middle East. In 2010, Nestlé announced its commitment to investing U.S. $136 million in a new manufacturing facility in Dubai aiming to serve Nestlé markets across the region. In addition, another investment to expand operations in the Middle East to meet the growing regional demand and eventually export to other regions is in the pipelines – Nestlé Middle East built a new Nestlé confectionery factory which is set to be the third largest KitKat plant worldwide.

The UAE is not the only country where Nestlé is interested in investing. In 2010, Nestlé created the first and only factory outside Europe for the production of Mövenpick Super Premium ice cream in Egypt. It will also be a base for products such as Cerelac infant cereal and Maggi soups and bouillons. Nestlé believes that Egypt—with a large population, diverse and energetic, of 90 million—is a good market. The ice cream produced is distributed locally as well as exported to countries like Jordan, Libya, Lebanon, and Tunisia and Malaysia. In future, mixing, processing, chocolate-coating and cone-filling equipment will be added to the factory.

Nestlé continues to expand in the emerging markets and is currently using a Popularly Positioned Products (PPP) model as a growth driver for the region. For targeting emerging consumers who are entering the cash economy and buying branded goods for the first time, Nestlé's PPPs are adapted to meet their needs in terms of price, accessibility and format, such as single-serve packets. In Egypt, Nestlé's research conducted on behalf of the food service industry is applied to Nestlé Professional strengthening – since consumption on-the-go and hence, out-of-home is steadily on the rise, there is scope for developing Nestlé's coffee machine vending business.

Satisfaction of the needs of consumers, from "emerging consumers to those looking for premium products," is the topmost priority and Nestlé aims to fill this gap. The Egyptian Revolution, also known as the Revolution of January 25th, did not stop Nestlé's investment; a week after the uprising it publicized a $160-million program for improvements across its manufacturing and distribution, and investment in skills over the next three to five years. Nestlé Egypt aims to attract and adapt to the cultural change in an innovative way – for instance, a new nutrition initiative called the "Healthy Kids" program aims to engage the target audience in the company's identity. It is an educational scheme with almost 30,000 children in 50 secondary schools around Egypt.

Finally, to emphasize the importance of marketing research, Nestlé is very keen on understanding the nutritional needs of its consumers so as to accelerate the development of products with an improved nutrition profile at the right price in emerging markets. For example, in South Africa, a new research partnership with South African scientists is being coordinated by the Council for Scientific and Industrial Research (CSIR), a part of the government's Department for Science and Technology (DST). It will allow scientists to explore and make use extensively of Nestlé's research capabilities and expertise in nutrition, food science and food safety. Moreover, part of Nestlé's global R&D efforts focuses on discovering new bioactive ingredients. Biodiversity is very important; some of the researches will work on studying how to make use of the locally sourced ingredients to create foods that provide health benefits. Researchers would examine "how well these ingredients target different tissues in the body once ingested, as well as their effectiveness in helping to promote health."

Discussion Questions

6-10. Critically examine Nestlé's positioning model.

6-11. Discuss the importance of investment in research with regards to the Nestlé case.

6-12. Explain the different ways in which market research can be applied to satisfy consumers.

Sources: A word from the Chairman and CEO, Nestlé Middle East, www.nestle-me.com/en/aboutus; Fact Sheet, Nestlé Middle East (2010), www.nestle.com/asset-library/Documents/Library/Events/2010-Inauguration-of-a-new-factory-in-Dubai/Fact_Sheet_2010_Nestle_Middle_East_EN_FINAL.pdf; "FMCG companies tap Middle East growth," Warc (May 8, 2013), www.warc.com/Content/News/FMCG_companies_tap_Middle_East_growth.content?ID=efe6d4d4-bd8c-44b7-9e1b-9700051a3718&q; "Nestlé opens new USD 136 million factory in Dubai," Nestlé (2010), www.nestle.com/media/newsandfeatures/nestle-opens-new-factory-dubai; "Nestlé invests CHF 160m and creates 500 new jobs in Egypt," Nestlé (2010), www.nestle.com/media/newsandfeatures/nestle-invests-chf-160m-and-creates-500-new-jobs-in-egypt; "Nestlé Egypt: The new Egypt," *Business Excellence*, (November 25, 2011), www.bus-ex.com/article/nestl%C3%A9-egypt; "Nestlé partners with South African scientists," *New Food Magazine* (March 6, 2012), www.newfoodmagazine.com/7099/news/nestle-partners-with-south-african-scientists/; "Egypt factory investment as appetite for ice cream soars," Nestlé (2013), www.nestle.com/Media/NewsAndFeatures/Ice-Cream-Egypt.

CASE 6-2
Research Helps Whirlpool Keep Its Cool at Home, Act Local in Emerging Markets

Whirlpool Corporation, headquartered in Benton Harbor, Michigan, is the world's number 1 appliance company. The company sells more than $18 billion worth of "white goods" each year; this category includes refrigerators, stoves, washing machines, dryers, and microwave ovens. Whirlpool's success has been achieved, in part, by offering a brand portfolio of products in different price ranges. These include the premium KitchenAid and Maytag brands as well as the medium-priced Amana and Whirlpool brands.

Not surprisingly, the global economic crisis translated into lower sales in North America and Europe, where Whirlpool generates nearly 75 percent of its revenues. By contrast, sales in Latin America and Asia are showing double-digit gains. Whirlpool is not new to foreign markets; for example, the company has had a presence in Latin America since 1957. Today, it is the market share leader there, offering global brands (Whirlpool, KitchenAid, and Maytag) as well as local (Brastemp) and regional ones (Consul).

At the beginning of 1993, David Whitwam, then-chairman and CEO of Whirlpool Corporation, told an interviewer, "Five years ago we were essentially a domestic company. Today about 40 percent of our revenues are overseas, and by the latter part of this decade, a majority will be." The former CEO's comments came 3 years after he had placed his first bet that the appliance industry was globalizing. By acquiring Philips Electronics' European appliance business for $1 billion, Whirlpool vaulted into the number 3 position in Europe. Whitwam pledged another $2 billion investment in Europe alone.

As the decade of the 1990s drew to a close, however, Whitwam's ambitious plans for expanding beyond Europe into Japan and the developing nations in Asia and Latin America hadn't achieved the desired results. Noting that Whirlpool stock underperformed in the bull market of the 1990s, analysts began questioning whether Whitwam's global vision was on target. As one analyst put it, "The strategy has been a failure. Whirlpool went big into global markets and investors have paid for it." Others faulted the company on execution. Another analyst said, "I respect Whirlpool's strategy. They just missed on the blocking and tackling."

The challenge Whirlpool faces is rooted partially in the structure of the appliance industry. In Europe, for example, the presence of more than 200 brands and 170 factories makes the appliance industry highly fragmented and highly competitive there. Electrolux, a Swedish company, ranks number 1. Whirlpool's various brands are available in 30 countries; however, European appliance sales have been flat for years, with sales volumes growing at a mere 1 or 2 percent; industry overcapacity is a major issue. Although analysts expect to see a surge in demand from Central and Eastern Europe within a few years, there will also be an influx of products from low-cost producers in those regions.

From its headquarters in Comerio, Italy, Whirlpool Europe operates manufacturing facilities in seven countries. In the 1990s, Whirlpool executives began the process of streamlining the European organization to cut costs and increase margins. When he was president of Whirlpool Europe BV, Hank Bowman cut fixed costs by closing many of the company's 30 warehouses. Today, the company even outsources management of some distribution functions; in 2010, for example, France's Norbert Dentressangle took over management of Whirlpool's national distribution center at Aylesford in Kent, England.

Bowman was confident that a global market segmentation approach was the key to success in Europe. Whirlpool relies heavily on market research to maintain its leadership in the United States; listening to consumers is important in Europe and Latin America as well. "Research tells us that the trends, preferences and biases of consumers, country by country, are reducing as opposed to increasing," Bowman said. He believed that European homemakers fall into distinct "Euro-segments"—traditionalists and aspirers, for example, allowing Whirlpool to duplicate its three-tiered approach to brands that has worked so well in the United States. The Bauknecht brand is positioned at the high end of the market, with Whirlpool in the middle and Ignis at the lower end. For example, appliance shoppers in Germany visiting a department store such as Saturn can choose a Bauknecht ECO 9.0 priced at €499 or a Whirlpool for €369.

Research has also indicated that consumers in different countries prefer different types of features. Thus, Whirlpool has begun emphasizing product platforms as a means to produce localized versions of ovens, refrigerators, and other appliance lines more economically. A platform is essentially a technological core underneath the metal casing of an appliance. The platform—for example, the compressor and sealant system in a refrigerator—can be the same throughout the world. Country- or region-specific capabilities can be added late in the production cycle. The goal was to cut 10 percent from Whirlpool's $200 million annual production development budget and achieve a 30 percent productivity increase among the company's 2,000 member product-development staff. Ultimately, the platform project team hopes to reduce the total number of platforms in the company from 135 to 65. Specific goals include reducing the number of dishwasher platforms from 6 to 3 and refrigerator platforms from 48 to 25.

Whirlpool also conducts usability studies that provide insight into the ways that consumers interact with its products. In one study, for example, engineers and designers stood behind a two-way mirror and watched as a volunteer put groceries away in a Kenmore Elite refrigerator. The Whirlpool team recorded a variety of data, such as the amount of time required for the volunteer to finish the task and the number of features she used. The results from these types of studies are used to help designers create appliances with a distinctive look and feel. Chuck Jones, Whirlpool's design guru, has made sure that each of Whirlpool's brands has its own "visual design language."

Jones has also been known to trust his gut rather than the data. For example, Jones wanted to sell a new front-loading, German-made washer and matching "Made in the USA" dryer in tandem. Priced at $2,000, the combo was known as the Duet. However, company research indicated that 80 percent of the time, consumers buy either a washer or a dryer, but not both together. To make matters worse, one-third of the members of a focus group did not like the design. Recalling that moment, Jones says, "In the past, that would have been the kiss of death. This was one of those watershed moments that tested the company's fiber. You can't expect consumers to articulate that leap to the next breakthrough idea. It's our job to lead them there."

Jones stood his ground during a review with senior-level executives. He even threatened to quit if the company didn't give the go-ahead to the Duet concept. In the end, management gave Jones the green light and the Duet was launched. Despite the fact that it is Whirlpool's most expensive washer-dryer pair, the Duet has a 20 percent market share in the premium front-loading washer category.

Market research also drives the search for new products that address the specific needs of developing markets. In Brazil, for example, Whirlpool's market-entry strategy included acquiring two local established appliance brands, Brastemp and Consul. However, with a basic washer priced at $300, even the low end of Whirlpool's product lines proved to be too expensive for many Brazilians. Economic data indicated that Brazil's 30 million low-income households, many with monthly incomes of about $220, account for about one-third of national consumption. Moreover, studies showed that these households ranked an automatic washer second only to a cell phone as an aspirational purchase. Whirlpool's researchers convened focus groups and made visits to representative low-income households. Marcele Rodrigues is director of laundry technology at Multibrás SA Eletrodomésticos, Whirlpool's Brazilian division. "It wasn't a matter of stripping down an existing model," he noted. "We had to innovate for the masses."

Whirlpool's response was to develop what it proudly calls the world's least expensive automatic washer, to be sold under the Consul brand. The company has a strong team of engineers and industrial designers in Brazil, as well as some of its most technologically advanced factories. Despite the fact that Brazil's economy was in turmoil, Whirlpool invested $30 million to develop the new washer, the Ideale, to meet the needs of a large class of consumers who still wash clothes by hand. One cost-saving design breakthrough was a patentable technology that allows the machine to switch from the wash cycle to the spin cycle without shifting gears. However, the design involves some performance compromises: Compared with more expensive models, the spin cycle takes longer and clothes come out damper. However, research indicated that these were not critical issues for most consumers.

Focus group research also indicated that consumers would find a smaller-capacity washer acceptable because low-income families do laundry more often. Because Brazilian housewives like to wash floors underneath furniture, the Ideale sits high on four legs as opposed to resting on the floor as most conventional units do. Perhaps the most significant thing that the Ideale design team learned from its research was that form matters, too. As Emerson do Valle, vice president of Multibrás, explained, "We realized the washer should be aesthetically pleasing; it's a status symbol for these people." The team selected a rounded design with a yellow start button and blue lettering on the control panel. Because white is widely associated with cleanliness in Brazil, the Ideale is available only in white.

Although the Ideale incorporates many design features that appeal to consumers in Brazil, adaptations of the Ideale platform are also being manufactured and marketed in China and India. In India, the color options include green, blue, and white; the setting for delicate fabrics is labeled "sari." Also, the Indian units are mounted on casters so they can be moved easily.

In China, an appliance with a white exterior would be undesirable because of the prevailing belief that white shows dirt easily. For that reason, the Chinese Ideale is available in light blue and gray.

In addition, the heavy-duty wash cycle in China is labeled "grease removal" for the simple reason that many Chinese use bicycles for daily transportation. Although the majority of Chinese washing machines have separate tubs for the wash and spin cycles, sales of single-drum washers such as the Ideale and a new front-loading model, the Sunrise, are growing. Overall, washer sales in China totaled 16.5 million units in 2005; Whirlpool expected that number to reach 22.2 million by 2011.

After a decade of losses, Whirlpool China finally posted a profit in 2006. The company first entered the market in the mid-1990s via joint ventures with local partners. Whirlpool called its strategy "T-4": offering refrigerators, washing machines, microwave ovens, and air conditioners, the four most-sought home appliances. Several of the ventures quickly went sour; as one executive recalls, "We quickly jumped into joint ventures without insights into Chinese consumers. We brought in North American know-how, but we also needed to distill local know-how." For one thing, Whirlpool underestimated the speed at which Haier and other local competitors were evolving into world-class manufacturers. Company executives note that since China joined the World Trade Organization in 2001, it has been easier for Western companies to do business there.

In 2006, Jeff M. Fettig succeeded David Whitwam as Whirlpool's CEO and chairman. If emerging markets are to be drivers of global growth under Fettig's leadership, Whirlpool will have to build brand recognition in countries such as Brazil, India, and China. Also, consumers in emerging markets must be persuaded to move beyond washing machines to purchase some of the company's other appliances. That trend is already gaining traction: Middle-class Chinese consumers are splurging on high-end appliances such as a side-by-side Whirlpool refrigerator that costs the equivalent of $2,500. Many of the units find their way into living rooms. As Michael Todman, president of Whirlpool International, noted, "Appliances can be furniture, too. It's a source of pride to own one: 'Gee, look what I can own. I'm doing well.'"

Discussion Questions

⭐ **6-13.** Describe Whirlpool's global marketing strategy. Does Whirlpool use an extension product strategy or an adaptation product strategy?

6-14. What is the primary reason people buy and own major appliances such as a washing machine? Is there a secondary reason as well?

⭐ **6-15.** What are the key lessons to be learned from Whirlpool's experience in emerging markets?

Sources: Anjali Athavely, "High-Tech Looks Put New Spin on Laundry," *The Wall Street Journal* (November 2, 2010); Calum MacLeod, "Whirlpool Spins China Challenge into Turnaround," *USA Today* (April 5, 2007), pp. 1B, 2B; Chuck Salter, "Whirlpool Finds Its Cool," *Fast Company* (June 1, 2005); Miriam Jordan and Jonathan Karp, "Machines for the Masses," *The Wall Street Journal* (December 9, 2003), pp. B1, B2; Katheryn Kranhold, "Whirlpool Conjures Up Appliance Divas," *The Wall Street Journal* (April 27, 2000), p. B1; Peter Marsh and Nikki Tait, "Whirlpool's Platform for Growth," *Financial Times* (March 26, 1998), p. 8; Peter Marsh and Nikki Tait, "Whirlpool Sticks to Its Global Guns," *Financial Times* (February 2, 1998), p. 4; Greg Steinmetz and Carl Quintanilla, "Tough Target: Whirlpool Expected Easy Going in Europe, and It Got a Big Shock," *The Wall Street Journal* (April 10, 1998), pp. A1, A6.

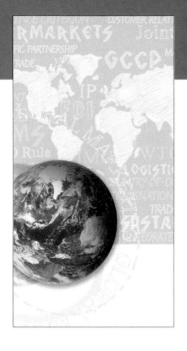

7

Segmentation, Targeting, and Positioning

CASE 7-1

Global Companies Target Low-Income Consumers (A)

"Frugal engineering." "Indovation." "Reverse innovation." These are some of the terms that marketers at GE, Procter & Gamble, Siemens, and Unilever are using to describe efforts to penetrate more deeply into emerging markets. As growth in mature markets slows, executives and managers at many global companies are realizing that the ability to serve the needs of the world's poorest consumers will be a critical source of competitive advantage in the decades to come.

Exhibit 7-1 In Africa and other emerging markets, many isolated villages lack basic services such as running water and electricity. The situation is improving as the cost of small-scale energy sources continues to fall. In Kenya, a low-cost solar panel mounted on the roof of a hut can provide enough electricity to charge a cellphone and provide light so that children can study at night.
Source: AfriPics.com/Alamy.

Procter & Gamble CEO Robert McDonald has set a strategic goal of introducing 800 million new consumers to the company's brands by 2015. This will require a better understanding of what daily life is like in, say, hundreds of thousands of rural villages in Africa, Latin America, and China.

Consider, for example, that two-thirds of the world's population—more than 4 billion people—live on less than $2 per day. This segment is sometimes referred to as the "bottom of the pyramid" and includes an estimated 1.5 billion people who live "off the grid"; that is, they have no access to electricity to provide light or to charge their cell phones. Often, a villager must walk several miles to hire a taxi for the trip to the nearest city with electricity. Such trips are costly in terms of both time and money.

This situation has provided an opportunity for companies to create innovative sources of renewable energy. Solutions include a small-scale, roof-mounted, Chinese-made solar power system that costs $80, underground biogas chambers that generate electricity from cow manure, and scaled-down hydroelectric dams that can power a village from a local stream or river (see Exhibit 7-1).

The efforts by global companies to reach low-income consumers in emerging markets highlight the importance of skillful global market segmentation and targeting. **Market segmentation** represents an effort to identify and categorize groups of customers and countries according to common characteristics. **Targeting** is the process of evaluating the segments and focusing marketing efforts on a country, region, or group of people that has significant potential to respond. Such targeting reflects the reality that a company should identify those consumers it can reach most effectively, efficiently, and profitably. Finally, proper **positioning** is required to differentiate the product or brand in the minds of target customers. The second part of Case 7-1, at the end of the chapter, explores the challenges and issues facing Procter & Gamble and other companies as they segment global markets by income and population and target hundreds of millions of poor consumers with innovative products and appropriate positioning strategies.

Global markets can be segmented according to buyer category (e.g., consumer, enterprise, government), age, gender, income, and a number of other criteria. Segmentation and targeting are two separate but closely related go-to-market activities. Together, they serve as the link between market needs and wants and tactical decisions by managers to develop marketing programs and value propositions that meet the specific needs of one or more segments. Segmentation, targeting, and positioning are all examined in this chapter.

LEARNING OBJECTIVES

1 Identify the variables that global marketers can use to segment global markets and give an example of each.

2 Explain the criteria that global marketers use to choose specific markets to target.

3 Understand how global marketers use a product-market grid to make targeting decisions.

4 Compare and contrast the three main target market strategy options.

5 Describe the various positioning options available to global marketers.

Global Market Segmentation

Global market segmentation has been defined as the process of identifying specific segments—whether they be country groups or individual consumer groups—of potential customers with homogeneous attributes who are likely to exhibit similar responses to a company's marketing mix.[1] Marketing practitioners and academics have been interested in global market segmentation for several decades. In the late 1960s, one observer suggested that the European market could be divided into three broad categories—international sophisticate, semi-sophisticate, and provincial—solely on the basis of consumers' presumed receptivity to a common advertising approach.[2] Another writer suggested that some themes—for example, the desire to be beautiful, the desire to

---

[1] Salah S. Hassan and Lea Prevel Katsanis, "Identification of Global Consumer Segments: A Behavioral Framework," *Journal of International Consumer Marketing* 3, no. 2 (1991), p. 17.
[2] John K. Ryans, Jr., "Is It Too Soon to Put a Tiger in Every Tank?" *Columbia Journal of World Business* (March–April 1969), p. 73.

be healthy and free of pain, and the love between mother and child—are universal and could be used in advertising around the globe.[3]

Consider the following examples:

- The personal computer market can be divided into home users, corporate (also known as "enterprise") users, and educational users. Dell originally targeted corporate customers; even today, sales of products for home use account for only 20 percent of revenues. After focusing only on the PC market, Dell then branched out into other computer categories, such as servers and storage hardware.
- After convening worldwide employee conferences to study women's shaving preferences, Schick-Wilkinson Sword introduced a shaving system for women that features a replaceable blade cartridge. Intuition, as the system is known, incorporates a "skin-conditioning solid" that allows a woman to lather and shave her legs simultaneously. Intuition is a premium product targeted directly at users of Venus, Gillette's three-blade razor system for women.[4]
- Dove, a division of Unilever, traditionally targeted women with its Dove-branded skin care products. Recently, the company launched a new brand, Men+Care. The move prompted marketers at rival Old Spice to launch humorous ads poking fun at guys who use "lady-scented body wash"—a clear jab at Dove.
- GM's original market-entry strategy for China called for targeting government and company officials who were entitled to a large sedan-style automobile. Today, GM's lineup for China includes the Buick Century, targeted at the country's middle class, and the $10,000 Buick Sail.

Four decades ago, Professor Theodore Levitt advanced the thesis that consumers in different countries increasingly seek variety and that the same new segments are likely to show up in multiple national markets. Thus, ethnic or regional foods such as sushi, falafel, or pizza might be in demand anywhere in the world. Levitt suggested that this trend, known variously as the *pluralization of consumption* and *segment simultaneity*, provides an opportunity for marketers to pursue one or more segments on a global scale. Frank Brown, president of MTV Networks Asia, acknowledged this trend in explaining MTV's success in Asia despite a business downturn in the region: "When marketing budgets are tight, advertisers look for a more effective buy, and we can deliver a niche audience with truly panregional reach," he said.[5] Authors John Micklethwait and Adrian Wooldridge sum up the situation this way:

> The audience for a new recording of a Michael Tippett symphony or for a nature documentary about the mating habits of flamingos may be minuscule in any one country, but round up all the Tippett and flamingo fanatics around the world, and you have attractive commercial propositions. The cheap distribution offered by the Internet will probably make these niches even more attractive financially.[6]

Global market segmentation is based on the premise that companies should attempt to identify consumers in different countries who share similar needs and desires. However, the fact that significant numbers of pizza-loving consumers are found in many countries does not mean that they are eating the exact same thing. In France, for example, Domino's serves pizza with goat cheese and strips of pork fat known as *lardoons*. In Taiwan, toppings include squid, crab, shrimp, and pineapple; Brazilians can order their pies with mashed bananas and cinnamon. As Patrick Doyle, executive vice president of Domino's international division, explains, "Pizza is beautifully adaptable to consumer needs around the world, simply by changing the toppings."[7]

---

[3] Arther C. Fatt, "The Danger of 'Local' International Advertising," *Journal of Marketing* 31, no. 1 (January 1967), pp. 60–62.

[4] Charles Forelle, "Schick Puts a Nick in Gillette's Razor Cycle," *The Wall Street Journal* (October 3, 2003), p. B7.

[5] Magz Osborne, "Second Chance in Japan," *Ad Age Global* 1, no. 9 (May 2001), p. 28.

[6] John Micklethwait and Adrian Wooldridge, *A Future Perfect: The Challenge and Hidden Promise of Globalization* (New York: Crown Publishers, 2000), p. 198.

[7] Neil Buckley, "Domino's Returns to Fast Food's Fast Lane," *Financial Times* (November 26, 2003), p. 10.

A. Coskun Samli developed a useful approach to global market segmentation that compares and contrasts "conventional" versus "unconventional" wisdom.[8] For example, conventional wisdom might assume that consumers in Europe and Latin America are interested in World Cup soccer, whereas those in America are not. Unconventional wisdom would note that the "global jock" segment exists in many countries, including the United States.[9] Similarly, conventional wisdom might assume that, because per capita income in India is about $1,420, all Indians have low incomes. Unconventional wisdom would note the presence of a higher-income, middle-class segment. As Sapna Nayak, a food analyst at Raobank India, noted, "The potential Indian customer base for a McDonald's or a Subway is larger than the size of entire developed countries."[10] The same is true of China; the average annual income of people living in eastern China is approximately $1,200. This is equivalent to a lower-middle-income country market with 470 million people, larger than every other single country market except India.[11]

Contrasting Views of Global Segmentation

As we have noted many times in this book, global marketers must determine whether a standardized or an adapted marketing mix is required to best serve consumers' wants and needs. By performing market segmentation, marketers can generate the insights needed to devise the most effective approach. The process of global market segmentation begins with the choice of one or more variables to use as a basis for grouping customers. Common variables include demographics (including national income and size of population), psychographics (values, attitudes, and lifestyles), behavioral characteristics, and benefits sought. It is also possible to cluster different national markets in terms of their environments—for example, the presence or absence of government regulation in a particular industry—to establish groupings.

Demographic Segmentation

Demographic segmentation is based on measurable characteristics of populations, such as income, population, age distribution, gender, education, and occupation. A number of global demographic trends—fewer married couples, smaller family size, changing roles of women, higher incomes and living standards, for example—have contributed to the emergence of global market segments. The following are several key demographic facts and trends from around the world:

- Asia is home to 500 million consumers aged 16 and younger.
- India has the youngest demographic profile among the world's large nations. More than half its population is younger than 25; the number of young people below the age of 14 is greater than the entire U.S. population.
- In the European Union (EU), the number of consumers aged 16 and under is rapidly approaching the number of consumers aged 60 and older.
- Half of Japan's population will be 50 years old or older by 2025.
- By 2030, 20 percent of the U.S. population—70 million Americans—will be 65 years old or older versus 13 percent (36 million) today.
- America's three main ethnic groups—African/Black Americans, Hispanic Americans, and Asian Americans—represent a combined annual buying power of $2.5 trillion.[12]
- The United States is home to 28.4 million foreign-born residents with a combined income of $233 billion.

Statistics such as these can provide valuable insights to marketers who are scanning the globe for opportunities. As noted in Chapter 4, for example, Disney hopes to capitalize on the huge number of young people—and their parents' rising incomes—in India. Managers at global companies must be alert to the possibility that marketing strategies will have to be adjusted in response to

[8] A. Coskun Samli, *International Consumer Behavior* (Westport, CT: Quorum, 1995), p. 130.
[9] Robert Frank, "When World Cup Soccer Starts, World-Wide Productivity Stalls," *The Wall Street Journal* (June 12, 1998), pp. B1, B2; Daniela Deane, "Their Cup Runneth Over: Ethnic Americans Going Soccer Crazy," *USA Today* (July 2, 1998), p. 13A.
[10] Saritha Rai, "Tastes of India in U.S. Wrappers," *The New York Times* (April 29, 2003), p. W7.
[11] Joseph Kahn, "Made in China, Bought in China," *The New York Times* (January 5, 2003), sec. 3, p. 10.
[12] Jeffrey M. Humphreys, *The Multicultural Economy 2010* (Athens, GA: Selig Center for Economic Growth, 2010).

the aging of the population and other demographic trends. For example, consumer products companies will need to convene focus groups consisting of people over 50 years old who are nearing retirement. These same companies will also have to target Brazil, Mexico, Vietnam, and other developing country markets to achieve growth objectives in the years to come.

Demographic changes can create opportunities for marketing innovation. In France, for example, two entrepreneurs began rewriting the rules of retailing years before Sam Walton founded the Walmart chain. Marcel Fournier and Louis Defforey opened the first Carrefour ("crossroads") hypermarket in 1963. At the time, France had a fragmented shop system that consisted of small, specialized stores with only about 5,000 square feet of floor space, such as the *boulangerie* and *charcuterie*. The shop system was part of France's national heritage, and shoppers developed personal relationships with a shop's proprietor. However, time-pressed, dual-parent-working families had less time to stop at several stores for daily shopping. The same trend was occurring in other countries. By 1993, Carrefour SA was a global chain with $21 billion in sales and a market capitalization of $10 billion. Sales totaled $121 billion in 2010, and today Carrefour operates more than 9,630 stores in 32 countries. As Adrian Slywotzky has noted, it was a demographic shift that provided the opportunity for Fournier and Defforey to create a novel, customer-matched, cost-effective business design.[13]

SEGMENTING GLOBAL MARKETS BY INCOME AND POPULATION When a company charts a plan for global market expansion, it often finds that income is a valuable segmentation variable. After all, a market consists of those who are willing and *able* to buy. For cigarettes, soft drinks, candy, and other consumer products that have a low per-unit cost, population is often a more valuable segmentation variable than income. Nevertheless, for a vast range of industrial and consumer products offered in global markets today, income is a valuable and important macro indicator of market potential. About two-thirds of world gross national income (GNI) is generated in the Triad; however, only about 12 percent of the world's population is located in Triad countries.

The concentration of wealth in a handful of industrialized countries has significant implications for global marketers. After segmenting in terms of a single demographic variable—income—a company can reach the most affluent markets by targeting fewer than 20 nations: half the EU, North America, and Japan. By doing so, however, the marketers are *not* reaching almost 90 percent of the world's population! A word of caution is in order here. Data about income (and population) have the advantage of being widely available and inexpensive to access. However, management may unconsciously "read too much" into such data. In other words, while providing some measure of market potential, such macro-level demographic data should not necessarily be used as the sole indicator of presence (or absence) of a market opportunity. This is especially true when an emerging country market or region is being investigated.

Ideally, gross domestic product (GDP) and other measures of national income converted to U.S. dollars should be calculated on the basis of purchasing power parities (i.e., what the currency will buy in the country of issue) or through direct comparisons of actual prices for a given product. This would provide an actual comparison of the standards of living in the countries of the world. Table 7-1 ranks the top 10 countries in terms of 2011 per capita income followed by the respective figure adjusted for purchasing power parity (PPP). Although the United States ranks sixth in per capita income, only Norway, Luxembourg, and Switzerland surpass its standard of living—as measured by what money can buy.[14] By most metrics, the U.S. market is enormous: $15 trillion in national income and a population that passed the 300 million milestone in 2006. Little wonder, then, that so many non-U.S. companies target and cater to American consumers and organizational buyers!

A case in point is Mitsubishi Motors, which had begun redesigning its Montero Sport sport utility vehicle (SUV) with the goal of creating a "global vehicle" that could be sold worldwide with little adaptation. Then the design program changed course; the new goal was to make the vehicle more "American" by providing more interior space and more horsepower. Hiroshi Yajima, a Mitsubishi executive in North America, attributed the change to the vibrancy and sheer size of the American auto market. "We wouldn't care if the vehicle didn't sell outside the U.S.," he said.[15]

[13] Adrian Slywotzky, *Value Migration* (Cambridge, MA: Harvard Business School Press, 1996), p. 37.
[14] For a more detailed discussion, see Malcolm Gillis et al., *Economics of Development* (New York: Norton, 1996), pp. 37–40.
[15] Norihiko Shirouzu, "Tailoring World's Cars to U.S. Tastes," *The Wall Street Journal* (January 1, 2001), p. B1.

TABLE 7-1 Per Capita Income, 2011 (excluding Liechtenstein and Monaco)

	2011 GNI per Capita	2011 Income Adjusted for Purchasing Power
1. Norway	$88,870	$61,450
2. Luxembourg	$77,390	$64,110
3. Switzerland	$76,350	$52,530
4. Denmark	$60,160	$41,920
5. Sweden	$53,170	$42,210
6. Netherlands	$49,660	$43,150
6. United States	$48,620	$48,820
7. Germany	$44,230	$40,190
8. France	$42,410	$35,910
9. Ireland	$39,150	$33,520
10. United Kingdom	$37,780	$35,950

The Montero was sold in the United States until 2004, when it was superceded by the Endeavor. The Endeavor, manufactured in Illinois, was part of Mitsubishi's "Project America" program, which focuses on producing cars targeting the U.S. market without concern for the preferences of drivers in export markets. The program is paying off: Mitsubishi's current SUV offering, the Outlander, has a "Recommended" rating from the influential *Consumer Reports.*

Despite having comparable per capita incomes, other industrialized countries are nevertheless quite small in terms of *total* annual income (see Table 7-2). In Sweden, for example, per capita GNI is about $53,170; however, Sweden's smaller population—9.4 million—means that, in relative terms, its market is limited. This helps explain why Ericsson, IKEA, Saab, and other Swedish companies have looked beyond their borders for significant growth opportunities.

While Table 7-1 highlights the differences between straightforward income statistics and the standard of living in the world's most affluent nations, such differences can be even more pronounced in less-developed countries. A visit to a mud house in Tanzania will reveal many of the things that money can buy: an iron bed frame, a corrugated metal roof, beer and soft drinks, bicycles, shoes, photographs, radios, and even televisions. What Tanzania's per capita income of $540 does not reflect is the fact that instead of utility bills, Tanzanians have the local well and the sun. Instead of nursing homes, tradition and custom ensure that families will take care of the elderly at home. Instead of expensive doctors and hospitals, villagers may utilize the services of witch doctors and healers.

TABLE 7-2 Top 10 Nations Ranked by GDP, 2011

Country	GDP (in millions)
1. United States	$14,900,000
2. China	7,318,000
3. Monaco	6,075,000
4. Japan	5,867,000
5. Liechtenstein	4,826,000
6. Germany	3,601,000
7. France	2,773,000
8. Brazil	2,477,000
9. United Kingdom	2,445,000
10. Italy	2,194,000

In industrialized countries, a significant portion of national income is the value of goods and services that would be free in a poor country. Thus, the standard of living in low- and lower-middle-income countries is often higher than income data might suggest; in other words, the *actual* purchasing power of the local currency may be much higher than that implied by exchange values. For example, the per capita income average for China of $4,940 equals 30,529 Chinese yuan at an exchange rate of 6.18 yuan = US$1.00. But, 30,529 yuan will buy much more in China than $4,940 will buy in the United States. Adjusted for PPP, per capita income in China is estimated to be $8,390; this amount is more than twice as high as the unadjusted figure suggests. Similarly, calculated in terms of purchasing power, per capita income in Tanzania is approximately $1,500. Indeed, a visit to the capital city of Dar Es Salaam reveals that stores are stocked with televisions and CD players, and businesspeople can be seen negotiating deals using their cell phones.[16]

In 2011, the 10 most populous countries in the world accounted for just over 50 percent of world income; the 5 most populous accounted for 39 percent (see Table 7-3). Although population is not as concentrated as income, there is, in terms of size of nations, a pattern of considerable concentration. The 10 most populous countries in the world account for roughly 60 percent of the world's population today. The concentration of income in the high-income and large-population countries means that a company can be "global" by targeting buyers in 10 or fewer countries. World population is now 7 billion; at the present rate of growth, it will reach 12 billion by the middle of the century. Simply put, global population will probably double during the lifetimes of many students using this textbook.

As noted previously, for products whose price is low enough, population is a more important variable than income in determining market potential. As former Kodak CEO George Fisher commented almost two decades ago, "Half the people in the world have yet to take their first picture. The opportunity is huge, and it's nothing fancy. We just have to sell yellow boxes of film."[17] Thus, China and India, with populations of 1.3 billion and 1 billion, respectively, represent attractive target markets. In a country like China, one segmentation approach would call for serving the existing mass market for inexpensive consumer products. Kao, Johnson & Johnson, Procter & Gamble, Unilever, and other packaged goods companies are targeting and developing the China market, lured in part by the presence of hundreds of millions of Chinese customers who are willing and able to spend a few cents for a single-use pouch of shampoo and other personal-care products.

TABLE 7-3 The 10 Most Populous Countries, 2011

Global Income and Population	2011 Population (millions)	Percent of World Population	2011 GDP (billions)	2011 per Capita GNI	Percent of World GDP
WORLD TOTAL	6,974	100.00%	$70,000	$9,514	100.0%
1. China	1,334	19%	7,318	4,940	10.0%
2. India	1,241	18%	1,873	1,420	2.0%
3. United States	312	4%	14,990	48,620	21.0%
4. Indonesia	242	3.4%	846	2,940	1.0%
5. Brazil	197	2.8%	2,477	10,720	3.0%
6. Pakistan	177	2.5%	210	1,120	.3%
7. Nigeria	162	2.3%	244	1,280	.3%
8. Bangladesh	150	2.1%	112	780	.2%
9. Russian Federation	143	2%	1,858	10,650	2.6%
10. Japan	128	1.8%	5,867	44,900	8.4%

[16] Robert S. Greenberger, "Africa Ascendant: New Leaders Replace Yesteryear's 'Big Men,' and Tanzania Benefits," *The Wall Street Journal* (December 10, 1996), pp. A1, A6.
[17] Mark Maremont, "Kodak's New Focus," *BusinessWeek* (January 30, 1995), p. 63.

McDonald's global expansion illustrates the significance of both income and population on marketing activities. As noted in Case 1-2, McDonald's operates in 118 countries. What this figure conceals, however, is that 80 percent of McDonald's restaurants are located in nine country markets: Australia, Brazil, Canada, China, France, Germany, Japan, the United Kingdom, and the United States. These nine countries generate about 75 percent of the company's total revenues. Seven of these countries appear in the top 10 rankings shown in Table 7-2; however, only four appear in the Table 7-3 population rankings. At present, the restaurants in the company's approximately 100 non-major-country markets contribute less than 20 percent to operating income. McDonald's is counting on an expanded presence in China and other high-population-country markets to drive corporate growth in the twenty-first century.

In rapidly growing economies, marketers must take care when using income, population, and other macro-level data during the segmentation process. For example, marketers should keep in mind that national income figures such as those cited for China and India are averages. Using averages alone, it is possible to underestimate a market's potential; fast-growing, higher-income segments are present in both of these countries. As Harold L. Sirkin and his coauthors point out in *Globality*, the income disparity in China and India is reflected in the diversity of their huge populations. In China, this diversity manifests itself in eight major languages and several dialects and minor languages; in addition, 30 Chinese cities have populations of 2 million people or more. The authors write:

> Mandarin is the dominant language in the main cities of northern China, while Cantonese is the dominant language in the south, particularly in Hong Kong. And behind each language is a unique regional history, culture, and economy that collectively give rise to radical differences in tastes, activities, and aspirations.
>
> Such differences present a major challenge for companies in the most fundamental of go-to-market activities: segmenting the population to understand motivations, expectations, and aspirations—and estimating how much spending power each segment has. It makes the term "mass market" almost meaningless. Yes, there is a mass of consumers in the rapidly developing economies, but they can hardly be addressed en masse, at least not through one set of product propositions or one campaign of spoken or written communications.[18]

The same is true in India, where more than 10 percent of the population can be classified as "upper middle class." Pinning down a demographic segment may require additional information; according to some estimates, India's middle class totals 300 million people. However, if the middle-class segment is defined more narrowly as "households that own cars, computers, and washing machines," the figure would be much lower. According to one Indian expert, India's population can be further segmented to include a "bike" segment of 25 million households in which telephones and motorbikes are present. However, the vast majority of India's population comprises a "bullock cart" segment whose households lack most comforts but typically own a television.[19] The lesson is clear: As Samli has suggested, to avoid being misled by averages, *do not assume* homogeneity.

AGE SEGMENTATION Age is another useful demographic variable in global marketing. One global segment based on demographics is **global teens**, young people between the ages of 12 and 19. Teens, by virtue of their shared interests in fashion, music, and a youthful lifestyle, exhibit consumption behavior that is remarkably consistent across borders (see Exhibit 7-2). As Renzo Rosso, creator of the Diesel brand and investor in Italy's H-Farm innovation incubator, explains, "A group of teenagers randomly chosen from different parts of the world will share many of the same tastes."[21] Young consumers may not yet have conformed to cultural norms; indeed, they may be rebelling against them. This fact, combined with shared universal wants, needs, desires, and fantasies (for name-brand, novelty, entertainment, trendy, and image-oriented products), make it possible to reach the global teen segment with a unified marketing program.

"Urban India is getting saturated. In the cities, everyone who can afford a television has one. If you want to maintain high growth, you have to penetrate into rural India."[20]

—K. Ramachandran, chief executive, Philips Electronics India

---

[18] Harold L. Sirkin, James W. Hemerling, and Arindam K. Bhattacharya, *Globality: Competing with Everyone from Everywhere for Everything* (New York: Boston Consulting Group, 2008), p. 117.
[19] Sundeep Waslekar, "India Can Get Ahead if It Gets on a Bike," *Financial Times* (November 12, 2002), p. 15.
[20] Chris Prystay, "Companies Market to India's Have-Littles," *The Wall Street Journal* (June 5, 2003), p. B1.
[21] Alice Rawsthorn, "A Hipster on Jean Therapy," *Financial Times* (August 20, 1998), p. 8.

Exhibit 7-2 Kurkure Desi Beats Rock On is a popular MTV show in India. Dubbed a "musical reality show," the program is a showcase for Indian rock bands. Presenting sponsor Kurkure markets a popular line brand of Namkeen savory snacks. Preliminary auditions are held in various cities, with finalists competing for the chance to make a music video, record an album, and receive $20,000 in prize money. Judges Pritan Chakraborty and Rahul Ram join anchors Elisabeth Hayden and Aykushmann Khurrana on the show, which airs on Saturday nights.
Source: bp1/ZUMA Press/Newscom.

This segment is attractive both in terms of its size (about 1.3 billion) and its multibillion-dollar purchasing power. According to London-based trend consultancy LS:NGlobal, the U.S. teen market represents roughly $200 billion in annual buying power; the United Kingdom's 7.5 million teens spend more than $10 billion each year.[22] Coca-Cola, Benetton, Swatch, and Sony are some of the companies pursuing the global teen segment. The global telecommunications revolution is a critical driving force behind the emergence of this segment. Global media such as MTV, Facebook, and Twitter are perfect vehicles for reaching this segment. Meanwhile, satellites are beaming Western programming and commercials to millions of viewers in China, India, and other emerging markets.

Another global segment is the so-called **global elite**, affluent consumers who are well traveled and have the money to spend on prestigious products with an image of exclusivity (see Exhibit 7-3). Although this segment is often associated with older individuals who have accumulated wealth over the course of a long career, it also includes movie stars, musicians, elite athletes, entrepreneurs, and others who have achieved great financial success at a relatively young age. This segment's needs and wants are spread over various product categories: durable goods (luxury automobiles such as Rolls-Royce or Mercedes-Benz), nondurables (upscale beverages such as Cristal champagne or Grey Goose vodka), and financial services (American Express Gold and Platinum cards).

GENDER SEGMENTATION For obvious reasons, segmenting markets by gender is an approach that makes sense for many companies. Less obvious, however, is the need to ensure that opportunities for sharpening the focus on the needs and wants of one gender or the other do not go unnoticed. Although some companies—fashion designers and cosmetics companies, for example—market primarily or exclusively to women, other companies offer different lines of products to both genders.

For example, in 2000 Nike generated $1.4 billion in global sales of women's shoes and apparel, a figure representing 16 percent of total Nike sales. Nike executives believe its global women's business is poised for big growth. To make it happen, Nike is opening concept shops

---

[22] Lucie Greene, "Pretty, Posh, and Profitable," *Financial Times* (May 14/15, 2011), p. 19.

Exhibit 7-3 Rolls-Royce, the automaker whose name is synonymous with exclusive luxury, sells about 1,000 vehicles each year. The United States accounts for about one-third of the overall market. Prices for the flagship Phantom start at about $400,000; the company's customers are typically members of the global elite, with more than $30 million in liquid assets. The introduction of the new $250,000 Ghost has jump-started sales for Rolls-Royce. Potential buyers can download an iPhone app that allows them to create their own vehicle. As one industry analyst noted recently, "One of the things that Rolls-Royce has been particularly good at is not corrupting its brand in the name of growth or profit."
Source: AFP/Getty Images.

inside department stores and creating free-standing retail stores devoted exclusively to women.[23] In Europe, Levi Strauss is taking a similar approach. In 2003, the company opened its first boutique for young women, Levi's for Girls, in Paris. As Suzanne Gallacher, associate brand manager for Levi's in Europe, the Middle East, and Africa, noted, "In Europe, denim is for girls."[24] The move is part of a broader strategy to boost Levi Strauss' performance in the face of strong competition from Calvin Klein and Gap in the United States and Diesel in Europe. Gallacher predicted that if Levi's for Girls was a success in France, similar stores would be opened in other European countries.

Psychographic Segmentation

Psychographic segmentation involves grouping people in terms of their attitudes, values, and lifestyles. Data are obtained from questionnaires that require respondents to indicate the extent to which they agree or disagree with a series of statements. Psychographics is primarily associated with SRI International, a market research organization whose original Values and Lifestyles (VALS) and updated VALS 2 analyses of consumers are widely known. Finland's Nokia relies heavily on psychographic segmentation of mobile phone users; its most important segments are Poseurs, Trendsetters, Social Contact Seekers, and Highfliers. By carefully studying these segments and tailoring products to each, Nokia once commanded 40 percent of the world's market for mobile communication devices.[25] Recently, however, Nokia's market share has declined due to intense competition from a new generation of Android-based phones.

Porsche AG, the German sports car maker, turned to psychographics after experiencing a worldwide sales decline from 50,000 units in 1986 to about 14,000 in 1993. Its U.S. subsidiary, Porsche Cars North America, already had a clear demographic profile of its typical customer: a 40-plus-year-old male college graduate whose annual income exceeded $200,000.

[23] Paula Stepanowsky, "Nike Tones up Its Marketing to Women with Concept Shops, New Apparel Lines," *The Wall Street Journal* (September 5, 2001), p. B19.

[24] John Tagliabue, "2 Sexes Separated by a Common Levi's," *The New York Times* (September 30, 2003), p. W1.

[25] John Micklethwait and Adrian Wooldridge, *Future Perfect: The Challenge and Hidden Promise of Globalization* (New York: Crown Business, 2000), p. 131.

A psychographic study showed that, demographics aside, Porsche buyers could be divided into several distinct categories. Top Guns, for example, buy Porsches and expect to be noticed; for Proud Patrons and Fantasists, however, such conspicuous consumption is irrelevant. Porsche used the profiles to develop advertising tailored to each type. As Richard Ford, Porsche vice president of sales and marketing, noted: "We were selling to people whose profiles were diametrically opposed. You wouldn't want to tell an elitist how good he looks in the car or how fast he could go." The results were impressive; Porsche's U.S. sales improved nearly 50 percent after a new advertising campaign was launched.[26]

Honda's experience in Europe demonstrates the potential value of using psychographic segmentation to supplement the use of more traditional variables such as demographics. When Honda executives were developing a communication strategy to support the European launch of the company's new HR-V sport-utility vehicle in the late 1990s, they brought together a panel of experts from the United Kingdom, Germany, France, and Italy. The goal was to develop a pan-European advertising campaign targeted squarely at a relatively young demographic. The researchers agreed that, irrespective of nationality, European youth exhibit more similarities than differences: They listen to the same music, enjoy the same films, and pursue the same recreational activities. The resulting ad campaign, dubbed "Joy Machine," was targeted at 25- to 35-year-olds. However, the HR-V proved to be popular with Europeans of *all* ages; in fact, one out of six buyers was a grandparent! Reflecting on this turn of events, Chris Brown, an advertising executive at Honda Motor Europe, noted, "The decision within advertising should be about attitudes, not ages. I was recently reminded that [former British Prime Minister] John Major and Mick Jagger of the Rolling Stones are the same age."[27]

Brown's statement underscores the insight that people of the same age don't necessarily have the same attitudes, just as people in one age bracket sometimes share attitudes with those in other age brackets. Sometimes it is preferable to market to a mind-set rather than to a particular age group; in such an instance, psychographic studies can help marketers arrive at a deeper understanding of consumer behavior than is possible with traditional segmentation variables such as demographics.

However, such understanding comes at a price. Psychographic market profiles are available from a number of different sources; companies may pay thousands of dollars to use these studies. SRI International has created psychographic profiles of the Japanese market; broader-scope studies have been undertaken by several global advertising agencies. For example, a research team at D'arcy Massius Benton & Bowles (DMBB) focused on Europe and produced a 15-country study entitled "The Euroconsumer: Marketing Myth or Cultural Certainty?"[28] The researchers identified four lifestyle groups: Successful Idealists, Affluent Materialists, Comfortable Belongers, and Disaffected Survivors. The first two groups represent the elite; the latter two, mainstream European consumers:

- **Successful Idealists.** Comprising from 5 to 20 percent of the population, this segment consists of persons who have achieved professional and material success while maintaining commitment to abstract or socially responsible ideals.
- **Affluent Materialists.** These status-conscious "up-and-comers"—many of whom are business professionals—use conspicuous consumption to communicate their success to others.
- **Comfortable Belongers.** Comprising one-fourth to one-half of a country's population, this group, like Global Scan's Adapters and Traditionals, is conservative and most comfortable with the familiar. Belongers are content with the comfort of home, family, friends, and community.
- **Disaffected Survivors.** Lacking power and affluence, this segment harbors little hope for upward mobility and tends to be either resentful or resigned. This segment is concentrated in high-crime, inner-city-type neighborhoods. Despite Disaffecteds' lack of societal status, their attitudes nevertheless tend to affect the rest of society.

---

[26] Alex Taylor III, "Porsche Slices Up Its Buyers," *Fortune* (January 16, 1995), p. 24.
[27] Ian Morton, "Target Advertising Is Not an Exact Science," *Automotive News Europe* (June 19, 2000), p. 28.
[28] The following discussion is adapted from Rebecca Piirto, *Beyond Mind Games: The Marketing Power of Psychographics* (Ithaca, NY: American Demographics Books, 1991).

TABLE 7-4 Sony's U.S. Consumer Segments

Segment	Description
Affluent	High-income consumers
CE Alphas	Early adopters of high-tech consumer electronics products, irrespective of age
Zoomers	55 years old or older
SoHo	Small office/home office
Families	35 to 54 years old
Young professionals/D.I.N.K.S.	Dual income, no kids, 25 to 34 years old
Gen Y	Younger than 25 years old (includes tweens, teens, college students)

The segmentation and targeting approach used by a company can vary from country to country. In Europe, Levi Strauss is relying heavily on gender segmentation. By contrast, former CEO Phil Marineau believed that a psychographic segmentation strategy was the key to revitalizing the venerable jeans brand in its home market. Marineau's team identified several different segments, including Fashionistas, Trendy Teens, Middle-Aged Men, and Budget Shoppers. The goal was to create different styles of jeans at different price points for each segment and to make them available at stores ranging from Walmart to Neiman Marcus.[29] Likewise, Sony Electronics, a unit of Sony Corp. of America, undertook a reorganization of its marketing function. Traditionally, Sony had approached marketing from a product category point of view. It changed its philosophy so that a new unit, the Consumer Segment Marketing Division, would be responsible for getting closer to consumers in the United States (see Table 7-4).[30] What variables did Sony use to develop these categories?

Behavior Segmentation

Behavior segmentation focuses on whether people buy and use a product, as well as how often and how much they use or consume. Consumers can be categorized in terms of **usage rates**: heavy, medium, light, or nonuser. Consumers can also be segmented according to **user status**: potential users, nonusers, ex-users, regulars, first-timers, or users of competitors' products. Marketers sometimes refer to the **80/20 rule** when assessing usage rates. This rule (also known as the *law of disproportionality* or *Pareto's Law*) suggests that 80 percent of a company's revenues or profits are accounted for by 20 percent of a firm's products or customers. As noted earlier, nine country markets generate about 80 percent of McDonald's revenues. This situation presents McDonald's executives with strategy alternatives: Should the company pursue growth in the handful of countries where it is already well known and popular? Or, should it focus on expansion and growth opportunities in the scores of countries that, as yet, contribute little to revenues and profits?

Benefit Segmentation

Global **benefit segmentation** focuses on the numerator of the value equation—the B in $V = B/P$. This approach is based on marketers' superior understanding of the problem a product solves, the benefit it offers, or the issue it addresses, regardless of geography. Food marketers are finding success creating products that can help parents create nutritious family meals with a minimal investment of time. Campbell Soup is making significant inroads into Japan's $500 million soup market as time-pressed homemakers place a premium on convenience. Marketers of health and beauty aids also use benefit segmentation. Many toothpaste brands are straightforward cavity fighters, and as such they reach a very broad market. However, as consumers become more

[29] Sally Beatty, "At Levi Strauss, Trouble Comes from All Angles," *The Wall Street Journal* (October 13, 2003), pp. B1, B3.
[30] Tobi Elkin, "Sony Marketing Aims at Lifestyle Segments," *Advertising Age* (March 18, 2002), pp. 1, 72.

EMERGING MARKETS BRIEFING BOOK

Market Segmentation in Russia

SYNC • THINK • LEARN

MyMarketingLab

In the early 1990s, following the collapse of the Soviet Union, the DMBB agency created a psychographic profile of the Russian market. The study divided Russians into five categories based on their outlook, behavior, and openness to Western products. The categories included *Kuptsy*, *Cossacks*, *Students*, *Business Executives*, and *Russian Souls*. Members of the largest group, the *Kuptsy* (the label comes from the Russian word for "merchant"), theoretically preferred Russian products but looked down on mass-produced goods of inferior quality. Nigel Clarke, the author of the study, noted that segmentation and targeting were appropriate in Russia, despite the fact that its broad consumer market was still in its infancy. "If you're dealing with a market as different as Russia is, even if you want to go 'broad,' it's best to think: 'Which group would go most for my brand? Where is my natural center of gravity?'"

The study's marketing implications became clearer in the late 1990s. Market share growth for many Western brands began to slow; the trend accelerated after the economic crisis of 1998. As Sergei Platinin, director of a Russian company that markets fruit juices, noted, "People used to want only to buy things that looked foreign. Now they want Russian." In the world of fashion, expensive blue jeans from designer Valentin Yudashkin supplanted Armani as *the* hip jeans. At the other end of the price spectrum, the local Nestlé subsidiary revived several brands of Russian chocolate candies. According to a survey conducted by Comcon 2, nearly two-thirds of upper-income Russians prefer to buy domestic chocolates even though they can afford to buy imported brands.

As for behavioral segmentation, Diageo PLC, V&S Vin & Spirit AB, Seagram, and other marketers of distilled spirits know that vodka consumption in Russia is the highest in the world; indeed, vodka has been described as "a mainstay of Russian life." Russians consume about 4.75 gallons of alcohol each year, a figure that is twice the level of consumption in the United States and much higher than the level deemed by the World Health Organization to be a health threat. Alcoholism is contributing to a population decline that could lead to a demographic crisis, and life expectancy for adult males is only 60 years. According to estimates, half a million Russians die each year of alcohol-related causes. The fine for public intoxication is 100 rubles—about $3.50.

The Kremlin has imposed limits on vodka advertising, and also restricts when and where it can be sold. Even so, production of home-made vodka, known as *samogon*, and illegal bootleg vodka from unlicensed distilleries, constitute a huge problem. Because illegal distilleries account for half the vodka Russians consume (see Exhibit 7-4), the Russian government loses billions in annual tax revenues. Some observers are calling for higher prices for vodka, including higher taxes, in order to curb consumption.

As a result of high duties, as well as a premium positioning, imports such as Smirnoff and Absolut are priced significantly higher than local brands. In the late 1990s, economic uncertainty was high, and workers went for months without being paid. In such an environment, price is a significant factor. An entrepreneur named Vladimir Dovgan prospered by launching several different brands of vodka priced between $5 and $10 per bottle. Meanwhile, Diageo PLC began producing Smirnoff in St. Petersburg. Ironically, Smirnoff's heritage is truly Russian, although for decades the brand was produced only in the West. As a company executive noted, "This should make Smirnoff seem more Russian. We want Russians to realize that Smirnoff came to Russia to produce for Russians."

Even as marketers of distilled spirits adjust their strategies, market preferences are changing; young Russians are turning to beer. In 2002, expenditures on beer surpassed vodka for the first time. Local brands are favored, as the weak ruble prices imports out of the reach of the average consumer. Some observers attribute the change to the influence of healthier, Western lifestyles. Also, vodka was associated with heavy drinking during Russia's tumultuous transition to a market economy in the 1990s. Even so, vodka is still an $11 billion market in Russia.

Sources: Clifford J. Levy, "Russia Tries, Once Again, to Rein in Vodka Habit," *The New York Times* (November 3, 2009), p. A4; Andrew Osborn, "Vodkas Reflect Allure of Power," *The Wall Street Journal* (March 10, 2009), p. B4; Nick Paton Walsh, "Russia Lite: Nyet to Vodka, Da to Beer," *The Observer* (October 20, 2002); Ernest Beck, "Absolut Frustration: Why Foreign Distillers Find It So Hard to Sell Vodka to the Russians," *The Wall Street Journal* (January 15, 1998), pp. A1, A9; Betsy McKay, "Vladimir Dovgan Is a Constant Presence in Capitalist Russia," *The Wall Street Journal* (March 20, 1998), pp. A1, A8; Stuart Elliot, "Figuring Out the Russian Consumer," *The New York Times* (April 1, 1992), pp. C1, C19; Betsy McKay, "In Russia, West No Longer Means Best; Consumers Shift to Home-Grown Goods," *The Wall Street Journal* (December 9, 1996), p. A9.

Exhibit 7-4 Home-brew vodka is a staple in Russia. Consider the following excerpt from Vladimir Voinovich's satirical novel *The Life and Extraordinary Adventures of Private Ivan Chonkin*:

"They clinked glasses. Ivan downed the contents of his glass and nearly fell off his chair. He instantly lost his breath, just as if he'd been punched in the stomach . . .

Gladishev, who had downed his own glass without any difficulty, looked over at Ivan with a sly grin. 'Well, Ivan, how's the home brew?'

'First rate stuff,' praised Chonkin, wiping the tears from his eyes with the palm of his hand. 'Takes your breath away.'"

Source: © DIZ Muenchen GmbH, Sueddeutsche Zeitung Photo / Alamy.

→ THE CULTURAL CONTEXT

Food Giants Target "Nutritional" Segment

MyMarketingLab   SYNC • THINK • LEARN

In response to increasing worldwide concerns about obesity, diabetes, and other food-related health issues, some of the world's largest food and beverage companies have stepped up efforts to develop new products and new product categories. Demographic trends point to a huge opportunity, with aging populations in the United States, Japan, and other

developed markets. According to Euromonitor International, the global market for foods that offer health benefits is currently worth about $600 billion in annual sales (see Exhibit 7-5).

Nestlé is in the vanguard of companies that are expanding offerings in the health-food category. The giant Swiss company recently established two new subsidiaries, Nestlé Health Science SA and the Nestlé Institute of Health Sciences, that will focus on products known as "medical foods," "functional foods," and "nutraceuticals." The goal is to create new food products that target diseases. Nestlé recently acquired CM&D Pharma, a U.K.-based startup that has developed a chewing gum that offers relief from kidney disease. Nestlé also acquired a stake in Accera; the company makes Axona®, a prescription medical food intended for the clinical dietary management of mild to moderate Alzheimer's disease.

Groupe Danone SA is pursuing similar types of opportunities. Its Nutricia division has developed Souvenaid, a beverage that Danone claims helps delay the onset of Alzheimer's disease by maintaining brain synapses. Two of Danone's most profitable brands are Activia, a digestive-health yogurt, and Actimel, a yogurt drink that can strengthen the body's immune system.

Thanks to the nature of the ingredients and the claims made in ads and on the product labels, many functional foods are not classified as drugs by government regulators. Even so, regulatory agencies such as the European Food Safety Authority are pressuring marketers to substantiate health-benefit claims. Although functional foods appear to have great commercial potential, some observers caution about exaggerated claims. Indeed, will food companies gain the upper hand in this new market, or will pharmaceutical companies become leaders? Teams of MBA students from Oxford and Cambridge addressed that question at a recent War Games business strategy competition. Teams devised strategies for four companies: Nestlé Health Science, Danone, Abbott Nutrition and GSK Consumer Healthcare. How did it go? Check out "Fuld War Game 2012: The European Battle for Designer Foods" on YouTube!

Sources: Shirley S. Wang, "'Medical Foods' and Supplements for Brain Health Advance," *The Wall Street Journal* (July 24, 2012), p. D2; John Revill, "Nestlé Buys U.S. Maker of 'Brain Health' Shake," *The Wall Street Journal* (July 20, 2012), p. B3; Paul Sonne, "Nestlé Buys 'Medical Food' Start-Up," *The Wall Street Journal* (February 2, 2011), p. B8; Laurie Burkitt, "Selling Health Food in China," *The Wall Street Journal* (December 13, 2010), p. A1; Clive Cookson, "Big Food Eyes Profits in Smaller Waistlines," *Financial Times* (October 1, 2010), p. 9; Goran Mijuk, "Nestlé Renews Push into Health Products," *The Wall Street Journal* (September 27, 2010).

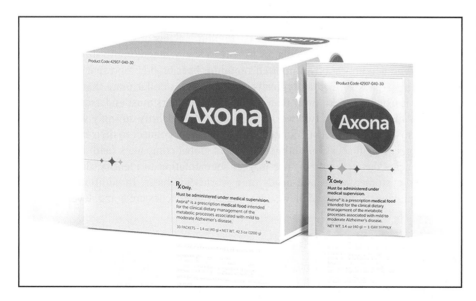

Exhibit 7-5 Only a handful of FDA-approved drugs are available to treat Alzheimer's patients in the United States. Some patients have sought alternative therapies such as Axona®, a medical food in milkshake form. In Alzheimer's patients, the brain loses its ability to metabolize glucose. Axona® provides an alternative "brain fuel" known as ketones.
Source: Courtesy of Accera Pharma.

concerned about whitening, sensitive teeth, gum disease, and other oral care issues, marketers are developing new toothpaste brand extensions suited to the different sets of perceived needs.

The European pet food market represents $30 billion in annual sales. Nestlé discovered that cat owners' attitudes toward feeding their pets are the same everywhere. In response, a pan-European campaign was created for Friskies Dry Cat Food. The appeal was that dry cat food better suits a cat's universally recognized independent nature. Likewise, many Europeans are concerned with improving the health and longevity of their pets. Accordingly, Procter & Gamble is marketing its Iams brand premium pet food as a way to improve pets' health.[31]

Ethnic Segmentation

In many countries, the population includes ethnic groups of significant size. In the United States, for example, the three major ethnic segments are African/Black Americans, Asian Americans, and Hispanic Americans. Each segment shows great diversity and can be further subdivided. For example, Asian Americans include Thai Americans, Vietnamese Americans, and Chinese Americans, and each group speaks a different language.

America's Hispanic population shares a common language but can also be segmented by place of origin: the Dominican Republic, Cuba, Central America, South America, Puerto Rico, and, of course, Mexico. The Hispanic American segment comprises nearly 50 million people, representing about 16 percent of the population and $978 billion in annual buying power. As a group, Hispanic Americans are hard working and exhibit strong family and religious orientations. However, the different segments are very diverse, and marketers need to beware of falling into the trap of thinking "All Hispanics are the same." Some call the new face of opportunity the "$1 trillion Latina." Indeed, the United States is home to 24 million women of Hispanic heritage; 42 percent are single, 35 percent are heads of households, and 54 percent are employed.

From a marketing point of view, the various Hispanic American segments represent a great opportunity. Companies in a variety of industry sectors, including food and beverages, consumer durables, and leisure and financial services, are recognizing the need to include these segments when preparing marketing programs for the United States. For example, companies based in Mexico are zeroing in on opportunities to the north. Three Mexican retailers—Famsa, Grupo Gigant SA, and Grupo Comercial Chedraui SA—have opened stores in the United States. As Famsa President Humberto Garza Valdez explained at the grand opening of a store in San Fernando, California, "We're not coming to the U.S. to face big companies like Circuit City or Best Buy. Our focus is the Hispanic market."[32]

From 1999 through 2000, new-vehicle registrations by Hispanics in the United States grew 20 percent, twice the overall national growth rate. Honda, Toyota, and other Japanese automakers have been courting U.S. Hispanics for years and have built up a great deal of brand loyalty. Ford and GM are playing catch-up, with mixed results; despite large increases in advertising targeting Hispanics, GM's market share is slipping.[33] Sales of Corona Extra beer in the United States have grown dramatically, thanks in part to savvy marketing to the Hispanic segment. In lower-income neighborhoods, imported premium beer brands represent "affordable luxuries." Although a six-pack of Corona typically costs at least a dollar more than Budweiser at a local bodega, it is usually priced lower than Heineken. Marketers must understand, though, that many Hispanic Americans live in two worlds; although they identify strongly with the United States, there is also a sense of pride associated with brands that connect to their heritage.[34]

The preceding discussion outlines the ways global companies (and the research and advertising agencies that serve them) use market segmentation to identify, define, understand, and respond to customer wants and needs on a worldwide basis. In addition to the segmentation variables previously discussed, new segmentation approaches are being developed in response to

---

[31] Sarah Ellison and Emily Nelson, "Pet-Food Companies Compete to Be the Pick of the Litter," *The Wall Street Journal* (July 31, 2001), p. B11.

[32] Joel Millman, "Mexican Retailers Enter U.S. to Capture Latino Dollars," *The Wall Street Journal* (February 8, 2001), p. A18.

[33] Eduardo Porter, "Ford, Other Auto Makers Target Hispanic Community," *The Wall Street Journal* (November 9, 2000), p. B4.

[34] Suein L. Hwang, "Corona Ads Target Hispanics in Effort to Hop to Head of U.S. Beer Market," *The Wall Street Journal Europe* (November 21–22, 1997), p. 9; Michael Barone, "How Hispanics Are Americanizing," *The Wall Street Journal* (February 6, 1998), p. A22.

today's rapidly changing business environment. For example, the widespread adoption of the Internet and other new technologies creates a great deal of commonality among global consumers. These consumer subcultures are composed of people whose similar outlooks and aspirations create a shared mind-set that transcends language and national differences. Consumer products giant Procter & Gamble is one company that is attuned to the changing times. As Melanie Healey, president of P&G's Global Health and Feminine Care unit, notes, "We're seeing global tribes forming around the world that are more and more interconnected through technology."[35]

Assessing Market Potential and Choosing Target Markets or Segments[36]

After segmenting the market by one or more of the criteria just discussed, the next step is to assess the attractiveness of the identified segments. This part of the process is especially important when sizing up emerging country markets as potential targets. It is at this stage that global marketers should be mindful of several potential pitfalls associated with the market segmentation process. First, there is a tendency to overstate the size and short-term attractiveness of individual country markets, especially when estimates are based primarily on demographic data such as income and population. For example, while China, India, Brazil, and other emerging markets undoubtedly offer potential in the long run, management must realize that short-term profit and revenue growth objectives may be hard to achieve. During the 1990s, Procter & Gamble and other consumer packaged goods companies learned this lesson in Latin America. By contrast, the success of McDonald's Russia during the same period is a case study in the rewards of persistence and long-term outlook.

A second trap that global marketers can set for themselves is to target a country because shareholders or competitors exert pressure on management not to "miss out" on a strategic opportunity. Recall from Chapter 2, for example, the statement by India's finance minister that the twenty-first century will be "the century of India." Such pronouncements can create the impression that management must "act now" to take advantage of a limited window of opportunity. Third, there is a danger that management's network of contacts will emerge as a primary criterion for targeting. The result can be market entry based on convenience rather than rigorous market analysis. For example, a company may enter into a distribution agreement with a non-national employee who wants to represent the company after returning to his or her home country. The issue of choosing the right foreign distributor will be discussed in detail in Chapter 12.

With these pitfalls in mind, marketers can utilize three basic criteria for assessing opportunity in global target markets: current size of the segment and anticipated growth potential, competition, and compatibility with the company's overall objectives and the feasibility of successfully reaching a designated target.

Current Segment Size and Growth Potential

Is the market segment currently large enough to present a company with the opportunity to make a profit? If the answer is "no" today, does it have significant growth potential to make it attractive in terms of a company's long-term strategy? Consider the following facts about India:

- India is the world's fastest-growing cell phone market. The industry is expanding at an annual rate of 50 percent, with 5 to 6 million new subscribers added every month. By mid-2008, India had 261 million cell phone users; that number approached 900 million by the end of 2011. Even so, barriers originating in the political and regulatory environments have shackled private-sector growth.[37]

---

[35] Carol Hymowitz, "Marketers Focus More on Global 'Tribes' Than on Nationalities," *The Wall Street Journal* (December 10, 2007), p. B1.

[36] Parts of the following discussion are adapted from David Arnold, *The Mirage of Global Markets* (Upper Saddle River, NJ: Pearson Education, 2004), Chapter 2.

[37] Amol Sharma and Jackie Range, "AT&T, Others Hit by Challenges in India," *The Wall Street Journal* (May 15, 2008), p. B8. See also Eric Bellman, "India's Cell Phone Boom May Lose Charge," *The Wall Street Journal* (August 25, 2006), p. A6.

- About 1.3 million cars are sold each year in India; in absolute terms, this is a relatively small number. However, industry observers forecast that the market will expand to 3 million cars within a decade. In 2008, India overtook China as the world's fastest-growing car market.[38]

- Approximately 70 percent of India's population is under the age of 35. This segment is increasingly affluent and today, young, brand-conscious consumers are buying $100 Tommy Hilfiger jeans and $690 Louis Vuitton handbags. Mohan Murjani owns the rights to the Tommy Hilfiger brand in India. Commenting on the country's decade-long economic boom, he notes, "Aspirationally, things changed dramatically. What we were seeing was huge growth in terms of consumers' assets, in terms of their incomes and in terms of their spending power through credit."[39]

As noted earlier, one of the advantages of targeting a market segment globally is that although the segment in a single-country market might be small, even a narrow segment can be served profitably if the segment exists in several countries. The billion-plus members of the global MTV Generation are a case in point. Moreover, by virtue of its size and purchasing power, the global teen segment is extremely attractive to consumer goods companies. In the case of a huge country market such as India or China, segment size and growth potential may be assessed in a different manner.

From the perspective of a consumer packaged goods company, for example, low incomes and the absence of a distribution infrastructure offset the fact that 75 percent of India's population lives in rural areas. The appropriate decision may be to target urban areas only, even though they are home to only 25 percent of the population. Visa's strategy in China perfectly illustrates this criterion as it relates to demographics: Visa is targeting persons with a monthly salary equivalent to $300 or more. The company predicted that by 2010, the number of people fitting that description could include as many as 200 million people (see Exhibit 7-6).

Thanks to a combination of favorable demographics and lifestyle-related needs, the United States has been a very attractive market for foreign automakers. For example, demand for SUVs exploded during the 1990s. From 1990 to 2000, SUV sales tripled, growing from nearly 1 million units in 1990 to 2 million units in 1996 and passing 3 million sold in 2000.

Exhibit 7-6 In China, only about 1 percent of the population currently owns a credit card. That means roughly 13 million cards for 1.3 billion people. Visa offers cards bearing the Chinese Olympic symbol: a dancing figure based on the Chinese character jing that means "capital." Visitors to the Beijing Olympics in 2008 were able to use their cards at many stores.
Source: NG Han Guan/ AP Images.

[38] Heather Timmons, "In India, a $2,500 Pace Car," *The New York Times* (October 12, 2007), p. C1.
[39] Eric Bellman, "As Economy Grows, India Goes for Designer Goods," *The Wall Street Journal* (March 27, 2007), pp. A1, A17. See also Christina Passariello, "Beauty Fix: Behind L'Oréal's Makeover in India: Going Upscale," *The Wall Street Journal* (July 13, 2007), pp. A1, A14.

TABLE 7-5 Global Automakers Targeting the U.S. Market with SUVs

Automaker	Select SUV Model	Country of Assembly or Manufacture	Year Introduced
Porsche	Cayenne	Germany	2003
Volkswagen	Touareg	Slovakia	2004
Honda	CR-V	Japan	1995
Toyota	RAV-4	Japan	1994
Kia	Sorento	South Korea	2003
BMW	X5	United States	2000
Mercedes-Benz	ML 350	United States	2003

Why are these vehicles so popular? Primarily it is the security of four-wheel drive and the higher clearance for extra traction in adverse driving conditions. They also typically have more space for hauling cargo.

Reacting to high demand for the Jeep Cherokee, Ford Explorer, and Chevy Blazer, manufacturers from outside the United States introduced models of their own at a variety of price points (see Table 7-5). Dozens of SUV models are available as Toyota, Mazda, Honda, Kia, Nissan, Rover, BMW, Mercedes, Volkswagen, and other global automakers target American buyers. Many manufacturers offer various SUV styles, including full-size, mid-size, compact, and crossover SUVs. Even as growth slows in the United States, SUVs are growing in popularity in many other countries. In China, for example, SUVs account for about 40 percent of auto imports and represent the fastest-growing sector in the auto industry. In 2008, GM started exporting its popular Escalade to China; the sticker price is the equivalent of about $150,000.

Potential Competition

A market segment or country market characterized by strong competition may be a segment to avoid. However, if the competition is vulnerable in terms of price or quality disadvantages, it is possible for a market newcomer to make significant inroads. Over the past several decades, for example, Japanese companies in a variety of industries targeted the U.S. market despite the presence of entrenched domestic market leaders. Some of the newcomers proved to be extremely adept at segmenting and targeting; as a result, they made significant inroads. In the motorcycle industry, for example, Honda first created the market for small-displacement dirt bikes. The company then moved upmarket with bigger bikes targeted at casual riders whose psychographic profiles were quite different from those of the hard-core Harley-Davidson rider. In document imaging, Canon outflanked Xerox by offering compact desktop copiers and targeting department managers and secretaries. Similar examples can be found in earthmoving equipment (Komatsu versus Caterpillar), photography (Fuji versus Kodak), and numerous other industries.

By contrast, there are also many examples of companies whose efforts to develop a position in an attractive country market ended in failure. For example, Germany's DHL tried to enter the U.S. package-delivery market in 2003; to achieve scale, DHL acquired Airborne Express. However, management underestimated the dominance of the entrenched incumbents FedEx and UPS. DHL finally withdrew from the United States market in 2008 after losses totaled about $10 billion. Likewise, Walmart pulled out of South Korea and Germany after failing to find the right positioning and product mix.

Virgin chief executive Richard Branson learned important lessons in the mid-1990s when he launched Virgin Cola, directly targeting Coca-Cola's core market (see Exhibit 7-7). In his book *Business Stripped Bare: Adventures of a Global Entrepreneur*, Branson recalls:

Starting a soft-drinks war with Coca-Cola was crazy. It was one of our highest profile business mistakes, though it was also one of the things that raised the profile of the Virgin name in America. Launching Virgin Cola in 1994, we were having fun and reveling in bravado, so pleased to be snapping at the heels of the biggest dog in town…. Taking on Coke taught

Exhibit 7-7 Virgin Group chief Sir Richard Branson has an uncanny knack for generating publicity. He has crossed the Atlantic Ocean by hot-air balloon and by speedboat—both sponsored by Virgin, of course. In 1998, Branson famously rode into Times Square on a military tank and crushed a pile of Coca-Cola cans for the launch of Virgin Cola. For Virgin Cola's Japanese launch, Branson donned a costume for a public appearance in Tokyo.
Source: YOSHIKAZU TSUNO/AFP/Newscom.

us two things: how to make a great cola with a different taste; and how to antagonize a global business that brought in $28 billion in 2007, with profits of $5 billion....Yes, we somehow contrived to blind ourselves completely to the power and the influence of a global brand that epitomizes the strength and reach of American capitalism.[40]

Feasibility and Compatibility

If a market segment is judged to be large enough, and if strong competitors are either absent or deemed to be vulnerable, then the final consideration is whether a company can and should target that market. The feasibility of targeting a particular segment can be negatively impacted by various factors. For example, significant regulatory hurdles may limit market access. This issue is especially important in China today. Other marketing-specific issues can arise; in India, for example, 3 to 5 years are required to build an effective distribution system for many consumer products. This fact may serve as a deterrent to foreign companies that would otherwise be attracted by the apparent potential of India's large population.[41]

Managers must decide how well a company's product or business model fits the country market in question—or, as noted, if the company does not currently offer a suitable product, can it develop one? To make this decision, a marketer must consider several criteria:

- Will adaptation be required? If so, is this economically justifiable in terms of the expected sales volume?
- Will import restrictions, high tariffs, or a strong home-country currency drive up the price of the product in the target market currency and effectively dampen demand?
- Is it advisable to source locally? In many cases, reaching global market segments requires considerable expenditures for distribution and travel by company personnel. Would it make sense to source products in the country for export elsewhere in the region?

Finally, it is important to address the question of whether targeting a particular segment is compatible with the company's overall goals, brand image, or established sources of competitive advantage. For example, BMW is one of the world's premium auto brands. Should BMW add a

[40] Richard Branson, *Business Stripped Bare: Adventures of a Global Entrepreneur* (London: Virgin Books, 2010), p. 178.
[41] Khozem Merchant, "Sweet Rivals Find Love in a Warm Climate," *Financial Times* (July 24, 2003), p. 9.

TABLE 7-6 Market Selection Framework

Market (population)	Market Size	Competitive Advantage		Market Potential	Terms of Access	Market Potential
China (1.3 billion)	100	.07	=	7	.50	3.5
Russia (141 million)	50	.10	=	5	.60	3.0
Mexico (108 million)	20	.20	=	4	.90	3.6

minivan to its product lineup? For now, management is responding to other competitive opportunities and threats. In 2013, BMW unveiled the i-Series electric sedan as an alternative for drivers shopping for a plug-in car such as the Tesla Model S. And, Maserati is taking aim at BMW's 5 Series; the Italian company has unveiled a $65,000 "entry-level" model. Management hopes that the appeal of Italian chic paired with a Ferrari engine will prove irresistible to luxury car buyers.[42]

A Framework for Selecting Target Markets

As one can infer from this discussion, it would be extremely useful to have formal tools or frameworks available when assessing emerging country markets. Table 7-6 presents a market selection framework that incorporates some of the elements just discussed. Suppose an American company has identified China, Russia, and Mexico as potential country target markets. The table shows the countries arranged in declining rank by market size. At first glance, China might appear to hold the greatest potential simply on the basis of size. However, the competitive advantage of our hypothetical firm is 0.07 in China, 0.10 in Russia, and 0.20 in Mexico. Multiplying the market size and competitive advantage index yields a market potential of 7 in China, 5 in Russia, and 4 in Mexico.

The next stage in the analysis requires an assessment of the various market access considerations. In Table 7-6, all these conditions or terms are reduced to an index number of terms of access, which is 0.50 for China, 0.60 for Russia, and 0.90 for Mexico. In other words, the "market access considerations" are more favorable in Mexico than in Russia, perhaps in this instance due to NAFTA. Multiplying the market potential by the terms of access index suggests that Mexico, despite its small size, holds greater market potential than China or Russia.

Although the framework in Table 7-6 should prove useful as a preliminary screening tool for intercountry comparisons, it does not go far enough in terms of assessing actual market potential. Global marketing expert David Arnold has developed a framework that goes beyond demographic data and considers other, marketing-oriented assessments of market size and growth potential. Instead of a "top-down" segmentation analysis beginning with, for example, income or population data from a particular country, Arnold's framework is based on a "bottom-up" analysis that begins at the product-market level.

As shown in Figure 7-1, Arnold's framework incorporates two core concepts: marketing model drivers and enabling conditions. **Marketing model drivers** are key elements or factors required for a business to take root and grow in a particular country market environment. The drivers may differ depending on whether a company serves consumer or industrial markets. Does success hinge on establishing or leveraging a brand name? In Vietnam, for example, Procter & Gamble promotes its Tide detergent brand as "Number 1 in America." Or, is distribution the key element? Or a tech-savvy sales staff? Marketing executives seeking an opportunity must arrive at insights into the true driving force(s) that will affect success for their particular product market.

Enabling conditions are structural market characteristics whose presence or absence can determine whether the marketing model can succeed. For example, in India, refrigeration is not widely available in shops and market food stalls. This creates challenges for Nestlé and Cadbury as they attempt to capitalize on Indians' increasing appetite for chocolate confections. Although Nestlé's KitKat and Cadbury's Dairy Milk bars have been reformulated to better withstand heat, the absence or rudimentary nature of refrigeration hampers the companies' efforts to ensure their products are in saleable condition.

After marketing model drivers and enabling conditions have been identified, the third step is for management to weigh the estimated costs associated with entering and serving the market with

---

[42] Tommaso Ebhardt, "Maserati Woos Drivers Bored With BMW," *Bloomberg BusinessWeek* (July 8, 2013), pp. 21–22.

FIGURE 7-1

Screening Criteria for Market Segments

Source: David Arnold, "The Mirage of Global Markets: How Globalizing Companies Can Succeed As Markets Localize," ©2004 Reprinted by Permission of Pearson Education, Inc. Upper Saddle River, NJ.

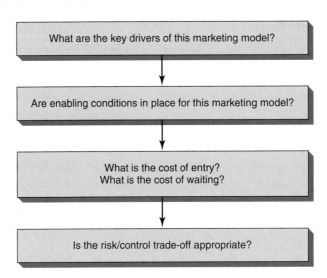

potential short- and long-term revenue streams. Does this segment or country market merit entry now? Or, would it be better to wait until specific enabling conditions are established? The issue of timing is often framed in terms of the quest for **first-mover advantage**. The conventional wisdom is that the first company to enter a market has the best chance of becoming the market leader.

Examples from the annals of global marketing that appear to support this notion include the Coca-Cola Company, which established itself globally during World War II. However, there are also first-mover *disadvantages*. The first company to enter a market often makes substantial investments in marketing only to find that a late-arriving competitor reaps some of the benefits. Ample evidence suggests that late entrants into global markets can also achieve success. One way they do this is by benchmarking established companies and then outmaneuvering them, first locally and then globally. Jollibee, the Philippines-based fast-food chain whose business model was influenced by McDonald's, is a case in point.

Late movers can also succeed by developing innovative business models. This approach was used by Stephen Millar, chief executive of Australian wine producer BRL Hardy. Millar's insight was that no leading global brand had emerged in the wine business; in other words, there was no equivalent to Coca-Cola in the wine business. During the 1990s, Millar established Hardy as a leading global brand. He accomplished this by moving on several fronts. First, he took control of the sales function. Second, he made sure Hardy's wines were crafted to appeal to a broader demographic than "wine snobs," who tend to favor bottles from France and Italy. Third, he supplemented Hardy's line of Australian wines with select brands from other countries. In 2002 Hardy sold 20 million cases of wine worldwide. Today, Hardy is one of the world's top 10 wine companies.[43]

One way to determine the marketing model drivers and enabling conditions is to create a product-market profile. The profile should address some or all of the following basic questions:

1. Who buys our product or brand?
2. Who does not buy our product or brand?
3. What need or function does our product serve? Does our product or brand address that need?
4. Is there a market need that is not being met by current product or brand offerings?
5. What problem does our product solve?
6. What are customers currently buying to satisfy the need, or solve the problem, that our product targets?
7. What price are they paying for the product they are currently buying?
8. When is our product purchased?
9. Where is our product purchased?

---

[43] Christopher A. Bartlett and Sumantra Ghoshal, "Going Global: Lessons from the Late Movers," *Harvard Business Review* 78, no. 2 (March–April 2000), pp. 138–140. See also Christopher Lawton, "Aussie Wines Star at Spirits Marketer Constellation Brands," *The Wall Street Journal* (January 16, 2004), pp. B1, B4.

Product-Market Decisions

The next step in assessing market segments is a company review of current and potential product offerings in terms of their suitability for the country market or segment. This assessment can be performed by creating a product-market grid that maps markets as horizontal rows on a spreadsheet and products as vertical columns. Each cell represents the possible intersection of a product and a market segment. In the case of the candy companies just discussed, both Nestlé and Cadbury determined that a liquid chocolate confection would be one way to address the issue of India's hot weather. The companies are also working to improve the enabling conditions for selling traditional chocolate treats by supplying coolers to merchants.

Table 7-7 shows a product-market matrix for Lexus. Toyota launched the Lexus brand in 1989 with two sedan models. In market segmentation terms, the luxury car buyer Lexus hoped to

TABLE 7-7 2012 Product-Market Grid for Lexus, Select Country Markets

Country Segment	Lexus Brand										
	IS	RX	CT	LS	GS	IS C	IS F	LX	ES	LFA	HS
Asia											
China	X	X	X	X	X	X		X	X	X	
Hong Kong	X	X	X	X	X	X				X	
Taiwan	X	X	X	X	X	X	X	X	X		
India											
North America											
Canada	X	X	X	X	X	X	X	X	X	X	X
USA	X	X	X	X	X	X	X	X	X	X	X
Latin America											
Brazil	X			X					X		
Europe											
Austria	X	X	X	X	X	X	X				
Belgium	X	X	X	X	X	X	X				
Denmark	X	X	X		X						
Finland	X	X	X	X	X	X	X				
France	X	X	X	X	X	X	X			X	
Germany	X	X	X	X	X	X	X			X	
Great Britain	X	X	X	X	X	X	X			X	
Greece	X	X	X		X						
Ireland	X	X	X	X		X	X				
Netherlands	X	X	X	X	X	X	X				
Portugal	X	X	X		X	X	X				
Russia	X	X	X	X	X	X	X	X	X		
Sweden	X	X	X	X	X	X	X				
Switzerland	X	X	X	X	X	X	X				
Middle East											
Israel	X	X	X	X	X	X					
UAE	X	X	X	X	X	X	X	X	X	X	
Kuwait	X	X	X	X	X	X	X	X	X	X	
Saudi Arabia	X	X	X	X	X	X	X	X	X		

Source: Used by permission of Toyota Motor Corporation.

attract is associated with an upper-income demographic. In 1996, Lexus launched its first SUV. The decision to enter the SUV product-market represented management's desire to reach upper-income consumers whose lifestyles required something other than a luxury sedan. In 2012, Lexus offered a total of 11 different models in the United States; these include the top-of-the line LX 470 luxury utility vehicle, the LS 430 luxury sedan, and, at the entry level, the IS series. Lexus vehicles are marketed in more than 60 countries; the United States is the number 1 market. Ironically, in Japan the vehicles were sold for years under the Toyota nameplate; the line was relaunched under the Lexus brand in 2005.[44]

Management intends to build Lexus into a global luxury brand; worldwide 2012 sales totaled 477,000 vehicles. Lexus has to target Germany, the largest market in Europe, where 4 in 10 vehicles sold are luxury models. Approximately 15 million cars are sold in Europe each year; Germany accounts for nearly one-quarter of the total. At the beginning of 2013, there were about 25,000 registered Lexus vehicles in Germany; by comparison, total vehicle registrations for Mercedes and BMW exceeded 6.8 million. Can Lexus succeed on the home turf of two of the world's leading luxury carmakers? Armed with the understanding that local brands comprise more than 90 percent of German auto sales in the premium segment, Lexus has made significant product adaptations. For example, because Germans want the option of buying vehicles with diesel engines, Lexus developed new diesel models as well as a gas-electric hybrid engine for the RX series. Note that in Europe, Lexus offers the top-of-the-line LX 470 SUV in only one country: Russia. Can you explain this situation? How do the model offerings vary among the BRICS countries?

Targeting and Target Market Strategy Options

After evaluating the identified segments in terms of the three criteria presented, a decision is made whether to pursue a particular opportunity. Not surprisingly, in global marketing one fundamental decision concerns which country or regional market(s) to enter. For example, Hershey, the U.S.-based confectionary company, recently targeted the United Kingdom, Europe, and the Middle East, where Mars and Kraft are the dominant players. Previously, Hershey's business was concentrated in North and South America and Asia. Consider also the following examples of targeting:

- The global home furnishings market can be segmented in terms of gender. Approximately 70 percent of IKEA's customers are women.
- India's vehicle market can be segmented into scooter and motorcycle drivers and those who can afford a vehicle with four wheels. The target market for Tata Motor's Nano microcar is two-wheeled drivers who are willing and able to upgrade to four wheels. When the Nano was launched in April 2009, Ratan Tata predicted sales of 20,000 vehicles per month.
- American car buyers can be segmented by age. Toyota's Scion is targeted at Generation Y—twentysomethings who are buying their first car.

If the decision is made to proceed, an appropriate targeting strategy must be developed. The three basic categories of target marketing strategies are standardized marketing, concentrated marketing, and differentiated marketing.

Standardized Global Marketing

Standardized global marketing is analogous to mass marketing in a single country. It involves creating the same marketing mix for a broad mass market of potential buyers. Standardized global marketing, also known as *undifferentiated target marketing*, is based on the premise that a mass market exists around the world. In addition, that mass market is served with a marketing mix of standardized elements. Product adaptation is minimized, and a strategy of intensive distribution ensures that the product is available in the maximum number of retail outlets. The appeal of standardized global marketing is clear: lower production costs. The same is true of standardized global communications.

---

[44] Jathon Sapsford, "Toyota Introduces a New Luxury Brand in Japan: Lexus," *The Wall Street Journal* (August 3, 2005), pp. B1, B5.

Concentrated Global Marketing

The second global targeting strategy, concentrated target marketing, involves devising a marketing mix to reach a **niche.** A niche is simply a single segment of the global market. In cosmetics, Estée Lauder, Chanel, and other cosmetics marketers have used this approach successfully to target the upscale, prestige segment of the market. As Leonard Lauder remarked recently, "The founders, who were my parents, had two very simple ideas: Product quality and narrow distribution to high-end retailers. We never went mass."[45]

Concentrated targeting is also the strategy employed by the hidden champions of global marketing: companies unknown to most people that have succeeded by serving a niche market that exists in many countries. These companies define their markets narrowly and strive for global depth rather than national breadth. For example, Germany's Winterhalter is a hidden champion in the dishwasher market, but the company has never sold a dishwasher to a consumer, hospital, or school. Instead, it focuses exclusively on dishwashers and water conditioners for hotels and restaurants. As Jürgen Winterhalter noted, "The narrowing of our market definition was the most important strategic decision we ever made. It is the very foundation of our success in the past decade."[46]

Differentiated Global Marketing

The third target marketing strategy, **differentiated global marketing**, represents a more ambitious approach than concentrated target marketing. Also known as **multisegment targeting**, this approach entails targeting two or more distinct market segments with multiple marketing mix offerings. This strategy allows a company to achieve wider market coverage. For example, Danone SA, the French food products company, targets consumers in developed countries with premium brands such as Evian and Badoit mineral water and the Dannon and Activia yogurt brands. However, Danone CEO Franck Riboud is also focusing on developing markets. In Bangladesh, Shoktidoi is an inexpensive yogurt brand sold by local women. In Senegal, Danone's offerings include 50-gram packets of Dolima drinkable yogurt that sell for 50 cents.[47] Positioning, which we discuss in the next section, is key to successful execution of this strategy. As CEO Riboud has noted:

> Our brands have different positionings within the same market. With our bottled waters, for example, Evian is strongly associated with health and beauty—a promise of youthful looks through drinking water—while Volvic promotes the same message but associates it with energy through replenishing the body during sports activities. They don't cannibalize each other, because they're marketed as promoting different qualities.[48]

In the cosmetics industry, Unilever pursues differentiated global marketing strategies by targeting both ends of the perfume market. Unilever targets the luxury market with Calvin Klein and Elizabeth Taylor's Passion; Wind Song and Brut are its mass-market brands. Mass marketer Procter & Gamble, known for its Old Spice and Incognito brands, also embarked upon this strategy with its 1991 acquisition of Revlon's EuroCos, marketer of Hugo Boss for men and Laura Biagiotti's Roma perfume. In the mid-1990s, it launched a new prestige fragrance, Venezia, in the United States and several European countries. Currently, Procter & Gamble also markets Envy, Rush, and other Gucci fragrances as a licensee of the Italian fashion house.

Positioning

The term *positioning* is attributed to marketing gurus Al Ries and Jack Trout, who first introduced it in a 1969 article published in *Industrial Marketing* magazine. As noted at the beginning of the chapter, positioning refers to the act of differentiating a brand in customers' minds in

---

[45] Natasha Singer, "What Would Estée Do?" *The New York Times* (March 26, 2011), p. BU 1.
[46] Hermann Simon, *Hidden Champions: Lessons from 500 of the World's Best Unknown Companies* (Boston: Harvard Business School Press, 1996), p. 54.
[47] Christina Passariello, "Danone Expands Its Pantry to Woo the World's Poor," *The Wall Street Journal* (June 29, 2010), p. A1.
[48] "Think Global, Act Local," *Outlook* no. 3 (2003), p. 9.

relation to competitors in terms of attributes and benefits that the brand does and does not offer. Put differently, positioning is the process of developing strategies for "staking out turf" or "filling a slot" in the mind of target customers.[49]

Positioning is frequently used in conjunction with the segmentation variables and targeting strategies discussed previously. For example, Unilever and other consumer goods companies often engage in differentiated target marketing, offering a full range of brands within a given product category. Unilever's various detergent brands include All, Wisk, Surf, and Persil; each is positioned slightly differently. In some instances, extensions of a popular brand can also be positioned in different ways. Colgate's Total toothpaste is positioned as the brand that addresses a full range of oral health issues, including gum disease. In most parts of the world, Total is available in several formulations, including Total Advanced Clean, Total Clean Mint Paste, and Total Whitening Paste. Effective positioning differentiates each variety from the others.

In the decades since Ries and Trout first focused attention on the importance of the concept, marketers have utilized a number of general positioning strategies. These include positioning by attribute or benefit, quality and price, use or user, or competitor.[50] Recent research has identified three additional positioning strategies that are particularly useful in global marketing: global consumer culture positioning, local consumer culture positioning, and foreign consumer culture positioning.

Attribute or Benefit

A frequently used positioning strategy exploits a particular product attribute, benefit, or feature. Economy, reliability, and durability are frequently used attribute/benefit positions. Volvo automobiles are known for solid construction that offers safety in the event of a crash. By contrast, BMW is positioned as "the ultimate driving machine," a reference that signifies high performance. In the ongoing credit card wars, Visa's long-running advertising theme "It's Everywhere You Want to Be" drew attention to the benefit of worldwide merchant acceptance. In global marketing, it may be deemed important to communicate the fact that a brand is imported. This approach is known as *foreign consumer culture positioning* (FCCP).

Quality and Price

This strategy can be thought of in terms of a continuum from high-fashion/quality and high price to good value (rather than "low quality") at a reasonable price. A legendary print ad campaign for Belgium's Stella Artois beer included various executions that positioned the brand at the premium end of the market. One ad juxtaposed a cap pried off a bottle of Stella with a close-up of a Steinway piano. The tagline "Reassuring expensive" was the only copy; upon close inspection of the Steinway, the reader could see that one of the keys was broken because it had been used to open the bottle! InBev, the world's biggest brewer in terms of volume, markets the Stella Artois brand. While Stella is regarded as an "everyday" beer in its local market of Belgium, the marketing team at InBev has repositioned it as a premium global brand.[51]

At the high end of the distilled spirits industry, marketers of imported vodkas such as Belvedere and Grey Goose have successfully positioned their brands as super-premium entities selling for twice the price of premium ("ordinary") vodka. Ads for several export vodka brands emphasize their national origins, demonstrating how FCCP can reinforce quality and price positioning. Marketers sometimes use the phrase "transformation advertising" to describe advertising that seeks to change the experience of buying and using a product—in other words, the product benefit—to justify a higher-price/quality position. Presumably, buying and drinking Grey Goose (from France), Belvedere (Poland), or Ketel One (the Netherlands) is a more gratifying consumption experience than that of buying and drinking a "bar brand" such as Popov (who knows where it's made?).

Use or User

Another positioning strategy represents how a product is used or associates the brand with a user or class of users. For example, to capitalize on the global success and high visibility of the *Lord of the Rings* trilogy, Gillette's Duracell battery unit ran print and TV ads proclaiming that when

---

[49] Al Ries and Jack Trout, *Positioning: The Battle for Your Mind* (New York: Warner Books, 1982), p. 44.
[50] David A. Aaker and J. Gary Shansby, "Positioning Your Product," *Business Horizons* 25, no. 2 (May–June 1982), pp. 56–62.
[51] "Head to Head," *The Economist* (October 29, 2005), pp. 66–69.

on location in remote areas of New Zealand, *Rings* director Peter Jackson and his crew used Duracell exclusively. Likewise, Max Factor makeup is positioned as "the makeup that makeup artists use." Pulsar watch associates the brand with a handsome man who is "addicted to reality TV" and enjoys reading Dostoevsky.

Competition

Implicit or explicit reference to competitors can provide the basis for an effective positioning strategy. For example, when Anita Roddick started The Body Shop International in the 1970s, she emphasized the difference between the principles pursued by "mainstream" health and beauty brands and those of her company. The Body Shop brand stands for natural ingredients, no animal testing, and recyclable containers. In addition, the company sources key ingredients via direct relationships with suppliers throughout the world; sustainable sourcing and paying suppliers fair-trade prices are integral to the brand's essence. Moreover, Roddick abandoned the conventional industry approach of promising miracles; instead, women are given realistic expectations of what health and beauty aids can accomplish.

Dove's "Campaign for Real Beauty" broke new ground by positioning the brand around a new definition of beauty. The campaign was based on research commissioned by Silvia Lagnado, Dove's global brand director. The research indicated that, worldwide, only 2 percent of women considered themselves to be beautiful. Armed with this insight, Ogilvy & Mather Worldwide's office in Dusseldorf developed the concept that was the basis of the Campaign for Real Beauty. To strengthen the connection between the Real Beauty campaign and Dove's products, Dove launched a Web community in 2008. Visitors to the site could watch "Fresh Takes," a miniseries that aired on MTV, as well as seek medical advice on skin care.[52]

Global, Foreign, and Local Consumer Culture Positioning[53]

As noted in Chapter 4 and discussed briefly in this chapter, global consumer culture positioning is a strategy that can be used to target various segments associated with the emerging global consumer culture. **Global consumer culture positioning (GCCP)** is defined as a strategy that identifies a brand as a symbol of a particular global culture or segment. It has proven to be an effective strategy for communicating with global teens, cosmopolitan elites, globe-trotting laptop warriors who consider themselves members of a "transnational commerce culture," and other groups. For example, Sony's brightly colored "My First Sony" line is positioned as *the* electronics brand for youngsters around the globe with discerning parents. Philips' current global corporate image campaign is keyed to the theme "Sense and Simplicity." Benetton uses the slogan "United Colors of Benetton" to position itself as a brand concerned with the unity of humankind. Heineken's strong brand equity around the globe can be attributed in good measure to a GCCP strategy that reinforces consumers' cosmopolitan self-images.

Certain categories of products lend themselves especially well to GCCP. High-tech and high-touch products are both associated with high levels of customer involvement and by a shared "language" among users.[54] *High-tech products* are sophisticated, technologically complex, and/or difficult to explain or understand. When shopping for them, consumers often have specialized needs or interests and rational buying motives. High-tech brands and products are frequently evaluated in terms of their performance against established, objective standards. Portable MP3 players, cell phones, personal computers, home theater audio/video components, luxury automobiles, and financial services are some of the high-tech product categories for which companies have established strong global positions. Buyers typically already possess—or wish to acquire—considerable technical information. Generally speaking, for example, computer buyers in all parts of the world are equally knowledgeable about Pentium microprocessors, 500-gigabyte hard drives, software RAM requirements, and high-resolution flat-panel displays. High-tech global consumer positioning also works well for special-interest products associated with leisure or recreation. Fuji bicycles, Adidas sports equipment, and Canon cameras are

[52] Suzanne Vranica, "Can Dove Promote a Cause and Sell Soap?" *The Wall Street Journal* (April 10, 2008), p. B6.

[53] The following discussion is adapted from Dana L. Alden, Jan-Benedict Steenkamp, and Rajeev Batra, "Brand Positioning through Advertising in Asia, North America, and Europe: The Role of Global Consumer Culture," *Journal of Marketing* 63, no. 1 (January 1999), pp. 75–87.

[54] Teresa J. Domzal and Lynette Unger, "Emerging Positioning Strategies in Global Marketing," *Journal of Consumer Marketing* 4, no. 4 (Fall 1987), pp. 26–27.

Exhibit 7-8 This Portuguese-language Bridgestone print ad underscores the point that although Bridgestone is a global company, it is a local one as well. Translation: "There is only one thing better than a Japanese tire. A Japanese tire made in Brazil. Made in Brazil with Japanese technology."

examples of successful global special-interest products. Because most people who buy and use high-tech products "speak the same language" and share the same mind-set, marketing communications should be informative and emphasize performance-related attributes and features to establish the desired GCCP (see Exhibit 7-8).

By contrast, when shopping for *high-touch products*, consumers are generally energized by emotional motives rather than rational ones. Consumers may feel an emotional or spiritual connection with high-touch products, the performance of which is evaluated in subjective, aesthetic terms rather than objective, technical terms. Acquisition of high-touch products may represent an act of personal indulgence, reflect the user's actual or ideal self-image, or reinforce interpersonal relationships between the user and family members or friends. High-touch products appeal to the senses more than the intellect; if a product comes with a detailed user's manual, it's probably high tech. By contrast, the consumption experience associated with a high-touch product probably does not entail referring to an instruction manual. Luxury perfume, designer fashions, and fine champagne are all examples of high-touch products that lend themselves to GCCP. Some high-touch products are linked with the joy or pleasure found in "life's little moments." Ads that show friends chatting over a cup of coffee in a café or someone's kitchen put the product at the center of everyday life. As Nestlé has convincingly demonstrated with its Nescafé brand, this type of high-touch, emotional appeal is understood worldwide.

A brand's GCCP can be reinforced by the careful selection of the thematic, verbal, or visual components that are incorporated into advertising and other communications. For marketers seeking to establish a high-touch GCCP, leisure, romance, and materialism are three themes that cross borders well. By contrast, professionalism and experience are advertising themes that work well for high-tech products such as global financial services. Several years ago, for example, Chase Manhattan bank launched a $75 million global advertising campaign geared to the theme "Profit from experience." According to Aubrey Hawes, a vice president and corporate director of marketing for the bank, Chase's business and private banking clients "span the globe and travel the globe. They can only know one Chase in their minds, so why should we try to confuse them?"[56] Presumably, Chase's target audience is sophisticated enough to appreciate the subtlety of the copywriter's craft—"profit" can be interpreted as either a noun ("monetary gain") or a verb ("reap an advantage").

In some instances, products may be positioned globally in a "bipolar" fashion as both high tech and high touch. This approach can be used when products satisfy buyers' rational criteria while evoking an emotional response. For example, audio/video components from Denmark's Bang & Olufsen (B&O), by virtue of their performance and elegant styling, are perceived as both high tech (i.e., advanced engineering and sonically superior) and high touch (i.e., sleek, modern design; see Exhibit 7-9). As former CEO Torben Ballegaard Sørensen explained, "Our brand is

"Chinese companies are certainly growing but they haven't yet acquired the skills that make their Western peers so successful in 'high tech and high touch' industries."[55]

—Pankaj Ghemwat, Professor of Global Strategy, IESE Business School, Barcelona

[55] Pankaj Ghemawat and Thomas M. Hout, "Softening the 'Red Edge,'" *The Wall Street Journal* (October 10, 2008).
[56] Gary Levin, "Ads Going Global," *Advertising Age* (July 22, 1991), p. 42.

Exhibit 7-9 The worldwide success of Apple's iPod digital music player (more than 350 million units sold) can be attributed to a superior global marketing strategy. The iPod product lineup includes the Shuffle, the Nano, the Classic, and the iPod Touch. Prices start at $49 and top out at $399. iPods are available directly from www.apple.com and Apple Stores, as well as a variety of other retail sources. Ads reinforce the message that the iPod is the ultimate in high-tech, high-touch "cool." The brand appeals to global teens, the global elite, and everyone in between.
Source: Katsumi Kasahara/ AP Images.

about feeling good at home, or where you feel at home—in a car or in a hotel. When daily life is cluttered, you can come home to a system that works and is tranquil. It cocoons you."[57] Nokia became the world's leading cell phone brand because the company combines state-of-the-art technical performance with a fashion orientation that allows users to view their phones as extensions of themselves. Likewise, as shown in Exhibit 7-10, Apple positions its products on the basis of both performance ("160GB of storage, holds 40,000 songs") and design (writing in the *Financial Times*, a reviewer called the iPod "an all-time design classic").

To the extent that English is the primary language of international business, mass media, and the Internet, one can make the case that English signifies modernism and a cosmopolitan outlook. Therefore, the use of English in advertising and labeling throughout the world is another way to achieve GCCP. Benetton's tagline "United Colors of Benetton" appears in English in all of the company's advertising. The implication is that fashion-minded consumers everywhere in the world shop at Benetton. English is often used as a marketing tool in Japan. Even though a native English speaker would doubtless find the syntax to be muddled, it is the symbolism associated with the use of English that counts rather than the specific meanings that the words might (or might not) convey. A third way to reinforce a GCCP is to use brand symbols whose interpretation defies association with a specific country culture. Examples include Nestlé's "little nest" logo with an adult bird feeding its babies, the Nike swoosh, and the Mercedes-Benz star.

A second option is **foreign consumer culture positioning (FCCP)**, which associates the brand's users, use occasions, or production origins with a foreign country or culture. A long-running campaign for Foster's Brewing Group's U.S. advertising proudly trumpeted the brand's national origin; print ads featured the tagline "Foster's. Australian for beer," while TV and radio spots were keyed to the theme "How to speak Australian." Needless to say, these ads were not used in Australia itself! Advertising for Grupo Modelo's Corona Extra brand is identified more generally with Latin America. The "American-ness" of Levi jeans, Marlboro cigarettes, American Apparel clothing, and Harley-Davidson motorcycles—sometimes conveyed with subtlety, sometimes not—enhances their brands' appeal to cosmopolitans around the world and offers opportunities for FCCP.

IKEA, the home furnishings retailer based in Sweden, wraps itself in the Swedish flag—literally. Inside and out, IKEA's stores are decorated in the national colors of blue and yellow. To reinforce the chain's Scandinavian heritage—and to encourage shoppers to linger—many stores feature cafeterias in which Swedish meatballs and other foods are served! Sometimes,

---

[57] John Gapper, "When High Fidelity Becomes High Fashion," *Financial Times* (December 20, 2005), p. 8.

Exhibit 7-10 Renowned worldwide for Danish craftsmanship and innovation, Bang & Olufsen is a textbook example of high-touch, high-tech global brand positioning. This print ad showcases Bang & Olufsen's Beosound 8 speaker dock. One reviewer called the Beosound 8 "a truly exceptional product . . . the coolest and most 'now' product B&O has made for years."
Source: Used by permission of Bang & Olufsen.

AT LAST... A DOCK
THAT MATCHES THE DEVICE

Dock your iPod, iPhone or iPad in BeoSound 8. Or connect an MP3 player, PC or Mac and rediscover your music collection all over again - only this time it will sound like you are sitting in the front row!

Start the experience at **www.bang-olufsen.com** or call **888 302 8192** for your closest showroom.

MSRP $999.00

iPod, iPhone and iPad are trademarks of Apple Inc., registered in the U.S. and other countries. Wall mount also available for BeoSound 8.

BANG & OLUFSEN

brand names suggest an FCCP even though a product is of local origin. For example, the name "Häagen-Dazs" was made up to imply Scandinavian origin even though an American company launched the ice cream. Conversely, a popular chewing gum in Italy marketed by Perfetti bears the brand name "Brooklyn."

Marketers can also utilize **local consumer culture positioning (LCCP)**, a strategy that associates the brand with local cultural meanings, reflects the local culture's norms, portrays the brand as consumed by local people in the national culture, or depicts the product as locally produced for local consumers. An LCCP approach can be seen in Budweiser's U.S. advertising; ads featuring the iconic Clydesdale horses, for example, associate the brand with small-town American culture. Researchers studying television advertising in seven countries found that LCCP predominated, particularly in ads for food, personal nondurables, and household nondurables.

Summary

The global environment must be analyzed before a company pursues expansion into new geographic markets. Through **global market segmentation**, a company can identify and group customers or countries according to common needs and wants. **Demographic segmentation** can be based on country income and population, age, ethnicity, or other variables. **Psychographic segmentation** groups people according to attitudes, interests, opinions, and lifestyles. **Behavior segmentation** utilizes **user status** and **usage rate** as segmentation variables. **Benefit segmentation** is based on the benefits buyers seek. **Global teens** and **global elites** are two examples of global market segments.

After marketers have identified segments, the next step is **targeting**: The identified groups are evaluated and compared, and one or more segments with the greatest potential are selected. The groups are then evaluated on the basis of several factors, including segment size and growth potential, competition, and compatibility and feasibility. Target market assessment also entails a thorough understanding of the **product market** in question and determining **marketing model drivers** and **enabling conditions** in the countries under study. The timing of market entry should take into account whether a **first-mover advantage** is likely to be gained. After evaluating the identified segments, marketers must decide on an appropriate targeting strategy. The three basic categories of global target marketing strategies are **standardized global marketing, niche** marketing, and **multisegment targeting**.

Positioning a product or brand to differentiate it in the minds of target customers can be accomplished in various ways: **positioning by attribute or benefit, positioning by quality/price, positioning by use or user**, and **positioning by competition. Global consumer culture positioning (GCCP), foreign consumer culture positioning (FCCP)**, and **local consumer culture positioning (LCCP)** are additional strategic options in global marketing.

MyMarketingLab

Go to **mymktlab.com** for the following Assisted-graded writing questions:

7-1. Compare and contrast the standardized, concentrated, and differentiated global marketing strategies. Illustrate each strategy with an example from a global company.

7-2. What is a high-touch product? Explain the difference between high-tech product positioning and high-touch product positioning. Can some products be positioned using both strategies? Explain.

7-3. Mymarketinglab Only – comprehensive writing assignment for this chapter.

MyMarketingLab

Go to **mymktlab.com** to complete the problems marked with this icon .

Discussion Questions

 7-4. In a recent interview, a brand manager at Procter & Gamble noted, "Historically, we used to be focused on discovering the common hopes and dreams within a country, but now we're seeing that the real commonalities are in generations across geographic borders." What is the significance of this comment in terms of segmenting and targeting?

7-5. Identify the five basic segmentation strategies. Give an example of a company that has used each one.

7-6. Explain the difference between segmenting and targeting.

7-7. What is positioning? Identify the different positioning strategies presented in the chapter and give examples of companies or products that illustrate each.

7-8. What is global consumer culture positioning (GCCP)? What other strategic positioning choices do global marketers have?

CASE 7-1 CONTINUED (REFER TO PAGE 220)
Global Companies Target Low-Income Consumers (A)

One of the most basic issues at the bottom of the pyramid is access to basic infrastructure. Historically, government-owned power-generation facilities, including massive solar projects and wind farms, have been the norm in emerging markets such as India. However, it is often not cost-effective to extend the power grid into rural areas. In fact, according to the International Energy Agency, less than two-thirds of the rural residents in the world's developing nations have access to electricity. One problem with the new renewable energy systems is the lack of scale. Rural markets are dispersed, and distribution is not well established. As a result, many investors consider rural renewable energy initiatives to be too risky.

The situation may be changing in Africa, where nearly 600 million people are included in the "off-grid segment." That is, they live without access to reliable sources of electricity. For years, small-scale organizations such as Solar Sisters have worked at the individual level to help provide renewable energy sources. Now large global companies such as Philips Electronics, DuPont, and Siemens are testing solar-powered systems at the village level. The companies hope that government officials will purchase the systems and bring power to rural areas. The systems include solar panels for charging batteries and overhead home lighting and lanterns that use efficient LEDs. As Philips has discovered in its pilot program in South Africa, the money that villagers save by not buying kerosene can be spent on necessities such as bread. If the pilot programs are successful and win government funding, enough power will be available to enable village households to have refrigerators and radios.

Lack of scale and a shortage of capital are just two of the problems associated with reaching the world's poor. For consumer products, Professor Aneel Karnani of the Ross School of Business has identified another stumbling block to market success. "The biggest problem is that prices are too high. Companies overestimate the size of the market and end up selling to the middle class, not the poor," he says. But there is a potential upside: Even as shoppers in mature markets cut back on discretionary spending, consumer spending on basic items such as food and soap remains stable and relatively unaffected by trends in the broader global economy. However, after companies have created the right product at the right price, another potential problem presents itself: communicating product benefits and persuading low-income consumers to change long-entrenched behaviors by paying for new products and integrating them into their lifestyles. In short, it is not enough to simply launch a low-cost product; markets for that product must be created.

Nestlé's experience in emerging markets illustrates how a painstaking approach can yield positive results. Indonesia is a case in point. As the data in Table 7-3 indicate, Indonesia is the world's fourth-most-populous country. Even though per capita income is only $3,420 per year, Nestlé Indonesia generates annual revenues of $1 billion. The company has enjoyed consistent sales growth for Milo, a chocolate sports drink mix for children. It can be prepared hot or cold and sells for about 10 cents per serving. Crunch, another new chocolate product, is a bite-sized snack wafer that also sells for 10 cents per package. Nestlé's food engineers managed to keep the cost low by using existing production processes utilized for the company's breakfast cereal lines. Because the Crunch packaging is inflated, the wafers don't melt or break into pieces.

Nestlé has also successfully targeted low-income consumers in Latin America. With a population of nearly 200 million people and a GDP of $2.25 trillion, Brazil dominates the region. Per capita income is $11,630, placing Brazil in the ranks of upper-middle-income countries. However, averages can be deceiving. Some 30 million Brazilians qualify as "bottom-of-the-pyramid" consumers, and an estimated 16 million Brazilians live on less than $600 per year. In the mid-2000s, the president of Nestlé do Brasil initiated a regionalization program. As Ivan Zurita explains, "In this country, which we consider to be a continent, there are different brands and different histories in each region. Anyone who tries to operate in Brazil with a single consumer profile is not going to run into many opportunities."

For example, northeastern Brazil is the poorest region in the country. There, Nestlé launched Leche Ideal, a powdered milk mix enriched with vitamins and iron that is sold in 200-gram packets that are easy to store. In the Brazilian state of Bahia, Nestlé opened a new plant in 2007 that has the capacity to produce 50,000 tons of food products each year. Crucially, the products can easily be adapted to local tastes, such as a smoother-tasting coffee. The success of the regionalization program in Brazil has prompted Nestlé executives to call for its expansion throughout the region. Notes Mr. Zurita, "I have worked practically everywhere in Latin America and there is not one place where we can't apply what we have done here in Brazil. Chile is an example in the region. If you leave Santiago you will find poverty, and the program can be applied."

Other well-known global marketers are also capitalizing on the opportunity to serve low-income consumers. For example, Kraft recently opened its first plant in northeastern Brazil. Adidas has developed a sneaker priced at one euro that it hopes to sell in Bangladesh. Unilever's Cubitos are seasoning cubes that sell for as little as two cents each. Danone has developed a variety of products for emerging markets, including Dolima drinkable yogurt, Dany Xprime jelly pouches, and Milky Start milk porridge.

Not every company has been successful targeting the low-income segment. For example, Procter & Gamble spent years developing PUR, a water purification powder that sells for 10 cents. Although market research indicated that villagers wanted clean water, PUR ultimately did not catch on with consumers. In the end, P&G chose to donate PUR to relief organizations and partner with other groups to educate villagers about the benefits of PUR.

Even as Procter & Gamble continues to target consumers at the bottom of the pyramid, its primary target is the middle-class consumer: a professional manager who lives in a modern high-rise apartment building and has enough discretionary income to dine out several times each month.

> **"Our innovation strategy is not just diluting the top-tier product for the lower-end consumer. You have to discretely innovate for every one of those consumers on that economic curve, and if you don't do that, you'll fail."**
>
> —Robert McDonald, CEO and chairman, Procter & Gamble

Procter & Gamble has also learned the value of local research and development programs. This is something that domestic companies in India and other emerging markets have known for a long time. In fact, as innovation guru Vijay Govindarajan has noted, "The biggest threat for U.S. multinationals is not existing competitors. It is going to be emerging-market competitors." In India, for example, entrepreneurial companies are creating a variety of low-cost products that meet the needs and fit the lifestyles of consumers at affordable prices.

The products include an improved $23 wood-burning stove created by a startup company called First Energy. Indian women spend many hours each day cooking, and there was a clear need for a stove that burned less wood and generated less smoke. The key was adapting technology used in power plants. Engineers at the Indian Institute of Science created a high-efficiency, perforated burning chamber equipped with a small fan. The engineers also found an innovative way to convert agricultural by-products into valuable resources: The new stove burns pellets made from corn husks and peanut shells.

Hindustan Unilever spent 4 years developing Pureit, a portable water purification system that costs $43. Rather than rely on traditional distribution channels, Unilever tapped its network of 45,000 sales representatives who demonstrate Unilever products in their own homes. The women follow up the demonstrations by delivering products door-to-door. Today, more than 3 million Indian homes have Pureit systems.

Godrej & Boyce Manufacturing offers Little Cool, a $70 portable refrigerator that uses minimal electricity. Only 20 percent of Indian households have refrigerators; to assess the opportunity, Godrej sent researchers to meet with farm families in rural India. The resulting product resembles a cooler with handles for easy transport. Instead of a power-hungry compressor, the units have cooling chips and fans. Because power outages are common in India, Little Cool can run on batteries, and it is heavily insulated so contents stay cool for hours.

Discussion Questions

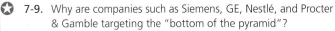 **7-9.** Why are companies such as Siemens, GE, Nestlé, and Procter & Gamble targeting the "bottom of the pyramid"?

7-10. Review the Chapter 4 discussion of diffusion theory. How might an understanding of the characteristics of innovations help marketers succeed in emerging markets?

7-11. What types of marketing communications may be necessary to launch an innovative product such as Procter & Gamble's PUR in emerging markets? What changes in consumer attitudes and behavior are required for successfully launching a product such as PUR?

7-12. What key concepts discussed in Chapter 1 apply to Nestlé's experience in Latin America?

Sources: Tio Kermeliotis, "'Solar Sisters' Spreading Light in Africa," *Marketplace Africa*, www.cnn.com, January 2, 2013; Eric Bellman, "Multinationals Market to the Poor," *The Wall Street Journal* (July 24, 2012), p. B8; Patrick McGroarty, "Power to More People," *The Wall Street Journal Report: Innovations* (June 18, 2012), p. R4; "Catching Up in a Hurry," *The Economist* (May 19, 2011); Jennifer Reinhold, "Can P&G Make Money in Places Where People Earn $2 a Day?" *Fortune* (January 17, 2011), pp. 58–63; Christina Passariello, "Danone Expands Its Pantry to Woo the World's Poor," *The Wall Street Journal* (June 25, 2010), pp. A1, A16; James Lamont, "The Age of 'Indovation' Dawns," *Financial Times* (June 15, 2010); Elisabeth Rosenthal, "African Huts Far from the Grid Glow with Renewable Power," *The New York Times* (December 25, 2010), p. A1; Erik Simanis, "At the Base of the Pyramid," *The Wall Street Journal* (October 26, 2009), p. R6; Eric Bellman, "Indian Firms Shift Focus to the Poor," *The Wall Street Journal* (October 21, 2009), p. A1; Carlos Adese, "In Good Taste: Nestlé Tweaks Products for Different Parts of Brazil—and Latin America—to Boost Sales," *Latin Trade* (July 1, 2007).

CASE 7-2
Cosmetics Giants Segment the Global Cosmetics Market

The world's best-known cosmetics companies are setting their sights on a lucrative new market segment: the emerging middle classes in countries such as Brazil, Russia, India, and China. For example, the Chinese spent $10.3 billion on cosmetics and toiletries in 2005; that figure has doubled in the last few years. Not surprisingly, marketers at L'Oréal, Procter & Gamble, Shiseido, and Estée Lauder Companies are moving quickly. William Lauder, president and CEO of Estée Lauder, calls China a "$100 billion opportunity."

Noting that there is no "one-size-fits-all" ideal of beauty, cosmetics marketers pride themselves on sensitivity to local cultural preferences. As Jean-Paul Agon, chief executive of L'Oréal, explains, "We have different customers. Each customer is free to have her own aspirations. Our intention is just to respond as well as possible to each customer aspiration. Some want to be gorgeous, some want to be natural, and we just have to offer them the best quality and the best product to satisfy their wishes and their dreams." For example, many Asian women use whitening creams to lighten and brighten their complexions; in China, white skin is associated with wealth. L'Oréal responded by creating White Perfect; Shiseido offers Aupres White.

> **"You can't just import cosmetics here. Companies have to understand what beauty means to Chinese women and what they look for, and product offerings and communication have to be adjusted accordingly. It's a lot harder than selling shampoo or skin care."**
>
> —Daisy Ching, regional group account director for Procter & Gamble, Grey Global Group

Market research is critical to understanding women's preferences in different parts of the world. According to Eric Bone, head of L'Oréal's Tokyo Research Center, "Japanese women prefer to use a compact foundation rather than a liquid. Humidity here is much higher and the emphasis is on long-lasting coverage." Armed with this knowledge, L'Oréal devotes more development time to compacts rather than liquids. The researchers have also learned that the typical Japanese woman cleanses her face twice a day.

In China, L'Oréal and its competitors have an opportunity to educate women about cosmetics, which were banned prior to 1982. Each year, L'Oréal observes and films 6,000 Chinese women applying and removing makeup. Alice Laurent, L'Oréal's skincare development manager in Shanghai, says, "In China, the number of products used in the morning and the evening is 2.2." At its Shanghai Innovation Centre, L'Oréal is also studying how to incorporate traditional Chinese medicine into new product lines.

L'Oréal offers a wide range of products in China, including both mass-market and premium brands. The company pursues a localization product strategy, with more than 80 percent of its Asian products developed specifically for the region. L'Oréal's Lancôme luxury brand is typically sold in exclusive shopping districts that have upscale shops and luxury malls. L'Oréal has also capitalized on the opportunity to target a new demographic: Chinese men. The Chinese market for men's skincare products is growing much faster than the market for women's skincare. Many of the purchases are made by women during shopping trips when couples go out together. Increasing numbers of Chinese men view appearance as a key to success, with skincare products playing an important role in male grooming.

Although mass-market cosmetic lines are exhibiting slow growth, the demand for luxury cosmetics is growing rapidly. This is especially true outside of China's main metropolitan centers. Consumers in Tier 1 cities such as Beijing and Shanghai have the highest incomes, but these cities represent only about 9 percent of China's population. As these markets become saturated, L'Oréal and other cosmetics marketers are targeting Tier 2 provincial capitals such as Nanjing. Tier 3 cities such as Zhenjiang are typically prefectural centers; China has approximately 260 such cities, with a combined population of more than 200 million people. An additional 300 million people live in Tier 4 and Tier 5 cities. Notes Stéphane Rinderknech, a L'Oréal general manager based in China, "Three-quarters of China's urban population live outside Tier-One and Tier-Two cities and they account for two-thirds of retail sales."

Estée Lauder's focus is on expensive prestige brands such as Estée Lauder, Clinique, and MAC, which are sold through upmarket department stores. Like its competitors, Lauder is achieving growth in China by targeting new cities. As a company spokesperson explained, "More of Estée Lauder's growth is expected to come from expansion and awareness-building in tier-two and three cities as tier-one cities begin to mature."

One research analyst cautions that Estée Lauder's targeting and positioning may be too narrow for China. According to Access Asia, Estée Lauder "is in danger of becoming too exclusively placed at the top end of the market and it may have to reposition itself more in the mass market to compete for a larger part of the Chinese market."

Estée Lauder's Carol Shen disagrees with that assessment. She views her company's brands as aspirational. "Chinese consumers are price sensitive but at the same time are willing to invest in products that are relatively expensive versus their income levels because they are so confident about the future," she says. Shen's views are shared by other industry leaders. As CEO William Lauder explains, "The Estée

Exhibit 7-11 L'Oréal is expanding distribution in China. After successful market tests at Walmart and Carrefour stores, L'Oréal Paris, Maybelline, Garnier, and other brands are now available in retail stores as well as Chinese supermarkets. In 2006, L'Oréal China launched a new advertising campaign for the Mininurse Professional UV cosmetics line targeting women 18 years of age to 25 years of age. The ads communicate the brand's core benefits: UV protection, daytime skin whitening action, and nighttime hydrating action.
Source: AP Images.

Lauder brand in China is exploding right now because it represents aspirational luxury but at a price that's much more affordable than Louis Vuitton." Nicolas Hieronimus, president of L'Oréal Luxury, concurs: "We're not in the super-premium luxury world. We are not selling €10,000 watches, but €300 creams at best."

In India, L'Oréal has recently shifted from a low-price, mass-market strategy to a premium-price, upscale strategy. Competitor Hindustan Lever rings up nearly $1 billion in annual sales by targeting the hundreds of millions of people who must live on the equivalent of $2 per day. This means body lotion priced at $0.70 and $0.90 bottles of perfume. Upon first entering India in 1991, L'Oréal used a similar strategy. However, its low-priced Garnier Ultra Doux shampoo failed to catch on with consumers. Offering no particular advantage relative to local brands, it was, in the words of Alain Evrard, L'Oréal's managing director for Africa, Orient, and the Pacific, "an absolute flop." Some shopkeepers were stuck with unsold inventories.

In the mid-1990s, Evrard was determined to gain a better understanding of the Indian market. He noted several different trends. The number of working women was increasing dramatically, and consumer attitudes were shifting. Thanks to cable television, CNN and MTV were finding large viewing audiences. To learn more about women's preferences, Evrard spoke with advertising executives and fashion magazine editors as well as L'Oréal's local employees. In doing so, Evrard arrived at a keen insight: Women in their twenties concerned about gray hair were not satisfied with existing do-it-yourself hair color products. Evrard responded by launching L'Oréal Excellence Crème in India. An innovative but expensive product popular in Europe, Excellence Crème was priced at $9 and positioned as a luxury purchase. To gain support among shopkeepers, a local L'Oréal staffer named Dinesh Dayal mounted an education campaign and went door-to-door to promote the product at local shops. Today, Excellence Crème is widely available in India. In 2004, after more than a decade of losses, L'Oréal's Indian operations became profitable.

Brazil is another important market for the global cosmetics giants. On a per capita basis, Brazilian women spend more on beauty products than their counterparts elsewhere. Overall, Brazil is the third-largest global cosmetics market, after the United States and Japan. Natura Cosméticos, a Brazilian company, and Avon are market-share leaders here; traditionally, Brazilians have bought their cosmetics from sales representatives who go door-to-door. This creates a challenge for L'Oréal and other companies that distribute their products through department stores, drug stores, and pharmacies.

Although L'Oréal has operated in Brazil for decades, the focus has been on hair-care products. Worldwide, makeup and skin care represent about 50 percent of L'Oréal's sales; by contrast, in Brazil these categories represent only about 15 percent of sales. To build its presence in makeup and skin care, L'Oréal has hired personal beauty advisors to offer shoppers in-store consultations about Maybelline and other brands. As L'Oréal CEO Jean-Paul Agon notes, "Our big bet here is to create a makeup business in retail from scratch. The more the market develops, the less important direct sales will be."

Meanwhile, Shinzo Maeda, president and CEO of Shiseido, does not intend to stay on the sidelines as Western cosmetics marketers penetrate deeper into emerging markets. Shiseido is Japan's second-largest cosmetics company; however, domestic sales are expected to grow only about 2 percent annually. Maeda notes, "The need to globalize our organization has come at an accelerated pace." Throughout the region, consumers associate the Shiseido brand with a company that understands skin issues specific to Asian women. The company also has a reputation for advanced research and development in key areas such as anti-aging products. In China, Shiseido uses a selling strategy that has been extremely effective in Japan. Highly trained beauty counselors offer advice on color coordination, moisture levels, and related topics. As one beauty counselor said, "It's a real delight to see my customers become happy."

Discussion Questions

7-13. How do women's preferences for cosmetics and beauty care vary from country to country?

7-14. Assess Estée Lauder's strategy for China. Does it make sense to focus on premium brands, or should the company launch a mass-market brand?

7-15. What is the best positioning strategy for Shiseido as the company expands in Asia? High touch? High tech? Both?

7-16. Do you think L'Oréal will succeed in changing the buying habits of Brazilian women?

Sources: Scheherazade Daneshkhu, "Cosmetics Groups Move Deeper into China," *Financial Times* (April 23, 2013), p. 15; Christina Passariello, "To L'Oréal, Brazil's Women Need Fresh Style of Shopping," *The Wall Street Journal* (January 21, 2011), p. B1; Patti Waldemeir, "L'Oréal Changes the Face of Men in China," *Financial Times* (May 29, 2010), p. 17; Miki Tanikawa, "A Personal Touch Counts in Cosmetics," *The New York Times* (February 17, 2009), p. B4; Passariello, "L'Oréal Net Gets New-Market Lift," *The Wall Street Journal* (February 14, 2008), p. C7; Ellen Byron, "Beauty, Prestige, and Worry Lines," *The Wall Street Journal* (August 20, 2007), p. B3; Passariello, "Beauty Fix: Behind L'Oréal's Makeover in India: Going Upscale," *The Wall Street Journal* (July 13, 2007), pp. A1, A14; Beatrice Adams, "Big Brands Are Watching You," *Financial Times* (November 4/5, 2006), p. W18; Adam Jones, "How to Make Up Demand," *Financial Times* (October 3, 2006), p. 8; Lauren Foster and Andrew Yeh, "Estée Lauder Puts on a New Face," *Financial Times* (March 23, 2006), p. 7; Laurel Wentz, "P&G Launches Cover Girl in China," *Advertising Age* (October 31, 2005), p. 22; Rebecca Rose, "Global Diversity Gets All Cosmetic," *Financial Times* (April 11/12, 2004), p. W11.

8

Importing, Exporting, and Sourcing

CASE 8-1

East-Asian Countries: Export-led Growth for Economic Success

Few countries have witnessed economic growth as sustained and incredible as the East-Asian countries in the last 30 years. If the 21st century were to be defined as the Asian Century, then the key to this achievement can be traced back to Japan's recipe for economic success. Soon after 1860, when the country was forced to open up, Japan's traditional cotton textile industry was wiped out by European goods. By 1914 however, the country was selling half of its automated cotton-spinner produced yarns abroad, accounting for about a quarter of the global cotton yarn exports.

Exhibit 8-1 Instead of closing up their economies, several countries in East Asia adopted trade policies that promoted exports in targeted industries. After witnessing Japan's astonishing growth, before and after World War II, Hong Kong, Singapore, South Korea, and Taiwan, the so-called Asian Tigers, replicated the model for trade and economic growth in the 1960s and 1970s. Since then, the Asian markets have been booming in spite of periods with financial instabilities, with Hong Kong leading the race.

This phenomenon represents the two competing theories of economic development in international trade – import-substitution industrialization (ISI) and export-led growth.

ISI is a model of trade and economic growth where a country reduces its share of imported goods by locally producing as much as it can. On the other hand, in a model of export-led growth a country specializes completely or substantially in export production. These products are normally goods in which the country enjoys comparative advantage.

It is an age-old debate – which one of these models is more suitable for assuring a sustainable and balanced economic growth? There is some factual evidence which tells us that low- and middle-income free trade countries have higher economic growth on an average. This is why, by the mid-1980s, many governments previously advocating ISI began liberalizing trade.

Following Japan's astounding growth vis-à-vis the trade models, the Asian Tigers adopted them. China followed suit by opening four SEZs (special economic zones) in 1979, with the coastal cities of Shenzhen and Zhuhai becoming centers of global manufacturing for export production. Later on, more Asian countries adopted the same model—to the point that, since 2000, the trade on GDP ratio of emerging Asia's exports has grown from 37 percent to 47 percent on an average.

Some economists have warned about the limitations of this model, especially in periods of general economic depressions or slumps, and the 2008-2009 global economic crisis has shown some proof of it. However, trade figures from the last 50 years speak for themselves: Asian share in world trade has increased from 13 percent in 1960 to over 30 percent in 2011 – not so bad for a controversial model of growth! Find the continuation of Case 8-1 at the end of the chapter.

This chapter provides an overview of import–export basics. We begin by explaining the difference between export selling and export marketing. Next is a survey of organizational export activities. An examination of national policies that support exports and/or discourage imports follows. After a discussion of tariff systems, we introduce key export participants. The next section provides an overview of organizational design issues as they pertain to exporting.

This is followed by a section devoted to material that can be extremely useful to undergraduates who are majoring in international business and international marketing: export financing and payment methods. For many students, that all-important first job may be in the import–export department. A familiarity with documentary credits and payment-related terminology can help you make a good impression during a job interview and, perhaps, lead to a job as an export/import coordinator (see Case 8-3). The chapter ends with a discussion of outsourcing, a topic that is becoming increasingly important as companies in many parts of the world cut costs by shifting both blue-collar and white-collar work to nations with low-wage workforces.

LEARNING OBJECTIVES

1 Understand the differences between export selling and export marketing.

2 Identify the stages a company goes through, and the problems it is likely to encounter, as it gains experience as an exporter.

3 Describe the various national policies that pertain to exports and imports.

4 Explain the structure of the Harmonized Tariff System.

5 Describe the various organizations that support and facilitate the export process.

6 Compare and contrast home-country and market-country export organization considerations.

7 Discuss the various payment methods that are typically used in trade financing.

8 Identify the factors that global marketers consider when making sourcing decisions.

Export Selling and Export Marketing: A Comparison

To better understand importing and exporting, it is important to distinguish between **export selling** and **export marketing**. First of all, export selling does not involve tailoring the product, the price, or the promotional material to suit the requirements of global markets. Also, the only marketing mix element that differs is the "place"; that is, the country where the product is sold. The export selling approach may work for some products or services; for unique products with little or no international competition, such an approach is feasible. Similarly, companies new to exporting may initially experience success with selling. Even today, the managerial mind-set in many companies still favors export selling. However, as companies mature in the global marketplace or as new competitors enter the picture, export *marketing* becomes necessary.

Export marketing targets the customer in the context of the total market environment. The export marketer does not simply take the domestic product "as is" and sell it to international customers. To the export marketer, the product offered in the home market represents a starting point. It is then modified as needed to meet the preferences of international target markets; this is the approach the Chinese have adopted in the U.S. furniture market. Similarly, the export marketer sets prices to fit the marketing strategy and does not merely extend home-country pricing to the target market. Charges incurred in export preparation, transportation, and financing must be taken into account in determining prices. Finally, the export marketer also adjusts strategies and plans for communication and distribution to fit the market. In other words, effective communication about product features or uses to buyers in different export markets may require creating brochures with different copy, photographs, or artwork. As the vice president of sales and marketing of one manufacturer noted, "We have to approach the international market with *marketing* literature as opposed to *sales* literature."

Export marketing is the integrated marketing of goods and services that are destined for customers in international markets. Export marketing requires:

1. An understanding of the target market environment
2. The use of marketing research and identification of market potential
3. Decisions concerning product design, pricing, distribution channels, advertising, and communications—the marketing mix

After the research effort has zeroed in on potential markets, there is no substitute for a personal visit to size up the market firsthand and begin the development of an actual export-marketing program. A market visit should do several things. First, it should confirm (or contradict) assumptions regarding market potential. A second major purpose is to gather the additional data necessary to reach the final go or no-go decision regarding an export-marketing program. Certain kinds of information simply cannot be obtained from secondary sources. For example, an export manager or international marketing manager may have a list of potential distributors provided by the U.S. Department of Commerce. In addition, he or she may have corresponded with distributors on the list and formed some tentative idea of whether they meet the company's international criteria.

However, it is difficult to negotiate a suitable arrangement with international distributors without actually meeting face-to-face to allow each side to appraise the capabilities and character of the other party. A third reason for a visit to the export market is to develop a marketing plan in cooperation with the local agent or distributor. Agreement should be reached on necessary product modifications, pricing, advertising and promotion expenditures, and a distribution plan. If the plan calls for investment, agreement on the allocation of costs must also be reached.

As shown in Exhibit 8-2, one way to visit a potential market is through a **trade show** or a state- or federally sponsored **trade mission**. Each year hundreds of trade fairs, usually organized

Exhibit 8-2 Milan is widely regarded as the design capitol of the world. 2011 marked the 50th anniversary of Salon Internazionale del Mobile di Milano ("Milan Furniture Fair"), the world's largest furniture and home furnishings trade fair. Every April, thousands of vendors and visitors from more than 160 countries converge on Milan to share the latest designs.
Source: Cosmit Spa.

around a product category or industry, are held in major markets. By attending these events, company representatives can conduct market assessment, develop or expand markets, find distributors or agents, or locate potential end users. Perhaps most important, attending a trade show enables company representatives to learn a great deal about competitors' technology, pricing, and depth of market penetration. For example, exhibits often offer product literature with strategically useful technological information. Overall, company managers or sales personnel should be able to get a good general impression of competitors in the marketplace as they try to sell their own company's product.

Organizational Export Activities

Exporting is becoming increasingly important as companies in all parts of the world step up their efforts to supply and service markets outside their national boundaries.[1] Research has shown that exporting is essentially a developmental process that can be divided into the following distinct stages:

1. The firm is unwilling to export; it will not even fill an unsolicited export order. This may be due to perceived lack of time ("too busy to fill the order") or to apathy or ignorance.
2. The firm fills unsolicited export orders but does not pursue unsolicited orders. Such a firm is an export seller.
3. The firm explores the feasibility of exporting (this stage may bypass stage 2).
4. The firm exports to one or more markets on a trial basis.
5. The firm is an experienced exporter to one or more markets.
6. After this success, the firm pursues country- or region-focused marketing based on certain criteria (e.g., all countries where English is spoken or all countries where it is not necessary to transport by water).
7. The firm evaluates global market potential before screening for the "best" target markets to include in its marketing strategy and plan. *All* markets—domestic and international—are regarded as equally worthy of consideration.

The probability that a firm will advance from one stage to the next depends on different factors. Moving from stage 2 to stage 3 depends on management's attitude toward the attractiveness of exporting and confidence in the firm's ability to compete internationally. However, *commitment* is the most important aspect of a company's international orientation. Before a firm can reach stage 4, it must receive and respond to unsolicited export orders. The quality and dynamism of management are important factors that can lead to such orders. Success in stage 4 can lead a firm to stages 5 and 6. A company that reaches stage 7 is a mature, geocentric enterprise that is relating global resources to global opportunity. To reach this stage requires management with vision and commitment.

One study noted that export procedural expertise and sufficient corporate resources are required for successful exporting. An interesting finding was that even the most experienced exporters express lack of confidence in their knowledge about shipping arrangements, payment procedures, and regulations. The study also showed that, although profitability is an important expected benefit of exporting, other advantages include increased flexibility and resiliency and improved ability to deal with sales fluctuations in the home market. Although research generally supports the proposition that the probability of being an exporter increases with firm size, it is less clear whether export intensity—the ratio of export sales to total sales—is positively correlated with firm size. Table 8-1 lists some of the export-related problems that a company typically faces.[2]

[1] This section relies heavily on Warren J. Bilkey, "Attempted Integration of the Literature on the Export Behavior of Firms," *Journal of International Business Studies* 8, no. 1 (1978), pp. 33–46. The stages are based on Rogers' adoption process. See Everett M. Rogers, *Diffusion of Innovations* (New York: Free Press, 1995).
[2] Masaaki Kotabe and Michael R. Czinkota, "State Government Promotion of Manufacturing Exports: A Gap Analysis," *Journal of International Business Studies* 23, no. 4 (Fourth Quarter 1992), pp. 637–658.

TABLE 8-1 Potential Export Problems

Logistics	Servicing Exports
Arranging transportation	Providing parts availability
Transport rate determination	Providing repair service
Handling documentation	Providing technical advice
Obtaining financial information	Providing warehousing
Distribution coordination	**Sales Promotion**
Packaging	Advertising
Obtaining insurance	Sales effort
Legal Procedures	Marketing information
Government red tape	**Foreign Market Intelligence**
Product liability	Locating markets
Licensing	Trade restrictions
Customs/duty	Competition overseas
Contract	
Agent/Distributor Agreements	

National Policies Governing Exports and Imports

It is hard to overstate the impact of exporting and importing on the world's national economies. In 1997, for example, total imports of goods and services by the United States passed the $1 trillion mark for the first time; in 2011, the combined total was $2.7 trillion. European Union (EU) imports, counting both intra-EU trade and trade with non-EU partners, totaled more than $3 trillion. Trends in both exports and imports reflect China's pace-setting economic growth in the Asia-Pacific region. Exports from China have grown significantly; they are growing even faster now that China has joined the World Trade Organization (WTO). As shown in Table 8-2, Chinese apparel exports surpass those of other countries by a wide margin. Historically, China protected its own producers by imposing double-digit import tariffs. These have been reduced as China complies with WTO regulations.

Needless to say, representatives of the apparel, footwear, furniture, and textile industries in many countries are deeply concerned about the impact increased trade with China will have

TABLE 8-2 Top 10 Clothing Exporters 2011 ($ billions)

1. China	153.8
2. Italy	23.3
3. Bangladesh	19.9
4. Germany	19.6
5. India	14.4
6. Turkey	13.9
7. Vietnam	13.2
8. France	11.0
9. Spain	9.2
10. Belgium	9.1

Source: The World Trade Organization.

on these sectors. As this example suggests, one word can summarize national policies toward exports and imports: contradictory. For centuries, nations have combined two opposing policy attitudes toward the movement of goods across national boundaries. On the one hand, nations directly encourage exports; the flow of imports, on the other hand, is generally restricted.

Government Programs That Support Exports

To see the economic boost that can come from a government-encouraged export strategy, consider Japan; Singapore; South Korea; and the so-called Greater-China or "China triangle" market, which includes Taiwan, Hong Kong, and the People's Republic of China. Japan totally recovered from the destruction of World War II and became an economic superpower as a direct result of export strategies devised by the Ministry for International Trade and Industry (MITI). The four tigers—Singapore, South Korea, Taiwan, and Hong Kong—learned from the Japanese experience and built strong export-based economies of their own. Although Asia's "economic bubble" burst in 1997 as a result of uncontrolled growth, Japan and the tigers are moving forward in the twenty-first century at a more moderate rate. China, an economy unto itself, has attracted increased foreign investment from Daimler AG, GM, Hewlett-Packard, and scores of other companies that are setting up production facilities to support local sales, as well as exports to world markets.

Any government concerned with trade deficits or economic development should focus on educating firms about the potential gains from exporting. Policymakers should also remove bureaucratic obstacles that hinder company exports. This is true at the national, regional, and local government levels. In India, for example, leaders in the state of Tamil Nadu gave Hyundai permission to operate its plant around the clock, making it the first Hyundai operation anywhere in the world to operate on a 24-hour basis (see Exhibit 8-3).[3] Governments commonly use four activities to support and encourage firms that engage in exporting. These are tax incentives, subsidies, export assistance, and free trade zones.

First, *tax incentives* treat earnings from export activities preferentially either by applying a lower rate to earnings from these activities or by refunding taxes already paid on income associated with exporting. The tax benefits offered by export-conscious governments include varying degrees of tax exemption or tax deferral on export income, accelerated depreciation of export-related assets, and generous tax treatment of overseas market development activities.

Exhibit 8-3 A worker finishes a K-Series engine at the Maruti Suzuki assembly line in Gurgaon, India. Maruti Suzuki is one of India's leading auto manufacturers. However, foreign investment in the automotive sector is exploding as Ford, Honda, Nissan, Toyota, and other companies rush to capitalize on growing Indian demand for passenger cars.
Source: AP Photo/Gurinder Osan.

[3] Anand Giridharadas, "Foreign Automakers See India as Exporter," *The New York Times* (September 12, 2006), p. C5.

From 1985 until 2000, the major tax incentive under U.S. law was the **foreign sales corporation (FSC)**, through which American exporters could obtain a 15 percent exclusion on earnings from international sales. Big exporters benefited the most from the arrangement; Boeing, for example, saved about $100 million per year, and Eastman Kodak saved about $40 million annually. However, in 2000 the WTO ruled that any tax break that was contingent on exports amounted to an illegal subsidy. Accordingly, the U.S. Congress has set about the task of overhauling the FSC system; failure to do so would entitle the EU to impose up to $4 billion in retaliatory tariffs. Potential winners and losers from a change in the FSC law are lobbying furiously. One proposed version of a new law would benefit GM, Procter & Gamble, Walmart, and other U.S. companies with extensive manufacturing or retail operations overseas. By contrast, Boeing would no longer benefit. As Rudy de Leon, a Boeing executive in charge of government affairs, noted, "As we look at the bill, the export of U.S. commercial aircraft would become considerably more expensive."[4]

Governments also support export performance by providing outright **subsidies**, which are direct or indirect financial contributions or incentives that benefit producers. Subsidies can severely distort trade patterns when less competitive but subsidized producers displace competitive producers in world markets. Organisation for Co-operation and Development (OECD) members spend nearly $400 billion annually on farm subsidies; currently, total annual farm support in the EU is estimated at $100 billion. With about $40 billion in annual support, the United States has the highest subsidies of any single nation. Agricultural subsidies are particularly controversial because, although they protect the interests of farmers in developed countries, they work to the detriment of farmers in developing areas such as Africa and India. The EU has undertaken an overhaul of its **Common Agricultural Policy (CAP)**, which critics have called "as egregious a system of protection as any" and "the single most harmful piece of protectionism in the world."[5] In May 2002, much to Europe's dismay, President George W. Bush signed a $118 billion farm bill that actually *increased* subsidies to American farmers over a 6-year period. The Bush administration took the position that, despite the increases, overall U.S. subsidies were still lower than those in Europe and Japan; Congress voted to extend the farm bill for another 5 years.

The third support area is *governmental assistance* to exporters. Companies can avail themselves of a great deal of government information concerning the location of markets and credit risks. Assistance may also be oriented toward export promotion. Government agencies at various levels often take the lead in setting up trade fairs and trade missions designed to promote sales to foreign customers.

The export–import process can also entail red tape and bureaucratic delays. This is especially true in emerging markets such as China and India. In an effort to facilitate exports, countries are designating certain areas as **free trade zones (FTZ)** or **special economic zones (SEZ)**. These are geographic entities that offer manufacturers simplified customs procedures, operational flexibility, and a general environment of relaxed regulations.

Governmental Actions to Discourage Imports and Block Market Access

Measures such as tariffs, import controls, and a host of nontariff barriers are designed to limit the inward flow of goods. **Tariffs** can be thought of as the "three Rs" of global business: rules, rate schedules (duties), and regulations of individual countries. Duties on individual products or services are listed in the schedule of rates (see Table 8-3). One expert on global trade defines **duties** as "taxes that punish individuals for making choices of which their governments disapprove."[6]

As noted in earlier chapters, a major U.S. objective in the Uruguay Round of General Agreement on Tariffs and Trade (GATT) negotiations was to improve market access for U.S. companies with major U.S. trading partners. When the Uruguay Round ended in December 1993, the United States had secured reductions or total eliminations of tariffs on 11 categories of U.S. goods exported to the EU, Japan, five of the EFTA nations (Austria, Switzerland, Sweden, Finland, and Norway), New Zealand, South Korea, Hong Kong, and Singapore. The categories affected included equipment for the construction, agricultural, medical, and scientific industry sectors, as well as steel, beer, brown

---

[4] Edmund L. Andrews, "A Civil War Within a Trade Dispute," *The New York Times* (September 20, 2002), pp. C1, C2.
[5] John Micklethwait and Adrian Wooldridge, *A Future Perfect: The Challenge and Hidden Promise of Globalization* (New York: Crown Publishers, 2000), p. 261.
[6] Edward L. Hudgins, "Mercosur Gets a 'Not Guilty' on Trade Diversion," *The Wall Street Journal* (March 21, 1997), p. A19.

TABLE 8-3 Examples of Trade Barriers

Country/Region	Tariff Barriers	Nontariff Barriers
European Union	16.5% antidumping tariff on shoes from China, 10% on shoes from Vietnam	Quotas on Chinese textiles
China	Tariffs as high as 28% on foreign-made auto parts	Expensive, time-consuming procedures for obtaining pharmaceutical import licenses

distilled spirits, pharmaceuticals, paper, pulp and printed matter, furniture, and toys. Most of the remaining tariffs were phased out over a 5-year period. A key goal of the ongoing Doha Round of WTO trade talks is the reduction in agricultural tariffs, which currently average 12 percent in the United States, 31 percent in the EU, and 51 percent in Japan.

Developed under the auspices of the Customs Cooperation Council (now the World Customs Organization), the **Harmonized Tariff System (HTS)** went into effect in January 1989 and has since been adopted by the majority of trading nations. Under this system, importers and exporters have to determine the correct classification number for a given product or service that will cross borders. With the Harmonized Tariff Schedule B, the export classification number for any exported item is the same as the import classification number. Also, exporters must include the Harmonized Tariff Schedule B number on their export documents to facilitate customs clearance. Accuracy, especially in the eyes of customs officials, is essential. The U.S. Census Bureau compiles trade statistics from the HTS system. Any HTS with a value of less than $2,500 is not counted as a U.S. export. However, *all* imports, regardless of value, are counted.

In spite of the progress made in simplifying tariff procedures, administering a tariff is an enormous burden. People who work with imports and exports must familiarize themselves with the different classifications and use them accurately. Even a tariff schedule of several thousand items cannot clearly describe every product traded globally. Plus, the introduction of new products and new materials used in manufacturing processes creates new problems. Often, determining the duty rate on a particular article requires assessing how the item is used or determining its main component material. Two or more alternative classifications may have to be considered. A product's classification can make a substantial difference in the duty applied. For example, is a Chinese-made *X-Men* action figure a doll or a toy? For many years, dolls were subject to a 12 percent duty when imported into the United States; the rate was 6.8 percent for toys. Moreover, action figures that represent nonhuman creatures such as monsters or robots were categorized as toys and thus qualified for lower duties than human figures that the Customs Service classified as dolls. Duties on both categories have been eliminated; however, the Toy Biz subsidiary of Marvel Enterprises spent nearly 6 years on an action in the U.S. Court of International Trade to prove that its *X-Men* action figures do not represent humans. Although the move appalled many fans of the mutant superheroes, Toy Biz hoped to be reimbursed for overpayment of past duties made when the U.S. Customs Service had classified imports of Wolverine and his fellow figures as dolls.[7]

A **nontariff barrier (NTB)** is any measure other than a tariff that is a deterrent or obstacle to the sale of products in a foreign market. Also known as *hidden trade barriers*, NTBs include quotas, discriminatory procurement policies, restrictive customs procedures, arbitrary monetary policies, and restrictive regulations.

A **quota** is a government-imposed limit or restriction on the number of units or the total value of a particular product or product category that can be imported. Generally, quotas are designed to protect domestic producers. In 2005, for example, textile producers in Italy and other European countries were granted quotas on 10 categories of textile imports from China. The quotas, which were scheduled to run through the end of 2007, were designed to give European producers an opportunity to prepare for increased competition.[8]

---

[7] Neil King, Jr., "Is Wolverine Human? A Judge Answers 'No'; Fans Howl in Protest," *The Wall Street Journal* (January 20, 2003), p. A1.
[8] Juliane von Reppert-Bismarck and Michael Carolan, "Quotas Squeeze European Boutiques," *The Wall Street Journal* (October 22, 2005), p. A9.

The High Cost of U.S. Sugar Subsidies and Quotas

SYNC • THINK • LEARN

MyMarketingLab

A turf war has been raging over one of the humblest commodities traded on world markets: sugar. On one side are small-scale farmers in some of the poorest regions of the world; desperate to increase their incomes and improve their living standards, these farmers want to export more sugar cane. On the other side are farmers

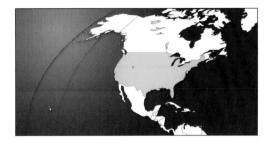

in some of the richest nations in the world who are equally intent on preserving a system of quotas and subsidies that support production of sugar cane and sugar beets. Caught in the middle are processed food and beverage companies that use sugar in baked goods, ice cream, soft drinks, and a range of other products. Consumers are also affected: Sugar subsidies and quotas result in higher prices for popular food and beverage products. The issue has become more prominent in recent years as prices for sugar and other agricultural commodities have been extremely volatile.

The debate over agricultural policy is at the heart of the struggle. Worldwide, agricultural subsidies amount to hundreds of billions of dollars each year. The subsidies issue has been central to the current round of global trade negotiations; it has also been debated at the World Summit on Sustainable Development. Brazil, Australia, and Thailand rank first, third, and fourth, respectively, among top sugar exporters; the EU ranks second.

The EU produces much more sugar than it can use; for decades, about 4 tons of European sugar sold on the world market each year. This situation prompted Australia and Thailand to join Brazil in challenging the EU's sugar export policy at the WTO. In 2004, the WTO ruled against the EU. The following year the WTO's Appellate Body upheld the ruling and gave the EU 15 months to bring sugar exports into compliance with global trade rules. The EU's reforms went into effect July 1, 2006.

In Europe, protection of the agricultural sector was a response to the shortages and rationing that occurred during World War II. Thanks to the Common Agricultural Policy (CAP), European farmers supply virtually all of Europe's food consumption needs. Agricultural producers also made gains in the 1960s in negotiations relating to the creation of the Common Market—the precursor to today's EU.

Europe's agricultural policies led to sugar beet production in Sweden and Finland—countries not renowned for favorable growing conditions—as well as France. The impact of the sugar regime was clear: European farmers operated with quotas that specified how much they could produce. The farmers were also guaranteed prices for their crops that were roughly three times higher than the world price. The 2006 reforms were aimed at reducing production, and uncompetitive sugar farmers in the EU were given incentives to leave the sector.

In the United States, the current sugar regime can be traced back to the Sugar Act of 1934. The act was designed to stabilize prices and protect sugar growers; in 2010 the U.S. price for raw sugar was about $.35 per pound compared with the world market price of less than $.20 per pound. The General Accounting Office estimates that the program costs Americans $2 billion annually in inflated sugar prices.

In addition, American consumers pay an estimated $826,000 for each job saved in the sugar sector. In contrast to Europe, however, the United States exports only a fraction of the 8 tons of sugar it produces each year. Current regulations concerning import quotas were put in place in 1990; critics point out that the quotas were based on trade statistics from the 1970s. In 2010, quotas limited sugar imports to about 1.3 million metric tons.

The U.S. government pays approximately $50 billion in farm aid each year; in May 2002, President George W. Bush signed a new farm bill that actually increased support to some farmers. Not surprisingly, the Europeans pointed to the bill as evidence that the United States is hypocritical on trade issues. U.S. sugar cane and sugar beet producers rank first in contributions to political campaigns, ahead of both tobacco farmers and dairy farmers. Florida, the key sugar-producing state, is a crucial swing state in national elections. However, sugar beets are also grown in North Dakota and other states in the northern Plains.

The Sugar Association heads the industry's lobbying effort in the United States. However, the industry flexes its political muscle in other ways. For example, the World Health Organization (WHO) and the Food and Agriculture Organization have identified sugar as a key contributor to obesity. A report titled *Diet, Nutrition and the Prevention of Chronic Diseases* recommended that no more than 10 percent of an individual's caloric intake should come from "added sugars." The Sugar Association assailed the "dubious nature" of the report and implied that more than $400 million in congressional funding to the WHO could be jeopardized. Andrew Briscoe, president of the association, said, "We are not opposed to a global strategy in the fight against obesity. No one, including the sugar industry, wants anybody to be obese and we want to be part of the solution. But we want that solution to be based on the preponderance of science."

The Bush administration actively pursued bilateral and regional trade agreements, a fact that also had the sugar industry up in arms. For example, as part of the Central American Free Trade Agreement, the United States agreed to import 100,000 tons of sugar—about 1 percent of the U.S. market—from Guatemala and its neighbors. Industry reaction was swift. Robert Coker, senior vice president of Florida-based U.S. Sugar Corporation, stated, "If the U.S. agrees in regional trade negotiations to open up the U.S. sugar market, American sugar producers, including our company, will be wiped out." The president of the American Sugarbeet Growers Association summed up the situation more succinctly: "If you go to free trade, Brazil wins and everybody else gets killed," he said.

Sources: Carolyn Cui, "Price Gap Puts Spice in Sugar-Quota Fight," *The Wall Street Journal* (March 15, 2010), pp. A1, A20; Tobia Buck, "EU to Consider Sugar Subsidy Reform," *Financial Times* (June 24, 2004), p. 7; Robert B. Zoellick, "Don't Get Bitter About Sugar," *The Wall Street Journal* (February 25, 2004), p. A14; Edward Alden and Neil Buckley, "Sweet Deals: 'Big Sugar' Fights Threats from Free Trade and a Global Drive to Limit Consumption," *Financial Times* (February 27, 2004), p. 11; Mary Anastasia O'Grady, "Clinton's Sugar Daddy Games Now Threaten NAFTA's Future," *The Wall Street Journal* (December 20, 2002), p. A15; Roger Thurow and Geoff Winestock, "Bittersweet: How an Addiction to Sugar Subsidies Hurts Development," *The Wall Street Journal* (September 16, 2002), pp. A1, A10.

Exhibit 8-4 In February 2009, U.S. President Barack Obama addressed workers at a Caterpillar plant in Peoria, Illinois. The appearance came one month after Caterpillar officials announced the elimination of 22,000 jobs. The President spoke about his economic recovery and reinvestment plan, noting, "What's happening at this company tells us a larger story about what's happening with our nation's economy—because, in many ways, you can measure America's bottom line by looking at Caterpillar's bottom line." The President added, "Caterpillar has shaped the American landscape, and shown the world what a great American company looks like." **Source:** bp3/ZUMA Press/Newscom.

Discriminatory procurement policies can take the form of government rules, laws, or administrative regulations requiring that goods or services be purchased from domestic companies. For example, the Buy American Act of 1933 stipulates that U.S. federal agencies and government programs must buy goods produced in the United States. The act does not apply if domestically produced goods are not available, if the cost is unreasonable, or if "buying local" would be inconsistent with the public interest. Similarly, the Fly American Act states that U.S. government employees must fly on domestic carriers whenever possible. One of the most controversial aspects of U.S. President Barack Obama's $885 billion economic stimulus bill was a proposed provision requiring that all manufactured goods purchased with stimulus money be "Made in the USA" (see Exhibit 8-4). Opponents alleged that the proposal's language violated U.S. trade agreements; the clause elicited strong protests from key trading partners, some of which announced that they would retaliate with protectionist measures of their own. Congress ultimately toned down the protectionist rhetoric, thus averting a possible trade war.[9]

Customs procedures are considered restrictive if they are administered in a way that makes compliance difficult and expensive. For example, the U.S. Department of Commerce might classify a product under a certain harmonized number; Canadian customs may disagree. The U.S. exporter may have to attend a hearing with Canadian customs officials to reach an agreement. Such delays cost time and money for both the importer and the exporter.

Discriminatory exchange rate policies distort trade in much the same way as selective import duties and export subsidies. As noted earlier, some Western policymakers have argued that China is pursuing policies that ensure an artificially weak currency. Such a policy has the effect of giving Chinese goods a competitive price edge in world markets.

Finally, **restrictive administrative** and **technical regulations** also can create barriers to trade. These may take the form of antidumping regulations, product size regulations, and safety and health regulations. Some of these regulations are intended to keep out foreign goods; others are directed toward legitimate domestic objectives. For example, the safety and pollution regulations being developed in the United States for automobiles are motivated almost entirely by legitimate concerns about highway safety and pollution. However, an effect of these regulations has been to make it so expensive to comply with U.S. safety requirements that some automakers have withdrawn certain models from the market. Volkswagen, for example, was forced to stop selling diesel automobiles in the United States for several years.

As discussed in earlier chapters, there is a growing trend to remove all such restrictive trade barriers on a regional basis. The largest single effort was undertaken by the EU and resulted in the creation of a single market starting January 1, 1993. The intent was to have one standard for all

---

[9] David Lynch, "'Buy American' Clause Stirs Up Controversy," *USA Today* (February 4, 2009), p. 3B.

EMERGING MARKETS BRIEFING BOOK

Clothing Factory Tragedies in Bangladesh

MyMarketingLab SYNC • THINK • LEARN

As shown in Table 8-2, Bangladesh ranks as the world's number 3 clothing exporter; the country has benefited from rising wages in China that have increased the cost of manufacturing there. As noted in Chapter 2, about 80 percent of Bangladesh's export earnings come from its network of more than 5,000 garment manufacturing operations. However, the garment industry has been roiled by a series of tragedies that have highlighted the often-dangerous conditions facing workers.

In 2010, dozens of Bangledeshis were killed in two separate fires in factories that made clothing for Western clients such as Hennes & Mauritz, JCPenney, and Gap. In November 2012, 112 garment workers were killed when a fire broke out at Tazreen Fashions, a clothing manufacturer in Dhaka, Bangladesh. Tazreen's clients included Walmart and other well-known global retail brands. The tragedy highlighted the Bangladesh Fire and Building Safety Agreement, a contract that increasing numbers of workers, unions, and marketers have signed.

In April 2013, tragedy struck another factory in Dhaka (see Exhibit 8-5). More than 500 people—most of them women—were killed. This time, however, fire was not the cause. Rather, the eight-story Rana Plaza building in Dhaka collapsed. The building housed garment factories that employed about 5,000 garment workers making clothing such as the Joe Fresh line for Loblaw, a Canadian retailer; Italy's Benetton was another customer.

In the aftermath of the tragedy, it was revealed that the building's owner was a local politician who had not obtained the necessary permits from Dhaka's building-safety authority. Some of the factories in the Rana Plaza building had been certified in audits conducted by the Business Social Compliance Initiative (BSCI). The Initiative was launched by the Foreign Trade Association, an agency that represents hundreds of European retailers. As it turned out, however, the BSCI's auditors were not engineers and had not made recommendations regarding building safety and stability.

The response from Western retailers was swift. For example, although Walmart had forbidden its contractors from using the Tazreen factory, some of its clothing was found at the scene of the 2012 fire. Walmart has since implemented a "zero-tolerance policy" for contractors who use factories without Walmart's authorization. Walmart has donated $1.6 million to provide fire-safety training to garment workers in Bangladesh.

Despite such efforts, the Workers Rights Consortium, the International Labor Organization, the Interfaith Center for Corporate Responsibility, and other groups that monitor labor issues are stepping up pressure on the companies that participate in the global garment supply chain. Too often, the activists charge, Western retailers pay lip service to concerns about factory safety; in reality, critics say, the retailers continue to focus on low prices rather than the welfare of workers. As the head of the Cambodian garment manufacturers association told the *Financial Times*, "The buyer and consumer must be willing to pay more."

Sources: Syed Zain Al-Mahmood, Christina Passariello, and Preetika Rana, "The Global Garment Trail: From Bangladesh to a Mall Near You," *The Wall Street Journal* (May 4–5, 2013), pp. A1, A11; Syed Zain Al-Mahmood and Tom Wright, "Collapsed Factory Was Built Without Permit," *The Wall Street Journal* (April 26, 2013), p. A9; Syed Zain Al-Mahmood and Shelly Banjo, "Deadly Collapse," *The Wall Street Journal* (April 25, 2013), pp. A1, A10; Shelly Banjo and Syed Zain Al-Mahmood, "Bangladesh Fire Spurs Rights Campaign," *The Wall Street Journal* (April 8, 2013), p. B3; Barney Jopson and Amy Kazmin, "Bangladeshis Pay Price of Cheap Goods," *Financial Times* (December 18, 2012); Rahul Jacob, "Lip Service to Workers Isn't Worth the Price," *Financial Times* (December 6, 2012), p. 10; Jonathan Birchall, "Western Brands in Bangladesh Face Safety Push," *Financial Times* (December 19, 2010).

Exhibit 8-5 Following the collapse of an eight-story building which housed several Bangladesh garment factories, relatives of missing workers argued and pleaded with army officials as the search for survivors continued.
Source: AP Photo/Kevin Frayer.

TABLE 8-4 Sample Rates of Duty for U.S. Imports

Column 1		Column 2
General	Special	Non-NTR
1.5%	Free (A, E, IL, J, MX)	30%
	0.4% (CA)	

A, Generalized System of Preferences
E, Caribbean Basin Initiative (CBI) Preference
IL, Israel Free Trade Agreement (FTA) Preference
J, Andean Agreement Preference
MX, NAFTA Canada Preference
CA, NAFTA Mexico Preference

of Europe's industry sectors, including automobile safety, drug testing and certification, and food and product quality controls. The introduction of the euro has also facilitated trade and commerce.

Tariff Systems

Tariff systems provide either a single rate of duty for each item, applicable to all countries, or two or more rates, applicable to different countries or groups of countries. Tariffs are usually grouped into two classifications.

The **single-column tariff** is the simplest type of tariff: a schedule of duties in which the rate applies to imports from all countries on the same basis. Under the **two-column tariff** (Table 8-4), column 1 includes "general" duties plus "special" duties indicating reduced rates determined by tariff negotiations with other countries. Rates agreed upon by "convention" are extended to all countries that qualify for **normal trade relations (NTR)** (formerly most-favored nation, or MFN) status within the framework of the WTO. Under the WTO, nations agree to apply their most favorable tariff or lowest tariff rate to all nations—subject to some exceptions—that are signatories to the WTO. Column 2 shows rates for countries that do not enjoy NTR status.

Table 8-5 shows a detailed entry from Chapter 89 of the Harmonized System pertaining to "Ships, Boats, and Floating Structures" (for explanatory purposes, each column has been

TABLE 8-5 Chapter 89 of the Harmonized System

A	B	C	D	E	F	G
8903		Yachts and other vessels for pleasure or sports; rowboats and canoes				
8903.10.00		Inflatable		2.4%	Free	
					(A, E, IL, J, MX)	
					0.4% (CA)	
		Valued over $500				
	15	With attached rigid hull	No			
	45	Other	No			
	60	Other	No			
8903.91.00		Other:		1.5%	Free	
		Sailboats, with or without auxiliary motors			(A, E, IL, J, MX)	
					0.3% (CA)	

A, Generalized System of Preferences
E, Caribbean Basin Initiative (CBI) Preference
IL, Israel Free Trade Agreement (FTA) Preference
J, Andean Agreement Preference
MX, NAFTA Canada Preference
CA, NAFTA Mexico Preference

identified with an alphabet letter). Column A contains the heading-level numbers that uniquely identify each product. For example, the product entry for heading level 8903 is "Yachts and other vessels for pleasure or sports; rowboats and canoes." Subheading level 8903.10 identifies "Inflatable"; 8903.91 designates "Sailboats with or without auxiliary motor." These six-digit numbers are used by more than 100 countries that have signed on to the HTS. Entries can extend to as many as 10 digits, with the last 4 used on a country-specific basis for each nation's individual tariff and data collection purposes. Taken together, E and F correspond to column 1 as shown in Table 8-4, and G corresponds to column 2.

The United States has given NTR status to some 180 countries around the world, so the name is really a misnomer. Only North Korea, Iran, Cuba, and Libya are excluded, showing that NTR is really a political tool more than an economic one. In the past, China had been threatened with the loss of NTR status because of alleged human rights violations. The landed prices of its exports—the cost after the goods have been delivered to a port, unloaded, and passed through customs—would have risen significantly. Thus, many Chinese products would have been priced out of the U.S. market. However, the U.S. Congress granted China permanent NTR as a precursor to its joining the WTO in 2001. Table 8-6 illustrates what a loss of NTR status would have meant to China.

A **preferential tariff** is a reduced tariff rate applied to imports from certain countries. GATT prohibits the use of preferential tariffs, with three major exceptions. First are historical preference arrangements such as the British Commonwealth preferences and similar arrangements that existed before GATT. Second, preference schemes that are part of a formal economic integration treaty, such as free trade areas or common markets, are excluded. Third, industrial countries are permitted to grant preferential market access to companies based in less-developed countries.

The United States is now a signatory to the GATT customs valuation code. U.S. customs value law was amended in 1980 to conform to the GATT valuation standards. Under the code, the primary basis of customs valuation is "transaction value." As the term implies, *transaction value* is defined as the actual individual transaction price paid by the buyer to the seller of the goods being valued. In instances where the buyer and seller are related parties (e.g., when Honda's U.S. manufacturing subsidiaries purchase parts from Japan), customs authorities have the right to scrutinize the transfer price to make sure it is a fair reflection of market value. If there is no established transaction value for the good, alternative methods that are used to compute the customs value sometimes result in increased values and, consequently, increased duties. In the late 1980s, the U.S. Treasury Department began a major investigation into the transfer prices charged by the Japanese automakers to their U.S. subsidiaries. It contended that the Japanese paid virtually no U.S. income taxes because of their "losses" on the millions of cars they imported into the United States each year.

During the Uruguay Round of GATT negotiations, the United States successfully sought a number of amendments to the Agreement on Customs Valuations. Most important, the United States wanted clarification of the rights and obligations of importing and exporting countries in cases where fraud was suspected. Two overall categories of products were frequently targeted for investigation. The first included exports of textiles, cosmetics, and consumer durables; the second included entertainment software such as videotapes, audiotapes, and compact discs. Such amendments improve the ability of U.S. exporters to defend their interests if charged with

TABLE 8-6 Tariff Rates for China, NTR Versus Non-NTR

	NTR	Non-NTR
Gold jewelry, such as plated neck chains	6.5%	80%
Screws, lock washers, misc. iron/steel parts	5.8%	35%
Steel products	0–5%	66%
Rubber footwear	0	66%
Women's overcoats	19%	35%

Source: U.S. Customs Service.

fraudulent practices. The amendments were also designed to encourage nonsignatories, especially developing countries, to become parties to the agreement.

Customs Duties

Customs duties are divided into two categories. They may be calculated either as a percentage of the value of the goods (ad valorem duty), as a specific amount per unit (specific duty), or as a combination of both of these methods. Before World War II, specific duties were widely used and the tariffs of many countries, particularly those in Europe and Latin America, were extremely complex. During the past half-century, the trend has been toward the conversion to ad valorem duties.

As noted, an **ad valorem duty** is expressed as a percentage of the value of goods. The definition of customs value varies from country to country. An exporter is well advised to secure information about the valuation practices applied to his or her product in the country of destination. The reason is simple: to be price competitive with local producers. In countries adhering to GATT conventions on customs valuation, the customs value is the value of cost, insurance, and freight (CIF) at the port of importation. This figure should reflect the arm's-length price of the goods at the time the duty becomes payable.

A *specific duty* is expressed as a specific amount of currency per unit of weight, volume, length, or other unit of measurement; for example, "50 cents U.S. per pound," "$1.00 U.S. per pair," or "25 cents U.S. per square yard." Specific duties are usually expressed in the currency of the importing country, but there are exceptions, particularly in countries that have experienced sustained inflation.

Both ad valorem and specific duties are occasionally set out in the custom tariff for a given product. Normally, the applicable rate is the one that yields the higher amount of duty, although there are cases where the lower amount is specified. Compound or mixed duties provide for specific, plus ad valorem, rates to be levied on the same articles.

Other Duties and Import Charges

Dumping, which is the sale of merchandise in export markets at unfair prices, is discussed in detail in Chapter 11. To offset the impact of dumping and to penalize guilty companies, most countries have introduced legislation providing for the imposition of **antidumping duties** if injury is caused to domestic producers. Such duties take the form of special additional import charges equal to the dumping margin. Antidumping duties are almost invariably applied to products that are also manufactured or grown in the importing country. In the United States, antidumping duties are assessed after the U.S. Commerce Department finds a foreign company guilty of dumping and the International Trade Commission (ITC) rules that the dumped products injured American companies.

Countervailing duties (CVDs) are additional duties levied to offset subsidies granted in the exporting country. In the United States, CVD legislation and procedures are very similar to those pertaining to dumping. The U.S. Commerce Department and the ITC jointly administer both the CVD and antidumping laws under provisions of the Trade and Tariff Act of 1984. Subsidies and countervailing measures received a great deal of attention during the Uruguay Round of GATT negotiations. In 2001, the ITC and the U.S. Commerce Department imposed both countervailing and antidumping duties on Canadian lumber producers. The CVDs were intended to offset subsidies to Canadian sawmills in the form of low fees for cutting trees in forests owned by the Canadian government. The antidumping duties on imports of softwood lumber, flooring, and siding were in response to complaints by American producers that the Canadians were exporting lumber at prices below their production cost.

Several countries, including Sweden and some other members of the EU, apply a system of **variable import levies** to certain categories of imported agricultural products. If prices of imported products would undercut those of domestic products, these levies raise the price of imported products to the domestic price level. **Temporary surcharges** have been introduced from time to time by certain countries, such as the United Kingdom and the United States, to provide additional protection for local industry and, in particular, in response to balance of payments deficits.

Key Export Participants

Anyone with responsibilities for exporting should be familiar with some of the entities that can assist with various export-related tasks. Some of these entities, including foreign purchasing agents, export brokers, and export merchants, have no assignment of responsibility from the client. Others, including export management companies, manufacturers' export representatives, export distributors, and freight forwarders, are assigned responsibilities by the exporter.

Foreign purchasing agents are variously referred to as *buyer for export, export commission house*, or *export confirming house*. They operate on behalf of, and are compensated by, an overseas customer known as a *principal*. They generally seek out a manufacturer whose price and quality match the specifications of their principal. Foreign purchasing agents often represent governments, utilities, railroads, and other large users of materials. Foreign purchasing agents do not offer the manufacturer or exporter stable volume except when long-term supply contracts are agreed upon. Purchases may be completed as domestic transactions, with the purchasing agent handling all export packing and shipping details, or the agent may rely on the manufacturer to handle the shipping arrangements.

The **export broker** receives a fee for bringing together the seller and the overseas buyer. The fee is usually paid by the seller, but sometimes the buyer pays it. The broker takes no title to the goods and assumes no financial responsibility. A broker usually specializes in a specific commodity, such as grain or cotton, and is less frequently involved in the export of manufactured goods.

Export merchants are sometimes referred to as *jobbers*. These are marketing intermediaries that identify market opportunities in one country or region and make purchases in other countries to fill these needs. An export merchant typically buys unbranded products directly from the producer or manufacturer. The export merchant then brands the goods and performs all other marketing activities, including distribution. For example, an export merchant might identify a good source of women's boots in a factory in China. The merchant then purchases a large quantity of the boots and markets them in, for example, the EU or the United States.

An **export management company (EMC)** is an independent marketing intermediary that acts as the export department for two or more manufacturers (principals) whose product lines do not compete with each other. The EMC usually operates in the name of its principals for export markets, but it may operate in its own name. It may act as an independent distributor, purchasing and reselling goods at an established price or profit margin. Alternatively, it may act as a commissioned representative, taking no title and bearing no financial risks in the sale. According to one survey of U.S.-based EMCs, the most important activities for export success are gathering marketing information, communicating with markets, setting prices, and ensuring parts availability. The same survey ranked export activities in terms of degree of difficulty; analyzing political risk, sales force management, setting pricing, and obtaining financial information were found to be the most difficult to accomplish. One of the study's conclusions was that the U.S. government should do a better job of helping EMCs and their clients analyze the political risk associated with foreign markets.[10]

Another type of intermediary is the **manufacturer's export agent (MEA)**. Much like an EMC, the MEA can act as an export distributor or as an export commission representative. However, the MEA does not perform the functions of an export department, and the scope of market activities is usually limited to a few countries. An **export distributor** assumes financial risk. The export distributor usually represents several manufacturers and is therefore sometimes known as a *combination export manager*. The firm usually has the exclusive right to sell a manufacturer's products in all or some markets outside the country of origin. The distributor pays for the goods and assumes all financial risks associated with the foreign sale; it handles all shipping details. The agent ordinarily sells at the manufacturer's list price abroad; compensation comes in the form of an agreed percentage of the list price. The distributor may operate in its own name or in the manufacturer's name.

The **export commission representative** assumes no financial risk. The manufacturer assigns some or all foreign markets to the commission representative. The manufacturer carries

---

[10] Donald G. Howard, "The Role of Export Management Companies in Global Marketing," *Journal of Global Marketing* 8, no. 1 (1994), pp. 95–110.

all accounts, although the representative often provides credit checks and arranges financing. Like the export distributor, the export commission representative handles several accounts and hence is also known as a *combination export management company*.

The **cooperative exporter**, sometimes called a *mother hen*, a *piggyback exporter*, or an *export vendor*, is an export organization of a manufacturing company retained by other independent manufacturers to sell their products in foreign markets. Cooperative exporters usually operate as export distributors for other manufacturers, but in special cases they operate as export commission representatives. They are regarded as a form of export management company.

Freight forwarders are licensed specialists in traffic operations, customs clearance, and shipping tariffs and schedules; simply put, they can be thought of as travel agents for freight. Minnesota-based C.H. Robinson Worldwide is one such company. Freight forwarders seek out the best routing and the best prices for transporting freight and assist exporters in determining and paying fees and insurance charges. Forwarders may also do export packing, when necessary. They usually handle freight from the port of export to the overseas port of import. They may also move inland freight from the factory to the port of export and, through affiliates abroad, handle freight from the port of import to the customer. In addition, freight forwarders perform consolidation services for land, air, and ocean freight. Because they contract for large blocks of space on a ship or airplane, they can resell that space to various shippers at a rate lower than is generally available to individual shippers dealing directly with the export carrier.

A licensed forwarder receives brokerage fees or rebates from shipping companies for booked space. Some companies and manufacturers engage in freight forwarding or some portion of it on their own, but they may not, under law, receive brokerage from shipping lines.

Organizing for Exporting in the Manufacturer's Country

Home-country issues involve deciding whether to assign export responsibility inside the company or to work with an external organization specializing in a product or geographic area. Most companies handle export operations within their own in-house export organization. Depending on the company's size, responsibilities may be incorporated into an employee's domestic job description. Alternatively, these responsibilities may be handled as part of a separate division or organizational structure.

The possible arrangements for handling exports include the following:

1. As a part-time activity performed by domestic employees
2. Through an export partner affiliated with the domestic marketing structure that takes possession of the goods before they leave the country
3. Through an export department that is independent of the domestic marketing structure
4. Through an export department within an international division
5. For multidivisional companies, each of the preceding options is available.

A company that assigns a sufficiently high priority to its export business will establish an in-house organization. It then faces the question of how to organize it effectively. This depends on two things: the company's appraisal of the opportunities in export marketing and its strategy for allocating resources to markets on a global basis. It may be possible for a company to make export responsibility part of a domestic employee's job description. The advantage of this arrangement is obvious: It is a low-cost arrangement requiring no additional personnel. However, this approach can work under only two conditions: First, the domestic employee assigned to the task must be thoroughly competent in terms of product and customer knowledge; second, that competence must be applicable to the target international market(s). The key issue underlying the second condition is the extent to which the target export market is different from the domestic market. If customer circumstances and characteristics are similar, the requirements for specialized regional knowledge are reduced.

The company that chooses not to perform its own marketing and promotion in-house has numerous external export service providers from which to choose. As described previously, these include EMCs, export merchants, export brokers, combination export managers, manufacturers' export representatives or commission agents, and export distributors. However, because these terms and labels may be used inconsistently, we urge the reader to check and confirm the services performed by a particular independent export organization.

Organizing for Exporting in the Market Country

In addition to deciding whether to rely on in-house or external export specialists in the home country, a company must also make arrangements to distribute the product in the target market country. Every exporting organization faces one basic decision: To what extent do we rely on direct market representation as opposed to representation by independent intermediaries?

The two major advantages to direct representation in a market are control and communications. Direct market representation enables decisions concerning program development, resource allocation, or price changes to be implemented unilaterally. Moreover, when a product is not yet established in a market, special efforts are necessary to achieve sales. The advantage of direct representation is that the marketer's investment ensures that these special efforts will be undertaken. With indirect or independent representation, such efforts and investment are often not forthcoming; in many cases, there is simply not enough incentive for independents to invest significant time and money in representing a product. The other great advantage to direct representation is that the possibilities for feedback and information from the market are much greater. This information can vastly improve export-marketing decisions concerning product, price, communications, and distribution.

Note that direct representation does not mean that the exporter is selling directly to the consumer or customer. In most cases, direct representation involves selling to wholesalers or retailers. For example, the major automobile exporters in Germany and Japan rely upon direct representation in the U.S. market in the form of their distributing agencies, which are owned and controlled by the manufacturing organization. The distributing agencies then sell products to franchised dealers.

In smaller markets, it is usually not feasible to establish direct representation because the low sales volume does not justify the cost. Even in larger markets, a small manufacturer usually lacks adequate sales volume to justify the cost of direct representation. Whenever sales volume is small, use of an independent distributor is an effective method of sales distribution. Finding "good" distributors can be the key to export success.

Trade Financing and Methods of Payment

The appropriate method of payment for a given international sale is a basic credit decision. A number of factors must be considered, including currency availability in the buyer's country, creditworthiness of the buyer, and the seller's relationship to the buyer. Finance managers at companies that have never exported often express concern regarding payment. However, many chief financial officers (CFOs) with international experience know that in a normal business environment, there are generally fewer collections problems on international sales than on domestic sales, provided the proper financial instruments are used. The reason is simple: A letter of credit can be used to guarantee payment for a product.

Unfortunately, the global financial crisis undermined the ability of firms of all sizes to get the financing they depend on for trade. Prior to the crisis, big lenders such as Citigroup and HSBC had thriving businesses setting up lines of credit and then assigning them to smaller banks. However, because of the financial crisis, these smaller banks have become more risk averse and are cutting their exposure to trade financing. Compounding the problem was the fact that trade finance was drying up in key emerging markets—the very markets that had the potential to boost the volume of global trade. In Brazil, for example, even large companies such as Embraer were finding that the cost of dollar-denominated financing had increased dramatically. To remedy the situation, Brazil's development bank and central bank both made funds available for trade financing.[11]

---

[11] John Lyons, "Trade-Financing Pinch Hurts the Healthy," *The Wall Street Journal* (December 22, 2008), p. A2.

With the constraints of the recent economic environment in mind, we will review the basics of trade financing. The export sale begins when the exporter-seller and the importer-buyer agree to do business. The agreement is formalized when the terms of the deal are set down in a pro forma invoice, contract, fax, or some other document. Among other things, the **pro forma invoice** spells out how much, and by what means, the exporter-seller wants to be paid.

Documentary Credit

Documentary credits (also known as *letters of credit*) are widely used as a payment method in international trade. A **letter of credit (L/C)** is essentially a document stating that a bank has substituted its creditworthiness for that of the importer-buyer. Next to cash in advance, an L/C offers the exporter the best assurance of being paid. That assurance arises from the fact that the payment obligation under an L/C lies with the buyer's bank and not with the buyer. The international standard by which L/Cs are interpreted is ICC Publication No. 500 of the Uniform Customs and Practice for Documentary Credits, also known as UCP 500.

The importer-buyer's bank is the "issuing" bank; the importer-buyer is, in essence, asking the issuing bank to extend credit. The importer-buyer is considered the applicant. The issuing bank may require that the importer-buyer deposit funds in the bank or use some other method to secure a line of credit. After agreeing to extend the credit, the issuing bank requests that the exporter-seller's bank advise and/or confirm the L/C. (A bank "confirms" an L/C by adding its name to the document.) The seller's bank becomes the "advising" and/or "confirming" bank. Whether it is advised or confirmed, the L/C represents a guarantee that ensures payment contingent on the exporter-seller (the beneficiary in the transaction) complying with the terms set forth in the L/C.

The actual payment process is set in motion when the exporter-seller physically ships the goods and submits the necessary documents as specified in the L/C. These could include a transportation bill of lading (which may represent title to the product), a commercial invoice, a packing list, a certificate of origin, or insurance certificates. For most of the world, a commercial invoice and bill of lading represent the minimum documentation required for customs clearance. If the pro forma invoice specifies a confirmed L/C as the method of payment, the exporter-seller receives payment at the time the correct shipping documents are presented to the confirming bank.

The confirming bank, in turn, requests payment from the issuing bank. In the case of an irrevocable L/C, the exporter-seller receives payment only after the advising bank negotiates the documents and requests payment from the issuing bank in accordance with terms set forth in the L/C. Once the shipper sends the documents to the advising bank, the advising bank negotiates those documents and is referred to as the negotiating bank. Specifically, it takes each shipping document and closely compares it to the L/C. If there are no discrepancies, the negotiating or confirming bank transfers the money to the exporter-seller's account.

The fee for an irrevocable L/C—for example, "1/8 of 1 percent of the value of the credit, with an $80 minimum"—is lower than that for a confirmed L/C. The higher bank fees associated with confirmation can drive up the final cost of the sale; fees are also higher when the transaction involves a country with a high level of risk. Good communication between the exporter-seller and the advising or confirming bank regarding fees is important; the selling price indicated on the pro forma invoice should reflect these and other costs associated with exporting. The process described here is illustrated in Figures 8-1 and 8-2.

Documentary Collections (Sight or Time Drafts)

After an exporter and an importer have established a good working relationship and the finance manager's level of confidence increases, it may be possible to move to a documentary collection or an open-account method of payment. A documentary collection is a method of payment that uses a bill of exchange, also known as a *draft*. A **bill of exchange** is a negotiable instrument that is easily transferable from one party to another. In its simplest form, it is a written order from one party (the *drawer*) directing a second party (the *drawee*) to pay to the order of a third party (the *payee*). Drafts are distinctly different from L/Cs; a **draft** is a payment instrument that transfers all the risk of nonpayment onto the exporter-seller. Banks are involved as intermediaries, but they do not bear financial risk. Because a draft is negotiable, however, a bank may be willing to buy

FIGURE 8-1

Flowchart of Documentary Credit

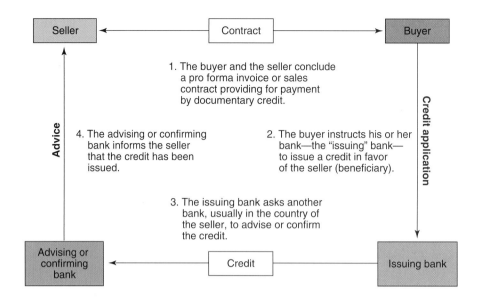

the draft from the seller at a discount and thus assume the risk. Also, because bank fees for drafts are lower than those for L/Cs, drafts are frequently used when the monetary value of an export transaction is relatively low.

With a documentary draft, the exporter-seller delivers documents such as the bill of lading, the commercial invoice, a certificate of origin, and an insurance certificate to a bank in the exporter-seller's country. The shipper or bank prepares a collection letter (draft) and sends it

FIGURE 8-2

Flowchart of documentary credit documents

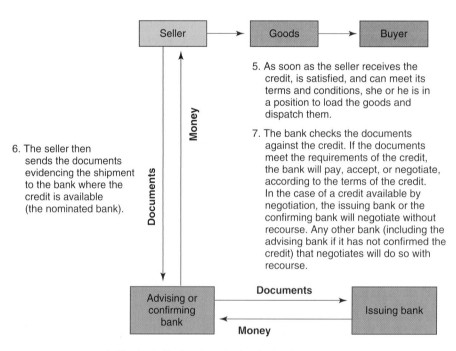

via courier to a correspondent bank in the importer-buyer's country. The draft is presented to the importer-buyer; payment takes place in accordance with the terms specified in the draft. In the case of a *sight draft* (also known as *documents against payment* or D/P), the importer-buyer is required in principle to make payment when presented with both the draft and the shipping documents even though the buyer may not have taken possession of the goods yet. *Time drafts* can take two forms. As the names imply, an *arrival draft* specifies that payment is due when the importer-buyer receives the goods; a *date draft* requires payment on a particular date, irrespective of whether the importer-buyer has the goods in hand.

Cash in Advance

A number of conditions may prompt the exporter to request cash payment—in whole or in part—in advance of shipment. Examples include times when credit risks abroad are high; when exchange restrictions within the country of destination may delay return of funds for an unreasonable period; or when, for any other reason, the exporter may be unwilling to sell on credit terms. Because of competition and restrictions against cash payment in many countries, the volume of business handled on a cash-in-advance basis is small. Note, however, that a company that manufactures a unique product for which there are no substitutes available can use cash in advance. For example, Compressor Control Corporation is a Midwestern firm that manufactures special equipment for the oil industry. It can stipulate cash in advance because no other company offers a competing product.

Sales on Open Account

Goods that are sold on open account are paid for after delivery. Intracorporate sales to branches or subsidiaries of an exporter are frequently on open-account terms. Open-account terms also generally prevail in areas where exchange controls are minimal and exporters have had long-standing relations with reputable buyers in nearby or long-established markets. For example, Jimmy Fand is the owner of the Tile Connection in Tampa, Florida. He imports high-quality ceramic tile from Italy, Spain, Portugal, Colombia, Brazil, and other countries. Fand takes pride in the excellent credit rating that he has built up with his vendors. The manufacturers from whom he buys no longer require an L/C; Fand's philosophy is "pay in time," and he makes sure that his payables are sent electronically on the day they are due.

The main objection to open-account sales is the absence of a tangible obligation. Normally, if a time draft is drawn and then dishonored after acceptance, it can be used as a basis of legal action. By contrast, if an open-account transaction is dishonored, the legal procedure may be more complicated. Starting in 1995, the Export-Import Bank expanded insurance coverage on open-account transactions to limit the risk for exporters.

Additional Export and Import Issues

In the post–September 11 business environment in the United States, national security concerns have resulted in increased scrutiny for imports. A number of initiatives have been launched to ensure that international cargo cannot be used for terrorism. One such initiative is the Customs Trade Partnership Against Terrorism (C-TPAT). As noted on the U.S. Customs and Border Protection Web site:

> C-TPAT recognizes that U.S. Customs and Border Protection (CBP) can provide the highest level of cargo security only through close cooperation with the ultimate owners of the international supply chain such as importers, carriers, consolidators, licensed customs brokers, and manufacturers. Through this initiative, CBP is asking businesses to ensure the integrity of their security practices and communicate and verify the security guidelines of their business partners within the supply chain.

CBP is responsible for screening import cargo transactions; the goal of C-TPAT is to secure voluntary cooperation from supply-chain participants in an effort to reduce inspection delays. Organizations that are C-TPAT certified are entitled to priority status for CBP inspections.

Another issue is *duty drawback*. This refers to refunds of duties paid on imports that are processed or incorporated into other goods and then re-exported. Drawbacks have long been used in the United States to encourage exports. However, when NAFTA was negotiated, the U.S. trade representative agreed to restrict drawbacks on exports to Canada and Mexico. As the United States negotiates new trade agreements, some industry groups are lobbying in favor of keeping drawbacks.[12] Duty drawbacks are also common in protected economies and represent a policy instrument that aids exporters by reducing the price of imported production inputs. China was required to remove duty drawbacks as a condition for joining the WTO. As duty rates around the world fall, the drawback issue will become less important.

Sourcing

In global marketing, the issue of customer value is inextricably tied to the **sourcing decision**: whether a company makes or buys its products as well as *where* it makes or buys its products. **Outsourcing** means shifting production jobs or work assignments to another company to cut costs. When the outsourced work moves to another country, the terms *global outsourcing* or *offshoring* are sometimes used. In today's competitive marketplace, companies are under intense pressure to lower costs; one way to do this is to locate manufacturing and other activities in China, India, and other low-wage countries. And why not? Many consumers do not know where the products they buy—athletic shoes, for example—are manufactured (see Exhibit 8-6). It is also true that, as Case 1-1 in Chapter 1 indicated, people often can't match corporate and brand names with particular countries.

In theory, this situation bestows great flexibility on companies. However, in the United States the sourcing issue has became highly politicized. At election time, candidates tap into Americans' fears and concerns over a "jobless" economic recovery. The first wave of non-manufacturing outsourcing primarily affected **call centers**. These are sophisticated telephone operations that provide customer support and other services to in-bound callers from around the world. Call centers also perform outbound services such as telemarketing (see Exhibit 8-7). Now, however, outsourcing is expanding and includes white-collar, high-tech service sector

Exhibit 8-6 Vietnam is home to dozens of state-run textile and apparel manufacturers that export $1 billion in clothing and footwear each year. The country's garment sector produces merchandise for Nike, Zara, The Limited, and other popular brands. Recently, Vietnam's National Textile-Garment Group (Vinatex) began working with Western consultants to transform the structure and culture of its affiliated companies.
Source: Richard Vogel/AP Images

---

[12] R. G. Edmonson, "Drawback Under Attack at USTR," *The Journal of Commerce* (August 11–17), 2003, p. 21.

Exhibit 8-7
Source: Cartoon Features Syndicate

jobs. Workers in low-wage countries are performing a variety of tasks including completing tax returns, processing insurance claims, performing research for financial services companies, reading medical scans and X-rays, and drawing up architectural blueprints. American companies that transfer work abroad are finding themselves in the spotlight. Table 8-7 lists the top 30 country destinations for global outsourcing, as determined by the Gartner Group.

As this discussion suggests, the decision of where to locate key business activities depends on factors besides cost. There are no simple rules to guide sourcing decisions. Thus the sourcing decision is one of the most complex and important decisions faced by a global company. Several factors may figure into the sourcing decision: management vision, factor costs and conditions, customer needs, public opinion, logistics, country infrastructure, the political environment, and exchange rates.

Management Vision

Some chief executives are determined to retain some or all manufacturing in their home country. The late Nicolas Hayek was one such executive. When he was head of the Swatch Group, Hayek presided over the spectacular revitalization of the Swiss watch industry. The Swatch Group's portfolio of brands includes Blancpain, Omega, Breguet, Rado, and, of course, the inexpensive Swatch brand itself. Hayek demonstrated that the fantasy and imagination of childhood and youth could be translated into breakthroughs that allow mass-market products to be manufactured in high-wage countries side by side with handcrafted luxury products. The Swatch story is a triumph of engineering, as well as a triumph of the imagination.

> "Twenty years ago we were in the process of moving every appliance manufacturing job to China or Mexico. But when I open up the safe under my desk I can't find the pennies that we have saved.... So the next generation of products are going to be made in the U.S."[13]
>
> —Jeff Immelt, CEO, GE

TABLE 8-7 Top 30 Country Destinations for Outsourcing

Region	Countries
Americas	Argentina, Brazil, Chile, Colombia, Costa Rica, Mexico, Panama, Peru
Asia/Pacific	Bangladesh, China, India, Indonesia, Malaysia, the Philippines, Sri Lanka, Thailand, Vietnam
Europe, Middle East, and Africa	Bulgaria, the Czech Republic, Egypt, Hungary, Mauritius, Morocco, Poland, Romania, Russia, Slovakia, South Africa, Turkey, Ukraine.

---

[13] Jeremy Lemer, "GE Plans to Return to U.S.-Made Products," *Financial Times* (October 19, 2010), p. 17.

Exhibit 8-8 In Bangalore, India and other locations, call centers such as this one specialize in "long-distance" or "arm's length" services. India's well-educated workforce and the growing availability of broadband Internet connections mean that more Western service jobs and industries are subject to global outsourcing. Among the tasks being outsourced to India are medical record transcription, tax return preparation, and technical writing. In fact, the book you are reading was typeset in Jawahar Nagar, Pondicherry, India.
Source: Sherwin Crasto/Reuters/Corbis Images

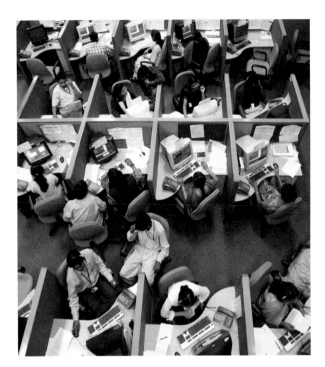

Similarly, top management at Canon has chosen to maintain a strategic focus on high-value-added products rather than manufacturing location. The company aims to keep 60 percent of its manufacturing at home in Japan. The company offers a full line of office equipment, including popular products such as printers and copiers; it is also one of the top producers of digital cameras. Instead of increasing the level of automation in its Japanese factories, it has transitioned from assembly lines to so-called cell production.[14]

Factor Costs and Conditions

Factor costs are land, labor, and capital costs (remember Economics 101!). Labor includes the cost of workers at every level: manufacturing and production, professional and technical, and management. Direct labor costs in basic manufacturing today range from less than $1 per hour in the typical emerging country to $6 to $12 per hour in the typical developed country. In certain industries in the United States, direct labor costs in manufacturing exceed $20 per hour without benefits. German hourly compensation costs for production workers in manufacturing are 160 percent of those in the United States, whereas those in Mexico are a fraction of those in the United States.

Volkswagen's business environment includes a significant wage differential between Mexico and Germany, the strength of the euro, and growing worldwide demand for compact and subcompact vehicles. Taken together, these factors dictate a Mexican manufacturing facility that builds models destined for the United States, China, Europe, and other key markets. Assembly-line wages for Mexican workers start at about $40 per day; by contrast, German auto workers average $60 per hour in pay and benefits. Volkswagen has invested $1 billion to design and produce the next-generation Jetta at a sprawling plant in Mexico City. Next up: Volkswagen will build a $1.3 billion plant to produce its popular Audi Q5 SUV. Volkswagen, Honda, Nissan, and other global automakers also benefit from the fact that Mexico has 45 free trade agreements (FTAs) with North America, Europe, Japan, and most of the countries of South America. These FTAs cut the costs of importing components as well as exporting finished vehicles. In addition, Mexico's car industry is now well developed and the labor pool is highly skilled and productive.[15]

---

[14] Sebastian Moffett, "Canon Manufacturing Strategy Pays Off with Strong Earnings," *The Wall Street Journal* (January 4, 2004), p. B3.
[15] Nicolas Casey, "In Mexico, Auto Plants Hit the Gas," *The Wall Street Journal* (November 20, 2012), pp. A1, A12; see also Adam Thomson, "Car Exports Power Mexico to Recovery," *Financial Times* (October 19, 2010), p. 17.

Do lower wage rates demand that a company relocate 100 percent of its manufacturing to low-wage countries? Not necessarily. During his tenure as chairman at VW, Ferdinand Piech improved his company's competitiveness by convincing unions to accept flexible work schedules. For example, during peak demand, employees work 6-day weeks; when demand slows, factories produce cars only 3 days per week. Labor costs in nonmanufacturing jobs are also dramatically lower in some parts of the world. For example, a software engineer in India may receive an annual salary of $12,000; by contrast, an American with the same education and experience might earn $80,000.

The other factors of production are land, materials, and capital. The costs of these factors depend on their availability and relative abundance. Often, the differences in factor costs will offset each other so that, on balance, companies have a level field in the competitive arena. For example, some countries have abundant land, and Japan has abundant capital. These advantages partially offset each other. When this is the case, the critical factor is management, professional, and worker team effectiveness.

The application of advanced computer controls and other new manufacturing technologies has reduced the proportion of labor relative to capital for many businesses. In formulating a sourcing strategy, company managers and executives should also recognize the declining importance of direct manufacturing labor as a percentage of total product cost. It is certainly true that, for many companies in high-wage countries, the availability of cheap labor is a prime consideration when choosing manufacturing locations; this is why China has become "the world's workplace." However, it is also true that direct labor cost may be a relatively small percentage of the total production cost. As a result, it may not be worthwhile to incur the costs and risks of establishing a manufacturing activity in a distant location.

Customer Needs

Although outsourcing can help reduce costs, sometimes customers are seeking something besides the lowest possible price. A few years ago, for example, Dell rerouted some of its call center jobs back to the United States after complaints from key business customers that Indian tech support workers were offering scripted responses and having difficulty answering complex problems. In such instances, the need to keep customers satisfied justifies the higher cost of home-country support operations.

Logistics

In general, the greater the distance between the product source and the target market, the greater the time delay for delivery and the higher the transportation cost. However, innovation and new transportation technologies are cutting both time and dollar costs. To facilitate global delivery, transportation companies such as CSX Corporation are forming alliances and becoming an important part of industry value systems. Manufacturers can take advantage of intermodal services that allow containers to be transferred among rail, boat, air, and truck carriers. In Europe, Latin America, and elsewhere, the trend toward regional economic integration means fewer border controls, which greatly speeds up delivery times and lowers costs.

Despite these overall trends, a number of specific issues pertaining to logistics can affect the sourcing decision. For example, in the wake of the 2001 terror attacks, importers are required to send electronic lists of cargo to the U.S. government prior to shipping. The goal is to help the U.S. Customs Service identify high-risk cargo that could be linked to the global terror network. In the fall of 2002, a 10-day strike on the West Coast shut down 29 docks and cost the U.S. economy an estimated $20 billion. Such incidents can delay shipments by weeks or even months.

Country Infrastructure

In order to present an attractive setting for a manufacturing operation, it is important that a country's infrastructure be sufficiently developed to support manufacturing and distribution. Infrastructure requirements will vary by company and by industry, but minimally, they will include power, transportation and roads, communications, service and component suppliers,

"Supply Chain 101 says the most important thing is continuity of supply. When you establish a supply line that is 12,000 miles long, you have to weigh the costs of additional inventory and logistics costs versus what you can save in terms of lower costs per unit or labor costs."[16]

—Norbert Ore, Institute for Supply Management

---

[16] Barbara Hagenbaugh, "Moving Work Abroad Tough for Some Firms," *USA Today* (December 3, 2003), p. 2B.

a labor pool, civil order, and effective governance. In addition, companies must have reliable access to foreign exchange for the purchase of necessary material and components from abroad. Additional requirements include a physically secure setting where work can be done and from which products can be shipped.

A country may have cheap labor, but does it have the necessary supporting services or infrastructure to support a high volume of business activities? Many countries offer these conditions, including Hong Kong, Taiwan, and Singapore. In scores of other low-wage countries, however, the infrastructure is woefully underdeveloped. In China, a key infrastructure weakness is the "cold chain," a food industry term for temperature-controlled trucks and warehouses. According to one estimate, an investment of $100 billion will be required to modernize China's cold chain.[17] Meanwhile, the Chinese government is spending hundreds of millions of dollars on a superhighway system that will eventually connect all 31 of China's provinces. When the project is completed in 2020, China will have about 53,000 miles of paved expressway—more than that of the United States.

Infrastructure improvement is a key issue in other emerging markets as well. In India, for example, it takes 8 days for cargo traveling by truck between Kolkata and Mumbai to make the trip of 1,340 miles![18] One of the challenges of doing business in the new Russian market is an infrastructure that is woefully inadequate to handle the increased volume of shipments.

Political Factors

As discussed in Chapter 5, political risk is a deterrent to investment in local sourcing. Conversely, the lower the level of political risk, the less likely it is that an investor will avoid a country or market. The difficulty of assessing political risk is inversely proportional to a country's stage of economic development: All other things being equal, the less developed a country, the more difficult it is to predict political risk. The political risk of the Triad countries, for example, is quite limited as compared to that of a less-developed country in Africa, Latin America, or Asia. The recent rapid changes in Central and Eastern Europe and the dissolution of the Soviet Union have clearly demonstrated the risks *and* opportunities resulting from political upheavals.

Other political factors may weigh on the sourcing decision. For example, with protectionist sentiment on the rise, the U.S. Senate passed an amendment that would prohibit the U.S. Treasury and Department of Transportation from accepting bids from private companies that use offshore workers. In a highly publicized move, the state of New Jersey changed a call center contract that had shifted jobs offshore. About one dozen jobs were brought back to the state—at a cost of about $900,000.

Market access is another type of political factor. If a country or a region limits market access because of local content laws, balance of payments problems, or any other reason, it may be necessary to establish a production facility within the country itself. For instance, the Japanese automobile companies invested in U.S. plant capacity because of concerns about market access. By producing cars in the United States, they have a source of supply that is not exposed to the threat of tariff or import quotas. Market access also figured heavily in Boeing's decision to produce airplane components in China. China ordered 100 airplanes valued at $4.5 billion; in return, Boeing is making investments and transferring engineering and manufacturing expertise.[19]

Foreign Exchange Rates

In deciding where to source a product or locate a manufacturing activity, managers must take into account foreign exchange rate trends in various parts of the world. Exchange rates are

"Ultimately, the best strategy is to build vehicles in the markets where we sell them."[20]

—Takahiko Ijichi, Senior Managing Director, Toyota

---

[17] Jane Lanhee Lee, "China Hurdle: Lack of Refrigeration," *The Wall Street Journal* (August 30, 2007), p. A7.

[18] Harold L. Sirkin, James W. Hemerling, and Arindam K. Bhattacharya, *Globality: Competing with Everyone from Everywhere for Everything* (New York: Boston Consulting Group, 2008), p. 23.

[19] Jeff Cole, Marcus W. Brauchli, and Craig S. Smith, "Orient Express: Boeing Flies into Flap Over Technology Shift in Dealings with China," *The Wall Street Journal* (October 13, 1995), pp. A1, A11. See also Joseph Kahn, "Clipped Wings: McDonnell Douglas's High Hopes for China Never Really Soared," *The Wall Street Journal* (May 22, 1996), pp. A1, A10.

[20] Jonathan Soble and Lindsay Whipp, "Yen's March Spoils the Party for Japan's Exporters," *Financial Times* (August 10, 2010), p. 14.

so volatile today that many companies pursue global sourcing strategies as a way of limiting exchange-related risk. At any point in time, what has been an attractive location for production may become much less attractive due to exchange rate fluctuation. For example, *endaka* is the Japanese term for a strong yen. In 2010, the yen strengthened to a 15-year high, trading at ¥85/$1. For every 1 yen increase relative to the American dollar, Canon's operating income declines by 6 billion yen! As noted earlier, Canon's management is counting on research-and-development investment to ensure that its products deliver superior margins that offset the strong yen. Also, Canon and other Japanese companies have become less reliant on the U.S. market as demand in emerging markets has increased.

The dramatic shifts in price levels of commodities and currencies are a major characteristic of the world economy today. Such volatility argues for a sourcing strategy that provides alternative country options for supplying markets. Thus, if the dollar, the yen, or the mark becomes seriously overvalued, a company with production capacity in other locations can achieve competitive advantage by shifting production among different sites.

Summary

A company's first business dealings outside the home country often take the form of exporting or importing. Companies should recognize the difference between **export marketing** and **export selling**. By attending **trade shows** and participating in **trade missions**, company personnel can learn a great deal about new markets.

Governments use a variety of programs to support exports, including tax incentives, subsidies, and export assistance. Governments also discourage imports with a combination of **tariffs** and **nontariff barriers**. A **quota** is one example of a nontariff barrier. Export-related policy issues include the status of **foreign sales corporations (FSCs)** in the United States, Europe's **Common Agricultural Policy (CAP)**, and **subsidies**. Governments establish **free trade zones** and **special economic zones** to encourage investment.

The **Harmonized Tariff System (HTS)** has been adopted by most countries that are actively involved in export–import trade. **Single-column tariffs** are the simplest; **two-column tariffs** include special rates such as those available to countries with **normal trade relations (NTR)** status. Governments can also impose special types of duties. These include **antidumping duties** imposed on products whose prices government officials deem too low and **countervailing duties (CVDs)** to offset government subsidies.

Key participants in the export–import process include **foreign purchasing agents, export brokers, export merchants, export management companies, manufacturer's export agents, export distributors, export commission representatives, cooperative exporters**, and **freight forwarders**.

A number of export–import payment methods are available. A transaction begins with the issue of a **pro forma invoice** or some other formal document. A basic payment instrument is the **letter of credit (L/C)**, which ensures payment from the buyer's bank. Sales may also be made using a **bill of exchange (draft)**, cash in advance, sales on open account, or a consignment agreement.

Exporting and importing are directly related to management's **sourcing decisions**. Concern is mounting in developed countries about job losses linked to **outsourcing** jobs, both skilled and unskilled, to low-wage countries. A number of factors determine whether a company makes or buys the products it markets as well as *where* it makes or buys those products.

MyMarketingLab

8-1. Discuss why exporting from the United States is dominated by large companies. What, if anything, could be done to increase exports from smaller companies?

8-2. What criteria should company management consider when making sourcing decisions?

8-3. Mymarketinglab Only – comprehensive writing assignment for this chapter.

MyMarketingLab

Go to **mymktlab.com** to complete the problems marked with this icon .

Discussion Questions

8-4. What is the difference between export marketing and export selling?

8-5. Describe the stages a company typically goes through as it learns about exporting.

 8-6. Governments often pursue policies that promote exports while limiting imports. What are some of those policies?

 8-7. What are the various types of duties that export marketers should be aware of?

8-8. How did the recent economic crisis affect financing for global trade?

8-9. What is the difference between an L/C and other forms of export–import financing? Why do sellers often require L/Cs in international transactions?

CASE 8-1   CONTINUED (REFER TO PAGE 254)

Hong Kong Trade and Investment Hub

A former British territory handed over to China in 1997, but still preserving a fairly autonomous and independent economy (according to the formula, "one country, two systems"), and one of the principal export-led growth Asian economies, the small Hong Kong SAR (special administrative region) has a central place in the East Asian production and distribution channels as one of the leading RDCs (regional distribution centers) together with Shanghai, Shenzhen and Singapore.

Hong Kong is the world's 10th largest trading economy, the second in Asia as recipient of FDIs after China and often the first port of call for Western companies approaching Asian markets, both to export and for sourcing. A very sophisticated service economy more than anything else – services account for more than 90 percent in terms of contribution – Hong Kong's GDP is based on four main sectors, trading and logistics (25.5 percent of GDP in 2011), tourism (4.5 percent), financial services (16.1 percent), and professional services of various kinds (12.4 percent).

What makes Hong Kong so attractive? History aside, there are many important factors which are of key relevance when a company decides to get global and enter Asian markets, now acknowledged as the engines of world growth.

First of all, Hong Kong is a free trade zone, in the sense that all products, with the exception of specific items, like tobacco and spirits, enjoy zero taxes in imports and exports. This has allowed a series of advantages, such as the offshoring of manufacturing to the neighboring Guangdong province in China since the 1970s, and then importing outputs to Hong Kong for packaging, advertising and further re-exports.

A rapid look at the Hong Kong Trade and Development Centre's trade statistics will show that the majority of the HK SAR's exports is actually re-exports of imported products, from China and abroad. In fact, total exports of Hong Kong were about U.S. $490 billion in 2012, where re-exports account for U.S. $432 billion. China, unsurprisingly, is the main supplier of imports, even if many countries take benefit of the free-trade regime. In the specific case of China, this has been made even easier since the signature of CEPA, Closer Economic Partnership Arrangement. The CEPA Treaty, signed in 2004 and first ever between the two entities, is now a building block of the progressively closer integration of Hong Kong's economy with the Chinese mainland, not only in the traditional manufacturing and logistics sectors, but in services too, which are generally off-limits to foreign companies. Thanks to CEPA's provisions, Hong Kong suppliers are enjoying preferential treatment when entering into the mainland market in various service areas, and can also have professional titles and qualifications recognized in China.

Infrastructures account for a lot of Hong Kong's success in international trade and investments.

First, it has an impressive network for exhibitions and conventions. It is considered one of the most efficient and organized in the world, with locations like the Hong Kong Convention and Exhibition Centre (HKCEC) in the main business district, the AsiaWorld-Expo near the international airport and the Hong Kong International Trade and Exhibition Centre in Kowloon area. According to government's statistics, the exhibition business contributed around U.S. $4.6 billion to Hong Kong's economy in 2010, i.e., 2.1 percent of Hong Kong's GDP, and it keeps growing steadily. Almost 60,000 companies exhibited in 2012 in one of Hong Kong's numerous trade fairs, with the number of visitors reaching 1.7 million (around one-fifth of the whole Hong Kong population, to give a fair idea); the sector also provides employment for about 60,000 full-time workers.

All these factors contribute to creating a very positive environment for external trade logistics, which is where Hong Kong's specialty lies.

A veritable trade hub, Hong Kong is now a key component in the Asian supply chains, and its deepwater port is one of the world's most competitive. Namely, it ranks as the world's busiest airport for international cargoes, and the third busiest container port, after Shanghai and Singapore, with 23.10 million TEU in 2012. Hong Kong International Airport (HKIA) at Chek Lap Kok is the busiest cargo gateway and one of the 10 passenger airports in the world. The world's most important for container traffic from 1987 to 1989, from 1992 to 1997, and from 1999 to 2004, the deepwater port operates nine container terminals in three locations – Kwai Chung, Stonecutters Island and the recently completed Tsing Yi. There are many important operators, like Modern Terminal (by Wharf and Swire), Hongkong International Terminals (owned by Hutchison Whanpoa) and COSCO (a Mainland China government-owned shipping company).

Many Western companies have started using Hong Kong not only as a hub, but also as a location to showcase brands to be sold later in Chinese markets, since it is known that in the fashion business especially, Hong Kong is the city of references for mainland customers who increasingly visit the SAR on shopping sprees (more than 48 million visitors have been recorded in 2012, with Mainland Chinese accounting for 72 percent of the total).

Nevertheless, there are challenges awaiting Hong Kong. The SAR is a late starter, compared to, say, Singapore or Taiwan, when it comes to RTA-partnerships, which are progressively becoming a fundamental tool in international trade. Unlike others, Hong Kong only has four of these agreements – CEPA; the one with the four-member European Free Trade Association (EFTA), i.e., Iceland, Liechtenstein, Norway and Switzerland; Chile; and New Zealand. One with the ASEAN bloc is only at its inception. Furthermore, given its free port status, Hong Kong has less to offer in terms of tariff cuts. However, given its privileged status with China, and its strengths in financial and legal services, odds are that the Hong Kong SAR will maintain its position as one of the world leading trading economies.

Discussion Questions

8-10. What are the elements that make Hong Kong so successful in terms of external trade?

8-11. Analyze the role of exhibition industry in Hong Kong.

8-12. Using the sources provided and with the help of online research, illustrate the main features of Hong Kong as a logistics hub, especially regarding its deepwater port.

8-13. Why do Western companies increasingly use Hong Kong to showcase their products?

8-14. What are the main challenges awaiting Hong Kong in its efforts to remain the world's 10th largest trading economy?

Sources: Hong Kong Trade and Development Centre, research.hktdc.com; CEPA partnership Agreement, www.tid.gov.hk/english/cepa/cepa_overview.html; World Bank Statistics on container port traffic's in TEU statistics, data.worldbank.org/indicator/IS.SHP.GOOD.TU; Hong Kong International Airport, www.hongkongairport.com/eng/index.html.

CASE 8-2
Turkish Cars: The Big Picture

In recent years, the automotive sector has become Turkey's leading exporter – exports worth U.S. $22 billion constitute over 17.4 percent of Turkey's total export revenues. Over the last decade the market was dominated by four main producers representing 85 percent of the production – Ford Otosan, Oyak-Renault, and Tofaş-Fiat, that are partnerships between Turkish and foreign carmakers, and Toyota, which is now wholly owned by Japan. Last year, Turkey was estimated to be the 6th largest producer in Europe and ranked 16th/17th worldwide, producing up to 1.2 million motor vehicles a year. Foreign direct investment has been the main entrance into the sector. In last 11 years production capacity has increased 1.7 times, exports 2.8 times, local market have grown 4.2 times, and imports 6.2 times. As a result, increased demand has been answered with imports. In 2013, 78 percent of all the automobiles sold in the local market were imported cars. However, there is yet to be an automotive brand completely owned by Turkey. While Turkey targets to produce and develop a local brand by 2023, sourcing all the components and technologies from within the country is highly unlikely, despite the availability of technological infrastructure (R&D centers, high level universities) and accumulation of skills, owing to a globalized economy and the role of automotive imports. So far, there aren't any brands in this sector with absolute local sourcing within the country of production. As such, it may not be a limitation for Turkey to not have its own car brand—instead, it has been opting to encourage further deepening of cooperation with major global manufacturers, with particular focus on electric batteries and design development—or to develop a brand that imports some of the required components. Automobile ownership per capita over the last decade has increased considerably in Turkey with a current level of 144 cars per 1,000 people compared to ownership in France and Germany, where there are approximately 500 cars per 1,000 people.

Yet, there are several challenges concerning nations worldwide that keep Turkey from achieving its annual export target. A recession in the global economy since 2008 has affected external demand negatively. The decreasing value of the Turkish Lira against the Euro and the Dollar adversely affected the sector and exporters, since other currencies also lost against the Dollar (especially in emerging markets). Interestingly, the change in exchange rates causes imported input prices to rise, thereby increasing export prices. Moreover, foreign luxury carmakers—like BMW, Audi, VW, Mercedes, Land Rover, Jaguar, and Porsche—reap exorbitant profits by selling luxury cars in Turkey, despite heavy import taxes. In addition, import prices of car parts and raw material (steel, energy) along with the luxury car sector, comprising vehicles not made in Turkey, are canceling out the positive effect of car export on the balance of payment. In 2012, incentives were introduced by the Ministry of Economy for the automobile sector to become a global player by 2023. Turkey began offering tax breaks of up to 60 percent and incentives—deductions on employee costs in the hopes of attracting investment in the automotive sector—in a bid to raise the sector's annual exports to $75 billion (from $20 billion this year) over the next decade. In the same year, however, a hike in the special consumption tax (SCT) took the sector by surprise – it was up from 84 percent to 130 percent on engines of two liters and over. Reacting to the rise in SCT and the global financial crisis, local automotive sales diminished since the beginning of 2012, with an estimated annual market contraction predicted to be around 15 percent year-on-year. Additionally, other factors must be considered: (a) while consumer loan applications (car credit) have not decreased much, the number of approved requests has, because banks are more selective now; and, (b) inflation and hike in unemployment were also noted in many reports as discouraging purchases.

Looking ahead, Turkey's automotive sector is expected to heavily depend on exports of finished products and imports of components and technological know-how. With Europe slowly recovering from the 2008 economic crisis, a moderate rise in demand is expected. Domestically, as indicated above, the number of cars per 1000 residents is still low, allowing production to be re-directed towards the home market, depending on credit and general economic conditions. For the automotive sector an average annual growth rate of 4.5 to 5 percent a year in 2013, continuing till 2015, is supported by the following forecast:

The (slowly) growing export volume, due to Turkey's close positioning to the EU, the Middle Eastern and North African markets, and aided by the growing strength of the Turkish economy (4.5 percent growth in 2013) and modern manufacturing capacity together with its competitive labor costs;

The emerging prospect at home, evidenced by the fact that 75 percent of the households in Turkey do not own a car;

Active foreign direct investment policy including various forms of tax exemptions, social security premium contribution to the employer's share, land allocation, R&D support, training and recruitment subsidies; and

Free trade zones, designed to encourage trade to and from Turkey, including the development of the required infrastructures—port, airport, fast rail links, third bridge in Istanbul—boosting the automotive sector.

This case demonstrates the importance of having a good understanding of country-specific factors, macro-factors, local legislation, and political strategy while dealing with international businesses. Working in the automotive sector in Turkey entails operating on an international level on a daily basis, while dealing with both internal and external changes in the ecosystem. When working in the transportation industry, it is easier to forget the big picture. Although the process may seem overwhelming—with specific jargons such as container load (CL), rate request, transit times, hazardous declarations, estimated time of departure (ETD) and estimated time of arrival (ETA), storage/disposal charges, letter of credit, shippers export declaration (SED), and bill of lading (B/L)—together with an array of agents—from vessel operating common carrier to local customs, trade associations and part suppliers networks—it is important to remember the counterintuitive factors that enhance or hinder import/export potentials.

Discussion Questions

8-15. What industry knowledge and skills are required to be successful as an export coordinator, especially in the automotive sector?

8-16. What do you think is the hardest type of macro-environmental factor to obtain? And how can you keep it up to date?

8-17. If you were working in the automotive industry in Turkey, what would your next move be?

CASE 8-3
A Day in the Life of an Export Coordinator

Mikkel Jakobsen works as an export coordinator with Shipco Transport, a subsidiary of Scan-Group, a major European transportation company. Shipco Transport has offices all over the world, including 12 branches in North America. Shipco has an extensive network of independent agents in most areas of the world. Shipco's core business is Less than a Container Load (LCL) ocean freight, but it also offers Full Container Load (FCL) ocean freight services, as well as airfreight. Mikkel and four other coworkers constitute the company's FCL Chicago branch export team.

As a Non-Vessel Operating Common Carrier (NVOCC), Shipco Transport operates similarly to shipping companies such as Maersk Sealand, Mediterranean Shipping Company, and others, with one key difference: Shipco has no vessels of its own. Instead, Shipco relies on favorable contracts with over 40 carriers, enabling Shipco to offer competitive rates on routings to destinations around the world. Most of Shipco's customers are freight forwarders, but the company also deals directly with exporting companies and, on occasion, private individuals. Because of its Midwest location, a significant number of containers come through Chicago on a daily basis and are railed to ports around the country.

In 2006, Mikkel earned a BA degree in international management and economics from a small liberal arts college in the Midwest. He is a citizen of Denmark, and currently works in the United States on a J-1 work visa sponsored by Shipco Transport. How did he get his first job after graduating? Mikkel explains, "In the spring of 2006, I contacted 15 different companies operating in the United States that had a connection to Denmark. I was offered a position in Shipco Transport's Chicago branch."

Mikkel's day begins at 8:30 A.M., and usually ends at 5:30 P.M., depending on the workload. Most customers are located in the Midwest, but overnight, he receives e-mails from overseas that he processes in the morning hours. Mikkel says, "In general, my job consists of quoting out shipping costs to customers, placing bookings with steamship lines, preparing export documentation, and dealing with problems that arise during the container's journey from shipper to consignee.

"A customer contacts me with a rate request on a certain routing," Mikkel continues. "He may wish to ship one 20-foot container with auto parts from Indianola, to the port of Ningbo, China. Based on our carrier contracts, I work up a quote including drayage from Indianola, Iowa, to the appropriate rail hub, rail transportation from hub to port, and ocean freight from U.S port to port of discharge Ningbo. Several things must be considered including what carrier is cheapest on the routing, differences in transit times, if the commodity is covered in the contract, and what profit level is appropriate. If the customer accepts the quote, the booking is placed with the steamship line, and a dispatch is sent to the chosen trucking company. Certain situations need additional attention. If the commodity is hazardous, the hazardous declaration must be approved by the steamship line. Also, certain goods, such as automobiles, must be cleared by customs before leaving the United States to avoid U.S. customs demanding the return of the container for inspection, at the expense of the party at fault.

"Although quoting and setting up bookings takes up a lot of my work day, the majority is spent addressing various problems and issues that arise. Problems such as carriers running out of equipment at their depots, loadings taking longer than expected, or rail delays are common and dealt with regularly. More serious issues are derailments, problems securing payment, and container abandonment. As an example, disposing of scrap materials in the United States can be expensive, and in the past, some have overcome the problem by loading it in a container and sending it to places like India as a collect shipment with a nonexistent consignee. This can become an extremely costly situation as demurrage [storage charges], unloading, and disposal charges may apply.

"In ocean freight, we work with ETDs [Estimated Time of Departure] and ETAs [Estimated Time of Arrival], because vessels crossing oceans tend to deviate from their schedule. Although this is a fact, customers sometimes have a difficult time understanding the concept. In the world of shipping, vessels running late, expected early, or even on time can be a problem. If so, I am contacted by my customer[,] who either needs an explanation or appropriate action taken. As a middleman, I will contact the specific carrier with the same request. Most of the time the problem is that the container hasn't reached its destination according to the ETA.

"Interestingly, sometimes a shipper is interested in a delay, and wants the container held up on its journey. This could be because more time is needed to secure payment, or it could represent an attempt to avoid a holiday in the destination country."

How did Mikkel's college studies prepare him for the job? "Incoterms, letter of credit, SED [Shippers Export Declaration], and B/L [bill of lading] are just some of the industry jargon used on a daily basis. Working with customers, familiarity is expected. The documentation part of export shipping is important, and demands attention to detail. As an NVOCC, Shipco produces both a House B/L and a Line B/L that holds information on the shipper and the consignee, and on the products shipped. Most of our containers are released on an express release basis, but some require the use of original bills of lading. In these instances, the original B/L must be presented before a container is released. Although I do not get directly involved in the intricacies of L/C [letter of credit] shipments, special attention must be given to the accuracy of B/L information because small deviations can be troublesome. When doing business internationally it is essential to recognize the differences in how business is conducted around the world. South America and Russia in particular are destinations where we rely heavily on our overseas offices and agents and their knowledge of local customs and regulations."

Summing up, Mikkel says, "I enjoy operating on an international level on a daily basis, while doing my part to alleviate the current American trade deficit. Working in the transportation industry, I am sometimes surprised by how many different and obscure items are exported around the world. Although the process may seem overwhelming, with the help of a shipping specialist such as Shipco, any company anywhere can view the entire world as a potential market."

Discussion Questions

8-18. What knowledge and skills are required to be successful as an export coordinator?

8-19. What do you think is the best part of Mikkel's job? The worst part?

8-20. If you were in Mikkel's position, what would your next career move be?

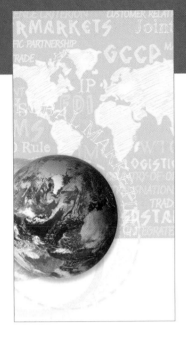

9
Global Market-Entry Strategies: Licensing, Investment, and Strategic Alliances

MyMarketingLab™

⭐ **Improve Your Grade!**

Over 10 million students improved their results using the Pearson MyLabs. Visit **mymktlab.com** for simulations, tutorials, and end-of-chapter problems.

CASE 9-1
Mo'men Launches Franchises in UAE

Mo'men, owned by the Mo'men Group, is one of the largest restaurant chains in Egypt. The name comes from the word *mo'men* or "believer" in Arabic which highlights the Islamic identity of the brand.

The Mo'men Group includes the Al Motaheda Foods, Mo'men, Pizza King, Three Chefs, and Planet Africa brands. The Mo'men brothers started the company in 1988 to meet the Egyptian market's need for a fast-food restaurant that offered high-quality foods, often on-the-go, at competitive prices. At present, Mo'men serves over 9 million customers annually in Egypt and holds about 15 percent share of the fast food market.

Since Mo'men is based in Egypt and has an Islamic identity, it only offers foods that are halal. As opposed to haram, halal stands for anything, object or action, that is permissible under the Islamic law. There is no pork on the menu; it is forbidden to eat pork in Islam. Similarly, bread is one of the important components in Egyptian cuisine. Thus, Mo'men makes sure that the quality of the bread

Exhibit 9-1 Mo'men restaurants today cater to more than 9 million customers annually in Egypt alone. In a little more than 20 years, the one-store restaurant has become a fast food chain spread over eight countries. At present, the company is aggressively seeking to expand in the UAE and Malaysia, the potential growth markets.
Source: Jasmine Merdan/Fotolia

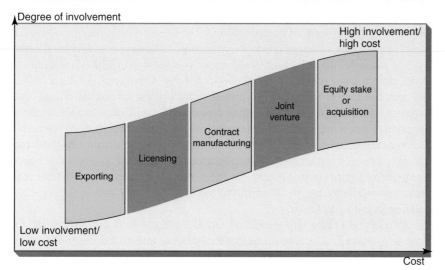

FIGURE 9-1

Investment Cost of Market-Entry Strategies

Degree of involvement

High involvement/ high cost

Equity stake or acquisition

Joint venture

Contract manufacturing

Licensing

Exporting

Low involvement/ low cost

Cost

in its sandwiches is high on taste as well as nutrients. It is worth noting that Egypt has the highest bread consumption worldwide.

Since its humble beginnings in 1988, Mo'men has grown from just one store to an international brand. However, such rapid growth has not been easy. The Mo'men Group has invested heavily in infrastructure and in the application of modern branding concepts. In 2008, it made the strategic decision to work with one of the world's largest branding agencies to create a reputable, well-respected name and to revive the brand's original spirit. The rebranding was reflected in its restaurants, customer experiences, and advertising. The retooling was a leap in Mo'men's history, taking it to an international level.

In addition to the Islamic identity that the company has built, Mo'men Group has also entered into a long-term joint venture with the Al Islami Group of the United Arab Emirates (UAE) to market Mo'men franchises. Al Islami Group is a leading halal food producer in the Middle East. The $21 million project will span 20 years.

The first franchised outlet in the UAE opened in Sharjah, and the goal is to open a total of 20 outlets across the Emirates. Mo'men Group sees the UAE as a regional hub from where it can expand and capitalize on the growing halal market in the Middle East and North Africa.

The Mo'men Group's goal is for Mo'men to be the consumers' favorite quick-service restaurant and an integral part of its clientele's daily lives, nationally and globally. Mo'men restaurants

are located in Egypt, Bahrain, Libya, Sudan, Malaysia, Qatar, Saudi Arabia, and the UAE, as per the franchise agreement. As it expands to the global market, Mo'men ensures that its food menu accounts for the local taste, while retaining the essence of the brand. This was the case when Mo'men penetrated the Malaysian market. The second part of this case aims to show how Mo'men adapted to the cultural differences in Malaysia and the method for operating in the Malaysian market. To learn more about Mo'men's international growth, particularly in Malaysia, see the continuation of Case 9-1 at the end of the chapter.

In this chapter, we discuss several additional entry mode options that form a continuum. As shown in Figure 9-1, the levels of involvement, risk, and financial reward increase as a company moves from market-entry strategies such as licensing to joint ventures and, ultimately, various forms of investment.

When a global company seeks to enter a developing country market, an additional strategy issue that must be addressed is whether to replicate, without significant adaptation, the strategy that served the company well in developed markets. Formulating a market-entry strategy means that management must decide which option or options to use in pursuing opportunities outside the home country. The particular market-entry strategy that company executives choose will depend on their vision, their attitude toward risk, the availability of investment capital, and the amount of control sought.

LEARNING OBJECTIVES

1 Explain the advantages and disadvantages of using licensing as a market-entry strategy.

2 Compare and contrast the different forms that a company's foreign investments can take.

3 Discuss the factors that contribute to the successful launch of a global strategic partnership.

4 Describe the special forms of cooperative strategies found in Asia.

5 Explain the evolution of the virtual corporation.

6 Use the market expansion strategies matrix to explain the strategies used by the world's biggest global companies.

Licensing

Licensing is a contractual arrangement whereby one company (the licensor) makes a legally protected asset available to another company (the licensee) in exchange for royalties, license fees, or some other form of compensation.[1] The licensed asset may be a brand name, company name, patent, trade secret, or product formulation. Licensing is widely used in the fashion industry. For example, the namesake companies associated with Bill Blass, Hugo Boss, and other global design icons typically generate more revenue from licensing deals for jeans, fragrances, and watches than from their high-priced couture lines. Organizations as diverse as Disney, Caterpillar Inc., the National Basketball Association, and Coca-Cola also make extensive use of licensing. Even though none is an apparel manufacturer, licensing agreements allow them to leverage their brand names and generate substantial revenue streams. As these examples suggest, licensing is a global market-entry and expansion strategy with considerable appeal. It can offer an attractive return on investment for the life of the agreement, provided that the necessary performance clauses are included in the contract. The only cost is signing the agreement and policing its implementation.

Two key advantages are associated with licensing as a market-entry mode. First, because the licensee is typically a local business that will produce and market the goods on a local or regional basis, licensing enables companies to circumvent tariffs, quotas, or similar export barriers discussed in Chapter 8. Second, when appropriate, licensees are granted considerable autonomy and are free to adapt the licensed goods to local tastes. Disney's success with licensing is a case in point. Disney licenses trademarked cartoon characters, names, and logos to producers of clothing, toys, and watches for sale throughout the world. Licensing allows Disney to create synergies based on its core theme park, motion picture, and television businesses. Its licensees are allowed considerable leeway to adapt colors, materials, or other design elements to local tastes (see Exhibit 9-2).

In China, licensed goods were practically unknown until a few years ago; by 2001, annual sales of all licensed goods totaled $600 million. Industry observers expect that figure to grow by 10 percent or more each of the next few years. Similarly, yearly worldwide sales of licensed Caterpillar merchandise are running at nearly $1 billion as consumers make a fashion statement of boots, jeans, and handbags bearing the distinctive black-and-yellow Cat label. Stephen Palmer is the head of London-based Overland Ltd., which holds the worldwide license for Cat apparel.

Exhibit 9-2 Licensed merchandise generates $30 billion in annual revenues for the Walt Disney Company. Thanks to the popularity of the company's theme parks, movies, and television shows, Mickey Mouse, Winnie the Pooh, and other popular characters are familiar faces throughout the world. The president of Disney Consumer Products recently predicted that the company's license-related revenues will eventually reach $75 billion.
Source: John Mocre/The Image Works.

[1] Franklin R. Root, *Entry Strategies for International Markets* (New York: Lexington Books, 1994), p. 107.

He noted, "Even if people here don't know the brand, they have a feeling that they know it. They have seen Caterpillar tractors from an early age. It's subliminal, and that's why it's working."[2]

Licensing is also associated with several disadvantages and opportunity costs. First, licensing agreements offer limited market control. Because the licensor typically does not become involved in the licensee's marketing program, potential returns from marketing may be lost. The second disadvantage is that the agreement may have a short life if the licensee develops its own know-how and begins to innovate in the licensed product or technology area. In a worst-case scenario (from the licensor's point of view), licensees—especially those working with process technologies—can develop into strong competitors in the local market and, eventually, into industry leaders. This is because licensing, by its very nature, enables a company to "borrow"— that is, leverage and exploit—another company's resources. A case in point is Pilkington, which has seen its leadership position in the glass industry erode as Glaverbel, Saint-Gobain, PPG, and other competitors have achieved higher levels of production efficiency and lower costs.[3]

Perhaps the most famous example of the opportunity costs associated with licensing dates back to the mid-1950s, when Sony cofounder Masaru Ibuka obtained a licensing agreement for the transistor from AT&T's Bell Laboratories. Ibuka dreamed of using transistors to make small, battery-powered radios. However, the Bell engineers with whom he spoke insisted that it was impossible to manufacture transistors that could handle the high frequencies required for a radio; they advised him to try making hearing aids instead. Undeterred, Ibuka presented the challenge to his Japanese engineers, who then spent many months improving high-frequency output. Sony was not the first company to unveil a transistor radio; a U.S.-built product, the Regency, featured transistors from Texas Instruments and a colorful plastic case. However, it was Sony's high-quality, distinctive approach to styling and marketing savvy that ultimately translated into worldwide success.

Companies may find that the upfront easy money obtained from licensing turns out to be a very expensive source of revenue. To prevent a licensor-competitor from gaining unilateral benefit, licensing agreements should provide for a cross-technology exchange among all parties. At the absolute minimum, any company that plans to remain in business must ensure that its license agreements include a provision for full cross-licensing (i.e., that the licensee shares its developments with the licensor). Overall, the licensing strategy must ensure ongoing competitive advantage. For example, license arrangements can create export market opportunities and open the door to low-risk manufacturing relationships. They can also speed diffusion of new products or technologies.

Special Licensing Arrangements

Companies that use **contract manufacturing** provide technical specifications to a subcontractor or local manufacturer. The subcontractor then oversees production. Such arrangements offer several advantages. First, the licensing firm can specialize in product design and marketing, while transferring responsibility for ownership of manufacturing facilities to contractors and subcontractors. Other advantages include limited commitment of financial and managerial resources and quick entry into target countries, especially when the target market is too small to justify significant investment.[4] One disadvantage, as already noted, is that companies may open themselves to public scrutiny and criticism if workers in contract factories are poorly paid or labor in inhumane circumstances. Timberland and other companies that source in low-wage countries are using image advertising to communicate their corporate policies on sustainable business practices.

Franchising is another variation of licensing strategy. A franchise is a contract between a parent company/franchiser and a franchisee that allows the franchisee to operate a business developed by the franchiser in return for a fee and adherence to franchise-wide policies and practices. Exhibit 9-3 shows an ad for Pollo Campero, a restaurant chain based in Central America that is using franchising to expand operations in the United States.

---

[2] Cecilie Rohwedder and Joseph T. Hallinan, "In Europe, Hot New Fashion for Urban Hipsters Comes from Peoria," *The Wall Street Journal* (August 8, 2001), p. B1.

[3] Charis Gresser, "A Real Test of Endurance," *Financial Times—Weekend* (November 1–2, 1997), p. 5.

[4] Franklin R. Root, *Entry Strategies for International Markets* (New York: Lexington Books, 1994), p. 138.

Exhibit 9-3 Executives at Guatemala's Pollo Campero SA know how to spot a market entry opportunity. It came to their attention that passengers flying to the United States from Guatemala City and San Salvador often carried packages of the company's spicy chicken on board the planes. The Campero team also recognized that the chain enjoyed high levels of brand awareness in Los Angeles, where there is a large Guatemalan population.
Source: Used by permission of Campero US.

Franchising has great appeal to local entrepreneurs anxious to learn and apply Western-style marketing techniques. Franchising consultant William Le Sante suggests that would-be franchisers ask the following questions before expanding overseas:

- Will local consumers buy your product?
- How tough is the local competition?
- Does the government respect trademark and franchiser rights?
- Can your profits be easily repatriated?
- Can you buy all the supplies you need locally?
- Is commercial space available and are rents affordable?
- Are your local partners financially sound and do they understand the basics of franchising?[5]

---

[5] Eve Tahmincioglu, "It's Not Only the Giants with Franchises Abroad," *The New York Times* (February 12, 2004), p. C4.

By addressing these issues, franchisers can gain a more realistic understanding of global opportunities. In China, for example, regulations require foreign franchisers to directly own two or more stores for a minimum of 1 year before franchisees can take over the business. Intellectual property protection is also a concern in China.

The specialty retailing industry favors franchising as a market-entry mode. For example, The Body Shop has more than 2,500 stores in 60 countries; franchisees operate about 90 percent of them. Franchising is also a cornerstone of global growth in the fast-food industry; McDonald's reliance on franchising to expand globally is a case in point. The fast-food giant has a well-known global brand name and a business system that can be easily replicated in multiple country markets. Crucially, McDonald's headquarters has learned the wisdom of leveraging local market knowledge by granting franchisees considerable leeway to tailor restaurant interior designs and menu offerings to suit country-specific preferences and tastes (see Case 1-2). Generally speaking, however, franchising is a market-entry strategy that is typically executed with less localization than is licensing.

When companies do decide to license, they should sign agreements that anticipate more extensive market participation in the future. Insofar as is possible, a company should keep options and paths open for other forms of market participation. Many of these forms require investment and give the investing company more control than is possible with licensing.

> "One of the key things licensees bring to the business is their knowledge of the local marketplace, trends, and consumer preferences. As long as it's within the guidelines and standards, and it's not doing anything to compromise our brand, we're very willing to go along with it."[6]
>
> —Paul Leech, chief operating officer, Allied Domecq Quick Service Restaurants

Investment

After companies gain experience outside the home country via exporting or licensing, the time often comes when executives desire a more extensive form of participation. In particular, the desire to have partial or full ownership of operations outside the home country can drive the decision to invest. **Foreign direct investment (FDI)** figures reflect investment flows out of the home country as companies invest in or acquire plants, equipment, or other assets. FDI allows companies to produce, sell, and compete locally in key markets. Examples of FDI abound: Honda built a $550 million assembly plant in Greensburg, Indiana; Hyundai invested $1 billion in a plant in Montgomery, Alabama; IKEA has spent nearly $2 billion to open stores in Russia; and South Korea's LG Electronics purchased a 58 percent stake in Zenith Electronics (see Exhibit 9-4). Each of these represents FDI.

The final years of the twentieth century were a boom time for cross-border mergers and acquisitions. At the end of 2000, cumulative foreign investment by U.S. companies totaled $1.2 trillion. The top three target countries for U.S. investment were the United Kingdom, Canada, and the Netherlands. Investment in the United States by foreign companies also totaled $1.2 trillion; the United Kingdom, Japan, and the Netherlands were the top three sources of investment.[7] Investment in developing nations also grew rapidly in the 1990s. For example, as noted in earlier chapters, investment interest in the BRICS (Brazil, Russia, India, China, and South Africa) nations is increasing, especially in the automobile industry and other sectors critical to the countries' economic development.

Foreign investments may take the form of minority or majority shares in joint ventures, minority or majority equity stakes in another company, or outright acquisition. A company may also choose to use a combination of these entry strategies by acquiring one company, buying an equity stake in another, and operating a joint venture with a third. In recent years, for example, UPS has made numerous acquisitions in Europe and has also expanded its transportation hubs.

Joint Ventures

A joint venture with a local partner represents a more extensive form of participation in foreign markets than either exporting or licensing. Strictly speaking, a **joint venture** is an entry strategy for a single target country in which the partners share ownership of a newly created business entity.[8] This strategy is attractive for several reasons. First and foremost is the sharing of risk. By

---

[6] Sarah Murray, "Big Names Don Camouflage," *Financial Times* (February 5, 2004), p. 9.
[7] Maria Borga and Raymond J. Mataloni, Jr., "Direct Investment Positions for 2000: Country and Industry Detail," *Survey of Current Business* 81, no. 7 (July 2001), pp. 16–29.
[8] Franklin R. Root, *Entry Strategies for International Markets* (New York: Lexington Books, 1994), p. 309.

Exhibit 9-4 "Drive your way" is the advertising slogan for Hyundai Motor Company, South Korea's leading automaker. In a press statement, Hyundai chairman Chung Mong Koo noted, "Our new brand strategy is designed to ensure that we reach industry-leading levels, not only in terms of size but also in terms of customer perception and overall brand value." To better serve the U.S. market, Hyundai recently invested $1 billion in an assembly plant in Montgomery, Alabama. The plant produces two models, the popular Sonata sedan and the Santa Fe SUV.
Source: Hyundai Motor America.

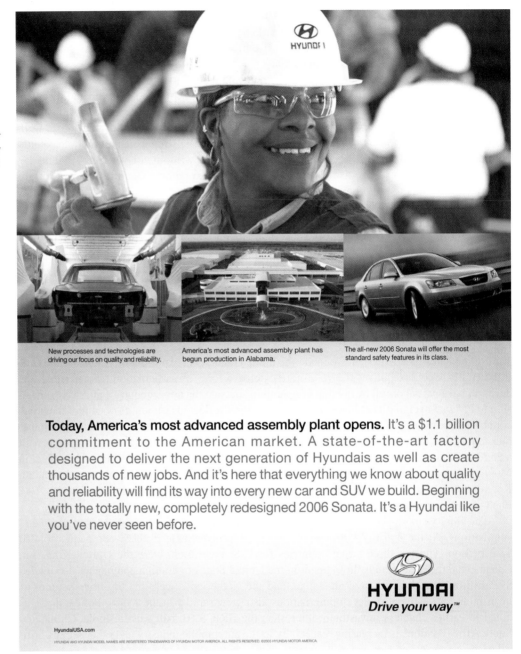

New processes and technologies are driving our focus on quality and reliability.

America's most advanced assembly plant has begun production in Alabama.

The all-new 2006 Sonata will offer the most standard safety features in its class.

Today, America's most advanced assembly plant opens. It's a $1.1 billion commitment to the American market. A state-of-the-art factory designed to deliver the next generation of Hyundais as well as create thousands of new jobs. And it's here that everything we know about quality and reliability will find its way into every new car and SUV we build. Beginning with the totally new, completely redesigned 2006 Sonata. It's a Hyundai like you've never seen before.

HYUNDAI
Drive your way™

HyundaiUSA.com

HYUNDAI AND HYUNDAI MODEL NAMES ARE REGISTERED TRADEMARKS OF HYUNDAI MOTOR AMERICA. ALL RIGHTS RESERVED. ©2005 HYUNDAI MOTOR AMERICA.

pursuing a joint venture entry strategy, a company can limit its financial risk as well as its exposure to political uncertainty. Second, a company can use the joint venture experience to learn about a new market environment. If it succeeds in becoming an insider, it may later increase the level of commitment and exposure. Third, joint ventures allow partners to achieve synergy by combining different value chain strengths. One company might have in-depth knowledge of a local market, an extensive distribution system, or access to low-cost labor or raw materials. Such a company might link up with a foreign partner possessing well-known brands or cutting-edge technology, manufacturing know-how, or advanced process applications. A company that lacks sufficient capital resources might seek partners to jointly finance a project. Finally, a joint venture may be the only way to enter a country or region if government bid award practices routinely favor local companies, if import tariffs are high, or if laws prohibit foreign control but permit joint ventures.

Many companies have experienced difficulties when attempting to enter the Japanese market. Anheuser-Busch's experience in Japan illustrates both the interactions of the entry modes discussed so far and the advantages and disadvantages of the joint venture approach. Access to distribution is critical to success in the Japanese market; Anheuser-Busch first entered by means of a licensing agreement with Suntory, the smallest of Japan's four top brewers. Although Budweiser became Japan's top-selling imported beer within a decade, Bud's market share in the early 1990s was still less than 2 percent. Anheuser-Busch then created a joint venture with Kirin Brewery, the market leader. Anheuser-Busch's 90 percent stake in the venture entitled it to market and distribute beer produced in a Los Angeles brewery through Kirin's channels. Anheuser-Busch also had the option to use some of Kirin's brewing capacity to brew Bud locally. For its part, Kirin was well positioned to learn more about the global market for beer from the world's largest brewer. By the end of the decade, however, Bud's market share hadn't increased and the venture was losing money. On January 1, 2000, Anheuser-Busch dissolved the joint venture and eliminated most of the associated job positions in Japan; it then reverted to a licensing agreement with Kirin. The lesson for consumer products marketers considering market entry in Japan is clear. It may make more sense to give control to a local partner via a licensing agreement than to make a major investment.[9]

The disadvantages of joint venturing can be significant. Joint venture partners must share rewards as well as risks. The main disadvantage associated with joint ventures is that a company incurs very significant control and coordination cost issues that arise when working with a partner. (However, in some instances country-specific restrictions limit the share of capital help by foreign companies.)

A second disadvantage is the potential for conflict between partners. These often arise out of cultural differences, as was the case in a failed $130 million joint venture between Corning Glass and Vitro, Mexico's largest industrial manufacturer. The venture's Mexican managers sometimes viewed the Americans as being too direct and aggressive; the Americans believed their partners took too much time to make important decisions.[10] Such conflicts can multiply when there are several partners in the venture. Disagreements about third-country markets where partners view each other as actual or potential competitors can lead to "divorce." To avoid this, it is essential to work out a plan for approaching third-country markets as part of the venture agreement.

A third issue, also noted in the discussion of licensing, is that a dynamic joint venture partner can evolve into a stronger competitor. Many developing countries are very forthright in this regard. Yuan Sutai, a member of China's Ministry of Electronics Industry, told *The Wall Street Journal*, "The purpose of any joint venture, or even a wholly-owned investment, is to allow Chinese companies to learn from foreign companies. We want them to bring their technology to the soil of the People's Republic of China."[11] GM and South Korea's Daewoo Group formed a joint venture in 1978 to produce cars for the Korean market. By the mid-1990s, GM had helped Daewoo improve its competitiveness as an auto producer, but Daewoo Chairman Kim Woo-Choong terminated the venture because its provisions prevented the export of cars bearing the Daewoo name.[12]

As one global marketing expert warns, "In an alliance you have to learn skills of the partner, rather than just see it as a way to get a product to sell while avoiding a big investment." Yet, compared with U.S. and European firms, Japanese and Korean firms seem to excel in their abilities to leverage new knowledge that comes out of a joint venture. For example, Toyota learned many new things from its partnership with GM—about U.S. supply and transportation and managing American workers—that Toyota subsequently applied at its Camry plant in Kentucky. However, some American managers involved in the venture complained that the manufacturing expertise Toyota gained was not applied broadly throughout GM.

---

[9] Yumiko Ono, "Beer Venture of Anheuser, Kirin Goes Down Drain on Tepid Sales," *The Wall Street Journal* (November 3, 1999), p. A23.

[10] Anthony DePalma, "It Takes More than a Visa to Do Business in Mexico," *The New York Times* (June 26, 1994), sec. 3, p. 5.

[11] David P. Hamilton, "China, with Foreign Partners' Help, Becomes a Budding Technology Giant," *The Wall Street Journal* (December 7, 1995), p. A10.

[12] "Mr. Kim's Big Picture," *The Economist* (September 16, 1995), pp. 74–75.

EMERGING MARKETS BRIEFING BOOK

Auto Industry Joint Ventures in Russia

SYNC • THINK • LEARN

MyMarketingLab

Russia represents a huge, barely tapped market for a number of industries, and the number of joint ventures is increasing. In 1997, GM became the first Western automaker to begin assembling vehicles in Russia. To avoid hefty tariffs that would have pushed the street price of an imported Blazer to $65,000 or more, GM invested in a 25-75 joint venture with the government of the autonomous Tatarstan republic. Elaz-GM assembled Blazer SUVs from imported components until the end of 2000. Young Russian professionals were expected to snap up the vehicles as long as the price was less than $30,000. However, after about 15,000 vehicles had been sold, market demand evaporated. At the end of 2001, GM terminated the joint venture.

GM has achieved better results with a joint venture with AvtoVAZ, the largest carmaker in Russia. Founded in 1966 in Togliatti, a city on the Volga River, AvtoVAZ is home to Russia's top technical design center and also has access to low-cost Russian titanium and other materials. The company was best known for being inefficient and for the outdated, boxy Lada, whose origins dated back to the Soviet era. GM originally intended to assemble a stripped-down, reengineered car based on its Opel model. However, market research revealed that a "Made in Russia" car would be acceptable only if it sported a very low sticker price; the same research pointed GM toward an opportunity to put the Chevrolet nameplate on a redesigned domestic model.

Developed with $100 million in funding from GM, the Chevrolet Niva was launched in the fall of 2002. Within a few years, however, the joint venture was struggling as AvtoVAZ installed a new management team that had the personal approval of then-President Vladimir Putin. The Russian government owns 25 percent of AvtoVAZ; in 2008, Renault paid $1 billion for a 25 percent stake. Renault's contribution consisted of technology transfer—specifically, its "B-Zero" auto platform—and production equipment. That same year, Russians bought a record 2.56 million vehicles. However, Russian auto sales collapsed as the global economic crisis deepened, and AvtoVAZ was close to bankruptcy. More than 40,000 workers were laid off, and Moscow was forced to inject $900 million into the company.

In 2009, an American, Jeffrey Glover, was sent from GM's Adam Opel division in Germany to run the Russian joint venture. By 2011, when AvtoVAZ celebrated its 45th anniversary, Russian automobile sales had rebounded. In 2012, sales reached pre-crisis levels of 3 million vehicles. Indeed, industry analysts expect Russia to surpass Germany as Europe's top auto market by 2014. And the Niva? More than 500,000 have been sold since 2002. As Jim Bovenzi, president of GM Russia explains, "Ten years ago, this was a difficult decision for GM. It was the first time in the 100-year history of the company that we would produce a fully locally designed and produced product, but when we look back now, it was the right decision."

Renault's Logan is already a big seller in Russia; executives are leveraging the investment in AvtoVAZ by producing cars under the Renault nameplate. Renault's plans call for increasing its stake to 50.1 percent by mid-2014. Nissan, which is an alliance partner with Renault, will take a 17 percent stake in the venture. Other automakers are hoping to capitalize on the growing Russian market. For example, Fiat scouted sites for a Jeep factory in Russia; expanded production was part of Fiat's goal to sell 800,000 Jeeps worldwide by 2014. In 2012, Jeep's worldwide sales totaled 700,000 vehicles. Some other recent joint venture alliances are outlined in Table 9-1.

The Russian market for imported premium vehicles is also exploding as the number of households that can afford luxury products exhibits rapid growth. Porsche (a division of Volkswagen) and BMW are both expanding the number of dealerships. Rolls-Royce (owned by BMW) now has two dealerships in Moscow; the only other city in the world with two dealerships is New York City. In addition, Nissan is assembling the Infiniti FX SUV in St. Petersburg.

Sources: Anatoly Temkin, "The Land of the Lada Eyes Upscale Rides," *Bloomberg Businessweek* (September 17, 2012), pp. 28–30; Luca I. Alpert, "Russia's Auto Market Shines," *The Wall Street Journal* (August 30, 2012), p. B3; John Reed, "AvtoVAZ Takes Stock of 45 Years of Ladas," *Financial Times* (July 22, 2011), p. 17; David Pearson and Sebastian Moffett, "Renault to Assist AvtoVAZ," *The Wall Street Journal* (November 28, 2009), p. A5; Guy Chazan, "Kremlin Capitalism: Russian Car Maker Comes Under Sway of Old Pal of Putin," *The Wall Street Journal* (May 19, 2006), p. A1; Keith Naughton, "How GM Got the Inside Track in China," *BusinessWeek* (November 6, 1995), pp. 56–57; Gregory L. White, "Off Road: How the Chevy Name Landed on SUV Using Russian Technology," *The Wall Street Journal* (February 20, 2001), pp. A1, A8.

Exhibit 9-5 Russia used to be known as "the land of the Lada," a reference to a Soviet-era car of dubious distinction. Today, Russia is on track to surpass Germany as Europe's largest car market. This is good news for global automakers such as BMW, Renault, and Volvo. Strong demand also means that GM's $100 million bet on a joint venture with AvtoVAZ is paying big dividends.
Source: © RIA Novosti / Alamy

TABLE 9-1 Market Entry and Expansion by Joint Venture

Companies Involved	Purpose of Joint Venture
GM (United States), Toyota (Japan)	NUMMI, a jointly operated plant in Freemont, California (venture was terminated in 2009).
GM (United States), Shanghai Automotive Industry (China)	A 50-50 joint venture to build an assembly plant to produce 100,000 mid-sized sedans for the Chinese market beginning in 1997 (total investment of $1 billion).
GM (United States), Hindustan Motors (India)	A joint venture to build up to 20,000 Opel Astras annually (GM's investment was $100 million).
GM (United States), governments of Russia and Tatarstan	A 25-75 joint venture to assemble Blazers from imported parts and, by 1998, to build a full assembly line for 45,000 vehicles (total investment of $250 million).
Ford (United States), Mazda (Japan)	AutoAlliance International 50-50 joint operation of a plant in Flat Rock, Michigan.
Ford (United States), Mahindra & Mahindra Ltd. (India)	A 50-50 joint venture to build Ford Fiestas in the Indian state of Tamil Nadu (total investment of $800 million).
Chrysler (United States), BMW (Germany)	A 50-50 joint venture to build a plant in South America to produce small-displacement 4-cylinder engines (total investment of $500 million).

Source: Compiled by authors.

Investment via Equity Stake or Full Ownership

The most extensive form of participation in global markets is investment that results in either an equity stake or full ownership. An **equity stake** is simply an investment; if the investor owns fewer than 50 percent of the shares, it is a minority stake; ownership of more than half the shares makes it a majority. **Full ownership**, as the name implies, means the investor has 100 percent control. This may be achieved by a startup of new operations, known as **greenfield investment**, or by merger or acquisition of an existing enterprise. For example, in 2008 the largest merger and acquisition (M&A) deal in the pharmaceutical industry was Roche's acquisition of Genentech for $43 billion. Prior to the onset of the global financial crisis, the media and telecommunications industry sectors were among the busiest for M&A worldwide. Ownership requires the greatest commitment of capital and managerial effort and offers the fullest means of participating in a market.

Companies may move from licensing or joint venture strategies to ownership in order to achieve faster expansion in a market, greater control, and/or higher profits. In 1991, for example, Ralston Purina ended a 20-year joint venture with a Japanese company to start its own pet food subsidiary. Monsanto and Bayer AG, the German pharmaceutical company, are two other companies that have also recently disbanded partnerships in favor of wholly owned subsidiaries in Japan. Home Depot used acquisition to expand in China; in 2006, the home improvement giant acquired the HomeWay chain. However, Chinese consumers did not embrace the big-box, do-it-yourself model. By the end of 2012, Home Depot had closed the last of its big-box stores in China; its two remaining Chinese retail locations are a paint and flooring specialty store and an interior design store.

If government restrictions prevent 100 percent ownership by foreign companies, the investing company will have to settle for a majority or minority equity stake. In China, for example, the government usually restricts foreign ownership in joint ventures to a 51 percent majority stake. However, a minority equity stake may suit a company's business interests. For example, Samsung was content to purchase a 40 percent stake in computer maker AST. As Samsung manager Michael Yang noted, "We thought 100 percent would be very risky, because any time you have a switch of ownership, that creates a lot of uncertainty among the employees."[13]

---

[13] Ross Kerber, "Chairman Predicts Samsung Deal Will Make AST a Giant," *The Los Angeles Times* (March 2, 1995), p. D1.

In other instances, the investing company may start with a minority stake and then increase its share. In 1991, Volkswagen AG made its first investment in the Czech auto industry by purchasing a 31 percent share in Skoda. By 1995, Volkswagen had increased its equity stake to 70 percent, with the government of the Czech Republic owning the rest. Volkswagen acquired full ownership in 2000. By 2011, Skoda's twentieth anniversary of its relationship with VW, the Czech automaker had evolved from a regional company to a global one, selling more than 750,000 vehicles in 100 countries.[14] Similarly, during the economic downturn of the late 2000s, Italy's Fiat acquired a 20 percent stake in Chrysler when the U.S. automaker was in bankruptcy proceedings. Fiat CEO Sergio Marchionne returned Chrysler to profitability and upped his company's stake to 53.5 and then 58.5 percent. Finally, in 2013, Fiat was set to acquire the remaining 41.5 percent and complete the full acquisition of Chrysler.[15]

Large-scale direct expansion by means of establishing new facilities can be expensive and require a major commitment of managerial time and energy. However, political or other environmental factors sometimes dictate this approach. For example, Japan's Fuji Photo Film Company invested hundreds of millions of dollars in the United States after the U.S. government ruled that Fuji was guilty of dumping (i.e., selling photographic paper at substantially lower prices than in Japan). As an alternative to greenfield investment in new facilities, acquisition is an instantaneous—and sometimes less expensive—approach to market entry or expansion. Although full ownership can yield the additional advantage of avoiding communication and conflict-of-interest problems that may arise with a joint venture or coproduction partner, acquisitions still present the demanding and challenging task of integrating the acquired company into the worldwide organization and coordinating activities.

Tables 9-2, 9-3, and 9-4 provide a sense of how companies in the automotive industry utilize a variety of market-entry options discussed previously, including equity stakes, investments to establish new operations, and acquisition. Table 9-2 shows that GM favors minority stakes in non-U.S. automakers; from 1998 through 2000, the company spent $4.7 billion on such deals, whereas Ford spent twice as much on acquisitions. Despite the fact that GM losses from the deals resulted in substantial write-offs, the strategy reflects management's skepticism about big mergers actually working. As former GM chairman and CEO Rick Wagoner said, "We could have bought 100 percent of somebody, but that probably wouldn't have been a good use of capital." Meanwhile, the company's investments in minority stakes have paid off: The company enjoys scale-related savings in purchasing, it has gained access to diesel technology, and Saab produced a new model in record time with the help of Subaru.[16] Following its bankruptcy filing in 2009, GM divested itself of several noncore businesses and brands, including Saab.

TABLE 9-2 Investment in Equity Stake

Investing Company (Home Country)	Investment (Share, Amount, Date)
Fiat (Italy)	Chrysler (United States, initial 20% stake, 2009; Fiat took Chrysler out of bankruptcy)
General Motors (United States)	Fuji Heavy Industries (Japan, 20% stake, $1.4 billion, 1999); Saab Automobiles AB (Sweden, 50% stake, $500 million, 1990; remaining 50%, 2000; following bankruptcy filing, sold Saab to Swedish consortium in 2009)
Volkswagen AG (Germany)	Skoda (Czech Republic, 31% stake, $6 billion, 1991; increased to 50.5%, 1994; currently owns 70% stake)
Ford (USA)	Mazda Motor Corp. (Japan, 25% stake, 1979; increased to 33.4%, $408 million, 1996; decreased stake to 13%, 2008, reduced to 3.5%, 2010)
Renault SA (France)	AvtoVaz (Russia, 25% stake, $1.3 billion, 2008); Nissan Motors (Japan, 35% stake, $5 billion, 2000)

[14] Andrew English, "Skoda Celebrates 20 Years of Success Under VW," *The Telegraph* (April 19, 2011); see also Gail Edmondson, "Skoda, Volkswagen's Hot Growth Engine," *BusinessWeek* (September 14, 2007), p. 30.
[15] Sharon Terlep and Christina Rogers, "Fiat Poised to Absorb Chrysler," *The Wall Street Journal* (April 25, 2013), p. B1.
[16] James Mackintosh, "GM Stands by Its Strategy for Expansion," *Financial Times* (February 2, 2004), p. 5.

TABLE 9-3 Investment to Establish New Operations

Investing Company (Headquarters Country)	Investment (Location, Date)
Honda Motor (Japan)	$550 million auto-assembly plant (Indiana, United States, 2006)
Hyundai (South Korea)	$1.1 billion auto-assembly and -manufacturing facility producing Sonata and Santa Fe models (Georgia, United States, 2005)
Bayerische Motoren Werke AG (Germany)	$400 million auto-assembly plant (South Carolina, United States, 1995)
Mercedes-Benz AG (Germany)	$300 million auto-assembly plant (Alabama, United States, 1993)
Toyota (Japan)	$3.4 billion manufacturing plant producing Camry, Avalon, and minivan models (Kentucky, United States); $400 million engine plant (West Virginia, United States)

What is the driving force behind many of these acquisitions? It is globalization. In cases like Gerber, management realizes that the path to globalization cannot be undertaken independently. Management at Helene Curtis Industries came to a similar realization and agreed to be acquired by Unilever. Ronald J. Gidwitz, president and CEO, said, "It was very clear to us that Helene Curtis did not have the capacity to project itself in emerging markets around the world. As markets get larger, that forces the smaller players to take action."[17] Still, management's decision to invest abroad sometimes clashes with investors' short-term profitability goals—or with the wishes of members of the target organization (see Exhibit 9-6).

Several of the advantages of joint ventures also apply to ownership, including access to markets and avoidance of tariff or quota barriers. Like joint ventures, ownership also permits important technology experience transfers and provides a company with access to new manufacturing techniques. For example, The Stanley Works, a toolmaker with headquarters in New Britain, Connecticut, has acquired more than a dozen companies. Among them is Taiwan's National Hand Tool/Chiro Company, a socket wrench manufacturer and developer of a "cold-forming" process that speeds up production and reduces waste. Stanley is now using that technology in the manufacture of other tools. Former Chairman Richard H. Ayers presided over the acquisitions and envisioned such global cross-fertilization and "blended technology" as a key benefit of globalization.[19] In 1998, former GE executive John Trani succeeded Ayers as CEO; Trani brought considerable experience with international acquisitions, and his selection was widely viewed as evidence that Stanley intended to boost global sales even more.

The alternatives discussed here—licensing, joint ventures, minority or majority equity stake, and ownership—are points along a continuum of alternative strategies for global market entry and expansion. The overall design of a company's global strategy may call for combinations of exporting–importing, licensing, joint ventures, and ownership among different operating units. Avon Products uses both acquisition and joint ventures to enter developing markets. A company's strategy preference may change over time. For example, Borden Inc. ended licensing and joint venture

> "We used to go into talks saying 'acquisition,' with joint ventures a distant second choice, but now we see joint ventures as a great way to dip a toe into a new market."[18]
>
> —Pamela Daley, senior vice president for corporate business development, GE

TABLE 9-4 Market Entry and Expansion by Acquisition

Acquiring Company	Target (Country, Amount, Date)
Tata Motors (India)	Jaguar and Land Rover (UK, $2.3 billion, 2008)
Volkswagen AG (Germany)	Sociedad Española de Automóviles de Turismo (SEAT, Spain, $600 million, purchase completed in 1990)
Zhejiang Geely (China)	Volvo car unit (Sweden, $1.3 billion, 2010)
Paccar (USA)	DAF Trucks (Netherlands, $543 million, 1996)

[17] Richard Gibson and Sara Calian, "Unilever to Buy Helene Curtis for $770 Million," *The Wall Street Journal* (February 19, 1996), p. A3.
[18] Claudia Deutsch, "The Venturesome Giant," *The New York Times* (October 5, 2007), p. C1.
[19] Louis Uchitelle, "The Stanley Works Goes Global," *The New York Times* (July 23, 1989), sec. 3, pp. 1, 10.

Exhibit 9-6 As we have seen in previous chapters, China's growing economic clout has contributed to increased antiglobalization sentiment in various parts of the world. For example, China offsets its huge trade surplus with the United States by investing in American securities and companies. As this cartoon implies, business schools may be next!
Source: Cartoon Features Syndicate.

"OK, but just suppose China *did* make a takeover move on our B-school."

arrangements for branded food products in Japan and set up its own production, distribution, and marketing capabilities for dairy products. Meanwhile, in nonfood products, Borden has maintained joint venture relationships with Japanese partners in flexible packaging and foundry materials.

Competitors within a given industry may pursue different strategies. For example, Cummins Engine and Caterpillar both face very high costs—in the $300 to $400 million range—for developing new diesel engines suited to new applications. However, the two companies vary in their strategic approaches to the world market for engines. Cummins management looks favorably on collaboration; also, the company's relatively modest $6 billion in annual revenues presents financial limitations. Thus, Cummins prefers joint ventures. The biggest joint venture between an American company and a Russian company linked Cummins with the KamAZ truck company in Tatarstan. The joint venture allowed the Russians to implement new manufacturing technologies while providing Cummins with access to the Russian market. Cummins also has joint ventures in Japan, Finland, and Italy. Management at Caterpillar, by contrast, prefers the higher degree of control that comes with full ownership. The company has spent more than $2 billion on purchases of Germany's MaK, British engine maker Perkins, and others. Management believes that it is often less expensive to buy existing firms than to develop new applications independently. Also, Caterpillar is concerned about safeguarding proprietary knowledge that is basic to manufacturing in its core construction equipment business.[20]

Global Strategic Partnerships

In Chapter 8 and the first half of this chapter, we surveyed the range of options—exporting, licensing, joint ventures, and ownership—traditionally used by companies wishing either to enter global markets for the first time or to expand their activities beyond present levels. However, recent changes in the political, economic, sociocultural, and technological environments of the global firm have combined to change the relative importance of those strategies. Trade barriers have fallen, markets have globalized, consumer needs and wants have converged, product life cycles have shortened, and new communications technologies and trends have emerged. Although these developments provide unprecedented marketing opportunities, they also have strong strategic implications for the global organization and new challenges for the global marketer. Such strategies will undoubtedly incorporate—or may even be structured around—a variety of collaborations. Once thought of only as joint ventures, with the more dominant party reaping most of the benefits (or losses) of the partnership, cross-border alliances are taking on surprising new configurations and even more surprising players.

---

[20] Peter Marsh, "Engine Makers Take Different Routes," *Financial Times* (July 14, 1998), p. 11.

Why would any firm—global or otherwise—seek to collaborate with another firm, be it local or foreign? For example, despite commanding a 37 percent share of the global cellular handset market, Nokia once announced that it would make the source code for its proprietary Series 60 software available to competing handset manufacturers such as Siemens AG. Why did Nokia's top executives decide to collaborate, thereby putting the company's competitive advantage in software development (and healthy profit margins) at risk? As noted, a "perfect storm" of converging environmental forces is rendering traditional competitive strategies obsolete.

Today's competitive environment is characterized by unprecedented degrees of turbulence, dynamism, and unpredictability; thus global firms must respond and adapt quickly. To succeed in global markets, firms can no longer rely exclusively on the technological superiority or core competence that brought them past success. In the twenty-first century, firms must look toward new strategies that will enhance environmental responsiveness. In particular, they must pursue "entrepreneurial globalization" by developing flexible organizational capabilities, innovating continuously, and revising global strategies accordingly.[21] In the second half of this chapter, we will focus on global strategic partnerships. In addition, we will examine the Japanese *keiretsu* and various other types of cooperation strategies that global firms are using today.

The Nature of Global Strategic Partnerships

The terminology used to describe the new forms of cooperation strategies varies widely. The terms **strategic alliances**, **strategic international alliances**, and **global strategic partnerships** **(GSPs)** are frequently used to refer to linkages among companies from different countries to jointly pursue a common goal. This terminology can cover a broad spectrum of interfirm agreements, including joint ventures. However, the strategic alliances discussed here exhibit three characteristics (see Figure 9-2):[22]

1. The participants remain independent subsequent to the formation of the alliance.
2. The participants share the benefits of the alliance as well as control over the performance of assigned tasks.
3. The participants make ongoing contributions in technology, products, and other key strategic areas.

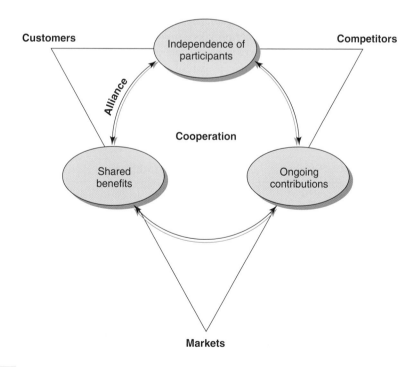

FIGURE 9-2

Three Characteristics of Strategic Alliances

[21] Michael Y. Yoshino and U. Srinivasa Rangan, *Strategic Alliances: An Entrepreneurial Approach to Globalization* (Boston: Harvard Business School Press, 1995), p. 51.
[22] Michael Y. Yoshino and U. Srinivasa Rangan, *Strategic Alliances: An Entrepreneurial Approach to Globalization* (Boston: Harvard Business School Press, 1995), p. 5. For an alternative description, see Riad Ajami and Dara Khambata, "Global Strategic Alliances: The New Transnationals," *Journal of Global Marketing* 5, no. 1/2 (1991), pp. 55–59.

Exhibit 9-7 The Star Alliance is a global network that brings together United Airlines and other carriers in a number of different countries. Passengers booking a ticket on any Alliance member can easily connect with other carriers for smooth travel to more than 130 countries. A further benefit for travelers is the fact that frequent-flyer miles earned can be redeemed with any Alliance member.
Source: © imagebroker / Alamy

According to estimates, the number of strategic alliances has been growing at a rate of 20 to 30 percent since the mid-1980s. The upward trend for GSPs comes, in part, at the expense of traditional cross-border mergers and acquisitions. Since the mid-1990s, a key force driving partnership formation is the realization that globalization and the Internet will require new, intercorporate configurations (see Exhibit 9-7). Table 9-5 lists examples of GSPs.

Like traditional joint ventures, GSPs have some disadvantages. Partners share control over assigned tasks, a situation that creates management challenges. Also, strengthening a competitor from another country can present a number of risks.

First, high product development costs in the face of resource constraints may force a company to seek one or more partners; this was part of the rationale for Sony's partnership with

TABLE 9-5 Examples of Global Strategic Partnerships

Name of Alliance or Product	Major Participants	Purpose of Alliance
Fiat/Chrysler	Fiat (Italy), Chrysler (United States)	Chrysler gains access to fuel-efficient small-car platforms (e.g., Dodge Dart); Fiat nameplate reintroduced into the U.S. market, starting with 500 subcompact.
S-LCD	Sony Corp., Samsung Electronics Co.	Produce flat-panel LCD screens for high-definition televisions
Beverage Partners Worldwide	Coca-Cola and Nestlé	Offer new coffee, tea, and herbal beverage products in "rejuvenation" category
Star Alliance	Adria, Aegean, Air Canada, Air China, Air New Zealand, ANA, Asiana Airlines, Austrian, Avianca Taca, Brussels Airlines, Copa Airlines, Croatia Airlines, EGYPTAIR, Ethiopian Airlines, LOT Polish Airways, Lufthansa, Scandinavian Airlines, Shenzhen Airlines, Singapore Airlines, South African Airways, SWISS, TAM, TAP Portugal, THAI, Turkish Airlines, United, US Airways	Create a global travel network by linking 27 airlines and providing improved service for international travelers

Samsung to produce flat-panel TV screens. Second, the technology requirements of many contemporary products mean that an individual company may lack the skills, capital, or know-how to go it alone.[23] Third, partnerships may be the best means of securing access to national and regional markets. Fourth, partnerships provide important learning opportunities; in fact, one expert regards GSPs as a "race to learn." Professor Gary Hamel of the London Business School has observed that the partner that proves to be the fastest learner can ultimately dominate the relationship.

As noted earlier, GSPs differ significantly from the market-entry modes discussed in the first half of the chapter. Because licensing agreements do not call for continuous transfer of technology or skills among partners, such agreements are not strategic alliances.[24] Traditional joint ventures are basically alliances focusing on a single national market or a specific problem. The Chinese joint venture described previously between GM and Shanghai Automotive fits this description; the basic goal is to make cars for the Chinese market. A true global strategic partnership is different and is distinguished by five attributes.[25] S-LCD, Sony's strategic alliance with Samsung, offers a good illustration of each attribute.[26]

1. *Two or more companies develop a joint long-term strategy aimed at achieving world leadership by pursuing cost leadership, differentiation, or a combination of the two.* Samsung and Sony are jockeying with each other for leadership in the global television market. One key to profitability in the flat-panel TV market is being the cost leader in panel production. S-LCD is a $2 billion joint venture that produces 60,000 panels per month.

2. *The relationship is reciprocal. Each partner possesses specific strengths that it shares with the other; learning must take place on both sides.* Samsung is a leader in the manufacturing technologies used to create flat-panel TVs. Sony excels at parlaying advanced technology into world-class consumer products; its engineers specialize in optimizing TV picture quality. Jang Insik, Samsung's chief executive, says, "If we learn from Sony, it will help us in advancing our technology."[27]

3. *The partners' vision and efforts are truly global, extending beyond home countries and the home regions to the rest of the world.* Sony and Samsung are both global companies that market global brands throughout the world.

4. *The relationship is organized along horizontal, not vertical, lines. Continual transfer of resources laterally between partners is required, with technology sharing and resource pooling representing norms.* Jang and Sony's Hiroshi Murayama speak by telephone on a daily basis; they also meet face-to-face each month to discuss panel making.

5. *When competing in markets excluded from the partnership, the participants retain their national and ideological identities.* Samsung markets a line of high-definition televisions that use digital light processing (DLP) technology. Sony does not produce DLP sets. When developing a DVD player and home theater sound system to match the TV, a Samsung team headed by head TV designer Yunje Kang worked closely with the audio/video division. At Samsung, managers with responsibility for consumer electronics and computer products report to digital media chief Gee-sung Choi. All the designers work side by side on open floors. As noted in a company profile, "the walls between business units are literally nonexistent."[28] By contrast, in recent years Sony has been plagued by a time-consuming, consensus-driven communication approach among divisions that have operated largely autonomously.

---

[23] Kenichi Ohmae, "The Global Logic of Strategic Alliances," *Harvard Business Review* 67, no. 2 (March–April 1989), p. 145.

[24] Michael A. Yoshino and U. Srinivasa Rangan, *Strategic Alliances: An Entrepreneurial Approach to Globalization* (Boston: Harvard Business School Press, 1995), p. 6.

[25] Howard V. Perlmutter and David A. Heenan, "Cooperate to Compete Globally," *Harvard Business Review* 64, no. 2 (March–April 1986), p. 137.

[26] This discussion is adapted from Phred Dvorak and Evan Ramstad, "TV Marriage: Behind Sony–Samsung Rivalry, an Unlikely Alliance Develops," *The Wall Street Journal* (January 3, 2006), pp. A1, A6.

[27] Phred Dvorak and Evan Ramstad, "TV Marriage: Behind Sony–Samsung Rivalry, an Unlikely Alliance Develops," *The Wall Street Journal* (January 3, 2006), pp. A1, A6.

[28] Frank Rose, "Seoul Machine," *Wired* (May 2005).

Success Factors

Assuming that a proposed alliance has these five attributes, it is necessary to consider six basic factors deemed to have significant impact on the success of GSPs: mission, strategy, governance, culture, organization, and management:[29]

1. *Mission.* Successful GSPs create win-win situations, where participants pursue objectives on the basis of mutual need or advantage.
2. *Strategy.* A company may establish separate GSPs with different partners; strategy must be thought out up front to avoid conflicts.
3. *Governance.* Discussion and consensus must be the norms. Partners must be viewed as equals.
4. *Culture.* Personal chemistry is important, as is the successful development of a shared set of values. The failure of a partnership between Great Britain's General Electric Company and Siemens AG was blamed in part on the fact that the former was run by finance-oriented executives, the latter by engineers.
5. *Organization.* Innovative structures and designs may be needed to offset the complexity of multicountry management.
6. *Management.* GSPs invariably involve a different type of decision making. Potentially divisive issues must be identified in advance and clear, unitary lines of authority established that will result in commitment by all partners.

Companies forming GSPs must keep these factors in mind. Moreover, the following four principles will guide successful collaborations. First, despite the fact that partners are pursuing mutual goals in some areas, partners must remember that they are competitors in others. Second, harmony is not the most important measure of success—some conflict is to be expected. Third, all employees, engineers, and managers must understand where cooperation ends and competitive compromise begins. Finally, as noted earlier, learning from partners is critically important.[30]

The issue of learning deserves special attention. As one team of researchers notes,

> The challenge is to share enough skills to create advantage vis-à-vis companies outside the alliance while preventing a wholesale transfer of core skills to the partner. This is a very thin line to walk. Companies must carefully select what skills and technologies they pass to their partners. They must develop safeguards against unintended, informal transfers of information. The goal is to limit the transparency of their operations.[31]

Alliances with Asian Competitors

Western companies may find themselves at a disadvantage in GSPs with an Asian competitor, especially if the latter's manufacturing skills are the attractive quality. Unfortunately for Western companies, manufacturing excellence represents a multifaceted competence that is not easily transferred. Non-Asian managers and engineers must also learn to be more receptive and attentive—they must overcome the "not-invented-here" syndrome and begin to think of themselves as students, not teachers. At the same time, they must learn to be less eager to show off proprietary lab and engineering successes. To limit transparency, some companies involved in GSPs establish a "collaboration section." Much like a corporate communications department, this department is designed to serve as a gatekeeper through which requests for access to people and information must be channeled. Such gatekeeping serves an important control function in guarding against unintended transfers.

A 1991 report by McKinsey and Company shed additional light on the specific problems of alliances between Western and Japanese firms.[32] Oftentimes, problems between partners have less to do with objective levels of performance than with a feeling of mutual disillusionment and missed opportunity. The study identified four common problem areas in alliances gone wrong. The first problem is that each partner has a "different dream"; the Japanese partner sees itself

[29] Howard V. Perlmutter and David A. Heenan, "Cooperate to Compete Globally," *Harvard Business Review* 64, no. 2 (March–April 1986), p. 137.
[30] Gary Hamel, Yves L. Doz, and C. K. Prahalad, "Collaborate with Your Competitors—and Win," *Harvard Business Review* 67, no. 1 (January–February 1989), pp. 133–139.
[31] Ibid., p. 136.
[32] Kevin K. Jones and Walter E. Schill, "Allying for Advantage," *The McKinsey Quarterly*, no. 3 (1991), pp. 73–101.

emerging from the alliance as a leader in its business or entering new sectors and building a new basis for the future; the Western partner seeks relatively quick and risk-free financial returns. Said one Japanese manager, "Our partner came in looking for a return. They got it. Now they complain that they didn't build a business. But that isn't what they set out to create."

A second area of concern is the balance between partners. Each must contribute to the alliance, and each must depend on the other to a degree that justifies participation in the alliance. The most attractive partner in the short run is likely to be a company that is already established and competent in the business but with the need to master, say, some new technological skills. The best long-term partner, however, is likely to be a less competent player or even one from outside the industry.

Another common cause of problems is "frictional loss" caused by differences in management philosophy, expectations, and approaches. All functions within the alliance may be affected, and performance is likely to suffer as a consequence. Speaking of his Japanese counterpart, a Western businessperson said, "Our partner just wanted to go ahead and invest without considering whether there would be a return or not." The Japanese partner stated that "The foreign partner took so long to decide on obvious points that we were always too slow." Such differences often lead to frustration and time-consuming debates that stifle decision making.

Last, the study found that short-term goals can result in the foreign partner limiting the number of people allocated to the joint venture. Those involved in the venture may perform only 2- or 3-year assignments. The result is "corporate amnesia"; that is, little or no corporate memory is built up on how to compete in Japan. The original goals of the venture will be lost as each new group of managers takes their turn. When taken collectively, these four problems will almost always ensure that the Japanese partner will be the only one in it for the long haul.

CFM International, GE, and Snecma: A Success Story

Commercial Fan Moteur (CFM) International, a partnership between GE's jet engine division and Snecma, a government-owned French aerospace company, is a frequently cited example of a successful GSP. GE was motivated, in part, by the desire to gain access to the European market so it could sell engines to Airbus Industrie; also, the $800 million in development costs was more than GE could risk on its own. While GE focused on system design and high-tech work, the French side handled fans, boosters, and other components. In 2004, the French government sold a 35 percent stake in Snecma; in 2005, Sagem, an electronics maker, acquired Snecma. The new business entity, known as Safran, had more than €13 billion ($18 billion) in 2012 revenues; slightly more than half was generated by the aerospace propulsion unit.

The alliance got off to a strong start because of the personal chemistry between two top executives, GE's Gerhard Neumann and the late General René Ravaud of Snecma. The partnership continues to thrive despite each side's differing views regarding governance, management, and organization. Brian Rowe, senior vice president of GE's engine group, has noted that the French like to bring in senior executives from outside the industry, whereas GE prefers to bring in experienced people from within the organization. Also, the French prefer to approach problem solving with copious amounts of data, and Americans may take a more intuitive approach. Still, senior executives from both sides of the partnership have been delegated substantial responsibility.

Boeing and Japan: A Controversy

In some circles, GSPs have been the target of criticism. Critics warn that employees of a company that becomes reliant on outside suppliers for critical components will lose expertise and experience erosion of their engineering skills. Such criticism is often directed at GSPs involving U.S. and Japanese firms. For example, a proposed alliance between Boeing and a Japanese consortium to build a new fuel-efficient airliner, the 7J7, generated a great deal of controversy. The project's $4 billion price tag was too high for Boeing to shoulder alone. The Japanese were to contribute between $1 billion and $2 billion; in return, they would get a chance to learn manufacturing and marketing techniques from Boeing. Although the 7J7 project was shelved in 1988, a new wide-body aircraft, the 777, was developed with about 20 percent of the work subcontracted out to Mitsubishi, Fuji, and Kawasaki.[33]

---

[33] John Holusha, "Pushing the Envelope at Boeing," *The New York Times* (November 10, 1991), sec. 3, pp. 1, 6.

Critics envision a scenario in which the Japanese use what they learn to build their own aircraft and compete directly with Boeing in the future—a disturbing thought considering that Boeing is a major exporter to world markets. One team of researchers developed a framework outlining the stages that a company can go through as it becomes increasingly dependent on partnerships:[34]

Step 1. Outsourcing of assembly for inexpensive labor

Step 2. Outsourcing of low-value components to reduce product price

Step 3. Growing levels of value-added components move abroad

Step 4. Manufacturing skills, designs, and functionally related technologies move abroad

Step 5. Disciplines related to quality, precision manufacturing, testing, and future avenues of product derivatives move abroad

Step 6. Core skills surrounding components, miniaturization, and complex systems integration move abroad

Step 7. Competitor learns the entire spectrum of skills related to the underlying core competence

Yoshino and Rangan have described the interaction and evolution of the various market-entry strategies in terms of cross-market dependencies.[35] Many firms start with an export-based approach, as described in Chapter 8. For example, the success of Japanese firms in the automobile and consumer electronics industries can be traced back to an export drive. Nissan, Toyota, and Honda initially concentrated production in Japan, thereby achieving economies of scale.

Eventually, an export-driven strategy gives way to an affiliate-based one. The various types of investment strategies—equity stake, investment to establish new operations, acquisitions, and joint ventures—create operational interdependence within the firm. By operating in different markets, firms have the opportunity to transfer production from place to place in response to fluctuating exchange rates, resource costs, or other considerations. Although at some companies foreign affiliates operate as autonomous fiefdoms (the prototypical multinational business with a polycentric orientation), other companies realize the benefits that operational flexibility can bring.

The third and most complex stage in the evolution of a global strategy comes with management's realization that full integration and a network of shared knowledge from different country markets can greatly enhance the firm's overall competitive position. As company personnel opt to pursue increasingly complex strategies, they must simultaneously manage each new interdependency as well as preceding ones. The stages described here are reflected in the evolution of South Korea's Samsung Group, as described in Case 1-3.

International Partnerships in Developing Countries

Central and Eastern Europe, Asia, India, and Mexico offer exciting opportunities for firms that seek to enter gigantic and largely untapped markets. An obvious strategic choice for entering these markets is the strategic alliance. Like the early joint ventures between U.S. and Japanese firms, potential partners will trade market access for know-how. Other entry strategies are also possible; in 1996, for example, Chrysler and BMW agreed to invest $500 million in a joint venture plant in Latin America capable of producing 400,000 small engines annually. Although then–Chrysler Chairman Robert Eaton was skeptical of strategic partnerships, he believed that limited forms of cooperation such as joint ventures make sense in some situations. Eaton said, "The majority of world vehicle sales are in vehicles with engines of less than 2.0 liters, outside of the United States. We have simply not been able to be competitive in those areas because of not having a smaller engine. In the international market, there's no question that in many cases such as this, the economies of scale suggest you really ought to have a partner."[36]

---

[34] David Lei and John W. Slocum, Jr., "Global Strategy, Competence-Building, and Strategic Alliances," *California Management Review* 35, no. 1 (Fall 1992), pp. 81–97.

[35] Michael A. Yoshino and U. Srinivasa Rangan, *Strategic Alliances: An Entrepreneurial Approach to Globalization* (Boston: Harvard Business School Press, 1995), pp. 56–59.

[36] Angelo B. Henderson, "Chrysler and BMW Team Up to Build Small-Engine Plant in South America," *The Wall Street Journal* (October 2, 1996), p. A4.

Assuming that risks can be minimized and problems overcome, joint ventures in the transition economies of Central and Eastern Europe could evolve at a more accelerated pace than past joint ventures with Asian partners. A number of factors combine to make Russia an excellent location for an alliance: It has a well-educated workforce, and quality is very important to Russian consumers. However, several problems are frequently cited in connection with joint ventures in Russia; these include organized crime, supply shortages, and outdated regulatory and legal systems in a constant state of flux. Despite the risks, the number of joint ventures in Russia is growing, particularly in the service and manufacturing sectors. In the early post-Soviet era, most of the manufacturing ventures were limited to assembly work, but higher value-added activities such as component manufacture are now being performed.

A Central European market with interesting potential is Hungary. Hungary already has the most liberal financial and commercial systems in the region. It has also provided investment incentives to Westerners, especially in high-tech industries. Like Russia, this former Communist economy does have its share of problems. Digital's recent joint venture agreement with the Hungarian Research Institute for Physics and the state-supervised computer systems design firm Szamalk is a case in point. Although the venture was formed so Digital would be able to sell and service its equipment in Hungary, the underlying impetus of the venture was to stop the cloning of Digital's computers by Central European firms.

Cooperative Strategies in Asia

As we have seen in earlier chapters, Asian cultures exhibit collectivist social values; cooperation and harmony are highly valued in both personal life and the business world. Therefore, it is not surprising that some of the Asia's biggest companies—including Mitsubishi, Hyundai, and LG—pursue cooperation strategies.

Cooperative Strategies in Japan: *Keiretsu*

Japan's *keiretsu* represent a special category of cooperative strategy. A **keiretsu** is an interbusiness alliance or enterprise group that, in the words of one observer, "resembles a fighting clan in which business families join together to vie for market share."[37] The *keiretsu* were formed in the early 1950s as regroupings of four large conglomerates—*zaibatsu*—that had dominated the Japanese economy until 1945. *Zaibatsu* were dissolved after the U.S. occupational forces introduced antitrust as part of the reconstruction following World War II.

Today, Japan's Fair Trade Commission appears to favor harmony rather than pursuing anticompetitive behavior. As a result, the U.S. Federal Trade Commission has launched several investigations of price fixing, price discrimination, and exclusive supply arrangements. Hitachi, Canon, and other Japanese companies have also been accused of restricting the availability of high-tech products in the U.S. market. The Justice Department has considered prosecuting the U.S. subsidiaries of Japanese companies if the parent company is found guilty of unfair trade practices in the Japanese market.[38]

Keiretsu exist in a broad spectrum of markets, including the capital, primary goods, and component parts markets.[39] *Keiretsu* relationships are often cemented by bank ownership of large blocks of stock and by cross-ownership of stock between a company and its buyers and nonfinancial suppliers. Further, *keiretsu* executives can legally sit on each other's boards, share information, and coordinate prices in closed-door meetings of "presidents' councils." Thus, *keiretsu* are essentially cartels that have the government's blessing. Although not a market-entry strategy per se, *keiretsu* played an integral role in the international success of Japanese companies as they sought new markets.

[37] Robert L. Cutts, "Capitalism in Japan: Cartels and Keiretsu," *Harvard Business Review* 70, no. 4 (July–August 1992), p. 49.

[38] Carla Rappoport, "Why Japan Keeps on Winning," *Fortune* (July 15, 1991), p. 84.

[39] Michael L. Gerlach, "Twilight of the *Keiretsu*? A Critical Assessment," *Journal of Japanese Studies* 18, no. 1 (Winter 1992), p. 79.

→ **MYLAB SYNC/THINK/LEARN: THE CULTURAL CONTEXT**

Will Beer Drinkers Toast SABMiller's Global Strategy?

MyMarketingLab   SYNC • THINK • LEARN

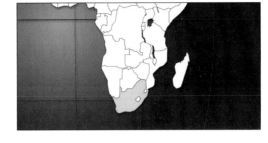

South African Breweries PLC had a problem. The company owned more than 100 breweries in 24 countries. South Africa, where the company had a commanding 98 percent share of the beer market, accounted for about 14 percent of annual revenues (see Exhibit 9-8). However, most of the company's brands, which include Castle Lager, Pilsner Urquell, and Carling Black Label, were sold on a local or regional basis; none had the global status of, say, Heineken, Amstel, or Guinness. Nor were the company's brands well known in the key U.S. market, where a growing number of the "echo boom"—the children of the nation's 75 million baby boomers—were reaching drinking age.

In 2002, a solution presented itself: South African Breweries had an opportunity to buy the Miller Brewing unit from Philip Morris. The $3.6 billion deal created SABMiller, a company that ranks as the world's number 2 brewer in terms of production volume; Anheuser-Busch InBev ranks first. Miller operates nine breweries in the United States, where its flagship brand, Miller Lite, has been losing market share for a number of years. The challenge facing SABMiller is to revitalize the Miller Lite brand in the United States and then launch Miller in Europe as a premium brand.

SABMiller and its competitors are also making strategic investment in China, the world's largest beer market, with $6 billion in annual sales. As Sylvia Mu Yin, an analyst with Euromonitor, noted, "Local brewers are keen to explore strategic alliances with large multinational companies. At the same time, foreign companies are eager to sell to the 1.3 billion Chinese, but lack local knowledge."

Meanwhile, some of SABMiller's local brands are being introduced in the United States. The company hopes to build Pilsner Urquell, the number 1 beer in the Czech Republic, into a national brand in the United States. If that effort succeeds, it can be the foundation for transforming Pilsner Urquell into a global premium brand that rivals Heineken. A pale lager, Pilsner Urquell has been produced at the Prazdroj brewery in Plzen ("Pilsen") since 1842. The brew has benefited from a trend that finds U.S. consumers graduating to craft beers that have stronger hops flavors. SABMiller's marketing program includes training bartenders to fill each draft pour with a thick head of foam.

Meanwhile, SABMiller and its competitors have set their sights on low-income consumers in key emerging markets such as Africa. According to industry forecasts, Africa's beer sector will grow by 5 percent annually; by contrast, beer consumption is shrinking in Europe and North America. The brewers are cutting costs by negotiating deals with local governments to lower taxes on beer sales. The brewers convince officials with a two-pronged argument. First, the low-cost beers use local crops such as sorghum and thus create jobs locally. And second, legal, branded brews from well-known companies are a safer alternative to illegal home brew.

Sources: Paul Sonne, "With West Flat, Big Brewers Peddle Cheap Beer in Africa," *The Wall Street Journal* (March 20, 2013), p. A1; Sean Carney, "Posh Beer Flows in U.S.," *The Wall Street Journal* (October 19, 2010), p. B10; Chris Buckley, "Battle Shaping Up for Chinese Brewery," *The New York Times* (May 6, 2004), pp. W1, W7; Maggie Urry and Adam Jones, "SABMiller Chief Preaches the Lite Fantastic," *Financial Times* (November 21, 2003), p. 22; Dan Bilefsky and Christopher Lawton, "SABMiller Has U.S. Hangover," *The Wall Street Journal* (November 20, 2003), p. B5; Lawton and Bilefsky, "Miller Lite Now: Haste Great, Less Selling," *The Wall Street Journal* (October 4, 2002), pp. B1, B6; Nicol Deglil Innocenti, "Fearless Embracer of Challenge," *Financial Times Special Report—Investing in South Africa* (October 2, 2003), p. 6; David Pringle, "Miller Deal Brings Stability to SAB," *The Wall Street Journal* (May 31, 2002), p. B6; John Willman, "Time for Another Round," *Financial Times* (June 21, 1999), p. 15.

Exhibit 9-8 A few years ago, South African Breweries was a local company that dominated its domestic market. Using joint ventures and acquisitions, the company expanded into the rest of Africa as well as key emerging markets such as China, India, and Central Europe. Today, following the acquisition of Miller, SABMiller is the world's second-largest brewer with a strong presence in the U.S. market.
Source: Bloomberg via Getty Images.

Some observers have disputed charges that *keiretsu* have an impact on market relationships in Japan and claim instead that the groups primarily serve a social function. Others acknowledge the past significance of preferential trading patterns associated with *keiretsu* but assert that the latter's influence is now weakening. Although it is beyond the scope of this chapter to address these issues in detail, there can be no doubt that, for companies competing with Japanese companies or wishing to enter the Japanese market, a general understanding of *keiretsu* is crucial. Imagine, for example, what it would mean in the United States if an automaker (e.g., GM), an electrical products company (e.g., GE), a steelmaker (e.g., USX), and a computer firm (e.g., IBM) were interconnected, rather than separate, firms. Global competition in the era of *keiretsu* means that competition exists not only among products, but among different systems of corporate governance and industrial organization.[40]

As the hypothetical example from the United States suggests, some of Japan's biggest and best-known companies are at the center of *keiretsu*. For example, several large companies with common ties to a bank are at the center of the Mitsui Group and the Mitsubishi Group. These and the Sumitomo, Fuyo, Sanwa, and DKB groups together make up the "big six" *keiretsu* (in Japanese, *roku dai kigyo shudan*, or "six big industrial groups"). The big six strive for a strong position in each major sector of the Japanese economy. Because intragroup relationships often involve shared stock holdings and trading relations, the big six are sometimes known as *horizontal keiretsu*.[41] Annual revenues in each group are in the hundreds of billions of dollars. In absolute terms, *keiretsu* constitute a small percentage of all Japanese companies. However, these alliances can effectively block foreign suppliers from entering the market and result in higher prices to Japanese consumers, while at the same time resulting in corporate stability, risk sharing, and long-term employment.

In addition to the big six, several other *keiretsu* have formed, bringing new configurations to the basic forms previously described. *Vertical* (i.e., supply and distribution) *keiretsu* are hierarchical alliances between manufacturers and retailers. For example, Matsushita controls a chain of National stores in Japan through which it sells its Panasonic, Technics, and Quasar brands. About half of Matsushita's domestic sales are generated through the National chain, 50 to 80 percent of whose inventory consists of Matsushita's brands. Japan's other major consumer electronics manufacturers, including Toshiba and Hitachi, have similar alliances. (Sony's chain of stores is much smaller and weaker by comparison.) All are fierce competitors in the Japanese market.[42]

Another type of manufacturing *keiretsu* consists of vertical hierarchical alliances between automakers and suppliers and component manufacturers. Intergroup operations and systems are closely integrated, with suppliers receiving long-term contracts. Toyota, for example, has a network of about 175 primary and 4,000 secondary suppliers. One supplier is Koito; Toyota owns about one-fifth of Koito's shares and buys about half of its production. The net result of this arrangement is that Toyota produces about 25 percent of the sales value of its cars, compared with 50 percent for GM. Manufacturing *keiretsu* show the gains that, in theory, can result from an optimal balance of supplier and buyer power. Because Toyota buys a given component from several suppliers (some are in the *keiretsu*, some are independent), discipline is imposed down the network. Also, because Toyota's suppliers do not work exclusively for Toyota, they have an incentive to be flexible and adaptable.[43]

The *keiretsu* system ensures that high-quality parts are delivered on a just-in-time basis, a key factor in the high quality for which Japan's auto industry is well known. However, as U.S. and European automakers have closed the quality gap, larger Western parts makers are building economies of scale that enable them to operate at lower costs than small Japanese parts makers. Moreover, the stock holdings that Toyota, Nissan, and others have in their supplier networks tie up capital that could be used for product development and other purposes.

---

[40] Ronald J. Gilson and Mark J. Roe, "Understanding the Japanese Keiretsu: Overlaps Between Corporate Governance and Industrial Organization," *The Yale Law Journal* 102, no. 4 (January 1993), p. 883.

[41] Kenichi Miyashita and David Russell, *Keiretsu: Inside the Hidden Japanese Conglomerates* (New York: McGraw-Hill, 1996), p. 9.

[42] However, the importance of the chain stores is eroding due to increasing sales at mass merchandisers not under the manufacturers' control.

[43] "Japanology, Inc.—Survey," *The Economist* (March 6, 1993), p. 15.

After Renault took a controlling stake in Nissan, for example, a new management team from France headed by Carlos Ghosn began divesting the company's 1,300 *keiretsu* investments. Nissan shifted to an open-source bidding process for parts suppliers, some of which were not based in Japan.[44] Eventually, Honda and Toyota adopted a similar approach and began seeking bids from non-*keiretsu* component suppliers. That, in turn, led to collusion among auto-parts makers that saw an opportunity to set higher prices. Recent antitrust charges brought by the U.S. Department of Justice resulted in fines totaling about $1 billion. Several Japanese auto-parts suppliers admitted that they had collaborated, and the Justice Department alleged that American car buyers paid higher prices for vehicles as a result. Even so, change comes slowly in Japan. As Mitsuhisa Kato, vice president for R&D at Toyota, said, "We feel a duty to protect our *keiretsu*. We are trying to incorporate more outside suppliers, but won't give up on our own way of doing business in Japan."[45]

HOW *KEIRETSU* AFFECT AMERICAN BUSINESS: TWO EXAMPLES Clyde Prestowitz provides the following example to show how *keiretsu* relationships have a potential impact on U.S. businesses. In the early 1980s, Nissan was in the market for a supercomputer to use in car design. Two vendors under consideration were Cray, the worldwide leader in supercomputers at the time, and Hitachi, which had no functional product to offer. When it appeared that the purchase of a Cray computer was pending, Hitachi executives called for solidarity; both Nissan and Hitachi are members of the same big six *keiretsu*, the Fuyo group. Hitachi essentially mandated that Nissan show preference to Hitachi, a situation that rankled U.S. trade officials. Meanwhile, a coalition within Nissan was pushing for a Cray computer; ultimately, thanks to U.S. pressure on both Nissan and the Japanese government, the business went to Cray.

Prestowitz describes the Japanese attitude toward this type of business practice:[46]

It respects mutual obligation by providing a cushion against shocks. Today Nissan may buy a Hitachi computer. Tomorrow it may ask Hitachi to take some of its redundant workers. The slightly lesser performance it may get from the Hitachi computer is balanced against the broader considerations. Moreover, because the decision to buy Hitachi would be a favor, it would bind Hitachi closer and guarantee slavish service and future Hitachi loyalty to Nissan products.... This attitude of sticking together is what the Japanese mean by the long-term view; it is what enables them to withstand shocks and to survive over the long term.[47]

Because *keiretsu* relationships are crossing the Pacific and directly affecting the American market, U.S. companies have reason to be concerned with *keiretsu* outside the Japanese market as well. According to data compiled by Dodwell Marketing Consultants, in California alone *keiretsu* own more than half of the Japanese-affiliated manufacturing facilities. But the impact of *keiretsu* extends beyond the West Coast. Illinois-based Tenneco Automotive, a maker of shock absorbers and exhaust systems, does a great deal of worldwide business with the Toyota *keiretsu*. In 1990, however, Mazda dropped Tenneco as a supplier to its U.S. plant in Kentucky. Part of the business was shifted to Tokico Manufacturing, a Japanese transplant and a member of the Mazda *keiretsu*; a non-*keiretsu* Japanese company, KYB Industries, was also made a vendor. A Japanese auto executive explained the rationale behind the change: "First choice is a *keiretsu* company, second choice is a Japanese supplier, third is a local company."[48]

[44] Norihiko Shirouzu, "U-Turn: A Revival at Nissan Shows There's Hope for Ailing Japan Inc.," *The Wall Street Journal* (November 16, 2000), pp. A1, A10.

[45] Chester Dawson and Brent Kendall, "Japan Probe Pops Car-Part Keiretsu," *The Wall Street Journal* (February 16–17, 2013), pp. B1, B4.

[46] For years, Prestowitz has argued that Japan's industry structure—*keiretsu* included—gives its companies unfair advantages. A more moderate view might be that any business decision must have an economic justification. Thus, a moderate would caution against overstating the effect of *keiretsu*.

[47] Clyde Prestowitz, *Trading Places: How We Are Giving Our Future to Japan and How to Reclaim It* (New York: Basic Books, 1989), pp. 299–300.

[48] Carla Rappoport, "Why Japan Keeps on Winning," *Fortune* (July 15, 1991), p. 84.

Cooperative Strategies in South Korea: *Chaebol*

South Korea has its own type of corporate alliance groups, known as *chaebol*. Like the Japanese *keiretsu*, **chaebol** are composed of dozens of companies that are centered on a central bank or holding company and dominated by a founding family. However, *chaebol* are a more recent phenomenon; in the early 1960s, Korea's military dictator granted government subsidies and export credits to a select group of companies in the auto, shipbuilding, steel, and electronics sectors. In the 1950s, for example, Samsung was best known as a woolen mill. By the 1980s, Samsung had evolved into a leading producer of low-cost consumer electronics products. Today, Samsung Electronics' Android-powered Galaxy S smartphone is a worldwide best seller.

The *chaebol* were a driving force behind South Korea's economic miracle; GNP increased from $1.9 billion in 1960 to $238 billion in 1990. After the economic crisis of 1997–1998, however, South Korean President Kim Dae Jung pressured *chaebol* leaders to initiate reform. Prior to the crisis, the *chaebol* had become bloated and heavily in debt; today, having improved corporate governance, changed their corporate cultures, and reduced debt loads, the *chaebol* are being transformed. For example, Samsung is diversifying into pharmaceuticals and green energy, and LG Electronics is moving into wastewater treatment. Samsung, LG, Hyundai, and other *chaebol* are building their brands by developing high-value-added branded products supported by sophisticated advertising.[49]

Twenty-First-Century Cooperative Strategies

One U.S. technology alliance, Sematech, is unique in that it is the direct result of government industrial policy. The U.S. government, concerned that key companies in the domestic semiconductor industry were having difficulty competing with Japan, agreed to subsidize a consortium of 14 technology companies beginning in 1987. Sematech originally had 700 employees, some permanent and some on loan from IBM, AT&T, Advanced Micro Devices, Intel, and other companies. The task facing the consortium was to save the U.S. chip-making equipment industry, whose manufacturers were rapidly losing market share in the face of intense competition from Japan. Although initially plagued by attitudinal and cultural differences among different factions, Sematech eventually helped chip makers try new approaches with their equipment vendors. By 1991, the Sematech initiative, along with other factors such as the economic downturn in Japan, reversed the market share slide of the semiconductor equipment industry.

Sematech's creation heralded a new era in cooperation among technology companies. As the company has expanded internationally, its membership roster has expanded to include Advanced Micro Devices, Hewlett-Packard, IBM, Infineon, Intel, Panasonic, Qualcomm, Samsung, and STMicroelectronics. Companies in a variety of industries are pursuing similar types of alliances.

The "relationship enterprise" is another possible stage of evolution of the strategic alliance. In a relationship enterprise, groupings of firms in different industries and countries are held together by common goals that encourage them to act as a single firm. Cyrus Freidheim, former vice chairman of the Booz Allen Hamilton consulting firm, outlined an alliance that, in his opinion, might be representative of an early relationship enterprise. He suggests that within the next few decades, Boeing, British Airways, Siemens, TNT, and Snecma might jointly build several new airports in China. As part of the package, British Airways and TNT would be granted preferential routes and landing slots, the Chinese government would contract to buy all its aircraft from Boeing/Snecma, and Siemens would provide air traffic control systems for all 10 airports.[50]

More than the simple strategic alliances we know today, relationship enterprises will be super-alliances among global giants, with revenues approaching $1 trillion. They would be able to draw on extensive cash resources; circumvent antitrust barriers; and, with home bases in all major markets, enjoy the political advantage of being a "local" firm almost anywhere. This type of alliance is not driven simply by technological change but by the political necessity of having multiple home bases.

---

[49] Christian Oliver and Song Jung-A, "Evolution Is Crucial to Chaebol Survival," *Financial Times* (June 3, 2011), p. 16.
[50] "The Global Firm: R.I.P.," *The Economist* (February 6, 1993), p. 69.

Another perspective on the future of cooperative strategies envisions the emergence of the "virtual corporation." As described in a *BusinessWeek* cover story, the virtual corporation "will seem to be a single entity with vast capabilities but will really be the result of numerous collaborations assembled only when they're needed."[51] On a global level, the virtual corporation could combine the twin competencies of cost-effectiveness and responsiveness; thus, it could pursue the "think globally, act locally" philosophy with ease. This reflects the trend toward "mass customization." The same forces that are driving the formation of the digital *keiretsu*—high-speed communication networks, for example—are embodied in the virtual corporation. As noted by William Davidow and Michael Malone in their book *The Virtual Corporation*, "The success of a virtual corporation will depend on its ability to gather and integrate a massive flow of information throughout its organizational components and intelligently act upon that information."[52]

Why did the virtual corporation burst onto the scene in the early 1990s? Previously, firms lacked the technology to facilitate this type of data management. Today's distributed databases, networks, and open systems make possible the kinds of data flow required for the virtual corporation. In particular, these data flows permit superior supply-chain management. Ford provides an interesting example of how technology is improving information flows among the far-flung operations of a single company. Ford's $6 billion "world car"—known as the Mercury Mystique and Ford Contour in the United States and the Mondeo in Europe—was developed using an international communications network linking computer workstations of designers and engineers on three continents.[53]

Market Expansion Strategies

Companies must decide whether to expand by seeking new markets in existing countries or, alternatively, by seeking new country markets for already identified and served market segments.[54] These two dimensions in combination produce four **market expansion strategy** options, as shown in Table 9-6. Strategy 1, **country and market concentration**, involves targeting a limited number of customer segments in a few countries. This is typically a starting point for most companies. It matches company resources and market investment needs. Unless a company is large and endowed with ample resources, this strategy may be the only realistic way to begin.

In strategy 2, **country concentration and market diversification**, a company serves many markets in a few countries. This strategy was implemented by many European companies that remained in Europe and sought growth by expanding into new markets. It is also the approach of the American companies that decide to diversify in the U.S. market as opposed to going international with existing products or creating new, global products. According to the U.S. Department of Commerce, the majority of U.S. companies that export limit their sales to five or fewer markets. This means that U.S. companies typically pursue strategy 1 or 2.

TABLE 9-6 Market Expansion Strategies

		MARKET	
		Concentration	Diversification
COUNTRY	**Concentration**	1. Narrow Focus	2. Country Focus
	Diversification	3. Country Diversification	4. Global Diversification

---

[51] John Byrne, "The Virtual Corporation," *BusinessWeek* (February 8, 1993), p. 103.
[52] William Davidow and Michael Malone, *The Virtual Corporation: Structuring and Revitalizing the Corporation for the 21st Century* (New York: HarperBusiness, 1993), p. 59.
[53] Julie Edelson Halpert, "One Car, Worldwide, with Strings Pulled from Michigan," *The New York Times* (August 29, 1993), sec. 3, p. 7.
[54] This section draws on I. Ayal and J. Zif, "Market Expansion Strategies in Multinational Marketing," *Journal of Marketing* 43 (Spring 1979), pp. 84–94; and "Competitive Market Choice Strategies in Multinational Marketing," *Columbia Journal of World Business* (Fall 1978), pp. 72–81.

Strategy 3, **country diversification and market concentration**, is the classic global strategy whereby a company seeks out the world market for a product. The appeal of this strategy is that by serving the world customer, a company can achieve a greater accumulated volume and lower costs than any competitor and therefore have an unassailable competitive advantage. This is the strategy of the well-managed business that serves a distinct need and customer category.

Strategy 4, **country and market diversification**, is the corporate strategy of a global, multibusiness company such as Matsushita. Overall, Matsushita is multicountry in scope, and its various business units and groups serve multiple segments. Thus, at the level of corporate strategy, Matsushita may be said to be pursuing strategy 4. At the operating business level, however, managers of individual units must focus on the needs of the world customer in their particular global market. In Table 9-6, this is strategy 3—country diversification and market concentration. An increasing number of companies all over the world are beginning to see the importance of market share not only in the home or domestic market but also in the world market. Success in overseas markets can boost a company's total volume and lower its cost position.

Summary

Companies that wish to move beyond exporting and importing can avail themselves of a wide range of alternative **market-entry strategies**. Each alternative has distinct advantages and disadvantages associated with it; the alternatives can be ranked on a continuum representing increasing levels of investment, commitment, and risk. **Licensing** can generate revenue flow with little new investment; it can be a good choice for a company that possesses advanced technology, a strong brand image, or valuable intellectual property. **Contract manufacturing** and **franchising** are two specialized forms of licensing that are widely used in global marketing.

A higher level of involvement outside the home country may involve **foreign direct investment (FDI)**. This can take many forms. **Joint ventures** offer two or more companies the opportunity to share risk and combine value chain strengths. Companies considering joint ventures must plan carefully and communicate with partners to avoid "divorce." FDI can also be used to establish company operations outside the home country through **greenfield investment**, acquisition of a minority or majority **equity stake** in a foreign business, or **full ownership** of an existing business entity through merger or outright acquisition.

Cooperative alliances known as **strategic alliances**, **strategic international alliances**, and **global strategic partnerships (GSPs)** represent an important market-entry strategy in the twenty-first century. GSPs are ambitious, reciprocal, cross-border alliances that may involve business partners in a number of different country markets. GSPs are particularly well suited to emerging markets in Central and Eastern Europe, Asia, and Latin America. Western businesspeople should also be aware of two special forms of cooperation found in Asia, namely, Japan's *keiretsu* and South Korea's *chaebol*.

To assist managers in thinking through the various alternatives, **market expansion strategies** can be represented in matrix form: **country and market concentration**, **country concentration and market diversification**, **country diversification and market concentration**, and **country and market diversification**. The preferred expansion strategy will be a reflection of a company's stage of development (i.e., whether it is international, multinational, global, or transnational). The stage 5 transnational combines the strengths of the prior three stages into an integrated network to leverage worldwide learning.

MyMarketingLab

9-1. What is meant by the phrase *global strategic partnership*? Discuss how this form of market-entry strategy differs from more traditional forms such as joint ventures.

9-2. Which strategic options for market entry or expansion would a small company be likely to pursue? A large company?

9-3. Mymarketinglab Only – comprehensive writing assignment for this chapter.

MyMarketingLab

Go to **mymktlab.com** to complete the problems marked with this icon .

Discussion Questions

 9-4. What are the advantages and disadvantages of using licensing as a market-entry tool? Give examples of companies from different countries that use licensing as a global marketing strategy.

9-5. The president of XYZ Manufacturing Company of Buffalo, New York, comes to you with a license offer from a company in Osaka. In return for sharing the company's patents and know-how, the Japanese company will pay a license fee of 5 percent of the ex-factory price of all products sold based on the U.S. company's license. The president wants your advice. What would you tell him?

9-6. What is foreign direct investment (FDI)? What forms can FDI take?

9-7. What are *keiretsu*? How does this form of industrial structure affect companies that compete with Japan or that are trying to enter the Japanese market?

CASE 9-1   **CONTINUED (REFER TO PAGE 284)**

Mo'men Launches Franchises in UAE

As discussed at the beginning of the chapter, Mo'men found success in its joint venture with the Al Islami Group in the UAE while developing a franchise network. Darul Rahmat Sdn Bhd (DRSB) was appointed the franchisee that managed and operated the Mo'men restaurants in Malaysia by the Mo'men Group (franchisor).

One of the advantages that Mo'men enjoyed was its religious inclination towards Islam. Egypt, the birthplace of the brand, is primarily an Islamic country, and since Malaysia also boasts of a significant percentage of followers of the Islamic faith, Mo'men found it easier to establish trust with the Malaysian consumers.

Mo'men offers a wide variety of sandwiches made with seafood, beef, and chicken in its extensive range of food items. Keen to abide by Islamic dietary rules, the brand has made sure not to serve pork in any of its branches worldwide and only serves halal foods.

Mo'men distinguishes itself from other fast food restaurants by offering unique products and excellent service. It provides a wide range of sandwiches to choose from that are tasty and affordable. Malaysia has various ethnicities, and its cuisine has been heavily influenced by a number of different cultures. Many different types of restaurants can be found in Malaysia, and Malaysian consumers are very accepting of new restaurant concepts and foods. However, adapting to cultural preferences is crucial, and an important ingredient in Malaysian cuisine is rice. Rice is a staple food in Malaysia, as well as in most countries in the region. The type of rice eaten in Malaysia tends to be a local variety or fragrant rice from Thailand. Sometimes, basmati and Japanese short-grain rice are consumed. Mo'men took these preferences into consideration and added a rice menu with a choice of lamb or chicken.

Seafood is another important component of Malay cuisine, and Mo'men's original restaurants in Egypt featured a shrimp sandwich. Mo'men's expertise in offering seafood sandwiches in Egypt might have given it an edge over competitors as it entered the Malaysian market.

Because the number of venues is currently small, Mo'men Malaysia offers a limited delivery service in order to reach more customers. Mo'men Malaysia also uses various promotions, loyalty cards, and discount cards, for example, offering 10 percent discounts to students who show their student ID card. Malaysian consumers seem to love Mo'men. One customer even expressed a wish for Mo'men to open in Indonesia.

The Mo'men restaurant chain is expanding globally and is doing its best to adapt its menus to the cultural taste of each country. A franchising strategy helps Mo'men Group get inside information on a country's food preferences and learn from previous experiences in the market.

Exhibit 9-9 Mo'men sandwiches have gained immense popularity in a very short time, with the chain rapidly spreading to the Middle East, North Africa and parts of Southeast Asia.

Source: stevem/Fotolia

Discussion Questions

9-8. What do you think sets Mo'men apart from the other fast food restaurants?

9-9. Do you believe that Mo'men Group's franchising strategy is the best way to expand internationally?

9-10. Is having a rice menu in the Malaysia franchises a good decision?

9-11. In the long run, who is more likely to garner the most market share in Malaysia—local restaurants, or will Mo'men be able to succeed and build a powerful brand? Give reasons for your answer.

Sources: This case was prepared by Dr. Hamed M. Shamma and Yosra Sourour, School of Business, The American University in Cairo, Egypt.

Additional Sources: "Mo'men (Egypt) Launches Franchise in UAE," *World Franchise Associations* (October 19, 2009); "Al Islami Foods Launches Mo'men Chain of Restaurant in UAE," *AMEInfo.com* (October 14, 2009); "Al Islami Foods Signs AED 80 Million Joint Venture with Mo'men Group of Egypt," *AMEInfo.com* (May 10, 2007); Mo'men Egypt, momen.co/egypt.html (accessed December 16, 2011); Mo'men Malaysia, momenmalaysia.wordpress.com/our-product/ (accessed December 16, 2011); Mo'men Malaysia Facebook page, www.facebook.com/momen.malaysia (accessed December 16, 2011).

CASE 9-2
Jaguar's Passage to India

In 2008, Tata Motors paid the Ford Motor Company $2.3 billion for UK-based automakers Land Rover and Jaguar. The deal came about as Detroit's automakers faced one of the worst business environments in decades. The Big Three posted losses in the billions of dollars; by 2008, with the global recession and credit crunch causing a sharp decline in demand, executives from GM and Chrysler appealed to Washington for a bailout. Meanwhile industry observers called for Ford to shed some of its luxury brands.

When Ford acquired Jaguar in 1989, the American company lacked a high-end luxury model. Executives were betting that they could leverage an exclusive nameplate by launching a new, less expensive line of Jaguar and selling it to more people. The challenge was to execute this strategy without diminishing Jaguar's reputation. Daniel Jones, a professor at the University of Cardiff and an auto industry expert, noted that the Ford name is synonymous with "bread and butter" cars. Meanwhile, Ford's Japanese competitors, including Honda, Nissan, and Toyota, pursued a different strategy: They launched new nameplates and upgraded their dealer organizations. Status- and quality-conscious car buyers embraced Lexus, Infiniti, and other new luxury sedans that offer high performance and outstanding dealer organizations.

Despite Jaguar's classy image and distinguished racing heritage, the cars were also legendary for their unreliability. Gears sometimes wouldn't shift, headlights wouldn't light, and the brakes sometimes caught fire. Part of the problem could be traced to manufacturing. To remedy the situation, Ford invested heavily to update and upgrade Jaguar's plant facilities and improve productivity. As a benchmark, Ford's manufacturing experts knew that German luxury carmakers could build a vehicle in 80 hours; in Japan, the figure was 20 hours. If Jaguar were ever to achieve world-class status, Jaguar's assembly time of 110 hours per car had to be drastically reduced.

As the 1990s came to an end, Jaguar introduced several new vehicles. In 1997, amid industry estimates that Ford's cumulative investment had reached $6 billion, Jaguar launched the $64,900 XK8 coupe and roadster. Styling cues clearly identified this model as the successor to Jaguar's legendary XK-E, or E-Type. In the spring of 1999, the S-Type sedan was introduced to widespread acclaim. One observer called the S-Type a "handsome car, instantly recognizable as a Jaguar, yet totally contemporary." In 2001, the long-awaited "baby Jaguar," the $30,000 X-Type compact sports sedan, was unveiled. Company executives hoped to attract a new generation of drivers and capture a significant share of the entry-level luxury market dominated by the BMW 3-series and the Mercedes C-Class. The X-Type was built on the same platform as the Ford Contour.

The early signs were positive. In 2002, first-year sales of the X-Type boosted Jaguar's worldwide sales to a record 130,000 vehicles, a 29 percent increase. Unfortunately, the company was not able to sustain the momentum. A backlash began to develop. For example, critics of the X-Type derided it as a "warmed-over Ford." Critics also found fault with Ford for failing to move Jaguar's styling forward enough. As one longtime Jaguar owner explained, "They lost their way in what the public wanted. Instead of making Jaguar a niche player, where it should be, they tried to go the mass-production route." In 2005, bowing to pressures to move the venerable nameplate upmarket again, it was announced that the least expensive Jaguar model, the 2.5 liter X-Type, would be discontinued. In 2008, the curtain came down on Jaguar's two decades under American ownership.

Jaguar Land Rover's new owner, Tata Motors, faced challenges of its own. The global economic crisis led to a slump in demand for cars in

Exhibit 9-10 *The Wall Street Journal* auto critic Dan Neill praised the XJ's massiveness, width, and stance. "From a low side angle this thing is a torpedo, a hollow-point bullet scattering shards of moonbeams, a blunt hypodermic of adrenaline," he writes. "It's completely bad-ass."
Source: image stock & people / Newscom.

India; in fact, in its first year of ownership, Tata Motors lost $500 million on Jaguar Land Rover. Then, as the global economy began to rebound, so did sales of luxury cars. Jaguar's XF and XJ sedans won rave reviews from auto critics; two decades of restructuring under Ford were finally paying off. Company forecasts call for 300,000 units of combined Land Rover and Jaguar sales within a few years, up from 250,000 today. As John Edwards, brand director for Land Rover, noted, "Ford laid out a good foundation for us, but I think we are more nimble." For its part, Ford management isn't second-guessing its decision to sell the Jaguar and Land Rover brands. As Lewis Booth, Ford's CFO, explained, "We didn't have enough capital resources to look after them. But we found an owner that had the resources to continue what we started."

Discussion Questions

9-12. Do you think Jaguar and Land Rover will prosper under the ownership of Tata Motors?

9-13. What do you think are the biggest challenges facing the Jaguar and Land Rover in the next few years?

9-14. Tata Motors recently introduced the Nano, the world's least-expensive car. The Nano fits Tata's strategic goal of building a low-cost car for the Indian market. Can Tata succeed in targeting both the very low end of the auto market as well as the high end?

Sources: Vikas Bajaj, "Burnishing British Brands," *The New York Times* (August 31, 2012), pp. B1, B4; Vanessa Fuhrmans, "Cast-Off Car Brands Find a Road Back," *The Wall Street Journal* (April 6, 2011), pp. B1, B5; Bill Neill, "Jaguar XJ: The Hottest Cat on the Road," *The Wall Street Journal* (April 30, 2010), p. B8; Sharon Silke Carty, "Ford Plans to Park Jaguar, Land Rover with Tata Motors," *USA Today* (March 26, 2008), pp. 1B, 2B; Gordon Fairclough, "Bill Ford Jr.: For Auto Makers, China Is the New Frontier," *The Wall Street Journal* (October 27, 2006), p. B5; James Mackintosh, "Ford's Luxury Unit Hits Problems," *Financial Times* (October 24, 2006), p. 23; Silke Carty, "Will Ford Make the Big Leap?" *USA Today* (August 31, 2006), pp. 1B, 2B; Mackintosh, "Jaguar Still Aiming to Claw Back Market Share," *Financial Times* (July 20, 2006), p. 14; "Reinventing a '60s Classic," *The Wall Street Journal* (May 5, 2006), p. W9; James R. Healy, "Cheapest Jags Get Kicked to the Curb," *USA Today* (March 29, 2005), p. 1B; Danny Hakim, "Restoring the Heart of Ford," *The New York Times* (November 14, 2001), pp. C1, C6.

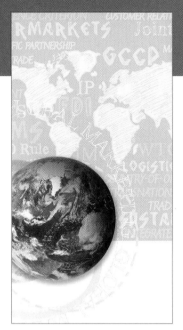

10
Brand and Product Decisions in Global Marketing

CASE 10-1
The Beatles Story, Liverpool

Exhibit 10-1 The Beatles Story is a museum with a permanent exhibition of artifacts, memorabilia, and collector's items from the lives of the Fab Four in their hometown of Liverpool. With other special exhibitions and learning-oriented programs, the place receives a crowd of 300,000 annually.
Source: Tutti Frutti/Shutterstock

The global music business is a major industry; annual global sales of recorded music are valued at over $15 billion. Worldwide interest in legendary artists such as Elvis Presley and the Beatles has also led to growth in music-based visitor attractions and music tourism in the United States and the United Kingdom, two countries that are strongly associated with the music and entertainment industries. Elvis Presley's home, the Graceland Mansion in Memphis, Tennessee, attracts over 600,000

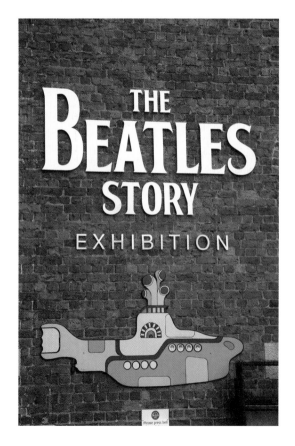

visitors each year. The Beatles Story, Liverpool tells the story of the band from its early days through the height of Beatlemania and attracts large numbers of visitors from all over the world. Fans also visit locations made famous by album covers, such as the iconic crosswalk featured on the album cover of the Beatles' "Abbey Road" album. These consumers are buying into world famous music brands; they are buying the songs, the experience, and the merchandise; and, in the case of the Beatles and Elvis, they are buying into musical and cultural memories shared by millions of music fans worldwide.

The growth and success of the global music industry illustrates the point that products are the most important part of a company's marketing offering. It is the product, the brand, its packaging, and the services supplied with the product that together meet the needs of the consumer and offer the unique added value that the consumer is willing to pay for. In Part 3, we studied the topics that directly affect product decisions when an organization is formulating a marketing strategy for global markets. Global marketing research information guides the development of products suitable for international markets. The market must be segmented and the global consumer's profile understood so that appropriate product positioning can be developed. Global marketers also have to make appropriate market entry and distribution decisions to ensure that their product is fully available to the consumer. As we will see in Part 4, every element of the global marketing mix must support and fit with the product. This chapter examines the main aspects of global product and brand decisions. We begin with a review of product and brand concepts, followed by a discussion of how products can be adapted to meet the needs of international markets. The guidelines for global brand leadership are discussed and attitudes towards foreign products are explored. Finally the strategic alternatives in global marketing are identified and new product development processes are discussed. Once you have read the chapter, turn to Case 10-1 at the end of the chapter to learn more about the branding and marketing of the Beatles Story, Liverpool.

LEARNING OBJECTIVES

1 Review the basic product concepts that underlie a successful global marketing product strategy.

2 Compare and contrast local products and brands, international products and brands, and global products and brands.

3 Explain how Maslow's needs hierarchy helps global marketers understand the benefits sought by buyers in different parts of the world.

4 Outline the importance of "country of origin" as a brand element.

5 List the five strategic alternatives that marketers can utilize during the global product planning process.

6 Explain the new-product continuum and compare and contrast the different types of innovation.

Basic Product Concepts

The product *P* of the marketing mix is at the heart of the challenges and opportunities facing global companies today: Management must develop product and brand policies and strategies that are sensitive to market needs, competition, and the company's ambitions and resources on a global scale. Effective global marketing often entails finding a balance between the payoff from extensively adapting products and brands to local market preferences and the benefits that come from concentrating company resources on relatively standardized global products and brands.

A **product** is a good, service, or idea with both tangible and intangible attributes that collectively create value for a buyer or user. A product's *tangible* attributes can be assessed in physical terms, such as weight, dimensions, or materials used. Consider, for example, a flat-panel TV with an LCD screen that measures 42 inches across. The unit weighs 22 pounds, is 3 inches deep, features four high-definition media interface (HDMI) connections, has a built-in tuner capable of receiving high-definition TV signals over the air, and delivers a screen resolution of 1080p with a 120 Hz screen-refresh rate. These tangible, physical features and attributes translate into benefits that enhance the enjoyment of watching HDTV broadcasts and DVD movies. Accessories such as wall mounts and floor stands enhance the value offering by enabling great flexibility in placing the set in a living room or home theater. *Intangible* product attributes, including the status associated with product ownership, a manufacturer's service commitment, and a brand's overall reputation or mystique, are also important. When shopping for a new TV, for example, many people want "the best": They want a TV loaded with features (tangible product elements), as well as one that is "cool" and makes a status statement (intangible product element).

Product Types

A frequently used framework for classifying products distinguishes between consumer and industrial goods. For example, Samsung offers products and services to both consumers and businesses worldwide. Consumer and industrial goods, in turn, can be further classified on the basis of criteria such as buyer orientation. Buyer orientation is a composite measure of the amount of effort a customer expends, the level of risk associated with a purchase, and buyer involvement in the purchase. The buyer orientation framework includes such categories as convenience, preference, shopping, and specialty goods. Electronics products are often high-involvement purchases, and many shoppers will compare several brands before making a decision. Products can also be categorized in terms of their life span (durable, nondurable, and disposable). Samsung and other electronics companies market products that are meant to last for many years; in other words, they are durable goods. As these examples from the electronics industry suggest, traditional product classification frameworks are fully applicable to global marketing.

Product Warranties

A warranty can be an important element of a product's value proposition. An **express warranty** is a written guarantee that assures the buyer that he or she is getting what he or she has paid for or that provides recourse in case a product's performance falls short of expectations. In global marketing, warranties can be used as a competitive tool to position a company in a positive way. For example, in the late 1990s Hyundai Motor America chief executive Finbarr O'Neill realized that many American car buyers perceived Korean cars as "cheap" and were skeptical about the Hyundai nameplate's reliability. The company had made significant improvements in the quality and reliability of its vehicles, but consumer perceptions of the brand had not kept pace with the changes. O'Neill instituted a 10-year, 100,000-mile warranty program that represents the most comprehensive coverage in the auto industry. Concurrently, Hyundai launched several new vehicles and increased expenditures for advertising. The results have been impressive: Hyundai's U.S. sales jumped from about 90,000 vehicles in 1998 to more than 500,000 vehicles in 2011. Hyundai has also overtaken Toyota as Europe's best-selling Asian car brand.

Packaging

Oftentimes, packaging is an integral element of product-related decisions. Packaging is an especially important consideration for products that are shipped to markets in far-flung corners of the world. The term *consumer packaged goods* applies to a wide variety of products whose packaging is designed to protect or contain the product during shipping, at retail locations, and at the point of use or consumption. "Eco-packaging" is a key issue today, and package designers must address environmental issues such as recycling, biodegradability, and sustainable forestry.

Packaging also serves important communication functions: Packages (and the labels attached to them) offer communication cues that provide consumers with a basis for making a purchase decision. Today, many industry experts agree that packaging must engage the senses, make an emotional connection, and enhance a consumer's brand experience. According to Bernd Schmitt, director of Columbia University's Center on Global Brand Leadership, "Packages are creating an experience for the customer that goes beyond the functional benefits of displaying and protecting the object."[1] Absolut Vodka, Altoids breath mints, and Godiva chocolates are a few examples of brands whose value proposition includes "experiential packaging."

Brewers, soft drink marketers, distillers, and other beverage firms typically devote considerable thought to ensuring that packages speak to consumers or provide some kind of benefit beyond simply holding liquid. For example, a critical element in the success of Corona Extra beer in export markets was management's decision to retain the traditional package design,

---

[1] Queena Sook Kim, "The Potion's Power Is in Its Packaging," *The Wall Street Journal* (December 21, 2000), p. B12.

which consists of a tall transparent bottle with "Made in Mexico" etched directly on the glass. At the time, the conventional wisdom in the brewing industry was that export beer bottles should be short, green or brown in color, and have paper labels. In other words, the bottle should resemble Heineken's! The fact that consumers could see the beer inside the Corona Extra bottle made it seem more pure and natural. Today, Corona is the top-selling imported beer brand in the United States, Australia, Belgium, the Czech Republic, and several other countries.[2]

Coca-Cola's distinctive (and trademarked) contour bottle comes in both glass and plastic versions and helps consumers seek out the "real thing." The bottle design dates back to 1916, and was intended to differentiate Coke from other soft drinks. The design is so distinctive that a consumer could even use his or her sense of touch to identify the bottle in the dark! The Coke example also illustrates the point that packaging strategies can vary by country and region. In North America, where large refrigerators are found in many households, one of Coca-Cola's packaging innovations is the Fridge Pack, a long, slender carton that holds the equivalent of 12 cans of soda. The Fridge Pack fits on a refrigerator's lower shelf and includes a tab for easy dispensing. In Latin America, by contrast, Coca-Cola executives intend to boost profitability by offering Coke in several different-sized bottles. Until recently, for example, 75 percent of Coke's volume in Argentina was accounted for by 2-liter bottles priced at $0.45 each. Coke has also introduced cold, individual-serving bottles priced at $0.33 that are stocked in stores near the front; unchilled, 1.25-liter returnable glass bottles priced at $0.28 are available on shelves farther back in the store.[3] Other innovation examples include the following:

- Grey Goose, the world's top-selling super-premium vodka brand, is the brainchild of the late Sidney Frank. The owner of an importing business in New Rochelle, New York, Frank first devised the bottle design and name. Only then did he approach a distiller in Cognac, France, to create the actual vodka.[4]
- Nestlé's worldwide network of packaging teams contribute packaging improvement suggestions on a quarterly basis. Implemented changes include a plastic lid to make ice cream containers easier to open; slightly deeper indentations in the flat end of candy wrappers in Brazil that make them easier to rip open; and deeper notches on single-serve packets of Nescafé in China. Nestlé also asked suppliers to find a type of glue to make the clicking sound louder when consumers snap open a tube of Smarties brand chocolate candies.[5]
- When GlaxoSmithKline launched Aquafresh Ultimate in Europe, the marketing and design team wanted to differentiate the brand from category leader Colgate Total. Most tube toothpaste is sold in cardboard cartons that are stocked horizontally on store shelves. The team designed the Aquafresh Ultimate tube to stand up vertically. The tubes are distributed to stores in shelf-ready trays, and the box-free packaging saves hundreds of tons of paper each year.[6]

Labeling

One hallmark of the modern global marketplace is the abundance of multilanguage labeling that appears on many products. In today's self-service retail environments, product labels may be designed to attract attention, to support a product's positioning, and to help persuade consumers to buy. Labels can also provide consumers with various types of information. Obviously, care must be taken that all ingredient information and use and care instructions are properly translated. The content of product labels may also be dictated by country- or region-specific regulations. Regulations regarding mandatory label content vary in different parts of the world; for example, the EU now requires mandatory labeling for some foods containing genetically modified ingredients.

Regulators in Australia, New Zealand, Japan, Russia, and several other countries have also proposed similar legislation. In the United States, the Nutrition Education and Labeling Act that

[2] Sara Silver, "Modelo Puts Corona in the Big Beer League," *Financial Times* (October 30, 2002), p. 26.
[3] Betsy McKay, "Coke's Heyer Finds Test in Latin America," *The Wall Street Journal* (October 15, 2002), p. B4.
[4] Christina Passariello, "France's Cognac Region Gives Vodka a Shot," *The Wall Street Journal* (October 20, 2004), p. B1.
[5] Deborah Ball, "The Perils of Packaging: Nestlé Aims for Easier Openings," *The Wall Street Journal* (November 17, 2005), p. B1.
[6] Clare Dowdy, "GlaxoSmithKline's New Toothpaste," *Financial Times* (August 11, 2011), p. 8.

went into effect in the early 1990s was intended to make food labels more informative and easier to understand. Today, virtually all food products sold in the United States must present, in a standard format, information regarding nutrition (e.g., calories and fat content) and serving size. The use of certain terms such as *light* and *natural* is also restricted. Other examples of labeling in global marketing include the following:

- Mandatory health warnings on tobacco products are required in most countries.
- The American Automobile Labeling Act clarifies the country of origin, the final assembly point, and the percentages of the major sources of foreign content of every car, truck, and minivan sold in the United States (effective since October 1, 1994).
- Responding to pressure from consumer groups, in 2006 McDonald's began posting nutrition information on all food packaging and wrappers in approximately 20,000 restaurants in key markets worldwide. Executives indicated that issues pertaining to language and nutritional testing would delay labeling in 10,000 additional restaurants in smaller country markets.[7]
- Nestlé introduced Nan, an infant-formula brand that is popular in Latin America, in the American market. Targeted at Hispanic mothers, Nan's instructions are printed in Spanish on the front of the can. Other brands have English-language labeling on the outside; Spanish-language instructions are printed on the reverse side.[8]
- In 2008, the United States enacted a country-of-origin labeling (COOL) law. The law requires supermarkets and other food retailers to display information that identifies the country that meat, poultry, and certain other food products came from.[9]

Aesthetics

In Chapter 4, the discussion of aesthetics included perceptions of color in different parts of the world. Global marketers must understand the importance of *visual aesthetics* embodied in the color or shape of a product, label, or package. Likewise, *aesthetic styles*, such as the degree of complexity found on a label, are perceived differently in different parts of the world. For example, it has been said that German wines would be more appealing in export markets if the labels were simplified. Aesthetic elements that are deemed appropriate, attractive, and appealing in one's home country may be perceived differently elsewhere.

In some cases, a standardized color can be used in all countries; examples include the distinctive yellow color on Caterpillar's earthmoving equipment and its licensed outdoor gear, the red Marlboro chevron, and John Deere's signature green. In other instances, color choices should be changed in response to local perceptions. It was noted in Chapter 4 that white is associated with death and bad luck in some Asian countries; when General Motors (GM) executives were negotiating with China for the opportunity to build cars there, they gave Chinese officials gifts from upscale Tiffany & Company in the jeweler's signature blue box. The Americans astutely replaced Tiffany's white ribbons with red ones because red is considered a lucky color in China and white has negative connotations (see the Emerging Markets Briefing Book, p. 326).

Packaging aesthetics are particularly important to the Japanese. This point was driven home to the chief executive of a small U.S. company that manufactures an electronic device for controlling corrosion. After spending much time in Japan, the executive managed to secure several orders for the device. However, following an initial burst of success, Japanese orders dropped off; for one thing, the executive was told, the packaging was too plain. "We couldn't understand why we needed a five-color label and a custom-made box for this device, which goes under the hood of a car or in the boiler room of a utility company," the executive said. While waiting for the bullet train in Japan one day, the executive's local distributor purchased a cheap watch at the station and had it elegantly wrapped. The distributor asked the American executive to guess the value of the watch based on the packaging. Despite all that he had heard and read about the Japanese obsession with quality, it was the first time the American

---

[7] Steven L. Gray and Ian Brat, "Read It and Weep? Big Mac Wrapper to Show Fat, Calories," *The Wall Street Journal* (October 26, 2005), p. B1.
[8] Miriam Jordan, "Nestlé Markets Baby Formula to Hispanic Mothers in U.S.," *The Wall Street Journal* (March 4, 2004), p. B1.
[9] David Kesmodel and Julie Jargon, "Labels Will Say if Your Beef Was Born in the USA," *The Wall Street Journal* (September 23, 2008), p. B1.

understood that, in Japan, "a book is judged by its cover." As a result, the company revamped its packaging, seeing to such details as ensuring that the strips of tape used to seal the boxes are cut to precisely the same length.[10]

Basic Branding Concepts

A **brand** is a complex bundle of images and experiences in the customer's mind. Brands perform two important functions. First, a brand represents a promise by a particular company regarding a particular product; it is a type of quality certification. Second, brands enable customers to better organize their shopping experience by helping them seek out and find a particular product. Thus, an important brand function is to differentiate a particular company's offering from all other companies' offerings.

Customers integrate all their experiences of observing, using, or consuming a product with everything they hear and read about it. Information about products and brands comes from a variety of sources and cues, including advertising, publicity, word of mouth, sales personnel, and packaging. Perceptions of service after the sale, price, and distribution are also taken into account. The sum of these impressions is a **brand image**, defined as perceptions about a brand as reflected by brand associations that consumers hold in their memories.[11]

Brand image is one way that competitors in the same industry sector differentiate themselves. Take Apple and Nokia, for example. Both market smartphones. Former Apple CEO Steve Jobs was a constant media presence and a master at generating buzz; the iPhone, iPad, and other Apple products generally receive stellar reviews for their sleek designs, powerful functionality, and user-friendly features. Apple's retail stores reinforce the brand's hip, cool image. By contrast, Nokia's brand image is more heavily skewed toward technology; few Nokia users are likely to know the name of the company's chief executive.[12]

Another important brand concept is **brand equity**, which represents the total value that accrues to a product as a result of a company's cumulative investments in the marketing of the brand. Just as a homeowner's equity grows as a mortgage is paid off over the years, brand equity grows as a company invests in the brand. Brand equity can also be thought of as an asset representing the value created by the relationship between the brand and its customers over time. The stronger the relationship, the greater the equity. For example, the value of global megabrands such as Coca-Cola and Marlboro runs in the tens of *billions* of dollars.[13] As outlined by branding expert Kevin Keller, the benefits of strong brand equity include:

- Greater loyalty
- Less vulnerability to marketing actions
- Less vulnerability to marketing crises
- Larger margins
- More inelastic consumer response to price increases
- More elastic consumer response to price decreases
- Increased marketing communication effectiveness[14]

Warren Buffett, the legendary American investor who heads Berkshire Hathaway, asserts that the global power of brands such as Coca-Cola and Gillette permits the companies that own them to set up a protective moat around their economic castles. As Buffett once explained, "The average company, by contrast, does battle daily without any such means of protection."[15] That

---

[10] Nilly Landau, "Face to Face Marketing Is Best," *International Business* (June 1994), p. 64.

[11] Kevin Lane Keller, *Strategic Brand Management: Building, Measuring, and Managing Brand Equity* (Upper Saddle River, NJ: Prentice Hall, 1998), p. 93.

[12] Cassell Bryan-Low, "Apple, Nokia Face Off in UK Music-Phone Clash," *The Wall Street Journal* (October 18, 2007), p. B3.

[13] For a complete discussion of brand equity, see Kevin Lane Keller, *Strategic Brand Management: Building, Measuring, and Managing Brand Equity* (Upper Saddle River, NJ: Prentice Hall, 1998), Chapter 2.

[14] Kevin Lane Keller, *Strategic Brand Management: Building, Measuring, and Managing Brand Equity* (Upper Saddle River, NJ: Prentice Hall, 1998), p. 93.

[15] John Willman, "Labels That Say It All," *Financial Times—Weekend Money* (October 25–26, 1997), p. 1.

protection often yields added profit because the owners of powerful brand names can typically command higher prices for their products than can owners of lesser brands. In other words, the strongest global brands have tremendous brand equity.

Companies develop logos, distinctive packaging, and other communication devices to provide visual representations of their brands. A logo can take a variety of forms, starting with the brand name itself. For example, the Coca-Cola brand is expressed in part by a *word mark* consisting of the words *Coke* and *Coca-Cola* written in a distinctive white script. The "wave" that appears on red Coke cans and bottle labels is an example of a *nonword mark logo*, sometimes known as a *brand symbol.* Nonword marks such as the Nike swoosh, the three-pronged Mercedes star, and McDonald's golden arches have the great advantage of transcending language and are therefore especially valuable to global marketers. To protect the substantial investment of time and money required to build and sustain brands, companies register brand names, logos, and other brand elements as trademarks or service marks. As discussed in Chapter 5, safeguarding trademarks and other forms of intellectual property is a key issue in global marketing.

Local Products and Brands

A **local product** or **local brand** is one that has achieved success in a single national market. Sometimes a global company creates local products and brands in an effort to cater to the needs and preferences of particular country markets. For example, Coca-Cola has developed several branded drink products for sale only in Japan, including a noncarbonated, ginseng-flavored beverage; a blended tea known as Sokenbicha; and the Lactia-brand fermented milk drink. In India, Coca-Cola markets Kinely brand bottled water. The spirits industry often creates brand extensions to leverage popular brands without large marketing expenditures. For example, Diageo PLC markets Gordon's Edge, a gin-based ready-to-drink beverage in the United Kingdom. Allied Domecq created TG, a brand flavored with Teacher's Scotch and guaraná, in Brazil.[17]

Local products and brands also represent the lifeblood of domestic companies. Entrenched local products and brands can represent significant competitive hurdles to global companies entering new country markets. In China, for example, a sporting goods company started by Olympic gold medalist Li Ning sells more sneakers than global powerhouse Nike. In developing countries, global brands are sometimes perceived as overpowering local ones. Growing national pride can result in a social backlash that favors local products and brands. In China, a local TV manufacturer, Changhong Electric Appliances, has built its share of the Chinese market from 6 percent to more than 22 percent by cutting prices and using patriotic advertising themes such as "Let Changhong hold the great flag of revitalizing our national industries."

White-goods maker Haier Group has also successfully fought off foreign competition and now accounts for 40 percent of China's refrigerator sales. In addition, Haier enjoys a 30 percent share of both the washing machine and air conditioner markets. Slogans stenciled on office walls delineate the aspirations of company president Zhang Ruimin: "Haier—Tomorrow's Global Brand Name" and "Never Say 'No' to the Market."[18] In 2002, Haier Group announced a strategic alliance with Taiwan's Sampo Group. The deal, valued at $300 million, called for each company to manufacture and sell the other's refrigerators and telecommunications products both globally and locally.

International Products and Brands

International products and **international brands** are offered in several markets in a particular region. For example, a number of "Euro products" and "Euro brands" such as Daimler's two-seat Smart car are available in Europe; the Smart was recently launched in the United States as well (see Case 10-2). The experience of GM with its Corsa model in the early 1990s provides a case study in how an international product or brand can be taken global. The Opel Corsa was a new model originally introduced in Europe. GM then decided to build different versions of the Corsa for China, Mexico, and Brazil. As David Herman, chairman of Adam Opel AG, noted, "The

[16] John Willman, "Time for Another Round," *Financial Times* (June 21, 1999), p. 15.
[17] Deborah Ball, "Liquor Makers Go Local," *The Wall Street Journal* (February 13, 2003), p. B3.
[18] John Ridding, "China's Own Brands Get Their Acts Together," *Financial Times* (December 30, 1996), p. 6; Kathy Chen, "Global Cooling: Would America Buy a Refrigerator Labeled 'Made in Quingdao'?" *The Wall Street Journal* (September 17, 1997), pp. A1, A14.

original concept was not that we planned to sell this car from the tip of Tierra del Fuego to the outer regions of Siberia. But we see its possibilities are limitless." GM calls the Corsa its "accidental world car."[19] Honda had a similar experience with the Fit, a five-door hatchback built on the company's Global Small Car platform. Following Fit's successful Japanese launch in 2001, Honda rolled out the vehicle in Europe (where it is known as Jazz). Over the next few years, Fit was rolled out in Australia, South America, South Africa, and China. The Fit made its North American market debut in 2006.

Global Products and Brands

Globalization is putting pressure on companies to develop global products and to leverage brand equity on a worldwide basis. A **global product** meets the wants and needs of a global market. A true global product is offered in all world regions, including the Triad and in countries at every stage of development. A **global brand** has the same name and, in some instances, a similar image and positioning throughout the world. Some companies are well established as global brands. For example, when Nestlé asserts that it "Makes the very best," the quality promise is understood and accepted globally. The same is true for Gillette ("The best a man can get"), BMW ("The ultimate driving machine"), GE ("Imagination at work"), Harley-Davidson ("An American legend"), Visa International ("Life takes Visa"), and many other global companies (see Exhibit 10-2).

Former Gillette CEO Alfred Zeien explained his company's approach as follows:

A multinational has operations in different countries. A global company views the world as a single country. We know Argentina and France are different, but we treat them the same. We sell them the same products, we use the same production methods, we have the same corporate policies. We even use the same advertising—in a different language, of course.[20]

Zeien's remarks reflect the fact that Gillette creates competitive advantage by marketing global products and utilizing global branding strategies. Gillette reaps economies of scale associated with creating a single ad campaign for the world and the advantages of executing a single

Exhibit 10-2 In French (*"La perfection au masculin"*), German (*"Für das Besteim Mann"*), Italian (*"Il meglio di un uomo"*), Portuguese (*"O melhorpara o homem"*), or any other language, Gillette's trademarked brand promise is easy to understand.
Source: KARIM SAHIB/AFP/Getty Images

[19] Diana Kurylko, "The Accidental World Car," *Automotive News* (June 27, 1994), p. 4.
[20] Victoria Griffith, "As Close as a Group Can Get to Global," *Financial Times* (April 7, 1998), p. 21.

brand strategy. By contrast, Peter Brabeck-Letmathe, the former CEO of Nestlé, has a different perspective:

> We believe strongly that there isn't a so-called global consumer, at least not when it comes to food and beverages. People have local tastes based on their unique cultures and traditions—a good candy bar in Brazil is not the same as a good candy bar in China. Therefore, decision making needs to be pushed down as low as possible in the organization, out close to the markets. Otherwise, how can you make good brand decisions? A brand is a bundle of functional and emotional characteristics. We can't establish emotional links with consumers in Vietnam from our offices in Vevey.[21]

Whichever view prevails at headquarters, all global companies are trying to increase the visibility of their brands, especially in key markets such as the United States and China. Examples include Philips with its "Sense and simplicity" global image advertising and Siemens' recent "Siemens answers" campaign.

In the twenty-first century, global brands are becoming increasingly important. As one research team noted:

> People in different nations, often with conflicting viewpoints, participate in a shared conversation, drawing upon shared symbols. One of the key symbols in that conversation is the global brand. Like entertainment stars, sports celebrities, and politicians, global brands have become a lingua franca for consumers all over the world. People may love or hate transnational companies, but they can't ignore them.[22]

These researchers note that brands that are marketed around the world are endowed with both an aura of excellence and a set of obligations. Worldwide, consumers, corporate buyers, governments, activists, and other groups associate global brands with three characteristics; consumers use these characteristics as a guide when making purchase decisions:

- *Quality signal.* Global brands compete fiercely with each other to provide world-class quality. A global brand name differentiates product offerings and allows marketers to charge premium prices.
- *Global myth.* Global brands are symbols of cultural ideals. As noted in Chapter 7, marketers can use global consumer culture positioning (GCCP) to communicate a brand's global identity and link that identity to aspirations in any part of the world.
- *Social responsibility.* Customers evaluate companies and brands in terms of how they address social problems and how they conduct business (see Exhibit 10-3).

Note that a global brand is not the same thing as a global product. For example, personal stereos are a category of global product; Sony is a global brand. Many companies, including Sony, make personal stereos. However, Sony created the category 30 years ago when it introduced the Walkman in Japan. The Sony Walkman is an example of **combination** or **tiered branding**, whereby a corporate name (Sony) is combined with a product brand name (Walkman). By using combination branding, marketers can leverage a company's reputation while developing a distinctive brand identity for a line of products. The combination brand approach can be a powerful tool for introducing new products. Although Sony markets a number of local products, the company also has a stellar track record as a global corporate brand, a creator of global products, and a marketer of global brands. For example, using the Walkman brand name as a point of departure, Sony created the Discman portable CD player and the Watchman portable TV. Sony's current global product brand offerings include Bravia brand HDTVs, CyberShot digital cameras, PlayStation game consoles and portables, and the Xperia Z smartphone.

Co-branding is a variation on combination branding in which two or more *different* company or product brands are featured prominently on product packaging or in advertising.

[21] Suzy Wetlaufer, "The Business Case Against Revolution," *Harvard Business Review* 79, no. 2 (February 2001), p. 116.
[22] Douglas B. Holt, John A. Quelch, and Earl L. Taylor, "How Global Brands Compete," *Harvard Business Review* 82, no. 9 (September 2004), p. 69.

Exhibit 10-3 Nucor is a steel company best known for its pioneering use of the minimill. Minimills produce steel by melting scrap in electric arc furnaces. This process is much more efficient than that used by traditional integrated steel producers. Nucor uses print and online media for an integrated general branding campaign featuring the tagline "It's our nature." The campaign is designed to raise awareness about the company's stance on a variety of issues, including the environment, energy conservation, and the importance of creating a strong corporate culture.
Source: Nucor

Properly implemented, co-branding can engender customer loyalty and allow companies to achieve synergy. However, co-branding can also confuse consumers and dilute brand equity. The approach works most effectively when the products involved complement each other. Credit card companies were the pioneers, and today it is possible to use cards to earn frequent-flier miles and discounts on automobiles. Another well-known example of co-branding is the Intel Inside campaign promoting both the Intel Corporation and its Pentium-brand processors in conjunction with advertising for various brands of personal computers.

Global companies can also leverage strong brands by creating **brand extensions**. This strategy entails using an established brand name as an umbrella when entering new businesses or developing new product lines that represent new categories to the company. British entrepreneur Richard Branson is an acknowledged master of this approach: The Virgin brand has been attached to a wide range of businesses and products (www.virgin.com). Virgin is a global brand, and the company's businesses include an airline, a railroad franchise, retail stores, movie theaters, financial services, and health clubs. Some of these businesses are global, and some are local. For example, Virgin Megastores are found in many parts of the world, whereas Virgin Rail Group and Virgin Media operate only in the United Kingdom. The brand has been built on Branson's shrewd ability to exploit weaknesses in competitors' customer service skills, as well as his flair for self-promotion. Branson's business philosophy is that brands are built around reputation, quality, innovation, and price rather than image. Although Branson is intent on establishing Virgin as *the* British brand of the new millennium, some industry observers wonder if the brand has been spread too thin. Branson's newest ventures include Virgin America Airlines and Virgin Galactic.

The history of the Sony Walkman illustrates the fact that it is up to visionary marketers to create global brands. Initially, Sony's personal stereo was to be marketed under three brand names. In their book *Breakthroughs!*, Ranganath Nayak and John Ketteringham describe how the global brand as we know it today came into being when famed Sony Chairman Akio Morita realized that global consumers were one step ahead of his marketing staffers:

At an international sales meeting in Tokyo, Morita introduced the Walkman to Sony representatives from America, Europe, and Australia. Within 2 months, the Walkman was introduced in the United States under the name "Soundabout"; 2 months later, it was on sale in the United Kingdom as "Stowaway." Sony in Japan had consented to the name changes because their English-speaking marketing groups had told them the name "Walkman" sounded funny in English. Nevertheless, with tourists importing the Walkman from Japan and spreading the original name faster than any advertising could have done, Walkman became the name most people used when they asked for the product in a store. Thus,

TABLE 10-1 Product/Brand Matrix for Global Marketing

		PRODUCT	
		Local	Global
BRAND	**Local**	1. Local product/local brand	2. Global product/local brand
	Global	3. Local product/global brand	4. Global product/global brand

Sony managers found themselves losing sales because they had three different names for the same item. Morita settled the issue at Sony's U.S. sales convention in May 1980 by declaring that, "funny or not," Walkman was the name everybody had to use.[23]

Table 10-1 shows the four combinations of local and global products and brands in matrix form. Each represents a different strategy; a global company can use one or more strategies as appropriate. Some global companies pursue strategy 1 by developing local products and brands for individual country or regional markets. Coca-Cola makes extensive use of this strategy; Georgia canned coffee in Japan is one example. Coca-Cola's flagship cola brand is an example of strategy 4. In South Africa, Coca-Cola markets Valpre brand bottled water (strategy 2). The global cosmetics industry makes extensive use of strategy 3; the marketers of Chanel, Givenchy, Clarins, Guerlain, and other leading cosmetics brands create different formulations for different regions of the world. However, the brand name and the packaging may be uniform everywhere.

Global Brand Development

Table 10-2 shows global brands ranked in terms of their economic value as determined by analysts at the Interbrand consultancy and Citigroup. To be included in the rankings, the brand had to generate about one-third of sales outside the home country; brands owned by privately held companies, such as Mars, are not included. Not surprisingly, Coca-Cola tops the list. However, the rankings show that strong brand management is being practiced by companies in a wide range of industries, from consumer packaged goods to electronics to automobiles. Even top brands have their ups and downs; in the 2012 rankings, Nokia dropped out of the top ten. Stephen

TABLE 10-2 The World's Most Valuable Brands

Rank	Value ($ millions)	Rank	Value ($ millions)
1. Coca-Cola	77,839	14. Cisco	27,197
2. Apple	76,568	15. HP	26,087
3. IBM	75,532	16. Gillette	24,898
4. Google	69,726	17. Louis Vuitton	23,577
5. Microsoft	57,853	18. Oracle	22,126
6. GE	43,682	19. Nokia	21,009
7. McDonald's	40,062	20. Amazon	18,625
8. Intel	39,385	21. Honda	17,280
9. Samsung	32,893	22. Pepsi	16,594
10. Toyota	30,280	23. H&M	16,571
11. Mercedes-Benz	30,097	24. American Express	15,702
12. BMW	29,052	25. SAP	15,641
13. Disney	27,438		

Source: Adapted from "Best Global Brands: 2012 Rankings," www.interbrand.com/en/best-global-brands/Best-Global-Brands-2012-Brand-View.aspx (accessed April 29, 2013).

---

[23] Adapted from P. Ranganath Nayak and John M. Ketteringham, *Breakthroughs! How Leadership and Drive Create Commercial Innovations That Sweep the World* (San Diego, CA: Pfeiffer & Company, 1994), pp. 128–129. www.prnayak.org, where the whole of *Breakthroughs!* is available for free download.

Exhibit 10-4 Annual global cell phone sales have passed the one-billion-unit mark. Now, faced with saturated markets in the West, Nokia and its competitors are looking to emerging markets for new customers. Robust economic growth and rising incomes mean that consumers in China, India, and other emerging markets can buy cell phones as status symbols. As indicated by this billboard on the Grand Trunk Highway outside of Islamabad, Pakistan, many users are upgrading to new handsets with fashionable designs and the latest features, including color screens, cameras, and digital music players.
Source: Robert Nickelsberg/Getty Images

Elop, Nokia's new CEO, has partnered with Microsoft to develop a new generation of smartphones. Nokia is also looking to emerging markets to drive growth (see Exhibit 10-4).

Developing a global brand is not always an appropriate goal. As David Aaker and Erich Joachimsthaler note in the *Harvard Business Review*, managers who seek to build global brands must first consider whether such a move fits well with their company or their markets. First, managers must realistically assess whether anticipated scale economies will actually materialize. Second, they must recognize the difficulty of building a successful global brand team. Finally, managers must be alert to instances in which a single brand cannot be imposed on all markets successfully. Aaker and Joachimsthaler recommend that companies place a priority on creating strong brands in *all* markets through **global brand leadership**:

> Global brand leadership means using organizational structures, processes, and cultures to allocate brand-building resources globally, to create global synergies, and to develop a global brand strategy that coordinates and leverages country brand strategies.[24]

Mars Inc. confronted the global brand issue with its chocolate-covered caramel bar that was sold under a variety of national brand names, such as Snickers in the United States and Marathon in the United Kingdom. Management decided to transform the candy bar—already a global product—into a global brand. This decision entailed some risk, such as the possibility that consumers in the United Kingdom would associate the name Snickers with knickers, the British slang for a woman's undergarment. Mars also changed the name of its successful European chocolate biscuit from Raider to Twix, the same name used in the United States. In both instances, a single brand name gave Mars the opportunity to leverage all of its product communications across national boundaries. Managers were forced to think globally about the positioning of Snickers and Twix, something that they had not been obliged to do when the candy products were marketed under different national brand names. The marketing team rose to the challenge; as Lord Saatchi described it:

> Mars decided there was a rich commercial prize at stake in ownership of a single human need: hunger satisfaction. From Hong Kong to Lima, people would know that Snickers was "a meal in a bar." Owning that emotion would not give them 100 percent of the global confectionery market but it would be enough. Its appeal would be wide enough to make Snickers the number-one confectionery brand in the world, which it is today.[25]

---

[24] David Aaker and Erich Joachimsthaler, "The Lure of Global Branding," *Harvard Business Review* 77, no. 6 (November–December 1999), pp. 137–144.
[25] Lord Saatchi, "Battle for Survival Favours the Simplest," *Financial Times* (January 5, 1998), p. 19.

EMERGING MARKETS BRIEFING BOOK

China Gives Buick a New Lease on Life

SYNC • THINK • LEARN

MyMarketingLab

GMs' experience at home and abroad provides a good example of how a company's brand strategy must be adapted to cultural realities as well as the changing needs of the market. For example, in the 1990s GM was vying for the right to build a sedan in China. Company executives gave Chinese officials gifts from Tiffany's in the jeweler's signature blue boxes. However, the Americans replaced Tiffany's white ribbons with red ones because red is considered a lucky color in China and white has negative connotations.

GM ultimately won government approval of its proposal and was given the opportunity to produce Buick sedans for government and business (see Exhibit 10-5). Why was the Buick nameplate chosen from among GM's various vehicle brands? In an interview with *Fortune*, former GM CEO Rick Wagoner related the following story:

There is a straightforwardness to the way the Chinese negotiate things. What they are interested in becomes clear quickly. When we were ready to go into the China market, they said, "Okay, we will choose GM, and we want you to use Buick." We said, "It is not really one of our global brands. We'd probably rather use something else." They said, "We'd like you to use Buick." We said, "We'll use Buick." And it has worked great.

Back at home, Buick's image has been in decline for decades. The average Buick buyer is 61 years old; this stands in marked contrast to, say, Volvo, whose average buyer is only 50. Buick was once a popular aspirational brand among American drivers; one advertising tagline asked, "Wouldn't you really rather have a Buick?" The line was designed to motivate a Ford owner to take a step up in class by choosing a Buick LeSabre or Riviera. Another headline read, "Want the Big buy for Big families?"

Unfortunately, by the mid-1980s, Buick had fallen victim to corporate consolidation and cost cutting. The resulting design and engineering overlap meant that some car buyers found it difficult to distinguish among models from GM's different divisions. A case in point: the Riviera, the Oldsmobile Toronado, and the Cadillac Eldorado were all very similar. Even the breakthrough design of the 1995 Riviera could not breathe new life into the brand; despite rave reviews (*Autoweek* said the new design was "bound to make waves in the luxury coupe segment"), the Riviera model itself was retired in 1999.

By 2009, Buick's Chinese sales totaled 450,000, more than four times the U.S. sales figure. Moreover, the typical Chinese Buick owner is 35 years old. These facts help explain why the Buick nameplate is still in production. When the U.S. government took control of GM, it pressured GM chief Fritz Henderson to terminate Buick. Thanks to the brand's popularity in China, it was given a reprieve. Meanwhile, GM has phased out Oldsmobile, Pontiac, and Saturn.

One auto analyst summarized the situation by noting, "In China, GM has played a local strategy. They left the people running Buick alone, and they were extremely successful in building the brand there." Now the task facing American marketing managers is to revitalize the Buick brand at home. New models such as the mid-sized Regal and the Verano compact sedan are integral to the effort. The Regal is built in Germany, and some print ads position it as having European roots. For example, one ad suggests, "Listen closely and you might detect a German accent." As Craig Bierley, advertising and promotions director, told *Financial Times*, "The goal is about expanding the audience for the brand. Germany automatically says 'sports sedan' to people." There is evidence that Buick is on the right track: 2012 U.S. sales figures were among the highest ever for the brand.

Sources: James R. Healey, "Buick Tries to Buff Away Its Image as Inefficient Carmaker," *USA Today* (June 22, 2012), pp. 1B, 2B; Sharon Terlep, "GM Seeks Sway in China," *The Wall Street Journal* (April 19, 2012), pp. B1, B2; Bernard Simon, "Out with the Old," *Financial Times* (October 18, 2010); Jens Meiners, "Chinese Takeout," *Car and Driver* (October 2010), pp. 31–32; John D. Stoll, "East Meets West," *The Wall Street Journal* (June 23, 2008), p. R5; Alex Taylor III, "China Would Rather Have Buicks," *Fortune* (October 4, 2004), p. 98; Matt DeLorenzo, "Cruising in Style," *Autoweek* (December 6, 1993), pp. 13–14.

Exhibit 10-5 As General Motors sought aid from the U.S. government, the Barack Obama administration asked CEO Rick Wagoner to step down. The company has been aggressive about cost-cutting; among other concessions and remedies, the Saturn and Pontiac brands have been discontinued. Meanwhile, GM's Buick brand is one of the top-selling nameplates in China. GM's Chinese sales totaled more than 1 million vehicles in 2008.
Source: The Eng Koon/AFP/Newscom

The following six guidelines can assist marketing managers in their efforts to establish global brand leadership:[26]

1. Create a compelling value proposition for customers in every market entered, beginning with the home-country market. A global brand begins with this foundation of value.

2. Before taking a brand across borders, think about all elements of brand identity and select names, marks, and symbols that have the potential for globalization. Give special attention to the Triad and BRICS nations.

3. Develop a company-wide communication system to share and leverage knowledge and information about marketing programs and customers in different countries.

4. Develop a consistent planning process across markets and products. Make a process template available to all managers in all markets.

5. Assign specific responsibility for managing branding issues to ensure that local brand managers accept global best practices. This can take a variety of forms, ranging from a business management team or a brand champion (led by senior executives) to a global brand manager or brand management team (led by middle managers).

6. Execute brand-building strategies that leverage global strengths and respond to relevant local differences.

Coke is arguably the quintessential global product and global brand. Coke relies on similar positioning and marketing in all countries; it projects a global image of fun, good times, and enjoyment. The product itself, though, may vary to suit local tastes; for example, Coke increased the sweetness of its beverages in the Middle East, where customers prefer a sweeter drink. Also, prices may vary to suit local competitive conditions, and the channels of distribution may differ. In 2009, Coke adopted the global advertising theme "Open Happiness." The previous slogan, "The Coke Side of Life," was also global but required adaptation in emerging markets such as Russia and China.[27] However, the basic, underlying strategic principles that guide the management of the brand are the same worldwide. The issue is not exact uniformity but rather: Are we offering *essentially* the same product and brand promise? As discussed in the next few chapters, other elements of the marketing mix—for example, price, communications appeal and media strategy, and distribution channels—may also vary.

A Needs-Based Approach to Product Planning

Coca-Cola, McDonald's, Singapore Airlines, Mercedes-Benz, and Sony are a few of the companies that have transformed local products and brands into global ones. The essence of marketing is finding needs and filling them. **Maslow's needs hierarchy**, a staple of sociology and psychology courses, provides a useful framework for understanding how and why local products and brands can be extended beyond home-country borders. Maslow proposed that people's desires can be arranged into a hierarchy of five needs.[28] As an individual fulfills needs at each level, he or she progresses to higher levels (Figure 10-1). At the most basic level of human existence, physiological and safety needs must be met. People need food, clothing, and shelter, and a product that meets these basic needs has potential for globalization.

However, the basic human need to consume food and drink is not the same thing as wanting or preferring a Big Mac or a Coke. Before the Coca-Cola Company and McDonald's conquered the world, they built their brands and business systems at home. Because their products fulfilled basic human needs and because both companies are masterful marketers, they were able to cross geographic boundaries and build global brand franchises. At the same time, Coca-Cola and McDonald's have learned from experience that some food and drink preferences—China is a case in point—remain deeply embedded in culture.[29] Responding to those differences has meant

---

[26] Warren J. Keegan, "Global Brands: Issues and Strategies," Center for Global Business Strategy, Pace University, Working Paper Series, 2002.

[27] Betsy McKay and Suzanne Vranica, "Coca-Cola to Uncap 'Open Happiness' Campaign," *The Wall Street Journal* (January 14, 2009), p. B6.

[28] A. H. Maslow, "A Theory of Human Motivation," in *Readings in Managerial Psychology*, Harold J. Levitt and Louis R. Pondy, eds. (Chicago: University of Chicago Press, 1964), pp. 6–24.

[29] Jeremy Grant, "Golden Arches Bridge Local Tastes," *Financial Times* (February 9, 2006), p. 10.

FIGURE 10-1

Maslow's Hierarchy of Needs

Source: A. H. Maslow, "A Theory of Human Motivation," in *Readings in Managerial Psychology,* Harold J. Levitt and Louis R. Pondy, ads. (Chicago: University of Chicago Press, 1964), pp. 6-24. Original— *Psychological Review* 50 (1943).

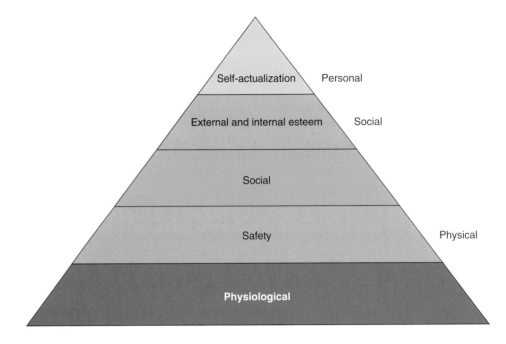

creating local products and brands for particular country markets. Sony has prospered for a similar reason. Audio and video entertainment products fulfill important social functions. Throughout its history, Sony's corporate vision has called for developing new products such as the transistor radio and the Walkman personal stereo that fulfill the need for mobile entertainment.

Mid-level needs in the hierarchy include self-respect, self-esteem, and the esteem of others. These social needs, which can create a powerful internal motivation driving demand for status-oriented products, cut across the various stages of country development. Gillette's Alfred Zeien understood this. Marketers in Gillette's Parker Pen subsidiary are confident that consumers in Malaysia and Singapore shopping for an upscale gift will buy the same Parker pen as Americans shopping at Neiman Marcus. "We are not going to come out with a special product for Malaysia," Zeien has said.[30] In Asia today, young women are taking up smoking as a status symbol—and showing a preference for Western brands such as Marlboro. However, smokers' needs and wants may be tempered by economic circumstances. Recognizing this, companies such as BAT create local brands that allow individuals to indulge their desire or need to smoke at a price they can afford to pay.

Luxury goods marketers are especially skilled at catering to esteem needs on a global basis. Rolex, Louis Vuitton, and Dom Perignon are just a few of the global brands that consumers buy in an effort to satisfy esteem needs. Some consumers flaunt their wealth by buying expensive products and brands that others will notice. Such behavior is referred to as *conspicuous consumption* or *luxury badging.* Any company with a premium product or brand that has proven itself in a local market by fulfilling esteem needs should consider devising a strategy for taking the product global.

Products can fulfill different needs in different countries. Consider the refrigerator as used in industrialized, high-income countries. The *primary function* of the refrigerator in these countries is related to basic needs as fulfilled in that society. These include storing frozen foods for extended periods; keeping milk, meat, and other perishable foods fresh between car trips to the supermarket; and making ice cubes. In lower-income countries, by contrast, frozen foods are not widely available. Homemakers shop for food daily rather than weekly. People are reluctant to pay for unnecessary features such as icemakers. These are luxuries that require high income levels to support. The function of the refrigerator in a lower-income country is to store small quantities of perishable food for one day and to store leftovers for slightly longer periods. Because the needs fulfilled by the refrigerator are limited in these countries, a relatively small refrigerator is quite adequate. In some developing countries, refrigerators have an important *secondary purpose*

[30] Louis Uchitelle, "Gillette's World View: One Blade Fits All," *The New York Times* (January 3, 1994), p. C3.

Exhibit 10-6 In India, Vietnam, and other emerging markets, many people cannot afford housing or automobiles. That means that amenities such as refrigerators or flush toilets are considered status symbols when a family welcomes visitors to their home. In public, cellphones serve a similar secondary purpose.

Now, some Indian companies are developing innovative new products that the country's poorest consumers can afford. For example, one company has created the Little Cool refrigerator. Selling for the equivalent of $70, the device is small and portable. It only has about 20 parts, about one-tenth the number of parts that are found in conventional full-sized units.

Source: David Turnley/Corbis Images

related to higher-order needs: They fulfill a need for prestige. In these countries, there is demand for the largest model available, which is prominently displayed in the living room rather than hidden in the kitchen (see Exhibit 10-6).

Hellmut Schütte has proposed a modified hierarchy to explain the needs and wants of Asian consumers (Figure 10-2).[32] Although the two lower-level needs are the same as in the traditional hierarchy, the three highest levels emphasize social needs. *Affiliation needs* in Asia are satisfied when an individual has been accepted by a group. Conformity with group norms becomes a key force driving consumer behavior. For example, when a cool new cell phone hits the market, every teenager who wants to fit in buys one. Knowing this, managers at Japanese companies develop local products specifically designed to appeal to teens. The next level is *admiration*, a higher-level need that can be satisfied through acts that command respect within a group. At the top of the Asian hierarchy is *status*, the esteem of society as a whole. In part, attainment of high status is character driven. However, the quest for status also leads to luxury badging. Support for Schütte's contention that status is the highest-ranking need in the Asian hierarchy can be seen in the geographic breakdown of the $200-plus billion global luxury goods market. Fully 20 percent of industry sales are generated in Japan alone, with another 22 percent of sales occurring in the rest of the Asia-Pacific region. Nearly half of all sales revenues of Italy's Gucci Group are generated in Asia.

> **"For Asians, face is very important, so you have to show you are up to date with the latest available product."[31]**
>
> —Alan Chang, View Sonic (Taiwan), explaining the popularity of flat-panel TVs in Japan

"Country of Origin" as Brand Element

One of the facts of life in global marketing is that perceptions about and attitudes toward particular countries often extend to products and brands known to originate in those countries. Such perceptions contribute to the **country-of-origin effect**; they become part of a brand's image and contribute to brand equity. This is particularly true for automobiles, electronics, fashion, beer, recorded music, and certain other product categories.

Perceptions and attitudes about a product's origins can be positive or negative. On the positive side, as one marketing expert pointed out in the mid-1990s, "'German' is synonymous with

---

[31] Andrew Ward, Kathrin Hille, Michiyo Nakamoto, and Chris Nuttal, "Flat Out for Flat Screens: The Battle to Dominate the $29 bn Market Is Heating Up but the Risk of Glut Is Growing," *Financial Times* (December 24, 2003), p. 9.
[32] Hellmut Schütte, *Consumer Behavior in Asia* (New York: NYU Press, 1998).

FIGURE 10-2

Maslow's Hierarchy: The Asian Equivalent

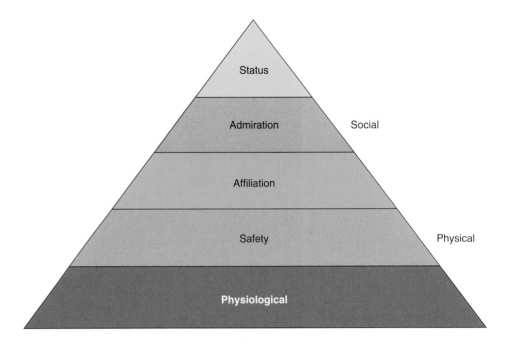

quality engineering, 'Italian' is synonymous with style, and 'French' is synonymous with chic."[33] Why is this still true today, especially in emerging markets? As Diego Della Valle, CEO of Italian luxury goods marketer Tod's, explains:

> "Made in Italy" will retain its luster because it is still the maximum guarantee of high quality for products such as ours. Like the French for perfume, the Swiss for watches. The Chinese do not want to buy "Made in China."[34]

"China is complex and becoming more so. But 'Made in Germany' still carries great appeal here and if you prepare seriously, there are few limits to what you can achieve."[35]

—Christian Sommer, German Centre for Industry and Trade

The manufacturing reputation of a particular country can change over time. Studies conducted during the 1970s and 1980s indicated that the "made in the USA" image lost ground to the "made in Japan" image. Today, however, U.S. brands are finding renewed acceptance globally. Examples include the Jeep Cherokee, clothing from Lands' End and American Apparel, and Budweiser beer, all of which are being successfully marketed with strong "USA" themes. American Apparel is building a global brand on the positioning "Made in Downtown LA." Its fashion items are available in the European Union (EU), Switzerland, Japan, and, most recently, China. Will the company's T-shirts and other logo-free basics appeal to fashion-conscious Chinese youth? CEO Dov Charney admits it will be a challenge. American Apparel sells understated, "well-designed basics," whereas luxury goods are a "bit bourgeoisie and nouveau riche," he said recently. But, he added, "The young people tend to like Audi better than the Bentley, so maybe it can work." As brand strategist Eli Portnoy points out, the fact that American Apparel's clothes are actually made in America appeals to Chinese consumers. "That is a distinction that will give it cachet to young fashion-oriented Chinese," Portnoy says.[36]

Finland is home to Nokia, which rose in stature from a local company to a global one in little more than a decade. However, as brand strategy expert Simon Anholt points out, other Finnish companies need to move quickly to capitalize on Nokia's success if Finland is to become a valuable nation-brand. For example, Raisio Oy's Benecol brand margarine has been proven to lower cholesterol levels. If large numbers of health-conscious consumers around the world embrace so-called nutraceutical products, Raisio and Benecol may become well-known brands and further raise Finland's profile on the global scene. Anholt also notes that Slovenia and other

[33] Dana Milbank, "Made in America Becomes a Boast in Europe," *The Wall Street Journal* (January 19, 1994), p. B1.

[34] Peter Aspden, "Diego Della Valle," *Financial Times* (August 12, 2011).

[35] Bertrand Benoit and Geoff Dyer, "The Mittelstand Is Making Money in the Middle Kingdom," *Financial Times* (June 6, 2006), p. 13.

[36] Leslie Earnest, "U.S. Clothing Firm Seeks Good Fit in China," *Los Angeles Times* (April 3, 2008).

Exhibit 10-7 Countries, like products, can be branded and positioned. For example, Slovenia recently launched an integrated brand image campaign that will be used by a variety of governmental and nongovernmental organizations. "Slovenian green" is the dominant color in the new logo. As the Government Communication Office explains, "It refers to the natural balance and calm diligence of Slovenes. One can feel Slovenia through the smell of the forest, the rushing of the creek, the fresh taste of water and the softness of wood . . ."
Source: Embassy of the Republic of Slovenia.

countries are "launch brands" in the sense that they lack centuries of tradition and foreign interaction upon which to build their reputations (see Exhibit 10-7):

> For a country like Slovenia to enhance its image abroad is a very different matter than for Scotland or China. Slovenia needs to be launched: Consumers around the world first must be taught where it is, what it makes, what it has to offer, and what it stands for. This in itself represents a powerful opportunity: The chance to build a modern country brand, untainted by centuries of possibly negative associations.[37]

Since the mid-1990s, the "Made in Mexico" image has gained in stature as local companies and global manufacturers have established world-class manufacturing plants in Mexico to supply world demand. For example, Ford, GM, Nissan, Volkswagen, and other global automakers have established Mexican operations that produce nearly 2 million vehicles per year, three-fourths of which are exported.[38] Similarly, consumer attitudes toward "Made in Japan" have come a long way since the mid-1970s. What about "Made in China" or "Made in India"? China and India take great pride in their manufacturing capabilities but, generally speaking, consumer perception lags behind the reality. The question for them is: How do you change that image?[39]

In some product categories, foreign products have a substantial advantage over their domestic counterparts simply because of their "foreign-ness." Global marketers have an opportunity to capitalize on the situation by charging premium prices. The import segment of the beer industry is a case in point. In one study of American attitudes about beer, subjects who were asked to taste beer with the labels concealed indicated a preference for domestic beers over imports. The same subjects were then asked to indicate preference ratings for beers in an open test with labels attached. In this test, the subjects preferred imported beer. Conclusion: The subjects' perceptions were positively influenced by the knowledge they were drinking an import. In 1997, thanks to a brilliant marketing campaign, Grupo Modelo's Corona Extra surpassed Heineken as the best-selling imported beer in America. With distribution in 150 countries, Corona is a textbook example of a local brand that has been built into a global powerhouse.

Scotland provides an interesting case study of a country that enjoys strong brand equity but is somewhat misunderstood. A study titled "Project Galore" was undertaken to discover which

"Consider labels such as 'Made in Brazil' and 'Made in Thailand.' Someday they may be symbols of high quality and value, but today many consumers expect products from those countries to be inferior."[40]

—Christopher A. Bartlett and Sumantra Ghoshal

[37] Simon Anholt, "The Nation as Brand," *Across the Board* 37, no. 10 (November–December 2000), pp. 22–27.
[38] Elliot Blair Smith, "Early PT Cruiser Took a Bruising," *USA Today* (August 8, 2001), pp. 1B, 2B; see also Joel Millman, "Trade Wins: The World's New Tiger on the Export Scene Isn't Asian; It's Mexico," *The Wall Street Journal* (May 9, 2000), pp. A1, A10.
[39] Vanessa Friedman, "Relocated Labels," *Financial Times* (September 1, 2010), p. 5.
[40] Christopher A. Bartlett and Sumantra Ghoshal, "Going Global: Lessons from Late Movers," *Harvard Business Review* 78, no. 2 (March–April 2000), p. 133.

Exhibit 10-8

"Not just a wheel, Trog, but a wheel of aged Parmigiano Reggiano!"

aspects of Scotland's equity could be leveraged for commercial advantage. Among other things, the researchers learned that high-quality goods and services such as whisky, wool, salmon, and golf courses were perceived as Scotland's core industries. In fact, Scotland's top export category is information technology! The researchers created a perceptual map that identified Scotland 's four key values: integrity, tenacity, inventiveness, and spirit.[41] In order to better position Scotland relative to Ireland and other neighboring countries, Scottish Development International recently launched an advertising campaign that incorporated some of the study's findings (see Exhibit 10-9).

Extend, Adapt, Create: Strategic Alternatives in Global Marketing

To capitalize on opportunities outside the home country, company managers must devise and implement appropriate marketing programs. Depending on organizational objectives and market needs, a particular program may consist of extension strategies, adaptation strategies, or a combination of the two. A company that has developed a successful local product or brand can implement an **extension strategy** that calls for offering a product virtually unchanged (i.e., "extending" it) in markets outside the home country. A second option is an **adaptation strategy**; this involves changing elements of design, function, or packaging in response to needs

---

[41] Kate Hamilton, "Project Galore: Qualitative Research and Leveraging Scotland's Brand Equity," *Journal of Advertising Research* 40, nos. 1/2 (January–April 2000), pp. 107–111. *Galore* is one of two English words that are taken from Gaelic. The other is *whisky*.

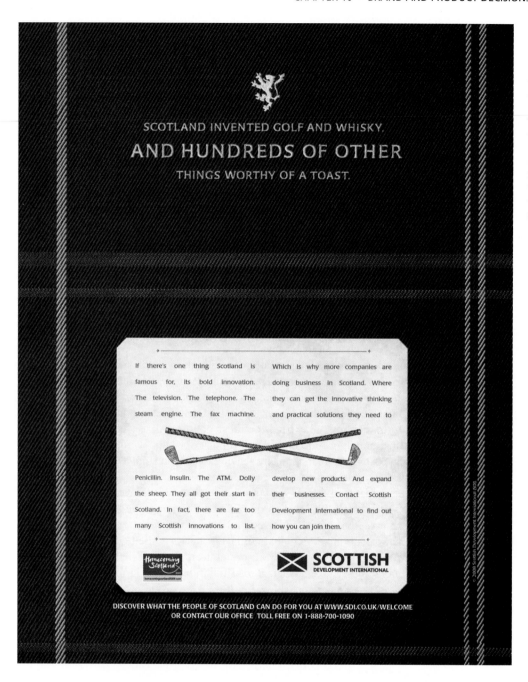

Exhibit 10-9 The body copy in this print ad positions Scotland in a positive light: "If there's one thing Scotland is known for, it's bold innovation. The television. The telephone. The steam engine. The fax machine. Penicillin. Insulin. The ATM. Dolly the sheep. They all got their start in Scotland. In fact, there are far too many Scottish innovations to name. Which is why more companies are doing business in Scotland. Where they can get the innovative thinking and practical solutions they need to develop new products."
Source: Scottish Development International

or conditions in particular country markets. These product strategies can be used in conjunction with extension or adaptation communication strategies. This is the type of strategic decision facing executives at a company such as Starbucks who build a brand and a product/service offering in the home-country market before expanding into global markets. A third strategic option, **product invention**, entails developing new products "from the ground up" with the world market in mind.

Laws and regulations in different countries frequently lead to obligatory product design adaptations. This may be seen most clearly in Europe, where one impetus for the creation of the single market was the desire to dismantle regulatory and legal barriers that prevented pan-European sales of standardized products. These were particularly prevalent in the areas of technical standards and health and safety standards. In the food industry, for example, there were 200 legal and regulatory barriers to cross-border trade within the EU in 10 food categories. Among these were prohibitions or taxes on products with certain ingredients and different packaging and labeling laws. As these barriers are dismantled, there will be less need to adapt product designs, and many companies will be able to create standardized "Euro-products."

Despite the trend toward convergence, many product standards that remain on the books have not been harmonized. This situation can create problems for companies not based in the EU. For example, Dormont Manufacturing, appropriately based in Export, Pennsylvania, makes hoses that hook up to deep-fat fryers and similar appliances used in the food industry. Dormont's gas hose is made of stainless-steel helical tubing with no covering. British industry requirements call for galvanized metal annular tubing and a rubber covering; Italian regulations specify stainless-steel annular tubing with no covering. The cost of complying with these regulations effectively shuts Dormont out of the European market.[42]

Moreover, the European Commission continues to set product standards that force many non-EU companies to adapt product or service offerings to satisfy domestic market regulations. For example, consumer safety regulations mean that McDonald's cannot include soft plastic toys in its Happy Meals in Europe. Microsoft has been forced to modify contracts with European software makers and Internet service providers to ensure that consumers in the EU have access to a wide range of technologies. The commission has also set stringent guidelines on product content as it affects recyclability. As Maja Wessels, a Brussels-based lobbyist for United Technologies Corporation (UTC), noted, "Twenty years ago, if you designed something to U.S. standards you could pretty much sell it all over the world. Now the shoe's on the other foot." Engineers at UTC's Carrier division have redesigned the company's air conditioners to comply with pending European recycling rules, which are tougher than U.S. standards.[43]

As noted in Chapter 1, the extension/adaptation/creation decision is one of the most fundamental issues addressed by a company's global marketing strategy. Although it pertains to all elements of the marketing mix, extension/adaptation is of particular importance in product and communications decisions. Earlier in the chapter, Table 10-1 displayed product and brand strategic options in matrix form. Figure 10-3 expands on those options: All aspects of promotion and communication—not just branding—are considered. Figure 10-3 shows four strategic alternatives available to Starbucks or any other company seeking to expand from its domestic base into new geographic markets.

Companies in the international, global, and transnational stages of development all employ extension strategies. The critical difference is one of execution and mind-set. In an international company, for example, the extension strategy reflects an ethnocentric orientation and the *assumption* that all markets are alike. A global company such as Gillette does not fall victim to such assumptions; the company's geocentric orientation allows it to thoroughly understand its markets and consciously take advantage of similarities in world markets. Likewise, a

FIGURE 10-3

Global Product Planning: Strategic Alternatives

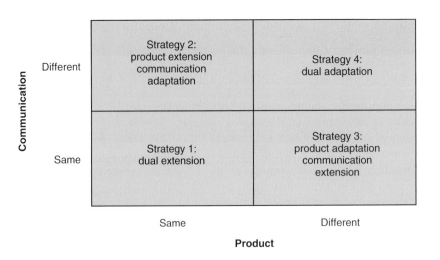

---

[42] Timothy Aeppel, "Europe's 'Unity' Undoes a U.S. Exporter," *The Wall Street Journal* (April 1, 1996), p. B1.
[43] Brandon Mitchener, "Standard Bearers: Increasingly, Rules of Global Economy Are Set in Brussels," *The Wall Street Journal* (April 23, 2002), p. A1.

multinational company utilizes the adaptation strategy because of its polycentric orientation and the assumption that all markets are different. By contrast, the geocentric orientation of managers and executives in a global company has sensitized them to actual, rather than assumed, differences between markets. The key, as one executive has noted, is to avoid being either "hopelessly local" or "mindlessly global."

Strategy 1: Product-Communication Extension (Dual Extension)

Many companies employ the **product-communication extension** strategy when pursuing global market opportunities. Under the right conditions, this is a very straightforward marketing strategy; it can be the most profitable one as well. Companies pursuing this strategy sell the same product with virtually no adaptation, using the same advertising and promotional appeals used domestically, in two or more country markets or segments. For this strategy to be effective, the advertiser's message must be understood across different cultures, including those in emerging markets. Examples of the dual-extension strategy include the following:

- Apple launched its iPhone in the United States in mid-2007. In the following months, it was gradually rolled out in several more markets, including France and the United Kingdom. When Apple brought its second-generation iPhone to market 1 year later, it was launched in 21 countries simultaneously.
- Henkel KGaA's family of Loctite-brand adhesive products are marketed globally using the dual-extension strategy (see Exhibit 10-10). The company's various lines—including medical adhesives and threadlockers—bear the Loctite brand name. Ads also include the Henkel corporate logo.
- Microsoft's Windows 7 operating system was launched in 2009 with the user-centric global advertising campaign keyed to the theme "I'm a PC and Windows 7 was my idea." The ads featured actual Microsoft customers and employees.

As a general rule, extension/standardization strategies are utilized more frequently with industrial (business-to-business) products than with consumer products. The reason is simple: Industrial products tend to be less deeply rooted in culture than are consumer goods. However, if this is so, how can Apple, a consummate consumer brand, utilize the dual-extension strategy to such good effect? One explanation is that, as discussed in Chapter 7, the brand's high-tech, high-touch image lends itself to GCCP. As these examples show, technology companies and industrial goods manufacturers should be especially alert to dual-extension possibilities. However, Henkel also markets hundreds of other glues, detergents, and personal-care products with different formulas and different brand names. Speaking about Loctite, Henkel CEO Ulrich Lehner explains, "There aren't many products like that. Usually, you have to adapt to local tastes. You have to balance between local insight and centralized economies of scale. It's a constant battle."[44]

Strategy 2: Product Extension–Communication Adaptation

In some instances, a product or brand can be successfully extended to multiple country markets with some modification of the communication strategy. Research may have revealed that consumer perceptions about one or more aspects of the value proposition are different from country to country. It may also turn out that a product fills a different need, appeals to a different segment, or serves a different function in a particular country or region. Whatever the reason, extending the product while adapting the marketing communications program may be the key to market success. The appeal of the **product extension–communication adaptation** strategy is its relatively low cost of implementation. Because the product itself is unchanged, expenditures for research and development (R&D), manufacturing setup, and inventory are avoided. The biggest costs associated with this approach are in researching the market and revising advertising, sales promotion efforts, point-of-sale material, and other communication elements as appropriate.

---

[44] Gerrit Wiesmann, "Brands That Stop at the Border," *Financial Times* (October 6, 2006), p. 10.

Exhibit 10-10 Germany's Henkel is a global company that markets products in three main categories: Adhesive technologies; laundry and home care; and cosmetics and toiletries. The Loctite family of adhesives and sealants has a wide range of applications in the home as well as medical and industrial settings. Henkel's portfolio also includes such popular consumer brands as Right Guard, Dial, and Purex.

Source: Henkel Corporation

Consider the following examples of product extension–communication adaptation:

- In Hungary, Slovakia, and other Central European countries, SABMiller positions Miller Genuine Draft as an international lifestyle brand (GCCP) rather than an American brand (FCCP). The communication adaptation strategy was chosen after focus group research showed that many Europeans have a low regard for American beer.[45]
- Before executives at Ben & Jerry's Homemade launched their ice cream in the United Kingdom, the company conducted extensive research to determine whether the package design effectively communicated the brand's "super-premium" position. The research

---

[45] Dan Bilefsky and Christopher Lawton, "In Europe, Marketing Beer as 'American' May Not Be a Plus," *The Wall Street Journal* (July 21, 2004), p. B1.

indicated that British consumers perceived the colors differently than U.S. consumers do. The package design was then changed, and Ben & Jerry's was launched successfully in the UK market.

- To promote its Centrino wireless chip, Intel launched a global ad campaign that features different combinations of celebrities. In print, TV, and online ads, one of the celebrities sits on the lap of a mobile computer user. The celebrities—including comedian John Cleese, actress Lucy Liu, and skateboard king Tony Hawk—were chosen because they are widely recognized in key world markets.[46]

- In the United States, Sony's TV ads for its Bravia high-definition TVs encourage viewers to log onto the Internet and choose different endings. In Europe, the ads are completely different: They feature bright images such as colored balls bouncing in slow motion. As Mike Fasulo, chief marketing officer at Sony Electronics, explains, "Consumer adoption as well as awareness of high-definition products, including our line of Bravia televisions, differs dramatically from region to region."[47]

- Targeting the 300 million farmers in India who still use plows harnessed to oxen, John Deere engineers created a line of relatively inexpensive, no-frills tractors. The Deere team then realized that the same equipment could be marketed to hobby farmers and acreage owners in the United States—a segment that they had previously overlooked.[48]

Marketers of premium American bourbon brands such as Wild Turkey have found that images of Delta blues music, New Orleans, and Route 66 appeal to upscale drinkers outside the United States. However, images that stress bourbon's rustic, backwoods origins do not appeal to Americans. As Gary Regan, author of *The Book of Bourbon*, has noted, "Europeans hate Americans when they think of them as being the policemen of the world, but they love Americans when they think about blue jeans and bourbon and ranches."[50]

Likewise, Jägermeister schnapps is marketed differently in different key country markets. Chief executive Hasso Kaempfe believes that a diversity of images has been a key element in the success of Jägermeister outside of Germany, where the brown, herb-based concoction originated. In the United States, Jägermeister was "discovered" in the mid-1990s by the college crowd. Kaempfe's marketing team has capitalized on the brand's cult status by hiring "Jägerettes," girls who pass out free samples; the company's popular T-shirts and orange banners are also distributed at rock concerts. By contrast, in Italy, the brand's second-largest export market, Jägermeister is considered an up-market digestive to be consumed after dinner. In Germany, Austria, and Switzerland, where beer culture predominates, Jägermeister and other brands of schnapps have more traditional associations as a remedy for coughs, stomachaches, or as a "morning after" elixir.[51]

Jägermeister is an example of **product transformation**: The same physical product ends up serving a different function or use than that for which it was originally designed or created. In some cases, a particular country or regional environment will allow local managers a greater degree of creativity and risk taking when approaching the communication task.

Strategy 3: Product Adaptation–Communication Extension

A third approach to global product planning is to adapt the product to local use or preference conditions while extending, with minimal change, the basic home-market communications strategy or brand name. This third strategy option is known as **product adaptation–communication extension**. For example:

- A new Cadillac model, the BLS, is built in Sweden; it is 6 inches shorter than the current CTS. A 4-cylinder engine is standard; buyers can also choose an available diesel engine.

- For many years, Ford sold the Escort, Focus, and other nameplates worldwide. However, the vehicles themselves often varied from region to region. In 2010, Ford launched a new

> "I can think of very few truly global ads that work. Brands are often at different stages around the world, and that means there are different advertising jobs to do."[49]
>
> —Michael Conrad, chief creative officer, Leo Burnett Worldwide

[46] Geoffrey A. Fowler, "Intel's Game: Play It Local, but Make It Global," *The Wall Street Journal* (September 30, 2005), p. B4.

[47] Jorge Valencia, "Sony Paints Lavish Hues to Sell LCDs," *The Wall Street Journal* (August 3, 2007), p. B3.

[48] Jenny Mero, "John Deere's Farm Team," *Fortune* (April 14, 2008), pp. 119–126.

[49] Vanessa O'Connell, "Exxon 'Centralizes' New Global Campaign," *The Wall Street Journal* (July 11, 2001), p. B6.

[50] Kimberly Palmer, "Rustic Bourbon: A Hit Overseas, Ho-Hum in the U.S.," *The Wall Street Journal* (September 2, 2003), p. B1.

[51] Bettina Wassener, "Schnapps Goes to College," *Financial Times* (September 4, 2003), p. 9.

Focus model in the United States that has 80 percent shared content with the European Focus. The 20 percent adapted content reflects regulations such as bumper crash test standards.[52]

- When Kraft Foods launched Oreo brand cookies in China in 1996, it used a product extension approach. Following several years of flat sales, Kraft's in-country marketing team launched a research study, which alerted the team to the fact that Oreos were too sweet for the Chinese palate and that the price—14 cookies for 72 cents—was too high. Oreos were then reformulated as a less-sweet, chocolate-covered, four-layer wafer filled with vanilla and chocolate cream. Packages of the new wafer Oreo contain fewer cookies but sell for about 29 cents. Today, Oreo is the best-selling cookie brand in China.[53]

Kraft's experience with Oreos in China is an example of changing from a product extension to a product adaptation strategy when an extension strategy does not yield the desired results. Conversely, managers at Ford, faced with strong competition from Toyota, Honda, and other automakers, are now seeking alternatives to product adaptation. In 2008, Ford unveiled the latest version of its Fiesta. It is designed to be manufactured in high volumes—as many as 1 million units annually—that can be sold worldwide with minimal adaptation. As Ford executive Mark Shields explained, "This is a real shift point for us in that it's a real global car."[54] In the case of GM's Cadillac, managers intended to achieve annual sales of 20,000 vehicles outside the United States by 2010, which required considerable adaptation of the Cadillac to European driving preferences and conditions. The BLS model is only sold in Europe; as James Taylor, general manager of GM's Cadillac division, noted, "There's no Cadillac guy in the U.S. who is going to buy a 4-cylinder low-displacement engine."[55]

Strategy 4: Product-Communication Adaptation (Dual Adaptation)

A company may also utilize the **product-communication adaptation (dual adaptation)** strategy. As the name implies, both the product and one or more promotional elements are adapted for a particular country or region. Sometimes marketers discover that environmental conditions or consumer preferences differ from country to country; the same may be true of the function a product serves or consumer receptivity to advertising appeals. In cases where country managers who have been granted considerable autonomy order adaptations, they may be simply exercising their power to act independently. If headquarters tries to achieve intercountry coordination, the result can be, in the words of one manager, "like herding cats." Consider Unilever's use of dual adaptation strategies. Unilever's Italian country managers discovered that, although Italian women spend more than 20 hours each week cleaning, ironing, and doing other tasks, they are not interested in labor-saving conveniences. The final result—a really clean, shiny floor, for example—is more important than saving time. For the Italian market, Unilever reformulated its Cif brand spray cleaner to do a better job on grease; several different varieties were also rolled out, as were bigger bottles. Television commercials portray Cif as strong rather than convenient.[56] Unilever's Rexona deodorant once had 30 different package designs and 48 different formulations. Advertising and branding were also executed on a local basis.[57] In the case of Cif in Italy, managers boosted sales by making product and promotion improvements based on business intelligence findings. By contrast, the multiple formulations of the Rexona brand were, for the most part, redundant and unnecessary. To address such issues, in 1999, Unilever initiated Path to Growth. This was a program designed to reduce country-by-country tinkering with product formulations and packaging.

---

[52] Joseph B. White, "One Ford for the Whole World," *The Wall Street Journal* (March 17, 2009), p. D2.

[53] Bruce Einhorn, "Want Some Milk with Your Green Tea Oreos?" *Bloomberg Businessweek* (May 7, 2012), pp. 25, 26.

[54] Bill Vlasic, "Ford Introduces One Small Car for a World of Markets," *The Wall Street Journal* (February 15, 2008), p. C3.

[55] Mark Landler, "Europe, Meet Cadillac and Dodge," *The Wall Street Journal* (March 2, 2005), p. C3.

[56] Deborah Ball, "Women in Italy Like to Clean but Shun the Quick and Easy," *The Wall Street Journal* (April 25, 2006), pp. A1, A12.

[57] Deborah Ball, "Too Many Cooks: Despite Revamp, Unwieldy Unilever Falls Behind Rivals," *The Wall Street Journal* (January 3, 2005), pp. A1, A5.

As noted previously, the four alternatives are not mutually exclusive. In other words, a company can simultaneously utilize different product-communication strategies in different parts of the world. For example, Nike has built a global brand by marketing technologically advanced, premium-priced athletic shoes in conjunction with advertising that emphasizes U.S.-style, in-your-face brashness and a "Just Do It" attitude. In the huge and strategically important China market, however, this approach had several limitations. For one thing, Nike's "bad boy" image is at odds with ingrained Chinese values such as respect for authority and filial piety. As a general rule, Nike advertisements in China do not show disruption of harmony; this is due, in part, to a government that discourages dissent. Price was another issue: A regular pair of Nike shoes cost the equivalent of $60–$78, while average annual family income ranges from about $200 in rural areas to $500 in urban areas. In the mid-1990s, Nike responded by creating a shoe that could be assembled in China specifically for the Chinese market using less expensive material and sold for less than $40. After years of running ads designed for Western markets by longtime agency Wieden & Kennedy, Nike hired Chinese-speaking art directors and copywriters working in WPP Group's J. Walter Thompson ad agency in Shanghai to create new advertising featuring local athletes that would appeal to Chinese nationalistic sentiments.[58]

Strategy 5: Innovation

Extension and adaptation strategies are effective approaches to many but not all global market opportunities. For example, they do not respond to markets where there is a need but not the purchasing power to buy either the existing or the adapted product. Global companies are likely to encounter this situation when targeting consumers in India, China, and other emerging markets. When potential customers have limited purchasing power, a company may need to develop an entirely new product designed to address the market opportunity at a price point that is within the reach of the potential customer. The converse is also true: Companies in low-income countries that have achieved local success may have to go beyond mere adaptation by "raising the bar" and bringing product designs up to world-class standards if they are to succeed in high-income countries. **Innovation**, the process of endowing resources with a new capacity to create value, is a demanding but potentially rewarding product strategy for reaching mass markets in less-developed countries as well as important market segments in industrialized countries.

Two entrepreneurs working independently recognized that millions of people around the globe need low-cost eyeglasses. Robert J. Morrison, an American optometrist, created Instant Eyeglasses. These glasses utilize conventional lenses, can be assembled in minutes, and sell for about $20 per pair. Joshua Silva, a physics professor at Oxford University, took a more high-tech approach and came up with glasses with transparent membrane lenses filled with clear silicone fluid. Using two manual adjusters, users can increase or decrease the power of the lenses by regulating the amount of fluid in them. Professor Silva is currently CEO of the Centre for Vision in the Developing World. The organization's mission is to sell low-cost, self-adjusting glasses in developing countries.[59] Another example of the innovation strategy is the South African company that licensed the British patent for a hand-cranked, battery-powered radio. The radio was designed by an English inventor responding to the need for radios in low-income countries. Consumers in these countries do not have electricity in their homes, and they cannot afford the cost of replacement batteries. His invention is an obvious solution: a hand-cranked radio. It is ideal for the needs of low-income people in emerging markets. Users simply crank the radio, and it will play for almost an hour on the charge generated by a short cranking session.

Sometimes manufacturers in developing countries that intend to go global also utilize the innovation strategy. For example, Thermax, an Indian company, had achieved great success in its domestic market with small industrial boilers. Engineers then developed a new design for the

[58] Sally Goll Beatty, "Bad-Boy Nike Is Playing the Diplomat in China," *The Wall Street Journal* (November 10, 1997), p. B1.

[59] Amy Borrus, "Eyeglasses for the Masses," *BusinessWeek* (November 20, 1995), pp. 104–105; Nicholas Thompson, "Self-Adjusted Glasses Could Be Boon to Africa," *The New York Times* (December 10, 2002), p. D6.

Indian market that significantly reduced the size of the individual boiler unit. However, the new design was not likely to succeed outside India because installation was complex and time-consuming. In India, where labor costs are low, relatively elaborate installation requirements are not an issue. The situation is different in higher-wage countries where industrial customers demand sophisticated, integrated systems that can be installed quickly. The managing director at Thermax instructed his engineers to revise the design for the world market with ease of installation as a key attribute. The gamble paid off: Today, Thermax is one of the world's largest producers of small boilers.[60]

The winners in global competition are the companies that can develop products offering the most benefits and, in turn, creating the greatest value for buyers anywhere in the world. In some instances, value is not defined in terms of performance, but rather in terms of customer perception. Product quality is essential—indeed, it is frequently a given—but it is also necessary to support the product quality with imaginative, value-creating advertising and marketing communications. Most industry experts believe that a global appeal and a global advertising campaign are more effective in creating the perception of value than a series of separate national campaigns.

How to Choose a Strategy

Most companies seek product-communications strategies that optimize company profits over the long term. Which strategy for global markets best achieves this goal? There is no one answer to this question. For starters, the considerations noted before must be addressed. In addition, it is worth noting that managers run the risk of committing two types of errors regarding product and communication decisions. One error is to fall victim to the **"not invented here" (NIH) syndrome** and *ignore* decisions made by subsidiary or affiliate managers. Managers who behave in this way are essentially abandoning any effort to leverage product-communication policies outside the home-country market. The other error is to *impose* policies upon all affiliate companies on the assumption that what is right for customers in the home market must also be right for customers everywhere.

To sum up, the choice of product-communication strategy in global marketing is a function of three key factors: (1) the product itself, defined in terms of the function or need it serves; (2) the market, defined in terms of the conditions under which the product is used, the preferences of potential customers, and customers' ability and willingness to buy; and (3) the adaptation and manufacturing costs to the company considering these product-communication approaches. Only after analysis of the product-market fit and of company capabilities and costs can executives choose the most profitable strategy.

New Products in Global Marketing

The matrix shown in Figure 10-3 provides a framework for assessing whether extension or adaptation strategies can be effective. However, the four strategic options described in the matrix do not necessarily represent the best possible responses to global market opportunities. To win in global competition, marketers, designers, and engineers must think outside the box and create innovative new products that offer superior value worldwide. In today's dynamic, competitive market environment, many companies realize that continuous development and introduction of new products are keys to survival and growth. That is the point of strategy 5, product invention. Similarly, marketers should look for opportunities to create global advertising campaigns to support the new product or brand.

Identifying New-Product Ideas

What is a new product? A product's newness can be assessed in terms of its relation to those who buy or use it. Newness may also be organizational, as when a company acquires an already existing product with which it has no previous experience. Finally, an existing product that is not new

---

[60] Christopher A. Bartlett and Sumantra Ghoshal, "Going Global: Lessons from Late Movers," *Harvard Business Review* 78, no. 2 (March–April 2000), p. 137.

➜ **THE CULTURAL CONTEXT**

Marketing Doughnuts Around the World

SYNC • THINK • LEARN

MyMarketingLab

It is tough to attribute the origin of doughnuts to any particular region, and in that it stayed true to the notion of the American melting pot. However, it is said that the first doughnut came to the United States with the Dutch settlers under the name *olykoeks* or "oily cakes." Since then, the proletariat snack has come a long way and if the makers were to see doughnuts being sold in countries throughout the world today, they would be amazed at how a simple treat can morph from culture to culture and over continents, in some instances becoming something Westerners could not readily recognize. The global market entry experiences of Dunkin' Donuts, an American doughnut chain, offer us good insights into how the American-style grub had to be tweaked to suit different palates as they ventured into Asian markets.

Dunkin' Donuts started off as a doughnut shop in Quincy, Massachusetts in 1950. It had by the end of 2012, 10,500 Dunkin' Donuts stores worldwide, including more than 7,000 franchised restaurants in 36 United States, in addition to more than 3,000 international shops in 30 countries. However, all these expansions have not come easy. In the early 2000s, it opened several stores in Beijing but soon had to retreat from the Chinese market. According to one source, the American version of doughnuts is like bread to the Chinese, which could not justify a higher price. It is also too sweet for the Chinese palate. However, with the help of a Taiwanese franchise partner, Dunkin' Donuts is back in China, opening seven stores in Shanghai in 2010. The re-entry was made possible by tapping the expertise of the Taiwanese partner which was familiar with Chinese tastes. Upon its advice, Dunkin' Donuts adapted its product and communication strategies for its re-entry. It used rice flour instead of wheat flour to give the doughnuts a chewy texture much like the sticky rice desserts that many Chinese preferred, and the sugar level was also lowered. Knowing that the Chinese loved fillings, the doughnuts sold in the Chinese stores have red bean paste, some are stuffed with vanilla pudding, some sliced in half to add a wedge of cheesecake, while some have toppings such as ham and cheese, red spaghetti sauce, salmon, spicy beef and seaweed flakes. Besides customizing the taste, the doughnuts are also shaped differently; for example, some could be shaped like pearl bracelets, displayed in showcases to look like deep-fried jewelry, and known by a different name—*Tian tian quan* or "sweet sweet rings." According to the Taiwanese partner, Dunkin' Donuts is thus, marketed as something special, as a new form of enjoyment rather than just doughnuts.

It was a different story for Dunkin' Donuts' entry into India in 2012, where it offered the same American version of its doughnuts. Pursuing a dual extension strategy, Dunkin' Donuts targeted the higher-spending urban Indians who were familiar with western snacks for its entry into the Indian market.

Sources: "Dunkin' Donuts enters India," *Business Times* (February 12, 2010), www.business-standard.com/article/companies/dunkin-donuts-enters-india-112050900069_1.html; "China discovers doughnuts, with salmons," *NBC News* (February 15, 2010), www.nbcnews.com/id/35394535/#.UpxXbtIW134.

to a company may be new to a particular market. The starting point for an effective worldwide new-product program is an information system that seeks new-product ideas from all potentially useful sources and channels these ideas to relevant screening and decision centers within the organization. Ideas can come from many sources, including customers, suppliers, competitors, company salespeople, distributors and agents, subsidiary executives, headquarters executives, documentary sources (e.g., information service reports and publications), and, finally, actual, firsthand observation of the market environment.

The product may be an entirely new invention or innovation that requires a significant amount of learning on the part of users. When such products are successful, they create new markets and new consumption patterns, and have a disruptive impact on industry structures. Sometimes referred to as **discontinuous innovations**, products that belong to this category of "new and different" literally represent a break with the past.[61] In short, they are game-changers.

---

[61] The terminology and framework described here are adapted from Thomas Robertson, "The Process of Innovation and the Diffusion of Innovation," *Journal of Marketing* 31, no. 1 (January 1967), pp. 14–19.

For example, the VCR's revolutionary impact in the 1970s can be explained by the concept of time shifting: The device's initial appeal was that it freed TV viewers from the tyranny of network programming schedules—and allowed viewers to fast-forward past commercials! Likewise, the personal computer revolution that began three decades ago resulted in the democratization of technology. When they were first introduced, PCs were a discontinuous innovation that dramatically transformed the way users live and work. Apple's brilliant string of new-product introductions in the 2000s—the iPod (2001), the iPhone (2007), and the iPad (2010)—likewise represents a hat trick of discontinuous innovation.

An intermediate category of newness is less disruptive and requires less learning on the part of consumers; such products are called **dynamically continuous innovations**. Products that embody this level of innovation share certain features with earlier generations while incorporating new features that offer added value, such as a substantial improvement in performance or greater convenience. Such products cause relatively smaller disruptions in previously existing consumption patterns. The Sensor, SensorExcel, and MACH3 shaving systems represent Gillette's ongoing efforts to bring new technology to bear on wet shaving, an activity that is performed today pretty much as it has been for centuries.

The consumer electronics industry has been the source of many dynamically continuous innovations. Personal stereos such as Sony's Walkman provide music on the go, something that people had been accustomed to since the transistor radio was introduced in the 1950s; the innovation was a miniaturized playback-only cassette tape system. The advent of the compact disc in the early 1980s provided an improved music listening experience but didn't require significant behavioral changes. Similarly, much to the delight of couch potatoes everywhere, wide-screen, flat-panel HDTVs offer viewers significantly improved performance. It must be noted that HDTV owners do have to order a high-definition service tier from cable or satellite companies.

Most new products fall into a third category, **continuous innovation**. Such products are typically "new and improved" versions of existing ones and require less R&D expenditure to develop than dynamically continuous innovations. Continuous innovations cause minimal disruption in existing consumption patterns and require the least amount of learning on the part of buyers. As noted previously, newness can be evaluated relative to a buyer or user. When a current PC user seeking an upgrade buys a new model with a faster processor or more memory, the PC can be viewed as a continuous innovation. However, to a first-time PC user, the same computer represents a discontinuous innovation. Consumer packaged goods companies and food marketers rely heavily on continuous innovation when rolling out new products. These often take the form of **line extensions**, such as new sizes, flavors, and low-fat versions. The three degrees of product newness can be represented in terms of a continuum, as shown in Figure 10-4.

New-Product Development

A major driver for the development of global products is the cost of product R&D. As competition intensifies, companies discover they can reduce the cost of R&D for a product by developing a global product design. Often the goal is to create a single **platform**, or core product design element or component, that can be quickly and cheaply adapted to various country markets. As Christopher Sinclair noted during his tenure as president and CEO of PepsiCo Foods and Beverages International, "What you really want to do is look at the four or five platforms that

FIGURE 10-4
New-Product Continuum

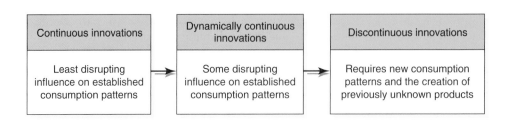

Continuous innovations	Dynamically continuous innovations	Discontinuous innovations
Least disrupting influence on established consumption patterns	Some disrupting influence on established consumption patterns	Requires new consumption patterns and the creation of previously unknown products

can allow you to cut across countries, become a scale operator, and do the things that global marketers do."[62]

Even automobiles, which must meet national safety and pollution standards, are now designed with global markets in mind. With a global product platform, automakers can offer an adaptation of a global design as needed instead of creating unique designs for individual countries or geographic regions. The first-generation Ford Focus, launched in Europe at the end of 1998 and in the United States in 1999, was marketed globally with a minimum of adaptation. The chief program engineer on the Focus project was from Great Britain, the chief technical officer was German, the project manager was Irish, and an Anglo-Australian was chief designer. Under Ford 2000, about $1,000 per vehicle was cut out of the development cost.[63]

A standardized platform was also a paramount consideration when GM set about the task of redesigning its minivan in the 1990s. GM's globally minded board directed the design team to create a vehicle that would be popular in both the United States and Europe. Because roads in Europe are typically narrower and fuel is more expensive, the European engineers lobbied for a vehicle that was smaller than the typical minivan. By using lightweight metals such as magnesium for some components, vehicle weight was minimized, with a corresponding improvement in fuel economy.[64] As it turned out, the resulting models—the Chevrolet Silhouette (United States), Opel Sentra (Germany), and Vauxhall Sintra (United Kingdom)—met with limited success in their respective markets. The lesson: It is one thing to formulate a global strategy. It is quite another thing to execute it successfully!

Other design-related costs, whether incurred by the manufacturer or the end user, must also be considered. *Durability* and *quality* are important product characteristics that must be appropriate for the proposed market. In the United States and Europe, car buyers do not wish to incur high service bills. Thus, the new Ford Focus was designed to be less expensive to maintain and repair. For example, engine removal takes only about 1.5 hours, about half the time required to remove the engine in the discontinued Escort. In addition, body panels are bolted together rather than welded, and the rear signal lights are mounted higher so they are less likely to be broken in minor parking lot mishaps.

The International New-Product Department

As noted previously, a high volume of information flow is required to scan adequately for new-product opportunities, and considerable effort is subsequently required to screen these opportunities to identify candidates for product development. The best organizational design for addressing these requirements is a new-product department. Managers in such a department engage in several activities. First, they ensure that all relevant information sources are continuously tapped for new-product ideas. Second, they screen these ideas to identify appropriate candidates for investigation. Third, they investigate and analyze these selected new-product ideas. Finally, they ensure that the organization commits resources to the most promising new-product candidates and is continuously involved in an orderly program of new-product introduction and development on a worldwide basis.

With the enormous number of possible new products, most companies establish screening grids in order to focus on those ideas that are the most appropriate for investigation. The following questions are relevant to this task:

1. How big is the market for this product at various prices?
2. What are the likely competitive moves in response to our activity with this product?
3. Can we market the product through our existing structure? If not, what changes will be required, and what costs will be incurred to make the changes?

[62] "Fritos 'Round the World," *Brandweek* (March 27, 1995), pp. 32, 35.
[63] Robert L. Simison, "Ford Hopes Its New Focus Will Be a Global Bestseller," *The Wall Street Journal* (October 8, 1998), p. B10.
[64] Rebecca Blumenstein, "While Going Global, GM Slips at Home," *The Wall Street Journal* (January 8, 1997), pp. B1, B4.

4. Given estimates of potential demand for this product at specified prices and estimated levels of competition, can we source the product at a cost that will yield an adequate profit?

5. Does this product fit our strategic development plan? (a) Is the product consistent with our overall goals and objectives? (b) Is the product consistent with our available resources? (c) Is the product consistent with our management structure? (d) Does the product have adequate global potential?

For example, the corporate development team at Virgin evaluates more than a dozen proposals each day from outside the company, as well as proposals from Virgin staff members. Brad Rosser, Virgin's former group corporate development director, headed the team for several years. When assessing new-product ideas, Rosser and his team looked for synergy with existing Virgin products, pricing, marketing opportunities, risk versus return on investment, and whether the idea "uses or abuses" the Virgin brand. Examples of ventures that have been given the green light are Virgin Jeans, a denim clothing store chain; Virgin Bride, a wedding consulting service; and Virgin Net, an Internet service provider.[65]

Testing New Products

The major lesson of new-product introduction outside the home market has been that whenever a product interacts with human, mechanical, or chemical elements, there is the potential for a surprising and unexpected incompatibility. Because virtually *every* product matches this description, it is important to test a product under actual market conditions before proceeding with full-scale introduction. A test does not necessarily involve a full-scale test-marketing effort. It may simply involve observing the actual use of the product in the target market.

Failure to assess actual use conditions can lead to big surprises, as Unilever learned when it rolled out a new detergent brand in Europe without sufficient testing. Unilever spent $150 million to develop the new detergent, which was formulated with a stain-fighting manganese complex molecule intended to clean fabrics faster at lower temperatures than competing products such as Procter & Gamble's (P&G) Ariel. Backed by a $300 million marketing budget, the detergent was launched in April 1994 as Persil Power, Omo Power, and other brand names. After a restructuring, Unilever had cut the time required to roll out new products in Europe from 3 years to 16 months. In this particular instance, the increased efficiency combined with corporate enthusiasm for the new formula resulted in a marketing debacle. Consumers discovered that some clothing items were damaged after being washed with Power. P&G, quick to capitalize on the situation, ran newspaper ads denouncing Power and commissioned lab tests to verify that the damage did, in fact, occur. Unilever chairman Sir Michael Perry called the Power fiasco, "the greatest marketing setback we've seen." Unilever reformulated Power, but it was too late to save the brand. The company lost the opportunity to gain share against P&G in Europe.[66]

Summary

The product is the most important element of a company's marketing program. Global marketers face the challenge of formulating coherent product and brand strategies on a worldwide basis. A **product** can be viewed as a collection of tangible and intangible attributes that collectively provide benefits to a buyer or user. A **brand** is a complex bundle of images and experiences in the mind of the customer. In most countries, **local brands** compete with **international brands** and **global brands**. A **local product** is available in a single country; an **international product** is available in several countries; a **global product** meets the wants and needs of a global market.

[65] Elena Bowes, "Virgin Flies in Face of Conventions," *Ad Age International* (January 1997), p. i4.
[66] Laurel Wentz, "Unilever's Power Failure a Wasteful Use of Haste," *Advertising Age* (May 6, 1995), p. 42.

A global brand has the same name and a similar image and positioning in most parts of the world. Many global companies leverage favorable **brand images** and high **brand equity** by employing **combination (tiered) branding**, **co-branding**, and **brand-extension** strategies. Companies can create strong brands in all markets through **global brand leadership**. **Maslow's needs hierarchy** is a needs-based framework that offers a way of understanding opportunities to develop local and global products in different parts of the world. Some products and brands benefit from the **country-of-origin effect**. Product decisions must also address packaging issues such as labeling and **aesthetics**. Also, **express warranty** policies must be appropriate for each country market.

Product and communications strategies can be viewed within a framework that allows for combinations of three strategies: **extension strategy**, **adaptation strategy**, and creation strategy. Five strategic alternatives are open to companies pursuing geographic expansion: **product-communication extension**, **product extension–communication adaptation**, **product adaptation–communication extension**, **product-communication adaptation (dual adaptation)**, and **product invention (innovation)**. The strategic alternative(s) that a particular company chooses will depend on the product and the need it serves, customer preferences and purchasing power, and the costs of adaptation versus standardization. **Product transformation** occurs when a product that has been introduced into new country markets serves a different function or is used differently than originally intended. When choosing a strategy, management should consciously strive to avoid the **"not invented here" (NIH) syndrome**.

Global competition has put pressure on companies to excel at developing standardized product **platforms** that can serve as a foundation for cost-efficient adaptations. New products can be classified as **discontinuous**, **dynamically continuous**, or **continuous innovations** such as **line extensions**. A successful product launch requires an understanding of how markets develop: sequentially over time or simultaneously. Today, many new products are launched in multiple national markets as product development cycles shorten and product development costs soar.

MyMarketingLab

Go to **mymktlab.com** for the following Assisted-graded writing questions:

10-1. Briefly describe the various combinations of product-communication strategies available to global marketers. When is it appropriate to use each?

10-2. Assess the U.S. market potential for the Smart. Do you think the car will be a success? Why or why not?

10-3. Mymarketinglab Only – comprehensive writing assignment for this chapter.

MyMarketingLab

Go to **mymktlab.com** to complete the problems marked with this icon .

Discussion Questions

10-4. What is the difference between a product and a brand?

10-5. How do local, international, and global products differ? Cite examples.

10-6. What are some of the elements that make up a brand? Are these elements tangible or intangible?

10-7. What criteria should global marketers consider when making product design decisions?

10-8. How can buyer attitudes about a product's country of origin affect marketing strategy?

10-9. Identify several global brands. What are some of the reasons for the global success of the brands you chose?

⭐**10-10.** Each year, the Interbrand consultancy compiles a ranking of global brands. The top-ranked brands for 2012 are shown in Table 10-2. Browse through the list and choose any brand that interests you. Compare its 2012 ranking with the most recent ranking, which you can find online at www.interbrand.com. How has the brand's ranking changed? Consult additional sources (e.g., articles from print media, annual reports, the company's Web site) to enhance your understanding of the factors and forces that contributed to the brand's move up or down in the rankings.

10-11. Hofstede's social values framework can be used to help explain the Asian version of Maslow's hierarchy. Which dimension from Table 4-2 (p. 137) is most relevant? In Chapter 4, we also noted the differences between innovation diffusion processes in Asia and the West. Review the discussion on pages 144 and 145 Can you relate it to Figure 10-1?

10-12. Compare and contrast the three categories of innovation discussed in the chapter. Which type of innovation do flat-panel wide-screen HDTVs represent? The iPad?

CASE 10-1 CONTINUED (REFER TO PAGE 314)

The Beatles Story, Liverpool

The Beatles Story, Liverpool, opened in 1990 in the Beatles' hometown of Liverpool, UK; it is a favorite visitor attraction for Beatles fans from all over the world. The Beatles' music and brand have had an enduring global appeal; the group broke up in 1970, but as the bestselling band of all time its music is acknowledged as having enduring international cultural significance.

The Beatles Story, Liverpool, offers visitors the chance to learn about the Beatles from the early days of the band through the height of Beatlemania by using themed rooms, film footage, music, and artifacts. Each visitor is issued an audio guide that tells the story of the band. Liverpool's thriving music scene of the 1950s and 1960s is recreated for the visitor through rooms furnished in 1960s style and crammed full of press cuttings, photographs, and memorabilia to reflect the fashion and atmosphere of the time.

The world famous Cavern Club where the Beatles had their first public performance has also been recreated, giving visitors the opportunity to sit and watch archive footage of Beatles' performances. Archive news coverage of the Beatles first tour to America in 1964, including footage of their appearance on the Ed Sullivan Show, is shown continuously. The displays of the artwork used for each album, the posters, sample records, and news coverage recreate the sights and sounds of the Beatles era. At the end of the tour, a range of Beatles merchandise is available for purchase; CDs, posters, clothing, and accessories provide lasting memories of the visit.

In 2008, to extend the success of the original attraction, a second Beatles Story opened on Liverpool's waterfront, offering a cinematic visitor experience targeted at families using computer-generated 3D animation and special effects, including music, motion, and aroma technologies. In the same year, the original Beatles Story, Liverpool, attraction was extended to include four special displays, each dedicated to the individual music and film achievements of each of the four band members: George Harrison, John Lennon, Sir Paul McCartney, and Ringo Starr.

Elvis and the Beatles are music brands with enduring global appeal. During 2011, archivists and curators from Elvis Presley's Graceland and the Beatles Story, Liverpool, worked together to host a joint interactive multimedia exhibition entitled "Elvis and Us." The unique groundbreaking exhibition tells the story of how Elvis' music influenced the early work of the Beatles and of their first meeting in 1965. It offers visitors the opportunity to view unique artifacts and rare film footage and to experience the music of two global music icons together for the first time in one visitor attraction.

The Beatles Story, Liverpool, offers a unique cultural experience for the visitor. It details the story of a unique band with a global fan base. The experience offers older consumers memories of their youth and of an important time in the development of popular music. For many of these consumers, a visit to the home city of the Beatles can be a nostalgic and emotional experience. For younger consumers, it offers the opportunity to learn about the most significant era in the development of the modern music business, to enjoy the music, and to catch a glimpse of the early days of rock and roll, whose enduring influence continues to be heard in the music of today.

Discussion Questions

10-13. What tangible and intangible attributes make up the Beatles Story, Liverpool experience?

10-14. Why does the Beatles brand continue to have global appeal?

10-15. To what extent do you feel that the Beatles Story, Liverpool, benefits from the country-of-origin effect?

Source: This case was prepared by Susan Scoffield, Department of Business and Management, Manchester Metropolitan University, UK.

Additional Sources: The Beatles Story, Liverpool, www.beatlesstory.com (accessed December 16, 2011); Elvis Presley, www.elvis.com (accessed December 16, 2011); Elvis and Us, www.elvisandus.com (accessed December 16, 2011); Alexandra Topping, "Music Tourism Adds Plenty of Notes to British Economy," *The Guardian, UK* (May 15, 2011).

CASE 10-2
The Smart Car

In the summer of 2006, DaimlerChrysler announced that the company's Smart car would be offered for sale in the United States the following year. Launched in Europe in 1998, the diminutive Smart had never turned a profit for its parent company. When Dieter Zetsche became DaimlerChrysler's CEO at the beginning of 2006, the Smart car issue was one of his top priorities.

At the time of the announcement, the Smart saga had been 15 years in the making. In 1991, Nicolas Hayek, chairman of Swatch, announced plans to develop a battery-powered "Swatch car" in conjunction with Volkswagen. At the time, Hayek said his goal was to build "an ecologically inoffensive, high-quality city car for two people" that would sell for about $6,400. The Swatchmobile concept was based on Hayek's conviction that consumers become emotionally attached to cars just as they do to watches. Like the Swatch, the Swatchmobile (officially named "Smart") was designed to be affordable, durable, and stylish.

Early on, Hayek noted that safety would be another key selling point, declaring, "This car will have the crash security of a Mercedes." Composite exterior panels mounted on a cage-like body frame would allow owners to change colors by switching panels. Further, Hayek envisioned a car that emitted almost no pollutants, thanks to its electric engine. The car would also offer gasoline-powered operation, using a highly efficient, miniaturized engine capable of achieving speeds of 80 miles per hour. Hayek predicted that worldwide sales would reach 1 million units, with the United States accounting for about half the market.

Then, in 1993, the alliance with Volkswagen was dissolved. In the spring of 1994, Hayek announced that he had lined up a new joint venture partner. The Mercedes-Benz unit of Daimler-Benz AG would invest 750 million Deutsche marks in a new factory in Hambach-Saargemuend, France. In November 1998, after several months of production delays and repeated cost overruns, Hayek sold Swatch's remaining 19 percent stake in the venture, officially known as Micro Compact Car GmBH (MCC), to Mercedes. A spokesman indicated that Mercedes' refusal to pursue the hybrid gasoline/battery engine was the reason Swatch withdrew from the project.

The decision by Mercedes executives to take full control of the venture was consistent with its strategy for leveraging its engineering skills and broadening the company's appeal beyond the luxury segment of the automobile market. As Mercedes chairman Helmut Werner said, "With the new car, Mercedes wants to combine ecology, emotion, and intellect." Approximately 80 percent of the Smart's parts are components and modules engineered by and sourced from outside suppliers and subcontractors known as "system partners." The decision to locate the assembly plant in France disappointed German labor unions, but Mercedes executives expected to save 500 marks per car. The reason: French workers are on the job 275 days per year, while German workers average only 242 days; also, overall labor costs are 40 percent lower in France than in Germany.

MCC claims that at Smart Ville, as the factory is known, only 7.5 hours are required to complete a vehicle—25 percent less time than that required by the world's best automakers. The first 3 hours of the process are performed by systems partners. A Canadian company, Magna International, starts by welding the structural components, which are then painted by Eisenmann, a German company. Both operations are performed outside the central assembly hall; a conveyer then transports the body into the main hall. There, VDO, another German company, installs the instrument panel. At this point, modules and parts manufactured by Krupp-Hoesch, Bosch, Dynamit Nobel, and Ymos are delivered for assembly by MCC employees. To encourage integration of MCC employees and system partners and to underscore the need for quality, both groups share a common dining room overlooking the main assembly hall.

The Smart City Coupe officially went on sale in Europe in October 1998. In an effort to create a distinct brand identity, a separate dealer network was established for Smart. In retrospect, this decision turned out to be an expensive one. Sales got off to a slow start amid concerns about the vehicle's stability. That problem was solved with a sophisticated electronics package that monitors wheel slippage. Late-night TV comedians gave the odd-looking car no respect and referred to it as "a motorized ski boot" and "a backpack on wheels." The sales picture was brightest in the United Kingdom; the brisk sales pace in Britain was especially noteworthy because MCC was building only left-hand-drive models (the United Kingdom is the only country in Europe in which right-hand-drive cars are the norm). Industry observers noted that Brits' affection for the Austin Mini, a tiny vehicle that first appeared in the 1960s, appeared to have been extended to the Smart.

Despite this success, MCC reduced its annual sales target from 130,000 to 100,000. Robert Eaton, joint chairman of DaimlerChrysler, went on record as being skeptical of the vehicle's future. In an interview with *Automotive News*, he said, "It's possible we'll conclude that it's a good idea but one whose time simply hasn't come."

In 2000, amid growing interest in the brand, the Smart exceeded its revised sales target. Wolf-Garten GmbH & Company, a German gardening equipment company, initiated a program to convert the Smart to a lawn mower suitable for use on golf courses. Both convertible and diesel-engine editions were added to the product line.

Exhibit 10-11 Thanks to the success of the Smart car in Europe, several new models have been added to the Smart family. These include the convertible Smart Roadster and the Smart forfour (a four-door model). An SUV—the Smart formore—was introduced in 2006. The original model will be rechristened the Smart City Coupé. As one observer noted, "Buying a Smart is less like buying a small car and more like buying an iMac, a Blackberry PDA, or a box of take-out sushi."

Source: Chitose Suzuki/AP Images

In 2001, executives at DaimlerChrysler initiated a program to research the U.S. market to determine prospects for the Smart. The announcement came as Americans were facing steep increases in gasoline prices. Between 2001 and 2006, several other small cars in the $10,000 to $14,000 range were introduced in the U.S. market, including the Chevrolet Aveo (manufactured by Daewoo), the Toyota Yaris, and the Honda Fit. In addition, Toyota had successfully launched the Scion, and BMW's new Mini was also proving to be hugely popular with U.S. drivers.

"The Smart brand is capable of sustainable profitability, and it will be profitable in 2007 and beyond. We are working on a cost basis that is almost 50 percent lower than it used to be. The production time at the Hambach plant in France and the assembly time for the new car are 20 percent shorter than with its predecessor."

—Ulrich Walker, chairman and CEO, Daimler Northeast Asia; president and CEO, Smart

One challenge in bringing the Smart across the Atlantic was the euro's strength relative to the dollar. To further complicate matters, the DaimlerChrysler merger ended with the sale of Chrysler to a private equity group. Going forward, Smart was under the ownership of Daimler AG. Moreover, distribution and promotion were critical to a successful U.S. launch.

Auto racing legend Roger Penske, chief executive of Penske Automotive Group, decided to gamble on the Smart. He snapped up the rights to serve as the sole U.S. distributor for the tiny car. Penske had assembled the second-largest auto retailing group in the United States by selling luxury cars and imports. The network included more than 300 franchised dealers in the United States and Europe. Penske's team set the goal of selling 16,000 Smart cars in the first year; as gasoline prices rose to $4 per gallon, the minicar's appeal seemed obvious. The company sold 24,622 cars in 2008.

In 2010, as gasoline prices moderated, car buyers began gravitating back toward large vehicles. Smart's sales fell from 14,595 cars in 2009 to 5,927 in 2010. Early in 2011, Penske Automotive Group announced that it was terminating its distribution agreement for the Smart and returning distribution to Mercedes-Benz USA. A company spokesperson attributed the move to a change in organizational structure for the Smart brand in Germany.

Meanwhile, Smart USA and the Strawberry Frog advertising agency launched a social media initiative to leverage the exploding popularity of Facebook and Twitter. The brand's Twitter handle is @smartcarusa; followers are reminded that "Smart is against dumb, mindless consumption." Sample tactics include "The Great Dumb Trade-In" and retweets of owner comments about their vehicles.

Today, Smart USA's page on Facebook has more than 100,000 "likes." The company has also mobilized street teams and produced viral videos.

Scott Goodson, the founder of Strawberry Frog, sums up the brand this way: "The Smart car is about living a flexible, agile life. Less is more." Asked how she would measure the success of the "Against Dumb" movement, Kim McGill, Smart's vice president of marketing and advertising, said:

> If it makes people just think about it, that will be a success.... We need to get people thinking of buying not for that one time, but buying for what we need most of the time. If we can get more people talking in that direction, it will be nothing but positive for this brand.

To learn more about the Smart, visit www.smartusa.com.

Discussion Questions

10-16. What is Smart's competitive advantage? Brand promise? Positioning?

⭐10-17. How does the Smart compare to the Honda Element, Scion iQ, Kia Soul, or Fiat 500? Are these models targeting the same consumers as the Smart? In view of the success of these brands, do you think the Smart's U.S. launch is too late?

10-18. As noted in the case, Penske Automotive Group is no longer the distributor for Smart USA. How will this affect Smart's fortunes in the United States?

⭐10-19. Evaluate Smart USA's social media strategy. Discuss what additional channels or tactics you would recommend.

Sources: Vanessa Fuhrmans and Matthew Dolan, "Daimler's Smart Gets Tuneup," *The Wall Street Journal* (January 11, 2012), p. B4; Max Ramsey, "Penske, Daimler End Smart-Minicar Deal," *The Wall Street Journal* (February 15, 2011), p. B3; Eleftheria Parpis, "Smart USA Refuels Brand," *Adweek* (November 24, 2010); Elaine Wong, "Why Smart (the Car) Wants Americans to Be 'Against Dumb,'" Forbes.com; D. Stoll, "Smart Car a Shrewd Move?" *The Wall Street Journal* (June 27, 2007), p. A8; Bernard Simon, "Daimler Weighs Smart's U.S. Appeal," *Financial Times* (March 28, 2006), p. 21; "Smart Shows Redesigned ForTwo," *The Wall Street Journal Online* (November 10, 2006); Neal E. Boudette and Stephen Power, "Will Chrysler's Move Be Smart?" *The Wall Street Journal* (June 24/25, 2006), p. A2; Dan McCosh, "Get Smart: Buyers Try to Jump the Queue," *The New York Times* (March 19, 2004), p. D1; Nicholas Foulkes, "Smart Set Gets Even Smarter," *Financial Times* (February 14–15, 2004), p. W10; Will Pinkston and Scott Miller, "DaimlerChrysler Steers Toward 'Smart' Debut in U.S.," *The Wall Street Journal* (August 20, 2001), pp. B1, B4; Scott Miller, "Daimler May Roll Out Its Tiny Car Here," *The Wall Street Journal* (June 9, 2001), p. B1; Miller, "DaimlerChrysler's Smart Car May Have a New Use," *The Wall Street Journal* (February 15, 2001), pp. B1, B4; Haig Simonian, "Carmakers' Smart Move," *Financial Times* (July 1, 1997), p. 12; William Taylor, "Message and Muscle: An Interview with Swatch Titan Nicolas Hayek," *Harvard Business Review* (March–April 1993), pp. 99–110; Kevin Helliker, "Swiss Movement: Can Wristwatch Whiz Switch Swatch Cachet to an Automobile?" *The Wall Street Journal* (March 4, 1994), pp. A1, A3; Ferdinand Protzman, "Off the Wrist, onto the Road: A Swatch on Wheels," *The New York Times* (March 4, 1994), p. C1.

11
Pricing Decisions

CASE 11-1
Global Companies Target Low-Income Consumers (B)

In the 1950s and 1960s, the space race pitted the Soviet Union against the United States in an effort to explore outer space. Half a century later, the International Space Station is a collaborative effort involving Russia, the United States, and other nations. Meanwhile, a new race is underway. This one is much more "down to earth" and does not involve superpowers in different hemispheres jostling for geopolitical advantage. Rather, this twenty-first-century competition involves efforts by leading automakers in Asia, Europe, and the United States to create inexpensive cars that can be sold in huge volumes to consumers in India and other developing countries.

Renault, the French automotive group, was a pioneer in the low-price segment with its Logan; launched in 2004, more than 1.2 million units have been sold (see Exhibit 11-1). Initially, the Logan

Exhibit 11-1 The Dacia Logan is one element center of Renault chief Carlos Ghosn's low-price strategy. The Logan doesn't have power steering or air conditioning; even so, it has proven to be very popular in both emerging and developed countries.

The Logan's success demonstrates a very simple marketing idea: Price sells cars. Many first-time buyers have discovered that they can own a new Logan for about the same price as a motorcycle. In 2009, government stimulus programs in France, Germany, and elsewhere that included "cash-for-clunkers" incentives kept demand high.
Source: ERIC PIERMONT/AFP/GettyImages

was produced at a single plant operated by Renault's Dacia affiliate in Romania. As Dacia chairman Luc-Alexandre Ménard explained, "At the time, we weren't too sure of what we would do with this car. It was meant to be a one-off, a Trojan horse to penetrate new markets in developing countries." Today, Logans are manufactured in several countries, including Iran, India, and Brazil; the cars are available for sale in more than 50 countries.

Two other automakers have joined the race to bring low-cost cars to the emerging-market masses. In 2009, India's Tata Motors launched the Nano, a radical new design with a rock-bottom sticker price of 1 lakh (equivalent to 100,000 rupees, or $2,500). The Nano has a rear-mounted, 2-cylinder engine that delivers 33 horsepower. The top speed is 60 miles per hour, and it delivers 50 miles per gallon of gas. Nissan recently announced that the venerable Datsun nameplate would be reborn in 2014 as a barebones car priced between $3,000 and $5,000. Like the Nano, the new Datsun's powertrain will feature a 2-cylinder engine mated to a manual transmission. Unlike the Nano, which has no airbags, the Datsun will be equipped with a driver's-side airbag.

In general, two basic factors determine the boundaries within which prices should be set. The first is product cost, which establishes a *price floor*, or minimum price. Although pricing a product below the cost boundary is certainly possible, few firms can afford to do this over the long run. Moreover, as we saw in Chapter 8, low prices in export markets can invite dumping investigations.

Second, prices for comparable substitute products create a *price ceiling*, or maximum price. In many instances, global competition puts pressure on the pricing policies and related cost structures of domestic companies. The imperative to cut costs—especially fixed costs—is one of the reasons for the growth of outsourcing. In some cases, local market conditions, such as low incomes, force companies to innovate by creating new products that can be profitably sold at low prices. For more on the auto industry's efforts to create low-cost cars, turn to the continuation of Case 11-1 at the end of the chapter.

Between the lower and upper boundaries for every product is an *optimum price*, which is a function of the demand for the product as determined by the willingness and ability of customers to buy it. In this chapter, we will first review basic pricing concepts and then discuss several pricing topics that pertain to global marketing. These include target costing, price escalation, and environmental considerations such as currency fluctuations and inflation. In the second half of the chapter, we will discuss gray market goods, dumping, price fixing, transfer pricing, and countertrade.

LEARNING OBJECTIVES

1 Review the basic pricing concepts that underlie a successful global marketing pricing strategy.

2 Identify the different pricing strategies and objectives that influence decisions about pricing products in global markets.

3 Summarize the various Incoterms that affect the final price of a product.

4 List some of the environmental influences that impact prices.

5 Apply the ethnocentric/polycentric/geocentric framework to decisions regarding price.

6 Explain some of the tactics global companies can use to combat the problem of gray market goods.

7 Assess the impact of dumping on prices in global markets.

8 Compare and contrast the different types of price fixing.

9 Explain the concept of transfer pricing.

10 Define *countertrade* and explain the various forms it can take.

Basic Pricing Concepts

Generally speaking, international trade results in lower prices for goods. Lower prices, in turn, help keep a country's rate of inflation in check. In a true global market, the **law of one price** would prevail: All customers in the market could get the best product available for the best price. As Lowell Bryan and his collaborators note in *Race for the World*, a global market exists for certain products such as crude oil, commercial aircraft, diamonds, and integrated circuits. All other things being equal, a Boeing 787 costs the same worldwide. By contrast, beer, compact discs, and many other products that are available around the world are actually offered in markets that are national rather than global in nature; that is, these are markets where national competition reflects differences in factors such as costs, regulations, and the intensity of the rivalry among industry members.[1] The beer market, for one, is extremely fragmented; even though Budweiser is the leading global brand, it commands less than 4 percent of the total market. The nature of the beer market explains why, for example, a six-pack of Heineken varies in price by as much as 50 percent (adjusted for purchasing power parity, transportation, and other transaction costs) depending on where it is sold. In Japan, for example, the price is a function of the competition between Heineken, other imports, and five national producers—Kirin, Asahi, Sapporo, Suntory, and Orion—which collectively command 60 percent of the market.

Because of these differences in national markets, the global marketer must develop pricing systems and pricing policies that take into account price floors, price ceilings, and optimum prices. A firm's pricing system and policies must also be consistent with other uniquely global opportunities and constraints. For example, many companies that are active in the 17 nations of the euro zone are adjusting to the new cross-border transparency of prices. Similarly, the Internet has made price information for many products available around the globe. Companies must carefully consider how customers in one country or region will react if they discover they are paying significantly higher prices for the same product than customers in other parts of the world.

There is another important internal organizational consideration besides cost. Within the typical corporation, there are many interest groups and, frequently, conflicting price objectives. Divisional vice presidents, regional executives, and country managers are all concerned about profitability at their respective organizational levels. Similarly, the director of global marketing seeks competitive prices in world markets. The controller and financial vice president are concerned about profits. The manufacturing vice president seeks long production runs for maximum manufacturing efficiency. The tax manager is concerned about compliance with government transfer pricing legislation. Finally, company counsel is concerned about the antitrust implications of global pricing practices. Ultimately, however, price generally reflects the goals set by members of the sales staff, product managers, corporate division chiefs, and/or the company's chief executive.

Global Pricing Objectives and Strategies

Whether dealing with a single home-country market or multiple country markets, marketing managers must develop pricing objectives as well as strategies for achieving those objectives. Remember: Price is an independent variable; as a marketing tactic, managers can raise, lower, or maintain prices as part of the overall marketing strategy. However, a number of pricing issues are unique to global marketing. The pricing strategy for a particular product may vary from country to country; a product may be positioned as a low-priced, mass-market product in some countries and a premium-priced, niche product in others. Stella Artois beer is a case in point: As noted in Chapter 7, it is a low-priced, "everyday" beer in Belgium but a premium brand ("Perfection Has Its Price") in export markets. Pricing objectives may also vary depending on a product's life-cycle stage and the country-specific competitive situation. In making global pricing decisions, it is additionally necessary to factor in external considerations such as the added cost associated with shipping goods long distances across national boundaries. The issue of global pricing can also be fully integrated in the product design process, an approach widely used by Japanese companies.

Market Skimming and Financial Objectives

Price can be used as a strategic variable to achieve specific financial goals, including return on investment, profit, and rapid recovery of product development costs. When financial criteria such as profit and maintenance of margins are the objectives, the product must be part of a superior value proposition for buyers; price is thus integral to the total positioning strategy. The **market skimming** pricing strategy is often part of a deliberate attempt to reach a market segment that is willing to pay a premium price for a particular brand or for a specialized or unique product (see Exhibit 11-2 and Exhibit 11-3). Companies that seek competitive advantage by pursuing

---

[1] Lowell Bryan, *Race for the World: Strategies to Build a Great Global Firm* (Boston: Harvard Business School Press, 1999), pp. 40–41.

Exhibit 11-2 Reebok dominates the footwear market in India, where its cricket shoes are a top seller. Reeboks are expensive; a shoe that costs Rs2,500 is equivalent of a month's salary for a junior civil servant. As Muktesh Pant, the first CEO of Reebok India, noted, "For Rs2,000 to Rs3,000, people feel they can really make a statement. It's cheaper than buying a new watch, for instance, if you want to make a splash at a party. And though our higher-priced shoes put us in competition with things like refrigerators and cows, the upside is that we're now being treated as a prestigious brand."
Source: AP Photo/Tsering Topgyal

differentiation strategies or positioning their products in the premium segment frequently use market skimming. LVMH and other luxury goods marketers that target the global elite market segment use skimming strategies (see Case 11-2). For years, Mercedes-Benz utilized a skimming strategy; however, this created an opportunity for Toyota to introduce its luxury Lexus line and undercut Mercedes.

The skimming pricing strategy is also appropriate in the introductory phase of the product life cycle, when both production capacity and competition are limited. By setting a high price, demand is limited to innovators and early adopters, who are willing and able to buy and who want to be among the first to own and use the product (see Exhibit 11-2). When the product enters the growth stage of the life cycle and competition increases, manufacturers start to cut prices. This strategy has been used consistently in the consumer electronics industry; for example, when Sony introduced the first consumer VCRs in the 1970s, the retail price exceeded $1,000. The same was true when compact disc players were launched in the early 1980s. Within a few years, though, prices for these products dropped well below $500. Today, the VCR is virtually obsolete while compact disc players are considered commodities.

A similar pattern is evident with HDTVs; in the fall of 1998, HDTVs went on sale in the United States with prices starting at about $7,000. This price maximized revenue on limited volume and matched demand to available supply. Now, prices for HDTVs have dropped significantly as consumers become more familiar with HDTV and its advantages and as next-generation factories in Asia allow for lower costs and increased production capacity. In 2005, Sony surprised the industry by launching a 40-inch HDTV for $3,500; by the end of 2006, comparable HDTVs were selling for about $2,000. Today, equivalent sets cost less than $1,000. The challenge facing manufacturers now is to hold the line on prices; if they do not succeed, HDTVs may also become commoditized.

> "For us, 'Made in Italy' is so important, the quality and the artisans and the material is so important, that if we feel any kind of pressure on our profitability we will raise prices. We've found that as long as our quality is maintained the customers are willing to pay a premium."[2]
>
> —Marco Bizzari, chairman and CEO, Bottega Veneta

Penetration Pricing and Nonfinancial Objectives

Some companies are pursuing nonfinancial objectives with their pricing strategy. Price can be used as a competitive weapon to gain or maintain market position. Market share or other sales-based objectives are frequently set by companies that enjoy cost-leadership positions in their industry. A **market penetration pricing strategy** calls for setting price levels that are low enough to quickly build market share. Historically, many companies that used this type of

[2] Rachel Sanderson, "Bottega Veneta Hits Luxury Sweet Spot," *Financial Times* (April 9, 2013), p. 17.

Exhibit 11-3 Canada's Imax Corporation is the world's premier provider of large-format motion picture projection technology. The company has identified 900 potential markets for new Imax theaters; two-thirds of those are global. Imax has developed a lower-cost projection system called Imax MPX that fits in existing movie theaters; by improving the economics for movie exhibitors, this innovation will expand the number of available market opportunities. China is Imax's fastest-growing market. At the end of 2012, there were 73 Imax theaters in China; the company plans to have 300 theaters in operation by 2016. Imax enjoys high brand awareness levels in China's Tier 1, Tier 2, and Tier 3 cities.
Source: Morton Beebe/Corbis Images

pricing were located in the Pacific Rim. Scale-efficient plants and low-cost labor allowed these companies to blitz the market.

It should be noted that a first-time exporter is unlikely to use penetration pricing. The reason is simple: Penetration pricing often means that the product may be sold at a loss for a certain length of time. Unlike Sony, many companies that are new to exporting cannot absorb such losses, nor are they likely to have the marketing system in place (including transportation, distribution, and sales organizations) that allows global companies like Sony to make effective use of a penetration strategy.

Companion Products: Captive Pricing, a/k/a "Razors and Blades" Pricing

When formulating pricing strategies for products such as video game consoles, DVD players, and smartphones, it is necessary to view these products in a broader context. The biggest profits in the video industry come from sales of game software; even though Sony and Microsoft may actually lose money on each console, sales of hit video titles generate substantial revenues and profits. Sony, Microsoft, and Nintendo also receive licensing fees from the companies that create the games. Moreover, typical households own only one or two consoles but dozens of games. Likewise, in the mobile phone business, substantial profits come from the services—app and music downloads, for example—that handset users purchase.

These examples illustrate the concept of *companion products*: A video game console has no value without video game software, and a DVD player has no value without movies on DVD. Additional examples abound. A razor handle has no value without blades; thus Gillette can sell a single Mach3 razor for less than $5—or even give the razor away for free. Over a period of years, the company will make significant profits from selling packages of replacement blades. As the saying goes, "If you make money on the blades, you can give away the razors."

Companion products pricing has long been the preferred strategy of Vodaphone, AT&T, and other cellular service providers. They buy handsets at prices set by Motorola, Nokia, and other manufacturers, and then subsidize the cost by offering significant discounts on (or even giving away) handsets to subscribers who sign long-term contracts. The carriers make up the price difference by charging additional fees for extras such as roaming, text messaging, and so on. However, this approach does not always work globally. For example, in the United States, Apple's iPhone is priced at the equivalent of $199. In India and other markets, however, consumers don't like to be locked into long-term contracts, and the iPhone sells for the equivalent of $600. Moreover, Apple distributes the iPhone in India exclusively through stores operated by Airtel, an Indian carrier, and Vodaphone. Indian sales of the iPhone have been slow because consumers choose lower-priced models from Nokia and Samsung that are distributed through more retailers. Also, a significant number of $199 iPhones are making the trip from the United States to India in tourist luggage![3] Industry observers expect that, in the near future, Apple will roll out a new, lower-priced version of the iPhone in emerging markets.

When Sony was developing the Walkman in the late 1970s, initial plans called for a retail price of ¥50,000 ($249) to achieve breakeven. However, it was felt that a price of ¥35,000 ($170) was necessary to attract the all-important youth market segment. After the engineering team conceded that it could trim costs to achieve breakeven volume at a price of ¥40,000, Chairman Akio Morita pushed them further and insisted on a retail price of ¥33,000 ($165) to commemorate Sony's 33rd anniversary. At that price, even if the initial production run of 60,000 units sold out, the company would lose $35 per unit.

The marketing department was convinced the product would fail: Who would want a tape recorder that couldn't record? Even Yasuo Kuroki, the project manager, hedged his bets: He ordered enough parts for 60,000 units but had only 30,000 produced. Although sales were slow immediately following the Walkman's launch in July 1979, they exploded in late summer. The rest, as the saying goes, is marketing history.[5]

Target Costing[6]

Japanese companies have traditionally approached cost issues in a way that results in substantial production savings and products that are competitively priced in the global marketplace. Toyota, Sony, Olympus, and Komatsu are some of the well-known Japanese companies that use target costing. The process, sometimes known as *design to cost*, can be described as follows:

> Target costing ensures that development teams will bring profitable products to market not only with the right level of quality and functionality but also with appropriate prices for the target customer segments. It is a discipline that harmonizes the labor of disparate participants in the development effort, from designers and manufacturing engineers to market researchers and suppliers.... In effect, the company reasons backward from customers' needs and willingness to pay instead of following the flawed but common practice of cost-plus pricing.[7]

Western companies are beginning to adopt some of these money-saving ideas. For example, target costing was used in the development of Renault's Logan, a car that retails for less than $10,000 in Europe. Nissan is also using target costing to develop a $3,000 Datsun (see Case 11-1). According to Luc-Alexandre Ménard, chief of Renault's Dacia unit, the design approach prevented technical personnel from adding features that customers did not consider absolutely necessary. For example, the Logan's side windows have relatively flat glass; curved glass is more attractive, but it adds to the cost. The Logan was originally targeted at consumers in Eastern Europe; to the company's surprise, it has also proven to be popular in Germany and France.[8]

The target costing approach can be used with inexpensive consumer nondurables as well. For example, in Mexico and other emerging markets, Procter & Gamble (P&G) managers know that workers are often paid a daily wage and that its Mexican customers generally carry 5- and

[3] Brian Caulfield, "iPhone's Pricing Problem in India," Forbes.com (November 18, 2008).
[4] Phred Dvorak and Merissa Marr, "Shock Treatment: Sony, Lagging Behind Rivals, Hands Reins to a Foreigner," *The Wall Street Journal* (March 7, 2005), p. A8.
[5] Adapted from P. Ranganath Nayak and John M. Ketteringham, *Breakthroughs! How Leadership and Drive Create Commercial Innovations That Sweep the World* (San Diego, CA: Pfeiffer, 1994), pp. 124–127.
[6] This section is adapted from Robin Cooper and W. Bruce Chew, "Control Tomorrow's Costs Through Today's Designs," *Harvard Business Review* 74, no. 1 (January–February 1996), pp. 88–97. See also Robin Cooper and Regine Slagmulder, "Develop Profitable New Products with Target Costing," *Sloan Management Review* 40, no. 4 (Summer 1999), pp. 23–33.
[7] Robin Cooper and W. Bruce Chew, "Control Tomorrow's Costs Through Today's Designs," *Harvard Business Review* 74, no. 1 (January–February 1996), pp. 88–97.
[8] Norihiko Shirouzu and Stephen Power, "Unthrilling but Inexpensive, the Logan Boosts Renault in Emerging Markets," *The Wall Street Journal* (October 14, 2006), pp. B1, B18.

> "Nobody buys a piece of hardware because they like hardware. They buy it to play movies or music content."[4]
>
> —Howard Stringer, chairman, Sony Corporation

10-peso coins. To keep prices of shampoo and detergent below, say, 11 or 12 pesos and still ensure satisfactory profit margins, P&G uses target costing (P&G calls it "reverse engineering"). Rather than create an item and then assign a price to it—the traditional cost-plus approach—the company first estimates what consumers in emerging markets can afford to pay. From there, product attributes and manufacturing processes are adjusted to meet various pricing targets. For example, to hold down the cost of its Ace Natural detergent, which is used to hand-wash clothes in Mexico, P&G reduced the product's enzyme content. The result: a product that costs a peso less than a single-use packet of regular Ace. Plus, the reformulated product is gentler on the skin.[9]

The target costing process begins with market mapping and product definition and positioning; this requires using concepts and techniques discussed in Chapters 6 and 7. The marketing team must do the following:

- Determine the segment(s) to be targeted, as well as the prices that customers in the segment will be willing to pay. Using market research techniques such as focus groups and conjoint analysis, the team seeks to better understand how customers will perceive product features and functionalities.
- Compute overall target costs with the aim of ensuring the company's future profitability.
- Allocate target costs to the product's various functions. Calculate the gap between the target cost and the estimated actual production cost. Think of debits and credits in accounting: Because the target cost is fixed, additional funds allocated to one subassembly team for improving a particular function must come from another subassembly team's funds.
- Obey the cardinal rule: If the design team can't meet the targets, the product should not be launched.

Only at this point are design, engineering, and supplier pricing issues dealt with; extensive consultation between all value chain members is used to meet the target. Once the necessary negotiations and trade-offs have been settled, manufacturing begins, followed by continuous cost reduction. In the United States, cost is typically determined after design, engineering, and marketing decisions have been made in sequential fashion; if the cost is too high, the process cycles back to square one—the design stage.

Calculating Prices: Cost-Plus Pricing and Export Price Escalation

Laptops, smartphones, tablets, and other popular consumer electronics products exemplify many characteristics of today's global supply chain: No matter what the brand—Acer, Apple, Dell, or Hewlett-Packard, for example—components are typically sourced in several different countries, and the products themselves are assembled in China, Taiwan, or Japan. Within a matter of days, the goods are sent via airfreight to the countries where they will be sold. As anyone who has studied managerial accounting knows, finished goods have a cost associated with the actual production. In global marketing, however, the total cost will depend on the ultimate market destination, the mode of transport, tariffs, various fees, handling charges, and documentations costs. **Export price escalation** is the increase in the final selling price of goods traded across borders that reflects these factors. The following is a list of eight basic considerations for those whose responsibility includes setting prices on goods that cross borders:[10]

1. Does the price reflect the product's quality?
2. Is the price competitive given local market conditions?
3. Should the firm pursue market penetration, market skimming, or some other pricing objective?
4. What type of discount (trade, cash, quantity) and allowance (advertising, trade-off) should the firm offer its international customers?
5. Should prices differ with market segment?

---

[9] Ellen Byron, "Emerging Ambitions: P&G's Global Target: Shelves of Tiny Stores," *The Wall Street Journal* (July 16, 2007), p. A1.

[10] Adapted from "Price, Quotations, and Terms of Sale Are Key to Successful Exporting," *Business America* (October 4, 1993), p. 12.

6. What pricing options are available if the firm's costs increase or decrease? Is demand in the international market elastic or inelastic?
7. Are the firm's prices likely to be viewed by the host-country government as reasonable? Exploitative?
8. Do the foreign country's dumping laws pose a problem?

Companies frequently use a method known as cost-plus or cost-based pricing when selling goods outside their home-country markets. **Cost-based pricing** is based on an analysis of internal (e.g., materials, labor, testing) and external costs. As a starting point, firms that comply with Western cost-accounting principles typically use the *full absorption cost method*; this defines the per-unit product cost as the sum of all past or current direct and indirect manufacturing and overhead costs. However, when goods cross national borders, additional costs and expenses such as transportation, duties, and insurance are incurred. If the manufacturer is responsible for those costs, they, too, must be included (we discuss Incoterms a bit later in this chapter). By adding the desired profit margin to the cost-plus figure, managers can arrive at a final selling price. It is important to note that in China and some other developing countries, many manufacturing enterprises are state run and state subsidized. This makes it difficult to calculate accurate cost figures and opens a country's exporters to charges that they are selling products for less than the "true" cost of producing them. The recent controversy over Chinese-made solar panel exports is a case in point.

Companies using *rigid cost-plus pricing* set prices without regard to the eight considerations listed previously. They make no adjustments to reflect market conditions outside the home country. The obvious advantage of rigid cost-based pricing is its simplicity: Assuming that both internal and external cost figures are readily available, it is relatively easy to arrive at a quote. The disadvantage is that this approach ignores demand and competitive conditions in target markets; the risk is that prices will be set either too high or too low. If the rigid cost-based approach results in market success, it is only by chance. Rigid cost-plus pricing is attractive to inexperienced exporters, who are frequently less concerned with financial goals than with assessing market potential. Such exporters are typically responding to global market opportunities in a reactive manner, rather than proactively seeking them.

An alternative method, *flexible cost-plus pricing*, is used to ensure that prices are competitive in the context of the particular market environment. This approach is frequently used by experienced exporters and global marketers. They realize that the rigid cost-plus approach can result in severe price escalation, with the unintended and unwanted result that exports are priced at levels above what customers can pay. Managers who utilize flexible cost-plus pricing are acknowledging the importance of the eight criteria listed earlier. Flexible cost-plus pricing sometimes incorporates the *estimated future cost method* to establish the future cost for all component elements. For example, the automobile industry uses palladium in catalytic converters. Because the market price of heavy metals is volatile and varies with supply and demand, component manufacturers might use the estimated future cost method to ensure that the selling price they set enables them to cover their costs.

Every commercial transaction is based on a contract of sale, and the trade terms in that contract specify the exact point at which the ownership of merchandise is transferred from the seller to the buyer and which party in the transaction pays which costs. The following activities must be performed when goods cross international boundaries:

1. Obtaining an export license, if required (in the United States, nonstrategic goods are exported under a general license that requires no specific permit)
2. Obtaining a currency permit, if required
3. Packing the goods for export
4. Transporting the goods to the place of departure (this would normally involve transport by truck or rail to a seaport or airport)
5. Preparing a land bill of lading
6. Completing necessary customs export papers
7. Preparing customs or consular invoices as required by the country of destination
8. Arranging for ocean freight and preparation
9. Obtaining marine insurance and certificate of the policy

→ **THE CULTURAL CONTEXT**

Ethics, Religion, and Sustainable Production

MyMarketingLab   SYNC • THINK • LEARN

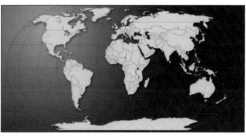

It's a basic law of economics: When supply goes up, price goes down. That is the situation that faced the coffee industry in the early twenty-first century, as a glut of coffee beans led to sharply lower prices on world commodities markets. Historically, coffee has been one of the most lucrative exports in many developing nations. Green, unroasted coffee beans are traded on the London and New York futures markets; Volcafe and Neumann Gruppe are large coffee traders that buy about 25 percent of the world's coffee supply. Other major players include Kraft, Nestlé, and Smuckers; all are key suppliers to the grocery industry, where the greatest percentage of coffee is purchased. Specialty coffees, such as those marketed by Starbucks, are regarded as niche products that account for only about 2 percent of the world's supply of coffee beans.

Since the mid-1990s, Starbucks has pursued a policy of improving the working conditions of its suppliers; however, in 2011, Starbucks' coffee purchases amounted to only 428 million pounds. Luckily, a number of different nongovernmental organizations have begun to address the situation faced by farmers who supply the broader coffee market. For example, the Rainforest Alliance works with big corporations to monitor environmental and working conditions in developing countries. It was a pioneer in certifying lumber sourced from forests in the tropics. It now certifies about $12.5 billion worth of coffee beans each year. Fairtrade International (FLO; www.fairtrade.net), a certification authority based in Bonn, Germany, represents more than 1 million farmers and workers. FLO licenses its trademark to organizations such as the UK's Fairtrade Foundation (www.fairtrade.org.uk). The Fairtrade label on a bag or can of coffee indicates that growers were paid a fair price for their crops. Fair Trade USA is a fair-trade certification organization in the United States (www.fairtradeusa.org).

Coffee bearing the Fairtrade label is often marketed with the help of charitable organizations; for example, Oxfam, a private charity in Britain, joined with Equal Exchange, a fair-trade distribution company; Traidcraft; and Twin to create a new coffee brand called Cafédirect (www.cafedirect.co.uk). In addition to providing price supports, such organizations also sponsor training and development programs to help growers become more knowledgeable about market prices and learn ways to reach export markets. Catholic Relief Services (CRS) recently launched an effort to encourage America's 65 million Catholics to buy fair-trade coffee (www.crsfairtrade.org/coffee). The CRS Coffee Project is part of a larger organization, the Interfaith Coffee Program of Equal Exchange; the latter includes participants from Lutheran, Presbyterian, and Methodist groups. The bottom line: Wholesale coffee buyers that participate in the fair-trade program agree to pay farmers a minimum of $1.40 per pound for regular coffee beans and more for higher-quality, organic beans.

The fair-trade coffee movement is gaining momentum among socially conscious consumers. For example, each year the interfaith partnership in the United States sells millions of dollars' worth of coffee at 7,500 houses of worship. However, these sales represent a mere drop in the bucket (or cup); per capita consumption of fair-trade coffee is only $2.50. Americans spend about $19 billion on coffee. However, as Paul Rice, president and CEO of Fair Trade USA, noted, "If we could get every Catholic in the country to drink fair-trade coffee, that would be a huge market right there." He added, "But it's the ripple effect—getting all those people kind of up to speed on what fair trade is all about and getting them to ask for it at their local stores—that's going to have a much broader effect on the market."

> "We've been in this business for 100 years and want to be in it for another 100.... This is not philanthropy. This is about incorporating sustainable coffee into our mainstream brands as a way to have a more efficient and competitive way of doing business."
>
> —Annemieke Wijm, senior director for Commodity Sustainability Programs, Kraft Foods

Kraft signed an accord with the Rainforest Alliance in which Kraft, the purchaser of about 10 percent of the world's coffee crop, agreed to buy beans that are certified as being produced with sustainable agricultural practices and then blend them into their mass-market brands. The purchases will amount to about $3.1 billion annually and will benefit farmers in Brazil, Colombia, Mexico, and Central America. Tensie Whelen, executive director for the Rainforest Alliance, hailed the accord, noting, "This step by Kraft marks the beginning of transforming the coffee industry. You have a company capable of shaping markets commit to buying a significant amount of coffee and to mainstreaming across their brands and not 'ghettoising' it in one brand."

Meanwhile, some entrepreneurial individuals are experimenting with new business models in an effort to return even *more* revenue to coffee farmers. Instead of selling unroasted, green coffee beans wholesale for a couple of dollars, why not capture an amount closer to the final retail price? Notes Kenneth Lander, "We're teaching a farmer that you don't have to relinquish control of your coffee. You can participate in the added value as coffee moves downstream to the customer." Lander should know: In addition to owning a coffee plantation in Costa Rica, he started Thrive Farmers Coffee. In this model, farmers have to wait to get paid until their beans have been exported, roasted, and sold at retail. However, waiting has its rewards; farmers receive fully 50 percent of the final price.

Sources: Nicole LaPorte, "Coffee's Economics, Rewritten by Farmers," *The New York Times* (March 17, 2013), pp. B1, B3; Sarah Murray, "Coffee Needs to Be Served with Credentials," *Financial Times Special Report: The Future of the Food Industry* (November 21, 2012), p. 4; Andrew Adam Newman, "This Wake-Up Cup Is Fair-Trade Certified," *The New York Times* (September 28, 2012), p. B3; Francis Percival, "No Bitter Aftertaste," *Financial Times* (February 28/March 1, 2009), p. 5; Elizabeth Weise, "Fair Trade Sweetens Pot," *USA Today* (February 9, 2005), p. 6D; Mary Beth Marklein, "Goodness—To the Last Drop," *USA Today* (February 16, 2004), pp. 1D, 2D; Tony Smith, "Difficult Times for the Coffee Industry," *The New York Times* (November 25, 2003), p. W1; Sara Silver, "Kraft Blends Ethics with Coffee Beans," *Financial Times* (October 7, 2003), p. 10; Tim Harford, "Fairtrade Tries a Commercial Blend for Coffee," *Financial Times* (September 12, 2003), p. 10; In-Sung Yoo, "Faith Organizations Throw Weight Behind 'Fair Trade' Coffee Movement," *USA Today* (December 2, 2003), p. 7D.

Who is responsible for performing these tasks? It depends on the terms of the sale. The internationally accepted terms of trade are known as International Commercial Terms (**Incoterms**). Incoterms are classified into four categories. **Ex-works (EXW)**, the sole "E-Term" or "origin" term among Incoterms, refers to a transaction in which the buyer takes delivery at the premises of the seller; the buyer bears all risks and expenses from that point on. In principle, ex-works affords the buyer maximum control over the cost of transporting the goods. Ex-works can be contrasted with several "D-Terms" ("post-main-carriage" or "arrival" terms). For example, under **delivered duty paid (DDP)**, the seller has agreed to deliver the goods to the buyer at the place the buyer names in the country of import, with all costs, including duties, paid. Under this contract, the seller is also responsible for obtaining the import license if one is required.

Another category of Incoterms is known as "F-Terms" or "pre-main-carriage terms." Because it is suited for all modes of transport, **free carrier (FCA)** is widely used in global sales. Under FCA, transfer from seller to buyer occurs when the goods are delivered to a specified carrier at a specified destination. Two additional F-terms apply to sea and inland waterway transportation only. **Free alongside ship (FAS) named port** is the Incoterm for a transaction in which the seller places the shipment alongside, or available to, the vessel upon which the goods will be transported out of the country. The seller pays all charges up to that point. The seller's legal responsibility ends once the goods have been cleared for export; the buyer pays the cost of actually loading the shipment. FAS is often used with *break bulk cargo*, which is noncontainerized, general cargo such as iron, steel, or machinery (often stowed in the hold of a vessel rather than in containers on the deck). With **free on board (FOB) named port**, the responsibility and liability of the seller do not end until the goods—typically in containers—have cleared the ship's rail. As a practical matter, access to the terminal and harbor areas in many modern ports may be restricted; in such an instance, FCA should be used instead.

Several Incoterms are known as "C-Terms" or "main-carriage" terms. When goods are shipped **cost, insurance, freight (CIF) named port**, the risk of loss or damage to goods is transferred to the buyer once the goods have passed the ship's rail. In this sense, CIF is similar to FOB. However, with CIF, the seller has to pay the expense of transportation for the goods up to the port of destination, including the expense of insurance. If the terms of the sale are **CFR (cost and freight)**, the seller is not responsible for risk or loss at any point outside the factory.

Table 11-1 is a typical example of the kind of export price escalation that can occur when some of these costs are added to the per-unit cost of the product itself. In this example, a Des Moines–based distributor of agricultural equipment is shipping a container load of agricultural tires to Yokohama, Japan, through the port of Seattle. A shipment of tires that costs ex-works $45,000 in Des Moines ends up with a total retail price in excess of $66,000 in Yokohama. A line-by-line analysis of this shipment shows how price escalation occurs. First, there is the total shipping charge of $2,715, which is 6 percent of the ex-works Des Moines price. The principal component of this shipping charge is a combination of land and ocean freight totaling $2,000.

All import charges are assessed against the landed price of the shipment (CIF value). Note that there is no line item for duty in this example; no duties are charged on agricultural equipment sent to Japan. Duties may be charged in other countries. A nominal distributor markup of 10 percent ($4,925.46) actually represents 12 percent of the CIF Yokohama price because it is a markup not only on the ex-works price, but on freight and value-added tax (VAT) as well. Finally, a dealer markup of 25 percent adds up to $12,313.64 (27 percent) of the CIF Yokohama price. Like distributor markups, dealer markup is based on the total landed cost.

The net effect of this add-on, accumulating process is a total retail price in Yokohama of $66,493.67, or 147 percent of the ex-works Des Moines price. This is price escalation. The example provided here is by no means an extreme case. Indeed, longer distribution channels or channels that require a higher operating margin, as are typically found in export marketing, can contribute to price escalation. Because of the layered distribution system in Japan, the markups in Tokyo could easily result in a price that is 200 percent of the CIF value. An example of price escalation for a single product is shown in Table 11-2. A right-hand-drive Jeep Grand

TABLE 11-1 Price Escalation: A 20-ft Container of Agricultural Equipment Shipped from Des Moines to Yokohama*

Item			Percentage of Ex-Works Price
Ex-works Des Moines		$45,000	100%
Inland and ocean freight from DSM to CY Yokohama	$1,475.00		4.44%
Bunker adjustment fee	300.00		0.67%
Destination charges	240.00		0.53%
Freight forwarding fee	150.00		0.33%
AES filing fee	25.00		0.06%
Total shipping charges	$2,715.00	$ 2,715.00	6.03%
Insurance (110% of CIF value) – $0.20 per $100		104.97	0.23%
Total CIF Yokohama value		$47,819.97	106.27%
VAT (3% of CIF value)		1,434.60	3.19%
Landed cost		49,254.57	109.45%
Distributor markup (10%)		4,925.46	10.95%
Dealer markup (25%)		12,313.64	27.36%
Total retail price		$66,493.67	147.76%

* This was loaded at the manufacturer's door, shipped by stack train to Seattle, and then transferred via ocean freight to Yokohama. Total transit time from factory door to foreign port was about 30 days. The authors are indebted to Terri Carter, Manager, Export Services, Bridgestone Americas Tire Operations LLC, for her assistance in creating this table.

Cherokee equipped with a V8 engine ends up costing ¥5 million—roughly $50,000—in Japan (see Exhibit 11-4). The final price represents 167 percent of the U.S. sticker price of $30,000.

These examples of cost-plus pricing show an approach that a beginning exporter might use to determine the CIF price. This approach could also be used for differentiated products such as the Jeep Cherokee for which buyers are willing to pay a premium. However, as noted earlier, experienced global marketers are likely to take a more flexible approach and view price as a strategic variable that can help achieve marketing and business objectives.[11]

TABLE 11-2 An American-Built Jeep Grand Cherokee Goes to Japan (estimates)

Item	Amount of Price Escalation	Total
Ex-works price	0	$30,000
Exchange rate adj.	$2,100	$32,100
Shipping	$300	$32,400
Customs fees	$1,000	$33,400
Distributor margin	$3,700	$37,100
Inspection, accessories	$1,700	$38,800
Added options, prep	$3,000	$41,800
Final sticker price	$8,200	$50,000

[11] Since the Uruguay Round of General Agreement on Tariffs and Trade (GATT) negotiations, Japan has lowered or eliminated duties on thousands of categories of imports. Japan's simple average duty rate for 2003 was 2.5 percent; approximately 60 percent of tariff lines (including for most industrial products) were rated 5 percent or lower.

Exhibit 11-4 Price escalation in China is a major issue for Chrysler's Jeep unit. Jeep established the first joint U.S./China auto operation in 1983; however, production ceased in 2006. Today, the Compass, Wrangler (pictured), and Cherokee models are all shipped from the United States and are subject to a 25 percent import tariff. The sticker price of a fully loaded Jeep Grand Cherokee SRT8 with a 6.4 liter V8 engine can top $200,000—more than triple the U.S. price of $62,790! Jeep enjoys high brand awareness in China, thanks in part to Jeep-branded clothing sold in specialty stores. Chrysler's market strategy for the brand includes restarting local production and doubling the number of dealers.
Source: AP Photo/Eugene Hoshiko

From a practical point of view, a working knowledge of Incoterms can be a source of competitive advantage to anyone seeking an entry-level job in global marketing. Beth Dorrell, an export coordinator at a U.S.-based company that markets industrial ink products, explains how terms of the sale affect price:[12]

> We actually use different Incoterms as incentives for larger orders. Instead of offering a "price break" price, we offer a better Incoterm based upon the size of a customer's order. We adhere to some general guidelines: Any order less than 1 ton is sold on an ex-works basis. Anything 1 ton or more is sold CIF port. All air freight is ex-factory. We will, of course, go to great lengths to ensure that our customers are happy. So, even though a product is sold ex-works, we'll often arrange shipping to destination port (CIF) or airport (CIP), or to the domestic port (FOB) and simply tag the freight cost onto the invoice. We end up with an ex-factory price, but a CIF or FOB invoice total. Sounds complicated, doesn't it? It keeps me busy arranging shipping.

Environmental Influences on Pricing Decisions

Global marketers must deal with a number of environmental considerations when making pricing decisions. Among them are currency fluctuations, inflation, government controls and subsidies, and competitive behavior. Some of these factors work in conjunction with others; for example, inflation may be accompanied by government controls. Each is discussed in detail in the following paragraphs.

Currency Fluctuations

In global marketing, fluctuating exchange rates complicate the task of setting prices. As we noted in Chapter 2, currency fluctuations can create significant challenges and opportunities for any company that exports. Management faces different decision situations, depending on whether

---

[12] Beth Dorrell, personal interview (December 20, 2008).

EMERGING MARKETS BRIEFING BOOK

Demand in Asia Drives Fine Wine Prices

MyMarketingLab SYNC • THINK • LEARN

As every student of microeconomics knows, when demand exceeds supply, prices tend to rise. The market for fine wine is a textbook example. Each year connoisseurs seek out wines from top estates such as France's Château Lafite Rothschild. A single bottle from a top vintage—for example, 2009—can cost $1,000 or more. The world's best wines need some time in the cellar and, as the years go by, the bottles appreciate in value.

Today, a new customer has joined the global wine culture: affluent collectors in China and other Asian countries. Several factors have contributed to this trend. In 2008, the Hong Kong government reduced tariffs on wine imports from 40 percent to zero. Since then, a flourishing wine auction scene has emerged within the Special Administrative Region. Although mainland China still imposes ad valorem taxes on wine, hand-carried bottles crossing the border from Hong Kong are not taxed. Needless to say, this has created a business opportunity for entrepreneurial individuals to hire "mules" to transport wine to the mainland. Also not surprisingly, considering the prices consumers are paying, there is a brisk trade in counterfeit wine.

As the Chinese economy has boomed, well-heeled consumers and collectors can't seem to get enough of Château Lafite and other wines. How many Chinese are willing and able to buy expensive wine? According to industry observers, the number is between 5,000 and 10,000. Chinese wine drinkers do their homework; they have been known to check out the tasting scores and prices of wines they have been served. This, of course, reflects the importance of status in Asian culture. Meanwhile, recession-weary buyers in Japan, the United States, and Europe are scaling back on their purchases of expensive wines. As one European wine exporter noted, "Every case of Château Lafite we purchase ends up in China."

Singapore and Indonesia are also vibrant markets for fine wine. Retail distribution in Singapore is streamlined compared to elsewhere, meaning that importers can sell directly to consumers. In addition, government regulations have been loosened somewhat, and two casinos have opened as part of the Resorts World Sentosa and Marina Bay Sands developments. Free-spending high rollers at these establishments want to drink the best. Demand for fine wine is growing in Indonesia as well even though the hot, humid climate creates challenges for members of the wine trade hoping to keep wine in saleable condition.

Sources: Jason Chow, "French Wines Are Tough Sell," *The Wall Street Journal* (April 26, 2013), p. B1; Jancis Robinson, "China's Viticultural Revolution," *Financial Times—Life & Arts* (February 12/13, 2011), p. 4; Gideon Rachman, "China Reaps a Vintage European Crop," *Financial Times* (November 30, 2010), p. 13; Kimberly Peterson, "New Whine: China Pushes Bordeaux Prices Higher," *The Wall Street Journal* (September 15, 2010), pp. B1, B2; John Stimpfig, "Demand from China Fuels Spectacular Performance," *Financial Times Special Report: Buying and Investing in Wine* (June 19, 2010), p. 6; Robinson, "A Continent of Connoisseurs," *Financial Times* (May 15, 2010); Laura Santini, "Wealthy Chinese Make Hong Kong a New Wine Hub," *The Wall Street Journal* (December 2, 2009), p. B9.

Exhibit 11-5 High auction prices in Hong Kong reflect skyrocketing Asian demand for top-rated French wines such as Château Lafite-Rothschild. China is the most important export market for Bordeaux wine producers, accounting for more than one-third of that region's exports. Chinese investors are also snapping up top estates in France.
Source: PHILIPPE LOPEZ/AFP/GettyImages

currencies in key markets have strengthened or weakened relative to the home-country currency. A weakening of the home-country currency swings exchange rates in a favorable direction: A producer in a weak-currency country can choose to cut export prices to increase market share, or maintain its prices and reap healthier profit margins. Overseas sales can result in windfall revenues when translated into the home-country currency.

It is a different situation when a company's home currency strengthens; this is an unfavorable turn of events for the typical exporter because overseas revenues are reduced when translated into the home-country currency. Now, suppose the U.S. dollar weakens relative to the Japanese yen. This is good news for American companies such as Boeing, Caterpillar, and GE, but bad news for Canon and Olympus (and Americans shopping for cameras). Indeed, according to Teruhisa Tokunaka, chief financial officer of Sony, a 1-yen shift in the yen–dollar exchange rate can raise or lower the company's annual operating profit by 8 billion yen (see Figure 11-1).[13] These examples underscore the point that "roller-coaster" or "yo-yo"–style swings in currency values, which may move in a favorable direction for several quarters and then abruptly reverse, characterize today's business environment.

The degree of exposure varies among companies. For example, Harley-Davidson exports all of its motorcycles from the United States. In every export market, the company's pricing decisions must take currency fluctuations into account. Similarly, 100 percent of German automaker Porsche's production takes place at home; Germany serves as its export base. However, for exports within the euro zone, Porsche is insulated from currency fluctuations.

In responding to currency fluctuations, global marketers can utilize other elements of the marketing mix besides price. In some instances, slight upward price adjustments due to the strengthening of a country's currency have little effect on export performance, especially if demand is relatively inelastic. Companies in the strong-currency country can also choose to absorb the cost of maintaining international market prices at previous levels—at least for a while. Other options include offering improved quality or after-sales service, improving productivity and cutting costs, and sourcing outside the home country.[14]

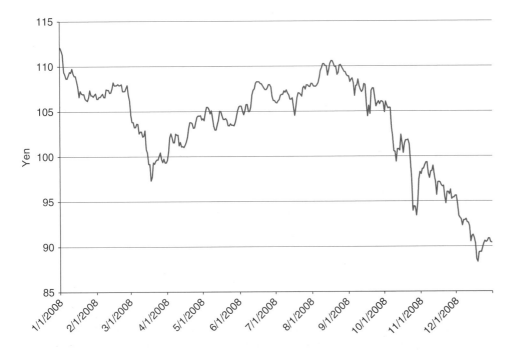

FIGURE 11-1

Value of U.S. Dollars Versus Japanese Yen

Source: Based on data gathered by the Board of Governors of the Federal Reserve (www.federalreserve.gov)

[13] Robert A. Guth, Michael M. Phillips, and Charles Hutzler, "On the Decline: As the Yen Keeps Dropping, a New View of Japan Emerges," *The Wall Street Journal* (April 24, 2002), pp. A1, A8.

[14] S. Tamer Cavusgil, "Pricing for Global Markets," *Columbia Journal of World Business* 31, no. 4 (Winter 1996), p. 69.

Companies using the rigid cost-plus pricing method described earlier may be forced to change to a more flexible approach. The use of the flexible cost-plus method to reduce prices in response to unfavorable currency swings is an example of a **market holding strategy** and is adopted by companies that do not want to lose market share. If, by contrast, large price increases are deemed unavoidable, managers may find that their products can no longer compete.

In the 3 years immediately after the euro zone was established, the euro declined in value more than 25 percent relative to the dollar. This situation forced American companies, in particular small exporters, to choose from among the options associated with strong currencies. The strategy chosen varies according to a company's particular circumstances. For example, Vermeer Manufacturing of Pella, Iowa, a midsized company with about $1 billion in annual sales, prices its products in euros for the European market. As 2000 came to an end, Vermeer had been forced to raise its European prices four times since the euro's introduction. Its subsidiary in the Netherlands pays employees in euros and also buys materials locally.

By contrast, Stern Pinball of Melrose Park, Illinois, prices its machines in dollars in export markets. Company president Gary Stern's product strategy also reflects a strong-currency strategy: To offset the higher cost to European customers who must convert euros before paying in dollars, the company developed new features such as pinball machines that "speak" several European languages. It has also produced new products such as a soccer game themed to European interests as well as an Austin Powers game targeted at the United Kingdom. As Stern commented, "If I were bright enough to know which way the euro was going, I sure wouldn't be making pinball machines. I'd be trading currency."[15]

> "We believe that our customers—especially our European customers—are just as willing to pay in pounds and may have more access to British pounds than dollars."[16]
>
> —Christine Russell, chief financial officer, Evans Analytical Group LLC, Santa Clara, California

As noted earlier, price discrepancies across the euro zone should gradually disappear because manufacturers will no longer be able to cite currency fluctuations as a justification for the discrepancies. **Price transparency** means that buyers will be able to comparison shop easily because goods will be priced in euros as opposed to marks, francs, or lira. The European Commission publishes an annual report comparing automobile price differences in the European Union (EU). Table 11-3 shows prices for 2008 and prices for 2010. A comparison of the figures shows that, although price discrepancies for some models have narrowed, prices for a Volkswagen Passat are as much as 39 percent higher depending on the country of purchase. Not surprisingly, these differences encourage cross-border shopping.

Some automobile price differences in Europe are due to different standards for safety equipment and different tax levels. For example, Denmark and Sweden have a VAT of 25 percent, the highest rate in the EU. Moreover, Denmark taxes luxury goods heavily. Taxes are also high in Finland, Belgium, Ireland, Austria, and Italy. Volkswagen has already begun to harmonize its wholesale prices for vehicles distributed in Europe.

Inflationary Environment

Inflation, or a persistent upward change in price levels, is a problem in many country markets. An increase in the money supply can cause inflation; as noted in the previous section,

TABLE 11-3 Automobile Price Differences in the EU, 2010/2008

Small Segment		Medium Segment		Large Segment	
Peugeot 206/207	39.7%/32.6%	Peugeot 308	36.0%/37.5%	VW Passat	28.1%/17.1%
Renault Clio	32.3%/23.4%	Ford Focus	27.9%/27.4%	Peugeot 407	20.5%/15.2%
Fiat Grande Punto	29.2%/21.4%	VW Golf	27.45%/24.3%	Mercedes C	14.2%/11.9%
VW Polo	28.1%/25.0%	Renault Mégane	26.8%/17.3%	Audi A4	13.1%/7.4%
Ford Fiesta	24.3%/21.4%	Audi A3	18.1%/14.5%	BMW 320D	10.6%/12%

Source: European Commission press releases. Available at http://europa.eu/press_room/index_en.htm (accessed November 2010).

---

[15] Christopher Cooper, "Euro's Drop Is Hardest for the Smallest," *The Wall Street Journal* (October 2, 2000), p. A21.
[16] Emily Chasan, "Currencies Pose New Risks," *The Wall Street Journal* (August 14, 2012), p. B5.

inflation is often reflected in the prices of imported goods in a country whose currency has been devalued. Spiraling commodities and raw materials costs have been putting upward pressure on prices for a variety of goods. For example, higher prices for corn and wheat force companies such as Kraft Foods to raise prices; similarly, higher prices for copper, oil, and other commodities mean that managers at United Technologies must review pricing for the helicopters, jet engines, and air conditioning systems the company makes. And, as anyone who has shopped for clothes lately can attest, prices for sweaters, jeans, and T-shirts have been going up. The reason? Cotton inventories are low worldwide, and the price of cotton has almost doubled.[17]

An essential requirement for pricing in an inflationary environment is the maintenance of operating profit margins. When present, inflation requires price adjustments for a simple reason: Rising costs must be covered by higher selling prices. Regardless of cost-accounting practices, if a company maintains its margins, it has effectively protected itself from the effects of inflation. This, in turn, requires manufacturers and retailers of all types to become more technologically adept. In Brazil, where the inflation rate was as high as 2,000 percent during the late 1980s, retailers sometimes changed prices several times each day. Shelf pricing, rather than individual unit pricing, became the norm throughout the retailing sector nearly 15 years before Walmart arrived in the region. Because their warehouses contained goods that had been bought at different prices, local retailers were forced to invest in sophisticated computer and communications systems to help them keep pace with the volatile financial environment. They thus utilized sophisticated inventory management software to help them maintain financial control. When Walmart came to Brazil in the mid-1990s, it discovered that local competitors had the technological infrastructure that allowed them to match its aggressive pricing policies.[18]

Low inflation presents pricing challenges of a different type. With inflation in the United States in the low single digits in the late 1990s and strong demand forcing factories to run at or near capacity, companies should have been able to raise prices. However, the domestic economic situation was not the only consideration. In the mid-1990s, excess manufacturing capacity in many industries, high rates of unemployment in many European countries, and the lingering recession in Asia made it difficult for companies to increase prices. As John Ballard, CEO of a California-based engineering firm, noted in 1994, "We thought about price increases. But our research of competitors and what the market would bear told us it was not worth pursuing." By the end of the decade, globalization, the Internet, a flood of low-cost exports from China, and a new cost-consciousness among buyers were also significant constraining factors.[19]

Government Controls, Subsidies, and Regulations

Governmental policies and regulations that affect pricing decisions include dumping legislation, resale price maintenance legislation, price ceilings, and general reviews of price levels. Government actions that limit management's ability to adjust prices can put pressure on margins. Under certain conditions, government actions pose a threat to the profitability of a subsidiary operation. In a country that is undergoing severe financial difficulties and is in the midst of a financial crisis (e.g., a foreign exchange shortage caused in part by runaway inflation), government officials are under pressure to take some type of action. This was true in Brazil for many years. In some cases, governments take expedient steps such as selective or broad price controls.

When selective controls are imposed, foreign companies are more vulnerable to control than local ones, particularly if the outsiders lack the political influence over government decisions that local managers have. For example, Procter & Gamble encountered strict price controls in

[17] John Shipman and Anjali Cordiero, "Dilemma Over Pricing," *The Wall Street Journal* (October 20, 2010), pp. B1, B4.

[18] Pete Hisey, "Walmart's Global Vision," *Retail Merchandiser* 41, no. 4 (April 2001), pp. 21–49.

[19] Lucinda Harper and Fred R. Bleakley, "Like Old Times: An Era of Low Inflation Changes the Calculus for Buyers and Sellers," *The Wall Street Journal* (January 14, 1994), p. A1. See also Jacob M. Schlesinger and Yochi J. Dreazen, "Counting the Cost: Firms Start to Raise Prices, Stirring Fear in Inflation Fighters," *The Wall Street Journal* (May 16, 2000), pp. A1, A8.

Venezuela in the late 1980s. Despite increases in the cost of raw materials, P&G was granted only about 50 percent of the price increases it requested; even then, months passed before permission to raise prices was forthcoming. As a result, by 1988, detergent prices in Venezuela were less than detergent prices in the United States.[20]

Government control can also take other forms. As discussed in Chapter 8, companies are sometimes required to deposit funds in a noninterest-bearing escrow account for a specified period of time if they wish to import products. In one case, Cintec International, an engineering firm that specializes in restoring historic structures, spent 8 years seeking the necessary approval from Egyptian authorities to import special tools to repair a mosque. In addition, the country's port authorities required a deposit of nearly $25,000 before they allowed Cintec to import diamond-tipped drills and other special tools. Why would Cintec's management accept such conditions? Cairo is the largest city in the Muslim world, and there are hundreds of centuries-old historic structures in need of refurbishment. By responding to the Egyptian government's demands with patience and persistence, Cintec was positioning itself as a leading contender for more contract work.[21]

Cash deposit requirements such as the one just described clearly create an incentive for a company to minimize the stated value of the imported goods; lower prices mean smaller deposits. Other government requirements that affect the pricing decision are profit transfer rules that restrict the conditions under which profits can be transferred out of a country. Under such rules, a high transfer price paid for imported goods by an affiliated company can be interpreted as a device for transferring profits out of a country.

Also discussed in Chapter 8 were government subsidies. As noted earlier, the topic of agricultural subsidies is a sensitive one in the current round of global trade talks. Brazil and a bloc of more than 20 other nations are pressing Washington to end agricultural subsidies. For example, Washington spends between $2.5 and $3 billion per year on cotton subsidies (the EU spends the equivalent of about $700 million), a fact that has contributed to delays in completing the Doha Round. Benin, Chad, Burkina Faso, and others complain that the subsidies keep U.S. cotton prices so low that it costs the African nations $250 million each year in lost exports.[22] Brazil recently won its Word Trade Organization (WTO) complaint against U.S. cotton subsidies.

Government regulations can also affect prices in other ways. In Germany, for example, price competition was historically severely restricted in a number of industries. This was particularly true in the service sector. The German government's recent moves toward deregulation have improved the climate for market entry by foreign firms in a range of industries, including insurance, telecommunications, and air travel. Deregulation is also giving German companies their first experience of price competition in the domestic market. In some instances, deregulation represents a *quid pro quo* that will allow German companies wider access to other country markets. For example, the United States and Germany recently completed an open-skies agreement that will allow Lufthansa to fly more routes within the United States. At the same time, the German air market has been opened to competition. As a result, air travel costs between German cities have fallen significantly. Change is slowly coming to the retail sector as well. The Internet and globalization have forced policymakers to repeal two archaic laws. The first, the *Rabattgesetz*, or Discount Law, limited discounts on products to 3 percent of the list price. The second, the *Zugabeverordung*, or Free Gift Act, banned companies from giving away free merchandise such as shopping bags.[23]

Competitive Behavior

Pricing decisions are bounded not only by cost and the nature of demand but also by competitive action. If competitors do not adjust their prices in response to rising costs, management—even if

---

[20] Alecia Swasy, "Foreign Formula: Procter & Gamble Fixes Aim on Tough Market: The Latin Americans," *The Wall Street Journal* (June 15, 1990), p. A7.

[21] Scott Miller, "In Trade Talks, the Gloves Are Off," *The Wall Street Journal* (July 15, 2003), p. A12. See also James Drummond, "The Great Conservation Debate," *Financial Times Special Report—Egypt* (October 22, 2003), p. 6.

[22] Neil King, Jr., and Scott Miller, "Trade Talks Fail Amid Big Divide Over Farm Issues," *The Wall Street Journal* (September 15, 2003), pp. A1, A18.

[23] Greg Steinmetz, "Mark Down: German Consumers Are Seeing Prices Cut in Deregulation Push," *The Wall Street Journal* (August 15, 1997), pp. A1, A4; David Wessel, "German Shoppers Get Coupons," *The Wall Street Journal* (April 5, 2001), p. A1.

acutely aware of the effect of rising costs on operating margins—will be severely constrained in its ability to adjust prices accordingly. Conversely, if competitors are manufacturing or sourcing in a lower-cost country, it may be necessary to cut prices to stay competitive.

In the United States, Levi Strauss & Company is under price pressure from several directions. First, Levi faces stiff competition from the Wrangler and Lee brands marketed by VF Corporation. A pair of Wrangler jeans retails for about $20 at JCPenney and other department stores, compared with about $30 for a pair of Levi 501s. Second, Levi's two primary retail customers, JCPenney and Sears, are aggressively marketing their own private-label brands. Finally, designer jeans from Calvin Klein, Polo, and Diesel are enjoying renewed popularity. Exclusive fashion brands such as Seven and Lucky retail for more than $100 per pair. Outside the United States, thanks to the heritage of the Levi brand and less competition, Levi jeans command premium prices—$80 or more for one pair of 501s.

To support the prestige image, Levi's are sold in boutiques. Levi's non-U.S. sales represent about one-third of revenues but more than 50 percent of profits. In an attempt to apply its global experience and enhance the brand in the United States, Levi has opened a number of Original Levi's Stores in select American cities. Despite such efforts, Levi rang up only $4.4 billion in sales in 2010, compared with $7.1 billion in 1996. A decade ago, officials closed six plants and moved most of the company's North American production offshore in an effort to cut costs.[24]

Using Sourcing as a Strategic Pricing Tool

The global marketer has several options for addressing the problem of price escalation or the environmental factors described in the last section. Product and market competition, in part, dictate the marketer's choices. Marketers of domestically manufactured finished products may be forced to switch to offshore sourcing of certain components to keep costs and prices competitive. In particular, China is quickly gaining a reputation as "the world's workshop." U.S. bicycle companies such as Huffy are relying more heavily on production sources in China and Taiwan.

Another option is a thorough audit of the distribution structure in the target markets. A rationalization of the distribution structure can substantially reduce the total markups required to achieve distribution in international markets. Rationalization may include selecting new intermediaries, assigning new responsibilities to old intermediaries, or establishing direct marketing operations. For example, Toys 'R' Us successfully targets the Japanese toy market by bypassing layers of distribution and adopting a warehouse style of selling similar to its U.S. approach. Toys 'R' Us was viewed as a test case of the ability of Western retailers—discounters in particular—to change the rules of distribution.

Global Pricing: Three Policy Alternatives

What pricing policy should a global company pursue? Remember that price is a strategic variable; pricing strategy can be developed using a rational, analytical approach or an intuitive one. For example, when Sydney Frank created Grey Goose vodka, he set the per-bottle price $10 higher than Stolichnaya or Absolut. Why? Because he could! Frank did not conduct any form of market analysis. Instead, he relied on instinct and insights gained during a long career in the liquor business. Similar examples of simple decision rules used in pricing include the following:

- "We have our competitor's price list on our desk....We know exactly what our competitors charge for certain products, and we calculate accordingly."
- "We differentiate simply because there are some countries where we can get a better price. Then there are countries where we can't."[25]

Viewed broadly, a company has three positions it can take on worldwide pricing.

---

[24] Leslie Kaufman, "Levi Strauss to Close 6 U.S. Plants and Lay Off 3,300," *The New York Times* (April 9, 2002), p. C2.
[25] Barbara Stöttinger, "Strategic Export Pricing: A Long and Winding Road," *Journal of International Marketing* 9, no. 1 (2001), pp. 40–63.

Extension or Ethnocentric Pricing

The first position can be called *extension* or *ethnocentric* pricing. **Extension** or **ethnocentric pricing** calls for the per-unit price of an item to be the same no matter where in the world the buyer is located. In such instances, the importer must absorb freight and import duties. The extension approach has the advantage of extreme simplicity because it does not require information on competitive or market conditions for implementation. The disadvantage of the ethnocentric approach is that it does not respond to the competitive and market conditions of each national market and, therefore, does not maximize the company's profits in each national market or globally. When toymaker Mattel adapted U.S. products for overseas markets, for example, little consideration was given to the price levels that would result when U.S. prices were converted to local currency prices. As a result, Holiday Barbie and some other toys were overpriced in global markets.[26]

Similarly, Mercedes executives moved beyond an ethnocentric approach to pricing. As Dieter Zetsche, chairman of Daimler AG, noted, "We used to say that *we* know what the customer wants, and he will have to pay for it …we didn't realize the world had changed."[27] Mercedes got its wake-up call when Lexus began offering "Mercedes quality" for $20,000 less. After assuming the top position in 1993, Mercedes CEO Helmut Werner boosted employee productivity, increased the number of low-cost outside suppliers, and invested in production facilities in the United States and Spain in an effort to move toward more customer- and competition-oriented pricing. The company also rolled out new, lower-priced versions of its E Class and S Class sedans. *Advertising Age* immediately hailed management's new attitude for transforming Mercedes from "a staid and smug purveyor into an aggressive, market-driven company that will go bumper-to-bumper with its luxury car rivals—even on price."[28]

Adaptation or Polycentric Pricing

The second policy, **adaptation** or **polycentric pricing**, permits subsidiary or affiliate managers or independent distributors to establish whatever price they feel is most appropriate in their market environment. There is no requirement that prices be coordinated from one country to the next. IKEA takes a polycentric approach to pricing: While it is company policy to have the lowest price on comparable products in every market, managers in each country set their own prices. These depend, in part, on local factors such as competition, wages, taxes, and advertising rates. Overall, IKEA's prices are lowest in the United States, where the company competes with large retailers. Prices are higher in Italy, where local competitors tend to be smaller, more upscale furniture stores than those in the U.S. market. Generally, prices are higher in countries where the IKEA brand is strongest. When IKEA opened its first stores in mainland China, the young professional couples who are the company's primary target segment considered the prices to be too high. Ian Duffy, an Englishman in charge of the stores, quickly increased the amount of Chinese-made furniture in the stores so that he could lower prices; today, the average Chinese customer spends ¥300—about $36—per visit.[29]

One recent study of European industrial exporters found that companies utilizing independent distributors were the most likely to utilize polycentric pricing. Such an approach is sensitive to local market conditions; however, valuable knowledge and experience within the corporate system concerning effective pricing strategies are not brought to bear on each local pricing decision. Because the distributors or local managers are free to set prices as they see fit, they may ignore the opportunity to draw upon company experience. Arbitrage is also a potential problem with the polycentric approach; when disparities in prices between different country markets exceed the transportation and duty costs separating the markets, enterprising individuals can purchase goods in the lower-price country market and then transport them for sale in markets where higher prices prevail.

> "The practice of selling U.S. products abroad at prices keyed to the local market is longstanding. It's not unusual, it doesn't violate public policy, and it's certainly not illegal."[30]
>
> —Allen Adler, American Association of Publishers

---

[26] Lisa Bannon, "Mattel Plans to Double Sales Abroad," *The Wall Street Journal* (February 11, 1998), pp. A3, A11.
[27] Alex Taylor III, "Speed! Power! Status!" *Fortune* (June 10, 1996), pp. 46–58.
[28] Raymond Serafin, "Mercedes-Benz of the '90s Includes Price in Its Pitch," *Advertising Age* (November 1, 1993), p. 1.
[29] Mei Fong, "IKEA Hits Home in China," *The Wall Street Journal* (March 3, 2006), pp. B1, B4. See also Eric Sylvers, "IKEA Index Indicates the Euro Is Not a Price Equalizer Yet," *The New York Times* (October 23, 2003), p. W1; and Paula M. Miller, "IKEA with Chinese Characteristics," *The China Business Review* (July–August 2004), pp. 36–38.
[30] Tamar Lewin, "Students Find $100 Textbooks Cost $50, Purchased Overseas," *The New York Times* (October 21, 2003), p. A16.

This is precisely what has happened in both the pharmaceutical and textbook publishing industries. Discounted drugs intended for AIDS patients in Africa have been smuggled into the EU and sold at a huge profit. Similarly, Pearson (which publishes this text), McGraw-Hill, Thomson, and other publishers typically set lower prices in Europe and Asia than in the United States. The reason is that the publishers use polycentric pricing: They establish prices on a regional or country-by-country basis using per capita income and economic conditions as a guide. (By the way, authors have no control over the prices university bookstores and other retailers charge for textbooks. Trust us on this one!)

Geocentric Pricing

The third approach, geocentric pricing, is more dynamic and proactive than the other two. A company using **geocentric pricing** neither fixes a single price worldwide, nor allows subsidiaries or local distributors to make independent pricing decisions. Instead, the geocentric approach represents an intermediate course of action. Geocentric pricing is based on the realization that unique local market factors should be recognized when arriving at pricing decisions. These factors include local costs, income levels, competition, and the local marketing strategy. Price must also be integrated with other elements of the marketing program. The geocentric approach recognizes that price coordination from headquarters is necessary in dealing with international accounts and product arbitrage. This approach also consciously and systematically seeks to ensure that accumulated national pricing experience is leveraged and applied wherever relevant.

Local costs plus a return on invested capital and personnel fix the price floor for the long term. In the short term, however, headquarters might decide to set a market penetration objective and price at less than the cost-plus return figure by using export sourcing to establish a market. This was the case described earlier with the Sony Walkman launch. Another short-term objective might be to arrive at an estimate of the market potential at a price that would be profitable given local sourcing and a certain volume of production. Instead of immediately investing in local manufacture, a decision might be made to supply the target market initially from existing higher-cost external supply sources. If the market accepts the price and product, the company can then build a local manufacturing facility to further develop the identified market opportunity in a profitable way. If the market opportunity does not materialize, the company can experiment with the product at other prices because it is not committed to a fixed sales volume by existing local manufacturing facilities.

Gray Market Goods

Gray market goods are trademarked products that are exported from one country to another and sold by unauthorized persons or organizations. Consider the following illustration:

> Suppose that a golf equipment manufacturer sells a golf club to its domestic distributors for $200; it sells the same club to its Thailand distributor for $100. The lower price may be due to differences in overseas demand or ability to pay. Or, the price difference may reflect the need to compensate the foreign distributor for advertising and marketing the club. The golf club, however, never makes it to Thailand. Instead, the Thailand distributor resells the club to a gray marketer in the United States for $150. The gray marketer can then undercut the prices charged by domestic distributors who paid $200 for the club. The manufacturer is forced to lower the domestic price or risk losing sales to gray marketers, driving down the manufacturer's profit margins. Additionally, gray marketers make liberal use of manufacturer's trademarks and often fail to provide warranties and other services that consumers expect from the manufacturer and its authorized distributors.[31]

This practice, known as **parallel importing**, occurs when companies employ a polycentric, multinational pricing policy that calls for setting different prices in different country markets. Gray markets can flourish when a product is in short supply, when producers employ skimming

---

[31] Adapted from Perry J. Viscounty, Jeff C. Risher, and Collin G. Smyser, "Cyber Gray Market Is Manufacturers' Headache," *The National Law Journal* (August 20, 2001), p. C3.

strategies in certain markets, or when the goods are subject to substantial markups. For example, in the European pharmaceuticals market, prices vary widely. In the United Kingdom and the Netherlands, for example, parallel imports account for as much as 10 percent of the sales of some pharmaceutical brands. The Internet is emerging as a powerful new tool that allows would-be gray marketers to access pricing information and reach customers.[32]

Gray markets impose several costs or consequences on global marketers, including the following:[33]

● *Dilution of exclusivity*. Authorized dealers are no longer the sole distributors. The product is often available from multiple sources and margins are threatened.

● *Free riding*. If the manufacturer ignores complaints from authorized channel members, those members may engage in *free riding*; that is, they may opt to take various actions to offset downward pressure on margins. These options include cutting back on presale service, customer education, and salesperson training.

● *Damage to channel relationships*. Competition from gray market products can lead to channel conflict as authorized distributors attempt to cut costs, complain to manufacturers, and file lawsuits against the gray marketers.

● *Undermining segmented pricing schemes*. As noted earlier, gray markets can emerge because of price differentials that result from multinational pricing policies. However, a variety of forces—including falling trade barriers, the information explosion on the Internet, and modern distribution capabilities—hamper a company's ability to pursue local pricing strategies.

● *Reputation and legal liability*. Even though gray market goods carry the same trademarks as goods sold through authorized channels, they may differ in quality, ingredients, or some other way. Gray market products can compromise a manufacturer's reputation and dilute brand equity, as when prescription drugs are sold past their expiration dates or electronics equipment is sold in markets where it is not approved for use or where manufacturers do not honor warranties.

Sometimes, gray marketers bring a product produced in a single country—French champagne, for example—into export markets in competition with authorized importers. The gray marketers sell at prices that undercut those set by the legitimate importers. In another type of gray marketing, a company manufactures a product in the home-country market as well as in foreign markets. In this case, products manufactured abroad by the company's foreign affiliate for sales abroad are sometimes sold by a foreign distributor to gray marketers. The latter then bring the products into the producing company's home-country market, where they compete with domestically produced goods.

As these examples show, the marketing opportunity that presents itself requires gray market goods to be priced lower than goods sold by authorized distributors or domestically produced goods. Clearly, buyers gain from lower prices and increased choice. In the United Kingdom alone, for example, total annual retail sales of gray market goods are estimated to be as high as $1.6 billion. A case in Europe resulted in a ruling that strengthened the rights of brand owners. Silhouette, an Austrian manufacturer of upscale sunglasses, sued the Hartlauer discount chain after the retailer obtained thousands of pairs of sunglasses that Silhouette had intended for sale in Eastern Europe. The European Court of Justice found in favor of Silhouette. In clarifying a 1989 directive, the court ruled that stores cannot import branded goods from outside the EU and then sell them at discounted prices without permission of the brand owner. However, the *Financial Times* denounced the ruling as "bad for consumers, bad for competition, and bad for European economies."[34]

In the United States, gray market goods are subject to the Tariff Act of 1930. Section 526 of the act expressly forbids importation of goods of foreign manufacture without the permission of

[32] Perry J. Viscounty, Jeff C. Risher, and Collin G. Smyser, "Cyber Gray Market Is Manufacturers' Headache," *The National Law Journal* (August 20, 2001), p. C3.

[33] Kersi D. Antia, Mark Bergen, and Shantanu Dutta, "Competing with Gray Markets," *MIT Sloan Management Review* 46, no. 1 (Summer 2004), pp. 65–67.

[34] Peggy Hollinger and Neil Buckley, "Grey Market Ruling Delights Brand Owners," *Financial Times* (July 17, 1998), p. 8.

the trademark owner. However, because courts have considerable leeway in interpreting the act, one legal expert has argued that the U.S. Congress should repeal Section 526. In its place, a new law should require gray market goods to bear labels clearly explaining any differences between them and goods that come through authorized channels. Other experts believe that instead of changing the laws, companies should develop proactive strategic responses to gray markets. One such strategy would be improved market segmentation and product differentiation to make gray market products less attractive; another would be to aggressively identify and terminate distributors that are involved in selling to gray marketers.

> "The gray market is the biggest threat we have. You can't develop this market properly and make investments in retailing, merchandising, after-sales service and distribution without a legal market."[35]
>
> —Pankaj Mohindroo, president, Indian Cellular Association

Dumping

Dumping is an important global pricing strategy issue. General Agreement on Tariff and Trade's (GATT) 1979 antidumping code defined *dumping* as the sale of an imported product at a price lower than that normally charged in a domestic market or country of origin. In addition, many countries have their own policies and procedures for protecting national companies from dumping. For example, China has retaliated against years of Western antidumping rules by introducing rules of its own. China's State Council passed the Antidumping and Antisubsidy Regulations in March 1997. The Ministry of Foreign Trade and Economic Cooperation and the State Economic and Trade Commission have responsibility for antidumping matters.[36]

The U.S. Congress has defined *dumping* as an unfair trade practice that results in "injury, destruction, or prevention of the establishment of American industry." Under this definition, dumping occurs when imports sold in the U.S. market are priced either at levels that represent less than the cost of production plus an 8 percent profit margin or at levels below those prevailing in the producing country. The U.S. Commerce Department is responsible for determining whether products are being dumped in the United States; the International Trade Commission (ITC) then determines whether the dumping has resulted in injury to U.S. firms. Many of the dumping cases in the United States involve manufactured goods from Asia and frequently target a single or very narrowly defined group of products. U.S. companies that claim to be materially damaged by the low-priced imports often initiate such cases. In 2000, the U.S. Congress passed the so-called **Byrd Amendment**; this law calls for antidumping revenues to be paid to U.S. companies harmed by imported goods sold at below-market prices.[37]

In Europe, the European Commission administers antidumping policy; a simple majority vote by the Council of Ministers is required before duties can be imposed on dumped goods. Six-month provisional duties can be imposed; more stringent measures include definitive, 5-year duties. Low-cost imports from Asia have been the subject of dumping disputes in Europe. Another issue concerned $650 million in annual imports of unbleached cotton from China, Egypt, India, Indonesia, Pakistan, and Turkey. A dispute pitted an alliance of textile importers and wholesalers against Eurocoton, which represents textile weavers in France, Italy, and other EU countries. Eurocoton supported the duties as a means of protecting jobs from low-priced imports; the job issue was particularly sensitive in France. British textile importer Broome & Wellington maintained, however, that imposing duties would drive up prices and cost even more jobs in the textile finishing and garment industries.[38] In January 2005, the global system of textile quotas was abolished. Almost overnight, Chinese textile exports to the United States and Europe increased dramatically. Within a few months, the U.S. government had re-imposed quotas on several categories of textile imports; in the EU, trade minister Peter Mandelson also imposed quotas for a period of 2 years.

Dumping was a major issue in the Uruguay Round of GATT negotiations. Many countries took issue with the U.S. system of antidumping laws, in part because historically, the U.S.

---

[35] Ray Marcelo, "Officials See Red Over Handset Sales," *Financial Times* (October 3, 2003), p. 16.

[36] Lester Ross and Susan Ning, "Modern Protectionism: China's Own Antidumping Regulations," *China Business Review* (May/June 2000), pp. 30–33.

[37] Philip Brasher, "Clarinda Plant Takes Hit in Dispute Over Imports," *The Des Moines Register* (November 16, 2005), p. D1.

[38] Neil Buckley, "Commission Faces Fight on Cotton 'Dumping,'" *Financial Times* (December 2, 1997), p. 5; Emma Tucker, "French Fury at Threat to Cotton Duties," *Financial Times* (May 19, 1997), p. 3.

Commerce Department almost always ruled in favor of the U.S. company that filed the complaint. For their part, U.S. negotiators were concerned that U.S. exporters were often targeted in antidumping investigations in countries with few formal rules for due process. The U.S. side sought to improve the ability of U.S. companies to defend their interests and understand the bases for rulings.

The result of the GATT negotiations was an agreement on interpretation of GATT Article VI. From the U.S. point of view, one of the most significant changes between the agreement and the 1979 code is the addition of a "standard of review" that will make it harder for GATT panels to dispute U.S. antidumping determinations. A number of procedural and methodological changes were also made. In some instances, these have the effect of bringing GATT regulations more in line with U.S. law. For example, in calculating "fair price" for a given product, any sales of the product at below-cost prices in the exporting country are not included in the calculations; inclusion of such sales would have the effect of exerting downward pressure on the fair price. The agreement also brought GATT standards in line with U.S. standards by prohibiting governments from penalizing differences between home-market and export-market prices of less than 2 percent.

For positive proof that dumping has occurred in the United States, both price discrimination and injury must be demonstrated. *Price discrimination* is the practice of setting different prices when selling the same quantity of "like-quality" goods to different buyers. The existence of either one without the other is an insufficient condition to constitute dumping. Companies concerned with running afoul of antidumping legislation have developed a number of approaches for avoiding the dumping laws. One approach is to differentiate the product sold from that in the home market so it does not represent "like quality." An example of this is an auto accessory that one company packaged with a wrench and an instruction book, thereby changing the "accessory" to a "tool." The duty rate in the export market happened to be lower on tools, and the company also acquired immunity from antidumping laws because the package was not comparable to competing goods in the target market. Another approach is to make nonprice competitive adjustments in arrangements with affiliates and distributors. For example, credit can be extended, which essentially has the same effect as a price reduction.

Price Fixing

In most instances, it is illegal for representatives of two or more companies to secretly set similar prices for their products. This practice, known as **price fixing**, is generally held to be an anticompetitive act. Companies that collude in this manner are generally trying to ensure higher prices for their products than would generally be available if markets were functioning freely. In *horizontal price fixing*, competitors within an industry that make and market the same product conspire to keep prices high. For example, in 2011 the European Commission determined that P&G, Unilever, and Henkel had conspired to set prices for laundry detergent. The term *horizontal* applies in this instance because P&G and its coconspirators are all at the same supply-chain "level" (i.e., they are manufacturers).

Vertical price fixing occurs when a manufacturer conspires with wholesalers or retailers (i.e., channel members at different "levels" from the manufacturer) to ensure certain retail prices are maintained. For example, the European Commission fined Nintendo nearly $150 million after it was determined that the video game company had colluded with European distributors to fix prices. During the 1990s, prices of Nintendo video game consoles varied widely across Europe. They were much more expensive in Spain than in Britain and other countries; however, distributors in countries with lower retail prices agreed not to sell to retailers in countries with higher prices.[39]

Another case of price fixing pits DeBeers SA, the South African diamond company, against the United States. At issue are prices for industrial diamonds, not gemstones; however, DeBeers is a well-known name in the United States thanks to a long-running advertising campaign keyed to the tagline "A Diamond Is Forever." Because the company itself has no American retail presence, DeBeers diamonds are marketed in the United States by intermediaries. DeBeers executives have indicated a willingness to plead guilty and pay a fine in exchange for access to the

[39] Paul Meller, "Europe Fines Nintendo $147 Million for Price Fixing," *The Wall Street Journal* (February 24, 2004), p. W1.

United States. As a spokesperson said, "The U.S. is the biggest market for diamond jewelry—accounting for 50 percent of global retail jewelry sales—and we would really, really like to resolve these issues."[40]

Transfer Pricing

Transfer pricing refers to the pricing of goods, services, and intangible property bought and sold by operating units or divisions of the same company. In other words, transfer pricing concerns *intracorporate exchanges*, which are transactions between buyers and sellers that have the same corporate parent. For example, Toyota subsidiaries both sell to, and buy from, each other. Transfer pricing is an important topic in global marketing because goods crossing national borders represent a sale; therefore, their pricing is a matter of interest both to the tax authorities, who want to collect a fair share of income taxes, and to the customs service, which wants to collect an appropriate duty on the goods. Joseph Quinlan, chief marketing strategist at Bank of America, estimates that U.S. companies have 23,000 overseas affiliates; about 25 percent of U.S. exports represent shipments by American companies to affiliates and subsidiaries outside the United States.

In determining transfer prices to subsidiaries, global companies must address a number of issues, including taxes, duties and tariffs, country profit transfer rules, conflicting objectives of joint venture partners, and government regulations. Tax authorities such as the Internal Revenue Service (IRS) in the United States, Inland Revenue in the United Kingdom, and Japan's National Tax Administration Agency take a keen interest in transfer pricing policies.[41] Transfer pricing is proving to be a key corporate issue in Europe as the euro makes it easier for tax authorities to audit transfer pricing policies.

Three major alternative approaches can be applied to transfer pricing decisions. The approach used will vary with the nature of the firm, the products, the markets, and the historical circumstances of each case. A **market-based transfer price** is derived from the price required to be competitive in the global marketplace. In other words, it represents an approximation of an arm's-length transaction. **Cost-based transfer pricing** uses an internal cost as the starting point in determining price. Cost-based transfer pricing can take the same forms as the cost-based pricing methods discussed earlier in the chapter. The way costs are defined may have an impact on tariffs and duties of sales to affiliates and subsidiaries. A third alternative is to allow the organization's affiliates to determine **negotiated transfer prices** among themselves. This method may be employed when market conditions are subject to frequent changes. Table 11-4 summarizes the ways that the different methods satisfy multiple managerial criteria.

TABLE 11-4 Comparison of Different Transfer Pricing Methods

Critiera	Market-Based	Cost-Based	Negotiated
Achieves goal congruence	Yes, when markets are competitive	Often, but not always	Yes
Motivates managerial effort	Yes	Yes, when based on budgeted costs	Yes
Useful for evaluating subunit performance	Yes, when markets are competitive	Difficult unless transfer price exceeds full cost	Yes, but transfer prices are affected by negotiating skills of buyer and seller.
Preserves subunit autonomy	Yes, when markets are competitive	No, because it is rule-based	Yes, because it is based on negotiations between subunits
Other factors	Markets may not exist or may be imperfect	Useful for determining full cost of products; easy to implement	Bargaining and negotiations take time and may need to be reviewed as conditions change.

Source: Adapted from Charles T. Horngren, Srikant M. Datar, George Foster, Madhav Rajan, and Christopher Ittner, *Cost Accounting: A Managerial Emphasis* (Upper Saddle River, NJ: Prentice Hall, 2009), p. 783.

---

[40] John R. Wilke, "DeBeers Is in Talks to Settle Price-Fixing Charge," *The Wall Street Journal* (February 24, 2004), pp. A1, A14.

[41] Matthew Saltmarsh, "Tax Enforcers Intensify Focus on Multinationals," *The New York Times* (January 5, 2010), p. B3.

Tax Regulations and Transfer Prices

Because global companies conduct business in a world characterized by different corporate tax rates, companies have an incentive to maximize income in countries with the lowest tax rates—Ireland, for example—and to minimize income in the United States and other countries with high tax rates. Governmental regulatory agencies are well aware that Apple and other companies formulate strategies for tax planning and tax avoidance.[42] In recent years, many governments have tried to maximize national tax revenues by examining company returns and mandating real-location of income and expenses. Some companies involved in transfer pricing cases include:

- Motorola may owe the Internal Revenue Service (IRS) as much as $500 million in taxes from earnings from global operations that were booked incorrectly.
- The U.S. Labor Department filed a complaint against Swatch Group alleging that the Swiss watchmaker improperly used transfer pricing to evade millions of dollars in customs duties and taxes.[43]
- The U.S. government spent years attempting to recover $2.7 billion plus interest from pharmaceutical giant GlaxoSmithKline (GSK). The IRS charged that GSK did not pay enough tax on profits from Zantac, its hugely successful ulcer medication. Between 1989 and 1999, U.S. revenues from Zantac totaled $16 billion; the IRS charged that GSK's American unit overpaid royalties to the British parent company, thus reducing taxable U.S. income. The case was scheduled for trial in 2007; however, in September 2006, GSK settled the case by agreeing to pay the IRS approximately $3.1 billion.[44]

Sales of Tangible and Intangible Property

Each country has its own set of laws and regulations for dealing with controlled intracompany transfers. Whatever the pricing rationale, executives and managers involved in global pricing policy decisions must familiarize themselves with the laws and regulations in the applicable countries. The pricing rationale must conform with the intention of these laws and regulations. Although the applicable laws and regulations often seem perplexingly inscrutable, ample evidence exists that most governments simply seek to prevent tax avoidance and to ensure fair distribution of income from the operations of companies doing business internationally.

Even companies that make a conscientious effort to comply with the applicable laws and regulations and that document this effort may find themselves in tax court. Should a tax auditor raise questions, executives should be able to make a strong case for their decisions. Fortunately, consulting services are available to help managers deal with the arcane world of transfer pricing. It is not unusual for large global companies to invest hundreds of thousands of dollars and hire international accounting firms to review transfer pricing policies.

Countertrade

In recent years, many exporters have been forced to finance international transactions by taking full or partial payment in some form other than money.[45] A number of alternative finance methods, known as *countertrade*, are widely used. In a **countertrade** transaction, a sale results in product flowing in one direction to a buyer; a separate stream of products and services, often flowing in the opposite direction, is also created. Countertrade generally involves a seller from the West and a buyer in a developing country; for example, the countries in the former Soviet bloc have historically relied heavily on countertrade. This approach, which reached a peak in popularity in the mid-1980s, is now used in some 100 countries. Within the former Soviet Union, countertrade flourished in the 1990s, following the collapse of the central planning system.

As one expert noted, countertrade flourishes when hard currency is scarce. Exchange controls may prevent a company from expatriating earnings; the company may be forced to spend

[42] Vanessa Houlder, "Apple Tax Probe in U.S. Spurs Plans For Global Regime," *Financial Times* (May 24, 2013), p. 3.

[43] Leslie Lopez and John D. McKinnon, "Swatch Faces Complaint Over Taxes," *The Wall Street Journal* (August 13, 2004), p. B2.

[44] Susannah Rodgers, "GlaxoSmithKline Gets Big Tax Bill," *The Wall Street Journal* (January 8, 2004), p. A8.

[45] Many of the examples in this section are adapted from Matt Schaffer, *Winning the Countertrade War: New Export Strategies for America* (New York: John Wiley & Sons, 1989).

money in-country for products that are then exported and sold in third-country markets. Historically, the single-most-important driving force behind the proliferation of countertrade was the decreasing ability of developing countries to finance imports through bank loans. This trend resulted in debt-ridden governments pushing for self-financed deals.[46] According to Pompiliu Verzariu, former director of the Financial Services and Countertrade Division at the International Trade Administration:

> In the 1990s, countertrade pressures abated in many parts of the world, notably Latin America, as a result of debt reduction induced by the Brady plan initiative, lower international interest rates, policies that liberalized trade regimes, and the emergence of economic blocs such as NAFTA and Mercosur, which integrate regional trade based on free-market principles.[47]

Generally, several conditions affect the probability that some form of countertrade will be used.

- *The priority attached to the import.* The higher the priority, the less likely it is that countertrade will be required.
- *The value of the transaction.* The higher the value, the greater the likelihood that countertrade will be involved.
- *The availability of products from other suppliers.* If a company is the sole supplier of a differentiated product, it can demand monetary payment.

The debt crisis in Europe has prompted some companies to consider using countertrade. For example, German chemical giant BASF has a contingency plan to accept countertrade deals with Greek buyers in the agricultural sector. Such deals are not new for BASF; in Eastern Europe, for example, the company has accepted minerals as payment for its chemical products. Some customers in Brazil even pay with molasses! Fried-Walter Muenstermann, the CFO for BASF in North America, says his company will be selective with new countertrade deals in Europe: "We don't need wine and olive oil."[48]

Two categories of countertrade are discussed here. Barter falls into one category; the mixed forms of countertrade, including counterpurchase, offset, compensation trading, and switch trading, belong in a separate category. They incorporate a real distinction from barter because the transaction involves money or credit.

Barter

The term **barter** describes the least complex and oldest form of bilateral, nonmonetized countertrade. Simple barter is a direct exchange of goods or services between two parties. Although no money is involved, both partners construct an approximate shadow price for products flowing in each direction. Companies sometimes seek outside help from barter specialists. For example, New York–based Atwood Richards engages in barter in all parts of the world. Generally, however, distribution is direct between trading partners, with no intermediary included.

One of the highest-profile companies involved in barter deals is PepsiCo, which has done business in the Soviet and post-Soviet market for decades. In the Soviet era, when the ruble could not be converted to dollars or other "hard" currencies, PepsiCo bartered soft drink syrup concentrate for Stolichnaya vodka. The vodka was exported to the United States by the PepsiCo Wines & Spirits subsidiary and marketed by M. Henri Wines. In the post-Soviet market economy, Russian rubles are freely convertible, and barter is not necessarily required. Today, Stolichnaya is imported into the United States and marketed by Carillon Importers, a unit of Diageo PLC. A cornerstone of late Venezuelan president Hugo Chávez's economic policy was bartering oil to foster closer relations with other Latin American countries. For example, Cuba sent doctors to Venezuela in exchange for oil; other countries "paid" for oil with bananas or sugar.

---

[46] Pompiliu Verzariu, "Trends and Developments in International Countertrade," *Business America* (November 2, 1992), p. 2.

[47] Janet Aschkenasy, "Give and Take," *International Business* (September 1996), p. 11.

[48] Emily Chasan, "Currencies Pose New Risks," *The Wall Street Journal* (August 14, 2012), p. B5.

Counterpurchase

The **counterpurchase** form of countertrade, also termed *parallel trading* or *parallel barter*, is distinguished from other forms of countertrade in that each delivery in an exchange is paid for in cash. For example, Rockwell International sold a printing press to Zimbabwe for $8 million. The deal went through, however, only after Rockwell agreed to purchase $8 million in ferrochrome and nickel from Zimbabwe, which it subsequently sold on the world market.

The Rockwell-Zimbabwe deal illustrates several aspects of counterpurchase. Generally, products offered by the foreign principal are not related to the Western firm's exports and cannot be used directly by the firm. In most counterpurchase transactions, two separate contracts are signed. In one contract, the supplier agrees to sell products for a cash settlement (the original sales contract); in the other, the supplier agrees to purchase and market unrelated products from the buyer (a separate, parallel contract). The dollar value of the counterpurchase generally represents a set percentage—and sometimes the full value—of the products sold to the foreign principal. When the Western supplier sells these goods, the trading cycle is complete.

Offset

Offset is a reciprocal arrangement whereby the government in the importing country seeks to recover large sums of hard currency spent on expensive purchases such as military aircraft or telecommunications systems. In effect, the government is saying, "If you want us to spend government money on your exports, you must import products from our country." Offset arrangements may also involve cooperation in manufacturing, some form of technology transfer, placing subcontracts locally, or arranging local assembly or manufacturing equal to a certain percentage of the contract value.[49] In one deal involving offsets, Lockheed Martin Corp. sold F-16 fighters to the United Arab Emirates for $6.4 billion. In return, Lockheed agreed to invest $160 million in the petroleum-related UAE Offsets Group.[50]

Offset may be distinguished from counterpurchase because the latter is characterized by smaller deals over shorter periods of time.[51] Another major distinction between offset and other forms of countertrade is that the agreement is not contractual but reflects a memorandum of understanding that sets out the dollar value of products to be offset and the time period for completing the transaction. In addition, there is no penalty on the supplier for nonperformance. Typically, requests range from 20 to 50 percent of the value of the supplier's product. Some highly competitive sales have required offsets exceeding 100 percent of the valuation of the original sale.

Offsets have become a controversial facet of today's trade environment. To win sales in important markets such as China, global companies can face demands for offsets even when transactions do not involve military procurement. For example, the Chinese government requires Boeing to spend 20 to 30 percent of the price of each aircraft on purchases of Chinese goods. As Boeing executive Dean Thornton explained:

> "Offset" is a bad word, and it's against GATT and a whole bunch of other stuff, but it's a fact of life. It used to be 20 years ago in places like Canada or the UK, it was totally explicit, down to the decimal point. "You will buy 20 percent offset of your value." Or 21 percent or whatever. It still is that way in military stuff. [With sales of commercial aircraft], it's not legal so it becomes less explicit.[52]

Compensation Trading

Compensation trading, also called *buyback*, is a form of countertrade that involves two separate and parallel contracts. In one contract, the supplier agrees to build a plant or provide plant equipment, patents or licenses, or technical, managerial, or distribution expertise for a hard-currency down payment at the time of delivery. In the other contract, the supplier company agrees to take

---

[49] The commitment to local assembly or manufacturing under the supplier's specifications is commonly termed a *coproduction agreement*, which is tied to the offset but does not, in itself, represent a type of countertrade.

[50] Daniel Pearl, "Arms Dealers Get Creative with 'Offsets,'" *The Wall Street Journal* (April 20, 2000), p. A18.

[51] Patricia Daily and S. M. Ghazanfar, "Countertrade: Help or Hindrance to Less-Developed Countries?" *Journal of Social, Political, and Economic Studies* 18, no. 1 (Spring 1993), p. 65.

[52] William Greider, *One World, Ready or Not: The Manic Logic of Global Capitalism* (New York: Simon & Schuster, 1997), p. 130.

payment in the form of the plant's output equal to its investment (minus interest) for a period of as many as 20 years.

Essentially, the success of compensation trading rests on the willingness of each firm to be both a buyer and a seller. The People's Republic of China has used compensation trading extensively. Egypt also used this approach to develop an aluminum plant. A Swiss company, Aluswiss, built the plant and also exports alumina (an oxide of aluminum found in bauxite and clay) to Egypt. Aluswiss takes back a percentage of the finished aluminum produced at the plant as partial payment for building the plant. As this example shows, compensation differs from counterpurchase in that the technology or capital supplied in the former is related to the output produced.[53] In counterpurchase, as noted before, the goods taken by the supplier typically cannot be used directly in its business activities.

Switch Trading

Also called *triangular trade* and *swap*, **switch trading** is a mechanism that can be applied to barter or countertrade. In this arrangement, a third party steps into a simple barter or other countertrade arrangement when one of the parties is not willing to accept all the goods received in a transaction. The third party may be a professional switch trader, a switch trading house, or a bank. The switching mechanism provides a "secondary market" for countertraded or bartered goods and reduces the inflexibility inherent in barter and countertrade. Fees charged by switch traders range from 5 percent of market value for commodities to 30 percent for high-technology items. Switch traders develop their own networks of firms and personal contacts and are generally headquartered in Vienna, Amsterdam, Hamburg, or London. If a party to the original transaction anticipates that the products received in a barter or countertrade deal will be sold eventually at a discount by the switch trader, the common practice is to price the original products higher, build in "special charges" for port storage or consulting, or require shipment by the national carrier.

Summary

Pricing decisions are a critical element of the marketing mix that must reflect costs, competitive factors, and customer perceptions regarding value of the product. In a true global market, the **law of one price** would prevail. Pricing strategies include **market skimming**, **market penetration**, and **market holding**. Novice exporters frequently use the cost-plus method when setting prices. International terms of a sale such as **ex-works**, **DDP**, **FCA**, **FAS**, **FOB**, **CIF**, and **CFR** are known as **Incoterms** and specify which party to a transaction is responsible for covering various costs. These and other costs lead to **export price escalation**, the accumulation of costs that occurs when products are shipped from one country to another.

Expectations regarding currency fluctuations, inflation, government controls, and the competitive situation must also be factored into pricing decisions. The introduction of the euro has impacted price strategies in the EU because of improved **price transparency**. Global companies can maintain competitive prices in world markets by shifting production sources as business conditions change. Overall, a company's pricing policies can be categorized as **ethnocentric**, **polycentric**, or **geocentric**.

Several additional pricing issues are related to global marketing. The issue of **gray market goods** arises because price variations between different countries lead to **parallel imports**. **Dumping** is another contentious issue that can result in strained relations between trading partners. **Price fixing** among companies is anticompetitive and illegal. **Transfer pricing** is an issue because of the sheer monetary volume of intracorporate sales and because country governments are anxious to generate as much tax revenue as possible. Various forms of **countertrade** play an important role in today's global environment. **Barter**, **counterpurchase**, **offset**, **compensation trading**, and **switch trading** are the main countertrade options.

---

[53] Patricia Daily and S. M. Ghazanfar, "Countertrade: Help or Hindrance to Less-Developed Countries?" *Journal of Social, Political, and Economic Studies* 18, no. 1 (Spring 1993), p. 66.

MyMarketingLab

Go to **mymktlab.com** for the following Assisted-graded writing questions:

11-1. What is dumping? Why was dumping such an important issue during the Uruguay Round of GATT negotiations?

11-2. Luxury goods marketers such as LVMH use distinctive logos to differentiate their brands. Discuss the risks associated with this marketing strategy.

11-3. Mymarketinglab Only – comprehensive writing assignment for this chapter.

MyMarketingLab

Go to **mymktlab.com** to complete the problems marked with this icon .

Discussion Questions

11-4. What are the basic factors that affect price in any market? What considerations enter into the pricing decision?

11-5. Define the various types of pricing strategies and objectives available to global marketers.

11-6. Identify some of the environmental constraints on global pricing decisions.

11-7. Why do price differences in world markets often lead to gray marketing?

11-8. What is a transfer price? Why is it an important issue for companies with foreign affiliates? Why did transfer pricing in Europe take on increased importance in 1999?

11-9. What is the difference among ethnocentric, polycentric, and geocentric pricing strategies? Which would you recommend to a company that has global market aspirations?

11-10. If you were responsible for marketing computerized tomography (CT) scanners worldwide (average price, $1,200,000) and your country of manufacture was experiencing a strong and appreciating currency against almost all other currencies, what options would be available to you to maintain your company's competitive advantage in world markets?

11-11. Compare and contrast the different forms of countertrade.

CASE 11-1 CONTINUED (REFER TO PAGE 350)

Global Companies Target Low-Income Consumers (B)

The Logan is a case study in driving down costs. Drivers turn on the ignition with an "old-fashioned," manual key; there is no cruise control. The windshield glass is nearly flat, which makes it less expensive to produce. The left and right outside mirrors are identical; the ashtrays are exactly the same as the ones used in another Renault model, the Espace. Similarly, Logan shares an engine and gearbox with Renault's Clio subcompact; for these and other components, high manufacturing volumes translate into economies of scale.

Production of the first Logan models began in Romania in 2004. The choice of an assembly site was dictated by simple economics: France's high labor rates and payroll taxes would have translated into an additional €1,000 ($1,400) cost per vehicle. The Logan was launched in India in April 2007 with a sticker price of about $10,000; the vehicle was manufactured by a joint venture between Renault and Mahindra & Mahindra (M&M), one of India's best-known industrial conglomerates. After a dispute between the partners, the joint venture was dissolved. Mahindra & Mahindra now produces Logans under a licensing agreement.

In 2008 a hatchback model, the Sandero, was introduced. This was followed in 2009 by the Duster sport-utility vehicle; the Lodgy debuted in 2012. In 2012, Renault sold a record 2.55 million vehicles; 25 percent were low-cost models. Sales are about evenly split between the Logan and entry-level Renault models. As it turned out, the geographic distribution of sales indicated that Renault's strategy was in trouble: Although the Logan was targeted at emerging markets, it was a big hit with consumers in affluent European countries.

How did this happen? Enterprising independent distributors bought Logans that were manufactured in Romania and exported them to France and other countries in Western Europe. This coincided with a shift in consumer attitudes; in light of the financial crisis, it was not surprising that many young Europeans were of the opinion that cutting back on spending was a sensible thing to do. Indeed, surveys showed that a high proportion of twentysomething Europeans were "interested" or "very interested" in buying a low-cost car.

Nano

Even as Renault continued to refine its low-cost-car strategy, some in the industry were asking a tantalizing question: Could the auto companies come up with the optimal value proposition—small, no-frills, four-door cars that are safe to drive, stylish enough to appeal to the aspirations of first-time buyers, and yet sell for *half* the price of a Logan (or less)? Under the best of circumstances, creating such a vehicle would test the prowess of the world's best automotive engineers. However, the challenge was especially daunting in a business environment characterized by record prices for steel, resin, and other commodities and components. As the general manager for a sourcing and procuring company noted, "There are so many legacy costs built into a design, and trying to engineer those out is difficult. It's better to start with a clean sheet of paper and engineer low costs in."

Top executives at India's Tata Motors believed their company was up to the task, and the Nano is the evidence. The Nano's instrument panel is clustered in the middle of the dashboard so that Tata can offer both right- and left-hand-drive versions for export. Tata's target market is consumers in emerging markets who currently travel by scooter. Some environmentalists have warned about the negative impact of hundreds of thousands of new vehicles on India's already congested roads. However, as Chairman Ratan Tata noted, low-income families should be given access to the freedom that a car provides. "Should they be denied the right to independent transport?" he asked.

After an initial flurry of industry interest and positive press, the Nano program fell victim to bad luck and changing attitudes. For one thing, protesters objected to the location of the first assembly plant. After production finally began, there were several well-publicized incidents in which cars caught fire. Many car buyers shopped the competition; one best-selling model was the $6,200 Maruti Suzuki Alto. It seemed that the market had spoken: Very few people wanted to be seen driving "the world's cheapest car." As Hormazd Sorabjee, editor of *India Autoweek*, noted, "The bottom of the pyramid continues to be where the action is, but the aspirations of people are moving up. People want to jump into something more substantial."

Datsun

Tata Motors' announcement about the Nano galvanized Carlos Ghosn, Nissan's chief executive. Nissan's Datsun relaunch had Ghosn's full support: He was born in Brazil and didn't own a car until his late teens. Datsun represented more than a business strategy or business model. Much more, in fact: It was a life mission, a make-or-break, billion-dollar decision that would determine his legacy and his reputation. In 2007, Ghosn convened a cadre of executives known as the Nissan Exploratory Team and dispatched members to India to study what consumers there sought in a car.

Industry observers noted that the Datsun nameplate was very popular in the United States in the 1960s and 1970s. The Datsun name was used for one simple reason: In the event the Japanese automaker did not succeed in the United States, the Nissan name would not be tarnished. However, in 1981, executives decided to unify the two brands, and so Datsun became Nissan. The result: Much confusion among consumers and a gradual erosion of Nissan's market position in the United States. The move is widely regarded as one of the worst decisions in the history of the automobile business.

Yukitoshi Funo, an executive vice president at rival Toyota Motor Corporation, has his doubts about Datsun's prospects. "It's a big mistake to think you can introduce a cheap car in emerging markets and be successful. People want a car they and their families can be proud of," he says.

Discussion Questions

11-12. What is the key to the Logan's low price?

11-13. Do you think Tata will be able to save the Nano? What steps should the company take?

11-14. Assess Carlos Ghosn's plans to revive the Datsun nameplate. Can a car that sells for $3,000 make a profit for the parent company?

11-15. Low-cost cars such as the Nano and Datsun lack the multilayered safety and quality features required by regulators in high-income markets. Is it appropriate to create "bare-bones" cars with fewer safety features for emerging markets?

Sources: Chester Dawson, "For Datsun Revival, Nissan Gambles on $3,000 Model," *The Wall Street Journal* (October 1, 2012), p. A1; Sebastian Moffett, "Renault's Low-Price Plan Turns Tricky," *The Wall Street Journal* (February 2, 2011), pp. B1, B2; Vikas Bajaj, "Tata's Nano, the Car That Few Want to Buy," *The New York Times* (December 10, 2010), p. B1; Simon Robinson, "The World's Cheapest Car," Time.com (January 10, 2008); Heather Timmons, "In India, a $2,500 Pace Car," *The New York Times* (October 12, 2007), pp. C1, C4; David Gauthier-Villars, "Ghosn Bets Big on Low-Cost Strategy," *The Wall Street Journal* (September 4, 2007), p. A8; John Reed and Amy Yee, "Thrills Without Frills," *Financial Times* (June 25, 2007), p. 9; Christopher Condon, "The Birth of a Frankenstein Car," *Financial Times* (July 20, 2004), p. 12.

CASE 11-2
LVMH and Luxury Goods Marketing

LVMH Moët Hennessy–Louis Vuitton SA is the world's largest marketer of luxury products and brands. Chairman Bernard Arnault has assembled a diverse empire of more than 60 brands, sales of which totaled $28 billion (€20.3 billion) in 2010 (see Figure 11-2). Arnault, whom some refer to as "the pope of high fashion," recently summed up the luxury business as follows: "We are here to sell dreams. When you see a couture show on TV around the world, you dream. When you enter a Dior boutique and buy your lipstick, you buy something affordable, but it has the dream in it."

Decades ago, the companies that today comprise LVMH were family-run enterprises focused more on prestige than on profit. Fendi, Pucci, and others sold mainly to a niche market comprised of very rich clientele. However, as markets began to globalize, the small luxury players struggled to compete. When Arnault set about acquiring smaller luxury brands, he had three goals in mind. First, he hoped that the portfolio approach would reduce the risk exposure in fashion cycles. According to this logic, if demand for watches or jewelry declined, clothing or accessory sales would offset any losses. Second, he intended to cut costs by eliminating redundancies in sourcing and manufacturing. Third, he hoped that LVMH's stable of brands would translate into a stronger bargaining position when managers negotiated leases for retail space or bought advertising.

Sales of luggage and leather fashion goods, including the 160-year-old Louis Vuitton brand, account for 35 percent of revenues (see Figure 11-2). The company's Selective Retailing group includes Duty Free Shoppers (DFS) and Sephora. DFS operates "travel retail" stores in international airports around the world; Sephora, which LVMH acquired in 1997, is Europe's second-largest chain of perfume and cosmetics stores. Driven by such well-known brands as Christian Dior, Givenchy, and Kenzo, perfumes and cosmetics generate nearly 15 percent of LVMH's revenues. LVMH's wine and spirits unit includes such prestigious Champagne brands as Dom Perignon, Moët & Chandon, and Veuve Clicquot.

Despite the high expenses associated with operating elegant stores and purchasing advertising space in upscale magazines, the premium retail prices that luxury goods command translate into handsome profits. The Louis Vuitton brand alone accounts for about 60 percent of

Exhibit 11-6
Source: Landon Media

LVMH's operating profit. However, unscrupulous operators have taken note of the high margins associated with Vuitton handbags, gun cases, and luggage displaying the distinctive beige-on-brown latticework LV monogram. Louis Vuitton SA spends $10 million annually battling counterfeiters in Turkey, Thailand, China, Morocco, South Korea, and Italy. Some of the money is spent on lobbyists who represent the company's interests in meetings with foreign government officials. Yves Carcelle, chairman of Louis Vuitton SA, recently explained, "Almost every month, we get a government somewhere in the world to destroy canvas, or finished products."

Another problem is a flourishing gray market. Givenchy and Christian Dior's Dune fragrance are just two of the luxury perfume brands that are sometimes diverted from authorized channels for sale at mass-market retail outlets. However, LVMH and other luxury goods marketers found a new way to combat gray market imports into the United States. In March 1995, the U.S. Supreme Court let stand an appeals court ruling prohibiting a discount drugstore chain from selling Givenchy perfume without permission. Parfums Givenchy USA had claimed that its distinctive packaging should be protected under U.S. copyright law. The ruling has meant that Costco, Walmart, and other discounters cannot sell some imported fragrances without authorization.

Opportunities and Challenges in Asia

Asia—particularly Japan—is a key region for LVMH and its competitors. The financial turmoil of the late 1990s and the subsequent currency devaluations and weakening of the yen translated into lower demand for luxury goods. Because price perceptions are a critical component of luxury goods' appeal, LVMH executives made a number of adjustments in response to changing business conditions. For example, Patrick Choel, president of the perfume and cosmetics division, raised wholesale prices in individual Asian markets. The goal was to discourage discount retailers from stocking up on designer products and then selling them to down-market consumers. Also, expenditures on perfume and cosmetics advertising were reduced to maintain profitability in the face of a possible sales decline.

Louis Vuitton chairman Yves Carcelle also made adjustments. He canceled plans for a new store in Indonesia, and group managers

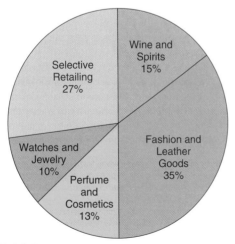

FIGURE 11-2
LVMH Operating Units by 2012 Net Sales

Wine and Spirits 15%
Selective Retailing 27%
Watches and Jewelry 10%
Perfume and Cosmetics 13%
Fashion and Leather Goods 35%

raised prices to counteract the effect of currency devaluations. Because the DFS chain depends on Japanese tourists in Asia and Hawaii for 75 percent of sales, Louis Vuitton managers also work with tour operators to predict the flow of Japanese tourists. When tourism is at a peak, price increases from 10 to 22 percent help maximize profits on merchandise sales.

Arnault was confident that the Asian crisis would not severely affect his company's performance in the long term. As Arnault explained in the spring of 1998, "One has to distinguish between Japan, where most of our business is, and the rest of Asia. Japan is in a growth slump, but it isn't going to have the same difficulties as Korea or Indonesia. And our business in Japan is doing very well." Because the Louis Vuitton unit controls its own distribution, management was even able to take advantage of the crisis by renegotiating store leases in key Asian cities. In some instances, the company secured longer lease terms plus reductions in rates by as much as one-third. Arnault's optimism was well founded; with interest rates at record lows and a gloomy outlook for the stock market, Japanese consumers had few other spending options. In 2001, executives actually raised prices at Louis Vuitton's Japanese stores.

> **"The big question for the future is, will the Chinese new entrant to the luxury market choose a Louis Vuitton as her first bag, as she has tended to do to date, or that of another brand?"**
>
> —Antoine Belge, luxury goods analyst, HSBC

Strategic Decisions at LVMH

Over the past decade, Arnault has leveraged his multibrand strategy by broadening the company's consumer base. In the late 1990s, Arnault sensed that cosmetics-buying habits were changing in key markets. He opened Sephora stores in New York, Chicago, and San Francisco in conjunction with a new Web site, Sephora.com. Today, there are more than 270 Sephora stores in the United States and Canada; the chain also has a presence in more than a dozen other countries, including China and Russia. Customers who visit Sephora USA stores are encouraged to wander freely and sample products on an open floor without waiting for sales clerks to assist them.

In 2001, Arnault paid more than $600 million for Donna Karan International Inc. and its trademarks. Arnault had tried without success to acquire Giorgio Armani; Donna Karan is LVMH's first American designer label. As Arnault noted, "What appealed to us is the fact that it is one of the best-known brand names in the world."

In January 2008, executives at Louis Vuitton announced a new corporate branding campaign using a 90-second ad that would appear on cable and satellite television and in cinemas. This was something new in the luxury goods sector; generally, advertising budgets are limited and television is viewed as too expensive. In addition, some in the industry believe that TV's status as a mass-marketing medium can undercut a luxury brand's aura of exclusivity. However, Louis Vuitton executives hoped audiences would connect with the brand's travel heritage. To achieve that connection, the company's ad agency proposed buying time on news channels that business travelers watch such as CNN. As Louis Vuitton marketing chief Pietro Beccari noted, "It is supposed to touch our clientele and viewers in ways that perhaps other media will not touch. This is a way to say Louis Vuitton is different. It is something éphémère, but also something that stays."

Arnault has also turned his attention to emerging markets. Louis Vuitton entered India in 2002 with a boutique at a luxury hotel; now, Fendi, Tag Heuer, and Dior are open for business as well. LVMH has a lock on prime locations at Emporio, an upscale shopping mall that

opened recently in New Delhi. Because LVMH has a group presence in the mall, it can negotiate favorable lease rates for retail space. Arnault's expansion coincided with the September 2007 launch of Vogue India. Once again, thanks to LVMH's diverse brand portfolio, the company is able to buy large blocks of advertising space from Condé Nast India at discounted prices.

The global economic crisis that gained traction in 2008 affected many retail sectors, and the luxury goods business was no exception. Overall purchases of luxury goods fell in the key U.S. market; sales slowed in Russia and other emerging markets as well. Although total sales in the luxury segment were expected to reach a record €175 billion ($218 billion) in 2008, industry observers expected the sales to drop significantly in 2009. For European-based luxury companies, there was some good news: The dollar was strengthening against the euro. As the 2008 holiday shopping season approached, many luxury goods makers reduced prices in the United States. At Chanel, the cuts ranged from 7 to 10 percent; as John Galantic, president of Chanel's U.S. unit, noted, "The dollar's recent strength has allowed us to pass on greater value to our customers." Louis Vuitton was a notable exception; in fact, during 2008, the company raised prices twice, resulting in an average increase of 10 percent. The price increases did not dampen sales; in fact, sales continued to increase.

Visit the Web site

www.lvmh.com
A complete PowerPoint presentation of the current year's financial results is available on the LVMH Web site.
www.sephora.com

Discussion Questions

11-16. What were the possible risks of Louis Vuitton's first-ever television advertising campaign?

11-17. In March 2008, the euro/dollar exchange rate was €1 = $1.50. By November, the dollar had strengthened to €1 = $1.25. Assume that a European luxury goods marketer cut the price of an $8,000 tweed suit by 10 percent to maintain holiday sales in December. How would revenues have been affected when dollar prices were converted to euros?

⭐**11-18.** Louis Vuitton executives raised prices in 2008, and sales continued to increase. What does this say about the demand curve of the typical Louis Vuitton customer?

11-19. Compare and contrast LVMH's pricing strategy with that of Coach.

Sources: Scheherazade Daneshkhu, "LVMH Faces Dilemma of Success," *Financial Times* (October 20/21, 2012), p. 11; Christina Passariello, "LVMH Sees Shift in China: Locals Go Abroad to Shop," *The Wall Street Journal* (April 19, 2012), pp. B1, B2; Rachel Dodes and Christina Passariello, "In Rare Move, Luxury-Goods Makers Trim Their Prices in U.S.," *The Wall Street Journal* (November 14, 2008), p. B1; Eric Pfanner, "Vuitton Is Embracing Medium of the Masses," *The New York Times* (January 30, 2008), p. C3; Passariello, "LVMH Books Passage to India for Vuitton, Dior, Fendi, Celine," *The Wall Street Journal* (May 8, 2007), pp. B1, B2; Lisa Bannon and Alessandra Galloni, "Brand Manager Deluxe," *The Wall Street Journal* (October 10, 2003), p. B1; John Carreyrou and Christopher Lawton, "Napoleon's Nightcap Gets a Good Rap from Hip-Hop Set," *The Wall Street Journal* (July 14, 2003), pp. A1, A7; Teri Agins and Deborah Ball, "Changing Outfits: Did LVMH Commit a Fashion Faux Pas Buying Donna Karan?" *The Wall Street Journal* (March 21, 2002), pp. A1, A8; Ball, "Despite Downturn, Japanese Are Still Having Fits for Luxury Goods," *The Wall Street Journal* (April 24, 2001), pp. B1, B4; Bonnie Tsui, "Eye of the Beholder: Sephora's Finances," *Advertising Age* (March 19, 2001), p. 20; Lucia van der Post, "Life's Brittle Luxuries," *Financial Times* (July 18–19, 1998), p. I; Gail Edmondson, "LVMH: Life Isn't All Champagne and Caviar," *BusinessWeek* (November 10, 1997), pp. 108+; Jennifer Steinhauer, "The King of Posh," *The New York Times* (August 17, 1997), sec. 3, pp. 1, 10–11; David Owen, "A Captain Used to Storms," *Financial Times* (June 21–22, 1997); Holly Brubach, "And Luxury for All," *The New York Times Magazine* (July 12, 1998), pp. 24–29+.

CASE 11-3
One Laptop Per Child

As director of the prestigious Media Lab at the Massachusetts Institute of Technology (MIT), Nicolas Negroponte had a unique opportunity to immerse himself in cutting-edge technology development projects. Robotic design, artificial intelligence, holographic video, and educational applications for PCs were just some of the areas the Lab's various departments explored. In 2005, after 20 years at the Lab, Negroponte announced he was leaving to pursue an ambitious vision: bridging the digital divide between developed and developing nations by providing powerful PCs to schoolchildren in sub-Saharan Africa and other impoverished parts of the world. Negroponte named his initiative One Laptop Per Child (OLPC); his goal was to develop a $100 laptop that governments could buy in large quantities and distribute to schools. As Negroponte said, "My goal is not selling laptops. OLPC is not in the laptop business. It's in the education business." In April 2007, Negroponte announced that he hoped to have between 50 and 150 million children using the new computer by the end of 2008.

> **"We do not view kids as a market, but as a mission."**
>
> —Nicolas Negroponte, founder, OLPC

The OLPC design team, which included Media Lab veteran Walter Bender, created a computer known as the XO that is rugged enough to stand up to heavy use and abuse. The XO is dust- and waterproof; a small solar panel can be used to recharge the battery. The laptop's high-resolution screen displays bright images even in sunlight; other features include a built-in video camera. Wi-Fi connectivity is provided by two small antennas on either side of the screen; some observers commented that the antennas look like ears on a friendly alien-type creature.

To keep the cost down, each computer was loaded with an open-source operating system known as Linux. Linux is nonproprietary; that is, it is available for free to anyone who wants to use it. Moreover, Linux users are encouraged to make improvements to it. The user interface, dubbed Sugar, could also be modified by the children using the computers. As described by its creators, Sugar captures students' "world of fellow learners and teachers as collaborators, emphasizing the connections within the community, among people, and their activities." The design team believed that Linux and Sugar would foster collaborative learning among schoolchildren, in line with OLPC's core mission. The laptops were powered by microprocessors from Advanced Micro Devices (AMD); these cost less than components from Intel.

Another factor affecting the final cost was the volume of production. Negroponte needed firm purchase commitments so that production could be scaled up quickly. Government officials in Libya and Nigeria initially pledged to buy about 1 million computers each for their respective citizens; however, by mid-2007 both countries had backed off those pledges. As a result, the manufacturer, Taiwan's Quanta Computer, only achieved an initial production volume of 300,000 units. The lower volume, plus microprocessor upgrades, translated into a higher per-unit cost. The $100 price—a key selling point—had to be abandoned. The new price target was in the $180 to $190 range.

The higher price was one reason that initial enthusiasm for OLPC did not translate into firm commitments for orders. Other issues surfaced as well. For example, some potential buyers worried about the lack of Microsoft's Windows operating system. Meanwhile, OLPC had attracted the attention of several industry heavyweights. In 2006, Intel officials demonstrated a laptop prototype called the Classmate that was designed to sell for $230 to $300. The Classmate featured Microsoft's Windows XP operating system, had four hours of battery life, and used a solid-state flash drive. In 2007, Microsoft chairman Bill Gates announced that his company would offer developing countries a

Exhibit 11-7 The non-profit One Laptop Per Child (OLPC) initiative has sold more than two million laptops since 2005. Today, however, OLPC faces competition from Intel's Classmate PC and Studybook tablet and others. The initiative has also faced criticism for its mission, and questions have been raised about assessable educational outcomes. Meanwhile, e-readers such as the Kindle are making inroads in Africa and developing countries in other parts of the world.
Source: © Joerg Boethling / Alamy

$3 software package that included Windows, Office, and educational software. The low-priced software was offered through Unlimited Potential Group, the Microsoft unit that targets developing countries; early customers included the governments of Libya and Egypt.

Negroponte accused Intel officials of trying to undermine his non-profit's efforts; for example, reports surfaced that Intel's sales force had made head-to-head comparisons between the Classmate and the OLPC laptop during presentations in Mongolia and Nigeria. Even so, Intel made a substantial financial contribution to OLPC and an Intel official joined the organization's board.

In November 2007, in an effort to increase production, OLPC announced a promotion called "Give One. Get One." Consumers in the United States and Canada were offered the opportunity to buy two OLPC computers for $399. Each buyer would keep one laptop; the second would go to a student in Haiti or another developing country.

In 2008, faced with disappointing sales, Negroponte struck a deal with Microsoft. Starting in 2010, the OLPC laptops would be delivered with both the Microsoft Windows operating system and the nonproprietary Linux OS. Microsoft would provide the software for about $3 per computer, bringing the total selling price of each laptop to $199.

Discussion Questions

11-20. Why are Microsoft, Intel, and other leading for-profit companies interested in low-cost computers for the developing world?

11-21. Do you agree with Negroponte's decision to partner with Microsoft?

11-22. Discuss the thinking behind the "Give One. Get One." promotion. Do you think this is a good marketing tactic?

Sources: Geoffrey A. Fowler and Nicholas Bariyo, "An E-Reader Revolution for Africa," *The Wall Street Journal* (June 16–17, 2012), p. C3; Nick Bilton, "One Laptop Per Child Project Works with Marvell to Produce a $100 Tablet," *The New York Times* (May 27, 2010), bits.blogs.nytimes.com; Randall Stross, "Two Billion Laptops? It May Not Be Enough," *The New York Times* (April 17, 2010), p. BU5; Steve Stecklow, "Laptop Program for Kids in Poor Countries Teams Up with Microsoft's Windows," *The Wall Street Journal* (May 16, 2008), pp. B1, B2; Steve Stecklow and James Bandler, "A Little Laptop with Big Ambitions: How a Computer for the Poor Got Stomped by Tech Giants," *The Wall Street Journal* (November 24–25, 2007), pp. A1, A7; David Pogue, "$100 Laptop a Bargain at $200," *The New York Times* (October 4, 2007), pp. C1, C8; Kevin Maney, "The Latest Cool Tool You Can't Have: Laptops So Cheap They're Disposable," *USA Today* (February 28, 2007), p. B8; John Markoff, "At Davos, the Squabble Resumes on How to Wire the Third World," *The New York Times* (January 29, 2007), pp. C1, C2.

12
Global Marketing Channels and Physical Distribution

Exhibit 12-1 There are various factors that led to the success of Carrefour in Dubai. One was its leadership position in the global market, which helps when entering new markets. Two, the in-house brand allowed Carrefour to lower its prices. Three, brand equity combined with good quality has further bolstered Carrefour's name. It is the second largest hypermarket globally, after Walmart. Carrefour also gained first-mover advantages when penetrating emerging markets.

 CASE 12-1
Carrefour's Entry in Dubai

Carrefour, a superstore that sells everything from groceries to hardware, is a French retail chain that has expanded exponentially since 1977. It is one of the biggest businesses in history—Carrefour was listed as the second largest hypermarket chain worldwide right behind Walmart in 2006—and was the one to introduce unbranded products as a substitute for well-known brands at competitive prices; their idea of unbranded products culminated in the company creating its own brand. The idea, once proven successful, led other supermarkets and hypermarkets around the world to explore the prospects of such ventures.

Expansion plans usually include emerging markets, and Carrefour is no different. Similar to Walmart's interest in the BRICS nations, Carrefour decided to expand to the Middle East and North

Africa (MENA). Carrefour had the first-mover advantage when it decided to open in Dubai and enjoys the distinction of being the first major foreign retailer to operate in the United Arab Emirates.

The UAE has been noted to have a strong economic growth and has attracted a lot of investments because of its rising retail industry and booming economy. Dubai's economy is known to provide support to businesses to encourage foreign investment. Zero corporate taxes, an excellent transportation network, low political risk, a well-defined legal system, positive retail conditions, and low transfer risks are among the many benefits that Dubai offers. Despite having one of the highest standards of living and per capita income in the world, Dubai has a smaller demographic as compared to other markets that Carrefour caters to. Yet, Dubai is the most populated emirate in the UAE and presents a rare composition of expatriates and local residents. It is easier to expand and open in the remaining six emirates after establishing a firm base in Dubai since it is the most competitive market among the other emirates. In 1995, after reviewing the laws and weighing all the pros and cons, Carrefour decided that the best way to penetrate an emerging market like the UAE was by entering into a joint venture with Majid Al Futtaim, a pan-regional conglomerate with retail experience in the Middle East.

Majid Al Futtaim was seen as a qualified partner to seek growth. The local partner helped to better understand the local taste and establish networks with local producers and suppliers. It started by adapting to the market—the store venues shifted to the shopping mall, but most importantly, it adapted food products to fit the socio-cultural needs. The venture is considered a success but

Carrefour still has to address some key problems such as customer grievance redressal and Dubai's long-term macroeconomic challenges. For more on Carrefour's entry to Dubai and the challenges it faces, see the continuation of Case 12-1 at the end of the chapter.

Supermarkets and convenience stores comprise just two of the many elements that make up distribution channels around the globe. Today, global supply chains connect producers in all parts of the world, and sophisticated logistics are utilized to ensure the smooth flow through the system. The American Marketing Association defines a **channel of distribution** as "an organized network of agencies and institutions that, in combination, perform all the activities required to link producers with users to accomplish the marketing task."[1] Physical distribution is the movement of goods through channels; as suggested by the definition, channels are made up of a coordinated group of individuals or firms that perform functions that add utility to a product or service.

Distribution channels are one of the most highly differentiated aspects of national marketing systems. Retail stores vary in size from giant hypermarkets to small stores in Latin America called *pulperías*. The diversity of channels and the wide range of possible distribution strategies and market-entry options can present challenges to managers responsible for designing global marketing programs. Channels and physical distribution are crucial aspects of the total marketing program; without them, a great product at the right price and effective communications mean very little.

---

[1] Peter D. Bennett, *Dictionary of Marketing Terms* (Chicago: American Marketing Association, 1988), p. 29.

LEARNING OBJECTIVES

1 Identify and compare the basic structure options for consumer channels and industrial channels.

2 List the guidelines companies should follow when choosing channel intermediaries in global markets.

3 Describe the different categories of retail operations that are found in various parts of the world.

4 Compare and contrast the six major international transportation modes and explain how they vary in terms of reliability, accessibility, and other performance metrics.

Distribution Channels: Objectives, Terminology, and Structure

Marketing channels exist to create utility for customers. The major categories of channel utility are **place utility** (the availability of a product or service in a location that is convenient to a potential customer), **time utility** (the availability of a product or service when desired by a customer), **form utility** (the availability of the product processed, prepared, in proper condition, and/or ready to use), and **information utility** (the availability of answers to questions and general communication about useful product features and benefits). Because these utilities can be a basic source of competitive advantage and comprise an important element of a firm's overall value proposition, choosing a channel strategy is one of the key policy decisions management must make. For example, the Coca-Cola Company's global marketing leadership position is based in part on its ability to put Coke "within an arm's reach of desire"; in other words, to create place utility.

The starting point in selecting the most effective channel arrangement is a clear focus of the company's marketing effort on a target market and an assessment of the way(s) in which distribution can contribute to the firm's overall value proposition. Who are the target customers, and where are they located? What are their information requirements? What are their preferences for service? How sensitive are they to price? Moreover, each market must be analyzed to determine the cost of providing channel services. What is appropriate in one country may not be effective in another. Even marketers concerned with a single-country program should study channel arrangements in different parts of the world for valuable information and insight into possible new channel strategies and tactics. For example, retailers in Europe and Asia studied self-service discount retailing in the United States and then introduced the self-service concept in their own countries. Similarly, governments and business executives from many parts of the world have examined Japanese trading companies to learn from their success. Walmart's formula has been closely studied and copied by competitors in the markets it has entered.

As defined previously, distribution channels are systems that link manufacturers to customers. Although channels for consumer products and industrial products are similar, there are also some distinct differences. In **business-to-consumer** (b-to-c or B2C) **marketing**, consumer channels are designed to put products in the hands of people for their own use. By contrast, **business-to-business** (b-to-b or B2B) **marketing** involves industrial channels that deliver products to manufacturers or other organizations that then use them as inputs in the production process or in day-to-day operations. Intermediaries play important roles in both consumer and industrial channels; a **distributor** is a wholesale intermediary that typically carries product lines or brands on a selective basis. An **agent** is an intermediary who negotiates exchange transactions between two or more parties but does not take title to the goods being purchased or sold.

Consumer Products and Services

Figure 12-1 summarizes six channel structure alternatives for consumer products. The characteristics of both buyers and products have an important influence on channel design. The first alternative is to market directly to buyers via the Internet, mail order, various types of door-to-door selling, or manufacturer-owned retail outlets. The other options use retailers and various combinations of sales

FIGURE 12-1

Marketing Channel Alternatives: Consumer Products

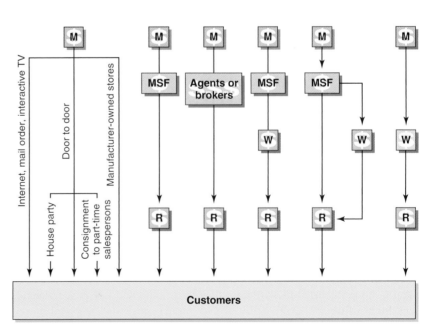

M = Manufacturer   MSF = Manufacturer's sales force
W = Wholesaler   R = Retailer

forces, agents/brokers, and wholesalers. The number of individual buyers and their geographic distributions, incomes, shopping habits, and reactions to different selling methods frequently vary from country to country and may require different channel approaches.

Product characteristics such as degree of standardization, perishability, bulk, service requirements, and unit price have an impact as well. Generally speaking, channels tend to be longer (require more intermediaries) as the number of customers to be served increases and the price per unit decreases. Bulky products usually require channel arrangements that minimize shipping distances and the number of times products change hands before they reach the ultimate customer.

The Internet and related forms of new media are dramatically altering the distribution landscape. eBay pioneered the **peer-to-peer** (p-to-p) **marketing** model, whereby individual consumers market products to other individuals. eBay's success was one reason that traditional merchants quickly recognized the Internet's potential. To sustain revenue growth, eBay began assisting large companies such as Disney and IBM in setting up online "storefronts" to sell items for fixed prices in addition to conducting b-to-c auctions. "As we evolved from auction-style bidding to adding Buy It Now, the logical next step for us was to give sellers a place to showcase their listings," said Bill Cobb, eBay's senior vice president for global marketing.[2] Some observers predict that interactive television (ITV) will also become a viable direct-distribution channel in the coming years as more households are wired with the necessary two-way technology. Time-pressed consumers in many countries are increasingly attracted to the time and place utility created by the Internet and similar new media technologies.

Low-cost mass-market products and certain services can be sold door-to-door via a direct sales force. Door-to-door and house-party selling is mature in the United States; however, it is now growing in popularity elsewhere. For example, Orlando, Florida–based Tupperware has a sales force of 170,000 in Indonesia. Brand-conscious consumers there have embraced the company's plastic food-storage containers, and Tupperware's direct-sales business model gives it an advantage in a country with a limited retail infrastructure (see Exhibit 12-2). Today, Indonesia is Tupperware's biggest market. As CEO Rick Goings notes, "This is an incredible sweet spot for us. It's where the population of the world is. You cannot fight that."[3]

Exhibit 12-2 Tupperware's direct sales force in Indonesia has grown from about 50,000 salespeople in 2008 to nearly 200,000 in 2013. Although emerging markets are important to Tupperware's growth, the brand is also resurgent in France and other high-income countries that have been hit hard by the global economic crisis. CEO Rick Goings has modernized the brand's image; in France, for example, the brand is associated with hip young women rather than traditional house-wives. There is also an emphasis on high-end cookware and cooking lessons. Check out Tupperware France's Facebook page–how many "likes" does it have? The answer may surprise you!
Source: Jean-Philippe Ksiazek/AFP/Getty Images

[2] Nick Wingfield, "Ebay Allows Sellers to Set Up Storefronts Online in Bid to Expand Beyond Auctions," *The Wall Street Journal* (June 12, 2001), p. B8.
[3] Eric Bellman, "Indonesia Serves Tasty Dish for Tupperware," *The Wall Street Journal* (April 25, 2013), p. B8.

In 1995, Mary Kay entered the Chinese market with its network of independent sales agents. After successfully penetrating China's first-tier cities, the company expanded into second- and third-tier locations.[4] In April 1998, China's state council imposed a blanket ban on all types of direct selling. Because the ban was aimed most directly at illegal pyramid schemes, several foreign companies, including Amway, Avon, Mary Kay, and Tupperware, were allowed to continue operations in China. However, they were forced to adapt their business models: Their sales agents had to be affiliated with brick-and-mortar retailers. The ban was lifted in 2005; because it had restricted competition, the handful of foreign direct-sales marketers that had maintained a presence in China had had a unique growth opportunity during the years the ban was in force. Mary Kay is a case in point: By 2011, Mary Kay's Chinese sales were more than 50 times higher than they'd been in 1999. Today, Mary Kay has 35 branch offices in China.

In Japan, the biggest barrier facing U.S. auto manufacturers isn't high tariffs; rather, it's the fact that half the cars that are sold each year are sold door-to-door. Toyota and its Japanese competitors do maintain showrooms, but they also employ more than 100,000 car salespeople. Unlike their American counterparts, many Japanese car buyers never visit dealerships. The close, long-term relationships between auto salespersons and the Japanese people can be thought of as a consumer version of the *keiretsu* system discussed in Chapter 9. Japanese car buyers expect numerous face-to-face meetings with a sales representative, during which trust is established. The relationship continues after the deal is closed; sales reps send cards and continually seek to ensure the buyer's satisfaction. American rivals such as Ford, meanwhile, try to generate showroom traffic. Nobumasa Ogura manages a Ford dealership in Tokyo. "We need to come up with some ideas to sell more cars without door-to-door sales, but the reality is that we haven't come up with any," he said.[5]

Another direct-selling alternative is the *manufacturer-owned store* or *independent franchise store*. One of the first successful U.S.-based international companies, Singer, established a worldwide chain of company-owned and -operated outlets to sell and service sewing machines. As noted in Chapter 9, Japanese consumer electronics companies integrate stores into their distribution groups. Apple, Levi Strauss, Nike, Sony, well-known fashion design houses, and other companies with strong brands sometimes establish flagship retail stores as product showcases or as a means of obtaining marketing intelligence (see Exhibit 12-3). Nokia and Motorola are among the cell phone marketers that have opened branded stores in London, Moscow, New York, Paris, and other major cities. The stores are designed to provide an interactive shopping

Exhibit 12-3 Apple operates more than 400 retails stores in the United States, Canada, Japan, the United Kingdom, and nine other countries. Each store features a Genius Bar where customers can seek one-on-one technical support with a knowledgeable employee. Many stores, such as this one in London, feature a signature glass staircase that Apple cofounder and former CEO Steve Jobs helped design.

Although Jobs died of cancer in 2011, his legacy includes a far-reaching impact on global retailing strategies and tactics.

Source: Hufton & Crow/Alamy Images

[4] Terence Tsai and Shubo Liu, "Mary Kay: Developing a Salesforce in China," *Financial Times* (January 8, 2013), p. 10.
[5] Valerie Reitman, "Toyota Calling: In Japan's Car Market, Big Three Face Rivals Who Go Door-to-Door," *The Wall Street Journal* (September 28, 1994), pp. A1, A6.

experience and build brand loyalty.[6] Such channels supplement, rather than replace, distribution through independent retail stores.

Other channel structure alternatives for consumer products include various combinations of a manufacturer's sales force and wholesalers calling on independent retail outlets that, in turn, sell to customers (retailing is discussed in detail later in the chapter). For mass-market consumer products such as ice cream novelties, cigarettes, and light bulbs that are bought by millions of consumers, a channel that links the manufacturer to distributors and retailers is generally required to achieve market coverage. A cornerstone of Walmart's phenomenal growth in the United States has been its ability to achieve significant economies by buying huge volumes of goods directly from manufacturers. By contrast, some companies elect to pursue very selective distribution strategies to ensure that products are displayed in attractive surroundings. UK-based Alfred Sargent has adopted this approach for distributing its handcrafted shoes throughout the world (see Exhibit 12-4).

Perishable goods impose special demands on channel members, who must ensure that the merchandise—e.g., fresh fruits and vegetables—is in satisfactory condition (form utility) at the time of customer purchase. In developed countries, a company's own sales force or independent channel members handle distribution of perishable food products; in either case, the distributor organization checks the stock to ensure that it is fresh. In less-developed countries, public marketplaces are important channels; they provide a convenient way for producers of vegetables, bread, and other food products to sell their goods directly. The high perishability rate for fresh produce is one of the biggest supply-chain issues in modern India.

Sometimes, a relatively simple channel innovation in a developing country can significantly increase a company's overall value proposition. In the early 1990s, for example, the Moscow Bread Company (MBC) needed to improve its distribution system. Russian consumers queue up daily to buy fresh loaves at numerous shops and kiosks. Unfortunately, MBC's staff was burdened by excessive paperwork, which resulted in the delivery of stale bread. Andersen Consulting found that as much as one-third of the bread the company produced was wasted. In developed countries, about 95 percent of food is sold packaged; the figure is much lower in the former Soviet Union. Whether a consumer bought bread at an outdoor market or in an enclosed store, it was displayed unwrapped. The consulting team thus devised a simple solution—plastic bags to

Exhibit 12-4 Alfred Sargent is a small manufacturer located in Northamptonshire, the heart of England's traditional shoemaking region. AS Handgrade is a semi-bespoke collection of made-to-order shoes and boots distributed through boutique shoe stores such as Leffot in New York City.
Source: © Alfred Sargent

---

[6] Cassell Bryan-Low and Li Yuan, "Selling Cellphone Buzz," *The Wall Street Journal* (February 23, 2006), pp. B1, B5.

Exhibit 12-5 Brazil's middle class is growing rapidly, but reaching consumers in far-flung rural areas can be a challenge for global marketers. Nestlé's channel strategy includes a floating supermarket. Nestlé Até Você a Bordo ("Nestlé Takes You On Board") is a boat that travels the Amazon by night and welcomes shoppers in 18 different municipalities by day. Consumers who don't have access to hypermarkets can stock up on dog food, chocolates, powdered milk, and nearly three hundred other Nestlé products and brands.
Source: Marcia Zoet/Bloomberg via Getty Images

keep the bread fresh. Russian consumers responded favorably to the change; not only do the bags guarantee freshness and significantly extend the bread's shelf life, but the bags themselves also create utility. In a country where such extras are virtually unknown, the bags constitute a reusable "gift."[7]

The retail environment in developing countries presents similar challenges for companies marketing nonperishable items. In affluent countries, Procter & Gamble (P&G), Kimberly-Clark, Unilever, Colgate-Palmolive, and other global consumer products companies are accustomed to catering to a "buy-in-bulk" consumer mentality. By contrast, in Mexico and other emerging markets, many consumers shop for food, soft drinks, and other items several times each day at tiny, independent "mom-and-pop" stores, kiosks, and market stalls (see Exhibit 12-5). The products offered, including shampoo, disposable diapers, and laundry detergent, are packaged in single-use quantities at a relatively high per-use cost.

At P&G, these operations are known as "high-frequency stores"; in Mexico alone, an estimated 70 percent of the population shops at such stores. To motivate shopkeepers to stock more of P&G's products, the company launched a "golden store" program. In exchange for a pledge to carry at least 40 different P&G products, participating stores receive regular visits from P&G representatives, who tidy display areas and arrange promotional material in prominent places. Although P&G initially used its own sales force, it has since begun relying on independent agents who buy inventory (paying in advance) and then resell the items to shop operators.[8] P&G's experience illustrates the fact that the channel structures shown in Figure 12-1 represent strategic alternatives; firms can and should vary their strategies as market conditions change.

Industrial Products

Figure 12-2 summarizes marketing channel alternatives for the industrial or business products company. As is true with consumer channels, product and customer characteristics have an impact on channel structure. Three basic elements are involved: the manufacturer's sales force, distributors or agents, and wholesalers. A manufacturer can reach customers with its own sales

---

[7] "Case Study: Moscow Bread Company," Andersen Consulting, 1993.
[8] Ellen Byron, "Emerging Ambitions: P&G's Global Target: Shelves of Tiny Stores," *The Wall Street Journal* (July 16, 2007), p. A1.

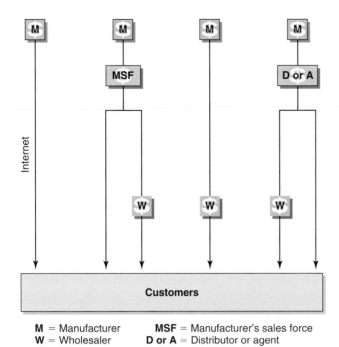

FIGURE 12-2
Marketing Channel Alternatives: Industrial Products

force, a sales force that calls on wholesalers who sell to customers, or a combination of these two arrangements. A manufacturer can also sell directly to wholesalers without using a sales force, and wholesalers, in turn, can supply customers.

Italy's Saeco distributes its products through both b-to-c and b-to-b channels. Marketing managers responsible for domestic appliances arrange for retail distribution for consumer purchase. Managers who service the vending and professional segments provide vending machines to organizational customers and professional espresso-making equipment to bars and cafés.

Channel innovation can be an essential element of a successful marketing strategy. Dell's rise to a leading position in the global PC industry was based on Michael Dell's decision to bypass conventional channels by selling direct and by building computers to customers' specifications. Dell began life as a b-to-b marketer; its business model proved so successful that the company then began marketing directly to the home PC market. Also consider Boeing aircraft; given the price, physical size, and complexity of a jet airliner, it is easy to understand why Boeing utilizes its own sales force. Other products sold in this way include mainframe computers and large photocopy systems; these are expensive, complicated products that require both explanation and applications analysis focused on each customer's needs. A company-trained salesperson, sales engineer, or sales team is well suited for the task of creating information utility for computer buyers.

Establishing Channels and Working with Channel Intermediaries

A global company expanding across national boundaries must utilize existing **distribution channels** or build its own. Channel obstacles are often encountered when a company enters a competitive market where brands and supply relationships are already established. If management chooses *direct involvement*, the company establishes its own sales force or operates its own retail stores. Kodak adopted the direct approach in Japan, where Kodak Japan is a company-owned distributor. The other option is *indirect involvement*, which entails utilizing independent agents, distributors, and retailers. In Asia, for example, Western luxury goods marketers have long relied on independent distributors such as Hong Kong–based Fairton, whose local market knowledge and networks of stores are keys to success. Similarly, as noted in Chapter 11, DeBeers uses independent intermediaries to market its diamonds in the United States.

Channel strategy in a global marketing program must fit the company's competitive position and overall marketing objectives in each national market. Direct involvement in distribution in a new market can entail considerable expense. Sales representatives and sales management must be hired and trained. The sales organization will inevitably be a massive loser in its early stages of operation in a new market because it will not have sufficient volume to cover its overhead costs. Therefore, any company contemplating establishing its own sales force should be prepared to underwrite its losses for a reasonable period of time.

Channel decisions are important because of the number and nature of relationships that must be managed. Channel decisions typically involve long-term legal commitments and obligations to various intermediaries. Such commitments are often extremely expensive to terminate or change, so it is imperative for companies to document the nature of the relationship with the foreign partner. As the saying goes, "The shortest pencil is better than the longest memory." At a minimum, the written agreement should include a definition of what constitutes "good cause" for termination. Also, as noted in Chapter 5, it is often preferable to settle business disputes through arbitration rather than in a local court. Thus, the distributor or agent agreement should also provide for arbitration in a neutral forum in a third country. In many instances, local laws protect agents and distributors; even in the absence of a formal written agreement, in a civil-law country the law will be applied. In addition to written obligations, commitments must be backed by good faith and feelings of mutual obligation. In short, the careful selection of distributors and agents in a target market is critically important.

Companies entering emerging markets for the first time must exercise particular care in choosing a channel intermediary. Typically, a local distributor is required because the market entrant lacks knowledge of local business practices and needs a partner with links to potential customers. In addition, newcomers to a particular market generally want to limit their risk and financial exposure. However, although initial results may be satisfactory, with time headquarters may become dissatisfied with the local distributor's performance. This is when managers from the global company often intervene and attempt to take control. Harvard professor David Arnold offers seven specific guidelines to help prevent such problems from arising:[9]

1. *Select distributors. Don't let them select you.* A company may link up with a distributor by default after being approached by representatives at a trade fair. In fact, such eager candidates may already be serving a company's competitors. Their objective may be to maintain control over the product category in a given market. A proactive market entrant can identify potential distributors by requesting a list from the U.S. Department of Commerce or its equivalent in other countries. The local chamber of commerce or trade association in a country can provide similar information.

2. *Look for distributors capable of developing markets, rather than those with a few good customer contacts.* A distributor with good contacts may appear to be the "obvious" choice in terms of generating quick sales and revenues. However, a better choice is often a partner willing to both make the investment necessary to achieve success and draw upon the marketing experience of the global company. Such a partner may, in fact, have no prior experience with a particular product category. In this case, the distributor may devote more effort and assign the new partner a higher priority simply because taking on the product line does not represent the status quo.

3. *Treat local distributors as long-term partners, not temporary market-entry vehicles.* A contractual agreement that provides strong financial incentives for customer acquisition, new-product sales, or other forms of business development is a signal to the distributor that the market entrant is taking a long-term perspective. Such development can take place with the input of managers from the global company.

4. *Support market entry by committing money, managers, and proven marketing ideas.* In addition to providing sales personnel and technical support, management should consider demonstrating its commitment early on by investing in a minority equity stake in an

---

[9] The following discussion is adapted from David Arnold, "Seven Rules of International Distribution," *Harvard Business Review* 78, no. 6 (November–December 2000), pp. 131–137.

independent distributor. Of course, the risks associated with such investment should be no greater than the risks associated with independent distribution systems in the manufacturer's home country. The earlier such a commitment is made, the better the relationship that is likely to develop.

5. *From the start, maintain control over marketing strategy.* To exploit the full potential of global marketing channels, the manufacturer should provide solid leadership for marketing in terms of which products the distributor should sell and how those products should be positioned. Again, it is necessary to have employees on site or to have country or regional managers monitor the distributor's performance. As one manager noted, "We used to give far too much autonomy to distributors, thinking that they knew their markets. But our value proposition is a tough one to execute, and time and again we saw distributors cut prices to compensate for failing to target the right customers or to sufficiently train salespeople." This is not to say that the intermediary should not be allowed to adapt the distribution strategy to suit local conditions. The point is for the manufacturer to take the lead.

6. *Make sure distributors provide you with detailed market and financial performance data.* Distributor organizations are often a company's best source—maybe the only source—of market information. The contract between a manufacturer and distributor should include specific language to the effect that local market information and financial data will be transferred back to the manufacturer. One sign that a successful manufacturer–distributor relationship can be established is the latter's willingness to provide such information.

7. *Build links among national distributors at the earliest opportunity.* A manufacturer should attempt to establish links between its networks of national distributors. This can be accomplished by setting up a regional corporate office or by establishing a distributor council. At any point in time, a company may have some excellent agents and distributors, others that are satisfactory, and a third group that is unsatisfactory. By creating opportunities for distributors to communicate, ideas for new product designs based on individual market results can be leveraged, and overall distributor performance can be improved.

When devising a channel strategy, it is necessary to be realistic about the intermediary's motives. It is the intermediary's responsibility to implement an important element of a company's marketing strategy. Left to their own devices, however, middlemen may seek to maximize their own profit rather than the manufacturer's. These agents sometimes engage in **cherry picking**, the practice of accepting orders only from manufacturers with established demand for certain products and brands. Cherry picking can also take the form of selecting only a few choice items from a vendor's product lines. The cherry picker is not interested in developing a market for a new product, which is a problem for an expanding international company. As noted previously, a manufacturer should provide leadership and invest resources to build the relationship with a desired distributor. A manufacturer with a new product or a product with a limited market share may find it more desirable to set up some arrangement for bypassing the cherry-picking channel member. In some cases, a manufacturer must incur the costs of direct involvement by setting up its own distribution organization to obtain a share of the market. When the company sales finally reach critical mass, management may decide to shift from direct involvement to a more cost-effective, independent intermediary.

An alternative method of dealing with the cherry-picking problem does not require setting up an expensive direct sales force. Rather, a company may decide to rely on a distributor's own sales force by subsidizing the cost of the sales representatives the distributor has assigned to the company's products. This approach has the advantage of holding down costs by tying in with the distributor's existing sales management team and physical distribution system. It is possible to place managed direct-selling support and distribution support behind a product at the expense of only one salesperson per selling area. The distributor's incentive for cooperating in this kind of arrangement is that he or she obtains a "free" sales representative for a new product that has the potential to be a profitable addition to his or her line. This cooperative arrangement is ideally suited to getting a new export-sourced product into distribution in a market. Alternatively, a company may decide to provide special incentives to independent channel agents.

Global Retailing

Global retailing is any retailing activity that crosses national boundaries. For centuries, entrepreneurial merchants have ventured abroad to seek out merchandise and ideas and to establish retail operations. During the nineteenth and early twentieth centuries, British, French, Dutch, Belgian, and German trading companies established retailing organizations in Africa and Asia. International trading and retail store operations were two of the economic pillars of that era's colonial system. In the twentieth century, Dutch apparel and footwear retailer C&A expanded across Europe. In 1909, Harry Gordon Selfridge traveled from Chicago to London to open a department store that ended up reshaping retailing. That same year, another American, Frank Woolworth took his five-and-dime concept across the Atlantic, opening his first British store in Liverpool.

Global retailers serve an important distribution function; when Carrefour, Tesco, and Walmart set up shop in developing countries, they provide customers with access to more products and lower prices than were available previously. As we have noted throughout the text, when global companies expand abroad, they often encounter local competitors. The retail sector is no exception; India is a case in point. *Organized retail*, a term that is used to describe modern, branded chain stores, currently comprises less than 5 percent of India's market. The sector is expected to exhibit double-digit growth, a fact that has attracted the giants of global retailing. However, they must compete with stores operated by local retail chains. One such company is Reliance Industries; its Reliance Retail division is opening thousands of modern supermarkets across India. What's more, Reliance itself is developing plans for global expansion.[10]

In some instances, it is a local retailer, rather than a global one, that breaks new ground by transforming the shopping experience. Nakumatt, a supermarket chain in Kenya, is a case in point. As Wambui Mwangi, a political science professor at the University of Toronto, notes, "Nakumatt is where you go to show you are educated and prosperous and cognizant of larger affairs. It's an aspirational space that appeals to everyone, especially the people who can't really afford to shop there."[11]

Retail business models may undergo significant adaptation outside the country in which they originated. For example, after the first 7-Eleven Japan franchise opened in 1973, the stores quickly attracted customers seeking convenience. Today, "conbinis" are ubiquitous in Japan, with more than 43,000 store locations. Seven & I Holdings, which operates 7-Eleven, is Japan's largest grocer. The convenience store operators use cutting-edge EPOS data to track customer behavior and ensure that perishable products and other merchandise is delivered on a just-in-time basis during high-traffic periods. Even in the recent difficult economic environment, convenience store sales remained strong. Now the operators are moving to further differentiate themselves; for example, 7-Eleven has Seven Bank ATMs in its stores and a lower-priced line of own-brand merchandise, Seven Premium.[12]

Today's global retailing scene is characterized by great diversity (Table 12-1 lists the top five companies by revenue). We will begin the discussion with a brief survey of some of the

TABLE 12-1 Top Five Global Retailers, 2012

Rank	Company	Country	Formats	Sales ($ millions)
1	Walmart Stores	United States	Discount store, wholesale club	$469,162
2	Carrefour	France	Hypermarket	100,601
3	Tesco PLC	UK	Supermarket/hypermarket	98,062
4	Metro AG	Germany	Diversified	86,372
5	Aldi	Germany	Discount store	73,000

Source: Company reports.

---

[10] Eric Bellman, "India's Reliance Looks Abroad," *The Wall Street Journal* (March 16, 2007), p. A8.
[11] Barney Jopson, "Consumerism for Kenya's As and Bs," *Financial Times* (July 8, 2008), p. 14.
[12] Michiyo Nakamoto, "Convenience Stores Pay Price of Success," *Financial Times Special Report—Japan* (October 14, 2008), p. 3. See also Juro Osawa, "Convenience Stores Score in Japan," *The Wall Street Journal* (August 19, 2008), p. B2.

TABLE 12-2 Department Stores with Global Branches

Store	Original Store Location	Global Locations
Harvey Nichols	United Kingdom	Saudi Arabia, Hong Kong, Ireland, Dubai
Saks Fifth Avenue	United States	Dubai, Saudi Arabia, Mexico
Barneys New York	United States	Japan
Lane Crawford	Hong Kong	China, Macao, Taiwan
Mitsukoshi	Japan	United States, Europe, Asia
H&M (Hennes & Mauritz)	Sweden	Austria, Germany, Kuwait, Slovakia, United States, 20 others

different forms retailing can take. Retail stores can be divided into categories according to the amount of square feet of floor space, the level of service offered, the width and depth of product offerings, or other criteria. Each represents a strategic option for a retailer considering global expansion.

Types of Retail Operations

Department stores literally have several departments under one roof, each representing a distinct merchandise line and staffed with a limited number of salespeople. Departments in a typical store might include men's, women's, children's, beauty aids, housewares, and toys. Table 12-2 lists major department stores that have expanded outside their home-country markets. However, in most instances, the expansion is limited to a few countries. As Maureen Hinton, a retail analyst with a London-based consultancy, notes, "It's quite difficult to transfer a department store brand abroad. You have to find a city with the right demographic for your offer. If you adapt your offer to the locality, you dilute your brand name." Marvin Traub, former chief executive of Bloomingdales, has a different perspective. "Conceptually, department stores are global brands already because we live in a world with an enormous amount of travel between cities and continents," he says.[13]

Specialty retailers offer less variety than department stores. They are more narrowly focused and offer a relatively narrow merchandise mix aimed at a particular target market. Specialty stores do offer a great deal of merchandise depth (e.g., many styles, colors, and sizes), high levels of service from knowledgeable staff, and a value proposition that is both clear and appealing to consumers. Laura Ashley, The Body Shop, Victoria's Secret, Gap, Starbucks, and the Disney Store are examples of global retail operators that have stores in many parts of the world. In some countries, local companies operate the stores. In Japan, for example, the giant Aeon Group runs Laura Ashley and The Body Shop stores and has a joint venture with Sports Authority.

Supermarkets are departmentalized, single-story retail establishments that offer a variety of food (e.g., produce, baked goods, meats) and nonfood items (e.g., paper products, health and beauty aids), mostly on a self-service basis. On average, supermarkets occupy between 50,000 square feet and 60,000 square feet of floor space. UK-based Tesco is one retailing group that is expanding globally. While home-country sales still account for approximately 80 percent of overall sales, the company has operations in more than a dozen foreign countries. Company officials typically study a country market for several years before choosing an entry strategy. Tesco's initial entry into Japan came via the acquisition of the C Two-Network, a chain of shops in Tokyo. As international operations chief David Reid explains, Tesco has succeeded globally because it does its homework and pays attention to details. However, as noted in Case 12-2, Tesco came up short in its effort to penetrate the U.S. market. Although Walmart is generating headlines as it moves around the globe, American retailers lag behind the Europeans in moving

---

[13] Cecilie Rohwedder, "Harvey Nichols's Foreign Affair," *The Wall Street Journal* (February 18, 2005), p. B3.

outside their home countries. One reason is the sheer size of the domestic U.S. market.[14] In fact, Walmart's lack of experience outside North America undoubtedly contributed to its failures in South Korea and Germany.

Convenience stores offer some of the same products as supermarkets, but the merchandise mix is limited to high-turnover convenience and impulse products. Prices for some products may be 15 to 20 percent higher than supermarket prices. In terms of square footage, these are the smallest organized retail stores discussed here. In the United States, for example, the typical 7-Eleven occupies 3,000 square feet. Typically, convenience stores are located in high-traffic locations and offer extended service hours to accommodate commuters, students, and other highly mobile consumers. 7-Eleven is the world's largest convenience store chain; it has a total of 26,000 locations, including franchisees, licensees, and stores the company operates itself. A trend in convenience store retailing is toward smaller stores placed inside malls, airports, office buildings, and in college and university buildings. As Jeff Lenard, spokesperson for the National Association of Convenience Stores, has noted, "All the good street corners are gone, and the competition is so fierce for the ones that are left."[15]

Discount retailers can be divided into several categories. The most general characteristic that they have in common is the emphasis on low prices. *Full-line discounters* typically offer a wide range of merchandise, including nonfood items and nonperishable food, in a limited-service format. As Table 12-1 clearly shows, Walmart is the reigning king of the full-line discounters. Many stores cover 120,000 square feet (or more) of floor space; food accounts for about a third of floor space and sales. Walmart stores typically offer a folksy atmosphere and value-priced brands. Walmart is also a leader in the *warehouse club* segment of discount retailing; shoppers "join" the club to take advantage of low prices on a limited range of products (typically 3,000 to 5,000 different items), many of which are displayed in their shipping cartons in a "no-frills" atmosphere.

When Walmart expands into a new country market, local discounters must respond to the competitive threat. In Canada, for example, Hudson Bay's Zellers is the largest discount store chain. After Walmart acquired a bankrupt Canadian chain, Zellers countered by brightening the décor in its stores, widening aisles, and catering to women with young children.[16] French discounter Tati is also going global; in addition to opening a store on New York's Fifth Avenue, Tati currently has stores in Lebanon, Turkey, Germany, Belgium, Switzerland, and the Côte d'Ivoire.

Dollar stores sell a select assortment of products at a single low price. In the United States, Family Dollar Stores and Dollar Tree Stores dominate the industry. However, a recent industry entrant, My Dollarstore, is experiencing rapid international growth. My Dollarstore Inc. has franchises in Eastern Europe, Central America, and Asia. To succeed in global markets, My Dollarstore has adapted its U.S. business model. For example, the typical U.S. dollar store has a "bargain basement" image. By contrast, in India, My Dollarstore targets affluent, middle-class shoppers who are attracted by the lure of low prices on brands associated with "the good life" in America. Goods are priced at 99 rupees—the equivalent of $2—and the stores are decorated in red, white, and blue with the Statue of Liberty on display. In the United States, dollar stores operate on a self-service basis with lean staffs; My Dollarstore's Indian locations have significantly higher staffing levels, the better to answer questions about new or unfamiliar products.[17]

Hard discounters include retailers such as Germany's Aldi and Lidl ("Where quality is cheaper!") and France's Leader Price ("Le Prix La Qualité en Plus!"), which sell a tightly focused selection of goods—typically 900 to 1,600 different items—at rock-bottom prices. Starting in 1976, Aldi began opening a few stores each year in the United States. The stores have a relatively small footprint; 17,500 square feet of floor space is typical. As Jason Hart, copresident of Aldi's U.S. operation, noted recently, "We carry 1,500 of the most popular grocery items out there.

[14] Michael Flagg, "In Asia, Going to the Grocery Increasingly Means Heading for a European Retail Chain," *The Wall Street Journal* (April 24, 2001), p. A21.

[15] Kortney Stringer, "Convenience Stores Turn a New Corner," *The Wall Street Journal* (June 1, 2004), p. B5.

[16] Elena Cherney and Ann Zimmerman, "Canada's Zellers Retools Itself in Bid to Battle Walmart," *The Wall Street Journal* (December 10, 2001), p. B4.

[17] Eric Bellman, "A Dollar Store's Rich Allure in India," *The Wall Street Journal* (January 23, 2007), pp. B1, B14.

When you look at the large supermarkets that may have 20- to 30,000 items, it's surprising to the customers how much of the shopping list we're able to fit in our smaller store." The company had plans for 80 new U.S. stores in 2011 and 2012.[18]

When Walmart entered the German market, hard discounters were already well entrenched. By mid-2006, after years of losses, Walmart decided to close up shop. In the recent economic downturn, hard discounters thrived as cash-strapped consumers sought ways to stretch household budgets. Hard-discount retailers, which account for about 10 percent of grocery sales in Europe, rely heavily on private brands. Some of these sell for half the price of well-known global brands. Carrefour and other large supermarket operators are responding by offering more own-brand products at lower prices. For example, Tesco recently began selling 350 new, cheaper products under its own brands, including tea bags, cookies, and shampoo. "If there is a war, we will win it," said Tesco's commercial director, Richard Brasher.[19]

Hypermarkets are a hybrid retailing format combining the discounter, supermarket, and warehouse club approaches under a single roof. Size-wise, hypermarkets are huge, ranging from 200,000 to 300,000 square feet.

Supercenters offer a wide range of aggressively priced grocery items plus general merchandise in a space that occupies about half the size of a hypermarket. Supercenters are an important aspect of Walmart's growth strategy, both at home and abroad. Walmart opened its first supercenter in 1988; today, it operates more than 2,600 supercenters, including hundreds of stores in Mexico and units in Argentina and Brazil. Some prices at Walmart's supercenters in Brazil are as much as 15 percent lower than competitors' prices, and some observers wondered if the company had taken the discount approach too far. Company officials insisted, though, that profit margins were in the 20 to 22 percent range.[20]

Superstores (also known as **category killers** and *big-box retail*) is the label many in the retailing industry use when talking about stores such as Toys 'R' Us, Home Depot, and IKEA (see Exhibit 12-6). The name refers to the fact that such stores specialize in selling vast assortments of a particular product category—toys or furniture, for example—in high volumes at low prices. In short, these stores represent retailing's "900-pound gorillas," which put pressure on smaller, more traditional competitors and prompt department stores to scale down merchandise sections that are in direct competition.

Shopping malls consist of a grouping of stores in one place. Developers such as Simon Property Group assemble an assortment of retailers that will create an appealing leisure destination; typically one or more large department stores serve as anchors. Shopping malls offer acres of free parking and easy access from main traffic thoroughfares. Historically, malls were enclosed, allowing shoppers to browse in comfort no matter the weather outside. However, a current trend is toward outdoor shopping centers, now called "lifestyle centers." Food courts and entertainment encourage families to spend several hours at the mall. In the United States, malls sprang up as people moved from city centers to the suburbs. Today, global mall development reflects the opportunity to serve emerging middle-class consumers who seek both convenience and entertainment.

Three of the world's five largest malls are in Asia (see Table 12-3). The reasons are clear-cut: Economic growth led to rising incomes; in addition, tourism is booming in the region. Some industry observers warn, however, that the megamalls and their glamorous global brand offerings are luring shoppers away from markets that sell goods produced by local craftspeople. Somewhere along the way, the thrill of discovering something new has been lost. Emil Pocock, a professor of American studies at Eastern Connecticut State University, is an expert on shopping malls. As he has noted, "I find it very disconcerting that shopping malls are more or less the same wherever you go in the world. I'm not sure I want 100 international companies determining our choices for consumer goods."[22]

> "There is a new middle class of savvy consumers in South Africa. A shopping mall in South Africa is not very different from an Australian shopping mall or a British shopping mall."[21]
>
> —Simon Susman, CEO Woolworths Holdings

[18] Stephanie Clifford, "Where Wal-Mart Failed, Aldi Succeeds," *The New York Times* (March 30, 2011), p. B1.

[19] Christina Passariello and Aaron O. Patrick, "Europe Eats on the Cheap," *The Wall Street Journal* (September 30, 2008), pp. B1, B7.

[20] Matt Moffett and Jonathan Friedland, "Walmart Won't Discount Its Prospects in Brazil, Though Its Losses Pile Up," *The Wall Street Journal* (June 4, 1996), p. A15; Wendy Zellner, "Walmart Spoken Here," *BusinessWeek* (June 23, 1997), pp. 138–139+.

[21] Robb M. Stewart, "Wal-Mart Checks Out a New Continent," *The Wall Street Journal* (October 27, 2010), p. B1.

[22] Stan Sesser, "The New Spot for Giant Malls: Asia," *The Wall Street Journal* (September 16/17, 2006), p. P6.

Exhibit 12-6 STIHL Inc. manufactures and markets chainsaws, trimmers, and other types of outdoor power equipment. The distribution "P" is an integral part of STIHL's marketing strategy: Its products are only available at independent dealers that provide full after-sale service. STIHL also sponsors "Independent We Stand," an initiative among independent businesses to help educate consumers about the importance of "buying local."
Source: Courtesy of STIHL Inc

Outlet stores are a variation on the traditional shopping mall: retail operations that allow companies with well-known consumer brands to dispose of excess inventory, out-of-date merchandise, or factory seconds. To attract large numbers of shoppers, outlet stores are often grouped together in **outlet malls**. The United States is home to hundreds of outlet malls such as the giant Woodbury Common mall in Central Valley, New York. Now, the concept is catching

TABLE 12-3 The World's Largest Shopping Malls (ranked by gross leasable retail space)

Rank	Mall	City/Country	Store Capacity
1	South China Mall	Dongguan, China	2,350
2	Great Gold Mall	Beijing, China	1,000
3	SM City North EDSA	Philippines	1100
4	1 Utama	Malaysia	700
5	Persian Gulf Complex	Iran	2,500[23]

[23] At printing The Persian Gulf Complex in Iran housed only one merchant.

Exhibit 12-7 McArthurGlen operates several upscale designer outlets in Europe. Retail tenants include popular American companies such as Nike. However, the majority of stores represent a veritable "Who's who" of exclusive European fashion brands: Fendi, Ferrari, Harmont & Blaine, Jil Sander, Prada, Salvatore Ferragamo, and Versace (to name just a few). Fashion-forward bargain hunters can find prices that represent discounts of 30 percent to 70 percent off regular retail prices.
Source: McArthurGlen

on in Europe and Asia as well. The acceptance reflects changing attitudes among consumers and retailers; in both Asia and Europe, brand-conscious consumers are eager to save money (see Exhibit 12-7).

Trends in Global Retailing

Currently, a variety of environmental factors have combined to push retailers out of their home markets in search of opportunities around the globe. Saturation of the home-country market, recession or other economic factors, strict regulation on store development, and high operating costs are some of the factors that prompt management to look abroad for growth opportunities. Walmart is a case in point; its international expansion in the mid-1990s coincided with disappointing financial results in its home market.

Even as the domestic retailing environment grows more challenging for many companies, an ongoing environmental scanning effort is likely to turn up markets in other parts of the world that are underdeveloped or where competition is weak. In addition, high rates of economic growth, a growing middle class, a high proportion of young people in the population, and less stringent regulation combine to make some country markets very attractive.[24] For example, Laura Ashley,

---

[24] Ross Davies and Megan Finney, "Retailers Rush to Capture New Markets," *Financial Times—Mastering Global Business, Part VII* (1998), pp. 2–4.

The Body Shop, Disney Stores, and other specialty retailers were lured to Japan by developers who needed established names to fill space in large, suburban, American-style shopping malls.[25] Such malls are being developed as some local and national restrictions on retail development are being eased and as consumers tire of the aggravations associated with shopping in congested urban areas.

However, the large number of unsuccessful cross-border retailing initiatives suggests that any chief executive contemplating a move into global retailing should do so with a great deal of caution and due diligence. A few years ago, Frank Blake, Home Depot's CEO, noted, "International expansion has proved to be a competitive advantage for us. In Canada, Mexico, and now, China, we've shown we can enter a market, tailor our model to the local customer and see the same sort of growth we saw in our early days here in the U.S."[26] Despite this pronouncement, by the end of 2012 Home Depot had been forced to scale back its China operations. Other failures include the following:

- Walmart pulled out of Germany and South Korea.
- Best Buy closed several stores in China.
- Mattel closed its six-story flagship Barbie store in Shanghai.
- Tesco shut down its Fresh & Easy stores in the United States after piling up $1.6 billion in losses (see Case 12-2).

These are just a few of the examples that illustrate that it's not always possible to export a retail business model that has proven successful in the domestic market. As one industry analyst noted, "It's awfully hard to operate across the water. It's one thing to open up in Mexico and Canada, but the distribution hassles are just too big when it comes to exporting an entire store concept overseas."[27]

The critical question for the would-be global retailer is, "What advantages do we have relative to local competition?" After taking into account competition, local laws governing retailing practice, distribution patterns, or other factors, the answer will often be, "Nothing." However, a company may possess competencies that can be the basis for competitive advantage in a particular retail market. A retailer may have several things to offer consumers, such as selection, price, and the overall manner and condition in which the goods are offered in the store setting. Store location, parking facilities, in-store atmosphere, and customer service also contribute to the value proposition. Competencies can also be found in less visible value chain activities such as distribution, logistics, and information technology. As Thomas Hübner, CEO of Metro Cash & Carry International, noted, "Stores are just the tip of the iceberg—90 percent of the work is under water."[28]

For example, Japanese retailers traditionally offered few extra services to their clientele. There were no special orders or returns, and stock was chosen not according to consumer demand but, rather, according to purchasing preferences of the stores. Typically, a store would buy limited quantities from each of its favorite manufacturers, leaving consumers with no recourse when the goods sold out. Instead of trying to capitalize on the huge market, many retailers simply turned a deaf ear to customer needs/desires. From the retailers' point of view, this came out fine in the end; most of their stock eventually sold because buyers were forced to purchase what was left over. They had no other choice. Then Gap, Eddie Bauer, and other Western retailers entered Japan, often by means of joint ventures. The stores offer liberal return policies, a willingness to take special orders, and a policy of replenishing stock; and many Japanese consumers switched loyalties. Also, thanks to economies of scale and modern distribution methods unknown to some Japanese department store operators, the foreign retailers offer a greater variety of goods at lower prices. Although this upscale foreign competition has hurt

[25] Norihiko Shirouzu, "Japanese Mall Mogul Dreams of American Stores," *The Wall Street Journal* (July 30, 1997), pp. B1, B10; Norihiko Shirouzu, "Jusco Bets that U.S.-Style Retail Malls Will Revolutionize Shopping in Japan," *The Wall Street Journal* (April 21, 1997), p. A8.

[26] Ann Zimmerman, "Home Depot Chief Renovates," *The Wall Street Journal* (June 5, 2008), p. B2.

[27] Neil King, Jr., "Kmart's Czech Invasion Lurches Along," *The Wall Street Journal* (June 8, 1993), p. A11.

[28] Eric Bellman and Cecilie Rohwedder, "Western Grocer Modernizes Passage to India's Markets," *The Wall Street Journal* (November 28, 2007), p. B2.

Japanese department store operators, Japan's depressed economy is another factor. Traditional retailers are also being squeezed from below as recession-pressed consumers flock to discounters such as the Y100 Shop chain.

JCPenney is expanding retailing operations internationally for a number of the reasons cited here. After touring several countries, JCPenney executives realized that retailers outside the United States often lack marketing sophistication when grouping and displaying products and locating aisles to optimize customer traffic. For example, a team visiting retailers in Istanbul in the early 1990s noted that one store featured lingerie next to plumbing equipment. As CEO William R. Howell noted at the time, Penney's advantage in such instances is its ability to develop an environment that invites the customer to shop. Although it struggled in Indonesia, the Philippines, and Chile, Penney's has met with great success in Brazil. In 1999, the American retailer purchased a controlling stake in Renner, a regional chain with 21 stores. Crucially, Penney's maintained the local name and local management team. Meanwhile, Renner, benefiting from Penney's expertise in logistics, distribution, and branding, has become Brazil's fastest-growing chain, with more than 60 stores.

Figure 12-3 shows a matrix-based scheme for classifying global retailers.[29] One axis represents a private- or own-label focus versus a manufacturer-brand focus. The other axis differentiates between retailers specializing in relatively few product categories and retailers that offer a wide product assortment. IKEA, in quadrant A, is a good example of a global retailer with a niche focus (assemble-yourself furniture for the home) as well as an own-label focus (IKEA sells its own brand). IKEA and other retailers in quadrant A typically use extensive advertising and product innovation to build a strong brand image.

In quadrant B, the private-label focus is retained, but many more product categories are offered. This is the strategy of Marks & Spencer (M&S), the British-based department store company whose St. Michael private label is found on a broad range of clothing, food, home furnishings, jewelry, and other items. Private-label retailers that attempt to expand internationally face a double-edged challenge: They must attract customers to both the store and the branded merchandise. M&S has succeeded by virtue of an entrepreneurial management style that has evolved over the last 100-plus years. M&S opened its first store outside the United Kingdom in 1974; it currently operates in 40 countries. In 1997, then-chairman Sir Richard Greenbury announced an ambitious plan to put M&S "well on its way to establishing a global business." It was his belief that consumer tastes are globalizing, at least with respect to fashion apparel. Food is a different story; because tastes are more localized, M&S executives anticipated that the

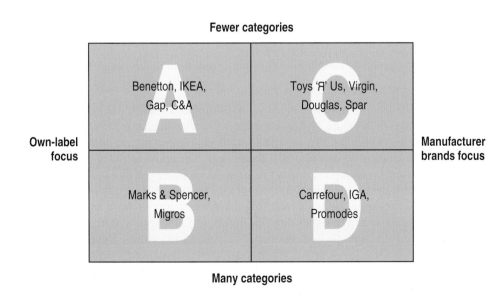

FIGURE 12-3

Global Retailing Categories

Source: Adapted from Jacques Horovitz and Nirmalya Kumar, "Strategies for Retail Globalization," *Financial Times-Mastering Global Business, Part VII* (1998), pp. 4–8.

[29] The discussion in this section is adapted from Jacques Horovitz and Nirmalya Kumar, "Strategies for Retail Globalization," *Financial Times—Mastering Global Business, Part VII* (1998), pp. 4–8.

proportion of revenues from global food sales would be lower than they are in Great Britain.[30] The difficulty of today's retailing environment is underscored by Marks & Spencer's financial woes. The company's profits and share price plunged in the late 1990s amid a sales slump and infighting between top executives; Sir Richard left the company in 1998. A turnaround strategy called for disposing of noncore properties such as the Brooks Brothers and Kings Super Markets chains in the United States.

Retailers in quadrant C offer many well-known brands in a relatively tightly defined merchandise range. Here, for example, we find Toys 'R' Us, which specializes in toys and includes branded products from Mattel, Nintendo, and other marketers. Additional examples include such category killers as Blockbuster Video and Virgin Megastores. As noted earlier, this type of store tends to quickly dominate smaller established retailers by out-merchandising local competition and offering customers superior value by virtue of extensive inventories and low prices. Typically, the low prices are the result of buyer power and sourcing advantages that local retailers lack.

The retailing environment in which Richard Branson built the Virgin Megastore chain illustrates once again the type of success that can be achieved through an entrepreneurial management style:

> It required little retailing expertise to see that the sleepy business practices of traditional record shops provided a tremendous opportunity. To rival the tiny neighborhood record shops, with their eclectic collections of records, a new kind of record store was coming into being. It was big; it was well-lit, and records were arranged clearly in alphabetical order by artist; it covered most tastes in pop music comprehensively; and it turned over its stock much faster than the smaller record retailer…. It was the musical equivalent of a supermarket.[31]

Starting with one megastore location on London's Oxford Street in 1975, Branson's Virgin Retail empire now extends throughout Europe, North America, Japan, Hong Kong, and Taiwan. Another of Branson's ventures, Virgin Atlantic Airlines, reflects the same effort to provide a different service experience. As Steve Ridgway, former CEO of Virgin Atlantic, explains, "Fundamentally it's around the value proposition and what consumers will pay for. Our single biggest innovation was always to try to wrong-foot the market. We've always positioned our products half a notch out of the convention."[32]

Carrefour, Promodès, Walmart, and other retailers in quadrant D offer the same type of merchandise available from established local retailers. What the newcomers bring to a market, however, is competence in distribution or some other value chain element. To date, Walmart's international division has established more than 3,000 stores outside the United States; it is already the biggest retailer in Mexico and Canada. Other store locations include Central America, South America, China, and, until recently, Germany.

Global Retailing Market Expansion Strategies

Retailers can choose from four market-entry expansion strategies when expanding outside the home country. As shown in Figure 12-4, these strategies can be diagrammed using a matrix that differentiates between (1) markets that are easy to enter versus those that are difficult to enter and (2) culturally close markets versus culturally distant ones. The upper half of the matrix encompasses quadrants A and D and represents markets in which shopping patterns and retail structures are similar to those in the home country. In the lower half of the matrix, quadrants B and C represent markets that are significantly different from the home-country market in terms of one or more cultural characteristics. The right side of the matrix, quadrants A and B, represents markets that are difficult to enter because of the presence of strong competitors, location restrictions,

[30] Rufus Olins, "M&S Sets Out Its Stall for World Domination," *The Sunday Times* (November 9, 1997), p. 6. See also Andrew Davidson, "The Andrew Davidson Interview: Sir Richard Greenbury," *Management Today* (November 2001), pp. 62–67; and Judi Bevan, *The Rise and Fall of Marks & Spencer* (London: Profile Books, 2001).
[31] Tim Jackson, *Virgin King: Inside Richard Branson's Business Empire* (London: HarperCollins, 1995), p. 277.
[32] Daniel Michaels, "No, the CEO Isn't Sir Richard Branson," *The Wall Street Journal* (July 30, 2007), pp. B1, B3.

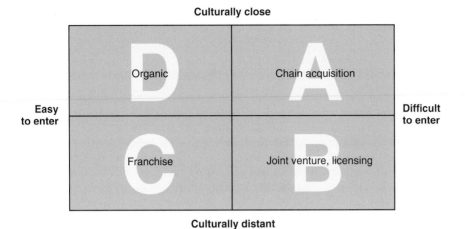

FIGURE 12-4

Global Retailing Market Entry Strategy Framework

Source: Adapted from Jacques Horovitz and Nirmalya Kumar, "Strategies for Retail Globalization," *Financial Times-Mastering Global Business, Part VII* (1998), p. 5.

excessively high rent or real estate costs, or other factors. In quadrants C and D, any barriers that exist are relatively easy to overcome. The four entry strategies indicated by the matrix are organic, franchise, chain acquisition, and joint ventures and licensing.

Organic growth occurs when a company uses its own resources to open a store on a green-field site or to acquire one or more existing retail facilities from another company. In 1997, for example, M&S announced plans to expand from one store to four in Germany via the purchase of three stores operated by Cramer and Meerman. When Richard Branson set up the first Virgin Megastore in Paris, he did so by investing millions of pounds in a spectacular retail space on the Champs-Élysées. From the perspectives of M&S and Virgin, the retail environments of Germany and France are both culturally close and easy to enter. The success of this strategy hinges on the availability of company resources to sustain the high cost of the initial investment.

Franchising, shown in quadrant C of Figure 12-4, is the appropriate entry strategy when barriers to entry are low yet the market is culturally distant in terms of consumer behavior or retailing structures. As defined in Chapter 9, franchising is a contractual relationship between two companies. The parent company–franchisor authorizes a franchisee to operate a business developed by the franchisor in return for a fee and adherence to franchise-wide policies and practices. The key to a successful franchise operation is the ability to transfer company know-how to new markets. Benetton, IKEA, and other focused, private-label retailers often use franchising as a market-entry strategy in combination with wholly owned stores that represent organic growth. IKEA has more than 100 company-owned stores across Europe and the United States; its stores in the Middle East and Hong Kong are franchise operations.

In global retailing, **acquisition** is a market-entry strategy that entails purchasing a company with multiple retail locations in a foreign country. This strategy can provide the buyer with quick growth as well as access to existing brand suppliers, distributors, and customers. For example, when Walmart first entered the Japanese market in 2002, it did so by acquiring a 6.1 percent stake in the Seiyu retail chain. In 2007, Walmart upped its stake to 95.1 percent; the following year, Seiyu and its 414 stores became a wholly owned subsidiary. Now Walmart is seeking to expand by making additional acquisitions. As Walmart Asia CEO Scott Price explained, "We see scale as being the next level of being able to change the value proposition for Japanese customers." Organic growth is not an option, however: "We do not want to build more retail in Japan. The last thing Japan needs is more retail space," Price said.[33]

Joint ventures and **licensing** were examined in detail in Chapter 9. Global retailers frequently use these strategies to limit their risk when targeting unfamiliar, difficult-to-enter markets. For example, Barneys New York licensed its name to Barneys Japan for a period of 10 years; Saks Fifth Avenue has licensed stores in the Middle East. In some countries, local regulations mandate the use of joint ventures. For example, prior to 2005, China had regulations that required foreign retailers entering the market to have local partners. Chinese authorities

---

[33] Mariko Sanchanta, "Wal-Mart Bargain Shops for Japanese Stores to Buy," *The Wall Street Journal* (November 15, 2010), p. B1.

INNOVATION, ENTREPRENEURSHIP, AND THE GLOBAL STARTUP

An American Retailer in London

Harry Gordon Selfridge was an entrepreneur. He was also an enthusiast and a dreamer. He developed an innovative product, created a brand, and started a business. And not just any business: He launched Selfridge & Company, called by some "the most beautiful department store the world has ever seen." By applying the basic tools and principles of marketing decades before modern marketing had emerged as a discipline, Selfridge achieved remarkable success. As is true with many entrepreneurs, Selfridge's idea was based on his own needs, wants, and vision. He declared, "We are going to show the world how to make shopping thrilling!" (See Exhibit 12-8.)

Retailers may have a difficult time crossing borders if they fail to appreciate differences in retailing environments and consumer behavior and preferences. However, just the opposite was true when Selfridge opened his department store just off Oxford Street. He broke with convention on a number of fronts. Noting that there were more horse-drawn carriages than cars at the time, he moved perfume and fragrances to the front of the store, putting them front and center. This arrangement served to neutralize any foul odors from horse dung that shoppers might track in on their shoes. In traditional British stores, articles were kept behind counters and shoppers had to ask clerks for help. By contrast, Selfridge put the goods out for people to see and touch. "The customer always comes first," Selfridge declared. Londoners had never seen anything like it.

If the Selfridge story sounds fascinating, well, it is! It has been the subject of a book, *Shopping, Seduction, and Mr Selfridge*, as well as a television series that aired on ITV in Great Britain and on public television in the United States. As the book and the TV series clearly demonstrate, Selfridge loved the theater, performers, and artists. Not surprisingly, there was more than a hint of theatricality in some of Selfridge's marketing tactics and publicity stunts. These included early-bird specials, an in-store appearance by Russian ballerina Anna Pavlova, and a display on the store's ground floor of the first airplane to cross the English Channel.

As it turns out, the human story ended badly; Selfridge fell victim to various demons and vices and was ousted from the company he had founded. His legacy endures, however, and in the twenty-first century, Selfridges continues to be at the forefront of retailing innovation. Its flagship London store is home to Europe's largest cosmetics department. Window displays have featured buzz-building "performances" such as humans in animal costumes modeling lingerie. As Peter Williams, CEO of Selfridges, said, "Our competitors are not just other department stores. Our competitors are restaurants, theaters, a weekend away, or other entertainment venues."

Sources: Mike Hale, "Fogging Up the Windows of a Big Store," *The New York Times* (March 30, 2013), p. C1; Nancy Dewolf Smith, "The Dawn of Shopping," *The Wall Street Journal* (March 29, 2013), p. D5; Vanessa O'Connell, "Department Stores Are Hard Sell Abroad," *The Wall Street Journal* (May 22, 2008), p. B3; Cecilie Rohwedder, "Harvey Nichols's Foreign Affair," *The Wall Street Journal* (February 18, 2005), pp. B1, B3; Erin White, "Dress for Success: After Long Slump, U.S. Retailers Look to Britain for Fashion Tips," *The Wall Street Journal* (April 22, 2004), pp. A1, A8; Rohwedder, "Selling Selfridges," *The Wall Street Journal* (May 5, 2003), p. B1.

Exhibit 12-8 Harry Gordon Selfridge was a marketing and retail genius. Actor Jeremy Piven, familiar to many viewers from his role as Ari Gold in the HBO series *Entourage*, portrays the American entrepreneur. *Mr. Selfridge* was produced in Great Britain by ITV Studios; it aired in the United States on PBS.
Source: Photo by Matt Sayles/Invision/AP

liberalized the country's retail climate in 2005, and today, IKEA and other retailers that initially used joint ventures as an entry strategy are shifting to wholly owned stores.

Virgin Group's retail expansion in Asia provides a case study in the appropriateness of the joint venture approach. In Japan, commercial landlords typically require millions in upfront payments before they will lease retail space. Accordingly, in 1992, Virgin established a joint venture called Virgin Megastores Japan with Marui, a local retailer with a good track record of catering to the preferences of young people. The first megastore was set up in the basement of an existing Marui department store in Japan's Shinjuku district. That and subsequent stores have been wildly successful; Virgin has duplicated the joint venture approach elsewhere in Asia, including Hong Kong, Taiwan, and South Korea. In each location, Virgin establishes a joint venture with a leading industrial group.[34]

Achieving retailing success outside the home-country market is not simply a matter of consulting a matrix and choosing the recommended entry strategy. Management must also be alert to the possibility that the merchandise mix, sourcing strategy, distribution, or other format elements will have to be adapted. Management at Crate & Barrel, for example, is hesitant to open stores in Japan. Part of the reason is research indicating that at least half the company's product line would have to be modified to accommodate local preferences. Another issue is whether the company will have the ability to transfer its expertise to new country markets.

Physical Distribution, Supply Chains, and Logistics Management

In Chapter 1, marketing was described as one of the activities in a firm's value chain. The distribution P of the marketing mix is a critical value chain activity. After all, Coca-Cola, IKEA, Nokia, P&G, Toyota, and other global companies create value by making sure their products are available where and when customers need and want to buy them. As defined in this chapter, physical distribution consists of activities involved in moving finished goods from manufacturers to customers. However, the value chain concept is much broader. The value chain is a useful tool for assessing an organization's competence as it performs value-creating activities within a broader **supply chain**. The latter includes *all* the firms that perform support activities by generating raw materials, converting them into components or finished products, and facilitating their delivery to customers.

The particular industry in which a firm competes (e.g., automobiles, consumer electronics, furniture, or pharmaceuticals) is characterized by a value chain. The specific activities an individual firm performs help define its position in the value chain. A company or activity that is somewhat removed from the final customer is said to be *upstream* in the value chain. Consider the following comment from Anders Moberg, the former CEO of IKEA: "At IKEA, we went out into the forest to see which were the right trees to pick to optimize production and cost efficiency in the saw mills."[35] That's a pretty good description of an upstream activity! A company or activity that is relatively close to customers—a retailer, for example—is said to be downstream in the value chain.

Logistics, in turn, is the management process that integrates the activities of all companies—both upstream and downstream—to ensure an efficient flow of goods through the supply chain. Logistics was not really a household term until UPS launched its global "We ♥ Logistics" advertising campaign. The TV ads utilize a catchy jingle: a Harry Warren–penned tune, "That's Amore," popularized by the 1953 motion picture *The Caddy* starring Jerry Lewis and Dean Martin. In the UPS ads, the original lyrics (e.g., "When the moon hits your eye like a big pizza pie, that's amore!") have been replaced by an ode to, well, logistics! Here's a sample:

"When it's planes in the sky for a chain of supply, that's logistics.
When the parts for the line come precisely on time, that's logistics."

---

[34] Tim Jackson, *Virgin King: Inside Richard Branson's Business Empire* (London: HarperCollins, 1995), pp. 289–291.
[35] Ian Bickerton, "'It Is All About the Value Chain,'" *Financial Times* (February 24, 2006), p. 10.

Whoa There! How Did Horse Meat Get in Europe's Food?

SYNC • THINK • LEARN

MyMarketingLab

Some people would be surprised to learn that in many countries, it is customary to eat horse meat. The flesh is lean, and high in iron and other nutrients. It is also much less expensive than beef. In Italy, for example, Pastissada de Caval is a traditional stew from northern Italy's Verona region in which horse meat is a key ingredient (*cavallo* is the Italian word for "horse"). In Europe alone, 60,000 tons of horse meat were sold in 2012.

Recently, however, a scandal broke out after horse DNA was found in frozen beefburgers sold in supermarkets in Ireland. Then, frozen lasagna sold in Great Britain and labeled as containing "beef" was also found to contain horse meat. Before long, the scandal had spread across Europe, and raised questions about the security of the region's food supply.

In Europe, horse meat is available from a variety of suppliers. The supply chain includes a network of slaughterhouses, brokers, and traders. Italy, for example, imports 50 million pounds of horse meat annually from Ireland, Poland, and a dozen other European countries. (It has been illegal to produce horse meat in the United States since 2006; horses are shipped to Mexico and Canada for slaughter. It can then be shipped to export markets such as Europe.) As authorities in several countries began investigations, it appeared that horse meat labeled as beef had come from processing facilities in France, Germany, and Ireland.

With the scandal gaining traction, several global food companies, restaurant chains, and retailers scrambled to respond. Taco Bell was forced to withdraw its beef products from its stores in the United Kingdom. Swedish furniture retailer IKEA pulled meatballs from its cafeterias and grocery sections in several countries after food inspectors found some samples that contained horse meat. Nestlé pulled some beef pasta products from stores in Italy and Spain. Philip Clark, CEO of Tesco, the UK's largest supermarket chain, pledged to source more of his company's food products from local suppliers. As Peter Kendall, president of the National Farmers Union, declared, "It's clear that the longer a supply chain and the more borders it crosses, the less traceable our food is and the more the chain is open to negligence at best, fraud and criminal activity at worst."

Ironically, the horse meat scandal comes just as the United States Department of Agriculture is relaxing a ban on imports of another kind of meat. A variety of pork-based, cured meat products from Northern Italy will finally be available in the United States for the first time in decades. With the lifting of the ban, it is estimated that imports of Italian cold cuts—currently valued at about $90 million annually—could rise as much as $13 million in the coming years. As Joseph Bastianich, a well-known restaurateur, noted, "It could open up a new world of Italian salami in the United States. Americans have been eating bad salami forever, but now the end is near."

Sources: Glenn Collins, "A Ban on Some Italian Cured Meats Is Ending," *The Wall Street Journal* (May 1, 2013), p. D3; John Revill and Inti Landauro, "Horse-Meat Scandal Hits Nestlé in Europe," *The Wall Street Journal* (February 20, 2013), p. B4; Anna Moline, "Horse-Meat Scandal Claims IKEA's Swedish Meatball," *The Wall Street Journal* (February 26, 2013), p. B1

Exhibit 12-9 In February 2013, supermarkets in London and other European cities posted recall notices for frozen meals that had tested positive for horse meat. The French government promised to punish those found responsible for selling horse meat in beef products.
Source: REUTERS/Suzanne Plunkett

You can find the U.S. version of the ad, plus Chinese and Spanish versions, on YouTube.

Analogy and metaphor can also help you gain a better understanding of logistics; consider the following passage from a book written in 1917:

> Strategy is to war what the plot is to the play. Tactics is represented by the role of the players; logistics furnishes the stage management, accessories, and maintenance. The audience, thrilled by the action of the play and the art of the performers, overlooks all of the cleverly hidden details of stage management.[36]

As this quote suggests, many activities associated with logistics and supply-chain management take place "behind the scenes." However, the supply chain's vital role in global marketing has become more evident in recent years. The catastrophic earthquake and tsunami that struck Japan in March 2011 resulted in a tragic loss of life. These natural disasters also disrupted supply chains for a variety of industries, including automobiles and consumer electronics.

The ongoing political upheaval in the Middle East has also highlighted the importance of flexibility in global supply-chain design. For example, in spring 2011, P&G was forced to briefly close plants in Egypt that supply products for South Africa. During the closure, production from plants in Hungary and Turkey was redirected to supply the South African market. Such incidents explain why supply-chain managers use another term borrowed from the military, VUCA, to describe places that are "volatile, uncertain, complex, and ambiguous."[37]

Walmart's mastery of logistics and supply-chain management is an important source of competitive advantage. The retailing giant's basic value proposition is simple: getting goods to people as efficiently as possible. To do this, Walmart exploits a core competency: leveraging its vast customer database to know and anticipate what customers want and getting it to them quickly and efficiently.

An industry's value chain can change over time. In pharmaceuticals, for example, research, testing, and delivery were the three steps that historically defined the industry from its beginnings in the early nineteenth century. Then, starting in the mid-1960s, after Crick and Watson published their groundbreaking work on DNA, two new upstream steps in the industry's value chain emerged: basic research into genes associated with specific diseases and identification of the proteins produced by those genes. More recently, with the mapping of the human genome largely complete, value in the pharmaceuticals industry is migrating downstream to identifying, testing, and producing molecules that operate on the proteins produced by genes.[39]

The value chain, logistics, and related concepts are extremely important as supply chains stretch around the globe. As export administrator Beth Dorrell notes, "A commodity raw material from Africa can be refined in Asia, then shipped to South America to be incorporated into a component of a final product that is produced in the Middle East and then sold around the world." Figure 12-5 illustrates some of these concepts and activities at IKEA, the global furniture marketer. IKEA purchases wood and other raw material inputs from a network of suppliers located

> "We are trying to take advantage of the global factory. We are a global company; we should have a supply chain that reflects our customer base."[38]
>
> —Keith Sherin, finance director, GE

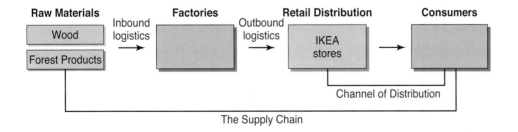

FIGURE 12-5

Supply Chain, Value Chain, and Logistics

[36] Lt. Col. George C. Thorpe, *Pure Logistics* (National Defense University Press, 1917; 1986).

[37] Barney Jopson, "Business Diary: Keith Harrison, Procter & Gamble," *Financial Times* (March 8, 2011).

[38] Francesco Guerrera, "GE to Shift Output from U.S.," *Financial Times* (July 27, 2006), p. 27.

[39] David Champion, "Mastering the Value Chain: An Interview with Mark Levin of Millennium Pharmaceuticals," *Harvard Business Review* 79, no. 6 (June 2001), pp. 108–115.

in dozens of countries; these suppliers are upstream in the value chain, and the process by which wood is transported to the factories is known as *inbound logistics*. IKEA's factories add value to the inputs by transforming them into furniture kits that are then shipped to IKEA's stores. The stores are downstream in IKEA's value chain; the activities associated with shipping furniture kits from factory to store are known as *outbound logistics*.[40]

Physical distribution and logistics are the means by which products are made available to customers when and where they want them. The most important distribution activities are order processing, warehousing, inventory management, and transportation.

Order Processing

Activities related to order processing provide information inputs that are critical in fulfilling a customer's order. **Order processing** includes *order entry*, in which the order is actually entered into the company's information system; *order handling*, which involves locating, assembling, and moving products into distribution; and *order delivery*, the process by which products are made available to the customer.

In some instances, the customer is a consumer, as is the case when you place an order with Amazon.com or Lands' End. In other instances, the customer is a channel member. Pepsi Bottling Group overhauled its supply chain in an effort to eliminate out-of-stock inventory problems. The company's handheld computers lacked wireless capability and required a hookup to a landline telephone service; by upgrading the technology, sales representatives can now enter orders wirelessly. Warehouse workers are equipped with barcode scanners and headsets so they can do a better job of ensuring that each pallet of drink products contains exactly what retailers ordered.[41]

Warehousing

Warehouses are used to store goods until they are sold; another type of facility, the *distribution center*, is designed to efficiently receive goods from suppliers and then fill orders for individual stores or customers. Modern distribution and warehousing is such an automated, high-tech business today that many companies outsource this function. For example, ODW Logistics Inc. operates several warehouses on behalf of Deere & Company, Limited Brands, and other customers. Much of ODW's capacity is in Columbus, Ohio, a major U.S. port of entry for textiles. One of the driving forces behind the growth of third-party warehousing is the need to reduce fixed costs and speed up delivery times to customers. ODW adds additional utility by tracking shipments from the time they leave the factory in, say, China, until they reach Columbus. This enables the company to alert retailers of possible delays due to weather or port congestion. In addition, as manufacturers ramp up efforts to use radio frequency identification (RFID) tags on shipments, ODW will split the cost of the new technology with its customers. As consultant John Boyd notes, "Right now, distribution warehousing is the next arena of corporate re-engineering and corporate cost-cutting."[42]

Inventory Management

Proper inventory management ensures that a company neither runs out of manufacturing components or finished goods nor incurs the expense and risk of carrying excessive stocks of these items. Another issue is balancing order-processing costs against inventory-carrying costs. The more often a product is ordered, the higher the order-processing costs associated with unloading, stocking, and related activities. The less frequently a product is ordered, the higher the inventory-carrying costs, because more product must be kept in inventory to cover the longer

---

[40] A detailed analysis of IKEA's approach to value creation is found in Richard Normann and Rafael Ramirez, "From Value Chain to Value Constellation: Designing Interactive Strategy," *Harvard Business Review* 71, no. 4 (July–August 1993), pp. 65–77.

[41] Chad Terhune, "Supply-Chain Fix for Pepsi," *The Wall Street Journal* (June 6, 2006), p. B3.

[42] Kris Maher, "Global Goods Jugglers," *The Wall Street Journal* (July 5, 2005), pp. A11, A12.

TABLE 12-4 Comparison of Major International Transportation Modes

Mode	Reliability	Cost	Speed	Accessibility	Capability	Ease of Tracing
Rail	Average	Average	Average	High	High	Low
Water	Low	Low	Slow	Low	High	Low
Truck	High	Varies	Fast	High	High	High
Air	High	High	Fast	Low	Moderate	High
Pipeline	High	Low	Slow	Low	Low	Moderate
Internet	High	Low	Moderate to fast	Moderate; increasing	Low	High

period between orders. As noted in Chapter 6, an important new tool for inventory management is RFID, which utilizes small tags that are attached to pallets, containers, or individual inventory items.

Transportation

Finally, transportation decisions concern the method, or *mode*, a company should utilize when moving products through domestic and global channels. The word *mode* implies a choice, and the major transportation mode choices are rail, truck, air, water, pipeline, and the Internet. Each of these modes has its advantages and disadvantages, as summarized in Table 12-4. However, a particular mode may be unavailable in some countries because of an underdeveloped infrastructure or geographic barriers. Pipelines are highly specialized and used by companies transporting energy-related resources such as oil and natural gas.

Rail provides an extremely cost-effective means for moving large quantities of merchandise long distances. In the United States, carriers such as CSX and Burlington Northern Santa Fe (BNSF) account for nearly half of all cargo moved when measured by ton-miles (see Exhibit 12-10). Rail's capability is second only to water in terms of the variety of products that can be transported. However, trains are less reliable than trucks. Poor track maintenance leads to derailments, and bottlenecks on heavily traveled lines can create delays.

Trucks are an excellent mode for both long-haul, transcontinental transport and local delivery of goods. In nations with well-developed highway systems, truck freight combines the advantage of fast delivery times with the highest level of accessibility of any mode. Thanks to modern information technology, truck shipments are also easily traced. However, in countries with poorly developed infrastructures, truck deliveries can move much more slowly. India is a case in point.

The two main types of water transportation are inland water and ocean transportation. *Inland water transportation* is an extremely low-cost mode generally used to move agricultural commodities, petroleum, fertilizers, and other goods that, by their nature, lend themselves to bulk shipping via barge. However, inland water transportation can be slow and subject to weather-related delays. Virtually any product can be shipped via *ocean transportation*. The world's deep-water ports can receive a variety of types of oceangoing vessels, such as container vessels; bulk and break-bulk vessels; and roll-on, roll-off (ro-ro) vessels. Although sailing times are not competitive with air transportation, it is generally more cost-effective to ship large quantities of merchandise via ocean than by air. Denmark's Maersk Sealand is the world's largest shipping container line (see Table 12-5).

Why is water rated "low" in reliability? In any given year, approximately 200 freighters sink due to bad weather or other factors. Compounding the tragic loss of human lives is the fact that the cargo ends up on the ocean floor. Cargo can also sometimes be lost without a ship sinking. For example, in 1997 a huge wave rocked the freighter *Tokio Express* in the waters off Land's End, England. Several dozen shipping containers were tossed overboard, including one

Exhibit 12-10 "How tomorrow moves" is the theme of a corporate brand-image advertising campaign from CSX. The company is one of the largest freight-hauling rail lines in the United States. This ad is a reminder that CSX is a critical link in the supply chain: Products that people use every day travel at least part of the way by rail as they move from producer to consumer.

Source: Photographer: Bruce DeBoer. Used by permission of CSX

TABLE 12-5 **Leading Container Shipping Lines**

Carrier	Number of Vessels
A.P. Moller-Maersk (Denmark)	600+
Mediterranean Shipping Company MSC (Switzerland)	458
CMA-CGM (France)	414
Evergreen Marine (Taiwan)	182
Cosco (China)	130+

Source: Compiled by authors from company reports.

containing nearly 5 million LEGO pieces. The container was bound for Connecticut, where the pieces were to be assembled in kits. One year later, LEGO pieces began washing ashore in Florida!

Losses can occur even when the cargo remains on board and the ship doesn't sink. For example, the *Cougar Ace*, a freighter loaded with 4,700 new Mazdas, narrowly avoided sinking in the Pacific in 2006. The cars were strapped down but the ship listed at a 60-degree angle for weeks before being righted. Concerned that the cars might not be saleable, management decided to destroy the entire shipment, which was valued at $100 million.[43] Piracy on the high seas is another factor affecting the reliability of water as a transport mode. In recent years, pirates operating in the Indian Ocean off the coast of Africa have fired upon and attempted to board dozens of commercial vessels. In some instances, the pirates have succeeded in boarding ships and hijacking the cargo. In one case, pirates captured the captain of an American-flagged ship carrying food aid to East Africa.

Air is the fastest transport mode and the carrier of choice for perishable exports such as flowers or fresh fish, but it is also the most expensive. The size and the weight of an item may indicate that it is more cost-effective to ship via air than ocean. If a shipment's delivery is time sensitive, such as an emergency parts replacement, air is also the logical mode.

Thanks to the digital revolution, the *Internet* is becoming an important transportation mode that is associated with several advantages and one major disadvantage. First, the bad news: The Internet's capability is low. As Nicolas Negroponte of MIT's Media Lab has famously observed, as long as something consists of atoms, it cannot be shipped via the Internet. However, anything that can be digitized—including text, voice, music, pictures, and video—can be sent via the Internet. Advantages include low cost and high reliability. Accessibility is increasing as global PC demand increases; today, it is estimated that approximately 1 billion households have Internet access. Accessibility is also growing thanks to telecommunications innovations that allow cell phones and other wireless digital devices to access the Internet. Speed depends on several factors, including bandwidth. As broadband technology becomes more widespread and compression technology improves, the speed at which large digital files such as full-length motion pictures can be downloaded will increase dramatically.

Channel strategy involves an analysis of each shipping mode to determine which mode, or combination of modes, will be both effective and efficient in a given situation. A number of firms specializing in third-party logistics are available to help companies with transportation logistics. For example, C. H. Robinson Worldwide matches shippers with trucking companies and other carriers in all parts of the world. An aspect of transportation technology that has revolutionized global trade is containerization—a concept that was first utilized in the United States starting in the mid-1950s. **Containerization** refers to the practice of loading oceangoing freight into steel boxes measuring 20 feet, 40 feet, or longer. Containerization offers many advantages, including flexibility in the product that can be shipped via container, as well as flexibility in shipping modes (see Exhibit 12-11).

Intermodal transportation of goods involves a combination of land and water shipping from producer to customer.[44] In the United States alone, railroads handle more than $150 billion in seaport goods, a statistic that is a testament to intermodal transportation's growing importance. Unfortunately, lack of investment in America's rail infrastructure has resulted in delays at seaports. As Bernard LaLonde, a professor of transportation and logistics, noted, "It's the Achilles' heel of global distribution. The ships keep getting bigger and faster. Trade keeps growing. But we don't have the rail links we need."[45]

The decision about which mode of transportation to use may be dictated by a particular market situation, by the company's overall strategy, or by conditions at the port of importation. For example, every November, winemakers from France's Beaujolais region participate in a promotion celebrating the release of the current vintage. Although wine destined for European

---

[43] Joel Millman, "A Crushing Issue: How to Destroy Brand-New Cars," *The Wall Street Journal* (April 29, 2008), pp. A1, A9.

[44] For an excellent case study of the evolution of intermodal technology in the United States, see Jon R. Katzenback and Douglas K. Smith, *The Wisdom of Teams: Creating the High-Performance Organization* (New York: HarperBusiness, 1994), Chapter 2.

[45] Daniel Machalaba, "Cargo Hold: As U.S. Seaports Get Busier, Weak Point Is a Surprise: Railroads," *The Wall Street Journal* (September 19, 1996), p. A1.

Exhibit 12-11 Prior to 1985, the Port of New York was the busiest container port in the world. Then New York went into decline as ports on the West Coast and the South courted freight lines. Now, thanks to a high tide of imports from Asia, the Port of New York is experiencing a resurgence of traffic. Giant freighters leave China and travel through the Panama Canal.
Source: © Randy Duchaine / Alamy

markets may travel by rail or truck, U.S.-bound wine is shipped via air freight. Normally, owing to weight and bulk considerations, French wine makes the transatlantic journey by water. Similarly, Acer Group ships motherboards and other high-tech components from Taiwan via air freight to ensure that the latest technology is incorporated into its computers. Bangladesh's primary port, Chittagong, is subject to frequent delays and strikes, which forces Gap and other clothing companies to ship via air.

Every Christmas, supplies of the season's hottest-selling toys and electronics products are shipped via air from factories in Asia to ensure just-in-time delivery by Santa Claus. Sony's PS3 is a case in point; in the fall of 2006, the company shipped hundreds of thousands of units by air to the United States. Likewise, in 2007, the first shipments of Apple's highly anticipated iPhone arrived from Asia via air freight. An estimated $1 billion is added to U.S. shipping costs each year because companies are forced to compensate for railway delays by keeping more components or parts in inventory or by shipping via air.

Logistics Management: A Brief Case Study

The term **logistics management** describes the integration of activities necessary to ensure the efficient flow of raw materials, in-process inventory, and finished goods from producers to customers. JCPenney provides a case study in the changing face of logistics, physical distribution, and retail supply chains in the twenty-first century. Several years ago, Penney's management team made a key decision to outsource most elements of its private-label shirt supply chain to TAL Apparel Ltd. of Hong Kong. Penney's North American stores carry virtually no extra inventory of house-brand shirts; when an individual shirt is sold, EPOS scanner data are transmitted directly to Hong Kong. TAL's proprietary computer model then determines whether to replenish the store with the same size, color, and style. Replacement shirts are sent directly to stores without passing through Penney's warehouse system; sometimes the shirts are sent via air, sometimes by ship. This approach represents a dramatic departure from past practices; Penney's typically carried 6 months' worth of inventory in its warehouses and 3 months' inventory in stores. By working closely with TAL, Penney's can lower its inventory costs, reduce the quantity of goods that have to be marked down, and respond more quickly to changing consumer tastes and fashion styles. However, as Wai-Chan Chan of McKinsey & Company Hong Kong noted, "You are giving away a pretty important function when you outsource your inventory management. That's something that not a lot of retailers want to part with."[46]

---

[46] Alexandra Harney, "Technology Takes the Wrinkles Out of Textiles Manufacturing," *Financial Times* (January 11, 2006), p. 11. See also Gabriel Kahn, "Made to Measure: Invisible Supplier Has Penney's Shirts All Buttoned Up," *The Wall Street Journal* (September 11, 2003), pp. A1, A9.

Summary

A **channel of distribution** is the network of agencies and institutions that links producers with users. **Physical distribution** is the movement of goods through channels. **Business-to-consumer marketing (b-to-c)** uses consumer channels; **business-to-business (b-to-b) marketing** employs industrial channels to deliver products to manufacturers or other types of organizations. **Peer-to-peer** marketing via the Internet is another channel. **Distributors** and **agents** are key intermediaries in both channel types. Channel decisions are difficult to manage globally because of the variation in channel structures from country to country. Marketing channels can create **place utility**, **time utility**, **form utility**, and **information utility** for buyers. The characteristics of customers, products, middlemen, and the environment all affect channel design and strategy.

Consumer channels may be relatively direct, utilizing direct mail or door-to-door selling, as well as manufacturer-owned stores. A combination of manufacturers' sales forces, agents/brokers, and wholesalers may also be used. Channels for industrial products are less varied, with manufacturers' sales forces, wholesalers, and dealers or agents used.

Global retailing is a growing trend as successful retailers expand around the world in support of growth objectives. Retail operations take many different forms, including **department stores**, **specialty retailers**, **supermarkets**, **convenience stores**, **discount retailers**, **hard discounters**, **hypermarkets**, **supercenters**, **superstores**, **shopping malls**, **outlet stores**, and **outlet malls**. Selection, price, store location, and customer service are a few of the competencies that can be used strategically to enter a new market. It is possible to classify retailers in a matrix that distinguishes companies offering few product categories with an own-label focus, many categories with an own-label focus, few categories with a manufacturer-brand focus, and many categories with a manufacturer-brand focus. Global retail expansion can be achieved via **organic growth**, **franchising**, **acquisition**, **joint venture**, and **licensing**.

Transportation and physical distribution issues are critically important in a company's value chain because of the geographical distances involved in sourcing products and serving customers in different parts of the world. A company's **supply chain** includes all the firms that perform support activities such as generating raw materials or fabricating components. **Logistics** and **logistics management** integrate the activities of all companies in a firm's value chain to ensure an efficient flow of goods through the supply chain. Important activities include **order processing**, **warehousing**, and **inventory management**. To cut costs and improve efficiency, many companies are reconfiguring their supply chains by outsourcing some or all of these activities. Six transportation modes—air, truck, water, rail, pipeline, and Internet—are widely used in global distribution. **Containerization** was a key innovation in physical distribution that facilitates **intermodal transportation**.

MyMarketingLab

12-1. What is *cherry picking*? What approaches can be used to deal with this problem?

12-2. Briefly discuss the global issues associated with physical distribution and transportation logistics. Cite one example of a company that is making efficiency improvements in its channel or physical distribution arrangements.

12-3. Mymarketinglab Only – comprehensive writing assignment for this chapter.

MyMarketingLab

Go to **mymktlab.com** to complete the problems marked with this icon .

Discussion Questions

12-4. In what ways can channel intermediaries create utility for buyers?

⭐ **12-5.** What factors influence the channel structures and strategies available to global marketers?

12-6. What is *cherry picking*? What approaches can be used to deal with this problem?

12-7. Compare and contrast the typical channel structures for consumer products and industrial products.

⭐ **12-8.** Identify the different forms of retailing, and cite an example of each. Identify retailers from as many different countries as you can.

12-9. Identify the four retail market expansion strategies discussed in the text. What factors determine the appropriate mode?

12-10. Many global retailers are targeting China, India, and other emerging markets. In terms of the strategies described in Figure 12-4, what would be the most likely entry strategies for these countries?

12-11. Briefly discuss the global issues associated with physical distribution and transportation logistics. Cite one example of a company that is making efficiency improvements in its channel or physical distribution arrangements.

⭐ **12-12.** What special distribution challenges exist in Japan? What is the best way for a non-Japanese company to deal with these challenges?

CASE 12-1   CONTINUED (REFER TO PAGE 384)

How Successful is Carrefour's Joint Venture in the UAE?

As noted previously in this chapter, the term *organized retail* is used to describe activity by large branded retail chains such as Woolworths, Tesco, and Walmart.

While gaining access to an emerging market such as the UAE in 1995, Carrefour decided to enter into a joint venture with Majid Al Futtaim after the evaluation of laws and market conditions. One of the major reasons for this kind of agreement was that in order to enjoy exclusive presence in the region and be protected from contract termination, the foreign companies needed to have a joint venture with nationals or commercial entities owned solely by UAE Emiratis. Carrefour saw the qualifying condition as a plus point since it would entail sharing the liability of ownership between the parties involved. In addition, the UAE is characterized by a strong food culture with religious and cultural restrictions; thus, if it operated as a joint undertaking with a local sponsor, it would be easier to obtain food health certificates like the halal slaughter certificate (for the slaughter of animals for meat as per the laws permissible under Islam) and to import food. Furthermore, Carrefour would be subject to the same barriers as the sponsors, or none at all, on most inventories, excluding some items such as cigarettes.

Although there are a lot of benefits to forming a joint venture, Carrefour had to face certain problems. To begin with, the biggest difficulty lay in finding the most suitable local partner who would be able to handle the complexity of local import statutes and pre-operational regulations, such as product licensing, providing access to product samples, and testing in the local municipal labs to make sure the cultural and health criteria are met. Secondly, operating costs are linked to the size of a particular location. Carrefour operates as large hypermarkets rather than smaller supermarkets, so it would have to pay huge sums of money on renting stock, shelving, and listing. The UAE is part of the Gulf Cooperation Council (GCC), which states that if the food products imported into the country do not have half or more of its shelf life remaining at the time of entrance, clearance cannot be issued. Thirdly, adapting to the local customs and traditions of working is imperative. For example, the weekly offs might vary and not fall on the conventional Western weekends (Saturdays and Sundays).

Partnering with Majid Al Futtaim (MAF) was a good decision since they are a major pan-regional company with ownership in shopping malls, hotels, and business communities. MAF offered Carrefour profitable locations such as high-traffic malls and properties which they already owned. Furthermore, this would limit direct competition since no other hypermarket would be able to open shop at the same mall. Carrefour wanted to expand throughout the Middle East and since MAF operated the region, it could facilitate the expansion under the same partnership. Most importantly, MAF had previous experience with foreign retailers and business enterprises, and was the candidate most likely to be able to handle Carrefour's operations.

Establishing a strategy in Dubai with MAF in order to adapt to the local culture was crucial. Dubai has a very strong mall culture primarily because of its harsh climate. The idea was to create a city within a city by locating Carrefour inside shopping malls instead of its usual location strategy of using a freestanding building. Dubai is a very diverse emirate with a sizeable population of expatriates, so accepting foreign credit cards, different GCC currencies, and international currencies like the Euro and the U.S. Dollar was a must. Language was not a problem; English is widely spoken in Dubai and Carrefour set up bilingual signs across all stores. MAF managed local promotions and coordinated regionally in the Middle East. Due to the overall high cost of living, sales promotion was really important for the different demographic segments. At the time of Carrefour's Dubai entry, the emirate's local demographic accounted for only 17 percent of the population, expatriate Asians (85 percent) and Westerners (3 percent) making up for the rest of it. The expatriates, who form the largest segment, have the lowest disposable income but are open to buying Western electronics and products.

Carrefour faces some challenges as well, particularly in the food segment, where competition is increasing and thus reducing profit margins. While Walmart is not yet considering the Middle East, some European hypermarkets are. For example, Union Coop in 2006 opened an 180,000-square-feet hypermarket in Dubai. Inflation in Dubai is a serious problem, especially with rapid growth, greater liquidity, high demand, and low supply; economists expect actual consumer price inflation to be at 20 percent per year. Inflation affects the revenues and raises the costs of inventory and staffing. Moreover, the dollar decline compared to other currencies translates to lower revenues when exchanged. Lately, the UAE government has implemented stricter regulations: it is now harder to obtain work permits and tourist visas, which has especially affected the tourism-dependant Dubai. Further, as Dubai depends on more foreign investment than any other emirate, it is more vulnerable to economic crisis.

To conclude, joint ventures seem to be a success given the increased number of stores opening in Dubai and their further expansion to other Middle Eastern and North African countries. It is said that Carrefour was successful only because it had the first-mover advantage and adapted so well that it was embraced by the locals. The aggressiveness with which Majid Al Futtaim pursued its growth added to the chain's prosperity. In 2005, the venture published sales worth $1 billion out of its 13 stores, around 1 percent of the global sales. In 2007, sales rose to $2.5 billion regionally.

Discussion Questions

12-13. What are the reasons behind Carrefour choosing joint venture as a method of entry?

12-14. Why do you think Carrefour chose UAE as a stepping stone to expand into the Middle East?

12-15. State Majid Al Futtaim's (MAF) characteristics that allow them to be a good partner?

12-16. Do you think Carrefour's joint venture was a good choice? Please validate your answer.

Source: Analysis of Carrefour's Dubai Market Entry, SIS International Research (February 2, 2009), thoughtleadership.sismarketresearch.com/middle-east-journal/2009/2/2/analysis-of-carrefours-dubai-market-entry.html.

CASE 12-2
Fail! Tesco Strikes Out in the United States

Tesco is the largest supermarket chain in the United Kingdom. The company's slogan is "Every Little Helps"; it executes on that claim in various ways, including its Clubcard loyalty program and an online grocery retailing operation that fulfills more than 100,000 orders every week. Tesco's supply chain—including relationships with suppliers and distributors—is one of the best in the industry. The retailer performed solidly during the recession, and the company is pursuing growth opportunities in nongrocery areas such as banking and broadband services. Tesco generates 70 percent of its profits in the United Kingdom, where it is the largest private-sector employer.

Despite these strengths, Tesco lags behind retailing giants Walmart and Carrefour in terms of global presence. To address this weakness, Sir Terry Leahy, Tesco CEO from 1996 to 2010, formulated and implemented an expansion strategy. For example, his executives initiated negotiations with India's Bharti Enterprises about possible joint ventures. Tesco is also expanding into China and Japan. Tesco currently has operations in 14 countries.

The United States represented a key expansion destination. Leahy committed hundreds of millions of dollars to open small stores in Nevada, Arizona, and California, a decision that industry observers described as "one of the most widely watched events in the global retailing sector." The former CEO's vision was to have 10,000 small convenience stores "on every junction, in every major city in the USA."

The first stores had 15,000 square feet of floor space and bore the name "Tesco Fresh & Easy"; they offered a focused selection of fresh foods, packaged goods, and prepared meals (see Exhibit 12-12). Commenting on the $1 trillion U.S. grocery market, Leahy noted, "Demand for convenience shopping is very well developed there. There are lots of wealthy and busy people and it's multicultural. You've got to start somewhere and it's important to do it in bite-sized chunks."

In its home market, Tesco operates more than 2,300 stores in four formats: supercenters (large stores with a limited range of non-food items), regular and compact supermarkets, and Tesco Express convenience stores. While the U.S. market entry was limited to small neighborhood markets, Tesco raised eyebrows with an ambitious plan to establish its own distribution network. Management expected prepared foods such as salads and chicken-based dishes to be big sellers. To execute its plan, Tesco brought two suppliers across the Atlantic: Natures Way Foods, which specializes in salads, and 2 Sisters Food Group, a leading UK poultry purveyor.

Management was confident it had identified an opportunity. The small-store format made it unlikely that Tesco would encounter the type of backlash that has been directed at Walmart in some communities. Speaking about the U.S. retail environment, Tim Mason, director of marketing and property at Tesco, noted, "Generally, shopping either means the big-box model, where you get in your car once a week and drive out of town to do your shopping, or the convenience store at the end of the street. We found that the [U.S.] market for convenience stores at the end of your street is not very well served. There is more consumer opportunity and more retail opportunity."

At the end of 2010, however, 6 years after the launch, it was clear that the Fresh & Easy venture was performing below expectations. Cumulative losses totaled more than $600 million. Only 145 stores were operating; the Tesco team had anticipated having 200 stores open by the end of 2009. Some industry observers questioned whether Tesco had fully understood American consumers. In a typical U.S. grocery store, for example, many fresh fruits and vegetables are stacked loose in coolers in the produce section. At Fresh & Easy, by contrast, most produce is displayed in bags. The emphasis on private-label brands was cited as another drawback. As one retail executive explained, "Fresh & Easy is very highly dependent on private label and

Exhibit 12-12 Tesco operated nearly 200 Fresh & Easy supermarkets in the United States. The first store opened in November 2007; as the economic environment deteriorated, Tesco was forced to adjust its strategy. To appeal to budget-conscious shoppers, Tesco used aggressive price promotions. By early 2013, however, executives decided to shut down the operation after losses totaling £1 billion ($1.6 billion).
Source: Paul Harris/padficco astnows/ Newscom

the U.S. consumer likes brands. Fresh & Easy was not a known brand, so by focusing on that, there was nothing for the consumer to hang on to."

In other cases, the company does have an impressive track record outside the United Kingdom; Tesco has even successfully penetrated markets that have proven to be difficult for Walmart and Carrefour. For example, Tesco entered South Korea in 1999. Samsung Tesco, an 89-11 joint venture, operates Homeplus "value store" hypermarkets. Homeplus is known for more than just shopping: The stores also feature coffee shops and restaurants. As one analyst noted, the joint venture approach has served Tesco well. "Thanks to its local partner, Tesco has tailored its service well to local tastes, while Walmart and Carrefour have struggled to win over consumers with their focus on prices," the analyst said. In 2008, Tesco acquired E-Land, a local chain with 36 stores. Today, Tesco has more than 300 stores in South Korea; annual sales of $6 billion make Korea Tesco's most successful global market entry to date.

Tesco has also been successful in Japan, although on a more limited scale. Before entering the market, a team was dispatched to live with Japanese consumers, accompany them on shopping trips, and observe their food preparation customs. As David Reid, chairman and head of Tesco's international operations, explained, "In America you have big cars, you can drive several miles in 5 minutes, you can buy in bulk and store it in your double garage. Chalk and cheese compared to Japan. In Japan we learned that some housewives shop on bikes and shop daily. They visit six or seven shops looking for deals." Armed with these insights, Tesco acquired C Two-Network, a small discount, convenience store chain with stores in Tokyo.

Back in America, at the end of 2011, Tesco announced a shakeup in the Fresh & Easy management ranks. Chief marketing officer Simon Uwins, one of the original members of the startup team, left the company. Fresh & Easy CEO Tim Mason reorganized the commercial and marketing units into a single team. The move came as the first Fresh & Easy store was opened in central Los Angeles. Tesco also introduced Friends of Fresh & Easy, a new loyalty card based on the company's highly regarded Clubcard.

At Tesco's UK headquarters, new CEO Philip Clark was intent on making the U.S. operation profitable by the end of the 2013 fiscal year. As the former head of Tesco's Asian and European divisions, he also saw important opportunities to leverage the company's online marketing expertise in China, the Czech Republic, Poland, and other key emerging markets. Explaining his strategy, the CEO noted, "I don't think you can afford to say it's all sequential, build out a store network and then do the Internet. I think what you've got to say is, 'We've got a good store network, we've got to do grocery home shopping, what about non-food? What next?'"

Discussion Questions

12-17. What are the keys to Tesco's success in the competitive global retailing industry?

12-18. In view of the tough retailing environment, what additional changes do you think Tesco might be forced to make to the Fresh & Easy concept?

12-19. Which of the market-entry strategies identified in the chapter was Tesco using in the United States? Do you think this was the appropriate strategy?

12-20. At the end of 2012, after £1 billion ($1.6 billion) in losses, Philip Clark announced he was closing Tesco's U.S. business down. Does this surprise you?

Sources: Paul Sonne, "Five Years, $1.6 Billion Later, Tesco Decides to Quit U.S.," *The Wall Street Journal* (December 6, 2012), p. B1; Elizabeth Rigby, "Tesco Aims to Expand Online Model Overseas," *Financial Times* (September 20, 2010), p. 7; Rigby, "Fresh Horizons Uneasily Scanned," *Financial Times* (September 20, 2010), p. 7; Rigby, "Tesco's American Dream Struggles to Fulfill Potential" (September 21, 2010), p. 19; Rigby, "Clarke to Take on Challenges at Tesco," *Financial Times* (June 9, 2010), p. 17; Christian Oliver, "Every Little Helps in the Local Culture," *Financial Times Special Report: Investing in South Korea* (May 21, 2009), p. 4; Cecilie Rohwedder, "Tesco Tries to Hit a U.S. Curveball," *The Wall Street Journal* (March 2, 2009), p. B1; Rohwedder, "Stores of Knowledge: No. 1 Retailer in Britain Uses 'Clubcard' to Thwart Walmart," *The Wall Street Journal* (June 6, 2006), pp. A1, A16; Jonathan Birchall, "Tesco Will Launch in LA and Phoenix," *Financial Times* (May 18, 2006), p. 17; Rigby, "Tesco Seeks to Gain Weight Abroad," *Financial Times* (May 2, 2006), p. 17; Song Jung-a, "One-Stop Model Gives Tesco Edge in Korea," *Financial Times* (March 22, 2006), p. 17; Sophy Buckley and Birchall, "Tesco Plans to Build Brand in US," *Financial Times* (February 10, 2006), p. 19; Rohwedder, "Tesco Jumps the Pond," *The Wall Street Journal* (February 10, 2006), p. B2; Susanna Voyle, "Tesco's Tough Act: With Record Profits, Britain's Biggest Retailer Prepares for Further Challenges at Home and Abroad," *Financial Times* (April 20, 2004), p. 13; Alastair Ray, "Own-Brand Broadcaster Tunes In," *Financial Times* (March 16, 2004), p. 10; Bayan Rahman, "Tesco's Japanese Shopping without the Hype," *Financial Times* (January 16, 2004), p. 20.

13

Global Marketing Communications Decisions I: Advertising and Public Relations

MyMarketingLab™

⭐ **Improve Your Grade!**

Over 10 million students improved their results using the Pearson MyLabs. Visit **mymktlab.com** for simulations, tutorials, and end-of-chapter problems.

CASE 13-1
The Gulf Oil Spill: BP's Public Relations Nightmare

It's not hard to figure out what keeps BP executives awake at night. The catastrophic explosion on the Deepwater Horizon oil-drilling platform in the Gulf of Mexico in April 2010 killed 11 workers and allowed millions of gallons of oil to spill into the waters off the Louisiana coast. Numerous efforts to stop the leak failed. As an estimated 30,000 barrels of oil leaked from the stricken well each day, Deepwater Horizon became the worst oil spill in U.S. history, surpassing the 1989 Exxon

Exhibit 13-1 Thousands of workers took part in a massive cleanup effort as oil washed ashore in Louisiana, Mississippi, Alabama, and Florida. One year after the spill, tar balls were still washing up on coastal beaches. The Gulf Coast Claims Facility was responsible for distributing $20 billion to individuals and businesses affected by the spill. Although economic repercussions are still being felt, fisheries have reopened and the shrimp catch has rebounded.
Source: Craig Ruttle/Alamy.

Valdez accident in Alaska (see Exhibit 13-1). As one newspaper noted in mid-2010, "BP has become public enemy number-one in the U.S."

BP, which was once known as British Petroleum, is the leading producer of gas and oil in the United States. Forty percent of its shareholders are in the United States. Ironically, in 2000, BP implemented an ecology-themed corporate identity campaign keyed to the theme "Beyond Petroleum." As the disaster unfolded, oil-contaminated oyster beds and fishing grounds threatened the livelihoods of thousands of fishermen. Images of oil-soaked, brown pelicans were widely circulated by the media. Hotel owners in Alabama, Florida, Louisiana, and Mississippi faced the prospect of fewer tourists as tar balls began to wash up on beaches.

While engineers struggled around the clock to plug the leak, BP tried to reassure the public that it was doing everything possible. Full-page print ads declared, "We will get it done. We will make this right." Even so, critics pounced on early comments by BP CEO Tony Hayward that the environmental impact of the spill would likely be "very, very modest." BP was also embarrassed over revelations that some photos of the spill operation posted on the company's Web site had been digitally altered.

As the crisis continued into the summer months, the rhetoric on both sides of the Atlantic escalated. U.S. President Barack Obama declared that he wanted to find out "whose ass to kick." In a televised address from the Oval Office, President Obama asserted that he would hold BP accountable. BP's board of directors canceled the company's dividend and pledged $20 billion in aid to those impacted by the spill. For more on BP's response to the Deepwater Horizon spill, see the continuation of Case 13-1 at the end of the chapter.

Advertising, public relations, and other forms of communication are critical tools in the marketing program. Marketing communications—the promotion P of the marketing mix—refers to all forms of communication used by organizations to inform, remind, explain, persuade, and influence the attitudes and buying behavior of customers and others. The primary purpose of marketing communications is to tell customers about the benefits and values that a company, nation, product, or service offers. The elements of the promotion mix are advertising, public relations, personal selling, and sales promotion.

Global marketers can use all of these elements, either alone or in varying combinations. BP's experience in the aftermath of the Deepwater Horizon oil spill highlights the critical importance of public relations to any entity—be it a nation or a business enterprise—that finds itself spotlighted on the world stage. This chapter examines advertising and public relations from the perspective of the global marketer. Chapter 14 examines sales promotion, personal selling, event marketing, and sponsorships. As you study these chapters, remember: All the communication tools described here should be used in a way that reinforces a consistent message.

LEARNING OBJECTIVES

1 Define *global advertising* and identify the top-ranked companies in terms of worldwide ad spending.

2 Explain the structure of the advertising industry and describe the difference between agency holding companies and individual agency brands.

3 Identify key ad agency personnel and describe their respective roles in creating global advertising.

4 Explain how media availability varies around the world.

5 Compare and contrast publicity and public relations and identify global companies that have recently been impacted by negative publicity.

Global Advertising

The environment in which marketing communications programs and strategies are implemented varies from country to country. The challenge of effectively communicating across borders is one reason that global companies and their advertising agencies are embracing a concept known as **integrated marketing communications (IMC)**. Adherents of an IMC approach explicitly recognize that the various elements of a company's communication strategy must be carefully coordinated.[1]

---

[1] Thomas R. Duncan and Stephen E. Everett, "Client Perception of Integrated Marketing Communications," *Journal of Advertising Research* (May–June 1993), pp. 119–122; see also Stephen J. Gould, Dawn B. Lerman, and Andreas F. Grein, "Agency Perceptions and Practices on Global IMC," *Journal of Advertising Research* 39, no. 1 (January–February 1999), pp. 7–20.

For example, Nike has embraced the IMC concept. Trevor Edwards, Nike's vice president for global brand and category management, notes:

> We create demand for our brand by being flexible about how we tell the story. We do not rigidly stay with one approach.…We have an integrated marketing model that involves all elements of the marketing mix from digital to sports marketing, from event marketing to advertising to entertainment, all sitting at the table driving ideas.[2]

Advertising is one element of an IMC program. **Advertising** may be defined as any sponsored, paid message that is communicated in a nonpersonal way. Some advertising messages are designed to communicate with consumers in a single country or market area. Regional or pan-regional advertising is created for audiences across several country markets, such as Europe or Latin America. **Global advertising** may be defined as messages whose art, copy, headlines, photographs, taglines, and other elements have been developed expressly for their worldwide suitability. Companies that have used global themes include McDonald's ("I'm lovin' it"), IBM ("Solutions for a small planet"), De Beers ("A diamond is forever"), BP ("Beyond Petroleum"), and Vodafone ("Your voice"). In Chapter 10, we noted that some global companies simultaneously offer local, international, and global products and brands to buyers in different parts of the world. The same is true with advertising: A global company may use single-country advertising in addition to campaigns that are regional and global in scope.

A global company possesses a critical marketing advantage with respect to marketing communications: It has the opportunity to successfully transform a domestic advertising campaign into a worldwide one. Alternatively, it can create a new global campaign from the ground up. The search for a global advertising campaign should bring together key company and ad agency personnel to share information, insights, and experience. McDonald's "I'm lovin' it" tagline is a case in point; it was developed after global marketing chief Larry Light called a meeting of representatives from all of McDonald's ad agencies. Global campaigns with unified themes can help to build long-term product and brand identities and offer significant savings by reducing the cost associated with producing ads. Regional market areas such as Europe are experiencing an influx of standardized global brands as companies align themselves for a united region by making acquisitions and evaluating production plans and pricing policies. From a marketing point of view, there is a great deal of activity going on that will make brands truly pan-European in a short period of time. This phenomenon is accelerating the growth of global advertising.

The potential for effective global advertising also increases as companies recognize and embrace new concepts such as "product cultures." An example is the globalization of beer culture, which can be seen in the popularity of German-style beer halls in Japan and Irish-style pubs in the United States. Similarly, the globalization of coffee culture has created market opportunities for companies such as Starbucks. Marketing managers also realize that some market segments can be defined on the basis of global demography—youth culture or an emerging middle class, for example—rather than ethnic or national culture. Athletic shoes and other clothing items, for instance, can be targeted to a worldwide segment of 18- to 25-year-old males. William Roedy, former global chairman of MTV Networks, sees clear implications of such product cultures for advertising. MTV is just one of the media vehicles that enable people virtually anywhere to see how the rest of the world lives and to learn about the latest electronic gadgets and fashion trends. As Roedy noted, "Eighteen-year-olds in Paris have more in common with 18-year-olds in New York than with their own parents. They buy the same products, go to the same movies, listen to the same music, sip the same colas. Global advertising merely works on that premise."[3]

According to data compiled by various industry groups, worldwide advertising expenditures in 2012 passed the $500 billion milestone. Because advertising is often designed to add psychological value to a product or brand, it plays a more important communications role in marketing consumer products than in marketing industrial products. Frequently purchased, low-cost products generally require heavy promotional support, which often takes the form of reminder advertising. Consumer products companies top the list of big global advertising spenders. Procter

---

[2] Gavin O'Malley, "Who's Leading the Way in Web Marketing? It's Nike, of Course," *Advertising Age* (October 26, 2006), p. D3.
[3] Ken Wells, "Selling to the World: Global Ad Campaigns, After Many Missteps, Finally Pay Dividends," *The Wall Street Journal* (August 27, 1992), p. A1.

& Gamble, Unilever, L'Oréal, and Nestlé are companies whose global scope can be inferred from the significant proportion of advertising expenditures outside the home-country markets.

Advertising Age magazine's ranking of global marketers in terms of advertising expenditures is shown in Table 13-1.[4] The United States is the world's top advertising market; the $160 billion spent on major media in 2012 represents one-third of the worldwide total. This figure represents a recovery of sorts; as the recession deepened in 2009, U.S. advertising spending fell by about 12 percent. Emerging markets are posting solid growth numbers; 2012 ad spending in Brazil totaled $18.6 billion; Russia, $9.7 billion; India, $6.1 billion; and China, $36.2 billion.[5] A close examination of Table 13-1 provides clues to the extent of a company's globalization efforts. For example, packaged goods giants Procter & Gamble and Unilever spend significant amounts in all major world regions. By contrast, the geographic scope of France's Peugeot Citroën is largely limited to Europe, with additional presence in Asia and Latin America.

Global advertising also offers companies economies of scale in advertising as well as improved access to distribution channels. Where shelf space is at a premium, a company has to convince retailers to carry its products rather than those of competitors. A global brand supported by global advertising may be very attractive because, from the retailer's standpoint, a global brand

TABLE 13-1 Top 25 Global Marketers by Ad Spending, 2011 ($ millions)

Company/Headquarters	Worldwide	United States	Asia*	Europe	Latin America
1. Procter & Gamble (United States)	$11,247	$3,134	$3,300	$3,324	$578
2. Unilever (United Kingdom, Netherlands)	7,358	694	2,474	2,407	963
3. L'Oréal (France)	5,533	1,380	1,149	2,612	210
4. General Motors Corp. (United States)	3,334	1,774	240	846	220
5. Nestlé (Switzerland)	2,977	828	463	1,207	244
6. Coca-Cola Co. (United States)	2,906	390	979	984	285
7. Toyota Motor Corp. (Japan)	2,828	1,088	973	598	44
8. Volkswagen (Germany)	2,823	511	313	1,688	233
9. McDonald's (United States)	2,647	963	567	862	102
10. Reckitt Benckiser (Great Britain)	2,616	434	462	1,181	298
11. Kraft Foods (United States)	2,490	791	324	1,016	176
12. Fiat (incl. Chrysler; Italy, United States)	2,347	1,286	21	723	222
13. Mars Inc. (United States)	2,251	568	447	993	20
14. Johnson & Johnson (United States)	2,167	1,041	306	579	108
15. Ford Motor Co. (United States)	2,127	1,060	69	661	178
16. Comcast Corp. (United States)	1,822	1,585	30	175	0
17. PepsiCo (United States)	1,803	652	285	201	116
18. Sony Corp. (Japan)	1,777	800	324	573	5
19. Pfizer (United States)	1,751	1,343	182	142	39
20. Nissan Motor (Japan)	1,750	630	437	506	93
21. PSA Peugeot Citroën (France)	1,623	1	11	1,430	159
22. Time Warner (United States)	1,607	1,280	21	264	4
23. GlaxoSmithKline (United Kingdom)	1,592	551	318	501	128
24. Honda Motor (Japan)	1,587	707	649	149	39
25. Walt Disney Company (United States)	1,501	991	149	302	19

*Asia includes Australia and New Zealand.
Source: Adapted from "100 Largest Global Marketers," *Advertising Age* (December 10, 2012), p. 18.

[4] To be included in the rankings, companies must report media spending on at least three continents.
[5] Adapted from "Global Marketers 2012: U.S. Versus BRIC," *Advertising Age* (December 10, 2012), p. 17.

is less likely to languish on the shelves. Landor Associates, a company specializing in brand identity and design, recently determined that Coke has the number 1 brand-awareness and esteem position in the United States, number 2 in Japan, and number 6 in Europe. However, standardization is not always required or even advised. Nestlé's Nescafé coffee is marketed as a global brand, even though advertising messages and product formulation vary to suit cultural differences.

Global Advertising Content: Standardization versus Adaptation

Communication experts generally agree that the overall requirements of effective communication and persuasion are fixed and do not vary from country to country. The same is true of the components of the communication process: The marketer is the source of the message; the message must be encoded, conveyed via the appropriate channel(s), and decoded by a member of the target audience. Communication takes place only when the intended meaning transfers from the source to the receiver. Four major difficulties can compromise an organization's attempt to communicate with customers in any location:

1. The message may not get through to the intended recipient. This problem may be the result of an advertiser's lack of knowledge about appropriate media for reaching certain types of audiences.
2. The message may reach the target audience but may not be understood or may even be misunderstood. This can be the result of an inadequate understanding of the target audience's level of sophistication or improper encoding.
3. The message may reach the target audience and may be understood but still may not compel the recipient to take action. This could result from a lack of cultural knowledge about a target audience.
4. The effectiveness of the message may be impaired by noise. *Noise*, in this case, is an external influence, such as competitive advertising, other sales personnel, or confusion at the receiving end, that can detract from the ultimate effectiveness of the communication.

The key question for global marketers is whether the *specific* advertising message and media strategy must be changed from region to region or country to country because of environmental requirements. Proponents of the "one world, one voice" approach to global advertising believe that the era of the global village has arrived and that tastes and preferences are converging worldwide. According to this standardization argument, people everywhere want the same products for the same reasons. This means that companies can achieve significant economies of scale by unifying advertising around the globe.

Advertisers who prefer the localized approach are skeptical of the global village argument. Instead, they assert that consumers still differ from country to country and must be reached by advertising tailored to their respective countries. Proponents of localization point out that most blunders occur because advertisers have failed to understand—and adapt to—foreign cultures. Ad industry veteran Nick Brien is currently CEO of Interpublic Group's McCann Worldgroup global agency network. As Brien observed in the late 1990s, the local/global debate does not necessarily have to be framed as an "either/or" proposition:

> As the potency of traditional media declines on a daily basis, brand building locally becomes more costly and international brand building becomes more cost effective. The challenge for advertisers and agencies is finding ads that work in different countries and cultures. At the same time as this global tendency, there is a growing local tendency. It's becoming increasingly important to understand the requirements of both.[6]

Nils Larsson, an external communications executive at IKEA, echoes Brien's view, but leans more toward the localized side of the debate:

> If we could find one message on a global basis it could be effective, but so far there are different needs in different countries. We have been in Sweden for 60 years and in China for only 4 or 5 so our feeling is that retail is local. It is important to take advantage of local humor, and the things on people's minds.[7]

---

[6] Meg Carter, "Think Globally, Act Locally," *Financial Times* (June 30, 1997), p. 12.
[7] Emma Hall and Normandy Madden, "IKEA Courts Buyers with Offbeat Ideas," *Advertising Age* (April 12, 2004), p. 1.

And consider this quote from Michael Conrad, the chief creative officer at Leo Burnett Worldwide:

> I can think of very few truly global ads that work. Brands are often at different stages around the world, and that means there are different advertising jobs to do.[8]

During the 1950s, the widespread opinion among advertising professionals was that effective international advertising required assigning responsibility for campaign preparation to a local agency. In the early 1960s, this idea of local delegation was challenged repeatedly. For example, Eric Elinder, head of a Swedish advertising agency, wrote: "Why should three artists in three different countries sit drawing the same electric iron and three copywriters write about what, after all, is largely the same copy for the same iron?"[9] Elinder argued that consumer differences among countries were diminishing and that he would more effectively serve a client's interest by putting top specialists to work devising a strong international campaign. The campaign would then be presented with insignificant modifications that mainly entailed translating the copy into language well suited for a particular country.

As the 1980s began, Pierre Liotard-Vogt, then-CEO of Nestlé, expressed similar views in an interview with *Advertising Age*:

> *Advertising Age:* Are food tastes and preferences different in each of the countries in which you do business?
>
> *Liotard-Vogt:* The two countries where we are selling perhaps the most instant coffee are England and Japan. Before the war they didn't drink coffee in those countries, and I heard people say that it wasn't any use to try to sell instant coffee to the English because they drink only tea and still less to the Japanese because they drink green tea and they're not interested in anything else.
>
> When I was very young, I lived in England and at that time, if you spoke to an Englishman about eating spaghetti or pizza or anything like that, he would just look at you and think that the stuff was perhaps food for Italians. Now on the corner of every road in London you find pizzerias and spaghetti houses.
>
> So I do not believe [preconceptions] about "national tastes." They are "habits," and they're not the same. If you bring the public a different food, even if it is unknown initially, when they get used to it, they will enjoy it too.
>
> To a certain extent we know that in the north they like a coffee milder and a bit acid and less roasted; in the south, they like it very dark. So I can't say that taste differences don't exist. But to believe that those tastes are set and can't be changed is a mistake.[10]

The "standardized versus localized" debate picked up tremendous momentum after the 1983 publication, noted in earlier chapters, of Professor Ted Levitt's *Harvard Business Review* article "The Globalization of Markets." Recently, global companies have embraced a technique known as **pattern advertising**. This is analogous to the concept of global product platforms discussed in Chapter 10. Representing a middle ground between 100 percent standardization and 100 percent adaptation, a pattern strategy calls for developing a basic pan-regional or global communication concept for which copy, artwork, or other elements can be adapted as required for individual country markets. For example, ads in a European print campaign for Boeing shared basic design elements, but the copy and the visual elements were localized on a country-by-country basis.

Much of the research on this issue has focused on the match between advertising messages and local culture. For example, Ali Kanso surveyed two different groups of advertising managers, those adopting localized approaches to advertising and those adopting standardized approaches. One finding was that managers who are attuned to cultural issues tend to prefer the localized approach, whereas managers less sensitive to cultural issues prefer a standardized approach.[11] Bruce Steinberg, ad sales director for MTV Europe, discovered that the people responsible for executing global campaigns locally can exhibit strong resistance to a global

---

[8] Vanessa O'Connell, "Exxon 'Centralizes' New Global Campaign," *The Wall Street Journal* (July 11, 2001), p. B6.

[9] Eric Elinder, "International Advertisers Must Devise Universal Ads, Dump Separate National Ones, Swedish Ad Man Avers," *Advertising Age* (November 27, 1961), p. 91.

[10] "A Conversation with Nestlé's Pierre Liotard-Vogt," *Advertising Age* (June 30, 1980), p. 31.

[11] Ali Kanso, "International Advertising Strategies: Global Commitment to Local Vision," *Journal of Advertising Research* 32, no. 1 (January–February 1992), pp. 10–14.

campaign. Steinberg reported that he sometimes had to visit as many as 20 marketing directors from the same company to get approval for a pan-European MTV ad.[12]

As Kanso correctly notes, the long-standing debate over advertising approaches will probably continue for years to come. Kanso's conclusion: What is needed for successful international advertising is a global commitment to local vision. In the final analysis, the decision of whether to use a global or a localized campaign depends on recognition by managers of the trade-offs involved. A global campaign will result in the substantial benefits of cost savings, increased control, and the potential creative leverage of a global **appeal**. It is also true that localized campaigns can focus on the most important attributes of a product or brand in each nation or culture.

As a practical matter, marketing managers may choose to run *both* global *and* local ads rather than adopt an "either/or" stance. For example, marketing and advertising managers at

Exhibit 13-2 These ads from DuPont Pioneer ran in the 2000s; they are a textbook example of pattern advertising. Overall, the layouts are similar. For example, the dominant visual elements appear on the left side, and the Better Bt™ brand name (in white sans serif type) is reversed out against a dark background. Additional elements common to the two ads are the trapezoid-shaped brand signature and the registered slogan "Technology That Yields.®" By contrast, the visuals themselves are entirely different, and the subheads and body copy have been localized, not simply translated.
Source: DuPont Pioneer.

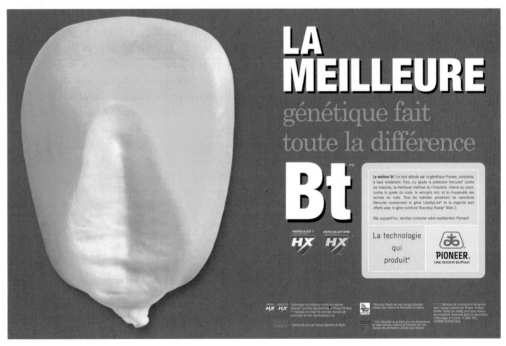

[12] Ken Wells, "Selling to the World: Global Ad Campaigns, After Many Missteps, Finally Pay Dividends," *The Wall Street Journal* (August 27, 1992), p. A1.

Pioneer Hi-Bred International frequently use both global and localized advertising executions. It is management's belief that some messages lend themselves to straight translation, whereas others need to be created in a way that best suits the farmers, marketplace, and style of the particular country or region. Of the ads shown in Exhibit 13-2, the top ad is for the United States; the ad at the bottom was created for Québec.

The question of *when* to use each approach depends on the product involved and a company's objectives in a particular market. The following generalizations can serve as guidelines:

- Standardized print campaigns can be used for industrial products or for high-tech consumer products. Examples: Apple's iPhone and iPad.
- Standardized print campaigns with a strong visual appeal often travel well. Example: Chivas Regal ("This is the Chivas Life"). Similarly, no text appears in the assembly instructions for IKEA furniture. Picture-based instructions can be used throughout the world without translation.
- TV commercials that use voiceovers instead of actors or celebrity endorsers speaking dialogue can use standardized visuals with translated copy for the voiceover. Examples: Gillette ("The best a man can get"); GE ("Imagination at work"); UPS ("We ♥ Logistics").

Advertising Agencies: Organizations and Brands

Advertising is a fast-paced business, and the ad agency world is fluid and dynamic. New agencies are formed, existing agencies are dismantled, and cross-border investments, spin-offs, joint ventures, and mergers and acquisitions are a fact of life. The industry is also very mobile, and executives and top talent move from one agency to another. The 20 largest global **advertising organizations** ranked by 2012 worldwide revenue are shown in Table 13-2. The key to understanding the table is the word *organization*; most of the firms identified in Table 13-2 are

TABLE 13-2 Top 20 Global Advertising Agency Companies

Organization and Headquarters Location	Worldwide Revenue 2012 ($ millions)
1. WPP Group (London)	$16,459
2. Omnicom Group (New York)	14,219
3. Publicis Groupe (Paris)	8,494
4. Interpublic Group of Cos. (New York)	6,956
5. Dentsu (Tokyo)	6,390
6. Havas (Puteaux, France)	2,287
7. Hakuhodo DY Holdings (Tokyo)	2,184
8. Epsilon (Irving, Texas)	1,223
9. MDC Partners (New York)	1,071
10. Experian Marketing Services (New York)	947
11. Acxiom (Little Rock, Arkansas)	823
12. Sapient Corp.'s SapientNitro (Boston)	772
13. IBM Corp.'s IBM Interactive (Chicago)	717
14. DJE Holdings (Chicago)	690
15. Cheil Worldwide (Seoul)	597
16. Asatsu-DK (Tokyo)	580
17. Aimia (Montréal)	486
18. Media Consulta (Berlin)	481
19. Grupo ABC (São Paulo)	402
20. Inventive Health Communications (New York)	388

Source: Adapted from "Agency Companies," *Advertising Age* (April 29, 2013), p. 34.

umbrella corporations or holding companies that include one or more "core" advertising agencies, as well as units specializing in direct marketing, marketing services, public relations, or research. A close inspection of the table reveals that IBM has gotten into the advertising business. Not surprisingly, IBM Interactive (ranked 13) is a digital specialist.

In 2013, the announcement that Omnicom and Publicis were merging rocked the advertising world. As shown in Figure 13-1, Publicis Omnicom Group will have worldwide revenues of more than $22 billion. This catapults the new company past WPP and makes it the world's largest advertising holding company. Both companies, in turn, own several global agency networks that represent a veritable "who's who" of global companies. For example, Omnicom is home to DDB Worldwide Communications Group, DDBO Worldwide, and TBWA Worldwide;

FIGURE 13-1

Omnicom Group, Publicis Group, and WPP: A Comparison

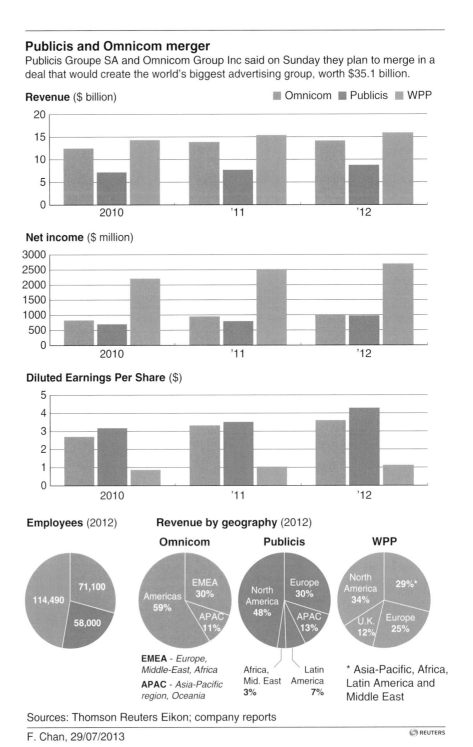

Publicis and Omnicom merger

Publicis Groupe SA and Omnicom Group Inc said on Sunday they plan to merge in a deal that would create the world's biggest advertising group, worth $35.1 billion.

Sources: Thomson Reuters Eikon; company reports

F. Chan, 29/07/2013

TABLE 13-3 Top 10 Advertising Agency Networks

Agency	Estimated Worldwide Revenue 2012 ($ millions)
1. Dentsu (Dentsu)	$3,577
2. Young & Rubicam Group (WPP)	3,400
3. McCann Worldgroup (Interpublic)	2,965
4. DDB Worldwide Communications Group (Omnicom)	2,655
5. Ogilvy & Mather (WPP)	2,413
6. BBDO Worldwide (Omnicom)	2,403
7. TBWA Worldwide (Omnicom)	1,797
8. Publicis Worldwide (Publicis)	1,524
9. Hakuhodo (Hakuhodo DY Holdings)	1,357
10. Havas Worldwide (Publicis)	1,327

Source: Adapted from "World's Largest Agency Networks," *Advertising Age* (April 29, 2013), p. 35.

its client roster includes Johnson & Johnson, Nissan, and Volkswagen. The key Publicis networks are Publicis Worldwide, Leo Burnett Worldwide, DigitasLBi, and Saatchi & Saatchi; clients include L'Oréal, Unilever, and Nestlé.

Table 13-3 presents the rankings of individual agencies (agency "brands") by 2012 worldwide revenue. Most of the agency brands identified in Table 13-3 are *full-service agencies*: In addition to creating advertising, they provide other services, such as market research, media buying, and direct marketing. The agencies listed in Table 13-3 are all owned by larger holding companies.

Selecting an Advertising Agency

Companies can create ads in-house, use an outside agency, or combine both strategies. For example, Chanel, Benetton, H&M, and Diesel rely on in-house marketing and advertising staffs for creative work; Coca-Cola has its own agency, Edge Creative, but also uses the services of outside agencies such as Leo Burnett. When one or more outside agencies are used, they can serve product accounts on a multicountry or even global basis. It is possible to select a local agency in each national market or an agency with both domestic and overseas offices. Like Coca-Cola, Levi Strauss and Polaroid also use local agencies.

Today, however, there is a growing tendency for Western clients to designate global agencies for product accounts to support the integration of the marketing and advertising functions; Japanese companies are less inclined to use this approach. For example, in 1995, Colgate-Palmolive consolidated its $500 million in global billings with Young & Rubicam. That same year, IBM consolidated its ad account with Ogilvy & Mather for the launch of the "Solutions for a small planet" global campaign. Similarly, Bayer AG consolidated most of its $300 million consumer products advertising with BBDO Worldwide; Bayer had previously relied on 50 agencies around the globe. Agencies are aware of this trend and are themselves pursuing international acquisitions and joint ventures to extend their geographic reach and their ability to serve clients on a global account basis. In an effort to remain competitive, many small, independent agencies in Europe, Asia, and the United States belong to the Transworld Advertising Agency Network (TAAN). TAAN enables member agencies to tap into worldwide resources that would not otherwise be available to them.

The following issues should be considered when selecting an advertising agency:

- *Company organization.* Companies that are decentralized typically allow managers at the local subsidiary to make ad agency selection decisions.
- *National responsiveness.* Is the global agency familiar with local culture and buying habits in a particular country, or should a local selection be made?
- *Area coverage.* Does the candidate agency cover all relevant markets?
- *Buyer perception.* What kind of brand awareness does the company want to project? If the product needs a strong local identification, it would be best to select a national agency.

→ **THE CULTURAL CONTEXT**

Smokers Fume About Limits on Tobacco Advertising

SYNC • THINK • LEARN

MyMarketingLab

According the World Health Organization (WHO), 5 million people die each year as a direct result of consuming tobacco products. A total of 172 countries are signatories to the Framework Convention on Tobacco Control (WHO FCTC), which aims to reduce global tobacco production as well as the consumption of tobacco products. The treaty entered into force in February 2005 (see Exhibit 13-3).

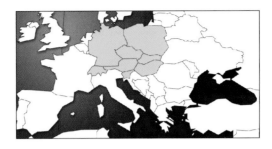

Even before the WHO FCTC, policymakers in various countries had taken steps to reduce the extent to which tobacco companies could promote their products and brands. In China, tobacco advertising has been banned from television and radio since 1994; the ban also extends to newspaper, magazine, and cinema ads. With a population of 1.3 billion people, including one-third of the world's smokers, China is a massive potential market for cigarette manufacturers at a time when Western markets are shrinking. The ban was part of China's first law regulating advertisements. The WHO asked Chinese leaders to launch antismoking campaigns and impose tougher controls on cigarette smuggling and higher taxes on domestic cigarette producers. China agreed to ratify the WHO FCTC.

The European Union (EU) spends about €16 million ($21 million) annually on antismoking initiatives. A tobacco ad ban proposal was introduced in mid-1991 with the aim of fulfilling the single-market rules of the Maastricht Treaty. The directive would have prohibited tobacco advertising on billboards as of July 2001; newspaper and magazine advertising was slated to end by 2002, with sports sponsorship banned by 2003 (such "world-level" sports as Formula One racing would be excluded until 2006). Not surprisingly, tobacco companies and advertising associations opposed the proposed ban. The European Commission justified the directive on the grounds that various countries had, or were considering, restrictions on tobacco advertising and that there was a need for common rules on cross-border trade.

Prior to the directive's implementation date, however, the German government took the issue to the European Court of Justice (ECJ). The Germans argued that the directive was illegal because tobacco advertising is a health issue; thus, the directive could be adopted only if the member states agreed unanimously. The EU's advocate general concurred with the German government. On October 5, 2000, the court ruled that the directive prohibiting tobacco ads should be annulled. A revised directive concerning cross-border tobacco advertising was adopted in December 2002.

However, the German government challenged the new directive at the ECJ on the grounds that it would restrict single-country print advertisements for local cigarette brands. Germany's argument, that most media operate on a local or national basis, was dismissed by the ECJ. Even as Germany set about complying with the ban, a retailer's association asserted that some 40,000 jobs would be lost across Germany after the ban was implemented.

For RJ Reynolds International, Philip Morris International, B.A.T., and other tobacco marketers, the receding threat of a pan-European ban on tobacco ads comes as welcome news. The industry spends between $600 million and $1 billion on advertising in the EU annually. An EU ban would have hurt them most in the countries where they compete with entrenched state tobacco monopolies, namely, France, Italy, and Spain.

Tobacco companies in Central Europe face the prospect of tougher marketing regulations as countries in the region work to meet requirements for entry into the EU. In Lithuania, authorities began to enforce the country's 3-year-old tobacco advertising ban on May 1, 2000; some newspapers printed blank pages in protest. Jurga Karmanoviene, media director for Saatchi & Saatchi Lithuania, interpreted the enforcement as evidence that the government is sending a signal that it is beginning to meet EU requirements. Similar developments are occurring in Poland, Hungary, Bulgaria, and Romania.

Sources: Enda Curran, "Australia Plans to Get Tougher on Tobacco," *The Wall Street Journal* (April 8, 2011), p. B2; Cailainn Barr, "Cigarette Factories Suck in €1.5 Million of Funds," *Financial Times* (December 2, 2010), p. 8; Rita Rubin, "Smoking Warnings More Graphic Elsewhere," *USA Today* (December 9, 2010), p. 13A; Farai Mutsaka, "Zimbabwe Enemies United on Tobacco," *The Wall Street Journal* (November 13–14, 2010), p. A8; Hugh Williamson, "Germany to Stub Out Most Tobacco Adverts," *Financial Times* (June 13, 2006); Geoffrey A. Fowler, "Treaty May Stub Out Cigarette Ads in China," *The Wall Street Journal* (December 2, 2003), pp. B1, B6; Joyce-Ann Gatsoulis, "EU Aspirants Shake Up Tobacco Marketing Scene," *Advertising Age International* (July 2000), p. 15; Tony Koenderman and Paul Meller, "EU Topples Tobacco Ad Rules," *Advertising Age* (October 9, 2000), pp. 4, 97; Juliana Koranteng, "EU Ad Ban on Tobacco Under Fire as Illegal," *Advertising Age* (July 10, 2000), pp. 4, 49; "Australia's Ad Ban Is Fought," *The New York Times* (June 7, 1994), p. 19; Marcus Brauchli, "China Passes Law in Move to Prohibit Ads for Tobacco," *The Wall Street Journal* (October 31, 1994), p. B10; Lili Cui, "Mass Media Boycott Tobacco Ads," *Beijing Review* (June 6, 1994), p. 8; "Tobacco Adverts: Fuming," *The Economist* (February 5, 1994), pp. 60–61.

Despite an unmistakable trend toward using global agencies to support global marketing efforts, companies with geocentric orientations will adapt to the global market requirements and select the best agency or agencies accordingly. Western agencies still find markets such as China and Japan to be very complex; Asian agencies find it just as difficult to establish a local agency presence in Western markets.

As noted later in the chapter, advertising professionals face escalating pressure to achieve new heights of creativity. Some critics of advertising complain that agencies sometimes try to create advertising that will win awards and generate acclaim and prestige rather than advertising

Exhibit 13-3 This anti-smoking billboard in Tehran is typical of efforts underway in many countries to curb consumption of tobacco products. An estimated 50,000 Iranians die each year from tobacco-related causes. In Iran, smoking is banned in all public places and on buses and other forms of public transportation.
Source: © Nick Cunard / Alamy.

that serves clients' needs. The search for fresh answers to promotion challenges has prompted some client companies to look to new sources for creative ideas. For example, McDonald's historically relied on American agencies for basic creative direction. However, Larry Light, McDonald's global marketing chief, staged a competition that included agencies from all over the world. A German agency devised the "I'm lovin' it" tagline.[13] Leo Burnett China's ideas included a hand signal for the McDonald's global campaign. As Light noted, "China just blew our minds. We didn't expect that kind of expression and joy. Our expectation was for more conservatism, much less individuality, and more caution."[14]

Creating Global Advertising

As suggested earlier in the discussion of the adaptation versus standardization debate, the *message* is at the heart of advertising. The particular message and the way it is presented will depend on the advertiser's objective. Is the ad designed to inform, entertain, remind, or persuade? Moreover, in a world characterized by information overload, ads must break through the clutter, grab the audience's attention, and linger in their minds. This requires developing an original and effective **creative strategy**, which is simply a statement or concept of what a particular message or campaign will say. Advertising agencies can be thought of as "idea factories"; in industry

---

[13] Erin White and Shirley Leung, "How Tiny German Shop Landed McDonald's," *The Wall Street Journal* (August 6, 2003), pp. B1, B3.
[14] Geoffrey A. Fowler, "Commercial Break: The Art of Selling," *Far Eastern Economic Review* (October 30, 2003), pp. 30–33.

parlance, the Holy Grail in creative strategy development is something known as the **big idea**. Legendary ad man John O'Toole defined the *big idea* as "that flash of insight that synthesizes the purpose of the strategy, joins the product benefit with consumer desire in a fresh, involving way, brings the subject to life, and makes the reader or audience stop, look, and listen."[15] In his book about Subaru of America, Randall Rothenberg describes the big idea in the following way:

> The Big Idea is easier to illustrate than define, and easier to illustrate by what it is not than by what it is. It is not a "position" (although the place a product occupies in the consumer's mind may be a part of it). It is not an "execution" (although the writing or graphic style of an ad certainly contributes to it). It is not a slogan (although a tagline may encapsulate it).
>
> The Big Idea is the bridge between an advertising strategy, temporal and worldly, and an image, powerful and lasting. The theory of the Big Idea assumes that average consumers are at best bored and more likely irrational when it comes to deciding what to buy.[16]

Some of the world's most memorable advertising campaigns have achieved success because they originate from an idea that is so big that the campaign offers opportunities for a seemingly unlimited number of new executions. Such a campaign is said to have *legs* because it can be used for long periods of time. The print campaign for Absolut Vodka is a perfect example: Over the course of two decades, Absolut's agency created hundreds of two-word puns on the brand name linked with various pictorial renderings of the distinctive bottle shape. Other campaigns based on big ideas include MSN ("Life's better with the butterfly") and MasterCard ("There are some things in life money can't buy"). In 2003, McDonald's executives launched a search for an idea big enough to be used in multiple country markets even as the company faced disapproval in some countries from consumers who link it to unpopular U.S. government policies (see Case 1-2).

The **advertising appeal** is the communications approach that relates to the motives of the target audience. For example, ads based on a **rational appeal** depend on logic and speak to the audience's intellect. Rational appeals are based on consumers' needs for information. The Pioneer Hi-Bred ads inform farmers about the attributes of pest-resistant seed varieties that will boost yields (see Exhibit 13-2). By contrast, ads using an **emotional appeal** may tug at the heartstrings or tickle the funny bone of the intended audience and evoke an emotional response that will direct purchase behavior. For example, a recent global campaign for IKEA, the Swedish home furnishings retailer, positioned houses as homes: "It's a place for love…a place for memories…a place for laughter. Home is the most important place in the world."[17]

The message elements in a particular ad will depend, in part, on which appeal is being employed. The **selling proposition** is the promise or claim that captures the reason for buying the product or the benefit that ownership confers. Because products are frequently at different stages in their life cycles in various national markets, and because of cultural, social, and economic differences that exist in those markets, the most effective appeal or selling proposition for a product may vary from market to market.

Effective global advertising may also require developing different presentations of the product's appeal or selling proposition. The way an appeal or proposition is presented is called the **creative execution**. In other words, there can be differences between *what* one says and *how* one says it. Ad agency personnel can choose from a variety of executions, including straight sell, scientific evidence, demonstration, comparison, testimonial, slice of life, animation, fantasy, and dramatization. The responsibility for deciding on the appeal, the selling proposition, and the appropriate execution lies with **creatives**, a term that applies to art directors and copywriters.

Art Direction and Art Directors

The visual presentation of an advertisement—the "body language"—is a matter of **art direction**. The individual with general responsibility for the overall look of an ad is known as an **art director**. This person chooses graphics, pictures, type styles, and other visual elements that

[15] John O'Toole, *The Trouble with Advertising* (New York: Random House, 1985), p. 131.

[16] Randall Rothenberg, *Where the Suckers Moon* (New York: Vintage Books, 1995), pp. 112–113.

[17] Suzanne Vranica, "IKEA to Tug at Heartstrings," *The Wall Street Journal* (September 18, 2007), p. B6.

→ EMERGING MARKETS BRIEFING BOOK

Localizing Ad Executions in China

MyMarketingLab SYNC • THINK • LEARN

A creative challenge presented to Ogilvy & Mather in China illustrates the relationship among creative strategy, appeal, and execution. The client, Coca-Cola's Fanta, wanted a national TV ad that would communicate to consumers that Fanta is an antidote to everyday pressures on Chinese youth. This was the overall creative strategy—in other words, what the message should say. What type of appeal would be appropriate? Not surprisingly, soft drinks lend themselves especially well to emotional appeals; that was the appeal Ogilvy & Mather preferred.

The next step was to choose a specific execution. Soft drink marketers often utilize slice-of-life and fantasy executions, usually injected with an element of fun or humor. As Jeff Delkin, Ogilvy's regional business director in Shanghai, notes, for a U.S. ad the creative strategy could be executed with a teen's fantasy or images of revenge on a mean teacher. However, in China it is not acceptable to challenge or undermine the position of authority figures. The completed ad shows that drinking Fanta can create a fun experience in a classroom. When a student opens a can of Fanta, oranges begin to rain down. The teacher catches the oranges and juggles them—much to the delight of the students.

Another example is a recent Nike campaign created by the AKQA digital agency. Nike's "Just Do It" ads typically showcase famous athletes and sports heroes and are legendary for their inspirational appeals. The Big Idea in much of Nike's advertising is presenting sports heroes—Michael Jordan, for example—as the product, rather than the shoes per se. The selling proposition is universal—Nike is a "cool" brand. However, to the Chinese, the sport of running is perceived differently than it is in the West. As Gavin Lum, strategy director at AKQA, explains, "It doesn't come with spectators like basketball and football, where you can show your stuff and how cool you are. There's no credibility earned through running." Compounding the problem is the fact that many of Asia's largest cities suffer from high levels of air pollution, and the streets are jammed with cars and other vehicles.

Nike's solution was to launch "Run For," a new video campaign on social media sites featuring runners discussing why they run. Viewers were encouraged to share their own stories about what motivates them. One Chinese woman explained her motivation by saying, "The city is always noisy and busy. This adds even more pressure to my day. I guess for me, running is about shutting out the noise." As Johan Vakidis, creative director at AKQA put it, "We needed to make sure it wasn't necessarily Nike telling people why running is good, so the whole entry point of the communication is really leveraging the stories of the few runners who are out there."

McDonald's used a localized campaign for the Chinese launch of the Quarter Pounder sandwich; ironically, the campaign came as the fast-food giant removed menu items such as an Asian-style chicken or beef wrap with rice created to appeal to Chinese tastes. Beef is considered a luxury, upscale item in China; beef also is perceived to boost energy and heighten sex appeal. In Chinese, the word *beef* connotes manliness, strength, and skill. Television commercials for the Quarter Pounder have sex appeal: They include close-ups of a woman's neck and mouth juxtaposed with images of fireworks and spraying water. The voiceover says, "You can feel it. Thicker. You can taste it. Juicier."

The McDonald's print ads also conveyed sexual innuendo. One execution featured a "beauty shot" of a Quarter Pounder with an extreme close-up of a woman's mouth in the background. The copy read, "Part of your body will be excited. You will feel 100 percent of the beef." As Jeffrey Schwartz, the head of McDonald's Chinese operations, explained, "Our customers are young, modern, and bilingual. If we're not edgy in communications, out front in technology, this consumer is going to blow right by us."

Sources: "Nike Faces Ultimate Marketing Challenge in China: Make Running Cool," *Advertising Age* (October 31, 2011), pp. 1, 56; Gordon Fairclough and Janet Adamy, "Sex, Skin, Fireworks, Licked Fingers—It's a Quarter Pounder Ad in China," *The Wall Street Journal* (September 21, 2006), pp. B1, B2; Geoffrey A. Fowler, "Commercial Break: The Art of Selling," *Far Eastern Economic Review* (October 30, 2003), p. 32.

---

appear in an ad. Some forms of visual presentation are universally understood. Revlon, for example, has used a French producer to develop television commercials in English and Spanish for use in international markets. These commercials are filmed in Parisian settings but communicate the universal appeals and specific benefits of Revlon products. By producing its ads in France, Revlon obtains effective television commercials at a much lower cost than it would pay for commercials produced in the United States. PepsiCo has used four basic commercials to communicate its advertising themes. The basic setting of young people having fun at a party or on a beach has been adapted to reflect the general physical environment and racial characteristics of North America, South America, Europe, Africa, and Asia. The music in these commercials has also been adapted to suit regional tastes, ranging from rock 'n' roll in North America to bossa nova in Latin America to the high life in Africa.

The global advertiser must make sure that visual executions are not extended inappropriately into certain markets. In the mid-1990s, Benetton's United Colors of Benetton campaign generated considerable controversy. The campaign appeared in scores of countries, primarily in print and on billboards. The art direction focused on striking, provocative interracial juxtapositions—a white hand and a black hand handcuffed together, for example. Another version of the campaign, depicting a black woman nursing a white baby, won advertising awards in France and Italy. However, because the image evoked the history of slavery in the United States, that particular creative execution was not used in the U.S. market.[18]

Copy and Copywriters

The words that are the spoken or written communication elements in advertisements are known as **copy**. **Copywriter**s are language specialists who develop the headlines, subheads, and body copy used in print advertising and the scripts containing the words that are delivered by spokespeople, actors, or hired voice talents in broadcast ads. As a general rule, copy should be relatively short and avoid slang and idioms. Languages vary in terms of the number of words required to convey a given message; thus the increased use of pictures and illustrations. Some global ads feature visual appeals that convey a specific message with minimal use of copy. Low literacy rates in many countries seriously compromise the use of print as a communications device and require greater creativity in the use of audio-oriented media.

It is important to recognize overlap in the use of languages in many areas of the world (e.g., the European Union (EU), Latin America, and North America). Capitalizing on this, global advertisers can realize economies of scale by producing advertising copy with the same language and message for these markets. The success of this approach will depend in part on avoiding unintended ambiguity in the ad copy. Then again, in some situations, ad copy must be translated into the local language. Translating copy has been the subject of great debate in advertising circles. Advertising slogans often present the most difficult translation problems. The challenge of encoding and decoding slogans and taglines in different national and cultural contexts can lead to unintentional errors. For example, the Asian version of Pepsi's "Come alive" tagline was rendered as a call to bring ancestors back from the grave.

Advertising executives may elect to prepare new copy for a foreign market in the language of the target country or to translate the original copy into the target language. A third option is to leave some (or all) copy elements in the original (home-country) language. In choosing from these alternatives, the advertiser must consider whether the intended foreign audience will be able to receive and comprehend a translated message. Anyone with knowledge of two or more languages realizes that the ability to think in another language facilitates accurate communication. For a message to be understood correctly after it is received, one must understand the connotations of words, phrases, and sentence structures, as well as their translated meaning.

The same principle applies to advertising—perhaps to an even greater degree. A copywriter who can think in the target language and understands the consumers in the target country will be able to create the most effective appeals, organize the ideas, and craft the specific language, especially if colloquialisms, idioms, or humor are involved. For example, in southern China, McDonald's is careful not to advertise prices with multiple occurrences of the number four. The reason is simple: In Cantonese, the pronunciation of the word *four* is similar to that of the word *death*.[19] In its efforts to develop a global brand image, Citicorp discovered that translations of its slogan "Citi never sleeps" conveyed that Citibank had a sleeping disorder such as insomnia. Company executives decided to retain the slogan but use English throughout the world.[20]

Cultural Considerations

Knowledge of cultural diversity, especially the symbolism associated with cultural traits, is essential for creating advertising. Local country managers can share important information, such as when to use caution in advertising creativity. Use of colors and man–woman relationships can often be stumbling blocks. For example, in Japan intimate scenes between men and women are

[18] Janet L. Borgerson, Jonathan E. Schroeder, Martin Escudero Magnusson, and Frank Magnusson, "Corporate Communication, Ethics, and Operational Identity: A Case Study of Benetton," *Business Ethics: A European Review* 18, no. 3 (July 2009), pp. 209–223.

[19] Jeanne Whalen, "McDonald's Cooks Worldwide Growth," *Advertising Age International* (July–August 1995), p. I4.

[20] Stephen E. Frank, "Citicorp's Big Account Is at Stake as It Seeks a Global Brand Name," *The Wall Street Journal* (January 9, 1997), p. B6.

in bad taste; they are outlawed in Saudi Arabia. Veteran adman John O'Toole offers the following insights to global advertisers:

> Transplanted American creative people always want to photograph European men kissing women's hands. But they seldom know that the nose must never touch the hand or that this rite is reserved solely for married women. And how do you know that the woman in the photograph is married? By the ring on her left hand, of course. Well, in Spain, Denmark, Holland, and Germany, Catholic women wear the wedding ring on the right hand.
>
> When photographing a couple entering a restaurant or theater, you show the woman preceding the man, correct? No. Not in Germany and France. And this would be laughable in Japan. Having someone in a commercial hold up his hand with the back of it to you, the viewer, and the fingers moving toward him should communicate "come here." In Italy it means "good-bye."[21]

Ads that strike viewers in some countries as humorous or irritating may not necessarily be perceived that way by viewers in other countries. American ads make frequent use of spokespeople and direct product comparisons; they use logical arguments to try to appeal to the reason of audiences. Japanese advertising is more image oriented and appeals to audience sentiment. In Japan, what is most important frequently is not what is stated explicitly, but rather what is implied. Nike's U.S. advertising is legendary for its irreverent, "in-your-face" style and relies heavily on celebrity sports endorsers such as Michael Jordan. In other parts of the world, where soccer is the top sport, some Nike ads are considered to be in poor taste, and its spokespeople have less relevance. Nike has responded by adjusting its approach; as Geoffrey Frost, former director of global advertising at Nike, noted over a decade ago, "We have to root ourselves in the passions of other countries. It's part of our growing up."[22] Some American companies have canceled television ads created for the Latin American market portraying racial stereotypes that were offensive to persons of color. Nabisco, Goodyear, and other companies are also being more careful about the shows during which they buy airtime; some very popular Latin American programs feature content that exploits class, race, and ethnic differences.[23]

Standards vary widely with regard to the use of sexually explicit or provocative imagery. Partial nudity and same-sex couples are frequently seen in ads in Latin America and Europe. In the U.S. market, however, network television decency standards and the threat of boycotts by conservative consumer activists constrain advertisers. Some industry observers note a paradoxical situation in which the programs shown on U.S. TV are frequently racy, but the ads that air during those shows are not. As Marcio Moreira, worldwide chief creative officer at the McCann-Erickson agency, noted, "Americans want titillation in entertainment but when it comes to advertising they stop being viewers and become consumers and critics."[24] However, it is certainly not the case that anything goes outside the United States. Women in Monterrey, Mexico, have complained about billboards for the Playtex unit of Sara Lee Corporation that featured supermodel Eva Herzegova wearing a Wonderbra. The campaign was created by a local agency, Perez Munoz Publicidad. Playtex responded by covering up the model on the billboards in some Mexican cities. French Connection UK made waves in the United States with print ads that prominently featured the British company's initials, that is, FCUK. Public outcry prompted the company to tone down the ads by spelling out the name.

Food is the product category most likely to elicit cultural sensitivity. Thus, marketers of food and food products must be alert to the need to localize their advertising. A good example of this is the effort by H. J. Heinz Company to develop the overseas market for ketchup. More than 20 years ago, marketing managers at Heinz formulated a strategy that called for adapting both

[21] John O'Toole, *The Trouble with Advertising* (New York: Random House, 1985), pp. 209–210.

[22] Roger Thurow, "Shtick Ball: In Global Drive, Nike Finds Its Brash Ways Don't Always Pay Off," *The Wall Street Journal* (May 5, 1997), p. A10.

[23] Leon E. Wynter, "Global Marketers Learn to Say 'No' to Bad Ads," *The Wall Street Journal* (April 1, 1998), p. B1.

[24] Melanie Wells and Dottie Enrico, "U.S. Admakers Cover It Up; Others Don't Give a Fig Leaf," *USA Today* (June 27, 1997), pp. B1, B2.

the product and the advertising to target country tastes.[25] In Greece, for example, ads show ketchup pouring over pasta, eggs, and cuts of meat. In Japan, they instruct Japanese homemakers on using ketchup as an ingredient in Western-style food such as omelets, sausages, and pasta. Barry Tilley, London-based general manager of Heinz's Western Hemisphere trading division, says Heinz uses focus groups to determine what foreign consumers want in the way of taste and image. Americans like a sweet ketchup, but Europeans prefer a spicier, more piquant variety. Significantly, Heinz's foreign marketing efforts are most successful when the company quickly adapts to local cultural preferences. In Sweden, the made-in-America theme is so muted in Heinz's ads that "Swedes don't realize Heinz is American. They think it is German because of the name," says Tilley. In contrast to this, American themes still work well in Germany. Kraft and Heinz are trying to outdo each other with ads featuring strong American images. In one of Heinz's TV ads, American football players in a restaurant become very angry when the 12 steaks they ordered arrive without ketchup. The ad ends happily, of course, with plenty of Heinz ketchup to go around.[26]

Much academic research has been devoted to the impact of culture on advertising. For example, Tamotsu Kishii identified seven characteristics that distinguish Japanese from American creative strategy:

1. Indirect rather than direct forms of expression are preferred in the messages. This avoidance of directness in expression is pervasive in all types of communication among the Japanese, including their advertising. Many television ads do not mention what is desirable about the brand in use and let the audience judge for themselves.
2. There is often little relationship between ad content and the advertised product.
3. Only brief dialogue or narration is used in television commercials, with minimal explanatory content. In the Japanese culture, the more one talks, the less others will perceive him or her as trustworthy or self-confident. A 30-second advertisement for young menswear shows five models in varying and seasonal attire, ending with a brief statement from the narrator: "Our life is a fashion show!"
4. Humor is used to create a bond of mutual feelings. Rather than slapstick, humorous dramatizations involve family members, neighbors, and office colleagues.
5. Famous celebrities appear as close acquaintances or everyday people.
6. Priority is placed on company trust rather than product quality. Japanese tend to believe that if the firm is large and has a good image, the quality of its products should also be outstanding.
7. The product name is impressed on the viewer with short, 15-second commercials.[27]

Green, Cunningham, and Cunningham conducted a cross-cultural study to determine the extent to which consumers of different nationalities use the same criteria to evaluate soft drinks and toothpaste. Their subjects were college students from the United States, France, India, and Brazil. Compared to the French and Indian respondents, the U.S. respondents placed more emphasis on the subjective, as opposed to the functional, product attributes. The Brazilian respondents appeared even more concerned with the subjective attributes than the Americans were. The authors concluded that advertising messages should not use the same appeal for these countries if the advertiser is concerned with communicating the most important attributes of its product in each market.[28]

[25] Gary Levin, "Ads Going Global," *Advertising Age* (July 22, 1991), pp. 4, 42.
[26] Gabriella Stern, "Heinz Aims to Export Taste for Ketchup," *The Wall Street Journal* (November 20, 1992), p. B1.
[27] C. Anthony di Benedetto, Mariko Tamate, and Rajan Chandran, "Developing Creative Advertising Strategy for the Japanese Marketplace," *Journal of Advertising Research* (January–February 1992), pp. 39–48. A number of studies have compared ad content in different parts of the world, including Mary C. Gilly, "Sex Roles in Advertising: A Comparison of Television Advertisements in Australia, Mexico, and the United States," *Journal of Marketing* (April 1988), pp. 75–85; and Marc G. Weinberger and Harlan E. Spotts, "A Situation View of Information Content in TV Advertising in the U.S. and UK," *Journal of Advertising* 53 (January 1989), pp. 89–94.
[28] Robert T. Green, William H. Cunningham, and Isabella C. M. Cunningham, "The Effectiveness of Standardized Global Advertising," *Journal of Advertising* (Summer 1975), pp. 25–30.

Global Media Decisions

The next issue facing advertisers is which medium or media to use when communicating with target audiences. Media availability can vary from country to country. Some companies use virtually the entire spectrum of available media; Coca-Cola is a good example. Other companies prefer to utilize one or two media categories. In some instances, the agency that creates the advertising also makes recommendations about media placement; however, many advertisers use the services of specialized media planning and buying organizations. Omnicom's OMD Worldwide, the Starcom Media Vest Group unit of Publicis, and WPP's MindShare Worldwide are three of the top media specialists.

The available alternatives can be broadly categorized as print media, electronic media, and other. Print media range from local daily and weekly newspapers to magazines and business publications with national, regional, or international audiences. Electronic media include broadcast television, cable television, radio, and the Internet. Additionally, advertisers may utilize various forms of outdoor, transit, and direct mail advertising. Globally, media decisions must take into account country-specific regulations. For example, France bans retailers from advertising on television.

Global Advertising Expenditures and Media Vehicles

Each year, more money is spent on advertising in the United States than anywhere else in the world. As noted previously, U.S. ad spending in 2012 totaled $160 billion. To put this figure in context, consider that 2012 ad spending in Japan, the second-largest advertising market, totaled approximately $52 billion. In addition, as one might expect, the largest per capita ad spending occurs in highly developed countries. However, much of the current growth in advertising expenditures—as much as one-third—is occurring in the BRICS countries. Russia alone represents a $9.7 billion advertising market; ad expenditures are growing at about 13 percent annually, compared with a rate between 3.5 percent and 4.5 percent in the United States and Europe. Top advertisers in Russia include Procter & Gamble, L'Oréal, PepsiCo, Nestlé, and Mars.

Worldwide, television is the number 1 advertising medium; with estimated ad revenues of $163 billion in 2012, television captured slightly more than 40 percent of global expenditures. Serbia leads the world in terms of watching the most television; daily viewership is 5 hours, 39 minutes each day. Macedonia ranks second, with 5:19; the United States is third with 5:04.[29] Newspapers rank second on a worldwide basis, accounting for about 27 percent of advertising spending. However, media consumption patterns vary from country to country. In developed countries, many households have more than one TV. By contrast, in China, only about 16 percent of households have a TV. Also, television is the number 1 medium in both the United States and Japan; by contrast, newspapers are the leading medium in Germany; television ranks second.

Television is also important in the Latin American market. Puerto Rico, Mexico, and Venezuela are all in the top 25 in terms of daily per capita viewership. In Brazil, expenditures on television advertising are nearly three times higher than those for newspapers. The availability of media and the conditions affecting media buys also vary greatly around the world. In Mexico, an advertiser that can pay for a full-page ad may get the front page, whereas in India, paper shortages may require booking an ad 6 months in advance. In some countries, especially those where the electronic media are government owned, television and radio stations can broadcast only a restricted number of advertising messages. In Saudi Arabia, no commercial television advertising was allowed prior to May 1986; currently, ad content and visual presentations are restricted.

Worldwide, radio continues to be a less important advertising medium than print and television. However, in countries where advertising budgets are limited, radio's enormous reach can provide a cost-effective means of communicating with a large consumer market. Also, radio can be effective in countries where literacy rates are low. One clear trend that is gaining traction throughout the world: Spending on CRM and Internet advertising is gaining ground at the expense of TV and print.

"The U.S. online advertising market is much bigger than Europe's, but it is a crowded market and the room for growth is shrinking. In Europe, online advertising is growing much faster and portals like Yahoo want to tap into that."[30]

—Jupiter Research

---

[29] "Global Media Habits: A TV in Every House," *Advertising Age* (October 3, 2011), p. 8.
[30] Dan Bilefsky, "Yahoo Tightens Control in Europe and Asia," *The New York Times* (November 8, 2005), p. C18.

Media Decisions

The availability of television, newspapers, and other forms of broadcast and print media varies around the world. Moreover, patterns of media consumption differ from country to country as well. In many developed countries, for example, newspapers are experiencing circulation and readership declines as consumers devote more time to new media options such as the Internet. In India, by contrast, print media are enjoying a revival as redesigned newspaper formats and glossy supplements lure a new generation of readers. India is home to nearly 300 daily newspapers, including the *Times of India* and the *Hindustan Times*; the price per copy is only 5 rupees—about 10 cents. Additional critical factors in India's media environment include the lack of penetration by cable television and the fact that only about 4 million Indians currently subscribe to an Internet service.[31] By contrast, billboards are the medium of choice in Moscow. As Thomas L. Friedman has pointed out, Moscow is a city built for about 30,000 cars; during the past decade, the number of cars has grown from 300,000 to 3 million.[32] The result is massive traffic jams and commuting delays; thus, affluent businesspeople spend hours in traffic and have little time to read the newspaper or watch TV.

Even when media availability is high, its use as an advertising vehicle may be limited. For example, in Europe, television advertising is very limited in Denmark, Norway, and Sweden. Regulations concerning content of commercials vary; Sweden bans advertising to children younger than 12 years of age. In 2001, when Sweden headed the EU, its policymakers tried to extend the ban to the rest of Europe. Although the effort failed, Sweden retained its domestic ban. This helps explain why annual spending on print media in Sweden is three times the annual spending for television.[33]

As noted earlier, cultural considerations often affect the presentation of the advertising message. One study comparing the content of magazine advertisements in the United States with those in the Arab world found the following:

- People are depicted less often in Arabic magazine ads. However, when people do appear, there is no difference in the extent to which women are depicted. Women appearing in ads in Arab magazines wear long dresses; their presence generally is relevant to the advertised product.
- U.S. ads tend to have more information content; by contrast, brevity is considered a virtue in the Arab world. Context plays a greater role in interpreting an Arab message than in the United States.
- U.S. ads contain more price information, and are more likely to include comparative appeals than Arabic ads.[34]

Public Relations and Publicity

In 2011, the Public Relations Society of America (PRSA) launched Public Relations Defined, an initiative to update the definition of public relations. The PRSA sought input from industry professionals, academics, and members of the general public. More than 900 definitions were submitted; according to the winning entry, **public relations (PR)** is a "strategic communication process that builds mutually beneficial relationships between organizations and their publics."[35]

[31] John Larkin, "Newspaper Nirvana? 300 Dailies Court India's Avid Readers," *The Wall Street Journal* (May 5, 2006), pp. B1, B3.

[32] Thomas L. Friedman, "The Oil-Addicted Ayatollahs," *The New York Times* (February 2, 2007), p. A19.

[33] John Tylee, "EC Permits Sweden to Continue Child Ad Ban," *Advertising Age* (July 11, 2003), p. 6.

[34] Fahad S. Al-Olayan and Kiran Karande, "A Content Analysis of Magazine Advertisements from the United States and the Arab World," *Journal of Advertising* 29, no. 3 (Fall 2000), pp. 69–82. See also Mushtag Luqmani, Ugur Yavas, and Zahir Quraeshi, "Advertising in Saudi Arabia: Content and Regulation," *International Marketing Review* 6, no. 1 (1989), pp. 59–72.

[35] Stuart Elliot, "Public Relations Defined, After an Energetic Public Discussion," *The New York Times* (March 2, 2012), p. B2.

Exhibit 13-4 Because of its size and presence in more than 200 countries, the Coca-Cola Company is often the target of antiglobalization protests. The Indian villagers shown here were protesting the company's water consumption in areas severely affected by drought. Coca-Cola chairman and CEO E. Neville Isdell has responded to this type of negative publicity by guiding the company toward greater transparency in its global operations. Isdell also wants to make sure that the public perceives Coke as a global leader in corporate social responsibility. To do this, he is forging relationships and partnerships with nongovernmental organizations (NGOs).
Source: RAVEENDRAN/AFP/Getty Images.

Public relations personnel are responsible for fostering goodwill, understanding, and acceptance among a company's various constituents and stakeholders. Along with advertising, PR is one of four variables in the promotion mix. One of the tasks of the PR practitioner is to generate favorable **publicity**. By definition, publicity is communication about a company or product for which the company does not pay. (In the PR world, publicity is sometimes referred to as *earned media*, and advertising and promotions are known as *unearned media*.)

PR professionals also play a key role in responding to unflattering media reports, crises, or controversies that arise because of a company's activities in different parts of the globe. In such instances, especially if a company's reputation is on the line, it is good PR practice to respond promptly and provide the public with facts (see Exhibit 13-4). The basic tools of PR include news releases, newsletters, media kits, press conferences, tours of plants and other company facilities, articles in trade or professional journals, company publications and brochures, TV and radio talk show interviews, special events, social media, and corporate Web sites.

Caterpillar's activities in China are a textbook example of the power of public relations. The Chinese market for industrial machinery is booming because the government is spending billions of dollars on infrastructure improvements. Caterpillar hopes to sell giant wheel tractor-scrapers that are more efficient to operate than the hydraulic excavators and trucks currently in use. However, a business intelligence team that contacted 100 customers and dealers across China found low levels of awareness and acceptance of Caterpillar's machines. Survey respondents were not persuaded by data from other countries about the machines' cost savings. To gain traction, Mike Cai, Caterpillar's man in China, staged product demonstrations—road shows—around the country. "Word-of-mouth is the best form of publicity for the construction industry in China," he says. Scott Kronick, president for Ogilvy Public Relations Worldwide/China, agrees. "Chinese customers are being introduced to a lot of products and services for the first time, so you can't advertise something that's intangible," he said. Reporters from the local and national media were invited to the demonstrations; in one instance, China Central Television ran a story that featured a clip of the tractor-scraper at work.[36]

Senior executives at some companies relish the opportunity to generate publicity. For example, Benetton's striking print and outdoor ad campaigns keyed to the "United Colors of Benetton" generate both controversy and widespread media attention. Richard Branson, the flamboyant founder of the Virgin Group, is a one-man publicity machine. His personal exploits as a hot-air balloon pilot have earned him and his company a great deal of free ink. The company does employ traditional media advertising; however, as Will Whitehorn, Virgin's head of brand development and corporate affairs, noted, "PR is the heart of the company. If we do things badly, it will reflect badly on the image of the brand more than most other companies." At Virgin, Whitehorn has said, "Advertising is a subset of PR, not the other way around."[37]

Not surprisingly, social media's importance as a PR tool is growing at many companies. PR professionals point to increasing consumer "engagement with the brand" on Facebook, Twitter, and other Web 2.0 platforms. Consider, for example, that as of mid-2013, Adidas Originals had 20 million Facebook "likes," and Heineken had 13 million. FedEx's "I am FedEx" Facebook page features "Team Member Stories from FedEx." This communication channel allows the company's 285,000 employees to share stories about their work and home lives. Joe Becker, an executive at Ketchum Digital, believes that the conversations that take place on Facebook can be leveraged as content that can be used to enhance the FedEx brand. He says, "The primary goal is about enabling employees to tell and create stories, which influences public opinion about the brand."[38] Another advantage: Because visitors to social media sites can immediately click on a link to an e-commerce site, it is easy to track return on investment (ROI). We discuss social media in more detail in Chapter 15.

As noted earlier, a company exerts complete control over the content of its advertising and pays for message placement in the media. However, the media typically receive many more press releases and other PR materials than they can use. Generally speaking, a company has little control over when, or if, a news story runs; nor can the company directly control the spin, slant, or tone of the story. To compensate for this lack of control, many companies utilize **corporate advertising**, which despite the name, is generally considered part of the PR function. As with "regular" advertising, a company or organization identified in the ad pays for corporate advertising. However, unlike regular advertising, the objective of corporate advertising is not to generate demand by informing, persuading, entertaining, or reminding customers. Rather, in the context of integrated marketing communications, corporate advertising is often used to call attention to the company's other communications efforts. In addition to the examples discussed in the following pages, Table 13-4 summarizes several instances of global publicity involving well-known firms.

Image advertising enhances the public's perception of a company; creates goodwill; or announces a major change, such as a merger, acquisition, or divestiture. In 2008, for example, Anheuser-Busch InBev placed full-page ads in the business press to announce their merger. Global companies frequently use image advertising in an effort to present themselves as good corporate citizens in foreign countries. BASF uses advertising to raise awareness about the company's innovative products that are used in the automotive, home construction, and pharmaceutical industries. Similarly, a campaign from Daimler AG was designed to raise awareness

---

[36] Jason Leow, "In China, Add a Caterpillar to the Dog and Pony Show," *The Wall Street Journal* (December 10, 2007), p. B1.

[37] Elena Bowes, "Virgin Flies in Face of Conventions," *Ad Age International* (January 1997), p. I.

[38] Matthew Schwartz, "Metrics of Success: PR's New Numbers," *Advertising Age* (November 29, 2010), p. S14.

TABLE 13-4 Negative Publicity Affecting Global Marketers

Company or Brand (home country)	Nature of Publicity
Boeing (United States)	Fires caused by faulty lithium-ion batteries on the new 787 Dreamliner resulted in all aircraft being grounded until the problem could be resolved.
Walmart (United States)	Fires and collapsed buildings at garment factories in Bangladesh revived concerns about the global supply chain and the human cost of low-price goods.
BP (Great Britain)	Massive oil spill in the Gulf of Mexico off the coast of Louisiana.
Apple (United States)	Suicides by employees at Chinese supplier Foxconn Technologies; injuries due to exposure to toxic chemicals at plant that makes glass screens for iPhone.
Google (United States)	Self-censorship of Chinese search engine.
Nike (United States)	Since the mid-1990s, Nike has been responding to the criticism that its subcontractors operate factories in which sweatshop conditions prevail. Filmmaker Michael Moore featured an interview with Nike CEO Phil Knight in the antiglobalization documentary *The Big One*.

of the company's eco-friendly electric drive vehicles. (see Exhibit 13-5). In **advocacy advertising**, a company presents its point of view on a particular issue. Consider the following examples of advocacy advertising:

- Japan's Fuji Photo Film asked its advertising agency to develop an advocacy campaign for the United States. At the time, Fuji was embroiled in a trade dispute with Kodak. Fuji had also invested more than $1 billion in U.S. production facilities and had won a long-term photofinishing contract with Walmart. The campaign was designed to appeal both to

Exhibit 13-5 Daimler AG is one of the world's leading producers of automobiles with alternative drive systems. This corporate image advertisement does not provide information about a specific car model; rather, it is about the company's leadership in developing electric passenger cars and commercial vehicles that allow for emission-free driving.

The ad positions Daimler both as an innovator and as a responsible corporate citizen. Because the message and the associated image have worldwide appeal, this ad lends itself to an extension strategy.
Source: Courtesy of Daimler Corporation.

Walmart and to the giant retailer's customers; as a Walmart spokesman said, "We've long said we buy American when we can. The more people understand how American Fuji is, the better."[39]

- In 1995, the American International Automobile Dealers Association (AIADA) hired Hill & Knowlton to create a PR campaign designed to convince then-President Bill Clinton, Congress, the media, and the general public that a proposed plan to impose a 100 percent tariff on 13 luxury cars was ill-advised. The campaign's central message was that foreign automakers account for a good number of U.S. jobs that would be jeopardized if the sanctions were enacted. Nissan and other companies also sent position papers and information packets to dealers and the media. Interviews with representatives from auto dealers were carried by both print and electronic media. Within a few weeks, the Clinton administration announced that the United States and Japan had reached an agreement. No sanctions were imposed, and the AIADA was able to claim an important PR victory.

Sometimes a company generates publicity simply by going about the business of global marketing activities. As noted in Table 13-4, Nike and other marketers have received a great deal of negative publicity regarding alleged sweatshop conditions in factories run by subcontractors. Today, Nike's PR team is doing a better job of counteracting the criticism by effectively communicating the positive economic impact Nike has had on the nations where it manufactures its sneakers (see Exhibit 13-6).

Any company that is increasing its activities outside the home country can utilize PR personnel as boundary spanners between the company and employees, unions, stockholders, customers, the media, financial analysts, governments, or suppliers. Many companies have their own in-house PR staff. Companies may also choose to engage the services of an outside PR firm. During the past few years, some of the large advertising holding companies discussed previously have acquired PR agencies. For example, Omnicom Group bought Fleishman-Hillard, WPP Group acquired Canada's Hill & Knowlton, and Interpublic Group bought Golin/Harris International. Other PR firms, including the London-based Shandwick

Exhibit 13-6 When making public appearances, Nike chairman Phil Knight and other executives frequently defend labor practices and policies in the Asian factories where the company's shoes are made. In the late 1990s, a protester filed a lawsuit against Nike alleging that the company's public assertions about working conditions constituted false advertising. Attorneys for Nike countered that statements made by executives are part of a public policy debate and therefore are protected by the First Amendment. After the California Supreme Court ruled against Nike, the company appealed. In 2003, the U.S. Supreme Court heard the case as protesters gathered outside. The Court later dismissed Nike's appeal, and the case was sent back to California.
Source: Chuck Kennedy/ Newscom.

[39] Wendy Bounds, "Fuji Considers National Campaign to Develop All-American Image," *The Wall Street Journal* (October 1, 1996), p. B8.

PLC and Edelman Public Relations Worldwide, are independent. Several independent PR firms in the United Kingdom, Germany, Italy, Spain, Austria, and the Netherlands have joined together in a network known as Globalink. The purpose of the network is to provide members with various forms of assistance such as press contacts, event planning, literature design, and suggestions for tailoring global campaigns to local needs in a particular country or region.[40]

The Growing Role of PR in Global Marketing Communications

PR professionals with international responsibility must go beyond media relations and serve as more than a company mouthpiece; they are called upon to simultaneously build consensus and understanding, create trust and harmony, articulate and influence public opinion, anticipate conflicts, and resolve disputes.[41] As companies become more involved in global marketing and the globalization of industries continues, company management must recognize the value of international PR. Today the industry faces a challenging business environment with a mixture of threats and opportunities. Many PR firms saw revenues and profits decline in 2009 as a result of the global recession. At the same time, the recession also increased the demand for PR services. Edelman Worldwide chief Richard Edelman recently noted that PR's status as a key input to corporate decision making has been improving. Edelman says, "We used to be the tail on the dog."[42]

Europe has a long-standing PR tradition; for example, the Deutsche Public Relations Gesellschaft (DPRG) recently commemorated its 50th anniversary. Many European PR practitioners and trade associations, including the DPRG, are members of the Confédération Européenne des Relations Publiques (www.cerp.org). The UK-based International Public Relations Association (www.ipra.org) has an Arabic Web site, an illustration of the way PR's importance is recognized in all parts of the world. An important factor fueling the growth of international PR is increased governmental relations between countries. Governments, organizations, and societies are dealing with broad-based issues of mutual concern, such as the aftermath of the recent global recession, trade relations, the environment, and world peace. The technology-driven communication revolution that has ushered in the Information Age makes public relations a profession with truly global reach. Smartphones, broadband Internet connectivity, social media, satellite links, and other channel innovations allow PR professionals to be in contact with media virtually anywhere in the world.

In spite of these technological advances, PR professionals must still build good personal working relationships with journalists and other media representatives, as well as with leaders of other primary constituencies. Therefore, strong interpersonal skills are needed. One of the most basic concepts of the practice of PR is to know the audience. For the global PR practitioner, this means knowing the audiences in both the home country and the host country or countries. Specific skills needed include the ability to communicate in the language of the host country and familiarity with local customs. A PR professional who is unable to speak the language of the host country will be unable to communicate directly with a huge portion of an essential audience. Likewise, the PR professional working outside the home country must be sensitive to nonverbal communication issues in order to maintain good working relationships with host-country nationals. Commenting on the complexity of the international PR professional's job, one expert noted that, in general, audiences are "increasingly more unfamiliar and more hostile, as well as more organized and powerful…more demanding, more skeptical and more diverse." International PR practitioners can play an important role as "bridges over the shrinking chasm of the global village."[43]

---

[40] Joe Mullich, "European Firms Seek Alliances for Global PR," *Business Marketing* 79 (August 1994), pp. 4, 31.

[41] Karl Nessman, "Public Relations in Europe: A Comparison with the United States," *Public Relations Journal* 21, no. 2 (Summer 1995), p. 154.

[42] "Good News: Other Firms' Suffering Has Bolstered the PR Business," *Economist* (January 14, 2010).

[43] Larissa A. Grunig, "Strategic Public Relations Constituencies on a Global Scale," *Public Relations Review* 18, no. 2 (Summer 1992), pp. 127–136.

How PR Practices Differ Around the World

Cultural traditions, social and political contexts, and economic environments in specific countries can affect public relations practices. As noted earlier in the chapter, the mass media and the written word are important vehicles for information dissemination in many industrialized countries. In developing countries, however, the best way to communicate might be through the gong man, the town crier, the market square, or the chief's courts. In Ghana, dance, songs, and storytelling are important communication channels. In India, where half of the population cannot read, issuing press releases will not be the most effective way to communicate.[44] In Turkey, the practice of PR is thriving in spite of that country's reputation for harsh treatment of political prisoners. Although the Turkish government still asserts absolute control as it has for generations, corporate PR and journalism are allowed to flourish so that Turkish organizations can compete globally.

Even in industrialized countries, PR practices differ. In the United States, the hometown news release comprises much of the news in a small, local newspaper. In Canada, in contrast, large metropolitan population centers have combined with Canadian economic and climatic conditions to thwart the emergence of a local press. The dearth of small newspapers means that the practice of sending out hometown news releases is almost nonexistent.[45] In the United States, PR is increasingly viewed as a separate management function. In Europe, this perspective has not been widely accepted; PR professionals are viewed as part of the marketing function rather than as distinct and separate specialists in a company. In Europe, fewer colleges and universities offer courses and degree programs in PR than in the United States. Also, European coursework in PR is more theoretical; in the United States, PR programs are often part of mass communication or journalism schools, and there is more emphasis on practical job skills.

A company that is ethnocentric in its approach to public relations will extend home-country PR activities into host countries. The rationale behind this approach is that people everywhere are motivated and persuaded in much the same manner. This approach does not take cultural considerations into account. A company adopting a polycentric approach to PR gives the host-country practitioner more leeway to incorporate local customs and practices into the PR effort. Although such an approach has the advantage of local responsiveness, the lack of global communication and coordination can lead to a PR disaster.[46]

The ultimate test of an organization's understanding of the power and importance of PR occurs during a time of environmental turbulence, especially a potential or actual crisis. When disaster strikes, a company or industry often finds itself thrust into the spotlight. A company's swift and effective handling of communications during such times can have significant implications. The best response is to be forthright and direct, reassure the public, and provide the media with accurate information.

China's ongoing trade-related friction with its trading partners highlights the need for a better PR effort on the part of the Chinese Foreign Ministry. Some sources of this friction have been discussed in earlier chapters, such as estimates that Chinese counterfeiting of copyrighted material costs foreign companies billions of dollars annually and that 98 percent of the computer software used in China is pirated. Such revelations reflect poorly on China. As Hong Kong businessman Barry C. Cheung noted in the mid-1990s, "China lacks skills in public relations generally and crisis management specifically, and that hurts them."[47] Part of the problem stems from the unwillingness of China's Communist leaders to publicly explain their views on these issues, to admit failure, and to accept advice from the West.

---

[44] Carl Botan, "International Public Relations: Critique and Reformulation," *Public Relations Review* 18, no. 2 (Summer 1992), pp. 150–151.
[45] Melvin L. Sharpe, "The Impact of Social and Cultural Conditioning on Global Public Relations," *Public Relations Review* 18, no. 2 (Summer 1992), pp. 103–107.
[46] Carl Botan, "International Public Relations: Critique and Reformulation," *Public Relations Review* 18, no. 2 (Summer 1992), p. 155.
[47] Marcus W. Brauchli, "A Change of Face: China Has Surly Image, but Part of the Reason Is Bad Public Relations," *The Wall Street Journal* (June 16, 1996), p. A1.

Summary

Marketing communications—the promotion P of the marketing mix—includes advertising, public relations, sales promotion, and personal selling. When a company embraces **integrated marketing communications (IMC)**, it recognizes that the various elements of a company's communication strategy must be carefully coordinated. **Advertising** is a sponsored, paid message that is communicated through nonpersonal channels. **Global advertising** consists of the same advertising appeals, messages, artwork, and copy in campaigns around the world. The effort required to create a global campaign forces a company to determine whether or not a global market exists for its product or brand. The trade-off between standardized and adapted advertising is often accomplished by means of **pattern advertising**, which can be used to create localized global advertising. Many advertising agencies are part of larger **advertising organizations**. Advertisers may place a single global agency in charge of worldwide advertising; it is also possible to use one or more agencies on a regional or local basis.

The starting point in ad development is the **creative strategy**, a statement of what the message will say. The people who create ads often seek a **big idea** that can serve as the basis for memorable, effective messages. The **advertising appeal** is the communication approach—rational or emotional—that best relates to buyer motives. **Rational appeals** speak to the mind; **emotional appeals** speak to the heart. The **selling proposition** is the promise that captures the reason for buying the product. The **creative execution** is the way an appeal or proposition is presented. **Art direction** and **copy** must be created with cultural considerations in mind. Perceptions of humor, male–female relationships, and sexual imagery vary in different parts of the world. Media availability varies considerably from country to country. When selecting media, marketers are sometimes as constrained by laws and regulations as by literacy rates.

A company utilizes **public relations (PR)** to foster goodwill and understanding among constituents both inside and outside the company. In particular, the PR department attempts to generate favorable **publicity** about the company and its products and brands. The PR department must also manage corporate communications when responding to negative publicity. Important PR tools include interviews, media kits, press releases, social media, and tours. Many global companies make use of various types of **corporate advertising**, including **image advertising** and **advocacy advertising**. PR is also responsible for providing accurate, timely information, especially in the event of a crisis.

MyMarketingLab

Go to **mymktlab.com** for the following Assisted-graded writing questions:

13-1. When creating advertising for world markets, what are some of the issues that art directors and copywriters should take into account?

13-2. How does public relations differ from advertising? Why is public relations especially important for global companies?

13-3. Mymarketinglab Only – comprehensive writing assignment for this chapter.

MyMarketingLab

Go to **mymktlab.com** to complete the problems marked with this icon .

Discussion Questions

⭐ **13-4.** In what ways can global brands and global advertising campaigns benefit a company?

⭐ **13-5.** How does the "standardized versus localized" debate apply to advertising?

13-6. What is the difference between an advertising appeal and creative execution?

13-7. Starting with Chapter 1, review the ads that appear in this text. Can you identify ads that use emotional appeals? Rational appeals? What is the communication task of each ad? To inform? To persuade? To remind? To entertain?

⭐ **13-8.** How do the media options available to advertisers vary in different parts of the world? What can advertisers do to cope with media limitations in certain countries?

13-9. What are some of the ways PR practices vary in different parts of the world?

CASE 13-1 CONTINUED (REFER TO PAGE 418)
The BP Oil Spill

BP was not the only global company with a PR problem in 2010. Japanese automaker Toyota found itself under fire for quality issues, and Wall Street investment firm Goldman Sachs was fined more than $500 million for securities fraud. As PR specialist Howard Rubenstein noted, "These were real reputational implosions. In all three cases, the companies found themselves under attack over the very traits that were central to their strong global brands and corporate identities."

BP chief executive Tony Hayward became a lightning rod for America's anger and frustration about the spill. At times, Hayward appeared in public in pin-striped suits; his attire was in stark contrast to the overalls worn by shrimp-boat operators and others whose livelihoods were threatened by the spill. Some of Hayward's public statements also appeared insensitive. For example, *The Guardian*, a British newspaper, quoted him as saying, "The Gulf of Mexico is a very big ocean. The amount of oil and the volume of dispersant we are putting into it is tiny in relation to the total water volume." Critics also pilloried Hayward for two other statements he made during a television interview: "There's no one who wants this thing over more than I do," he said. "I want my life back."

Some industry observers wondered whether the rhetoric directed against BP was motivated in part by the perception that the company is British. Global companies must ensure that they have successfully positioned themselves as diverse entities with representation in the various markets in which they have operations. As brand consultant Wally Olins noted, the BP disaster "shows you need people at, or near, the top of the business who can speak the language and use the style of the countries in which they operate." In this regard, many observers agreed that both BP and Hayward himself came up short.

Crisis management practitioners are in wide agreement that in times of crisis, it is imperative for company spokespersons to tell the truth and to take responsibility. Failure to do so can result in lost credibility. Rubenstein was especially critical of BP in this regard. The company's early assessment of the spill was that very little oil was leaking into the Gulf; these reports were contradicted by estimates from specialists outside BP. Also, BP tried to pin blame for the blowout on contactors. Rubenstein said, "It was one of the worst PR approaches I've seen in my 56 years of business. They tried to be opaque. They had every excuse in the book. Right away they should have accepted responsibility and recognized what a disaster they faced. They basically thought they could spin their way out of catastrophe. It doesn't work that way."

Another point of view is that some corporate crises are so monumental that traditional PR approaches will simply not suffice. Eric Dezenhall is a communications strategist who holds this view. According to Dezenhall, BP's attempts to win over the American public were bound to be futile as long as the oil was leaking. Dezenhall says, "Two things that are very hard to survive are hypocrisy and ridicule. It's the height of arrogance to assume that in the middle of a crisis the public yearns for chestnuts of wisdom from people they want to kill. The goal is not to get people not to hate them. It's to get people to hate them less."

Hoping to regain some credibility in Washington, BP assembled a team of consultants and lobbyists to help it prepare for congressional testimony and respond to government inquiries. The team included James Lee Witt, former director of the Federal Emergency Management Agency (FEMA). BP also tapped Hilary Rosen, a partner in the Brunswick Group public relations firm, for assistance. Some observers were dismayed that people with political connections would agree to be on BP's payroll. Robert Weissman, president of the Public Citizen Action Network, asked, "Do these people go to bed at night and think, 'I hope I get to wake up in the morning and represent a corporate criminal?'" In response to such criticism, Donna Brazile, a Democratic strategist, noted, "This is an enormous challenge and it doesn't matter who they hire to contain the spill, clean up the mess and compensate those who have lost so much."

Although the crippled well was finally shut down in August 2010, BP faces the prospect of criminal and civil suits that will likely keep the company in court for many years. For example, the U.S. government could prosecute BP for violating the Clean Water Act or the Refuse Act. Also, because the spill coincided with the spawning and nesting season for the Gulf's wildlife, the Migratory Bird Treaty Act could also be the basis for legal action. Thousands of private lawsuits are also pending. BP has established a $20 billion compensation fund; BP's lawyers hope that individuals whose livelihoods were harmed by the spill will apply to the fund rather than go to court. Finally, there is the prospect of shareholder suits from investors who saw the value of their BP holdings plummet in the wake of the crisis.

Discussion Questions

13-10. Some industry observers think that BP should not have spent money on print and TV ads to reassure the American public. Do you agree or disagree? Explain.

13-11. On October 1, 2010, an American, Bob Dudley, replaced Tony Hayward as chief executive of BP. Does this change surprise you?

13-12. How might the advice from BP's lawyers differ from the advice BP receives from PR professionals?

13-13. What factor(s) will affect whether BP's corporate reputation can be repaired?

Sources: Peter S. Goodman, "In Case of Emergency: What Not to Do," *The New York Times* (August 22, 2010), p. C1; Michael Peel, "Eagles and Vultures," *Financial Times* (July 2, 2010), p. 5; Mimi Hall, "BP Enlists Washington Elite to Help Image," *USA Today* (July 1, 2010); Morgen Witzel and Ravi Mattu, "The Perils of a Tarnished Brand," *Financial Times* (June 23, 2010); Stefan Stern, "Can Too Strong a National Identity Harm the Business?" *Financial Times* (June 16, 2010), p. 10; Ed Crooks, "BP's Disaster Manager," *Financial Times* (May 1–2, 2010), p. 7.

CASE 13-2

Samsung: Launching People

Electronics is a textbook example of global products. Discerning consumers do not hesitate to pay premium prices for top global brands such as Samsung. Moreover, electronics' consumers everywhere associate the products with aspirational goals such as success and achievement. In 2013, Samsung launched a global campaign featuring the program "Launching People" which focuses on discovering real stories, helping consumers and sharing their stories with the world.

Samsung Electronics Co. Ltd is a multinational electronics and information technology company headquartered in Suwon, South Korea. It is an important offshoot of the Samsung Group and employs 270,000 people across 79 countries, making it the global leader in technology with annual sales of US $187.8 billion. Through continuous innovation, Samsung has been changing lives and revolutionizing markets it operates in with its products which include everything electronic from televisions, smartphones, personal computers, printers, cameras, home appliances, medical devices, and semiconductors.

According to Interbrand's 'Best Global Brands 2013' report, there has been a marked progress in Samsung's brand—within three years of entering the top 20 in 2009, it reached the top 10 in 2012 and holds the 8th position as of 2013—and is recognized for its outstanding management, global growth in brand value through marketing initiatives, and continued market leadership. Samsung also ranked 2nd in the global strategic consulting firm, Boston Consulting Group's (BCG) report, 'The Most Innovative Companies 2013.'

Samsung strengthened its ranking as the best in the mobile and TV categories by delivering new technologically advanced products such as the Galaxy S4, Galaxy Note 3 and the world's first curved UHD TV. Samsung also created a new market with the launch of the ingenious wearable device, the Galaxy Gear. In addition, the company is leading the market in one-of-a-kind household appliances.

Samsung's objective is to become one of the top five global brands by 2020. To achieve this vision, Samsung has refreshed its brand strategy: "Accelerating Discoveries and Possibilities." This reflects the philosophy of a genuine global brand aiming to meet current consumer demand.

Regional and local Samsung subsidiaries began to make a strong impression on their customer base with localized consumer-centric marketing activities. Subsidiaries in Europe, for instance, were some of the first in Samsung Electronics to identify and carry out cultural marketing based around different local "passion points." As the name suggests, the term refers to any commodity that consumers relate to and generates excitement. Sports, fine arts, music, cinema, politics, and religion are all topical passion points.

Cultural marketing around passion points gives the subsidiary marketing team ample opportunity to proactively engage consumers and create linkages between Samsung and the most pertinent local passions. Whereas in England, the UK subsidiary found considerable success with football marketing (eventually leading to Samsung's sponsorship of Chelsea football), the French subsidiary focused on culture aspects like fashion, art, and gastronomy (cooking).

Another example of this marketing initiative is the global consumer engagement program "Launching People," a 2013 Samsung brand campaign which actively conveys the newly established Brand Ideal that various opportunities can be discovered and realized when new products and technology meet consumer potential.

To help people around the world realize their potential, Samsung's culture of innovation is reaching beyond products to technology, and aims to make a difference in people's lives and the lives of others by identifying and investing in inspiring individuals across a varied cross-section.

The campaign invites people passionate about their dreams to submit their ideas for several categories such as Sports, Art and Entrepreneurship for an opportunity to turn them into reality.

The campaign started from France in June 2013 with the goal of turning consumers' dreams and potentials into reality in 13 regions across Europe, Latin America and Middle East in 2013, and is expected to expand further in 2014.

The campaign has gained tremendous popularity in France, reaching around 60 million people in 5 weeks and discovering 2000 stories. It has made a significant impact on Samsung's brand, with an increase of 10 percent in brand attributes, such as 'friendly,' 'for me,' and 'differentiated,' compared to before the campaign was released.

The campaign promises to invest not only in technology, but also in the ideas of passionate people—whether this potential is related to a personal journey, a larger cause, or both.

Samsung will spread the word about "Launching People" with real consumer stories on Samsung.com and across all digital and social media channels, including Facebook and YouTube.

The focus will be on providing ambitious consumers with the chance to realize their potential by teaming them up with renowned regional mentors, start-up funding and products to help them on their journey.

Samsung has several objectives behind putting together this global creation competition: positioning itself as a dynamic structure by helping the young generation to get started, sponsoring prospective projects, and incubating talent.

Exhibit 13-7 An illustration of an ad from Samsung's "Launching People" campaign

Source: Samsung Gulf Electronics

Discussion Questions

13-14. What is the purpose behind Samsung's global "Launching People" campaign?

13-15. How can Samsung localize this campaign in emerging markets?

13-16. How can Samsung engage more consumers for this campaign in your country?

13-17. How does usage of electronics products vary from country to country?

13-18. What strategies should Samsung pursue in 2014 to make this a successful global campaign?

13-19. How can Samsung measure the success of this initiative?

Sources: Samsung Announces "Launching People" Campaign and Plan to Support Inspiring Ideas around the Globe, Samsung Tomorrow (October 28, 2013), global. samsungtomorrow.com/?p=29481; "Samsung Rises to No. 8 Position in Interbrand's 'Best Global Brands 2013' Report," *Pakistan Press International* (October 1, 2013), ppinewsagency.com/140392/samsung-rises-to-no-8-position-in-interbrands-best-global-brands-2013%E2%80%B2-report/; "Samsung No. 8 'Most Valuable Brand' worldwide," *Saudi Gazette* (October 7, 2013), www.saudigazette.com.sa/index. cfm?method=home.regcon&contentid=20131008182957; Launching People, Samsung (2013), www.samsung.com/ae/launchingpeople/landing.html.

14

Global Marketing Communications Decisions II:

Sales Promotion, Personal Selling, and Special Forms of Marketing Communication

CASE 14-1
Red Bull

It's a safe bet that most people reading this textbook are familiar with Red Bull. The $6.4 billion company that virtually created the market for energy drinks revels in its association with cultural events such as concerts and extreme sports including snowboarding and surfing. The company uses a variety of communication channels in addition to advertising and public relations to promote the brand. Red Bull's Facebook page has 38 million "likes," and 1 million people follow its Twitter feed.

Exhibit 14-1 Felix Baumgartner's historic free-fall from the edge of space was a spectacular sponsorship and public relations coup for Red Bull. The project also provided a laboratory for testing new spacesuit designs and escape procedures and for assessing various contingencies that can arise when a human being breaks the sound barrier.
Source: AP Photo/Red Bull Stratos, File.

At concerts and other events, street teams pass out free samples while driving specially modified cars with giant Red Bull cans mounted on them. Also, the company sponsors the Infiniti Red Bull Formula One racing team. In addition, the Red Bull Arena in Harrison, New Jersey, is home to the New York Red Bulls Major League Soccer team. Needless to say, Red Bull is not only high energy; it's high profile, too!

The brand's slogan, "Red Bull Gives You Wings," made Red Bull the perfect corporate partner for one of the biggest public relations coups in recent years. In fall 2012, Red Bull sponsored Felix Baumgartner's death-defying skydive from the edge of space (see Exhibit 14-1). After seven years of planning, Baumgartner jumped from a helium-filled balloon at an altitude of 24 miles. As a worldwide audience watched on television and YouTube, Baumgartner plummeted toward earth at speeds as high as Mach 1.24 (834 miles per hour) before landing safely. Needless to say, the Red Bull logo was prominently displayed on his uniform, and the event received extensive publicity in the press.

The success of the Red Bull Stratos project helps the Red Bull brand stand out from a crowded field of competitors that include Monster and Rockstar. As brand strategist Roger Addis noted, "It's a smart move because it's such a singular event. If the logo is buried in a sea of logos on a NASCAR car, you're completely diluted by all the others." The ad industry seems to agree; Red Bull topped *Advertising Age* magazine's 2012 Best of Creativity rankings in the integrated/interactive category.

Sponsorships and event marketing are critical marketing tools for global companies such as Red Bull. When developing IMC solutions and strategies, global companies and advertising agencies are giving these and other special forms of promotion an increasingly prominent role in the communication mix; in the first decades of the twenty-first century, worldwide expenditures on sales promotion have been growing at double-digit rates. Sales promotion, direct marketing, and specialized forms of marketing communication such as infomercials and the Internet are also growing in importance. Personal selling remains an important promotional tool as well. Taken together, the marketing mix elements discussed in this chapter and Chapter 13 can be used to create highly effective, integrated promotional campaigns that support global brands.

LEARNING OBJECTIVES

1 Define *sales promotion* and identify the most important promotion tactics and tools used by global marketers.

2 List the steps in the strategic/consultative selling model.

3 Explain the contingency factors that must be considered when making decisions about sales force nationality.

4 Explain direct marketing's advantages and identify the most common types of direct marketing channels.

5 Identify special forms of marketing communication and explain how global marketers integrate them into the overall promotion mix.

Sales Promotion

Sales promotion refers to any paid consumer or trade communication program of limited duration that adds tangible value to a product or brand. In a *price promotion*, tangible value may take the form of a price reduction, coupon, or mail-in refund. *Nonprice promotions* may take the form of free samples, premiums, "buy one, get one free" offers, sweepstakes, and contests. **Consumer sales promotions** may be designed to make consumers aware of a new product, to stimulate nonusers to sample an existing product, or to increase overall consumer demand. **Trade sales promotions** are designed to increase product availability in distribution channels. At many companies, expenditures for sales promotion activities have surpassed expenditures for media advertising. At any level of expenditure, however, sales promotion is only one of several marketing communication tools. Sales promotion plans and programs should be integrated and coordinated with those for advertising, public relations (PR), and personal selling.

Worldwide, several explanations have been offered for the increasing popularity of sales promotion as a marketing communication tool. In addition to providing a tangible incentive to buyers, sales promotions also reduce the perceived risk buyers may associate with purchasing

Exhibit 14-2 When it comes to iconic figures that embody heroism, nothing beats an astronaut. That's the message from brand managers for Unilever's Axe Apollo. A marketing promotion created by the London-based Bartle Bogle Hegarty advertising agency partnered Axe with legendary American astronaut Buzz Aldrin and offered 22 prize winners a free trip in space. In 1969, Aldrin piloted the Apollo 11 lunar-landing module, and he was the second human to set foot on the moon.
Source: Getty Images for AXE.

the product. From the point of view of the marketer, sales promotion provides accountability; the manager in charge of the promotion can immediately track its results. Overall, promotional spending is increasing at many companies as they shift advertising spending away from traditional print and broadcast advertising. Exhibit 14-2 shows how marketing managers responsible for Axe Apollo use sales promotions; additional examples are listed in Table 14-1.

TABLE 14-1 Sales Promotions by Global Marketers

Company/Country Market for Promotion	Promotion
Unilever/Global	In a contest in 45 different languages covering 60 countries, marketers for Axe Apollo invited consumers to fill out an "astronaut profile." Twenty-two finalists will have the opportunity to travel into space on the Lynx suborbital airship.
Walt Disney Company/China	To fight counterfeiting, the "Disney Magical Journey" promotion was keyed to mail-in hologram stickers on genuine Disney products. Participants could win Disney DVDs, TV sets, and trips to Hong Kong Disneyland.*
Mars/Global	The Global Color Vote promotion invited consumers in 200 countries to vote on whether a new M&M candy should be purple, aqua, or pink. Purple won.
Guinness/Worldwide	The "Arthur's Day" concert series honored the 250th anniversary of the birth of Arthur Guinness, founder of the Dublin, Ireland–based Guinness brewery.

* Geoffrey A. Fowler, "Disney Fires a Broadside at Pirates," *The Wall Street Journal* (May 31, 2006), p. B3.

Sweepstakes, rebates, and other promotional tools may require consumers to divulge personal information, which companies can add to their databases. For example, the French Ministry of Agriculture recently launched a global promotion aimed at boosting exports of French wine and cheese. Acknowledging that some consumers are intimidated by France's culinary heritage, the Ministry sponsored the promotion to demonstrate that French cuisine can be relaxed and laid back. Spoexa, a food-marketing company, was hired to organize cocktail parties in 19 countries, including Canada, Spain, and the United States. House Party Inc., an American marketing firm, promoted the U.S. parties through its Web site. Would-be hosts registered online; from that applicant pool, House Party chose 1,000 people. The winners received discount coupons good for purchases of French wine; they also were entitled to free gifts when ordering French cheeses from select Web sites. Each winner also received a basket of party supplies, including a corkscrew and an apron. In return, the hosts agreed to take photos and blog about their party. After the parties, the hosts answered questionnaires to provide sponsors with feedback about the featured food and wine. Finally, in-store promotions on party-related French goods were featured at various shops and supermarkets.[1]

A global company can sometimes leverage experience gained in one country market and use it in another market. For example, PepsiCo experienced great success in Latin America with its Numeromania contest. When soft drink sales stalled in Poland in the mid-1990s, Pepsi rolled out Numeromania there; lured by the promise of big cash prizes, many economically squeezed Poles rushed out to buy Pepsi so they could enter the contest.[2] International managers can learn about American-style promotion strategies and tactics by attending seminars such as those offered by the Promotional Marketing Association of America (PMAA). Sometimes adaptation to country-specific conditions is required; for example, TV ads in France cannot have movie tie-ins. Ads must be designed to focus on the promotion rather than the movie. Such regulations would have an impact on Disney, for example.

As with other aspects of marketing communication, a key issue is whether headquarters should direct promotion efforts or leave those decisions to local country managers. The authors of one study noted that Nestlé and other large companies that once had a polycentric approach to consumer and trade sales promotion have redesigned their efforts. Kashani and Quelch identify four factors that contribute to more headquarters' involvement in the sales promotion effort: cost, complexity, global branding, and transnational trade:[3]

1. As sales promotions command ever-larger budget allocations, headquarters naturally takes a greater interest.
2. The formulation, implementation, and follow-up of a promotion program may require skills that local managers lack.
3. The increasing importance of global brands justifies headquarters involvement to maintain consistency from country to country and to ensure that successful local promotion programs are leveraged in other markets.
4. As mergers and acquisitions lead to increased concentration in the retail industry and as the industry globalizes, retailers will seek coordinated promotional programs from their suppliers.

The level of headquarters' involvement notwithstanding, in most cases local managers in the market know the specific local situation. Therefore, they should be consulted before a promotion is launched. A number of factors must be taken into account when determining the extent to which the promotion must be localized:

- In countries with low levels of economic development, low incomes limit the range of promotional tools available. In such countries, free samples and demonstrations are more likely to be used than coupons or on-pack premiums.
- Market maturity can also be different from country to country; consumer sampling and coupons are appropriate in growing markets, but mature markets might require trade allowances or loyalty programs.

[1] Max Colchester, "French Recipe for Launching 1,000 Parties," *The Wall Street Journal* (April 24, 2009), p. B7.
[2] Roderick Oram, "Brand Experiences," *Financial Times* (October 30, 1996), FT Survey, p. III.
[3] Kamran Kashani and John A. Quelch, "Can Sales Promotion Go Global?" *Business Horizons* 33, no. 3 (May–June 1990), pp. 37–43.

- Local perceptions of a particular promotional tool or program can vary. Japanese consumers, for example, are reluctant to use coupons at the checkout counter. A particular premium can be a waste of money.
- Local regulations in certain countries may rule out the use of a particular promotion such as in-pack coupons or price-off coupons by mail.
- Trade structure in the retailing industry can affect the use of sales promotions. For example, in the United States and parts of Europe, the retail industry is highly concentrated (i.e., dominated by a few key players such as Walmart). This situation requires significant promotional activity at both the trade and the consumer levels. By contrast, in countries where retailing is more fragmented—Japan is a case in point—there is less pressure to engage in promotional activities.

Sampling

Sampling is a sales promotion technique that provides potential customers with the opportunity to try a product or service at no cost. As Marc Pritchard, vice president of global cosmetics and personal care at Procter & Gamble (P&G), noted, "The most fundamental thing that consumers want to do is try before they buy."[4] A typical sample is an individual portion of a consumer packaged good, such as breakfast cereal, shampoo, cosmetics, or detergent, distributed through the mail, door-to-door, or at a retail location.

Fifty years ago, Kikkoman brand soy sauce was unknown in the United States. Yuzaburo Mogi, currently honorary CEO and chairman of the Board of Directors, took part in a sampling program that Kikkoman had started in American supermarkets. Mogi and his employees passed out free samples of food seasoned with Kikkoman; today, the U.S. market accounts for about 70 percent of Kikkoman's profits from international operations (see Exhibit 14-3).[5] The company continues to make extensive use of shopper marketing as a communication tool. During grilling season, for example, Kikkoman's promotional strategy calls for dispensing recipes for marinades and coupons from shelf displays in the supermarket meat aisle. Before Thanksgiving, the strategy calls for placing turkey brining recipes in the poultry section.[6]

The average cost per sample can range from $0.10 to $0.50; 2 to 3 million samples are distributed in a typical sampling program. Cost is one of the major disadvantages associated with sampling; another problem is that it is sometimes difficult for marketing managers to assess the contribution a sampling program makes to return on investment. Today, many companies utilize *event marketing* and *sponsorships* to distribute samples at concerts, sports events, and special events such as food and beverage festivals attended by large numbers of people. In the Information Age, sampling may also consist of a week's free viewing of a cable TV channel or a no-cost trial subscription to an online computer service; Internet users can also request free samples through a company's Web site.

Compared with other forms of marketing communication, sampling is more likely to result in actual trials of the product. To ensure a trial, consumer products companies are increasingly using a technique known as "point-of-use" sampling. For example, Starbucks dispatches "Chill Patrols" in the summertime to pass out samples of ice-cold Frappuccinos to overheated commuters during rush hour in busy metropolitan areas. In an example of "point-of-dirt" sampling, Unilever hired a promotional marketing firm to pass out Lever2000 hand wipes in food courts and petting zoos. As Michael Murphy, director of home and personal-care promotions at Unilever, noted, "We're getting smarter. You must be much more precise in what, where, and how you deliver samples."[7]

Sampling can be especially important if consumers are not persuaded by claims made in advertising or other channels. In China, for example, shoppers are reluctant to buy full-sized packages of imported consumer products that they haven't tried—especially because the price may be several times higher than the price of local brands. P&G's dominance in China's shampoo market can be attributed to the company's skillful use of market segmentation coupled with an aggressive sampling program. P&G offers four shampoo brands in China: Rejoice ("soft and

[4] Sarah Ellison, "Taking the 'Free' Out of Free Samples," *The Wall Street Journal* (September 25, 2002), p. D1.
[5] Mariko Sanchanta, "Soy Sauce Seeps into the Culture," *Financial Times* (August 10, 2006), p. 6.
[6] Andrew Adam Newman, "Taking Pickles Out of the Afterthought Aisle," *The New York Times* (April 26, 2011), p. B3.
[7] Geoffrey A. Fowler, "When Free Samples Become Saviors," *The Wall Street Journal* (August 14, 2001), p. B1.

beautiful hair"), Pantene ("nutrition"), Head & Shoulders ("dandruff relief"), and Vidal Sassoon ("fashion").[8] P&G distributed millions of free samples of its shampoo products; after the no-risk trial, many consumers became adopters.

Couponing

A **coupon** is a printed certificate that entitles the bearer to a price reduction or some other special consideration for purchasing a particular product or service. In the United States and Great Britain, marketers rely heavily on newspapers to deliver coupons; nearly 90 percent of all coupons are distributed in a printed, ride-along vehicle known as a *free-standing insert* (FSI). Sunday papers carry the vast majority of FSIs. *On-pack coupons* are attached to, or part of, the product

---

[8] "Winning the China FMCG Market," ATKearney, 2003.

package; they can frequently be redeemed immediately at checkout. *In-pack coupons* are placed inside the package. Coupons can also be handed out in stores, offered on a self-service basis from on-shelf dispensers, delivered to homes by mail, or distributed electronically at the checkout counter. Also, the number of coupons distributed via the Internet is growing. *Cross coupons* are distributed with one product but redeemable for another. For example, a toothpaste coupon might be distributed with a toothbrush. The United States leads the world in the number of coupons issued, by a wide margin. NCH Marketing Services, which tracks coupon trends, reports that about 300 billion coupons are distributed in the United States each year; only about 1 percent are actually redeemed. Online coupon distribution is growing at a rapid rate; Google is among the players experimenting with them.[9]

Coupons are a favorite promotion tool of consumer packaged goods companies such as P&G and Unilever. The goal is to reward loyal users and stimulate product trial by nonusers. In the European Union (EU), couponing is widely used in the United Kingdom and Belgium. Couponing is not as prevalent in Asia, where saving face is important. Although Asian consumers have a reputation for thriftiness, some are reluctant to use coupons, because doing so might bring shame upon them or their families. According to Joseph Potacki, who teaches a "Basics of Promotion" seminar for the PMAA, couponing is the aspect of the promotion mix for which the practices in the United States differ the most from those in other countries. In the United States, couponing accounts for 70 percent of consumer promotion spending. Elsewhere, the percentage is much lower. As Potacki explained, "It is far less—or nonexistent—in most other countries simply because the cultures don't accept couponing." Potacki has noted that one reason couponing is gaining importance in countries such as the United Kingdom is because retailers are learning more about its advantages.[10]

Social couponing is one of hottest online sales promotion trends today. Industry leader Groupon offers its followers deal-of-the-day coupons that are sponsored by local businesses. Followers then share their experiences via social networks. The local business gets customers, and Groupon takes a share of the coupon proceeds. Groupon has grown at a dizzying pace, expanding from 1 country to 35 in a single year. Much of that growth has come via acquisition. By the end of 2012, Groupon had more than 40 million users in 48 countries. More than half of Groupon's Web site visitors live in Europe; 33 percent are in North America. A key investor is Russian Internet investment group Digital Sky Technologies (DST); Groupon's founders recently rejected a $6 billion takeover offer from Google![11]

Sales Promotion: Issues and Problems

As noted earlier, many companies are being more strategic in targeting their sampling programs. In the case of coupons, retailers must bundle the redeemed coupons together and ship them to a processing point. Many times, coupons are not validated at the point of purchase; in addition, fraudulent redemption costs marketers hundreds of millions of dollars each year. Fraud can take other forms as well. For example, during the 2004 Super Bowl broadcast, PepsiCo launched a joint promotion with Apple's iTunes Music Store. Apple planned to give away 100 million songs for free (regular price: $0.99); consumers could obtain a code from the caps of Pepsi bottles and enter the code online to qualify for the download. The promotion was designed so that anyone purchasing a bottle of Pepsi had a one-in-three chance of being a winner. However, many people discovered that by tilting the bottles to one side, they could tell whether the bottle was a winner. Moreover, they could read the code without having to pay for the Pepsi![12]

Companies must thus take extreme care when formulating and executing sales promotions. In some emerging markets, sales promotion efforts can raise eyebrows if companies appear to be exploiting regulatory loopholes and lack of consumer resistance to intrusion. Sales promotion in Europe is highly regulated. Sales promotions are popular in Scandinavia because of restrictions on broadcast advertising, but promotions in the Nordic countries are subject to regulations. If such regulations are relaxed as the single market develops in Europe and are harmonized, companies may be able to roll out pan-European promotions.

---

[9] Steve Lohr, "Clip and Save Holds Its Own Against Point and Click," *The New York Times* (August 30, 2006), p. C1.

[10] Leslie Ryan, "Sales Promotion: Made in America," *Brandweek* (July 31, 1995), p. 28.

[11] Kunur Patel, "What's Next for Groupon?" *Advertising Age* (December 13, 2010).

[12] Ina Fried, "Pepsi's iTunes Promotion Goes Flat," *cnetNews* (April 28, 2004). news.cnet.com. Accessed June 1, 2010.

A study examined coupon usage and attitudes toward both coupons and sweepstakes in Taiwan, Thailand, and Malaysia. The study has particular relevance to global companies that are targeting these and other developing nations in Asia, where consumers have relatively little experience with coupons. The study utilized Hofstede's social values framework as a guide. All three countries in the study are collectivist, and the researchers found that positive attitudes of family members and society as a whole influenced in an individual a positive attitude toward coupons and coupon usage.

However, consumers in the three nations showed some differences in value orientation. For example, Malaysia has higher power distance and lower uncertainty avoidance than the other countries. For Malaysians, the fear of public embarrassment was a constraint on coupon usage. In all three countries, media consumption habits were also a factor; persons who were not regular readers of magazines or newspapers were less likely to be aware that coupons were available in the periodicals. Consumers in Taiwan and Thailand looked more favorably on coupons than sweepstakes. The impact of religion surprised the researchers. In Malaysia, where the population is primarily Muslim, the researchers assumed that consumers would avoid sweepstakes promotions. Sweepstakes can be likened to gambling, which is frowned on by Islam. However, Malaysians showed a preference for sweepstakes over coupons. In Taiwan, where Buddhism, Confucianism, and Taoism are all practiced, religion appeared to have little impact on attitudes toward promotions. One implication for marketing in developing countries is that, despite cultural differences, increased availability of promotions will result in higher levels of consumer utilization.[13]

Personal Selling

Personal selling is person-to-person communication between a company representative and a prospective buyer. The seller's communication effort is focused on informing and persuading the prospect, with the short-term goal of making a sale and the longer-term goal of building a relationship with that buyer. The salesperson's job is to correctly understand the buyer's needs, match those needs to the company's product(s), and then persuade the customer to buy. Because selling provides a two-way communication channel, it is especially important in marketing industrial products that may be expensive and technologically complex. Sales personnel can often provide headquarters with important customer feedback that can be used in design and engineering decisions.

Effective personal selling in a salesperson's home country requires building a relationship with the customer; global marketing presents additional challenges because the buyer and seller may come from different national or cultural backgrounds. In addition to such challenges, it is difficult to overstate the importance of a face-to-face, personal selling effort for industrial products in global markets. For example, when Spain's Iberia Airlines was modernizing its long-haul fleet, salespeople from Boeing and rival Airbus met numerous times with Enrique Dupuy de Lome, Iberia's chief financial officer. At stake was a 12-plane order worth about $2 billion. The aircraft under consideration were the Boeing 777-300ER ("Extended Range") and the Airbus A340-600. After each sales team presented initial bids, the negotiations began; Toby Bright, Boeing's top salesperson for jets, faced off against John Leahy of Airbus. Iberia's demands included discounts off list prices and resale value guarantees for the aircraft. After months of meetings and revised proposals, Airbus was awarded the contract.[14]

Personal selling is also a popular marketing communication tool in countries with various restrictions on advertising. It is difficult to obtain permission to present product comparisons in any type of advertising in Japan. In such an environment, personal selling is the best way to provide hard-hitting, side-by-side comparisons of competing products. Personal selling is also used frequently in countries where low wage rates allow large local sales forces to be hired. For example, HBO built its core of subscribers in Hungary by selling door-to-door.

---

[13] Lenard C. Huff and Dana L. Alden, "An Investigation of Consumer Response to Sales Promotions in Developing Markets: A Three Country Analysis," *Journal of Advertising Research* 38, no. 3 (May/June 1998), pp. 47–57.
[14] Daniel Michaels, "Dogfight: In the Secret World of Airplane Deals, One Battle Up Close," *The Wall Street Journal* (March 10, 2003), pp. A1, A9.

The cost-effectiveness of personal selling in certain parts of the world has been a key driver behind the decision at many U.S.-based firms to begin marketing products and services overseas. A company is more likely to test a new territory or product if the entry price is relatively low. For example, some high-tech firms have utilized lower-cost sales personnel in Latin America to introduce new product features to their customers. Only if the response is favorable do the firms commit major resources to a U.S. rollout.

The challenge to companies that wish to pursue low-cost personal selling overseas, however, is to establish and maintain acceptable quality among members of the sales team. The old saying "You get what you pay for" has come to haunt more than one company that has undertaken global expansion. When MCI Communications first entered Latin America several decades ago, it was attracted, in part, by the prospect of achieving inexpensive market penetration for its large, multinational client companies. Management's initial enthusiasm quickly gave way to an alarming realization that the quality of support in this part of the world was not equal to what MCI's major accounts were used to in the United States. As a result, there was a period when both MCI and its competition chose the costlier sales approach of using U.S.-based personnel to provide remote, but higher-quality, support to the Latin American sites of their respective global customer bases. However, MCI's upper management ultimately decided to invest more to create in-country sales and service teams whose output would more closely mirrored that of their U.S. counterparts.

The risks inherent in establishing a personal selling structure overseas remain today. The crucial issue is not whether in-country sales and marketing people can provide more benefit than a remote force. It's a given that, in the vast majority of scenarios, they can. Instead, the issue is whether the country team should consist of in-country nationals or **expatriates** (also known as *expats*)—that is, employees who are sent from their respective home countries to work abroad. It should be noted that many of the environmental issues and challenges identified in earlier chapters often surface as a company completes the initial stages of implementing a personal selling strategy. These include:

- *Political risks.* Unstable or corrupt governments can completely change the rules for the sales team. Establishing new operations in a foreign country is especially tricky if a coup is imminent or if a dictator demands certain "considerations" (which has been the case in many developing countries). Today, for example, Colombia offers great market potential, and its government projects an image of openness; this was not always the case, however. In the not-so-distant past, many companies found the unspoken rules of the cabal to be inordinately burdensome. In a country ruled by a dictatorship, the target audience and accompanying message of the sales effort tend to be far narrower and restricted because government planners mandate how business will be conducted. Firms selling in Hong Kong, for example, were concerned that China would impose its will and dramatically alter the selling environment after the transfer of power in 1997. In response to such concerns, British Telecom brought many members of its Hong Kong sales staff back to London prior to the changeover. However, to the great relief of Hong Kong's business community, Chinese officials ultimately recognized that a policy of minimal intervention would be the wisest approach.
- *Regulatory hurdles.* Governments sometimes set up quota systems or impose tariffs that affect entering foreign sales forces. In part, governments consider such actions to be an easy source of revenue, but, even more important, policymakers want to ensure that sales teams from local firms retain a competitive edge in terms of what they can offer and at what price. Regulations can also take the form of rules that restrict certain types of sales activities. In 1998, for example, the Chinese government banned door-to-door selling, effectively thwarting Avon's business model. Avon responded by establishing a network of store representatives. When direct selling was legalized in 2006, CEO Andrea Jung expected that China would soon be adding $1 billion a year to Avon's bottom line. As it turns out however, Avon has incurred losses in China in connection with the transition from stores to the direct-sales business model. Compounding the situation is a bribery scandal that originated in China and spread to other markets; the ongoing investigation has tarnished the company's reputation and cost it tens of millions of dollars.[15]

---

[15] Ellen Byron, "Avon Bribery Investigation Widens," *The Wall Street Journal* (May 5, 2011), p. B1.

- *Currency fluctuations.* There have been many instances where a company's sales effort has been derailed not by ineffectiveness or lack of market opportunity but by fluctuating currency values. In the mid-1980s, for example, Caterpillar's global market share declined when the dollar's strength allowed Komatsu to woo U.S. customers away. Then, while Caterpillar's management team was preoccupied with domestic issues, competitors chipped away at the firm's position in global markets.

- *Market unknowns.* When a company enters a new region of the world, its selling strategy may unravel because of a lack of knowledge of market conditions, the accepted way of doing business, or the positioning of its in-country competitors. When a game plan is finally crafted to counter the obstacles, it is sometimes too late for the company to succeed. On the other hand, if management devotes an inordinate amount of time conducting market research prior to entry, it may discover that its window of opportunity has been lost to a fast-moving competitor that did not fall victim to the "analysis paralysis" syndrome. Thus, it is difficult to make generalizations about the optimal time to enter a new country.

If all of these challenges can be overcome, or at least minimized, the personal selling endeavor can be implemented with the aid of a tool known as the *strategic/consultative selling model.*

The Strategic/Consultative Selling Model

Figure 14-1 shows the **strategic/consultative selling model**, which has gained wide acceptance in the United States. The model consists of five interdependent steps, each with three

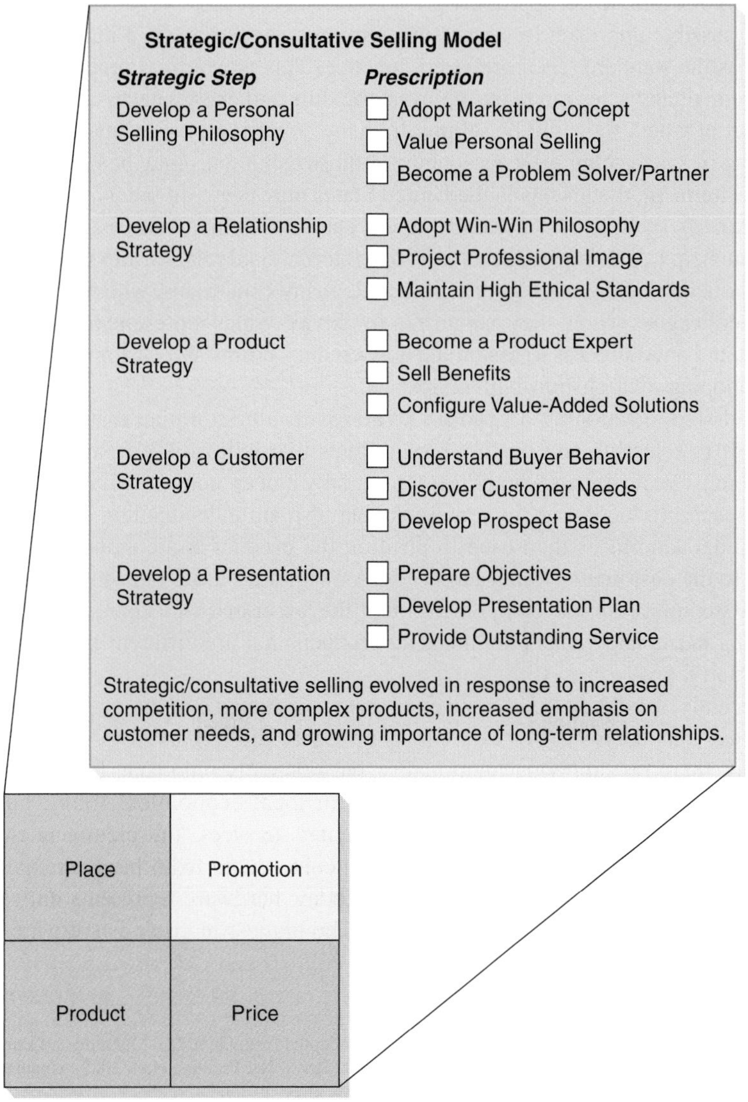

Strategic/Consultative Selling Model

Strategic Step	Prescription
Develop a Personal Selling Philosophy	☐ Adopt Marketing Concept ☐ Value Personal Selling ☐ Become a Problem Solver/Partner
Develop a Relationship Strategy	☐ Adopt Win-Win Philosophy ☐ Project Professional Image ☐ Maintain High Ethical Standards
Develop a Product Strategy	☐ Become a Product Expert ☐ Sell Benefits ☐ Configure Value-Added Solutions
Develop a Customer Strategy	☐ Understand Buyer Behavior ☐ Discover Customer Needs ☐ Develop Prospect Base
Develop a Presentation Strategy	☐ Prepare Objectives ☐ Develop Presentation Plan ☐ Provide Outstanding Service

Strategic/consultative selling evolved in response to increased competition, more complex products, increased emphasis on customer needs, and growing importance of long-term relationships.

Place	Promotion
Product	Price

FIGURE 14-1

The Strategic/Consultative Selling Model

Source: Gerald L. Manning and Barry L. Reece, *Selling Today: Creating Customer Value*, 10th ed. © 2007, pp. 15, 18, 238. Reprinted/Adapted by permission of Pearson Education, Inc., Upper Saddle River, NJ.

prescriptions that can serve as a checklist for sales personnel.[16] Many U.S. companies have begun developing global markets and have established face-to-face sales teams either directly, using their own personnel, or indirectly, through contracted sales agents. As a result, the strategic/consultative selling model is increasingly used on a worldwide basis. The key to ensuring that the model produces the desired outcome—quality partnerships with customers—is to have it implemented and followed on a consistent basis. This is far more difficult to achieve with international sales teams than it is with U.S.-based units, which are much more accessible to corporate headquarters.

First, a sales representative must develop a **personal selling philosophy**. This requires a commitment to the marketing concept and a willingness to take on the role of problem solver or partner in helping customers. A sales professional must also be secure in the belief that selling is a valuable activity. The second step is to develop a **relationship strategy**, which is a game plan for establishing and maintaining high-quality relationships with prospects and customers. The relationship strategy provides a blueprint for creating the rapport and mutual trust that will serve as the basis of a lasting partnership. This step connects sales personnel directly to the concept of *relationship marketing*, an approach that stresses the importance of developing long-term partnerships with customers. Many U.S.-based companies have adopted the relationship marketing approach to selling in the American market; it is equally relevant—perhaps even more so—to any company hoping to achieve success in global marketing.

In developing personal and relationship strategies on an international level, the representative is wise to take a step back and understand how these strategies will likely fit in the foreign environment. For example, an aggressive, "I'll do whatever it takes to get your business" attitude is the worst possible approach to use in some cultures, even though in many large U.S. cities, it is viewed as the standard, even preferred, practice. This is why it is prudent for a company's sales management and sales rep teams to invest the time and energy necessary to learn about the global market in which they will be selling. In many countries, people have only a rudimentary understanding of sales techniques; acceptance of those techniques may be low as well. A sophisticated sales campaign that excels in the United States may never hit the mark in other countries. In-country experts such as consultants or agents can be excellent sources of real-world intelligence that can help a sales rep create an effective international relationship strategy. Such people are especially helpful if the sales force will include many expatriates, who will not have resident nationals as colleagues whom they can turn to for advice. Sales representatives must understand that patience and a willingness to assimilate host-country norms and customs are important attributes in developing relationships built on respect.

The third step, developing a **product strategy**, results in a plan that can assist the sales representative in selecting and positioning products that will satisfy customer needs. A sales professional must be an expert who possesses not only a deep understanding of the features and attributes of each product he or she represents, but also an understanding of competitive offerings. That understanding is then used to position the product and communicate benefits that are relevant to the customers' wants and needs. As with the selling philosophy and relationship strategy, this step must include comprehension of the target market's characteristics and the fact that prevailing needs and wants may mandate products that are different from those offered in the home country.

Until recently, most American companies that were engaged in international selling offered products rather than services. For example, John Deere did a marvelous job of increasing its global market share by supplying high-quality, but relatively mundane, farming equipment to countries where agriculture remains a mainstay of local economies. Today, however, with exploding worldwide demand for technology-related services, the picture is changing. For example, in 2000, 24 percent of IBM's pretax income came from hardware sales. Services accounted for 40 percent; software, 24 percent. Today, hardware represents only 8 percent of pretax income; services account for 39 percent. The biggest increase is software, which now

---

[16] This discussion of the strategic/consultative selling model is adapted from Gerald L. Manning and Barry L. Reece, *Selling Today: Creating Customer Value*, 10th ed. (Upper Saddle River, NJ: Prentice Hall, 2007), Chapter 1. The authors are also indebted to Larry Sirhall, a marketing consultant based in Bend, Oregon.

accounts for 44 percent of income.[17] When IBM turned 100 in 2011, *The Economist* summarized the success formula the company has perfected over the years:

> From the beginning, as a maker of complex machines, IBM had no choice but to explain its products to its customers and thus to develop a strong understanding of their business requirements. From that followed close relationships between customers and supplier.[18]

In short, IBM's success is due in no small part to superior execution of a **customer strategy**, a plan that ensures that the sales professional will be maximally responsive to customer needs. Doing so requires a general understanding of consumer behavior; in addition, the salesperson must collect and analyze as much information as possible about the needs of each customer or prospect. The customer strategy step also includes building a prospect base consisting of current customers as well as potential customers (or leads). A *qualified lead* is someone whose probability of wanting to buy the product is high. Many sales organizations diminish their own productivity by chasing after too many nonqualified leads. This issue can be extremely challenging for an international sales unit, because customer cues or "buying signs" may not coincide with those that have been proven in the sales rep's home country.

The final step, the actual face-to-face selling situation, requires a **presentation strategy**. This consists of setting objectives for each sales call and establishing a presentation plan to meet those objectives. The presentation strategy must be based on the sales representative's commitment to provide outstanding service to customers. As shown in Figure 14-2, when these five strategies are integrated into an appropriate personal selling philosophy, the result is a high-quality partnership.

The **presentation plan** that is at the heart of the presentation strategy is typically divided into six stages: approach, presentation, demonstration, negotiation, closing, and servicing the sale (Figure 14-3). The relative importance of each stage can vary by country or region. As mentioned several times already, the global salesperson *must* understand cultural norms and proper protocol, from proper exchange of business cards to the proper volume of one's voice during a discussion to the proper amount of eye contact made with the decision maker. In some countries, the approach is prolonged as the buyer gets to know or takes the measure of the salesperson on a personal level, with no mention of the pending deal. In such instances, the presentation comes only after rapport has been firmly established. In some regions of Latin America and Asia, for example, rapport development may take weeks, even months. The customer may also place more importance on what occurs *following* work than on what is accomplished during the formal work hours of 8 A.M. to 5 P.M.

In the six-step presentation plan, the first step, *approach*, is the sales representative's initial contact with the customer or prospect. The most crucial element of this step is to completely

FIGURE 14-2

Building a High-Quality Sales Partnership

Source: Gerald L. Manning and Barry L. Reece, *Selling Today: Creating Customer Value*, 10th ed. © 2007, pp. 15, 18, 238. Reprinted/Adapted by permission of Pearson Education, Inc., Upper Saddle River, NJ.

---

[17] *IBM 2010 Annual Report* (Armonk, New York), p. 10.
[18] "1100100 and Counting," *The Economist* (June 11, 2011), p. 60.

FIGURE 14-3

The Six-Step Presentation Plan

Source: Gerald L. Manning and Barry L. Reece, *Selling Today: Creating Customer Value*, 10th ed. © 2007, pp. 15, 18, 238. Reprinted/Adapted by permission of Pearson Education, Inc., Upper Saddle River, NJ.

Step One: Approach	☐ Review Strategic/Consultative Selling Model ☐ Initiate customer contact
Step Two: Presentation	☐ Determine prospect needs ☐ Select product or service ☐ Initiate sales presentation
Step Three: Demonstration	☐ Decide what to demonstrate ☐ Select selling tools ☐ Initiate demonstration
Step Four: Negotiation	☐ Anticipate buyer concerns ☐ Plan negotiating methods ☐ Initiate win-win negotiations
Step Five: Close	☐ Plan appropriate closing methods ☐ Recognize closing clues ☐ Initiate closing methods
Step Six: Servicing the Sale	☐ Suggestion selling ☐ Follow through ☐ Follow-up calls

Service, retail, wholesale, and manufacturer selling

understand the decision-making process and the roles of each participant, such as decision maker, influencer, ally, or blocker. In some societies, it is difficult to identify the highest-ranking individual based on observable behavior during group meetings. This crucial bit of strategic information often is uncovered only after the sales rep has spent considerable time developing rapport and getting to know the overall customer organization from various perspectives and in various contexts.

In the *presentation* step, the prospect's needs are assessed and matched to the company's products. To communicate effectively with a foreign audience, the style and message of the presentation must be carefully thought out. In the United States, the presentation is typically designed to sell and persuade, whereas the intent of the international version should be to educate and inform. High-pressure tactics rarely succeed in global selling, despite the fact that they are natural components of many American sales pitches. The message is equally critical because what may be regarded as fully acceptable in U.S. discussions may either offend or confuse the overseas sales audience. A humorous example of this occurred during a session between representatives from Adolph Coors Company and a foreign prospect. The first slide in the presentation contained a translation of Coors's slogan "Turn It Loose," but within seconds of this slide being shown, the audience began to chuckle. As translated, the slogan described diarrhea—obviously something that the presenters had no desire to convey to this group!

Next comes the *sales demonstration*, during which the salesperson has the opportunity to tailor the communication effort to the customer and alternately tell and show how the product can meet the customer's needs. This step represents one of personal selling's important advantages as a promotional tool. The prospect's senses become involved, and he or she can actually see the product in action, and touch it, taste it, or hear it, as the case may be.

During the presentation, the prospect may express concerns or objections about the product itself, the price, or some other aspect of the sale. Dealing effectively with objections in an international setting is a learned art. In some cases, this is simply part of the sales ritual, and the customer expects the representative to be prepared for a lively debate on the pros and cons of the product in question. In some instances, it is taboo to initiate an open discussion where any form of disagreement is apparent; such conversations are to be handled in a one-to-one situation or in a small group with a few key individuals present. A common theme in sales training is the concept of *active listening*; naturally, in global sales, verbal and nonverbal communication barriers of the type discussed in Chapter 4 present special challenges. When objections are successfully overcome, serious negotiations can begin.

Negotiation is required to ensure that both the customer and the salesperson come away from the presentation as winners. Experienced American sales representatives know that persistence during the negotiation stage is one tactic often needed to win an order in the United States. However, some foreign customers consider American-style persistence (implying tenacity) or arm-twisting rude and offensive. This can end the negotiations quickly—or, in the worst case, can be taken as a display of self-perceived American superiority, which then must be countered aggressively or brought to an immediate end. Inappropriate application of American-style negotiation tactics has plagued some U.S. sales representatives attempting to assertively close deals with Canadian companies. Conversely, in other countries, persistence often means endurance, a willingness to patiently invest months or years before the efforts result in an actual sale. For example, a company wishing to enter the Japanese market must be prepared for negotiations to take several years.

Having completed the negotiation step, the sales representative is able to move on to the *close*, and thus ask for the order. Attitudes toward the degree of bluntness that is acceptable in making this request vary among countries. In Latin America, a bold closing statement is respected, whereas in Asia, the closing must be done with more deference toward the decision maker. As with objection handling and negotiation, the close is a selling skill that comes with both knowledge and experience in global business and sales.

The final step is *servicing the sale*. A sale does not end when the order is written; to ensure customer satisfaction with the purchase, an implementation process (which may include delivery and installation) must be outlined and a customer service program established (see Exhibit 14-4). Implementation can be complicated because of logistical and transportation issues as well as potential problems with the in-country resources to handle all the necessary steps. Transportation alternatives were discussed in Chapter 12. Decisions regarding resources for implementation and after-sale service are similar to decisions about the personal selling structure described in the following paragraphs. There are cost benefits to using in-country nationals for implementation, but quality control is more difficult to guarantee. Establishing expatriates for the primary function of implementation is costly and normally cannot be justified until international operations are more mature and profitable. But sending an implementation team to the host country creates a variety of expense and regulatory concerns. Even when implementation has been adequately addressed, the

Exhibit 14-4 This pair of print advertisements for DuPont Pioneer communicates the fact that the company's global network of sales agents is dedicated to top-notch customer service. Worldwide, the Pioneer brand is associated with expert advice and customer support: It is important for farmers to have the right seeds for their particular soil and climatic conditions. Pioneer's sales agents go into the field equipped with tablet devices on which they record and store data about each farmer's needs and search Pioneer's database for the product that will give the best yield per acre. Compare these ads with the pair that appears in Chapter 13. Which exhibits more adaptation?"
Source: DuPont Pioneer.

requirement of solid customer service raises all of the same questions again: in-country nationals, expatriates, or third-country nationals?

Sales Force Nationality

As just noted, a basic issue for companies that sell globally is the composition of the sales force in terms of nationality. It is possible to utilize expatriate salespersons, hire host-country nationals, or recruit third-country sales personnel (see Exhibit 14-5). The staffing decision is contingent on several factors, including management's orientation, the technological sophistication of the product, and the stage of economic development exhibited by the target country. Not surprisingly, a company with an ethnocentric orientation is likely to prefer expatriates and adopt a standardized approach without regard to technology or the level of economic development in the target country. Polycentric companies selling in developed countries should opt for expatriates to sell technologically sophisticated products; a host-country sales force can be used when technological sophistication is lower. In less-developed countries, host-country nationals should be used for products in which technology is a factor; host-country agents should be used for low-tech products. The widest diversity of sales force nationality is found in a company in which a regiocentric orientation prevails. Except in the case of high-tech products in developed countries, third-country nationals are likely to be used in all situations.[19]

In addition to the factors just cited, management must also weigh the advantages and disadvantages of each option. First, because they come from the home country, expatriates often possess a high level of product knowledge and are likely to be thoroughly versed in their company's commitment to after-sales service. They also come with corporate philosophies and culture well ingrained. In addition, they are better able to institute the acceptable practices and follow the policies of the home office and, generally, there is less potential for control or loyalty issues to arise. Finally, a foreign assignment can provide employees with valuable experience that can enhance promotion prospects.

However, utilizing expatriates has several disadvantages. If the headquarters' mind-set is *too* firmly ingrained, the expat may have a difficult time understanding the foreign environment and assimilating into it. This can eventually lead to significant losses; the sales effort may be poorly received in the market, or homesickness can lead to a costly reversal of the relocation process. Maintaining expat sales personnel is also extremely expensive; the average annual cost to post employees and their families overseas exceeds $250,000. In addition to paying expat salaries, companies must pay moving expenses, cost-of-living adjustments, and host-country

Exhibit 14-5 In global marketing, sales meetings and presentations typically involve people from various nationalities. These may include expatriates (from the headquarters country), host-country nationals, and third-country nationals. A successful salesperson takes the time to adapt the strategic/consultative selling model to the specific selling situation. The various elements of the six-step presentation plan may also need to be adapted. Can you think of any characteristics of your home-country communication patterns that may require adaptation?
Source: Harry Maynard/zefa/Corbis Images.

---

[19] Earl D. Honeycutt, Jr., and John B. Ford, "Guidelines for Managing an International Sales Force," *Industrial Marketing Management* 24 (March 1995), p. 139.

taxes. Despite the high investment, many expats fail to complete their assignments because of inadequate training and orientation prior to the cross-border transfer.

An alternative is to build a sales force with host-country personnel. Locals offer several advantages, including intimate knowledge of the market and business environment, language skills, and superior knowledge of local culture. The last consideration can be especially important in Asia and Latin America. In addition, because in-country personnel are already in place in the target country, there is no need for expensive relocations. However, host-country nationals may possess work habits or selling styles that do not mesh with those of the parent company. Furthermore, a firm's corporate sales executives tend to have less control over an operation that is dominated by host-country nationals. Headquarters executives may also experience difficulty cultivating loyalty, and host-country nationals are likely to need hefty doses of training and education regarding both the company and its products.

A third option is to hire persons who are not natives of either the headquarters country or the host country; such persons are known as *third-country nationals.* For example, a U.S.-based company might hire someone from Thailand to represent it in China. This option has many advantages in common with the host-country-national approach. In addition, if conflict, diplomatic tension, or some other form of disagreement has driven a wedge between the home country and the target sales country, a sales representative from a third country may be perceived as sufficiently neutral or at "arm's length" to enable the company to continue its sales effort. However, the third-country option has several disadvantages. For one thing, sales prospects may wonder why they have been approached by someone who is neither a local national nor a native of the headquarters country. Third-country nationals may lack motivation if they are compensated less generously than expats or host-country sales personnel; also, they may find themselves passed over for promotions as coveted assignments go to others.

After much trial and error in creating sales forces, most companies today attempt to establish a hybrid sales force composed of a balanced mix of expatriates and in-country nationals. The operative word for this approach is *balanced*, because the potential always remains for conflict between the two groups. It is also the most expensive proposition in terms of upfront costs, because both relocation of expats and extensive training of in-country nationals are required. However, the short-term costs are usually deemed necessary in order to do business and conduct personal selling overseas.

After considering the options, management may question the appropriateness of trying to create personal selling units made up of their own people. A fourth option is to utilize the services of **sales agents**. Agents work under contract rather than as full-time employees. From a global perspective, it often makes a great deal of sense to set up one or more agent entities to at least gain entry into a selected country or region. In some cases, because of the remoteness of the area or the lack of revenue opportunity (beyond servicing satellite operations of customers headquartered elsewhere), agents are retained on a fairly permanent level. To this day, the majority of U.S., Asian, and European companies with an Africa-based sales presence maintain agent groups to represent their interests.

Agents are less expensive than full-time, in-country national sales representatives; at the same time, they possess the same market and cultural knowledge. If agents are used initially and the sales effort gains traction, they can be phased out and replaced by the manufacturer's sales force. Conversely, a company may use its own sales force initially and then convert to agents. P&G's Golden Store program in Mexico is an excellent illustration of the various sales force options. As discussed in Chapter 12, company representatives visit participating stores to tidy display areas and arrange promotional material in prominent places. At first, P&G used its own sales force; now it relies on independent agents, who buy inventory (paying in advance) and then resell the items to shopkeepers.

Other international personal selling approaches that fall somewhere between sales agents and full-time employee teams include the following:

- *Exclusive license arrangements* in which a firm will pay commissions to an in-country company's sales force to conduct personal selling on its behalf. For example, when Canada's regulatory agency prevented U.S. telephone companies from entering the market on their own, AT&T, MCI, Sprint, and other firms crafted a series of exclusive license arrangements with Canadian telephone companies.

- *Contract manufacturing or production* with a degree of personal selling made available through warehouses or showrooms that are open to potential customers. Sears has employed this technique in various overseas markets, with the emphasis placed on manufacturing and production but with the understanding that opportunities for some sales results do exist.
- *Management-only agreements* through which a corporation will manage a foreign sales force in a mode that is similar to franchising. Hilton Hotels has these types of agreements all over the world, not only for hotel operations, but also for personal selling efforts aimed at securing conventions, business meetings, and other large-group events.
- *Joint ventures* with an in-country (or regional) partner. Because many countries place restrictions on foreign ownership within their borders, partnerships can serve as the best way for a company to obtain both a personal sales capability as well as an existing base of customers.

Special Forms of Marketing Communications: Direct Marketing, Support Media, Event Sponsorship, and Product Placement

The Direct Marketing Association defines **direct marketing** as any communication with a consumer or business recipient that is designed to generate a response in the form of an order, a request for further information, and/or a visit to a store or other place of business. Companies use direct mail, telemarketing, television, print, and other media to generate responses and build databases filled with purchase histories and other information about customers. By contrast, mass-marketing communications are typically aimed at broad segments of consumers with certain demographic, psychographic, or behavioral characteristics in common. Table 14-2 shows other differences between direct marketing and "regular" marketing.

Although direct marketing dates back decades, more sophisticated techniques and tools are being used today. For example, Don Peppers and Martha Rogers advocate an approach known as **one-to-one marketing**. Building on the notion of customer relationship management (CRM), one-to-one marketing calls for treating different customers differently based on their previous purchase histories or past interactions with the company. Peppers and Rogers describe the four steps in one-to-one marketing as follows:[20]

1. *Identify* customers and accumulate detailed information about them.
2. *Differentiate* customers and rank them in terms of their value to the company.
3. *Interact* with customers and develop more cost-efficient and -effective forms of interaction.
4. *Customize* the product or service offered to the customer (e.g., by personalizing direct mail offers).

TABLE 14-2 Comparison of Direct Marketing and Mass Marketing

Direct Marketing	Mass Marketing
Marketer adds value (creates place utility) by arranging for delivery of product to customer's door.	Product benefits do not typically include delivery to customer's door.
Marketer controls the product all the way through to delivery.	Marketer typically loses control as product is turned over to distribution channel intermediaries.
Direct-response advertising is used to generate an immediate inquiry or order.	Advertising is used for cumulative effect over time to build image, awareness, loyalty, and benefit recall. Purchase action is deferred.
Repetition is used within the ad/offer.	Repetition is used over a period of time.
Customer perceives higher risk because product is bought unseen. Recourse may be viewed as distant or inconvenient.	Customer perceives less risk due to direct contact with product. Recourse is viewed as less distant.

---

[20] Don Peppers, Martha Rogers, and Bob Dorf, "Is Your Company Ready for One-to-One Marketing?" *Harvard Business Review* 77, no. 1 (January–February 1999).

Worldwide, the popularity of direct marketing has been steadily increasing in recent years. One reason is the availability of credit cards—widespread in some countries, growing in others—as a convenient payment mechanism for direct-response purchases. (Visa, American Express, and MasterCard generate enormous revenues by sending direct mail offers to their cardholders.) Another reason is societal: Whether in Japan, Germany, or the United States, dual-income families have money to spend but less time to shop outside the home. Technological advances have made it easier for companies to reach customers directly. Cable and satellite television allow advertisers to reach specific audiences on a global basis. MTV reaches hundreds of millions of households worldwide and attracts a young viewership. A company wishing to reach business-people can buy time on CNN, Fox News Network, or CNBC.

Direct marketing's popularity in Europe increased sharply during the 1990s. The European Commission expects investment in direct marketing to surpass expenditures for traditional advertising in the near future. One reason is that direct marketing programs can be readily made to conform to the "think global, act local" philosophy. As Tony Coad, managing director of a London-based direct marketing and database company, noted two decades ago, "Given the linguistic, cultural, and regional diversity of Europe, the celebrated idea of a Euro-consumer is Euro-baloney. Direct marketing's strength lies in addressing these differences and adapting to each consumer."[21] Obstacles still remain, however, including the European Commission's concerns about data protection and privacy, high postal rates in some countries, and the relatively limited development of the mailing list industry. Rainer Hengst of Deutsche Post offers the following guidelines for U.S.-based direct marketers that wish to go global:[22]

- The world is full of people who are not Americans. Be sure not to treat them like they are.
- Like politics, all marketing is local. Just because your direct mail campaign worked in Texas, do not assume it will work in Toronto.
- Although there may be a EU, there is no such thing as a "European."
- Pick your target, focus on one country, and do your homework.
- You'll have a hard time finding customers in Paris, France, if your return address is Paris, Texas. Customers need to be able to return products locally or at least believe there are services available in their country.

Direct Mail

Direct mail uses the postal service as a vehicle for delivering a personally addressed offer to a prospect targeted by a marketer. Direct mail is popular with banks, insurance companies, and other financial services providers. As customers respond to direct mail offers, the marketer adds information to its database. That information, in turn, allows the marketer to refine subsequent offers and generate more precisely targeted lists. The United States is home to a well-developed mailing list industry. A company can rent a list to target virtually any type of buyer; naturally, the more selective and specialized the list, the more expensive it is. The availability of good lists and the sheer size of the market are important factors in explaining why Americans receive more direct mail than anyone else. However, on a per capita basis, German consumers are world-leader mail-order shoppers, buying more than $500 each in merchandise annually.

Compared with the United States, list availability in Europe and Japan is much more limited. The lists that are available may be lower in quality and contain more errors and duplications than lists from the United States. Despite such problems, direct mail is growing in popularity in some parts of the world. In Europe, for example, regulators are concerned about the extent that children are exposed to, or even targeted by, traditional cigarette advertising. Faced with the threat of increased restrictions on its advertising practices, the tobacco industry is making a strategy shift toward direct mail. As David Robottom, development director at the Direct Marketing Association, noted, "Many of the promotions on cigarette packets are about collected data. [The tobacco companies] are working very hard at building up loyalty."

Following the economic crisis in Asia, a number of companies in that region turned to direct mail in an effort to use their advertising budgets more effectively. Historically, the Asian direct marketing sector has lagged behind its counterparts in the United States and Europe. Grey

---

[21] Bruce Crumley, "European Market Continues to Soar," *Advertising Age* (February 21, 1994), p. 22.
[22] Rainer Hengst, "Plotting Your Global Strategy," *Direct Marketing* 63, no. 4 (August 2000), pp. 52–57.

Global Group established a Kuala Lumpur office of Grey Direct Interactive in 1997; OgilvyOne Worldwide is the Malaysian subsidiary of Ogilvy & Mather Group specializing in direct marketing. Companies in the banking and telecommunications sectors have been at the forefront of direct marketing initiatives in Asia, using their extensive databases to target individual consumers by mail or Internet.

Catalogs

A **catalog** is a magazine-style publication that features photographs, illustrations, and extensive information about a company's products. (The term *magalog* is sometimes used to describe this communication medium.) The global catalog retail sector generates revenues of several hundred billion dollars each year. Catalogs have a long and illustrious history as a direct marketing tool in both Europe and the United States. The European catalog market flourished after World War II as consumers sought convenience, bargain prices, and access to a wider range of goods. U.S.-based catalog marketers include JCPenney, Lands' End, L.L.Bean, and Victoria's Secret; in Europe, Otto GmbH & Co KG (Germany) is the leading catalog retailer. Catalogs are widely recognized as an important part of an IMC program, and many companies use catalogs in tandem with traditional retail distribution and e-commerce channels. The catalog retail sector in the United States represents about one-third of the total global market; more than 17 billion catalogs were mailed in 2008.[23]

Historically, catalogers in the United States benefited from the ability to ship goods from one coast to the other, crossing multiple state boundaries with relatively few regulatory hurdles. By contrast, prior to the advent of the single market, catalog sales in Europe were hindered by the fact that mail-order products passing through customs at national borders were subject to value-added taxes (VAT). Because VAT drove up prices of goods that crossed borders, a particular catalog tended to be targeted at intracountry buyers. In other words, Germans bought from German catalogs, French consumers bought from French catalogs, and so on. Market-entry strategies were also affected by customs regulations; catalogers' business grew by acquiring existing companies in various countries. For example, Otto GmbH & Co KG distributes hundreds of different catalogs in 20 countries (see Exhibit 14-6).

Exhibit 14-6 German supermodel Yvonne Catterfeld poses with Otto's spring/summer 2011 catalog, which features her photo on the cover. Shoppers can choose from Pure Wear, Kind To Your Skin, and other eco-friendly fashion lines made from organic cotton. As Otto Group CEO Dr. Michael Otto explains, "Conscious buying and consumption behavior are an important contribution toward promoting environmentally friendly and socially compatible ways of manufacturing goods worldwide."
Source: imago stock&people/Newscom.

---

[23] Jeffrey Ball, "In Digital Era, Marketers Still Prefer Paper Trail," *The Wall Street Journal* (October 16, 2009), p. B1.

Today, the single market means that mail-order goods can move freely throughout the EU without incurring VAT charges. Also, since January 1993, VAT exemptions have been extended to goods bound for the European Free Trade Area countries (Norway, Iceland, Switzerland, and Liechtenstein). Some predict robust growth in Europe's mail-order business, thanks to the increased size of the potential catalog market and the VAT-free environment. The single market is also attracting American catalog retailers even though they will face higher costs for paper, printing, and shipping as well as the familiar issue of whether to adapt their offerings to local tastes. Stephen Miles, director of international development at Lands' End, said, "The most difficult thing is to know in which areas to be local. We're proud that we're an American sportswear company, but that doesn't mean your average German consumer wants to pick up the phone and speak English to someone."[24]

In Japan, the domestic catalog industry is well developed. Leading catalog companies include Cecile, with $1 billion in annual sales of women's apparel and lingerie; Kukutake Publishing, which sells educational materials; and Shaddy, a general merchandise company. As noted in Chapter 12, Japan's fragmented distribution system represents a formidable obstacle to market entry by outsiders. An increasing number of companies use direct marketing to circumvent the distribution bottleneck. Annual revenues for all forms of consumer and business direct-response advertising in Japan passed the $1 trillion mark in the mid-1990s; they declined to $525 billion in 2000 as Japan's economic difficulties continued. Success can be achieved using different strategies. For example, Patagonia dramatically increased sales after publishing a Japanese-language catalog, whereas L.L.Bean offers a Japanese-language insert in its traditional catalog.

Even as they continue to develop the Japanese market, Western catalogers are now turning their attention to other Asian countries. In Hong Kong and Singapore, efficient postal services, highly educated populations, wide use of credit cards, and high per capita income are attracting the attention of catalog marketers. Notes Michael Grasee, the former director of international business development at Lands' End, "We see our customer in Asia as pretty much the same customer we have everywhere. It's the time-starved, traveling, hardworking executive."[25] Catalogers are also targeting Asia's developing countries. Otto GmbH & Co KG, with 2012 revenues of $15.3 billion and about 6 percent of global mail-order sales, is planning to enter China, Korea, and Taiwan. Because these countries have few local mail-order companies that could be acquisition targets, executives at Otto have mapped out an entry strategy based on acquiring a majority stake in joint ventures with local retailers.

Infomercials, Teleshopping, and Interactive Television

An **infomercial** is a form of paid television programming in which a particular product is demonstrated, explained, and offered for sale to viewers who call a toll-free number shown on the screen. Thomas Burke, president of Saatchi & Saatchi's infomercial division, calls infomercials "the most powerful form of advertising ever created." The cost of producing a single infomercial can reach $3 million; advertisers then pay as much as $500,000 for time slots on U.S. cable and satellite systems and local TV channels. Because infomercials are typically 30 minutes in length and often feature studio audiences and celebrity announcers, many viewers believe they are watching regular talk show–type programming. Although originally associated with personal care, fitness, and household products, such as those from legendary direct-response pitchman Ron Popeil, infomercials have gone upmarket in recent years. For example, Lexus generated more than 40,000 telephone inquiries after launching its used-car program with an infomercial; 2 percent of respondents ultimately purchased a Lexus automobile.

In Asia, infomercials generate several hundred million dollars in annual sales. Costs for a late-night time slot range from $100,000 in Japan to $20,000 in Singapore. Infomercials are also playing a part in the development of China's market. The government has given its blessing by allowing China Central Television, the state-run channel, to air infomercials and give Chinese consumers access to Western goods. Despite low per capita incomes, Chinese consumers are thought to achieve a savings rate as high as 40 percent because housing and health care are

[24] Cecilie Rohwedder, "U.S. Mail-Order Firms Shake Up Europe," *The Wall Street Journal* (January 6, 1998), p. A15.
[25] James Cox, "Catalogers Expand in Asia," *USA Today* (October 18, 1996), p. 4B.

Exhibit 14-7 QVC ("Quality, Value, and Convenience"), the U.S.-based home shopping channel, is available in nearly 250 million homes worldwide. Shoppers can order jewelry, house-wares, clothing, and other merchandise around the clock, both on QVC's cable TV channels and online. QVC has inter-national retailing operations in China (via joint venture), Germany, Italy, Japan, and the United Kingdom. As Jeff Charney, chief marketing officer at QVC, noted, "The essence of the brand is the feeling you get when you open the package."

Oliver Mallman is a popular on-air personality and program host for QVC Germany. His specialty is presenting kitchenware, chef's tools, and other household helpers. Mallman loves QVC's round-the-clock format, noting that "you never know what's coming at you and it's always different."
Source: Courtesy of QVC, Inc.

provided by the state. China Shop-A-Vision is in the vanguard, signing up 20,000 "TV shopping members" in its first year of airing infomercials. As these and other pioneers in Chinese direct-response television have learned, however, many obstacles remain, including the limited number of private telephones, low penetration of credit cards, and problems with delivery logistics in crowded cities such as Shanghai.[26]

With **teleshopping**, home-shopping channels such as QVC and the Home Shopping Network (HSN) take the infomercial concept one step further; the round-the-clock programming is *exclusively* dedicated to product demonstration and selling (see Exhibit 14-7). Worldwide, home shopping is a multibillion-dollar industry. The leading home-shopping channels are also leveraging the Internet. For example, in addition to operating home-shopping channels in the United States, China, Germany, and Japan, HSN Inc. also offers an online shopping experience at www.hsn.com.

QVC's agreement with Rupert Murdoch's British Sky Broadcasting (BSkyB) satellite company enables it to reach Germany, Italy, and the United Kingdom; it is also available in Japan. As QVC executive Francis Edwards explained, "European customers respond in differ-ent ways, though the basic premise and concept is the same. The type of jewelry is different. German consumers wouldn't buy 14-karat gold. They go for a higher karat. We can sell wine in Germany, but not in the U.S."[27] A number of local and regional teleshopping channels have sprung up in Europe. Germany's HOT (Home Order Television) is a joint venture with Quelle Schickedanz, a mail-order company. Sweden's TV-Shop is available in more than one dozen European countries. Typically, Europeans are more discriminating than the average American teleshopping customer.

Industry observers expect the popularity of home shopping to increase during the next few years as **interactive television** (ITV or t-commerce) technology is introduced into more house-holds. As the term implies, ITV allows television viewers to interact with the programming content that they are viewing. ITV has a greater presence in Europe than in the United States; in the United Kingdom alone, more than half of all Pay TV subscribers make use of ITV services.

---

[26] Jon Hilsenrath, "In China, a Taste of Buy-Me TV," *The New York Times* (November 17, 1996), Sec. 3, pp. 1, 11.
[27] Michelle Pentz, "Teleshopping Gets a Tryout in Europe but Faces Cultural and Legal Barriers," *The Wall Street Journal* (September 9, 1996), p. A8.

TABLE 14-3 Expenditures for Outdoor Advertising as Percentage of Total Ad Spending

Country	Percentage
France	11.7%
United Kingdom	5.8
Spain	5.4
Italy	4.3
Canada	4.2
United States	4.0
Germany	4.0
Worldwide	5.9

The remote control units provided by Pay TV service providers in the United Kingdom have a red button that viewers press to order products from home-shopping channels, choose different camera angles during sports broadcasts, vote during audience participation shows such as *Big Brother*, or order free samples of advertised products. In 2005, Diageo tested an interactive ad for Smirnoff vodka; after the first 60 seconds, viewers were required to press the button two more times to see the ad in its entirety. Comparing traditional TV ads with the new format, James Pennefather, Smirnoff brand manager for the United Kingdom, noted, "Interactive advertising is a lot more unproven and untested, and it is a calculated risk for us. We have to do this kind of thing to learn if it will be a success or not."[28]

Support Media

Traditional support media include transit and billboard advertising. As shown in Table 14-3, in most parts of the world outdoor advertising is growing at a faster rate than the overall advertising market. Exhibit 14-8 illustrates how, as governments in China and other emerging markets add

Exhibit 14-8 The popularity of transit and billboard advertising is boosting the fortunes of JCDecaux, the outdoor advertising group. The market leader in Europe, the company operates in about 45 countries. Outdoor advertising is experiencing explosive growth in China, where JCDecaux competes with Tom Group, Clear Media, and thousands of other local companies. This is especially true in large cities such as Beijing, Shanghai, and Guangzhou. The same trend is evident in Russia, especially in Moscow.
Source: Jiri Rezac/Alamy.

[28] Aaron O. Patrick, "Selling Vodka with an Interactive Twist," *The Wall Street Journal* (October 11, 2005), p. B3. See also "Europe Wants Its ITV," *Chain Store Age* 77, no. 7 (July 2001), pp. 76–78.

EMERGING MARKETS BRIEFING BOOK

Billboards Banned in Brazil!

MyMarketingLab   SYNC • THINK • LEARN

Score one for environmental activists: On January 1, 2007, *Lei Cidade Limpa* ("Clean City Law") went into effect in São Paulo, Brazil. The main effect of the law, which was championed by Mayor Gilberto Kassab, is to ban various forms of outdoor advertising in the city of 11 million people. As Kassab asserted, "The Clean City Law came about from a necessity to combat pollution….pollution of water, sound, air, and the visual. We decided that we should start combating pollution with the most conspicuous sector: visual pollution."

The ban means that São Paulo's giant billboards and video screens—some 15,000 in all—have come down. What's left is a mishmash of skeleton frames devoid of posters (see Exhibit 14-9). In addition, transit ads on buses and taxis are no longer allowed. Store signs are still permitted, but the maximum size of a given sign is determined by a formula based on the dimensions of the store's facade.

Applauding the ban, a local journalist wrote that the new law "is a rare victory of the public interest over private; of order over disorder; of aesthetics over ugliness; of cleanliness over trash." That view, however, was not shared by the chief economist of the 32,000-member Commercial Association of São Paulo. Denouncing the ban, Marcel Solimeo said, "This is a radical law that damages the rules of a market economy and respect for the rule of law. We live in a consumer society and the essence of capitalism is the availability of information about products."

Some advertisers even acknowledge that, in Brazil, traditional outdoor advertising may not be the best communication channel. Marcio Santoro, an executive at Agência Africa, is blunt when he describes the advertising environment before the Clean City Law went into effect. He says, "It was terrible. There came a point that for you to be noticed you had to buy a lot of ads, because there was so much noise." Anna Freitag, a marketing manager for Hewlett-Packard in Brazil, concurs. "A billboard is media on the road. In rational purchases it means less effectiveness…as people are involved in so many things that it makes it difficult to execute the call to action," she says.

Denied access to traditional outdoor advertising for now, companies have devised a number of alternative ways to communicate with prospective customers. For example, Citibank uses the color blue in much of its advertising, so its main branch in São Paulo was painted blue to help it stand out. Innovative indoor approaches such as placing ads in elevators and bathrooms are also being adopted. Brazilians have embraced social media, so online channels are a natural fit. As Nizan Guanaes of agency network Grupo ABC says, "The Internet is the next frontier, for reasons I don't have to explain. Brazil is very sophisticated in digital and social media."

City leaders have indicated that, eventually, special zones will be created in which a limited amount of outdoor advertising will be permitted. Even so, many advertisers have adjusted to the new reality. With the vast majority of São Paulo residents supporting the ban, advertisers understand that it does not make sense to puts ads where they are not welcome.

Sources: Vincent Bevins, "São Paulo Advertising Goes Underground," *Financial Times* (September 7, 2010), p. 10; David Evan Harris, "São Paulo: A City Without Ads," *Adbusters*, no. 73 (September/October 2007); Larry Rohter, "Billboard Ban in São Paulo Angers Advertisers," *The New York Times* (December 12, 2006), p. C1.

Exhibit 14-9 Billboards were once ubiquitous in Brazil's most populous city. Now that the Clean City Law has taken effect, empty frames are all that remain.
Source: Bloomberg via Getty Images.

mass transportation systems and build and improve their highway infrastructures, advertisers are utilizing more indoor and outdoor posters and billboards to reach the buying public. Japan's population relies heavily on public transportation; the average Tokyo resident spends 70 minutes commuting to work. Consequently, spending on outdoor and transit advertising in Japan is much higher than in most other countries; an estimated $4.4 billion annual expenditures on outdoor media amounts to as much as 12 percent of total ad spending.[29]

Worldwide spending on outdoor advertising amounts to about 6 percent of total ad spending; in Europe, 6.4 percent of advertising spending is allocated to outdoor advertising, compared with 4 percent in the United States. The two largest players in the industry are Texas-based Clear Channel Outdoor Holdings, with more than 900,000 outdoor and transit displays worldwide, and France's JCDecaux.

Sponsorship

Sponsorship is an increasingly popular form of marketing communications whereby a company pays a fee to have its name associated with a particular event, team or athletic association, or sports facility. Sponsorship combines elements of PR and sales promotion. From a PR perspective, sponsorship generally ensures that a corporate or brand name will be mentioned numerous times by on-air or public-address commentators. Large-scale events also draw considerable media attention that typically includes multiple mentions of the sponsoring company or brand in news reports or talk shows (see Exhibit 14-10). Because event sponsorship typically provides numerous contact points with large numbers of people, it is a perfect vehicle for sampling and other sales promotion opportunities.

Olympic Games or World Cup soccer sponsorships can help companies reach a global audience; sponsors are also drawn to professional team sports, car racing, hot-air balloon competitions, rodeos, music concerts, and other events that appeal to national or regional audiences. For example, the Coca-Cola Company views World Cup sponsorship as a key promotional opportunity. During the 2010 World Cup in South Africa, Coca-Cola spent an estimated $124 million for sponsorship rights plus another $475 million on advertising and promotions. The beverage giant used an IMC approach, running Africa-themed ads on TV, online, and in restaurants. When World Cup matches were broadcast, Coke's Powerade sports drink brand was featured on the

Exhibit 14-10 In September 2005, with 150 days to go before the opening ceremonies of the 2006 Olympic Winter Games in Torino, Italy, Lenovo Chairman Yuanqing Yang and Vice President of Marketing Philippe Davy kicked off the company's computing equipment sponsorship in New York City. Lenovo was the official computing equipment partner for the 2006 Olympic Winter Games; it was also the partner for the 2008 Olympic Games in Beijing.
Source: Jason Lee/Reuters/Landov Media.

[29] Geoffrey A. Fowler and Sebastian Moffett, "Adidas's Billboard Ads Give a Kick to Japanese Pedestrians," *The Wall Street Journal* (August 29, 2003), pp. B1, B4.

EMERGING MARKETS BRIEFING BOOK

Expo 2010 Shanghai China

SYNC • THINK • LEARN

MyMarketingLab

For marketers of the world's biggest corporate and national brands, all roads led to Shanghai in 2010. The reason? The Shanghai Expo, the latest in a series of massive Universal Exhibitions that date back to the mid-nineteenth century. London's Great Exhibition of the Works of Industry of All Nations in 1851 was the first; others include the Exhibition Universelle in Paris (1889), the World's Columbian Exposition in Chicago (1893), and the New York World's Fair (1939 and 1964).

Shanghai Expo, which opened May 1, 2010, enjoyed the distinction of being the biggest expo of them all. It was mounted at an expense of $55 billion, twice the amount Beijing spent on the 2008 Olympics. However, there was a key difference between the Beijing Olympics and the Shanghai Expo; as one observer noted, the Olympics was a show that China put on for the world. By contrast, the Expo was a performance that the world put on for China (see Exhibit 14-11).

A total of 192 countries participated, and exhibitors welcomed about 73 million visitors—most of them Chinese—by the time the Expo closed at the end of October 2010. What did these visitors find? Shanghai Expo's theme was "Better City, Better Life"; the entire Expo site used water from the Huangpu River for the cooling system. Now that the Expo is closed, Shanghai's residents have continued to benefit from the investment in infrastructure improvements. For example, the neighborhood where the Expo was staged has newly paved streets, and 150 new subway stops were built.

At one time Shanghai was known as the "Paris of the Orient." After the Cultural Revolution, however, glamour and individuality gave way to uniforms and conformity. But things have come full circle now, with Shanghai once again celebrating its status as China's financial center and an up-and-coming, cosmopolitan city. China as a whole now represents the world's second-largest market for luxury goods. It is no surprise, therefore, that numerous global fashion companies and brands were present at Expo 2010. Chanel, Prada, and Versace were among the exhibitors; staff at the Italian Pavilion wore Prada. Prada created a special line of Expo-themed consumer products, including windbreakers, baseball caps, and key chains.

The theme of Expo 2010 was "Better City, Better Life," and many exhibits by corporate and national sponsors were designed to show how technology can improve quality of life. Exhibits in the Urban Best Practices Area embodied this overarching theme. For example, the German city of Hamburg chose the theme "Balancity"—a city in balance—and showcased a "passive house" designed to maintain year-round comfortable interior temperatures without conventional heating or air conditioning systems. The guiding philosophy was that "A city can be a good place to live—if it provides a balance between renewal and preservation, innovation and tradition, urbanity and nature, community and individual development, and work and leisure." Among the innovations that held promise for everyday living were "ecological toilets" that collect rainwater for flushing; these were particularly welcome in a country where public sanitation is problematic.

The Swiss Pavilion, which was sponsored in part by Nestlé, was keyed to the theme "Rural–Urban Interaction" and featured walls made of soybeans. The "intelligent facade" was covered with 10,000 solar cells; when the pavilion was dismantled, the cells were given away. Spain's $2.6 million pavilion offered 8,500 square feet of floor space encased by a steel structure covered with wicker that was handwoven into various patterns. Spain's exhibit also included a five-story house made from bamboo.

The queues and visitor tallies at the various exhibits indicated the high level of interest. People would sometimes wait 8 hours to see Saudi Arabia's IMAX theater attraction, which offered an immersive flight over the Kingdom's treasures. Saudi Arabia's pavilion also showcased four types of cities, including the "City of Energy" and the "City of Fast-Growing Economy." Chinese visitors referred to Japan's exhibit as "Purple Silkworm Island"; the semicircular structure was covered with a double-layered, purple membrane. Solar collectors were incorporated into the membrane, and indentations called "caves" collected rainwater, which was then sprayed on the membrane to promote cooling. The exhibit was designed to express "harmony between the human heart and technology." A total of 5.5 million visitors poured into Denmark's pavilion to see the iconic Little Mermaid statue. Chile showcased the Phoenix 1 capsule that had been used in the dramatic rescue of 33 miners trapped in a collapsed mine.

General Motors (GM) has been an exhibitor at many previous expos. At the 1939 New York World's Fair, for example, GM proposed the interstate highway system that was eventually built by the U.S. government. Airbags and car seats for children are two GM innovations from the 1974 Spokane Expo that have become commonplace. In Shanghai, General Motors and its Chinese joint venture partner, SAIC, showcased electric mini-cars so compact and light that they could park themselves in the closets of high-rise apartments.

GM was not the only Western corporate exhibitor with a branded Pavilion at Expo 2010. Cisco, the California-based maker of Internet networking equipment, created the SMART+CONNECTED LIFE (S+CL) Pavilion. S+CL was created to showcase a triple bottom line of economic, social, and environmental benefits. The Cisco exhibit included an automated drink dispenser that can offer refreshments when, say, a child returns home from school.

Coca-Cola's red-and-white pavilion—"The Happiness Factory"—featured animated characters and creatures that introduced visitors to "a world refreshed by happiness." In addition, Coke showcased PlantBottle, a packaging innovation that uses plastic and plant-based material. Visitors were also treated to cans of Coke that froze when they were opened. Why was Coke represented at Expo 2010? As Ted Ryan, a manager at Coca-Cola, said, "Our goal is to be considered the premier drinks brand; who else would be there? It has got to be Coca-Cola."

Of course, Chinese companies were also very much in evidence at the Expo. The exterior of their pavilion, dubbed the Dream Cube, changed its colors in response to the movement of the people inside. What kind of return on investment did exhibitors enjoy? National exhibitors hoped for a tourism boost; although only about 3 percent of Chinese citizens have passports, there is a growing trend toward global travel. Paris is one city that is experiencing a big increase in the number of Chinese visitors. According to the French tourism agency Atout, in 2010 alone, 550,000 tourists visited from China and spent $890 billion. Popular shopping destinations include Galeries Lafayette and Au Printemps, two department stores that are very well known in China. Both stores advertise in China; in addition, they employ Chinese-speaking staff members and distribute store maps that have been translated into Chinese.

Sources: Steven Erlanger, "After Long March, Chinese Surrender to Capitalist Shrine," *The New York Times* (September 14, 2011), p. A10; James T. Areddy, "What Makes a Crowd? In Shanghai, 73 Million," *The Wall Street Journal* (October 29, 2010), p. B1; Edwin Heathcote, "Special Effects," *Financial Times* (June 5–6, 2010), p. 8; Patti Waldmeir, "A Luxury Invasion," *Financial Times* (June 5–6, 2010), p. 8; Claire Wrathall, "A City in the Mood for Celebration," *Financial Times* (June 5–6, 2010), p. 9; Waldmeir, "Grand Vision of Shanghai Expo Set to Redream the Past," *Financial Times* (May 1–2, 2010), p. 4.

Exhibit 14-11 One of the six cone-shaped Sun Valleys features in the Expo Axis, the main entrance to the 2010 Shanghai World Exp Park, Pudon, Shanghai, China.
Source: Stan Rohrer/Alamy.

Exhibit 14-12 Shanghai Expo Ticket.

electronic billboards that surrounded the pitch. Scott McCune, Coke's integrated marketing chief, predicted a 5 percent sales increase for Coke in the months leading up to the match. His company plans to invest $12 billion in Africa between now and 2020. As McCune said, "The continent is critically important to us."[30]

As the Coca-Cola Company's participation in World Cup soccer demonstrates, sponsorship can be an effective component of an IMC program. It can be used in countries where regulations limit the extent to which a company can use advertising or other forms of marketing communication. In China, for example, where tobacco advertising is prohibited, B.A.T. and Philip Morris spent tens of millions of dollars sponsoring events such as a Hong Kong–Beijing car rally and China's national soccer tournament. However, in 2005, Chinese authorities ratified the World Health Organization's (WHO) Framework Convention on Tobacco Controls; all forms of tobacco promotion and sponsorship were phased out in 2010. Sponsorship was also popular in the United Kingdom, where Benson & Hedges paid £4 million ($6 million) for a 5-year contract to sponsor cricket matches and Rothman's spent £15 million ($23 million) annually to sponsor a Formula One racing team. However, to comply with the EU directive on tobacco advertising, tobacco sponsorship of all sports—including Formula One racing—has been phased out.

Product Placement: Motion Pictures, Television Shows, and Public Figures

Companies can achieve a unique kind of exposure by using **product placement**, arranging for their products and brand names to appear in popular television programs, movies, and other

---

[30] Valerie Baurlein and Robb M. Stewart, "Coca-Cola Hopes to Score with World Cup Campaign," *The Wall Street Journal* (June 29, 2010), pp. B1, B2.

types of performances. Marketers can also lend or donate products to celebrities or other public figures; the products get publicity when the celebrity appears in public using the product (see Exhibit 14-13).

This tactic is especially popular with auto manufacturers and fashion designers and is often used in conjunction with popular annual television events such as the Academy Awards and the Grammys that garner media attention. For example, Celeste Atkinson is a lifestyle and entertainment manager for Audi. Her job is to create buzz by ensuring that vehicles such as the Audi A8L, the 12-cylinder A8L, and the S8 sports sedan figure in paparazzi photos.[31] For the premiere of *Superman Returns* in 2006, Atkinson arranged for 35 Audis to chauffer Kevin Spacey and other stars to the event. And, let's not forget the Audi R8 Spyder that Robert Downey, Jr.'s Tony Stark character drives in the *Iron Man* movies!

Worldwide audience figures for a blockbuster movie can equal tens of millions of people. In many instances, product placements generate considerable media interest and result in additional publicity. Placements can be arranged in several different ways. Sometimes companies pay a fee for the placement; alternatively, a show's producers will write the product into the script in exchange for marketing and promotion support of the new production. A brand's owners can also strike a barter agreement whereby the company (Sony, for example) supplies the filmmakers with products that serve as props in exchange for licensing rights to, say, the James Bond name in retail promotions (see Exhibit 14-13). Product placement agencies such as Propaganda, Hero Product Placement, and Eon function like talent agencies for products. As such, the agencies fulfill several important functions, among them obtaining legal clearances from a brand's owners, promoting their clients' products to producers, and arranging for products to be delivered to a soundstage.

In the case of television placement, the blurring of advertising and programming content comes as companies increasingly question the effectiveness of traditional advertising. In fact, some evidence suggests that a prominent product placement in a television program leads to better recall than a traditional advertisement. Moreover, many viewers use digital video recorders

Exhibit 14-13 Some global marketers are able to generate publicity for their brands from an unlikely source: Pope Benedict XVI. In this photo taken during the pope's installment mass, for example, His Holiness was wearing red shoes supplied by Italian shoemaker Geox. The pope also has been seen wearing Serengeti sunglasses, and he travels in a customized sport-utility vehicle with a bulletproof bubble that Mercedes-Benz donated to the Vatican. One global branding consultant notes that the pope's devoted following— one billion Catholics—makes a brand's association with him far more valuable than association with even an A-list celebrity.
Source: Jasper Juinen/AP Images.

---

[31] Chris Woodyard, "Audi Works the Ropes to Put Stars in Its Cars," *USA Today* (February 22, 2007), p. 3B.

(DVRs) to "skip" through commercials; consumers are, in effect, ignoring commercials. This trend is forcing advertisers to find new ways to expose viewers to their messages. Sometimes called *branded entertainment*, the effective integration of products and brands into entertainment can be seen on the monster TV hit *American Idol*.

In addition to the effectiveness issue, prop masters and set dressers facing budget pressures are compelled to obtain props for free whenever possible. Moreover, as the cost of marketing major feature films has increased—it is not unusual for a studio to spend $20 to $30 million on marketing alone—studios are increasingly looking for partnerships to share the cost and attract the broadest possible viewing audience. However, product placement raises an interesting issue for global marketers, especially consumer packaged goods companies. This tactic virtually dictates a product standardization approach, because once footage of a scene is shot and incorporated into a movie or television program, the image of the product is "frozen" and will be seen without adaptation everywhere in the world.[32]

For better or for worse, product placements have even reached the world of live theater and opera: In fall 2002, a new Broadway production of Puccini's *La Bohème* was set in Paris circa 1957. The stage set included billboards for luxury pen maker Montblanc and Piper-Heidsieck champagne; during a crowd scene at Café Momus, Piper-Heidsieck was served. Some industry observers warn of a backlash. Ethical concerns are sometimes raised when controversial products such as cigarettes are featured prominently or glamorized. When advertising appears in conventional forms such as broadcast commercials, most consumers are aware of the fact that they are being exposed to an ad. This is not necessarily the case with product placement; in effect, viewers are being marketed to subliminally without their consent. What constitutes proper use of product placement? As Joe Uva, an executive of Omnicom's media planning group, noted, "It shouldn't be forced; it shouldn't be intrusive. If people say 'It's a sell out, it's product placement,' it didn't work." Eugene Secunda, a media studies professor at New York University, is also skeptical. "I think it's a very dangerous plan. The more you get the audience to distrust the content of your programming, to look at it with suspicion in terms of your real agenda, the less likely they are to be responsive to the message because they're going to be looking at everything cynically and with resistance."[33]

Source: Cartoon Features Syndicate.

"It's only until tourism picks up."

---

[32] Stephen J. Gould, Pola B. Gupta, and Sonja Grabner-Krauter, "Product Placements in Movies: A Cross-Cultural Analysis of Austrian, French and American Consumers' Attitudes Toward This Emerging, International Promotional Medium," *Journal of Advertising* 29, no. 4 (Winter 2000), pp. 41–58.

[33] Richard Tompkins, "How Hollywood Brings Brands into Your Home," *Financial Times* (November 5, 2002), p. 15.

→ **THE CULTURAL CONTEXT**

Products Star in Bond Films

SYNC • THINK • LEARN

MyMarketingLab

Lieutenant Commander James Bond—better known as Agent 007—first appeared on film in 1962. Fifty years later, the Bond franchise is stronger than ever, and the films have become famous for integrating well-known brand names into the action. The 23 films featuring the suave British agent have grossed more than $5 billion in worldwide ticket sales. However, the most recent film in the series, *Skyfall*, cost more than $100 million to produce. The series' popularity, plus the high cost of making the films, makes Bond a perfect vehicle for showcasing products and brands.

Many companies are eager to be associated with a high-profile project like a Bond film. In 1996, when BMW introduced a sporty new Z3 convertible, it wanted to make a major global splash. BMW garnered extensive publicity by placing the Z3 in *GoldenEye*, the 18th James Bond film. In the film, gadget chief Q gives 007 a Z3 in place of his Aston Martin; the Z car also figured prominently in movie previews and print ads. BMW dealers were provided with "BMW 007 kits" that allowed prospective buyers to learn more about both the movie and the car before either was available. As *Advertising Age* observed, "BMW has shaken, not just stirred, the auto industry with unprecedented media exposure and awareness for the Z3 and BMW in the U.S."

Tomorrow Never Dies, the follow-up to *GoldenEye*, featured global brand promotional tie-ins worth an estimated $100 million. Ericsson, Heineken, Omega, Brioni, and Visa International all placed products in the film. Bond star Pierce Brosnan also appeared as Agent 007 in specially filmed television commercials. However, when *Die Another Day*, the 20th installment in the series, was released at the end of 2002, BMW took a back seat to Ford. The U.S. automaker persuaded the producers to bring back the Aston Martin (the nameplate was owned by Ford at the time); Jaguars and the new Thunderbird were also prominent in the film.

The 21st Bond film, *Casino Royale*, featured actor Daniel Craig in the role of 007. To avoid a backlash from fans and marketing executives, the film's producers deliberately limited the number of official global partners in the film to six: Sony Electronics, Sony Ericsson, Omega, Heineken, Ford, and Smirnoff. As Myles Romero, Ford's global brand entertainment director, noted, "It's great for brand awareness. The film takes us where we don't have marketing."

The producers' decision to cast Craig as the sixth Bond proved to be a brilliant choice. *Casino Royale* raked in nearly $600 million at the box office, making it the number 1 moneymaker in the franchise. For the next installment, 2008's *Quantum of Solace*, several companies hitched their brands to Bond for the first time. These included Coke Zero and Avon. Speaking of Coke Zero, Derk Hendriksen explained, "We're in more than 100 markets. We thought the tie-in would be very appropriate for two irreverent and global personalities." For its part, Avon coordinated the launch of Bond Girl 007 Fragrance with the film's release. Tracy Haffner, global vice president for marketing, called the film "a great platform to develop a beautiful fragrance and connect with women worldwide."

As the Bond franchise celebrated its 50th anniversary, 2012's *Skyfall* continued the product placement tradition. Heineken spent tens of millions of dollars on a product placement for its flagship beer; star Daniel Craig also appeared in television commercials for the brand. A Sony Vaio laptop and Xperia mobile phone got some screen time, too. And there were the cars: nameplates in evidence included Audi, Jaguar, Land Rover, Volkswagen, Range Rover, and, of course, Aston Martin.

Sources: Edward Helmore, "Happy Birthday, Mr. Bond," *The Wall Street Journal* (July 7–8, 2012), p. D11; Theresa Howard, "Brands Cozy Up to Bond," *USA Today* (October 20, 2008), p. 3B; Emiko Terazono, "Brand New Bond Has a License to Sell," *Financial Times* (November 14, 2006), p. 10; Tim Burt, "His Name's Bond, and He's Been Licensed to Sell," *Financial Times* (October 5–6, 2002), p. 22; Jon Rappoport, "BMW Z3," *Advertising Age* (June 24, 1996), p. S37.

Exhibit 14-14 The Aston Martin DB5 is closely identified with Agent 007. The car's big screen debut was in 1962's *Dr. No*, with Sean Connery starring as James Bond. Things came full circle in fall 2012 as Daniel Craig, the actor who has taken over the Bond role, was paired with a vintage silver DB5.
Source: REUTERS/Chris Helgren.

Summary

Sales promotion is any paid, short-term communication program that adds tangible value to a product or brand. **Consumer sales promotions** are targeted at the ultimate consumers; **trade sales promotions** are used in business-to-business marketing. **Sampling** gives prospective customers a chance to try a product or service at no cost. A **coupon** is a certificate that entitles the bearer to a price reduction or other value-enhancing consideration when purchasing a product or service.

Personal selling is face-to-face communication between a prospective buyer and a company representative. The **strategic/consultative selling model** that is widely used in the United States is also being utilized worldwide. The model's five strategic steps call for developing a **personal selling philosophy**, a **relationship strategy**, a **product strategy**, a **customer strategy**, and a **presentation strategy**. The six steps in the **presentation plan** are approach, presentation, demonstration, negotiation, close, and servicing the sale. Successful global selling may require adaptation of one or more steps in the presentation plan. An additional consideration in global selling is the composition of the sales force, which may include **expatriates**, host-country natives, or **sales agents**.

Several other forms of communication can be used in global marketing. These include **direct marketing**, a measurable system that uses one or more media to start or complete a sale. **One-to-one marketing** is an updated approach to direct marketing that calls for treating each customer in a distinct way based on his or her previous purchase history or past interactions with the company. **Direct mail**, **catalogs**, **infomercials**, **teleshopping**, and **interactive television** are some of the direct marketing tools that have been successfully used on a global basis. Global marketers frequently try to place their products in blockbuster movies that will reach global audiences. **Sponsorships** and **product placement** are also becoming vital communication tools that can be used on a global basis.

MyMarketingLab

Go to **mymktlab.com** for the following Assisted-graded writing questions:

14-1. Identify the five steps in the strategic/consultative selling model and the outlined six-step presentation plan. Do these steps have global applicability, or can they be used only for selling in the home-country market? What special challenges face a sales representative outside his or her home country?

14-2. Some industry observers think that BP should not have spent money on print and TV ads to reassure the American public. Do you agree or disagree? Explain.

14-3. Mymarketinglab Only – comprehensive writing assignment for this chapter.

MyMarketingLab

Go to **mymktlab.com** to complete the problems marked with this icon .

Discussion Questions

14-4. Briefly review how the main tools of sales promotion (e.g., sampling and couponing) can be used in global markets. What issues and problems can arise in different country markets?

14-5. What potential environmental challenges must be taken into account by a company that uses personal selling as a promotional tool outside the home country?

⭐ **14-6.** How does management's orientation (e.g., ethnocentric, polycentric, or regiocentric) correlate with decisions about sales force nationality? What other factors affect sales force composition?

14-7. As mentioned earlier in this chapter, P&G has a "Golden Store" program in Mexico and other emerging markets. P&G's representatives visit participating stores to tidy display areas and arrange promotional material in prominent places. At first, P&G used its own sales force; now it relies on independent agents who buy inventory (paying in advance) and then resell the items to shopkeepers. Is this approach in line with the chapter's discussion?

14-8. What role does direct marketing have in a global company's promotion mix? Name three companies that have successfully used direct mail or other forms of direct-response advertising.

⭐ **14-9.** Why are infomercials, sponsorship, and product placement growing in importance for global marketers?

CASE 14-1   CONTINUED (REFER TO PAGE 448)

Red Bull

Dietrich Mateschitz, Red Bull's creator, trusted his entrepreneurial instincts instead of relying on traditional marketing research. As Mateschitz recalls, "When we first started, we said that there is not an existing market for Red Bull, but Red Bull will create it. And this is what finally became true." In other words, Mateschitz succeeded at accomplishing one of the most basic goals in marketing: He discovered a market segment with needs that weren't being met by any existing product. Today, Red Bull's blue-and-silver cans emblazoned with the iconic charging bulls logo are recognized around the globe. Mateschitz's marketing instincts have made him a wealthy man; in 2005, for example, he was featured in *Forbes* magazine's cover story on billionaires.

With typical entrepreneurial flair, Mateschitz pursues alternatives to orthodox advertising strategies and tactics. "We were always looking for a different, more creative point of view," he says. For example, Red Bull utilizes a communication tool known as marketer-produced media. *The Red Bulletin* is a monthly magazine produced by Red Bull Media House. Red Bull distributes more than 3 million copies of each issue through newsstand sales, subscriptions, and as a free iPad app. The magazine is available in Austria, Germany, Great Britain, Kuwait, New Zealand, Poland, and South Africa. In 2011, *The Red Bulletin* was launched in the United States; 1.2 million free copies were distributed in major newspapers such as *The Los Angeles Times*, *The Chicago Tribune*, and *The New York Daily News*. The first U.S. issue featured San Francisco Giants pitcher Tim Lincecum, one of hundreds of athletes who are sponsored by Red Bull. As publisher Raymond Roker put it, "We are entering a new age of media in terms of what consumers of content want and expect."

Since 1998, Red Bull has been involved in another high-profile initiative. The Red Bull Music Academy is a series of concerts, workshops, art installations, and other cultural events that rotate from year to year among different international cities. Red Bull Music Academy also sponsors stages at international music festivals such as Montreaux Jazz; RBMA Radio is a Web resource where listeners can access new music, live concerts, interviews, and other content. Despite the name, Red Bull plays down its participation in the Academy; according to the Web site, "The Red Bull Music Academy is not a sponsored event, but a long-term music initiative, commit[t]ed to fostering creative exchange amongst those who have made and continue to make a difference in the world of sound." Needless to say, the Red Bull logo is visible everywhere, and coolers filled with the drink are placed in strategic locations.

In its first two years of existence, the Academy was held in Berlin; subsequent host cities have included Dublin, Rome, London, Cape Town, and New York City. Songwriters, DJs, producers, and musicians are invited to apply to the Academy; out of thousands of applicants, 62 people are selected to participate each year. The participants attend workshops and lectures during the day; in the evenings, they break into teams to write and record music. Red Bull makes no ownership claims on any music that is produced at the Academy. As Torsten Schmidt, one of the Academy's founders, explains, "That's part of the opening speech: there is no catch. We are going to offer you nothing in the end but inspiration and this chance of being here together."

In 2013, the Red Bull Music Academy returned to New York City for the first time since 2001. Many of the workshops and lectures were open to the public; for example, a panel discussion featuring veteran music producers Nile Rodgers, Tony Visconti, and Ken Scott was devoted to David Bowie's studio recordings. There were presentations and performances by industry legends such as ambient music pioneer Brian Eno and Giorgio Moroder, who was Donna Summer's producer.

One enthusiastic alumnus of the Academy explained its impact and importance this way: "The people behind the academy, they're not just 'suits'; they are really special people who are passionate about artists. Above them they have some 'suits' to deal with, but I've never dealt with them." Still, there are some dissenting voices. Matthew Herbert is a British electronic musican whose recordings include "One Pig," an album cataloging the life (and death) of, well, one pig. He has participated in the Red Bull Music Academy in the past, but has no plans to do so in the future. "My overriding impression of any music industry Red Bull tie-in is that the brand is always louder than the art. I don't think one would come away from any interaction with them thinking that they were interested in anything else other than selling caffeinated sugary drinks," he said.

Nirmalya Kumar, a marketing professor at the London Business School, has written a case study on Red Bull titled "The Anti-Brand Brand." Kumar gives Red Bull high marks for its nontraditional marketing communication strategy. As Kumar explains, "Part of being a great brand is conveying what you stand for in an authentic manner so consumers find it believeable. The music academy and the [Baumgartner] air show have given Red Bull a lot of that."

Discussion Questions

14-10. What is the critical thinking issue raised by the case?

⭐14-11. Summarize the different types of marketing communications that Red Bull uses. Are these "traditional" or "nontraditional"?

⭐14-12. What communication goal does each of Red Bull's marketing communication tools accomplish? Are you familiar with any additional brand touch points that aren't mentioned in the case?

14-13. What is the risk of sponsoring a special event such as Felix Baumgartner's historic skydive?

14-14. Red Bull and other energy drinks have generated negative publicity regarding possible health hazards. Discuss.

14-15. What makes Red Bull, in Professor Kumar's words, an "anti-brand brand"?

Sources: Ben Sesario, "Live Music and a Canned Patron," *The New York Times* (April 26, 2013), p. C1; William M. Welch, "Skydiver's Space Jump Pays Off for Red Bull," *USA Today* (October 21, 2012); Nat Ives, "Red Bull Brings Its Monthly Magazine, *Red Bulletin*, to the U.S.," *Advertising Age* (May 8, 2011); Kerry A. Dolan, "The Soda with Buzz," *Forbes* (March 28, 2005), pp. 126–130.

CASE 14-2
Marketing an Industrial Product in Latin America

Management at a large manufacturer located in the Mexican state of Nuevo León decided to improve productivity at one of its subsidiaries by investing several million dollars in state-of-the-art production equipment. As word circulated about the planned investment, vendors in Asia, Europe, and North America put together proposals. One such vendor was an American company that had a global reputation for quality products and service. Management at the American firm reviewed the size of the order and decided to bypass its regular Latin American representative and send its international sales manager instead. The following describes what took place.

The sales manager arrived and checked into a prominent hotel. He immediately had some difficulty pinning down just who his business contact was. After several days without results, he called the American Embassy, where he learned that the commercial attaché had the necessary, up-to-the-minute information. The commercial attaché listened to the sales manager's story. The attaché realized that the sales manager had already made a number of mistakes but, figuring that the locals were used to American blundering, he reasoned that all was not lost. The attaché informed the sales manager that the company's global purchasing manager was the key man and that whoever got the nod from him would get the contract. He also briefed the sales manager on methods of conducting business in Latin America and offered some pointers about dealing with the purchasing manager.

The attaché's advice ran somewhat as follows:

14-16. "You don't do business here the way you do in the States; it is necessary to spend much more time. You have to get to know your man and vice versa."

14-17. "You must meet with him several times before you talk business. I will tell you at what point you can bring up the subject. Take your cues from me." (At this point, the American sales manager made a few observations to himself about "cookie pushers" and wondered how many payrolls had been met by the commercial attaché.)

14-18. "Take that price list and put it in your pocket. Don't get it out until I tell you to. Down here price is only one of the many things taken into account before closing a deal. In the United States, your past experience will prompt you to act according to a certain set of principles, but many of these principles will not work here. Every time you feel the urge to act or to say something, look at me. Suppress the urge and take your cues from me. This is very important."

14-19. "Down here people like to do business with men who are somebody. 'Being somebody' means having written a book, lectured at a university, or developed your intellect in some way. The man you are going to see is a poet. He has published several volumes of poetry. Like many Latin Americans, he prizes poetry highly. You will find that he will spend a good deal of business time quoting his poetry to you, and he will take great pleasure in this."

14-20. "You will also note that the people here are very proud of their past and of their Spanish blood, but they are also exceedingly proud of their liberation from Spain and their independence. The fact that they are a democracy, that they are free, and also that they are no longer a colony is very, very important to them. They are warm and friendly and enthusiastic if they like you. If they don't, they are cold and withdrawn."

14-21. "And another thing, time down here means something different. It works in a different way. You know how it is back in the States when a certain type blurts out whatever is on his mind without waiting to see if the situation is right. He is considered an impatient bore and somewhat egocentric. Well, down here you have to wait much, much longer, and I really mean much, *much* longer, before you can begin to talk about the reason for your visit."

14-22. "There is another point I want to caution you about. Back in the States, it is normal for the sales representative to take the initiative. Here, the *buyer* will tell you when he is ready to do business. But most of all, don't discuss price until you are asked and don't rush things."

The Presentation

The next day the commercial attaché took the sales manager to meet the purchasing manager. First, there was a long wait in the outer office while people went in and out of the purchasing manager's office. The sales manager looked at his watch, fidgeted, and finally asked whether the purchasing manager was really expecting him. The reply he received was scarcely reassuring: "Oh yes, he is expecting you but several things have come up that require his attention. Besides, one gets used to waiting here." The sales manager irritably replied, "But doesn't he know I flew all the way down here from the United States to see him, and I have spent over a week already of my valuable time trying to find him?" "Yes, I know," was the answer, "but things just move much more slowly here."

At the end of about 30 minutes, the purchasing manager emerged from his office and greeted the commercial attaché with a double *abrazo* (embrace), throwing his arms around him and patting him on the back as though they were long-lost brothers. Now, turning and smiling, the purchasing manager extended his hand to the sales manager, who, by this time, was feeling rather miffed because he had been kept in the outer office so long. As the purchasing manager ushered both men into his corporate suite, the attaché discreetly pointed to paintings by Diego Rivera, Joaquin Clausell, and other Mexican artists that were displayed on the walls. The sales manager looked but had no comment.

As the sales manager took a seat, the telephone rang. The purchasing manager took the call; as he was speaking, an administrative assistant walked in carrying several checks and other documents that needed the manager's signature. Then a second telephone call came in on another line; the purchasing manager quickly finished the first call and picked up the second call.

Finally, after what seemed to be an all-too-short chat with many interruptions, the purchasing manager rose and suggested a well-known café where they might meet for dinner the next evening. The sales manager had expected, of course, that considering the nature of their business and the size of the order, he might be taken to the purchasing manager's home, not realizing that the Latin American home is reserved for family and very close friends.

Until now, nothing at all had been said about the reason for the sales manager's visit, a fact that bothered him somewhat. The whole setup seemed wrong; additionally, he did not like the idea of wasting another day in town. He had told the home office before he left that he would be gone for a week or 10 days at most, and made a mental note that he would clean this order up in 3 days and enjoy a few days in Acapulco or Mexico City. Now the week was already gone and he would be lucky if he made it home in 10 days.

Voicing his misgivings to the commercial attaché, he wanted to know if the purchasing manager really meant business, and if he did, why could they not get together and talk about it? The commercial attaché by now was beginning to show the strain of constantly having to reassure the sales manager. Nevertheless, he tried again: "What you don't realize is that part of the time we were waiting, the purchasing manager was rearranging a very tight schedule so that he could spend tomorrow night with you. You see, here they don't delegate responsibility the way companies do in the States. They exercise much tighter control than American companies do. As a consequence, this man spends up to 15 hours a day at his desk. It may not look like it to you, but I assure you he really means business. He wants to give your company the order; if you play your cards right, you will get it."

The next evening was more of the same. Much conversation about food and music, about many people the sales manager had never heard of. They went to a nightclub, where the sales manager brightened up and began to think that perhaps he and the purchasing manager might have something in common after all. It bothered him, however, that the principal reason for his visit was not even hinted at. But every time he started to talk about electronics, the commercial attaché would nudge him and change the subject.

The next meeting was held over morning coffee at a café. By now the sales manager was having difficulty hiding his impatience. To make matters worse, the purchasing manager had a mannerism that he did not like. When they talked, the purchasing manager was likely to put his hand on him; he would take hold of his arm and get so close that he nearly spit in his face. Consequently, the sales manager kept trying to dodge and put more distance between himself and the purchasing manager.

Following coffee, they walked in a nearby park. The purchasing manager expounded on the shrubs, the birds, and the beauties of nature, and at one spot he stopped to point at a statue and said: "There is a statue of the world's greatest hero, the liberator of mankind!" At this point, the worst happened. The sales manager asked whom the statue depicted and, when told the name of the famous Latin American patriot, said, "I've never heard of him" and walked on. After this meeting, the American sales manager was never able to see the purchasing manager again. The order went to a Swedish company.

Discussion Questions

14-23. What impression do you think the sales manager made on the purchasing manager?

14-24. How would you critique the quality of the communication among all parties in this case?

14-25. Is a high-context culture or a low-context culture at work in this case? Explain your answer.

Sources: Special thanks to Jeff Wilson, Global Project Manager, Becker Underwood, Inc., for his contributions to this case. Additional sources: Edward T. Hall, "The Silent Language in Overseas Business," *Harvard Business Review* (May–June 1960), pp. 93–96; Alan Riding, *Distant Neighbors: A Portrait of the Mexicans* (New York: Vintage, 1989); Philip R. Harris and Robert T. Moran, *Managing Cultural Differences: High Performance Strategies for a New World of Business*, 3rd ed. (Houston: Gulf Publishing Company, 1991), Chapter 14; Paul Leppert, *Doing Business with Mexico* (Fremont, CA: Jain Publishing Company, 1995); Lawrence Tuller, *Doing Business in Latin America and the Caribbean* (Chicago: Amacom, 1993).

15
Global Marketing and the Digital Revolution

CASE 15-1
Africa 3.0

Have you heard of the Cheetah generation? Here's a hint: It is the opposite of the Hippo generation. As you might infer, we are talking about Africa, a continent with 53 countries and a population of 1.03 billion. According to Ghanaian economist George Ayittey, the Cheetah generation is composed of fast-moving citizens who don't accept corruption and who believe that democracy and transparency lead to better governance. Cell phones are powerful tools for the Cheetahs; notes Michael Joseph, CEO of Kenya's Safaricom, "The mobile phone has revolutionized lives and transformed society."

Exhibit 15-1 Africa's economy is rebounding from the global financial crisis faster than the developed world. This is particularly true in sub-Saharan Africa, where the widespread adoption of cell phones has spawned mobile-banking networks and other innovations.
Source: Trevor Snapp/Bloomberg via Getty Images.

482

Deregulation of the telecommunications sector has been driving that transformation, and market liberalization helps explain why Africa's gross domestic product (GDP) growth rate is averaging between 5 and 6 percent. Overall, there are more than 650 million mobile phone subscribers in Africa; between 2000 and 2011, mobile use grew at an average annual rate of 41 percent. This explosive growth is easy to understand: Cell phones make life easier. In villages that lack running water and electricity, a cell phone is a person's most important possession (see Exhibit 15-1). Improved communication has also led to increased economic activity; for example, a peasant farmer can check crop prices to determine where and when to sell his harvest.

Africa's widespread adoption of the cell phone and the explosive growth of the telecom sector have also corrected a common misperception among global marketers: that the market opportunity in Africa is limited because the people are too poor and it is too risky to do business there. To find out more about the challenges facing telecommunications companies and the impact cell phones are having in Africa, turn to the continuation of Case 15-1 at the end of the chapter.

The digital revolution is driving the creation of new companies, industries, and markets in Africa and the rest of the world. It is also contributing to the transformation and, in some cases, the destruction of companies, industries, and markets. In short, the revolution is dramatically transforming the world in which we live. As the revolution gains traction and picks up speed, global marketers will be forced to adapt to an evolutionary world in which cell phone tablets and other mobile devices play an important role.

This chapter appears after the five-chapter sequence devoted to the marketing mix. Why? Because all the elements of the marketing mix—the four Ps—converge in the world of Internet connectivity and commerce. For example, the product "P" includes Facebook, Google, Pinterest, Twitter, Wikipedia, and the myriad other Web sites that can be accessed worldwide. The Web also functions as a distribution channel, and a very efficient one at that. Case in point: Apple's iTunes, the digital-only entertainment retailer that has rewritten the rules of music and video distribution.

The Internet has also become a key communication platform. Today, virtually every company and organization has a presence in the online space. The Internet can be used as an advertising channel, as a public relations (PR) tool, as a means for running a contest or sales promotion, and as support for the personal selling effort. Finally, there is price. Comparison-shopping Web sites make it easy to check and compare prices for products and services. Moreover, the marginal cost of storing and distributing digitized products—music files, for example—is practically nothing. This has led to some interesting pricing strategy experiments. For example, Radiohead, the innovative rock band from Oxford, England, harnessed the efficiency of the Web to offer free downloads of their 2007 album *In Rainbows*.

We begin by briefly reviewing the key innovations that served as precursors to the digital revolution. In the next two sections, convergence and the disruptive nature of Internet technology, and their effects on global companies, are discussed. Next, key e-commerce issues that face global marketers are examined. The discussion continues with an overview of Web site design issues as they pertain to global marketing. The final section of the chapter examines some of the products and service innovations that are driving the digital revolution.

LEARNING OBJECTIVES

1 List the major innovations and trends that underlie the digital revolution.

2 Define *value network* and explain the differences between sustaining technologies and disruptive technologies.

3 Identify current trends in global e-commerce and explain how global companies are expanding their presence on the Web.

4 Identify the most important new products and services that have been introduced in the past decade.

The Digital Revolution: A Brief History

The **digital revolution** is a paradigm shift resulting from technological advances that allow for the digitization (i.e., conversion to binary code) of analog sources of information, sounds, and images. The origins of the digital revolution can be traced back to the mid-twentieth century. Over a 5-year period between 1937 and 1942, John Vincent Atanasoff and Clifford Berry developed the world's first electromechanical digital computer at Iowa State University. The Atanasoff-Berry Computer (ABC) incorporated several major innovations in computing, including the use of binary arithmetic, regenerative memory, parallel processing, and separation of the memory and computing functions.

In 1947, William Shockley and two colleagues at AT&T's Bell Laboratories invented a "solid state amplifier," or **transistor**, as it became known. This was a critical innovation, because the vacuum tubes used in computers and electronics products at that time were large, consumed a large amount of power, and generated a great deal of heat. Shockley and collaborators John Bardeen and William Brattain were awarded the Nobel Prize in physics in 1956 for their invention.

In 1948, a Bell Labs researcher named Claude Shannon wrote a technical report titled "A Mathematical Theory of Communication" in which he proposed that all information media could be encoded in *binary digits*, or bits. Earlier, in 1940, Shannon had argued in his doctoral dissertation that the logical values "true" and "false" could be denoted by "1" and "0," respectively, and that streams of 1s and 0s could transmit media over a wire. Thanks to his pioneering work, Shannon is regarded as the inventor of information theory.

In the mid-1950s, Sony licensed the transistor from Bell Labs; Sony engineers boosted the yield of the transistor and created the market for transistor radios. The sound was "lo-fi" but the devices were portable and stylish, which is what consumers—especially teenagers—wanted. Also during the 1950s, Robert Noyce and Jack Kilby independently invented the silicon chip (also known as the **integrated circuit**, or **IC**).[1] In essence, the IC put the various parts of an electrical circuit—including resistors, diodes, and capacitors—on a single piece of material. The IC gave the transistor its modern form and allowed its power to be harnessed in a reliable, low-cost way.

The IC and the concept of binary code permitted the development of the **personal computer (PC)**, a compact, affordable device whose advent marked the next phase of the digital revolution. Many of the events and people associated with this era have become the stuff of legend. Some observers credit Alan Kay with the research that permitted the development of the first PCs. During the 1970s, Kay was director of the Learning Research Group at the Xerox Palo Alto Research Center (PARC). Then, between 1981 and 1983, Kay worked at Atari, which, along with other pioneering PC companies such as Osborne and Commodore, have long since disappeared from the scene.

Kay's work at Xerox PARC had a strong impact on Steve Jobs who, with partner Steve Wozniak, started Apple Computer in a garage in the late 1970s. The company's Apple II is widely regarded as the first "true" PC; the Apple II's popularity received a big boost in 1979 when a spreadsheet program known as VisiCalc was introduced. A computer **spreadsheet** is an electronic ledger that automatically calculates the effect of a change to one figure on other figures across rows and down columns; previously, these changes had to be done manually. While such powerful, time-saving functionality is taken for granted today, VisiCalc was a true milestone in the digital revolution.[2]

IBM brought its first PC to market in 1981; Bill Gates initially declined an offer to create an **operating system**—the software code that provides basic instructions—for IBM's new machine. Gates later changed his mind and developed the Microsoft Disk Operating System (MS-DOS). In 1984, Apple introduced the revolutionary Macintosh, with its user-friendly graphical interface and point-and-click mouse. A few years later, Microsoft replaced MS-DOS with Windows. Meanwhile, component manufacturers were innovating as well; Intel began marketing the 286 microprocessor in 1982. This was followed in quick succession by the 386 and 486 versions; in 1993, Intel unveiled the Pentium processor.

The rise of the Internet and the World Wide Web marks the next phase of the digital revolution. The Internet's origins can be traced back to an initiative by the **Defense Advanced Research Projects Agency (DARPA)**, which created a computer network that could maintain lines of communication in the event of a war. In 1969, the ARPANET was unveiled; this was a network linking computer research centers at colleges and universities. E-mail within a computer network was made possible by the creation of a file-transfer program in 1972. There was a problem, however; it was not possible to send e-mail that was created on one network to a computer

---

[1] Noyce founded Fairchild Semiconductor and, later, Intel. His Intel cofounder was Gordon Moore, who is famous for formulating "Moore's Law," according to which computer power doubles every 18 months. Kilby was the founder of Texas Instruments. See Evan Ramstad, "At the End of an Era, Two Tech Pioneers Are Remembered," *The Wall Street Journal* (August 15, 2005), p. B1.

[2] For more on the development of VisiCalc, see Dan Bricklin, "Natural Born Entrepreneur," *Harvard Business Review* 79, no. 8 (September 2001), pp. 53–59.

on a different network. This problem was solved the following year when Vinton Cerf and Robert Kahn created a software framework known as TCP/IP (Transmission Control Protocol/Internet Protocol). Launched in 1973, this cross-network protocol paved the way for a "network of networks," and the **Internet** was born.

The ability to exchange e-mail messages on the Internet had a revolutionary impact on society, as technology guru Stewart Brand noted in the late 1980s:

> Marshall McLuhan used to remark, "Gutenberg made everybody a reader. Xerox made everybody a publisher." Personal computers are making everybody an author. E-mail, word processing programs that make revising as easy as thinking, and laser printers collapse the whole writing–publishing–distributing process into one event controlled entirely by the individual. If, as alleged, the only real freedom of the press is to own one, the fullest realization of the First Amendment is being accomplished by technology, not politics.[3]

Of course, the Internet revolution did not end with the advent of e-mail. More innovations were yet to come. In 1990, a software consultant named Tim Berners-Lee invented the **Uniform Resource Locator (URL)**, an Internet site's address on the World Wide Web; **Hypertext Markup Language (HTML)**, a format language that controls the appearance of Web pages; and **Hypertext Transfer Protocol (HTTP)**, which enables hypertext files to be transferred across the Internet.[4] These innovations allowed Web sites to be linked and visually rich content to be posted and accessed. In short, Berners-Lee is the father of the **World Wide Web** (see Exhibit 15-2).

In the mid-1990s, a computer scientist at the University of Illinois named Marc Andreessen developed a Web browser; called Mosaic, it combined images and words together on the same screen and allowed users to search for and view resources on the Web. Andreessen joined forces with Jim Clark, one of the founders of Silicon Graphics, to form Mosaic Communications. Renamed Netscape Communications, the company became one of the brightest stars in the dot-com era as commercial demand for the Netscape browser software

> "There are certain limitations that are part of the network, and we are struggling with that. We're worried that in the zeal to address localization that people will not be able to communicate any more. If someone gives you a business card with the e-mail address in Chinese, what are you to do?"[5]
>
> —Vinton G. Cerf, Internet pioneer and former chairman of ICANN

Exhibit 15-2 Tim Berners-Lee invented the World Wide Web, and today he is the Director of the World Wide Web Consortium. W3C is a foundation that helps develop standards that allow the full potential of the Web to be realized. Berners-Lee is an advocate for open standards and Web neutrality, two topics that he discussed at the SXSW Interactive Festival in Austin, Texas, in March 2013.
Source: Photo by Amy E. Price/Getty Images for SXSW.

---

[3] Stewart Brand, *The Media Lab: Inventing the Future at MIT* (New York: Penguin Books, 1988), p. 253.
[4] Hypertext is any text that contains links to other documents.
[5] John Markoff, "Control the Internet? A Futile Pursuit, Some Say," *The New York Times* (November 24, 2005), p. C4.

exploded. As Thomas L. Friedman notes, "Marc Andreessen did not invent the Internet, but he did as much as any single person to bring it alive and popularize it."[6]

Within 5 years of the Web's debut, the number of users increased from 600,000 to 40 million. In the following decade, search engines such as Yahoo! and Google emerged and encryption and security features were built into the Web. Search engines have also been dramatically improved; for example, Google's novel "page ranking" superseded an earlier technology known as "link analysis." Recent upgrades to Google's search capabilities include the introductions of Universal Search (2007) and Knowledge Graph (2012). Surprisingly, Microsoft had not been a major player in the search market. To remedy this situation, in 2009 the software giant unveiled Bing, which is designed to provide a superior experience for shopping-, travel-, and health-related searches.

Meanwhile, Google has added new capabilities and businesses: Its Motorola Mobility unit makes smartphones and tablets, and its Android operating system is the world's leading smartphone software. Google also owns YouTube, the popular video-sharing site, and has launched the Google+ social network. Today, almost 3 billion people—nearly half of the world's population—are using the Internet. However, because residents in developing countries lag in terms of Internet access, Google is working to build wireless networks in areas—especially outside large cities—that are beyond the reach of wired networks. In addition, Google Glass is a new project centering on wearable computers, and the company also recently launched a music-streaming service called All Access (see Exhibit 15-3).[7]

However, the technology's powerful capabilities and increasing importance have resulted in a backlash that manifests itself in various ways. For example, the Chinese government, alarmed by the free flow of information across the Internet, closely monitors the content on Web sites that its citizens access. Facebook, Twitter, and many other social media sites are blocked in China.

Who controls the Internet? Good question! The first Internet Governance Forum (IGF) was held in Athens, Greece, in 2006. The IGF will guide "the development and application by governments, the private sector, and civil society, in their respective roles, of shared principles, norms, rules, decision-making procedures, and programs that shape the evolution and use of the Internet." Many in the global Internet community are concerned about the inclusion of the

Exhibit 15-3 Many in the tech world are predicting that wearable devices are going to be the "next big thing." Google Glass is one such device; resembling a pair of eyeglasses, the device enables the wearer to photograph whatever he or she is looking at. Google Glass can perform other tasks such as providing directions and language translation. Meanwhile, Apple is expected to launch an iWatch in the near future.
Source: Photo by Justin Sullivan/Getty Images.

---

[6] Thomas L. Friedman, *The World Is Flat* (New York: Farrar, Straus and Giroux, 2005), p. 58.
[7] Amir Efrati, "Google Pushes into Emerging Markets," *The Wall Street Journal* (May 25–26, 2013), pp. B1, B2.

→ THE CULTURAL CONTEXT

South Korea Embraces the Digital Revolution

SYNC • THINK • LEARN

MyMarketingLab

According to a recent "digital opportunity index" published by the United Nations, South Korea leads the world in providing its citizens with access to information and communications technologies (ICT). The country's high-tech infrastructure takes a variety of forms. The availability of broadband Internet connections is one example. In South Korea, 94 percent of households are broadband subscribers.

As Stephen Ward, a consultant with Deloitte, explains, "Koreans tend to be early adopters of technology and, more significantly, are fast followers. They are always conscious of the need not to get left behind by the Japanese and the young have a great desire to conform with the gadget-carrying norm of their peers" (see Exhibit 15-4). Ninety percent of Koreans in their teens and early twenties regularly log onto Cyworld ("Cyber World"), South Korea's leading social network site. Subscribers create virtual worlds and blog in a rich 3D environment. Although the site is free, users pay for virtual furniture, BGM (BackGroundMusic), and other items to customize their "rooms."

The desire for speed also seems to be ingrained in South Korea's culture; as one university student noted, Koreans tend to be "fast, fast, and fast." To bring the speed, South Korea's government is committing significant financial resources. It budgeted $50 billion in an effort to link 80 major cities and towns via broadband; moreover, South Korea's network is extremely fast, offering standard speeds of up to 100 megabits per second (Mbps). Korea's Communication Commission planned to boost the network's speed to 1 gigabit per second (Gbps) by 2012.

However, South Korea's digital future includes much more than broadband connections. For example, policymakers are aggressively pursuing applications for radio frequency identification tags (RFID); the South Korean government is spending nearly $300 million to build an RFID research center.

The RFID center will be part of an even more ambitious effort: the construction of a ubiquitous city on a 1,500-acre man-made island near the Incheon Free Economic Zone. What makes New Songdo City a "ubiquitous city" (or, more simply, U-city)? For one thing, all major information systems—commercial, residential, and government—share data, and computers are designed into all buildings. With an estimated price tag of $25 billion, New Songdo City was scheduled for completion in 2014. Complementing its high-tech features will be high-touch elements inspired by the world's major cities. These elements include a central park (inspired by New York City) and a canal system similar to that in Venice.

John Kim is in charge of planning for the U-city, which he says will exemplify "U-life." Kim explains, "U-life will become its own brand, its own lifestyle." Residents will be able to communicate via videoconferencing and everyone will have access to video on demand. Smartcard house keys will also function as payment devices for subways, parking meters, movie tickets, and myriad other uses. The challenge now is to make sure that all Koreans—even those who don't live in U-city—can benefit from the development's innovations.

Sources: Mark McDonald, "For South Korea, Internet at Blazing Speeds Is Still Not Fast Enough," *The New York Times* (February 22, 2011), p. B3; Christian Oliver, "S Korea's Dream City Entangled in Red Tape," *Financial Times* (August 12, 2009), p. 13; Song Jung-a, "Korean Site Tackles Might of MySpace," *Financial Times* (September 1, 2006), p. 16; Tom Braithwaite, "The Young Guns of Broadband," *Financial Times* (May 29, 2006), p. 8; Pamela Licalzi O'Connell, "Korea's High-Tech Utopia, Where Everything Is Observed," *The New York Times* (October 5, 2005).

Exhibit 15-4 Songdo has been hailed as a prototype of the aerotropolis, an urban development concept that showcases ways that travel can be made more efficient. One of Songdo's key features is the airport in the center of the development. Songdo was created as a model of sustainability, and the United Nations selected it as the home of the Green Climate Fund.
Source: © Robert Koehler/Getty Images.

word "governments" in this statement. The nonprofit Internet Corporation for Assigned Names and Numbers (ICANN) is based in Marina del Ray, California. ICANN maintains a database of Web addresses, approves new suffixes for Web addresses (e.g., .info and .tv), and performs other behind-the-scenes procedures that are critical for keeping the Internet functioning properly. ICANN's advisory body includes international members, but the U.S. Department of Commerce retains veto power over all decisions. For example, after ICANN tentatively approved the domain name .xxx for pornography sites, the U.S. Department of Commerce blocked the decision.

Policymakers in some countries are concerned about U.S. control of the Internet. For example, China, India, Brazil, and the European Union (EU) have taken the position that, because the Internet is global, no single country should be in control of it. Accordingly, these nations have sought to have the United Nations assume a role in Internet governance.[8] Privacy is another issue. As companies become more adept at using the Internet to gather, store, and access information about customers, privacy issues are becoming a focal point of concern among policymakers and the general public. In the EU, for example, a privacy protection directive was established in 1995; in 2002, the EU adopted a privacy and electronic communications directive.

Convergence

The digital revolution is causing dramatic, disruptive changes in industry structures. Writing in *The New York Times* at the beginning of 2010, columnist Jon Pareles summarized some of these changes as follows:

> The 2000s were the broadband decade, the disintermediation decade, the file-sharing decade, the digital recording (and image) decade, the iPod decade, the long-tail decade, the blog decade, the user-generated decade, the on-demand decade, the all-access decade. Inaugurating the new millennium, the Internet swallowed culture whole and delivered it back—cheaper, faster, and smaller—to everyone who can get online.[9]

Convergence is a term that refers to the coming together of previously separate industries and product categories (see Figure 15-1). New technologies affect the business sector(s) in which a company competes. What business is Sony in? Originally, Sony was a consumer electronics company best known for innovative products such as transistor radios, Trinitron televisions, VCRs, stereo components, and the Walkman line of personal music players. Then, Sony entered new businesses by acquiring CBS Records and Columbia Motion Pictures. These acquisitions themselves did not represent convergence, however, because they occurred in the early days of the digital revolution, when motion pictures, recorded music, and consumer electronics were still separate industries. Today, however, Sony is in the "bits" business: Its core businesses incorporate digital technology and involve digitizing and distributing sound, images, and data. Now, Sony's competitors include Apple (music players, smartphones), Dell (computers), Canon (cameras), and Nokia (smartphones).

What kinds of challenges does convergence present? Consider the case of Kodak, the undisputed leader in photography-related products for more than a century. The company struggled to remake its business model as its sales of digital-related products grew from zero to $1 billion in 5 years. Because of convergence, Kodak's competitors came to include companies such as Dell and Hewlett-Packard. Moreover, Kodak's core businesses—film, photographic paper, and chemicals—were disrupted. Competition also came from the telecommunications industry. The cell phone camera was invented in 1997; a key benefit was the ability to download digital photos from the camera and post them on the Web or e-mail them to friends. Ironically, Motorola, a key player in the cell phone business, could have been one of the first companies to market a cell phone camera. However, management's attention was distracted by the ill-fated launch of the Iridium satellite phone (see Chapter 6). As a result, inventor Philippe Kahn took his idea to

---

[8] Christopher Rhoads, "EU, Developing Nations Challenge U.S. Control of Internet," *The Wall Street Journal* (October 25, 2005), pp. B1, B2. See also "A Free Internet," *Financial Times* (November 14, 2003), p. 15.
[9] Jon Pareles, "A World of Megabeats and Megabytes," *The New York Times* (January 3, 2010), p. AR1.

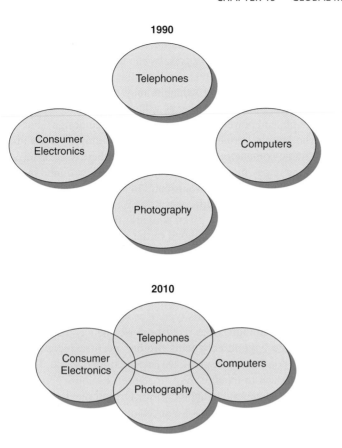

FIGURE 15-1
Industry Convergence

Japan, where the first cell phone cameras were introduced in 1999.[10] In 2010, annual sales of camera-equipped cell phones passed the 1-billion-unit mark.

Value Networks and Disruptive Technologies[12]

As noted in the chapter introduction, the digital revolution has created both opportunities and threats. Dell, Kodak, Motorola, Xerox, and Sony are just a few examples of global companies that have struggled to remake their businesses in the face of technological innovation. IBM missed out on the minicomputer market, in part because management believed minicomputers promised lower profit margins and represented a smaller market opportunity. DEC, Data General, and Prime created the minicomputer market, but these companies, in turn, missed the PC revolution. This time, however, IBM's executive team demonstrated that it had learned its lesson: It set up an independent organizational unit to create the company's first PC. However, IBM subsequently was slow to recognize growing market demand for laptops; new entrants included Apple, Dell, Toshiba, Sharp, and Zenith. Recently, IBM exited the PC market altogether.

How is it that managers at many companies fail to respond to change in a timely manner? According to Harvard professor Clayton Christensen, the problem is that executives become so committed to a current, profitable technology that they fail to provide adequate levels of investment in new, apparently riskier technologies. Ironically, companies fall into this trap by adhering to prevailing marketing orthodoxy, namely, listening to and responding to the needs of established customers. Christensen calls this situation the **innovator's dilemma**.

"I think there will be an increasing convergence between content and commerce, that it will be about following consumers instead of making consumers come to you, and I am especially excited about the various platforms that will allow more and more access to customers."[11]

—Natalie Massenet, founder, Net-a-Porter

---

[10] Kevin Maney, "Baby's Arrival Inspires Birth of Cell Phone Camera—and Societal Evolution," *USA Today* (January 24, 2007), p. 3B.

[11] Vanessa Friedman, "Ready for the Next Chapter in E-Tailing," *Financial Times* (April 5, 2010), p. 18.

[12] Much of the material in this section is adapted from Clayton Christensen, *The Innovator's Dilemma* (New York: HarperBusiness, 2003). See also Simon London, "Digital Discomfort: Companies Struggle to Deal with the 'Inevitable Surprise' of the Transition from Atoms to Bits," *Financial Times* (December 17, 2003), p. 17.

In every industry, companies are embedded in a **value network**. Each value network has a cost structure associated with it that dictates the margins needed to achieve profitability. The boundaries of the network are defined, in part, by the unique rank ordering of the importance of various product performance attributes. Parallel value networks, each built around a different definition of what makes a product valuable, may exist within the same broadly defined industry. Each network has its own "metrics of value" (e.g., for laptop computers, the metrics are small size, low weight and power consumption, and rugged design). For example, during the 1980s, customers who bought portable computers were willing to pay a premium for smaller size; buyers of mainframe computers did not value this attribute. Conversely, mainframe buyers valued (i.e., were willing to pay more for) memory capacity as measured by megabytes; portable computer buyers placed less value on this attribute. In short, the value networks for mainframe computers and portable computers are different.

As firms gain experience within a given network, they are likely to develop capabilities, organizational structures, and cultures tailored to the distinctive requirements of their respective value networks. The industry's dominant firms—typically those with reputations as "well-managed" firms—lead in developing and/or adopting **sustaining technologies**; that is, incremental or radical innovations that improve product performance. According to Christensen, most new technologies developed by established companies are sustaining in nature; indeed, the vast majority of innovations are of this type. However, new entrants to an industry lead in developing **disruptive technologies** that redefine performance. The benefits associated with disruptive technologies go beyond enhancing product performance; disruptive technologies enable something to be done that was previously deemed impossible. Disruptive technologies typically enable new markets to emerge. As Christensen explains, "An innovation that is disrupting to one firm can be sustaining to another firm. The Internet was sustaining technology to Dell, which already sold PCs via direct marketing channels. But it was disruptive technology to Compaq, whose major distribution channel was retailers."[13]

To help managers recognize the innovator's dilemma and develop appropriate responses to environmental change, Christensen has developed five principles of disruptive innovations:

1. Companies depend on customers and investors for resources. As management guru Rosabeth Moss Kanter points out, the best innovations are user-driven; paradoxically, however, if management listens to established customers, opportunities for disruptive innovation may be missed.[14]

2. Small markets don't solve the growth needs of large companies. Small organizations can most easily respond to the opportunities for growth in a small market. This fact may require large organizations to create independent units to pursue new technologies, as IBM did in developing its PC.

3. Markets that don't exist can't be analyzed. Christensen recommends that companies embrace *agnostic marketing*. This is the explicit assumption that *no one*—not company personnel, not the company's customers—can know whether, how, or in what quantities a disruptive product can or will be used before they have experienced using it.

4. An organization's capabilities define its disabilities. For example, Microsoft was once an industry trendsetter. Today, however, while it remains firmly committed to its Windows operating system, Microsoft lags behind new industry entrants in high-growth, consumer-oriented areas such as search and social networking.[15]

5. Technology supply may not equal market demand. Some products offer a greater degree of sophistication than the market requires. For example, developers of accounting software for small businesses overshot the functionality required by the market, thus creating an opportunity for a disruptive software technology that provided adequate, not superior, functionality and was simple and more convenient to use. This was the opportunity seized by Scott Cook, developer of Quicken and QuickBooks.

---

[13] Simon London, "Why Disruption Can Be Good for Business," *Financial Times* (October 3, 2003), p. 8.
[14] Rosabeth Moss Kanter, John Kao, and Fred Wiersema, *Innovation: Breakthrough Thinking at 3M, DuPont, GE, Pfizer, and Rubbermaid* (New York: HarperBusiness, 1997), p. 24.
[15] "Middle-Aged Blues," *The Economist* (June 11, 2011), p. 59.

Global E-Commerce

The term **e-commerce** refers to the general exchange of goods and services using the Internet or a similar online network as a marketing channel. According to Forrester Research, U.S. online retail sales revenues totaled $192 billion in 2011, a figure that represents about 7 percent of total U.S. retail sales. Internet penetration in the United States is currently about 75 percent of the population; in Norway, Greenland, and Sweden, more than 90 percent of the population is online. South Korea is currently undergoing a dramatic upgrade in its Internet infrastructure (see The Cultural Context feature in this chapter).[16] Consider the following:

- Every 48 hours, Yahoo! records more than 24 terabytes of data about its users' online activities. That is the equivalent of all the information contained in all the books in the Library of Congress.[17]
- Between 2003 and 2010, the number of Internet users in China increased from 68 million to 450 million. This makes China the world's largest e-commerce market; in Shanghai, Beijing, and Guangzhou, more than one-third of all residents use the Internet. Local companies such as Dangdang.com are proving to be formidable competitors against global rivals such as Yahoo!, Google, and eBay.[18]
- According to Forrester Research, online retail and travel sales in Western Europe would grow at a compound annual rate of 8 percent between 2008 and 2014. In 2008, 37 percent of European adults—136 million people—shopped online.[19]

E-commerce activities can be divided into three broad categories: business-to-consumer (B2C or b-to-c), business-to-business (B2B or b-to-b), and consumer-to-consumer (or peer-to-peer or P2P). Many people associate e-commerce with well-known consumer-oriented sites such as Amazon.com, Apple's iTunes Store, and eBay. Overall, however, B2B commerce constitutes the biggest share of the Internet economy and will likely continue to do so for the foreseeable future. About three-fourths of 2001 b-to-c revenue was generated in North America; that figure is expected to drop to 50 percent as online sales in Europe and elsewhere increase over the next few years (see Table 15-1).

Problems can arise when a transaction site that is not designed to serve foreign customers nevertheless attracts them. Customer service can be a problem when customers are located in different time zones. For example, BlueTie is a small company based in Rochester, New York, that markets e-mail and office-software applications by subscription. The company's servers

TABLE 15-1 Forecast, Online Retail and Travel Sales, Select European Countries, 2008–2014 (millions)

Country	2008	2009	2010	2011	2012	2013	2014
Germany[a]	€ 27,581	€ 31,311	€ 34,021	€ 37,131	€ 39,662	€ 41,901	€ 43,723
France[b]	14,795	16,990	19,594	22,334	24,373	26,256	27,948
Spain[c]	5,961	6,976	9,031	11,281	13,247	15,286	17,353
Western Europe[d]	116,009	128,606	146,636	164,046	177,781	190,960	202,799

[a] Forrester Research, *German Online Retail and Travel Sales, 2008–2014* (March 2, 2009), p. 8.
[b] Forrester Research, *French Online Retail and Travel Sales, 2008–2014* (March 2, 2009), p. 8.
[c] Forrester Research, *Spanish Online Retail and Travel Sales, 2008–2014* (March 6, 2009), p. 9.
[d] Forrester Research, *Western European Online Retail and Travel Sales, 2008–2014* (March 16, 2009), p. 8. Data is for EU-17: Austria, Belgium, Denmark, Finland, France, Germany, Greece, Ireland, Italy, Luxembourg, the Netherlands, Norway, Portugal, Spain, Sweden, Switzerland, and the United Kingdom.

---

[16] Internet World Stats, www.internetworldstats.com (accessed June 1, 2011).
[17] Kevin J. Delaney, "Lab Test: Hoping to Overtake Its Rivals, Yahoo Stocks Up on Academics," *The Wall Street Journal* (August 26, 2006), p. A8.
[18] Jason Dean, "China's Web Retailers Beat U.S. Rivals at Their Own Game," *The Wall Street Journal* (August 22, 2006), p. B1.
[19] Forrester Research, *Western European Online Retail and Travel Sales, 2008–2014* (March 16, 2009), p. 2.

continually update customer calendars and e-mail. When non-U.S. orders began to come in, BlueTie managers found it challenging to deliver correct times and dates. Fixing the problem required spending tens of thousands of dollars and tied up precious employee time.

Web sites can be classified by purpose: **Promotion sites** provide marketing communications about a company's goods or services, **content sites** provide news and entertainment and support a company's PR efforts, and **transaction sites** are online retail operations that allow customers to purchase goods and services. In many instances, Web sites combine the three functions. Web sites can also be categorized in terms of content and audience focus.

For example, international students at your college or university may have learned about your school via the Internet, even though home-country prospective students constitute the primary target audience for the Web site. Similarly, Pandora, the online music service, only serves American listeners; Deezer, the French online music-streaming company, is only operational in its domestic market. The reason? International copyright laws make it difficult to license performance rights for songs. As former Pandora CEO Joe Kennedy recently remarked, "The good news is that the Internet is global, but the bad news is that copyright law is country by country."[20] Apple's iTunes Music Store began as a U.S.-only retailer. During the past several years, the service has been rolled out in Germany, France, the United Kingdom, and elsewhere. Netflix, the online movie distributor, has evolved from domestic to international in a similar way.

Companies such as FedEx and Gucci are global in scope, and the Internet constitutes a powerful, cost-effective communication tool. Similarly, the interactive marketing staff at Unilever PLC understands that the Web represents an important low-cost medium for promoting products. Unilever's vast archive of TV commercials has been digitized; Web surfers can download the videos for products such as Salon Selectives shampoo and watch them anytime. Recently, Unilever launched a 12-week series on Yahoo! Food titled *In Search of Real Food*. Hosted by Food Network TV star David Lieberman, the show was created around Hellman's mayonnaise. As Doug Scott, executive director of entertainment at the Ogilvy & Mather ad agency explained, "Content for broadband costs significantly less than TV productions and it allows you to distribute to a much larger audience."[21]

Companies can also seek e-commerce transactions with customers on a worldwide basis. Amazon.com is the most successful example of the transaction business model. Online book shoppers can choose from millions of book titles; many carry discounted prices. After assessing a number of potential products in terms of their suitability for online sales, company founder Jeffrey Bezos settled on books for two reasons. First, there are too many titles for any one "brick-and-mortar" store to carry. The second reason is related to industry structure: The publishing industry is highly fragmented, with 4,200 publishers in the United States alone. That means that no single publisher has a high degree of supplier power. Bezos' instincts proved sound: Sales exploded after Amazon.com's Web site became operational in mid-1995. Within a year, orders were coming in from dozens of countries. Today, Amazon.com is the world's largest online retail site, with hundreds of millions of annual visitors. Amazon.com's nine international sites—Brazil, Canada, China, France, Germany, Italy, Japan, Spain, and the United Kingdom—generate 50 percent of total sales.

As noted earlier, online retail in the United States passed the $200-billion-mark in 2011. According to Forrester Research, by 2016 online retail sales will total $327 billion and constitute nearly 10 percent of retail sales. These figures include orders from abroad; Abercrombie & Fitch, Aéropostale, J. Crew, Macy's, Timberland, and Saks Fifth Avenue are just some of the U.S. retailers targeting foreign buyers by adding international shipping to their Web sites. The trend was fueled by a variety of factors, including the slowdown in U.S. consumer spending and a weak dollar, which translates into savings for shoppers paying in euros or other currencies. Of course, adding international shipping capabilities requires some effort; for example, warehouse software must be updated to recognize foreign postal codes. To keep shipping costs and import duties down, some retailers are considering opening distribution centers in Europe and elsewhere.[22]

[20] Joe Mullin, "Pandora CEO: The Complexity of International Copyright Law Is a Big Problem," PaidContent.org (March 30, 2011). Accessed June 1, 2011.
[21] Susanne Vranica, "Hellman's Targets Yahoo for Its Spread," *The Wall Street Journal* (June 27, 2007), p. B4.
[22] Stephanie Clifford, "U.S. Stores Learn How to Ship to Foreign Shoppers," *The New York Times* (March 21, 2012), pp. B1, B7; Vanessa O'Connell and Rachel Dodes, "Going Online to Lure Foreign Shoppers," *The Wall Street Journal* (February 8, 2008), p. B1.

Some products are inherently not suitable candidates for sale via the Internet; for example, McDonald's doesn't sell hamburgers from its Web site. In some instances, global marketers make the strategic decision to establish a presence on the Web without offering transaction opportunities even though the product could be sold that way. Rather, such companies limit their Web activities to promotion and information in support of offline retail distribution channels. There are several reasons for this. First, many companies lack the infrastructure necessary to process orders from individual customers. Second, it can cost anywhere from $20 million to $30 million to establish a fully functioning e-commerce site. There may be other, product-specific reasons. The Web site for Godin Guitars, for example, provides a great deal of product information and a directory of the company's worldwide dealer network. However, company founder Robert Godin believes that the best way for a person to select a guitar is to play one, and that requires a visit to a music store.

For consumer products giant Procter & Gamble (P&G), the Internet represents a global promotion and information channel that is an integral part of its brand strategy. For example, Pampers is P&G's number 1 brand, with annual global sales of $8.5 billion. Pampers' online presence at www.pampers.com represents a new conceptualization of the brand. Previously, brand managers viewed Pampers disposable diapers as a way of keeping babies happy; the new view is that the Pampers brand is a child development aid. Visitors to the Pampers Village online community can read advice from the Pampers Parenting Institute as well as tips from mothers. Discount coupons are also available.

After P&G launched Pampers Dry Max in March 2010, the company got a tutorial in the power of social media. The new diaper was designed to be the "driest and thinnest" Pampers ever. The Pampers brand management team sent free samples to authors of various "mommy blogs," including The Shopping Momma. P&G was surprised by what happened next: Some bloggers complained that babies wearing Dry Max were developing severe diaper rash. The U.S. Consumer Products Safety Commission (CSPC) announced that it would investigate the matter.

At first, P&G responded to customer complaints on a case-by-case basis. Then, with negative publicity spreading, P&G's North American baby care chief Jodi Allen appeared on morning talk shows and denounced the "growing but completely false rumors fueled by social media." In P&G's view, some of the negative blogs came from parents who were unhappy that Dry Max had replaced a familiar but older version of Pampers. Other parents, Allen asserted, advocated using cloth diapers, and "sought to promote the myth that our product causes 'chemical burns.'"

Some industry observers were taken aback by the tone of the response. Kathy Marsh Lord, who blogs as The Shopping Mama, noted, "When I first read their press release, it felt a bit cold. It did not help put out the fire or make people feel their voices were being heard." In an effort to mend fences, P&G invited Marsh Lord and other bloggers to the company's Cincinnati headquarters. The visitors spent the day talking with the Dry Max development team. Going forward, P&G intended to convey the message that Dry Max diapers are safe, while also communicating "all that we're doing to listen and act to help moms and dads."

P&G launched www.thankyoumom.com to position P&G as "a proud sponsor of moms." In 2010, P&G used the site to award $100,000 in travel vouchers to help moms reunite with their families. P&G has also launched a retail Web site to sell Pantene shampoo, Pampers baby products, and other brands to U.S. consumers. This online strategy change brings P&G into direct competition with Walmart, Target, and other retailers that complement brick-and-mortar stores with Internet selling.[23]

Until recently, visitors to Web sites for most luxury goods purveyors were not given the opportunity to buy. The reason is simple: Top design houses strive to create an overall retail shopping experience that enhances the brand. This objective is basically at odds with e-commerce. As Forrester Research analyst Sucharita Mulpuru explained recently, "There was a belief that there was no way you could communicate your brand essence online."[24] This belief is changing, however. Some luxury goods marketers have developed smartphone and iPad apps to help consumers shop. Burberry, Chanel, Coach, Gucci, and many other luxury brands are cultivating official online communities on Facebook. According to Reggie Bradord, CEO of a

[23] Ellen Byron, "P&G Goes on the Defensive for Pampers," *The Wall Street Journal* (June 15, 2010), p. B5.
[24] David Gelles, "Innovation Brings a Touch of Class to Online Shopping," *Financial Times Special Report: Business of Luxury* (June 14, 2010), p. 7.

social media management company, they are doing the right thing. He says, "Luxury brands should be thinking about 'how can we create a dialogue and get consumers connecting with our brand?'"[25]

As the Internet has developed into a crucial global communication tool, decision makers in virtually all organizations are realizing that they must include this new medium in their communications planning. Many companies purchase banner ads on popular Web sites; the ads are linked to the company's homepage or product- or brand-related sites. Advertisers pay when users click the link. Although creative possibilities are limited with banner ads and **click-through rates**—the percentage of users who click on an advertisement that has been presented—are typically low, the number of companies that use the Web as a medium for global advertising is expected to increase dramatically over the next few years.

An important trend is **paid search advertising**, whereby companies pay to have their ads appear when users type certain search terms. Yahoo! paid $1.6 billion to acquire Overture, a company specializing in paid search advertising. As a Yahoo! spokesperson noted, "Paid search is just starting to take off globally. So this acquisition wasn't just part of our strategy for search, it was important for our international strategy as well."[26]

One of the most interesting aspects of the digital revolution has been noted by Chris Anderson, the editor of *Wired* magazine and author of *The Long Tail*. The book's title refers to the use of the efficient economics of online retail to aggregate a large number of relatively slow-selling products. *The Long Tail* helps explain the success of eBay, Amazon.com, Netflix, and iTunes, all of which offer far more variety and choice than traditional retailers can. As Anderson explains, "The story of the Long Tail is really about the economics of abundance—what happens when the bottlenecks that stand between supply and demand in our culture start to disappear and everything becomes available to everyone." Anderson notes that "below-the-radar" products— for example, obscure books, movies, and music—are driving revenues at e-commerce merchants such as Amazon.com, Netflix, and iTunes. He says, "These millions of fringe sales are an efficient, cost-effective business....For the first time in history, hits and niches are on equal economic footing."[27]

Web Site Design and Implementation[28]

To fully exploit the Internet's potential, company executives must be willing to integrate interactive media into their marketing mixes. Web sites can be developed in-house, or an outside firm can be contracted to do the job. During the past few years, a new breed of interactive advertising agency has emerged to help companies globalize their Internet offerings (see Table 15-2). Some

TABLE 15-2 Top Five Digital Agency Networks by 2012 Interactive Marketing Revenue

Agency (Parent Company)	Headquarters	Clients
Wunderman (WPP)	New York	Land Rover, Ford, Coca-Cola
Digital@Ogilvy (WPP)	New York	Louis Vuitton
Digitas LBi (Publicis)	Boston	Xperia, Coca-Cola, Puma
SapientNitro (Sapient Corp.)	Boston	Fiat, Lufthansa, Victorianox
IBM Interactive (IBM)	Chicago	Coca-Cola, Masters Golf Tournament

Source: Adapted from "World's 15 Largest Digital Agency Networks," *Advertising Age* (April 25, 2013), p. 32.

---

[25] Jonathan Birchall, "Criticism That Spread Like a Rash," *Financial Times* (May 27, 2010), p. 10; see also Birchall, "P&G Starts Direct Sale of Brands Online," *Financial Times* (May 20, 2010); Gary Silverman, "How May I Help You?" *Financial Times* (February 4–5, 2006), p. W2.
[26] Bob Tedeschi, "E-Commerce Report," *The New York Times* (January 12, 2004), p. C6.
[27] Chris Anderson, *The Long Tail: Why the Future of Business Is Selling Less of More* (New York: Hyperion, 2006), p. 13.
[28] Much of the discussion in this section is adapted from Alexis D. Gutzman, *The E-Commerce Arsenal* (New York: Amacom, 2001).

TABLE 15-3 Amazon.com Domain Names

Domain Name	Country
amazon.com.br	Brazil
amazon.ca	Canada
amazon.cn	China
amazon.fr	France
amazon.de	Germany
amazon.it	Italy
amazon.co.jp	Japan
amazon.es	Spain
amazon.co.uk	United Kingdom

of these agencies are independent; others are affiliated with other advertising agency brands and holding companies (see Chapter 13). Whether Web development is handled in-house or by an outside agency, several issues must be addressed when setting up for global e-commerce. These include choosing domain names, arranging payment, localizing sites, addressing privacy issues, and setting up a distribution system.

A critical first step is registering a country-specific domain name. Thus, Amazon.com has a family of different domain names, one for each country in which it operates (see Table 15-3). Although it is certainly possible for European consumers to browse Amazon.com's U.S. site, they may prefer a direct link to a site with a local domain name. From both a marketing and a consumer perspective, this makes sense: The Web site of choice will be one that quotes prices in euros rather than dollars, offers a product selection tailored to local tastes, and ships from local distribution points. However, as noted earlier, the weak dollar may make it less expensive for shoppers in, say, Europe, to order from U.S. online retailers.

Moreover, research suggests that visitors spend more time at sites that are in their own language; they also tend to view more pages and make more purchases. Many people will seek information about sites on local versions of well-known search engines. For example, in France, Yahoo!'s local site is http://fr.Yahoo.com. The same principle applies to non-U.S. companies targeting the American online consumer market. Waterford Wedgwood PLC, Harrods, Johnnie Boden, and other well-known companies have acquired U.S. domain names and created sites with prices listed in dollars.[29]

While registering a ".com" domain name is a relatively straightforward procedure in the United States, requirements can vary elsewhere. In some countries, for example, a company must establish a legal entity before it can register a site with a local domain-name extension. **Cybersquatting**—the practice of registering a particular domain name for the express purpose of reselling it to the company that should rightfully use it—is also a problem. Avon, Panasonic, and Starbucks are some of the companies that have been victims of cybersquatting.

Payment can be another problem; in some countries, including China, credit card use is low. In such situations, e-commerce operators must arrange payment by bank check or postal money order; cash on delivery is also an option. Another issue is credit card fraud; Indonesia, Russia, Croatia, and Bosnia are among the countries where fraud is rampant. Extra identity measures may have to be taken, such as requiring buyers to fax the actual credit card they are using as well as photo IDs.[30] In Japan, consumers pay for online purchases at convenience stores (*konbini*). After selecting an item online, the buyer goes to a nearby convenience store (e.g., a 7-Eleven) and pays cash for the item; the clerk transfers the money to the online seller's account. However,

---

[29] Jessica Vascellaro, "Foreign Shopping Sites Cater to U.S. Customers," *The Wall Street Journal* (October 12, 2005), pp. D1, D14.
[30] Peter Loftus, "Internet Turns Firms into Overseas Businesses," *The Wall Street Journal* (December 16, 2003), p. B4. See also Matt Richtel, "Credit Card Theft Is Thriving Online as Global Market," *The New York Times* (May 13, 2002), p. A1.

foreign companies can't participate in the *konbini* system; this means that a foreign online retailer must establish an alliance with a local company.

Ideally, each country-specific site should reflect local culture, language usage, customs, and aesthetic preferences. Logos and other elements of brand identity should be included on the site, with adjustments for color preferences and meaning differences when necessary. For example, the shopping cart icon is familiar to online shoppers in the United States and many European countries. However, online companies must determine whether that icon is appropriate in all country markets. Subtle but important language differences can also occur even in English-speaking countries. For example, www.figleaves.com and www.figleaves.com/uk are, respectively, the American and British Web addresses for a UK-based lingerie marketer. However, the U.S. site refers to "panties," whereas the UK site has a listing for "briefs." When two or more different languages are involved, translators should be used to ensure that copy reflects current language usage. It is also important not to "reinvent the wheel" by translating the same terms over and over again. Local translators should have access to an in-house dictionary that contains preferred translations of company-specific terms. The database system should be capable of identifying content that has already been translated and then reusing that content. Product descriptions may also vary from country to country; as noted in Chapter 4, American-themed merchandise is very popular in Japan.

After Yao Ming joined the Houston Rockets in 2002, www.nba.com/china was launched in conjunction with www.SOHU.com, China's leading Internet portal. Written entirely in Chinese characters, www.nba.com/china is designed to capitalize on basketball's increasing popularity in the world's largest market. The NBA has also launched several other country- and language-specific sites, including www.nba.com/uk, www.nba.com/Canada, and www.nba.com/espanol.

As the NBA's Chinese site illustrates, it is not enough to simply translate a Web site from the home-country language into other languages. Thus, another basic step is localizing a Web site in the native language and business nomenclature of the target country. From a technical point of view, Web sites designed to support English, French, German, and other languages that use the Latin alphabet store only a maximum of 256 characters in the American Standard Code for Information Interchange (ASCII) format. Even so, there are language-specific needs; for example, a German-language Web site requires more than double the capacity of an English language site because German copy takes more space.[31] However, languages such as Japanese and Chinese require a database that supports double-ASCII. For this reason, it is wise to start with a double-ACSII platform when designing a Web site's architecture. The site's architecture should also be flexible enough to allow different date, currency, and money formatting. For example, to someone living in the United Kingdom, "7/10/10" means October 7, 2010. To an American, it means July 10, 2010.

Another critical global e-commerce issue is privacy. The EU's regulations are among the world's strictest; companies are limited in terms of how much personal information—a customer's age, marital status, and buying patterns, for example—can be gathered and how long the information can be retained. In 2012, EU Justice Commissioner Viviane Reding announced an overhaul of the EU's data collection rules (see Exhibit 15-5). The rules will apply to companies based outside the EU—Apple, Google, and Facebook, for example—if they offer services to EU citizens. Customers living in the EU have the "right to be forgotten"—i.e., they can request to have their personal data deleted. Moreover, EU citizens must give explicit consent before companies can share their data.[32] By contrast, Washington's reluctance to protect privacy is due in part to First Amendment issues as well as to national security concerns stemming from the terror attacks of 2001. To help ensure compliance with privacy laws, American companies have created a new executive-level job position: chief privacy officer.[33]

A number of issues are related to physical distribution decisions. As online sales increase in a particular country or region, it may be necessary to establish local warehouse facilities to speed delivery and reduce shipping costs. In the United States, such a step has tax implications,

[31] Patricia Riedman, "Think Globally, Act Globally," *Advertising Age* (June 19, 2000), p. 48.
[32] Frances Robinson, "EU Unveils Web-Privacy Rules," *The Wall Street Journal* (January 26, 2012), p. B9.
[33] David Scheer, "For Your Eyes Only: Europe's New High-Tech Role: Playing Privacy Cop to the World," *The Wall Street Journal* (October 10, 2003), p. A1.

Exhibit 15-5 Viviane Reding is the European Commissioner for Justice, Fundamental Rights, and Citizenship. In her official capacity, Reding has spoken out about data privacy issues. One concern is the widespread corporate practice of gathering and using consumer data without permission. The privacy issue made headlines in 2013 after an American, Edward Snowden, revealed that the U.S. National Security Agency had been spying on e-mails and telephone calls in Europe.
Source: © epa european pressphoto agency b.v. / Alamy.

meaning that the marketer may have to collect sales tax. To allay consumer concerns about ordering merchandise online, companies may opt to waive shipping fees and offer free returns and money-back guarantees.

New Products and Services

The digital revolution has spurred innovations in many different industries. Companies in all parts of the world are developing a new generation of products, services, and technologies. These include broadband networks, mobile commerce, wireless connectivity, and smartphones (see Exhibit 15-6).

Broadband

A **broadband** communication system is one that has sufficient capacity to carry multiple voice, data, or video channels simultaneously. *Bandwidth* determines the range of frequencies that can pass over a given transmission channel. For example, traditional telephone networks offered quite limited bandwidth compared with state-of-the art digital telephone networks. As a result, a traditional telephone call sounds "lo-fi." Bandwidth is measured in bits-per-second (Bps); a full page of English text is about 16,000 bits. For example, a 56 Kbs modem connected to a conventional telephone line can move 16,000 bits per second; by comparison, a broadband Internet connection that utilizes coaxial cable can move up to 10 gigabits per second.

As noted in The Cultural Context feature, South Korea currently boasts the world's fastest average Internet speeds. However, technology upgrades currently underway will mean even higher speeds: The government intends to ensure that every Korean household has a 1-gigabit Internet connection. As Choi Gwang-gi, the engineer overseeing the project, explains, "A lot of Koreans are early adopters, and we thought we needed to be prepared for things like 3D TV, Internet Protocol TV, high-definition multimedia, gaming and videoconferencing, ultra-high definition TV, and cloud computing."[35] Consumers won't be the only beneficiaries of the upgrade; corporations will also be able to harness gigabit Internet connections for high-definition global videoconferencing and other applications.

> "Increased broadband penetration is opening up possibilities that didn't exist even 2 years ago.... We need to realize that online is now an important part of the overall communications mix.... We are not an online business. We're a beverage business. But we have to develop compelling marketing platforms that are relevant to the lives of young people."[34]
>
> —Tim Kopp, vice president of global interactive marketing, Coca-Cola

---

[34] Andrew Ward, "Coke Taps into Brand New Internet Craze," *Financial Times* (August 8, 2006), p. 15.
[35] Mark McDonald, "Home Internet May Get Even Faster in South Korea," *The New York Times* (February 22, 2011), p. B3.

Exhibit 15-6 The Linux open source operating system was created by Linus Tovalds, shown here with the software's iconic penguin mascot. Although Linux is distributed for free, annual sales of Linux-related software, hardware, and support services total about $15 billion. The Linux Foundation was created to deal with competitive issues pertaining to Microsoft and its Windows operating system. It also deals with technical, legal, and standards issues.
Source: Paul Sakuma/AP Images.

As South Korea and other countries forge ahead with massive investment in broadband infrastructure upgrades, politicians and union leaders in laggard countries are taking a keen interest in the issue. A recent study declared that South Korea and several other countries are "ready for tomorrow" in terms of Internet speed. A second tier of countries falls into the category "below today's applications threshold." The United States, Germany, and Hong Kong all fall into this category.[36] U.S. President Barack Obama responded to this situation in 2011 by promising $18.7 billion to improve America's broadband network.

Why are policymakers following the broadband race so closely? Broadband offers multiple marketing opportunities to companies in a variety of industries. Broadband also allows Internet users to access **streaming media** such as **streaming audio** and **streaming video**. Personalized radio services such as Pandora, Spotify, and iHeartRadio allow users to list their favorite artists and songs. Pandora uses a proprietary technology called the Music Genome Project to make recommendations for new music that are similar to a listener's current favorites. Streaming media is having a profound impact on the television industry, with Amazon.com, iTunes, Netflix, and other services offering movie and TV show downloads and streaming as viewing options.

Streaming media represents a major market opportunity for the video game industry, which includes electronics companies (e.g., Microsoft and Sony), game publishers (e.g., Electronic Arts), and Internet portals (e.g., Google). Gamers in different locations, even different countries, can compete against each other using PCs or Xbox or PlayStation consoles. These are sometimes called *massively multiplayer online games* (MMOG); the most popular MMOG is *World of Warcraft*. Microsoft's Xbox Live service has more than 10 million subscribers worldwide. Consumer interest in online gaming has been fueled by powerful next-generation game consoles such as Microsoft's Xbox One and Sony's PlayStation 4.

Cloud Computing

In the preceding section, *cloud computing* was referenced as one driver of higher broadband speeds. The term refers to next-generation computing that is performed "in the cloud." Rather than installing software such as iTunes or Microsoft Office on a computer hard drive, such applications will be delivered through a Web browser. Cloud computing means that archives—including music and movie files, photos, and documents—are stored on massive remote servers and data

---

[36] Alan Cane, "Leaders Look to Future in Broadband Race," *Financial Times* (October 23, 2009).

⑥ INNOVATION, ENTREPRENEURSHIP, AND THE GLOBAL STARTUP

Reed Hastings/Netflix

MyMarketingLab   SYNC • THINK • LEARN

Reed Hastings is an entrepreneur. He developed an innovative service, created a brand, and started a company to market it. By applying the basic tools and principles of modern marketing, Hastings has achieved remarkable success. As is true with many entrepreneurs, Hastings' idea was based on his recognition of a problem that needed to be solved and his own experience as a consumer. Like many people, he had forgotten to return some videocassettes that he had rented. When he finally did take them back to the video store, he had to pay some hefty late fees. He said to himself, "There has to be a better way." A business model that seemed to make more sense was the one used by many health clubs: In return for a monthly fee, members can use the club anytime they want. With this in mind, in 1997 Hastings started Netflix, a mail-order DVD rental service.

Within a few years, red-and-white Netflix envelopes were appearing in mailboxes throughout the United States. The company enjoyed robust subscriber growth, and by mid-2011 its stock had soared to nearly $300 per share. Netflix's popularity was due in part to its "star ratings" recommendation feature that helped subscribers find new shows and movies based on prior viewing habits and the ratings they gave to the programming that they watched. Netflix's success came at the expense of competitors in the brick-and-mortar video rental business; in 2010, for example, Blockbuster filed for bankruptcy.

Hastings was at the forefront in a video industry that was undergoing rapid transformation. However, more change was to come: As the user base of household broadband and lightning-fast 4G mobile networks reached critical mass, streaming video was supplanting physical DVDs as the viewing medium of choice. Hastings responded by offering streaming-content subscriptions for $7.99 per month in addition to DVD rentals. However, Netflix faced competition from Redbox, an upstart DVD rental company with very low prices, as well as from streaming services such as Hulu.

In mid-2011, Hastings announced a plan to rebrand its DVD rental service as Qwikster, and to separate its subscription base from subscribers who wanted only streaming movies and TV shows. But consumers were confused and the strategy backfired; Netflix lost hundreds of thousands of subscribers. With the stock dipping as low as $53.80 per share, Hastings had to find new sources of growth. As one analyst said, "The only option for Netflix is to go international."

That is exactly what Hastings had in mind. Canada was Netflix's first international market entry, with operations commencing in 2010. In 2011, Latin America was added, and in 2012 the United Kingdom, Ireland, Denmark, Finland, Norway, and Sweden came online as well. However, global expansion is expensive. Copyright laws require licensing content on a country-by-country basis, and marketing costs are significant as well. One of Hastings' goals is to negotiate worldwide licensing deals that will provide better terms than the country-by-country approach.

Today, Netflix has 36 million subscribers in 40 countries. Irrespective of location, streaming subscribers pay roughly the equivalent of the U.S. subscription rate—about $8.00 per month. Netflix content can also be accessed on more than 1,000 different devices, including smartphones, tablets, and, of course, televisions. Meanwhile, Hastings is moving ahead with plans to create original content. A 13-episode political thriller, *House of Cards*, was introduced to popular and critical acclaim. Subscribers returned, the company's fortunes turned around, and the stock has more than quadrupled from its 2011 lows. As *BloombergBusinessweek* put it, Netflix mounted "one of the all-time great comebacks." Says Hastings, "We think of the technology as a vehicle for creating a better, more modern experience for the content we have. What we're really competing for quite broadly is people's time."

Sources: Ashlee Vance, "The Man Who Ate the Internet (Cover Story)," *BloombergBusinessweek* (May 13, 2013), pp. 56–60+; Amol Sharma and Nathalie Tadena, "Viewers Stream to Netflix," *The Wall Street Journal* (April 23, 2013), pp. B1, B4; Greg Bensinger, "Netflix Transition Rattles Investors," *The Wall Street Journal* (July 26, 2012), p. B3.

Exhibit 15-7 Netflix shares slumped in mid-2011 after company founder Reed Hastings announced plans to separate the streaming video business from the DVD rental business. Less than two years later, however, the stock rebounded sharply as original Netflix programs such as *House of Cards* and *Orange Is the New Black* were well received by viewers and critics alike.
Source: © ZUMA Press, Inc. / Alamy.

centers rather than on individual users' computers. Computer files can be accessed remotely, via the Internet, from any location and from any computer.

Google's Chrome operating system, which has been described as "a new computing paradigm," is designed to exploit the opportunities of cloud computing. Another industry trendsetter, Amazon.com, has set up Amazon Web Services (AWS) to offer cloud-computing resources to businesses. AWS is a variation on the outsourcing trend that was discussed in Chapter 8; Netflix, Foursquare, and thousands of other companies use the service instead of running their own data centers. However, cloud computing is still in its infancy; a recent service interruption of AWS caused widespread disruptions among its clients. Despite such setbacks, cloud computing is expected to grow at an annual torrid pace of 25 percent over the next several years.[37]

Smartphones

Cell phones have been one of the biggest new-product success stories of the digital revolution. Worldwide, 1.75 billion cellular handsets were sold in 2012. Soaring demand has boosted the fortunes of manufacturers such as Apple, HTC, Motorola, RIM, and Samsung, as well as AT&T, Deutsche Telekom, U.S. Cellular, Verizon, and other service providers. New features and functionality give consumers a reason to upgrade their handsets on a regular basis. Conventional cell phones (sometimes called feature phones) allow text messaging via **short message service (SMS)**, a globally accepted wireless standard for sending alphanumeric messages of up to 160 characters. SMS is the technology platform that is the basis for Twitter's microblogging service. Industry experts expect marketers to integrate SMS with communication via other digital channels, such as interactive digital TV, the Internet, and e-mail.

Smartphones have much greater functionality than feature phones, incorporating some of the capabilities of computers. Worldwide, smartphones represent about one-fourth of all cell phone sales. Case in point: Apple's wildly successful iPhone comes equipped with a full-blown version of the company's iOS and Web browser. The popularity of smartphones is due, in part, to the availability of applications, or apps, such as Instagram, Action Movie FX, and Angry Birds. In 2013, Apple's iTunes store sold its 50 billionth iPhone app. Apple commemorated the milestone with a "50 Billion Apps Download Promotion": the lucky person who downloaded the 50 billionth app won a $10,000 gift card—to be redeemed on iTunes, of course! Many of Apple's rivals use Android, a phone operating system developed by Google.

Mobile Advertising and Mobile Commerce

Mobile advertising and **mobile commerce (m-commerce)** are terms that describe the use of cell phones as channels for delivering advertising messages and conducting product and service transactions. Most smartphone users can access the Internet via **Wi-Fi**; in addition, cell phone service providers typically offer data plans that allow Internet connections via 3G or 4G networks. This allows Apple, Crisp Wireless, Google, Medialets, Mobext, and other companies to offer clients mobile ad services. For example, Unilever, Nissan, and other companies use Apple's iAd service to place interactive ads inside iPhone and iPod apps.[38]

Total worldwide spending for mobile ads was only about $1 billion in 2007, but industry experts expected that figure to reach $10 billion to $20 billion by 2013. Mobile ad spending in the United States totaled $2.3 billion in 2012. Messaging campaigns allow advertisers to engage customers in conversations and connect them with brands. Mobile search and mobile display advertising are growing in importance; industry forecasters expect them to pass SMS-based advertising in the near future. This is especially true given the popularity of, and degree of engagement with, mobile Internet today. Another driving force is the torrid growth of the tablet format, which includes Apple's iPad, Samsung's Galaxy Tab, RIM's PlayBook, and several other devices.

---

[37] Steve Lohr, "Amazon's Trouble Raises Cloud Computing Doubts," *The New York Times* (April 23, 2011), p. B1.

[38] Yukari Iwatani Kane and Emily Steel, "Apple's iAd Helping Rivals," *The Wall Street Journal* (November 11, 2010), p. B4.

Smartphones that are equipped with **global positioning systems (GPS)** can determine the user's exact geographic position. This capability has created new opportunities for location-based mobile platforms, such as foursquare. The popularity of GPS-equipped mobile devices is driving interest in *location-based advertising.* For example, Alcatel-Lucent, the French telecommunications equipment manufacturer, has launched a service that sends tailored text messages when smartphone users are near a specific location, such as a store, hotel, or restaurant. The service, which is managed by San Francisco–based 1020 Placecast, provides addresses and telephone numbers of the businesses and can also provide links to coupons or other types of sales promotions. Users "opt in" by signing up to receive ads.

NAVTEQ Media Solutions is a digital-map data company owned by Nokia. NAVTEQ provides location-based advertising services using the company's proprietary technology, LocationPoint Advertising (Exhibit 15-8). NAVTEQ's global clients include Best Western Germany, Domino's Pizza India, and McDonald's Finland. Recent campaigns for a variety of

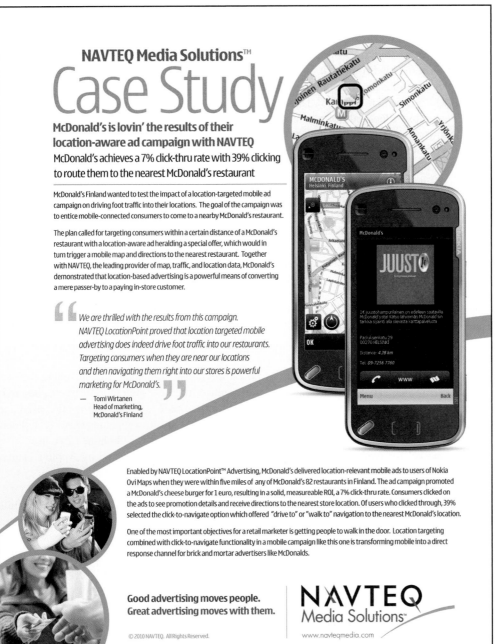

Exhibit 15-8 NAVTEQ provides digital map data for location-based devices such as smartphones. NAVTEQ data is also used in vehicle navigation devices from Garmin.
Source: NAVTEQ Media Solutions.

clients have demonstrated that mobile campaigns can provide marketers with important metrics that can be used to calculate return on investment (ROI).

In one campaign, mobile users who were within a 5-mile radius of any McDonald's location in Finland received an offer to buy a cheeseburger for 1 euro. The result was a 7 percent click-through rate. Of those users, 39 percent used the ad's click-to-navigate option to request walking or driving directions to the nearest McDonald's. In India, a campaign to reach existing and prospective Domino's customers was also successful. Ads were delivered to smartphone users; banner ads were also placed on Nokia's Ovi Services portal. The results were impressive: 22.6 percent of users clicked for the map, 10.8 percent clicked to call for home-delivery options, and 8 percent used the ad to access Domino's Web site.[39]

Cell phone usage is exploding in India. As Manoj Dawane, CEO of Mumbai software company People Infocom, explains, "In India, mobile phone penetration is high compared to other forms of media like television or the Internet. You can't have a better place than India for mobile advertising." One factor driving mobile ads in India is the low rates that subscribers pay—as little as 2 cents per minute. Demographics play an important role, too. About two-thirds of the Indian population lives in rural areas where television ownership and newspaper readership are low. Cellular operators such as BPL Mobile have built networks that reach tens of thousands of Indian villages. Arif Ali, head of brand communications at BPL, has ideas that will keep subscriber costs low. "We are thinking of providing 30- to 60-second commercials over the phone where we will pass on some kind of benefit," he said.[40]

Another popular mobile communication technology, **Bluetooth**, has the advantage of consuming less power than Wi-Fi.[41] This makes Bluetooth well suited for use with cell phones. Many people use Bluetooth to transfer photos from their phones to their computers. However, Bluetooth works over shorter distances than Wi-Fi. Bluetooth technology has thus been incorporated into automobiles and home appliances such as refrigerators and microwave ovens. Current Wi-Fi technology can only handle data, not voice. However, many industry observers expect that in the near future, hotspots will allow cell phones to switch to the Internet for telephone calls.

Wireless technology is also being used in other ways. In the automotive world, there is a trend toward **telematics**, which is a car's ability to exchange information about its location or mechanical performance. Cars are also being equipped with online access; BMW Assist, BMW Online, and BMW TeleServices illustrate some of telematics' potential. The system provides access to a wide range of information and services, including the availability of parking spaces. The service also assists users who wish to book hotel rooms or make restaurant reservations. Mercedes-Benz is rolling out a similar service. Similarly, Microsoft's SYNC is a voice-activated communication system that is available on Ford vehicles. It can be used in conjunction with Bluetooth-equipped cell phones.

Mobile Music

Because of rampant illegal sharing of music files, the music companies are searching for new sources of revenue. Thanks to technology convergence, the new generation of cell phones is leading to changes in the mobile music industry. **Mobile music** is music that is purchased and played on a cell phone or other mobile device. One way that music companies have created new revenue streams is by licensing the rights to popular songs for use as cell phone ringtones.

The market for paid, legal, full-track music downloads is dominated by Apple's iTunes Store. Music purchased from iTunes can be played back on computers and mobile devices such as Apple's iPod, iPhone, and iPad. In 2006, iTunes reached a milestone of 1 billion song downloads; today, Apple is the world's number 1 music seller, with a cumulative total of 25 billion downloads. (The 25 billionth song was downloaded in Germany in 2013, and the lucky iTunes

---

[39] Sara Silver and Emily Steel, "Alcatel Gets into Mobile Ads," *The Wall Street Journal* (May 21, 2009), p. B9; NAVTEQ, "Domino's," http://navteqmedia.com/mobile/case-studies/dominos (accessed May 24, 2011); NAVTEQ, "McDonald's," http://navteqmedia.com/mobile/case-studies/mcdonalds (accessed May 24, 2011).

[40] Eric Bellman and Tariq Engineer, "India Appears Ripe for Cell Phone Ads," *The Wall Street Journal* (March 10, 2008), p. B3.

[41] *Bluetooth* is the Anglicized version of a Scandinavian epithet for Harald Blatand, a Danish Viking and king who lived in the tenth century.

EMERGING MARKETS BRIEFING BOOK

New Media in China

MyMarketingLab   SYNC • THINK • LEARN

China is home to the world's largest population of Internet users—nearly 600 million in all, with new users coming online every day. So it is no surprise that Google, Yahoo!, and other Internet companies are flocking there. However, strict government control over information presents major challenges. Regulations regarding the Internet require search engine companies to filter out content that Beijing finds objectionable. Also, the government blocks access to popular sites such as Facebook, Twitter, and YouTube (which is owned by Google).

The vast amount of user data compiled by Google is supposed to be private. However, authorities in countries where Google has operations occasionally request access to data that will be used in government investigations. In other instances, government officials determine that some information is erroneous and ask that it be removed. The Chinese government does not allow Google to publish figures regarding its requests, on the grounds that such information is a state secret. Excluding China, Google's figures show that Brazil's government has made the most requests for user information: 3,663 at last count. In addition, Brazilian authorities filed nearly 300 requests for data removal; Google complied with 81 percent of those requests. One can assume that the Chinese government has made more requests than Brazil's government.

Google was granted a local Internet license in 2005 and began operating in mainland China in 2006. The company censored search results in accordance with Chinese law; searches on forbidden topics yielded a message that read, "According to local laws, regulations, and policies, some search results could not be displayed." In 2009, the Chinese government alleged that pornographic images were available on Google and insisted that the content be removed. Then, early in 2010, hackers based in China attacked Google. In the wake of the attack, Google announced it would no longer censor searches. In March, Google shut down www.google.cn; visitors to the site were automatically redirected to www.google.com.hk in Hong Kong. In June 2010, Google's Chinese operating license expired.

Despite the restrictions, new media startups are thriving in China. For example, Sina Weibo, Tencent, and Baidu are microblogging sites; Renren is a popular social networking site that has been called "the Chinese Facebook." Sina Weibo, a unit of SINA, is a microblogging site that is similar to Twitter. Despite government censorship of content that could be interpreted as antigovernment, Sina Weibo and similar sites have attracted more than 200 million registered users. What's the attraction? For one thing, these sites offer the opportunity for self-expression, which young people value in an environment of state-run media. Also, users hang on every word from Sina Weibo's celebrity bloggers, which include movie stars and athletes.

Sources: David Barboza, "Despite Restrictions, Twitter-Like Microblogs Catch on in China," *The New York Times* (March 16, 2011), p. B3; Kathrin Hille, "Google Searches for Truce in China," *Financial Times* (June 30, 2010), p. 17; Jon Swartz, "Google to Stop Censoring Search Results in China," *USA Today* (March 22, 2010), p. 1B; Hille, "Google Has a Rude Awakening in China," *Financial Times* (June 20/21, 2009), p. 10.

customer won a €10,000 Apple Gift Card.) Apple's competitors have tried, without much success, to develop music players and download services to rival the iPod/iTunes combination. Music players include Microsoft's Zune and Dell's Digital Jukebox (DJ) Music Players. Besides the iTunes Store, other online music services are available, including Amazon.com, Napster 2.0, RealNetworks' Rhapsody and RealPlayer Music Store, Slacker, Spotify, and Xbox Music.

These online music services use a variety of pricing strategies. Rhapsody is primarily a subscription service, with rates starting at $9.99 per month. Napster has different rate plans, ranging from $5 to $10 per month. By contrast, iTunes uses "à la carte" pricing, charging for each song track or album download. Originally, individual songs cost $0.99 each on iTunes. Recently, however, Apple introduced a variable pricing policy; popular songs from the Top 100 are $1.29 each, while millions of older titles are $0.69. Other songs still sell for $0.99. The new pricing policy coincided with Apple's decision to abandon digital rights management (DRM) copy protection on the song files it sells. This change means that songs purchased on iTunes can be played back on devices other than the iPod and iPhone.

The worldwide success of Apple's iTunes Store has generated a backlash of sorts. In Japan, the music industry was unsuccessful in its 2005 attempt to persuade the government to charge a royalty fee on each iPod sold. The money generated would have been distributed to record companies, songwriters, and recording artists as partial compensation for financial losses due to illegal music file downloading. In France, the National Assembly approved a bill that would require Apple to share the iTunes software codes with other companies so that music downloads would play on all digital music players, not just iPods. In January 2007, Norway's consumer ombudsman ruled that iPod's lack of interoperability was illegal. In response, Apple issued a statement that the company "hopes that European governments will encourage a competitive environment that allows innovation to thrive, protects intellectual property and allows consumers to decide which products are successful."

Cloud computing, which was discussed earlier in the chapter, is expected to have a major impact on the mobile music business. Cloud-based music services represent a hybrid of the subscription and online store business models; the new approach addresses some of the shortcomings of the existing methods. For example, iPod owners must sync their iPods to their computers or other devices. Also, the pricing schemes for the various subscription services can be confusing. By contrast, cloud-based music services offer users a music locker; the locker is "in the cloud," and music files that have been purchased or uploaded can be accessed from a variety of mobile devices. Currently, Amazon.com, Apple, and Google all have launched cloud-based music services.

Mobile Gaming[42]

Mobile gaming is gaining in popularity; according to industry estimates, revenues will reach $17.6 billion in 2015, up from $3.77 billion in 2010. Worldwide, Apple's iPhone, iPod, and iPad are the dominant mobile-gaming platforms. Zynga, founded by entrepreneur Mark Pincus in 2007, is one of the best-known developers of mobile games. Each month, some 240 million users play Zynga Poker, Words With Friends, and other games. Other popular games include puzzles such as Sudoku; solitaire, blackjack, and other card and casino games; and board games such as Monopoly. Some games are available on a free-to-play basis; others sell for the equivalent of a few dollars. How can a marketer monetize a free game? For a small fee, many free games can be upgraded to premium versions; in addition, many games offer users the opportunity to make in-game purchases of virtual goods. Indeed, the word "free" can be misleading, as network operators typically charge fees for downloading the games.

Early generations of smartphones had small screens and limited storage space and computing power, so mobile gaming originally appealed more to occasional users such as commuters rather than hard-core gamers. Industry growth was also slowed by the varying technical standards incorporated into different brands of cell phones. However, mobile games are quickly becoming more sophisticated as phone makers improve compatibility, add more features and functionality, and build high-speed 4G networks. GPS capabilities will also lead to location-based games in which players compete by trying to physically approach their opponents.

Internet Phone Service

For the telecommunications industry, Internet telephone service is the "next big thing." **Voice over Internet Protocol (VoIP)** technology allows the human voice to be digitized and broken into data packets that can be transmitted over the Internet and converted back into normal speech. If a call is placed to a conventional phone, it must be switched from the Internet to a traditional phone network; local telephone companies generally own the lines into residences and businesses. However, if the call is made between two subscribers to the same VoIP provider, it bypasses the traditional network altogether. The implications are clear: VoIP has the potential to render the current telecommunications infrastructure—consisting primarily of twisted copper and fiber optic cable—obsolete.

Currently, VoIP accounts for only a small percentage of global calls. However, it has the potential to be a disruptive innovation that will upset the balance of power in the telecommunications industry. The promise of a global growth market has resulted in soaring stock values for startups. In Europe, Niklas Zennström, cofounder of the Kazaa music file-sharing service, started Skype Ltd. to offer Internet telephone service. As hundreds of thousands of new users—many in China, India, and Sweden—joined each day, Skype became a global phenomenon. In 2005, eBay acquired Skype for $2.6 billion. However, eBay struggled to create synergies between the communication system and the company's core auction business. In 2009, eBay spun off Skype as a separate company. In 2011, Microsoft bought Skype for $8.6 billion.

---

[42] This section is based on Daisuke Wakabayashi and Spencer E. Ante, "Mobile Game Fight Goes Global," *The Wall Street Journal* (June 14, 2012), p. B1.

Exhibit 15-9 Amazon.com founder and CEO Jeff Bezos unveils the Kindle Fire, the latest version of his company's wireless reading device. Amazon.com's e-book sales recently overtook sales of titles in traditional paperback and hardback formats. Bezos is hoping that the Kindle will gain acceptance among college students.
Source: © ZUMA Press, Inc. / Alamy.

Digital Books and Electronic Reading Devices

The digital revolution has had a dramatic impact on traditional print media such as newspapers and magazines. Publishers are experiencing dramatic downturns in readership as people spend more time online. At the same time, the global recession forced many companies to cut back on print advertising. Caught in a squeeze, magazines are folding and newspapers are declaring bankruptcy. However, electronic readers (e-readers) such as the Amazon.com's Kindle, Sony's Reader Digital Book, and Apple's iPad may help lure subscribers back.

Amazon.com sold the first Kindle for $359; the new, larger Kindle DX costs $379, holds 3,500 e-books, and has a 9.7-inch display screen (see Exhibit 15-9). Amazon.com has taken the Kindle global with the launch of a smaller, less expensive version that can be used in more than 100 countries. Apple launched the iPad in March 2010; by the end of the year, 15 million units had been sold. By the end of 2012, Apple had sold more than 100 million of the devices.

Industry observers think that colleges and universities will be instrumental in building awareness and encouraging adoption of e-readers and e-books. The reason is simple: electronic versions of textbooks represent a huge market opportunity. For example, the textbook you are reading is available directly from the publisher in the form of an electronic "subscription" at www.coursesmart.com. The online version requires users to be connected to the Internet; the text can be accessed from an unlimited number of computers. Buyers can use the e-book for 180 days before the subscription expires. The price is approximately half of what bookstores charge for a new copy of the physical textbook. Usually, students can print as many as 10 pages at a time; it is also possible to cut and paste, highlight, and take notes directly on the computer.

As is the case with music and movies, digital piracy is a growing problem with e-books. A number of Web sites and file-sharing services distribute unauthorized copies of popular copyrighted material. What do authors themselves think of the problem? Some view digital piracy as a way to gain new readers. Others say that they simply want fair compensation for their work. A third camp includes authors who don't think pursuing the pirates is worth the effort. As best-selling author Stephen King said recently, "The question is, how much time and energy do I want to spend chasing these guys? And to what end? My sense is that most of them live in basements floored with carpeting remnants, living on Funions and discount beer."[43]

---

[43] Motoko Rich, "New Target for Digital Pirates: The Printed Word," *The New York Times* (May 12, 2009), p. A1.

Summary

The **digital revolution** has created a global electronic marketplace. The revolution has gained momentum over the course of 70-plus years, during which time technological breakthroughs included the digital mainframe computer; the **transistor**; the **integrated circuit (IC)**; the **personal computer (PC)**; the **spreadsheet**; the PC **operating system**; and the **Internet**, which originated as an initiative of the **Defense Advanced Research Projects Agency (DARPA)**. Three key innovations by Tim Berners-Lee—**URLs**, **HTTP**, and **HTML**—led to the creation in the early 1990s of the **World Wide Web**.

The digital revolution has resulted in a process known as **convergence**, meaning that previously separate industries and markets are coming together. In this environment, the **innovator's dilemma** means that company management must decide whether to invest in current technologies or try to develop new technologies. Although leading firms in an industry often develop **sustaining technologies** that result in improved product performance, the revolution has also unleashed a wave of **disruptive technologies** that are creating new markets and reshaping industries and **value networks**.

E-commerce is growing in importance for both consumer and industrial goods marketers. Generally, commercial Web sites can have a domestic or a global focus; in addition, they can be classified as **promotion sites**, **content sites**, or **transaction sites**. Global marketers must take care when designing Web sites. Country-specific domain names must be registered and local-language sites developed. In addition to addressing issues of technology and functionality, content must reflect local culture, customs, and aesthetic preferences. **Cybersquatting** can hinder a company's effort to register its corporate name as an Internet destination.

The Internet is a powerful tool for advertisers; **click-through rates** are one measure of effectiveness. Another trend is **paid search advertising**. New products and services spawned by the digital revolution include **broadband**, which permits transmission of **streaming media** over the Internet; **mobile commerce (m-commerce)**, which is made possible by **Wi-Fi**, **Bluetooth**, and other forms of wireless connectivity; **telematics** and **global positioning systems (GPS)**; and **short message service (SMS)**. **Smartphones** are creating new markets for **mobile music** downloads, including ringtones, **truetones**, and full-track music files; smartphones can also be used for mobile gaming and Internet phone service using **VoIP**.

MyMarketingLab

Go to **mymktlab.com** for the following Assisted-graded writing questions:

15-1. What key issues must be addressed by global companies that engage in e-commerce?

15-2. Briefly outline Web design issues as they pertain to global marketing.

15-3. Mymarketinglab Only – comprehensive writing assignment for this chapter.

MyMarketingLab

Go to **mymktlab.com** to complete the problems marked with this icon .

Discussion Questions

15-4. Briefly review the key innovations that culminated in the digital revolution. What is the basic technological process that made the revolution possible?

 15-5. What is convergence? How is convergence affecting Sony? Kodak? Nokia?

15-6. What is the innovator's dilemma? What is the difference between a sustaining technology and a disruptive technology? Briefly review Christensen's five principles of disruptive innovation.

15-7. What is the Long Tail? What implications does this have for market segmentation?

⭐ **15-8.** Review the key products and services that have emerged during the digital revolution. What are some new products and services that are not mentioned in the chapter?

15-9. You have the option of purchasing electronic editions of many of your college textbooks. Is this something that you are interested in doing?

⭐ **15-10.** Which pricing model do you think is better for music downloads, the iTunes Store's "pay-per-track" or Rhapsody's subscription service? Do you think cloud-based music services will be successful?

CASE 15-1 CONTINUED (REFER TO PAGE 482)

Africa 3.0

Investment in telecommunications and other sectors in Africa is being driven by a variety of factors. Several demographic trends are clear. For example, nearly half the population is under the age of 15. The World Bank reports that half the population lives on $1.25 per day. However, according to a study by the African Development Bank, Africa's middle class now comprises 34 percent of the population, some 313 million people in all. The report defines "middle class" as those who spend between $2 and $20 per day. A narrower definition would include the 120 million people (21 percent) who spend between $4 and $20 per day.

Demand from this emerging middle class has been a boon to telecommunications companies. Between 2006 and 2010, compound revenue growth in the sector averaged 40 percent. In Africa, a cell phone is often a person's most valuable possession, and there are more than 450 million cell phone subscribers. In Kenya, for example, there are more than 21 million active phone numbers for a population of 40 million people. In most parts of Africa, mobile networks suffer service interruptions. As a result, many people use more than one cell phone and have multiple providers.

Key industry players include Safaricom, Kenya's leading mobile phone service provider and the largest, most profitable company in East Africa. South Africa's MTN Group is the continent's leading mobile provider in terms of subscribers. MTN gained prominence in 2010 when it became the first African company to have a sponsorship for World Cup soccer. Globacon is in Nigeria.

One of the biggest African success stories involves Celtel International, a telecom created by Sudanese businessman Mo Ibrahim. In 2005, Ibraham sold the company to Zain, based in Kuwait, for $3.4 billion. In 2010, India's Bharti Airtel paid $10.7 billion for Zain's African assets. Zain has operations in 15 African countries, including Malawi, Chad, and Zambia. The acquisition makes Bharti the world's largest mobile provider—165 million subscribers in all—with operations only in emerging markets.

Not surprisingly, the market opportunity is also attracting investment from other global telecom operators. For example, France Telecom has 55 million users in 22 countries in Africa and the Middle East. Executives are extending the company's African reach to span the entire continent; the goal is to become the "champion of rural Africa" by rolling out a range of new, low-cost mobile services under the Orange brand. For example, the company's E-Recharge service lets users exchange credits via text messaging. Price discounts of up to 99 percent for off-peak calls are also very popular.

Kenya has become a key battleground, as service providers cut prices to attract customers. Airtel Kenya has squared off against Safaricom, Orange Kenya, and other rivals; Airtel recently cut rates by 50 percent, to $0.03 per minute for voice calls and $0.01 for text messages. Parent company Bharti Airtel had previously used this tactic in India, where customers are making longer calls because airtime is less expensive. For his part, Safaricom CEO Robert Collymore says his company will focus on data and mobile banking services.

Arguably the biggest mobile innovation in Africa is M-Pesa (M for "mobile"; *pesa* is Swahili for "money"). M-Pesa is a mobile phone–based money transfer service developed by Safaricom Kenya and Vodaphone, with backing from Britain's Department for International Development. With millions of registered users, M-Pesa is transforming the banking industry in Africa. Just a decade ago, many

mainstream banks would not have found it feasible to do business with low-income customers; the meager returns would not have justified opening branch networks or setting ATMs. As a result, a person with a city job would have to give money to a friend or a bus driver to deliver to relatives at home. Needless to say, highway robbery was a constant threat.

Today, however, banks can work with shopkeepers and bar owners who dispense or collect cash and then credit or debit a customer's mobile phone account. The target market is the "unbanked"; that is, people who do not have bank accounts. In Kenya alone, 70 percent of adults have access to financial services today, compared with only 5 percent in 2006. In Nigeria, a country of 150 million people, only 20 percent of the population has a bank account. Nigeria's Central Bank (CBN) is taking the lead, creating a system in which telecommunications companies will provide the infrastructure for offering financial services. This approach is necessary because there are several dominant cell phone service providers in Nigeria.

Price wars are just one of the challenges of doing business on the continent. Africa is at the bottom of the World Bank's "Ease of Doing Business" rankings. Widespread corruption is part of the problem; as Sudanese telecom magnate Ibrahim puts it, "There is a crisis of leadership and governance in Africa and we must face it." Moreover, he notes, "These guys know that millions of children are going to bed without dinner. The blood of those children is on the hands of those who spend the money on arms and private jets."

Data compiled by Global Financial Integrity, a nongovernmental organization, support Ibrahim's assessment of the business environment. According to a recent report, more than $350 billion flowed out of Africa as a result of corruption and illicit deals.

Discussion Questions

15-11. Will Zain be a good fit for Bharti Airtel? Is the Indian market similar to the African market?

15-12. Further economic liberalization in Africa depends, in part, on government leaders overcoming suspicions that foreign companies want to exploit Africa. How quickly is this likely to happen?

15-13. If marketers "think local and act local," what are some of the new products and services that are likely to emerge from Africa in the next few years?

Sources: Kevin J. O'Brien, "Microsoft and Huawei of China to Unite to Sell Low-Cost Windows Smartphones in Africa," *The New York Times* (February 5, 2013), p. B2; Peter Wonacott, "A New Class of Consumers Grows in Africa," *The Wall Street Journal* (May 2, 2011), p. A8; Sarah Childress, "Telecom Giants Battle for Kenya," *The Wall Street Journal* (January 14, 2011), pp. B1, B7; Ben Hall, "France Telecom Targets Rural Africa for Growth," *Financial Times* (November 10, 2010), p. 16; Parselelo Kantai, "Telecoms: Mobile May Be the Future of Banking," *Financial Times* (September 29, 2010); Gordon Brown, "To Combat Poverty, Get Africa's Children to School," *Financial Times* (September 20, 2010), p. 9; William Wallis and Tom Burgis, "Attitudes Change to Business in Region," *Financial Times* (June 4, 2010), p. 6; Wallis, "Outlook Brightens for Frontier Market," *Financial Times* (June 2, 2010), p. 7; Robb M. Stewart and Will Connors, "For Bharti, Africa Potential Outweighs Hurdles," *The Wall Street Journal* (February 17, 2010), pp. B1, B2; Jamie Anderson, Martin Kupp, and Ronan Moaligou, "Lessons from the Developing World," *The Wall Street Journal* (August 17, 2009), p. R6; Tom Burgis, "Case Study: Text Messages Give Shopkeepers the Power to Bulk Buy," *Financial Times Special Report: Digital Business* (May 29, 2009), p. 8; Cassell Bryan-Low, "New Frontiers for Cellphone Service," *The Wall Street Journal* (February 13, 2007), pp. B1, B5.

CASE 15-2
Global Marketers Discover Social Media

What do Chris Anderson, Sir Richard Branson, George Colony, and Tony Hsieh have in common? Besides being influential and successful business leaders, thinkers, and public figures, they all use the microblogging Web site known as Twitter. Twitter is one of many social media Web sites that have burst onto the scene and quickly gone global within the span of just a few short years. Other popular social networking Web sites include Facebook, MySpace, and YouTube; LinkedIn is a social network for professionals.

These sites, which are sometimes collectively referred to as *Web 2.0*, enable individuals and companies to interact using the Internet. Twitter users post short messages ("tweets") of 140 characters or fewer from computers and mobile devices such as cell phones and BlackBerries. Once an individual has signed up for Twitter, he or she can attract "followers," who read the tweets. But how can global marketers use Web 2.0? To help answer that question, many companies are turning to social media consultancies for help in navigating the new digital landscape.

Sir Richard Branson, the charismatic founder and chairman of the Virgin Group, typifies the type of corporate leader who uses Twitter. Two of his companies, Virgin Atlantic and Virgin America, have their own presence on Twitter (www.twitter.com/virginatlantic and www.twitter.com/virginamerica, respectively). As Sir Richard told *BusinessWeek*, "With more than 200 Virgin companies worldwide, my days and nights are filled with exciting service launches, product announcements, parties, events, and consumer opportunities. I'm regularly asked what a day in the life of Richard Branson looks like, and Twitter helps me answer that. It also enables communication no matter where I am."

Other corporate chiefs report similar experiences. Mozilla's John Lilly says, "Mozilla is a huge community of people all around the world—different time zones, countries, companies—and Twitter lets me follow both the mood and the substance of the community sort of in my peripheral vision." Tony Hsieh, CEO of Internet shoe retailer Zappos.com, confesses that he is hooked on Twitter as well. Hsieh uses Twitter as a media-sharing device; many Twitter postings include links to articles of interest from various news sources. "I generally get all my news through Twitter," Hsieh says.

Despite such enthusiastic endorsements, many people aren't sure what Twitter is, why they would want to use it, and how it is different from, say, Facebook. This is understandable; as noted in the *Financial Times*, "Operating at the juncture of blogging, texting, and social networking, the service defies easy categorization." Descriptions of Twitter often include "community," "conversation," "engagement," and similar words.

Twitter was launched in 2006 by Silicon Valley entrepreneurs Biz Stone and Evan Williams. The service has some interesting features. For example, Twitter is integrated with Facebook, so users can choose to have their status-update tweets automatically appear on their Facebook pages. Twitter is also designed to work with third-party apps. For example, TwitPic is an app that allows users to share photos via a link in their tweets. Twitterific is an app available from the iTunes Store that gives iPhone users direct access to Twitter.

Users must master some new terms and symbols. Members of Twitter's online community are known as "tweeps." "Tweet" can be both a noun and a verb; when users update their pages, they are "tweeting"; each individual entry is a "tweet." It is possible to "retweet" ("RT"), that is, to forward someone else's tweet. Each Twitter user can choose other users to follow. Twitter is searchable; entries marked with a # symbol (a *hashtag*) are a group of tweets about a particular subject. The @ symbol is used to link a tweet to another user.

Twitter has been embraced around the globe. According to industry estimates, Twitter's reach is broadest in Brazil, where nearly one-quarter of the population uses the service. By contrast, Twitter reaches only about 10 percent of the U.S. population. Twitter is also growing quickly in Japan, thanks in part to media coverage and its adoption by public figures, such as Prime Minister Yukio Hatoyama. Also, a smartphone app developed by Softbank, a fast-growing cell phone company, is attracting new users. Twitter has been a key communication channel for breaking news stories such as the political turmoil in the Middle East and the death of Osama bin Laden.

Even so, it is unclear whether Twitter will achieve the levels of global popularity enjoyed by, say, Facebook. Although the founders insist that they will never charge for the basic service, they may ultimately charge business users for access to premium services. A redesigned homepage helps people understand how they can use the site to discover what is happening around them. As Stone explains, "In the long run, we need to make Twitter the product more relevant to more people."

Discussion Questions

15-14. Twitter seems to have a polarizing effect on people; some are excited by it, others seem angry or even scared. What is the explanation for this?

15-15. You have just been hired as director of social media at a global company. This is a newly created position. What will you do during your first week on the job?

15-16. In the long run, how will Twitter generate revenues? Will it be through advertising, promoted tweets, or some other source?

Exhibit 15-10 Nathan Wright is a social media strategist at Lava Row, a consultancy based in Des Moines, Iowa. Wright helps companies of all sizes formulate and implement online engagement strategies. At a typical workshop, he and his associates explain best practices that illustrate how companies should behave and participate within online social channels and what to expect in terms of ROI.
Source: Garrett Cornelison.

Sources: Hiroko Tabuchia, "Twitter to Get Even Bigger in Japan," *The International Herald Tribune* (May 19, 2010); Jessica E. Vascellaro, "Twitter Trips on Its Rapid Growth," *The Wall Street Journal* (May 26, 2009), p. B1; Vascellaro, "Firms Seek Profits in Twitter's Chatter," *The Wall Street Journal* (March 25, 2009), p. B1; Richard Waters, "Sweet to Tweet," *Financial Times* (February 27, 2009), p. 8.

16
Strategic Elements of Competitive Advantage

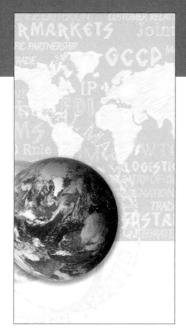

CASE 16-1
Volkswagen Aims for the Top

In May 2011, production began at Volkswagen's new $1 billion assembly plant in Chattanooga, Tennessee. The Passat sedans coming off the line are a striking symbol of the German automaker's ambitious strategic goal: Volkswagen CEO Martin Winterkorn intends to overtake both Toyota and GM and become the world's number 1 automaker by 2018. Winterkorn has vowed that VW will sell 1 million cars in the United States by 2018.

Exhibit 16-1 VW's 20-story "Autostadt storage tower" in Wolfsburg.
Source: John MacDougall/AFP/Getty Images/Newscom.

Volkswagen's sole previous U.S. plant, in Westmoreland, Pennsylvania, was closed in 1988. Several factors explain Winterkorn's decision to once again establish a manufacturing operation in the United States. For one thing, the strength of the euro—1 euro was equal to $1.40 when the plant opened—makes it difficult to export cars from Germany to the United States and sell them profitably (Exhibit 16-1). A "German-engineered, American-made" value proposition should also strengthen VW's place in the U.S. auto industry. And, by locating the new plant in the South, VW is taking advantage of much lower wage rates than at older plants operated by GM, Ford, and Chrysler in Detroit.

Winterkorn's declaration caused quite a stir in the auto industry. Volkswagen Auto Group of America markets both the VW and Audi nameplates in the United States; in 2012, unit sales for the group totaled a record 580,286 cars. However, the VW brand has been hampered by perceptions of hit-and-miss quality;

in a recent J.D. Power Initial Quality Study, VW ranked 31st out of 33 brands. In addition to a new model produced in Chattanooga, VW is also launching a revamped version of its iconic Bug as well as a new Jetta. To find out more about VW's global marketing strategy, turn to the continuation of Case 16-1 at the end of the chapter.

The essence of marketing strategy is successfully relating the strengths of an organization to its environment. As the horizons of marketers have expanded from domestic to regional and global, so, too, have the horizons of competitors. The reality in almost every industry today, including auto manufacturing, is global competition. This fact of life puts an organization under increasing pressure to master techniques for conducting industry analysis and competitor analysis and understanding competitive advantage at both the industry and the national levels. This chapter covers these topics in detail.

LEARNING OBJECTIVES

1 Identify the forces that shape competition in an industry and illustrate each force with a specific company or industry example.

2 Define *competitive advantage* and identify the key conceptual frameworks that guide decision makers in the strategic planning process.

3 Explain how a nation can achieve competitive advantage, and list the forces that may be present in a national "diamond."

4 Define *hypercompetitive industry* and list the key arenas in which dynamic strategic interactions take place.

Industry Analysis: Forces Influencing Competition

A useful way of gaining insight into competitors is through industry analysis. As a working definition, an *industry* can be defined as a group of firms that produce products that are close substitutes for each other. In any industry, competition works to drive down the rate of return on invested capital toward the rate that would be earned in the economist's "perfectly competitive" industry. Rates of return that are greater than this so-called "competitive" rate will stimulate an inflow of capital either from new entrants or from existing competitors making additional investments. The global smartphone industry is a case in point: Apple's success with the iPhone prompted Samsung and others to enter the market. Rates of return below this competitive rate will result in withdrawal from the industry and a decline in the levels of activity and competition.

Harvard University's Michael E. Porter, a leading authority on competitive strategy, developed a **five forces model** that explains competition in an industry: the threat of new entrants, the threat of substitute products or services, the bargaining power of buyers, the bargaining power of suppliers, and the competitive rivalry among current members of the industry. In industries such as soft drinks, pharmaceuticals, and cosmetics, the favorable nature of the five forces has resulted in attractive returns for competitors. However, pressure from any of the forces can limit profitability, as evidenced by the recent fortunes of some competitors in the PC and semiconductor industries. A discussion of each of the five forces follows.

Threat of New Entrants

New entrants to an industry bring new capacity; a desire to gain market share and position; and, quite often, new approaches to serving customer needs. The decision to become a new entrant in an industry is often accompanied by a major commitment of resources. New players mean prices will be pushed downward and margins squeezed, resulting in reduced industry profitability in the long run. Porter describes eight major sources of barriers to entry, the presence or absence of which determines the extent of threat of new industry entrants.[1]

The first barrier, **economies of scale**, refers to the decline in per-unit product costs as the absolute volume of production per period increases. Although the concept of scale economies is frequently associated with manufacturing, it is also applicable to research and development (R&D), general administration, marketing, and other business functions. Honda's efficiency at engine R&D, for example, results from the wide range of products it produces that feature gasoline-powered engines. When existing firms in an industry achieve significant economies of scale, it becomes difficult for potential new entrants to be competitive.

Product differentiation, the second major entry barrier, is the extent of a product's perceived uniqueness; in other words, whether it is a commodity. Differentiation can be achieved as a result of unique product attributes or effective marketing communications, or both. Product differentiation and brand loyalty "raise the bar" for would-be industry entrants who are required to make substantial investments in R&D or advertising. For example, Intel achieved differentiation and erected a barrier in the microprocessor industry with its "Intel Inside" advertising campaign and logo that appears on many brands of PCs.

A third entry barrier relates to *capital requirements*. Capital is required not only for manufacturing facilities (fixed capital) but also for financing R&D, advertising, field sales and service, customer credit, and inventories (working capital). The enormous capital requirements in such industries as pharmaceuticals, mainframe computers, chemicals, and mineral extraction present formidable entry barriers.

A fourth barrier to entry is the one-time *switching costs* resulting from the need to change suppliers and products. These might include retraining costs, ancillary equipment costs, the cost of evaluating a new source, and so on. The perceived cost to customers of switching to a new competitor's product may present an insurmountable obstacle, preventing industry newcomers from achieving success. For example, Microsoft's huge installed base of Windows operating systems and applications presented a formidable entry barrier for many years.

A fifth barrier to entry is access to *distribution channels*. If channels are full, or unavailable, the cost of entry is substantially increased because a new entrant must invest time and money to gain access to existing channels or to establish new channels. Some Western companies have encountered this barrier in Japan.

Government policy is frequently a major entry barrier. In some cases, the government will restrict competitive entry. This is true in a number of industries, especially those outside the United States, that have been designated as "national" industries by their respective governments. Japan's postwar industrialization strategy was based on a policy of preserving and protecting national industries in their development and growth phases. The result was a market that proved difficult for non-Japanese competitors to enter, an issue that was targeted by the Bill Clinton administration. American business executives in a wide range of industries urged adoption of a government policy that would reduce some of these barriers and open the Japanese market to more U.S. companies.

Established firms may also enjoy *cost advantages independent of scale economies* that present barriers to entry. Access to raw materials, a large pool of low-cost labor, favorable locations, and government subsidies are several examples.

Finally, expected *competitor response* can be a major entry barrier. If new entrants expect existing competitors to strongly oppose the entry, the entrants' expectations about the rewards of entry will certainly be affected. A potential competitor's belief that entry into an industry or market will be an unpleasant experience may serve as a strong deterrent. Bruce Henderson, former president of the Boston Consulting Group, used the term "brinkmanship" to describe a recommended approach for deterring competitive entry. Brinkmanship occurs when industry leaders convince potential competitors that any market-entry effort will be countered with vigorous and unpleasant responses. This is an approach that Microsoft has used many times to maintain its dominance in software operating systems and applications.

---

[1] Michael E. Porter, *Competitive Strategy* (New York: Free Press, 1980), pp. 7–33.

In the three decades since Porter first described the five forces model, the digital revolution appears to have altered the entry barriers in many industries. First and foremost, technology has lowered the cost for new entrants. For example, Barnes & Noble watched an entrepreneurial upstart, Amazon.com, storm the barriers protecting traditional brick-and-mortar booksellers. Amazon.com founder Jeff Bezos identified and exploited a glaring inefficiency in book distribution: Bookstores ship unsold copies of books back to publishers to be shredded and turned into pulp. Amazon.com's centralized operations and increasingly personalized online service enable customers to select from millions of different titles at discount prices and have them delivered to their homes within days. For a growing number of book-buying consumers, Amazon.com eclipses the value proposition of local bookstores that offer "only" a few thousand titles and gourmet coffee bars. Since Bezos founded Amazon.com in 1995, sales have grown to $61 billion and the company has expanded into new product lines, including CDs, DVDs, streaming movies and music, and e-books. The company serves tens of millions of customers in more than 160 countries. Barnes & Noble responded by entering the online book market itself even as it continues to be profitable in its traditional bricks-and-mortar business. In the meantime, Bezos has repositioned Amazon.com as an Internet superstore selling electronics and general merchandise.

Threat of Substitute Products

A second force influencing competition in an industry is the threat of substitute products. The availability of substitute products places limits on the prices market leaders can charge in an industry; high prices may induce buyers to switch to the substitute. Once again, the digital revolution is dramatically altering industry structures. In addition to lowering entry barriers, the digital era means that certain types of products can be converted to bits and distributed in pure digital form. For example, the development of the MP3 file format for music was accompanied by the increased popularity of peer-to-peer (p-to-p) file swapping among music fans. Napster and other online music services offered a substitute to consumers who were tired of paying $15 or more for a CD. Although a U.S. court severely curtailed Napster's activities, other services—including several outside the United States—sprang up in its place. The top players in the music industry were taken by surprise, and today, Sony BMG, Warner Music, and Universal Music Group are still struggling to develop new strategies in response to the changing business environment.

Bargaining Power of Buyers

In Porter's model, "buyers" refers to manufacturers (e.g., General Motors [GM]) and retailers (e.g., Walmart) rather than consumers. The ultimate aim of such buyers is to pay the lowest possible price to obtain the products or services that they require. Usually, therefore, if they can, buyers drive down profitability in the supplier industry. To accomplish this, the buyers have to gain leverage over their vendors. One way they can do this is to purchase in such large quantities that supplier firms are highly dependent on the buyers' business. Second, when the suppliers' products are viewed as commodities—that is, as standard or undifferentiated—buyers are likely to bargain hard for low prices because many firms can meet their needs. Buyers will also bargain hard when the supplier industry's products or services represent a significant portion of the buying firm's costs. A fourth source of buyer power is the willingness and ability to achieve backward integration.

For example, because it purchases massive quantities of goods for resale, Walmart is in a position to dictate terms to any vendor wishing to distribute its products through the retail giant's stores. Walmart's influence also extends to the recorded music industry; Walmart refuses to stock CDs bearing parental advisory stickers for explicit lyrics or violent imagery. Recording artists who want their recordings available at Walmart have the option of altering lyrics and song titles or deleting offending tracks. Likewise, artists are sometimes asked to change album cover art if Walmart deems it offensive (see Exhibit 16-2). In addition, Walmart has launched Soundcheck, which consists of performances by up-and-coming recording artists that are broadcast every Friday night on the in-house television network found in each store. Exclusive tracks featuring special versions of songs by the Soundcheck sessions' artists are also available.[3]

> "Walmart is the 800-pound gorilla. You're going to want to do more things for a customer who is growing as fast as Walmart is."[2]
>
> —Ted Taft, Meridian Consulting Group

---

[2] Melanie Warner, "Its Wish, Their Command," *The New York Times* (March 3, 2006), p. C1.
[3] Jonathan Birchall, "Walmart, the Record Label," *Financial Times* (January 31, 2006), p. 17.

Exhibit 16-2 For many years, Walmart was the biggest seller of recorded music in the United States. In the late 1990s, "big-box retail" only accounted for about 20 percent of recorded music sales; a few years later, the figure was about 65 percent. Much of the discounter's growth in this area came at the expense of specialty music stores.

Walmart has exercised its buying power by refusing to stock CDs bearing "Parental Advisory" stickers warning of controversial or potentially offensive lyrics; Slipknot's debut CD is one example. In 2008, data compiled by NPD MusicWatch confirmed that Apple's iTunes Music Store had surpassed Walmart to become the top music retailer.

In response to the "corporatization" of record retailing, independent shop owners have launched an annual international promotion called Record Store Day. On the third Saturday in April, discerning music fans are urged to patronize their local indie shop. Slipknot vocalist/lyricist Corey Taylor acknowledges that many of the band's fans have little choice but to shop at their local Walmart. To prove that he could do it, Taylor intentionally wrote lyrics that avoided profanity on *Vol. 3: (The Subliminal Verses)*.

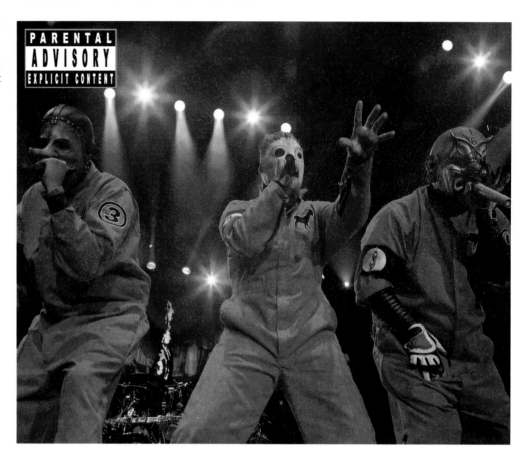

Bargaining Power of Suppliers

Supplier power in an industry is the converse of buyer power. If suppliers have enough leverage over industry firms, they can raise prices high enough to significantly influence the profitability of their organizational customers. Several factors determine suppliers' ability to gain leverage over industry firms. Suppliers will have the advantage if they are large and relatively few in number. Second, when the suppliers' products or services are important inputs to user firms, are highly differentiated, or carry switching costs, the suppliers will have considerable leverage over buyers. Suppliers will also enjoy bargaining power if alternative products do not threaten their business. A fourth source of supplier power is their willingness and ability to develop their own products and brand names if they are unable to get satisfactory terms from industry buyers.

In the tech world, Microsoft and Intel are two companies with substantial supplier power. Because about 90 percent of the world's 1-billion-plus PCs run on Microsoft's operating systems and 80 percent use Intel's microprocessors, the two companies enjoy a great deal of leverage relative to Dell, Hewlett-Packard, and other computer manufacturers. Microsoft's industry dominance prompted both the U.S. government and the European Union (EU) to launch separate antitrust investigations. Today, the shift is to new electronic devices such as smartphones, netbooks, and tablets. Many of these new products use the Apple, Android, or Linux operating systems instead of Windows; the chips are from competitors such as Qualcomm and Texas Instruments. As these trends take hold, Microsoft and Intel will find their supplier power diminishing.[4]

---

[4] Olga Kharif, Peter Burrows, and Cliff Edwards, "Windows and Intel's Digital Divide," *BusinessWeek* (February 23, 2009), p. 58.

→ **EMERGING MARKETS BRIEFING BOOK**

Cemex

SYNC • THINK • LEARN

MyMarketingLab

Mexico's S.A.B. de C.V. Cemex is a global building solutions company with operations in more than 50 countries. Chief executive Lorenzo Zambrano, the grandson of the company's founder, holds an MBA from Stanford University. To help drive sales in Mexico, where Cemex commands more than 50 percent of the market, the company devised an innovative payment method. Migrant workers in the United States can pay for cement that their friends and relatives in Mexico can pick up at a local store.

Zambrano introduced sophisticated technology to the company's operations. For example, satellites and computer software allow company engineers in Mexico to monitor temperatures in kilns across the ocean in Spain. As Zambrano explained, "A cement company is not supposed to be high-tech, but we showed it can be. It is supposed to be boring, but we showed it is not." Under Zambrano's leadership, Cemex had 2010 revenues of $14 billion.

Starting in the early 1990s, Zambrano began extending Cemex's global reach by acquiring Spain's two largest cement companies for $1 billion. Other acquisitions followed in Indonesia, Panama, the Philippines, the United States,

Venezuela, and elsewhere. Unfortunately, after a string of successes, one acquisition turned out to be disastrous. In 2007, Zambrano paid more than $15 billion to acquire Australia's Rinker Materials Corp. Rinker was a major supplier to the U.S. housing market; as the economic crisis worsened, sales to the United States declined.

There was more bad news; the global credit crunch made it very difficult for Zambrano to refinance some of the debt burden that Cemex had taken on. Moreover, as investors sought security by holding dollars, the greenback's value rose while other currencies weakened. The weaker peso meant that Cemex's dollar-denominated debt was even more of a burden. Rossana Fuentes Berain, author of a biography of the Cemex chief, summed up Zambrano's predicament this way: "For 20 years, he managed Cemex flawlessly. Now people are obviously asking why such brilliant people like Lorenzo could not see this coming. Why weren't they more cautious? Why didn't they ask the right questions?"

Sources: Amy Kamzin and James Fontanella-Khan, "Mexico's Cemex Eyes Indian Cement Group," *Financial Times* (November 23, 2010); Joel Millman, "Hard Times for Cement Man," *The Wall Street Journal* (December 11, 2008), pp. A1, A14.

Rivalry Among Competitors

Rivalry among firms refers to all the actions taken by firms in an industry to improve their positions and gain advantage over each other. Rivalry manifests itself in price competition, advertising battles, product positioning, and attempts at differentiation. To the extent that rivalry among firms forces companies to rationalize costs, it is a positive force. To the extent that it drives down prices (and therefore profitability) and creates instability in the industry, it is a negative factor. Several factors can create intense rivalry. Once an industry becomes mature, firms focus on market share and how it can be gained at the expense of other firms. Second, industries characterized by high fixed costs are always under pressure to keep production at full capacity to cover the fixed costs. Once the industry accumulates excess capacity, the drive to fill capacity will push prices—and profitability—down. A third factor affecting rivalry is lack of differentiation or an absence of switching costs, which encourages buyers to treat the products or services as commodities and shop for the best prices. Again, there is downward pressure on prices and profitability. Fourth, firms with high strategic stakes in achieving success in an industry generally are destabilizing because they may be willing to accept below-average profit margins to establish themselves, hold position, or expand.

The PC industry is a case in point. For years, demand for PCs grew at an annual rate of 15 percent. When the tech bubble burst in early 2000, however, the computer industry experienced a worldwide slowdown in demand; recent growth has been in the single digits. Dell responded by aggressively cutting prices in a bid to boost share. With profit margins collapsing, competitors struggled to adjust. Dell is legendary for its lean operating philosophy; just $0.115 cents of every sales dollar go toward overhead, compared with $0.225 cents at Hewlett-Packard.

Dell's factories can assemble a complete PC in 3 minutes. With a build-to-order strategy at the heart of its business model, Dell's sales staff maintains close ties with customers. This approach gives Dell a great deal of flexibility when making pricing decisions.[5] The price war has already claimed two victims; in mid-2001, key rival Compaq was acquired by Hewlett-Packard. Then, in 2007, Taiwan's Acer acquired Gateway. Today, Dell faces new competitive threats as the

---

[5] Gary McWilliams, "Lean Machine: How Dell Fine-Tunes Its PC Pricing to Gain Edge in a Slow Market," *The Wall Street Journal* (June 8, 2001), p. A1.

global recession slammed the brakes on industry growth. Businesses began ordering fewer computers and many consumers are opting for tablet devices rather than laptops. Founder Michael Dell is currently pursuing a plan to take Dell private.

Competitive Advantage

Competitive advantage exists when there is a match between a firm's distinctive competencies and the factors critical for success within its industry. Any superior match between company competencies and customers' needs permits the firm to outperform competitors. Competitive advantage can be achieved in two ways. First, a firm can pursue a low-cost strategy that enables it to offer products at lower prices than competitors' prices. Competitive advantage may also be gained by a strategy of differentiating products so that customers perceive unique benefits, often accompanied by a premium price. Note that both strategies have the same effect: They both contribute to the firm's overall value proposition. Porter explored these issues in two landmark books, *Competitive Strategy* (1985) and *Competitive Advantage* (1990); the latter is widely considered to be one of the most influential management books in recent years.

Ultimately, customer perception decides the quality of a firm's strategy. Operating results such as sales and profits are measures that depend on the level of psychological value created for customers: The greater the perceived consumer value, the better the strategy. A firm may market a better mousetrap, but the ultimate success of the product depends on customers deciding for themselves whether to buy it. Value is like beauty; it's in the eye of the beholder. In sum, creating more value than the competition achieves competitive advantage, and customer perception defines value.

Two different models of competitive advantage have received considerable attention. The first offers "generic strategies," four routes or paths that organizations choose to offer superior value and achieve competitive advantage. According to the second model, generic strategies alone did not account for the astonishing success of many Japanese companies in the 1980s and 1990s. The more recent model, based on the concept of "strategic intent," proposes four different sources of competitive advantage. Both models are discussed in the following paragraphs.

Generic Strategies for Creating Competitive Advantage

In addition to the "five forces" model of industry competition, Porter has developed a framework of so-called generic business strategies based on the two types or sources of competitive advantage mentioned previously: *low cost* and *differentiation*. The relationship of these two sources with the scope of the target market served (narrow or broad) or product mix width (narrow or wide) yields four **generic strategies**: *cost leadership*, *product differentiation*, *cost focus*, and *focused differentiation*.

Generic strategies aiming at the achievement of competitive advantage or superior marketing strategy demand that a firm make choices. The choices concern the *type of competitive advantage* it seeks to attain (based on cost or differentiation) and the *market scope* or *product mix width* within which competitive advantage will be attained.[7] The nature of the choice between types of advantage and market scope is a gamble, and it is the nature of every gamble that it entails *risk*: By choosing a given generic strategy, a firm always risks making the wrong choice.

BROAD MARKET STRATEGIES: COST LEADERSHIP AND DIFFERENTIATION **Cost leadership** is competitive advantage based on a firm's position as the industry's low-cost producer, in broadly defined markets or across a wide mix of products. This strategy has gained widespread appeal in recent years as a result of the popularization of the experience curve concept. In general, a firm that bases its competitive strategy on overall cost leadership must construct the most efficient facilities (in terms of scale or technology) and obtain the largest share of market so that its cost per unit is the lowest in the industry. These advantages, in turn, give the producer a

> "The only way to gain lasting competitive advantage is to leverage your capabilities around the world so that the company as a whole is greater than the sum of its parts. Being an international company—selling globally, having global brands or operations in different countries—isn't enough."[6]
>
> —David Whitwam, former CEO, Whirlpool

---

[6] Regina Fazio Maruca, "The Right Way to Go Global: An Interview with Whirlpool CEO David Whitwam," *Harvard Business Review* 72, no. 2 (March–April 1994), p. 135.

[7] Michael E. Porter, *Competitive Advantage: Creating and Sustaining Superior Performance* (New York: Free Press, 1985), p. 12.

substantial lead in terms of experience with building the product. Experience then leads to more refinements of the entire process of production, delivery, and service, which lead to further cost reductions.

Whatever its source, cost leadership advantage can be the basis for offering lower prices (and more value) to customers in the late, more-competitive stages of the product life cycle. In Japan, companies in a range of industries—photography and imaging, consumer electronics and entertainment equipment, motorcycles, and automobiles—have achieved cost leadership on a worldwide basis.

Cost leadership, however, is a sustainable source of competitive advantage only if barriers exist that prevent competitors from achieving the same low costs. In an era of increasing technological improvements in manufacturing, manufacturers constantly leapfrog over one another in pursuit of lower costs. At one time, for example, IBM enjoyed the low-cost advantage in the production of computer printers. Then the Japanese took the same technology and, after reducing production costs and improving product reliability, gained the low-cost advantage. IBM fought back with a highly automated printer plant in North Carolina, where the number of component parts was slashed by more than 50 percent and robots were used to snap many components into place. Despite these changes, IBM ultimately chose to exit the business.

When a firm's product has an actual or perceived uniqueness in a broad market, it is said to have achieved competitive advantage by **differentiation**. This can be an extremely effective strategy for defending market position and obtaining superior financial returns; unique products often command premium prices (see Exhibit 16-3). Examples of successful differentiation include Maytag in large home appliances, Caterpillar in construction equipment, and almost any successful branded consumer product. Maytag has been called "the Rolls-Royce of washers and dryers"; half the washers sold in the United States are priced at $399 or less, and Maytag does offer a model at that price point. However, Maytag also markets Neptune, a high-tech, water-saving machine; the Neptune line is priced substantially higher than "regular" washers. IBM traditionally has differentiated itself with a strong sales/service organization and the security of the IBM standard in a world of rapid obsolescence. Among athletic shoe manufacturers, Nike has positioned itself as the technological leader thanks to unique product features found in a wide array of shoes.

NARROW TARGET STRATEGIES: COST FOCUS AND FOCUSED DIFFERENTIATION The preceding discussion of cost leadership and differentiation considered only the impact on broad markets. By contrast, strategies to achieve a narrow-focus advantage target a narrowly defined market or customer. This advantage is based on an ability to create more customer value for a narrowly targeted segment and results from a better understanding of customer needs and wants. A narrow-focus strategy can be combined with either cost- or differentiation-advantage strategies. In other words, whereas a *cost focus* means offering low prices to a narrow target market, a firm pursuing *focused differentiation* will offer a narrow target market the perception of product uniqueness at a premium price.

Germany's *Mittelstand* companies have been extremely successful in pursuing **focused differentiation** strategies backed by a strong export effort. The world of "high-end" audio equipment offers another example of focused differentiation. A few hundred small companies design speakers, amplifiers, and related hi-fi gear that cost thousands of dollars per component. While audio components represent a $21 billion market worldwide, annual sales in the high-end segment are only about $1.1 billion. American companies such as Audio Research, Conrad-Johnson, Krell, Mark Levinson, Martin-Logan, and Thiel dominate the segment, which also includes hundreds of smaller enterprises with annual sales of less than $10 million (see Exhibit 16-4). The state-of-the-art equipment these companies offer is distinguished by superior craftsmanship and performance and is highly sought after by audiophiles in Asia (especially Japan and Hong Kong) and Europe. Industry growth is occurring as companies learn more about overseas customers and build relationships with distributors in other countries.[8]

"We're living in a very polarized world now. You're either an absolute price leader—you're a Ryanair, a Southwest Airlines, a Walmart and you're just hugely efficient and you will not be touched on price or cost. Or you're over on the quality end of the market with the Guccis and the Pradas and you're a quality leader."[9]

—Steve Ridgway, CEO of Virgin Atlantic Airways

---

[8] Personal communication from Kerry Moyer, Senior Director, Industry Programs, Consumer Electronics Association, Arlington, Virginia.
[9] Daniel Michaels, "No, the CEO Isn't Sir Richard Branson," *The Wall Street Journal* (July 30, 2007), pp. B1, B3.

Exhibit 16-3 With annual revenues of $100.6 billion, Munich-based Siemens AG is a key global player in a variety of engineering sectors. Worldwide, public interest in energy-related issues has increased significantly. This advertisement for Siemens' U.S. unit underscores the company's commitment to innovation in power generation, transmission, and distribution to ensure that the nation's energy needs are met.
Source: Courtesy of Siemens Corporation.

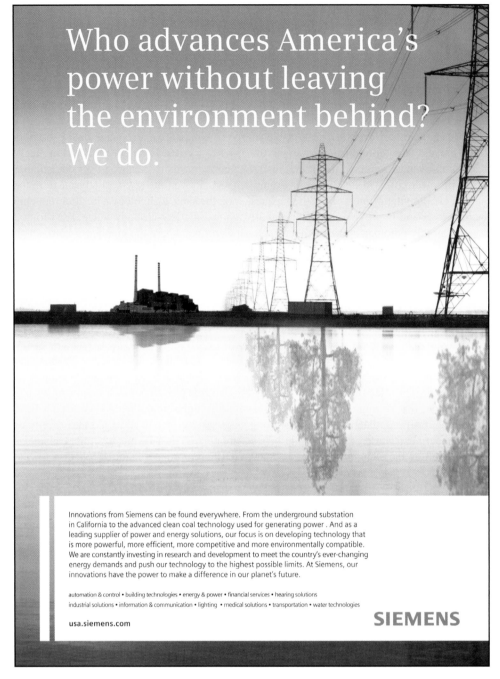

The final strategy is **cost focus**, which is when a firm's lower-cost position enables it to focus on a narrow target market and offer lower prices than the competition (see Exhibit 16-5). In the shipbuilding industry, for example, Polish and Chinese shipyards offer simple, standard vessel types at low prices that reflect low production costs.[10] Germany's Aldi, a no-frills "hard discounter" with operations in numerous countries, offers a very limited selection of household goods at extremely low prices. In 1976, Aldi opened its first U.S. stores in southeastern Iowa. It expanded slowly, opening a handful of stores each year. Private-label products help keep costs and prices down, allowing Aldi to expand in the key U.S. markets despite the recent poor economic climate. Recently, Aldi opened its first store in New York City.[11]

---

[10] Michael E. Porter, *The Competitive Advantage of Nations* (New York: Free Press, 1990), p. 39.
[11] Cecilie Rohwedder and David Kesmodel, "Aldi Looks to U.S. for Growth," *The Wall Street Journal* (January 13, 2009), p. B1. For an excellent discussion of Aldi's corporate history, see Michael J. Silverstein, *Treasure Hunt: Inside the Mind of the New Consumer* (New York: Portfolio, 2006), Chapter 3, pp. 66–75.

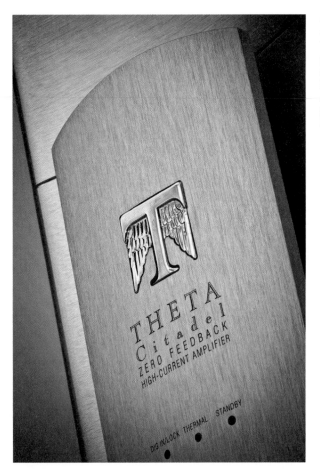

Exhibit 16-4 In keeping with the aesthetics of high-end audio gear, Theta Digital's Citadel 1.5 monoblock power amplifier is the epitome of classic, minimalist design. A pair of these beauties—one for each channel—will set you back $25,000.
Source: Copyright © Amplifier Technologies, Inc. All Rights Reserved.

IKEA, the Swedish furniture company, has grown into a successful global company by using the cost-focus strategy (see Case 16-2). As George Bradley, president of Levitz Furniture in Boca Raton, Florida, noted two decades ago, "[IKEA] has really made a splash. They're going to capture their niche in every city they go into." Such a strategy can be risky. As Bradley explained, "Their market is finite because it is so narrow. If you don't want contemporary,

Exhibit 16-5 For more than 100 years, Germany's Aldi has offered shoppers a tightly focused assortment of unbranded merchandise at very low prices in a no-frills setting. Now, taking a cue from its Trader Joe unit in the United States, Aldi is making major improvements in its home-country market. German shoppers want more than low prices; they also want a nice ambience and a more appealing atmosphere.
Source: © Lannis Waters/The Palm Beach Post/ZUMAPRESS.com/Alamy.

knock-down furniture, it's not for you. So it takes a certain customer to buy it. And remember, fashions change."[12]

The issue of sustainability is central to this strategy concept. As noted, cost leadership is a sustainable source of competitive advantage only if barriers exist that prevent competitors from achieving the same low costs. Sustained differentiation depends on continued perceived value and the absence of imitation by competitors.[13] Several factors determine whether focus can be sustained as a source of competitive advantage. First, a cost focus is sustainable if a firm's competitors are defining their target markets more broadly. A focuser doesn't try to be all things to all people: Competitors may diminish their advantage by trying to satisfy the needs of a broader market segment—a strategy that, by definition, means a blunter focus. Second, a firm's differentiation focus advantage is sustainable only if competitors cannot define the segment even more narrowly. Also, focus can be sustained if competitors cannot overcome barriers that prevent imitation of the focus strategy, and if consumers in the target segment do not migrate to other segments that the focuser doesn't serve.

The Flagship Firm: The Business Network with Five Partners[14]

According to Professors Alan Rugman and Joseph D'Cruz, Porter's model is too simplistic given the complexity of today's global environment. Rugman and D'Cruz have thus developed an alternative framework based on business networks that they call the **flagship model**. Japanese vertical *keiretsu* and Korean *chaebol* have succeeded, Rugman and D'Cruz argue, by adopting strategies that are mutually reinforcing within a business system and by fostering a collective long-term outlook among partners in the system. Moreover, the authors note, "long-term competitiveness in global industries is less a matter of rivalry between firms and more a question of competition between business systems."

A major difference between the flagship model and Porter's is that Porter's is based on the notion of corporate individualism and individual business transactions. For example, as discussed previously, Microsoft's tremendous supplier power allows it to dictate to, and even prosper at the expense of, the computer manufacturers it supplies with operating systems and applications. The flagship model, by contrast, is evident in the strategies of Ford, Volkswagen, and other global automakers; Sweden's IKEA and Italy's Benetton are additional examples (see Exhibit 16-6).

The flagship firm is at the center of a collection of five partners; together, they form a business system that consists of two types of relationships. The flagship firm provides the leadership, vision, and resources to "lead the network in a successful global strategy." *Key suppliers* are those that perform some value-creating activities, such as manufacturing of critical components, better than the flagship. This is a network relationship, with a sharing of strategies, resources, and responsibility for the success of the network. Other suppliers are kept at "arm's length." Likewise, the flagship has network relationships with *key customers* and more traditional, arm's-length commercial relationships with *key consumers*.

In the case of Volkswagen, for example, dealers are its key customers while individual car buyers are its key consumers; in other words, strictly speaking, Volkswagen sells to dealers, and dealers sell to consumers. Similarly, Benetton's key customers are its retail outlets while the individual clothes shopper is the key consumer. *Selected competitors* are companies with which the flagship develops alliances, such as those described at the end of Chapter 9. The fifth partner is the *non-business infrastructure* (NBI), composed of universities, governments, trade unions, and other entities that can supply the network with intangible inputs such as intellectual property and technology. In the flagship model, flagship firms often play a role in the development of a country's industrial policy.

Benetton's success in the global fashion industry illustrates the flagship model. Benetton is the world's largest purchaser of wool, and its centralized buying enables the company to reap

---

[12] Jeffrey A. Trachtenberg, "Home Economics: IKEA Furniture Chain Pleases with Its Prices, Not with Its Service," *The Wall Street Journal* (September 17, 1991), pp. A1, A5.
[13] Michael E. Porter, *Competitive Advantage: Creating and Sustaining Superior Performance* (New York: Free Press, 1985), p. 158.
[14] The following discussion is adapted from Alan M. Rugman and Joseph R. D'Cruz. *Multinationals as Flagship Firms* (Oxford, England: Oxford University Press, 2000).

Exhibit 16-6 Luciano Benetton is one of four siblings who founded the Italian fashion company that bears the family's name. Luciano recently stepped down as chairman of the Benetton Group and turned over control of the company to son Alessandro. The change comes as Benetton faces increased competition from fleet-footed global rivals such as Sweden's Hennes & Mauritz (H&M) and Spain's Zara. Some industry observers note that Benetton's business model, which involves partnerships with regional sales agents, will need to be adjusted to reflect the business environments in key emerging markets such as China and India.
Source: Marcelo del Pozo/Reuters/Corbis Images.

scale economies. The core activities of cutting and dyeing are retained in-house, and Benetton has made substantial investments in computer-assisted design and manufacturing. However, Benetton is linked to approximately 400 subcontractors that produce finished garments in exclusive supply relationships with the company. In turn, a network of 80 agents who find investors, train managers, and assist with merchandising link the subcontractors to the 6,000 Benetton retail shops. As Rugman and D'Cruz note, "Benetton is organized to reward cooperation and relationship building and the company's structure has been created to capitalize on the benefits of long-term relationships."

Creating Competitive Advantage via Strategic Intent

An alternative framework for understanding competitive advantage focuses on competitiveness as a function of the pace at which a company implants new advantages deep within its organization. This framework identifies **strategic intent**, growing out of ambition and obsession with winning, as the means for achieving competitive advantage. Writing in the *Harvard Business Review*, Gary Hamel and C. K. Prahalad note:

> Few competitive advantages are long lasting. Keeping score of existing advantages is not the same as building new advantages. The essence of strategy lies in creating tomorrow's competitive advantages faster than competitors mimic the ones you possess today. An organization's capacity to improve existing skills and learn new ones is the most defensible competitive advantage of all.[15]

This approach is founded on the principles of W. E. Deming, who stressed that a company must commit itself to continuing improvement in order to be a winner in a competitive struggle. For years, Deming's message fell on deaf ears in the United States, while the Japanese heeded his message and benefited tremendously. Japan's most prestigious business award is named after him. Eventually, however, U.S. manufacturers responded, and Detroit's current resurgence is evidence that they have made much progress.

The significance of Hamel and Prahalad's framework becomes evident when comparing Caterpillar and Komatsu. As noted earlier, Caterpillar is a classic example of differentiation: The

---

[15] Gary Hamel and C. K. Prahalad, "Strategic Intent," *Harvard Business Review* 67, no. 3 (May–June 1989), pp. 63–76. See also Hamel and Prahalad, "The Core Competence of the Corporation," *Harvard Business Review* 68, no. 3 (May–June 1990), pp. 79–93.

company became the largest manufacturer of earthmoving equipment in the world because it was fanatical about quality and service. Caterpillar's success as a global marketer has enabled it to achieve a 40 percent share of the worldwide market for earthmoving equipment, more than half of which represents sales to developing countries. The differentiation advantage was achieved with product durability, global spare parts service (including guaranteed parts delivery anywhere in the world within 48 hours), and a strong network of loyal dealers.

However, Caterpillar has faced a very challenging set of environmental pressures over the last several decades. Many of Caterpillar's plants were closed by a lengthy strike in the early 1980s; a worldwide recession at the same time caused a downturn in the construction industry. This hurt companies that were Caterpillar customers. In addition, the strong dollar gave a cost advantage to foreign rivals.

Compounding Caterpillar's problems was a new competitive threat from Japan. Komatsu was the world's number 2 construction equipment company and had been competing with Caterpillar in the Japanese market for years. Komatsu's products were generally acknowledged to offer a lower level of quality. The rivalry took on a new dimension after Komatsu adopted the slogan "*Maru-c*," meaning "encircle Caterpillar." Emphasizing quality and taking advantage of low labor costs and the strong dollar, Komatsu surpassed Caterpillar as number 1 in earthmoving equipment in Japan and made serious inroads in the United States and other markets. However, the company continued to develop new sources of competitive advantage even after it achieved world-class quality. For example, new-product development cycles were shortened and manufacturing was rationalized. Caterpillar struggled to sustain its competitive advantage because many customers found that Komatsu's combination of quality, durability, and lower price created compelling value. Yet even as the recession and a strong yen put new pressure on Komatsu, the company sought new opportunities by diversifying into machine tools and robots.[16]

The Komatsu/Caterpillar saga illustrates the fact that global competitive battles can be shaped by factors other than the pursuit of generic strategies. Many firms have gained competitive advantage by *disadvantaging* rivals through "competitive innovation." Hamel and Prahalad define *competitive innovation* as "the art of containing competitive risks within manageable proportions" and identify four successful approaches used by Japanese competitors. These are *building layers of advantage*, *searching for loose bricks*, *changing the rules of engagement*, and *collaborating*.

LAYERS OF ADVANTAGE A company faces less risk in competitive encounters if it has a wide portfolio of advantages. Successful companies steadily build such portfolios by establishing layers of advantage on top of one another. Komatsu is an excellent example of this approach. Another is the TV industry in Japan. By 1970, Japan was not only the world's largest producer of black-and-white TV sets but was also well on its way to becoming the leader in producing color sets. The main competitive advantage for such companies as Matsushita at that time was low labor costs.

Because they realized that their cost advantage might be temporary, the Japanese also added an additional layer of *quality and reliability* advantages by building plants large enough to serve world markets. Much of this output did not carry the manufacturer's brand name. For example, Matsushita Electric sold products to other companies such as RCA, which then marketed them under their own brand names. Matsushita was pursuing a simple idea: A product sold was a product sold, no matter whose label it carried.[17]

In order to build the next layer of advantage, the Japanese spent the 1970s investing heavily in marketing channels and Japanese brand names to gain recognition. This strategy added yet another layer of competitive advantage: the *global brand franchise*, that is, a global customer base. By the late 1970s, channels and brand awareness were established well enough to support the introduction of new products that could benefit from global marketing—VCRs and photocopy machines, for example. Finally, many companies have invested in *regional manufacturing* so their products can be differentiated and better adapted to customer needs in individual markets.

---

[16] Robert L. Rose and Masayoshi Kanabayashi, "Komatsu Throttles Back on Construction Equipment," *The Wall Street Journal* (May 13, 1992), p. B4.
[17] James Lardner, *Fast Forward: Hollywood, the Japanese, and the VCR Wars* (New York: New American Library, 1987), p. 135.

The process of building layers illustrates how a company can move along the value chain to strengthen competitive advantage. The Japanese began with manufacturing (an upstream value activity) and moved on to marketing (a downstream value activity) and then back upstream to basic R&D. All of these sources of competitive advantage represent mutually reinforcing layers that are accumulated over time.

LOOSE BRICKS A second approach takes advantage of the "loose bricks" left in the defensive walls of competitors whose attention is narrowly focused on a market segment or a geographic area to the exclusion of others. For example, Caterpillar's attention was focused elsewhere when Komatsu made its first entry into the Eastern Europe market. Similarly, as discussed in Case 1-3, Taiwan's Acer prospered by following founder Stan Shih's strategy of approaching the world computer market from the periphery. Shih's inspiration was the Asian board game *Go*, in which the winning player successfully surrounds opponents. Shih gained experience and built market share in countries overlooked by competitors such as IBM and Compaq. By the time Acer was ready to target the United States in earnest, it was already the number 1 PC brand in key countries in Latin America, Southeast Asia, and the Middle East.

Intel's loose brick was its narrow focus on complex microprocessors for PCs. The world's biggest chip maker in terms of sales, it currently commands about 80 percent of the global market for PC processors. However, even as it built its core business, demand for non-PC consumer electronics products began to explode. The new non-PC products, such as set-top boxes for televisions, digital cameras, smartphones, and tablets, require chips that are cheaper and use less power than those produced by Intel. Competitors such as LSI Logic and Arm Holdings recognized the opportunity and beat Intel into an important new market. Intel has responded by developing new chips incorporating 3D technology that use half as much power as current designs.[18]

CHANGING THE RULES A third approach involves **changing the rules of engagement** and refusing to play by the rules set by industry leaders. For example, in the copier market, IBM and Kodak imitated the marketing strategies used by market leader Xerox. Meanwhile, Canon, a Japanese challenger, wrote a new rulebook.

While Xerox built a wide range of copiers, Canon built standardized machines and components, reducing manufacturing costs. While Xerox employed a huge direct-sales force, Canon chose to distribute through office-product dealers. Canon also designed serviceability, as well as reliability, into its products so that it could rely on dealers for service rather than incurring the expense required to create a national service network. Canon further decided to sell rather than lease its machines, freeing the company from the burden of financing the lease base. In another major departure, Canon targeted its copiers at secretaries and department managers rather than at the heads of corporate duplicating operations.[19]

Canon introduced the first full-color copiers and the first copiers with "connectivity"— the ability to print images from such sources as video camcorders and computers. The Canon example shows how an innovative marketing strategy—with fresh approaches to the product, pricing, distribution, and selling—can lead to overall competitive advantage in the marketplace. Canon is not invulnerable, however; in 1991 Tektronix, a U.S. company, leapfrogged past Canon in the color copier market by introducing a plain-paper color copier that offered sharper copies at a much lower price.[20]

COLLABORATING A final source of competitive advantage is using know-how developed by other companies. Such *collaboration* may take the form of licensing agreements, joint ventures, or partnerships. History has shown that the Japanese have excelled at using the collaborating strategy to achieve industry leadership. As noted in Chapter 9, one of the legendary licensing agreements of modern business history is Sony's licensing of transistor technology from AT&T's Bell Labs subsidiary in the 1950s for $25,000. This agreement gave Sony access to the transistor and allowed the company to become a world leader. Building on its initial successes in the manufacturing and marketing of portable radios, Sony has grown into a superb global

---

[18] Chris Nuttal, Robin Kwong, and Maija Palmer, "Intel Wants to Get a Grip on Mobile Market," *Financial Times* (May 6, 2011), p. 17.
[19] Gary Hamel and C. K. Prahalad, "Strategic Intent," *Harvard Business Review* 67, no. 3 (May–June 1989), p. 69.
[20] G. Pascal Zachary, "Color Printer Gives Tektronix Jump on Canon," *The Wall Street Journal* (June 14, 1991), p. B1.

marketer whose name is synonymous with a wide assortment of high-quality consumer electronics products.

More recent examples of Japanese collaboration are found in the aircraft industry. Today, Mitsubishi Heavy Industries Ltd. and other Japanese companies manufacture airplanes under license to U.S. firms and also work as subcontractors for aircraft parts and systems. Many observers fear that the future of the American aircraft industry may be jeopardized as the Japanese gain technological expertise. The next section discusses various examples of "collaborative advantage."[21]

Global Competition and National Competitive Advantage[22]

An inevitable consequence of the expansion of global marketing activities is the growth of competition on a global basis. In industry after industry, global competition is a critical factor affecting success. As Yoshino and Rangan have explained, **global competition** occurs when a firm takes a global view of competition and sets about maximizing profits worldwide, rather than on a country-by-country basis. If, when expanding abroad, a company encounters the same rival in market after market, then it is engaged in global competition.[23] In some industries, global companies have virtually excluded all other companies from their markets. An example is the detergent industry, in which three companies—Colgate, Unilever, and Procter & Gamble—dominate an increasing number of detergent markets in Latin America and the Pacific Rim. Many companies can make a quality detergent, but brand-name muscle and the skills required for quality packaging overwhelm local competition in market after market.[24]

The automobile industry has also become fiercely competitive on a global basis. Part of the reason for the initial success of foreign automakers in the United States was the reluctance—or inability—of U.S. manufacturers to design and manufacture high-quality, inexpensive small cars. The resistance of U.S. manufacturers was based on the economics of car production: bigger cars equaled bigger profits. Under this formula, small cars meant smaller unit profits. Sadly, U.S. car manufacturers mostly ignored the increasing preference of U.S. drivers for smaller cars, a classic case of ethnocentrism and management myopia. European and Japanese manufacturers always offered cars smaller than those made in the United States, in part because market conditions were much different: less space, higher taxes on engine displacement and fuel, and greater market interest in functional design and engineering innovations.

First Volkswagen, then Japanese automakers such as Nissan and Toyota discovered a growing demand for their cars in the U.S. market. For most of the past twenty years, the Toyota Camry has been the best-selling passenger car in North America. Ironically, the Camry plants are located in Kentucky and Indiana, and Cars.com rates the Camry as "the most American car" in its American-Made Index! But the competitive environment continues to evolve. Today, South Korea's Hyundai and Kia have joined the ranks of world-class automakers. Meanwhile, Korea's Automobile Journalist Association named Camry the "Korea Car of the Year" for 2013; however, those Korea-bound Camrys come from U.S. plants. Doubly ironic! And, as noted in Case 16-1, for Volkswagen to achieve its strategic goal of becoming the world's top automaker, it must significantly boost U.S. sales.

---

[21] Hamel and Prahalad have continued to refine and develop the concept of strategic intent since it was first introduced in their groundbreaking 1989 article. During the 1990s, the authors outlined five broad categories of resource leverage that managers can use to achieve their aspirations: Concentrating resources on strategic goals via convergence and focus; accumulating resources more efficiently via extracting and borrowing; complementing one resource with another by blending and balancing; conserving resources by recycling, co-opting, and shielding; and rapid recovery of resources in the marketplace. Gary Hamel and C. K. Prahalad, "Strategy as Stretch and Leverage," *Harvard Business Review* 71, no. 2 (March–April 1993), pp. 75–84.
[22] This section draws heavily on Chapter 3, "Determinants of National Competitive Advantage," and Chapter 4, "The Dynamics of National Advantage," in Porter, *The Competitive Advantage of Nations*, 1990. For an extended country analysis based on Porter's framework, see Michael Enright, Antonio Francés, and Edith Scott Assavedra, *Venezuela: The Challenge of Competitiveness* (New York: St. Martin's Press, 1996).
[23] Michael Y. Yoshino and U. Srinivasa Rangan, *Strategic Alliances: An Entrepreneurial Approach to Globalization* (Boston: Harvard Business School Press, 1995), p. 56.
[24] See Joseph Kahn, "Cleaning Up: P&G Viewed China as a National Market and Is Conquering It," *The Wall Street Journal* (September 12, 1995), pp. A1, A6.

The effect of global competition has been highly beneficial to consumers around the world. In the two examples cited, detergents and automobiles, consumers have benefited. In Central America, detergent prices have fallen as a result of global competition. Global automakers provide consumers with the models, performance, and price characteristics they want. If smaller, lower-priced imported cars had not been available, it is unlikely that Detroit's manufacturers would have responded as quickly to the changing market conditions. What is true for automobiles in the United States is true for every product category around the world: Global competition expands the range of products available and increases the likelihood that consumers will get what they want.

The downside of global competition is its impact on the producers of goods and services. Global competition creates value for consumers, but it also has the potential to destroy jobs and profits. When a company—Toyota, for example—offers consumers in other countries a better product at a lower price, it takes customers away from domestic firms such as GM. Unless the domestic firm can create new values and find new customers, the jobs and livelihoods of the domestic supplier's employees are threatened.

This section addresses the following issue: Why is a particular nation a good home base for specific industries? Why, for example, is the United States the home base for the leading competitors in tablets and smartphones, software, credit cards, and filmed entertainment? Why is Germany home to so many world leaders in printing presses, chemicals, and luxury cars? Why are so many leading pharmaceutical, chocolate/confectionery, and trading companies located in Switzerland? How does one account for Italy's success in wool textiles, knitwear, and apparel?

Harvard professor Michael E. Porter explored these issues in his groundbreaking 1990 book *The Competitive Advantage of Nations*. The book was hailed as a valuable guide for shaping national policies on competitiveness. According to Porter, the presence or absence of particular attributes in individual countries influences industry development, not just the ability of individual firms to create core competencies and competitive advantage.[25] Porter describes these attributes in terms of a national "diamond." You can visualize these attributes relative to a baseball diamond; demand conditions are on "first base"; firm strategy, structure, and rivalry occupy the "second base" position; factor conditions are on "third base"; and related and supporting industries are at "home plate." The diamond shapes the environment in which firms compete. Activity in any one of the four points of the diamond impacts all the other points, and vice versa.

Factor Conditions

Factor conditions refers to a country's endowment with resources. Factor resources may have been created or inherited. *Basic factors* may be inherited or created without much difficulty; because they can be replicated in other nations, they are not sustainable sources of **national advantage**. Specialized factors, by contrast, are more advanced and provide a more sustainable source for advantage. Porter describes five categories of factor conditions: human, physical, knowledge, capital, and infrastructure.

HUMAN RESOURCES The quantity of workers available, the skills possessed by these workers, the wage levels, and the overall work ethic of the workforce together constitute a nation's human resource factor. Countries with a plentiful supply of low-wage workers have an obvious advantage in the production of labor-intensive products. However, such countries may be at a *disadvantage* when it comes to the production of sophisticated products requiring highly skilled workers capable of working without extensive supervision.

PHYSICAL RESOURCES The availability, quantity, quality, and cost of land, water, minerals, and other natural resources determine a country's physical resources (see Exhibit 16-7). A country's size and location are also included in this category, because proximity to markets and sources of supply, as well as transportation costs, are strategic considerations. These factors are important advantages—or disadvantages—to industries dependent on natural resources. Brazil is a case in point. With a large landmass, temperate climate, and abundant water supply, Brazil is a leading producer of agricultural commodities, including coffee, soybeans, and sugar.

---

[25] Michael E. Porter, *The Competitive Advantage of Nations* (New York: Free Press, 1990).

Exhibit 16-7 As Michael Porter discusses in his book *The Competitive Advantage of Nations*, Italy's strength as an exporter is due in part to clusters of successful industries including textiles and apparel; glass, ceramics, and stone products; and many others. A case in point is the town of Impruneta in the Italian province of Florence. Impruneta is a source of high-quality terracotta; the high iron content of the area's clay means that the finished pieces can withstand temperatures as low as -20 degrees F. Many artisan pieces are rolled by hand, including those imported in the United States by Seibert & Rice.

Source: © Kristoffer Tripplaar / Alamy.

KNOWLEDGE RESOURCES The availability within a nation of a significant portion of the population having scientific, technical, and market-related knowledge means that the nation is endowed with knowledge resources. The presence of this factor is usually a function of the number of research facilities and universities—both government and private—operating in the country. This factor is important to success in sophisticated products and services, and to doing business in sophisticated markets. This factor relates directly to Germany's leadership in chemicals; for nearly 200 years, Germany has been home to top university chemistry programs, advanced scientific journals, and apprenticeship programs.

CAPITAL RESOURCES Countries vary in the availability, amount, cost, and types of capital available to the country's industries. The nation's savings rate, interest rates, tax laws, and government deficit all affect the availability of this factor. The advantage enjoyed by industries in countries with low capital costs versus those located in nations with relatively high capital costs is sometimes decisive. Firms paying high capital costs are frequently unable to stay in a market where the competition comes from a nation with low capital costs. The firms with the low cost of capital can keep their prices low and force the firms paying high costs to either accept low returns on investment or leave the industry.

INFRASTRUCTURE RESOURCES Infrastructure includes a nation's banking system, health care system, transportation system, and communications system, as well as the availability and cost of using these systems. More sophisticated industries are more dependent on advanced infrastructures for success.

Competitive advantage accrues to a nation's industry if the mix of factors available to the industry is such that it facilitates pursuit of a generic strategy (i.e., low-cost production or the production of a highly differentiated product or service). Nations that have selective factor *disadvantages* may also indirectly create competitive advantage. For example, the absence of suitable labor may force firms to develop forms of mechanization or automation that give the nation an advantage. High transportation costs may motivate firms to develop new materials that are less expensive to transport.

Demand Conditions

The nature of home demand conditions for the firm's or industry's products and services is important because it determines the rate and nature of improvement and innovation by the firms in the nation. **Demand conditions** are the factors that either train firms for world-class competition or that fail to adequately prepare them to compete in the global marketplace. Four characteristics of home demand are particularly important to the creation of competitive advantage: the composition of home demand, the size and pattern of the growth of home demand, the rapid home-market

INNOVATION, ENTREPRENEURSHIP, AND THE GLOBAL STARTUP

Italian Entrepreneurs Combine Fashion and Function

SYNC • THINK • LEARN

MyMarketingLab

As Michael Porter notes in *The Competitive Advantage of Nations*:

> Entrepreneurship thrives in Italy, feeding rivalry in existing industries and the formation of clusters. Italians are risk takers. Many are individualistic and desire independence. They aspire to have their own company. They like to work with people they know well, as in the family, and not as part of a hierarchy....Recently, the entrepreneur has become celebrated in Italy, and a number of business magazines are full of nothing but profiles of successful entrepreneurs. (p. 447)

So, what is an entrepreneur? Management guru Peter Drucker used the term to describe someone who introduces innovations. Entrepreneurs, by definition, are always pioneers in introducing new products. Drucker writes:

> They are people with exceptional abilities who seize opportunities that others are oblivious to or who create opportunities through their own daring and imagination.... Innovation is the specific instrument of entrepreneurship. Innovation is the act that endows resources with a new capacity to create wealth....Through innovation, entrepreneurs create new satisfactions or new consumer demand.

Leonardo del Vecchio is an entrepreneur. He developed an innovative approach to an existing product and, in 1961, founded a company that manufactures and markets it. By applying the basic tools and principles of modern marketing, del Vecchio has achieved remarkable success. He grew up in an orphanage, but today he is one of Europe's richest men. His insight: While eyeglasses are critical for vision, they also reflect the wearer's personality. As a product, then, eyeglass frames serve two purposes; one is functional, the other is aesthetic. This insight fueled the growth of del Vecchio's company, Luxottica, into the world's top producer of eyeglass frames.

In the 1960s, del Vecchio approached Milan-based designer Giorgio Armani and asked, "Have you ever thought about glasses and your brand name and your style?" Armani's response? "Great idea! Let's go!" he said. The rest, as they say, is history. Today, Luxottica has 60,000 employees worldwide, and is vertically integrated. It designs and manufactures frames in its own factories, and also is involved in distribution through fully owned chains such as Sunglass Hut, LensCrafters, and Pearle Vision. It owns top eyewear brands including Oakley, Ray-Ban, and Vogue. The company also produces frames under license for a veritable who's who of luxury brands: Burberry, Dolce & Gabbana, Donna Karan, Prada, Ralph Lauren, Versace, and

many others. Ray-Ban is Luxottica's biggest-selling brand, with more than €2 billion in sales each year. Del Vecchio's business principles include the following (see Exhibit 16-8):

- "Made in Italy" is important!
- Must cut costs to keep production at home.
- Invest in automation: Robots, not workers, weld on hinges, set rhinestones, affix brand logos.

Diego Della Valle is another Italian entrepreneur. He developed an innovative approach to an existing product and then leveraged his family's business to manufacture and market it. By applying the basic tools and principles of modern marketing, Della Valle and his family have achieved remarkable success. As is true with many entrepreneurs, Della Valle's idea was based on his recognition that "there had to be a better way." While visiting the United States as a young man, he spotted "these strange, very badly made shoes from Portugal." They were marketed as a driving accessory. He brought a pair back to Italy and showed his father, Dorino. The elder Della Valle thought they were "horrible" and told his son to throw them away. Dorino Della Valle then reconsidered. His son says, "He changed the way we think about shoes. In the past, expensive shoes were rigid, heavy. So he had the idea of making them soft, to fit like a glove, using the best quality leather."

Today, Tod's S.p.A., the family business that was started in 1920s, is closely identified with its iconic driving shoe. The company's strategic focus is on shoes and handbags; annual sales are $1 billion. CEO Diego Della Valle says, "We want to guarantee our customers we're giving them the best." The CEO continues, "Pure Italian style is identifiable anywhere in the world. When I am walking in Central Park, I recognize the Italians because an Italian, even when he jogs, he's dressed perfect." The need to maintain a quality image is one reason that all Tod's production—including six sewing factories—takes place in Italy. Analyst Davide Vimercati notes, "Tod's is proof that if you manage your brand consistently and you build brand equity over the years, you reach a stage where demand remains strong, even in tough times."

Sources: Bill Emmott, *Good Italy, Bad Italy: Why Italy Must Conquer Its Demons to Face the Future* (New Haven, CT: Yale University Press, 2012), Chapter 7; Liz Alderman, "A Shoemaker That Walks but Never Runs," *The New York Times* (October 10, 2010), p. B1; Vincent Boland, "Italy's Entrepreneur with Sole," *Financial Times* (April 22, 2009); "Employment, Italian Style," *The Wall Street Journal* (June 26, 2012), p. A14; Christina Passariello, "Fitting Shades for Chinese," *The Wall Street Journal* (April 21, 2011), p. B5; Rachel Sanderson, "The Real Value of Being 'Made in Italy,'" *Financial Times* (January 19, 2011); Emanuela Scarpellini, *Material Nation: A Consumer's History of Modern Italy* (New York: Oxford University Press, 2011); David Segal, "Is Italy Too Italian?" *The New York Times* (August 1, 2010), p. B1; Michael E. Porter, *The Competitive Advantage of Nations* (New York: The Free Press, 1990), Chapter 8.

growth, and the means by which a nation's home demand pushes or pulls the nation's products and services into foreign markets.

COMPOSITION OF HOME DEMAND This demand element determines how firms perceive, interpret, and respond to buyer needs. Competitive advantage can be achieved when the home demand sets the quality standard and gives local firms a better picture of buyer needs, at an earlier time, than what is available to foreign rivals. This advantage is enhanced when home buyers pressure the nation's firms to innovate quickly and frequently. The basis for advantage is the fact that the

Exhibit 16-8 Luxottica, the world's leading eyewear manufacturer, also owns and operates retail chains in key global markets. Generally speaking, customers in the United States tend to emphasize function—e.g., brands such as Ray-Ban and Oakley—and are somewhat more conservative and traditional in their tastes. By contrast, European and Asian customers share the desire for an emotional connection with the things they buy—including eyeglass frames. Luxottica CEO Andrea Guerra is ramping up efforts to expand in Brazil, India, Turkey, and China.

nation's firms can stay ahead of the market when the firms are more sensitive and more responsive to home demand and when that demand, in turn, reflects or anticipates world demand.

SIZE AND PATTERN OF GROWTH OF HOME DEMAND These are important only if the composition of the home demand is sophisticated and anticipates foreign demand. Large home markets offer opportunities to achieve economies of scale and learning while dealing with familiar, comfortable markets. There is less apprehension about investing in large-scale production facilities and expensive R&D programs when the home market is sufficient to absorb the increased capacity. If the home demand accurately reflects or anticipates foreign demand, and if the firms do not become content with serving the home market, the existence of large-scale facilities and programs will be an advantage in global competition.

RAPID HOME-MARKET GROWTH This is yet another incentive to invest in and adopt new technologies faster and to build large, efficient facilities. The best example of this is in Japan, where rapid home-market growth provided the incentive for Japanese firms to invest heavily in modern, automated facilities. *Early home demand*, especially if it anticipates international demand, gives local firms the advantage of getting established in an industry sooner than foreign rivals. Equally important is *early market saturation*, which puts pressure on a company to expand into international markets and innovate. Market saturation is especially important if it coincides with rapid growth in foreign markets.

MEANS BY WHICH A NATION'S PRODUCTS AND SERVICES ARE PUSHED OR PULLED INTO FOREIGN COUNTRIES The issue here is whether a nation's people and businesses go abroad and then demand the home nation's products and services in those second countries. For example, when the U.S. auto companies set up operations in foreign countries, the auto parts industry followed. The same is true for the Japanese auto industry. Similarly, when overseas demand for the services of U.S. engineering firms skyrocketed after World War II, those firms, in turn, established demand for U.S. heavy construction equipment. This provided an impetus for Caterpillar to establish foreign operations.

A related issue is that of a nation's people going abroad for training, pleasure, business, or research. After returning home, they are likely to demand the products and services with which they became familiar while abroad. Similar effects can result from professional, scientific, and political relationships between nations. Those involved in the relationships begin to demand the products and services of the recognized leaders.

It is the interplay of demand conditions that produces competitive advantage. Of special importance are those conditions that lead to initial and continuing incentives to invest and innovate and to continuing competition in increasingly sophisticated markets.

Related and Supporting Industries

A nation has an advantage when it is home to globally competitive companies in business sectors that comprise **related and supporting industries**. Globally competitive supplier industries provide inputs to downstream industries. The latter, in turn, are likely to be globally competitive in terms of price and quality and thus gain competitive advantage from this situation. Downstream industries will have easier access to these inputs and the technology that produced them, and to the managerial and organizational structures that made them competitive. Access is a function of proximity both in terms of physical distance and cultural similarity. It is not the inputs themselves that give advantage. It is the *contact* and *coordination* with the suppliers, the opportunity to structure the value chain so that linkages with suppliers are optimized. These opportunities may not be available to foreign firms.

Similar advantages are present when there are globally competitive, related industries in a nation. Opportunities are available for coordinating and sharing value chain activities. Consider, for example, the opportunities for sharing between computer hardware manufacturers and software developers. Related industries also create "pull through" opportunities, as described previously. For example, non-U.S. sales of PCs from Hewlett-Packard, Lenovo, Dell, Acer, and others have bolstered demand for software from Microsoft and other U.S. companies. Porter notes that the development of the Swiss pharmaceuticals industry can be attributed, in part, to Switzerland's large synthetic dye industry; the discovery of the therapeutic effects of dyes, in turn, led to the development of pharmaceutical companies.[26]

Firm Strategy, Structure, and Rivalry

The **nature of firm strategy, structure, and rivalry** is the final determinant of a nation's diamond. Domestic rivalry in a single national market is a powerful influence on competitive advantage. The PC industry in the United States is a good example of how a strong domestic rivalry keeps an industry dynamic and creates continual pressure to improve and innovate. The rivalry between Dell, Hewlett-Packard, and Apple forces all the players to develop new products, improve existing ones, lower costs and prices, develop new technologies, and continually improve quality and service to keep customers happy. Rivalry with foreign firms may lack this intensity. Domestic rivals have to fight each other not just for market share, but also for employee talent, R&D breakthroughs, and prestige in the home market. Eventually, strong domestic rivalry will push firms to seek international markets to support expansions in scale and R&D investments, as Japan amply demonstrates. In contrast, the absence of significant domestic rivalry can lead to complacency in the home firms and eventually cause them to become noncompetitive in the world markets.

It is not the number of domestic rivals that is important; rather, it is the intensity of the competition and the quality of the competitors that make the difference. It is also important that there be a fairly high rate of new business formation to create new competitors and prevent the older companies from becoming comfortable with their market positions and products and services. As noted earlier in the discussion of the five forces model, new industry entrants bring new perspectives and new methods. They frequently define and serve new market segments that established companies have failed to recognize.

Differences in management styles, organizational skills, and strategic perspectives also create advantages and disadvantages for firms competing in different types of industries, as do differences in the intensity of domestic rivalry (see Exhibit 16-9). In Germany, for example, company structure and management style tend to be hierarchical. Managers tend to come from technical backgrounds and to be most successful when dealing with industries that demand highly disciplined structures, like chemicals and precision machinery. Italian firms, in contrast, tend to look like, and be run like, small family businesses that stress customized over standardized products, niche markets, and substantial flexibility in meeting market demands.

[26] Michael E. Porter, *The Competitive Advantage of Nations* (New York: Free Press, 1990), p. 324.

Exhibit 16-9 Well-known and highly esteemed in its own country, India's Tata Group participates in a variety of industries, including heavy vehicles, cars, department stores, and tea. Now the group's management team is hoping to maintain that brand image as an international strategy is implemented. Historically, Tata's Group's competitive advantage was based on scouring the globe to find the lowest-cost, highest-quality production inputs—be they raw materials or skilled labor—and then selling them in the global marketplace at a substantial profit. In 2006, the Group's Taj Hotels Resorts and Palaces subsidiary announced plans to buy the Ritz-Carlton Hotel in Boston.
Source: Kuni/AP Images.

There are two final external variables to consider in the evaluation of national competitive advantage—chance and government.

Chance

Chance events play a role in shaping the competitive environment. Chance events are occurrences that are beyond the control of firms, industries, and usually governments. Included in this category are such things as wars and their aftermaths; major technological breakthroughs; sudden, dramatic shifts in a factor or an input cost, like an oil crisis; dramatic swings in exchange rates; and so on.

Chance events are important because they create major discontinuities in technologies that allow nations and firms that were not competitive to leapfrog over former competitors and become competitive, even leaders, in the changed industry. For example, the development of microelectronics allowed many Japanese firms to overtake U.S. and German firms in industries that had been based on electromechanical technologies—areas traditionally dominated by the Americans and Germans.

From a systemic perspective, the importance of chance events lies in the fact that they alter conditions in the diamond. The nation with the most favorable "diamond," however, will be the one most likely to take advantage of these chance events and convert them into competitive advantage. For example, Canadian researchers were the first to isolate insulin, but they could not convert this breakthrough into a globally competitive product. However, firms in the United States and Denmark were able to make that conversion because of their respective national "diamonds."

Government

Although it is often argued that government is a major determinant of national competitive advantage, in actuality, government is not a determinant but rather an influence on determinants. Government influences determinants by virtue of its roles as a buyer of products and services and a maker of policies on labor, education, capital formation, natural resources, and product standards. It also influences determinants by its role as a regulator of commerce—for example, by telling banks and telephone companies what they can and cannot do.

By reinforcing determinants in industries where a nation has competitive advantage, government improves the competitive position of the nation's firms. Governments devise legal systems that influence competitive advantage by means of tariffs and nontariff barriers and laws requiring local content and labor. In the United States, for example, the dollar's decline over the past decade has been due, in part, to a deliberate policy to enhance U.S. export flows and stem imports. In other words, government can improve or lessen competitive advantage, but it cannot create it.

Current Issues in Competitive Advantage

Porter's work on national competitive advantage has stimulated a great deal of further research. The Geneva-based World Economic Forum issues an annual report ranking countries in terms of their competitiveness. A decade and a half ago, Morgan Stanley used the Porter framework to identify 238 companies with a sustainable competitive advantage worldwide. "National advantage" was then assessed by analyzing how many of these companies were headquartered in a particular country. The United States ranked first, with 125 companies identified as world leaders (see Table 16-1). Among the world's automakers, Morgan Stanley's analysts considered only BMW, Toyota, and Honda to have worldwide competitive advantage.[27]

Hypercompetitive Industries

In a book published in the mid-1990s, Dartmouth College professor Richard D'Aveni suggests that the Porter strategy frameworks fail to adequately address the dynamics of competition in the 1990s and the new millennium.[28] D'Aveni also takes a different approach. He notes that in today's business environment, short product life cycles, short product design cycles, new technologies, and globalization undermine market stability. The result is an escalation and acceleration of competitive forces. In light of these changes, D'Aveni believes the goal of strategy has shifted from sustaining to disrupting advantages. The limitation of the Porter models, D'Aveni argues, is that they are static; that is, they provide a snapshot of competition at a given point in time. Acknowledging that Hamel and Prahalad broke new ground in recognizing that few advantages are sustainable, D'Aveni aims to build upon their work in order to shape "a truly dynamic approach to the creation and destruction of traditional advantages." D'Aveni uses the term **hypercompetition** to describe a dynamic competitive world in which no action or advantage can be sustained for long. In such a world, D'Aveni argues, "everything changes" because of the dynamic maneuvering and strategic interactions by hypercompetitive firms such as Microsoft and Gillette.

TABLE 16-1 Location of Companies with Global Competitive Advantage

Country	Number of Companies
1. United States	125
2. United Kingdom	21
3. Japan	19
4. France	12
5. Germany	10
6. Netherlands	7
7. Canada	6
8. Switzerland	6
9. Sweden	3
10. Finland	3

---

[27] Tony Jackson, "Global Competitiveness Observed from an Unfamiliar Angle," *Financial Times* (November 21, 1996), p. 18.
[28] Richard D'Aveni, *Hypercompetition: Managing the Dynamics of Strategic Maneuvering* (New York: Free Press, 1994).

According to D'Aveni's model, competition unfolds in a series of dynamic strategic interactions in four areas: cost/quality, timing and know-how, entry barriers, and deep pockets. Each of these arenas is "continuously destroyed and recreated by the dynamic maneuvering of hypercompetitive firms." Also, according to D'Aveni, the only source of a truly sustainable competitive advantage is a company's ability to manage its dynamic strategic interactions with competitors by means of frequent movements and countermovements that maintain a relative position of strength in each of the four arenas (see Table 16-2).

COST/QUALITY Competition in the first arena, cost/quality, occurs via seven dynamic strategic interactions: price wars, quality and price positioning, "the middle path," "cover all niches," outflanking and niching, the move toward an ultimate value marketplace, and escaping from the ultimate value marketplace by restarting the cycle. D'Aveni cites the global watch industry as an example of hypercompetitive behavior in the cost/quality arena. In the 1970s, the center of the watch industry shifted from Switzerland to Japan as the Japanese created high-quality quartz watches that could be sold cheaply. In the early 1980s, the merger of two Swiss companies into

TABLE 16-2 Dynamic Strategic Interactions in Hypercompetitive Industries

Arena	Dynamic Strategic Interaction
1. Cost/Quality	**1.** Price wars
	2. Quality and price positioning
	3. "The middle path"
	4. "Cover all niches"
	5. Outflanking and niching
	6. The move toward an ultimate value marketplace
	7. Escaping from the ultimate value marketplace by restarting the cycle
2. Timing and know-how	**1.** Capturing first-mover advantages
	2. Imitation and improvement by followers
	3. Creating impediments to imitation
	4. Overcoming the impediments
	5. Transformation or leapfrogging
	6. Downstream vertical integration
3. Entry barriers	**1.** Building a geographic stronghold by creating and reinforcing entry barriers
	2. Targeting the product market strongholds of competitors in other countries
	3. Incumbents make short-term counter-responses to guerrilla attacks
	4. Incumbents realize they must respond fully to the invaders by making strategic responses to create new hurdles
	5. Competitors react to new hurdles
	6. Long-run counter-responses via defensive or offensive moves
	7. Competition between the incumbent and entrant is exported to entrant's home turf
	8. An unstable standoff between the competitors is established
4. Deep pockets	**1.** "Drive 'em out"
	2. Smaller competitors use courts or Congress to derail deep-pocketed firm
	3. Large firm thwarts antitrust suit
	4. Small firms neutralize the advantage of the deep pocket
	5. The rise of a countervailing power

Exhibit 16-10 Swatch Group was an Official Partner of the 2011 Venice Biennale International Art Exposition. Swatch often commissions new styles from well-known artists. Nick Hayek, the son of Swatch founder Nicolas Hayek, is the company's current CEO; Swatch recently introduced a new mechanical watch, the Sistem 51, that will be targeted at the Asian market. Nayla Hayek, Nick's sister, is the group's chairwoman. She was recently named CEO of Harry Winston, the luxury jeweler that Swatch acquired in 2013.
Source: Fabrice Coffrini/AFP/Getty Images.

Société Suisse Microélectronique et d'Horlogerie SA (SMH) was followed by a highly automated manufacturing innovation that allowed a quartz movement to be integrated into a stylish plastic case. As a result of this innovation and a strong marketing effort in support of the Swatch brand, the center of the watch industry shifted back to Switzerland. Today, the Swatch Group is the world's largest watchmaker. The watch industry continues to be highly segmented, with prestige brands competing on reputation and exclusivity; as with many other luxury goods, higher prices are associated with higher perceived quality. In the low-cost segment, brands compete on price and value (see Exhibit 16-10).

TIMING AND KNOW-HOW The second arena for hypercompetition is based on organizational advantages derived from timing and know-how. As described by D'Aveni, a firm that has the skills to be a "first mover" and arrive first in a market has achieved a *timing advantage*. A *know-how advantage* is the technological knowledge—or other knowledge of a new method of doing business—that allows a firm to create an entirely new product or market.[29]

D'Aveni identifies six dynamic strategic interactions that drive competition in this arena: capturing first-mover advantages, imitation and improvement by followers, creating impediments to imitation, overcoming the impediments, transformation or leapfrogging, and downstream vertical integration. As the consumer electronics industry has globalized, Sony and its competitors have exhibited hypercompetitive behavior in this second arena. Sony has an enviable history of first-mover achievements based on its know-how in audio technology: first pocket-sized transistor radio, first consumer VCR, first portable personal stereo, and first compact disc player.

Although each of these innovations literally created an entirely new market, Sony has fallen victim to the risks associated with being a first mover. The second dynamic strategic interaction—imitation and improvement by followers—can be seen in the successful efforts of JVC and Matsushita to enter the home VCR market a few months after Sony's Betamax launch. VHS technology offered longer recording times and was the dominant consumer format worldwide until the advent of the DVD era.

After years of moves and countermoves among Sony and its imitators, Sony progressed to downstream vertical integration with the 1988 purchase of CBS Records for $2 billion and

---

[29] Richard D'Aveni, *Hypercompetition: Managing the Dynamics of Strategic Maneuvering* (New York: Free Press, 1994), p. 71.

then, later, the purchase of Columbia Pictures. The acquisitions, which represent the sixth dynamic strategic interaction, were intended to complement Sony's core "hardware" businesses (e.g., TVs, VCRs, and hi-fi equipment) with "software" (e.g., videocassettes and CDs). However, Matsushita quickly imitated Sony by paying $6 billion for MCA Inc. Initially, neither Sony nor Matsushita proved successful at managing their acquisitions. More recently, however, Sony Pictures Entertainment has enjoyed huge successes with the *Spider-Man* movies and *Skyfall*, the latest James Bond film.

Sony is also facing serious challenges to its core electronics businesses. The digital revolution rendered Sony's core competencies in analog audio technology obsolete. The company must develop new know-how resources if it is to continue to lead in the Information Age. Sony has found technological leaps harder to achieve, as evidenced by the fact that Apple's iPod is now the world's best-selling portable music player. Sony was also slow to grasp the speed with which consumers would embrace flat-panel TV technology; its home entertainment and sound businesses have been losing money for years. In fact, a hedge fund manager has called for top management to spin off a portion of the entertainment business to boost profitability.[30]

Hypercompetition is showing up in other ways, too. For example, after 20 years, sales of Sony's Handycam camcorders started to decline. Meanwhile, an inexpensive device called the Flip from startup Pure Digital Technologies quickly became a best seller after its launch in 2006. Belatedly, Sony rolled out the Webbie Internet-ready camcorder. During the product's development, the U.S.-based marketing director for the design team asked Tokyo for permission to make the camcorder available in orange and purple.[31] More competitive challenges loom. Although Sony's Blu-ray high-definition DVD format triumphed over Toshiba's HD-DVD to become the industry standard, the victory may be fleeting as on-demand video downloads gain in popularity. Sony is also learning that technological breakthroughs are not necessarily the key to market leadership. For example, Sony's PlayStation 3 (PS3) has a powerful chip that provides new levels of realism; PS3 also contains a Blu-ray DVD player. However, the less complex, less expensive Nintendo Wii initially outsold Sony's game system by a margin of 3-to-1.

ENTRY BARRIERS Industries in which barriers to entry have been built up comprise the third arena in which hypercompetitive behavior is exhibited. As described earlier in the chapter, these barriers include economies of scale, product differentiation, capital investments, switching costs, access to distribution channels, cost advantages other than scale, and government policies. D'Aveni describes how aggressive competitors erode these traditional entry barriers via eight strategic interactions. For example, a cornerstone of Dell's global success in the PC industry is a direct-sales approach that bypasses dealers and other distribution channels.

The first dynamic strategic interaction comes as a company builds a geographic "stronghold" by creating and reinforcing barriers. After securing a market—especially the home-country market—competitors begin to seek markets outside the stronghold. Thus, the second dynamic strategic interaction takes place when companies target the product market strongholds of competitors in other countries. Honda's geographic expansion outside Japan with motorcycles and automobiles—a series of forays utilizing guerrilla tactics—is a case in point. The third dynamic strategic interaction comes when incumbents make short-term counterresponses to the guerrilla attacks. Strong incumbents may try to turn back the invader with price wars, factory investment, or product introductions, or they may adopt a wait-and-see attitude before responding. In the case of both Harley-Davidson and the Detroit-based U.S. auto industry, management originally underestimated and rationalized away the full potential of the threat from Honda and other Japanese companies. Realizing that their company was a weak incumbent, Harley-Davidson management then had little choice but to appeal for government protection. The resulting "breathing room" allowed Harley to put its house in order. Similarly, the U.S. government heeded Detroit's pleas for relief and imposed tariffs and quotas on Japanese auto imports. This gave the Big Three time to develop higher-quality, fuel-efficient models to offer U.S. consumers.

The fourth dynamic strategic interaction occurs when the incumbent realizes it must respond fully to the invader by making strategic responses to create new hurdles. U.S. automakers, for

---

[30] Hiroko Tabuchi, "Investor's Next Target Is Sony," *The New York Times* (May 15, 2013), p. B1.

[31] Daisuke Wakabayashi and Christopher Lawton, "At Sony, Culture Shift Yields a Low-Cost Video Camera," *The Wall Street Journal* (April 16, 2009), p. B1.

example, waged a PR campaign urging U.S. citizens to "Buy American." The fifth dynamic strategic interaction takes place when competitors react to these new hurdles. In an effort to circumvent import quotas as well as co-opt the "Buy American" campaign, the Japanese automakers built plants in the United States. The sixth dynamic strategic interaction consists of long-run counterresponses to the attack via defensive or offensive moves. GM's 1990 introduction of Saturn is a good illustration of a well-formulated and executed defensive move. As the second decade of the twenty-first century continues, GM is launching another defensive move; in an effort to defend its Cadillac nameplate from Lexus, Acura, and Infiniti, GM is developing a global strategy for Cadillac. Competition in the third arena continues to escalate; in the seventh dynamic strategic interaction, competition between the incumbent and the entrant is exported to the entrant's home turf. President Clinton's threat of trade sanctions against Japanese automakers in 1995 was intended to send a message that Japan needed to open its auto market. In 1997, GM intensified its assault on Japan by exporting right-hand-drive Saturns to the Japanese market. The eighth and final dynamic strategic interaction in this arena consists of an unstable standoff between the competitors. Over time, the stronghold erodes as entry barriers are overcome, leading competitors to the fourth arena.

As the preceding discussion shows, the irony and paradox of the hypercompetition framework is that in order to achieve a sustainable advantage, companies must seek a series of *unsustainable* advantages! D'Aveni is thus in agreement with the late Peter Drucker, who long counseled that the roles of marketing are innovation and the creation of new markets. Innovation begins with abandonment of the old and obsolete. Sumantra Ghoshal and Christopher Bartlett make a similar point in *The Individualized Corporation*:

> Managers are forced to refocus their attention from a preoccupation with defining defensible product-market positions to a newly awakened interest in how to develop the organizational capability to sense and respond rapidly and flexibly to change....Managers worldwide have begun to focus less on the task of forecasting and planning for the future and more on the challenge of being highly sensitive to emerging changes. Their broad objective is to create an organization that is constantly experimenting with appropriate responses, then is able to quickly diffuse the information and knowledge gained so it can be leveraged by the entire organization. The age of strategic planning is fast evolving into the era of organizational learning.[32]

Likewise, D'Aveni urges managers to reconsider and reevaluate the use of what he believes are old strategic tools and maxims. He warns of the dangers of commitment to a given strategy or course of action. The flexible, unpredictable player may have an advantage over the inflexible, committed opponent. D'Aveni notes that, in hypercompetition, pursuit of generic strategies results in short-term advantage, at best. The winning companies are the ones that successfully move up the ladder of escalating competition, not the ones that lock into a fixed position. D'Aveni is also critical of the five forces model. The best entry barrier, he argues, is one that maintains the initiative, not mounts a defensive attempt to exclude new entrants.

Additional Research on Comparative Advantage

Other researchers have challenged Porter's thesis that a firm's home-base country is the main source of core competencies and innovation. For example, Indiana University Professor Alan Rugman argues that the success of companies based in small economies such as Canada and New Zealand stems from the "diamonds" found in a particular set or combination of home and related countries. For example, a company based in an EU nation may rely on the national "diamond" of one of the 27 other EU members. Similarly, one impact of NAFTA on Canadian firms is to make the U.S. "diamond" relevant to competency creation. Rugman argues that, in such cases, the distinction between the home nation and the host nation becomes blurred. He proposes that Canadian managers must look to a "double-diamond" and assess the attributes of both Canada and the United States when formulating corporate strategy.[33] In other words, he argues

---

[32] Sumantra Ghoshal and Christopher Bartlett, *The Individualized Corporation* (New York: HarperBusiness, 1997), p. 71.
[33] Alan M. Rugman and Lain Verbeke, "Foreign Subsidiaries and Multinational Strategic Management: An Extension and Correction of Porter's Single Diamond Framework," *Management International Review* 3, no. 2 (1993), pp. 71–84.

that, for smaller countries, the nation is not the relevant unit of analysis in formulating strategy. Rather, corporate strategists must look beyond the nation to the region or to sets of closely linked countries. Other critics have argued that Porter generalized inappropriately from the American experience, while confusing industry-level competition with trade at the national level. In the *Journal of Management Studies*, Howard Davies and Paul Ellis assert that nations can, in fact, achieve sustained prosperity without becoming innovation driven; the authors also note the absence of strong diamonds in the home bases of many global industries.[34]

As for Michael Porter, his views on corporate strategy and competitive advantage have evolved during the last three decades. In a 1997 interview with the *Financial Times*, he emphasized the difference between operational efficiency and corporate strategy. The former, in Porter's view, concerns improvement via time-based competition or total quality management; the latter entails "making choices." Porter explains, "'Choice' arises from doing things differently from the rival. And strategy is about trade-offs, where you decide to do this and not that. Strategy is the deliberate choice not to respond to some customers, or choosing which customer needs you are going to respond to." Porter is not convinced of the validity of competitive advantage models based on core competency or hypercompetitive industries. He feels that a nation has an advantage when it is home to globally competitive companies in business sectors that are related and supporting industries. As for core competencies, Porter notes:

> Any individual thing that a company does can usually be imitated. The whole notion that you should rest your success on a few core competencies is an idea that invites destructive competition. Successful companies don't compete that way. They fit together the things they do in a way that is very hard to replicate. [Competitors] have to match everything, or they've basically matched nothing.

On the subject of hypercompetition, Porter says:

> I don't think we're moving towards a hypercompetitive world in which there are no trade-offs. We're probably moving in the other direction. There are more customer segments than ever before, more technological options, more distribution channels. That ought to create lots of opportunities for unique positions.[35]

In 2008, Porter revisited his five forces model in an article in the *Harvard Business Review*. Despite all the changes and challenges brought about by the global financial crisis, Porter believes his model is as relevant and robust as ever. As he told the *Financial Times* in 2011, the five forces are:

> …more and more and more fundamentally important and visible, because a lot of the barriers and the distortions that would blunt or mitigate these distortions and the need for strategy and competitive advantage…have been swept away.

The factors contributing to this, Porter says, are globalization, increased transparency of information, and the reduction in trade barriers.[36]

Summary

In this chapter, we focused on the factors that help industries and countries achieve **competitive advantage**. According to Porter's **five forces model**, industry competition is a function of the threat of new entrants, the threat of substitutes, the bargaining power of suppliers and buyers, and the rivalry among existing competitors. Managers can use Porter's **generic strategies** model to conceptualize possible sources of competitive advantage. A company can pursue broad market strategies of **cost leadership** and **differentiation** or the more targeted approaches of **cost focus** and **focused differentiation**. Rugman and D'Cruz have developed a framework known as the

[34] Howard Davies and Paul Ellis, "Porter's Competitive Advantage of Nations: Time for the Final Judgment?" *Journal of Management Studies* 37, no. 8 (December 2000), pp. 1189–1213.
[35] Tony Jackson, "Why Being Different Pays," *Financial Times* (June 23, 1997), p. 14.
[36] Andrew Hill, "An Academic Who Shares His Values," *Financial Times* (September 25, 2011), p. 14.

flagship model to explain how networked business systems have achieved success in global industries. For pursuing competitive advantage, Hamel and Prahalad have proposed an alternative framework that grows out of a firm's **strategic intent** and use of competitive innovation. A firm can build *layers of advantage*, search for **loose bricks** in a competitor's defensive walls, *change the rules of engagement*, or *collaborate with competitors* and utilize their technology and know-how.

Today, **global competition** is a reality in many industry sectors. Thus, competitive analysis must also be carried out on a global scale. Global marketers must also have an understanding of national sources of competitive advantage. Porter has described four determinants of *national advantage*. **Factor conditions** include human, physical, knowledge, capital, and infrastructure resources. **Demand conditions** include the composition, size, and growth pattern of home demand. The rate of home-market growth and the means by which a nation's products are pulled into foreign markets also affect demand conditions. The final two determinants are the presence of **related and supporting industries** and the **nature of firm strategy, structure, and rivalry**. Porter notes that chance and government also influence a nation's competitive advantage. Porter's work has been the catalyst for promising new research into strategy issues, including D'Aveni's work on **hypercompetition** and Rugman's recent **double-diamond framework** for national competitive advantage.

MyMarketingLab

Go to **mymktlab.com** for the following Assisted-graded writing questions:

16-1. How can a company measure its competitive advantage? How does a firm know if it is gaining or losing competitive advantage? Cite a global company and its source of competitive advantage.

16-2. Give an example of a company that illustrates each of the four generic strategies that can lead to competitive advantage: overall cost leadership, cost focus, differentiation, and focused differentiation.

16-3. Mymarketinglab Only – comprehensive writing assignment for this chapter.

MyMarketingLab

Go to **mymktlab.com** to complete the problems marked with this icon .

Discussion Questions

16-4. Outline Porter's five forces model of industry competition. How are the various barriers to entry relevant to global marketing?

 16-5. How does the five partners (flagship) model developed by Rugman and D'Aveni differ from Porter's five forces model?

16-6. Briefly describe Hamel and Prahalad's framework for competitive advantage.

 16-7. How can a nation achieve competitive advantage?

16-8. According to current research on competitive advantage, what are some of the shortcomings of Porter's model?

 16-9. What is the connection, if any, between *national* competitive advantage and *company* competitive advantage? Explain.

CASE 16-1 CONTINUED (REFER TO PAGE 510)

Volkswagen

CONTINUED (REFER TO PAGE 510)

Volkswagen executives acknowledge that if they are to triple the number of vehicles sold in the United States, they must make cars that appeal to American drivers. A potential stumbling block in Volkswagen's quest for global leadership in the auto industry is the fact that the company unveiled new versions of several key vehicles within the span of just a few months.

Company Background

Historically, one of VW's sources of competitive advantage has been its core competence in the design and manufacture of small, fuel-efficient gasoline engines. Diesel engines are another strength; both types of engines offer the kind of money-saving performance that drivers seek when gasoline prices are high. Several VW models also rank high for crash safety. Given these strengths, why does VW currently rank only third among global automakers? And why has it captured only 3 percent of the U.S. car market? Christian Klinger, Volkswagen Group board member and the executive in charge of sales and marketing for the Volkswagen brand, offers this explanation: "We need the right products and local production," he says. "In the past maybe we had the right product but not the right price. Or the right price and not the right product."

Volkswagen enjoys the distinction of being the number 1 carmaker in Europe and the third largest in the world. Worldwide, the company sold 9.07 million vehicles in 2012. The compact Golf is the best-selling car in Europe. Volkswagen's market share in Western Europe is 24.4 percent; in Central and Eastern Europe, its share is 15.4 percent. When the new midsize Passat was introduced, initial European demand for it was so strong that there was an eight-month waiting list. The company can boast that its giant Wolfsburg plant is home to the most automated production line in the world, capable of completing 80 percent of a car's assembly by machine. Outside Europe, Volkswagen has also achieved considerable success. In Mexico, for example, the company's share of the passenger car market is 16.7 percent. Volkswagen is also the number 1 Western auto manufacturer in China, where it commands nearly 21 percent of the market.

A deeper understanding of Volkswagen's place in the auto industry requires an overview of then-chairman Carl Hahn's attempts to implement his vision of VW as Europe's first global automaker. Indeed, management guru Peter Drucker credited Volkswagen for developing the first truly global strategy more than 30 years ago. By 1970, the Beetle was a mature product in Europe; sales were still moderately strong in the United States and were booming in Brazil. Drucker described what happened next:

> The chief executive officer of Volkswagen proposed switching the German plants entirely to the new model, the successor to the Beetle, which the German plants would also supply to the United States market. But the continuing demand for Beetles in the United States would be satisfied out of Brazil, which would then given Volkswagen do Brasil the needed capability to enlarge its plants and to maintain for another ten years the Beetle's leadership in the growing Brazilian market. To assure the American customers of the "German quality" that was one of the Beetle's main attractions, the critical parts such as engines and transmissions for all cars sold in North America would, however, still be made in Germany. The finished car for the North American market would be assembled in the United States.

Unfortunately, this visionary strategy failed. One problem was resistance on the part of German unions. A second problem was confusion among American dealers about a car that was equally "made in Germany," "made in Brazil," and "made in the USA." Two decades later, as described in an interview with the *Harvard Business Review*, Hahn's strategic plan for the 1990s and beyond called for a decentralized structure of four autonomous divisions. In pursuit of this vision, Hahn invested tens of billions of dollars in Czechoslovakia's Skoda autoworks and SEAT in Spain. The Volkswagen, Audi, Skoda, and SEAT units each would have its own chief executive. As a whole, the company would be capable of turning out more than 4 million cars annually in low-cost plants located close to buyers. The company's R&D center, however, would continue to be in Germany. Highly automated plants in Germany would provide components such as transmissions, engines, and axles to assembly operations in other parts of the world.

In Spain, VW hoped to take advantage of labor rates 50 percent lower than those in West Germany and roughly on par with those paid by Japanese companies with factories in Britain. Because labor makes up a larger share of production costs for subcompacts than for larger models, and because annual demand in Spain amounted to 500,000 cars, Spain was an attractive location for small-car production. Besides serving the domestic market, VW intended to use Spain as a production source that would allow it to cut prices and boost margins in Europe. Between 1986 and 1990, VW paid the Spanish government a total of $600 million in exchange for 100 percent ownership of SEAT. The company increased Spanish production from 350,000 to 500,000 vehicles; the popular Golf model represented about one-quarter of the output. VW then invested $1.9 billion in a new plant in Martorell capable of producing 300,000 cars each year.

Similar reasoning was behind VW's 1991 purchase of a 31 percent stake in Skoda from the Czechoslovak government. Located northeast of Prague in the city of Mlada Boleslav, the Skoda works enjoyed the distinction of being the most efficient plant in the former Soviet bloc. However, product quality was low, and the plant was a major source of pollution. With an eye to doubling production to 450,000 cars, VW pledged to invest $5 billion by the end of the decade. VW's presence also persuaded TRW, Rockwell International, and other parts suppliers interested in serving Skoda and other automakers in Central and Eastern Europe to establish operations in the Czech Republic.

However, to maintain their low-cost position and ensure quality control, VW and Skoda executives went a step beyond the Japanese-style "lean production" system that emphasizes just-in-time delivery from nearby suppliers: Several different suppliers manufactured components such as seats, instrument panels, and rear axles *inside* the plant itself. As Skoda CFO Volkhard Kohler explained in 1994, "We have to organize better than in the Western world and use supplier integration. Wages will increase, so we have to find other ways of being cost-effective. Supplier integration is part of the new thinking and what we do here can be a model for the West." Professor Daniel Jones of the Cardiff University Business School supported the effort: "It's physically integrated, but in terms of management and performance each runs his own show. It makes a lot of sense because you have the direct integration of [the] people making the parts and the people putting them in the car," he said in an interview.

Hahn also earmarked $3 billion for a project in which he took a keen personal interest: investment in the former East Germany, where he was born. On October 3, 1990, German reunification added 16 million people to Volkswagen's home-country market virtually overnight. Under communism, the citizens of East Germany had a choice of basically one car: the notoriously low-quality Trabant. Hahn's strategy for a reunited Germany included building a new, $1.9 billion factory that would employ 6,500 workers and produce a quarter of a million Golf and Polo models each year. The investment was justified in part by forecasts that East Germans would buy 750,000 cars each year; VW aimed to capture a third of that market, equal to its share in West Germany.

Ferdinand Piech, an autocratic leader with an engineering background who was "steely eyed and intense," succeeded Hahn as chairman in 1993. At the time, the company still had stakes in SEAT and Skoda. He immediately declared a state of crisis in the company and began taking drastic actions; cost cutting topped the list. Piech trimmed VW's worldwide employment, starting with 20,000 jobs in 1993. Piech also pledged to slash the number of auto platforms underlying VW's nameplates from 16 to 4 within a few years. During his tenure, a new car, the Passat, was launched, as were redesigned Jetta and Beetle models. He acquired three luxury automakers: Lamborghini, Bugatti, and Bentley. Piech also elevated the status of engineering in the company, and spending on R&D soared. Piech quickly gained a reputation for making key decisions himself.

With great fanfare, VW announced in March 1993 that it had succeeded in luring a new production chief away from General Motors. José Ignacio López de Arriortúa was expected to play a major role in cost cutting at VW, but he arrived amid accusations of industrial espionage. The controversy did not stop López from doing what he had been hired to do. He broke long-term contracts with many of VW's suppliers and put new contracts up for bid; as a result, a higher percentage of components were now sourced outside Germany. At VW's new General Pachecho plant in Buenos Aires, López subcontracted various aspects of production to a dozen outside companies. VW workers built a few crucial parts such as the chassis and power train; suppliers were responsible for various other tasks such as assembling instrument panels. In the end, however, the espionage controversy cost López his job, and Piech settled the civil case by agreeing to pay GM $100 million and buy $1 billion in GM parts.

Even though his tenure at VW was brief and stormy, the positive aspects of the López legacy endured. Maryann Kellar, author of a book about VW, calls the Czech experiment "something that has been talked about for years as the next great productivity and cost enhancement move by the industry." In 1996, Skoda rolled out the Octavia, the first new car developed by the Czech plant during the Volkswagen era and the first to use a VW chassis platform. Piech also won concessions from IG Metall, the German autoworkers union. The union agreed to 2.5 percent annual pay raises and a pledge of job security. In addition, the workday for many assembly-line workers was reduced to five hours and 46 minutes—in essence, a four-day week. CFO Bruno Adelt estimated that all the agreed-upon changes would boost productivity 4 to 5 percent.

Even as VW expanded production in emerging markets and introduced production efficiencies, it was devising a comeback strategy for the United States. Mexican production of a new version of the legendary Beetle began in 1997, with a U.S. launch in 1998. As board member Jens Neumann said, "The Beetle is the core of the VW soul. If we put it back in people's minds, they'll think of our products more." Like its predecessor, the new Beetle had curved body panels and running boards. However, it was a front-wheel-drive model with more headroom and legroom. Despite being priced at about $15,000, 10 percent higher than the company's entry-level Golf, the new Beetle was initially a huge success. Sales were strong through 2000; then, as the buzz surrounding the vehicle died down, sales began to slip. In 2003, hoping to recapture some "cool" and reenergize the Beetle brand, a convertible model was introduced.

Volkswagen in the Twenty-First Century

After Bernd Pischetsrieder became chairman of Volkswagen AG in April 2002, he presided over the launch of several key new vehicles. The $35,000 Volkswagen Touareg was the company's first SUV. Named after a nomadic African tribe that makes an annual journey across the Sahara, the Touareg was introduced just as SUV sales were starting to decline in the United States. *Car and Driver* magazine named the Touareg the "best luxury SUV" of 2003. Another new vehicle was the Phaeton, the first superluxury model to bear the VW nameplate. Developed at a cost of $700 million, Phaeton boasted the world's finest automotive air conditioning system and carried a price tag of $85,000. Together, the Touareg and Phaeton were compelling evidence that Volkswagen intended to move upmarket.

For Pischetsrieder, 2006 was a turbulent year; he lost a boardroom battle with Chairman Piech over the ongoing efforts to cut costs and remain competitive in the face of increased Asian competition. At the beginning of 2007, another key executive resigned. Wolfgang Bernhard, chairman of the Volkswagen brand group, had initiated a series of cost-cutting measures; both Germany's powerful labor unions and Chairman Piech were opposed to some of his actions.

In 2007, Martin Winterkorn took the helm at VW. Winterkorn moved swiftly to reboot the cost-cutting efforts of his predecessors. A production technology pioneered by Scania, the Swedish truck manufacturer, utilizes a modular approach. Because it reduces both complexity and costs, modular architecture is being used in a variety of industrial settings. In addition to Volkswagen, Daimler, Siemens, and Electrolux are also using modular designs and production processes. As a Volkswagen spokesperson put it, "With the modular production toolbox we will in the future be able to build different models and different brands on the same production line."

In essence, the approach means that cars will be assembled from common building blocks that have standard interfaces. VW will use four core modular *baukasten* (toolboxes) as the basis for four vehicle types across eleven brands: small city cars, midsize cars, mid-engine sports cars, and large vehicles. However, the commonality will not result in a standardized, "one-size-fits-all" product design. Rather, it will allow VW to create vehicles such as the new Audi Q3 that respond to specific regional needs and preferences. It is the responsibility of Walter de Silva, VW's design chief, to make sure all the company's cars share a common design language without losing their distinctive identities. And, how does an Italian designer fit in with the corporate culture at a German car company? As de Silva notes, "There is obviously a very special chemistry between German engineering and Italian creativity—it's something you can't explain."

Product Strategy: Jetta

Having conquered key emerging markets and modernized its production processes, VW must now shore up its U.S. business. To accomplish this, executives are determined to "Americanize" VW's cars; the first example of this effort was the 2011 Jetta. Developed at a cost of $1 billion, the new model was produced at VW's N80 assembly plant in Mexico City. The new Jetta arrived at dealers in fall 2010 backed by an advertising campaign that emphasized the $15,995 sticker price. The advertising tagline was "Great. For the price of good." The 2011 model was bigger than its 2010 predecessor, and cost-cutting changes were made to the rear brakes and suspension.

Product Strategy: Beetle

Industry observers are closely following the launch of the third-generation Beetle. The original Beetle (also known as the Bug) featured an air-cooled engine (no radiator!) that was located above the rear tires. The Beetle was very popular in both Europe and the United States, where about 5 million were sold between 1949 and 1979. In the American market, an advertising campaign created by Bill Bernbach has achieved mythic status in the industry. Bernbach is credited with launching the Creative Revolution by "telling the truth" about cars and encouraging buyers to "Think Small."

After VW retooled its German plant for a successor to the Beetle, production was shifted to Brazil. The Beetle was absent from the U.S. market from 1979 until 1999, at which time the second-generation Beetle was launched. The United States was the primary target market for the New Beetle, which was produced at VW's plant in Puebla, Mexico. The designers retained the distinctive, iconic profile of the original so that the new version would be instantly recognizable. It also featured whimsical touches such as a flower vase on the dashboard; however, the launch ad campaign promised, "Less flower. More power."

Other automakers rushed to capitalize on the nostalgia craze that VW was tapping; the BMW Mini Cooper was one notable success. The New Beetle was especially popular with women, but it was discontinued in 2010. The third-generation Beetle went on sale in the fall of 2011. The new Bug was designed for the global market; besides the United States, China, Europe, and Mexico are expected to be key. The new car has a bigger engine and is more sporty in appearance than its predecessors. VW hopes to attract more male buyers while still appealing to women.

Product Strategy: Passat

As noted at the beginning of the chapter, the first cars rolling off the line at VW's new Chattanooga plant were Passat sedans. However, production will soon shift to an NMS—"New Midsize Sedan." This entails risks, as David Sargent, a vice president at J.D. Power and Associates, notes: "Brand-new plants with brand-new models historically have struggled to produce world-class quality. Not to say a plant can't do that, but it's a struggle."

The new plant is also capable of producing diesel-powered cars; however, diesel versions of its current offerings account for only about one-quarter of VW's U.S. sales. Although diesel engines get higher mileage than gasoline engines, they are simply not popular with the majority of U.S. drivers. By contrast, diesels are very popular in Europe. However, it remains to be seen whether VW can change entrenched American attitudes toward diesels, especially since diesel models typically carry a price premium compared to their gasoline-powered counterparts.

Christoph Stürmer is a director at IHS Global Insight consultancy. Summarizing the strategic challenges facing Volkswagen, he said, "VW has to get it right. Get adjusted to American standards of what on-the-road quality is. It's a big challenge for a company so deep-dyed German."

Discussion Questions

16-10. CEO Winterkorn intends to make VW the world's number 1 automaker by 2018. Do you think this is an attainable goal, or is it an "exaggerated" or "stretch" goal designed to motivate employees?

16-11. In VW's advertising, the "Das Auto" tagline encourages potential buyers to associate the brand with its German heritage. Is this the right approach for VW?

16-12. Which rivals present the strongest competitive threats to VW's strategic plans?

16-13. Do you think, as some critics do, that the modular approach will lead to monotonous designs?

Sources: Chris Bryant, "Building Blocks to Cut Output Costs," *Financial Times* (May 20, 2013), p. 17; Dan Neil, "At Geneva, the Promise and Perils of Sharing," *The Wall Street Journal* (March 10/11, 2013), p. D9; John Reed, "Design Through Discipline," *Financial Times* (May 25, 2012), p. 10; Patrick Olsen, "Success Is Sweeter the 2nd Time for VW," *USA Today* (April 12, 2012), p. 3B; Ed Crooks, "Volkswagen Flags Up Its Plans for U.S. Market," *Financial Times* (May 26, 2011), p. 20; Chris Woodyard, "VW Takes Risks with 3G Beetle," *USA Today* (April 18, 2011), pp. 1A, 1B; James R. Healey, "2012 VW Beetle Gets Bigger, Ditches 'Girls' Car' Image," *USA Today* (April 18, 2011); Healey, "VW Plans to Be No. 1 Car Seller in the World by 2018," *USA Today* (September 3, 2010), pp. 1A, 1B; Healey, "Volkswagen Wants to Be the No. 1 Automaker," *USA Today* (November 30, 2009), pp. 1A, 1B; Stephen Power, "Aggressive Driver: Top Volkswagen Executive Tries U.S.-Style Turnaround Tactics," *The Wall Street Journal* (July 18, 2006), p. 1; Peter F. Drucker, *Innovation and Entrepreneurship: Practice and Principles* (New York: Harper & Row, 1985), p. 87.

CASE 16-2
IKEA

IKEA has been called "one of the most extraordinary success stories in the history of postwar European business." However, the first few years of the twenty-first century were difficult for IKEA, the $31 billion global furniture powerhouse based in Sweden. The euro's strength dampened financial results, as did an economic downturn in Central Europe. The company faces increasing competition from hypermarkets, "do-it-yourself" retailers such as Walmart, and supermarkets that are expanding into home furnishings. During his tenure as CEO from 1999 to 2009, Anders Dahlvig stressed three areas for improvement: product assortment, customer service, and product availability.

With stores in 40 countries, the company's success reflects founder Ingvar Kamprad's "social ambition" of selling a wide range of stylish, functional home furnishings at prices so low that the majority of people could afford to buy them. The store exteriors are painted bright blue and yellow, Sweden's national colors. Shoppers view furniture on the main floor in scores of realistic-looking settings arranged throughout the cavernous showrooms.

At IKEA, shopping is a self-service activity; after browsing and writing down the names of desired items, shoppers can pick up their furniture on the lower level. There, they find "flat packs" containing the furniture in kit form; one of the cornerstones of IKEA's low-cost strategy is having customers take their purchases home in their own vehicles and assemble the furniture themselves. The lower level of a typical IKEA store also contains a restaurant, a grocery store called the Swede Shop, a supervised play area for children, and a baby care room.

IKEA's unconventional approach to the furniture business has enabled it to rack up impressive growth in an industry in which overall sales have been flat. Sourcing furniture from a network of more than 1,600 suppliers in 55 countries helps the company maintain its low-cost, high-quality position. During the 1990s, IKEA expanded into Central and Eastern Europe. Because consumers in those regions have relatively little purchasing power, the stores offer a smaller selection of goods; some furniture is designed specifically for the cramped living styles typical in former Soviet bloc countries.

Throughout Europe, IKEA benefits from the perception that Sweden is a source of high-quality products and efficient service. Currently, Germany and the United Kingdom (UK) are IKEA's top two markets. The United Kingdom represents IKEA's fastest-growing market in Europe. Although Britons initially viewed the company's less-is-more approach as cold and "too Scandinavian," they were eventually won over. IKEA currently has 18 stores in the UK, and plans call for opening more in this decade. As Allan Young, creative director of London's St. Luke's advertising agency, noted, "IKEA is anticonventional. It does what it shouldn't do. That's the overall theme for all IKEA ads: liberation from tradition."

In 2005, IKEA opened two stores near Tokyo; more stores are on the way as the company expands in Asia. IKEA's first attempt to develop the Japanese market in the mid-1970s resulted in failure. Why? As Tommy Kullberg, former chief executive of IKEA Japan, explained, "In 1974, the Japanese market from a retail point of view was closed. Also, from the Japanese point of view, I do not think they were ready for IKEA, with our way of doing things, with flat packages and asking the consumers to put things together and so on." However, demographic and economic trends are much different today. After years of recession, consumers are seeking alternatives to paying high prices for quality goods. Also, IKEA's core customer segment—post–baby boomers in their thirties—grew nearly 10 percent between 2000 and 2010. In Japan, IKEA will offer home delivery and an assembly service option.

The coming years will bring big changes at IKEA. In 2013, Peter Agnefjäll became the company's new chief executive. He plans to continue the company's sustainability initiatives, including the possibility

Exhibit 16-11 IKEA currently has eleven stores in China; the Xu Hui store in Shanghai is one of the Swedish company's top performers by revenues. In keeping with IKEA's standardized global retail concept, the Chinese stores are spacious and clean. All locations feature restaurants where visitors can enjoy Swedish meatballs and other meal items. In some cases, the restaurants have also become a favorite meeting place for dating clubs that allow older Chinese to socialize.
Source: Doug Kanter/Bloomberg via Getty Images.

of leasing kitchens to consumers. As Steve Howard, chief sustainability officer, said, "We want a smarter consumption, and maybe people are less attached to ownership." However, some observers question IKEA's sustainability bona fides, noting that its low-priced furniture contributes to a "throw it away" mentality when a piece breaks. Howard responds to such criticism by noting that "People have needs to be met—they need wardrobes, sofas, kitchens. The most important thing is to meet those needs in the most sustainable way possible." For example, in France, one factory sources half its wood from recycled IKEA products that are ground up and repurposed as bookshelves, tables, and other new products.

Discussion Questions

16-14. Review the characteristics of global and transnational companies in Chapter 1. Based on your reading of the case, would IKEA be described as a global firm or a transnational firm?

16-15. At the end of Chapter 11, it was noted that managers of IKEA stores have a great deal of discretion when it comes to setting prices. In terms of the ethnocentric/polycentric/regiocentric/geocentric (EPRG) framework, which management orientation is in evidence at IKEA?

16-16. What does it mean to say that, in terms of Porter's generic strategies, IKEA pursues a strategy of "cost focus"?

Sources: Richard Milne, "Against the Grain," *Financial Times* (November 14, 2012), p. 7; Milne, "IKEA Eyes Kitchen Recycling in Green Push," *Financial Times* (October 23, 2012), p. 19; Mei Fong, "IKEA Hits Home in China," *The Wall Street Journal* (March 3, 2006), pp. B1, B4; Richard Tomkins, "How IKEA Has Managed to Treat Us Mean and Keep Us Keen," *Financial Times* (January 14/January 15, 2006), p. 7; Kerry Capell, "IKEA: How the Swedish Retailer Became a Global Cult Brand," *BusinessWeek* (November 14, 2005), pp. 96–106; Theresa Howard, "IKEA Builds on Furnishings Success," *USA Today* (December 29, 2004), p. 3B; Mariko Sanchanta, "IKEA's Second Try at Japan's Flat-Pack Fans," *Financial Times* (March 4, 2004), p. 11; Paula M. Miller, "IKEA with Chinese Characteristics," *The China Business Review* (July–August, 2004), pp. 36–38; Christopher Brown-Humes, "An Empire Built on a Flat Pack," *Financial Times* (November 24, 2003), p. 8.

CASE 16-3

LEGO

The LEGO Company is a $4 billion global business built out of the humblest of materials: interlocking plastic toy bricks. From its base in Denmark, the family-owned LEGO empire extends around the world and has at times included theme parks, clothing, and computer-controlled toys. Each year, the company produces about 15 billion molded plastic blocks as well as tiny human figures to populate towns and operate gizmos that spring from the imaginations of young people. LEGO products, which are especially popular with boys, are available in more than 130 countries; in the key North American market, the company's overall share of the construction-toy market has been as high as 85 percent.

Kjeld Kirk Kristiansen, the grandson of the company's founder as well as the main shareholder, served as CEO from 1979 until 2004. Kristiansen says that LEGO products stand for "exuberance, spontaneity, self-expression, concern for others, and innovation." (The company's name comes from the Danish phrase *leg godt*, which means "play well.") Kristiansen also attributes his company's success to the esteem the brand enjoys among parents. "Parents consider LEGO not as just a toy company but as providing products that help learning and developing new skills," he says.

LEGO has always been an innovator. For example, Mybots was a $70 toy set that included blocks with computer chips embedded to provide lights and sound. A $200 Mindstorms Robotics Invention System allows users to build computer-controlled creatures. To further leverage the LEGO brand, the company also formed alliances with Walt Disney Company and Lucasfilms, creator of the popular *Star Wars* series. For several years, sales of licensed merchandise relating to the popular *Harry Potter* and *Star Wars* movie franchises sold extremely well.

After a disappointing Christmas 2003 season, LEGO was left with millions of dollars worth of unsold goods. The difficult retail situation was compounded by the dollar's weakness relative to the Danish krone; LEGO posted a record loss of $166 million for 2003. The company then unveiled a number of new initiatives aimed at restoring profitability. A new line, Quattro, consisting of large, soft bricks, is targeted directly at the preschool market. Clikits is a line of pastel-colored bricks targeted at young girls who want to create jewelry.

In 2004, after LEGO had posted several years of losses, Jørgen Vig Knudstorp succeeded Kristiansen as LEGO's chief executive. Knudstorp convened a task force consisting of company executives and outside consultants to review the company's operations and business model. The task force discovered that LEGO's sources of competitive advantage—creativity, innovation, and superior quality—were also sources of weakness. The company had become overly complex, with 12,500 stock-keeping units (SKUs), a palette of 100 different block colors, and 11,000 suppliers.

Acknowledging that the company's forays into theme parks, children's clothing, and software games had been the wrong strategy, Knudstorp launched a restructuring initiative known as "Shared Vision." Within a few months, cross-functional teams collaborated to reduce the number of SKUs to 6,500; the number of color options was slashed by 50 percent. Production was outsourced to a Singaporean company with production facilities in Mexico and the Czech Republic, resulting in the elimination of more than 2,000 jobs.

Knudstorp also decided to focus on the company's retail customers, which include Toys 'R' Us, Metro, Karstadt, and Galeria. After surveying these customers, Knudstorp and his task force learned that the customers do not require express product deliveries. This insight prompted a change to once-weekly deliveries of orders that are placed in advance. The result: Improved customer service and lower costs. In the 3-year period from 2005 to 2008, on-time deliveries increased by 62 percent to 92 percent. LEGO also logged improvements in other key performance indicators, such as package quality and quantity. In 2008, LEGO was awarded the European Supply Chain Excellence Award in the category "Logistics and Fulfillment."

In terms of competitive advantage, Knudstorp has noted, "A bucket of bricks is the core of the core." Still, he adds, "There's more to being a global successful company than being able to build a plastic brick." Evidence of the company's magic touch can be found in LEGO Friends, a new theme targeting girls that has sold extremely well. Moreover, the company's forays into video games such as *Lego Batman 2*, children's books such as *The Lego Ideas Book*, and TV series on the Cartoon Network have proven to be successful as well.

Discussion Questions

16-17. Jørgen Vig Knudstorp became CEO in 2004. Assess the key strategic decisions he has made, including outsourcing and divesting the theme parks.

16-18. LEGO's movie-themed products, keyed to popular film franchises such as *Harry Potter*, *Lord of the Rings*, and *Spider-Man*, include detailed construction plans. Do you think this is the right strategy?

16-19. Using Porter's generic strategies framework, assess LEGO in terms of the company's pursuit of competitive advantage.

16-20. What risk, if any, is posed by LEGO's movement into multimedia categories such as video games and television?

Sources: Jens Hansegard, "What It Takes to Build a Lego Hobbit (and Gollum and More)," *The Wall Street Journal* (December 20, 2012), p. D1; Matt Richtel and Jesse McKinley, "Has Lego Sold Out?" *The New York Times* (December 23, 2012), p. SR4; Carlos Cordon, Ralf Seifert, and Edwin Wellian, "Case Study: LEGO," *Financial Times* (November 24, 2010); Kim Hjelmgaard, "Lego, Refocusing on Bricks, Builds an Image," *The Wall Street Journal* (December 24, 2009); David Robertson and Per Hjuler, "Innovating a Turnaround at LEGO," *Harvard Business Review* (September 2009); John Tagliabue, "Taking Their Blocks and Playing Toymaker Elsewhere," *The New York Times* (November 20, 2006), p. A4; Lauren Foster and David Ibison, "Spike the Robot Helps LEGO Rebuild Strategy," *Financial Times* (June 22, 2006), p. 18; Ian Austen, "Building a Legal Case, Block by Block," *The New York Times* (February 2, 2005), p. C6; Joseph Pereira and Christopher J. Chipello, "Battle of the Block Makers," *The Wall Street Journal* (February 4, 2004), pp. B1, B4; Clare MacCarthy, "Deputy Chief Sacked as LEGO Tries to Rebuild," *Financial Times* (January 9, 2004), p. 19; Majken Schultz and Mary Jo Hatch, "The Cycles of Corporate Branding: The Case of the LEGO Company," *California Management Review* 46, no. 1 (Fall 2003), pp. 6–26; Meg Carter, "Building Blocks of Success," *Financial Times* (October 30, 2003), p. 8.

Exhibit 16-12
Source: AP Images.

17

Leadership, Organization, and Corporate Social Responsibility

 CASE 17-1
A Changing of the Guard at Unilever

Unilever, the global food and consumer packaged goods powerhouse, markets a brand portfolio that includes such well-known names as Axe, Ben & Jerry's, Dove, Hellmann's, Lipton, and Rexona. The company has approximately 167,000 employees and annual sales of almost $59 billion; Unilever can trace its roots, in part, to the northern English town of Port Sunlight on the River Mersey. There, in 1888, Lever Brothers founder William Hesketh Lever created a garden village for the benefit of his employees.

Before retiring at the end of 2008, Unilever Group Chief Executive Patrick Cescau wanted to reconnect the company with its heritage of sustainability and concern for the environment (see Exhibit 17-1). These and other values reflect Unilever's philosophy of "doing well by doing good." One example: the "Campaign for Real Beauty," which was launched by managers at the company's

Exhibit 17-1 Patrick Cescau (left) put corporate social responsibility at the top of his agenda during his tenure as CEO of Unilever. The company's current chief executive, Paul Polman (right), is bulding on Cescau's initiatives while expanding into key emerging markets.
Sources: Unilever/AFP/Newscom and Peter Cavanagh/Alamy.

Dove brand. To prepare for their first presentation to management, Dove team members videotaped interviews with teen girls who talked about the pressures they felt to conform to a certain look and body type. The interviewees included Cescau's daughter as well as the daughters of Unilever's directors. Later, when the CEO recalled watching the video, he explained, "It suddenly becomes personal. You realize your own children are impacted by the beauty industry, and how stressed they are by this image of unattainable beauty which is imposed on them every day." The Dove team was given the green light to launch a new advertising campaign based on this insight; in the years since, Dove has won numerous awards and accolades.

Cescau's vision of "doing well by doing good" manifested itself in other ways, too. For example, he guided the company's detergent business toward using fewer chemicals and less water, plastic, and packaging. In addition, he recognized that today's "conscience consumers" look to a company's reputation when deciding which brands to purchase.

Paul Polman, Cescau's successor, has built on another of the former chief executive's priorities: business opportunities in emerging markets such as India and China. However, Polman also took the top job in the middle of the recent global recession. To find out more about Unilever's commitment to global social responsibility while dealing with tough economic challenges, turn to Case 17-1 at the end of the chapter.

This chapter focuses on the integration of each element of the marketing mix into a total plan that addresses opportunities and threats in the global marketing environment. Cescau's achievements as the head of Unilever illustrate some of the challenges facing business leaders in the twenty-first century: They must be able to articulate a coherent global vision and strategy that integrate global efficiency, local responsiveness, and leverage. The leader is also the architect of an organizational design that is appropriate for the company's strategy. For large global enterprises such as ABB, GE, Royal Philips Electronics, Tesco, Toyota, and Unilever, the leader must ensure that size and scale are assets that can be leveraged rather than encumbrances that slow response times and stifle innovation. Finally, the leader must ensure that the organization takes a proactive approach to corporate social responsibility.

LEARNING OBJECTIVES

1 Identify the names and nationalities of the chief executives at five global companies discussed in the text.

2 Describe the different organizational structures that companies can adopt as they grow and expand globally.

3 Discuss the attributes of lean production and identify some of the companies that have been pioneers in this organizational form.

4 List some of the lessons regarding corporate social responsibility that global marketers can take away from Starbucks' experience with Global Exchange.

Leadership

Global marketing demands exceptional leadership. As noted throughout this book, the hallmark of a global company is its capacity to formulate and implement global strategies that leverage worldwide learning, respond fully to local needs and wants, and draw on the talent and energy of every member of the organization. This daunting task requires global vision and sensitivity to local needs. Overall, the leader's challenge is to direct the efforts and creativity of everyone in the company toward a global effort that best utilizes organizational resources to exploit global opportunities. As Carly Fiorina, former CEO of Hewlett-Packard, said in her 2002 commencement address at the Massachusetts Institute of Technology:

> Leadership is not about hierarchy or title or status: It is about having influence and mastering change. Leadership is not about bragging rights or battles or even the accumulation of wealth; it's about connecting and engaging at multiple levels. It's about challenging minds and capturing hearts. Leadership in this new era is about empowering others to decide for themselves. Leadership is about empowering others to reach their full potential. Leaders can no longer view strategy and execution as abstract concepts, but must realize that both elements are ultimately about people.[1]

[1] Carleton "Carly" S. Fiorina, Commencement Address, Massachusetts Institute of Technology, Cambridge, MA, June 2, 2002. See also "It's Death if You Stop Trying New Things," *Financial Times* (November 20, 2003), p. 8.

An important leadership task is articulating beliefs, values, policies, and the intended geographic scope of a company's activities. Using the mission statement or similar document as a reference and guide, members of each operating unit must address their immediate responsibilities and at the same time cooperate with functional, product, and country experts in different locations. However, it is one thing to spell out a vision and another thing entirely to secure commitment to it throughout the organization. As noted in Chapter 1, global marketing further entails engaging in significant business activities outside the home country. This means an exposure to different languages and cultures. In addition, global marketing involves the skillful application of specific concepts, insights, and strategies. Such endeavors may represent substantial change, especially in U.S. companies with a long tradition of a domestic focus. When the "go global" initiative is greeted with skepticism, the CEO must be a change agent who prepares and motivates employees.

Former Whirlpool CEO David Whitwam described his own efforts in this regard in the early 1990s after he had approved the acquisition of Royal Philips Electronics' European home appliance division:

> When we announced the Philips acquisition, I traveled to every location in the company, talked with our people, explained why it was so important. Most opposed the move. They thought, "We're spending a billion dollars on a company that has been losing money for 10 years? We're going to take resources we could use right here and ship them across the Atlantic because we think this is becoming a 'global' industry? What the hell does that mean?"[2]

Jack Welch encountered similar resistance at GE: "The lower you are in the organization, the less clear it is that globalization is great," he said. As Paolo Fresco, a former GE vice chairman, explained:

> To certain people, globalization is a threat without rewards. You look at the engineer for X-ray in Milwaukee and there is no upside on this one for him. He runs the risk of losing his job, he runs the risk of losing authority—he might find his boss is a guy who does not even know how to speak his language.[3]

In addition to "selling" their visions, top management at Whirlpool, GE, Nokia, Boeing, Tata Group, and other companies face the formidable task of building a cadre of globally oriented managers. Similar challenges face corporate leaders in all parts of the world. For example, Uichiro Niwa, former president of Japan's ITOCHU Corp., took steps to ensure that more of the trading company's $115 billion in annual transactions were conducted online.[4] He also radically changed the way he communicated with employees and began relying more on e-mail, a practice that until recently was virtually unknown in Japan. He also convened face-to-face meetings and conferences with employees to solicit suggestions and to hear complaints. This too represented a dramatic change in the way some Japanese companies were being led; traditionally, low-level employees were expected to accept the edicts of top management without questioning them.

Top Management Nationality

Many globally minded companies realize that the best person for a top management job or board position is not necessarily someone born in the home country. Speaking of U.S. companies, Christopher Bartlett of the Harvard Business School has noted:

> Companies are realizing that they have a portfolio of human resources worldwide, that their brightest technical person might come from Germany, or their best financial manager from England. They are starting to tap their worldwide human resources. And as they do, it will not be surprising to see non-Americans rise to the top.[5]

---

[2] William C. Taylor and Alan M. Webber, *Going Global: Four Entrepreneurs Map the New World Marketplace* (New York: Penguin Books USA, 1996), p. 12.

[3] Noel M. Tichy and Stratford Sherman, *Control Your Destiny or Someone Else Will* (New York: HarperBusiness, 1994), p. 227.

[4] Robert Guth, "Facing a Web Revolution, a Mighty Japanese Trader Reinvents Itself," *The Wall Street Journal* (March 27, 2000), p. B1.

[5] Kerry Peckter, "The Foreigners Are Coming," *International Business* (September 1993), p. 53.

The ability to speak foreign languages is one difference between managers born and raised in the United States and those born and raised elsewhere. For example, the U.S. Department of Education has reported that 200 million Chinese children are studying English; by contrast, only 24,000 American children are studying Chinese! Fluency in English is a prerequisite for managerial success in many global organizations, irrespective of the language of the headquarters country. For example, Yong Nam, CEO of LG, recently stipulated that English would be required throughout the company. He explained:

> English is essential. The speed of innovation that is required to compete in the world mandates that we must have seamless communication. We cannot depend on a small group of people who are holding the key to all communication throughout the world. That really impedes information sharing and decision making. I want everybody's wisdom instead of just a few.[6]

Sigismundus W. W. Lubsen, the former president and CEO of Quaker Chemical Corporation, is a good example of today's cosmopolitan executive. Born in the Netherlands and educated in Rotterdam as well as New York, Lubsen speaks Dutch, English, French, and German. He recalled, "I was lucky to be born in a place where if you drove for an hour in any direction, you were in a different country, speaking a different language. It made me very comfortable traveling in different cultures."[7] PepsiCo's Indra Nooyi is also bilingual (see Exhibit 17-2). Table 17-1 shows additional examples of corporate leaders who are not native to the headquarters country.

As noted in this chapter's The Cultural Context feature, Howard Stringer is the chief executive at Sony. Generally speaking, however, Japanese companies have been reluctant to place non-Japanese nationals in top positions. For years, only Sony, Mazda, and Mitsubishi had foreigners on their boards. In March 1999, however, after Renault SA bought a 36.8 percent stake in Nissan Motor, the French company installed a Brazilian, Carlos Ghosn, as president. An outsider, Ghosn was required to move aggressively to cut costs and make drastic changes in Nissan's structure. He also introduced two new words into Nissan's lexicon: *speed* and *commitment*. Ghosn's turnaround effort was so successful that his life story and exploits have been celebrated in *Big Comic Story*, a comic that is popular with Japan's salarymen.[8]

Exhibit 17-2 Indra Nooyi, chair and chief executive of PepsiCo, is faced with rising commodity prices and weak demand for carbonated soft drinks in the United States. Despite these threats, Nooyi believes the snack-and-beverage giant's current strategy is on track. In recent quarters, the strongest results have come from PepsiCo's fast-growing international division. Snack sales are particularly strong in Mexico and Russia; international sales volume for beverage brands is also increasing, particularly in the Middle East, Argentina, China, and Brazil.
Source: Manish Swarup/AP Images.

---

[6] Evan Ramstad, "CEO Broadens Vistas at LG," *The Wall Street Journal* (May 21, 2008), pp. B1, B2.

[7] Kerry Peckter, "The Foreigners Are Coming," *International Business* (September 1993), p. 58.

[8] Norihiko Shirouzu, "U-Turn: A Revival at Nissan Shows There's Hope for Ailing Japan Inc.," *The Wall Street Journal* (November 16, 2000), pp. A1, A10. See also Todd Zaun, "Look! Up in the Sky! It's Nissan's Chief Executive!" *The Wall Street Journal* (December 27, 2001), p. B1.

TABLE 17-1 Who's in Charge? Executives of 2013

Company (Headquarters Country)	Executive/Nationality	Position
3M (United States)	Inge G. Thulin (Sweden)	CEO
ABB (Switzerland)	Joe Hogan (United States)	CEO
Chrysler (United States)	Sergio Marchionne (Italy)	CEO
Dow Chemical (United States)	Andrew Liveris (Australia)	CEO
Eastman Kodak (United States)	Antonio Perez (Spain)	Chairman and CEO
Electrolux (Sweden)	Keith McLoughlin (United States)	CEO
Molton Brown (Great Britain)	Amy Nelson-Bennett (United States)	CEO
Monsanto (United States)	Hugh Grant (United Kingdom–Scotland)	Chairman, CEO, and President
Nippon Sheet Glass (Japan)	Craig Naylor (United States)	President and CEO
Nissan Motor (Japan)	Carlos Ghosn (Brazil)	Chairman, President, and CEO
PepsiCo (United States)	Indra K. Nooyi (India)	CEO
Reckitt Benckiser (Great Britain)	Rakesh Kapoor (India)	CEO
Sony (Japan)	Howard Stringer (United Kingdom–Wales)	Chairman
Wolters Kluwer NV (Netherlands)	Nancy McKinstry (United States)	Chairman and CEO

Leadership and Core Competence

Core competence, a concept developed by global strategy experts C. K. Prahalad and Gary Hamel, was introduced in Chapter 16. In the 1980s, many business executives were assessed on their ability to reorganize their corporations. In the 1990s, Prahalad and Hamel believed instead that executives would be better judged on their abilities to identify, nurture, and exploit the core competencies that make growth possible. Simply put, **core competence** is something that an organization can do better than its competitors. Prahalad and Hamel note that a core competence has three characteristics:

- It provides potential access to a wide variety of markets.
- It makes a significant contribution to perceived customer benefits.
- It is difficult for competitors to imitate.

Few companies are likely to build world leadership in more than five or six fundamental competencies. In the long run, an organization derives its global competitiveness from its ability to bring high-quality, low-cost products to market faster than its competitors. To do this, an organization must be viewed as a portfolio of competencies rather than as a portfolio of businesses. In some instances, a company has the technical resources to build competencies, but key executives lack the vision to do so. Sometimes the vision is present, but is rigidly focused on existing competencies even as market conditions are changing rapidly.

For example, in the early 2000s Jorma Ollila, then-chairman of Finland's Nokia, noted, "Design is a fundamental building block of the [Nokia] brand. It is central to our product creation and is a core competence integrated into the entire company."[9] The chairman was right—10 years ago. Design did help Nokia secure its position as the worldwide leader in handset sales. However, Apple's introduction of the game-changing iPhone in 2007 caught Nokia off guard. Nokia clung to its proprietary Symbian operating system even as smartphones running Google's Android operating system exploded in popularity. Nokia responded by launching new, mid-priced smartphone models; in addition, new CEO Steven Elop announced an alliance with Microsoft to develop new phones using Windows OS. Despite such changes, however, by early 2011 the company was issuing profit warnings.

---

[9] Neil McCartney, "Squaring Up to Usability at Nokia," *Financial Times—IT Review Telecom World* (October 13, 2003), p. 4.

TABLE 17-2 Responsibility for Global Marketing

Company (Headquarters Country)	Executive	Position/Title
Amway (United States)	Candace Matthews	Global Chief Marketing Officer
Apple (United States)	Greg Joswiak	Vice President of Worldwide iPod Product Marketing
Coca-Cola (United States)	Joseph Tripodi	Chief Marketing and Commercial Officer
Ford (United States)	Jim Farley	Executive Vice President–Global Marketing
Gap (United States)	Seth Farbman	Global Chief Marketing Officer
General Motors (United States)	Joel Ewanick	Global Chief Marketing Officer
Levi's (United States)	Rebecca Van Dyck	Global Chief Marketing Officer
L'Oréal (France)	Marc Menesguen	Global Chief Marketing Officer
McDonald's (United States)	Kevin Newell	Global Chief Brand Officer
Procter & Gamble (United States)	Marc Pritchard	Global Marketing Officer
SAP AG (Germany)	Martin Homlish	Global Chief Marketing Officer
Starbucks (United States)	Annie Young-Scrivner	Global Chief Marketing Officer
Warner Music (United States)	John Reid	Executive Vice President, Warner Music International
Yum! Brands (United States)	Muktesh Pant	Worldwide Chief Marketing Officer

Nokia's reversal of fortune at the hands of Apple and Google underscores the fact that today's executives must rethink the concept of the corporation if they wish to operationalize the concept of core competencies. In addition, the task of management must be viewed as building both competencies and the administrative means for assembling resources spread across multiple businesses.[10] Table 17-2 lists some of the individuals responsible for global marketing at select companies.

Organizing for Global Marketing

The goal in **organizing** for global marketing is to find a structure that enables the company to respond to relevant market environment differences while ensuring the diffusion of corporate knowledge and experience from national markets throughout the entire corporate system. The struggle between the value of centralized knowledge and coordination and the need for individualized response to the local situation creates a constant tension in the global marketing organization. A key issue in global organization is how to achieve a balance between autonomy and integration. Subsidiaries need autonomy to adapt to their local environments, but the business as a whole needs to be integrated in order to implement global strategy.[11]

When management at a domestic company decides to pursue international expansion, the issue of how to organize arises immediately. Who should be responsible for this expansion? Should product divisions operate independently or should an international division be established? Should individual country's subsidiaries report directly to the company president or should a special corporate officer be appointed to take full-time responsibility for international activities? After the decision of how to organize initial international operations has been reached, a growing company is faced with a number of reappraisal points during the development of its international business activities. Should a company abandon its international division, and, if so, what alternative structure should be adopted? Should it form an area or regional headquarters? What should be the relationship among staff executives at corporate, regional, and subsidiary offices? Specifically, how should the company organize the marketing function? To what extent

---

[10] C. K. Prahalad and Gary Hamel, "The Core Competence of the Corporation," *Harvard Business Review* 68, no. 3 (May–June 1990), pp. 79–86.
[11] George S. Yip, *Total Global Strategy* (Upper Saddle River, NJ: Prentice Hall, 1992), p. 179.

should regional and corporate marketing executives become involved in subsidiary marketing management?

Even companies with years of experience competing around the globe find it necessary to adjust their organizational designs in response to environmental changes. It is perhaps not surprising that, during his tenure at Quaker Chemical, Sigismundus Lubsen favored a global approach to organizational design over a domestic/international approach. He advised Peter A. Benoliel, his predecessor CEO, to have units in Holland, France, Italy, Spain, and England report to a regional vice president in Europe. "I saw that it would not be a big deal to put all of the European units under one common denominator," Lubsen recalled.[12]

As markets globalize and as Japan opens its own market to more competition from overseas, more Japanese companies are likely to break from traditional organization patterns. Many of the Japanese companies discussed in this text qualify as global or transnational companies because they serve world markets, source globally, or do both. Typically, however, knowledge is created at headquarters in Japan and then transferred to other country units. For example, Canon enjoys a strong reputation for world-class, innovative imaging products such as bubble-jet printers and laser printers. In the past two decades, Canon has shifted more control to subsidiaries, hired more non-Japanese staff and management personnel, and assimilated more innovations that were not developed in Japan. In 1996, for example, research and development (R&D) responsibility for software was shifted from Tokyo to the United States, responsibility for telecommunication products to France, and computer-language translation to Great Britain. As Canon President Fujio Mitarai explained, "The Tokyo headquarters cannot know everything. Its job should be to provide low-cost capital, to move top management between regions, and come up with investment initiatives. Beyond that, the local subsidiaries must assume total responsibility for management. We are not there yet, but we are moving step by step in that direction." Toru Takahashi, director of R&D, shared this view: "We used to think that we should keep research and development in Japan, but that has changed," he said. Despite these changes, Canon's board of directors includes only Japanese nationals.[13]

No single correct organizational structure exists for global marketing. Even within a particular industry, worldwide companies have developed different strategic and organizational responses to changes in their environments.[14] Still, it is possible to make some generalizations. Leading-edge global competitors share one key organizational design characteristic: Their corporate structure is flat and simple, rather than tall and complex. The message is clear: The world is complicated enough, so there is no need to add to the confusion with complex internal structuring. Simple structures increase the speed and clarity of communication and allow for the concentration of organizational energy and valuable resources on learning, rather than on controlling, monitoring, and reporting.[15] According to David Whitwam, former CEO of Whirlpool, "You must create an organization whose people are adept at exchanging ideas, processes, and systems across borders, people who are absolutely free of the 'not-invented-here' syndrome, people who are constantly working together to identify the best global opportunities and the biggest global problems facing the organization."[16]

A geographically dispersed company cannot limit its knowledge to product, function, and the home territory. Company personnel must acquire knowledge of the complex set of social, political, economic, and institutional arrangements that exist within each international market. Many companies start with ad hoc arrangements such as having all foreign subsidiaries report to a designated vice president or to the president. Eventually, such companies establish an international division to manage their geographically dispersed new businesses. It is clear, however, that the international division in the multiproduct company is an unstable organizational arrangement. As a company grows, this initial organizational structure frequently gives way to various alternative structures.

[12] Kerry Peckter, "The Foreigners Are Coming," *International Business* (September 1993), p. 58.

[13] William Dawkins, "Time to Pull Back the Screen," *Financial Times* (November 18, 1996), p. 12. See also Sumantra Ghoshal and Christopher A. Bartlett, *The Individualized Corporation* (New York: Harper Perennial, 1999), pp. 179–181.

[14] Christopher Bartlett and Sumantra Ghoshal, *Managing Across Borders: The Transnational Solution* (Boston: Harvard Business School Press, 1989), p. 3.

[15] Vladimir Pucik, "Globalization and Human Resource Management," in V. Pucik, N. Tichy, and C. Barnett (eds.), *Globalizing Management: Creating and Leading the Competitive Organization* (New York: J. Wiley & Sons, 1992), p. 70.

[16] Regina Fazio Maruca, "The Right Way to Go Global: An Interview with Whirlpool CEO David Whitwam," *Harvard Business Review* 72, no. 2 (March–April 1994), p. 137.

In the fast-changing, competitive global environment of the twenty-first century, corporations will have to find new, more creative ways to organize. New forms of flexibility, efficiency, and responsiveness are required to meet the demands of globalizing markets. The need to be cost-effective, to be customer driven, to deliver the best quality, and to deliver that quality quickly are some of today's global realities. Recently, several authors have described new organization designs that represent responses to today's competitive environment. These designs acknowledge the need to find more responsive and flexible structures, to flatten the organization, and to employ teams. There is also the recognition of the need to develop networks, to develop stronger relationships among participants, and to exploit technology. These designs reflect an evolution in approaches to organizational effectiveness. Early in the twentieth century, Frederick Taylor claimed that all managers had to see the world the same way. Then came the contingency theorists, who said that effective organizations design themselves to match their conditions. These two basic theories are reflected in today's popular management writings. As Henry Mintzberg observed, "To Michael Porter, effectiveness resides in strategy, while to Tom Peters it is the operations that count—executing any strategy with excellence."[17]

Kenichi Ohmae has written extensively on the implications of globalization on organization design. He recommends a type of "global superstructure" at the highest level that provides a view of the world as a single unit. The staff members at this level are responsible for ensuring that work is performed in the best location and coordinating efficient movement of information and products across borders. Below this level, Ohmae envisions organizational units assigned to regions "governed by economies of service and economies of scale in information." In Ohmae's view of the world, there are 30 regions with populations ranging from 5 million to 20 million people. For example, China would be viewed as several distinct regions; the same would be true of the United States. The first task of the CEO in such an organization is to become oriented to the single unit that is the borderless business sphere, much as an astronaut might view the earth from space. Then, zooming in, the CEO attempts to identify differences. As Ohmae explained:

A CEO has to look at the entire global economy and then put the company's resources where they will capture the biggest market share of the most attractive regions. Perhaps as you draw closer from outer space you see a region around the Pacific Northwest, near Puget Sound, that is vibrant and prosperous. Then you recognize the region stretching from New York to Boston that is still doing awful. You might see a booming concentration of computer companies and software publishers around Denver, and similar concentrations around Dallas-Fort Worth. Along the coast of California and in parts of New England you will see regions that are strong centers for health care and biotechnology. As a CEO, that's where you put your resources and shift your emphasis.[18]

Your authors believe that successful companies, the real global winners, must have both good strategies and good execution.

Patterns of International Organizational Development

Organizations vary in terms of the size and potential of targeted global markets and local management competence in different country markets. Conflicting pressures may arise from the need for product and technical knowledge; functional expertise in marketing, finance, and operations; and area and country knowledge. Because the constellation of pressures that shape organizations is never exactly the same, no two organizations pass through organizational stages in exactly the same way, nor do they arrive at precisely the same organizational pattern. Nevertheless, some general patterns hold.

A company engaging in limited export activities often has a small in-house export department as a separate functional area. Most domestically oriented companies undertake initial foreign expansion by means of foreign sales offices or subsidiaries that report directly to the company president or other designated company officer. This person carries out his or her responsibilities

---

[17] Henry Mintzberg, "The Effective Organization: Forces and Forms," *Sloan Management Review* 32, no. 2 (Winter 1991), pp. 54–55.

[18] William C. Taylor and Alan M. Webber, *Going Global: Four Entrepreneurs Map the New World Marketplace* (New York: Penguin, 1996), pp. 48–58.

THE CULTURAL CONTEXT

Can a New Leader Reinvent Sony, the "Apple of the 1980s," in the Twenty-First Century?

SYNC • THINK • LEARN

MyMarketingLab

Sony Corporation is a legend in the global consumer electronics industry. Its reputation for innovation and engineering has made it the envy of rivals. For decades, quality-conscious consumers paid premium prices for the company's Trinitron color televisions. In 1979, Sony created the personal stereo category with its iconic Walkman.

By the early 2000s, however, Sony's vaunted innovation and marketing machine was faltering. The company had not anticipated the rapid consumer acceptance of flat-panel, widescreen TV sets, and the Sony Walkman was eclipsed by Apple's iPod and iTunes Music Store. In 2005, tumbling stock prices resulted in the resignation of chairman and CEO Nobuyuki Idei. Sir Howard Stringer, a Welsh-born American who had been knighted in 2000, was named as Idei's replacement (see Exhibit 17-3).

One of Stringer's first priorities was to bridge the divide between Sony's media businesses, which included music, games, and motion pictures, and its hardware businesses. As Stringer himself declared, "We've got to get the relationship between content and devices seamlessly managed."

Management writers often use terms like *silos*, *stovepipes*, or *chimneys* to describe an organization in which autonomous business units operate with their own agendas and a minimum of horizontal interdependence. This was the situation at Sony, where the internal rivalries between different engineering units—the PC and Walkman groups, for example—were ingrained in the corporate culture and regarded as healthy. As Osamu Katayama, author of several books about Sony, notes, "Instead of working together, the managers of the different businesses fought to keep their independence."

Because Sony's consumer products businesses have historically accounted for a significant proportion of Sony's worldwide sales, breathing new life into the home entertainment and mobile products units was important. To do this, Sir Howard developed a restructuring plan: He cut 28,000 jobs, reduced the number of manufacturing sites, and eliminated some unprofitable products.

Cost cutting was only part of the story. Boosting revenues with new products was also crucial to Sony's recovery. Sir Howard was convinced that Sony's TV business would recover, thanks in part to the new Bravia line of HDTVs. As it turned out, however, the television business continued to lose money. The company also launched an e-book reader. Although Sir Howard had high hopes for the launch of the PlayStation 3 (PS3) game console in mid-2006, production issues delayed the introduction until November 2006. By 2011, Microsoft's Xbox 360 was the top-selling console, thanks in part to its new Kinect controller.

After seven years, it was clear that Sir Howard's turnaround effort was still a work in progress. He had successfully negotiated Sony's withdrawal from a smartphone partnership with Sweden's Ericsson. He had restructured the TV business and ended an expensive LCD screen partnership with Samsung. Sony's Blu-ray DVD format has gained widespread acceptance. However, Sony, Sharp, Panasonic, and other Japanese manufacturers are all experiencing declining sales of traditional electronics products. Meanwhile, Apple and Samsung have risen to prominence in the competitive landscape once dominated by the Japanese. In 2011, Sony's stock price fell 54 percent.

In 2012, Sir Howard relinquished the chief executive role to Kazuo Hirai. In 2013, Hirai presided over the launch of a new smartphone, the Xperia Z, that provides tangible evidence of a reduction in divisional rivalries. Sony's management is also being pressured by a key investor to spin off part of the highly profitable Sony Entertainment unit.

Sources: Daisuke Wakabayashi, "Japan's Electronics Under Siege," *The Wall Street Journal* (May 15, 2013), pp. B1, B4; Andrew Edgecliffe-Johnson and Jonathan Soble, "Channels to Choose," *Financial Times* (February 28, 2012), p. 9; Soble, "Sony Chief Looks to Secure Legacy," *Financial Times* (May 23, 2011); Yukari Iwatani Kane, "Sony Expects to Trim PS3 Losses, Plans More Games, Online Features," *The Wall Street Journal* (May 18, 2007), p. B4; Phred Dvorak, "Sony Aims to Cut Costs, Workers to Revive Its Electronics Business," *The Wall Street Journal* (September 23, 2005), p. A5; Dvorak, "Out of Tune: At Sony, Rivalries Were Encouraged; Then Came iPod," *The Wall Street Journal* (June 29, 2005), pp. A1, A6; Lorne Manly and Andrew Ross Sorkin, "Choice of Stringer Aims to Prevent Further Setbacks," *The New York Times* (March 8, 2005), pp. C1, C8.

Exhibit 17-3 In 2012, Kazuo Hirai was named President and CEO of Sony Corporation; Sir Howard Stringer is Chairman. The new boss faces many challenges, as Japan's once-vaunted electronics industry has fallen behind in the fast-changing tech world. For example, Sony lost its lead in flat-panel television technology to Samsung; meanwhile, the one-two punch of Apple's iPod/iTunes combination upstaged Sony's Walkman personal stereo brand. Part of Sony's problem was that different divisions—e.g., Home Entertainment and Sound; Mobile Products and Communication; and Entertainment—did not work well together.
Source: © Hajime Takashi/Jana Press/ZUMAPRESS.com/Alamy.

Exhibit 17-4 With more than 7 million U.S. subscribers, *Better Homes and Gardens* is the flagship publication of Des Moines, Iowa-based Meredith Corporation. Meredith licenses *BH&G* and other titles in numerous international markets, including Europe, the Middle East, and Asia. At left is the Chinese edition of the magazine, published under license by SEEC Media.

Source: November 2012 *Better Homes and Gardens*® Magazine China edition. Photography by Edmund Barr. Photo courtesy of Meredith Corporation ©2012. All rights reserved.

without assistance from a headquarters staff group. Many other design options are available to companies that seek to extend their reach internationally without creating separate divisions. For example, Des Moines, Iowa-based Meredith Corporation participates in international markets by means of licensing agreements developed and managed by the Corporate Development group, and further supported by various operating departments within the company (Exhibit 17-4).

INTERNATIONAL DIVISION STRUCTURE As a company's international business grows, the complexity of coordinating and directing this activity extends beyond the scope of a single person. Pressure is created to assemble a staff that will have responsibility for coordination and direction of the growing international activities of the organization. Eventually, this process leads to the creation of the international division, as illustrated in Figure 17-1. Best Buy, Hershey, Levi Strauss, Under Armour, Walmart, and Walt Disney are some examples of companies whose structures include international divisions.

FIGURE 17-1

Functional Corporate Structure, Domestic Corporate Staff Orientation, International Division

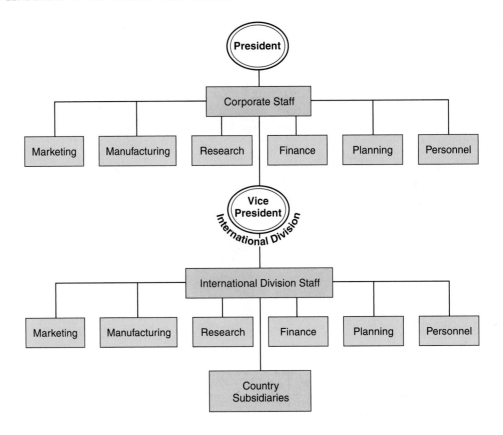

When Hershey announced the creation of its international division in 2005, J. P. Bilbrey, the division's senior vice president, noted that Hershey would no longer utilize the extension strategy of exporting its chocolate products from the United States. Instead, the company would tailor products to local markets and also manufacture locally. As Bilbrey explained, "We're changing our business model in Asia. The product was not locally relevant and it also got there at an unattractive cost."[19] Currently, international sales make up only 10 percent of Hershey's sales; the company's strategic goal is to boost that figure to 25 percent by 2017. China is the world's fastest-growing candy market, so it is no surprise that Hersey is ramping up efforts to penetrate the Middle Kingdom. Until recently, Hershey had only about a 2.2 percent share of China's chocolate market; by contrast, Mars commands 43 percent with its M&M's and Dove brands. In 2013, Hershey rolled out a new line of condensed-milk candies specifically targeting China's premium candy segment. Lancaster (as in "Lancaster, Pennsylvania," the company's hometown) is the English-language name; in Chinese, the brand is Yo-man. Hershey has opened its second-largest R&D facility, Asia Innovation Center, in Shanghai.[20]

Four factors contribute to the establishment of an international division. First, top management's commitment to global operations has increased enough to justify an organizational unit headed by a senior manager. Second, the complexity of international operations requires a single organizational unit whose management has sufficient authority to make its own determinations on important issues such as which market-entry strategy to employ. Third, an international division is frequently formed when the firm has recognized the need for internal specialists to deal with the special demands of global operations. A fourth contributing factor is management's recognition of the importance of strategically scanning the global horizon for opportunities and aligning them with company resources rather than simply responding on an ad hoc basis to opportunities as they arise.

---

[19] Jeremy Grant, "Hershey Chews Over Growth Strategy," *Financial Times* (December 14, 2005), p. 23.
[20] Colum Murphy and Laurie Burkitt, "Hershey Launches New Brand in China," *The Wall Street Journal* (May 21, 2013), p. B8.

REGIONAL MANAGEMENT CENTERS When business is conducted in a single region that is characterized by similarities in economic, social, geographical, and political conditions, there is both justification and need for a management center. Thus, another stage of organizational evolution is the emergence of an area or regional headquarters as a management layer between the country organization and the international division headquarters. The increasing importance of the European Union (EU) as a regional market has prompted a number of companies to change their organizational structures by setting up regional headquarters there. In the mid-1990s, for example, Quaker Oats established its European headquarters in Brussels; Electrolux, the Swedish home appliance company, has also regionalized its European operations.[21] In 2012, Procter & Gamble (P&G) began to shift its global skin, cosmetics, and personal-care unit from Cincinnati to Singapore; Asia-Pacific countries account for about half of the $100 billion global skin-care market.[22] A regional center typically coordinates decisions on pricing, sourcing, and other matters. Executives at the regional center also participate in the planning and control of each country's operations with an eye toward applying company knowledge on a regional basis and optimally utilizing corporate resources on a regional basis. This organizational design is illustrated in Figure 17-2.

Regional management can offer a company several advantages. First, many regional managers agree that an on-the-scene regional management unit makes sense where there is a real need for coordinated, pan-regional decision making. Coordinated regional planning and control are becoming necessary as the national subsidiary continues to lose its relevance as an independent operating unit. Regional management can probably achieve the best balance of geographical,

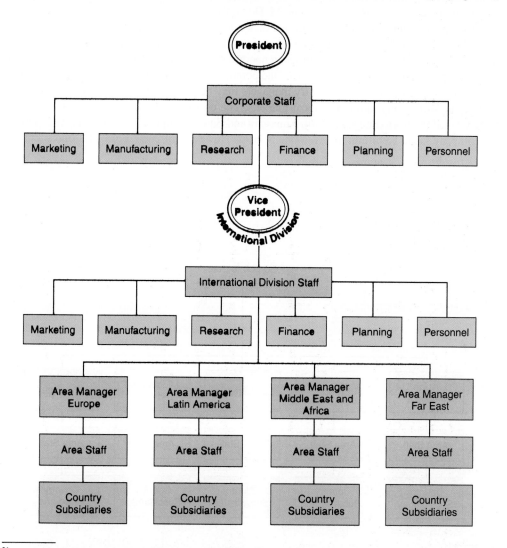

FIGURE 17-2

Functional Corporate Structure, Domestic Corporate Staff Orientation, International Division, Area Divisions

[21] "…And Other Ways to Peel the Onion," *The Economist* (January 7, 1995), pp. 52–53.
[22] Emily Glazer, "P&G Unit Bids Goodbye to Cincinnati, Hello to Asia," *The Wall Street Journal* (May 11, 2012), p. B1.

product, and functional considerations required to implement corporate objectives effectively. By shifting operations and decision making to the region, the company is better able to maintain an insider advantage.[23]

However, a major disadvantage of a regional center is its cost. The cost of a two-person office could exceed $600,000 per year. The scale of regional management must be in line with the scale of operations in a region. A regional headquarters is inappropriate if the size of the operations it manages is inadequate to cover the costs of the additional layer of management. The basic issue with regard to the regional headquarters is "Does it contribute enough to organizational effectiveness to justify its cost and the complexity of another layer of management?"

GEOGRAPHICAL AND PRODUCT DIVISION STRUCTURES As a company becomes more global, management frequently faces the dilemma of whether to organize by geography or by product lines. The geographically organized structure involves the assignment of operational responsibility for geographic areas of the world to line managers. The corporate headquarters retains responsibility for worldwide planning and control, and each area of the world—including the "home" or base market—is organizationally equal. For the company with French origins, for example, France is simply another geographic market under this organizational arrangement. This structure is most common in companies with closely related product lines that are sold in similar end-use markets around the world. For example, the major international oil companies utilize the geographical structure, which is illustrated in Figure 17-3. McDonald's organizational design integrates the international division and geographical structures. McDonald's U.S. has five geographical operating divisions, and McDonald's International has four.

When an organization assigns regional or worldwide product responsibility to its product divisions, manufacturing standardization can result in significant economies. For example, Whirlpool recently reorganized its European operations, switching from a geographic or country orientation to one based on product lines. One potential disadvantage of the product approach is that local input from individual country managers may be ignored, with the result that products will not be sufficiently tailored to local markets. The essence of the Ford 2000 reorganization initiated in 1995 was to integrate North American and European operations. Over a 3-year period, the company saved $5 billion in development costs. However, by 2000, Ford's European market

FIGURE 17-3

Geographic Corporate Structure, World Corporate Staff Orientation, Area Divisions Worldwide

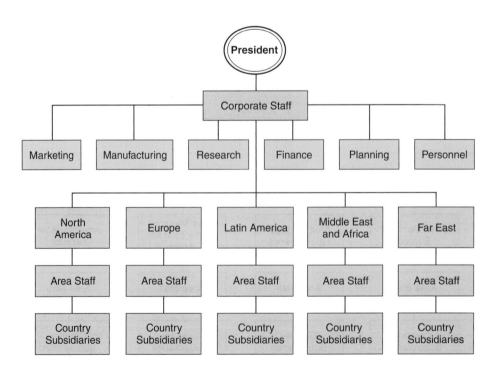

[23] Allen J. Morrison, David A. Ricks, and Kendall Roth, "Globalization Versus Regionalization: Which Way for the Multinational?" *Organizational Dynamics* (Winter 1991), pp. 17–29.

share had slipped nearly 5 percent. In a shift back toward the geographic model, then-CEO Jacques Nasser returned to regional executives some of the authority they had lost.[24]

The challenges associated with devising the structure that is best suited to improving global sales can be seen in Procter & Gamble's ambitious Organization 2005 plan. Initiated by then-CEO Durk Jager in 1999, this reorganization entailed replacing separate country organizations with five global business units for key product categories such as paper products and feminine hygiene. A number of executives were reassigned; in Europe alone, 1,000 staff members were transferred to Geneva. Many managers, upset about the transfers and news that P&G intended to cut 15,000 jobs worldwide, quit the company; the resulting upheaval cost Jager his job. To appease middle managers, new CEO A. G. Lafley restored some of the company's previous geographic focus.[25]

THE MATRIX DESIGN In the fully developed large-scale global company, product or business, function, area, and customer know-how are simultaneously focused on the organization's worldwide marketing objectives. This type of total competence is a **matrix organization**. Management's task in the matrix organization is to achieve an organizational balance that brings together different perspectives and skills to accomplish the organization's objectives. In 1998, both Gillette and Ericsson announced plans to reorganize into matrix organizations. Ericsson's matrix is focused on three customer segments: network operators, private consumers, and commercial enterprises.[27] Gillette's matrix structure separates product-line management from geographical sales and marketing responsibility.[28] Likewise, Boeing has reorganized its commercial transport design and manufacturing engineers into a matrix organization built around five platform or aircraft model–specific groups. Previously, Boeing was organized along functional lines; the new design was expected to lower costs and quicken updates and problem solving. It was also expected to unite essential design, engineering, and manufacturing processes between Boeing's commercial transport factories and component plants, enhancing product consistency.[29] Why are executives at these and other companies implementing matrix designs? The matrix form of organization is well suited to global companies because it can be used to establish a multiple-command structure that gives equal emphasis to functional and geographical departments.

Professor John Hunt of the London Business School has suggested four considerations regarding the matrix organizational design. First, the matrix is appropriate when the market is demanding and dynamic. Second, employees must accept higher levels of ambiguity and understand that policy manuals cannot cover every eventuality. Third, in country markets where the command-and-control model persists, it is best to overlay matrices on only small portions of the workforce. Finally, management must be able to clearly state what each axis of the matrix can and cannot do. However, this must be accomplished without creating a bureaucracy.[30]

Having established that the matrix is appropriate, management can expect the matrix to integrate four basic competencies on a worldwide basis:

1. *Geographic knowledge.* An understanding of the basic economic, social, cultural, political, and governmental market and competitive dimensions of a country is essential. The country subsidiary is the major structural device employed today to enable the corporation to acquire geographical knowledge.
2. *Product knowledge and know-how.* Product managers with a worldwide responsibility can achieve this level of competence on a global basis. Another way of achieving global product competence is simply to duplicate product management organizations in domestic and international divisions, achieving high competence in both organizational units.

> "GE is managing its worldwide organization as a network, not a centralized hub with foreign appendages."[26]
>
> —Christopher A. Bartlett

---

[24] Joann S. Lublin, "Division Problem: Place vs. Product: It's Tough to Choose a Management Model," *The Wall Street Journal* (June 27, 2001), pp. A1, A4.

[25] Emily Nelson, "Rallying the Troops at P&G: New CEO Lafley Aims to End Upheaval by Revamping Program of Globalization," *The Wall Street Journal* (August 31, 2000), pp. B1, B4.

[26] Claudia Deutsch, "At Home in the World," *The New York Times* (February 14, 2008), p. C1.

[27] "Ericsson to Simplify Business Structure," *Financial Times* (September 29, 1998), p. 21.

[28] Mark Maremont, "Gillette to Shut 14 of Its Plants, Lay Off 4,700," *The Wall Street Journal* (September 29, 1998), pp. A3, A15.

[29] Paul Proctor, "Boeing Shifts to 'Platform Teams,'" *Aviation Week & Space Technology* (May 17, 1999), pp. 63–64.

[30] John W. Hunt, "Is Matrix Management a Recipe for Chaos?" *Financial Times* (January 12, 1998), p. 10.

3. *Functional competence in such fields as finance, production, and, especially, marketing.* Corporate functional staff with worldwide responsibility contributes toward the development of functional competence on a global basis. In some companies, the corporate functional manager, who is responsible for the development of his or her functional activity on a global basis, reviews the appointment of country subsidiary functional managers.

4. *A knowledge of the customer or industry and its needs.* Certain large and extremely sophisticated global companies have staff with the responsibility for serving industries on a global basis to assist the line managers in the country organizations in their efforts to penetrate specific customer markets.

Under this arrangement, instead of designating national organizations or product divisions as profit centers, both are responsible for profitability—the national organization for country profits and the product divisions for national and worldwide product profitability. Figure 17-4 illustrates the matrix organization. This organization chart starts with a bottom section that represents a single-country responsibility level, moves to representing the area or international level, and finally moves to representing global responsibility from the product divisions to the corporate staff, to the chief executive at the top of the structure.

At Whirlpool, North American operations are organized in matrix form. Former CEO David Whitwam expected to extend this structure into Europe and other regional markets. Whirlpool

FIGURE 17-4

The Matrix Structure

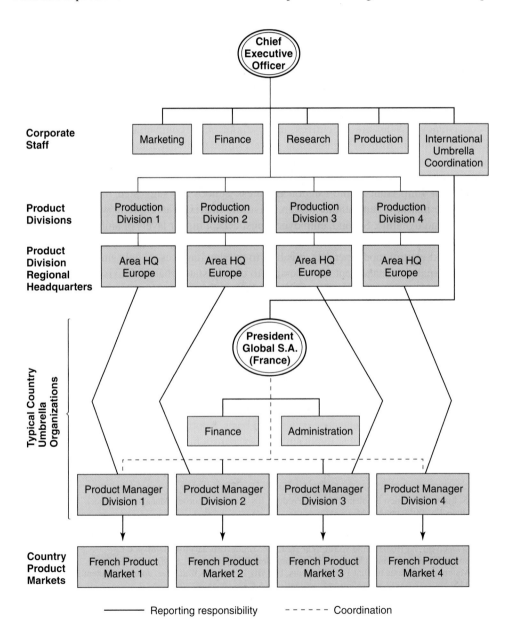

managers from traditional functions such as operations, marketing, and finance also work in teams devoted to specific products, such as dishwashers or ovens. To encourage interdependence and integration, the cross-functional teams are headed by "brand czars," such as the brand chief for Whirlpool or Kenmore. As Whitwam explained, "The Whirlpool-brand czar still worries about the Whirlpool name. But he also worries about all the refrigerator brands that we make because he heads that product team. It takes a different mind-set."[31]

The key to successful matrix management is ensuring that managers are able to resolve conflicts and achieve integration of organization programs and plans. The mere adoption of a matrix design or structure does not create a matrix organization. The matrix organization requires fundamental changes in management behavior, organizational culture, and technical systems. In a matrix, influence is based on technical competence and interpersonal sensitivity, not on formal authority. In a matrix culture, managers recognize the absolute need to resolve issues and choices at the lowest possible level and do not rely on higher authority.

Some companies are moving away from the matrix in response to changing competitive conditions. Heineken and EMI are two examples; ABB is another.[32] For nearly a decade, ABB was a matrix organized along regional lines. Local business units—factories that make motors or power generators, for example—reported both to a country manager and to a business area manager who set strategy for the whole world. This structure allowed ABB to execute global strategies while still thriving in local markets. However, in 1998, new chairman Göran Lindahl dissolved the matrix. As the chairman explained in a press release, "This is an aggressive move aimed at greater speed and efficiency by further focusing and flattening the organization. This step is possible now thanks to our strong, decentralized presence in all local and global markets around the world."

In January 2001, Lindahl stepped down and his successor, Jorgen Centerman, revamped the organizational structure yet again. The new design was intended to improve the focus on industries and large corporate customers; Centerman wanted to ensure that all of ABB's products were designed to the same systems standards. However, in 2002, with the chief executive under pressure to sell assets, ABB's board replaced Centerman with Jürgen Dorman. Dorman stepped down in 2005 and was succeeded by Fred Kindle. Although ABB returned to profitability under his leadership, Kindle left after 3 years. The official reason: irreconcilable differences about leading the company. Michel Demaré, ABB's chief financial officer, was named interim CEO. Then, in fall 2008, Joe Hogan was selected as ABB's new CEO. Hogan, an American, was a 23-year veteran of GE whose most recent assignment had been running GE Healthcare. ABB's board was impressed by Hogan's performance at the U.S. industrial giant: During his 8 years at GE Healthcare, the unit's sales more than doubled, from $7 billion to $18 billion. These results were due, in part, to several major acquisitions engineered by Hogan.[33]

In the twenty-first century, an important task of top management is to eliminate a one-dimensional approach to decisions and to encourage the development of multiple management perspectives and an organization that will sense and respond to a complex and fast-changing world. The challenges facing Sony, discussed earlier, are a case in point. By thinking in terms of changing behavior rather than changing structural design, management can free itself from the limitations of the structural chart and focus instead on achieving the best possible results with the available resources.

Lean Production: Organizing The Japanese Way

In the automobile industry, a comparison of early craft production processes, mass production, and modern "lean" production provides an interesting case study of the effectiveness of new organizational structures in the twenty-first century.[34] Dramatic productivity differences existed

[31] William C. Taylor and Alan M. Webber, *Going Global: Four Entrepreneurs Map the New World Marketplace* (New York: Penguin USA, 1996), p. 25.

[32] Andrew Edgecliffe-Johnson, "Case Study: EMI," *Financial Times* (September 23, 2011), p. 4.

[33] Haig Simonian, "The GE Man Who Generated a Buzz," *Financial Times* (June 8, 2009).

[34] This section is adapted from the following sources: James P. Womack, Daniel T. Jones, and Daniel Roos, *The Machine That Changed the World: The Story of Lean Production* (New York: HarperCollins, 1990); Ranganath Nayak and John M. Ketteringham, *Breakthroughs!* (San Diego, CA: Pfeiffer, 1994), Chapter 9; and Michael Williams, "Back to the Past: Some Plants Tear Out Long Assembly Lines, Switch to Craft Work," *The Wall Street Journal* (October 24, 1994), pp. A1, A4.

between craft and mass producers in the first part of the twentieth century. The mass producers—most notably Ford Motor Company—gained their substantial advantage by changing their value chains so that each worker was able to do far more work each day than the craft producers. The innovation that made this possible was the moving assembly line, which required the originators to conceptualize the production process in a totally new way. The assembly line also required a new approach to organizing people, production machinery, and supplies. By rearranging their value chain activities, the mass producers were able to achieve reductions in effort ranging from 62 to 88 percent over the craft producers. These productivity improvements provided an obvious competitive advantage.

The advantage of the mass producers lasted until the Japanese auto companies further revised the value chain and created **lean production**, thereby gaining for themselves the kinds of dramatic competitive advantages that mass producers had previously gained over craft producers. For example, the Toyota Production System (TPS), as the Japanese company's manufacturing methods are known, achieves efficiencies of about 50 percent over typical mass production systems. Even with the reduced assembly time, the lean producer's vehicles have significantly fewer defects than mass-produced vehicles. The lean producer is also using about 40 percent less factory space and maintaining only a fraction of the inventory stored by the mass producer. Again, the competitive advantages are obvious. Whether the strategy is based on differentiation or low cost, the lean producer has the advantage.

To achieve these gains at Toyota, production gurus Taiichi Ohno and Shigeo Shingo challenged several assumptions traditionally associated with automobile manufacturing. First, they made changes to operations within the auto company itself, such as reducing setup times for machinery. The changes also applied to operations within supplier firms and the interfaces between Toyota and its suppliers and to the interfaces with distributors and dealers. Ohno and Shingo's innovations have been widely embraced in the industry; as a result, individual producer's value chains have been modified, and interfaces between producers and suppliers have been optimized to create more effective and efficient value systems.

Assembler Value Chains

Employee ability is emphasized in a lean production environment. Before being hired, people seeking jobs with Toyota participate in the Day of Work, a 12-hour assessment test to determine who has the right mix of physical dexterity, team attitude, and problem-solving ability. Once hired, workers receive considerable training to enable them to perform any job in their section of the assembly line or area of the plant, and they are assigned to teams in which all members must be able to perform the functions of all other team members. Workers are also empowered to make suggestions and to take actions aimed at improving quality and productivity. Quality control is achieved through *kaizen*, a devotion to continuous improvement that ensures that every flaw is isolated, examined in detail to determine the ultimate cause, and then corrected (see Exhibit 17-5).

Mechanization, and particularly flexible mechanization, is a hallmark of lean production. For example, a single assembly line in Georgetown, Kentucky, that produces Toyota's Camry sedan also produces the Sienna minivan. The Sienna and Camry share the same basic chassis and 50 percent of their parts. Of the 300 different stations on the line, only 26 stations require different parts to assemble minivans. Similarly, Honda has invested hundreds of millions of dollars to introduce flexible production technology in its U.S. plants. In an era of volatile gasoline prices and fluctuating exchange rates, production flexibility becomes a source of competitive advantage. For example, when the weak dollar put pressure on margins for vehicles imported into the United States, Honda shifted production of CR-V crossovers from the United Kingdom to a plant in Ohio. Within a matter of minutes, Honda can switch from producing Civic compacts to CR-V crossovers as demand or other market conditions dictate.[35]

In contrast to the lean producers, U.S. mass producers typically maintain operations with greater direct labor content, less mechanization, and much less flexible mechanization. They also divide their employees into a large number of discrete specialties with no overlap. Employee initiative and teamwork are not encouraged. In addition, quality control is expressed as an acceptable number of defects per vehicle.

―――――――――
[35] Kate Linebaugh, "Honda's Flexible Plants Provide Edge," *The Wall Street Journal* (September 23, 2008), p. B1.

Exhibit 17-5 The Toyota Production System (TPS) is based on two concepts. First is *jidoka*, which involves visualizing potential problems. Jidoka also means that quality is built into the company's vehicles during the manufacturing process. "Just-in-time," the second pillar of the TPS, means that Toyota only produces what is needed, when it is needed, in the amount that is needed. Toyota's training programs ensure that all employees understand the Toyota Way. Future factory workers attend the Toyota Technical Skills Academy in Toyota City, Japan. Executive training takes place at the Toyota Institute.
Source: Ko Sasaki/Redux Pictures.

Even when the comparisons are based on industry averages, the Japanese lean producers continue to enjoy substantial productivity and quality advantages. Again, these advantages put the lean producers in a better position to exploit low-cost or differentiation strategies. They are getting better productivity out of their workers and machines, and they are making better use of their factory floor space. The relatively small size of the repair area reflects the higher quality of their products. A high number of "suggestions per employee" provides some insight into why lean producers outperform mass producers. First, they invest a great deal more in the training of their workers. They also rotate all workers through all jobs for which their teams are responsible. Finally, all workers are encouraged to make suggestions, and management acts on those suggestions. These changes to the value chain translate into major improvements in the value of the lean producers' products.

It should come as no surprise that many of the world's automakers are studying lean production methods and introducing them in both existing and new plants throughout the world. In 1999, for example, General Motors (GM) announced plans to spend nearly $500 million to overhaul its Adam Opel plant in Germany. Pressure for change came from several sources, including increasingly intense rivalry in Europe's car market, worldwide overcapacity, and a realization that price transparency in the euro zone will exert downward pressure on prices. GM's goal was to transform the plant into a state-of-the-art lean production facility with a 40 percent workforce reduction. As GM Europe President Michael J. Burns said at the time, "Pricing is more difficult today....You have to work on product costs, structural costs...everything."[36]

Downstream Value Chains

The differences between lean producers and U.S. mass producers in the way they deal with their respective dealers, distributors, and customers are as dramatic as the differences in the way they deal with their suppliers. U.S. mass producers follow the basic industry model and maintain an "arm's-length" relationship with dealers that is often characterized by a lack of cooperation and even open hostility. There is often no sharing of information because there is no incentive to do so. The manufacturer is often trying to force on the dealer models the dealer knows will not sell. The dealer, in turn, is often trying to pressure the customer into buying models he or she does not want. All parties are trying to keep from the others information about what they really want. This does little to ensure that the industry is responsive to market needs.

---

[36] Joseph B. White, "GM Plans to Invest $445 Million, Cut Staff," *The Wall Street Journal* (May 27, 1999), p. A23.

→ EMERGING MARKETS BRIEFING BOOK

Western Business Executives Scold China

MyMarketingLab   SYNC • THINK • LEARN

What happened when the chief executives of some of the world's biggest global companies got a chance to meet face-to-face with China's Premier Wen Jiabao? They gave him an earful, that's what. The CEOs, Jürgen Hambrecht of BASF and Peter Loescher of Siemens, were accompanying Germany chancellor Angela Merkel on a four-state visit. The criticisms reflected broader concerns among Western business and government leaders about China's business environment.

One issue is bidding procedures that appear to discriminate against foreign companies. For example, government procurement practices in China often favor local producers. Market access is another issue; CEO Hambrecht expressed frustration that foreign companies are forced to transfer technology to their Chinese partners in exchange for the opportunity to do business. Hambrecht said, "That does not exactly correspond to our views of a partnership."

GE's Jeff Immelt is another well-known CEO who has directed criticism at Beijing. At a private meeting in Rome with Italian business leaders, Immelt expressed his concern about China's increasingly protectionist tendencies. He reportedly told the group, "I am not sure that, in the end, they want any of us to win, or any of us to be successful." While acknowledging China's strategic importance to GE, Immelt also made it clear that the Middle East, Africa, and Latin America are emerging as key world markets. "The[y] don't all want to be colonized by the Chinese. They want to develop themselves," he said.

Manufacturing executives are not the only ones speaking out about China. Google CEO Eric Schmidt has also made his voice heard. Addressing the Council on Foreign Relations in New York recently, Schmidt expressed concern about Beijing's ongoing efforts to censor the Internet. For much of 2010, Google and the Chinese government clashed over issues concerning filtering content accessed via search engines. Beijing is also struggling to keep control over new media. In one instance, a Chinese woman was sent to a labor camp for retweeting a message that the authorities disapproved of. Using fewer than 140 characters, Dick Costolo, CEO of Twitter, tweeted his objections to the case. He wrote, "Dear Chinese Government, year-long detentions for sending a sarcastic tweet are neither the way forward nor the future of your great people."

Sources: Mark Millan, "Twitter CEO Chides China," *CNN Tech* (November 19, 2010); Qichen Zhang, "Google CEO Criticizes Chinese Internet Censorship," *OpenNet Initiative* (November 11, 2010); Jamil Anderlini, "German Industrialists Attack China," *Financial Times* (July 18, 2010); Guy Dinmore and Geoff Dyer, "Immelt Hits Out at China and Obama," *Financial Times* (July 1, 2010).

The problem starts with the market research, which is often in error. It is compounded by lack of feedback from dealers regarding real customer desires. It continues to worsen when the product-planning divisions make changes to the models without consulting the marketing divisions or the dealers. This process invariably results in production of models that are unpopular and almost impossible to sell. The manufacturer then uses incentives and other schemes, such as making a dealer accept one unpopular model for every five hot-selling models it orders, to persuade the dealers to accept the unpopular models. The dealer then has the problem of persuading customers to buy the unpopular models.

Within the mass assembler's value chain, the linkage between the marketing elements and the product planners is broken. The external linkage between the sales divisions and the dealers is also broken. The production process portion of the value chain is broken as well in that it relies on the production of thousands of models that won't sell and that will then sit on dealer lots, at enormous cost, while the dealer works to find customers. Within the dealerships, there are even more problems. The relationship between the salesperson and the customer is based on sparring and trying to outsmart each other on price. When the salesperson gets the upper hand, the customer gets stung. It is very much like the relationship between the dealer and the manufacturer. Each is withholding information from the other in the hope of outsmarting the other. Too often, salespeople do not investigate customers' real needs and try to find the best product to satisfy those needs. Rather, they provide only as much information as is needed to close the deal. Once the deal is closed, the salesperson has virtually no further contact with the customer. No attempt is made to optimize the linkage between dealers and manufacturers or the linkage between dealers and customers.

The contrast with the lean producer is again striking. In Japan, the dealer's employees are true product specialists. They know their products and deal with all aspects of the products, including financing, service, maintenance, insurance, registration and inspection, and delivery. A customer deals with one person in the dealership, and that person takes care of everything from the initial contact through eventual trade-in and replacement and all the problems in between. Further, dealer representatives are included on the manufacturer's product development teams and provide continuous input regarding customer desires. The linkages between dealers, marketing divisions, and product development teams are totally optimized.

The stress caused by large inventories of unsold cars is also absent. A car is not built until there is a customer order for it. Each dealer has only a stock of models for the customer to view. Once the customer has decided on the car he or she wants, the order is sent to the factory and in a matter of a couple of weeks, the salesperson delivers the car to the customer's house.

Once a Japanese dealership gets a customer, it is absolutely determined to hang on to that customer for life. It is also determined to acquire all of that customer's family members as customers. A joke among the Japanese says that the only way to escape the salesperson who sold a person a car is to leave the country. Japanese dealers maintain extensive databases on actual and potential customers. These databases deal with demographic data and preference data. Customers are encouraged to help keep the information in the database current, and they do so. This elaborate store of data becomes an integral part of the market research effort and helps ensure that products match customer desires. The fact that there are no inventories of unpopular models because every car is custom ordered for each customer and the fact that the dealer has elaborate data on the needs and desires of its customers change the whole nature of the interaction between the customer and the dealer. The customer literally builds the car she or he wants and can afford. There is no need for the salesperson and the customer to try to outsmart each other.

The differences between U.S. mass producers and Japanese lean producers reflect their fundamental differences in business objectives. The U.S. producers focus on short-term income and return on investment. Today's sale is a discrete event that is not connected to upstream activities in the value chain and has no value in tomorrow's activities. Efforts are made to reduce the cost of the sales activities. In contrast, the Japanese see the process in terms of the long-term perspective. There are two major goals of the sales process. The first is to maximize the income stream from each customer over time. The second is to use the linkage with the production processes to reduce production and inventory costs and to maximize quality and therefore differentiation.

Ethics, Corporate Social Responsibility, and Social Responsiveness in the Globalization Era

Today's chief executive must be a proactive steward of the reputation of the company he or she is leading. This entails, in part, understanding and responding to the concerns and interests of a variety of stakeholders. A **stakeholder** is any group or individual that is affected by, or takes an interest in, the policies and practices adopted by an organization (see Exhibit 17-6).[37] Top management, employees, customers, persons or institutions that own the company's stock, and suppliers constitute a company's *primary stakeholders*. *Secondary stakeholders* include the media, the general business community, local community groups, and **nongovernmental organizations (NGOs)**. The latter focus on human rights, political justice, and environmental issues; examples include Global Exchange, Greenpeace, Oxfam, and others. **Stakeholder analysis** is the process of formulating a "win-win" outcome for all stakeholders.[38]

The leaders of global companies must practice **corporate social responsibility (CSR)**, which can be defined as a company's obligation to pursue goals and policies that are in society's best interests. A key issue becomes: Whose interests come first? How does a company find the balance between competing points of view? Peter Brabeck, chairman and CEO of Nestlé, summarizes the situation this way:

> There are tensions in a multinational company between what I call the financial fundamentalists, who just want to stress short-term profits, and the ethical fundamentalists, who don't think we should make profits at all....As stewards of large amounts of capital, both

---

[37] The English term *stakeholder* is sometimes hard to convey in different languages, especially in developing countries. See Neil King, Jr., and Jason Dean, "Untranslatable Word in U.S. Aide's Speech Leaves Beijing Baffled," *The Wall Street Journal* (December 7, 2005), pp. A1, A8.

[38] Archie B. Carroll and Ann K. Buchholtz, *Business and Society: Ethics and Stakeholder Management*, 5th ed. (Cincinnati: South-Western, 2003).

Exhibit 17-6 U2 singer Bono and Bobby Shriver are cofounders of Product (RED)™, a partnership with several well-known global companies to raise money to fight disease in Africa. Apple, American Express, Emporio Armani, Converse, Gap, and Motorola are all offering (RED)-themed merchandise and services to their customers. The partners are demonstrating their commitment to corporate social responsibility by pledging to donate a percentage of the profits generated to the Global Fund to Fight AIDS, Tuberculosis, and Malaria. To launch its (RED) line, Gap's advertising campaign used celebrities and one-word headlines consisting of verbs that end in "-red." For example, one ad featured the word "INSPI(RED)" superimposed over a photo of director Steven Spielberg wearing a Product (RED) leather jacket.

Source: Tony Cenicola/Redux Pictures.

monetary and human, the unique role of business—and what no other institution can duplicate—is to create social, economic and environmental value for the countries where we operate. But this most challenging goal—of creating value for society—can only be successful in the long run if it has a relationship to creating shareholder value.[39]

Organizations can demonstrate their commitment to CSR in a variety of ways, including cause-marketing efforts or a commitment to sustainability (see Exhibit 17-7). In some companies, such policies play an important internal role with primary stakeholders, especially employees drawn from the ranks of Generation Y. As Kevin Havelock, president of Unilever U.S., has noted:

We are seeing, particularly with the new generation of young businesspeople and young marketers, that they are only attracted to companies that fit with their own value set. And the value set of the new generation is one that says this company must take a positive and global view on the global environment.…The ethical positions we take on brands like Dove, the positions we take on not using [fashion] models of size zero across any of our brands, the positions we take in terms of adding back to communities…these all underpin an attractive proposition for marketers.[40]

Similarly, Starbucks founder and CEO Howard Schultz's enlightened human resources policies have played a key part in the company's success. Partners, as the company's employees are known, who work 20 hours or more per week are offered health benefits; partners can also take advantage of an employee stock option plan known as Bean Stock. As noted on the company's Web site:

Consumers are demanding more than "'product" from their favorite brands. Employees are choosing to work for companies with strong values. Shareholders are more inclined to invest in businesses with outstanding corporate reputations. Quite simply, being socially responsible is not only the right thing to do; it can distinguish a company from its industry peers.

[39] Haig Simonian, "Nestlé Charts Low-Income Territory," *Financial Times* (July 14, 2006), p. 15.
[40] Jack Neff, "Unilever, P&G War Over Which Is Most Ethical," *Advertising Age* (March 3, 2008), p. 67.

Exhibit 17-7 The Subaru nameplate is synonymous with the company's Symmetrical All-Wheel Drive and Partial Zero Emissions Vehicle (PZEV) engineering. The company's U.S. assembly plant, Subaru of Indiana Automotive, Inc., has won awards for its zero landfill approach to manufacturing. Subaru, a unit of Japan's Fuji Heavy Industries, is enjoying strong demand in North America for its new Crosstrek hatchback and revamped Forester SUV. The Indiana plant currently produces 200,000 vehicles per year; plans call for increasing annual capacity to 300,000 vehicles by 2016.
Source: Subaru of America.

Schultz takes advantage of every opportunity to repeat his message. In interviews and personal appearances, CSR is a constant theme. Here's a typical example, from a 2005 interview with *Financial Times*:

> Perhaps we have the opportunity to be a different type of global company, a global brand that can build a different model, a company that is a global business, that makes a profit, but at the same time demonstrates a social conscience and gives back to the local market.[41]

---

[41] John Murray Brown and Jenny Wiggins, "Coffee Empire Expands Reach by Pressing Its Luck in Ireland," *Financial Times* (December 15, 2005), p. 21.

As noted in Chapter 1, one of the forces restraining the growth of global business and global marketing is resistance to globalization. In a wired world, a company's reputation can quickly be tarnished if activists target its policies and practices. The antiglobalization movement constitutes an important secondary stakeholder for global companies; the movement takes a variety of forms and finds expression in various ways. In developed countries, the movement's concerns and agenda include cultural imperialism (e.g., the French backlash against McDonald's), the loss of jobs due to offshoring and outsourcing (e.g., the furniture industry in the United States), and a distrust of global institutions (e.g., anti-World Trade Organization [WTO] protesters in Hong Kong).

In developing countries, globalization's opponents accuse companies of undermining local cultures, placing intellectual property rights ahead of human rights, promoting unhealthy diets and unsafe food technologies, and pursuing unsustainable consumption.[43] Environmental degradation and labor exploitation are also key issues (see Exhibit 17-8).

> "Coke has become a whipping boy for globalization, just as Nike and McDonald's have been for years."[42]
>
> —Tom Pirko, president, BevMark
> Courtesy of Johnson & Johnson.

Exhibit 17-8 The Timberland Company, based in Stratham, New Hampshire, is best known for its popular hiking boots and work boots. Timberland is a truly global brand; each year, the company sells outdoor gear, accessories, and apparel (2012 revenue was $1.4 billion) through a network of 200 franchised and company-owned stores as well as department and sporting goods stores.

However, the company stands for more than just rugged authenticity; Timberland is a mission-centered company as well. CEO Jeff Swartz, the grandson of Timberland's founder, is deeply concerned with social justice issues. In 2006, Timberland unveiled a "nutritional label" on its footwear boxes as a means of communicating its CSR commitment to consumers. The label (in both English and French) addresses issues of interest to many consumers, including "Percent of factories assessed against Code of Conduct—100%" and "Child labor—0%."

Source: Used with permission of Timberland.

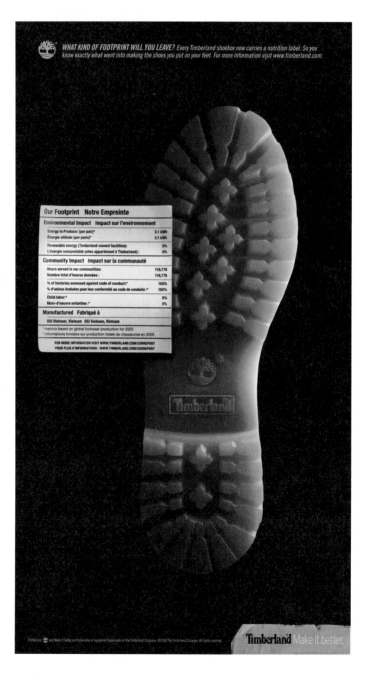

---

[42] Andrew Ward, "Coke Struggles to Defend Positive Reputation," *Financial Times* (January 6, 2006), p. 15.

[43] Terrence H. Witkowski, "Antiglobal Challenges to Marketing in Developing Countries: Exploring the Ideological Divide," *Journal of Public Policy and Marketing* 24, no. 1 (Spring 2005), pp. 7–23.

In a socially responsible firm, employees conduct business in an ethical manner. In other words, they are guided by moral principles that enable them to distinguish between right and wrong. At many companies, a formal statement or **code of ethics** summarizes core ideologies, corporate values, and expectations. GE, Boeing, and United Technologies Corp. are some of the American companies offering training programs that specifically address ethics issues. For many years, Jack Welch, the legendary former CEO of GE, challenged his employees to take an informal "mirror test." The challenge: "Can you look in the mirror every day and feel proud of what you're doing?"[44] Today, GE uses more formal approaches to ethics and compliance; it has produced training videos and instituted an online training program, and also provides employees with a 64-page guide to ethical conduct titled *The Spirit & The Letter*. The document provides guidance on potentially illegal payments, security and crisis management, and other issues. At Johnson & Johnson, the ethics statement is known as "Our Credo"; first introduced in 1943, the Credo has been translated into dozens of languages for Johnson & Johnson employees around the world (see Figure 17-5 and the Appendix at the end of this chapter).

As we have seen, the issue of corporate social responsibility becomes complicated for the global company with operations in multiple markets. When the chief executive of a global firm in a developed country or government policymakers attempt to act in "society's best interests," the question arises: Which society? That of the home-country market (see Exhibit 17-9)? Other developed countries? Developing countries? For example, in the late 1990s, in an effort to address the issue of child labor, the U.S. government threatened trade sanctions against the garment industry in Bangladesh. Thousands of child workers lost their jobs, and their plight

FIGURE 17-5

As management guru Jim Collins notes in his book *Built to Last*, Johnson & Johnson's (J&J) credo is a "codified ideology" that guides managerial actions. J&J operationalizes the credo in various ways, including its organizational structure and its planning and decision-making processes. The credo also serves as a crisis management guide. For example, during the Tylenol crisis of the early 1980s, J&J's adherence to the credo enabled the company to mount a swift, decisive, and transparent response.

Source: Courtesy of Johnson & Johnson.

Our Credo

We believe our first responsibility is to the doctors, nurses and patients, to mothers and fathers and all others who use our products and services. In meeting their needs everything we do must be of high quality. We must constantly strive to reduce our costs in order to maintain reasonable prices. Customers' orders must be serviced promptly and accurately. Our suppliers and distributors must have an opportunity to make a fair profit.

We are responsible to our employees, the men and women who work with us throughout the world. Everyone must be considered as an individual. We must respect their dignity and recognize their merit. They must have a sense of security in their jobs. Compensation must be fair and adequate, and working conditions clean, orderly and safe. We must be mindful of ways to help our employees fulfill their family responsibilities. Employees must feel free to make suggestions and complaints. There must be equal opportunity for employment, development and advancement for those qualified. We must provide competent management, and their actions must be just and ethical.

We are responsible to the communities in which we live and work and to the world community as well. We must be good citizens – support good works and charities and bear our fair share of taxes. We must encourage civic improvements and better health and education. We must maintain in good order the property we are privileged to use, protecting the environment and natural resources.

Our final responsibility is to our stockholders. Business must make a sound profit. We must experiment with new ideas. Research must be carried on, innovative programs developed and mistakes paid for. New equipment must be purchased, new facilities provided and new products launched. Reserves must be created to provide for adverse times. When we operate according to these principles, the stockholders should realize a fair return.

Johnson & Johnson

---

[44] Stratford Sherman and Noel Tichy, *Control Your Destiny or Someone Else Will* (New York: HarperBusiness, 2001), Chapter 9, "The Mirror Test."

Exhibit 17-9 New Balance Athletic Shoe, Inc., is the only major footwear company in the United States that manufactures athletic shoes domestically. Management believes that creating jobs at home is an important aspect of corporate citizenship. As a company spokesman has noted, if maximizing profit were the sole objective, it would be more advantageous to source shoes in low-wage countries. This corporate image print ad encourages other U.S. companies to follow New Balance's example.

Source: Courtesy of New Balance Athletic Shoe, Inc.

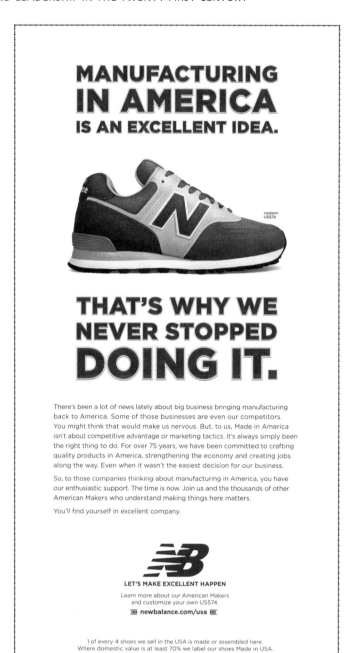

worsened. Whose interests were served by this turn of events? In addition, as noted in Chapter 1, companies that do business around the globe may be in different stages of evolution. Thus, a multinational firm may rely on individual country managers to address CSR issues on an ad hoc basis, while a global or transnational firm may create a policy at headquarters.

Consider the following:

- Nike came under fire from critics who alleged poor working conditions in the factories that made the company's athletic shoes.
- In 2005, Walmart became the target of criticism for a variety of reasons. Well-publicized lawsuits put the company's compensation policies in the public spotlight. A documentary film titled *The High Cost of Low Prices* examined the social repercussions of the retailer's presence in American communities. Two separate Web sites—WakeUpWalMart.com and WalMartWatch.com—were established by organizations representing U.S. labor unions.
- As retail gasoline prices soared in the United States following the devastation of Hurricane Katrina, BP, Royal Dutch Shell, and other companies were accused of price gouging. The

TABLE 17-3 Global Marketing and Corporate Social Responsibility

Company (Headquarters Country)	Nature of CSR Initiative
IKEA (Sweden)	IKEA's primary carpet supplier in India monitors subcontractors to ensure that they do not employ children (see Exhibit 17-10). IKEA also helps lower-caste Indian women reduce their indebtedness to moneylenders. In an effort to create a more child-friendly environment in Indian villages, IKEA sponsors "bridge schools" to increase literacy so young people—including girls and untouchables—can enroll in regular schools.*
Avon (USA)	The company's Breast Cancer Awareness Crusade has raised hundreds of millions of dollars for cancer research. The money funds research in 50 countries.
Subaru (Japan)	Subaru's assembly plant in Indiana is the first "zero landfill" auto plant in the United States. More than 99 percent of the packaging taken in by the plant is recycled. Subaru also partners with key organizations such as the Leave No Trace Center for Outdoor Ethics and United By Blue, the ocean-friendly apparel brand.

*Edward Luce, "IKEA's Grown-Up Plan to Tackle Child Labor," *Financial Times* (September 15, 2004), p. 7.

American Petroleum Institute, the industry's trade group, launched a national TV advertising campaign aimed at explaining its business and urging conservation.[45]
- CEO pay in the United States is rising faster than average salaries and much faster than inflation. One study found that in 2004, CEOs were paid 431 times more than the average worker.

What is the best way for a global firm to respond to such issues? Table 17-3 provides several examples. Using Starbucks as a case study, Paul A. Argenti explains how global companies can work collaboratively with NGOs to arrive at a "win-win" outcome. As previously noted, with no external prompting, Starbucks CEO Schultz uses enlightened compensation and benefits packages to attract and retain employees. Despite the fact that Starbucks is widely admired for such forward-thinking management policies, Global Exchange pressed the company to further demonstrate its commitment to social responsibility by selling Fair Trade coffee. Schultz was faced with three options: Ignore Global Exchange's demands, fight back, or capitulate. In the end, Schultz pursued a middle ground: He agreed to offer Fair Trade coffee in Starbucks' company-owned U.S. stores. He also launched several other initiatives, including establishing long-term, direct relationships with suppliers. Argenti offers seven lessons from the Starbucks case study:[46]

- Realize that socially responsible companies are likely targets but also attractive candidates for collaboration.
- Don't wait for a crisis to collaborate.
- Think strategically about relationships with NGOs.
- Recognize that collaboration involves some compromise.
- Appreciate the value of the NGOs' independence.
- Understand that building relationships with NGOs takes time and effort.
- Think more like an NGO by using communication strategically.

In an article in *Business Ethics Quarterly*, Arthaud-Day proposed a three-dimensional framework for analyzing the social behavior of international, multinational, global, and

[45] Jean Halliday, "Slick: Big Oil Tries Image Makeover," *Advertising Age* (November 7, 2005), pp. 1, 56.
[46] Paul A. Argenti, "Collaborating with Activists: How Starbucks Works with NGOs," *California Management Review* 47, no. 1 (Summer 2004), pp. 91–116.

FIGURE 17-6

Sources of Conflict in Global CSR

Source: *Business Ethics Quarterly* 15, no. 1 (2005). Used with permission of *Business Ethics Quarterly.*

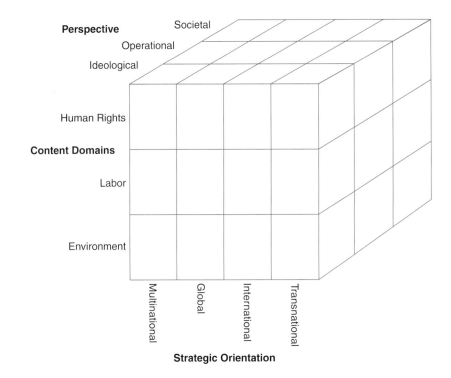

transnational firms; these different stages of development constitute the first dimension.[47] The second dimension of the model includes CSR's three "content domains": human rights, labor, and the environment. These are the universal concerns for global companies established by the United Nations Global Compact. The third dimension in Arthaud-Day's framework consists of three perspectives. The *ideological dimension* of CSR pertains to the things a firm's management believes it should be doing. The *societal dimension* consists of the expectations held by the firm's external stakeholders. The *operational dimension* includes the actions and activities actually taken by the firm. As illustrated in Figure 17-6, the interaction between the dimensions can result in several conflict scenarios. Conflict may arise if there is an incongruity between those

Exhibit 17-10 In India's carpet belt, IKEA operationalizes the concept of corporate global responsibility by sponsoring bridge schools. The school programs are intended to reduce child labor in India's carpet industry by preparing village children to enroll in mainstream schools. To date, the bridge school program has helped an estimated 21,000 children learn to read and write.

Source: Pallava Bagla/Corbis.

[47] Marne Arthaud-Day, "Transnational Corporate Social Responsibility: A Tri-Dimensional Approach to International CSR Research," *Business Ethics Quarterly* 15, no. 1 (January 2005), pp. 1–22.

things a company's leadership believes it should be doing and the expectations of stakeholders. Conflict can also arise when there is an incongruity between those things a company's leadership believes it should be doing and the things it actually is doing. A third scenario is conflict that arises from an incongruity between society's expectations and actual corporate practices and activities.

Summary

To respond to the opportunities and threats in the global marketing environment, organizational leaders must develop a global vision and strategy. Leaders must also be able to communicate that vision throughout the organization and build **core competencies** on a worldwide basis. Global companies are increasingly realizing that the "right" person for a top job is not necessarily a home-country national.

In **organizing** for the global marketing effort, the goal is to create a structure that enables the company to respond to significant differences in international market environments and to extend valuable corporate knowledge. Alternatives include an international division structure, regional management centers, geographical structure, regional or worldwide product division structure, and the **matrix organization**. Whichever form of organization is chosen, balance between autonomy and integration must be established. Many companies are adopting the organizational principle of **lean production** that was pioneered by Japanese automakers.

Many global companies are paying attention to the issue of **corporate social responsibility (CSR)**. A company's **stakeholders** may include **nongovernmental organizations (NGOs)**; **stakeholder analysis** can help identify others. Consumers throughout the world expect that the brands and products they buy and use are marketed by companies that conduct business in an ethical, socially responsible way. Socially conscious companies should include human rights, labor, and environmental issues in their agendas. These values may be spelled out in a **code of ethics**. Ideological, societal, and organizational perspectives can all be brought to bear on CSR.

MyMarketingLab

Go to **mymktlab.com** for the following Assisted-graded writing questions:

17-1. Identify some of the factors that lead to the establishment of an international division as an organization increases its global business activities.

17-2. Identify and explain the three dimensions that provide different perspectives on CSR.

17-3. Mymarketinglab Only – comprehensive writing assignment for this chapter.

MyMarketingLab

Go to **mymktlab.com** to complete the problems marked with this icon .

Discussion Questions

17-4. Are top executives of global companies likely to be home-country nationals?

17-5. In a company involved in global marketing, which activities should be centralized at headquarters and which should be delegated to national or regional subsidiaries?

17-6. "A matrix structure integrates four competencies on a worldwide scale." Explain.

17-7. In the automobile industry, how does "lean production" differ from the traditional assembly-line approach?

17-8. Identify some of the ways the global companies discussed in this text demonstrate their commitment to CSR.

CASE 17-1 CONTINUED (REFER TO PAGE 544)
Unilever

After Cescau was elevated to the top job, Unilever's board streamlined the company's management structure. Now there is a single chief executive; previously, there had been one in Rotterdam and one in London. Cescau asserted that, with a single chief executive, the need for consensus was replaced by speed at making decisions. As noted, many of those decisions concerned "doing good." However, some observers were skeptical of Cescau's determination to operationalize a responsible business philosophy. Cescau recalled, "The company was not doing well. There was an article saying that I was draping myself in a flag of corporate social responsibility to excuse poor performance. I was so angry with that."

Cescau's commitment was put to the test in 2008, his final year as CEO. Greenpeace launched an advertising campaign alleging that Unilever's purchases of Indonesian palm oil were contributing to rain forest destruction. Palm oil, a key ingredient in Dove soap, Magnum ice cream bars, and Vaseline lotion, comes from oil palm trees that grow in Indonesia and Malaysia. Unilever is the world's biggest palm oil customer, buying about 1.4 million tons each year. Rising world prices for the commodity prompted Indonesian farmers to cut down large swaths of old-growth rain forest and plant fast-growing oil palms. Specifically, Greenpeace identified the operations of Sinar Mas, an Indonesian company that is a major palm oil supplier, as contributing to deforestation.

The media strategy for the Greenpeace campaign included newspaper ads in London and a video on YouTube. Fliers parodied Unilever's Campaign for Real Beauty; for example, they showed pictures of orangutans juxtaposed with the headline "Gorgeous or gone?" John Sauven, executive director of Greenpeace, explained why his organization had targeted Unilever: "Everyone has heard of those brands. They are the public face of the company" (see Exhibit 17-11).

Cescau responded by calling for a moratorium on rain forest destruction by Indonesian oil producers. The Unilever chief also pledged that his company would buy palm oil only from producers who could prove that the rain forest had not been sacrificed in the production process. The move allied Unilever with the Roundtable on Sustainable Palm Oil (RSPO), an organization that certifies palm oil producers. A Unilever spokesperson also indicated that the proposed change in Unilever's palm oil sourcing strategy had been in the works for months. Nevertheless, Greenpeace and other NGOs claimed victory.

Unilever brought its message to the public with a print ad campaign featuring the headline "What you buy in the supermarket can change the world." The body copy outlined Unilever's pledge that "by 2015 all our palm oil will come from sustainable sources." The ads ended with the tagline "Small actions, big difference." By 2011, however, only about 2 percent of Unilever's palm oil purchases were coming from traceable sources. Even so, as chief procurement officer Marc Engel said, "I'm not aware of anyone else who has made that commitment, particularly on our scale."

"Doing well" is also part of the leadership equation at Unilever. Cescau understood the importance of improving Unilever's profitability. To this end, he continued a restructuring drive that was initiated by his predecessor, cochairman Niall FitzGerald. Specific actions included reducing Unilever's bureaucracy by removing several management layers. Cescau also reduced the top management head count from 25 people to 7 and narrowed the vertical distance between management and marketing. In addition, the company shed hundreds of brands and closed dozens of factories in France, Germany, and elsewhere. In Cescau's view, the new, leaner structure would translate into a more rapid response to changing market trends and consumer preferences and ensure quicker rollouts of new products.

Cescau also bet heavily on emerging markets to jump-start sales growth. Rising incomes mean that many people purchase consumer

Exhibit 17-11 Unilever has been targeted by activist groups concerned about sustainability issues. For example, palm oil is a key ingredient in several of Unilever's brands; however, orangutan habitat in Indonesia has been cleared to make room for oil palm plantations. Greenpeace and other NGOs have staged protests; here, an activist dressed as an orangutan is shown outside Unilever House in London. Unilever has pledged that, by 2015, all its palm oil will come from sustainable sources.
Source: REUTERS/Stephen Hird (BRITAIN.)

packaged goods for the first time. One scenario: As increasing numbers of people in developing countries buy their first washing machines, they will need to buy laundry detergent. To capitalize on such trends, Cescau shifted budgetary resources out of mature markets such as Europe; those funds were then used to support research in India and other emerging markets. Brand managers were instructed to innovate by taking a "clean slate" approach to developing new products for emerging markets. As Steph Carter, packaging director for deodorant brands, noted, "Traditionally, we would have taken existing products and then tried to fathom how to adapt them for the developing world. Our thinking has changed."

The Polman Era Begins

Paul Polman took over as CEO in January 2009; a former Nestlé executive, he is the first outsider to lead Unilever in its 80-year history. In his first months on the job, Polman initiated a shift in Unilever's core strategy. In the past, the company generated sales growth by increasing prices. Noting that this was the wrong strategy for recessionary times, Polman said the new priority would be to increase sales volumes. The change entailed some risk: Holding the line on prices could put pressure on margins, given the trend of rising costs for the agricultural commodities that are key ingredients in Unilever's products.

Polman was also keenly aware that many budget-conscious shoppers were choosing less expensive, private-label supermarket products instead of well-known name brands. Polman vowed to improve product quality across the board and to boost marketing and advertising spending. To support the increased investment, he accelerated some of the cost-cutting measures that his predecessor had initiated. For example, the timetable for planned factory closures and job cuts was moved up; Polman also froze executive salaries and changed the bonus policy. He established 30-day action plans for managers of brands with flagging sales. He also replaced about one-third of Unilever's top 100 executives, including the chief marketing officer.

When it comes to demonstrating Unilever's commitment to its customers, Polman sends clear signals to his employees. He spends about 50 percent of his time on the road, with regular stops in Asia, Latin America, and, of course, Europe. In a recent interview, he noted, "There's not one visit in a country when I don't meet a consumer. If we want to make this company passionate about consumers and customers, the example starts at the top."

That passion is evident in a flurry of marketing activities orchestrated by Polman. One is the quick pace of new-product rollouts, especially in emerging markets. For example, Unilever's home care unit was the first to market with liquid laundry detergent in China; it also introduced a dishwashing liquid in Turkey in less than 30 days. Innovation has also become a key element for shoring up the value proposition of Unilever's brands, with existing brands such as Surf laundry detergent getting an upgrade in the African market.

Driving growth in the personal-care category is another priority for Polman. By itself, the global deodorant segment represents an estimated $17 billion in annual sales. To tap into that market, the Dove brand has been extended to men's products. Dove for Men has been rolled out in dozens of countries. Meanwhile, Dove's product managers devised a new strategy for persuading women to switch deodorant brands. Dove Ultimate Go Sleeveless resulted from company research designed to discover insights about consumer attitudes toward underarms. What the researchers learned is that 93 percent of women think their armpits are not attractive. Dove Ultimate Go Sleeveless is formulated with moisturizers that, the company claims, will result in nicer-looking underarms after just a few days' use.

The ice cream and beverage unit is also on the move. Unilever's Magnum brand premium ice cream bars are the world's top-selling ice cream novelty. Although Magnum enjoys great popularity in Europe, it was not introduced in the United States until 2011. Häagen-Dazs and Mars were already entrenched in the market; undaunted, the Magnum marketing team is confident its brand will stand out. One manager explained that an important part of the brand's equity is the loud cracking sound heard when someone bites through Magnum's thick chocolate shell.

Renewing the Commitment to Sustainability

Even as he oversees these and other marketing activities, Polman is making sure that former CEO Cescau's commitment to corporate social responsibility is maintained. Summarizing his views on sustainability and environmental impact, Polman said:

> ... the road to well-being doesn't go via reduced consumption. It has to be done via more responsible consumption. . . . So that's why we're taking such a stand on moving the world to sustainable palm oil. That's why we go to natural refrigerants for our ice-cream cabinets. That's why we work with small-hold farmers, to be sure that people who don't have sufficient nutrition right now have a chance to have a better life. Because at the end of the day, I think companies that take that approach have a right to exist.

In 2012, Unilever announced plans to build a $100 million palm oil processing plant in Indonesia. Having a company-controlled plant near the source should make the task of tracing oil to sustainable sources easier. It is currently common practice at processing plants to combine oil from different sources—both sustainable and not—in the same vat. That makes it difficult to trace any individual batch of oil to its origins. Marc Engel, the procurement officer, draws an analogy between palm oil processing and crude oil processing used to make gasoline. "When you actually want to know where the gas in your car is coming from—from which oil well—it's very hard to see," he says. To hedge its bets, Unilever has also invested in Solazyme, a California-based company that produces oil from algae. What kind of potential does this technology hold? "We've made all kinds of food products," says Solazyme CEO and cofounder Jonathan Wolfson. "We've used the oil for frying. We've made mayonnaises, ice creams. And they work, taste good and are functional."

Discussion Questions

17-9. If a company such as Unilever has to make trade-offs between being a good corporate citizen and making a profit, which should be the higher priority?

17-10. Assess Cescau's response to the Greenpeace palm oil protest. Was it appropriate? What type of relationships should Unilever cultivate with Greenpeace and other NGOs in the future?

17-11. Do you think that a streamlined management structure and emphasis on emerging markets will enable current CEO Polman to lead Unilever to improved performance?

Sources: Paul Sonne, "Unilever Takes Palm Oil in Hand," *The Wall Street Journal* (April 24, 2012), p. B3; Louise Lucas, "Growing Issue for Palm Oil Producers," *Financial Times* (May 23, 2011), p. 22; Ellen Byron, "Unilever Takes on the Ugly Underarm," *The Wall Street Journal* (March 30, 2011), p. B1; Sonne, "To Wash Hands of Palm Oil, Unilever Embraces Algae," *The Wall Street Journal* (September 7, 2010), p. B1; Lucas, "Investors Skeptical as Unilever Pursues Bold Growth Plan," *Financial Times* (November 16, 2010), p. 20; Stefan Stern, "The Outsider in a Hurry to Shake Up His Company," *Financial Times* (April 5, 2010); Jenny Wiggins, "Unilever Vows to Focus on Cheaper Products," *Financial Times* (August 7, 2009), p. 17; Wiggins, "Unilever's New Chief Prepares to Brew Up Changes," *Financial Times* (February 6, 2009), p. 15; Michael Skapinker, "Taking a Hard Line on Soft Soap," *Financial Times* (July 7, 2008), p. 12; Aaron O. Patrick, "After Protests, Unilever Does an About-Face on Palm Oil," *The Wall Street Journal* (May 2, 2008), p. B1.

Nosso Credo

Cremos que nossa primeira responsabilidade é para com os médicos, enfermeiras e pacientes,
para com as mães, pais e todos os demais que usam nossos produtos e serviços.
Para atender suas necessidades, tudo o que fizermos deve ser de alta qualidade.
Devemos constantemente nos esforçar para reduzir nossos custos,
a fim de manter preços razoáveis.
Os pedidos de nossos clientes devem ser pronta e corretamente atendidos.
Nossos fornecedores e distribuidores devem ter a oportunidade
de auferir um lucro justo.

Somos responsáveis por nossos empregados,
homens e mulheres que conosco trabalham em todo o mundo.
Todos devem ser considerados em sua individualidade.
Devemos respeitar sua dignidade e reconhecer o seu mérito.
Eles devem se sentir seguros em seus empregos.
A remuneração pelo seu trabalho deve ser justa e adequada
e o ambiente de trabalho limpo, ordenado e seguro.
Devemos ter em mente maneiras de ajudar nossos empregados
a atender às suas responsabilidades familiares.
Os empregados devem se sentir livres para fazer sugestões e reclamações.
Deve haver igual oportunidade de emprego, desenvolvimento
e progresso para os qualificados.
Devemos ter uma administração competente,
e suas ações devem ser justas e éticas.

Somos responsáveis perante as comunidades nas quais vivemos e trabalhamos,
bem como perante a comunidade mundial.
Devemos ser bons cidadãos – apoiar boas obras sociais e de caridade
e pagar corretamente os tributos.
Devemos encorajar o desenvolvimento do civismo e a melhoria da saúde e da educação.
Devemos manter em boa ordem
as propriedades que temos o privilégio de usar,
protegendo o meio ambiente e os recursos naturais.

Nossa responsabilidade final é para com os acionistas.
Os negócios devem proporcionar lucros adequados.
Devemos experimentar novas idéias.
Pesquisas devem ser levadas avante. Programas inovadores desenvolvidos
e os erros corrigidos.
Novos equipamentos devem ser adquiridos, novas fábricas construídas
e novos produtos lançados.
Reservas devem ser criadas para enfrentar tempos adversos.
Ao operarmos de acordo com esses princípios,
nossos acionistas devem
receber justa recompensa.

Johnson & Johnson

Наше Кредо

Наша основная ответственность – перед врачами и медицинскими сестрами,
перед пациентами, перед отцами и матерями, перед всеми,
кто пользуется нашей продукцией и услугами. В соответствии с их
потребностями мы должны обеспечивать высокие стандарты качества во всем,
что мы делаем. Мы должны постоянно стремиться к снижению затрат,
чтобы поддерживать приемлемый уровень цен. Заказы клиентов должны
выполняться точно и в срок. Наши поставщики и дистрибьюторы
должны иметь возможность получать достойную прибыль.

Мы несем ответственность перед нашими сотрудниками,
мужчинами и женщинами, которые работают у нас по всему миру.
Мы должны ценить индивидуальность в каждом из них.
Мы должны уважать их достоинство и признавать их заслуги;
нам важно поддерживать в них чувство уверенности в завтрашнем дне.
Вознаграждение должно быть справедливым и соразмерным,
а условия труда обеспечивать чистоту, порядок и безопасность.
Нам важно, чтобы сотрудники имели возможность заботиться о семье.
Сотрудники должны чувствовать, что они могут свободно
выступать с предложениями и замечаниями.
У всех квалифицированных специалистов должны быть
равные возможности для получения работы, развития и продвижения.
Мы должны обеспечивать компетентное управление,
действия руководителей должны быть справедливыми и этичными.

Мы несем ответственность перед обществом,
в котором живем и работаем, а также перед мировым сообществом.
Мы должны выполнять свой гражданский долг –
поддерживать добрые начинания и благотворительные акции,
честно платить налоги. Мы должны содействовать улучшениям
в социальной сфере, здравоохранении и образовании.
Мы должны бережно относиться к вверенной нам собственности,
сохраняя природные ресурсы и защищая окружающую среду.

И, наконец, мы несем ответственность перед нашими акционерами.
Бизнес должен приносить существенную прибыль.
Мы должны экспериментировать с новыми идеями,
вести научно-исследовательскую работу,
внедрять инновации, учиться на своих ошибках.
Мы должны приобретать новое оборудование, обеспечивать современные
условия работы и выводить на рынок новую продукцию.
Мы должны быть готовы к сложным ситуациям и иметь резервы
для их решения. Придерживаясь этих принципов,
мы обеспечим нашим акционерам достойный доход.

हमारी नीति

हम यह मानते हैं कि हमारी पहली ज़िम्मेदारी डाक्टरों, नर्सों, रोगियों, माताओं, पिताओं तथा
उन सभी लोगों के प्रति है जो हमारे उत्पादनों और सेवाओं का उपयोग करते हैं।
उनकी आवश्यकताओं की पूर्ति के लिए जो कुछ भी हम करें, वह उत्तम दर्जे का हो।
हमें अपने उत्पादनों की कीमत घटाने की लगातार कोशिश करनी चाहिए
ताकि वे उचित कीमतों में उपलब्ध हों।
ग्राहकों की माँगें सही तौर पर तथा तत्परता से पूरी की जानी चाहिए।
हमारे विक्रेताओं और वितरकों को उचित लाभ मिलने का अवसर मिले।

हम अपने उन सभी और पुरुष कर्मचारियों के प्रति
ज़िम्मेदार हैं जो हमारे साथ संसार के हर देश में काम करते हैं।
हर व्यक्ति को व्यक्तिगत रूप से देखा जाय।
हमें उनकी प्रतिष्ठा और योग्यता का आदर करना चाहिए।
उन्हें अपनी नौकरी की सुरक्षा का विश्वास रहे।
उनका वेतन उचित और पर्याप्त हो।
काम करने का वातावरण स्वच्छ, सुव्यवस्थित और सुरक्षित हो।
पारिवारिक ज़िम्मेदारियाँ निभानेके लिए हमें अपने कर्मचारियोंको दक्षतापूर्वक मार्ग दिखाना चाहिए।
कर्मचारियों को उनके सुझाव और शिकायतें उचित ढंग से प्रस्तुत करने की स्वतंत्रता हो।
योग्य लोगों को सेवा, प्रगति और विकास का समान अवसर मिले।
हमारा व्यवस्थापन निपुण हो और प्रबंधकों की कृति उचित और न्यायपूर्ण हो।

हम जिस समाज में रहते और काम करते हैं और जिस विश्व समाज के हम भाग हैं
उस समाज के प्रति हमारी ज़िम्मेदारी है।
हमें अच्छा नागरिक होना चाहिए – दान, धर्म और दूसरे अच्छे कार्यों में
भाग लेना चाहिए तथा अपने हिस्से के कर बराबर देते रहना चाहिए।
हम नगर-सुधार, स्वास्थ्य और शिक्षा को प्रोत्साहित करें।
वातावरण और नैसर्गिक उपलब्धियों को सुरक्षित रखते हुए, जिस संपत्ति का उपयोग
करने का हमें सुअवसर मिला है इसे हम अच्छी तरह संभाल कर रखें।

हमारी आखरी ज़िम्मेदारी भागधारकों के प्रति है।
व्यापार में पर्याप्त लाभ होना चाहिए।
हमें नये-नये विचारों को अमल में लाना चाहिए।
अनुसंधान किए जाय, आन्वेषिक योजनाओं का विकास किया जाय और
भूलों से हुई हानि का मूल्य चुकाया जाय।
नये यंत्र खरिदे जाय, नई सुविधाएं उपलब्ध हों और नये उत्पादनों का
निर्माण किया जाय ताकि बुरे दिनों के लिए प्रबंध हो।
यदि हम उन सिद्धांतों के अनुसार कार्य करते हैं तो
भागधारकों को पर्याप्त लाभ मिल सकता है।

जॉनसन ऍण्ड जॉनसन

我们的信条

我们相信我们首先要对医生、护士和病人，
对父母亲以及所有使用我们的产品和接受我们服务的人负责。
为了满足他们的需求，我们所做的一切都必须是高质量的。
我们必须不断地致力于降低成本，以保持合理的价格。
客户的订货必须迅速而准确地供应，
我们的供应商和经销商应该有机会获得合理的利润。

我们要对世界各地和我们一起共事的男女同仁负责。
每一位同仁都应视为独立的个体。
我们必须维护他们的尊严，赞赏他们的优点，
要使他们对其工作有一种安全感。
薪酬必须公平合理。
工作环境必须清洁、整齐和安全。
我们必须设法帮助员工履行他们对家庭的责任。
必须让员工在提出建议和申诉时畅所欲言。
对于合格的人必须给予平等的聘用、发展和升迁的机会，
我们必须具备称职的管理人员，
他们的行为必须公正并符合道德。

我们要对我们所生活和工作的社会、对整个世界负责。
我们必须做好公民－支持对社会有益的活动和慈善事业，
要纳我们应付的税款，
我们必须鼓励全民进步，促进健康和教育事业，
我们必须很好地维护我们所使用的财产，
保护环境和自然资源。

最后，我们要对全体投东负责。
企业经营必须获取可靠的利润，
我们必须尝试新的构想，
必须坚持研究工作，开发革新项目，
承担错误的代价并加以改正。
必须购置新设备，提供新设施，推出新产品。
必须设立储备金，以备不时之需。
如果我们依据这些原则进行经营，
股东们就会获得合理的回报。

Johnson & Johnson

Source: Courtesy of Johnson & Johnson.

Glossary

The chapter number(s) follow(s) the definition.

80/20 rule In behavioral market segmentation, the rule of thumb that 20 percent of a company's products or customers account for 80 percent of revenues or profits. (7)

acquisition A market-entry strategy that entails investing in assets outside the home country. (12)

adaptation approach Management's use of highly localized marketing programs in different country markets. (1)

adaptation strategy A global market approach that involves changing elements of design, function, or packaging in response to needs or conditions in particular country markets. (10)

adopter categories In the adoption process developed by Everett Rogers, a typology of buyers at different stages of the "adoption" or product life cycle. The categories are innovators, early adopters, early majority, late majority, and laggards. (4)

adoption process A model developed by Everett Rogers that describes the "adoption" or purchase decision process. The stages consist of awareness, interest, evaluation, trial, and adoption. (4)

ad valorem duty A duty that is expressed as a percentage of the value of goods. (8)

advertising Any sponsored, paid message that is communicated through a nonpersonal channel. Advertising is one of the four variables in the promotion mix. (13)

advertising appeal The communications approach that relates to the motives of the target audience. (13)

advertising organization A corporation or holding company that includes one or more "core" advertising agencies, as well as units specializing in direct marketing, marketing services, public relations, or research. (13)

advocacy advertising A form of corporate advertising in which a company presents its point of view on a particular issue. (13)

aesthetics A shared sense within a culture of what is beautiful as opposed to not beautiful and what represents good taste as opposed to tastelessness. (4)

agent An intermediary who negotiates transactions between two or more parties but does not take title to the goods being purchased or sold. (12)

Andean Community A customs union comprised of Bolivia, Colombia, Ecuador, Peru, and Venezuela. (3)

antidumping duties Duties imposed on products whose prices government officials deem too low. (8)

arbitration A negotiation process between two or more parties to settle a dispute outside of the court system. (5)

art direction The visual presentation of an advertisement. (13)

art director An ad agency "creative" with general responsibility for the overall look of an advertisement. The art director chooses graphics, pictures, type styles, and other visual elements. (13)

Association of Southeast Asian Nations (ASEAN) A trade bloc comprised of Brunei, Cambodia, Indonesia, Malaysia, Laos, Myanmar, the Philippines, Singapore, Thailand, and Vietnam. (3)

attitude In culture, a learned tendency to respond in a consistent way to a given object or entity. (4)

balance of payments The record of all economic transactions between the residents of a country and the rest of the world. (2)

barter The least complex and oldest form of bilateral, nonmonetized countertrade consisting of a direct exchange of goods or services between two parties. (11)

behavior segmentation The process of performing market segmentation utilizing user status, usage rate, or some other measure of product consumption. (7)

belief In culture, an organized pattern of knowledge that an individual holds to be true about the world. (4)

benefit segmentation The process of segmenting markets on the basis of the benefits sought by buyers. (7)

big idea A concept that can serve as the basis for a memorable, effective advertising message. (13)

bill of exchange A written order from one party directing a second party to pay to the order of a third party. (8)

Bluetooth Technology that permits access to the Internet from a cell phone when the user is within the range of a hotspot. (15)

brand A representation of a promise by a particular company about a particular product; a complex bundle of images and experiences in the customer's mind. (10)

brand equity The reflection of the brand's value to a company as an intangible asset. (10)

brand extensions A strategy that uses an established brand name as an umbrella when entering new businesses or developing new product lines that represent new categories to the company. (10)

brand image A single, but often complex, mental image about both the physical product and the company that markets it. (10)

bribery The corrupt business practice of demanding or offering some type of consideration—typically a cash payment—when negotiating a cross-border deal. (5)

BRICS Brazil, Russia, India, China, and South Korea; the four fastest-growing markets that represent important opportunities. (2)

broadband A digital communication system with sufficient capacity to carry multiple voice, data, or video channels simultaneously. (15)

business-to-business (b-to-b or B2B) marketing Marketing products and services to other companies and organizations. Contrasts with business-to-consumer (b-to-c or B2C) marketing. (12)

business-to-consumer (b-to-c or B2C) marketing Marketing products and services to people for their own use. Contrasts with business-to-business (b-to-b or B2B) marketing. (12)

Byrd Amendment Law that calls for antidumping revenues to be paid to U.S. companies harmed by imported goods sold at below-market prices. (11)

call centers Sophisticated telephone operations that provide customer support and other services to in-bound callers from around the world. May also provide outsourcing services such as telemarketing. (8)

call option The right to buy a specified amount of foreign currency at a fixed price, up to the option's expiration date. (2)

capital account In a country's balance of payments, the record of all long-term direct investment, portfolio investment, and other short- and long-term capital flows. (2)

CARICOM (Caribbean Community and Common Market) Formed in 1973, a free trade area whose members include Antigua and Barbuda, Bahamas, Barbados, Belize, Dominica, Grenada, Guyana, Haiti, Jamaica, Montserrat, St. Kitts and Nevis, St. Lucia, St. Vincent and the Grenadines, and Trinidad and Tobago. (3)

cartel A group of separate companies or countries that collectively set prices, control output, or take other actions to maximize profits. (5)

catalog A magazine-style publication that features photographs, illustrations, and extensive information about a company's products. (14)

category killer A store that specializes in a particular product category and offers a vast selection at low prices. (12)

Central American Integration System A customs union comprised of El Salvador, Honduras, Guatemala, Nicaragua, Costa Rica, and Panama. (3)

centrally planned capitalism An economic system characterized by command resource allocation and private resource ownership. (2)

centrally planned socialism An economic system characterized by command resource allocation and state resource ownership. (2)

CFR (cost and freight) A contract in which the seller is not responsible for risk or loss at any point outside the factory. (11)

chaebol In South Korea, a type of corporate alliance group composed of dozens of companies and centered around a central bank or holding company and dominated by a founding family. (9)

changing the rules of engagement A strategy for creating competitive advantage that involves breaking these rules and refusing to play by the rules set by industry leaders. (16)

channel of distribution An organized network of agencies and institutions that, in combination, perform all the activities required to link producers with users to accomplish the marketing task. (12)

characteristics of innovations One element of Everett Rogers' diffusion of innovations framework. The other elements in the framework are the five-stage innovation adoption process and innovation adopter categories. (4)

cherry picking In distribution, a situation in which a channel intermediary such as a distributor accepts new lines only from manufacturers whose products and brands already enjoy strong demand. (12)

CIF (cost, insurance, freight) named port The Incoterm for a contract requiring the seller to retain responsibility and liability for goods until they have physically passed over the rail of a ship. (11)

civil-law country A country in which the legal system reflects the structural concepts and principles of the Roman Empire in the sixth century. (5)

click-through rate The percentage of visitors to an Internet site who click on an advertisement link presented on the computer screen. (15)

cluster analysis In market research, a quantitative data analysis technique that groups variables into clusters that maximize within-group similarities and between-group differences. Can be used in psychographic segmentation. (6)

co-branding A variation of combination branding in which two or more different company or product brands are featured prominently on product packaging or in advertising. (10)

code of ethics A formal statement that summarizes a company's core ideologies, corporate values, and expectations. (17)

collectivist culture In Geert Hofstede's social values typology, a culture in which group cohesiveness and harmony are emphasized. A shared concern for the well-being of all members of society is also evident. (4)

combination branding A strategy in which a corporate name is combined with a product brand name; also called tiered or umbrella branding. (10)

Common Agricultural Policy (CAP) Legislation adopted by European countries after World War II to aid and protect the interests of farmers. (8)

common external tariff (CET) A tariff agreed upon by members of a preferential trading bloc. Implementation of a CET marks the transition from a free trade area to a customs union. (3)

common-law country A country in which the legal system relies on past judicial decisions (cases) to resolve disputes. (5)

common market A preferential trade agreement that builds on the foundation of economic integration provided by a free trade area and a customs union. (3)

Common Market of the South (Mercosur) A customs union comprised of Argentina, Brazil, Paraguay, Uruguay, and Venezuela. (3)

compensation trading (buyback) A countertrade deal typically involving the sale of plant equipment or technology licensing in which the seller or licensor agrees to take payment in the form of the products produced using the equipment or technology for a specified number of years. (11)

competitive advantage The result of a match between a firm's distinctive competencies and the factors critical for creating superior customer value in an industry. (1, 16)

concentrated global marketing The target market strategy that calls for creating a marketing mix to reach a niche segment of global consumers. (7)

confiscation Governmental seizure of a company's assets without compensation. (5)

conjoint analysis In market research, a quantitative data analysis technique that can be used to gain insights into the combination of product features that will be attractive to potential buyers. (6)

consumer panel Primary data collection using a sample of consumers or households whose behavior is tracked over time; frequently used for television audience measurement. (6)

consumer sales promotions Promotion designed to make consumers aware of a new product, to stimulate nonusers to sample an existing product, or to increase overall consumer demand. (14)

containerization In physical distribution, the practice of loading oceangoing freight into steel boxes measuring 20 feet, 40 feet, or longer. (12)

content site A Web site that provides news and entertainment and supports a company's PR efforts. (15)

continuous innovation A product that is "new and improved" and requires little research and development (R&D) expenditure to develop, causes minimal disruption in existing consumption patterns, and requires the least amount of learning on the part of buyers. (10)

contract manufacturing A licensing arrangement in which a global company provides technical specifications to a subcontractor or local manufacturer. (9)

convenience stores A form of retail distribution that offers some of the same products as supermarkets, but the merchandise mix is limited to high-turnover convenience products. (12)

convergence The aspect of the digital revolution that pertains to the merging, overlapping, or coming together of previously distinct industries or product categories. (15)

cooperative exporter An export organization of a manufacturing company retained by other independent manufacturers to sell their products in some or all foreign markets. (8)

copy The words that are the spoken or written communication elements in advertisements. (13)

copyright The establishment of ownership of a written, recorded, performed, or filmed creative work. (5)

core competence Something that an organization can do better than its competitors. (17)

corporate advertising Advertising that is not designed to directly stimulate demand for a specific product. Image advertising and advocacy advertising are two types of corporate advertising. (13)

corporate social responsibility (CSR) A company's obligation and commitment to the pursuit of goals and policies that are in society's best interests. (17)

cost-based pricing Pricing based on an analysis of internal costs (e.g., materials, labor, etc.) and external costs. (11)

cost-based transfer pricing A transfer pricing policy that uses costs as a basis for setting prices in intracorporate transfers. (11)

cost focus In Michael Porter's generic strategies framework, one of four options for building competitive advantage. When a firm that serves a small (niche) market has a lower cost structure than its competitors, it can offer customers the lowest prices in the industry. (16)

cost leadership A competitive advantage based on a firm's position as the industry's low-cost producer. (16)

counterfeiting The unauthorized copying and production of a product. (5)

counterpurchase A monetized countertrade deal in which the seller agrees to purchase products of equivalent value that it must then sell in order to realize revenue from the original deal. (11)

countertrade An export transaction in which a sale results in product flowing in one direction to a buyer, and a separate stream of products and services, often flowing in the opposite direction. (11)

countervailing duties (CVDs) Additional duties levied to offset subsidies granted in the exporting country. (8)

country and market concentration A market expansion strategy that involves targeting a limited number of customer segments in a few countries. (9)

country and market diversification The corporate market expansion strategy of a global, multibusiness company. (9)

country concentration and market diversification A market expansion strategy in which a company serves many markets in a few countries. (9)

country diversification and market concentration A market expansion strategy whereby a company seeks out the world market for a product. (9)

country-of-origin effect Perceptions of, and attitudes toward, products or brands on the basis of the country of origin or manufacture. (10)

coupon A sales promotion tool consisting of a printed certificate that entitles the bearer to a price reduction or some other value-enhancing consideration when purchasing a particular product or service. (14)

creative execution In advertising, the way an appeal or selling proposition is presented. Creative execution is the "how," and creative strategy is the "what." (13)

creative strategy A statement or concept of what a particular advertising message or campaign will say. (13)

culture A society's ways of living transmitted from one generation to another. Culture's manifestations include attitudes, beliefs, values, aesthetics, dietary customs, and language. (4)

current account A record of all recurring trade in merchandise and services, private gifts, and public aid transactions between countries. (2)

customer relationship management (CRM) The process of storing and analyzing data collected from customer "touchpoints" for the purpose of identifying a firm's best customers and serving their needs as efficiently, effectively, and profitably as possible. (6)

customer strategy A sales representative's plan for collecting and analyzing information about the needs of each customer or prospect. (14)

customs union A preferential trade bloc whose members agree to seek a greater degree of economic integration than is provided by a free trade agreement. In addition to reducing tariffs and quotas, a customs union is characterized by a common external tariff (CET). (3)

cybersquatting The practice of registering a particular domain name for the express purpose of reselling it to the company that should rightfully use it. (15)

data warehouse A database, part of a company's MIS, that is used to support management decision making. (6)

Defense Advanced Research Projects Agency (DARPA) Agency that created a computer network that could maintain lines of communication in the event of a war. (15)

delivered duty paid (DDB) A type of contract in which the seller has agreed to deliver the goods to the buyer at the place the buyer names in the country of import, with all costs, including duties, paid. (11)

demand conditions In Michael Porter's framework for national competitive advantage, conditions that determine the rate and nature of improvement and innovations by the firms in the nation. (16)

demographic segmentation The process of segmenting markets on the basis of measurable characteristics such as country, income, population, age, or some other measure. (7)

department store A category of retail operations characterized by multiple sections or areas under one roof, each representing a distinct merchandise line and staffed with a limited number of salespeople. (12)

devaluation The decline in value of a currency relative to other currencies. (2)

developed countries Countries that can be assigned to the high-income category. (2)

developing countries Countries that can be assigned to the upper ranks of the low-income category, the lower-middle-income category, or the upper-middle-income category. (2)

differentiated global marketing A strategy that calls for targeting two or more distinct market segments with multiple marketing mix offerings. (7)

differentiation In Porter's generic strategies framework, one of four options for building competitive advantage. Differentiation advantage is present when a firm serves a broad market and its products are perceived as unique; this allows the firm to charge premium prices compared with the competition. (16)

diffusion of innovations A framework developed by Everett Rogers to explain the way that new products are adopted by a culture over time. The framework includes the five-stage innovation adoption process, characteristics of innovations, and innovation adopter categories. (4)

digital revolution The paradigm shift resulting from technological advances allowing for the digitization (i.e., conversion to binary code) of analog sources of information, sounds, and images. (15)

direct mail A direct marketing technique that uses the postal service as a vehicle for delivering an offer to prospects targeted by a marketer. (14)

direct marketing Any communication with a consumer or business recipient that is designed to generate a response in the form of an order, a request for further information, and/or a visit to a store or other place of business. (14)

discontinuous innovation A new product that, when it is widely adopted, creates new markets and new consumption patterns. (10)

discount retailers A category of retail operations that emphasizes low merchandise prices. (12)

discriminatory procurement policies Policies that can take the form of government rules and administrative regulations, as well as formal or informal company policies that discriminate against foreign suppliers. (8)

disruptive technology A technology that redefines product or industry performance and enables new markets to emerge. (15)

distribution One of the four Ps of the marketing mix; the physical flow of goods through channels. (12)

distribution channels A barrier to entry into an industry created by the need to create and establish new channels. (12)

distributor A channel intermediary, frequently a wholesaler, that aggregates products from manufacturers and delivers them to retail channel members. (12)

domestic company A company that limits the geographic scope of its resource commitment and marketing activities to opportunities in the home country. (1)

domestic market A company's "home turf," generally the country or countries in which the organization's headquarters is located. (1)

double-diamond framework A framework for understanding national competitive advantage in terms of a "double diamond" instead of the single diamond found in Michael Porter's national advantage model. (16)

draft A payment instrument that transfers all the risk of nonpayment onto the exporter-seller. (8)

dumping The sale of a product in an export market at a price lower than that normally charged in the domestic market or country of origin. (8, 11)

duties Rate schedule; can sometimes be thought of as a tax that punishes "individuals for making choices of which their governments disapprove." (8)

dynamically continuous innovation An intermediate category of newness that is somewhat disruptive and requires a moderate amount of learning on the part of consumers. (10)

e-commerce The general exchange of goods and services using the Internet or a similar online network as a marketing channel. (15)

Economic Community of West African States (ECOWAS) An association of 16 nations that includes Benin, Burkina Faso,

Cape Verde, Gambia, Ghana, Guinea, Guinea-Bissau, Ivory Coast, Liberia, Mali, Mauritania, Niger, Nigeria, Senegal, Sierra Leone, and Togo. (3)

economic freedom index A table of country rankings based on key economic variables such as trade policy, taxation policy, government consumption, monetary policy, capital flows, and foreign investment, etc. (2)

economic union A highly evolved form of cross-border economic integration involving reduced tariffs and quotas, a common external tariff, reduced restrictions on the movement of labor and capital, and the creation of unified economic policies and institutions such as a central bank. (3)

economies of scale The decline in per-unit product costs as the absolute volume of production per period increases. (16)

efficient consumer response (ECR) An MIS tool that enables retailers to work more closely with vendors to facilitate stock replenishment. (6)

electronic data interchange (EDI) An MIS tool that allows a company's business units to submit orders, issue invoices, and conduct business electronically with other company units as well as with outside companies. (6)

electronic point of sale (EPOS) Purchase data gathered by checkout scanners that help retailers identify product sales patterns and the extent to which consumer preferences vary with geography. (6)

emic analysis Global market research that analyzes a country in terms of its local system of meanings and values. (6)

emotional appeal In advertising, an appeal intended to evoke an emotional response (as opposed to an intellectual response) that will direct purchase behavior. (13)

enabling conditions Structural market characteristics whose presence or absence can determine whether the marketing model can succeed. (7)

environmental sensitivity A measure of the extent to which products must be adapted to the culture-specific needs of different country markets. Generally, consumer products show a higher degree of environmental sensitivity than industrial products. (4)

EPRG framework A developmental framework for analyzing organizations in terms of four successive management orientations: ethnocentric, polycentric, regiocentric, and geocentric. (1)

equity stake Market-entry strategy involving foreign direct investment for the purpose of establishing partial ownership of a business. (9)

ethnocentric orientation The first level in the EPRG framework: the conscious or unconscious belief that one's home country is superior. (1)

ethnocentric pricing The practice of extending a product's home-country price to all country markets. Also known as extension pricing. (11)

etic analysis Global market research that analyzes a country from an outside perspective. (6)

euro zone Sixteen countries that use the euro: Austria, Belgium, Cyprus, Finland, Ireland, the Netherlands, France, Germany, Greece, Italy, Luxembourg, Malta, Portugal, Slovakia, Slovenia, and Spain. (3)

expanded Triad The dominant economic centers of the world: the Pacific region, North America, and Europe. (2)

expatriate An employee who is sent from his or her home country to work abroad. (14)

export broker A broker who receives a fee for bringing together the seller and the overseas buyer. (8)

export commission representative Representative assigned to all or some foreign markets by the manufacturer. (8)

export distributor An individual or organization that has the exclusive right to sell a manufacturer's products in all or some markets outside the country of origin. (8)

export management company (EMC) Term used to designate an independent export firm that acts as the export department for more than one manufacturer. (8)

export marketing Exporting using the product offered in the home market as a starting point and modifying it as needed to meet the preferences of international target markets. (8)

export merchants Merchants who seek out needs in foreign markets and make purchases in world markets to fill these needs. (8)

export price escalation The increase in an imported product's price due to expenses associated with transportation, currency fluctuations, etc. (11)

export selling Exporting without tailoring the product, the price, or the promotional material to suit individual country requirements. (8)

express warranty A written guarantee that assures a buyer that he or she is getting what was paid for or provides recourse in the event that a product's performance falls short of expectations. (10)

expropriation Governmental seizure of a company's assets in exchange for compensation that is generally lower than market value. (5)

extension approach Management's use of domestic country marketing programs and strategies when entering new country markets. (1)

extension strategy A global strategy of offering a product virtually unchanged (i.e., "extending" it) in markets outside the home country. (10)

ex-works (EXW) A type of contract in which the seller places goods at the disposal of the buyer at the time specified in the contract. (11)

factor analysis In market research, a computerized quantitative data analysis technique that is used to perform data reduction. Responses from questionnaires that contain multiple items about a product's benefits serve as input; the computer generates factor loadings that can be used to create a perceptual map. (6)

factor conditions A country's endowment with resources. (16)

FAS (free alongside ship) named port The Incoterm for a contract that calls for the seller to place goods alongside, or available to, the vessel or other mode of transportation and pay all charges up to that point. (11)

femininity In Geert Hofstede's social values framework, the extent to which the social roles of men and women overlap in a culture. (4)

first-mover advantage Orthodox marketing wisdom suggesting that the first company to enter a country market has the best chance of becoming the market leader. (7)

five forces model Model developed by Michael Porter that explains competition in an industry: the threat of new entrants, the threat of substitute products or services, the bargaining power of buyers, the bargaining power of suppliers, and the competitive rivalry among current members of the industry. (16)

flagship model A model of competitive advantage developed by Alan Rugman and Joseph D'Cruz that describes how networked business systems can create competitive advantage in global industries. (16)

FOB (free on board) named port The Incoterm for a contract in which the responsibility and liability of the seller do not end until the goods have actually been placed aboard a ship. (11)

focus The concentration of resources on a core business or competence. (1)

focused differentiation In Michael Porter's generic strategies framework, one of four options for building competitive advantage. When a firm serves a small (niche) market and its products are perceived as unique, the firm can charge premium prices. (16)

focus group Primary data collection method involving a trained moderator who facilitates discussion among the members of a group at a specially equipped research facility. (6)

foreign consumer culture positioning (FCCP) A positioning strategy that seeks to differentiate a product, brand, or company by associating it with its country or culture of origin. (7)

Foreign Corrupt Practices Act (FCPA) A law that makes it illegal for U.S. corporations to bribe an official of a foreign government or political party to obtain or retain business. (5)

foreign direct investment (FDI) The market-entry strategy in which companies invest in or acquire plants, equipment, or other assets outside the home country. (9)

foreign purchasing agents Purchasing agents who operate on behalf of, and are compensated by, an overseas customer. (8)

foreign sales corporation (FSC) Provision in the U.S. tax code that allowed American exporters to exclude 15 percent of international sales from reported earnings. (8)

form utility The availability of the product processed, prepared, in proper condition, and/or ready to use. (12)

forward market A mechanism for buying and selling currencies at a preset price for future delivery. (2)

franchising A contract between a parent company–franchisor and franchisee that allows the franchisee to operate a business developed by the franchisor in return for a fee and adherence to franchise-wide policies and practices. This

is an appropriate entry strategy when barriers to entry are low yet the market is culturally distant in terms of consumer behavior or retailing structures. (9, 12)

free carrier (FCA) The Incoterm for a contract where transfer from seller to buyer is effected when the goods are delivered to a specified carrier at a specified destination. (11)

free trade agreement (FTA) An agreement that leads to the creation of a free trade area (also abbreviated FTA). A FTA represents a relatively low level of economic integration. (3)

free trade area (FTA) A preferential trade bloc whose members have signed a free trade agreement (also abbreviated FTA) that entails reducing or eliminating tariffs and quotas. (3)

free trade zone (FTZ) A geographical entity that may include a manufacturing facility and a warehouse. (8)

freight forwarders Specialists in traffic operations, customs clearance, and shipping tariffs and schedules. (8)

full ownership Market-entry strategy involving foreign direct investment for the purpose of establishing 100 percent control of a business. (9)

General Agreement on Tariffs and Trade (GATT) The organization established at the end of World War II to promote free trade; also, the treaty signed by member nations. (3)

generic strategies Michael Porter's model describing four different options for achieving competitive advantage: cost leadership, product differentiation, cost focus, focused differentiation. (16)

geocentric orientation The fourth level in the EPRG framework: the understanding that the company should seek market opportunities throughout the world. Management also recognizes that country markets may be characterized by both similarities and differences. (1)

geocentric pricing The practice of using both extension and adaptation pricing policies in different country markets. (11)

global advertising An advertising message whose art, copy, headlines, photographs, taglines, and other elements have been developed expressly for their worldwide suitability. (13)

global brand A brand that has the same name and a similar image and positioning throughout the world. (10)

global brand leadership The act of allocating brand-building resources globally with the goal of creating global synergies and developing a global brand strategy that coordinates and leverages country brand strategies. (10)

global company A company exhibiting a geocentric orientation that pursues marketing opportunities in all parts of the world using one of two strategies: either serving world markets by exporting goods manufactured in the home-country market or by sourcing products from a variety of different countries with the primary goal of serving the home-country market. Global operations are integrated and coordinated. (1)

global competition A success strategy in which a firm takes a global view of competition and sets about maximizing profits worldwide, rather than on a country-by-country basis. (16)

global consumer culture positioning (GCCP) A positioning strategy that seeks to differentiate a product, brand, or company as a symbol of, or association with, a global culture or a global market segment. (4, 7)

global elite A global market segment comprised of well-traveled, affluent consumers who spend heavily on prestige or luxury products and brands that convey an image of exclusivity. (7)

global industry An industry in which competitive advantage can be achieved by integrating and leveraging operations on a worldwide scale. (1)

global marketing The commitment of organizational resources to pursuing global market opportunities and responding to environmental threats in the global marketplace. (1)

global marketing strategy (GMS) A firm's blueprint for pursuing global market opportunities that addresses four issues: whether a standardization approach or a localization approach will be used; whether key marketing activities will be concentrated in relatively few countries or widely dispersed around the globe; the guidelines for coordinating marketing activities around the globe; and the scope of global market participation. (1)

global market research The project-specific gathering and analysis of data on a global basis or in one or more markets outside the home country. (6)

global market segmentation The process of identifying specific segments of potential customers with homogeneous attributes who are likely to exhibit similar buying behavior irrespective of their countries of residence. (7)

global positioning system (GPS) A digital communication system that uses satellite feeds to determine the geographic position of a mobile device. (15)

global product A product that satisfies the wants and needs of buyers in all parts of the world. (10)

global retailing Engaging in or owning retail operations in multiple national markets. (12)

global strategic partnerships (GSPs) A sophisticated market-entry strategy via an alliance with one or more business partners for the purpose of serving the global market. (9)

global teens A global market segment comprised of persons 12 to 19 years old whose shared interests in fashion, music, and youthful lifestyle issues shape purchase behavior. (7)

gray market goods Products that are exported from one country to another without authorization from the trademark owner. (11)

greenfield investment A market-entry strategy that entails foreign direct investment in a factory, retail outlet, or some other form of new operations in a target country. Also known as greenfield operations. (9)

gross domestic product (GDP) A measure of a nation's economic activity calculated by adding consumer spending (C), investment spending (I), government purchases (G), and net exports (NX): $C + I + G + NX = $ GDP. (2)

gross national income (GNI) A measure of a nation's economic activity that includes gross domestic product (GDP) plus income generated by nonresident sources. (2)

Group of Eight (G-8) Eight nations—the United States, Japan, Germany, France, Great Britain, Canada, Italy, and Russia—whose representatives meet regularly to deal with global economic issues. (2)

Group of Seven (G-7) Seven nations—the United States, Japan, Germany, France, Great Britain, Canada, and Italy—whose representatives meet regularly to deal with global economic issues. (2)

Group of Twenty (G-20) Twenty nations whose representatives meet regularly to discuss global economic and financial issues. Objectives include restoring global economic growth and strengthening the global financial system. (2)

Gulf Cooperation Council (GCC) An association of oil-producing states that includes Bahrain, Kuwait, Oman, Qatar, Saudi Arabia, and the United Arab Emirates. (3)

hard discounter A retailer that sells a tightly focused selection of goods at very low prices, often relying heavily on private brands. (12)

harmonization The coming together of varying standards and regulations that affect the marketing mix. (3)

Harmonized Tariff System (HTS) A system in which importers and exporters have to determine the correct classification number for a given product or service that will cross borders. (8)

hedging An investment made to protect a company from possible financial losses due to fluctuating currency exchange rates. (2)

hierarchy of effects A model of consumer response that shows the stages—cognitive, affective, and conative—that individuals move through when considering purchasing a product or service. (4)

high-context culture A culture in which a great deal of information and meaning reside in the context of communication, including the background, associations, and basic values of the communicators. (4)

high-income country A country in which per capita gross national income (GNI) is $12,476 or greater. (2)

hypercompetition A strategy framework developed by Richard D'Aveni that views competition and the quest for competitive advantage in terms of the dynamic maneuvering and strategic interactions by hypercompetitive firms in an industry. (16)

hypermarket A category of retail operations characterized by very large-scale facilities that combine elements of discount store, supermarket, and warehouse club approaches. (12)

hypertext markup language (HTML) A format language that controls the appearance of Web pages. (15)

hypertext transfer protocol (HTTP) A protocol that enables hypertext files to be transferred across the Internet. (15)

image advertising A type of corporate advertising that informs the public about a major event, such as a name change, merger, etc. (13)

incipient market A market in which demand will materialize if particular economic, demographic, political, or sociocultural trends continue. (6)

Incoterms Internationally accepted terms of trade that impact prices. (11)

individualist culture In Geert Hofstede's social values typology, a society in which each member is primarily concerned with his or her interests and those of the immediate family. (4)

infomercial A form of paid television programming in which a particular product is demonstrated, explained, and offered for sale to viewers who call a toll-free number shown on the screen. (14)

information technology (IT) An organization's processes for creating, storing, exchanging, using, and managing information. (6)

information utility The availability of answers to questions and general communication about useful product features and benefits. (12)

innovation The process of endowing resources with a new capacity to create value. (10)

innovator's dilemma Executives become so committed to a current, profitable technology that they fail to provide adequate levels of investment in new, apparently riskier technologies. (15)

integrated circuit (IC) The silicon chip that gave modern form to the transistor and represented a milestone in the digital revolution. (15)

integrated marketing communications (IMC) An approach to the promotion element of the marketing mix that values coordination and integration of a company's marketing communication strategy. (13)

interactive television (ITV) Allows television viewers to interact with the programming content that they are viewing. (14)

intermodal transportation The aspect of physical distribution that involves transferring shipping containers between land and water transportation modes. (12)

international brand A brand that is available throughout a particular world region. Also known as an international product. (10)

international company A company that pursues market opportunities outside the home country via an extension strategy. (1)

international law The body of international law that pertains to noncommercial disputes between nations. (5)

Internet A network of computer networks across which e-mail and other digital files can be sent. (15)

intranet An electronic system that allows authorized company personnel or outsiders to share information electronically in a secure fashion while reducing the amount of paper generated. (6)

inventory management The distribution activity that ensures companies carry the optimum amount of manufacturing components or finished goods. The objective is to avoid running out of stock without incurring excessive inventory carrying costs. (12)

Islamic law A legal system used in the Middle East that is based on a comprehensive code known as *sharia*. (5)

joint venture A market-entry strategy in which two companies share ownership of a newly created business entity. (9, 12)

jurisdiction The aspect of a country's legal environment that deals with a court's authority to rule on particular types of controversies arising outside of a nation's borders or exercise power over individuals or entities from different countries. (5)

keiretsu In Japan, an enterprise alliance consisting of businesses that are joined together in mutually reinforcing ways. (9)

latent market An undiscovered market segment in which demand for a product would materialize if an appropriate product were offered. (6)

law of one price A market in which all customers have access to the best product at the best price. (11)

lean production An extremely effective, efficient, and streamlined manufacturing system such as the Toyota Production System. (17)

least-developed countries (LDCs) Terminology adopted by the United Nations to refer to the 50 countries that rank lowest in per capita gross national product (GNP). (2)

legal environment A nation's system of laws, courts, attorneys, legal customs, and practices. (5)

letter of credit (L/C) A payment method in export/import in which a bank substitutes its creditworthiness for that of the importer-buyer. (8)

leverage Some type of advantage—for example, experience transfers, know-how, or scale economies—that a company enjoys by accumulating experience in multiple country markets. (1)

licensing A contractual market-entry strategy whereby one company makes an asset available to another company in exchange for royalties or some other form of compensation. (9, 12)

line extension A variation of an existing product such as a new flavor or new design. (10)

local brand A brand that is available in a single country market. Also known as a local product. (10)

local consumer culture positioning A positioning strategy that seeks to differentiate a product, brand, or company in terms of its association with local culture, local production, or local consumption. (7)

localization (adaptation) approach The pursuit of global market opportunities using an adaptation strategy of significant marketing mix variations in different countries. (1)

logistics The management process that integrates the activities of various suppliers and distribution intermediaries to ensure an efficient flow of goods through a firm's supply chain. (12)

logistics management The management activity responsible for planning, implementing, and controlling the flow of components and finished goods between the point of origin and the point of assembly or final consumption. (12)

long-term orientation (LTO) The fifth dimension in Geert Hofstede's social values framework, LTO is a reflection of a society's concern with immediate gratification versus persistence and thrift over the long term. (4)

loose bricks A strategy for creating competitive advantage by taking advantage of a competitor whose attention is narrowly focused on a market segment or geographic area to the exclusion of others. (16)

low-context culture A culture in which messages and knowledge are more explicit and words carry most of the information in communication. (4)

lower-middle-income country A country with gross national income (GNI) per capita between $1,026 and $4,035. (2)

low-income country A country with per capita gross national income (GNI) of less than $1,025. (2)

Maastricht Treaty The 1991 treaty that set the stage for the transition from the European monetary system to an economic and monetary union. (3)

Madrid Protocol A system of trademark protection that allows intellectual property registration in multiple countries with a single application and fee. (5)

management information system (MIS) A system that provides managers and other decision makers with a continuous flow of information about company operations. (6)

manufacturer's export agent (MEA) One who can act as an export distributor or as an export commission representative. (8)

market People or organizations with needs and wants and both the ability and the willingness to buy. (2)

market-based transfer price A transfer pricing policy that sets prices for intracorporate transactions at levels that are competitive in the global market. (11)

market capitalism An economic system characterized by market allocation of resources and private resource ownership. (2)

market-entry strategy The manner in which company management decides to pursue market opportunities outside the home country. (9)

market expansion strategy The particular combination of product-market and geographic alternatives that management chooses when expanding company operations outside the home country. (9)

market holding strategy A pricing strategy that allows management to maintain market share; prices are adjusted up or down as competitive or economic conditions change. (11)

marketing An organizational function and a set of processes for creating, communicating, and delivering value to customers and for managing customer relationships in ways that benefit the organization and its stakeholders. (1)

marketing mix The four factors—product, price, place, and promotion—that represent strategic variables controlled by the marketer. (1)

marketing model drivers Key elements or factors that must be taken into account when evaluating countries as potential target markets. (7)

market penetration pricing strategy A pricing strategy that calls for setting price levels that are low enough to quickly build market share. (11)

market research The project-specific, systematic gathering of data in the search scanning mode. (6)

market segmentation An effort to identify and categorize groups of customers and countries according to common characteristics. (7)

market skimming A pricing strategy designed to reach customers willing to pay a premium price for a particular brand or for a specialized product. (11)

market socialism An economic system characterized by limited market resource allocation within an overall environment of state ownership. (2)

masculinity In Geert Hofstede's social values framework, the extent to which a culture's male population is expected to be assertive, competitive, and concerned with material success. (4)

Maslow's needs hierarchy A classic framework for understanding how human motivation is linked to needs. (10)

matrix organization A pattern of organization design in which management's task is to achieve an organizational balance that brings together different perspectives and skills to accomplish the organization's objectives. (17)

merchandise trade In balance of payments statistics, entries that pertain to manufactured goods. (2)

mobile advertising Persuasive or informative communication that uses a smartphone or other handheld device as the channel. (15)

mobile commerce (m-commerce) Conducting commercial transactions using wireless handheld devices such as cell phones and tablets. (15)

mobile music Music that is purchased and played on a cell phone. (15)

multidimensional scaling (MDS) In market research, a quantitative data analysis technique that can be used to create perceptual maps. MDS helps marketers gain insights into consumer perceptions when a large number of products or brands are available. (6)

multinational company A company that pursues market opportunities outside the home-country market via an adaptation strategy (i.e., different product, price, place, and/or promotion strategies than used in the domestic market). In a typical multinational, country managers are granted considerable autonomy; there is little integration or coordination of marketing activities across different country markets. (1)

multisegment targeting A marketing strategy that entails targeting two or more distinct market segments with multiple marketing mix offerings. (7)

national advantage Strategy guru Michael Porter's competitive advantage framework for analysis at the nation-state level. The degree to which a nation develops competitive advantage depends on four elements: factor conditions, demand conditions, the presence of related and supporting industries, and the nature of firm strategy. (16)

nationalization Broad transfer of industry management and ownership in a particular country from the private sector to the government. (5)

nature of firm strategy, structure, and rivalry In Michael Porter's framework for national competitive advantage, the fourth determinant of a national "diamond." (16)

negotiated transfer price A transfer pricing policy that establishes prices for intracorporate transactions on the basis of the organization's affiliations. (11)

newly industrializing economies (NIEs) Upper-middle-income countries with high rates of economic growth. (2)

niche A single segment of the global market. (7)

nongovernmental organization (NGO) A secondary stakeholder that focuses on human rights, political justice, and environmental issues. (17)

nontariff barriers (NTBs) Any restriction besides taxation that restricts or prevents the flow of goods across borders, ranging from "buy local" campaigns to bureaucratic obstacles that make it difficult for companies to gain access to some individual country and regional markets. (1, 8)

normal trade relations (NTR) A trading stratus under World Trade Organization (WTO) rules that entitles a country to low tariff rates. (8)

North American Free Trade Agreement (NAFTA) A free trade area encompassing Canada, the United States, and Mexico. (3)

"not invented here" (NIH) syndrome An error made in choosing a strategy by ignoring decisions made by subsidiary or affiliate managers. (10)

observation A method of primary data collection using trained observers who watch and record the behavior of actual or prospective customers. (6)

offset A countertrade deal in which a government recoups hard-currency expenditures by requiring some form of cooperation from the seller, such as importing products or transferring technology. (11)

one-to-one marketing An updated framework for direct marketing that calls for treating each customer in a distinct way based on his or her previous purchase history or past interactions with the company. (14)

operating system A software code that provides basic instructions for a computer. (15)

option In foreign currency trading, a contract confirming the right to buy or sell a specific amount of currency at a fixed price. (2)

order processing The aspect of physical distribution that includes order entry, order handling, and order delivery. (12)

organic growth In global retailing, a market expansion strategy whereby a company uses its own resources to open a store on a greenfield site or to acquire one or more existing retail facilities or sites from another company. (12)

Organization for Economic Cooperation and Development (OECD) A group of 33 nations that work together to aid in the development of economic systems based on market capitalism and pluralistic democracy. (2)

organizing The goal of creating a structure that enables the company to respond to significant differences in international market environments and to extend valuable corporate knowledge. (17)

outlet mall A grouping of outlet stores. (12)

outlet store A category of retail operations that allows marketers of well-known consumer brands to dispose of excess inventory, out-of-date merchandise, or factory seconds. (12)

outsourcing Shifting jobs or work assignments to another company to cut costs. When the work moves abroad to a low-wage country such as India or China, the term *offshoring* is sometimes used. (8)

paid search advertising An Internet communication tactic in which companies pay to have their ads appear when users type certain search terms. (15)

parallel importing The act of importing goods from one country to another without authorization from the trademark owner. Parallel import schemes exploit price differentials among country markets. (11)

patent A formal legal document that gives an inventor the exclusive right to make, use, and sell an invention for a specified period of time. (5)

pattern advertising A communication strategy that calls for developing a basic pan-regional or global concept for which copy, artwork, or other elements can be adapted as required for individual country markets. (13)

peer-to-peer (p-to-p) marketing A marketing model whereby individual consumers market products to other individuals. (12)

peoplemeter An electronic device used by companies such as Nielsen to collect national television audience data. (6)

personal computer (PC) A compact, affordable computing device whose advent marked the next phase of the digital revolution. (15)

personal interview Primary data collection via interactive communication (e.g., face-to-face, telephone, etc.) that allows interviewers to ask "why"-type questions. (6)

personal selling One of four variables in the promotion mix; face-to-face communication between a prospective buyer and a company sales representative. (14)

personal selling philosophy A sales representative's commitment to the marketing concept coupled with a willingness to take on the role of problem solver or partner in helping customers. The first step in the strategic/consultative selling model. (14)

physical distribution All activities involved in moving finished goods from manufacturers to customers. Includes order processing, warehousing, inventory management, and transportation. (12)

place utility The availability of a product or service in a location that is convenient to a potential customer. (12)

platform A core product design element or component that can be quickly and cheaply adapted to various country markets. (10)

political environment The set of governmental institutions, political parties, and organizations that are the expression of the people in the nations of the world. (5)

political risk The risk of a change in political environment or government policy that would adversely affect a company's ability to operate effectively and profitably. (5)

polycentric orientation The second level in the EPRG framework: the view that each country in which a company does business is unique. In global marketing, this orientation results in high levels of marketing mix adaptation, often implemented by autonomous local managers in each country market. (1)

polycentric pricing The practice of setting different price levels for a given product in different country markets. Also known as adaptation pricing. (11)

positioning The act of differentiating a product or brand in the minds of customers or prospects relative to competing products or brands. (7)

positioning by attribute or benefit A positioning strategy that seeks to differentiate a company, product, or brand in terms of one or more specific benefits (e.g., reliability) offered to buyers. (7)

positioning by competition A positioning strategy that seeks to differentiate a company, product, or brand by comparing it to the competition. (7)

positioning by quality/price A positioning strategy that seeks to differentiate a product, brand, or company in terms of expensiveness/exclusivity, acceptable quality/good value, etc. (7)

positioning by use or user A positioning strategy that seeks to differentiate a product by associating it with users whose expertise or accomplishments potential buyers admire. (7)

power distance In Geert Hofstede's social values typology, the cultural dimension that reflects the extent to which it is acceptable for power to be distributed unequally in a society. (4)

preferential tariff A reduced tariff rate applied to imports from certain countries. (8)

preferential trade agreement (PTA) A trade agreement between a relatively small number of signatory nations, often on a regional or subregional basis. Different levels of economic integration can characterize such trade agreements. (3)

presentation plan In personal selling, the heart of the presentation strategy. The plan has six stages: approach, presentation, demonstration, negotiation, closing, and servicing the sale. (14)

presentation strategy Setting objectives for each sales call and establishing a presentation plan to meet those objectives. (14)

price fixing Secret agreements between representatives of two or more companies to set prices. (11)

price transparency Euro-denominated prices for goods and services that enable consumers and organizational buyers to comparison shop across Europe. (11)

primary data In market research, data gathered through research pertaining to the particular problem, decision, or issue under study. (6)

product One of the four Ps of the marketing mix: a good, service, or idea with tangible and/or intangible attributes that collectively create value for a buyer or user. (10)

product adaptation–communication extension A strategy of extending, with minimal change, the basic home-market communications strategy while adapting the product to local use or preference conditions. (10)

product-communication adaptation (dual adaptation) A dual-adaptation strategy that uses a combination of marketing conditions. (10)

product-communication extension A strategy for pursuing opportunities outside the home market. (10)

product extension–communications adaptation The strategy of marketing an identical product by adapting the marketing communications program. (10)

product invention In global marketing, developing new products with the world market in mind. (10)

product market A market defined in terms of a particular product category (e.g., in the automotive industry, "the SUV market," "the sports car market," etc.). (7)

product placement A marketing communication tool that involves a company paying a fee to have one or more products and brand names appear in popular television programs, movies, and other types of performances. (14)

product saturation level The percentage of customers or households that own a product in a particular country market; a measure of market opportunity. (2)

product strategy In personal selling, a sales representative's plan for selecting and positioning products that will satisfy customer needs. The third step in the strategic/consultative selling model. (14)

product transformation When a product that has been introduced into multiple country markets via a product extension–communication adaptation strategy serves a different function or use than originally intended. (10)

pro forma invoice A document that sets an export/import transaction into motion. The document specifies the amount and the means by which an exporter-seller wants to be paid; it also specifies the items to be purchased. (8)

promotion site A Web site that provides marketing communications about a company's goods or services. (15)

psychographic segmentation The process of assigning people to market segments on the basis of their attitudes, interests, opinions, and lifestyles. (7)

publicity Communication about a company or product for which the company does not pay. (13)

public relations (PR) One of four variables in the promotion mix. Within an organization, the department or function responsible for evaluating public opinion about, and attitudes toward, the organization and its products and brands. PR personnel also are responsible for fostering goodwill, understanding, and acceptance among a company's various constituents and the public. (13)

purchasing power parity (PPP) A concept that permits adjustment of national income measurements in various countries to reflect what a unit of each country's currency can actually buy. (2)

put option The right to sell a specified number of foreign currency units at a fixed price, up to the option's expiration date. (2)

quota Government-imposed limit or restriction on the number of units or the total value of a particular product or product category that can be imported. (8)

rational appeal In advertising, an appeal to the target audience's logic and intellect. (13)

regiocentric orientation The third level in the EPRG framework: the view that similarities as well as differences characterize specific regions of the world. In global marketing, a regiocentric orientation is evident when a company develops an integrated strategy for a particular geographic area. (1)

regulatory environment Governmental and nongovernmental agencies and organizations that enforce laws or establish guidelines for conducting business. (5)

related and supporting industries In Michael Porter's framework for national competitive advantage, one of the four determinants of a national "diamond." (16)

relationship strategy In personal selling, a sales representative's game plan for establishing and maintaining high-quality relationships with prospects and customers. The second step in the Strategic/Consultative Selling Model. (14)

restrictive administrative and technical regulations Regulations that can create barriers to trade; they may take the form of antidumping, size, or safety and health regulations. (8)

revaluation The strengthening of a country's currency. (2)

ringtone A digital sound file for cell phones that is an instrumental version of a song or composition. (15)

rules of origin A system of certification that verifies the country of origin of a shipment of goods. (3)

sales agent An agent who works under contract rather than as a full-time employee. (14)

sales promotion One of the four elements of the promotion mix. A paid, short-term communication program that adds tangible value to a product or brand. (14)

sampling A sales promotion technique that provides potential customers with the opportunity to try a product or service at no cost. (14)

secondary data Existing data in personal files, published sources, and databases. (6)

self-reference criterion (SRC) The unconscious human tendency to interpret the world in terms of one's own cultural experience and values. (4)

selling proposition In advertising, the promise or claim that captures the reason for buying the product or the benefit that product ownership confers. (13)

services trade The buying and selling of intangible, experience-based economic output. (2)

shopping mall A group of stores in one place, typically with one or more large department stores serving as anchors and with easy access and free parking. (12)

short message service (SMS) A globally accepted wireless standard for sending alphanumeric messages of up to 160 characters. (15)

short-term orientation One of the dimensions in Geert Hofstede's social values typology. Contrasts with long-term orientation. (4)

single-column tariff A schedule of duties in which the rate applies to imports from all countries on the same basis; the simplest type of tariff. (8)

smartphone A phone that offers some of the capabilities of computers, such as a Web browser. (15)

social values typology A study by Dutch organizational anthropologist Geert Hofstede that classifies national cultures according to five dimensions: individualism versus collectivism, masculinity versus femininity, power distance, uncertainty avoidance, and long-term orientation versus short-term orientation. (4)

sourcing decision A strategic decision that determines whether a company makes a product itself or buys products from other manufacturers as well as where it makes or buys its products. (8)

Southern African Development Community (SADC) An association whose member states are Angola, Botswana, Democratic Republic of Congo, Lesotho, Malawi, Mauritius, Mozambique, Namibia, Seychelles, South Africa, Swaziland, Tanzania, Zambia, and Zimbabwe. (3)

sovereignty A country's supreme and independent political authority. (5)

special economic zone (SEZ) A geographic entity that offers manufacturers simplified customs procedures, operational flexibility, and a general environment of relaxed regulations. (8)

specialty retailer A category of retail operations characterized by a more narrow focus than a department store and offering a relatively narrow merchandise mix aimed at a particular target market. (12)

sponsorship A form of marketing communication that involves payment of a fee by a company to have its name associated with a particular event, team or athletic association, or sports facility. (14)

spreadsheet A software application in the form of an electronic ledger that automatically calculates the effect of changes made to figures entered in rows and columns. (15)

stakeholder Any group or individual that is affected by, or takes an interest in, the policies and practices adopted by an organization. (17)

stakeholder analysis The process of formulating a "win-win" outcome for all stakeholders. (17)

standardized (extension) approach The pursuit of a global market opportunity using an extension strategy of minimal marketing mix variation in different countries. (1)

standardized global marketing A target market strategy that calls for creating the same marketing mix for a broad mass market of potential buyers. (7)

strategic alliance A partnership among two or more firms created to minimize risk while maximizing leverage in the marketplace. (9)

strategic/consultative selling model A five-step framework for approaching the personal selling task: personal selling philosophy, relationship strategy, product strategy, customer strategy, and presentation strategy. (14)

strategic intent A competitive advantage framework developed by strategy experts Gary Hamel and C. K. Prahalad. (16)

strategic international alliances A form of mutually beneficial collaboration among two or more companies doing business globally. The goal is to leverage complementary resources and competencies in order to achieve competitive advantage. (9)

streaming audio Transmission that allows users to listen to Internet radio stations. (15)

streaming media The transmission of combined audio and video content via a broadband network. (15)

streaming video A sequence of moving images sent in compressed form via the Internet and displayed on a computer screen. (15)

subculture Within a culture, a small group of people with their own shared subset of attitudes, beliefs, and values. (4)

subsidies Direct or indirect financial contributions or incentives that benefit producers. (8)

supercenter A category of retail operations that combines elements of discount stores and supermarkets in a space that occupies about half the size of a hypermarket. (12)

supermarket A category of retail operations characterized by a departmentalized, single-story retail establishment that offers a variety of food and nonfood items on a self-service basis. (12)

superstore A store that specializes in selling vast assortments of a particular product category in high volumes at low prices. (12)

supply chain A group of firms that perform support activities by generating raw materials, converting them into components or finished goods, and making them available to buyers. (12)

survey research Primary data collection via questionnaire-based studies designed to generate qualitative responses, quantitative responses, or both. (6)

sustaining technologies Incremental or radical innovations that improve product performance. (15)

switch trading A transaction in which a professional switch trader, switch trading house, or bank steps into a simple barter arrangement or other countertrade arrangement in which one of the parties is not willing to accept all the goods received in the transaction. (11)

targeting The process of evaluating market segments and focusing marketing efforts on a country, region, or group of people. (7)

tariffs The rules, rate schedules (duties), and regulations of individual countries affecting goods that are imported. (8)

telematics A car's ability to exchange information about its location or mechanical performance via a wireless Internet connection. (15)

teleshopping Round-the-clock programming exclusively dedicated to product demonstration and selling. (14)

temporary surcharge Surcharges introduced from time to time to provide additional protection for local industry and, in particular, in response to balance of payments deficits. (8)

tiered branding A strategy in which a corporate name is combined with a product brand name; also called combination or umbrella branding. (10)

time utility The availability of a product or service when desired by a customer. (12)

trade deficit A negative number in the balance of payments showing that the value of a country's imports exceeds the value of its exports. (2)

trademark A distinctive mark, motto, device, or emblem that a manufacturer affixes to a particular product or package to distinguish it from goods produced by other manufacturers. (5)

trade mission A state- or federally sponsored show outside the home country organized around a product, a group of products, an industry, or an activity at which company personnel can learn about new markets as well as competitors. (8)

trade sales promotion Promotion designed to increase product availability in distribution channels. (14)

trade show A gathering of company representatives organized around a product, a group of products, or an industry, at which company personnel can meet with prospective customers and gather competitor intelligence. (8)

trade surplus A positive number in the balance of payments showing that the value of a country's exports exceeds the value of its imports. (2)

transaction site A cyberspace retail operation that allows customers to purchase goods and services. (15)

Transatlantic Trade and Investment Partnership (TTIP) A proposed free-trade area that includes the United States and the EU. (3)

transfer pricing The pricing of goods, services, and intangible property bought and sold by operating units or divisions of a company doing business with an affiliate in another jurisdiction. (11)

transistor A "solid state amplifier" that replaced vacuum tubes in electronics products; it was a milestone in the digital revolution. (15)

transnational company A company exhibiting a geocentric orientation that pursues marketing opportunities in all parts of the world. However, a transnational company differs from a global company by fully integrating and coordinating two strategies: both sourcing products from a variety of different countries and serving multiple country markets across most world regions. (1)

Trans-Pacific Partnership (TPP) A proposed 12-nation free-trade area that includes Japan and the United States. (3)

transparency Openness in business dealings, financial disclosures, pricing, or other situations where the goal is to remove layers of secrecy or other obstacles to clear the way for understanding and decision making. (3)

Triad The three regions of Japan, Western Europe, and the United States, which represent the dominant economic centers of the world. (2)

truetone A digital sound file of a song or composition for a cell phone featuring the original recording artist. (15)

two-column tariff General duties plus special duties indicating reduced rates determined by tariff negotiations with other countries. (8)

uncertainty avoidance In Geert Hofstede's social values framework, the extent to which members of a culture are uncomfortable with unclear, ambiguous, or unstructured situations. (4)

uniform resource locator (URL) An Internet site's address on the World Wide Web. (15)

upper-middle-income country A country with gross national income (GNI) per capita between $4,036 and $12,475. (2)

usage rate In behavioral market segmentation, an assessment of the extent to which a person uses a product or service. (7)

user status In behavioral market segmentation, an assessment of whether a person is a present user, potential user, nonuser, former user, etc. (7)

value A customer's perception of a firm's product or service offering in terms of the ratio of benefits (product, place, promotion) relative to price. This ratio can be represented by the value equation $V = B/P$. (1)

value chain The various activities that a company performs (e.g., research and development, manufacturing, marketing, physical distribution, and logistics) in order to create value for customers. (1)

value equation $V = B/P$, where V stands for "perceived value," B stands for "product, price, and place," and P stands for "price." (1)

value network The cost structure in a particular industry that dictates the margins needed to achieve profitability. A broadly defined industry (e.g., computers) may have parallel value networks, each with its own metrics of value. (15)

values In culture, enduring beliefs or feelings that a specific mode of conduct is personally or socially preferable to another mode of conduct. (4)

variable import levies A system of levies applied to certain categories of imported agricultural products. (8)

Voice over Internet Protocol (VoIP) Technology that allows the human voice to be digitized and broken into data packets that can be transmitted over the Internet and converted back into normal speech. (15)

warehousing The aspect of physical distribution that involves the storage of goods. (12)

Wi-Fi (wireless fidelity) Technology based on a low-power radio signal that permits access to the Internet from a laptop computer or smartphone when the user is within range of a base station transmitter ("hotspot"). (15)

World Trade Organization (WTO) The successor to the General Agreement on Tariffs and Trade (GATT). (3)

World Wide Web Global computer network connecting Internet sites that contain text, graphics, and streaming audio and video resources. (15)

Author/Name Index

Note: Page numbers with *e*, *f*, or *t* represent exhibits, figures, and tables, respectively.

Subject/Organization Index

Note: Page numbers with *e*, *f*, or *t* represent exhibits, figures, and tables, respectively.